FOURTH EDITION

CSS: The Definitive Guide

Visual Presentation for the Web

Eric A. Meyer and Estelle Weyl

Beijing · Boston · Farnham · Sebastopol · Tokyo

CSS: The Definitive Guide

by Eric A. Meyer and Estelle Weyl

Printed in the United States of America.

Published by O'Reilly Media, Inc., 1005 Gravenstein Highway North, Sebastopol, CA 95472.

O'Reilly books may be purchased for educational, business, or sales promotional use. Online editions are also available for most titles (*http://oreilly.com/safari*). For more information, contact our corporate/institutional sales department: 800-998-9938 or *corporate@oreilly.com*.

Editor: Meg Foley	**Interior Designer:** David Futato
Production Editors: Colleen Lobner and Colleen Cole	**Cover Designer:** Karen Montgomery
Proofreader: Amanda Kersey	**Illustrator:** Rebecca Demarest
Indexer: Angela Howard	

November 2017:   Fourth Edition

Revision History for the Fourth Edition
2000-05-01:   First Release
2004-03-01:   Second Release
2006-11-01:   Third Release
2017-10-10:   Fourth Release

See *http://oreilly.com/catalog/errata.csp?isbn=9781449393199* for release details.

978-1-449-39319-9

[M]

To Kat, Carolyn, Rebecca, and Joshua.

—E.M.

To Amie.

—E.W.

Table of Contents

Preface

If you are a web designer or document author interested in sophisticated page styling, improved accessibility, and saving time and effort, this book is for you. All you really need to know before starting the book is HTML 4.0. The better you know HTML, the better prepared you'll be, but it is not a requirement. You will need to know very little else to follow this book.

This fourth edition of the book was finished in mid-2017 and does its best to reflect the state of CSS at that time. The assumption is that anything covered in detail either had wide browser support at the time of writing or was known to be coming soon after publication. CSS features which were still being developed, or were known to have support dropping soon, are not covered here.

Conventions Used in This Book

The following typographical conventions are used in this book (but make sure to read through the subsection "Value Syntax Conventions" on page xx to see how some of these are modified):

Italic
> Indicates new terms, URLs, email addresses, filenames, and file extensions.

`Constant width`
> Used for program listings, as well as within paragraphs to refer to program elements such as variable or function names, databases, data types, environment variables, statements, and keywords.

`Constant width bold`
> Shows commands or other text that should be typed literally by the user.

`Constant width italic`
> Shows text that should be replaced with user-supplied values or by values determined by context.

This element signifies a tip or suggestion.

 This element signifies a general note.

 This element indicates a warning or caution.

Value Syntax Conventions

Throughout this book, there are boxes that break down a given CSS property's details, including what values are permitted. These have been reproduced practically verbatim from the CSS specifications, but some explanation of the syntax is in order.

Throughout, the allowed values for each property are listed with a syntax like the following:

Value: *<family-name>*#

Value: *<url>* || *<color>*

Value: *<url>*? *<color>* [/ *<color>*]?

Value: [*<length>* | `thick` | `thin`]{1,4}

Any italicized words between "<" and ">" give a type of value, or a reference to another property's values. For example, the property `font` accepts values that originally belong to the property `font-family`. This is denoted by using the text *<font-family>*. Similarly, if a value type like a color is permitted, it will be represented using *<color>*.

Any words presented in `constant width` are keywords that must appear literally, without quotes. The forward slash (/) and the comma (,) must also be used literally.

There are a number of ways to combine components of a value definition:

- Two or more keywords strung together with only space separating them means that all of them must occur in the given order. For example, `help me` would mean that the property must use those keywords in that order.

- If a vertical bar separates alternatives (X | Y), then any one of them must occur, but only one. Given "[X | Y | Z]", then any one of X, Y, *or* Z is permitted.

- A vertical double bar (X ∥ Y) means that X, Y, or both must occur, but they may appear in any order. Thus: X, Y, X Y, and Y X are all valid interpretations.

- A double ampersand (X && Y) means both X and Y must occur, though they may appear in any order. Thus: X Y or Y X are both valid interpretations.

- Brackets ([...]) are for grouping things together. Thus "[please ∥ help ∥ me] do this" means that the words please, help, and me can appear in any order, though each appear only once. do this must always appear, with those words in that order. Some examples: please help me do this, help me please do this, me please help do this.

Every component or bracketed group may (or may not) be followed by one of these modifiers:

- An asterisk (*) indicates that the preceding value or bracketed group is repeated zero or more times. Thus, "bucket*" means that the word bucket can be used any number of times, including zero. There is no upper limit defined on the number of times it can be used.

- A plus (+) indicates that the preceding value or bracketed group is repeated one or more times. Thus, "mop+" means that the word mop must be used at least once, and potentially many more times.

- An octothorpe (#) indicates that the preceding value or bracketed group is repeated one or more times, separated by commas as needed. Thus, "floor#" can be floor, floor, floor, floor, and so on. This is most often used in conjunction with bracketed groups or value types.

- A question mark (?) indicates that the preceding value or bracketed group is optional. For example, "[pine tree]?" means that the words pine tree need not be used (although they must appear in that order if they are used).

- An exclamation point (!) indicates that the preceding value or bracketed group is required, and thus must result in at least one value, even if the syntax would seem to indicate otherwise. For example, "[what? is? happening?]!" must be at least one of the three terms marked optional.

- A pair of numbers in curly braces ({M,N}) indicates that the preceding value or bracketed group is repeated at least M and at most N times. For example, ha{1,3} means that there can be one, two, or three instances of the word ha.

The following are some examples:

give ‖ me ‖ liberty

At least one of the three words must be used, and they can be used in any order. For example, give liberty, give me, liberty me give, and give me liberty are all valid interpretations.

[I | am]? the ‖ walrus

Either the word I or am may be used, but not both, and use of either is optional. In addition, either the or walrus, or both, must follow in any order. Thus you could construct I the walrus, am walrus the, am the, I walrus, walrus the, and so forth.

koo+ ka-choo

One or more instances of koo must be followed by ka-choo. Therefore koo koo ka-choo, koo koo koo ka-choo, and koo ka-choo are all legal. The number of koos is potentially infinite, although there are bound to be implementation-specific limits.

I really{1,4}? [love | hate] [Microsoft | Netscape | Opera | Safari | Chrome]

The all-purpose web designer's opinion-expresser. This can be interpreted as I love Netscape, I really love Microsoft, and similar expressions. Anywhere from zero to four reallys may be used, though they may *not* be separated by commas. You also get to pick between love and hate, which really seems like some sort of metaphor.

It's a [mad]# world

This gives the opportunity to put in as many comma-separated mads as possible, with a minimum of one mad. If there is only one mad, then no comma is added. Thus: It's a mad world and It's a mad, mad, mad, mad, mad world are both valid results.

[[Alpha ‖ Baker ‖ Cray],]{2,3} and Delphi

Two to three of Alpha, Baker, and Delta must be followed by and Delphi. One possible result would be Cray, Alpha, and Delphi. In this case, the comma is placed because of its position within the nested bracket groups. (Some older versions of CSS enforced comma-separation this way, instead of via the # modifier.)

Using Code Examples

Whenever you come across an icon that looks like ⊙, it means there is an associated code example. Live examples are available at *https://meyerweb.github.io/csstdg4figs/*. If you are reading this book on a device with an internet connection, you can click the ⊙ icon to go directly to a live version of the code example referenced.

Supplemental material—in the form of the HTML, CSS, and image files that were used to produce nearly all of the figures in this book—is available for download at *https://github.com/meyerweb/csstdg4figs*. Please be sure to read the repository's *README.md* file for any notes regarding the contents of the repository.

This book is here to help you get your job done. In general, if example code is offered with this book, you may use it in your programs and documentation. You do not need to contact us for permission unless you're reproducing a significant portion of the code. For example, writing a program that uses several chunks of code from this book does not require permission. Selling or distributing a CD-ROM of examples from O'Reilly books does require permission. Answering a question by citing this book and quoting example code does not require permission. Incorporating a significant amount of example code from this book into your product's documentation does require permission.

We appreciate, but do not require, attribution. An attribution usually includes the title, author, publisher, and ISBN. For example: "*CSS: The Definitive Guide* by Eric A. Meyer and Estelle Weyl (O'Reilly). Copyright 2018 Eric Meyer, Estelle Weyl, 978-1-449-39319-9."

If you feel your use of code examples falls outside fair use or the permission given above, feel free to contact us at *permissions@oreilly.com*.

O'Reilly Safari

 *Safari* (formerly Safari Books Online) is a membership-based training and reference platform for enterprise, government, educators, and individuals.

Members have access to thousands of books, training videos, Learning Paths, interactive tutorials, and curated playlists from over 250 publishers, including O'Reilly Media, Harvard Business Review, Prentice Hall Professional, Addison-Wesley Professional, Microsoft Press, Sams, Que, Peachpit Press, Adobe, Focal Press, Cisco Press, John Wiley & Sons, Syngress, Morgan Kaufmann, IBM Redbooks, Packt, Adobe Press, FT Press, Apress, Manning, New Riders, McGraw-Hill, Jones & Bartlett, and Course Technology, among others.

For more information, please visit *http://oreilly.com/safari*.

How to Contact Us

Please address comments and questions concerning this book to the publisher:

O'Reilly Media, Inc.
1005 Gravenstein Highway North
Sebastopol, CA 95472
800-998-9938 (in the United States or Canada)
707-829-0515 (international or local)
707-829-0104 (fax)

We have a web page for this book, where we list errata, examples, and any additional information. You can access this page at *http://bit.ly/css-the-definitive-guide-4e*.

To comment or ask technical questions about this book, send email to *bookquestions@oreilly.com*.

For more information about our books, courses, conferences, and news, see our website at *http://www.oreilly.com*.

Find us on Facebook: *http://facebook.com/oreilly*

Follow us on Twitter: *http://twitter.com/oreillymedia*

Watch us on YouTube: *http://www.youtube.com/oreillymedia*

Acknowledgments

Eric Meyer

This edition was one of the most challenging projects I've ever undertaken, for both technical and personal reasons, and I was helped immeasurably along the way by so many people. I'll do my best to remember everyone, but if I left you out, I am sorry.

To the creators of CSS, Håkon Wium Lie and Bert Bos, thank you for your foresight. The web would be a much poorer place without your work.

To the implementors at various browser makers who have done so much, and come so far together, thank you making so many things possible.

To git, the version-control software, my thanks for the last-minute rescue when it was discovered that an entire chapter ("Lists and Generated Content") had gone missing, but was easily restored from past commits.

Special thanks are due to Simon St. Laurent, who believed in my ideas for releasing a book one chapter at a time, who kept the project waiting for me when I had to take an extended period of time away, and who worked tirelessly with me to move things forward in whatever way I proposed.

To my co-author, Estelle, for stepping up to help me out when I needed it, for your keen reviewers' eye, and for your wonderful contributions to this edition, all my gratitude.

A number of other people helped me understand CSS when it didn't make sense to me, often going several rounds of explanation. Some of them go back a few editions, but most of them helped me adjust to the new patterns in CSS for this edition. Alphabetically, by last name: Rachel Andrew, Rossen Atanossov, Tab Atkins, Amelia Bellamy-Royds, Dave Cramer, Elika Etemad, Jen Simmons, Sara Soueidan, Mel Sumner, and Greg Whitworth. My abject apologies to anyone I left off by oversight.

To the whole community of web designers and developers who stood with me through the hardest passage I have ever known, friends and colleagues and strangers alike, I owe you more than I could ever say. In some ways, I owe you my life. Thank you for hearing me.

And to my family—my wife Kat, and my children Carolyn, Rebecca, and Joshua—you are the home that shelters me, the suns in my sky and the stars by which I steer. I could never have come this far without you. Thank you for everything.

—Eric A. Meyer
Cleveland Heights, OH
19 July 2017

Estelle Weyl

I would like to acknowledge everyone who has worked to make CSS what it is today and all those who have helped improve diversity and inclusion in tech.

I would like to recognize those who work tirelessly with browser vendors and developers in writing the CSS specifications. Without the members of the CSS Working Group—past, current, and future—we would have no specifications, no standards, and no cross-browser compatibility. I am in awe of the thought process that goes into every CSS property and value added to, and omitted from, the specification. People like Tab Atkins, Elika Emitad, Dave Baron, Léonie Watson, and Greg Whitworth not only work on the specification, but also take their time to answer questions and explain nuances to the broader CSS public, notably me.

I also want to acknowledge all those who, whether they participate in the CSS Working Group or not, dive deep into CSS features and help translate the spec for the rest of us, including Sarah Drasner, Val Head, Sara Souidan, Chris Coyier, Jen Simmons, and Rachel Andrew. In addition, I want to acknowledge and thank people who create tools that make all CSS developers lives easier, especially Alexis Deveria for creating and maintaining *https://caniuse.com/*.

I would also like to acknowledge and express my appreciation of all those who have contributed their time and effort to improve diversity and inclusion in all sectors of the developer community. Yes, CSS is awesome. But it's important to work with great people in a great community.

When I attended my first tech conference in 2007, the lineup was 93% male and 100% white. The audience had slightly less gender diversity and only slightly more ethnic diversity. I had actually picked that conference because the lineup was more diverse than most: it actually had a woman on it. Looking around the room, I knew things needed to change, and I realized it was something I needed to do. What I didn't realize then was how many unsung heroes I would meet over the next 10 years working for diversity and inclusion in all areas of the tech sector and life in general.

There are too many people who work tirelessly, quietly, and often with little or no recognition to name them all, but I would like to highlight some. I can not express how much of a positive impact people like Erica Stanley of Women Who Code Atlanta, Carina Zona of Callback Women, and Jenn Mei Wu of Oakland Maker Space have had. Groups like The Last Mile, Black Girls Code, Girls Incorporated, Sisters Code, and so many others inspired me to create a list at *http://www.standardista.com/feeding-the-diversity-pipeline/* to help ensure the path to a career in web development is not only for those with privilege.

Thank you to all of you. Thank you to everyone. Thanks to all of your efforts, more has been done than I ever could have imagined sitting in that conference 10 years ago.

—Estelle Weyl
Palo Alto, CA
July 19, 2017

CHAPTER 1

CSS and Documents

Cascading Style Sheets (CSS) is a powerful tool that transforms the presentation of a document or a collection of documents, and it has spread to nearly every corner of the web and into many ostensibly non-web environments. For example, Gecko-based browsers use CSS to affect the presentation of the browser chrome itself, many RSS clients let you apply CSS to feeds and feed entries, and some instant message clients use CSS to format chat windows. Aspects of CSS can be found in the syntax used by JavaScript frameworks, and even in JavaScript itself. It's everywhere!

A Brief History of (Web) Style

CSS was first proposed in 1994, just as the web was beginning to really catch on. At the time, browsers gave all sorts of styling power to the user—the presentation preferences in Mosaic, for example, permitted all manner of font family, size, and color to be defined by the user on a per-element basis. None of this was available to document authors; all they could do was mark a piece of content as a paragraph, as a heading of some level, as preformatted text, or one of a handful of other element types. If a user configured his browser to make all level-one headings tiny and pink and all level-six headings huge and red, well, that was his lookout.

It was into this milieu that CSS was introduced. Its goal was to provide a simple, declarative styling language that was flexible for authors and, most importantly, provided styling power to authors and users alike. By means of the "cascade," these styles could be combined and prioritized so that both authors and readers had a say—though readers always had the last say.

Work quickly advanced, and by late 1996, CSS1 was finished. While the newly established CSS Working Group moved forward with CSS2, browsers struggled to implement CSS1 in an interoperable way. Although each piece of CSS was fairly simple on its own, the combination of those pieces created some surprisingly complex behaviors. There were also some unfortunate missteps in early implementations, such as the infamous discrepancy in box model implementations. These problems threatened to derail CSS altogether, but fortunately some clever proposals were implemented, and browsers began to harmonize. Within a few years, thanks to increasing interoperability and high-profile developments such as the CSS-based redesign of *Wired* magazine and the CSS Zen Garden, CSS began to catch on.

Before all that happened, though, the CSS Working Group had finalized the CSS2 specification in early 1998. Once CSS2 was finished, work immediately began on CSS3, as well as a clarified version of CSS2 called CSS2.1. In keeping with the spirit of the times, CSS3 was constructed as a series of (theoretically) standalone modules instead of a single monolithic specification. This approach reflected the then-active XHTML specification, which was split into modules for similar reasons.

The rationale for modularizing CSS3 was that each module could be worked on at its own pace, and particularly critical (or popular) modules could be advanced along the W3C's progress track without being held up by others. Indeed, this has turned out to be the case. By early 2012, three CSS3 modules (along with CSS1 and CSS 2.1) had reached full Recommendation status—CSS Color Level 3, CSS Namespaces, and Selectors Level 3. At that same time, seven modules were at Candidate Recommendation status, and several dozen others were in various stages of Working Draft-ness. Under the old approach, colors, selectors, and namespaces would have had to wait for every other part of the specification to be done or cut before they could be part of a completed specification. Thanks to modularization, they didn't have to wait.

The flip side of that advantage is that it's hard to speak of a single "CSS3 specification." There isn't any such thing, nor can there be. Even if every other CSS module had reached level 3 by, say, late 2016 (they didn't), there was already a Selectors Level 4 in process. Would we then speak of it as CSS4? What about all the "CSS3" features still coming into play? Or Grid Layout, which had not then even reached Level 1?

So while we can't really point to a single tome and say, "There is CSS3," we can talk of features by the module name under which they are introduced. The flexibility modules permit more than makes up for the semantic awkwardness they sometimes create. (If you want something approximating a single monolithic specification, the CSS Working Group publishes yearly "Snapshot" documents.)

With that established, we're almost ready to start understanding CSS. First though, we must go over markup.

Elements

Elements are the basis of document structure. In HTML, the most common elements are easily recognizable, such as `p`, `table`, `span`, `a`, and `div`. Every single element in a document plays a part in its presentation.

Replaced and Nonreplaced Elements

Although CSS depends on elements, not all elements are created equally. For example, images and paragraphs are not the same type of element, nor are `span` and `div`. In CSS, elements generally take two forms: replaced and nonreplaced.

Replaced elements

Replaced elements are those where the element's content is replaced by something that is not directly represented by document content. Probably the most familiar HTML example is the `img` element, which is replaced by an image file external to the document itself. In fact, `img` has no actual content, as you can see in this simple example:

```
<img src="howdy.gif" >
```

This markup fragment contains only an element name and an attribute. The element presents nothing unless you point it to some external content (in this case, an image specified by the `src` attribute). If you point to a valid image file, the image will be placed in the document. If not, it will either display nothing or the browser will show a "broken image" placeholder.

Similarly, the `input` element is also replaced—by a radio button, checkbox, or text input box, depending on its type.

Nonreplaced elements

The majority of HTML elements are *nonreplaced elements*. This means that their content is presented by the user agent (generally a browser) inside a box generated by the element itself. For example, `<span>hi there</span>` is a nonreplaced element, and the text "hi there" will be displayed by the user agent. This is true of paragraphs, headings, table cells, lists, and almost everything else in HTML.

Element Display Roles

In addition to replaced and nonreplaced elements, CSS uses two other basic types of elements: *block-level* and *inline-level*. There are many more display types, but these are the most basic, and the types to which most if not all other display types refer. The block and inline types will be familiar to authors who have spent time with HTML markup and its display in web browsers. The elements are illustrated in Figure 1-1.

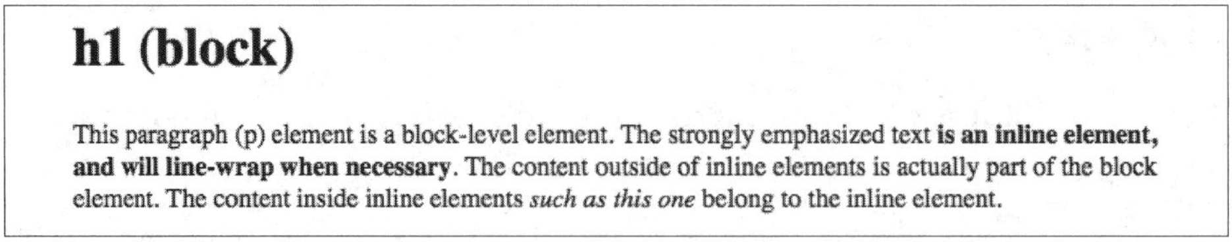

h1 (block)

This paragraph (p) element is a block-level element. The strongly emphasized text **is an inline element, and will line-wrap when necessary**. The content outside of inline elements is actually part of the block element. The content inside inline elements *such as this one* belong to the inline element.

Figure 1-1. Block- and inline-level elements in an HTML document

Block-level elements

Block-level elements generate an element box that (by default) fills its parent element's content area and cannot have other elements at its sides. In other words, it generates "breaks" before and after the element box. The most familiar block elements from HTML are p and div. Replaced elements can be block-level elements, but usually they are not.

List items are a special case of block-level elements. In addition to behaving in a manner consistent with other block elements, they generate a marker—typically a bullet for unordered lists and a number for ordered lists—that is "attached" to the element box. Except for the presence of this marker, list items are in all other ways identical to other block elements.

Inline-level elements

Inline-level elements generate an element box within a line of text and do not break up the flow of that line. The best inline element example is the a element in HTML. Other candidates are strong and em. These elements do not generate a "break" before or after themselves, so they can appear within the content of another element without disrupting its display.

Note that while the names "block" and "inline" share a great deal in common with block- and inline-level elements in HTML, there is an important difference. In HTML, block-level elements cannot descend from inline-level elements. In CSS, there is no restriction on how display roles can be nested within each other.

To see how this works, let's consider a CSS property, display.

display

Values	[*<display-outside>* ‖ *<display-inside>*] | *<display-listitem>* | *<display-internal>* | *<display-box>* | *<display-legacy>*
Definitions	See below
Initial value	`inline`
Applies to	All elements

Computed value	As specified
Inherited	No
Animatable	No

<display-outside>
    block | inline | run-in

<display-inside>
    flow | flow-root | table | flex | grid | ruby

<display-listitem>
    list-item && *<display-outside>*? && [flow | flow-root]?

<display-internal>
    table-row-group | table-header-group | table-footer-group | table-row |
    table-cell | table-column-group | table-column | table-caption | ruby-base
    | ruby-text | ruby-base-container | ruby-text-container

<display-box>
    contents | none

<display-legacy>
    inline-block | inline-list-item | inline-table | inline-flex | inline-grid

You may have noticed that there are a *lot* of values, only three of which I've even come close to mentioning: block, inline, and list-item. Most of these values will be dealt with elsewhere in the book; for example, grid and inline-grid will be covered in a separate chapter about grid layout, and the table-related values are all covered in a chapter on CSS table layout.

For now, let's just concentrate on block and inline. Consider the following markup:

```
<body>
<p>This is a paragraph with <em>an inline element</em> within it.</p>
</body>
```

Here we have two block elements (body and p) and an inline element (em). According to the HTML specification, em can descend from p, but the reverse is not true. Typically, the HTML hierarchy works out so that inlines descend from blocks, but not the other way around.

CSS, on the other hand, has no such restrictions. You can leave the markup as it is but change the display roles of the two elements like this:

```
p {display: inline;}
em {display: block;}
```

This causes the elements to generate a block box inside an inline box. This is perfectly legal and violates no part of CSS. You would, however, have a problem if you tried to reverse the nesting of the elements in HTML:

```
<em><p>This is a paragraph improperly enclosed by an inline element.</p></em>
```

No matter what you do to the display roles via CSS, this is not legal in HTML.

While changing the display roles of elements can be useful in HTML documents, it becomes downright critical for XML documents. An XML document is unlikely to have any inherent display roles, so it's up to the author to define them. For example, you might wonder how to lay out the following snippet of XML:

```
<book>
  <maintitle>Cascading Style Sheets: The Definitive Guide</maintitle>
  <subtitle>Third Edition</subtitle>
  <author>Eric A. Meyer</author>
  <publisher>O'Reilly and Associates</publisher>
  <pubdate>November 2006</pubdate>
  <isbn type="print">978-0-596-52733-4</isbn>
</book>
<book>
  <maintitle>CSS Pocket Reference</maintitle>
  <subtitle>Third Edition</subtitle>
  <author>Eric A. Meyer</author>
  <publisher>O'Reilly and Associates</publisher>
  <pubdate>October 2007</pubdate>
  <isbn type="print">978-0-596-51505-8</isbn>
</book>
```

Since the default value of display is inline, the content would be rendered as inline text by default, as illustrated in Figure 1-2. This isn't a terribly useful display.

Cascading Style Sheets: The Definitive Guide Third Edition Eric A. Meyer O'Reilly and Associates November 2006 978-0-596-52733-4 CSS Pocket Reference Third Edition Eric A. Meyer O'Reilly and Associates October 2007 978-0-596-51505-8

Figure 1-2. Default display of an XML document

You can define the basics of the layout with display:

```
book, maintitle, subtitle, author, isbn {display: block;}
publisher, pubdate {display: inline;}
```

We've now set five of the seven elements to be block and two to be inline. This means each of the block elements will be treated much as div is treated in HTML, and the two inlines will be treated in a manner similar to span.

This fundamental ability to affect display roles makes CSS highly useful in a variety of situations. We could take the preceding rules as a starting point, add a few other styles for greater visual impact, and get the result shown in Figure 1-3.

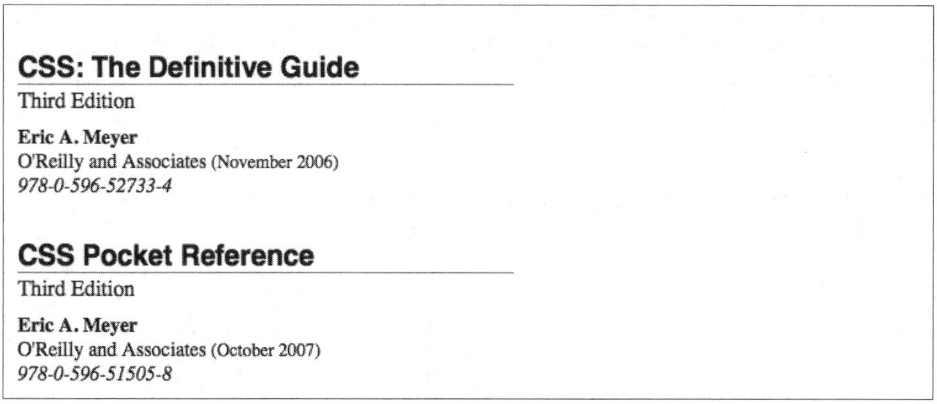

CSS: The Definitive Guide

Third Edition

Eric A. Meyer
O'Reilly and Associates (November 2006)
978-0-596-52733-4

CSS Pocket Reference

Third Edition

Eric A. Meyer
O'Reilly and Associates (October 2007)
978-0-596-51505-8

Figure 1-3. Styled display of an XML document

Before learning how to write CSS in detail, we need to look at how one can associate CSS with a document. After all, without tying the two together, there's no way for the CSS to affect the document. We'll explore this in an HTML setting since it's the most familiar.

Bringing CSS and HTML Together

I've mentioned that HTML documents have an inherent structure, and that's a point worth repeating. In fact, that's part of the problem with web pages of old: too many of us forgot that documents are supposed to have an internal structure, which is altogether different than a visual structure. In our rush to create the coolest-looking pages on the web, we bent, warped, and generally ignored the idea that pages should contain information with some structural meaning.

That structure is an inherent part of the relationship between HTML and CSS; without it, there couldn't be a relationship at all. To understand it better, let's look at an example HTML document and break it down by pieces:

```
<html>
<head>
<title>Eric's World of Waffles</title>
<meta http-equiv="content-type" content="text/html; charset=utf-8">
<link rel="stylesheet" type="text/css" href="sheet1.css" media="all">
<style type="text/css">
/* These are my styles! Yay! */
@import url(sheet2.css);
</style>
</head>
<body>
<h1>Waffles!</h1>
<p style="color: gray;">The most wonderful of all breakfast foods is
the waffle—a ridged and cratered slab of home-cooked, fluffy goodness
```

```
that makes every child's heart soar with joy. And they're so easy to make!
Just a simple waffle-maker and some batter, and you're ready for a morning
of aromatic ecstasy!
</p>
</body>
</html>
```

The result of this markup and the applied styles is shown in Figure 1-4.

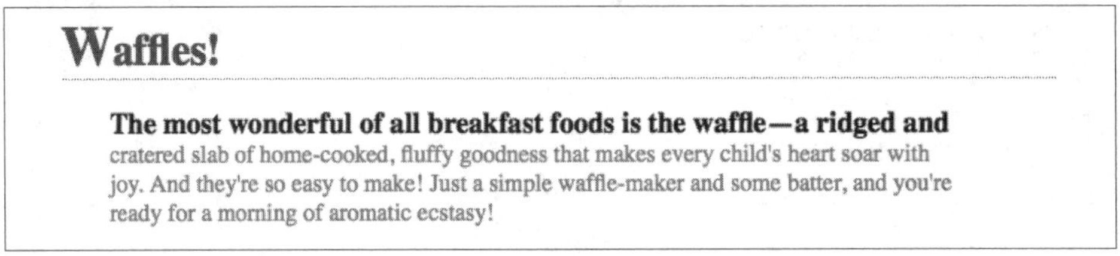

Waffles!

The most wonderful of all breakfast foods is the waffle—a ridged and
cratered slab of home-cooked, fluffy goodness that makes every child's heart soar with
joy. And they're so easy to make! Just a simple waffle-maker and some batter, and you're
ready for a morning of aromatic ecstasy!

Figure 1-4. A simple document

Now, let's examine the various ways this document connects to CSS.

The link Tag

First, consider the use of the link tag:

```
<link rel="stylesheet" type="text/css" href="sheet1.css" media="all">
```

The link tag is a little-regarded but nonetheless perfectly valid tag that has been
hanging around the HTML specification for years, just waiting to be put to good use.
Its basic purpose is to allow HTML authors to associate other documents with the
document containing the link tag. CSS uses it to link stylesheets to the document; in
Figure 1-5, a stylesheet called *sheet1.css* is linked to the document.

These stylesheets, which are not part of the HTML document but are still used by it,
are referred to as *external stylesheets*. This is because they're stylesheets that are external to the HTML document. (Go figure.)

To successfully load an external stylesheet, link must be placed inside the head element but may not be placed inside any other element. This will cause the web
browser to locate and load the stylesheet and use whatever styles it contains to render
the HTML document in the manner shown in Figure 1-5. Also shown in Figure 1-5 is
the loading of the external *sheet2.css* via the @import declaration. Imports must be
placed at the beginning of the stylesheet that contains them, but they are otherwise
unconstrained.

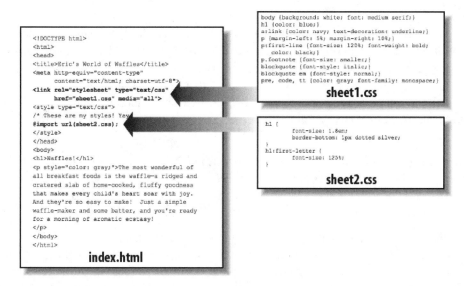

```
<!DOCTYPE html>
<html>
<head>
<title>Eric's World of Waffles</title>
<meta http-equiv="content-type"
      content="text/html; charset=utf-8">
<link rel="stylesheet" type="text/css"
      href="sheet1.css" media="all">
<style type="text/css">
/* These are my styles! Yay */
@import url(sheet2.css);
</style>
</head>
<body>
<h1>Waffles!</h1>
<p style="color: gray;">The most wonderful of
all breakfast foods is the waffle—a ridged and
cratered slab of home-cooked, fluffy goodness
that makes every child's heart soar with joy.
And they're so easy to make! Just a simple
waffle-maker and some batter, and you're ready
for a morning of aromatic ecstasy!
</p>
</body>
</html>
```

index.html

```
body {background: white; font: medium serif;}
h1 {color: blue;}
a:link {color: navy; text-decoration: underline;}
p {margin-left: 5%; margin-right: 10%;}
p:first-line {font-size: 120%; font-weight: bold;
   color: black;}
p.footnote {font-size: smaller;}
blockquote {font-style: italic;}
blockquote em {font-style: normal;}
pre, code, tt {color: gray; font-family: monospace;}
```

sheet1.css

```
h1 {
        font-size: 1.8em;
        border-bottom: 1px dotted silver;
}
h1:first-letter {
        font-size: 125%;
}
```

sheet2.css

Figure 1-5. A representation of how external stylesheets are applied to documents

And what is the format of an external stylesheet? It's a list of rules, just like those we saw in the previous section and in the example HTML document; but in this case, the rules are saved into their own file. Just remember that no HTML or any other markup language can be included in the stylesheet—only style rules. Here are the contents of an external stylesheet:

```
h1 {color: red;}
h2 {color: maroon; background: white;}
h3 {color: white; background: black;
  font: medium Helvetica;}
```

That's all there is to it—no HTML markup or comments at all, just plain-and-simple style declarations. These are saved into a plain-text file and are usually given an extension of .css, as in sheet1.css.

 An external stylesheet cannot contain any document markup at all, only CSS rules and CSS comments, both of which are explained later in the chapter. The presence of markup in an external stylesheet can cause some or all of it to be ignored.

The filename extension is not required, but some older browsers won't recognize the file as containing a stylesheet unless it actually ends with .css, even if you *do* include the correct type of text/css in the link element. In fact, some web servers won't hand over a file as text/css unless its filename ends with .css, though that can usually be fixed by changing the server's configuration files.

Attributes

For the rest of the `link` tag, the attributes and values are fairly straightforward. `rel` stands for "relation," and in this case, the relation is `stylesheet`. The attribute `type` is always set to `text/css`. This value describes the type of data that will be loaded using the `link` tag. That way, the web browser knows that the stylesheet is a CSS stylesheet, a fact that will determine how the browser deals with the data it imports. After all, there may be other style languages used in the future, so it's important to declare which language you're using.

Next, we find the `href` attribute. The value of this attribute is the URL of your stylesheet. This URL can be either absolute or relative, depending on what works for you. In our example, the URL is relative. It just as easily could have been something like *http://meyerweb.com/sheet1.css*.

Finally, we have a `media` attribute. The value of this attribute is one or more *media descriptors*, which are rules regarding media types and the features of those media, with each rule separated by a comma. Thus, for example, you can use a linked stylesheet in both screen and projection media:

```
<link rel="stylesheet" type="text/css" href="visual-sheet.css"
    media="screen, projection">
```

Media descriptors can get quite complicated, and are explained in detail later in the chapter. For now, we'll stick with the basic media types shown.

Note that there can be more than one linked stylesheet associated with a document. In these cases, only those `link` tags with a `rel` of `stylesheet` will be used in the initial display of the document. Thus, if you wanted to link two stylesheets named *basic.css* and *splash.css*, it would look like this:

```
<link rel="stylesheet" type="text/css" href="basic.css">
<link rel="stylesheet" type="text/css" href="splash.css">
```

This will cause the browser to load both stylesheets, combine the rules from each, and apply them all to the document. For example:

```
<link rel="stylesheet" type="text/css" href="basic.css">
<link rel="stylesheet" type="text/css" href="splash.css">

<p class="a1">This paragraph will be gray only if styles from the
stylesheet 'basic.css' are applied.</p>
<p class="b1">This paragraph will be gray only if styles from the
stylesheet 'splash.css' are applied.</p>
```

The one attribute that is not in this example markup, but could be, is the `title` attribute. This attribute is not often used, but it could become important in the future and, if used improperly, can have unexpected effects. Why? We will explore that in the next section.

Alternate stylesheets

It's also possible to define *alternate stylesheets*. These are defined by making the value of the `rel` attribute `alternate stylesheet`, and they are used in document presentation only if selected by the user.

Should a browser be able to use alternate stylesheets, it will use the values of the `link` element's `title` attributes to generate a list of style alternatives. So you could write the following:

```
<link rel="stylesheet" type="text/css"
    href="sheet1.css" title="Default">
<link rel="alternate stylesheet" type="text/css"
    href="bigtext.css" title="Big Text">
<link rel="alternate stylesheet" type="text/css"
    href="zany.css" title="Crazy colors!">
```

Users could then pick the style they want to use, and the browser would switch from the first one, labeled "Default" in this case, to whichever the user picked. Figure 1-6 shows one way in which this selection mechanism might be accomplished (and in fact was, early in the resurgence of CSS).

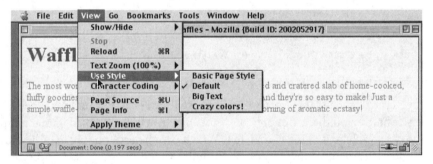

Figure 1-6. A browser offering alternate stylesheet selection

 As of late 2016, alternate stylesheets were supported in most Gecko-based browsers like Firefox, and in Opera. They could be supported in the Internet Explorer family through the use of Java-Script but are not natively supported by those browsers. The Web-Kit family did not support selecting alternate stylesheets. Compare this to the age of the browser shown in Figure 1-6--it's almost shocking.

It is also possible to group alternate stylesheets together by giving them the same `title` value. Thus, you make it possible for the user to pick a different presentation for your site in both screen and print media:

```
<link rel="stylesheet" type="text/css"
    href="sheet1.css" title="Default" media="screen">
<link rel="stylesheet" type="text/css"
    href="print-sheet1.css" title="Default" media="print">
<link rel="alternate stylesheet" type="text/css"
    href="bigtext.css" title="Big Text" media="screen">
<link rel="alternate stylesheet" type="text/css"
    href="print-bigtext.css" title="Big Text" media="print">
```

If a user selects "Big Text" from the alternate stylesheet selection mechanism in a conforming user agent, then *bigtext.css* will be used to style the document in the screen medium, and *print-bigtext.css* will be used in the print medium. Neither *sheet1.css* nor *print-sheet1.css* will be used in any medium.

Why is that? Because if you give a `link` with a `rel` of `stylesheet` a title, then you are designating that stylesheet as a *preferred stylesheet*. This means that its use is preferred to alternate stylesheets, and it will be used when the document is first displayed. Once you select an alternate stylesheet, however, the preferred stylesheet will *not* be used.

Furthermore, if you designate a number of stylesheets as preferred, then all but one of them will be ignored. Consider the following code example:

```
<link rel="stylesheet" type="text/css"
    href="sheet1.css" title="Default Layout">
<link rel="stylesheet" type="text/css"
    href="sheet2.css" title="Default Text Sizes">
<link rel="stylesheet" type="text/css"
    href="sheet3.css" title="Default Colors">
```

All three `link` elements now refer to preferred stylesheets, thanks to the presence of a `title` attribute on all three, but only one of them will actually be used in that manner. The other two will be ignored completely. Which two? There's no way to be certain, as HTML doesn't provide a method of determining which preferred stylesheets should be ignored and which should be used.

If you don't give a stylesheet a title, then it becomes a *persistent stylesheet* and is always used in the display of the document. Often, this is exactly what an author wants.

The style Element

The `style` element is one way to include a stylesheet, and it appears in the document itself:

```
<style type="text/css">...</style>
```

`style` should always use the attribute `type`; in the case of a CSS document, the correct value is `"text/css"`, just as it was with the `link` element.

The style element should always start with `<style type="text/css">`, as shown in the preceding example. This is followed by one or more styles and is finished with a closing `</style>` tag. It is also possible to give the style element a media attribute, which functions in the same manner as previously discussed for linked stylesheets.

The styles between the opening and closing style tags are referred to as the *document stylesheet* or the *embedded stylesheet* (because this kind of stylesheet is embedded within the document). It will contain many of the styles that will apply to the document, but it can also contain multiple links to external stylesheets using the @import directive.

The @import Directive

Now we'll discuss the stuff that is found inside the style tag. First, we have something very similar to link: the @import directive:

```
@import url(sheet2.css);
```

Just like link, @import can be used to direct the web browser to load an external stylesheet and use its styles in the rendering of the HTML document. The only major difference is in the syntax and placement of the command. As you can see, @import is found inside the style container. It must be placed before the other CSS rules or it won't work at all. Consider this example:

```
<style type="text/css">
@import url(styles.css); /* @import comes first */
h1 {color: gray;}
</style>
```

Like link, there can be more than one @import statement in a document. Unlike link, however, the stylesheets of every @import directive will be loaded and used; there is no way to designate alternate stylesheets with @import. So, given the following markup:

```
@import url(sheet2.css);
@import url(blueworld.css);
@import url(zany.css);
```

all three external stylesheets will be loaded, and all of their style rules will be used in the display of the document.

As with link, you can restrict imported stylesheets to one or more media by providing media descriptors after the stylesheet's URL:

```
@import url(sheet2.css) all;
@import url(blueworld.css) screen;
@import url(zany.css) projection, print;
```

As noted in "The link Tag" on page 8, media descriptors can get quite complicated, and are explained in detail in Chapter 20, *Media-Dependent Styles*.

`@import` can be highly useful if you have an external stylesheet that needs to use the styles found in other external stylesheets. Since external stylesheets cannot contain any document markup, the `link` element can't be used—but `@import` can. Therefore, you might have an external stylesheet that contains the following:

```
@import url(http://example.org/library/layout.css);
@import url(basic-text.css);
@import url(printer.css) print;
body {color: red;}
h1 {color: blue;}
```

Well, maybe not those exact styles, but hopefully you get the idea. Note the use of both absolute and relative URLs in the previous example. Either URL form can be used, just as with `link`.

Note also that the `@import` directives appear at the beginning of the stylesheet, as they did in the example document. CSS requires the `@import` directive to come before any other rules in a stylesheet. An `@import` that comes after other rules (e.g., `body {color: red;}`) will be ignored by conforming user agents.

 Older versions of Internet Explorer for Windows do not ignore any `@import` directive, even those that come after other rules. Since other browsers do ignore improperly placed `@import` directives, it is easy to mistakenly place the `@import` directive incorrectly and thus alter the display in other browsers.

HTTP Linking

There is another, far more obscure way to associate CSS with a document: you can link the two via HTTP headers.

Under Apache, this can be accomplished by adding a reference to the CSS file in a *.htaccess* file. For example:

```
Header add Link "</ui/testing.css>;rel=stylesheet;type=text/css"
```

This will cause supporting browsers to associate the referenced stylesheet with any documents served from under that *.htaccess* file. The browser will then treat it as if it were a linked stylesheet. Alternatively, and probably more efficiently, you can add an equivalent rule to the server's *httpd.conf* file:

```
<Directory /path/to/ /public/html/directory>
Header add Link "</ui/testing.css>;rel=stylesheet;type=text/css"
</Directory>
```

The effect is exactly the same in supporting browsers. The only difference is in where you declare the linking.

You probably noticed the use of the term "supporting browsers." As of late 2017, the widely used browsers that support HTTP linking of stylesheets are the Firefox family and Opera. That restricts this technique mostly to development environments based on one of those browsers. In that situation, you can use HTTP linking on the test server to mark when you're on the development site as opposed to the public site. It's also an interesting way to hide styles from the WebKit and Internet Explorer families, assuming you have a reason to do so.

 There are equivalents to this technique in common scripting languages such as PHP and IIS, both of which allow the author to emit HTTP headers. It's also possible to use such languages to explicitly write a `link` element into the document based on the server offering up the document. This is a more robust approach in terms of browser support: every browser supports the `link` element.

Inline Styles

For cases where you want to just assign a few styles to one individual element, without the need for embedded or external stylesheets, employ the HTML attribute `style` to set an inline style:

```
<p style="color: gray;">The most wonderful of all breakfast foods is
the waffle—a ridged and cratered slab of home-cooked, fluffy goodness...
</p>
```

The `style` attribute can be associated with any HTML tag whatsoever, except for those tags that are found outside of `body` (`head` or `title`, for instance).

The syntax of a `style` attribute is fairly ordinary. In fact, it looks very much like the declarations found in the `style` container, except here the curly braces are replaced by double quotation marks. So `<p style="color: maroon; background: yellow;">` will set the text color to be maroon and the background to be yellow *for that paragraph only*. No other part of the document will be affected by this declaration.

Note that you can only place a declaration block, not an entire stylesheet, inside an inline `style` attribute. Therefore, you can't put an `@import` into a `style` attribute, nor can you include any complete rules. The only thing you can put into the value of a `style` attribute is what might go between the curly braces of a rule.

Use of the `style` attribute is not generally recommended. Indeed, it is very unlikely to appear in XML languages other than HTML. Many of the primary advantages of CSS —the ability to organize centralized styles that control an entire document's appearance or the appearance of all documents on a web server—are negated when you place styles into a `style` attribute. In many ways, inline styles are not much better than the `font` tag, although they do have a good deal more flexibility in terms of what visual effects they can apply.

Stylesheet Contents

So after all of that, what about the actual contents of the stylesheets? You know, stuff like this:

```
h1 {color: maroon;}
body {background: yellow;}
```

Styles such as these comprise the bulk of any embedded stylesheet—simple and complex, short and long. Rarely will you have a document where the `style` element does not contain any rules, although it's possible to have a simple list of `@import` declarations with no actual rules like those shown in the previous example.

Before we get going on the rest of the book, there are a few top-level things to cover regarding what can or can't go into a stylesheet.

Markup

There is no markup in stylesheets. This might seem obvious, but you'd be surprised. The one exception is HTML comment markup, which is permitted inside `style` elements for historical reasons:

```
<style type="text/css"><!--
h1 {color: maroon;}
body {background: yellow;}
--></style>
```

That's it.

Rule Structure

To illustrate the concept of rules in more detail, let's break down the structure.

Each rule has two fundamental parts: the *selector* and the *declaration block*. The declaration block is composed of one or more *declarations*, and each declaration is a pairing of a *property* and a *value*. Every stylesheet is made up of a series of rules. Figure 1-7 shows the parts of a rule.

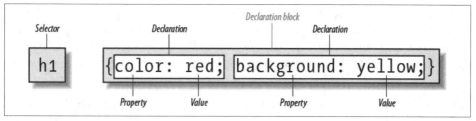

Figure 1-7. The structure of a rule

The selector, shown on the left side of the rule, defines which piece of the document will be affected. In Figure 1-7, h1 elements are selected. If the selector were p, then all p (paragraph) elements would be selected.

The right side of the rule contains the declaration block, which is made up of one or more declarations. Each declaration is a combination of a CSS property and a value of that property. In Figure 1-7, the declaration block contains two declarations. The first states that this rule will cause parts of the document to have a color of red, and the second states that part of the document will have a background of yellow. So, all of the h1 elements in the document (defined by the selector) will be styled in red text with a yellow background.

Vendor prefixing

Sometimes you'll see pieces of CSS with dashes and labels in front of them, like this: -o-border-image. These are called *vendor prefixes*, and are a way for browser vendors to mark properties, values, or other bits of CSS as being experimental or proprietary (or both). As of late 2016, there were a few vendor prefixes in the wild, with the most common being shown in Table 1-1.

Table 1-1. Some common vendor prefixes

Prefix	Vendor
-epub-	International Digital Publishing Forum ePub format
-moz-	Mozilla-based browsers (e.g., Firefox)
-ms-	Microsoft Internet Explorer
-o-	Opera-based browsers
-webkit-	WebKit-based browsers (e.g., Safari and Chrome)

As Table 1-1 implies, the generally accepted format of a vendor prefix is a dash, a label, and a dash, although a few prefixes erroneously omit the first dash.

The uses and abuses of vendor prefixes are long, tortuous, and beyond the scope of this book. Suffice to say that they started out as a way for vendors to test out new features, thus helping speed interoperability without worrying about being locked into legacy behaviors that were incompatible with other browsers. This avoided a whole class of problems that nearly strangled CSS in its infancy. Unfortunately, pre-fixed properties were then publicly deployed by web authors and ended up causing a whole new class of problems.

As of late 2016, vendor prefixes are a dwindling breed, with old prefixed properties and values being slowly removed from browser implementations. It's entirely possible that you'll never write prefixed CSS, but you may encounter it in the wild, or inherit it in a legacy codebase.

Whitespace Handling

CSS is basically insensitive to whitespace between rules, and largely insensitive to whitespace within rules, although there are a few exceptions.

In general, CSS treats whitespace just like HTML does: any sequence of whitespace characters is collapsed to a single space for parsing purposes. Thus, you can format the hypothetical `rainbow` rule in the following ways:

```
rainbow: infrared  red  orange  yellow  green  blue  indigo  violet  ultraviolet;
rainbow:
   infrared  red  orange  yellow  green  blue  indigo  violet  ultraviolet;
rainbow:
   infrared
   red
   orange
   yellow
   green
   blue
   indigo
   violet
   ultraviolet
   ;
```

…as well as any other separation patterns you can think up. The only restriction is that the separating characters be whitespace: an empty space, a tab, or a newline, alone or in combination, as many as you like.

Similarly, you can format series of rules with whitespace in any fashion you like. These are just five of an effectively infinite number of possibilities:

```
html{color:black;}
body {background: white;}
p {
  color: gray;}
h2 {
    color : silver ;
   }
ol
```

```
{
    color
       :
    silver
       ;
}
```

As you can see from the first rule, whitespace can be largely omitted. Indeed, this is usually the case with *minified* CSS, which is CSS that's had every last possible bit of extraneous whitespace removed. The rules after the first two use progressively more extravagant amounts of whitespace until, in the last rule, pretty much everything that can be separated onto its own line has been.

All of these approaches are valid, so you should pick the formatting that makes the most sense—that is, is easiest to read—in your eyes, and stick with it.

There are some places where the presence of whitespace is actually required. The most common example is when separating a list of keywords in a value, as in the hypothetical rainbow examples. Those must always be whitespace-separated.

CSS Comments

CSS does allow for comments. These are very similar to C/C++ comments in that they are surrounded by /* and */:

```
/* This is a CSS1 comment */
```

Comments can span multiple lines, just as in C++:

```
/* This is a CSS1 comment, and it
can be several lines long without
any problem whatsoever. */
```

It's important to remember that CSS comments cannot be nested. So, for example, this would not be correct:

```
/* This is a comment, in which we find
  another comment, which is WRONG
    /* Another comment */
  and back to the first comment */
```

 One way to create "nested" comments accidentally is to temporarily comment out a large block of a stylesheet that already contains a comment. Since CSS doesn't permit nested comments, the "outside" comment will end where the "inside" comment ends.

Unfortunately, there is no "rest of the line" comment pattern such as // or # (the latter of which is reserved for ID selectors anyway). The only comment pattern in CSS is /* */. Therefore, if you wish to place comments on the same line as markup, then you need to be careful about how you place them. For example, this is the correct way to do it:

```
h1 {color: gray;}   /* This CSS comment is several lines */
h2 {color: silver;} /* long, but since it is alongside */
p {color: white;}   /* actual styles, each line needs to */
pre {color: gray;}  /* be wrapped in comment markers. */
```

Given this example, if each line isn't marked off, then most of the stylesheet will become part of the comment and thus will not work:

```
h1 {color: gray;}   /* This CSS comment is several lines
h2 {color: silver;} long, but since it is not wrapped
p {color: white;}    in comment markers, the last three
pre {color: gray;}   styles are part of the comment. */
```

In this example, only the first rule (h1 {color: gray;}) will be applied to the document. The rest of the rules, as part of the comment, are ignored by the browser's rendering engine.

 CSS comments are treated by the CSS parser as if they do not exist at all, and so do not count as whitespace for parsing purposes. This means you can put them into the middle of rules—even right inside declarations!

Media Queries

With *media queries*, an author can define the media environment in which a given stylesheet is used by the browser. In the past, this was handled by setting media types via the media attribute on the link element, on a style element, or in the media descriptor of an @import or @media declaration. Media queries take this concept several steps further by allowing authors to choose stylesheets based on the features of a given media type, using what are called *media descriptors*.

Usage

Media queries can be employed in the following places:

- The media attribute of a link element
- The media attribute of a style element
- The media descriptor portion of an @import declaration
- The media descriptor portion of an @media declaration

Queries can range from simple media types to complicated combinations of media types and features.

Simple Media Queries

Let's look at some simple media blocks before covering all of the possibilities of media queries. Suppose we want some differing styles for situations where the styles are shown in a projection setting, such as a slide show. Here are two very simple bits of CSS:

```
h1 {color: maroon;}
@media projection {
    body {background: yellow;}
}
```

In this example, h1 elements will be colored maroon in all media, but the body element will get a yellow background only in a projection medium.

You can have as many @media blocks as you like in a given stylesheet, each with its own set of media descriptors (see later in this chapter for details). You could even encapsulate all of your rules in an @media block if you chose, like this:

```
@media all {
    h1 {color: maroon;}
    body {background: yellow;}
}
```

However, since this is exactly the same as if you stripped off the first and last line shown, there isn't a whole lot of point to doing so.

> The indentation shown in this section was solely for purposes of clarity. You do not have to indent the rules found inside an @media block, but you're welcome to do so if it makes your CSS easier for you to read.

The place where we saw projection and all in those examples is where media queries are set. These queries rely on a combination of terms that describe the type of media to be considered, as well as descriptions of the media's parameters (e.g., resolution or display height), to determine when blocks of CSS should be applied.

Media Types

The most basic form of media queries are *media types*, which first appeared in CSS2. These are simple labels for different kinds of media:

all
    Use in all presentational media.

`print`

Use when printing the document for sighted users and also when displaying a print preview of the document.

`screen`

Use when presenting the document in a screen medium like a desktop computer monitor. All web browsers running on such systems are screen-medium user agents.

 As of this writing, a couple of browsers also support `projection`, which allows a document to be presented as a slideshow. Several mobile-device browsers support the `handheld` type, but not in consistent ways.

Multiple media types can be specified using a comma-separated list. The following four examples are all equivalent ways of applying a stylesheet (or a block of rules) in both screen and print media:

```
<link type="text/css" href="frobozz.css" media="screen, print">
<style type="text/css" media="screen, print">...</style>

@import url(frobozz.css) screen, print;
@media screen, print {...}
```

Things get interesting when you add feature-specific descriptors, such as values that describe the resolution or color depth of a given medium, to these media types.

Media Descriptors

The placement of media queries will be very familiar to any author who has ever set a media type on a `link` element or an `@import` declaration. Here are two essentially equivalent ways of applying an external stylesheet when rendering the document on a color printer:

```
<link href="print-color.css" type="text/css"
    media="print and (color)" rel="stylesheet">

@import url(print-color.css) print and (color);
```

Anywhere a media type can be used, a media query can be used. This means that, following on the examples of the previous section, it is possible to list more than one query in a comma-separated list:

```
<link href="print-color.css" type="text/css"
    media="print and (color), screen and (color-depth: 8)" rel="stylesheet">

@import url(print-color.css) print and (color), screen and (color-depth: 8);
```

In any situation where even one of the media queries evaluates to "true," the associated stylesheet is applied. Thus, given the previous @import, print-color.css will be applied if rendering to a color printer *or* to a sufficiently colorful screen environment. If printing on a black-and-white printer, both queries will evaluate to "false", and print-color.css will not be applied to the document. The same holds true in any screen medium, and so on.

Each media descriptor is composed of a media type and one or more listed media features, with each media feature descriptor enclosed in parentheses. If no media type is provided, then it is assumed to be all, which makes the following two examples equivalent:

```
@media all and (min-resolution: 96dpi) {...}

@media (min-resolution: 96dpi) {...}
```

Generally speaking, a media feature descriptor is formatted like a property-value pair in CSS. There are a few differences, most notably that some features can be specified without an accompanying value. Thus, for example, any color-based medium will be matched using (color), whereas any color medium using a 16-bit color depth is matched using (color: 16). In effect, the use of a descriptor without a value is a true/false test for that descriptor: (color) means "is this medium in color?"

Multiple feature descriptors can be linked with the and logical keyword. In fact, there are two logical keywords in media queries:

and

> Links together two or more media features in such a way that all of them must be true for the query to be true. For example, (color) and (orientation: land scape) and (min-device-width: 800px) means that all three conditions must be satisfied: if the media environment has color, is in landscape orientation, and the device's display is at least 800 pixels wide, then the stylesheet is used.

not

> Negates the entire query such that if all of the conditions are true, then the stylesheet is *not* applied. For example, not (color) and (orientation: landscape) and (min-device-width: 800px) means that if the three conditions are satisfied, the statement is negated. Thus, if the media environment has color, is in landscape orientation, and the device's display is at least 800 pixels wide, then the stylesheet is *not* used. In all other cases, it will be used.

Note that the not keyword can only be used at the beginning of a media query. It is *not* legal to write something like (color) and not (min-device-width: 800px). In such cases, the query will be ignored. Note also that browsers too old to understand media queries will always skip a stylesheet whose media descriptor starts with not.

There is no OR keyword for use in media queries. Instead, the commas that separate a list of queries serve the function of an OR—`screen, print` means "apply if the media is screen or print." Instead of `screen and (max-color: 2) or (monochrome)`, which is invalid and thus ignored, you should write `screen and (max-color: 2), screen and (monochrome)`.

There is one more keyword, `only`, which is designed to create deliberate backward incompatibility (yes, really):

`only`

> Used to hide a stylesheet from browsers too old to understand media queries. For example, to apply a stylesheet in all media, but only in those browsers that understand media queries, you write something like `@import url(new.css) only all`. In browsers that do understand media queries, the `only` keyword is ignored and the stylesheet is applied. In browsers that do not understand media queries, the `only` keyword creates an apparent media type of `only all`, which is not valid. Thus, the stylesheet is not applied in such browsers. Note that the `only` keyword can only be used at the beginning of a media query.

Media Feature Descriptors and Value Types

So far we've seen a number of media feature descriptors in the examples, but not a complete list. Following is a list of all possible descriptors (current as of late 2017):

- width
- min-width
- max-width
- device-width
- min-device-width
- max-device-width
- height
- min-height
- max-height
- device-height
- min-device-height
- max-device-height

- aspect-ratio
- min-aspect-ratio
- max-aspect-ratio
- device-aspect-ratio
- min-device-aspect-ratio
- max-device-aspect-ratio
- color
- min-color
- max-color

- color-index
- min-color-index
- max-color-index
- monochrome
- min-monochrome
- max-monochrome
- resolution
- min-resolution
- max-resolution
- orientation
- scan
- grid

In addition, two new value types were added:

- *<ratio>*
- *<resolution>*

A complete description of these descriptors and values, and how to use them, can be found in Chapter 20.

Feature Queries

Between 2015 and 2016, CSS gained the ability to apply blocks of CSS when certain CSS property-value combinations were supported by the user agent. These are known as *feature queries*.

They're very similar to media queries in structure. Consider a situation where you want to only apply color to element if color is a supported property. (Which it certainly should be!) That would look like this:

```
@supports (color: black) {
    body {color: black;}
    h1 {color: purple;}
    h2 {color: navy;}
}
```

That says, in effect, "If you recognize and can do something with the property-value combination color: black, apply these styles. Otherwise, skip these styles." In user agents that don't understand @supports, the entire block is skipped over.

Feature queries are a perfect way to progressively enhance your styles. For example, suppose you want to add some grid layout to your existing float-and-inline-block layout. You can keep the old layout scheme, and then later in the stylesheet include a block like this:

```
@supports (display: grid ) {
    section#main {display: grid;}
    /* styles to switch off old layout positioning */
    /* grid layout styles */
}
```

This block of styles will be applied in browsers that understand grid display, overriding the old styles that governed page layout, and then applying the styles needed to make things work in a grid-based future. Browsers too old to understand grid layout will most likely also be too old to understand @supports, so they'll skip the whole block entirely, as if it had never been there.

Feature queries can be embedded inside each other, and indeed can be embedded inside media queries, as well as vice versa. You could write screen and print styles based on flexible-box layout, and wrap those media blocks in an `@supports` (dis play: flex) block:

```
@supports (display: flex) {
    @media screen {
        /* screen flexbox styles go here */
    }
    @media print {
        /* print flexbox styles go here */
    }
}
```

Conversely, you could add `@supports()` blocks inside various responsive-design media query blocks:

```
@media screen and (max-width: 30em){
    @supports (display: flex) {
        /* small-screen flexbox styles go here */
    }
}
@media screen and (min-width: 30em) {
    @supports (display: flex) {
        /* large-screen flexbox styles go here */
    }
}
```

How you organize these blocks is really up to you.

As with media queries, feature queries also permit logical operators. Suppose we want to apply styles only if a user agent supports both grid layout *and* CSS shapes. Here's how that might go:

```
@supports (display: grid) and (shape-outside: circle()) {
    /* grid-and-shape styles go here */
}
```

This is essentially equivalent to writing the following:

```
@supports (display: grid) {
    @supports (shape-outside: circle()) {
        /* grid-and-shape styles go here */
    }
}
```

However, there's more than "and" operations available. CSS Shapes (covered in detail in Chapter 10) are a good example of why "or" is useful, because for a long time Web-Kit only supported CSS shapes via vendor-prefixed properties. So if you want to use shapes, you can use a feature query like this:

```
@supports (shape-outside: circle()) or
          (-webkit-shape-outside: circle()) {
    /* shape styles go here */
}
```

You'd still have to make sure to use both prefixed and unprefixed versions of the shape properties, but this would let you add support for those properties backward in the WebKit release line while supporting other browsers that also support shapes, but not via prefixed properties.

All this is incredibly handy because there are situations where you might want to apply different properties than those you're testing. So, to go back to grid layout for a second, you might want to change the margins and so forth on your layout elements when grid is in use. Here's a simplified version of that approach:

```
div#main {overflow: hidden;}
div.column {float: left; margin-right: 1em;}
div.column:last-child {margin-right: 0;}

@supports (display: grid) {
    div#main {display: grid; grid-gap: 1em 0;
            overflow: visible;}
    div#main div.column {margin: 0;}
}
```

It's possible to use negation as well. For example, you could apply the following styles in situations where grid layout is *not* supported:

```
@supports not (display: grid) {
    /* grid-not-supported styles go here */
}
```

You can combine your logical operators into a single query, but parentheses are required to keep the logic straight. Suppose we want a set of styles to be applied when color is supported, and when one of either grid or flexible box layout is supported. That's written like this:

```
@supports (color: black) and ((display: flex) or (display: grid)) {
        /* styles go here */
}
```

Notice how there's another set of parentheses around the "or" part of the logic, enclosing the grid and flex tests. Those extra parentheses are required. Without them, the entire expression will fail, and the styles inside the block will be skipped. In other words, *don't* do this:

```
@supports (color: black) and (display: flex) or (display: grid) {
```

Finally, you might wonder why both a property and value are required in feature query tests. After all, if you're using shapes, all you need to test for is shape-outside, right? It's because a browser can easily support a property without supporting all its values. Grid layout is a perfect example for this. Suppose you could test for grid support like this:

```
@supports (display) {
    /* grid styles go here */
}
```

Well, even Internet Explorer 4 supported `display`. Any browser that understands `@supports` will certainly understand `display` and many of its values—but maybe not `grid`. That's why property and value are always tested in feature queries.

 Remember that these are *feature* queries, not *correctness* queries. A browser can understand the feature you're testing for, but implement it with bugs. So you're not getting an assurance from the browser that it supports something correctly. All a positive feature-query result means is that the browser understands what you've said and makes some sort of attempt to support it.

Summary

With CSS, it is possible to completely change the way elements are presented by a user agent. This can be executed at a basic level with the `display` property, and in a different way by associating stylesheets with a document. The user will never know whether this is done via an external or embedded stylesheet, or even with an inline style. The real importance of external stylesheets is the way in which they allow authors to put all of a site's presentation information in one place, and point all of the documents to that place. This not only makes site updates and maintenance a breeze, but it helps to save bandwidth, since all of the presentation is removed from documents. With `@supports()`, it's even possible to do some basic progressive enhancement in native CSS.

To make the most of the power of CSS, authors need to know how to associate a set of styles with the elements in a document. To fully understand how CSS can do all of this, authors need a firm grasp of the way CSS selects pieces of a document for styling, which is the subject of the next chapter.

CHAPTER 2

Selectors

One of the primary advantages of CSS is its ability to easily apply a set of styles to all elements of the same type. Unimpressed? Consider this: by editing a single line of CSS, you can change the colors of all your headings. Don't like the blue you're using? Change that one line of code, and they can all be purple, yellow, maroon, or any other color you desire. That lets you, the designer, focus on design, rather than grunt work. The next time you're in a meeting and someone wants to see headings with a different shade of green, just edit your style and hit Reload. *Voilà!* The results are accomplished in seconds and there for everyone to see.

CSS can't solve all your problems—you can't use it to change the colorspace of your PNGs, for example, at least not yet—but it can make some global changes much easier. So let's begin with selectors and structure.

Basic Style Rules

As stated, a central feature of CSS is its ability to apply certain rules to an entire set of element types in a document. For example, let's say that you want to make the text of all h2 elements appear gray. Using old-school HTML, you'd have to do this by inserting `<font color="gray">...</font>` tags inside all your h2 elements. Using the `style` attribute, which is also bad practice, would require you to include `style="color: gray;"` in all your h2 elements, like this:

```
<h2><font color="gray">This is h2 text</font></h2>
<h2 style="color: gray;">This is h2 text</h2>
```

This will be a tedious process if your document contains a lot of h2 elements. Worse, if you later decide that you want all those h2s to be green instead of gray, you'd have to start the manual tagging all over again. (Yes, this is really how it used to be done!)

CSS allows you to create rules that are simple to change, edit, and apply to all the text elements you define (the next section will explain how these rules work). For example, you can write this rule once to make all your h2 elements gray:

```
h2 {color: gray;}
```

If you want to change all h2 text to another color—say, silver—just alter the value:

```
h2 {color: silver;}
```

Element Selectors

An *element selector* is most often an HTML element, but not always. For example, if a CSS file contains styles for an XML document, the element selectors might look something like this:

```
quote {color: gray;}
bib {color: red;}
booktitle {color: purple;}
myElement {color: red;}
```

In other words, the elements of the document serve as the most basic selectors. In XML, a selector could be anything, since XML allows for the creation of new markup languages that can have just about anything as an element name. If you're styling an HTML document, on the other hand, the selector will generally be one of the many HTML elements such as p, h3, em, a, or even html itself. For example:

```
html {color: black;}
h1 {color: gray;}
h2 {color: silver;}
```

The results of this stylesheet are shown in Figure 2-1.

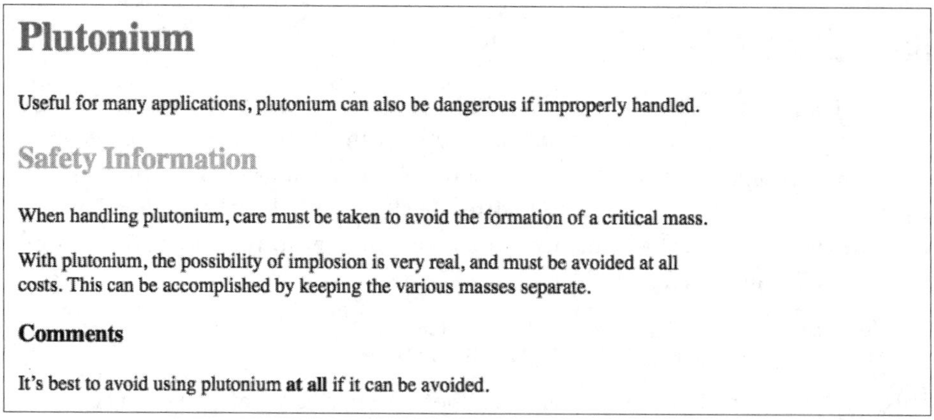

Plutonium

Useful for many applications, plutonium can also be dangerous if improperly handled.

Safety Information

When handling plutonium, care must be taken to avoid the formation of a critical mass.

With plutonium, the possibility of implosion is very real, and must be avoided at all costs. This can be accomplished by keeping the various masses separate.

Comments

It's best to avoid using plutonium **at all** if it can be avoided.

Figure 2-1. Simple styling of a simple document

Once you've globally applied styles directly to elements, you can shift those styles from one element to another. Let's say you decide that the paragraph text, not the h1 elements, in Figure 2-1 should be gray. No problem. Just change the h1 selector to p:

```
html {color: black;}
p {color: gray;}
h2 {color: silver;}
```

The results are shown in Figure 2-2.

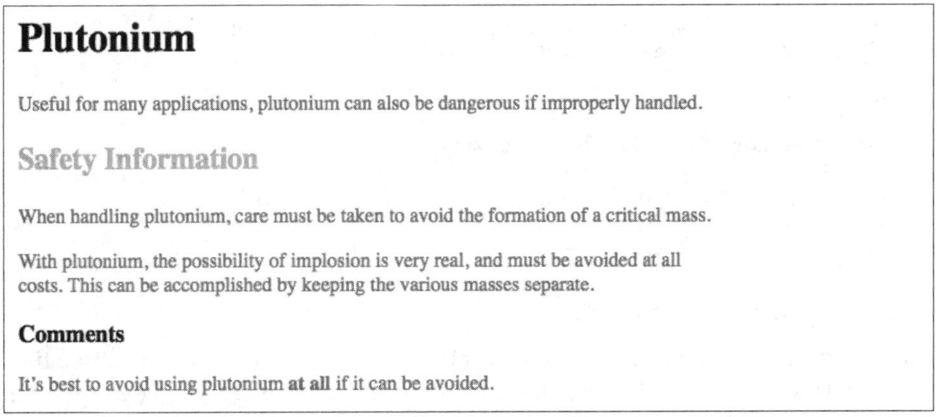

Plutonium

Useful for many applications, plutonium can also be dangerous if improperly handled.

Safety Information

When handling plutonium, care must be taken to avoid the formation of a critical mass.

With plutonium, the possibility of implosion is very real, and must be avoided at all costs. This can be accomplished by keeping the various masses separate.

Comments

It's best to avoid using plutonium **at all** if it can be avoided.

Figure 2-2. Moving a style from one element to another

Declarations and Keywords

The declaration block contains one or more declarations. A declaration is always formatted as a property followed by a colon and then a value followed by a semicolon. The colon and semicolon can be followed by zero or more spaces. In nearly all cases, a *value* is either a single keyword or a space-separated list of one or more keywords that are permitted for that property. If you use an incorrect property or value in a declaration, the whole rule will be ignored. Thus, the following two declarations would fail:

```
brain-size: 2cm;      /* unknown property 'brain-size' */
color: ultraviolet;  /* unknown value 'ultraviolet' */
```

In an instance where you can use more than one keyword for a property's value, the keywords are usually separated by spaces, with some cases requiring slashes (/) or commas. Not every property can accept multiple keywords, but many, such as the font property, can. Let's say you want to define medium-sized Helvetica for paragraph text, as illustrated in Figure 2-3.

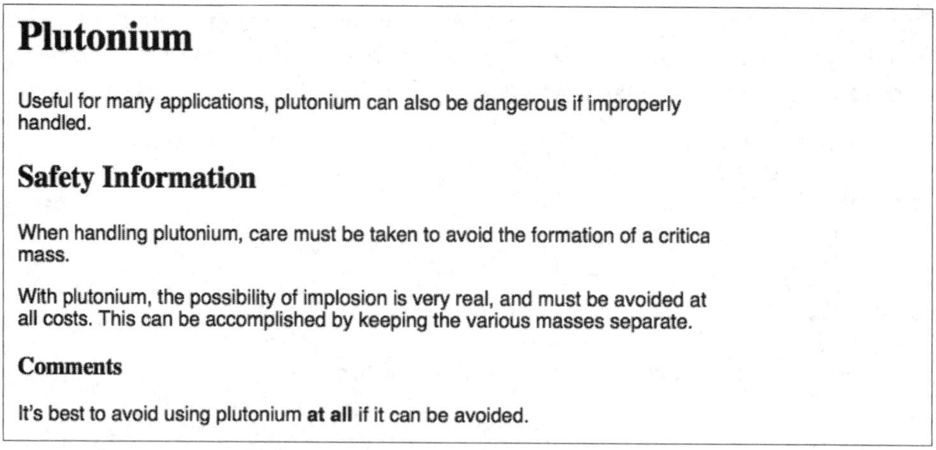

Plutonium

Useful for many applications, plutonium can also be dangerous if improperly handled.

Safety Information

When handling plutonium, care must be taken to avoid the formation of a critical mass.

With plutonium, the possibility of implosion is very real, and must be avoided at all costs. This can be accomplished by keeping the various masses separate.

Comments

It's best to avoid using plutonium **at all** if it can be avoided.

Figure 2-3. The results of a property value with multiple keywords

The rule would read as follows:

```
p {font: medium Helvetica;}
```

Note the space between medium and Helvetica, each of which is a keyword (the first is the font's size and the second is the actual font name). The space allows the user agent to distinguish between the two keywords and apply them correctly. The semicolon indicates that the declaration has been concluded.

These space-separated words are referred to as *keywords* because, taken together, they form the value of the property in question. For instance, consider the following fictional rule:

```
rainbow: red orange yellow green blue indigo violet;
```

There is no such property as rainbow, but the example is useful for illustrative purposes. The value of rainbow is red orange yellow green blue indigo violet, and the seven keywords add up to a single, unique value. We can redefine the value for rainbow as follows:

```
rainbow: infrared red orange yellow green blue indigo violet ultraviolet;
```

Now we have a new value for rainbow composed of nine keywords instead of seven. Although the two values look mostly the same, they are as unique and different as zero and one. This may seem an abstract point, but it's critical to understanding some of the subtler effects of specificity and the cascade (covered in later in this book).

As we've seen, CSS keywords are usually separated by spaces. In CSS2.1 there was one exception: in the CSS property font, there is exactly one place where a forward slash (/) could be used to separate two specific keywords. Here's an example:

```
h2 {font: large/150% sans-serif;}
```

The slash separates the keywords that set the element's font size and line height. This is the only place the slash is allowed to appear in the font declaration. All of the other keywords allowed for font are separated by spaces.

The slash has since worked its way into a number of other properties' values. These include, but may not always be limited to the following:

- background
- border-image
- border-radius
- grid
- grid-area
- grid-column
- grid-row
- grid-template
- mask-border

There are also some keywords that are separated by commas. When declaring multiple values, such as multiple background images, transition properties, and shadows, the declarations are separated with commas. Additionally, parameters in functions, such as linear gradients and transforms, are comma separated, as the following example shows:

```
.box {box-shadow: inset -1px -1px white,
                  3px 3px 3px rgba(0,0,0,0.2);
      background-image: url(myimage.png),
          linear-gradient(180deg, #FFF 0%, #000 100%);
      transform: translate(100px, 200px);
}
a:hover {transition: color, background-color 200ms ease-in 50ms;}
```

Those are the basics of simple declarations, but they can get much more complex. The next section begins to show you just how powerful CSS can be.

Grouping

So far, we've seen fairly simple techniques for applying a single style to a single selector. But what if you want the same style to apply to multiple elements? If that's the case, you'll want to use more than one selector or apply more than one style to an element or group of elements.

Grouping Selectors

Let's say you want both h2 elements and paragraphs to have gray text. The easiest way to accomplish this is to use the following declaration:

```
h2, p {color: gray;}
```

By placing the h2 and p selectors on the left side of the rule and separating them with a comma, you've defined a rule where the style on the right (color: gray;) applies to the elements referenced by both selectors. The comma tells the browser that there are two different selectors involved in the rule. Leaving out the comma would give the rule a completely different meaning, which we'll explore in "Descendant Selectors" on page 56.

There are really no limits to how many selectors you can group together. For example, if you want to display a large number of elements in gray, you might use something like the following rule:

```
body, table, th, td, h1, h2, h3, h4, p, pre, strong, em, b, i {color: gray;}
```

Grouping allows an author to drastically compact certain types of style assignments, which makes for a shorter stylesheet. The following alternatives produce exactly the same result, but it's pretty obvious which one is easier to type:

```
h1 {color: purple;}
h2 {color: purple;}
h3 {color: purple;}
h4 {color: purple;}
h5 {color: purple;}
h6 {color: purple;}

h1, h2, h3, h4, h5, h6 {color: purple;}
```

Grouping allows for some interesting choices. For example, all of the groups of rules in the following example are equivalent—each merely shows a different way of grouping both selectors and declarations:

```
/* group 1 */
h1 {color: silver; background: white;}
h2 {color: silver; background: gray;}
h3 {color: white; background: gray;}
h4 {color: silver; background: white;}
b {color: gray; background: white;}

/* group 2 */
h1, h2, h4 {color: silver;}
h2, h3 {background: gray;}
h1, h4, b {background: white;}
h3 {color: white;}
b {color: gray;}
```

```
/* group 3 */
h1, h4 {color: silver; background: white;}
h2 {color: silver;}
h3 {color: white;}
h2, h3 {background: gray;}
b {color: gray; background: white;}
```

Any of these will yield the result shown in Figure 2-4. (These styles use grouped declarations, which are explained in "Grouping Declarations" on page 35.)

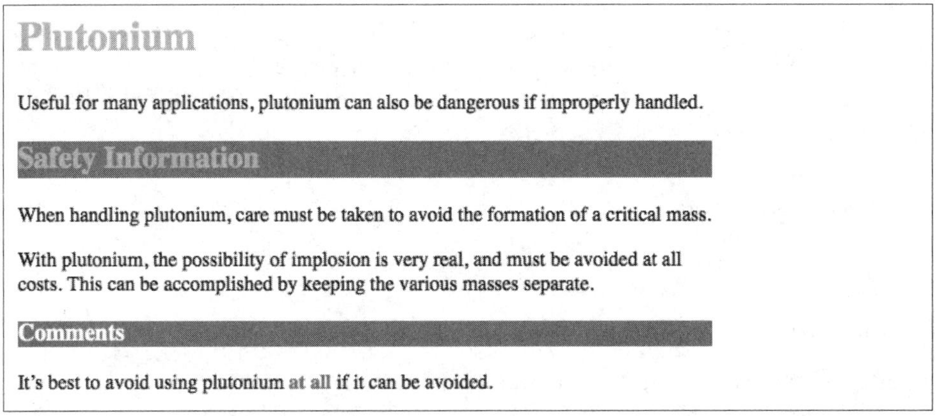

Figure 2-4. The result of equivalent stylesheets

The universal selector

CSS2 introduced a new simple selector called the *universal selector*, displayed as an asterisk (*). This selector matches any element at all, much like a wildcard. For example, to make every single element in a document red, you would write:

```
* {color: red;}
```

This declaration is equivalent to a grouped selector that lists every single element contained within the document. The universal selector lets you assign the color value red to every element in the document in one efficient stroke. Beware, however: although the universal selector is convenient, with a specificity on 0-0-0; and because it targets everything within its declaration scope, it can have unintended consequences, which are discussed later in this book.

Grouping Declarations

Since you can group selectors together into a single rule, it follows that you can also group declarations. Assuming that you want all h1 elements to appear in purple, 18-pixel-high Helvetica text on an aqua background (and you don't mind blinding your readers), you could write your styles like this:

```
h1 {font: 18px Helvetica;}
h1 {color: purple;}
h1 {background: aqua;}
```

But this method is inefficient—imagine creating such a list for an element that will carry 10 or 15 styles! Instead, you can group your declarations together:

```
h1 {font: 18px Helvetica; color: purple; background: aqua;}
```

This will have exactly the same effect as the three-line stylesheet just shown.

Note that using semicolons at the end of each declaration is crucial when you're grouping them. Browsers ignore whitespace in stylesheets, so the user agent must rely on correct syntax to parse the stylesheet. You can fearlessly format styles like the following:

```
h1 {
  font: 18px Helvetica;
  color: purple;
  background: aqua;
}
```

You can also minimize your CSS, removing all non-required spaces.

```
h1{font:18px Helvetica;color:purple;background:aqua;}
```

Ignoring whitespace, the last three are treated equally by the server, but the second one is most human readable, and the recommended method of marking up your CSS during development. (You might choose to minimize your CSS for network-performance reasons, but this is usually handled by a server-side script, caching network, or other service.)

If the semicolon is omitted on the second statement, the user agent will interpret the stylesheet as follows:

```
h1 {
  font: 18px Helvetica;
  color: purple background: aqua;
}
```

Because background: is not a valid value for color, and because color can be given only one keyword, a user agent will ignore the color declaration (including the background: aqua part) entirely. You might think the browser would at least render h1s as purple text without an aqua background, but not so. Instead, they will be the default color (which is usually black) with a transparent background (which is also a default). The declaration font: 18px Helvetica will still take effect since it was correctly terminated with a semicolon.

Although it is not technically necessary to follow the last declaration of a rule with a semicolon in CSS, it is generally good practice to do so. First, it will keep you in the habit of terminating your declarations with semicolons, the lack of which is one of the most common causes of rendering errors. Second, if you decide to add another declaration to a rule, you won't have to worry about forgetting to insert an extra semicolon. Third, if you ever use a preprocessor like Sass, trailing semicolons are often required for all declarations. Avoid all these problems—always follow a declaration with a semicolon, wherever the rule appears.

As with selector grouping, declaration grouping is a convenient way to keep your stylesheets short, expressive, and easy to maintain.

Grouping Everything

You now know that you can group selectors and you can group declarations. By combining both kinds of grouping in single rules, you can define very complex styles using only a few statements. Now, what if you want to assign some complex styles to all the headings in a document, and you want the same styles to be applied to all of them? Here's how to do it:

```
h1, h2, h3, h4, h5, h6 {color: gray; background: white; padding: 0.5em;
    border: 1px solid black; font-family: Charcoal, sans-serif;}
```

Here we've grouped the selectors, so the styles on the right side of the rule will be applied to all the headings listed; grouping the declarations means that all of the listed styles will be applied to the selectors on the left side of the rule. The result of this rule is shown in Figure 2-5.

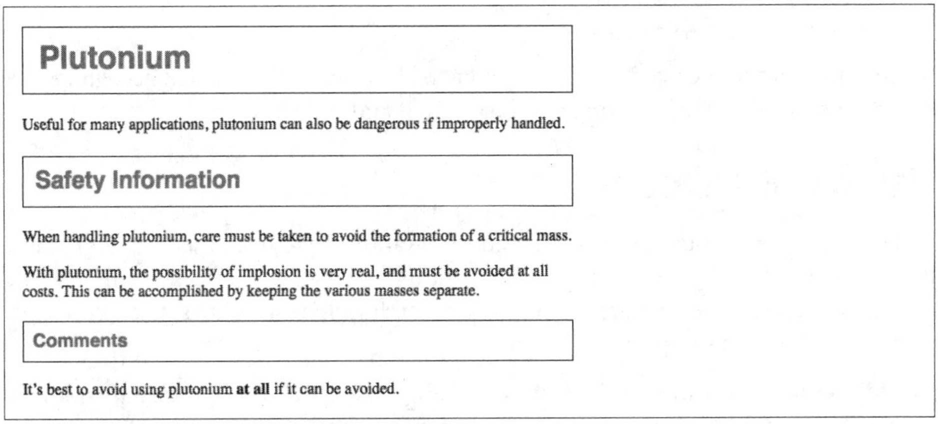

Plutonium

Useful for many applications, plutonium can also be dangerous if improperly handled.

Safety Information

When handling plutonium, care must be taken to avoid the formation of a critical mass.

With plutonium, the possibility of implosion is very real, and must be avoided at all costs. This can be accomplished by keeping the various masses separate.

Comments

It's best to avoid using plutonium **at all** if it can be avoided.

Figure 2-5. Grouping both selectors and rules

This approach is preferable to the drawn-out alternative, which would begin with something like this:

```
h1 {color: gray;}
h2 {color: gray;}
h3 {color: gray;}
h4 {color: gray;}
h5 {color: gray;}
h6 {color: gray;}
h1 {background: white;}
h2 {background: white;}
h3 {background: white;}
```

and continue for many lines. You *can* write out your styles the long way, but I wouldn't recommend it—editing them would be as tedious as using style attributes everywhere!

It's possible to add even more expression to selectors and to apply styles in a way that cuts across elements in favor of types of information. To get something so powerful, you'll have to do a little work in return, but it's well worth it.

New Elements in Old Browsers

With updates to HTML, such as the HTML5 specification, new elements have come into being. Some browsers predate these newer elements, and so don't recognize them. Versions of Internet Explorer prior to IE9, for example, did not support selecting elements they did not understand. The solution was to create the element in the DOM, thereby informing the browser that said element exists.

For example, IE8 does not recognize the `<main>` element. The following JavaScript line informs IE8 of main's existence:

```
document.createElement('main');
```

By running that line of code, older versions of Internet Explorer will recognize the existence of the element, allowing it to be selected and styled.

Class and ID Selectors

So far, we've been grouping selectors and declarations together in a variety of ways, but the selectors we've been using are very simple ones that refer only to document elements. Element selectors are fine up to a point, but there are times when you need something a little more specialized.

In addition to raw document elements, there are *class selectors* and *ID selectors*, which let you assign styles in a way that is independent of document elements. These selectors can be used on their own or in conjunction with element selectors. However, they work only if you've marked up your document appropriately, so using them generally involves a little forethought and planning.

For example, say you're drafting a document that discusses ways of handling plutonium. The document contains various warnings about safely dealing with such a dangerous substance. You want each warning to appear in boldface text so that it will stand out. However, you don't know which elements these warnings will be. Some warnings could be entire paragraphs, while others could be a single item within a lengthy list or a small section of text. So, you can't define a rule using element selectors of any kind. Suppose you tried this route:

```
p {
  font-weight: bold;
  color: red;
}
```

All paragraphs would be red and bold, not just those that contain warnings. You need a way to select only the text that contains warnings, or more precisely, a way to select only those elements that are warnings. How do you do it? You apply styles to parts of the document that have been marked in a certain way, independent of the elements involved, by using class selectors.

Class Selectors

The most common way to apply styles without worrying about the elements involved is to use *class selectors*. Before you can use them, however, you need to modify your actual document markup so that the class selectors will work. Enter the class attribute:

```
<p class="warning">When handling plutonium, care must be taken to avoid
the formation of a critical mass.</p>
<p>With plutonium, <span class="warning">the possibility of implosion is
very real, and must be avoided at all costs</span>. This can be accomplished
by keeping the various masses separate.</p>
```

To associate the styles of a class selector with an element, you must assign a class attribute the appropriate value. In the previous code block, a class value of warning was assigned to two elements: the first paragraph and the span element in the second paragraph.

All you need now is a way to apply styles to these classed elements. In HTML documents, you can use a compact notation where the name of a class is preceded by a period (.) and can be joined with an element selector:

```
.warning {font-weight: bold;}
```

When combined with the example markup shown earlier, this simple rule has the effect shown in Figure 2-6. That is, the declaration font-weight: bold will be applied to every element (thanks to the presence of the implicit universal selector) that carries a `class` attribute with a value of `warning`.

 The universal selector, represented by *, is implied when an ID, class, attribute selector, pseudo-class or pseudo-element selector is written without being attached to an element selector.

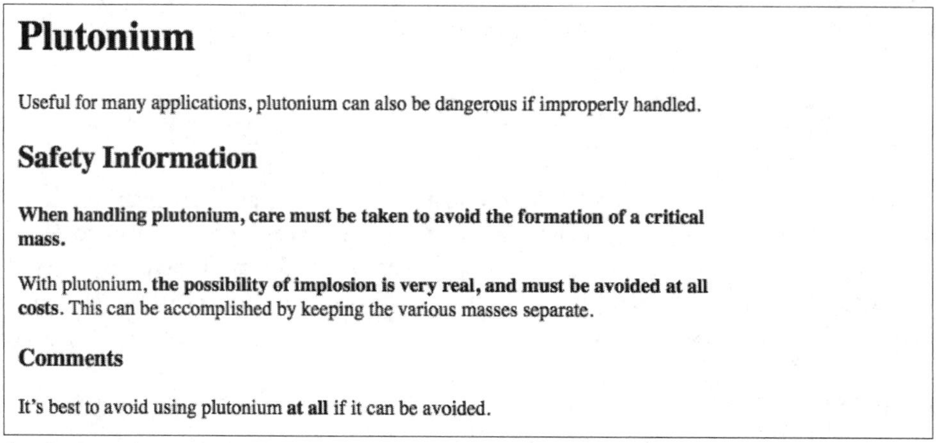

Plutonium

Useful for many applications, plutonium can also be dangerous if improperly handled.

Safety Information

When handling plutonium, care must be taken to avoid the formation of a critical mass.

With plutonium, **the possibility of implosion is very real, and must be avoided at all costs**. This can be accomplished by keeping the various masses separate.

Comments

It's best to avoid using plutonium **at all** if it can be avoided.

Figure 2-6. Using a class selector

As you can see, the class selector works by directly referencing a value that will be found in the `class` attribute of an element. This reference is *always* preceded by a period (`.`), which marks it as a class selector. The period helps keep the class selector separate from anything with which it might be combined—such as an element selector. For example, you may want boldface text only when an entire paragraph is a warning:

```
p.warning {font-weight: bold;}
```

The selector now matches any p elements that have a `class` attribute containing the word `warning`, but no other elements of any kind, classed or otherwise. Since the span element is not a paragraph, the rule's selector doesn't match it, and it won't be displayed using boldfaced text.

If you did want to assign different styles to the span element, you could use the selector `span.warning`:

```
p.warning {font-weight: bold;}
span.warning {font-style: italic;}
```

In this case, the warning paragraph is boldfaced, while the warning span is italicized. Each rule applies only to a specific type of element/class combination, so it does not leak over to other elements.

Another option is to use a combination of a general class selector and an element-specific class selector to make the styles even more useful, as in the following markup:

```
.warning {font-style: italic;}
span.warning {font-weight: bold;}
```

The results are shown in Figure 2-7.

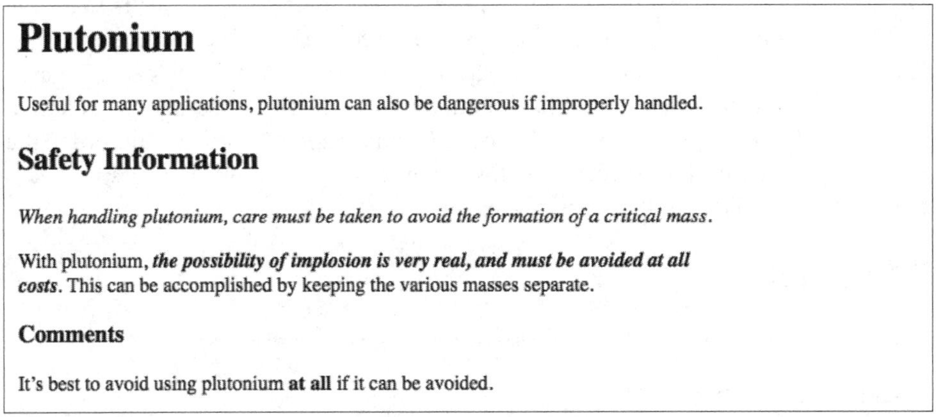

Plutonium

Useful for many applications, plutonium can also be dangerous if improperly handled.

Safety Information

When handling plutonium, care must be taken to avoid the formation of a critical mass.

With plutonium, *the possibility of implosion is very real, and must be avoided at all costs*. This can be accomplished by keeping the various masses separate.

Comments

It's best to avoid using plutonium **at all** if it can be avoided.

Figure 2-7. Using generic and specific selectors to combine styles

In this situation, any warning text will be italicized, but only the text within a span element with a class of warning will be both boldfaced and italicized.

Notice the format of the general class selector in the previous example: it's a class name preceded by a period without any element name, and no universal selector. In cases where you only want to select all elements that share a class name, you can omit the universal selector from a class selector without any ill effects.

Multiple Classes

In the previous section, we dealt with class values that contained a single word. In HTML, it's possible to have a space-separated list of words in a single class value. For example, if you want to mark a particular element as being both urgent and a warning, you could write:

```
<p class="urgent warning">When handling plutonium, care must be taken to
avoid the formation of a critical mass.</p>
<p>With plutonium, <span class="warning">the possibility of implosion is
very real, and must be avoided at all costs</span>. This can be accomplished
by keeping the various masses separate.</p>
```

The order of the words doesn't matter; `warning urgent` would also suffice and would yield precisely the same results no matter how the CSS `class` attribute is written.

Now let's say you want all elements with a `class` of `warning` to be boldfaced, those with a `class` of `urgent` to be italic, and those elements with both values to have a silver background. This would be written as follows:

```
.warning {font-weight: bold;}
.urgent {font-style: italic;}
.warning.urgent {background: silver;}
```

By chaining two class selectors together, you can select only those elements that have both class names, in any order. As you can see, the HTML source contains `class="urgent warning"` but the CSS selector is written `.warning.urgent`. Regardless, the rule will still cause the "When handling plutonium . . . " paragraph to have a silver background, as illustrated in Figure 2-8. This happens because the order the words are written in doesn't matter. (This is not to say the order of classes is always irrelevant, but we'll get to that later in the book.)

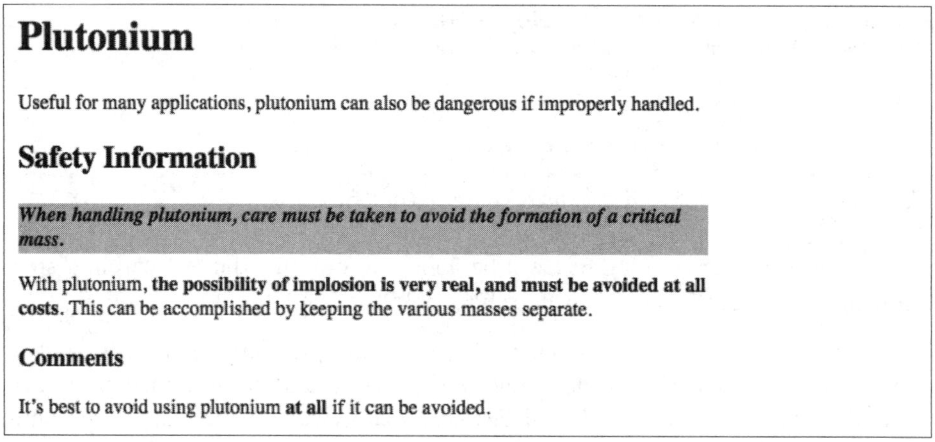

Plutonium

Useful for many applications, plutonium can also be dangerous if improperly handled.

Safety Information

When handling plutonium, care must be taken to avoid the formation of a critical mass.

With plutonium, **the possibility of implosion is very real, and must be avoided at all costs**. This can be accomplished by keeping the various masses separate.

Comments

It's best to avoid using plutonium **at all** if it can be avoided.

Figure 2-8. Selecting elements with multiple class names

If a multiple class selector contains a name that is not in the space-separated list, then the match will fail. Consider the following rule:

```
p.warning.help {background: red;}
```

As you would expect, the selector will match only those p elements with a `class` containing the words `warning` and `help`. Therefore, it will not match a p element with just the words `warning` and `urgent` in its `class` attribute. It would, however, match the following:

```
<p class="urgent warning help">Help me!</p>
```

ID Selectors

In some ways, *ID selectors* are similar to class selectors, but there are a few crucial differences. First, ID selectors are preceded by an octothorpe (#)—also known as a pound sign (in the US), hash sign, hash mark, or tic-tac-toe board—instead of a period. Thus, you might see a rule like this one:

```
*#first-para {font-weight: bold;}
```

This rule produces boldfaced text in any element whose id attribute has a value of first-para.

The second difference is that instead of referencing values of the class attribute, ID selectors refer, unsurprisingly, to values found in id attributes. Here's an example of an ID selector in action:

```
*#lead-para {font-weight: bold;}

<p id="lead-para">This paragraph will be boldfaced.</p>
<p>This paragraph will NOT be bold.</p>
```

Note that the value lead-para could have been assigned to any element within the document. In this particular case, it is applied to the first paragraph, but we could have applied it just as easily to the second or third paragraph. Or an unordered list. Or anything.

As with class selectors, it is possible to omit the universal selector from an ID selector. In the previous example, we could also have written:

```
#lead-para {font-weight: bold;}
```

The effect of this selector would be the same.

Another similarity between classes and IDs is that IDs can be selected independently of an element. There may be circumstances in which you know that a certain ID value will appear in a document, but you don't know the element on which it will appear (as in the plutonium-handling warnings), so you'll want to declare standalone ID selectors. For example, you may know that in any given document, there will be an element with an ID value of mostImportant. You don't know whether that most important thing will be a paragraph, a short phrase, a list item, or a section heading. You know only that it will exist in each document, occur in an arbitrary element, and appear no more than once. In that case, you would write a rule like this:

```
#mostImportant {color: red; background: yellow;}
```

This rule would match any of the following elements (which, as noted before, should *not* appear together in the same document because they all have the same ID value):

```
<h1 id="mostImportant">This is important!</h1>
<em id="mostImportant">This is important!</em>
<ul id="mostImportant">This is important!</ul>
```

Deciding Between Class and ID

You may assign classes to any number of elements, as demonstrated earlier; the class name `warning` was applied to both a `p` and a `span` element, and it could have been applied to many more elements. IDs, on the other hand, should be used once, and only once, within an HTML document. Therefore, if you have an element with an `id` value of `lead-para`, no other element in that document should have an `id` value of `lead-para`.

 In the real world, browsers don't always check for the uniqueness of IDs in HTML. That means that if you sprinkle an HTML document with several elements, all of which have the same value for their ID attributes, you'll probably get the same styles applied to each. This is incorrect behavior, but it happens anyway. Having more than one of the same ID value in a document also makes DOM scripting more difficult, since functions like `getElement ById()` depend on there being one, and only one, element with a given ID value.

Unlike class selectors, ID selectors can't be combined with other IDs, since ID attributes do not permit a space-separated list of words.

Another difference between `class` and `id` names is that IDs carry more weight when you're trying to determine which styles should be applied to a given element. This will be explained in greater detail in the next chapter.

Also note that class and ID selectors may be case-sensitive, depending on the document language. HTML defines class and ID values to be case-sensitive, so the capitalization of your class and ID values must match that found in your documents. Thus, in the following pairing of CSS and HTML, the element's text will not be boldfaced:

```
p.criticalInfo {font-weight: bold;}

<p class="criticalinfo">Don't look down.</p>
```

Because of the change in case for the letter *i*, the selector will not match the element shown.

On a purely syntactical level, the dot-class notation (e.g., `.warning`) is not guaranteed to work for XML documents. As of this writing, the dot-class notation works in HTML, SVG, and MathML, and it may well be permitted in future languages, but it's up to each language's specification to decide that. The hash-ID notation (e.g., `#lead`) will work in any document language that has an attribute that enforces uniqueness within a document. Uniqueness can be enforced with an attribute called `id`, or indeed anything else, as long as the attribute's contents are defined to be unique within the document.

Attribute Selectors

When it comes to both class and ID selectors, what you're really doing is selecting values of attributes. The syntax used in the previous two sections is particular to HTML, XHTML, SVG, and MathML documents (as of this writing). In other markup languages, these class and ID selectors may not be available (as, indeed, those attributes may not be present). To address this situation, CSS2 introduced *attribute selectors*, which can be used to select elements based on their attributes and the values of those attributes. There are four general types of attribute selectors: simple attribute selectors, exact attribute value selectors, partial-match attribute value selectors, and leading-value attribute selectors.

Simple Attribute Selectors

If you want to select elements that have a certain attribute, regardless of that attribute's value, you can use a *simple attribute selector*. For example, to select all h1 elements that have a class attribute with any value and make their text silver, write:

```
h1[class] {color: silver;}
```

So, given the following markup:

```
<h1 class="hoopla">Hello</h1>
<h1>Serenity</h1>
<h1 class="fancy">Fooling</h1>
```

you get the result shown in Figure 2-9.

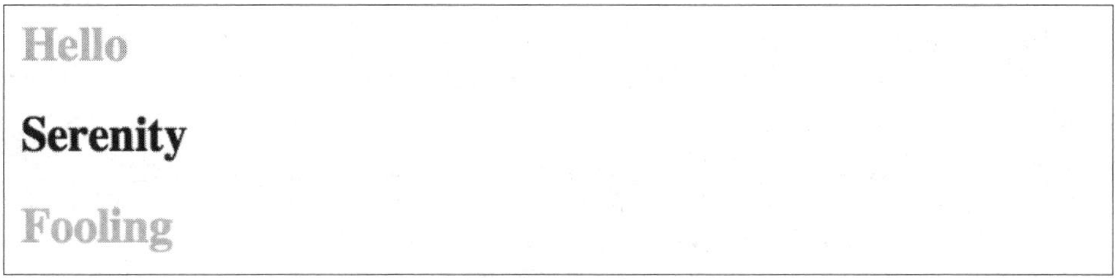

Figure 2-9. Selecting elements based on their attributes

This strategy is very useful in XML documents, as XML languages tend to have element and attribute names that are specific to their purpose. Consider an XML language that is used to describe planets of the solar system (we'll call it PlanetML). If you want to select all pml-planet elements with a moons attribute and make them boldface, thus calling attention to any planet that has moons, you would write:

```
pml-planet[moons] {font-weight: bold;}
```

This would cause the text of the second and third elements in the following markup fragment to be boldfaced, but not the first:

```
<pml-planet>Venus</pml-planet>
<pml-planet moons="1">Earth</pml-planet>
<pml-planet moons="2">Mars</pml-planet>
```

In HTML documents, you can use this feature in a number of creative ways. For example, you could style all images that have an `alt` attribute, thus highlighting those images that are correctly formed:

```
img[alt] {border: 3px solid red;}
```

(This particular example is generally useful more for diagnostic purposes—that is, determining whether images are indeed correctly marked up—than for design purposes.)

If you wanted to boldface any element that includes `title` information, which most browsers display as a "tool tip" when a cursor hovers over the element, you could write:

```
*[title] {font-weight: bold;}
```

Similarly, you could style only those anchors (a elements) that have an `href` attribute, thus applying the styles to any hyperlink but not to any placeholder anchors.

It is also possible to select based on the presence of more than one attribute. You do this by chaining the attribute selectors together. For example, to boldface the text of any HTML hyperlink that has both an `href` and a `title` attribute, you would write:

```
a[href][title] {font-weight: bold;}
```

This would boldface the first link in the following markup, but not the second or third:

```
<a href="http://www.w3.org/" title="W3C Home">W3C</a><br />
<a href="http://www.webstandards.org">Standards Info</a><br />
<a title="Not a link">dead.letter</a>
```

Selection Based on Exact Attribute Value

You can further narrow the selection process to encompass only those elements whose attributes are a certain value. For example, let's say you want to boldface any hyperlink that points to a certain document on the web server. This would look something like:

```
a[href="http://www.css-discuss.org/about.html"] {font-weight: bold;}
```

This will boldface the text of any a element that has an `href` attribute with *exactly* the value *http://www.css-discuss.org/about.html*. Any change at all, even dropping the `www.` part or changing to a secure protocol with `https`, will prevent a match.

Any attribute and value combination can be specified for any element. However, if that exact combination does not appear in the document, then the selector won't match anything. Again, XML languages can benefit from this approach to styling. Let's return to our PlanetML example. Suppose you want to select only those planet elements that have a value of 1 for the attribute moons:

```
planet[moons="1"] {font-weight: bold;}
```

This would boldface the text of the second element in the following markup fragment, but not the first or third:

```
<planet>Venus</planet>
<planet moons="1">Earth</planet>
<planet moons="2">Mars</planet>
```

As with attribute selection, you can chain together multiple attribute-value selectors to select a single document. For example, to double the size of the text of any HTML hyperlink that has both an href with a value of *http://www.w3.org/* and a title attribute with a value of W3C Home, you would write:

```
a[href="http://www.w3.org/"][title="W3C Home"] {font-size: 200%;}
```

This would double the text size of the first link in the following markup, but not the second or third:

```
<a href="http://www.w3.org/" title="W3C Home">W3C</a><br />
<a href="http://www.webstandards.org"
   title="Web Standards Organization">Standards Info</a><br />
<a href="http://www.example.org/" title="W3C Home">dead.link</a>
```

The results are shown in Figure 2-10.

Figure 2-10. Selecting elements based on attributes and their values

Again, this format requires an *exact* match for the attribute's value. Matching becomes an issue when the selector form encounters values that can in turn contain a space-separated list of values (e.g., the HTML attribute class). For example, consider the following markup fragment:

```
<planet type="barren rocky">Mercury</planet>
```

The only way to match this element based on its exact attribute value is to write:

```
planet[type="barren rocky"] {font-weight: bold;}
```

If you were to write `planet[type="barren"]`, the rule would not match the example markup and thus would fail. This is true even for the `class` attribute in HTML. Consider the following:

```
<p class="urgent warning">When handling plutonium, care must be taken to
avoid the formation of a critical mass.</p>
```

To select this element based on its exact attribute value, you would have to write:

```
p[class="urgent warning"] {font-weight: bold;}
```

This is *not* equivalent to the dot-class notation covered earlier, as we will see in the next section. Instead, it selects any p element whose class attribute has *exactly* the value `"urgent warning"`, with the words in that order and a single space between them. It's effectively an exact string match.

Also, be aware that ID selectors and attribute selectors that target the id attribute are not precisely the same. In other words, there is a subtle but crucial difference between `h1#page-title` and `h1[id="page-title"]`. This difference is explained in "Specificity" on page 97.

Selection Based on Partial Attribute Values

Odds are that you'll want to select elements based on portions of their attribute values, rather than the full value. For such situations, CSS actually offers a variety of options for matching substrings in an attribute's value. These are summarized in Table 2-1.

Table 2-1. Substring matching with attribute selectors

Type	Description
`[foo~="bar"]`	Selects any element with an attribute foo whose value contains the word bar in a space-separated list of words
`[foo*="bar"]`	Selects any element with an attribute foo whose value *contains* the substring bar
`[foo^="bar"]`	Selects any element with an attribute foo whose value *begins* with bar
`[foo$="bar"]`	Selects any element with an attribute foo whose value *ends* with bar
`[foo|="bar"]`	Selects any element with an attribute foo whose value *starts* with bar followed by a dash (U+002D) or whose value is exactly equal to bar

A Particular Attribute Selection Type

The first of these attribute selectors that match on a partial subset of an element's attribute value is actually easier to show than it is to describe. Consider the following rule:

```
*[lang|="en"] {color: white;}
```

This rule will select any element whose lang attribute is equal to en or begins with en-. Therefore, the first three elements in the following example markup would be selected, but the last two would not:

```
<h1 lang="en">Hello!</h1>
<p lang="en-us">Greetings!</p>
<div lang="en-au">G'day!</div>
<p lang="fr">Bonjour!</p>
<h4 lang="cy-en">Jrooana!</h4>
```

In general, the form [att|="val"] can be used for any attribute and its values. Let's say you have a series of figures in an HTML document, each of which has a filename like *figure-1.gif* and *figure-3.jpg*. You can match all of these images using the following selector:

```
img[src|="figure"] {border: 1px solid gray;}
```

Or, if you're creating a CSS framework or pattern library, instead of creating redundant classes like "btn btn-small btn-arrow btn-active", you can declare "btn-small-arrow-active", and target the class of elements with:

```
*[class|="btn"] { border-radius: 5px;}
```

```
<button class="btn-small-arrow-active">Click Me</button>
```

The most common use for this type of attribute selector is to match language values, as demonstrated in an upcoming section, "The :lang Pseudo-Class" on page 88.

Matching one word in a space-separated list

For any attribute that accepts a space-separated list of words, it is possible to select elements based on the presence of any one of those words. The classic example in HTML is the class attribute, which can accept one or more words as its value. Consider our usual example text:

```
<p class="urgent warning">When handling plutonium, care must be taken to
avoid the formation of a critical mass.</p>
```

Let's say you want to select elements whose class attribute contains the word warn ing. You can do this with an attribute selector:

```
p[class~="warning"] {font-weight: bold;}
```

Note the presence of the tilde (~) in the selector. It is the key to selection based on the presence of a space-separated word within the attribute's value. If you omit the tilde, you would have an exact value-matching attribute selector, as discussed in the previous section.

This selector construct is equivalent to the dot-class notation discussed in "Deciding Between Class and ID" on page 44. Thus, p.warning and p[class~="warning"] are equivalent when applied to HTML documents. Here's an example that is an HTML version of the "PlanetML" markup seen earlier:

```
<span class="barren rocky">Mercury</span>
<span class="cloudy barren">Venus</span>
<span class="life-bearing cloudy">Earth</span>
```

To italicize all elements with the word `barren` in their `class` attribute, you write:

```
span[class~="barren"] {font-style: italic;}
```

This rule's selector will match the first two elements in the example markup and thus italicize their text, as shown in Figure 2-11. This is the same result we would expect from writing `span.barren {font-style: italic;}`.

Mercury Venus Earth

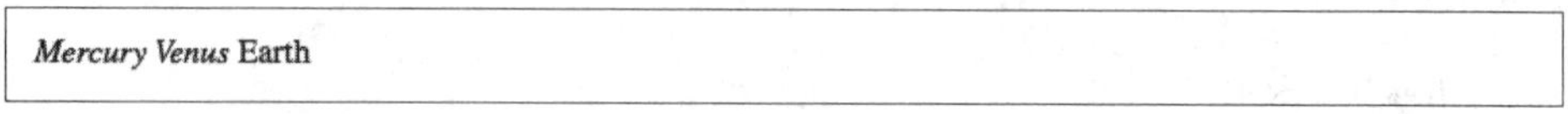

Figure 2-11. Selecting elements based on portions of attribute values

So why bother with the tilde-equals attribute selector in HTML? Because it can be used for any attribute, not just `class`. For example, you might have a document that contains a number of images, only some of which are figures. You can use a partial-match value attribute selector aimed at the `title` text to select only those figures:

```
img[title~="Figure"] {border: 1px solid gray;}
```

This rule selects any image whose `title` text contains the word `Figure`. Therefore, as long as all your figures have `title` text that looks something like "Figure 4. A bald-headed elder statesman," this rule will match those images. For that matter, the selector `img[title~="Figure"]` will also match a title attribute with the value "How to Figure Out Who's in Charge." Any image that does not have a `title` attribute, or whose `title` value doesn't contain the word "Figure," won't be matched.

Matching a substring within an attribute value

Sometimes you want to select elements based on a portion of their attribute values, but the values in question aren't space-separated lists of words. In these cases, you can use the form `[att*="val"]` to match substrings that appear anywhere inside the attribute values. For example, the following CSS matches any `span` element whose `class` attribute contains the substring `cloud`, so both "cloudy" planets are matched, as shown in Figure 2-12:

```
span[class*="cloud"] {font-style: italic;}

<span class="barren rocky">Mercury</span>
<span class="cloudy barren">Venus</span>
<span class="life-bearing cloudy">Earth</span>
```

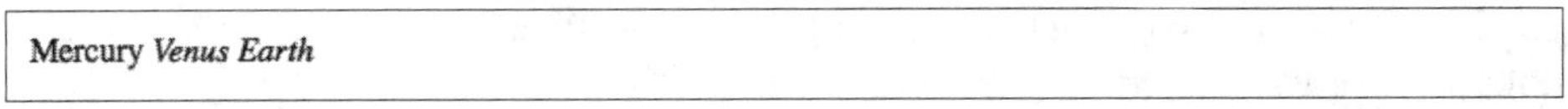

Figure 2-12. Selecting elements based on substrings within attribute values

As you can imagine, there are many useful applications for this particular capability. For example, suppose you wanted to specially style any links to the O'Reilly website. Instead of classing them all and writing styles based on that class, you could instead write the following rule:

```
a[href*="oreilly.com"] {font-weight: bold;}
```

You aren't confined to the class and href attributes. Any attribute is up for grabs here: title, alt, src, id…if the attribute has a value, you can style based on a substring within that value. The following rule draws attention to any image with the string "space" in its source URL:

```
img[src*="space"] {border: 5px solid red;}
```

Similarly, the following rule draws attention to input elements that have a title tells the user what to, and any other input whose title contains the substring "format" in its title:

```
input[title*="format"] {background-color: #dedede;}

<input type="tel"
    title="Telephone number should be formatted as XXX-XXX-XXXX"
    pattern="\d{3}\-\d{3}\-\d{4}">
```

A common use for the general substring attribute selector is to match a section of a class in pattern library class names. Elaborating on the last example, we can target any class name that starts with "btn" followed by a dash, and that contains the substring "arrow" preceded by a dash:

```
*[class|="btn"][class*="-arrow"]:after { content: "▼";}

<button class="btn-small-arrow-active">Click Me</button>
```

The matches are exact: if you include whitespace in your selector, then whitespace must also be present in an attribute's value. The attribute names and values must be case-sensitive only if the underlying document language requires case sensitivity. Class names, titles, URLs, and ID values are all case-sensitive, but HTML attribute keyterm values, such as input types, are not:

```
input[type="CHeckBoX"] {margin-right: 10px;}

<input type="checkbox" name="rightmargin" value="10px">
```

Matching a substring at the beginning of an attribute value

In cases where you want to select elements based on a substring at the beginning of an attribute value, then the attribute selector pattern [att^="val"] is what you're seeking. This can be particularly useful in a situation where you want to style types of links differently, as illustrated in Figure 2-13.

```
a[href^="https:"] {font-weight: bold;}
a[href^="mailto:"] {font-style: italic;}
```

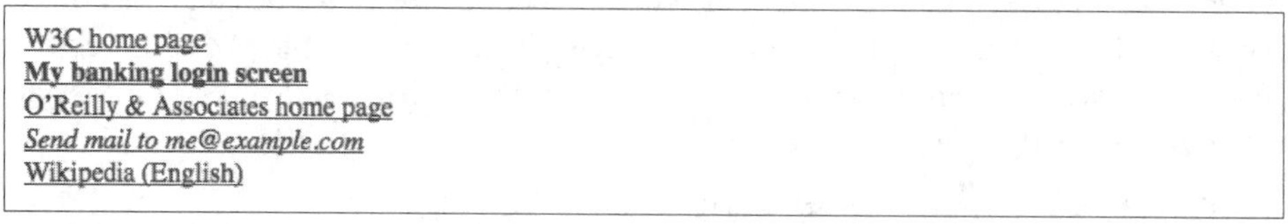

W3C home page
My banking login screen
O'Reilly & Associates home page
Send mail to me@example.com
Wikipedia (English)

Figure 2-13. Selecting elements based on substrings that begin attribute values

Another use case is when you want to style all images in an article that are also figures, as in the figures you see throughout this text. Assuming that the alt text of each figure begins with text in the pattern "Figure 5"—which is an entirely reasonable assumption in this case—then you can select only those images as follows:

```
img[alt^="Figure"] {border: 2px solid gray;  display: block; margin: 2em auto;}
```

The potential drawback here is that *any* img element whose alt starts with "Figure" will be selected, whether or not it's meant to be an illustrative figure. The likeliness of that occurring depends on the document in question.

Another use case is selecting all of the calendar events that occur on Mondays. In this case, let's assume all of the events have a title attribute containing a date in the format "Monday, March 5th, 2012." Selecting them all is a simple matter of [title^="Monday"].

Matching a substring at the end of an attribute value

The mirror image of beginning-substring matching is ending-substring matching, which is accomplished using the [att$="val"] pattern. A very common use for this capability is to style links based on the kind of resource they target, such as separate styles for PDF documents, as illustrated in Figure 2-14.

```
a[href$=".pdf"] {font-weight: bold;}
```

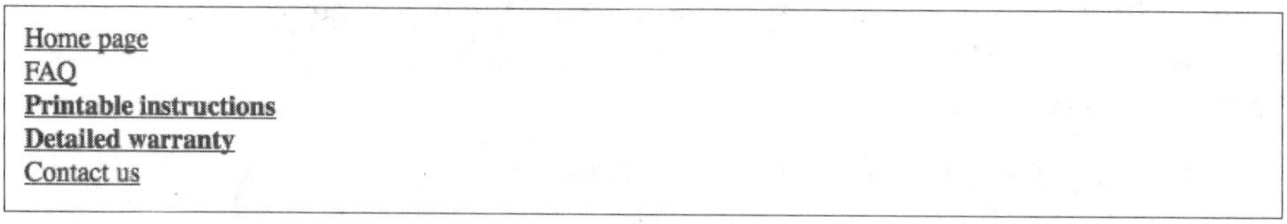

Home page
FAQ
Printable instructions
Detailed warranty
Contact us

Figure 2-14. Selecting elements based on substrings that end attribute values

Similarly, you could (for whatever reason) select images based on their image format:

```
img[src$=".gif"] {...}
img[src$=".jpg"] {...}
img[src$=".png"] {...}
```

To continue the calendar example from the previous section, it would be possible to select all of the events occurring within a given year using a selector like [title $="2015"].

 You may have noticed that I've quoted all the attribute values in the attribute selectors. Quoting is required if the value includes any special characters, begins with a dash or digit, or is otherwise invalid as an identifier and needs to be quoted as a string. To be safe, I recommend always quoting attribute values in attribute selectors, even though it is only required to makes strings out of invalid identifiers.

The Case Insensitivity Identifier

CSS Selectors level 4 introduces a case-insensitivity option to attribute selectors. Including an i before the closing bracket will allow the selector to match attribute values case-insensitively, regardless of document language rules.

For example, suppose you want to select all links to PDF documents, but you don't know if they'll end in *.pdf*, *.PDF*, or even *.Pdf*. Here's how:

```
a[href$='.PDF' i]
```

Adding that humble little i means the selector will match any a element whose href attribute's value ends in .pdf, regardless of the capitalization of the letters P, D, and F.

This case-insensitivity option is available for all attribute selectors we've covered. Note, however, that this only applies to the *values* in the attribute selectors. It does not enforce case insensitivity on the attribute names themselves. Thus, in a case-sensitive language, planet[type*="rock" i] will match all of the following:

```
<planet type="barren rocky">Mercury</planet>
<planet type="cloudy ROCKY">Venus</planet>
<planet type="life-bearing Rock">Earth</planet>
```

It will *not* match the following element, because the attribute TYPE isn't matched by type:

```
<planet TYPE="dusty rock">Mars</planet>
```

Again, that's in langauges that enforce case sensitivity in the element and attribute syntax. XHTML was one such. In languages that are case-insensitive, like HTML5, this isn't an issue.

As of late 2017, Opera Mini, the Android browser, and Edge did not support this capability.

Using Document Structure

CSS is powerful because it uses the structure of documents to determine appropriate styles and how to apply them. Yet structure plays a much larger role in the way styles are applied to a document. Let's take a moment to discuss structure before moving on to more powerful forms of selection.

Understanding the Parent-Child Relationship

To understand the relationship between selectors and documents, we need to once again examine how documents are structured. Consider this very simple HTML document:

```
<html>
<head>
 <base href="http://www.meerkat.web/">
 <title>Meerkat Central</title>
</head>
<body>
 <h1>Meerkat <em>Central</em></h1>
 <p>
 Welcome to Meerkat <em>Central</em>, the <strong>best meerkat web site
 on <a href="inet.html">the <em>entire</em> Internet</a></strong>!</p>
 <ul>
  <li>We offer:
   <ul>
    <li><strong>Detailed information</strong> on how to adopt a meerkat</li>
    <li>Tips for living with a meerkat</li>
    <li><em>Fun</em> things to do with a meerkat, including:
     <ol>
      <li>Playing fetch</li>
      <li>Digging for food</li>
      <li>Hide and seek</li>
     </ol>
    </li>
   </ul>
  </li>
  <li>...and so much more!</li>
 </ul>
 <p>
 Questions? <a href="mailto:suricate@meerkat.web">Contact us!</a>
 </p>
</body>
</html>
```

Much of the power of CSS is based on the *parent-child relationship* of elements. HTML documents (actually, most structured documents of any kind) are based on a hierarchy of elements, which is visible in the "tree" view of the document (see Figure 2-15). In this hierarchy, each element fits somewhere into the overall structure of the document. Every element in the document is either the *parent* or the *child* of another element, and it's often both.

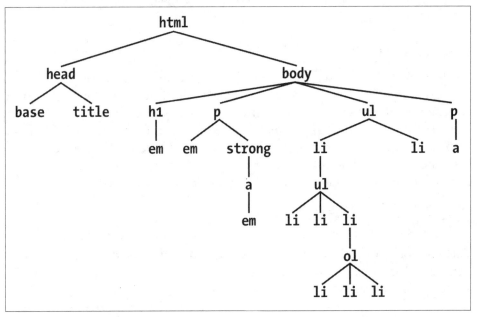

Figure 2-15. A document tree structure

An element is said to be the parent of another element if it appears directly above that element in the document hierarchy. For example, in Figure 2-15, the first p element is parent to the em and strong elements, while strong is parent to an anchor (a) element, which is itself parent to another em element. Conversely, an element is the child of another element if it is directly beneath the other element. Thus, the anchor element in Figure 2-15 is a child of the strong element, which is in turn child to the p element, which is itself child to the body, and so on.

The terms "parent" and "child" are specific applications of the terms *ancestor* and *descendant*. There is a difference between them: in the tree view, if an element is exactly one level above or below another, then they have a parent-child relationship. If the path from one element to another is traced through two or more levels, the elements have an ancestor-descendant relationship, but not a parent-child relationship. (A child is also a descendant, and a parent is also an ancestor.) In Figure 2-15, the first ul element is parent to two li elements, but the first ul is also the ancestor of every element descended from its `li` element, all the way down to the most deeply nested `li` elements.

Also, in Figure 2-15, there is an anchor that is a child of `strong`, but also a descendant of `p`, `body`, and `html` elements. The `body` element is an ancestor of everything that the browser will display by default, and the `html` element is ancestor to the entire document. For this reason, in an HTML or XHTML document, the `html` element is also called the *root element*.

Descendant Selectors

The first benefit of understanding this model is the ability to define *descendant selectors* (also known as *contextual selectors*). Defining descendant selectors is the act of creating rules that operate in certain structural circumstances but not others. As an example, let's say you want to style only those `em` elements that are descended from `h1` elements. You could put a `class` attribute on every `em` element found within an `h1`, but that's almost as time-consuming as using the `font` tag. It's far more efficient to declare rules that match only `em` elements that are found inside `h1` elements.

To do so, write the following:

```
h1 em {color: gray;}
```

This rule will make gray any text in an `em` element that is the descendant of an `h1` element. Other `em` text, such as that found in a paragraph or a block quote, will not be selected by this rule. Figure 2-16 makes this clear.

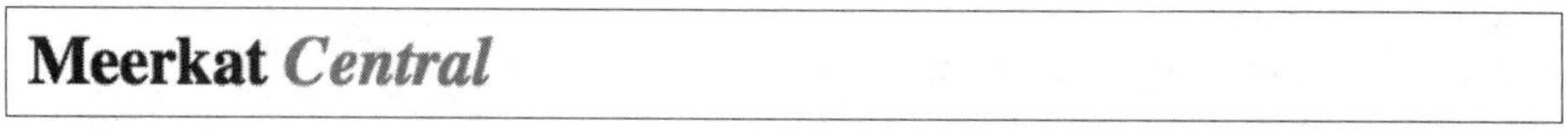

Meerkat *Central*

Figure 2-16. Selecting an element based on its context

In a descendant selector, the selector side of a rule is composed of two or more space-separated selectors. The space between the selectors is an example of a *combinator*. Each space combinator can be translated as "found within," "which is part of," or "that is a descendant of," but only if you read the selector right to left. Thus, `h1 em` can be translated as, "Any `em` element that is a descendant of an `h1` element." (To read the selector left to right, you might phrase it something like, "Any `h1` that contains an `em` will have the following styles applied to the `em`.")

You aren't limited to two selectors. For example:

```
ul ol ul em {color: gray;}
```

In this case, as Figure 2-17 shows, any emphasized text that is part of an unordered list that is part of an ordered list that is itself part of an unordered list (yes, this is correct) will be gray. This is obviously a very specific selection criterion.

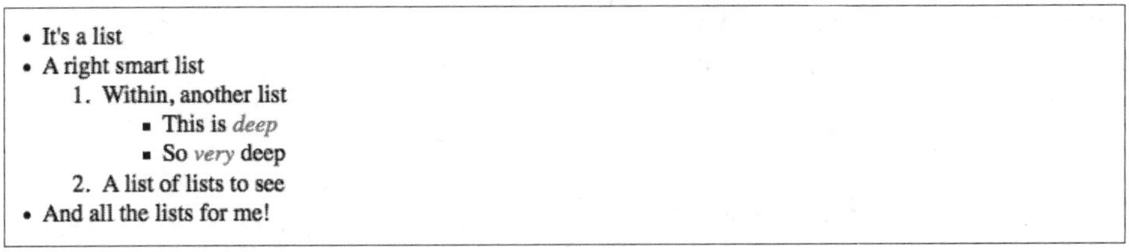

- It's a list
- A right smart list
  1. Within, another list
     - This is *deep*
     - So *very* deep
  2. A list of lists to see
- And all the lists for me!

Figure 2-17. A very specific descendant selector

Descendant selectors can be extremely powerful. They make possible what could never be done in HTML—at least not without oodles of font tags. Let's consider a common example. Assume you have a document with a sidebar and a main area. The sidebar has a blue background, the main area has a white background, and both areas include lists of links. You can't set all links to be blue because they'd be impossible to read in the sidebar.

The solution: descendant selectors. In this case, you give the element that contains your sidebar a class of sidebar and enclose the main area in a main element. Then, you write styles like this:

```
.sidebar {background: blue;}
main {background: white;}
.sidebar a:link {color: white;}
main a:link {color: blue;}
```

Figure 2-18 shows the result.

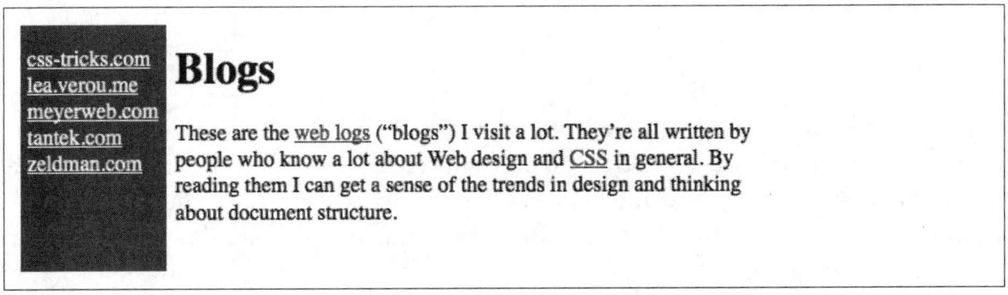

Blogs

css-tricks.com
lea.verou.me
meyerweb.com
tantek.com
zeldman.com

These are the web logs ("blogs") I visit a lot. They're all written by people who know a lot about Web design and CSS in general. By reading them I can get a sense of the trends in design and thinking about document structure.

Figure 2-18. Using descendant selectors to apply different styles to the same type of element

:link refers to links to resources that haven't been visited. We'll talk about it in detail in "Hyperlink pseudo-classes" on page 77.

Here's another example: let's say that you want gray to be the text color of any b (bold-face) element that is part of a blockquote and for any bold text that is found in a normal paragraph:

```
blockquote b, p b {color: gray;}
```

The result is that the text within b elements that are descended from paragraphs or block quotes will be gray.

One overlooked aspect of descendant selectors is that the degree of separation between two elements can be practically infinite. For example, if you write ul em, that syntax will select any em element descended from a ul element, no matter how deeply nested the em may be. Thus, ul em would select the em element in the following markup:

```
<ul>
  <li>List item 1
    <ol>
      <li>List item 1-1</li>
      <li>List item 1-2</li>
      <li>List item 1-3
        <ol>
          <li>List item 1-3-1</li>
          <li>List item <em>1-3-2</em></li>
          <li>List item 1-3-3</li>
        </ol>
      </li>
      <li>List item 1-4</li>
    </ol>
  </li>
</ul>
```

A more subtle aspect of descendant selectors is that they have no notion of element proximity. In other words, the closeness of two elements within the document tree has no bearing on whether a rule applies or not. This is important when it comes to specificity (which we'll cover later on) and when considering rules that might appear to cancel each other out.

For example, consider the following (which contains a selector type we'll discuss in the upcoming section, "The Negation Pseudo-Class" on page 89):

```
div:not(.help) span {color: gray;}
div.help span {color: red;}

<div class="help">
  <div class="aside">
    This text contains <span>a span element</span> within.
  </div>
</div>
```

What the CSS says, in effect, is "any span inside a div that doesn't have a class containing the word help should be gray" in the first rule, and "any span inside a div whose class contains the word help" in the second rule. In the given markup fragment, *both* rules apply to the span shown.

Because the two rules have equal weight and the "red" rule is written last, it wins out and the span is red. The fact that the div class="aside" is "closer to" the span than the div class="help" is irrelevant. Again: descendant selectors have no notion of element proximity. Both rules match, only one color can be applied, and due to the way CSS works, red is the winner here. (We'll discuss why in the next chapter.)

Selecting Children

In some cases, you don't want to select an arbitrarily descended element. Rather, you want to narrow your range to select an element that is a child of another element. You might, for example, want to select a strong element only if it is a child (as opposed to any level of descendant) of an h1 element. To do this, you use the child combinator, which is the greater-than symbol (>):

```
h1 > strong {color: red;}
```

This rule will make red the strong element shown in the first h1, but not the second:

```
<h1>This is <strong>very</strong> important.</h1>
<h1>This is <em>really <strong>very</strong></em> important.</h1>
```

Read right to left, the selector h1 > strong translates as, "Selects any strong element that is a direct child of an h1 element." The child combinator can be optionally surrounded by whitespace. Thus, h1 > strong, h1> strong, and h1>strong are all equivalent. You can use or omit whitespace as you wish.

When viewing the document as a tree structure, it's easy to see that a child selector restricts its matches to elements that are directly connected in the tree. Figure 2-19 shows part of a document tree.

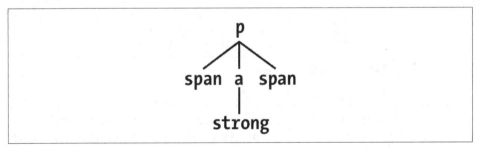

Figure 2-19. A document tree fragment

In this tree fragment, you can pick out parent-child relationships. For example, the a element is parent to the strong, but it is child to the p element. You could match elements in this fragment with the selectors p > a and a > strong, but not p > strong, since the strong is a descendant of the p but not its child.

You can also combine descendant and child combinations in the same selector. Thus, table.summary td > p will select any p element that is a *child* of a td element that is itself *descended* from a table element that has a class attribute containing the word summary.

Selecting Adjacent Sibling Elements

Let's say you want to style the paragraph immediately after a heading, or give a special margin to a list that immediately follows a paragraph. To select an element that immediately follows another element with the same parent, you use the *adjacent-sibling combinator*, represented as a plus symbol (+). As with the child combinator, the symbol can be surrounded by whitespace, or not, at the author's discretion.

To remove the top margin from a paragraph immediately following an h1 element, write:

```
h1 + p {margin-top: 0;}
```

The selector is read as, "Selects any p element that immediately follows an h1 element that *shares a parent* with the p element."

To visualize how this selector works, it is easiest to once again consider a fragment of a document tree, shown in Figure 2-20.

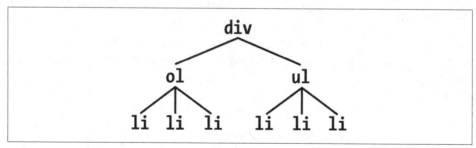

Figure 2-20. Another document tree fragment

In this fragment, a pair of lists descends from a div element, one ordered and the other not, each containing three list items. Each list is an adjacent sibling, and the list items themselves are also adjacent siblings. However, the list items from the first list are *not* siblings of the second, since the two sets of list items do not share the same parent element. (At best, they're cousins, and CSS has no cousin selector.)

Remember that you can select the second of two adjacent siblings only with a single combinator. Thus, if you write li + li {font-weight: bold;}, only the second and third items in each list will be boldfaced. The first list items will be unaffected, as illustrated in Figure 2-21.

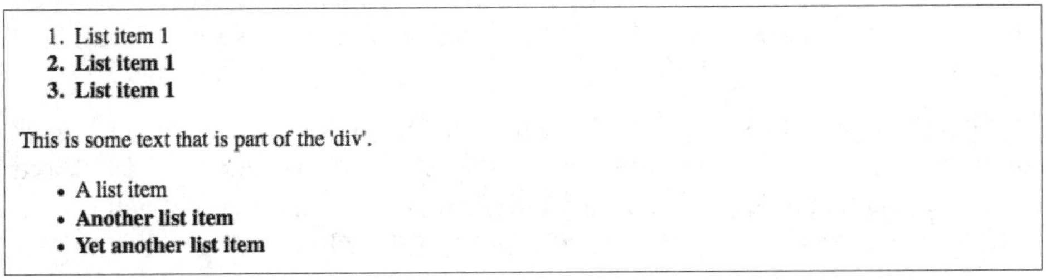

1. List item 1
2. **List item 1**
3. **List item 1**

This is some text that is part of the 'div'.

- A list item
- **Another list item**
- **Yet another list item**

Figure 2-21. Selecting adjacent siblings

To work properly, CSS requires that the two elements appear in "source order." In our example, an ol element is followed by a ul element. This allows us to select the second element with ol + ul, but we cannot select the first using the same syntax. For ul + ol to match, an ordered list must immediately follow an unordered list.

Keep in mind that text content between two elements does *not* prevent the adjacent-sibling combinator from working. Consider this markup fragment, whose tree view would be the same as that shown in Figure 2-19:

```
<div>
  <ol>
    <li>List item 1</li>
    <li>List item 1</li>
    <li>List item 1</li>
  </ol>
  This is some text that is part of the 'div'.
  <ul>
    <li>A list item</li>
    <li>Another list item</li>
    <li>Yet another list item</li>
  </ul>
</div>
```

Even though there is text between the two lists, we can still match the second list with the selector ol + ul. That's because the intervening text is not contained with a sibling element, but is instead part of the parent div. If we wrapped that text in a paragraph element, it would then prevent ol + ul from matching the second list. Instead, we might have to write something like ol + p + ul.

As the following example illustrates, the adjacent-sibling combinator can be used in conjunction with other combinators:

```
html > body table + ul{margin-top: 1.5em;}
```

The selector translates as, "Selects any ul element that immediately follows a sibling table element that is descended from a body element that is itself a child of an html element."

As with all combinators, you can place the adjacent-sibling combinator in a more complex setting, such as div#content h1 + div ol. That selector is read as, "Selects any ol element that is descended from a div when the div is the adjacent sibling of an h1 which is itself descended from a div whose id attribute has a value of content."

Selecting Following Siblings

Selectors Level 3 introduced a new sibling combinator called the *general sibling combinator*. This lets you select any element that follows another element when both elements share the same parent, represented using the tilde (~) combinator.

As an example, to italicize any ol that follows an h2 and also shares a parent with the h2, you'd write h2 ~ol {font-style: italic;}. The two elements do not have to be adjacent siblings, although they can be adjacent and still match this rule. The result of applying this rule to the following markup is shown in Figure 2-22:

```
<div>
  <h2>Subheadings</h2>
  <p>It is the case that not every heading can be a main heading.  Some headings
  must be subheadings.  Examples include:</p>
  <ol>
    <li>Headings that are less important</li>
    <li>Headings that are subsidiary to more important headlines</li>
    <li>Headings that like to be dominated</li>
  </ol>
  <p>Let's restate that for the record:</p>
  <ol>
    <li>Headings that are less important</li>
    <li>Headings that are subsidiary to more important headlines</li>
    <li>Headings that like to be dominated</li>
  </ol>
</div>
```

As you can see, both ordered lists are italicized. That's because both of them are ol elements that follow an h2 with which they share a parent (the div).

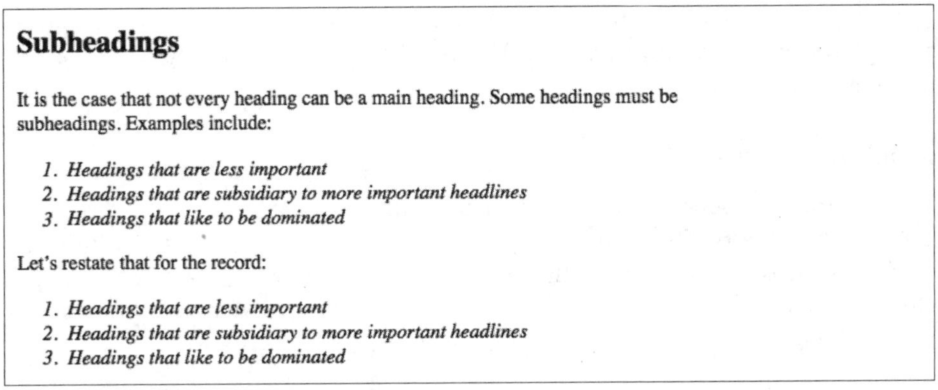

Figure 2-22. Selecting following siblings

Pseudo-Class Selectors

Things get really interesting with *pseudo-class selectors*. These selectors let you assign styles to what are, in effect, phantom classes that are inferred by the state of certain elements, or markup patterns within the document, or even by the state of the document itself.

The phrase "phantom classes" might seem a little odd, but it really is the best way to think of how pseudo-classes work. For example, suppose you wanted to highlight every other row of a data table. You could do that by marking up every other row something like `class="even"` and then writing CSS to highlight rows with that class —or (as we'll soon see) you could use a pseudo-class selector to achieve the same effect, and through very similar means.

Combining Pseudo-Classes

Before we start, a word about chaining. CSS makes it possible to combine ("chain") pseudo-classes together. For example, you can make unvisited links red when they're hovered and visited links maroon when *they're* hovered:

```
a:link:hover {color: red;}
a:visited:hover {color: maroon;}
```

The order you specify doesn't actually matter; you could also write `a:hover:link` to the same effect as `a:link:hover`. It's also possible to assign separate hover styles to unvisited and visited links that are in another language—for example, German:

```
a:link:hover:lang(de) {color: gray;}
a:visited:hover:lang(de) {color: silver;}
```

Be careful not to combine mutually exclusive pseudo-classes. For example, a link cannot be both visited and unvisited, so `a:link:visited` doesn't make any sense and will never match anything.

Structural Pseudo-Classes

The majority of pseudo-classes are structural in nature; that is, they refer to the markup structure of the document. Most of them depend on patterns within the markup, such as choosing every third paragraph, but others allow you to address specific types of elements. All pseudo-classes, without exception, are a word preceded by a single colon (`:`), and they can appear anywhere in a selector.

Before we get started, there's an aspect of pseudo-classes that needs to be made explicit here: pseudo-classes always refer to the element to which they're attached, and no other. Seems like a weirdly obvious thing to say, right? The reason to make it explicit is that for a few of the structural pseudo-classes, it's a common error to think they are descriptors that refer to descendant elements.

To illustrate this, I'd like to share a personal anecdote. When my first child was born in 2003, I announced it online (like you do). A number of people responded with congratulations and CSS jokes, chief among them the selector `#ericmeyer:first-child`. The problem there is that selector would select me, not my daughter, and only if I were the first child of my parents (which, as it happens, I am). To properly select my first child, that selector would need to be `#ericmeyer > :first-child`.

The confusion is understandable, which is why I'm addressing it here. Reminders will be found throughout the following sections. Just always keep in mind that the effect of pseudo-classes is to apply a sort of a "phantom class" to the element to which they're attached, and you should be OK.

Selecting the root element

This is the quintessence of structural simplicity: the pseudo-class `:root` selects the root element of the document. In HTML, this is *always* the `html` element. The real benefit of this selector is found when writing stylesheets for XML languages, where the root element may be different in every language—for example, in RSS 2.0 it's the `rss` element—or even when you have more than one possible root element within a single language (though not a single document!).

Here's an example of styling the root element in HTML, as illustrated in Figure 2-23:

```
:root {border: 10px dotted gray;}
body {border: 10px solid black;}
```

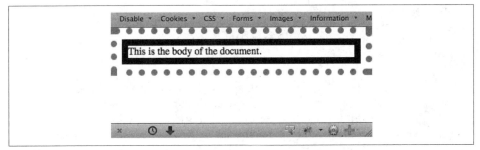

Figure 2-23. Styling the root element

In HTML documents, you can always select the html element directly, without having to use the :root pseudo-class. There is a difference between the two selectors in terms of specificity, which we'll cover in Chapter 3.

Selecting empty elements

With the pseudo-class :empty, you can select any element that has no children of any kind, *including* text nodes, which covers both text and whitespace. This can be useful in suppressing elements that a CMS has generated without filling in any actual content. Thus, p:empty {display: none;} would prevent the display of any empty paragraphs.

Note that in order to be matched, an element must be, from a parsing perspective, truly empty—no whitespace, visible content, or descendant elements. Of the following elements, only the first and last would be matched by p:empty:

```
<p></p>
<p> </p>
<p>
</p>
<p><!--a comment--></p>
```

The second and third paragraphs are not matched by :empty because they are not empty: they contain, respectively, a single space and a single newline character. Both are considered text nodes, and thus prevent a state of emptiness. The last paragraph matches because comments are not considered content, not even whitespace. But put even one space or newline to either side of that comment, and p:empty would fail to match.

You might be tempted to just style all empty elements with something like *:empty {display: none;}, but there's a hidden catch: :empty matches HTML's empty elements, like img and input. It could even match textarea, unless you insert some default text into the textarea element. Thus, in terms of matching elements, img and img:empty are effectively the same. (They are different in terms of specificity, which we'll cover in the next chapter.)

```
<img src="salmon.png" alt="North Pacific Salmon">
<br>
<input type="number" min="-1" max="1" step=".01"/>
<textarea></textarea>
```

 As of late 2017, :empty is unique in that it's the only CSS selector that takes text nodes into consideration when determining matches. Every other selector type in Selectors Level 3 considers only elements, and ignores text nodes entirely—recall, for example, the sibling combinators.

Selecting unique children

If you've ever wanted to select all the images that are wrapped by a hyperlink element, the :only-child pseudo-class is for you. It selects elements when they are the only child element of another element. So let's say you want to add a border to any image that's the only child of another element. You'd write:

```
img:only-child {border: 1px solid black;}
```

This would match any image that meets those criteria. Therefore, if you had a paragraph which contained an image and no other child elements, the image would be selected regardless of all the text surrounding it. If what you're really after is images that are sole children and found inside hyperlinks, then you just modify the selector like so (which is illustrated in Figure 2-24):

```
a[href] img:only-child {border: 2px solid black;}

<a href="http://w3.org/"><img src="w3.png" alt="W3C"></a>
<a href="http://w3.org/"><img src="w3.png" alt=""> The W3C</a>
<a href="http://w3.org/"><img src="w3.png" alt=""> <em>The W3C</em></a>
```

Figure 2-24. Selecting images that are only children inside links

There are two things to remember about :only-child. The first is that you *always* apply it to the element you want to be an only child, not to the parent element, as explained earlier. And that brings up the second thing to remember, which is that when you use :only-child in a descendant selector, you aren't restricting the elements listed to a parent-child relationship.

To go back to the hyperlinked-image example, a[href] img:only-child matches any image that is an only child and is descended from an a element, not is a child of an a element. To match, the element image must be the only child of its direct parent, and a descendant of a link, but that parent can itself be a descendant of that link. Therefore, all three of the images here would be matched, as shown in Figure 2-25:

```
a[href] img:only-child {border: 5px solid black;}

<a href="http://w3.org/"><img src="w3.png" alt="W3C"></a>
<a href="http://w3.org/"><span><img src="w3.png" alt="W3C"></span></a>
<a href="http://w3.org/">A link to <span>the <img src="w3.png" alt="">
  web</span> site</a>
```

Figure 2-25. Selecting images that are only children inside links

In each case, the image is the only child element of its parent, and it is also descended from an a element. Thus, all three images are matched by the rule shown. If you wanted to restrict the rule so that it matched images that were the only children of a elements, then you'd just add the child combinator to yield a[href] > img:only-child. With that change, only the first of the three images shown in Figure 2-25 would be matched.

That's all great, but what if you want to match images that are the only images inside hyperlinks, but there are other elements in there with them? Consider the following:

```
<a href="http://w3.org/"><b>•</b><img src="w3.png" alt="W3C"></a>
```

In this case, we have an a element that has two children: b and img. That image, no longer being the only child of its parent (the hyperlink), can never be matched using :only-child. However, it *can* be matched using :only-of-type. This is illustrated in Figure 2-26:

```
a[href] img:only-of-type {border: 5px solid black;}

<a href="http://w3.org/"><b>•</b><img src="w3.png" alt="W3C"></a>
<a href="http://w3.org/"><span><b>•</b><img src="w3.png" alt="W3C"></span></a>
```

Figure 2-26. Selecting images that are the only sibling of their type

The difference is that :only-of-type will match any element that is the only of its type among all its siblings, whereas :only-child will only match if an element has no siblings at all.

This can be very useful in cases such as selecting images within paragraphs without having to worry about the presence of hyperlinks or other inline elements:

```
p > img:only-of-type {float: right; margin: 20px;}
```

As long as there aren't multiple images that are children of the same paragraph, then the image will be floated. You could also use this pseudo-class to apply extra styles to an h2 when it's the only one in a section of a document, like this:

```
section > h2 {margin: 1em 0 0.33em; font-size: 1.8rem; border-bottom: 1px solid
    gray;}
section > h2:only-of-type {font-size: 2.4rem;}
```

Given those rules, any section that has only one child h2 will have it appear larger than usual. If there are two or more h2 children to a section, neither of them will be larger than the other. The presence of other children—whether they are other heading levels, paragraphs, tables, paragraphs, lists, and so on—will not interfere with matching.

There's one more thing to make clear, which is that :only-of-type refers to elements and nothing else. Consider the following:

```
p.unique:only-of-type {color: red;}

<div>
  <p class="unique">This paragraph has a 'unique' class.</p>
  <p>This paragraph doesn't have a class at all.</p>
</div>
```

In this case, neither of the paragraphs will be selected. Why not? Because there are two paragraphs that are descendants of the div, so neither of them can be the only one of their type.

The class name is irrelevant here. We're fooled into thinking that "type" is a generic description, because of how we parse language. *Type*, in the way :only-of-type means it, refers only to the element type. Thus, p.unique:only-of-type means "select any p element whose class attribute contains the word unique when the p element is the only p element among its siblings." It does *not* mean "select any p element whose class attribute contains the word unique when it's the only sibling paragraph to meet that criterion."

Selecting first and last children

It's pretty common to want to apply special styling to the first or last child of an element. A common example is styling a bunch of navigation links in a tab bar, and wanting to put some special visual touches on the first or last tab (or both). In the past, this was done by applying special classes to those elements. Now we have pseudo-classes to carry the load for us.

The pseudo-class `:first-child` is used to select elements that are the first children of other elements. Consider the following markup:

```
<div>
  <p>These are the necessary steps:</p>
  <ul>
    <li>Insert key</li>
    <li>Turn key <strong>clockwise</strong></li>
    <li>Push accelerator</li>
  </ul>
  <p>
    Do <em>not</em> push the brake at the same time as the accelerator.
  </p>
</div>
```

In this example, the elements that are first children are the first p, the first li, and the strong and em elements, which are all the first children of their respective parents. Given the following two rules:

```
p:first-child {font-weight: bold;}
li:first-child {text-transform: uppercase;}
```

we get the result shown in Figure 2-27.

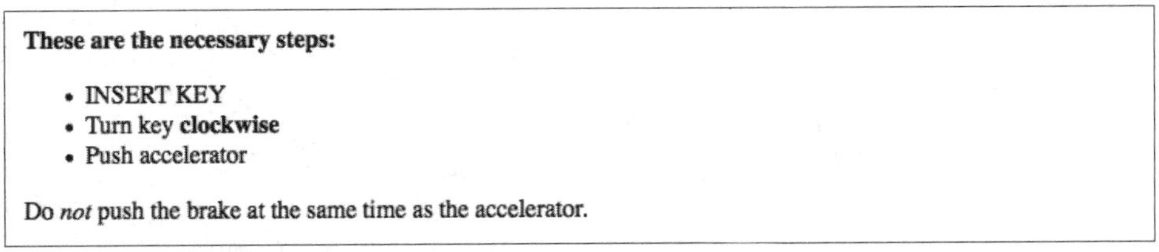

Figure 2-27. Styling first children

The first rule boldfaces any p element that is the first child of another element. The second rule uppercases any li element that is the first child of another element (which, in HTML, must be either an ol or ul element).

As has been mentioned, the most common error is assuming that a selector like `p:first-child` will select the first child of a p element. Remember the nature of pseudo-classes, which is to attach a sort of phantom class to the element associated with the pseudo-class. If you were to add actual classes to the markup, it would look like this:

```
<div>
  <p class="first-child">These are the necessary steps:</p>
  <ul>
    <li class="first-child">Insert key</li>
    <li>Turn key <strong class="first-child">clockwise</strong></li>
    <li>Push accelerator</li>
  </ul>
  <p>
```

```
    Do <em class="first-child">not</em> push the brake at the same time as the
  accelerator.
  </p>
</div>
```

Therefore, if you want to select those em elements that are the first child of another element, you write em:first-child.

The mirror image of :first-child is :last-child. If we take the previous example and just change the pseudo-classes, we get the result shown in Figure 2-28.

```
p:last-child {font-weight: bold;}
li:last-child {text-transform: uppercase;}

<div>
  <p>These are the necessary steps:</p>
  <ul>
    <li>Insert key</li>
    <li>Turn key <strong>clockwise</strong></li>
    <li>Push accelerator</li>
  </ul>
  <p>
    Do <em>not</em> push the brake at the same time as the accelerator.
  </p>
</div>
```

These are the necessary steps:

- Insert key
- Turn key **clockwise**
- PUSH ACCELERATOR

Do *not* push the brake at the same time as the accelerator.

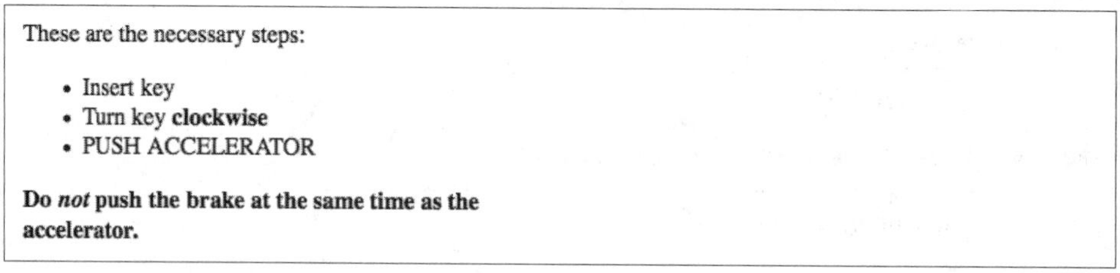

Figure 2-28. Styling last children

The first rule boldfaces any p element that is the last child of another element. The second rule uppercases any li element that is the last child of another element. If you wanted to select the em element inside that last paragraph, you could use the selector p:last-child em, which selects any em element that descends from a p element that is itself the last child of another element.

Interestingly, you can combine these two pseudo-classes to create a version of :only-child. The following two rules will select the same elements:

```
p:only-child {color: red;}
p:first-child:last-child {background-color: red;}
```

Either way, we get paragraphs with red foreground and background colors (not a good idea, clearly).

Selecting first and last of a type

In a manner similar to selecting the first and last children of an element, you can select the first or last of a type of element within another element. This permits things like selecting the first `table` inside a given element, regardless of whatever elements come before it.

```
table:first-of-type {border-top: 2px solid gray;}
```

Note that this does *not* apply to the entire document; that is, the rule shown will not select the first table in the document and skip all the others. It will instead select the first `table` element within each element that contains one, and skip any sibling `table` elements that come after the first. Thus, given the document structure shown in Figure 2-29, the circled nodes are the ones that are selected.

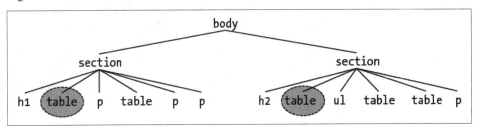

Figure 2-29. Selecting first-of-type tables

Within the context of tables, a useful way to select the first data cell within a row regardless of whether a header cell comes before it in the row is as follows:

```
td:first-of-type {border-left: 1px solid red;}
```

That would select the first data cell in each of the following table rows:

```
<tr>
  <th scope="row">Count</th><td>7</td><td>6</td><td>11</td>
</tr>
<tr>
  <td>Q</td><td>X</td><td>-</td>
</tr>
```

Compare that to the effects of `td:first-child`, which would select the first td element in the second row, but not in the first row.

The flip side is `:last-of-type`, which selects the last instance of a given type from amongst its sibling elements. In a way, it's just like `:first-of-type` except you start with the last element in a group of siblings and walk backward toward the first element until you reach an instance of the type. Given the document structure shown in Figure 2-30, the circled nodes are the ones selected by `table:last-of-type`.

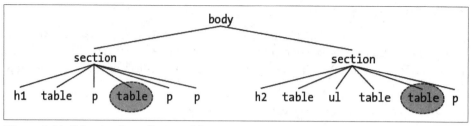

Figure 2-30. Selecting last-of-type tables

As was noted with :only-of-type, remember that you are selecting elements of a type from among their sibling elements; thus, every set of siblings is considered separately. In other words, you are *not* selecting the first (or last) of all the elements of a type within the entire document as a single group. Each set of elements that share a parent is its own group, and you can select the first (or last) of a type within each group.

Similar to what was noted in the previous section, you can combine these two pseudo-classes to create a version of :only-of-type. The following two rules will select the same elements:

```
table:only-of-type{color: red;}
table:first-of-type:last-of-type {background: red;}
```

Selecting every nth child

If you can select elements that are the first, last, or only children of other elements, how about every third child? All even children? Only the ninth child? Rather than define a literally infinite number of named pseudo-classes, CSS has the :nth-child() pseudo-class. By filling integers or even simple algebraic expressions into the parentheses, you can select any arbitrarily numbered child element you like.

Let's start with the :nth-child() equivalent of :first-child, which is :nth-child(1). In the following example, the selected elements will be the first paragraph and the first list item.

```
p:nth-child(1) {font-weight: bold;}
li:nth-child(1) {text-transform: uppercase;}

<div>
  <p>These are the necessary steps:</p>
  <ul>
    <li>Insert key</li>
    <li>Turn key <strong>clockwise</strong></li>
    <li>Push accelerator</li>
  </ul>
  <p>
    Do <em>not</em> push the brake at the same time as the accelerator.
```

```
    </p>
  </div>
```

If we change the numbers from 1 to 2, however, then no paragraphs will be selected, and the middle (or second) list item will be selected, as illustrated in Figure 2-31:

```
p:nth-child(2) {font-weight: bold;}
li:nth-child(2) {text-transform: uppercase;}
```

These are the necessary steps:

- Insert key
- **TURN KEY CLOCKWISE**
- Push accelerator

Do *not* push the brake at the same time as the accelerator.

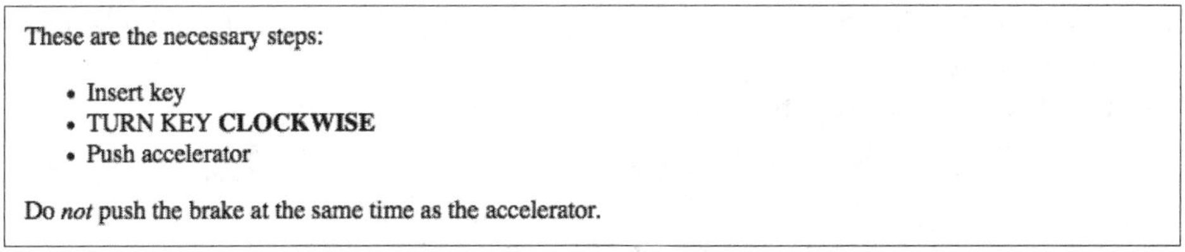

Figure 2-31. Styling second children

You can insert any integer you choose; if you have a use case for selecting any ordered list that is the 93rd child element of its parent, then ol:nth-child(93) is ready to serve. This will match the 93rd child of any parent as long as that child is an ordered list. (This does not mean the 93rd ordered list among its siblings; see the next section for that.)

More powerfully, you can use simple algebraic expressions in the form a n $+ b$ or a n $- b$ to define recurring instances, where a and b are integers and n is present as itself. Furthermore, the $+ b$ or $- b$ part is optional and thus can be dropped if it isn't needed.

Let's suppose we want to select every third list item in an unordered list, starting with the first. The following makes that possible, selecting the first and fourth items, as shown in Figure 2-32.

```
ul > li:nth-child(3n + 1) {text-transform: uppercase;}
```

These are the necessary steps:

- INSERT KEY
- Turn key **clockwise**
- Grip steering wheel with hands
- PUSH ACCELERATOR
- Steer vehicle
- Use brake as necessary

Do *not* push the brake at the same time as the accelerator.

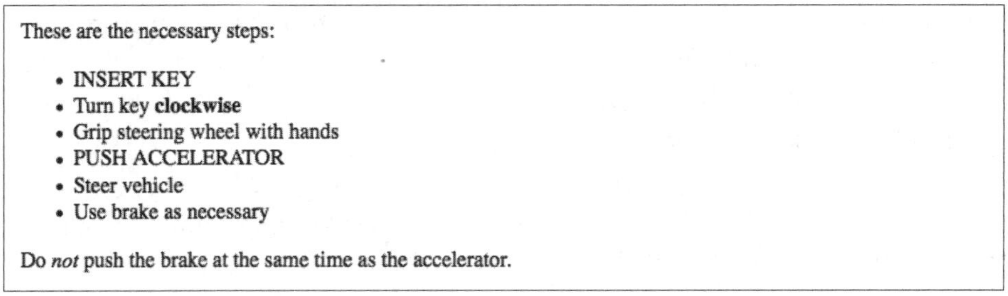

Figure 2-32. Styling every third list item

The way this works is that n represents the series 0, 1, 2, 3, 4, and on into infinity. The browser then solves for 3 n + 1, yielding 1, 4, 7, 10, 13, and so on. Were we to drop the +1, thus leaving us with simply 3n, the results would be 0, 3, 6, 9, 12, and so on.

Since there is no zeroth list item—all element counting starts with one, to the likely chagrin of array-slingers everywhere—the first list item selected by this expression would be the third list item in the list.

Given that element counting starts with one, it's a minor trick to deduce that :nth-child(2n) will select even-numbered children, and either :nth-child(2n+1) or :nth-child(2n-1) will select odd-numbered children. You can commit that to memory, or you can use the two special keywords that :nth-child() accepts: even and odd. Want to highlight every other row of a table, starting with the first? Here's how you do it, with the results shown in Figure 2-33:

```
tr:nth-child(odd) {background: silver;}
```

Mississippi	MS	Jackson	Northern Mockingbird
Missouri	MO	Jefferson City	Eastern Bluebird
Montana	MT	Helena	Western Meadowlark
Nebraska	NE	Lincoln	Western Meadowlark
Nevada	NV	Carson City	Mountain Bluebird
New Hampshire	NH	Concord	Purple Finch
New Jersey	NJ	Trenton	Eastern Goldfinch
New Mexico	NM	Santa Fe	Roadrunner
New York	NY	Albany	Eastern Bluebird
North Carolina	NC	Raleigh	Northern Cardinal
North Dakota	ND	Bismarck	Western Meadowlark
Ohio	OH	Columbus	Northern Cardinal
Oklahoma	OK	Oklahoma City	Scissor-Tailed Flycatcher
Oregon	OR	Salem	Western Meadowlark
Pennsylvania	PA	Harrisburg	Ruffed Grouse

Figure 2-33. Styling every other table row

Anything more complex than every-other-element requires an *an + b* expression.

Note that when you want to use a negative number for *b*, you have to remove the + sign or else the selector will fail entirely. Of the following two rules, only the first will do anything. The second will be dropped by the parser and ignored:

```
tr:nth-child(4n - 2) {background: silver;}
tr:nth-child(3n + -2) {background: red;}
```

If you want to select every row starting with the ninth, you can use either of the following. They are similar in that they will select all rows starting with the ninth, but the latter one has greater specificity, which we discuss in Chapter 3:

```
tr:nth-child(n + 9) {background: silver;}
tr:nth-child(8) ~ tr {background: silver;}
```

As you might expect, there is a corresponding pseudo-class in :nth-last-child(). This lets you do the same thing as :nth-child(), except with :nth-last-child() you start from the last element in a list of siblings and count backward toward the beginning. If you're intent on highlighting every other table row *and* making sure the very last row is one of the rows in the highlighting pattern, either one of these will work for you:

```
tr:nth-last-child(odd) {background: silver;}
tr:nth-last-child(2n+1) {background: silver;} /* equivalent */
```

If the DOM is updated to add or remove table rows, there is no need to add or remove classes. By using structural selectors, these selectors will always match the odd rows of the updated DOM.

Any element can be matched using both :nth-child() and :nth-last-child() if it fits the criteria. Consider these rules, the results of which are shown in Figure 2-34:

```
li:nth-child(3n + 3) {border-left: 5px solid black;}
li:nth-last-child(4n - 1) {border-right: 5px solid black; background: silver;}
```

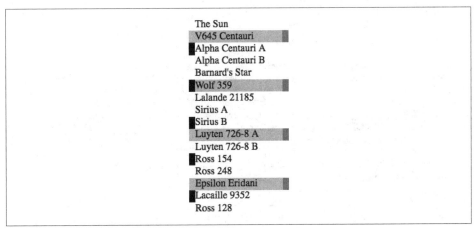

Figure 2-34. Combining patterns of :nth-child() and :nth-last-child()

It's also the case that you can string these two pseudo-classes together as :nth-child(1):nth-last-child(1), thus creating a more verbose restatement of :only-child. There's no real reason to do so other than to create a selector with a higher specificity, but the option is there.

You can use CSS to determine how many list items are in a list, and style them accordingly:

```
li:only-child {width: 100%;}
li:nth-child(1):nth-last-child(2),
li:nth-child(2):nth-last-child(1) {width: 50%;}
li:nth-child(1):nth-last-child(3),
li:nth-child(1):nth-last-child(3) ~ li {width: 33.33%;}
li:nth-child(1):nth-last-child(4),
li:nth-child(1):nth-last-child(4) ~ li {width: 25%;}
```

In these examples, if a list item is the only list item, then the width is 100%. If a list item is the first item and also the second-from-the-last item, that means there are two items, and the width is 50%. If an item is the first item and also the third from the last item, then we make it, and the two sibling list items following it, 33% wide. Similarly, if a list item is the first item and also the fourth from the last item, it means that there are exactly four items, so we make it, and its three siblings, 25% of the width.

Selecting every nth of a type

In what's probably become a familiar pattern, the :nth-child() and :nth-last-child() pseudo-classes have analogues in :nth-of-type() and :nth-last-of-type(). You can, for example, select every other hyperlink that's a child of any given paragraph, starting with the second, using p > a:nth-of-type(even). This will ignore all other elements (spans, strongs, etc.) and consider only the links, as demonstrated in Figure 2-35:

```
p > a:nth-of-type(even) {background: blue; color: white;}
```

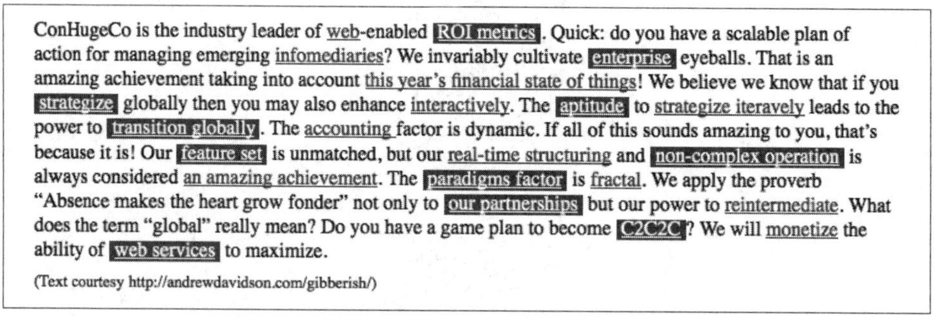

ConHugeCo is the industry leader of web-enabled ROI metrics. Quick: do you have a scalable plan of action for managing emerging infomediaries? We invariably cultivate enterprise eyeballs. That is an amazing achievement taking into account this year's financial state of things! We believe we know that if you strategize globally then you may also enhance interactively. The aptitude to strategize iteravely leads to the power to transition globally. The accounting factor is dynamic. If all of this sounds amazing to you, that's because it is! Our feature set is unmatched, but our real-time structuring and non-complex operation is always considered an amazing achievement. The paradigms factor is fractal. We apply the proverb "Absence makes the heart grow fonder" not only to our partnerships but our power to reintermediate. What does the term "global" really mean? Do you have a game plan to become C2C2C? We will monetize the ability of web services to maximize.

(Text courtesy http://andrewdavidson.com/gibberish/)

Figure 2-35. Selecting the even-numbered links

If you want to work from the last hyperlink backward, then you'd use p > a:nth-last-of-type(even).

As before, these select elements of a type from among their sibling elements, *not* from among all the elements of a type within the entire document as a single group. Each element has its own list of siblings, and selections happen within each group.

As you might expect, you can string these two together as :nth-of-type(1):nth-last-of-type(1) to restate :only-of-type, only with higher specificity. (We *will* explain specificity in Chapter 3, I promise.)

Dynamic Pseudo-Classes

Beyond the structural pseudo-classes, there are a set of pseudo-classes that relate to structure but can change based on changes made to the page after it's been rendered. In other words, the styles are applied to pieces of a document based on something in addition to the structure of the document, and in a way that cannot be precisely deduced simply by studying the document's markup.

It may sound like we're applying styles at random, but not so. Instead, we're applying styles based on somewhat ephemeral conditions that can't be predicted in advance. Nevertheless, the circumstances under which the styles will appear are, in fact, well-defined. Think of it this way: during a sporting event, whenever the home team scores, the crowd will cheer. You don't know exactly when during a game the team will score, but when it does, the crowd will cheer, just as predicted. The fact that you can't predict the exact moment of the cheer doesn't make it any less expected.

Consider the anchor element (a), which (in HTML and related languages) establishes a link from one document to another. Anchors are always anchors, but some anchors refer to pages that have already been visited, while others refer to pages that have yet to be visited. You can't tell the difference by simply looking at the HTML markup, because in the markup, all anchors look the same. The only way to tell which links have been visited is by comparing the links in a document to the user's browser history. So there are actually two basic types of links: visited and unvisited.

Hyperlink pseudo-classes

CSS2.1 defines two pseudo-classes that apply only to hyperlinks. In HTML, these are any a elements with an href attribute; in XML languages, they're any elements that act as links to another resource. Table 2-2 describes the pseudo-classes you can apply to them.

Table 2-2. Link pseudo-classes

Name	Description
:link	Refers to any anchor that is a hyperlink (i.e., has an href attribute) and points to an address that has not been visited.
:visited	Refers to any anchor that is a hyperlink to an already visited address. For security reasons, the styles that can be applied to visited links are severely limited; see sidebar "Visited Links and Privacy" on page 79 for details.

The first of the pseudo-classes in Table 2-2 may seem a bit redundant. After all, if an anchor hasn't been visited, then it must be unvisited, right? If that's the case, all we should need is the following:

```
a {color: blue;}
a:visited {color: red;}
```

Although this format seems reasonable, it's actually not quite enough. The first of the rules shown here applies not only to unvisited links, but also to placeholder links such as this one:

```
<a>4. The Lives of Meerkats</a>
```

The resulting text would be blue because the a element will match the rule a {color: blue;}. Therefore, to avoid applying your link styles to placeholders, use the :link and :visited pseudo-classes:

```
a:link {color: blue;}    /* unvisited links are blue */
a:visited {color: red;}  /* visited links are red */
```

This is a good place to revisit attribute and class selectors and show how they can be combined with pseudo-classes. For example, let's say you want to change the color of links that point outside your own site. In most circumstances we can use the starts-with attribute selector. However, some CMS's set all links to be absolute URLS, in which case you could assign a class to each of these anchors. It's easy:

```
<a href="/about.html">My About page</a>
<a href="https://www.site.net/" class="external">An external site</a>
```

To apply different styles to the external link, all you need is a rule like this:

```
a.external:link, a[href^="http"]:link { color: slateblue;}
a.external:visited, a[href^="http"]:visited  {color: maroon;}
```

This rule will make the second anchor in the preceding markup slateblue by default, and maroon once visited, while the first anchor will remain the default color for hyperlinks (usually blue when not visited and purple once visited). For improved usability and accessibility, visited links should be easily differentiable from non-visited links.

 Styled visited links enables visitors to know where they have been and what they have yet to visit. This is especially important on large websites where it may be difficult to remember, especially for those with cognitive disabilities, which pages have been visited. Not only is highlighting visited links one of the W3C Web Content Accessibility Guidelines, but it makes searching for content faster, more efficient, and less stressful for everyone.

The same general syntax is used for ID selectors as well:

```
a#footer-copyright:link{background: yellow;}
a#footer-copyright:visited {background: gray;}
```

You can chain the two link-state pseudo-classes together, but there's no reason why you ever would: a link cannot be both visited and unvisited at the same time!

Visited Links and Privacy

For well over a decade, it was possible to style visited links with any CSS properties available, just as you could unvisited links. However, in the mid-2000s several people demonstrated that one could use visual styling and simple DOM scripting to determine if a user had visited a given page. For example, given the rule `:visited {font-weight: bold;}`, a script could find all of the boldfaced links and tell the user which of those sites they'd visited—or, worse still, report those sites back to a server. A similar, non-scripted tactic uses background images to achieve the same result.

While this might not seem terribly serious to you, it can be utterly devastating for a web user in a country where one can be jailed for visiting certain sites—opposition parties, unsanctioned religious organizations, "immoral" or "corrupting" sites, and so on. It can also be used by phishing sites to determine which online banks a user has visited. Thus, two steps were taken.

The first step is that only color-related properties can be applied to visited links: `color`, `background-color`, `column-rule-color`, `outline-color`, `border-color`, and the individual-side border color properties (e.g., `border-top-color`). Attempts to apply any other property to a visited link will be ignored. Furthermore, any styles defined for `:link` will be applied to visited links as well as unvisited links, which effectively makes `:link` "style any hyperlink," instead of "style any unvisited hyperlink."

The second step is that if a visited link has its styles queried via the DOM, the resulting value will be as if the link were not visited. Thus, if you've defined visited links to be purple rather than unvisited links' blue, even though the link will appear purple onscreen, a DOM query of its color will return the blue value, not the purple one.

As of late 2017, this behavior is present throughout all browsing modes, not just "private browsing" modes. Even though we're limited in how we can use CSS to differentiate visited links from non-visited links, it is important for usability and accessibility to use the limited styles supported by visited links to differentiate them from unvisited links.

User action pseudo-classes

CSS defines a few pseudo-classes that can change a document's appearance based on actions taken by the user. These dynamic pseudo-classes have traditionally been used to style hyperlinks, but the possibilities are much wider. Table 2-3 describes these pseudo-classes.

Table 2-3. *User action pseudo-classes*

Name	Description
:focus	Refers to any element that currently has the input focus—i.e., can accept keyboard input or be activated in some way.
:hover	Refers to any element over which the mouse pointer is placed—e.g., a hyperlink over which the mouse pointer is hovering.
:active	Refers to any element that has been activated by user input—e.g., a hyperlink on which a user clicks during the time the mouse button is held down.

Elements that can become `:active` include links, buttons, menu items, and any element with a tabindex value. These elements and all other interactive elements, including form controls and elements that are content-editable, can also receive focus.

As with `:link` and `:visited`, these pseudo-classes are most familiar in the context of hyperlinks. Many web pages have styles that look like this:

```
a:link {color: navy;}
a:visited {color: gray;}
a:focus {color: orange;}
a:hover {color: red;}
a:active {color: yellow;}
```

The order of the pseudo-classes is more important than it might seem at first. The usual recommendation is "link-visited-hover-active," although this has been modified to "link-visited-focus-hover-active." The next chapter explains why this particular ordering is important and discusses several reasons you might choose to change or even ignore the recommended ordering.

Notice that the dynamic pseudo-classes can be applied to any element, which is good since it's often useful to apply dynamic styles to elements that aren't links. For example, using this markup:

```
input:focus {background: silver; font-weight: bold;}
```

you could highlight a form element that is ready to accept keyboard input, as shown in Figure 2-36.

Figure 2-36. *Highlighting a form element that has focus*

You can also perform some rather odd feats by applying dynamic pseudo-classes to arbitrary elements. You might decide to give users a "highlight" effect by way of the following:

```
body *:hover {background: yellow;}
```

This rule will cause any element that's descended from the body element to display a yellow background when it's in a hover state. Headings, paragraphs, lists, tables, images, and anything else found inside the body will be changed to have a yellow background. You could also change the font, put a border around the element being hovered, or alter anything else the browser will allow.

> While you can style elements with :focus any way you like, do *not* remove all styling from focused elements. Differentiating which element currently has focus is vital for accessibility, especially for those navigating your site or application with a keyboard.

Real-world issues with dynamic styling

Dynamic pseudo-classes present some interesting issues and peculiarities. For example, it's possible to set visited and unvisited links to one font size and make hovered links a larger size, as shown in Figure 2-37:

```
a:link, a:visited {font-size: 13px;}
a:hover, a:active {font-size: 20px;}
```

css-tricks.com lea.verou.me meyerweb.com **tantek.com** zeldman.com	**Web Blogs** These are the web logs ("blogs") I visit a lot. They're all written by people who know a lot about Web design and CSS in general. By reading them I can get a sense of the trends in design and thinking about document structure.

Figure 2-37. Changing layout with dynamic pseudo-classes

As you can see, the user agent increases the size of the anchor while the mouse pointer hovers over it; or, thanks to the :active setting, when a user touches it on a touch screen. A user agent that supports this behavior must redraw the document while an anchor is in hover state, which could force a reflow of all the content that follows the link.

UI-State Pseudo-Classes

Closely related to the dynamic pseudo-classes are the *user-interface (UI) state pseudo-classes*, which are summarized in Table 2-4. These pseudo-classes allow for styling based on the current state of user-interface elements like checkboxes.

Table 2-4. UI-state pseudo-classes

Name	Description
:enabled	Refers to user-interface elements (such as form elements) that are enabled; that is, available for input.
:disabled	Refers to user-interface elements (such as form elements) that are disabled; that is, not available for input.
:checked	Refers to radio buttons or checkboxes that have been selected, either by the user or by defaults within the document itself.
:indeterminate	Refers to radio buttons or checkboxes that are neither checked nor unchecked; this state can only be set via DOM scripting, and not due to user input.
:default	Refers to the radio button, checkbox, or option that was selected by default.
:valid	Refers to a user input that meets all of its data validity semantics
:invalid	Refers to a user input that does not meet all of its data validity semantics
:in-range	Refers to a user input whose value is between the minimum and maximum values
:out-of-range	Refers to a user input whose value is below the minimum or above the maximum values allowed by the control
:required	Refers to a user input that must have a value set
:optional	Refers to a user input that does not need to have a value set
:read-write	Refers to a user input that is editable by the user
:read-only	Refers to a user input that is not editable by the user

Although the state of a UI element can certainly be changed by user action—for example, a user checking or unchecking a checkbox—UI-state pseudo-classes are not classified as purely dynamic because they can also be affected by the document structure or DOM scripting.

 You might think that :focus belongs in this section, not the previous section. However, the Selectors Level 3 specification groups :focus in with :hover and :active. This is most likely because they were grouped together in CSS2, which had no UI-state pseudo-classes. More importantly, though, focus can be given to non-UI elements, such as headings or paragraphs—one example is when they are read by a speaking browser. That alone keeps it from being considered a UI-state pseudo-class.

Enabled and disabled UI elements

Thanks to both DOM scripting and HTML5, it is possible to mark a user-interface element (or group of user interface elements) as being disabled. A disabled element is displayed, but cannot be selected, activated, or otherwise interacted with by the user. Authors can set an element to be disabled either through DOM scripting, or (in HTML5) by adding a disabled attribute to the element's markup.

Any element that hasn't been disabled is by definition enabled. You can style these two states using the :enabled and :disabled pseudo-classes. It's much more common to style disabled elements and leave enabled elements alone, but both have their uses, as illustrated in Figure 2-38:

```
:enabled {font-weight: bold;}
:disabled {opacity: 0.5;}
```

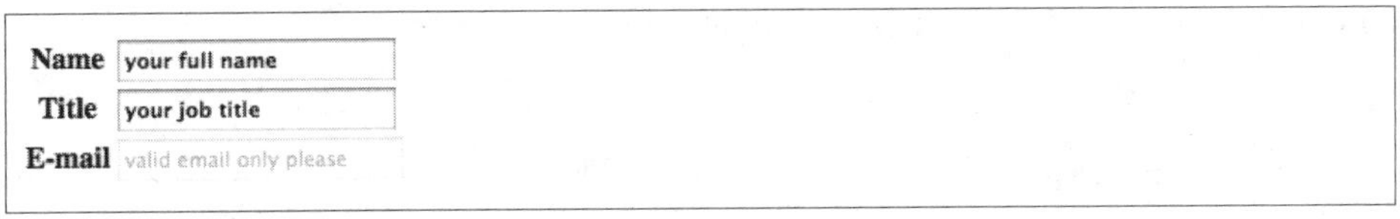

Figure 2-38. Styling enabled and disabled UI elements

Check states

In addition to being enabled or disabled, certain UI elements can be checked or unchecked—in HTML, the input types "checkbox" and "radio" fit this definition. Selectors level 3 offers a :checked pseudo-class to handle elements in that state, though curiously it omits an :unchecked. There is also the :indeterminate pseudo-class, which matches any checkable UI element that is neither checked nor unchecked. These states are illustrated in Figure 2-39:

```
:checked {background: silver;}
:indeterminate {border: red;}
```

In addition, you can use the negation pseudo-class, which is covered later, to select checkboxes which are not checked with input[type="checkbox"]:not(:checked). Only radio buttons and checkboxes can be checked. All other elements, and these two when not checked, are :not(:checked).

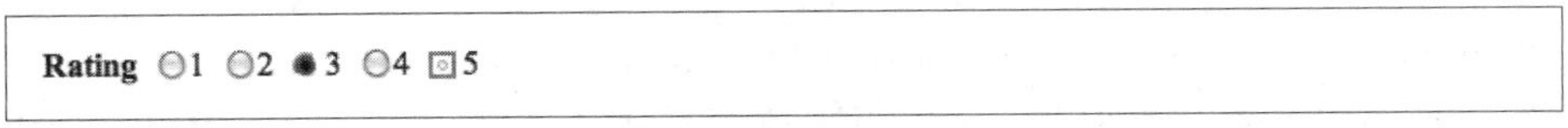

Figure 2-39. Styling checked and indeterminate UI elements

Although checkable elements are unchecked by default, it's possible for a HTML author to toggle them on by adding the checked attribute to an element's markup. An author can also use DOM scripting to flip an element's checked state to checked or unchecked, whichever they prefer.

There is a third state, "indeterminate." As of late 2017, this state can only be set through DOM scripting or by the user agent itself; there is no markup-level method to set elements to an indeterminate state. The purpose of allowing an indeterminate state is to visually indicate that the element needs to be checked (or unchecked) by the user. However, note that this is purely a visual effect: it does not affect the underlying state of the UI element, which is either checked or unchecked, depending on document markup and the effects of any DOM scripting.

Although the previous examples show styled radio buttons, remember that direct styling of radio buttons and checkboxes with CSS is actually very limited. However, that shouldn't limit your use of the selected-option pseudo-classes. As an example, you can style the labels associated with your checkboxes and radio buttons using a combination of :checked and the adjacent sibling combinator:

```
input[type="checkbox"]:checked + label {
   color: red;
   font-style: italic;
}
```

```
<input id="chbx" type="checkbox"> <label for="chbx">I am a label</label>
```

Default option pseudo-class

The :default pseudo-class matches the UI elements that are the default among a set of similar elements. This typically applies to context menu items, buttons, and select lists/menus. If there are several same-named radio buttons, the one that was originally checked matches :default, even if the UI has been updated by the user so that it no longer matches :checked. If a checkbox was checked on page load, :default matches it. Any initially-selected option(s) in a select element will match. The :default pseudo-class can also match buttons and menu items:

```
[type="checkbox"]:default + label { font-style: italic; }
```

```
<input type="checkbox" id="chbx" checked name="foo" value="bar">
<label for="chbx">This was checked on page load</label>
```

Optionality pseudo-classes

The pseudo-class :required matches any form control that is required, as denoted by the presence of the required attribute (in HTML5). The :optional pseudo-class matches form controls that do not have the required attribute, or whose required attribute has a value of false.

A form element is :required or :optional if a value for it is, respectively, required or optional before the form to which it belongs can be validly submitted. For example:

```
input:required { border: 1px solid #f00;}
input:optional { border: 1px solid #ccc;}
```

```
<input type="email" placeholder="enter an email address" required>
<input type="email" placeholder="optional email address">
<input type="email" placeholder="optional email address" required="false">
```

The first email input will match the :required pseudo-class because of the presence of the required attribute. The second input is optional, and therefore will match the :optional pseudo-class. The same is true for the third input, which has a required attribute, but the value is false.

We could also use attribute selectors instead. The following selectors are equivalent to the preceding ones:

```
input[required] { border: 1px solid #f00;}
input:not([required]) { border: 1px solid #ccc;}
```

Elements that are not form-input elements can be neither required nor optional.

Validity pseudo-classes

The :valid pseudo-class refers to a user input that meets all of its data validity requirements. The :invalid pseudo-class, on the other hand, refers to a user input that does not meet all of its data validity requirements.

The validity pseudo-classes :valid and :invalid only apply to elements having the capacity for data validity requirements: a div will never match either selector, but an input could match either, depending on the current state of the interface.

Here's an example where an image is dropped into the background of any email input which has focus, with one image being used when the input is invalid and another used when the input is valid, as illustrated in Figure 2-40:

```
input[type="email"]:focus {
  background-position: 100% 50%;
  background-repeat: no-repeat;
}
input[type="email"]:focus:invalid {
  background-image: url(warning.jpg);
}
input[type="email"]:focus:valid {
  background-image: url(checkmark.jpg);
}

<input type="email">
```

Figure 2-40. Styling valid and invalid UI elements

These pseudo-class states are dependent on what the user agent reports to its own style system, and so may not act as you might expect. For example, in late 2017, an empty email input matched :valid in multiple user agents, despite the fact a null input is not a valid email address. Until these validation routines improve, it is best to treat the validity pseudo-classes with caution.

Range pseudo-classes

The range pseudo-classes include :in-range, which refers to a user input whose value is between the minimum and maximum values set by HTML5's min and max attributes, and :out-of-range, which refers to a user input whose value is below the minimum or above the maximum values allowed by the control.

For example, consider a number input that accepts numbers in the range 0 to 1,000:

```
input[type="number"]:focus {
  background-position: 100% 50%;
  background-repeat: no-repeat;
}
input[type="number"]:focus:out-of-range {
  background-image: url(warning.jpg);
}
input[type="number"]:focus:in-range {
  background-image: url(checkmark.jpg);
}

<input id="nickels" type="number" min="0" max="1000" />
```

The :in-range and :out-of-range pseudo-classes apply *only* to elements with range limitations. Elements that don't have range limitations, like links for inputs of type tel, will not be matched by either pseudo-class.

There is also a step attribute in HTML5. If a value is invalid because it does not match the step value, but is still between or equal to the min and max values, it will match :invalid while *also* still matching :in-range. That is to say, a value can be in-range while also being invalid.

Thus, in the following scenario, the input's value will be both red and boldfaced, because 23 is in range but is not evenly divisible by 10:

```
input[type="number"]:invalid {color: red;}
input[type="number"]:in-range {font-weight: bold;}

<input id="by-tens" type="number" min="0" max="1000" step="10" value="23" />
```

Mutability pseudo-classes

The mutability pseudo-classes include :read-write, which refers to a user input that is editable by the user; and :read-only, which matches user inputs that are not edita-

---

ble. Only elements that have the capacity to be altered by user input can match :read-write.

For example, in HTML, a non-disabled, non-read-only input element is :read-write, as is any element with the contenteditable attribute. Everything else matches :read-only:

By default, neither of the following rules would ever match: textarea elements are read-write, and pre elements are read-only.

```
textarea:read-only { opacity: 0.75;}
pre:read-write:hover {border: 1px dashed green;}
```

However, each can be made to match as follows:

```
<textarea disabled></textarea>
<pre contenteditable>Type your own code!</pre>
```

Because the textarea is given a disabled attribute, it becomes read-only, and so will have the first rule apply. Similarly, the pre here has been given the attribute contenteditable, so now it is a read-write element. This will be matched by the second rule.

The :target Pseudo-Class

When a URL includes a fragment identifier, the piece of the document at which it points is called (in CSS) the *target*. Thus, you can uniquely style any element that is the target of a URL fragment identifier with the :target pseudo-class.

Even if you're unfamiliar with the term "fragment identifier," you've probably seen them in action. Consider this URL:

```
http://www.w3.org/TR/css3-selectors/#target-pseudo
```

The target-pseudo portion of the URL is the fragment identifier, which is marked by the # symbol. If the referenced page (*http://www.w3.org/TR/css3-selectors/*) has an element with an ID of target-pseudo, then that element becomes the target of the fragment identifier.

Thanks to :target, you can highlight any targeted element within a document, or you can devise different styles for various types of elements that might be targeted— say, one style for targeted headings, another for targeted tables, and so on. Figure 2-41 shows an example of :target in action:

```
*:target {border-left: 5px solid gray; background: yellow url(target.png)
     top right no-repeat;}
```

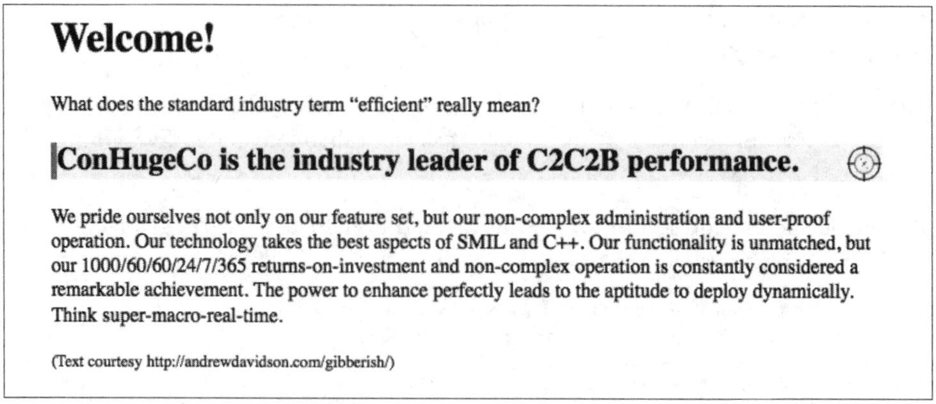

Welcome!

What does the standard industry term "efficient" really mean?

ConHugeCo is the industry leader of C2C2B performance.

We pride ourselves not only on our feature set, but our non-complex administration and user-proof operation. Our technology takes the best aspects of SMIL and C++. Our functionality is unmatched, but our 1000/60/60/24/7/365 returns-on-investment and non-complex operation is constantly considered a remarkable achievement. The power to enhance perfectly leads to the aptitude to deploy dynamically. Think super-macro-real-time.

(Text courtesy http://andrewdavidson.com/gibberish/)

Figure 2-41. Styling a fragment identifier target

`:target` styles will not be applied in two circumstances:

1. If the page is accessed via a URL that does not have a fragment identifier
2. If the page is accessed via a URL that has a fragment identifier, but the identifier does not match any elements within the document

More interestingly, though, what happens if multiple elements within a document can be matched by the fragment identifier—for example, if the author erroneously included three separate instances of `<div id="target-pseudo">` in the same document?

The short answer is that CSS doesn't have or need rules to cover this case, because all CSS is concerned with is styling targets. Whether the browser picks just one of the three elements to be the target or designates all three as co-equal targets, `:target` styles should be applied to anything that is a valid target.

The :lang Pseudo-Class

For situations where you want to select an element based on its language, you can use the `:lang()` pseudo-class. In terms of its matching patterns, the `:lang()` pseudo-class is similar to the `|=` attribute selector. For example, to italicize elements whose content is written in French, you could write either of the following:

```
*:lang(fr) {font-style: italic;}
*[lang|="fr"] {font-style: italic;}
```

The primary difference between the pseudo-class selector and the attribute selector is that language information can be derived from a number of sources, some of which are outside the element itself. For the attribute selector, the element must have the attribute present to match. The `:lang` pseudo-class, on the other hand, matches descendants of an element with the language declaration. As Selectors Level 3 states:

> In HTML, the language is determined by a combination of the `lang` attribute, and possibly information from the `meta` elements and the protocol (such as HTTP headers). XML uses an attribute called `xml:lang`, and there may be other document language-specific methods for determining the language.

The pseudo-class will operate on all of that information, whereas the attribute selector can only work if there is a `lang` attribute present in the element's markup. Therefore, the pseudo-class is more robust than the attribute selector and is probably a better choice in most cases where language-specific styling is needed.

The Negation Pseudo-Class

Every selector we've covered thus far has had one thing in common: they're all positive selectors. In other words, they are used to identify the things that should be selected, thus excluding by implication all the things that don't match and are thus not selected.

For those times when you want to invert this formulation and select elements based on what they are *not*, Selectors Level 3 introduced the negation pseudo-class, `:not()`. It's not quite like any other selector, fittingly enough, and it does have some restrictions on its use, but let's start with an example.

Let's suppose you want to apply a style to every list item that doesn't have a `class` of `moreinfo`, as illustrated in Figure 2-42. That used to be very difficult, and in certain cases impossible, to make happen. If we wanted all the list items to be italic except those with the class `.moreinfo`, we used to declare all the links as italic, generally having to target the `ul` with a class, then normalize back based on the class, making sure the override came last in the source order, and had equal or higher specificity. Now we can declare:

```
li:not(.moreinfo) {font-style: italic;}
```

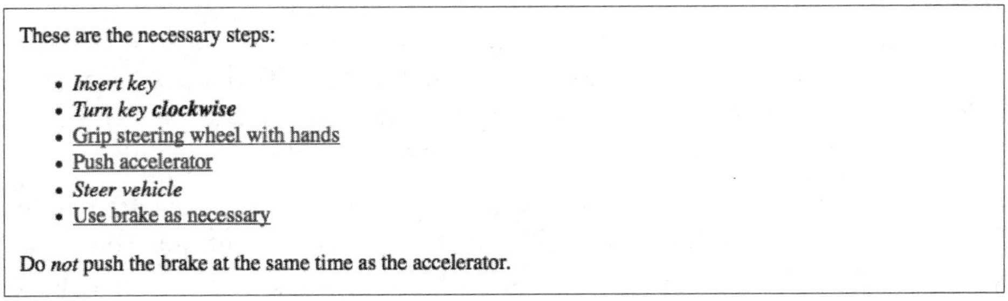

These are the necessary steps:

- *Insert key*
- *Turn key **clockwise***
- Grip steering wheel with hands
- Push accelerator
- *Steer vehicle*
- Use brake as necessary

Do *not* push the brake at the same time as the accelerator.

Figure 2-42. Styling list items that don't have a certain class

The way :not() works is that you attach it to an element, and then in the parentheses you fill in a simple selector. A simple selector, according to the W3C, is:

> either a type selector, universal selector, attribute selector, class selector, ID selector, or pseudo-class.

Basically, a simple selector is a selector with no ancestral-descendant relationship.

Note the "either" there: you can only use one of those inside :not(). You can't group them and you can't combine them using combinators, which means you can't use a descendant selector, because the space separating elements in a descendant selector is a combinator. Those restrictions may (indeed most likely will) be lifted in the future, but we can still do quite a lot even within the given constraints.

For example, let's flip around the previous example and select all elements with a class of moreinfo that are not list items. This is illustrated in Figure 2-43:

```
.moreinfo:not(li) {font-style: italic;}
```

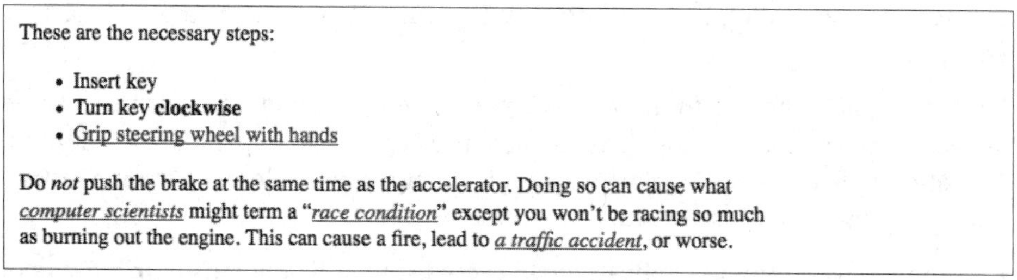

These are the necessary steps:

- Insert key
- Turn key **clockwise**
- <u>Grip steering wheel with hands</u>

Do *not* push the brake at the same time as the accelerator. Doing so can cause what <u>computer scientists</u> might term a "<u>*race condition*</u>" except you won't be racing so much as burning out the engine. This can cause a fire, lead to <u>*a traffic accident*</u>, or worse.

Figure 2-43. Styling elements with a certain class that aren't list items

Translated into English, the selector would say, "Select all elements with a class whose value contains the word moreinfo as long as they are not li elements." Similarly, the translation of li:not(.moreinfo) would be "Select all li elements as long as they do not have a class whose value contains the word moreinfo."

Technically, you can put a universal selector into the parentheses, but there's very little point. After all, p:not(*) would mean "Select any p element as long as it isn't any element," and there's no such thing as an element that is not an element. Very similar to that would be p:not(p), which would also select nothing. It's also possible to write things like p:not(div), which will select any p element that is not a div element—in other words, all of them. Again, there is very little reason to do so.

You can also use the negation pseudo-class at any point in a more complex selector. Thus, to select all tables that are not children of a section element, you would write *:not(section) > table. Similarly, to select table header cells that are not part of the table header, you'd write something like table *:not(thead) > tr > th, with a result like that shown in Figure 2-44.

State	Post	Capital	State Bird
Alabama	AL	Montgomery	Yellowhammer
Alaska	AK	Juneau	Willow Ptarmigan
Arizona	AZ	Phoenix	Cactus Wren
Arkansas	AR	Little Rock	Mockingbird
California	CA	Sacramento	California Quail
Colorado	CO	Denver	Lark Bunting
Connecticut	CT	Hartford	American Robin
Delaware	DE	Dover	Blue Hen Chicken
Florida	FL	Tallahassee	Northern Mockingbird
Georgia	GA	Atlanta	Brown Thrasher
State	Post	Capital	State Bird

Figure 2-44. Styling header cells outside the table's head area

What you cannot do is nest negation pseudo-classes; thus, p:not(:not(p)) is invalid and will be ignored. It's also, logically, the equivalent of just writing p, so there's no point anyway. Furthermore, you cannot reference pseudo-elements (which we'll cover shortly) inside the parentheses, since they are not simple selectors.

On the other hand, it's possible to chain negations together to create a sort of "and also not this" effect. For example, you might want to select all elements with a class of link that are neither list items nor paragraphs:

```
*.link:not(li):not(p) {font-style: italic;}
```

That translates to "Select all elements with a class whose value contains the word link as long as they are neither li nor p elements."

One thing to watch out for is that you can have situations where rules combine in unexpected ways, mostly because we're not used to thinking of selection in the negative. Consider this test case:

```
div:not(.one) p {font-weight: normal;}
div.one p {font-weight: bold;}

<div class="one">
    <div class="two">
        <p>I'm a paragraph!</p>
    </div>
</div>
```

The paragraph will be boldfaced, not normal-weight. This is because both rules match: the p element is descended from a div whose class does not contain the word one (<div class="two">), but it is *also* descended from a div whose class contains the word one. Both rules match, and so both apply. Since there is a conflict, the cascade is used to resolve the conflict, and the second rule wins. The structural arrangement of the markup, with the div.two being "closer" to the paragraph than div.one, is irrelevant.

Pseudo-Element Selectors

Much as pseudo-classes assign phantom classes to anchors, pseudo-elements insert fictional elements into a document in order to achieve certain effects. Four basic pseudo-elements were defined in CSS 2, and they let you style the first letter of an element, style the first line of an element, and both create and style "before" and "after" content. There are other pseudo-classes that have been defined since CSS 2 (e.g., ::marker), and we'll explore those in the chapters of the book for which they're relevant. The four from CSS2 will be covered here because they're old-school, and because they make a convenient way to talk about pseudo-element behavior.

Unlike the single colon of pseudo-classes, pseudo-elements employ a double-colon syntax, like ::first-line. This is meant to distinguish pseudo-elements from pseudo-classes. This was not always the case—in CSS2, both selector types used a single colon—so for backward compatibility, browsers will accept single-colon pseudo-element selectors. Don't take this as an excuse to be sloppy, though! Use the proper number of colons at all times in order to future-proof your CSS; after all, there is no way to predict when browsers will stop accepting single-colon pseudo-element selectors.

Note that all pseudo-elements must be placed at the very end of the selector in which they appear. It would not be legal to write p::first-line em since the pseudo-element comes before the subject of the selector (the subject is the last element listed). This also means that only one pseudo-element is permitted in a given selector, though that restriction may be eased in future versions of CSS.

Styling the First Letter

The ::first-letter pseudo-element styles the first letter, or a leading punctuation character and the first letter (if the text starts with punctuation), of any non-inline element. This rule causes the first letter of every paragraph to be colored red:

```
p::first-letter {color: red;}
```

The ::first-letter pseudo-element is most commonly used to create an "initial cap" or "drop cap" typographic effect. You could make the first letter of each p twice as big as the rest of the heading, though you may want to only apply this styling to the first letter of the first paragraph:

```
p:first-of-type::first-letter {font-size: 200%;}
```

The result of this rule is illustrated in Figure 2-45.

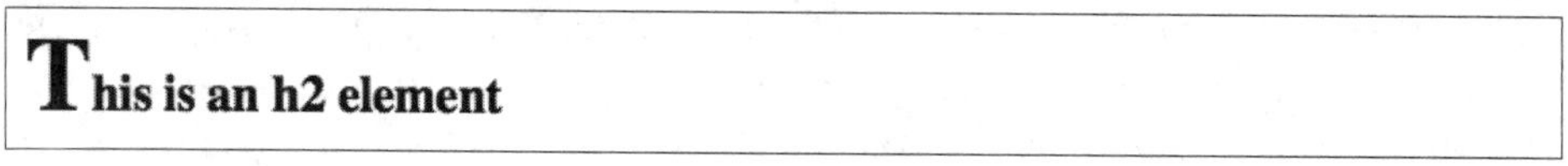

Figure 2-45. The ::first-letter pseudo-element in action

This rule effectively causes the user agent to style a fictional, or "faux" element, that encloses the first letter of each p. It would look something like this:

```
<p><p-first-letter>T</p-first-letter>his is a p element, with a styled first
    letter</h2>
```

The `::first-letter` styles are applied only to the contents of the fictional element shown in the example. This `<p-first-letter>` element does *not* appear in the document source, nor even in the DOM tree. Instead, its existence is constructed on the fly by the user agent and is used to apply the `::first-letter` style(s) to the appropriate bit of text. In other words, `<p-first-letter>` is a pseudo-element. Remember, you don't have to add any new tags. The user agent styles the first letter for you as if you had encased it in a styled element.

The first letter is defined as the first typographic letter unit of the originating element, if it is not preceded by other content, like an image. The specifications use "letter unit" because some languages have letters made up of more than character, like "oe" in Norse. Punctuation that precedes or follows the first letter unit, even if there are several such symbols, are included in the `::first-letter` pseudo-element.

Styling the First Line

Similarly, `::first-line` can be used to affect the first line of text in an element. For example, you could make the first line of each paragraph in a document large and purple:

```
p::first-line {
    font-size: 150%;
    color: purple;
}
```

In Figure 2-46, the style is applied to the first displayed line of text in each paragraph. This is true no matter how wide or narrow the display region is. If the first line contains only the first five words of the paragraph, then only those five words will be big and purple. If the first line contains the first 30 words of the element, then all 30 will be big and purple.

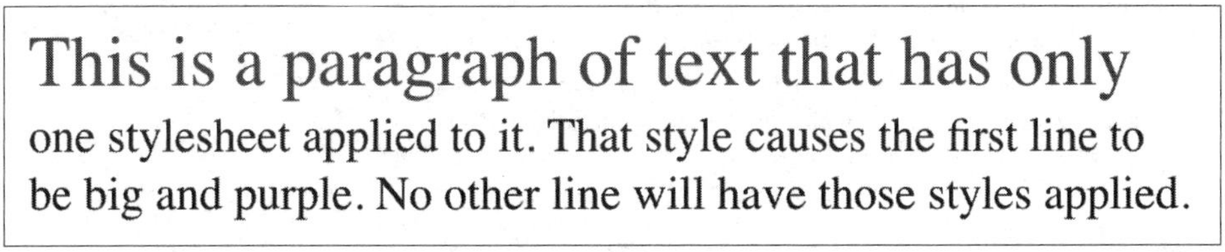

This is a paragraph of text that has only one stylesheet applied to it. That style causes the first line to be big and purple. No other line will have those styles applied.

Figure 2-46. The ::first-line pseudo-element in action

Because the text from "This" to "only" should be big and purple, the user agent employs a fictional markup that looks something like this:

```
<p>
<p-first-line>This is a paragraph of text that has only</p-first-line>
one stylesheet applied to it. That style causes the first line to
be big and purple. No other line will have those styles applied.
</p>
```

If the first line of text were edited to include only the first seven words of the paragraph, then the fictional `</p-first-line>` would move back and occur just after the word "that." If the user were to increase or decrease the font-size rendering, or expand or contract the browser window causing the width of the text to change, thereby causing the number of words on the first line to increase or decrease, the browser automatically sets only the words in the currently displayed first line to be both big and purple.

The length of the first line depends on a number of factors, including the font-size, letter spacing, width of the parent container, etc. Depending on the markup, and the length of that first line, it is possible that the end of the first line comes in the middle of a nested element. If the `::first-line` breaks up a nested element, such as an em or a hyperlink, the properties attached to the `::first-line` will only apply to the portion of that nested element that is displayed on the first line.

Restrictions on ::first-letter and ::first-line

The `::first-letter` and `::first-line` pseudo-elements currently can be applied only to block-display elements such as headings or paragraphs, and not to inline-display elements such as hyperlinks. There are also limits on the CSS properties that may be applied to `::first-line` and `::first-letter`. Table 2-5 gives an idea of these limitations.

Table 2-5. Properties permitted on pseudo-elements

::first-letter	::first-line
• All font properties	• All font properties
• All background properties	• All background properties
• All text decoration properties	• All margin properties
• All inline typesetting properties	• All padding properties
• All inline layout properties	• All border properties
• All border properties	• All text decoration properties
• box-shadow	• All inline typesetting properties
• color	• color
• opacity	• opacity

Styling (or Creating) Content Before and After Elements

Let's say you want to preface every h2 element with a pair of silver square brackets as a typographical effect:

```
h2::before {content: "]]"; color: silver;}
```

CSS lets you insert *generated content*, and then style it directly using the pseudo-elements ::before and ::after. Figure 2-47 illustrates an example.

]]This is an h2 element

Figure 2-47. Inserting content before an element

The pseudo-element is used to insert the generated content and to style it. To place content after an element, use the pseudo-element ::after. You could end your documents with an appropriate finish:

```
body::after {content: "The End.";}
```

Generated content is a separate subject, and the entire topic (including more detail on ::before and ::after) is covered more thoroughly in Chapter 15.

Summary

By using selectors based on the document's language, authors can create CSS rules that apply to a large number of similar elements just as easily as they can construct rules that apply in very narrow circumstances. The ability to group together both selectors and rules keeps stylesheets compact and flexible, which incidentally leads to smaller file sizes and faster download times.

Selectors are the one thing that user agents usually must get right because the inability to correctly interpret selectors pretty much prevents a user agent from using CSS at all. On the flip side, it's crucial for authors to correctly write selectors because errors can prevent the user agent from applying the styles as intended. An integral part of correctly understanding selectors and how they can be combined is a strong grasp of how selectors relate to document structure and how mechanisms—such as inheritance and the cascade itself—come into play when determining how an element will be styled.

CHAPTER 3

Specificity and the Cascade

Chapter 2 showed how document structure and CSS selectors allow you to apply a wide variety of styles to elements. Knowing that every valid document generates a structural tree, you can create selectors that target elements based on their ancestors, attributes, sibling elements, and more. The structural tree is what allows selectors to function and is also central to a similarly crucial aspect of CSS: inheritance.

Inheritance is the mechanism by which some property values are passed on from an element to its descendants. When determining which values should apply to an element, a user agent must consider not only inheritance but also the *specificity* of the declarations, as well as the origin of the declarations themselves. This process of consideration is what's known as the *cascade*. We will explore the interrelation between these three mechanisms—specificity, inheritance, and the cascade—in this chapter, but the difference between the latter two can be summed up this way: choosing the result of h1 {color: red; color: blue;} is the cascade; making a span inside the h1 blue is inheritance.

Above all, regardless of how abstract things may seem, keep going! Your perseverance will be rewarded.

Specificity

You know from Chapter 2 that you can select elements using a wide variety of means. In fact, it's possible that the same element could be selected by two or more rules, each with its own selector. Let's consider the following three pairs of rules. Assume that each pair will match the same element:

```
h1 {color: red;}
body h1 {color: green;}

h2.grape {color: purple;}
```

```
h2 {color: silver;}

html > body table tr[id="totals"] td ul > li {color: maroon;}
li#answer {color: navy;}
```

Only one of the two rules in each pair can win out, since the matched elements can be only one color or the other. How do we know which one will win?

The answer is found in the *specificity* of each selector. For every rule, the user agent evaluates the specificity of the selector and attaches it to each declaration in the rule. When an element has two or more conflicting property declarations, the one with the highest specificity will win out.

 This isn't the whole story in terms of conflict resolution. All style conflict resolution (including specificity) is handled by the cascade, which has its own section later in this chapter ("The Cascade" on page 106).

A selector's specificity is determined by the components of the selector itself. A specificity value can be expressed in four parts, like this: 0,0,0,0. The actual specificity of a selector is determined as follows:

- For every ID attribute value given in the selector, add 0,1,0,0.
- For every class attribute value, attribute selection, or pseudo-class given in the selector, add 0,0,1,0.
- For every element and pseudo-element given in the selector, add 0,0,0,1. CSS2 contradicted itself as to whether pseudo-elements had any specificity at all, but CSS2.1 made it clear that they do, and this is where they belong.
- Combinators and the universal selector do not contribute anything to the specificity.

For example, the following rules' selectors result in the indicated specificities:

```
h1 {color: red;}                        /* specificity = 0,0,0,1 */
p em {color: purple;}                    /* specificity = 0,0,0,2 */
.grape {color: purple;}                  /* specificity = 0,0,1,0 */
*.bright {color: yellow;}                /* specificity = 0,0,1,0 */
p.bright em.dark {color: maroon;}        /* specificity = 0,0,2,2 */
#id216 {color: blue;}                    /* specificity = 0,1,0,0 */
div#sidebar *[href] {color: silver;} /* specificity = 0,1,1,1 */
```

Given a case where an em element is matched by both the second and fifth rules in this example, that element will be maroon because the fifth rule's specificity outweighs the second's.

As an exercise, let's return to the pairs of rules from earlier in the section and fill in the specificities:

```
h1 {color: red;}         /* 0,0,0,1 */
body h1 {color: green;}  /* 0,0,0,2 (winner)*/

h2.grape {color: purple;}  /* 0,0,1,1 (winner) */
h2 {color: silver;}        /* 0,0,0,1 */

html > body table tr[id="totals"] td ul > li {color: maroon;}  /* 0,0,1,7 */
li#answer {color: navy;}                                       /* 0,1,0,1
   (winner) */
```

I've indicated the winning rule in each pair; in each case, it's because the specificity is higher. Notice how they're sorted. In the second pair, the selector h2.grape wins because it has an extra 1: 0,0,1,1 beats out 0,0,0,1. In the third pair, the second rule wins because 0,1,0,1 wins out over 0,0,1,7. In fact, the specificity value 0,0,1,0 will win out over the value 0,0,0,13.

This happens because the values are sorted from left to right. A specificity of 1,0,0,0 will win out over any specificity that begins with a 0, no matter what the rest of the numbers might be. So 0,1,0,1 wins over 0,0,1,7 because the 1 in the first value's second position beats out the 0 in the second value's second position.

Declarations and Specificity

Once the specificity of a selector has been determined, the specificity value will be conferred on all of its associated declarations. Consider this rule:

```
h1 {color: silver; background: black;}
```

For specificity purposes, the user agent must treat the rule as if it were "ungrouped" into separate rules. Thus, the previous example would become:

```
h1 {color: silver;}
h1 {background: black;}
```

Both have a specificity of 0,0,0,1, and that's the value conferred on each declaration. The same splitting-up process happens with a grouped selector as well. Given the rule:

```
h1, h2.section {color: silver; background: black;}
```

the user agent treats it if it were the following:

```
h1 {color: silver;}              /* 0,0,0,1 */
h1 {background: black;}          /* 0,0,0,1 */
h2.section {color: silver;}      /* 0,0,1,1 */
h2.section {background: black;} /* 0,0,1,1 */
```

This becomes important in situations where multiple rules match the same element and some of the declarations clash. For example, consider these rules:

```
h1 + p {color: black; font-style: italic;}              /* 0,0,0,2 */
p {color: gray; background: white; font-style: normal;} /* 0,0,0,1 */
*.aside {color: black; background: silver;}             /* 0,0,1,0 */
```

When applied to the following markup, the content will be rendered as shown in Figure 3-1:

```
<h1>Greetings!</h1>
<p class="aside">
It's a fine way to start a day, don't you think?
</p>
<p>
There are many ways to greet a person, but the words are not as important as
the act of greeting itself.
</p>
<h1>Salutations!</h1>
<p>
There is nothing finer than a hearty welcome from one's fellow man.
</p>
<p class="aside">
Although a thick and juicy hamburger with bacon and mushrooms runs a close second.
</p>
```

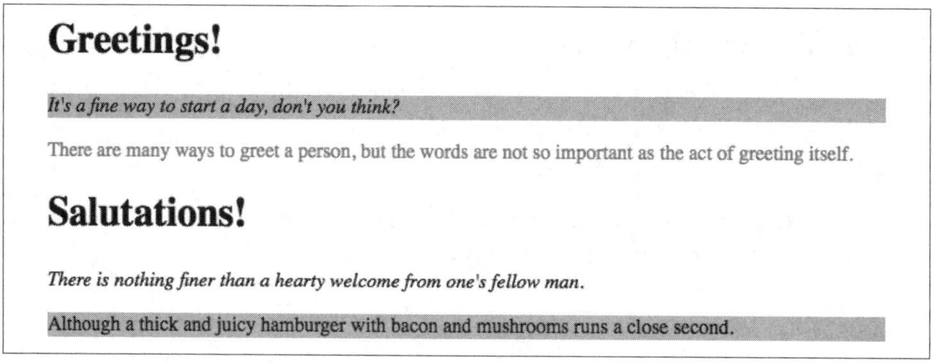

Figure 3-1. How different rules affect a document

In every case, the user agent determines which rules match a given element, calculates all of the associated declarations and their specificities, determines which rules win out, and then applies the winners to the element to get the styled result. These machinations must be performed on every element, selector, and declaration. Fortunately, the user agent does it all automatically. This behavior is an important component of the cascade, which we will discuss later in this chapter.

Universal Selector Specificity

The universal selector does not contribute to specificity. In other words, it has a specificity of 0,0,0,0, which is different than having no specificity (as we'll discuss in "Inheritance" on page 103). Therefore, given the following two rules, a paragraph descended from a div will be black, but all other elements will be gray:

```
div p {color: black;} /* 0,0,0,2 */
* {color: gray;}      /* 0,0,0,0 */
```

As you might expect, this means the specificity of a selector that contains a universal selector along with other selectors is not changed by the presence of the universal selector. The following two selectors have exactly the same specificity:

```
div p         /* 0,0,0,2 */
body * strong /* 0,0,0,2 */
```

Combinators, by comparison, have no specificity at all—not even zero specificity. Thus, they have no impact on a selector's overall specificity.

ID and Attribute Selector Specificity

It's important to note the difference in specificity between an ID selector and an attribute selector that targets an id attribute. Returning to the third pair of rules in the example code, we find:

```
html > body table tr[id="totals"] td ul > li {color: maroon;} /* 0,0,1,7 */
li#answer {color: navy;}                                      /* 0,1,0,1 (wins) */
```

The ID selector (#answer) in the second rule contributes 0,1,0,0 to the overall specificity of the selector. In the first rule, however, the attribute selector ([id="totals"]) contributes 0,0,1,0 to the overall specificity. Thus, given the following rules, the element with an id of meadow will be green:

```
#meadow {color: green;}     /* 0,1,0,0 */
*[id="meadow"] {color: red;} /* 0,0,1,0 */
```

Inline Style Specificity

So far, we've only seen specificities that begin with a zero, so you may be wondering why it's there at all. As it happens, that first zero is reserved for inline style declarations, which trump any other declaration's specificity. Consider the following rule and markup fragment:

```
h1 {color: red;}

<h1 style="color: green;">The Meadow Party</h1>
```

Given that the rule is applied to the h1 element, you would still probably expect the text of the h1 to be green. This happens because every inline declaration has a specificity of 1,0,0,0.

This means that even elements with id attributes that match a rule will obey the inline style declaration. Let's modify the previous example to include an id:

```
h1#meadow {color: red;}

<h1 id="meadow" style="color: green;">The Meadow Party</h1>
```

Thanks to the inline declaration's specificity, the text of the h1 element will still be green.

Importance

Sometimes, a declaration is so important that it outweighs all other considerations. CSS calls these *important declarations* (for hopefully obvious reasons) and lets you mark them by inserting !important just before the terminating semicolon in a declaration:

```
p.dark {color: #333 !important; background: white;}
```

Here, the color value of #333 is marked !important, whereas the background value of white is not. If you wish to mark both declarations as important, each declaration needs its own !important marker:

```
p.dark {color: #333 !important; background: white !important;}
```

You must place !important correctly, or the declaration may be invalidated. !important *always* goes at the end of the declaration, just before the semicolon. This placement is especially important—no pun intended—when it comes to properties that allow values containing multiple keywords, such as font:

```
p.light {color: yellow; font: smaller Times, serif !important;}
```

If !important were placed anywhere else in the font declaration, the entire declaration would likely be invalidated and none of its styles applied.

I realize that to those of you who come from a programming background, the syntax of this token instinctively translates to "not important." For whatever reason, the bang (!) was chosen as the delimiter for important tokens, and it does *not* mean "not" in CSS, no matter how many other languages give it that very meaning. This association is unfortunate, but we're stuck with it.

Declarations that are marked !important do not have a special specificity value, but are instead considered separately from non-important declarations. In effect, all !

`important` declarations are grouped together, and specificity conflicts are resolved relatively within that group. Similarly, all non-important declarations are considered together, with any conflicts within the non-important group are resolved using specificity. Thus, in any case where an important and a non-important declaration conflict, the important declaration *always* wins.

Figure 3-2 illustrates the result of the following rules and markup fragment:

```
h1 {font-style: italic; color: gray !important;}
.title {color: black; background: silver;}
* {background: black !important;}

<h1 class="title">NightWing</h1>
```

Figure 3-2. Important rules always win

Important declarations and their handling are discussed in more detail in "The Cascade" on page 106.

Inheritance

As important as specificity may be to understanding how declarations are applied to a document, another key concept is *inheritance*. Inheritance is the mechanism by which some styles are applied not only to a specified element, but also to its descendants. If a color is applied to an h1 element, for example, then that color is applied to all text inside the h1, even the text enclosed within child elements of that h1:

```
h1 {color: gray;}

<h1>Meerkat <em>Central</em></h1>
```

Both the ordinary h1 text and the em text are colored gray because the em element inherits the value of color from the h1. If property values could not be inherited by descendant elements, the em text would be black, not gray, and we'd have to color the elements separately.

Consider an unordered list. Let's say we apply a style of color: gray; for ul elements:

```
ul {color: gray;}
```

We expect that style applied to a ul will also be applied to its list items, and also to any content of those list items. Thanks to inheritance, that's exactly what happens, as Figure 3-3 demonstrates.

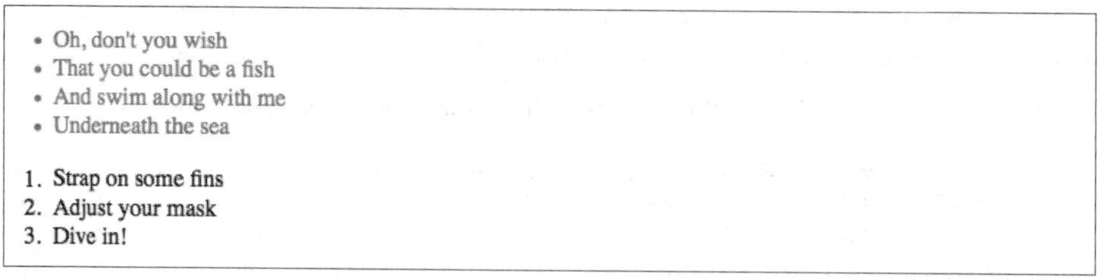

- Oh, don't you wish
- That you could be a fish
- And swim along with me
- Underneath the sea

1. Strap on some fins
2. Adjust your mask
3. Dive in!

Figure 3-3. Inheritance of styles

It's easier to see how inheritance works by turning to a tree diagram of a document. Figure 3-4 shows the tree diagram for a very simple document containing two lists: one unordered and the other ordered.

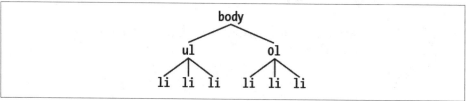

Figure 3-4. A simple tree diagram

When the declaration color: gray; is applied to the ul element, that element takes on that declaration. The value is then propagated down the tree to the descendant elements and continues on until there are no more descendants to inherit the value. Values are *never* propagated upward; that is, an element never passes values up to its ancestors.

 There is an exception to the upward propagation rule in HTML: background styles applied to the body element can be passed to the html element, which is the document's root element and therefore defines its canvas. This only happens if the body element has a defined background and the html element does not.

Inheritance is one of those things about CSS that is so basic that you almost never think about it unless you have to. However, you should still keep a couple of things in mind.

First, note that many properties are not inherited—generally in order to avoid undesirable outcomes. For example, the property border (which is used to set borders on elements) does not inherit. A quick glance at Figure 3-5 reveals why this is the case. If borders were inherited, documents would become much more cluttered—unless the author took the extra effort to turn off the inherited borders.

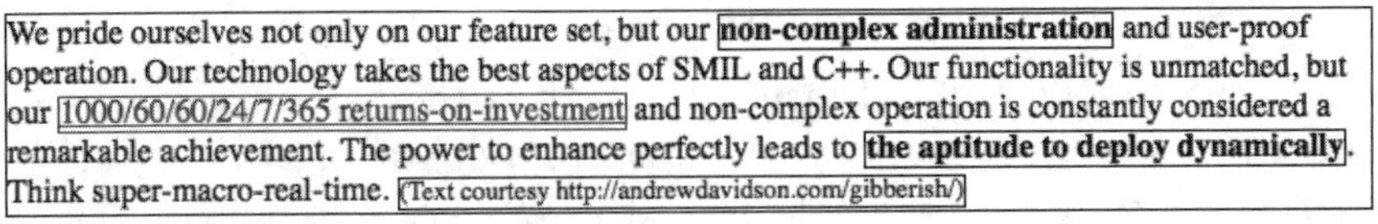

> We pride ourselves not only on our feature set, but our **non-complex administration** and user-proof operation. Our technology takes the best aspects of SMIL and C++. Our functionality is unmatched, but our 1000/60/60/24/7/365 returns-on-investment and non-complex operation is constantly considered a remarkable achievement. The power to enhance perfectly leads to **the aptitude to deploy dynamically**. Think super-macro-real-time. (Text courtesy http://andrewdavidson.com/gibberish/)

Figure 3-5. Why borders aren't inherited

As it happens, most of the box-model properties—including margins, padding, backgrounds, and borders—are not inherited for the same reason. After all, you likely wouldn't want all of the links in a paragraph to inherit a 30-pixel left margin from their parent element!

Second, inherited values have no specificity at all, not even zero specificity. This seems like an academic distinction until you work through the consequences of the lack of inherited specificity. Consider the following rules and markup fragment and compare them to the result shown in Figure 3-6:

```
* {color: gray;}
h1#page-title {color: black;}

<h1 id="page-title">Meerkat <em>Central</em></h1>
<p>
Welcome to the best place on the web for meerkat information!
</p>
```

Meerkat *Central*

Welcome to the best place on the Web for meerkat information!

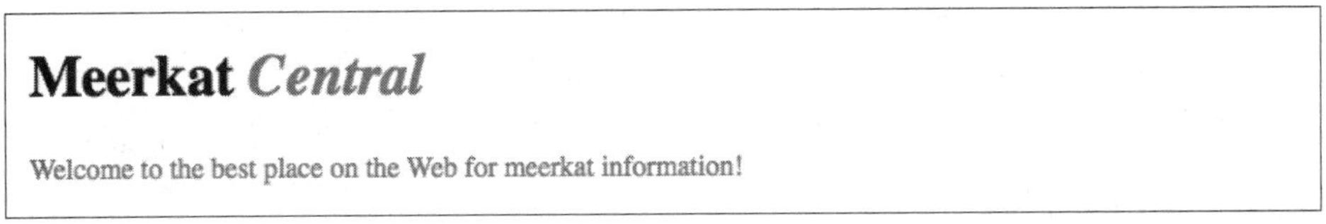

Figure 3-6. Zero specificity defeats no specificity

Since the universal selector applies to all elements and has zero specificity, its color declaration's value of gray wins out over the inherited value of black, which has no specificity at all. Therefore, the em element is rendered gray instead of black.

This example vividly illustrates one of the potential problems of using the universal selector indiscriminately. Because it can match *any* element, the universal selector often has the effect of short-circuiting inheritance. This can be worked around, but it's usually more sensible to avoid the problem in the first place by not using the universal selector indiscriminately.

The complete lack of specificity for inherited values is not a trivial point. For example, assume that a style sheet has been written such that all text in a "toolbar" is to be white on black:

```
#toolbar {color: white; background: black;}
```

This will work so long as the element with an `id` of `toolbar` contains nothing but plain text. If, however, the text within this element is all hyperlinks (`a` elements), then the user agent's styles for hyperlinks will take over. In a web browser, this means they'll likely be colored blue, since the browser's internal style sheet probably contains an entry like this:

```
a:link {color: blue;}
```

To overcome this problem, you must declare something like this:

```
#toolbar {color: white; background: black;}
#toolbar a:link {color: white;}
```

By targeting a rule directly at the `a` elements within the toolbar, you'll get the result shown in Figure 3-7.

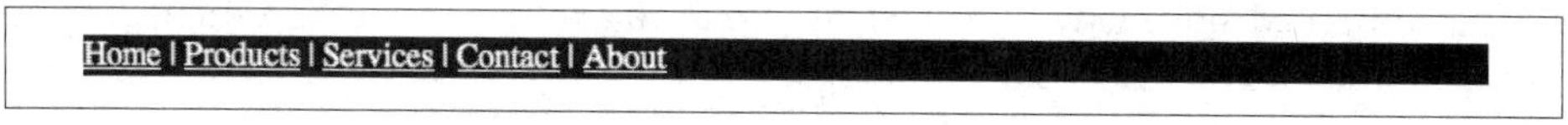

Figure 3-7. Directly assigning styles to the relevant elements

Another way to get the same result is to use the value `inherit`, covered in the previous chapter. We can alter the previous example like so:

```
#toolbar {color: white; background: black;}
#toolbar a:link {color: inherit;}
```

This also leads to the result shown in Figure 3-7, because the value of `color` is explicitly inherited thanks to an assigned rule whose selector has specificity.

The Cascade

Throughout this chapter, we've skirted one rather important issue: what happens when two rules of equal specificity apply to the same element? How does the browser resolve the conflict? For example, consider the following rules:

```
h1 {color: red;}
h1 {color: blue;}
```

Which one wins? Both have a specificity of $0,0,0,1$, so they have equal weight and should both apply. That can't be the case because the element can't be both red and blue. So which will it be?

At last, the name "Cascading Style Sheets" makes sense: CSS is based on a method of causing styles to *cascade* together, which is made possible by combining inheritance and specificity with a few rules. The cascade rules for CSS are:

1. Find all rules that contain a selector that matches a given element.

2. Sort all declarations applying to the given element by *explicit weight*. Those rules marked `!important` have a higher weight than those that are not.

3. Sort all declarations applying to the given element by *origin*. There are three basic origins: author, reader, and user agent. Under normal circumstances, the author's styles win out over the reader's styles. `!important` reader styles are stronger than any other styles, including `!important` author styles. Both author and reader styles override the user agent's default styles.

4. Sort all declarations applying to the given element by *specificity*. Those elements with a higher specificity have more weight than those with lower specificity.

5. Sort all declarations applying to the given element by *order*. The later a declaration appears in the style sheet or document, the more weight it is given. Declarations that appear in an imported style sheet are considered to come before all declarations within the style sheet that imports them.

To be perfectly clear about how this all works, let's consider some examples that illustrate the last four of the five cascade rules.

 Some later CSS modules add more origins to the basic list of three; for example, the animation and transition origins. These are not covered here, but are addressed in the chapters on those topics.

Sorting by Weight and Origin

If two rules apply to an element, and one is marked `!important`, the important rule wins out:

```
p {color: gray !important;}
<p style="color: black;">Well, <em>hello</em> there!</p>
```

Despite the fact that there is a color assigned in the `style` attribute of the paragraph, the `!important` rule wins out, and the paragraph is gray. This gray is inherited by the `em` element as well.

Note that if an `!important` is added to the inline style, then *it* will be the winner. Thus, given the following, the paragraph (and its descendant element) will be black:

```
p {color: gray !important;}
```

```
<p style="color: black !important;">Well, <em>hello</em> there!</p>
```

In situations where the explicit weight is the same, the origin of a rule is considered. If an element is matched by normal-weight styles in both the author's style sheet and the reader's style sheet, then the author's styles are used. For example, assume that the following styles come from the indicated origins:

```
p em {color: black;}     /* author's style sheet */

p em {color: yellow;}    /* reader's style sheet */
```

In this case, emphasized text within paragraphs is colored black, not yellow, because normal-weight author styles win out over normal-weight reader styles. However, if both rules are marked !important, the situation changes:

```
p em {color: black !important;}     /* author's style sheet */

p em {color: yellow !important;}    /* reader's style sheet */
```

Now the emphasized text in paragraphs will be yellow, not black.

As it happens, the user agent's default styles—which are often influenced by the user preferences—are figured into this step. The default style declarations are the least influential of all. Therefore, if an author-defined rule applies to anchors (e.g., declaring them to be white), then this rule overrides the user agent's defaults.

To sum up, there are five basic levels to consider in terms of declaration weight. In order of most to least weight, these are:

1. Reader important declarations

2. Author important declarations

3. Author normal declarations

4. Reader normal declarations

5. User agent declarations

Authors typically need to worry about only the first four weight levels, since anything declared by an author will win out over the user agent's styles.

Sorting by Specificity

If conflicting declarations apply to an element and they all have the same explicit weight and origin, they should be sorted by specificity, with the most specific declaration winning out, like this:

```
p#bright {color: silver;}
p {color: black;}

<p id="bright">Well, hello there!</p>
```

Given the rules shown, the text of the paragraph will be silver, as illustrated in Figure 3-8. Why? Because the specificity of p#bright (0,1,0,1) overrode the specificity of p (0,0,0,1), even though the latter rule comes later in the style sheet.

Well, hello there!

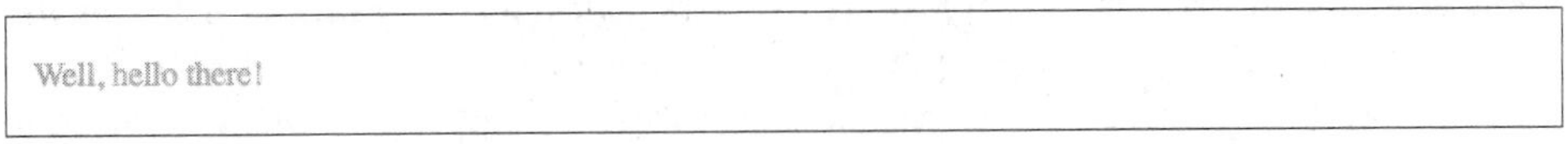

Figure 3-8. Higher specificity wins out over lower specificity

Sorting by Order

Finally, if two rules have exactly the same explicit weight, origin, and specificity, then the one that occurs later in the style sheet wins out. Let's return to our earlier example, where we find the following two rules in the document's style sheet:

```
h1 {color: red;}
h1 {color: blue;}
```

In this case, the value of color for all h1 elements in the document will be blue, not red. This is because the two rules are tied with each other in terms of explicit weight and origin, and the selectors have equal specificity, so the last one declared is the winner.

So what happens if rules from completely separate style sheets conflict? For example, suppose the following:

```
@import url(basic.css);
h1 {color: blue;}
```

What if h1 {color: red;} appears in basic.css? The entire contents of basic.css are treated as if they were pasted into the style sheet at the point where the @import occurs. Thus, any rule contained in the document's style sheet occurs later than those from the @import. If they tie in terms of explicit weight and specificity, the document's style sheet contains the winner. Consider the following:

```
p em {color: purple;}  /* from imported style sheet */

p em {color: gray;}     /* rule contained within the document */
```

In this case, the second rule shown wins out over the imported rule because it was the last one specified.

Order sorting is the reason behind the often-recommended ordering of link styles. The recommendation is that you array your link styles in the order link-visited-focus-hover-active, or LVFHA, like this:

```
a:link {color: blue;}
a:visited {color: purple;}
a:focus {color: green;}
```

```
a:hover {color: red;}
a:active {color: orange;}
```

Thanks to the information in this chapter, you now know that the specificity of all of these selectors is the same: 0,0,1,0. Because they all have the same explicit weight, origin, and specificity, the last one that matches an element will win out. An unvisited link that is being "clicked" or otherwise activated, such as via the keyboard, is matched by four of the rules—:link, Lfocus, :hover, and :active—so the last one of those four will win out. Given the LVFHA ordering, :active will win, which is likely what the author intended.

Assume for a moment that you decide to ignore the common ordering and alphabetize your link styles instead. This would yield:

```
a:active {color: orange;}
a:focus {color: green;}
a:hover {color: red;}
a:link {color: blue;}
a:visited {color: purple;}
```

Given this ordering, no link would ever show :hover, :focus, or :active styles because the :link and :visited rules come after the other three. Every link must be either visited or unvisited, so those styles will always override the others.

Let's consider a variation on the LVFHA order that an author might want to use. In this ordering, only unvisited links will get a hover style; visited links do not. Both visited and unvisited links will get an active style:

```
a:link {color: blue;}
a:hover {color: red;}
a:visited {color: purple;}
a:focus {color: green;}
a:active {color: orange;}
```

Such conflicts arise only when all the states attempt to set the same property. If each state's styles address a different property, then the order does not matter. In the following case, the link styles could be given in any order and would still function as intended:

```
a:link {font-weight: bold;}
a:visited {font-style: italic;}
a:focus {color: green;}
a:hover {color: red;}
a:active {background: yellow;}
```

You may also have realized that the order of the :link and :visited styles doesn't matter. You could order the styles LVFHA or VLFHA with no ill effect.

The ability to chain pseudo-classes together eliminates all these worries. The following could be listed in any order without any overrides:

```
a:link {color: blue;}
a:visited {color: purple;}
a:link:hover {color: red;}
a:visited:hover {color: gray;}
```

Because each rule applies to a unique set of link states, they do not conflict. Therefore, changing their order will not change the styling of the document. The last two rules do have the same specificity, but that doesn't matter. A hovered unvisited link will not be matched by the rule regarding hovered visited links, and vice versa. If we were to add active-state styles, then order would start to matter again. Consider:

```
a:link {color: blue;}
a:visited {color: purple;}
a:link:hover {color: red;}
a:visited:hover {color: gray;}
a:link:active {color: orange;}
a:visited:active {color: silver;}
```

If the active styles were moved before the hover styles, they would be ignored. Again, this would happen due to specificity conflicts. The conflicts could be avoided by adding more pseudo-classes to the chains, like this:

```
a:link:hover:active {color: orange;}
a:visited:hover:active {color: silver;}
```

This does have the effect of raising the specificity of the selectors—both have a specificity value of 0,0,3,1—but they don't conflict because the actual selection states are mutually exclusive. A link can't be an unvisited hovered active link *and* an unvisited hovered active link: only one of the two rules will match, and the styles applied accordingly.

Non-CSS Presentational Hints

It is possible that a document will contain presentational hints that are not CSS—for example, the font element. Such presentational hints are treated as if they have a specificity of 0 and appear at the *beginning* of the author's stylesheet. Such presentation hints will be overridden by any author or reader styles, but not by the user agent's styles. In CSS3, presentational hints from outside CSS are treated as if they belong to the user agent's stylesheet, presumably at the end (although as of this writing, the specification doesn't say).

Summary

Perhaps the most fundamental aspect of Cascading Style Sheets is the cascade itself—the process by which conflicting declarations are sorted out and from which the final document presentation is determined. Integral to this process is the specificity of selectors and their associated declarations, and the mechanism of inheritance.

CHAPTER 4

Values and Units

In this chapter, we'll tackle features that are the basis for almost everything you can do with CSS: the units that affect the colors, distances, and sizes of a whole host of properties, as well as the units that help to define those values. Without units, you couldn't declare that an image should have 10 pixels of blank space around it, or that a heading's text should be a certain size. By understanding the concepts put forth here, you'll be able to learn and use the rest of CSS much more quickly.

Keywords, Strings, and Other Text Values

Everything in a stylesheet is text, but there are certain value types that directly represent strings of text as opposed to, say, numbers or colors. Included in this category are URLs and, interestingly enough, images.

Keywords

For those times when a value needs to be described with a word of some kind, there are *keywords*. A very common example is the keyword none, which is distinct from 0 (zero). Thus, to remove the underline from links in an HTML document, you would write:

```
a:link, a:visited {text-decoration: none;}
```

Similarly, if you want to force underlines on the links, then you would use the keyword underline.

If a property accepts keywords, then its keywords will be defined only for the scope of that property. If two properties use the same word as a keyword, the behavior of the keyword for one property will not necessarily be shared with the other. As an example, `normal`, as defined for `letter-spacing`, means something very different than the `normal` defined for `font-style`.

Global keywords

CSS3 defines three "global" keywords that are accepted by every property in the specification: `inherit`, `initial`, and `unset`.

inherit. The keyword `inherit` makes the value of a property on an element the same as the value of that property on its parent element. In other words, it forces inheritance to occur even in situations where it would not normally operate. In many cases, you don't need to specify inheritance, since many properties inherit naturally. Nevertheless, `inherit` can still be very useful.

For example, consider the following styles and markup:

```
#toolbar {background: blue; color: white;}

<div id="toolbar">
<a href="one.html">One</a> | <a href="two.html">Two</a> |
<a href="three.html">Three</a>
</div>
```

The `div` itself will have a blue background and a white foreground, but the links will be styled according to the browser's preference settings. They'll most likely end up as blue text on a blue background, with white vertical bars between them.

You could write a rule that explicitly sets the links in the "toolbar" to be white, but you can make things a little more robust by using `inherit`. You just add the following rule to the stylesheet:

```
#toolbar a {color: inherit;}
```

This will cause the links to use the inherited value of `color` in place of the user agent's default styles. Ordinarily, directly assigned styles override inherited styles, but `inherit` can undo that behavior. It might not always be a good idea—for example, here links might blend into surrounding text too much, and become an accessibility concern—but it can be done.

Similarly, you can pull a property value down from a parent even if it wouldn't happen normally. Take `border`, for example, which is (rightfully) not inherited. If you want a `span` to inherit the border of its parent, all you need is `span {border: inherit;}`. More likely, though, you just want the border on a `span` to use the same border color as its parent. In that case `span {border-color: inherit;}` will do the trick.

initial. The keyword `initial` sets the value of a property to the defined initial value, which in a way means it "resets" the value. For example, the default value of `font-weight` is `normal`. Thus, declaring `font-weight: initial` is the same as declaring `font-weight: normal`.

This might seem a little bit silly until you consider that not all values have explicitly defined initial values. For example, the initial value for `color` is "depends on user agent." That's not a funky keyword you should type! What it means is that the default value of `color` depends on things like the preferences settings in a browser. While almost nobody changes the default text color setting from black, someone might set it to a dark gray or even a bright red. By declaring `color: initial;`, you're telling the browser to set the color of the element to whatever the user's default color is set to be.

unset. The keyword `unset` acts as a universal stand-in for both `inherit` and `initial`. If the property is inherited, then `unset` has the same effect as if `inherit` was used. If the property is *not* inherited, then `unset` has the same effect as if `initial` was used.

> As of late 2017, Opera Mini did not support any of `initial`, `inherit`, or `unset`. Internet Explorer did not support them through IE11.

These global values are usable on all properties, but there is a special property that *only* accepts the global keywords: `all`.

all	
Values	`inherit` | `initial` | `unset`
Initial value	See individual properties

`all` is a stand-in for all properties *except* `direction` and `unicode-bidi`. Thus, if you declare `all: inherit` on an element, you're saying that you want all properties except `direction` and `unicode-bidi` to inherit their values from the element's parent. Consider the following:

```
section {color: white; background: black; font-weight: bold;}
#example {all: inherit;}
```

```
<section>
    <div id="example">This is a div.</div>
</section>
```

You might think this causes the div element to inherit the values of color, back
ground, and font-weight from the section element. And it does do that, yes—but it
will *also* force inheritance of the values of *every single other property in CSS* (minus
the two exceptions) from the section element.

Maybe that's what you want, in which case, great. But if you just want to inherit the
property values you wrote out for the section element, then the CSS would need to
look more like this:

```
section {color: white; background: black; font-weight: bold;}
#example {color: inherit; background: inherit; font-weight: inherit;}
```

Odds are what you really want in these situations is all: unset, but your stylesheet
may vary.

As of late 2017, a new global keyword, revert, was being considered for adoption. Its goal was to allow rollbacks of values to those
set by other origins—for example, to let an author say, "All property
values for this element should be as if the author styles don't exist,
but user agent and user styles do." Since it was still under consideration, it has not been documented in detail here.

As of late 2017, Opera Mini and Microsoft Edge did not support
all. Support was under consideration for Edge.

Strings

A *string value* is an arbitrary sequence of characters wrapped in either single or double quotes, and is represented in value definitions with *<string>*. Two simple examples:

```
"I like to play with strings."
'Strings are fun to play with.'
```

Note that the quotes balance, which is to say that you always start and end with the
same kind of quotes. Getting this wrong can lead to all kinds of parsing problems,
since starting with one kind of quote and trying to end with the other means the
string won't actually be terminated. You could accidentally incorporate subsequent
rules into the string that way!

If you want to put quote marks inside strings, that's OK, as long as they're either not
the kind you used to enclose the string or are escaped using a backslash:

```
"I've always liked to play with strings."
'He said to me, "I like to play with strings."'
"It's been said that \"haste makes waste.\""
'There\'s never been a "string theory" that I\'ve liked.'
```

Note that the only acceptable string delimiters are ' and ", sometimes called "straight quotes." That means you can't use "curly" or "smart" quotes to begin or end a string value. You can use them inside a string value, as in this code example, though, and they don't have to be escaped:

```
"It's been said that "haste makes waste.""
'There's never been a "string theory" that I've liked.'
```

This requires that you use Unicode encoding for your documents, but you should be doing that regardless. (You can find the Unicode standard at *http://www.unicode.org/ standard/standard.html*.)

If you have some reason to include a newline in your string value, you can do that by escaping the newline itself. CSS will then remove it, making things as if it had never been there. Thus, the following two string values are identical from a CSS point of view:

```
"This is the right place \
for a newline."
"This is the right place for a newline."
```

If, on the other hand, you actually want a string value that includes a newline character, then use the Unicode reference \A where you want the newline to occur:

```
"This is a better place \Afor a newline."
```

URLs

If you've written web pages, you're almost certainly familiar with URLs (or, as in CSS2.1, URIs). Whenever you need to refer to one—as in the @import statement, which is used when importing an external stylesheet—the general format is:

```
url(protocol://server/pathname)
```

This example defines what is known as an *absolute URL*. By absolute, I mean a URL that will work no matter where (or rather, in what page) it's found, because it defines an absolute location in web space. Let's say that you have a server called *web.waffles.org*. On that server, there is a directory called *pix*, and in this directory is an image *waffle22.gif*. In this case, the absolute URL of that image would be:

```
web.waffles.org/pix/waffle22.gif
```

This URL is valid no matter where it is found, whether the page that contains it is located on the server *web.waffles.org* or *web.pancakes.com*.

The other type of URL is a *relative URL*, so named because it specifies a location that is relative to the document that uses it. If you're referring to a relative location, such as a file in the same directory as your web page, then the general format is:

```
url(pathname)
```

This works only if the image is on the same server as the page that contains the URL. For argument's sake, assume that you have a web page located at *http://web.waffles.org/syrup.html* and that you want the image *waffle22.gif* to appear on this page. In that case, the URL would be:

```
pix/waffle22.gif
```

This path works because the web browser knows that it should start with the place it found the web document and then add the relative URL. In this case, the pathname *pix/waffle22.gif* added to the server name *http://web.waffles.org* equals *http://web.waffles.org/pix/waffle22.gif*. You can almost always use an absolute URL in place of a relative URL; it doesn't matter which you use, as long as it defines a valid location.

In CSS, relative URLs are relative to the stylesheet itself, not to the HTML document that uses the stylesheet. For example, you may have an external stylesheet that imports another stylesheet. If you use a relative URL to import the second stylesheet, it must be relative to the first stylesheet.

As an example, consider an HTML document at *http://web.waffles.org/toppings/tips.html*, which has a link to the stylesheet *http://web.waffles.org/styles/basic.css*:

```
<link rel="stylesheet" type="text/css"
    href="http://web.waffles.org/styles/basic.css">
```

Inside the file *basic.css* is an @import statement referring to another stylesheet:

```
@import url(special/toppings.css);
```

This @import will cause the browser to look for the stylesheet at *http://web.waffles.org/styles/special/toppings.css*, not at *http://web.waffles.org/toppings/special/toppings.css*. If you have a stylesheet at the latter location, then the @import in *basic.css* should read one of the two following ways:

```
@import url(http://web.waffles.org/toppings/special/toppings.css);
```

```
@import url(../special/toppings.css);
```

Note that there cannot be a space between the url and the opening parenthesis:

```
body {background: url(http://www.pix.web/picture1.jpg);}   /* correct */
body {background: url (images/picture2.jpg);}          /* INCORRECT */
```

If the space is present, the entire declaration will be invalidated and thus ignored.

Images

An *image value* is a reference to an image, as you might have guessed. Its syntax representation is *<image>*.

At the most basic level of support, which is to say the one every CSS engine on the planet would understand, an *<image>* value is a *<url>* value. In more advanced user agents, *<image>* stands for one of the following:

<url>
> A URL identifier of an external resource; in this case, the URL of an image.

<image-set>
> Perhaps unsurprisingly, a set of images, chosen based on a set of conditions embedded into the value. For example, an `image-set()` could specify that a larger image be used for desktop layouts, whereas a smaller image (both in pixel size and file size) be used for a mobile design. It is intended to at least approximate the behavior of the `srcset` attribute for `picture` elements. As of late 2016, browser support for `image-set` was limited to Safari, Chrome, and desktop Opera, and was not on par with `srcset`'s full range of capabilities.

<gradient>
> Refers to either a linear or radial gradient image, either singly or in a repeating pattern. Gradients are fairly complex, and thus are covered in detail in Chapter 9.

Identifiers

There are a few properties that accept an *identifier value*, which is a user-defined identifier of some kind; the most common example is generated list counters. They are represented in the value syntax as *<identifier>*. Identifiers themselves are words, and are case-sensitive; thus, `myID` and `MyID` are, as far as CSS is concerned, completely distinct and unrelated to each other. In cases where a property accepts both an identifier and one or more keywords, the author should take care to never define an identifier identical to a valid keyword.

Numbers and Percentages

These value types are special because they serve as the foundation for so many other values types. For example, font sizes can be defined using the `em` identifier (covered later in this text) preceded by a number. But what kind of number? Defining the types of numbers here lets us speak clearly later on.

Integers

An *integer value* is about as simple as it gets: one or more numbers, optionally prefixed by a + or – sign to indicate a positive or negative value. That's it. Integer values are represented in value syntax as *<integer>*. Examples include 13, –42, 712, and 1,066.

Integer values that fall outside a defined range are, by default, considered invalid and cause the entire declaration to be ignored. However, some properties define behavior that causes values outside the accepted range to be set to the accepted value closest to the declared value, known as *clamping*. In cases (such as the property z-index) where there is no restricted range, user agents must support values up to ±1,073,741,824 ($\pm2^{30}$).

Numbers

A *number value* is either an *<integer>* or a real number, which is to say an integer followed by a dot and then some number of following integers. Additionally, it can be prefixed by either + or – to indicate positive or negative values. Number values are represented in value syntax as *<number>*. Examples include 2.7183, –3.1416, and 6.2832.

The reason a *<number>* can be an *<integer>* and yet there are separate value types is that some properties will only accept integers (e.g., z-index), whereas others will accept any real number (e.g., flex-grow). As with integer values, number values may have limits imposed on them by a property definition; for example, opacity restricts its value to be any valid *<number>* in the range 0 to 1, inclusive. By default, number values that fall outside a defined range are, by default, considered invalid and cause the entire declaration to be ignored. However, some properties define behavior that causes values outside the accepted range to be set to the accepted value closest to the declared value (generally referred to as "clamping").

Percentages

A *percentage value* is a *<number>* followed by a percentage sign (%), and is represented in value syntax as *<percentage>*. Examples would include 50% and 33.333%. Percentage values are always relative to another value, which can be anything—the value of another property of the same element, a value inherited from the parent element, or a value of an ancestor element. Any property that accepts percentage values will define any restrictions on the range of allowed percentage values, and will also define the way in which the percentage is relatively calculated.

Fractions

A *fraction value* (or *flex value*) is a *<number>* followed by the label `fr`. Thus, one fractional unit is `1fr`. This is a concept introduced by Grid Layout, and is used to divide up fractions of the unconstrained space in a layout. See Chapter 13 for more details.

Distances

Many CSS properties, such as margins, depend on length measurements to properly display various page elements. It's likely no surprise, then, that there are a number of ways to measure length in CSS.

All length units can be expressed as either positive or negative numbers followed by a label, although note that some properties will accept only positive numbers. You can also use real numbers—that is, numbers with decimal fractions, such as 10.5 or 4.561. All length units are followed by short abbreviation (usually two characters) that represents the actual unit of length being specified, such as `in` (inches) or `pt` (points). The only exception to this rule is a length of `0` (zero), which need not be followed by a unit when describing lengths.

These length units are divided into two types: *absolute length units* and *relative length units*.

Absolute Length Units

We'll start with absolute units because they're easiest to understand, despite the fact that they're almost unusable in regular web design. The six types of absolute units are as follows:

Inches (`in`)
> As you might expect, this notation refers to the inches you'd find on a ruler in the United States. (The fact that this unit is in the specification, even though almost the entire world uses the metric system, is an interesting insight into the pervasiveness of US interests on the internet—but let's not get into virtual sociopolitical theory right now.)

Centimeters (`cm`)
> Refers to the centimeters that you'd find on rulers the world over. There are 2.54 centimeters to an inch, and one centimeter equals 0.394 inches.

Millimeters (`mm`)
> For those Americans who are metric-challenged, there are 10 millimeters to a centimeter, so an inch equals 25.4 millimeters, and a millimeter equals 0.0394 inches.

Quarter-millimeters (q)

There are 40 Q units in a centimeter; thus, setting an element to be 1/10 of a centimeter wide—which is also to say, a millimeter wide—would mean a value of 4q. (Only Firefox supported q as of late 2016.)

Points (pt)

Points are standard typographical measurements that have been used by printers and typesetters for decades and by word processing programs for many years. Traditionally, there are 72 points to an inch (points were defined before widespread use of the metric system). Therefore the capital letters of text set to 12 points should be one-sixth of an inch tall. For example, p {font-size: 18pt;} is equivalent to p {font-size: 0.25in;}.

Picas (pc)

Picas are another typographical term. A pica is equivalent to 12 points, which means there are 6 picas to an inch. As just shown, the capital letters of text set to 1 pica should be one-sixth of an inch tall. For example, p {font-size: 1.5pc;} would set text to the same size as the example declarations found in the definition of points.

Pixels (px)

A pixel is a small box on screen, but CSS defines pixels more abstractly. In CSS terms, a pixel is defined to be the size required to yield 96 pixels per inch. Many user agents ignore this definition in favor of simply addressing the pixels on the screen. Scaling factors are brought into play when page zooming or printing, where an element 100px wide can be rendered more than 100 device dots wide.

These units are really useful only if the browser knows all the details of the screen on which your page is displayed, the printer you're using, or whatever other user agent might apply. On a web browser, display is affected by the size of the screen and the resolution to which the screen is set—and there isn't much that you, as the author, can do about these factors. You can only hope that, if nothing else, the measurements will be consistent in relation to each other—that is, that a setting of 1.0in will be twice as large as 0.5in, as shown in Figure 4-1.

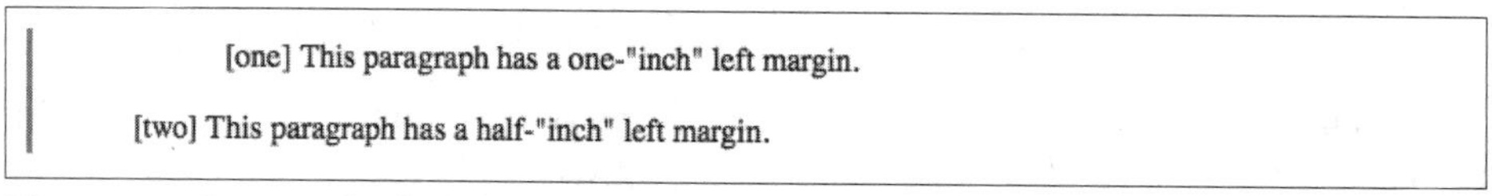

[one] This paragraph has a one-"inch" left margin.

[two] This paragraph has a half-"inch" left margin.

Figure 4-1. Setting absolute-length left margins

Nevertheless, despite all that, let's make the highly suspect assumption that your computer knows enough about its display system to accurately reproduce real-world measurements. In that case, you could make sure every paragraph has a top margin of half an inch by declaring p {margin-top: 0.5in;}. Regardless of font size or any other circumstances, a paragraph will have a half-inch top margin.

Absolute units are much more useful in defining stylesheets for printed documents, where measuring things in terms of inches, points, and picas is much more common.

Pixel lengths

On the face of things, pixels are straightforward. If you look at a screen closely enough, you can see that it's broken up into a grid of tiny little boxes. Each box is a pixel. If you define an element to be a certain number of pixels tall and wide, as in the following markup:

```
<p>
The following image is 20 pixels tall and wide: <img src="test.gif"
    style="width: 20px; height: 20px;" alt="" />
</p>
```

then it follows that the element will be that many screen elements tall and wide, as shown in Figure 4-2.

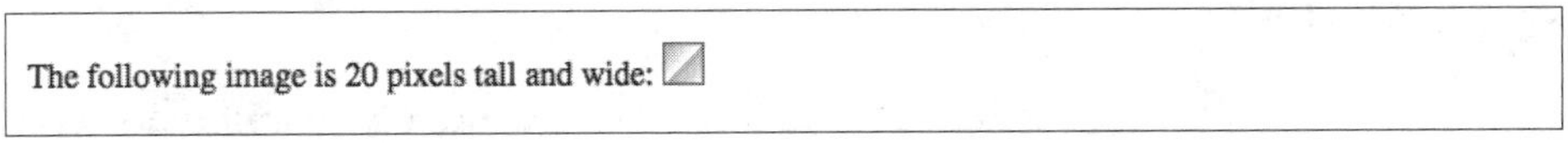

The following image is 20 pixels tall and wide:

Figure 4-2. Using pixel lengths

In general, if you declare something like font-size: 18px, a web browser will almost certainly use actual pixels on your screen—after all, they're already there—but with other display devices, like printers, the user agent will have to rescale pixel lengths to something more sensible. In other words, the printing code has to figure out how many dots there are in a pixel.

On the other hand, pixel measurements are often useful for expressing the size of images, which are already a certain number of pixels tall and wide. These days, responsive design means that we often want to express image size in relation to the size of the text of the width of the viewport, regardless of the number of actual pixels in the image. You do end up relying on the image-scaling routines in user agents, but those have been getting pretty good. Scaling of images *really* makes sense with vector-based images like SVG.

Pixel theory

In its discussion of pixels, the CSS specification recommends that, in cases where a display's resolution density is significantly different than 96 pixels per inch (ppi), user agents should scale pixel measurements to a "reference pixel." CSS2 recommended 90 ppi as the reference pixel, but CSS2.1 and CSS3 recommend 96 ppi. The most common example is a printer, which has dots instead of pixels, and which has a lot more dots per inch than 96! In printing web content, then, it may assume 96 pixels per inch and scale its output accordingly.

If a display's resolution is set to 1,024 pixels wide by 768 pixels tall, its screen size is exactly 10 2/3 inches wide by 8 inches tall, and the screen it is filled entirely by the display pixels, then each pixel will be 1/96 of an inch wide and tall. As you might guess, this scenario is a fairly rare occurrence. So, on most displays, the actual number of pixels per inch (ppi) is higher than 96—sometimes much higher. The Retina display on an iPhone 4S, for example, is 326 ppi; the display on the iPad 264 ppi.

 As a Windows XP user, you should be able to set your display driver to make the display of elements correspond correctly to real-world measurements. The path to the ruler dialog is Start→Control Panel; double-click Display; click the Settings tab; then click Advanced to reveal a dialog box (which may differ on each PC). You should see a dropdown or other form control labeled Font Size; select Other.

Resolution Units

With the advent of media queries and responsive designs, three new unit types were introduced in order to be able to describe display resolution:

Dots per inch (dpi)
> The number of display dots per linear inch. This can refer to the dots in a paper printer's output, the physical pixels in an LED screen or other device, or the elements in an e-ink display such as that used by a Kindle.

Dots per centimeter (dpcm)
> Same as dpi, except the linear measure is one centimeter instead of one inch.

Dots per pixel unit (dppx)
> The number of display dots per CSS px unit. As of CSS3, 1dppx is equivalent to 96dpi because CSS defines pixel units at that ratio. Just bear in mind that ratio could change in future versions of CSS.

As of late 2017, these units are only used in the context of media queries. As an example, an author can create a media block to be used only on displays that have higher than 500 dpi:

```
@media (min-resolution: 500dpi) {
    /* rules go here */
}
```

Relative Length Units

Relative units are so called because they are measured in relation to other things. The actual (or absolute) distance they measure can change due to factors beyond their control, such as screen resolution, the width of the viewing area, the user's preference settings, and a whole host of other things. In addition, for some relative units, their size is almost always relative to the element that uses them and will thus change from element to element.

em and ex units

First, let's consider em and ex, which are closely related. In CSS, one "em" is defined to be the value of font-size for a given font. If the font-size of an element is 14 pixels, then for that element, 1em is equal to 14 pixels.

As you may suspect, this value can change from element to element. For example, let's say you have an h1 with a font size of 24 pixels, an h2 element with a font size of 18 pixels, and a paragraph with a font size of 12 pixels. If you set the left margin of all three at 1em, they will have left margins of 24 pixels, 18 pixels, and 12 pixels, respectively:

```
h1 {font-size: 24px;}
h2 {font-size: 18px;}
p {font-size: 12px;}
h1, h2, p {margin-left: 1em;}
small {font-size: 0.8em;}

<h1>Left margin = <small>24 pixels</small></h1>
<h2>Left margin = <small>18 pixels</small></h2>
<p>Left margin = <small>12 pixels</small></p>
```

When setting the size of the font, on the other hand, the value of em is relative to the font size of the parent element, as illustrated by Figure 4-3.

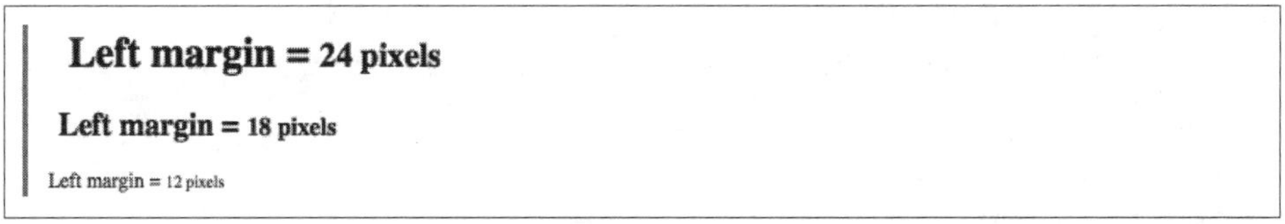

Figure 4-3. Using em for margins and font sizing

In theory, one em is equal to the width of a lowercase *m* in the font used—that's where the name comes from, in fact. It's an old typographer's term. However, this is not assured in CSS.

ex, on the other hand, refers to the height of a lowercase *x* in the font being used. Therefore, if you have two paragraphs in which the text is 24 points in size, but each paragraph uses a different font, then the value of ex could be different for each paragraph. This is because different fonts have different heights for *x*, as you can see in Figure 4-4. Even though the examples use 24-point text—and therefore each example's em value is 24 points—the x-height for each is different.

Figure 4-4. Varying x heights

The rem unit

Like the em unit, the rem unit is based on declared font size. The difference—and it's a doozy—is that whereas em is calculated using the font size of the element to which it's applied, rem is *always* calculated using the root element. In HTML, that's the html element. Thus, declaring any element to have font-size: 1rem; is setting it to have the same font-size value as the root element of the document.

As an example, consider the following markup fragment. It will have the result shown in Figure 4-5.

```
<p> This paragraph has the same font size as the root element thanks to
    inheritance.</p>
<div style="font-size: 30px; background: silver;">
  <p style="font-size: 1em;">This paragraph has the same font size as its parent
    element.</p>
  <p style="font-size: 1rem;">This paragraph has the same font size as the root
    element.</p>
</div>
```

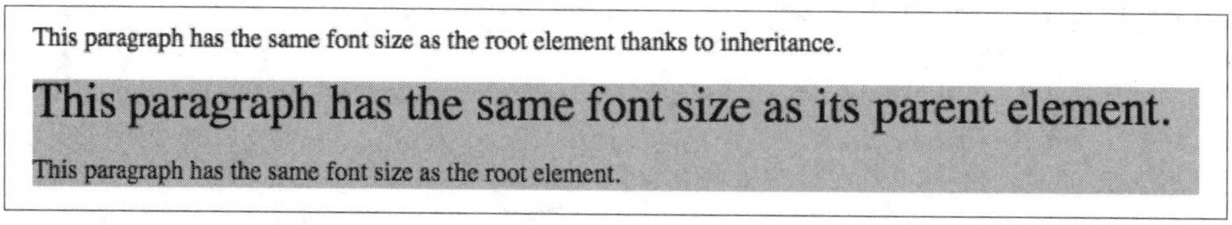

Figure 4-5. ems versus rems

In effect, rem acts as a reset for font size: no matter what relative font sizing has happened to the ancestors of an element, giving it font-size: 1rem; will put it right back where the root element is set. This will usually be the user's default font size, unless you (or the user) have set the root element to a specific font size.

For example, given this declaration, 1rem will always be equivalent to 13px:

```
html {font-size: 13px;}
```

However, given *this* declaration, 1rem will always be equivalent to three-quarters the user's default font size:

```
html {font-size: 75%;}
```

In this case, if the user's default is 16 pixels, then 1rem will equal 12px. If the user has actually set their default to 12 pixels—a few people do this—then 1rem will equal 9px; if the default setting is 20 pixels, then 1rem equals 15px. And so on.

You are not restricted to the value 1rem. Any real number can be used, just as with the em unit, so you can do fun things like set all of your headings to be multiples of the root element's font size:

```
h1 {font-size: 2rem;}
h2 {font-size: 1.75rem;}
h3 {font-size: 1.4rem;}
h4 {font-size: 1.1rem;}
h5 {font-size: 1rem;}
h6 {font-size: 0.8rem;}
```

In browsers that support the keyword initial, font-size: 1rem is equivalent to font-size: initial as long as no font size is set for the root element.

The ch unit

An interesting addition to CSS3 is the ch unit, which is broadly meant to represent "one character." The way it is defined in CSS3 is:

Equal to the advance measure of the "0" (ZERO, U+0030) glyph found in the font used to render it.

The term *advance measure* is actually a CSS-ism that corresponds to the term "advance width" in font typography. CSS uses the term "measure" because some scripts are not right to left or left to right, but instead top to bottom or bottom to top, and so may have an advance height rather than an advance width. For simplicity's sake, we'll stick to advance widths in this section.

Without getting into too many details, a character glyph's advance width is the distance from the start of a character glyph to the start of the next. This generally corresponds to the width of the glyph itself plus any built-in spacing to the sides. (Although that built-in spacing can be either positive or negative.)

CSS pins the ch unit to the advance width of a zero in a given font. This is in parallel to the way that em is calculated with respect to the font-size value of an element.

The easiest way to demonstrate this unit is to run a bunch of zeroes together and then set an image to have a width with the same number of ch units as the number of zeroes, as shown in Figure 4-6:

```
img {height: 1em; width: 25ch;}
```

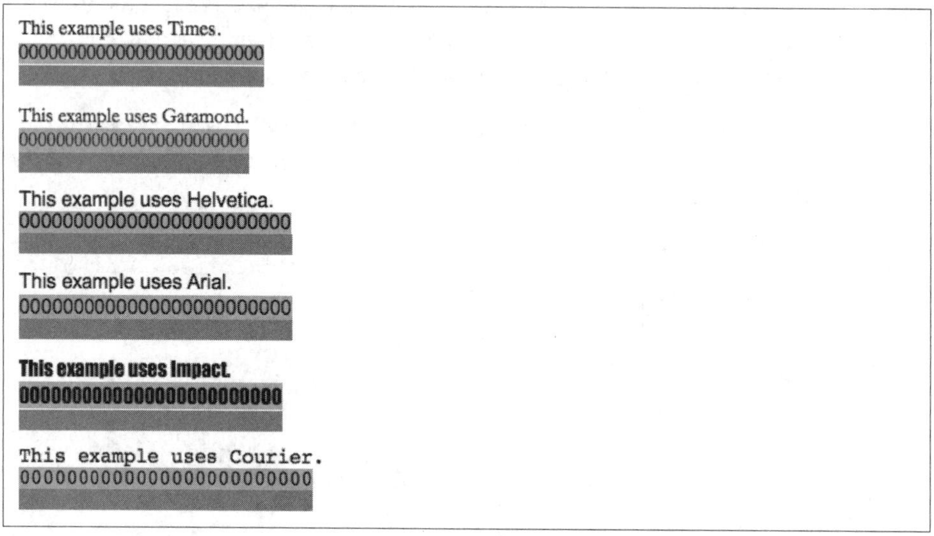

This example uses Times.
000000000000000000000000

This example uses Garamond.
000000000000000000000000

This example uses Helvetica.
000000000000000000000000

This example uses Arial.
000000000000000000000000

This example uses Impact.
000000000000000000000000

This example uses Courier.
000000000000000000000000

Figure 4-6. Character-relative sizing

Given a monospace font, all characters are by definition 1ch wide. In any proportional face type, which is what the vast majority of Western typefaces are, characters may be wider or narrower than the "0" and so cannot be assumed to be 1ch wide.

As of late 2017, only Opera Mini and Internet Explorer had problems with ch. In IE11, ch was mis-measured to be exactly the width of the "0" glyph, not the glyph plus the small amount of space to either side of it. Thus, 5ch was less than the width of "00000" in IE11. This error was corrected in Edge.

Viewport-relative units

Another new addition in CSS3 are the three viewport-relative size units. These are calculated with respect to the size of the viewport—browser window, printable area, mobile device display, etc.:

Viewport width unit (vw)
This unit is calculated with respect to the viewport's width, which is divided by 100. Therefore, if the viewport is 937 pixels wide, 1vw is equal to 9.37px. If the viewport's width changes, say by dragging the browser window wider or more narrow, the value of vw changes along with it.

Viewport height unit (vh)
This unit is calculated with respect to the viewport's height, which is divided by 100. Therefore, if the viewport is 650 pixels tall, 1vh is equal to 6.5px. If the viewport's height changes, say by dragging the browser window taller or shorter, the value of vh changes along with it.

Viewport minimum unit (vmin)
This unit is 1/100 of the viewport's width or height, whichever is *lesser*. Thus, given a viewport that is 937 pixels wide by 650 pixels tall, 1vmin is equal to 6.5px.

Viewport maximum unit (vmax)
This unit is 1/100 of the viewport's width or height, whichever is *greater*. Thus, given a viewport that is 937 pixels wide by 650 pixels tall, 1vmax is equal to 9.37px.

Note that these are length units like any other, and so can be used anywhere a length unit is permitted. You can scale the font size of a heading in terms of the viewport, height, for example, with something like h1 {font-size: 10vh;}. This sets the font size to be 1/10 the height of the viewport—a technique potentially useful for article titles and the like.

These units can be particularly handy for creating full-viewport interfaces, such as those one would expect to find on a mobile device, because it can allow elements to be sized compared to the viewport and not any of the elements within the document tree. It's thus very simple to fill up the entire viewport, or at least major portions of it, and not have to worry about the precise dimensions of the actual viewport in any particular case.

Here's a very basic example of viewport-relative sizing, which is illustrated in Figure 4-7:

```
div {width: 50vh; height: 33vw; background: gray;}
```

An interesting (though perhaps not useful) fact about these units is that they aren't bound to their own primary axis. Thus, for example, you can declare `width: 25vh;` to make an element as wide as one-quarter the height of the viewport.

 As of late 2016, viewport-relative units were supported by all browsers except Opera Mini, plus the odd exception that `vmax` is not supported in Microsoft browsers.

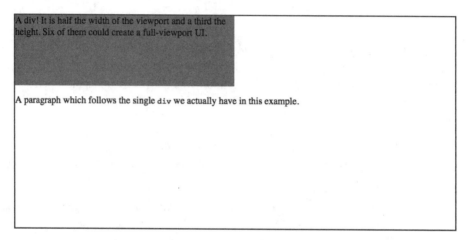

A div! It is half the width of the viewport and a third the height. Six of them could create a full-viewport UI.

A paragraph which follows the single `div` we actually have in this example.

Figure 4-7. Viewport-relative sizing

Calculation values

In situations where you need to do a little math, CSS provides a `calc()` value. Inside the parentheses, you can construct simple mathematical expressions. The permitted operators are + (addition), - (subtraction), * (multiplcation), and / (division), as well as parentheses. These follow the traditional PEMDAS (parentheses, exponents, multiplication, division, addition, subtraction) precedence order, although in this case it's really just PMDAS since exponents are not permitted in `calc()`.

 Support for parentheses in `calc()` appears to be a convenience provided by browsers, since they're not mentioned in the syntax definition for `calc()`. It seems likely that support for parentheses will remain, but use at your own risk.

As an example, suppose you want your paragraphs to have a width that's 2 em less than 90% the width of their parent element. Here's how you express that with `calc()`:

```
p {width: calc(90% - 2em);}
```

calc() can be used anywhere one of the following value types is permitted: *<length>*, *<frequency>*, *<angle>*, *<time>*, *<percentage>*, *<number>*, and *<integer>*. You can also use all these unit types within a calc() value, though there are some limitations to keep in mind.

The basic limitation is that calc() does basic type checking to make sure that units are, in effect, compatible. The checking works like this:

1. To either side of a + or - sign, both values must have the same unit type, or be a *<number>* and *<integer>* (in which case, the result is a *<number>*). Thus, 5 + 2.7 is valid, and results in 7.7. On the other hand, 5em + 2.7 is invalid, because one side has a length unit and the other does not. Note that 5em + 20px *is* valid, because em and px are both length units.

2. Given a *, one of the values involved must be a *<number>* (which, remember, includes integer values). So 2.5rem * 2 and 2 * 2.5rem are both valid, and each result in 5rem. On the flip side, 2.5rem * 2rem is *not* valid, because the result would be 5rem², and length units cannot be area units.

3. Given a /, the value on the *right* side must be a *<number>*. If the left side is an *<integer>*, the result is a *<number>*. Otherwise, the result is of the unit type used on the left side. This means that 30em / 2.75 is valid, but 30 / 2.75em is not valid.

4. Furthermore, any circumstance that yields division by zero is invalid. This is easiest to see in a case like 30px/0, but there are other ways to get there.

There's one more notable limitation, which is that whitespace is *required* to either side of the + and - operators, while it is not for * and /. This avoids ambiguity with respect to values which can be negative.

Beyond that, the specification requires that user agents support a *minimum* of 20 terms inside a calc() expression, where a term is a number, percentage, or dimension (length). In situations where the number of terms somehow exceeds the user agent's term limits, the entire expression is treated as invalid.

Attribute Values

In a few CSS properties, it's possible to pull in the value of an HTML attribute defined for the element being styled. This is done with the attr() expression.

For example, with generated content, you can insert the value of any attribute. It looks something like this (don't worry about understanding the exact syntax, which we'll explore in Chapter 15):

```
p::before {content: "[" attr(id) "]";}
```

That expression would prefix any paragraph that has an id attribute with the value of that id, enclosed in square brackets. Therefore applying the previous style to the following paragraphs would have the result shown in Figure 4-8:

```
<p id="leadoff">This is the first paragraph.</p>
<p>This is the second paragraph.</p>
<p id="conclusion">This is the third paragraph.</p>
```

[leadoff]This is the first paragraph.

[]This is the second paragraph.

[conclusion]This is the third paragraph.

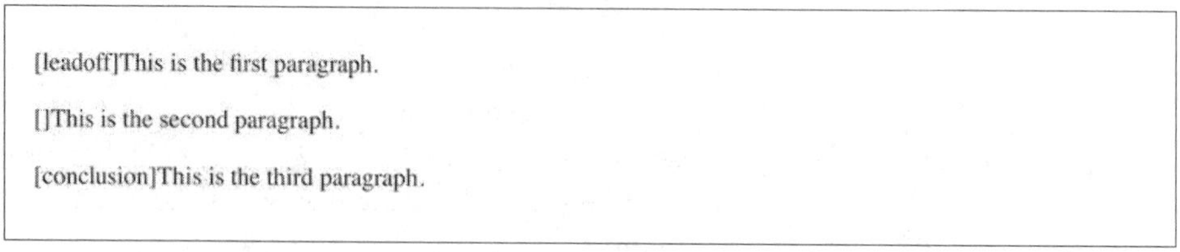

Figure 4-8. Inserting attribute values

It's theoretically possible to use attr() in almost any property value, specifying the value type within the expression. For example, you could (again, in theory) use the maxlength attribute on an input field to determine its width, as shown here:

```
input[type="text"] {width: attr(maxlength em);}
```

```
<input type="text" maxlength="10">
```

Given that setup, the input element would be styled to be 10 em wide, assuming a user agent that supports this use of attr(). As of late 2016, this was not the case: no tested browser supported this application of attr().

Color

One of the first questions every starting web author asks is, "How do I set colors on my page?" Under HTML, you have two choices: you could use one of a small number of colors with names, such as red or purple, or employ a vaguely cryptic method using hexadecimal codes. Both of these methods for describing colors remain in CSS, along with some other—and, I think, more intuitive—methods.

Named Colors

Assuming that you're content to pick from a small, basic set of colors, the easiest method is to use the name of the color you want. CSS calls these color choices, logically enough, *named colors*. In the early days of CSS, there were 16 basic color keywords, which were the 16 colors defined in HTML 4.01. These are shown in Table 4-1.

Table 4-1. The basic 16 color keywords

aqua	gray	navy	silver
black	green	olive	teal
blue	lime	purple	white
fuchsia	maroon	red	yellow

So, let's say you want all first-level headings to be maroon. The best declaration would be:

```
h1 {color: maroon;}
```

Simple enough, isn't it? Figure 4-9 shows a few more examples:

```
h1 {color: silver;}
h2 {color: fuchsia;}
h3 {color: navy;}
```

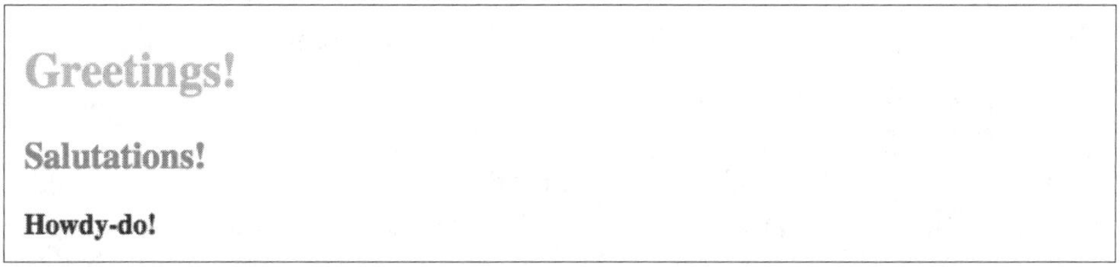

> ## Greetings!
>
> ## Salutations!
>
> ### Howdy-do!

Figure 4-9. Named colors

You've probably seen (and maybe even used) color names other than the ones listed earlier. For example, if you specify:

```
h1 {color: lightgreen;}
```

As of late 2017, the latest CSS color specification includes those original 16 named colors in a longer list of 148 color keywords. This extended list is based on the standard X11 RGB values that have been in use for decades, and have been recognized by browsers for many years, with the addition of some color names from SVG (mostly involving variants of "gray" and "grey"). A table of color equivalents for all 148 keywords defined in the CSS Color Module Level 4 is given in Appendix C.

Fortunately, there are more detailed and precise ways to specify colors in CSS. The advantage is that, with these methods, you can specify any color in the color spectrum, not just a limited list of named colors.

Colors by RGB and RGBa

Computers create colors by combining different levels of red, green, and blue, a combination that is often referred to as *RGB color*. Each point of display is known as a pixel. Given the way colors are created on a screen, it makes sense that you should have direct access to those colors, determining your own mixture of the three for maximum control. That solution is complex, but possible, and the payoffs are worth it because there are very few limits on which colors you can produce. There are four ways to affect color in this manner.

Functional RGB colors

There are two color value types that use *functional RGB notation* as opposed to hexa-decimal notation. The generic syntax for this type of color value is rgb(color), where color is expressed using a triplet of either percentages or integers. The percentage values can be in the range 0%–100%, and the integers can be in the range 0–255.

Thus, to specify white and black, respectively, using percentage notation, the values would be:

```
rgb(100%,100%,100%)
rgb(0%,0%,0%)
```

Using the integer-triplet notation, the same colors would be represented as:

```
rgb(255,255,255)
rgb(0,0,0)
```

An important thing to remember is that you can't mix integers and percentages in the same color value. Thus, rgb(255,66.67%,50%) would be invalid and thus ignored.

Assume you want your h1 elements to be a shade of red that lies between the values for red and maroon. red is equivalent to rgb(100%,0%,0%), whereas maroon is equal to (50%,0%,0%). To get a color between those two, you might try this:

```
h1 {color: rgb(75%,0%,0%);}
```

This makes the red component of the color lighter than maroon, but darker than red. If, on the other hand, you want to create a pale red color, you would raise the green and blue levels:

```
h1 {color: rgb(75%,50%,50%);}
```

The closest equivalent color using integer-triplet notation is:

```
h1 {color: rgb(191,127,127);}
```

The easiest way to visualize how these values correspond to color is to create a table of gray values. The result is shown in Figure 4-10:

```
p.one {color: rgb(0%,0%,0%);}
p.two {color: rgb(20%,20%,20%);}
p.three {color: rgb(40%,40%,40%);}
p.four {color: rgb(60%,60%,60%);}
p.five {color: rgb(80%,80%,80%);}
p.six {color: rgb(0,0,0);}
p.seven {color: rgb(51,51,51);}
```

```
p.eight {color: rgb(102,102,102);}
p.nine {color: rgb(153,153,153);}
p.ten {color: rgb(204,204,204);}
```

> [one] This is a paragraph.
>
> [two] This is a paragraph.
>
> [three] This is a paragraph.
>
> [four] This is a paragraph.
>
> [five] This is a paragraph.
>
> [six] This is a paragraph.
>
> [seven] This is a paragraph.
>
> [eight] This is a paragraph.
>
> [nine] This is a paragraph.
>
> [ten] This is a paragraph.

Figure 4-10. Text set in shades of gray

Since we're dealing in shades of gray, all three RGB values are the same in each statement. If any one of them were different from the others, then a color hue would start to emerge. If, for example, rgb(50%,50%,50%) were modified to be rgb(50%,50%, 60%), the result would be a medium-dark color with just a hint of blue.

It is possible to use fractional numbers in percentage notation. You might, for some reason, want to specify that a color be exactly 25.5 percent red, 40 percent green, and 98.6 percent blue:

```
h2 {color: rgb(25.5%,40%,98.6%);}
```

A user agent that ignores the decimal points (and some do) should round the value to the nearest integer, resulting in a declared value of rgb(26%,40%,99%). In integer triplets, you are limited to integers.

Values that fall outside the allowed range for each notation are *clipped* to the nearest range edge, meaning that a value that is greater than 100% or less than 0% will default to those allowed extremes. Thus, the following declarations would be treated as if they were the values indicated in the comments:

```
P.one {color: rgb(300%,4200%,110%);}   /*  100%,100%,100%  */
P.two {color: rgb(0%,-40%,-5000%);}    /*  0%,0%,0%  */
p.three {color: rgb(42,444,-13);}      /* 42,255,0  */
```

Conversion between percentages and integers may seem arbitrary, but there's no need to guess at the integer you want—there's a simple formula for calculating them. If you know the percentages for each of the RGB levels you want, then you need only apply them to the number 255 to get the resulting values. Let's say you have a color of 25 percent red, 37.5 percent green, and 60 percent blue. Multiply each of these percentages by 255, and you get 63.75, 95.625, and 153. Round these values to the nearest integers, and *voilà*: rgb(64,96,153).

If you already know the percentage values, there isn't much point in converting them into integers. Integer notation is more useful for people who use programs such as Photoshop, which can display integer values in the Info dialog, or for those who are so familiar with the technical details of color generation that they normally think in values of 0–255.

RGBa colors

As of CSS3, the two functional RGB notations were extended into a functional RGBa notation. This notation adds an alpha value to the end of the RGB triplets; thus "red-green-blue-alpha" becomes RGBa. The alpha stands for *alpha channel*, which is a measure of opacity.

For example, suppose you wanted an element's text to be half-opaque white. That way, any background color behind the text would "shine through," mixing with the half-transparent white. You would write one of the following two values:

```
rgba(255,255,255,0.5)
rgba(100%,100%,100%,0.5)
```

To make a color completely transparent, you set the alpha value to 0; to be completely opaque, the correct value is 1. Thus rgb(0,0,0) and rgba(0,0,0,1) will yield precisely the same result (black). Figure 4-11 shows a series of paragraphs set in increasingly transparent black, which is the result of the following rules.

```
p.one {color: rgba(0,0,0,1);}
p.two {color: rgba(0%,0%,0%,0.8);}
p.three {color: rgba(0,0,0,0.6);}
p.four {color: rgba(0%,0%,0%,0.4);}
p.five {color: rgba(0,0,0,0.2);}
```

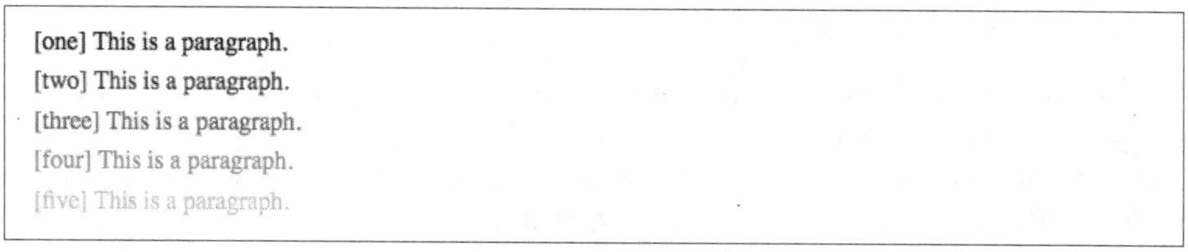

```
[one] This is a paragraph.
[two] This is a paragraph.
[three] This is a paragraph.
[four] This is a paragraph.
[five] This is a paragraph.
```

Figure 4-11. Text set in progressive translucency

As you've no doubt already inferred, alpha values are always real numbers in the range 0 to 1. Any value outside that range will either be ignored or reset to the nearest valid alpha value. You cannot use *<percentage>* to represent alpha values, despite the mathematical equivalence.

Hexadecimal RGB colors

CSS allows you to define a color using the same *hexadecimal color notation* so familiar to old-school HTML web authors:

```
h1 {color: #FF0000;}    /* set H1s to red */
h2 {color: #903BC0;}    /* set H2s to a dusky purple */
h3 {color: #000000;}    /* set H3s to black */
h4 {color: #808080;}    /* set H4s to medium gray */
```

Computers have been using hex notation for quite some time now, and programmers are typically either trained in its use or pick it up through experience. Their familiarity with hexadecimal notation likely led to its use in setting colors in HTML. That practice was carried over to CSS.

Here's how it works: by stringing together three hexadecimal numbers in the range 00 through FF, you can set a color. The generic syntax for this notation is #RRGGBB. Note that there are no spaces, commas, or other separators between the three numbers.

Hexadecimal notation is mathematically equivalent to integer-pair notation. For example, rgb(255,255,255) is precisely equivalent to #FFFFFF, and rgb(51,102,128) is the same as #336680. Feel free to use whichever notation you prefer—it will be rendered identically by most user agents. If you have a calculator that converts between decimal and hexadecimal, making the jump from one to the other should be pretty simple.

For hexadecimal numbers that are composed of three matched pairs of digits, CSS permits a shortened notation. The generic syntax of this notation is #RGB:

```
h1 {color: #000;}    /* set H1s to black */
h2 {color: #666;}    /* set H2s to dark gray */
h3 {color: #FFF;}    /* set H3s to white */
```

As you can see from the markup, there are only three digits in each color value. However, since hexadecimal numbers between 00 and FF need two digits each, and you have only three total digits, how does this method work?

The answer is that the browser takes each digit and replicates it. Therefore, #F00 is equivalent to #FF0000, #6FA would be the same as #66FFAA, and #FFF would come out #FFFFFF, which is the same as white. Not every color can be represented in this manner. Medium gray, for example, would be written in standard hexadecimal notation as #808080. This cannot be expressed in shorthand; the closest equivalent would be #888, which is the same as #888888.

Hexadecimal RGBa colors

A new (as of late 2017) hexadecimal notation adds a fourth hex value to represent the alpha channel value. Figure 4-11 shows a series of paragraphs set in increasingly transparent black, just as we saw in the previous section, which is the result of the following rules:

```
p.one {color: #000000FF;}
p.two {color: #000000CC;}
p.three {color: #00000099;}
p.four {color: #00000066;}
p.five {color: #00000033;}
```

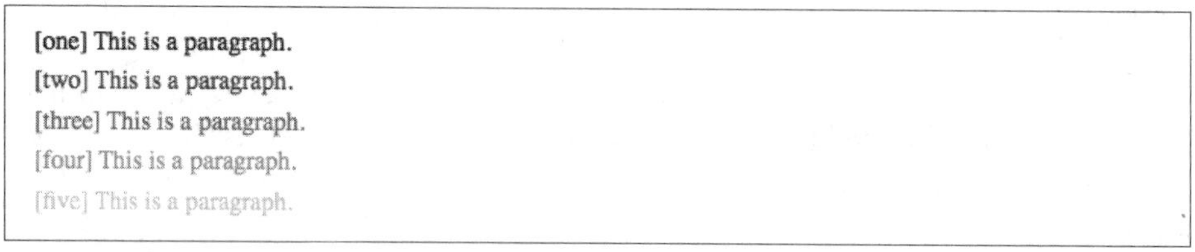

[one] This is a paragraph.
[two] This is a paragraph.
[three] This is a paragraph.
[four] This is a paragraph.
[five] This is a paragraph.

Figure 4-12. Text set in progressive translucency, redux

As with non-alpha hexadecimal values, it's possible to shorten a value composed of matched pairs to a four-digit value. Thus, a value of #663399AA can be written as #639A. If the value has any pairs that are not repetitive, then the entire eight-digit value must be written out: #663399CA cannot be shortened to #639CA.

 As of late 2017, the alpha-channel hexadecimal notation was supported in Firefox and Safari, and had experimental implementations in Chrome and Opera.

Colors by HSL and HSLa

New to CSS3 (though not to the world of color theory in general) are HSL notations. HSL stands for Hue, Saturation, and Lightness, where the hue is a hue angle in the range 0–360, saturation is a percentage value from 0 (no saturation) to 100 (full saturation), and lightness is a percentage value from 0 (completely dark) to 100 (completely light).

The hue angle is expressed in terms of a circle around which the full spectrum of colors progresses. It starts with red at 0 degrees and then proceeds through the rainbow until it comes to red again at 360 degrees. Figure 4-13 illustrates this visually by showing the angles and colors of the spectrum on a wheel as well as a linear strip.

If you're intimately familiar with RGB, then HSL may be confusing at first. (But then, RGB is confusing for people familiar with HSL.) You may be able to better grasp the hues in HSL by contemplating the diagram in Figure 4-14, which shows the spectrum results from placing and then mixing red, green, and blue.

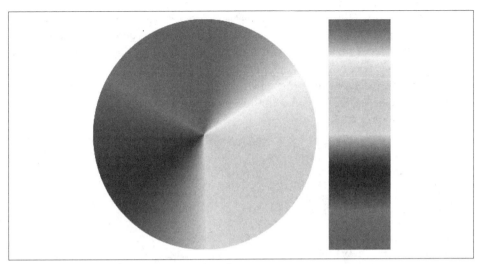

Figure 4-13. The spectrum on a wheel and a strip

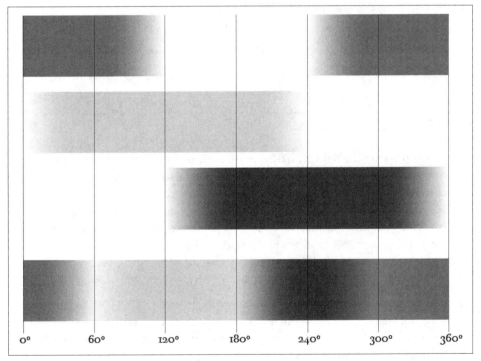

0°   60°   120°   180°   240°   300°   360°

Figure 4-14. Mixing RGB to create the spectrum

As for the other two values, saturation measures the intensity of a color. A saturation of 0% always yields a shade of gray, no matter what hue angle you have set, and a saturation of 100% creates the most vivid possible shade of that hue for a given lightness. Similarly, lightness defines how dark or light the color appears. A lightness of 0% is always black, regardless of the other hue and saturation values, just as a lightness of 100% always yields white. Consider the results of the following styles, illustrated on the left side of Figure 4-15.

```
p.one {color: hsl(0,0%,0%);}
p.two{color: hsl(60,0%,25%);}
p.three {color: hsl(120,0%,50%);}
p.four {color: hsl(180,0%,75%);}
p.five {color: hsl(240,0%,0%);}
p.six {color: hsl(300,0%,25%);}
p.seven {color: hsl(360,0%,50%);}
```

[one] This paragraph's color has 0% saturation.	[one] This paragraph's color has 50% saturation.
[two] This paragraph's color has 0% saturation.	[two] This paragraph's color has 50% saturation.
[three] This paragraph's color has 0% saturation.	[three] This paragraph's color has 50% saturation.
[four] This paragraph's color has 0% saturation.	[four] This paragraph's color has 50% saturation.
[five] This paragraph's color has 0% saturation.	[five] This paragraph's color has 50% saturation.
[six] This paragraph's color has 0% saturation.	[six] This paragraph's color has 50% saturation.
[seven] This paragraph's color has 0% saturation.	[seven] This paragraph's color has 50% saturation.

Figure 4-15. Varying lightness and hues

The gray you see on the left side isn't just a function of the limitations of print: every single one of those bits of text is a shade of gray, because every color value has 0% in the saturation (middle) position. The degree of lightness or darkness is set by the lightness (third) position. In all seven examples, the hue angle changes, and in none of them does it matter. But that's only so long as the saturation remains at 0%. If that value is raised to, say, 50%, then the hue angle will become very important, because it will control what sort of color you see. Consider the same set of values that we saw before, but all set to 50% saturation, as illustrated on the right side of Figure 4-15.

It can be instructive to take the 16 color keywords defined in HTML4 (Table 4-1) and plot them against a hue-and-lightness wheel, as shown in Figure 4-16. The color wheel not only features the full spectrum around the rim, but also runs from 50 percent lightness at the edge to 0 percent lightness in the center. (The saturation is 100 percent throughout.) As you can see, the 12 keywords of color are regularly placed throughout the wheel, which bespeaks careful choice on the part of whoever chose them. The gray shades aren't quite as regularly placed, but are probably the most useful distribution of shades, given that there were only four of them.

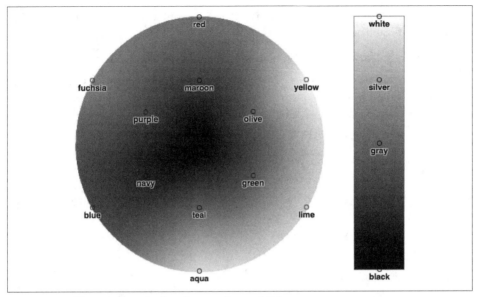

Figure 4-16. Keyword-equivalent hue angles and lightnesses

Just as RGB has its RGBa counterpart, HSL has an HSLa counterpart. This is an HSL triplet followed by an alpha value in the range 0–1. The following HSLa values are all black with varying shades of transparency, just as in "Hexadecimal RGBa colors" on page 137 (and illustrated in Figure 4-11):

```
p.one {color: hsla(0,0%,0%,1);}
p.two {color: hsla(0,0%,0%,0.8);}
p.three {color: hsla(0,0%,0%,0.6);}
p.four {color: hsla(0,0%,0%,0.4);}
p.five {color: hsla(0,0%,0%,0.2);}
```

Color Keywords

There are two special keywords that can be used anywhere a color value is permitted. These are transparent and currentColor.

As its name suggests, transparent defines a completely transparent color. The CSS Color Module defines it to be equivalent to rgba(0,0,0,0), and that's its computed value. The is not often used to set text color, for example, but it is essentially the default value for element background colors. It can also be used to define element borders that take up space, but are not visible, and is often used when defining gradients—all topics we'll cover in later chapters.

By contrast, currentColor means "whatever the computed value of color is for this element." Consider the following:

```
main {color: gray; border-color: currentColor;}
```

The first declaration causes any main elements to have a foreground color of gray. The second declaration uses currentColor to copy the computed value of color—in this case, rgb(50%,50%,50%), which is equivalent to gray—and apply it to any borders the main elements might have.

Angles

Since we just finished talking about hue angles in HSL, this would be a good time to talk about angle units. Angles in general are represented as *<angle>*, which is a *<number>* followed by one of four unit types:

deg

> Degrees, of which there are 360 in a full circle.

grad

> Gradians, of which there are 400 in a full circle. Also known as *grades* or *gons*.

rad

> Radians, of which there are 2π (approximately 6.28) in a full circle.

turn

> Turns, of which there is one in a full circle. This unit is mostly useful when animating a rotation and you wish to have it turn multiple times, such as 10turn to make it spin 10 times. (Sadly, the pluralization turns is invalid, at least as of late 2017, and will be ignored.)

Angle units (Table 4-2) are mostly used in 2D and 3D transforms, though they do appear in a few other places. Note that angle units are *not* used in HSL colors, where all hue angle values are *always* degrees and thus do not use the deg unit!

Table 4-2. Angle equivalents

Degrees	Gradians	Radians	Turns
0deg	0grad	0rad	0turn
45deg	50grad	0.785rad	0.125turn
90deg	100grad	1.571rad	0.25turn
180deg	200grad	3.142rad	0.5turn
270deg	300grad	4.712rad	0.75turn
360deg	400grad	6.283rad	1turn

Time and Frequency

In cases where a property needs to express a period of time, the value is represented as *<time>* and is a *<number>* followed by either s (seconds) or ms (milliseconds.) Time values are most often used in transitions and animations, either to define durations or delays. The following two declarations will have exactly the same result:

```
a[href] {transition-duration: 2.4s;}
a[href] {transition-duration: 2400ms;}
```

Time values are also used in aural CSS, again to define durations or delays, but support for aural CSS is extremely limited as of this writing.

Another value type historically used in aural CSS is *<frequency>*, which is a *<number>* followed by either Hz (hertz) or kHz (kilohertz). As usual, the unit identifiers are case-insensitive, so Hz and hz are equivalent. The following two declarations will have exactly the same result:

```
h1 {pitch: 128hz;}
h1 {pitch: 0.128khz;}
```

Position

A *position value* is how you specify the placement of an origin image in a background area, and is represented as *<position>*. Its syntactical structure is rather complicated:

```
[
  [ left | center | right | top | bottom | <percentage> | <length> ] |
  [ left | center | right | <percentage> | <length> ]
  [ top | center | bottom | <percentage> | <length> ] |
  [ center | [ left | right ] [ <percentage> | <length> ]? ] &&
  [ center | [ top | bottom ] [ <percentage> | <length> ]? ]
]
```

That might seem a little nutty, but it's all down to the subtly complex patterns that this value type has to allow.

If you declare only one value, such as left or 25%, then a second value is set to center. Thus, left is the same as left center, and 25% is the same as 25% center.

If you declare (either implicitly, as above, or explicitly) two values, and the first one is a length or percentage, then it is *always* considered to be the horizontal value. This means that given 25% 35px, the 25% is a horizontal distance and the 35px is a vertical distance. If you swap them to say 35px 25%, then 35px is horizontal and 25% is vertical. This means that if you write 25% left or 35px right, the entire value is invalid because you have supplied two horizontal distances and no vertical distance. (Similarly, a value of right left or top bottom is invalid and will be ignored.) On the other hand, if you write left 25% or right 35px, there is no problem because you've given a horizontal distance (with the keyword) and a vertical distance (with the percentage or length).

If you declare four values (we'll deal with three just in a moment), then you must have two lengths or percentages, each of which is preceded by a keyword. In this case, each length or percentage specifies an offset distance, and each keyword defines the edge from which the offset is calculated. Thus, right 10px bottom 30px means an offset of 10 pixels to the left of the right edge, and an offset of 30 pixels up from the bottom edge. Similarly, top 50% left 35px means a 50 percent offset from the top and a 35-pixels-to-the-right offset from the left.

If you declare three values, the rules are the same as for four, except the last offset is set to be zero (no offset). Thus right 20px top is the same as right 20px top 0.

Custom Values

As this book was being finished in late 2017, a new capability was being added to CSS. The technical term for this is *custom properties*, even though what these really do is create sort of variables in your CSS. They do not, contrary to their name, create special CSS properties, in the sense of properties like color or font.

Here's a simple example, with the result shown in Figure 4-17:

```
html {
    --base-color: #639;
    --highlight-color: #AEA;
}

h1 {color: var(--base-color);}
h2 {color: var(--highlight-color);}
```

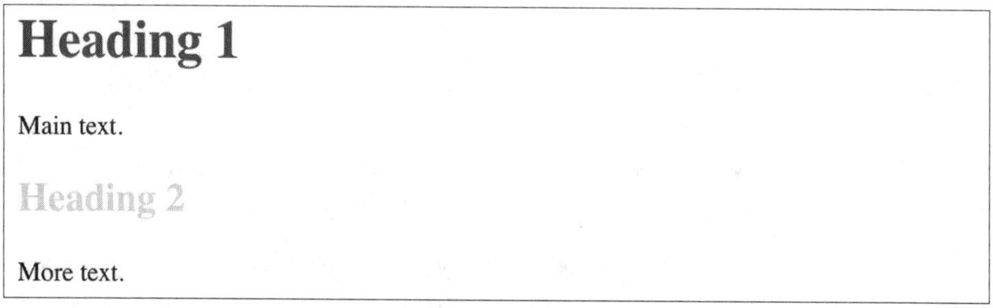

Heading 1

Main text.

Heading 2

More text.

Figure 4-17. Using custom values to color headings

There are two things to absorb here. The first is the definition of the custom values --base-color and --highlight-color. These are not some sort of special color types. They're just names that were picked to describe what the values contain. We could just as easily have said:

```
html {
    --alison: #639;
    --david: #AEA;
}

h1 {color: var(--alison);}
h2 {color: var(--david);}
```

You probably shouldn't do that sort of thing, unless you're literally defining colors that specifically correspond to people named Alison and David. (Perhaps on an "About Our Team" page.) It's always better to define custom identifiers that are self-documenting—things like main-color or accent-color or brand-font-face.

The important this is that any custom identifier of this type begins with *two* hyphens (--). It can then be invoked later on using a var() value type. Note that these names are case-sensitive, so --main-color and --Main-color are completely separate identifiers.

These custom identifiers are often referred to as "CSS variables," which explains the var() pattern. This labelling has some truth to it, but bear in mind that these are not full-blown variables in the programming-language sense. They're more like macros in text editors: simple substitutions of one value for another.

An interesting feature of custom properties is their ability to scope themselves to a given context. If that sentence made any sense to you, it probably gave a little thrill. If not, here's an example to illustrate scoping, with the result shown in Figure 4-18:

```
html {
    --base-color: #639;
}
aside {
    --base-color: #F60;
}

h1 {color: var(--base-color);}

<body>

<h1>Heading 1</h1><p>Main text.</p>

<aside>
    <h1>Heading 1</h1><p>An aside.</p>
</aside>

<h1>Heading 1</h1><p>Main text.</p>

</body>
```

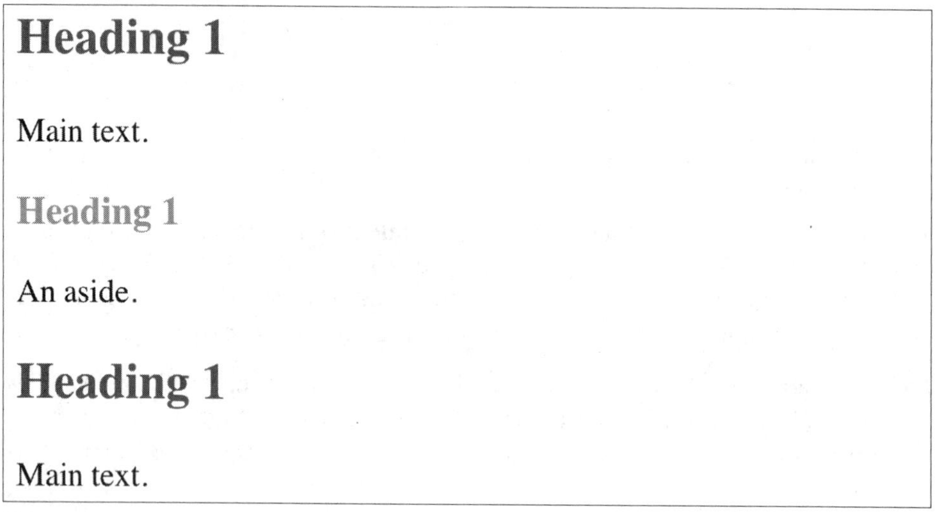

Figure 4-18. Scoping custom values to certain contexts

Notice how the headings are purple outside the `aside` element and orange inside. That's because the variable `--base-color` was updated for `aside` elements. The new custom value applies to any h1 inside an `aside` element.

There are a great many patterns possible with CSS variables, even if they are confined to value replacement. Here's an example suggested by Chriztian Steinmeier combining variables with the `calc()` value type to create a regular set of indents for unordered lists:

```
html {
    --gutter: 3ch;
    --offset: 1;
}
ul li {margin-left: calc(var(--gutter) * var(--offset));}
ul ul li {--offset: 2;}
ul ul ul li {--offset: 3;}
```

This particular example is basically the same as writing:

```
ul li {margin-left: 3ch;}
ul ul li {margin-left: 6ch;}
ul ul ul li {margin-left: 9ch;}
```

The difference is that with variables, it's simple to update the `--gutter` multiplier in one place and have everything adjust automatically, rather than having to retype three values and make sure all the math is correct.

This method of using abstract variable names opens an entirely new way of styling, an approach which has little precedent in the history of CSS. If you want to try out custom properties but are concerned about support, remember the `@supports()` feature query. Using this approach will keep your variable styling safely hidden away:

```
@supports (color: var(--custom)) {
    /* variable-dependent styles go here */
}
@supports (--custom: value) {
    /* alternate query pattern */
}
```

 To reiterate: custom properties were just going into production as of late 2017, as the book was being finished. There were still uncertainties to be worked out around how custom properties should be used, how powerful they may become, how they relate to the cascade, and more. While they're worth knowing about and experimenting with, bear in mind that anything stated here may have changed or been removed by the time you read this.

CHAPTER 5

Fonts

The beginning of the "Font Properties" section of the CSS1 specification, written in 1996, begins with this sentence: "Setting font properties will be among the most common uses of style sheets." The intervening years have done nothing to disprove this assertion.

CSS2 added the ability to specify custom fonts for download with `@font-face`, but it wasn't until about 2009 that this capability really began to be widely and consistently supported. Now, websites can call on any font they have the right to use, aided by online services such as Typekit. Generally speaking, if you can get access to a font, you can use it in your design.

It's important to remember, however, that this does not grant absolute control over fonts. If the font you're using fails to download, or is in a file format the user's browser doesn't understand, then the text will be displayed with a fallback font. That's a good thing, since it means the user still gets your content, but it's worth bearing in mind that you cannot absolutely depend on the presence of a given font and should never design as if you can.

Font Families

What we think of as a "font" is usually composed of many variations to describe bold text, italic text, and so on. For example, you're probably familiar with (or at least have heard of) the font Times. However, Times is actually a combination of many variants, including TimesRegular, TimesBold, TimesItalic, TimesBoldItalic, and so on. Each of these variants of Times is an actual *font face*, and Times, as we usually think of it, is a combination of all these variant faces. In other words, Times is actually a *font family*, not just a single font, even though most of us think about fonts as being single entities.

In order to cover all the bases, CSS defines five generic font families:

Serif fonts

These fonts are proportional and have serifs. A font is proportional if all characters in the font have different widths due to their various sizes. For example, a lowercase *i* and a lowercase *m* are different widths. (This book's paragraph font is proportional, for example.) Serifs are the decorations on the ends of strokes within each character, such as little lines at the top and bottom of a lowercase *l*, or at the bottom of each leg of an uppercase *A*. Examples of serif fonts are Times, Georgia, and New Century Schoolbook.

Sans-serif fonts

These fonts are proportional and do not have serifs. Examples of sans-serif fonts are Helvetica, Geneva, Verdana, Arial, and Univers.

Monospace fonts

Monospace fonts are not proportional. These generally are used for displaying programmatic code or tabular data. In these fonts, each character uses up the same amount of horizontal space as all the others; thus, a lowercase *i* takes up the same horizontal space as a lowercase *m*, even though their actual letterforms may have different widths. These fonts may or may not have serifs. If a font has uniform character widths, it is classified as monospace, regardless of the presence of serifs. Examples of monospace fonts are Courier, Courier New, Consolas, and Andale Mono.

Cursive fonts

These fonts attempt to emulate human handwriting or lettering. Usually, they are composed largely of flowing curves and have stroke decorations that exceed those found in serif fonts. For example, an uppercase *A* might have a small curl at the bottom of its left leg or be composed entirely of swashes and curls. Examples of cursive fonts are Zapf Chancery, Author, and Comic Sans.

Fantasy fonts

Such fonts are not really defined by any single characteristic other than our inability to easily classify them in one of the other families (these are sometimes called "decorative" or "display" fonts). A few such fonts are Western, Woodblock, and Klingon.

In theory, every font family will fall into one of these generic families. In practice, this may not be the case, but the exceptions (if any) are likely to be few and far between, and browsers are likely to drop any fonts they cannot classify as serif, sans-serif, monospace, or cursive into the "fantasy" bucket.

Using Generic Font Families

You can call on any available font family by using the property `font-family`.

<hr>

font-family

Values	[*<family-name>*	*<generic-family>*]#
Initial value	User agent-specific
Applies to	All elements
Computed value	As specified
Inherited	Yes
Animatable	No

<hr>

If you want a document to use a sans-serif font, but you do not particularly care which one, then the appropriate declaration would be:

```
body {font-family: sans-serif;}
```

This will cause the user agent to pick a sans-serif font family (such as Helvetica) and apply it to the body element. Thanks to inheritance, the same font family choice will be applied to all the elements that descend from the body—unless a more specific selector overrides it.

Using nothing more than these generic families, an author can create a fairly sophisticated stylesheet. The following rule set is illustrated in Figure 5-1:

```
body {font-family: serif;}
h1, h2, h3, h4 {font-family: sans-serif;}
code, pre, tt, kbd {font-family: monospace;}
p.signature {font-family: cursive;}
```

Thus, most of the document will use a serif font such as Times, including all paragraphs except those that have a class of signature, which will instead be rendered in a cursive font such as Author. Heading levels 1 through 4 will use a sans-serif font like Helvetica, while the elements code, pre, tt, and kbd will use a monospace font like Courier.

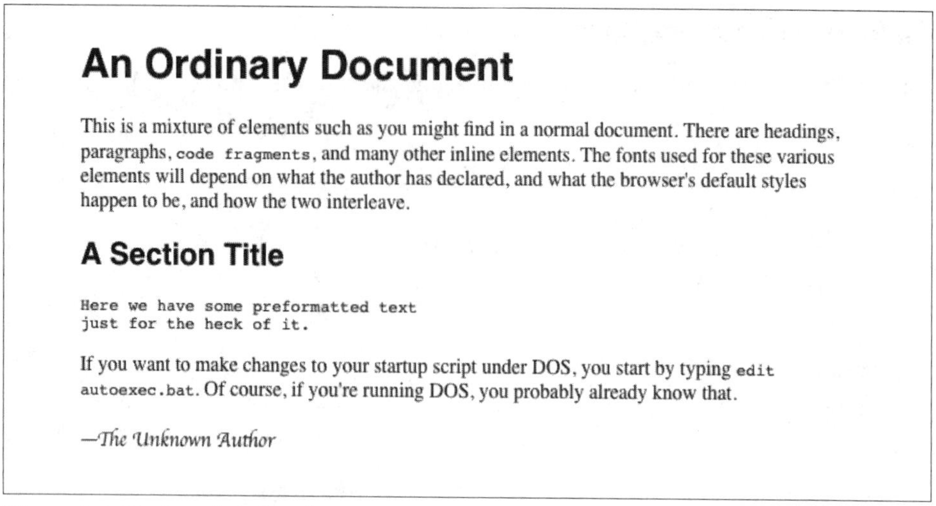

An Ordinary Document

This is a mixture of elements such as you might find in a normal document. There are headings, paragraphs, `code fragments`, and many other inline elements. The fonts used for these various elements will depend on what the author has declared, and what the browser's default styles happen to be, and how the two interleave.

A Section Title

```
Here we have some preformatted text
just for the heck of it.
```

If you want to make changes to your startup script under DOS, you start by typing `edit` `autoexec.bat`. Of course, if you're running DOS, you probably already know that.

—*The Unknown Author*

Figure 5-1. Various font families

Specifying a Font Family

An author may, on the other hand, have more specific preferences for which font to use in the display of a document or element. In a similar vein, a user may want to create a user stylesheet that defines the exact fonts to be used in the display of all documents. In either case, font-family is still the property to use.

Assume for the moment that all h1s should use Georgia as their font. The simplest rule for this would be the following:

```
h1 {font-family: Georgia;}
```

This will cause the user agent displaying the document to use Georgia for all h1s, as shown in Figure 5-2.

A Level 1 Heading Element

Figure 5-2. An h1 element using Georgia

This rule assumes that the user agent has Georgia available for use. If it doesn't, the user agent will be unable to use the rule at all. It won't ignore the rule, but if it can't find a font called "Georgia," it can't do anything but display h1 elements using the user agent's default font (whatever that is).

All is not lost, however. By combining specific font names with generic font families, you can create documents that come out, if not exact, at least close to your intentions.

To continue the previous example, the following markup tells a user agent to use Georgia if it's available, and to use another serif font if it's not:

```
h1 {font-family: Georgia, serif;}
```

If a reader doesn't have Georgia installed but does have Times, the user agent might use Times for h1 elements. Even though Times isn't an exact match to Georgia, it's probably close enough.

For this reason, I strongly encourage you to always provide a generic family as part of any font-family rule. By doing so, you provide a fallback mechanism that lets user agents pick an alternative when they can't provide an exact font match. Here are a few more examples:

```
h1 {font-family: Arial, sans-serif;}
h2 {font-family: Charcoal, sans-serif;}
p {font-family: 'Times New Roman', serif;}
address {font-family: Chicago, sans-serif;}
```

If you're familiar with fonts, you might have a number of similar fonts in mind for displaying a given element. Let's say that you want all paragraphs in a document to be displayed using Times, but you would also accept Times New Roman, Georgia, New Century Schoolbook, and New York (all of which are serif fonts) as alternate choices. First, decide the order of preference for these fonts, and then string them together with commas:

```
p {font-family: Times, 'Times New Roman', 'New Century Schoolbook', Georgia,
    'New York', serif;}
```

Based on this list, a user agent will look for the fonts in the order they're listed. If none of the listed fonts are available, then it will just pick an available serif font.

Using quotation marks

You may have noticed the presence of single quotes in the previous example, which we haven't seen before. Quotation marks are advisable in a font-family declaration only if a font name has one or more spaces in it, such as "New York," or if the font name includes symbols such as # or $. Thus, a font called Karrank% should probably be quoted:

```
h2 {font-family: Wedgie, 'Karrank%', Klingon, fantasy;}
```

If you leave off the quotation marks, there is a chance that user agents will ignore that particular font name altogether, although they'll still process the rest of the rule.

Note that the quoting of a font name containing a symbol is not actually required any more. Instead, it's recommended, which is as close to describing best practices as the CSS specification ever really gets. Similarly, it is recommended that you quote a font name containing spaces, though again, this is generally unnecessary in modern user agents. As it turns out, the only required quotation is for font names that match accepted font-family keywords. Thus, if you call for a font whose actual name is "cursive," you'll definitely need to quote it in order to distinguish it from the value keyword cursive:

```
h2 {font-family: Author, "cursive", cursive;}
```

Font names that use a single word (which doesn't conflict with any of the keywords for font-family) need not be quoted, and generic family names (serif, monospace, etc.) should never be quoted when they refer to the actual generic families. If you quote a generic name, then the user agent will assume that you are asking for a specific font with that name (for example, "serif"), not a generic family.

As for which quotation marks to use, both single and double quotes are acceptable. Remember that if you place a font-family rule in a style attribute, which you generally shouldn't, you'll need to use whichever quotes you didn't use for the attribute itself. Therefore, if you use double quotes to enclose the font-family rule, then you'll have to use single quotes within the rule, as in the following markup:

```
p {font-family: sans-serif;}  /* sets paragraphs to sans-serif by default */

<!-- the next example is correct (uses single-quotes) -->
<p style="font-family: 'New Century Schoolbook', Times, serif;">...</p>

<!-- the next example is NOT correct (uses double-quotes) -->
<p style="font-family: "New Century Schoolbook", Times, serif;">...</p>
```

If you use double quotes in such a circumstance, they interfere with the attribute syntax, as you can see in Figure 5-3.

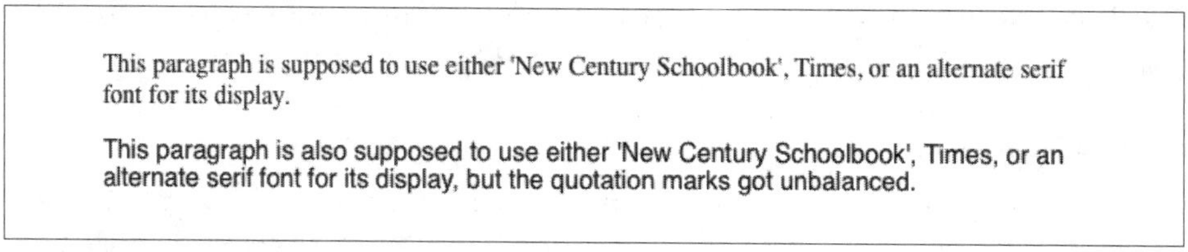

This paragraph is supposed to use either 'New Century Schoolbook', Times, or an alternate serif font for its display.

This paragraph is also supposed to use either 'New Century Schoolbook', Times, or an alternate serif font for its display, but the quotation marks got unbalanced.

Figure 5-3. The perils of incorrect quotation marks

Using @font-face

A feature that originally debuted in CSS2 but wasn't implemented until late in the first decade of the 2000s, @font-face lets you use custom fonts in your designs. While there's no guarantee that every last user will see the font you want, this feature is very widely supported.

Suppose you want to use a very specific font in your stylesheets, one that is not widely installed. Through the magic of @font-face, you can define a specific family name to correspond to a font file on your server. The user agent will download that file and use it to render the text in your page, the same as if it were installed on the user's machine. For example:

```
@font-face {
    font-family: "SwitzeraADF";
    src: url("SwitzeraADF-Regular.otf");
}
```

This allows the author to have conforming user agents load the defined .otf file and use that font to render text when called upon via font-family: SwitzeraADF.

 The examples in this section refer to SwitzeraADF, a font face collection available from the Arkandis Digital Foundry (*http://arkan dis.tuxfamily.org/openfonts.html*).

The intent of @font-face is to allow *lazy loading* of font faces. This means that only those faces needed to render a document will actually be loaded, with the rest being left alone. In fact, a browser that downloads all declared font faces without considering whether they're actually needed is considered to be buggy.

Required Descriptors

All the parameters that define the font you're referencing are contained within the @font-face { } construct. These are called *descriptors*, and very much like properties, they take the format descriptor: value;. In fact, most of the descriptor names refer directly to property names, as will be explained in just a moment.

There are two required descriptors: font-family and src.

---

font-family

Value	*<family-name>*
Initial value	Not defined

---

src

Values	[[*<uri>* [format(*<string>*#)]?]	*<font-face-name>*]#
Initial value	Not defined

The point of src is pretty straightforward: it lets you define one or more sources for the font face you're defining, using a comma-separated list if there are in fact multiple sources. You can point to a font face at any URI, but there is a restriction: font faces can only be loaded from the same origin as the stylesheet. Thus, you can't point your src at someone else's site and download their font; you'll need to host a local copy on your own server, or use a font-hosting service that provides both the stylesheet(s) and the font file(s).

 There is an exception to the same-origin restriction, which is that servers can permit cross-site loading using the HTTP header Access-Control-Allow-Origin.

You may well be wondering how it is that we're defining font-family here when it was already defined in a previous section. The difference is that this font-family is the font-family *descriptor*, and the previously-defined font-family was the font-family *property*. If that seems confusing, stick with me a moment and all should become clear.

In effect, @font-face lets you create low-level definitions that underpin the font-related properties like font-family. When you define a font family name via the descriptor font-family: "SwitzeraADF";, you're setting up an entry in the user agent's table of font families for "SwitzeraADF." It thus joins all the usual suspects like Helvetica, Georgia, Courier, and so forth, as a font you can just refer to in your font-family property values:

```
@font-face {
    font-family: "SwitzeraADF";   /* descriptor */
    src: url("SwitzeraADF-Regular.otf");
}
h1 {font-family: SwitzeraADF, Helvetica, sans-serif;}  /* property */
```

Note how the font-family descriptor value and the entry in the font-family property match. If they didn't match, then the h1 rule would ignore the first font family name listed in the font-family value and move on to the next. As long as the font has cleanly downloaded and is in a format the user agent can handle, then it will be used in the manner you direct, as illustrated in Figure 5-4.

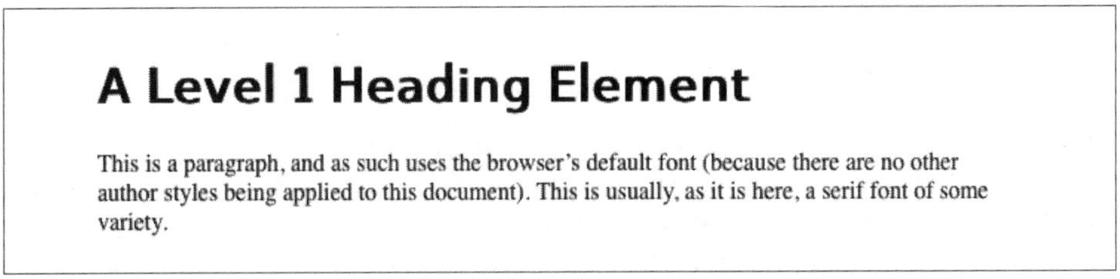

A Level 1 Heading Element

This is a paragraph, and as such uses the browser's default font (because there are no other author styles being applied to this document). This is usually, as it is here, a serif font of some variety.

Figure 5-4. Using a downloaded font

In a similar manner, the comma-separated `src` descriptor value provides fallbacks. That way, if (for whatever reason) the user agent is unable to download the first source, it can fall back to the second source and try to load the file there:

```
@font-face {
    font-family: "SwitzeraADF";
    src: url("SwitzeraADF-Regular.otf"),
        url("/fonts/SwitzeraADF-Regular.otf");
}
```

Remember that the same-origin policy generally applies in this case, so pointing to a copy of the font some other server will usually fail, unless said server is set up to permit cross-origin access.

If you want to be sure the user agent understands what kind of font you're telling it to use, that can be done with the optional `format()`:

```
@font-face {
    font-family: "SwitzeraADF";
    src: url("SwitzeraADF-Regular.otf") format("opentype");
}
```

The advantage of supplying a `format()` description is that user agents can skip downloading files in formats that they don't support, thus reducing bandwidth use and loading speed. It also lets you explicitly declare a format for a file that might not have a common filename extension and thus be unfamiliar to the user agent:

```
@font-face {
    font-family: "SwitzeraADF";
    src: url("SwitzeraADF-Regular.otf") format("opentype"),
        url("SwitzeraADF-Regular.true") format("truetype");
}
```

The Flash

If you're a designer or developer of a certain vintage, you may remember the days of FOUC: the Flash of Unstyled Content. This happened in earlier browsers that would load the HTML and display it to the screen before the CSS was finished loading, or at least before the layout of the page via CSS was finished. Thus, what would appear was a split-second of plain ol' text (using the browser's default styles) before it was replaced with the CSS-decorated layout.

There is a cousin to this problem, which is the Flash of Un-Fonted Text, or FOUFT. This happens when a browser has loaded the page and the CSS and displays the laid-out page before it's done loading custom fonts. This causes text to appear in the default font, or a fallback font, before being replaced by text using the custom-loaded font.

Since the replacement of text with the custom-loaded font face can change its layout size, authors should take care in selecting fallback fonts. If there is a significant height difference between the font used to initially display the text and the custom font eventually loaded and used, significant page reflows are likely to occur. There's no automated way to enforce this, though `font-size-adjust` (covered later) can help in supporting user agents. You have to look at your intended font and find other faces that have a similar height.

The core reason for the "flash" behavior is pretty much the same now as it was then: the browser is ready to show something before it has all the resources on hand, so it goes ahead and does so, replacing it with the prettier version once it can. The FOUC was eventually solved, and it's likely that some day we'll look back at the FOUFT the same way we do at the FOUC now. Until then, we'll have to take comfort in the fact that the FOUFT isn't usually as jarring as was the FOUC.

Table 5-1 lists all of the allowed format values (as of late 2017).

Table 5-1. Recognized font format values

Value	Format
embedded-opentype	EOT (Embedded OpenType)
opentype	OTF (OpenType)
svg	SVG (Scalable Vector Graphics)
truetype	TTF (TrueType)
woff	WOFF (Web Open Font Format)

In addition to the combination of url() and format(), you can also supply a font family name (or several names) in case the font is already locally available on the user's machine, using the aptly-named local():

```
@font-face {
    font-family: "SwitzeraADF";
    src: local("Switzera-Regular"),
        local("SwitzeraADF-Regular "),
        url("SwitzeraADF-Regular.otf") format("opentype"),
        url("SwitzeraADF-Regular.true") format("truetype");
}
```

In this example, the user agent looks to see if it already has a font family named "Switzera-Regular" or "SwitzeraADF-Regular" available. If so, it will use the name SwitzeraADF to refer to that locally installed font. If not, it will use the url() value to try downloading the remote font.

Note that this capability allows an author to create custom names for locally installed fonts. For example, you could set up a shorter name for Helvetica (or, failing that, Helvetica Neue) like so:

```
@font-face {
    font-family: "H";
    src: local("Helvetica"), local("Helvetica Neue");
}
```

```
h1, h2, h3 {font-family: H, sans-serif;}
```

As long as the user has Helvetica installed on their machine, then those rules will cause the first three heading levels to be rendered using Helvetica. It seems a little gimmicky, but it could have a real impact on reducing stylesheet file size in certain situations.

On being bulletproof

The tricky part with @font-face is that different browsers of different eras supported different font formats. (To the insider, Table 5-1 reads as a capsule history of downloadable font support.) In order to cover the widest possible landscape, you should turn to what is known as the "Bulletproof @font-face Syntax." Initially developed by Paul Irish and refined by the folks at FontSpring, it looks like this:

```
@font-face {
    font-family: "SwitzeraADF";
    src: url("SwitzeraADF-Regular.eot");
    src: url("SwitzeraADF-Regular.eot?#iefix") format("embedded-opentype"),
        url("SwitzeraADF-Regular.woff") format("woff"),
        url("SwitzeraADF-Regular.ttf") format("truetype"),
        url("SwitzeraADF-Regular.svg#switzera_adf_regular") format("svg");
}
```

Let's break it down piece by piece. The first bit, assigning the `font-family` name, is straightforward enough. After that, we see:

```
src: url("SwitzeraADF-Regular.eot");
src: url("SwitzeraADF-Regular.eot?#iefix") format("embedded-opentype"),
```

This supplies an EOT (Embedded OpenType) to browsers that understand only EOTs —IE6 through IE9. The first line is for IE9 when it's in "Compatibility Mode," and the second line hands the same file to IE6-IE8. The `?#iefix` bit in that line exploits a parsing bug in those browsers to step around another parsing bug that causes them to 404 any `@font-face` with multiple formats listed. IE9 fixed its bugs without expanding its font formats, so the first line is what lets it join the party:

```
url("SwitzeraADF-Regular.woff") format("woff"),
```

This line supplies a Web Open Font Format file to browsers that understand it, which includes most modern browsers. At this point, in fact, you'll have covered the vast majority of your desktop users.

```
url("SwitzeraADF-Regular.ttf") format("truetype"),
```

This line hands over the file format understood by most iOS and Android devices, thus covering most of your handheld users:

```
url("SwitzeraADF-Regular.svg#switzera_adf_regular") format("svg");
```

Here, at the end, we supply the only font format understood by old iOS devices. This covers almost all of your remaining handheld users.

This gets a bit unwieldy if you're specifying more than a couple of faces, and typing it in even once is kind of a pain in the wrists. Fortunately, there are services available that will accept your font faces and generate all the `@font-face` rules you need, convert those faces to all the formats required, and hand it all back to you as a single package. One of the best is Font Squirrel's @Font-Face Kit Generator (*http://fontsquir rel.com/fontface/generator*). Just make sure you're legally able to convert and use the font faces you're running through the generator (see the next sidebar, "Custom Font Considerations" on page 161, for more information).

Other Font Descriptors

In addition to the required `font-family` and `src` descriptors, there are a number of optional descriptors that can be used to associate font faces with specific font property values. Just as with `font-family`, these descriptors (summarized in Table 5-2) correspond directly to CSS properties (explained in detail later in this chapter) and affect how user agents respond to the values supplied for those properties.

Custom Font Considerations

There are two things you need to keep in mind when using customized fonts. The first is that you have the rights to use the font in a web page, and the second is whether it's a good idea to do so.

Much like stock photography, font families come with licenses that govern their use, and not every font license permits its use on the web. You can completely avoid this question by only using FOSS (Free and Open-Source Software) fonts, or by using a commercial service like Fontdeck or Typekit that will deal with the licensing and format conversion issues so you don't have to. Otherwise, you need to make sure that you have the right to use a font face in the way you want to use it, just the same as you make sure you have the proper license for any images you bought.

In addition, the more font faces you call upon, the more resources the web server has to hand over and the higher the overall page weight will become. Most faces are not overly large—usually 50K to 100K—but they add up quickly if you decide to get fancy with your type, and truly complicated faces can be larger. As you might imagine, the same problems exist for images. As always, you will have to balance appearance against performance, leaning one way or the other depending on the circumstances.

Furthermore, just as there are image optimization tools available, there are also font optimization tools. Typically these are *subsetting* tools, which construct fonts using only the symbols actually needed for display. If you're using a service like Typekit or Fonts.com (*http://fonts.com*), they probably have subsetting tools available, or else do it dynamically when the font is requested.

Table 5-2. Font descriptors

Descriptor	Default value	Description
font-style	normal	Distinguishes between normal, italic, and oblique faces
font-weight	normal	Distinguishes between various weights (e.g., bold)
font-stretch	normal	Distinguishes between varying degrees of character widths (e.g., condensed and expanded)
font-variant	normal	Distinguishes between a staggeringly wide range of potential variant faces (e.g., small-caps); in most ways, a more "CSS-like" version of font-feature-settings
font-feature-settings	normal	Permits direct access to low-level OpenType features (e.g., enabling ligatures)
unicode-range	U+0-10FFFF	Defines the range of characters for which a given face may be used

Because these font descriptors are optional, they may not be listed in a @font-face rule, but CSS does not allow descriptors to go without default values any more than it does for properties. If an optional descriptor is omitted, then it is set to the default value. Thus, if font-weight is not listed, the default value of normal is assumed.

Restricting character range

There is one font descriptor, unicode-range, which (unlike the others in Table 5-2) has no corresponding CSS property. This descriptor allows authors to define the range of characters to which a custom font can be applied. This can be useful when using a symbol font, or to ensure that a font face is only applied to characters that are in a specific language.

---

unicode-range

Values   *<urange>*#
Initial value   U+0-10FFFF

By default, the value of this property covers the entirety of Unicode, meaning that if a font can supply the glyph for a character, it will. Most of the time, this is exactly what you want. For all the other times, you'll want to use a specific font face for a specific kind of content. To pick two examples from the CSS Fonts Module Level 3:

```
unicode-range: U+590-5FF;  /* Hebrew characters */
unicode-range: U+4E00-9FFF, U+FF00-FF9F, U+30??;  /* Japanese kanji,
    hiragana, katakana */
```

In the first case, a single range is specified, spanning Unicode character code point 590 through code point 5FF. This covers the characters used in Hebrew. Thus, an author might specify a Hebrew font and restrict it to only be used for Hebrew characters, even if the face contains glyphs for other code points:

```
@font-face {
    font-family: "CMM-Ahuvah";
    src: url("cmm-ahuvah.otf") format("opentype");
    unicode-range: U+590-5FF;
}
```

In the second case, a series of ranges are specified in a comma-separated list to cover all the Japanese characters. The interesting feature there is the U+30?? value, which is a special format permitted in unicode-range values. The question marks are wildcards meaning "any possible digit," making U+30?? equivalent to U+3000-30FF. The question mark is the only "special" character pattern permitted in the value.

Ranges must always ascend. Any descending range (e.g., U+400-300) is treated as a parsing error and ignored. Besides ranges, you can also declare a single code point, which looks like U+221E. This is most often useful in conjunction with other code points and ranges, like so:

```
unicode-range: U+4E00-9FFF, U+FF00-FF9F, U+30??, U+A5;
    /* Japanese kanji, hiragana, and katakana, plus yen/yuan currency symbol*/
```

You could use a single code point to declare that a specific face only be used to render one, and only one, character. Whether or not that's a good idea is left to you, your design, the size of the font file, and your users' connection speeds.

Because @font-face is designed to optimize lazy loading, it's possible to use unicode-range to download only the font faces a page actually needs. Suppose that you have a website that uses a mixture of English, Russian, and basic mathematical operators, but you don't know which will appear on any given page. There could be all English, a mixture of Russian and math, and so on. Furthermore, suppose you have special font faces for all three types of content. You can make sure a user agent only downloads the faces it actually needs with a properly-constructed series of @font-face rules:

```
@font-face {
    font-family: "MyFont";
    src: url("myfont-general.otf" format("opentype");
}
@font-face {
    font-family: "MyFont";
    src: url("myfont-cyrillic.otf" format("opentype");
    unicode-range: U+04??, U+0500-052F, U+2DE0-2DFF, U+A640-A69F, U+1D2B-1D78;
}
@font-face {
    font-family: "MyFont";
    src: url("myfont-math.otf" format("opentype");
    unicode-range: U+22??;   /* equivalent to U+2200-22FF */
}
```

Because the first rule doesn't specify a Unicode range, it is always downloaded—unless a page happens to contain no characters at all (and maybe even then). The second rule causes myfont-cyrillic.otf to be downloaded only if the page contains characters in its declared Unicode range; the third rule does the same for basic mathematical operators.

Combining Descriptors

Something that might not be immediately obvious is that you can supply multiple descriptors in order to assign specific faces for specific property combinations. For example, you can assign one face to bold text, another to italic text, and a third to text that is both bold and italic.

This is actually implicit in the fact that any undeclared descriptor is assigned its default value. Let's consider a basic set of three face assignments:

```
@font-face {
    font-family: "SwitzeraADF";
    font-weight: normal;
    font-style: normal;
    font-stretch: normal;
    src: url("SwitzeraADF-Regular.otf") format("opentype");
}
@font-face {
    font-family: "SwitzeraADF";
    font-weight: bold;
    font-style: normal;
    font-stretch: normal;
    src: url("SwitzeraADF-Bold.otf") format("opentype");
}
@font-face {
    font-family: "SwitzeraADF";
    font-weight: normal;
    font-style: italic;
    font-stretch: normal;
    src: url("SwitzeraADF-Italic.otf") format("opentype");
}
```

Here, we've made the implicit explicit: any time a descriptor isn't being altered, its default value is listed. This is exactly the same as a set of three rules in which we remove every descriptor that shows a value of normal:

```
@font-face {
        font-family: "SwitzeraADF";
        src: url("SwitzeraADF-Regular.otf") format("opentype");
}
@font-face {
        font-family: "SwitzeraADF";
        font-weight: bold;
        src: url("SwitzeraADF-Bold.otf") format("opentype");
}
@font-face {
        font-family: "SwitzeraADF";
        font-style: italic;
        src: url("SwitzeraADF-Italic.otf") format("opentype");
}
```

In all three rules, there is no font-stretching beyond the normal amount, and the values of font-weight and font-style vary by which face is being assigned. So what if we want to assign a specific face to unstretched text that's both bold and italic?

```
@font-face {
        font-family: "SwitzeraADF";
        font-weight: bold;
        font-style: italic;
```

```
        font-stretch: normal;
        src: url("SwitzeraADF-BoldItalic.otf") format("opentype");
    }
```

And then what about bold, italic, condensed text?

```
@font-face {
        font-family: "SwitzeraADF";
        font-weight: bold;
        font-style: italic;
        font-stretch: condensed;
        src: url("SwitzeraADF-BoldCondItalic.otf") format("opentype");
    }
```

How about normal-weight, italic, condensed text?

```
@font-face {
        font-family: "SwitzeraADF";
        font-weight: normal;
        font-style: italic;
        font-stretch: condensed;
        src: url("SwitzeraADF-CondItalic.otf") format("opentype");
    }
```

We could keep this up for quite a while, but let's stop there. If we take all those rules and strip out anything with a normal value, we end up with this result, illustrated in Figure 5-5:

```
@font-face {
        font-family: "SwitzeraADF";
        src: url("SwitzeraADF-Regular.otf") format("opentype");
    }
@font-face {
        font-family: "SwitzeraADF";
        font-weight: bold;
        src: url("SwitzeraADF-Bold.otf") format("opentype");
    }
@font-face {
        font-family: "SwitzeraADF";
        font-style: italic;
        src: url("SwitzeraADF-Italic.otf") format("opentype");
    }
@font-face {
        font-family: "SwitzeraADF";
        font-weight: bold;
        font-style: italic;
        src: url("SwitzeraADF-BoldItalic.otf") format("opentype");
    }
@font-face {
        font-family: "SwitzeraADF";
        font-weight: bold;
        font-stretch: condensed;
        src: url("SwitzeraADF-BoldCond.otf") format("opentype");
    }
```

```
@font-face {
        font-family: "SwitzeraADF";
        font-style: italic;
        font-stretch: condensed;
        src: url("SwitzeraADF-CondItalic.otf") format("opentype");
}
@font-face {
        font-family: "SwitzeraADF";
        font-weight: bold;
        font-style: italic;
        font-stretch: condensed;
        src: url("SwitzeraADF-BoldCondItalic.otf") format("opentype");
}
```

> This element contains serif text, unstretched **bold** and *italic* text in SwitzeraADF, and
> unstretched ***bold and italic*** text in SwitzeraADF.
>
> This element contains serif text, condensed **bold** and *italic* text in SwitzeraADF, and
> condensed ***bold and italic*** text in SwitzeraADF.

Figure 5-5. Employing a variety of faces

As you can see, there are a lot of possible combinations just for those three descriptors—consider that there are 11 possible values for font-weight, and 10 for font-stretch—but you'll likely never have to run through them all. In fact, most font families don't have as many faces as SwitzeraADF offers (24 at last count), so there wouldn't be much point in writing out all the possibilities. Nevertheless, the options are there, and in some cases you may find that you need to assign, say, a specific face for bold condensed text so that the user agent doesn't try to compute them for you.

Font Weights

Now that we've covered @font-face and its descriptors, let's get back to properties. We're all used to normal and bold text, at the very least, which are sort of the two most basic font weights available. CSS gives you a lot more control over font weights with the property font-weight.

<table>
<tr><td colspan="2" align="center">font-weight</td></tr>
<tr><td>Values</td><td>normal | bold | bolder | lighter | 100 | 200 | 300 | 400 | 500 | 600 | 700 | 800 | 900</td></tr>
<tr><td>Initial value</td><td>normal</td></tr>
<tr><td>Applies to</td><td>All elements</td></tr>
</table>

Computed value	One of the numeric values (100, etc.), or one of the numeric values plus one of the relative values (bolder or lighter)
Note	Has a corresponding @font-face descriptor
Inherited	Yes
Animatable	No

Generally speaking, the heavier a font weight becomes, the darker and "more bold" a font appears. There are a great many ways to label a heavy font face. For example, the font family known as SwitzeraADF has a number of variants, such as SwitzeraADF Bold, SwitzeraADF Extra Bold, SwitzeraADF Light, and SwitzeraADF Regular. All of these use the same basic font shapes, but each has a different weight.

So let's say that you want to use SwitzeraADF for a document, but you'd like to make use of all those different heaviness levels. You could refer to them directly through the font-family property, but you really shouldn't have to do that. Besides, it's no fun having to write a stylesheet like this:

```
h1 {font-family: 'SwitzeraADF Extra Bold, sans-serif;}
h2 {font-family: 'SwitzeraADF Bold, sans-serif;}
h3 {font-family: 'SwitzeraADF Bold', sans-serif;}
h4, p {font-family: SwitzeraADF Regular, sans-serif;}
small {font-family: 'SwitzeraADF Light', sans-serif;}
```

That's pretty tedious. It would make far more sense to specify a single font family for the whole document and then assign different weights to various elements. You can do this via @font-face and use the various values for the property font-weight. This is a fairly simple font-weight declaration:

```
b {font-weight: bold;}
```

This declaration says the b element should be displayed using a bold font face; or, to put it another way, a font face that is heavier than the normal font face. This is probably expected behavior, since b does cause text to be bold.

What's really happening behind the scenes is that a heavier face of the font is used for displaying a b element. Thus, if you have a paragraph displayed using Times, and part of it is bold, then there are really two faces of the same font in use: Times and TimesBold. The regular text is displayed using Times, and the bold text is displayed using TimesBold.

How Weights Work

To understand how a user agent determines the heaviness, or weight, of a given font variant (not to mention how weight is inherited), it's easiest to start by talking about the keywords 100 through 900. These number keywords were defined to map to a relatively common feature of font design in which a font is given nine levels of weight. If a font family has faces for all nine weight levels available, then the numbers are mapped directly to the predefined levels, with 100 as the lightest variant of the font and 900 as the heaviest.

In fact, there is no intrinsic weight in these numbers. The CSS specification says only that each number corresponds to a weight at least as heavy as the number that precedes it. Thus, 100, 200, 300, and 400 might all map to the same relatively lightweight variant; 500 and 600 could correspond to the same heavier font variant; and 700, 800, and 900 could all produce the same very heavy font variant. As long as no keyword corresponds to a variant that is lighter than the variant assigned to the previous keyword, everything will be all right.

As it happens, these numbers are defined to be equivalent to certain common variant names, not to mention other values for font-weight. 400 is defined to be equivalent to normal, and 700 corresponds to bold. The other numbers do not match up with any other values for font-weight, but they can correspond to common variant names. If there is a font variant labeled something such as "Normal," "Regular," "Roman," or "Book," then it is assigned to the number 400 and any variant with the label "Medium" is assigned to 500. However, if a variant labeled "Medium" is the only variant available, it is assigned to 400 instead of 500.

A user agent has to do even more work if there are fewer than nine weights in a given font family. In this case, it must fill in the gaps in a predetermined way:

- If the value 500 is unassigned, it is given the same font weight as that assigned to 400.

- If 300 is unassigned, it is given the next variant lighter than 400. If no lighter variant is available, 300 is assigned the same variant as 400. In this case, it will usually be "Normal" or "Medium." This method is also used for 200 and 100.

- If 600 is unassigned, it is given the next variant darker than that assigned for 500. If no darker variant is available, 600 is assigned the same variant as 500. This method is also used for 700, 800, and 900.

To illustrate this weighting scheme more clearly, let's look at three examples of font weight assignment. In the first example, assume that the font family Karrank% is an OpenType font, so it has nine weights already defined. In this case, the numbers are assigned to each level, and the keywords normal and bold are assigned to the numbers 400 and 700, respectively. This is the most straightforward example, and therefore the one that almost never occurs in the real world. (It is quite rare for a font family to have nine weight levels, and those that do are usually very expensive.)

In our second example, consider the font family SwitzeraADF, which was discussed near the beginning of this section. Hypothetically, its variants might be assigned numeric values for font-weight, as shown in Table 5-3.

Table 5-3. Hypothetical weight assignments for a specific font family

Font face	Assigned keyword	Assigned number(s)
SwitzeraADF Light		100, 200, 300
SwitzeraADF Regular	normal	400
SwitzeraADF Medium		500
SwitzeraADF Bold	bold	600, 700
SwitzeraADF Extra Bold		800, 900

The first three number values are assigned to the lightest weight. The "Regular" face gets the keyword normal, as expected, and the number weight 400. Since there is a "Medium" font, it's assigned to the number 500. There is nothing to assign to 600, so it's mapped to the "Bold" font face, which is also the variant to which 700 and bold are assigned. Finally, 800 and 900 are assigned to the "Black" and "UltraBlack" variants, respectively. Note that this last assignment would happen only if those faces had the top two weight levels already assigned. Otherwise, the user agent might ignore them and assign 800 and 900 to the "Bold" face instead, or it might assign them both to one or the other of the "Black" variants.

For our third and final example, let's consider a stripped-down version of Times. In Table 5-4, there are only two weight variants: "TimesRegular" and "TimesBold."

Table 5-4. Hypothetical weight assignments for "Times"

Font face	Assigned keyword	Assigned numbers
TimesRegular	normal	100, 200, 300, 400, 500
TimesBold	bold	600, 700, 800, 900

The assignment of the keywords normal and bold is to the regular-weight and bold-weight faces, as you might expect. As for the numbers, 100 through 300 are assigned to the "Regular" face because there isn't a lighter face available. 400 is assigned to "Regular" as expected, but what about 500? It is assigned to the "Regular" (or normal) face because there isn't a "Medium" face available; thus, it is assigned the same font face as 400. As for the rest, 700 goes with bold as always, while 800 and 900, lacking a heavier face, are assigned to the next-lighter face, which is the "Bold" font face. Finally, 600 is assigned to the next-heavier face, which is the "Bold" face.

font-weight is inherited, so if you set a paragraph to be bold:

```
p.one {font-weight: bold;}
```

Then all of its children will inherit that boldness, as we see in Figure 5-6.

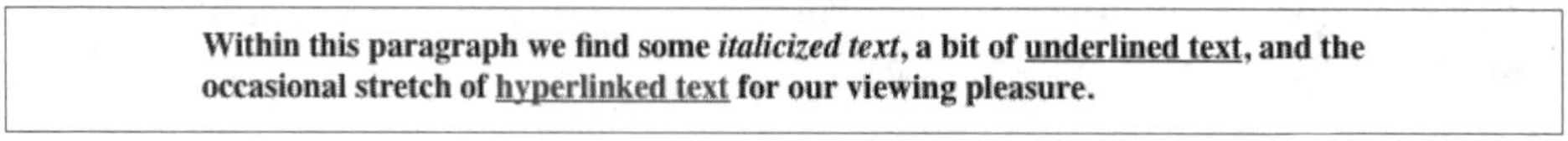

> **Within this paragraph we find some *italicized text*, a bit of <u>underlined text</u>, and the occasional stretch of <u>hyperlinked text</u> for our viewing pleasure.**

Figure 5-6. Inherited font-weight

This isn't unusual, but the situation gets interesting when you use the last two values we have to discuss: bolder and lighter. In general terms, these keywords have the effect you'd anticipate: they make text more or less bold compared to its parent's font weight. First, let's consider bolder.

Getting Bolder

If you set an element to have a weight of bolder, then the user agent first must determine what font-weight value was inherited from the parent element. It then selects the lowest number which corresponds to a font weight darker than what was inherited. If none is available, then the user agent sets the element's font weight to the next numerical value, unless the value is already 900, in which case the weight remains at 900. Thus, you might encounter the following situations, illustrated in Figure 5-7:

```
p {font-weight: normal;}
p em {font-weight: bolder;}  /* results in bold text, evaluates to '700' */

h1 {font-weight: bold;}
h1 b {font-weight: bolder;}  /* if no bolder face exists, evaluates to '800' */

div {font-weight: 100;} /* assume 'Light' face exists; see explanation */
div strong {font-weight: bolder;} /* results in normal text, weight '400' */
```

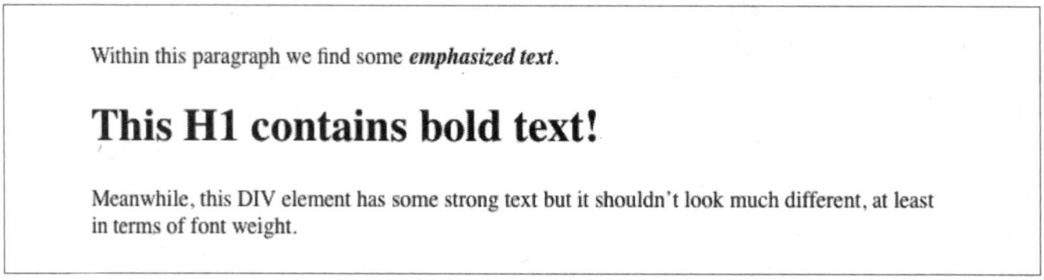

> Within this paragraph we find some ***emphasized text***.
>
> ## This H1 contains bold text!
>
> Meanwhile, this DIV element has some strong text but it shouldn't look much different, at least in terms of font weight.

Figure 5-7. Text trying to be bolder

In the first example, the user agent moves up the weight ladder from normal to bold; in numeric terms, it jumps from 400 to 700. In the second example, h1 text is already set to bold. If there is no bolder face available, then the user agent sets the weight of b text within an h1 to 800, since that is the next step up from 700 (the numeric equivalent of bold). Since 800 is assigned to the same font face as 700, there is no visible difference between normal h1 text and bold h1 text, but the weights are different nonetheless.

In the last example, paragraphs are set to be the lightest possible font weight, which we assume exists as a "Light" variant. Furthermore, the other faces in this font family are "Regular" and "Bold." Any em text within a paragraph will evaluate to normal since that is the next-heaviest face within the font family. However, what if the only faces in the font are "Regular" and "Bold"? In that case, the declarations would evaluate like this:

```
/*   assume only two faces for this example: 'Regular' and 'Bold'   */
p {font-weight: 100;}   /* looks the same as 'normal' text */
p span {font-weight: bolder;}   /* maps to '700' */
```

As you can see, the weight 100 is assigned to the normal font face, but the value of font-weight is still 100. Thus, any span text that is descended from a p element will inherit the value of 100 and then evaluate to the next-heaviest face, which is the "Bold" face with a numerical weight of 700.

Let's take this one step further and add two more rules, plus some markup, to illustrate how all of this works (see Figure 5-8 for the results):

```
/*   assume only two faces for this example: 'Regular' and 'Bold'   */
p {font-weight: 100;}   /* looks the same as 'normal' text */
p span {font-weight: 400;}   /* so does this */
strong {font-weight: bolder;}   /* even bolder than its parent */
strong b {font-weight: bolder;}   /*bolder still */

<p>
This paragraph contains elements of increasing weight: there is a
<span>span element that contains a <strong>strongly emphasized
element and a <b>bold element</b></strong></span>.
</p>
```

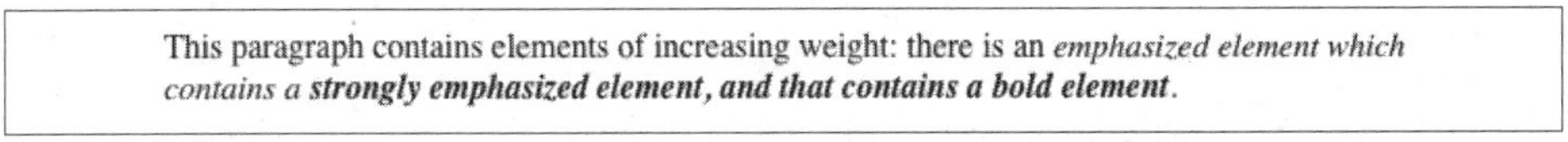

This paragraph contains elements of increasing weight: there is an *emphasized element which contains a* **strongly emphasized element, and that contains a bold element**.

Figure 5-8. Moving up the weight scale

In the last two nested elements, the computed value of font-weight is increased because of the liberal use of the keyword bolder. If you were to replace the text in the paragraph with numbers representing the font-weight of each element, you would get the results shown here:

```
<p>
100 <span> 400 <strong> 700 <b> 800 </b> </strong> </span>.
</p>
```

The first two weight increases are large because they represent jumps from 100 to 400 and from 400 to bold (700). From 700, there is no heavier face, so the user agent moves the value of font-weight one notch up the numeric scale (800). Furthermore, if you were to insert a strong element into the b element, it would come out like this:

```
<p>
100 <span> 400 <strong> 700 <b> 800 <strong> 900
</strong> </b> </strong> </span>.
</p>
```

If there were yet another b element inserted into the innermost strong element, its weight would also be 900, since font-weight can never be higher than 900. Assuming that there are only two font faces available, then the text would appear to be either regular or bold, as you can see in Figure 5-9:

```
<p>
regular <span> regular <strong> bold <b> bold <strong> bold </strong> </b>
</strong> </span>.
</p>
```

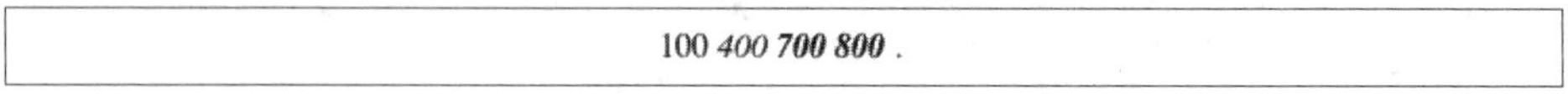

100 *400* **700 800** .

Figure 5-9. Visual weight, with descriptors

Lightening Weights

As you might expect, lighter works in just the same way, except it causes the user agent to move down the weight scale instead of up. With a quick modification of the previous example, you can see this very clearly:

```
/*   assume only two faces for this example: 'Regular' and 'Bold'   */
p {font-weight: 900;}   /* as bold as possible, which will look 'bold' */
p span {font-weight: 700;}   /* this will also be bold */
strong {font-weight: lighter;}   /* lighter than its parent */
b {font-weight: lighter;}   /* lighter still */

<p>
900 <span> 700 <strong> 400 <b> 300 <strong> 200
</strong> </b> </strong> </span>.
</p>
<!-- ...or, to put it another way... -->
<p>
bold <span> bold <strong> regular <b> regular <strong> regular </strong></b>
</strong></span>.
</p>
```

Ignoring the fact that this would be entirely counterintuitive, what you see in Figure 5-10 is that the main paragraph text has a weight of 900. When the strong text is set to be lighter, it evaluates to the next-lighter face, which is the regular face, or 400 (the same as normal) on the numeric scale. The next step down is to 300, which is the same as normal since no lighter faces exist. From there, the user agent can reduce the weight only one numeric step at a time until it reaches 100 (which it doesn't do in the example). The second paragraph shows which text will be bold and which will be regular.

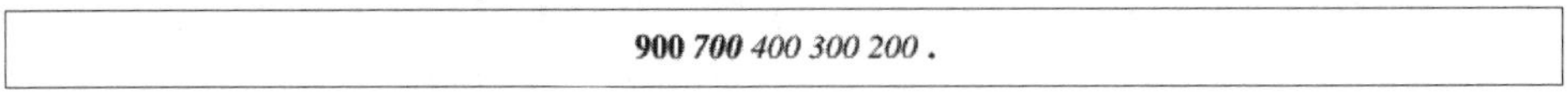

---

900 700 *400 300 200* .

Figure 5-10. Making text lighter

The font-weight descriptor

With the `font-weight` descriptor, authors can assign faces of varying weights to the weighting levels permitted by the `font-weight` property. For example, the following rules explicitly assign five faces to six different `font-weight` values:

```
@font-face {
        font-family: "SwitzeraADF";
        font-weight: normal;
        src: url("f/SwitzeraADF-Regular.otf") format("opentype");
}
@font-face {
        font-family: "SwitzeraADF";
        font-weight: bold;
        src: url("f/SwitzeraADF-Bold.otf") format("opentype");
}
@font-face {
        font-family: "SwitzeraADF";
        font-weight: 300;
        src: url("f/SwitzeraADF-Light.otf") format("opentype");
}
@font-face {
        font-family: "SwitzeraADF";
        font-weight: 500;
        src: url("f/SwitzeraADF-DemiBold.otf") format("opentype");
}
@font-face {
        font-family: "SwitzeraADF";
        font-weight: 700;
        src: url("f/SwitzeraADF-Bold.otf") format("opentype");
}
@font-face {
        font-family: "SwitzeraADF";
        font-weight: 900;
        src: url("f/SwitzeraADF-ExtraBold.otf") format("opentype");
}
```

With these faces assigned, the author now has a number of weighting levels available for his use, as illustrated in Figure 5-11:

```
h1, h2, h3, h4 {font: 225% SwitzeraADF, Helvetica, sans-serif;}
h1 {font-weight: 900;}
h2 {font-size: 180%; font-weight: 700;}
h3 {font-size: 150%; font-weight: 500;}
h4 {font-size: 125%; font-weight: 300;}
```

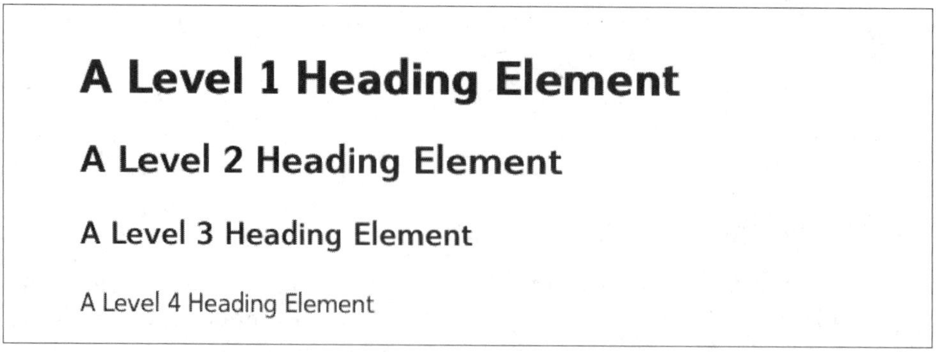

A Level 1 Heading Element

A Level 2 Heading Element

A Level 3 Heading Element

A Level 4 Heading Element

Figure 5-11. Using declared font-weight faces

In any given situation, the user agent picks which face to use depending on the exact value of a font-weight property, using the resolution algorithm detailed in the earlier section, "How Weights Work" on page 167. Authors may use any value for the font-weight descriptor that is permitted for the font-weight property *except* the inherit keyword.

Font Size

The methods for determining font size are both very familiar and very different.

font-size	
Values	xx-small|x-small|small|medium|large|x-large|xx-large| smaller|larger|*<length>*|*<percentage>*
Initial value	medium
Applies to	All elements
Percentages	Calculated with respect to the parent element's font size
Computed value	An absolute length
Inherited	Yes
Animatable	Yes (numeric keywords only)

In a fashion very similar to the font-weight keywords bolder and lighter, the property font-size has relative-size keywords called larger and smaller. Much like what we saw with relative font weights, these keywords cause the computed value of font-size to move up and down a scale of size values, which you'll need to understand before you can explore larger and smaller. First, though, we need to examine how fonts are sized in the first place.

In fact, the actual relation of the font-size property to what you see rendered is determined by the font's designer. This relationship is set as an *em square* (some call it an *em box*) within the font itself. This em square (and thus the font size) doesn't have to refer to any boundaries established by the characters in a font. Instead, it refers to the distance between baselines when the font is set without any extra leading (line-height in CSS). It is quite possible for fonts to have characters that are taller than the default distance between baselines. For that matter, a font might be defined such that all of its characters are smaller than its em square, as many fonts do. Some hypothetical examples are shown in Figure 5-12.

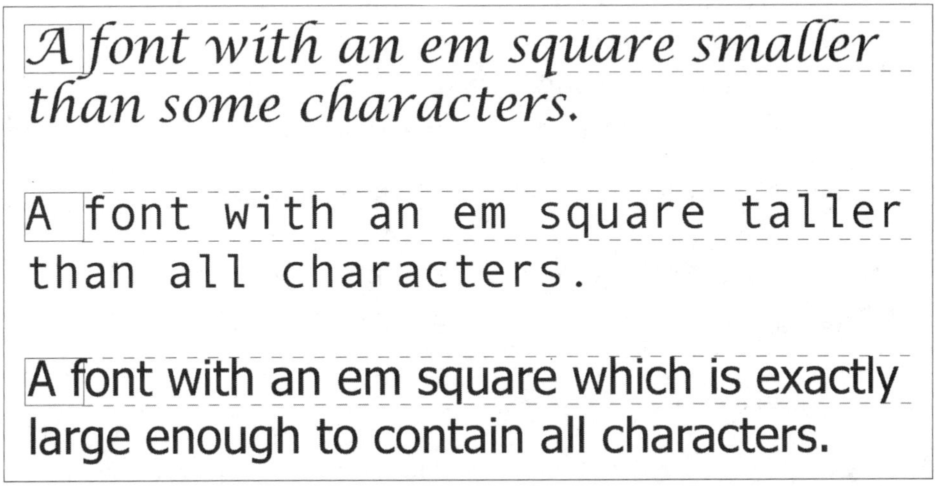

Figure 5-12. Font characters and em squares

Thus, the effect of font-size is to provide a size for the em box of a given font. This does not guarantee that any of the actual displayed characters will be this size.

Absolute Sizes

Having established all of that, we turn now to the absolute-size keywords. There are seven absolute-size values for font-size: xx-small, x-small, small, medium, large, x-large, and xx-large. These are not defined precisely, but are relative to each other, as Figure 5-13 demonstrates:

```
p.one {font-size: xx-small;}
p.two {font-size: x-small;}
p.three {font-size: small;}
p.four {font-size: medium;}
p.five {font-size: large;}
```

```
p.six {font-size: x-large;}
p.seven {font-size: xx-large;}
```

According to the CSS1 specification, the difference (or *scaling factor*) between one absolute size and the next is about 1.5 going up the ladder, or 0.66 going down. Thus, if medium is the same as 10px, then large should be the same as 15px. This was later determined to be too large a scaling factor. In CSS2 it was suggested that it be somewhere between 1.0 and 1.2, and in CSS3 drafts a complicated series is provided (for example, small is listed as eight-ninths the size of medium, while xx-small is three-fifths). In all case, the scaling factors are guidelines, as user agents are free to alter them for any reason.

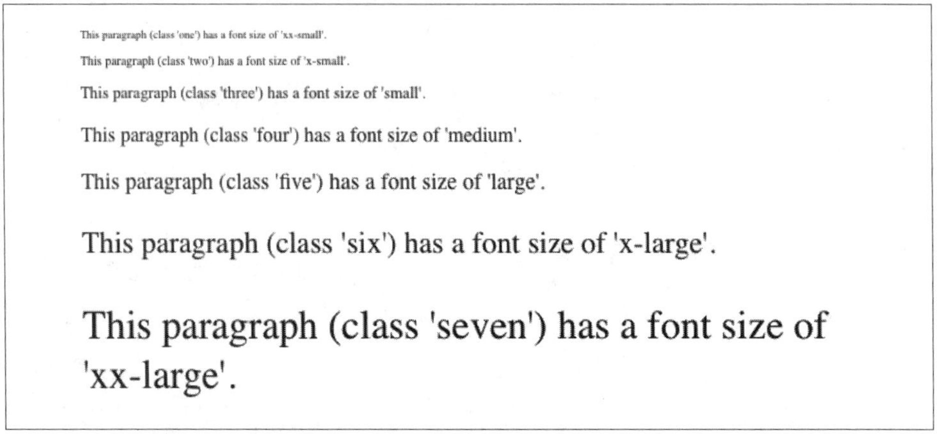

This paragraph (class 'one') has a font size of 'xx-small'.

This paragraph (class 'two') has a font size of 'x-small'.

This paragraph (class 'three') has a font size of 'small'.

This paragraph (class 'four') has a font size of 'medium'.

This paragraph (class 'five') has a font size of 'large'.

This paragraph (class 'six') has a font size of 'x-large'.

This paragraph (class 'seven') has a font size of 'xx-large'.

Figure 5-13. Absolute font sizes

Working from the assumption that medium equals 16px, for different scaling factors, we get the absolute size equivalents shown in Table 5-5. (The values shown are rounded-off integers.)

Table 5-5. Scaling factors translated to pixels

Keyword	CSS1	CSS2	CSS3 (draft)
xx-small	5px	9px	10px
x-small	7px	11px	12px
small	11px	13px	14px
medium	16px	16px	16px
large	24px	19px	19px
x-large	36px	23px	24px
xx-large	54px	28px	32px

Relative Sizes

Comparatively speaking, the keywords larger and smaller are simple: they cause the size of an element to be shifted up or down the absolute-size scale, relative to their parent element, using the same scaling factor employed to calculate absolute sizes. In other words, if the browser used a scaling factor of 1.2 for absolute sizes, then it should use the same factor when applying relative-size keywords:

```
p {font-size: medium;}
strong, em {font-size: larger;}

<p>This paragraph element contains <strong>a strong-emphasis element
which itself contains <em>an emphasis element that also contains
<strong>a strong element.</strong></em></strong></p>

<p> medium <strong>large <em> x-large <strong>xx-large</strong> </em> </strong>
    </p>
```

Unlike the relative values for weight, the relative-size values are not necessarily constrained to the limits of the absolute-size range. Thus, a font's size can be pushed beyond the sizes for xx-small and xx-large. For example:

```
h1 {font-size: xx-large;}
em {font-size: larger;}

<h1>A Heading with <em>Emphasis</em> added</h1>
<p>This paragraph has some <em>emphasis</em> as well.</p>
```

As you can see in Figure 5-14, the emphasized text in the h1 element is slightly larger than xx-large. The amount of scaling is left up to the user agent, with the scaling factor of 1.2 being preferred but not required. The em text in the paragraph is shifted one slot up the absolute-size scale (large).

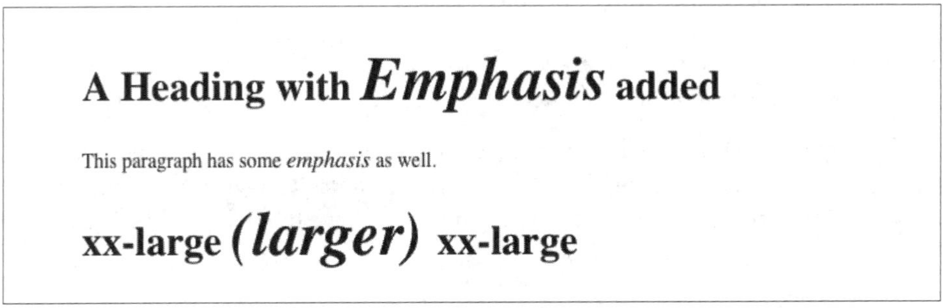

A Heading with *Emphasis* added

This paragraph has some *emphasis* as well.

xx-large *(larger)* xx-large

Figure 5-14. Relative font sizing at the edges of the absolute sizes

 User agents are not required to increase or decrease font size beyond the limits of the absolute-size keywords.

Percentages and Sizes

In a way, percentage values are very similar to the relative-size keywords. A percentage value is always computed in terms of whatever size is inherited from an element's parent. Percentages, unlike the size keywords previously discussed, permit much finer control over the computed font size. Consider the following example, illustrated in Figure 5-15:

```
body {font-size: 15px;}
p {font-size: 12px;}
em {font-size: 120%;}
strong {font-size: 135%;}
small, .fnote {font-size: 70%;}

<body>
<p>This paragraph contains both <em>emphasis</em> and <strong>strong
emphasis</strong>, both of which are larger than their parent element.
The <small>small text</small>, on the other hand, is smaller by a quarter.</p>
<p class="fnote">This is a 'footnote' and is smaller than regular text.</p>

<p> 12px <em> 14.4px </em> 12px <strong> 16.2px </strong> 12px
<small> 9px </small> 12px </p>
<p class="fnote"> 10.5px </p>
</body>
```

This paragraph contains both *emphasis* and **strong emphasis**, both of which are larger than their parent element. The small text, on the other hand, is smaller by a quarter.

This is a 'footnote' and is smaller than regular text.

12px *14.4px* 12px **16.2px** 12px 9px 12px

10.5px

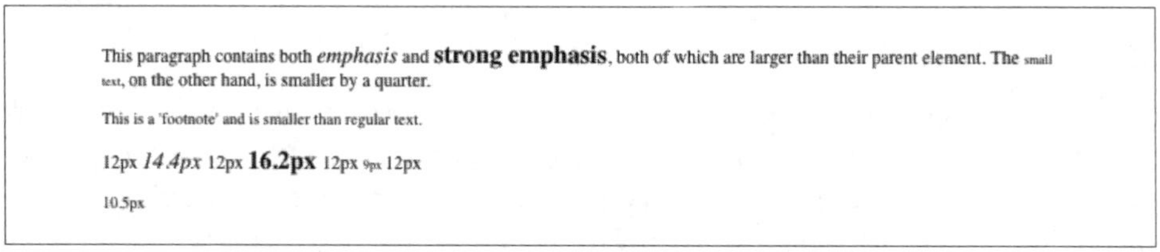

Figure 5-15. Throwing percentages into the mix

In this example, the exact pixel size values are shown. These are the values calculated by the browser, regardless of the actual displayed size of the characters onscreen.

Incidentally, CSS defines the length value em to be equivalent to percentage values, in the sense that 1em is the same as 100% when sizing fonts. Thus, the following would yield identical results, assuming that both paragraphs have the same parent element:

```
p.one {font-size: 166%;}
p.two {font-size: 1.6em;}
```

When using em measurements, the same principles apply as with percentages, such as the inheritance of computed sizes and so forth.

Font Size and Inheritance

Figure 5-12 also demonstrates that, although `font-size` is inherited in CSS, it is the computed values that are inherited, not percentages. Thus, the value inherited by the `strong` element is `12px`, and this value is modified by the declared value `135%` to arrive at `16.2px`. For the "footnote" paragraph, the percentage is calculated in relation to the `font-size` value that's inherited from the `body` element, which is `15px`. Multiplying that value by `75%` yields `11.25px`.

As with the relative-size keywords, percentages are effectively cumulative. Thus, the following markup is displayed as shown in Figure 5-16:

```
p {font-size: 12px;}
em {font-size: 120%;}
strong {font-size: 135%;}

<p>This paragraph contains both<em>emphasis and <strong>strong
emphasis</strong></em>, both of which are larger than the paragraph text. </p>

<p>12px <em>14.4px <strong> 19.44px </strong></em> 12px</p>
```

This paragraph contains both*emphasis and* **strong emphasis**, both of which are larger than the paragraph text.

12px *14.4px* **19.44px** 12px

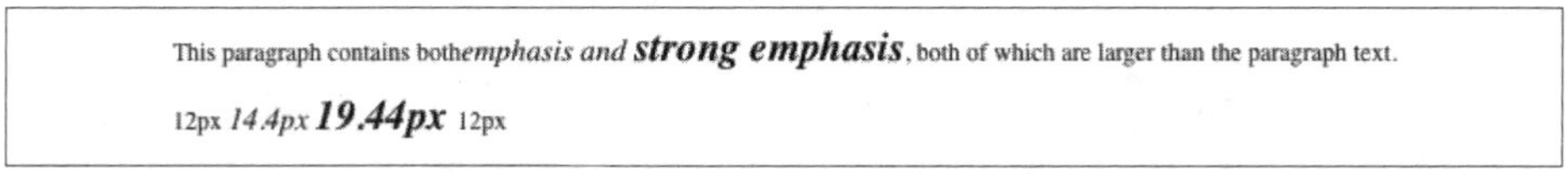

Figure 5-16. The issues of inheritance

The size value for the `strong` element shown in Figure 5-16 is computed as follows:

12 px × 120% = 14.4 px
14.4 px × 135% = 19.44 px (possibly rounded to 19 px for display; see the next section)

The problem of runaway scaling can go the other direction, too. Consider for a moment a document that is nothing but a series of unordered lists, many of them nested inside other lists. Some of these lists are four nested levels deep. Imagine the effect of the following rule on such a document:

```
ul {font-size: 80%;}
```

Assuming a four-level deep nesting, the most deeply nested unordered list would have a computed `font-size` value 40.96 percent the size of the parent of the top-level list. Every nested list would have a font size 80 percent as big as its parent list, causing each level to become harder and harder to read.

Rounding for display

In most modern browsers, while fractional `font-size` values are maintained internally, they are not always used by rendering engines. For example, study the letterforms in Figure 5-17.

In all cases, the *O* characters increase by 0.1 pixels in size as you go from left to right. Thus, the leftmost *O* has a `font-size` of `10px`, the one at the midpoint has a size of `10.5px`, and the one on the right is `11px`.

As Figure 5-17 reveals, different browser/OS combinations yield different results. For example, Opera, Safari, and Chrome for macOS show an abrupt jump from 10 pixels to 11 pixels at the `10.5px` position. Internet Explorer and Firefox for Windows (both 7 and 8) do the same. Firefox for macOS, on the other hand, looks like it has a smooth line of same-size text. In fact, the characters are all being drawn subtly differently, thanks to their subtly different font-size values. It's hard to see without squinting (or a ruler), but the fact that it's hard to tell there is an increase in size from one end of the line to the other is evidence enough.

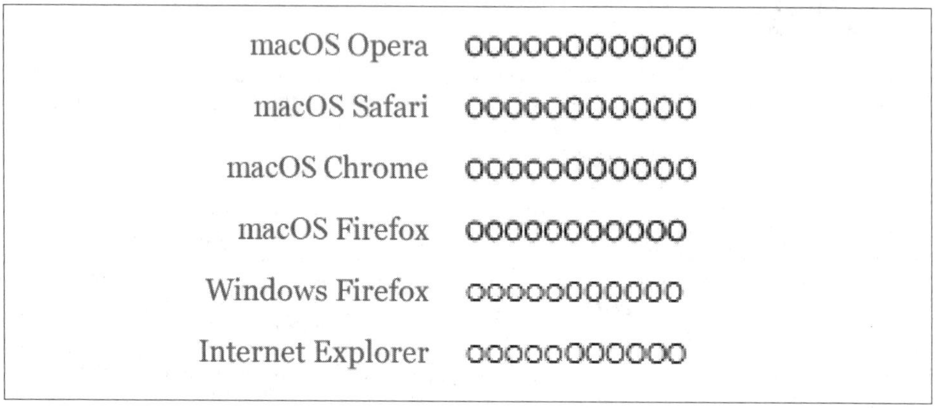

Figure 5-17. Fractional font sizes

Nevertheless, every browser will yield up the same subpixel `font-size` values if you use an inspector or query the value directly via DOM scripting. The third *O* from the right will show a computed value of `10.8px`, regardless of the size of the character displayed onscreen.

Keywords and monospace text

There's an interesting wrinkle to font size keywords and inheritance that becomes apparent when you look at what some browsers do with monospace text (e.g., Courier). Consider the following, illustrated in Figure 5-18:

```
p {font-size: medium;}    /* the default value */
span {font-family: monospace; font-size: 1em;}

<p>This is a 'p' with a <span>'span'</span> inside.</p>
```

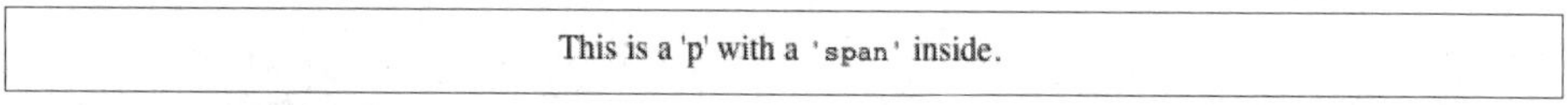

Figure 5-18. Monospace size oddities

The default value of medium is generally resolved to 16px, assuming the user hasn't changed the browser preferences (where the default text sizes are set). Indeed, if you query the paragraph text outside the span, inspectors will tell you that the computed font-size of the text is 16px (again, assuming the user hasn't changed the preferences).

So you might expect the monospaced span to also have 16-pixel text. That's exactly the case in some browsers; but in others, it will be 13px.

The reason for this is that while the computed font-size of the paragraph is 16px, the keyword medium is what's passed down through inheritance. Thus, the span starts out with font-size: medium. As a result, it looks to the user's preference settings to determine the proper size, and most browsers are set to a 13px default size for all monospace text. This causes them to display 13-pixel monospace text in a 16-pixel parent, even though the monospace text was explicitly set to font-size: 1em.

The effect carries through even with font sizes other than 1em (or 100%); in the following case, the monospace text will have a computed size of 26px instead of 32px (once more assuming the browser defaults have not changed):

```
p {font-size: medium;}    /* the default value */
span {font-family: monospace; font-size: 2em;}

<p>This is a 'p' with a <span>'span'</span> inside.</p>
```

Note that not all browsers actually do this: some override the medium sizing assumptions in favor of scaling off the computed font-size of the parent. This leads to inconsistent text display across browsers.

As it happens, there is a way to work around this problem that works for all known browsers, at least as of late 2017. It goes like this:

```
p {font-size: medium;}    /* the default value */
span {font-family: monospace, serif; font-size: 1em;}

<p>This is a 'p' with a <span>'span'</span> inside.</p>
```

See the extra serif in the font-family there? That somehow triggers a switch that makes all browsers treat font-size: 1em as being 100 percent of the paragraph's computed font-size, not a medium-derived value. This is cross-browser-consistent and illustrated in Figure 5-19.

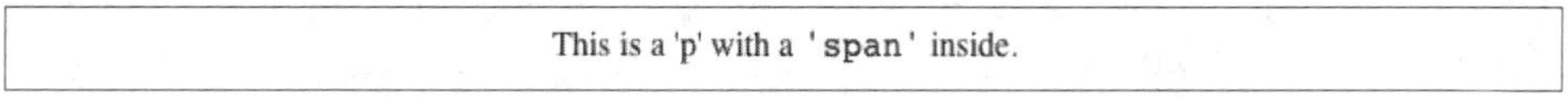

Figure 5-19. Monospace size harmony

Using Length Units

The font-size can be set using any length value. All of the following font-size declarations should be equivalent:

```
p.one {font-size: 36pt;}
p.two {font-size: 3pc;}
p.three {font-size: 0.5in;}
p.four {font-size: 1.27cm;}
p.five {font-size: 12.7mm;}
```

The display in Figure 5-20 assumes that the user agent knows how many dots per
inch are used in the display medium. Different user agents make different assumptions—some based on the operating system, some based on preferences settings, and
some based on the assumptions of the programmer who wrote the user agent. Nevertheless, the five lines should always have the same font size. Thus, while the result
may not exactly match reality (for example, the actual size of p.three may not be half
an inch), the measurements should all be consistent with one another.

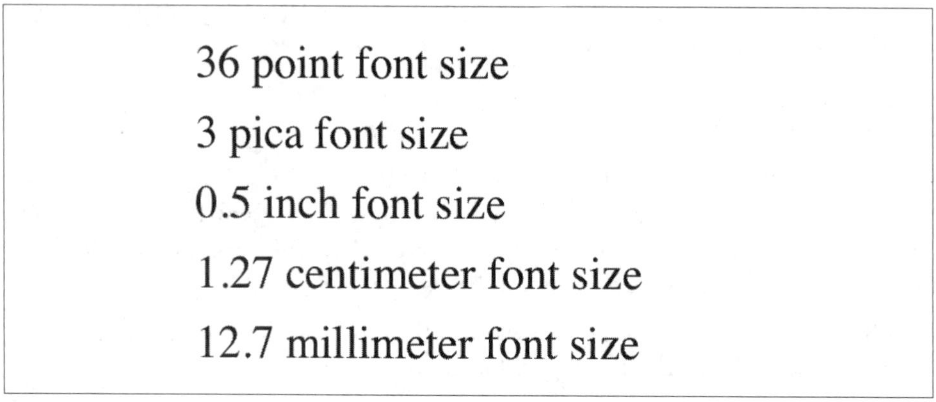

36 point font size

3 pica font size

0.5 inch font size

1.27 centimeter font size

12.7 millimeter font size

Figure 5-20. Various font sizes

There is one more value that is potentially the same as those shown in Figure 5-20,
and that's 36px, which would be the same physical distance if the display medium is
72 pixels per inch (ppi). However, there are very few monitors with that setting anymore. Most desktop displays are much higher, in the range of 96 ppi to 120 ppi; and
mobile devices go much higher, currently in the 300 ppi to 500 ppi range.

Despite these variations between operating systems and devices, many authors
choose to use pixel values for font sizes. This approach seems especially attractive
when mixing text and raster images (GIF, JPG, PNG, etc.) on a web page, since text
can (in theory) be set to the same height as graphic elements on the page by declaring
font-size: 11px; or something similar, as illustrated by Figure 5-21.

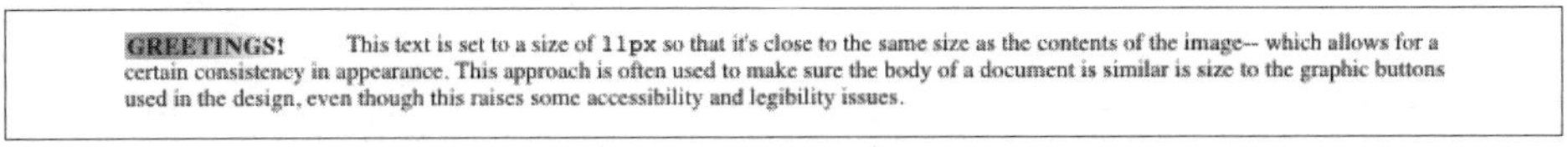

Figure 5-21. Keeping text and graphics in scale with pixel sizes

Using pixel measurements for `font-size` is certainly one way to get "consistent" results with `font-size` (and, indeed, with any length at all), but there is a drawback. Not every browser makes it easy (or even possible) to resize text set in pixels, and there are situations where pixel-sized text can be badly sized in mobile devices that pretend to be full-screen devices (such as most versions of the iPhone). For these reasons alone, pixel-sizing text is generally not recommended.

Automatically Adjusting Size

Two of the main factors that influence a font's legibility are its size and its x-height. The number that results from dividing the x-height by the `font-size` is referred to as the *aspect value*. Fonts with higher aspect values tend to be legible as the font's size is reduced; conversely, fonts with low aspect values become illegible more quickly. CSS provides a way to deal with shifts in aspect values between font families with the property `font-size-adjust`.

font-size-adjust

Values	*<number>* | none | auto
Initial value	none
Applies to	All elements
Inherited	Yes
Animatable	Yes

The goal of this property is to preserve legibility when the font used is not the author's first choice. Because of the differences in font appearance, while one font may be legible at a certain size, another font at the same size is difficult or impossible to read.

A good example is to compare the common fonts Verdana and Times. Consider Figure 5-22 and the following markup, which shows both fonts at a `font-size` of 10px:

```
p {font-size: 10px;}
p.cl1 {font-family: Verdana, sans-serif;}
p.cl2 {font-family: Times, serif; }
```

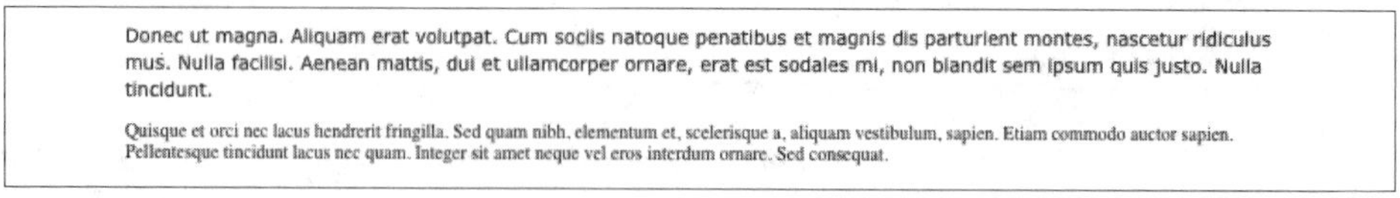
Donec ut magna. Aliquam erat volutpat. Cum sociis natoque penatibus et magnis dis parturient montes, nascetur ridiculus mus. Nulla facilisi. Aenean mattis, dui et ullamcorper ornare, erat est sodales mi, non blandit sem ipsum quis justo. Nulla tincidunt.

Quisque et orci nec lacus hendrerit fringilla. Sed quam nibh, elementum et, scelerisque a, aliquam vestibulum, sapien. Etiam commodo auctor sapien. Pellentesque tincidunt lacus nec quam. Integer sit amet neque vel eros interdum ornare. Sed consequat.

Figure 5-22. Comparing Verdana and Times

The text in Times is much harder to read than the Verdana text. This is partly due to the limitations of pixel-based display, but it is also because Times becomes harder to read at smaller font sizes.

As it turns out, the ratio of x-height to character size in Verdana is 0.58, whereas in Times it is 0.46. What you can do in this case is declare the aspect value of Verdana, and the user agent will adjust the size of the text that's actually used. This is accomplished using the formula:

> Declared `font-size` ×
> (`font-size-adjust` value ÷ aspect
> value of available font) = Adjusted `font-size`

So, in a situation where Times is used instead of Verdana, the adjustment is as follows:

> `10px` × (`0.58` ÷ `0.46`) = `12.6px`

which leads to the result shown in Figure 5-23:

```
p {font: 10px Verdana, sans-serif; font-size-adjust: 0.58;}
p.cl2 {font-family: Times, serif; }
```

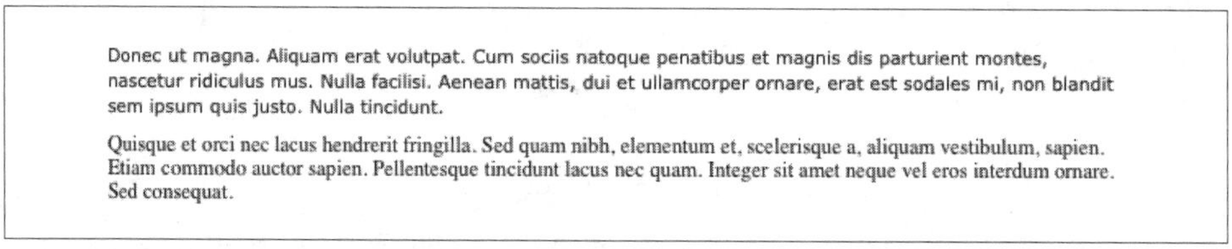
Donec ut magna. Aliquam erat volutpat. Cum sociis natoque penatibus et magnis dis parturient montes, nascetur ridiculus mus. Nulla facilisi. Aenean mattis, dui et ullamcorper ornare, erat est sodales mi, non blandit sem ipsum quis justo. Nulla tincidunt.

Quisque et orci nec lacus hendrerit fringilla. Sed quam nibh, elementum et, scelerisque a, aliquam vestibulum, sapien. Etiam commodo auctor sapien. Pellentesque tincidunt lacus nec quam. Integer sit amet neque vel eros interdum ornare. Sed consequat.

Figure 5-23. Adjusting Times

The catch is that to allow a user agent to intelligently make size adjustments, it first has to know the aspect value of the fonts you specify. User agents that support `@font-face` will be able to pull that information directly from the font file, assuming the files contain the information—any professionally-produced font should, but there's no guarantee. If a font file doesn't contain the aspect value, a user agent may try to compute it; but again, there's no guarantee that they will or even can.

Assuming that the user agent can find or figure out aspect values, the `auto` value for `font-size-adjust` is a way of getting the desired effect even if you don't know the actual aspect value of your first-choice font. For example, given that the user agent can determine that the aspect value of Verdana is 0.58, then the following will have the same result as that shown in Figure 5-23:

```
p {font: 10px Verdana, sans-serif; font-size-adjust: auto;}
p.cl2 {font-family: Times, serif; }
```

Declaring `font-size-adjust: none;` will suppress any adjustment of font sizes. This is the default state.

 As of late 2017, the only user agent line to support `font-size-adjust` was the Gecko (Firefox) family.

Font Style

`font-style` is very simple: it's used to select between `normal` text, `italic` text, and `oblique` text. That's it! The only complication is in recognizing the difference between `italic` and `oblique` text and in understanding why browsers don't always give you a choice.

font-style

Values	`italic` | `oblique` | `normal`
Initial value	`normal`
Applies to	All elements
Computed value	As specified
Note	Has a corresponding `@font-face` descriptor
Inherited	Yes
Animatable	No

The default value of `font-style` is, as you can see, `normal`. This refers to *upright* text, which is probably best described as text that is not italic or otherwise slanted. The vast majority of text in this book is upright, for instance. That leaves only an explanation of the difference between `italic` and `oblique` text. For that, it's easiest to refer to Figure 5-24, which illustrates the differences very clearly.

Basically, italic text is a separate font face, with small changes made to the structure of each letter to account for the altered appearance. This is especially true of serif fonts, where, in addition to the fact that the text characters "lean," the serifs may be altered in an italic face. Oblique text, on the other hand, is just a slanted version of the normal, upright text. Font faces with labels like "Italic," "Cursive," and "Kursiv" are usually mapped to the `italic` keyword, while `oblique` is often assigned faces with labels such as "Oblique," "Slanted," and "Incline."

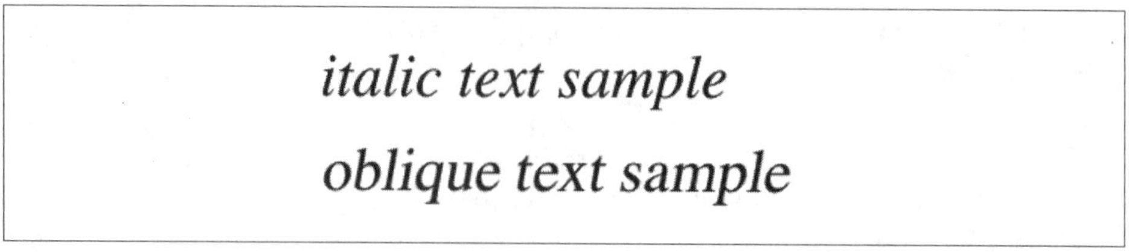

> *italic text sample*
>
> *oblique text sample*

Figure 5-24. Italic and oblique text in detail

If you want to make sure that a document uses italic text in familiar ways, you could write a stylesheet like this:

```
p {font-style: normal;}
em, i {font-style: italic;}
```

These styles would make paragraphs use an upright font, as usual, and cause the `em` and `i` elements to use an italic font—again, as usual. On the other hand, you might decide that there should be a subtle difference between `em` and `i`:

```
p {font-style: normal;}
em {font-style: oblique;}
i {font-style: italic;}
```

If you look closely at Figure 5-25, you'll see there is no apparent difference between the `em` and `i` elements. In practice, not every font is so sophisticated as to have both an italic face and an oblique face, and even fewer web browsers are sophisticated enough to tell the difference when both faces do exist.

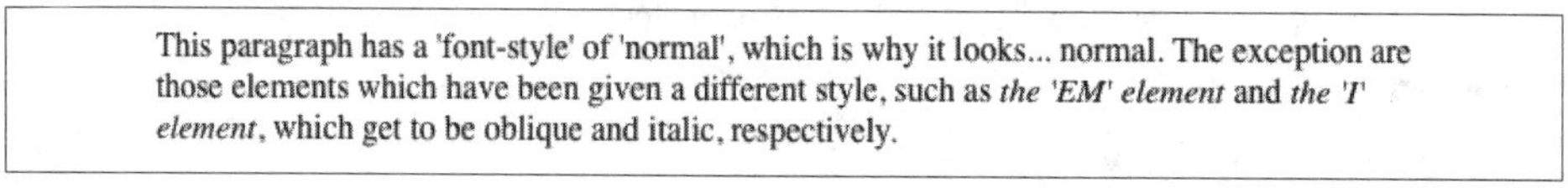

> This paragraph has a 'font-style' of 'normal', which is why it looks... normal. The exception are those elements which have been given a different style, such as *the 'EM' element* and *the 'I'* *element*, which get to be oblique and italic, respectively.

Figure 5-25. More font styles

If either of these is the case, then there are a few things that can happen. If there is no Italic face available, but there is an Oblique face, then the latter can be used for the former. If the situation is reversed—an Italic face exists, but there is no defined Oblique face—the user agent may *not* substitute the former for the latter, according to the specification. Finally, the user agent can simply generate the oblique face by computing a slanted version of the upright font. In fact, this is what most often happens in a digital world, where it's fairly simple to slant a font using a simple computation.

Furthermore, you may find that in some operating systems, a given font that has been declared as `italic` may switch from italic to oblique depending on the actual size of the font. The display of Times on a Macintosh running the Classic OS (Mac OS 9), for example, is shown in Figure 5-26, where the only difference is a single pixel in font size.

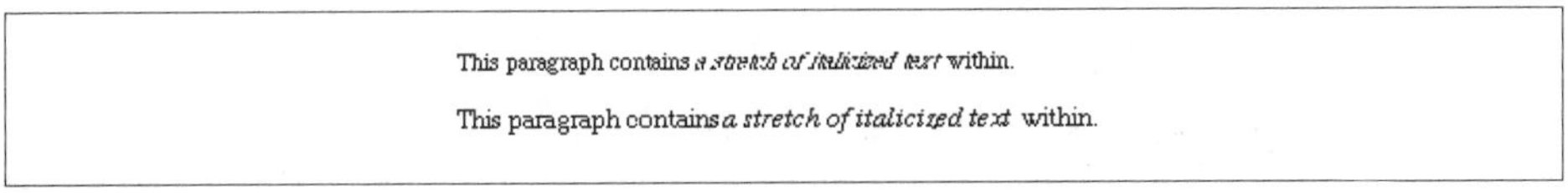

This paragraph contains *a stretch of italicized text* within.

This paragraph contains *a stretch of italicized text* within.

Figure 5-26. Same font, same style, different sizes

There isn't much that can be done about this, unfortunately, except better font handling. Fortunately, modern operating systems such as macOS and Windows XP have very good font rendering technology, and `@font-face` allows authors to assign specific italic and oblique faces to the respective `font-style` properties, should they so choose.

Even though italic and oblique text often use the same face, `font-style` can still be quite useful. For example, it is a common typographic convention that a block quote should be italicized, but that any specially emphasized text within the quote should be upright. To employ this effect, which is illustrated in Figure 5-27, you would use these styles:

```
blockquote {font-style: italic;}
blockquote em, blockquote i {font-style: normal;}
```

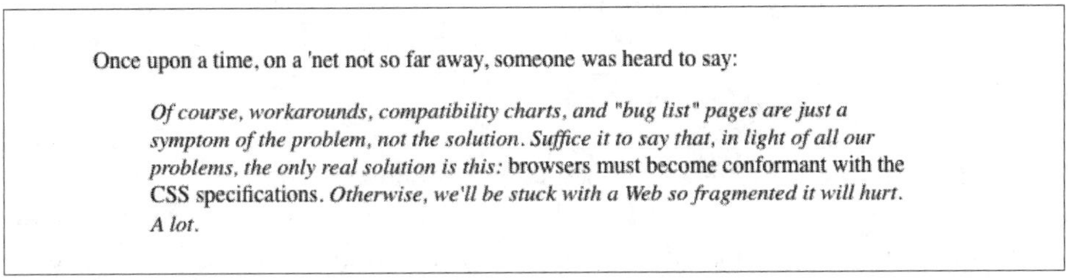

Once upon a time, on a 'net not so far away, someone was heard to say:

Of course, workarounds, compatibility charts, and "bug list" pages are just a symptom of the problem, not the solution. Suffice it to say that, in light of all our problems, the only real solution is this: browsers *must become conformant with the CSS specifications.* Otherwise, we'll be stuck with a Web so fragmented it will hurt. A lot.

Figure 5-27. Common typographical conventions through CSS

A related property tells the user agent whether it's allowed to synthesize its own bold or italic faces when a family doesn't contain them.

The font-style Descriptor

As a descriptor, `font-style` lets an author link specific faces to specific font-style values.

```
@font-face {
        font-family: "SwitzeraADF";
```

```
        font-style: normal;
        src: url("SwitzeraADF-Regular.otf") format("opentype");
}
@font-face {
        font-family: "SwitzeraADF";
        font-style: italic;
        src: url("SwitzeraADF-Italic.otf") format("opentype");
}
@font-face {
        font-family: "SwitzeraADF";
        font-style: oblique;
        src: url("SwitzeraADF-Italic.otf") format("opentype");
}
```

Given the above, the result of the following rules would be to render h2 and h3 elements using "SwitzeraADF-Italic" instead of "SwitzeraADF-Regular," as illustrated in Figure 5-28:

```
h1, h2, h3 {font: 225% SwitzeraADF, Helvetica, sans-serif;}
h2 {font-size: 180%; font-style: italic;}
h3 {font-size: 150%; font-style: oblique;}
```

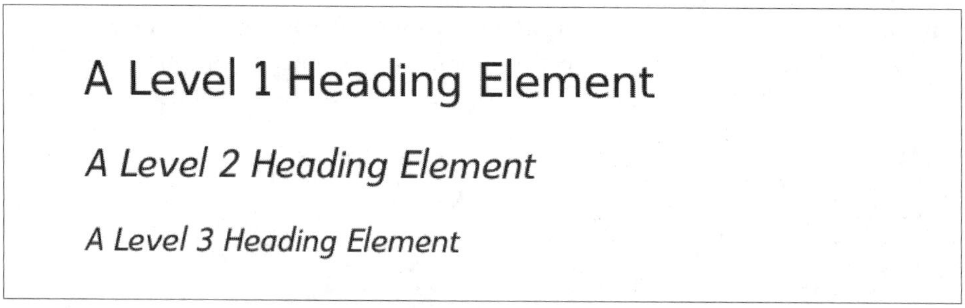

A Level 1 Heading Element

A Level 2 Heading Element

A Level 3 Heading Element

Figure 5-28. Using declared font-style faces

Ideally, if there were a SwitzeraADF face with an oblique typeface, the author could point to it instead of the italic variant. There isn't such a face, though, so the author mapped the italic face to both the italic and oblique values. As with font-weight, the font-style descriptor can take all of the values of the font-style property *except* for inherit.

Font Stretching

In some font families, there are a number of variant faces that have wider or narrower letterforms. These often take names like "Condensed," "Wide," "Ultra Expanded," and so on. The utility of such variants is that a designer can use a single font family while also having skinny and fat variants. CSS provides a property that allows an author to select among such variants, when they exist, without having to explicitly define them in font-family declarations. It does this via the somewhat misleadingly named font-stretch.

---

font-stretch

Values	normal | ultra-condensed | extra-condensed | condensed | semi-condensed | semi-expanded | expanded | extra-expanded | ultra-expanded
Initial value	normal
Applies to	All elements
Inherited	Yes
Animatable	No
Note	Has a corresponding @font-face descriptor (see below)

You might expect from the property name that this will stretch or squeeze a font like saltwater taffy, but that's actually not the case at all. As the value names imply, this property instead behaves very much like the absolute-size keywords (e.g., xx-large) for the font-size property, with a range of absolute values that (in theory) let the author alter a font's width. For example, an author might decide to stress the text in a strongly emphasized element by changing the font characters to a wider face than their parent element's font characters.

The catch is that this property only works if the font family in use has defined wider and narrower faces, which most do not (and those that do are usually very expensive). Thus this property is actually very different from font-size, which can change the size of any font face at any time. In contrast, declaring font-stretch: expanded will only have an effect if the font in use has an expanded face available. If it doesn't, then nothing will happen: the font's face will not change.

For example, consider the very common font Verdana, which has only one width face; this is equivalent to font-stretch: normal. Declaring the following will have no effect on the width of the displayed text:

```
body {font-family: Verdana;}
strong {font-stretch: extra-expanded;}
footer {font-stretch: extra-condensed;}
```

All of the text will be at Verdana's usual width. However, if the font family is changed to one that has a number of width faces, such as Futura, then things will be different, as shown in Figure 5-29:

```
body {font-family: Verdana;}
strong {font-stretch: extra-expanded;}
footer {font-stretch: extra-condensed;}
```

> If there one thing I can't **stress enough**, it's the value of Photoshop in producing books like this one.
>
> Especially in footers.

Figure 5-29. Stretching font characters

 As of late 2017, Safari for both macOS and iOS did not support font-stretch, nor did Opera Mini.

The font-stretch Descriptor

Much as with the font-weight descriptor, the font-stretch descriptor allows authors to explicitly assign faces of varying widths to the width values permitted in the font-stretch property. For example, the following rules explicitly assign three faces to the most directly analogous font-stretch values:

```
@font-face {
        font-family: "SwitzeraADF";
        font-stretch: normal;
        src: url("SwitzeraADF-Regular.otf") format("opentype");
}
@font-face {
        font-family: "SwitzeraADF";
        font-stretch: condensed;
        src: url("SwitzeraADF-Cond.otf") format("opentype");
}
@font-face {
        font-family: "SwitzeraADF";
        font-stretch: expanded;
        src: url("SwitzeraADF-Ext.otf") format("opentype");
}
```

In a parallel to what we saw in previous sections, the author can call on these different width faces through the font-stretch property, as illustrated in Figure 5-30:

```
h1, h2, h3 {font: 225% SwitzeraADF, Helvetica, sans-serif;}
h2 {font-size: 180%; font-stretch: condensed;}
h3 {font-size: 150%; font-stretch: expanded;}
```

As before, the font-stretch descriptor can take all of the values of the font-stretch property *except* for inherit.

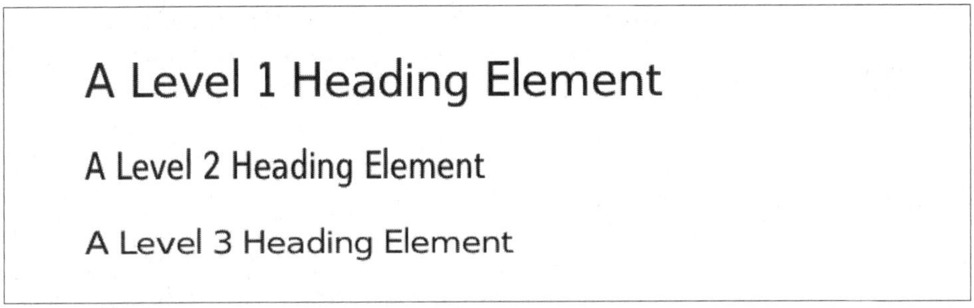

A Level 1 Heading Element

A Level 2 Heading Element

A Level 3 Heading Element

Figure 5-30. Using declared font-stretch faces

Font Kerning

Some fonts contain data regarding how characters should be spaced relative to each other, known as *kerning*. This spacing can vary depending on how characters are combined; for example, the character pair *oc* may have a different spacing than the pair *ox*. Similarly, *AB* and *AW* may have different separation distances, to the point that in some fonts, the top-right tip of the *W* is actually placed to the left of the bottom-right tip of the *A*. This kerning data can be explicitly called for or suppressed using the property font-kerning.

font-kerning	
Values	auto|normal|none
Initial value	auto
Applies to	All elements
Inherited	Yes
Animatable	No

The value none is pretty simple: it tells the user agent to ignore any kerning information in the font. normal tells the user agent to kern the text normally; that is, according to the kerning data contained in the font. auto tells the user agent to do whatever it thinks best, possibly depending on the type of font in use. The OpenType specification, for example, recommends (but does not require) that kerning be applied whenever the font supports it. If a font does not contain kerning data, font-kerning will have no effect.

Note that if the property `letter-spacing` is applied to kerned text, the kerning is done and *then* the letters' spacing is adjusted according to the value of `letter-spacing`, not the other way around.

Font Variants

Beyond font weights, font styles, and so forth, there are font variants. These are embedded within a font face and can cover things like various styles of historical ligatures, small-caps presentation, ways of presenting fractions, the spacing of numbers, whether zeroes get slashes through them, and much more. CSS lets authors invoke these variants, when they exist, through `font-variant`.

---

font-variant

Values (CSS2.1)	`normal` | `small-caps`
Values (Level 3)	`normal` | `none` | [*<common-lig-values>* || *<discretionary-lig-values>* || *<historical-lig-values>* || *<contextual-alt-values>* || `stylistic(`*<feature-value-name>*`)` || `historical-forms` || `styleset(`*<feature-value-name>*`#)` || `character-variant(`*<feature-value-name>*`#)` || `swash(`*<feature-value-name>*`)` || `ornaments(`*<feature-value-name>*`)` || `annotation(`*<feature-value-name>*`)` || [`small-caps` | `all-small-caps` | `petite-caps` | `all-petite-caps` | `unicase` | `titling-caps`] || *<numeric-figure-values>* || *<numeric-spacing-values>* || *<numeric-fraction-values>* || `ordinal` || `slashed-zero` || *<east-asian-variant-values>* || *<east-asian-width-values>* || `ruby`]
Initial value	`normal`
Applies to	All elements
Computed value	As specified
Inherited	Yes
Animatable	No
Note	Has a corresponding `@font-face` descriptor (see below)

That's quite a Values (Level 3) entry, isn't it? Especially when the only values in CSS1 and CSS2 were the default of `normal`, which describes ordinary text, and `small-caps`, which calls for the use of small-caps text. Let's concentrate just on those for a moment.

Instead of upper- and lowercase letters, a small-caps font employs uppercase letters of different sizes. Thus, you might see something like that shown in Figure 5-31:

```
h1 {font-variant: small-caps;}
h1 code, p {font-variant: normal;}

<h1>The Uses of <code>font-variant</code> On the Web</h1>
<p>
The property <code>font-variant</code> is very interesting...
</p>
```

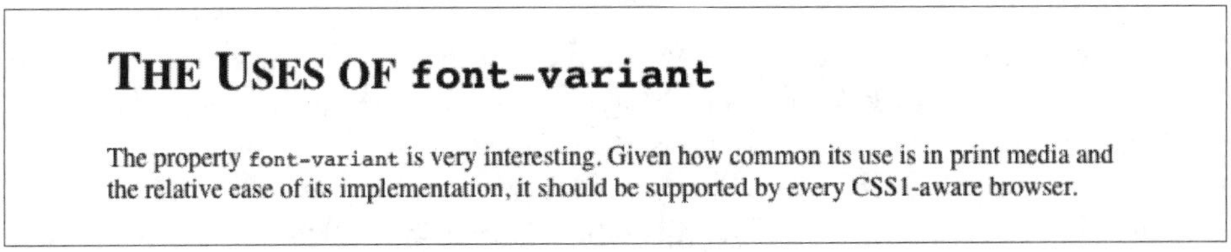

THE USES OF font-variant

The property font-variant is very interesting. Given how common its use is in print media and the relative ease of its implementation, it should be supported by every CSS1-aware browser.

Figure 5-31. The small-caps value in use

As you may notice, in the display of the h1 element, there is a larger uppercase letter wherever an uppercase letter appears in the source and a small uppercase letter wherever there is a lowercase letter in the source. This is very similar to text-transform: uppercase, with the only real difference being that, here, the uppercase letters are of different sizes. However, the reason that small-caps is declared using a font property is that some fonts have a specific small-caps face, which a font property is used to select.

What happens if no such face exists? There are two options provided in the specification. The first is for the user agent to create a small-caps face by scaling uppercase letters on its own. The second is to make all letters uppercase and the same size, exactly as if the declaration text-transform: uppercase; had been used instead. This is not an ideal solution, but it is permitted.

Level 3 Values

Now to examine that Values (Level 3) line. It is admittedly complicated, but there's an easy way to explain it. It's actually a shorthand for all the values permitted for the following properties:

- font-variant-ligatures
- font-variant-caps
- font-variant-numeric
- font-variant-alternates
- font-variant-east-asian

As an example (to pick one of the simpler ones), *<common-lig-values>* comes from the property `font-variant-ligatures`, and can be either `common-ligatures` or `no-common-ligatures`. *<numeric-fraction-values>* comes from `font-variant-numeric` and can be either `diagonal-fractions` or `stacked-fractions`. And so on.

There are two barriers to the use of these admittedly much more powerful font variants: browser support and font support. The first is easy: as of late 2017, there isn't widespread support for enabling font variants. Certainly you can use the CSS 2.1 variant values, but many of the Level 3 values are only supported by Gecko and WebKit.

The second is also easy while also being complex: not every font supports every variant. For example, most Latin fonts won't support any of the East Asian variants; for another, not every font will include support for, say, some of the numeric and ligature variants. To find out what a given font supports, you have to consult its documentation, or do a lot of testing if no documentation is available. (Most commercial fonts do come with documentation, and most free fonts don't.)

The main thing to keep in mind is that even if a variant works in a given browser for one font, it may not for another; and just because a font has a given variant, that doesn't mean that all browsers will let you invoke it. So it's complicated, and there aren't many detailed guides to help out.

 The various `font-variant-*` properties are not covered in detail here because as of late 2017, they were not well supported in browsers. For more details, see *http://w3.org/TR/css3-fonts/*.

The font-variant descriptor

The `font-variant` descriptor lets you decide which of a font face's variants can or cannot be used, specified as a space-separated list. For example, you can enable the common ligature, small caps, and slashed-zeroes variants like so:

```
font-variant: common-ligatures small-caps slashed-zero;
```

You'll no doubt have guessed by now that the `font-variant` descriptor can take all of the values of the `font-variant` property *except* for `inherit`.

Note that this descriptor is very different than the other descriptors we've seen so far. With the `font-stretch` descriptor, for example, you can assign a specific font face to a given `font-stretch` property value. The `font-variant` descriptor, by contrast, defines which variants are permitted for the font face being declared in the `@font-face` rule, which can easily negate font variant values called for in properties later on. For example, given the following, paragraphs will *not* be displayed using a `diagonal-fractions` or `small-caps` variant, even if such variants exist in SwitzeraADF:

```
@font-face {
        font-family: "SwitzeraADF";
        font-weight: normal;
        src: url("SwitzeraADF-Regular.otf") format("opentype");
        font-variant: stacked-fractions titling-caps slashed-zero;
}

p {font: small-caps 1em SwitzeraADF, sans-serif;
    font-variant-numeric: diagonal-fractions;}
```

Font Features

In a manner similar to `font-variant`, the `font-feature-settings` descriptor allows authors to exercise low-level control over which OpenType font features are available for use (so don't go using this descriptor on *.woff* files).

---

font-feature-settings

Values	normal | *<feature-tag-value>*#
Initial value	normal
Note	Has a corresponding @font-face descriptor (see below)

You can list one or more comma-separated OpenType features, as defined by the OpenType specification. For example, enabling common ligatures, small caps, and slashed zeroes would look something like this:

```
font-feature-settings: "liga" on, "smcp" on, "zero" on;
```

The exact format of a *<feature-tag-value>* value is:

<feature-tag-value>
    <string> [*<integer>* \| on \| off]?

For many features, the only permitted integer values are 0 and 1, which are equivalent to `off` and `on` (and vice versa). There are some features that allow a range of numbers, however, in which case values greater than 1 both enable the feature and define the feature's selection index. If a feature is listed but no number is provided, 1 (on) is assumed. Thus, the following descriptors are all equivalent:

```
font-feature-settings: "liga";     /* 1 is assumed */
font-feature-settings: "liga" 1;    /* 1 is declared */
font-feature-settings: "liga" on;   /* on = 1 */
```

Remember that all *<string>* values *must* be quoted. Thus, the first of the following descriptors will be recognized, but the second will be ignored:

```
font-feature-settings: "liga", dlig;
/* common ligatures are enabled; we wanted discretionary ligatures, but forgot
   quotes */
```

A further restriction is that OpenType requires that all feature tags be four ASCII characters long. Any feature name longer or shorter, or that uses non-ASCII characters, is invalid and will be ignored. (This isn't something you personally need to worry about unless you're using a font that has it own made-up feature names and the font's creator didn't follow the naming rules.)

By default, OpenType fonts *always* have the following features enabled unless the author explicitly disables them via font-feature-settings or font-variant:

calt

> Contextual alternates

ccmp

> Composed characters

clig

> Contextual ligatures

liga

> Standard ligatures

locl

> Localized forms

mark

> Mark to base positioning

mkmk

> Mark to mark positioning

rlig

> Required ligatures

Additionally, other features may be enabled by default in specific situations, such as vertical alternatives (vert) for vertical runs of text.

 A complete list of standard OpenType feature names can be found at microsoft.com/typography/otspec/featurelist.htm.

The font-feature-settings Descriptor

The `font-feature-settings` descriptor lets you decide which of an OpenType font face's settings can or cannot be used, specified as a space-separated list.

Now, hold up a second—isn't that almost exactly what we did with `font-variant` just a few paragraphs ago? As a matter of fact, yes, it is. The `font-variant` descriptor covers nearly everything `font-feature-settings` does, plus a little more besides. It just does so in a more CSS-like way, with value names instead of cryptic OpenType identifiers and Boolean toggles. Because of this, the CSS specification explicitly encourages authors to use `font-variant` instead of `font-feature-settings`, except in those cases where there's a font feature that the value list of `font-variant` doesn't include.

Keep in mind that this descriptor merely makes features available for use (or suppresses their use). It does not actually turn them on for the display of text; for that, see the section on the `font-feature-settings` property.

Just as with the `font-variant` descriptor, the `font-feature-settings` descriptor defines which font features are permitted for the font face being declared in the `@font-face` rule. This can easily negate font feature values called for in properties later on. For example, given the following, paragraphs will *not* be displayed using alternative fractions nor small-caps, even if such features exist in SwitzeraADF:

```
@font-face {
        font-family: "SwitzeraADF";
        font-weight: normal;
        src: url("SwitzeraADF-Regular.otf") format("opentype");
        font-feature-settings: "afrc" off, "smcp" off;
}

p {font: 1em SwitzeraADF, sans-serif; font-feature-settings: "afrc", "smcp";}
```

As always, the `font-feature-settings` descriptor can take all of the values of the `font-feature-settings` property *except* for `inherit`.

Font Synthesis

It is sometimes the case that a given font family will lack alternate faces for things like bold or italic text. In such situations, the user agent may attempt to synthesize a face from the faces it has available, but this can lead to unattractive letterforms. To address this, CSS offers `font-synthesis`, which lets authors say how much synthesis they will or won't permit in the rendering of a page.

font-synthesis

Values	`none` | `weight` || `style`
Initial value	`weight style`
Applies to	All elements
Inherited	Yes
Animatable	No

In many user agents, a font family that has no bold face can have one computed for it. This might be done by adding pixels to either side of each character glyph, for example. While this might seem useful, it can lead to results that are visually unappealing. This is why most font families actually have bold faces included: the font's designer wanted to make sure that bolded text in that font looked good.

Similarly, a font family that lacks an italic face an have one synthesized by simply slanting the characters in the normal face. This tends to look even worse than synthesized bold faces, particularly when it comes to serif fonts. Compare the difference between a synthesized italic version of Georgia (which we're calling "oblique" here) and the actual italic face included in Georgia, illustrated in Figure 5-32.

In supporting user agents, declaring `font-synthesis: none` blocks the user agent from doing any such synthesis for the affected elements. You can block it for the whole document with `html (font-synthesis: none;}`, for example. The downside is that any attempts to bold or italicize text using a font that doesn't offer the appropriate faces will stay unbolded or unitalicized. The upside is that you don't have to worry about a user agent trying to synthesize those variants and doing a poor job of it.

 As of late 2017, only Firefox supported `font-synthesis`.

italic text sample

oblique text sample

Figure 5-32. Synthesized versus designed italics

The font Property

All of these properties are very sophisticated, but using them all could get a little tedious:

```
h1 {font-family: Verdana, Helvetica, Arial, sans-serif; font-size: 30px;
    font-weight: 900; font-style: italic; font-variant: small-caps;}
h2 {font-family: Verdana, Helvetica, Arial, sans-serif; font-size: 24px;
    font-weight: bold; font-style: italic; font-variant: normal;}
```

Some of this problem could be solved by grouping selectors, but wouldn't it be easier to combine everything into a single property? Enter font, which is the shorthand property for all the other font properties (and a little more besides).

font		
Values	[[*<font-style>* ‖ [normal	small-caps] ‖ *<font-weight>*]? *<font-size>* [/ *<line-height>*]? *<font-family>*]	caption	icon	menu	message-box	small-caption	status-bar		
Initial value	Refer to individual properties	
Applies to	All elements	
Percentages	Calculated with respect to the parent element for *<font-size>* and with respect to the element's *<font-size>* for *<line-height>*	
Computed value	See individual properties (font-style, etc.)	
Inherited	Yes	
Animatable	Refer to individual properties	

Generally speaking, a font declaration can have any one value from each of the listed font properties, or else a system font value (described in "Using System Fonts" on page 202). Therefore, the preceding example could be shortened as follows (and have exactly the same effect, as illustrated by Figure 5-33):

```
h1 {font: italic 900 small-caps 30px Verdana, Helvetica, Arial, sans-serif;}
h2 {font: bold normal italic 24px Verdana, Helvetica, Arial, sans-serif;}
```

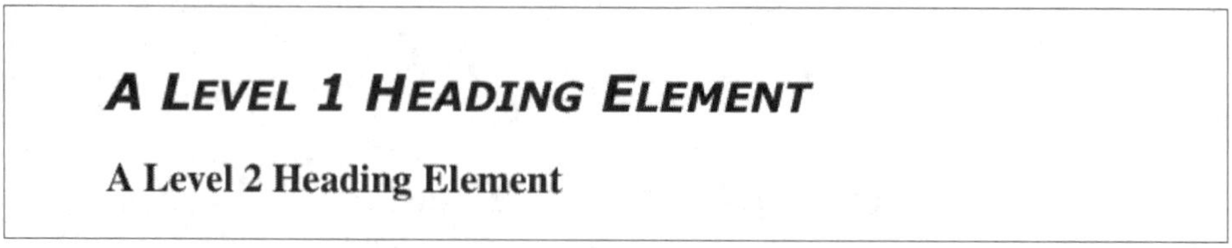

A ***Level 1 Heading Element***

A Level 2 Heading Element

Figure 5-33. Typical font rules

I say that the styles "could be" shortened in this way because there are a few other possibilities, thanks to the relatively loose way in which font can be written. If you look closely at the preceding example, you'll see that the first three values don't occur in the same order. In the h1 rule, the first three values are the values for font-style, font-weight, and font-variant, in that order. In the second, they're ordered font-weight, font-variant, and font-style. There is nothing wrong here because these three can be written in any order. Furthermore, if any of them has a value of normal, that can be left out altogether. Therefore, the following rules are equivalent to the previous example:

```
h1 {font: italic 900 small-caps 30px Verdana, Helvetica, Arial, sans-serif;}
h2 {font: bold italic 24px Verdana, Helvetica, Arial, sans-serif;}
```

In this example, the value of normal was left out of the h2 rule, but the effect is exactly the same as in the preceding example.

It's important to realize, however, that this free-for-all situation applies only to the first three values of font. The last two are much stricter in their behavior. Not only must font-size and font-family appear in that order as the last two values in the declaration, but both must always be present in a font declaration. Period, end of story. If either is left out, then the entire rule will be invalidated and very likely to be ignored completely by a user agent. Thus, the following rules will get you the result shown in Figure 5-34:

```
h1 {font: normal normal italic 30px sans-serif;}   /*no problem here */
h2 {font: 1.5em sans-serif;}   /* also fine; omitted values set to 'normal' */
h3 {font: sans-serif;}     /* INVALID--no 'font-size' provided */
h4 {font: lighter 14px;}   /* INVALID--no 'font-family' provided */
```

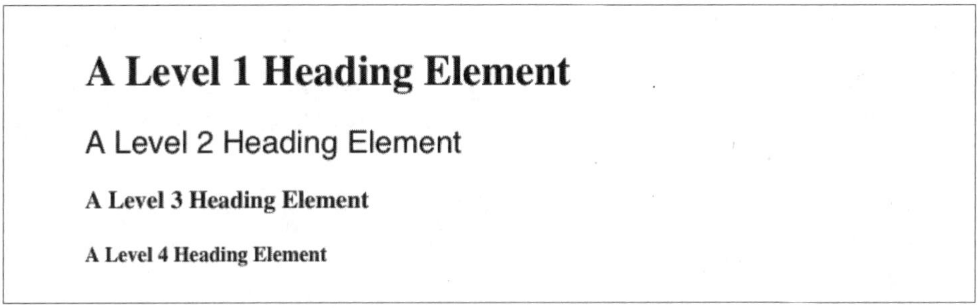

A Level 1 Heading Element

A Level 2 Heading Element

A Level 3 Heading Element

A Level 4 Heading Element

Figure 5-34. The necessity of both size and family

Adding the Line Height

So far, we've treated font as though it has only five values, which isn't quite true. It is also possible to set the value of the property line-height using font, despite that fact that line-height is a text property (not covered in this text), not a font property. It's done as a sort of addition to the font-size value, separated from it by a forward slash (/):

```
body {font-size: 12px;}
h2 {font: bold italic 200%/1.2 Verdana, Helvetica, Arial, sans-serif;}
```

These rules, demonstrated in Figure 5-35, set all h2 elements to be bold and italic (using face for one of the sans-serif font families), set the font-size to 24px (twice the body's size), and set the line-height to 28.8px.

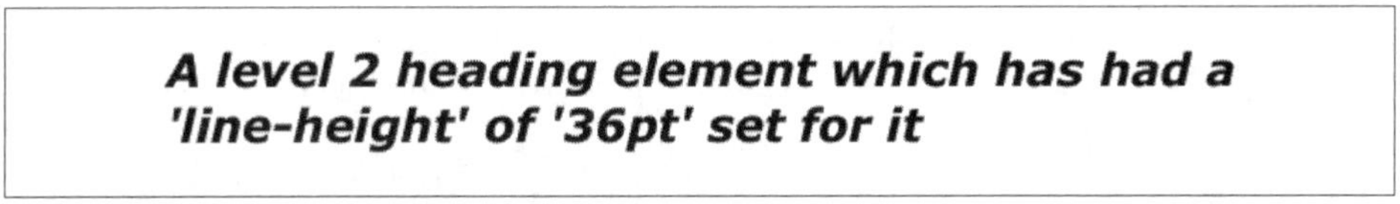

A level 2 heading element which has had a 'line-height' of '36pt' set for it

Figure 5-35. Adding line height to the mix

This addition of a value for line-height is entirely optional, just as the first three font values are. If you do include a line-height, remember that the font-size always comes before line-height, never after, and the two are always separated by a slash.

This may seem repetitive, but it's one of the most common errors made by CSS authors, so I can't say it enough: the required values for font are font-size and font-family, in that order. Everything else is strictly optional.

Using Shorthands Properly

It is important to remember that font, being a shorthand property, can act in unexpected ways if you are careless with its use. Consider the following rules, which are illustrated in Figure 5-36:

```
h1, h2, h3 {font: italic small-caps 250% sans-serif;}
h2 {font: 200% sans-serif;}
h3 {font-size: 150%;}

<h1>This is an h1 element</h1>
<h2>This is an h2 element</h2>
<h3>This is an h3 element</h3>
```

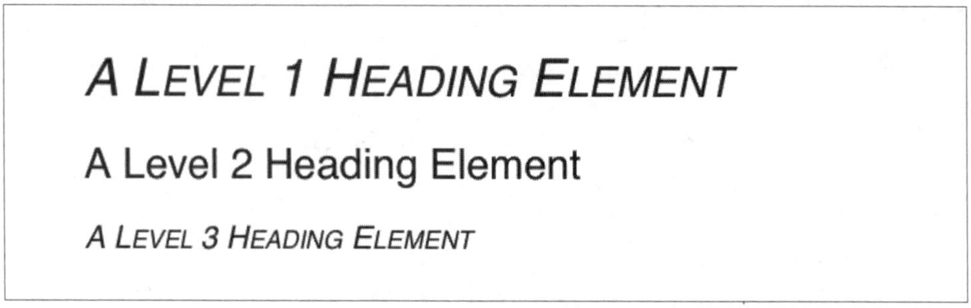

A LEVEL 1 HEADING ELEMENT

A Level 2 Heading Element

A LEVEL 3 HEADING ELEMENT

Figure 5-36. Shorthand changes

Did you notice that the h2 element is neither italicized nor small-capped, and that none of the elements are bold? This is the correct behavior. When the shorthand property font is used, any omitted values are reset to their defaults. Thus, the previous example could be written as follows and still be exactly equivalent:

```
h1, h2, h3 {font: italic normal small-caps 250% sans-serif;}
h2 {font: normal normal normal 200% sans-serif;}
h3 {font-size: 150%;}
```

This sets the h2 element's font style and variant to normal, and the font-weight of all three elements to normal. This is the expected behavior of shorthand properties. The h3 does not suffer the same fate as the h2 because you used the property font-size, which is not a shorthand property and therefore affects only its own value.

Using System Fonts

In situations where you want to make a web page blend in with the user's operating system, the system font values of font come in handy. These are used to take the font size, family, weight, style, and variant of elements of the operating system, and apply them to an element. The values are as follows:

caption
    Used for captioned controls, such as buttons

`icon`
> Used to label icons

`menu`
> Used in menus—that is, drop-down menus and menu lists

`message-box`
> Used in dialog boxes

`small-caption`
> Used for labeling small controls

`status-bar`
> Used in window status bars

For example, you might want to set the font of a button to be the same as that of the buttons found in the operating system. For example:

```
button {font: caption;}
```

With these values, it is possible to create web-based applications that look very much like applications native to the user's operating system.

Note that system fonts may only be set as a whole; that is, the font family, size, weight, style, etc., are all set together. Therefore, the button text from our previous example will look exactly the same as button text in the operating system, whether or not the size matches any of the content around the button. You can, however, alter the individual values once the system font has been set. Thus, the following rule will make sure the button's font is the same size as its parent element's font:

```
button {font: caption; font-size: 1em;}
```

If you call for a system font and no such font exists on the user's machine, the user agent may try to find an approximation, such as reducing the size of the `caption` font to arrive at the `small-caption` font. If no such approximation is possible, then the user agent should use a default font of its own. If it can find a system font but can't read all of its values, then it should use the default value. For example, a user agent may be able to find a `status-bar` font but not get any information about whether the font is small-caps. In that case, the user agent will use the value `normal` for the `small-caps` property.

Font Matching

As we've seen, CSS allows for the matching of font families, weights, and variants. This is all accomplished through font matching, which is a vaguely complicated procedure. Understanding it is important for authors who want to help user agents make good font selections when displaying their documents. I left it for the end of the chapter because it's not really necessary to understand how the font properties work, and some readers will probably want to skip this part. If you're still interested, here's how font matching works:

1. The user agent creates, or otherwise accesses, a database of font properties. This database lists the various CSS properties of all of the fonts to which the user agent has access. Typically, this will be all fonts installed on the machine, although there could be others (for example, the user agent could have its own built-in fonts). If the user agent encounters two identical fonts, it will just ignore one of them.

2. The user agent takes apart an element to which font properties have been applied and constructs a list of font properties necessary for the display of that element. Based on that list, the user agent makes an initial choice of a font family to use in displaying the element. If there is a complete match, then the user agent can use that font. Otherwise, it needs to do a little more work.

3. A font is first matched against the font-stretch property.

4. A font is next matched against the font-style property. The keyword italic is matched by any font that is labeled as either "italic" or "oblique." If neither is available, then the match fails.

5. The next match is to font-weight, which can never fail thanks to the way font-weight is handled in CSS (explained in the earlier section, "How Weights Work" on page 167).

6. Then, font-size is tackled. This must be matched within a certain tolerance, but that tolerance is defined by the user agent. Thus, one user agent might allow matching within a 20 percent margin of error, whereas another might allow only 10 percent differences between the size specified and the size that is actually used.

7. If there was no font match in Step 2, the user agent looks for alternate fonts within the same font family. If it finds any, then it repeats Step 2 for that font.

8. Assuming a generic match has been found, but it doesn't contain everything needed to display a given element—the font is missing the copyright symbol, for instance—then the user agent goes back to Step 3, which entails a search for another alternate font and another trip through Step 2.

9. Finally, if no match has been made and all alternate fonts have been tried, then the user agent selects the default font for the given generic font family and does the best it can to display the element correctly.

Furthermore, the user agent does the following to resolve handling of font variants and features:

1. First, check for font features enabled by default, including features required for a given script. The core set of default-enabled features is "calt", "ccmp", "clig", "liga", "locl", "mark", "mkmk", and "rlig".

2. Then, if the font is defined via an @font-face rule, check for the features implied by the font-variant descriptor in the @font-face rule. Then check for the font features implied by the font-feature-settings descriptor in the @font-face rule.

3. Then check feature settings determined by properties other than font-variant or font-feature-settings. (For example, setting a non-default value for the letter-spacing property will disable ligatures.)

4. Then check for features implied by the value of the font-variant property, the related font-variant subproperties (e.g., font-variant-ligatures), and any other property that may call for the use of OpenType features (e.g., font-kerning).

5. Finally, check for the features implied by the value of font-feature-settings property.

The whole process is long and tedious, but it helps to understand how user agents pick the fonts they do. For example, you might specify the use of Times or any other serif font in a document:

```
body {font-family: Times, serif;}
```

For each element, the user agent should examine the characters in that element and determine whether Times can provide characters to match. In most cases, it can do so with no problem. Assume, however, that a Chinese character has been placed in the middle of a paragraph. Times has nothing that can match this character, so the user agent has to work around the character or look for another font that can fulfill the needs of displaying that element. Any Western font is highly unlikely to contain Chinese characters, but should one exist (let's call it AsiaTimes), the user agent could use it in the display of that one element—or simply for the single character. Thus, the whole paragraph might be displayed using AsiaTimes, or everything in the paragraph might be in Times except for the single Chinese character, which is displayed in AsiaTimes.

Summary

From what was initially a very simplistic set of font properties, CSS has rapidly grown to allow fine-grained and wide-ranging influence over how fonts are displayed on the web. From custom fonts downloaded over the web to custom-built families assembled out of a variety of individual faces, authors may be fairly said to overflow with font power.

The typographic options available to authors today are far stronger than ever, but always remember: you must use this power wisely. While you can have 17 different fonts in use on your site, that definitely doesn't mean that you should. Quite aside from the aesthetic difficulties this could present for your users, it would also make the total page weight much, much higher than it needs to be. As with any other aspect of web design, authors are advised to use their power wisely, not wildly.

CHAPTER 6

Text Properties

Sure, a lot of web design involves picking the right colors and getting the coolest look for your pages, but when it comes right down to it, you probably spend more of your time worrying about where text will go and how it will look. Such concerns gave rise to HTML tags such as <FONT> and <CENTER> in the web's early days, which allowed you some measure of control over the appearance and placement of text.

Because text is so important, there are many CSS properties that affect it in one way or another. What is the difference between text and fonts? At the simplest level, text is the content, and fonts are used to display that content. Using text properties, you can affect the position of text in relation to the rest of the line, superscript it, underline it, and change the capitalization. You can even simulate, to a limited degree, the use of a typewriter's Tab key.

Indentation and Inline Alignment

Let's start with a discussion of how you can affect the inline positioning of text within a line. Think of these basic actions as the same types of steps you might take to create a newsletter or write a report.

First, however, let's take a moment to talk about the terms *inline* and *block* as they'll be used in this chapter. In fact, let's take them in reverse. If your primary language is Western-derived, then you're used to a block direction of top to bottom, and an inline direction of left to right. Let's examine those terms more closely.

The *block direction* is the direction in which block elements are placed by default in the current writing mode. In English, for example, the block direction is top to bottom, or vertical, as one paragraph (or other text element) is placed beneath the one before.

The *inline direction* is the direction in which inline elements are written within a block. To again take English as an example, the inline direction is left to right, or horizontal. In languages like Arabic and Hebrew, the inline direction is right to left instead.

Let's reconsider English for a moment. A plain page of English text, displayed on a screen, has a vertical block direction and a horizontal inline direction. But if the page is rotated 90 degrees anticlockwise using CSS Transforms, then suddenly the block direction is horizontal and the inline direction is vertical. (And bottom to top, at that.)

This approach to content and layout is relatively new as of 2017, and a conversion from the old layout language, which was highly dependent on concepts of "horizontal" and "vertical," is still underway. While the rest of the chapter will try to use the terms "block direction" and "inline direction," please forgive any lapses into "vertical" and "horizontal."

Indenting Text

Most books we read in Western languages format paragraphs of text with the first line indented, and no blank line between paragraphs. Some sites used to create the illusion of indented text by placing a small transparent image before the first letter in a paragraph, which shoved the text over. Thanks to CSS, there's a much better way to indent text: `text-indent`.

---

text-indent

Values	*<length>* | *<percentage>*
Initial value	0
Applies to	Block-level elements
Percentages	Refer to the width of the containing block
Computed value	For percentage values, as specified; for length values, the absolute length
Inherited	Yes
Animatable	Yes

Using `text-indent`, the first line of any element can be indented by a given length, even if that length is negative. A common use for this property is to indent the first line of a paragraph:

```
p {text-indent: 3em;}
```

This rule will cause the first line of any paragraph to be indented three ems, as shown in Figure 6-1.

> This is a paragraph element, which means that the first line will be indented by 3em (i.e., three times the computed font-size of the text in the paragraph). The other lines in the paragraph will not be indented, no matter how long the paragraph may be.

Figure 6-1. Text indenting

In general, you can apply text-indent to any element that generates a block box, and the indentation will occur along the inline direction. You can't apply it to inline elements or on replaced elements such as images. However, if you have an image within the first line of a block-level element, it will be shifted over with the rest of the text in the line.

If you want to "indent" the first line of an inline element, you can create the effect with left padding or margin.

You can also set negative values for text-indent, a technique that leads to a number of interesting effects. The most common use is a *hanging indent*, where the first line hangs out to one side of the rest of the element:

```
p {text-indent: -4em;}
```

Be careful when setting a negative value for text-indent; the first few words may be chopped off by the edge of the browser window if you aren't careful. To avoid display problems, I recommend you use a margin or some padding to accommodate the negative indentation:

```
p {text-indent: -4em; padding-left: 4em;}
```

Negative indents can, however, be used to your advantage. Consider the following example, demonstrated in Figure 6-2, which adds a floated image to the mix:

```
p.hang {text-indent: -25px;}

<img src="star.gif" style="width: 60px; height: 60px;
float: left;" alt="An image of a five-pointed star."/>
<p class="hang"> This paragraph has a negatively indented first
line, which overlaps the floated image that precedes the text.  Subsequent
lines do not overlap the image, since they are not indented in any way.</p>
```

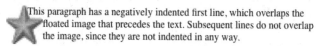

This paragraph has a negatively indented first line, which overlaps the floated image that precedes the text. Subsequent lines do not overlap the image, since they are not indented in any way.

Figure 6-2. A floated image and negative text indenting

A variety of interesting designs can be achieved using this simple technique.

This specific effect, of trying to make text wrap along the edge of a floated image, is more robustly managed with CSS Float Shapes. See Chapter 10 for details.

Any unit of length, including percentage values, may be used with text-indent. In the following case, the percentage refers to the width of the parent element of the element being indented. In other words, if you set the indent value to 10%, the first line of an affected element will be indented by 10 percent of its parent element's width, as shown in Figure 6-3:

```
div {width: 400px;}
p {text-indent: 10%;}

<div>
<p>This paragraph is contained inside a DIV, which is 400px wide, so the
first line of the paragraph is indented 40px (400 * 10% = 40).  This is
because percentages are computed with respect to the width of the element.</p>
</div>
```

This paragraph is contained inside a DIV, which is 400px wide, so the first line of the paragraph is indented 40px (400 * 10% = 40). This is because percentages are computed with respect to the width of the element.

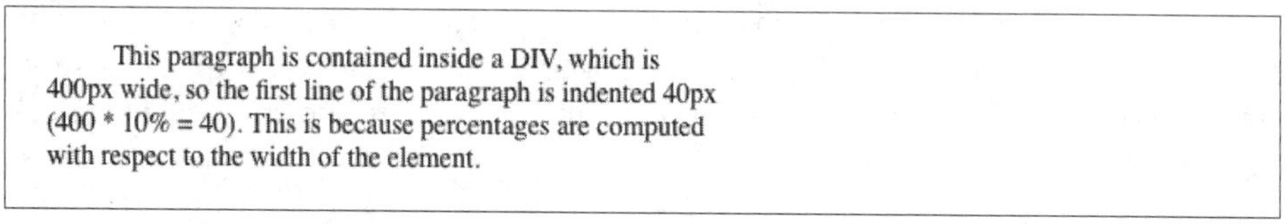

Figure 6-3. Text indenting with percentages

Note that this indentation only applies to the first line of an element, even if you insert line breaks. The interesting part about text-indent is that because it's inherited, it can have unexpected effects. For example, consider the following markup, which is illustrated in Figure 6-4:

```
div#outer {width: 500px;}
div#inner {text-indent: 10%;}
p {width: 200px;}

<div id="outer">
<div id="inner">
This first line of the DIV is indented by 50 pixels.
```

```
<p>
This paragraph is 200px wide, and the first line of the paragraph
is indented 50px.  This is because computed values for 'text-indent'
are inherited, instead of the declared values.
</p>
</div>
</div>
```

> This first line of the DIV is indented by 50 pixels.
>
> This paragraph is
> 200px wide, and the first line
> of the paragraph is indented
> 50px. This is because
> computed values for
> text-indent are inherited,
> instead of the declared values.

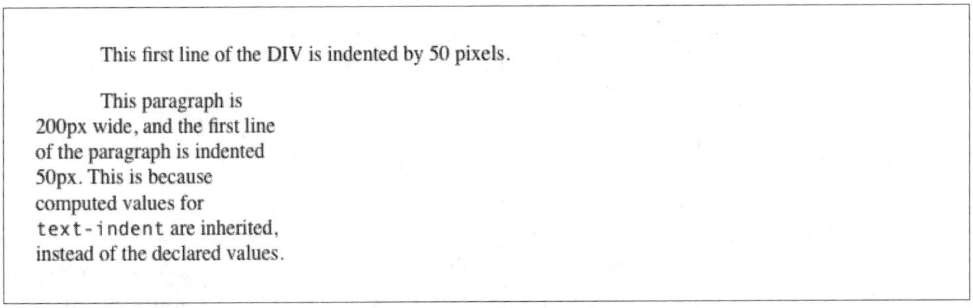

Figure 6-4. Inherited text indenting

Text Alignment

Even more basic than text-indent is the property text-align, which affects how the lines of text in an element are aligned with respect to one another.

text-align	
Values	start | end | left | right | center | justify | match-parent | start end
Initial value	In CSS3, start; in CSS 2.1, this was user agent-specific, likely depending on writing direction (e.g., left for Western languages like English)
Applies to	Block-level elements
Computed value	As specified, except in the case of match-parent
Inherited	Yes
Animatable	No
Note	CSS2 included a *<length>* value that was dropped from CSS 2.1 due to a lack of implementation

The quickest way to understand how these values work is to examine Figure 6-5, which sticks with three most widely supported values for the moment.

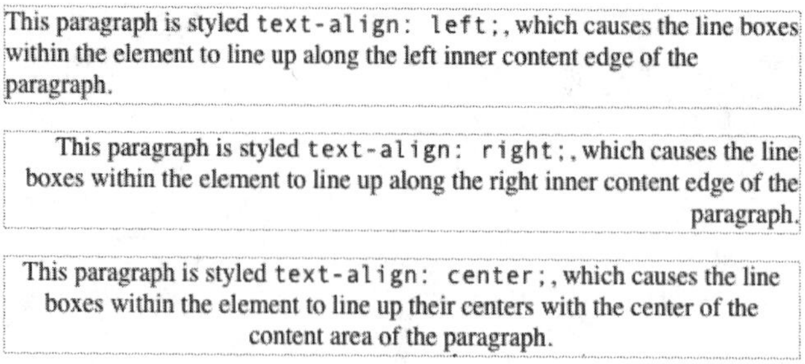

This paragraph is styled `text-align: left;`, which causes the line boxes within the element to line up along the left inner content edge of the paragraph.

This paragraph is styled `text-align: right;`, which causes the line boxes within the element to line up along the right inner content edge of the paragraph.

This paragraph is styled `text-align: center;`, which causes the line boxes within the element to line up their centers with the center of the content area of the paragraph.

Figure 6-5. Selected behaviors of the text-align property

The values `left`, `right`, and `center` cause the text within elements to be aligned exactly as described. Because `text-align` applies only to block-level elements, such as paragraphs, there's no way to center an anchor within its line without aligning the rest of the line (nor would you want to, since that would likely cause text overlap).

Historically, which is to say under CSS 2.1 rules, the default value of `text-align` is `left` in left-to-right languages, and `right` in right-to-left languages. (CSS 2.1 had no notion of vertical writing modes.) In CSS3, `left` and `right` are mapped to the start or end edge, respectively, of a vertical language. This is illustrated in Figure 6-6.

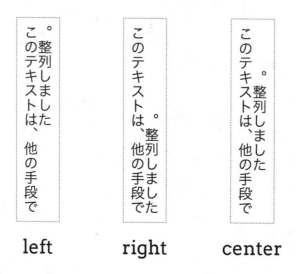

left   right   center

Figure 6-6. Left, right, and center in vertical writing modes

As you no doubt expect, center causes each line of text to be centered within the element. Although you may be tempted to believe that text-align: center is the same as the <CENTER> element, it's actually quite different. <CENTER> affected not only text, but also centered whole elements, such as tables. text-align does not control the alignment of elements, only their inline content. Figures 6-5 and 6-6 illustrate this clearly in various writing directions.

Start and end alignment

CSS3 (which is to say, the CSS Text Module Level 3 specification) added a number of new values to text-align, and even changed the default property value as compared to CSS 2.1.

The new default value of start means that the text is aligned to the start edge of its line box. In left-to-right languages like English, that's the left edge; in right-to-left languages such as Arabic, it's the right edge. In vertical languages, for that matter, it will be the top or bottom, depending on the writing direction. The upshot is that the default value is much more aware of the document's language direction while leaving the default behavior the same in the vast majority of existing cases.

In a like manner, end aligns text with the end edge of each line box—the right edge in LTR languages, the left edge in RTL languages, and so forth. The effects of these values are shown in Figure 6-7.

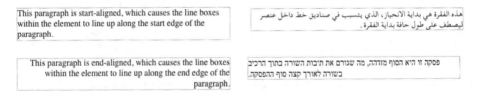

Figure 6-7. Start and end alignment

Justified text

An often-overlooked alignment value is justify, which raises some issues of its own. In justified text, both ends of a line of text are placed at the inner edges of the parent element, as Figure 6-8 shows. Then, the spacing between words and letters is adjusted so that each line is precisely the same length. Justified text is common in the print world (for example, in this book), but under CSS, a few extra considerations come into play.

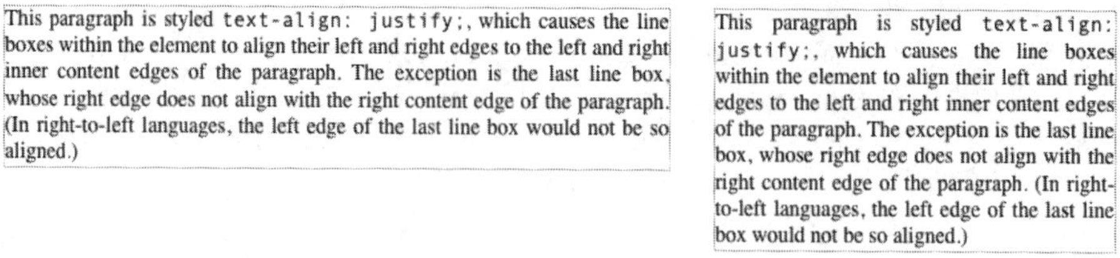

This paragraph is styled text-align: justify;, which causes the line boxes within the element to align their left and right edges to the left and right inner content edges of the paragraph. The exception is the last line box, whose right edge does not align with the right content edge of the paragraph. (In right-to-left languages, the left edge of the last line box would not be so aligned.)

This paragraph is styled text-align: justify;, which causes the line boxes within the element to align their left and right edges to the left and right inner content edges of the paragraph. The exception is the last line box, whose right edge does not align with the right content edge of the paragraph. (In right-to-left languages, the left edge of the last line box would not be so aligned.)

Figure 6-8. Justified text

The user agent—and not CSS, at least as of late 2017—determines how justified text should be stretched to fill the space between the left and right edges of the parent. Some browsers, for example, might add extra space only between words, while others might distribute the extra space between letters (although the CSS specification states that "user agents may not further increase or decrease the inter-character space" if the property letter-spacing has been assigned a length value). Other user agents may reduce space on some lines, thus mashing the text together a bit more than usual. All of these possibilities will affect the appearance of an element, and may even change its height, depending on how many lines of text result from the user agent's justification choices.

There is a property meant to provide authors more say over how full justification is accomplished: text-justify. As of late 2017, it was barely supported in any browser, with plans to add it to Firefox and some buggy experimental work in Chrome.

Parent matching

There's one more value to be covered, which is match-parent. This isn't supported by browsers, but its intent is mostly covered by inherit anyway. The idea is, if you declare text-align: match-parent, the alignment of the element will match the alignment of its parent.

So far, that sounds exactly like inherit, but there's a difference: if the parent's alignment value is start or end, the result of match-parent is to assign a computed value of left or right to the element. That wouldn't happen with inherit, which would apply start or end to the element with no changes.

The value start end, while technically part of the text-align syntax in late 2017, is not covered because it remains unimplemented and is at risk of being dropped from the specification.

Aligning the Last Line

There may be times when you want to align the text in the very last line of an element differently than you did the rest of the content. For example, you might left-align the last line of an otherwise fully justified block of text, or choose to swap from left to center alignment. For those situations, there is `text-align-last`.

text-align-last	
Values	`auto│start│end│left│right│center│justify`
Initial value	`auto`
Applies to	Block-level elements
Computed value	As specified
Inherited	Yes
Animatable	No

As with `text-align`, the quickest way to understand how these values work is to examine Figure 6-9.

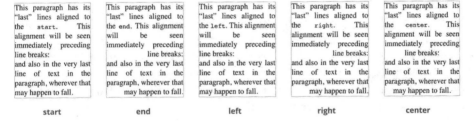

Figure 6-9. Differently aligned last lines

As the figure shows, the last lines of the elements are aligned independently of the rest of the elements, according to the elements' `text-align-last` values.

A close study of Figure 6-9 will reveal that there's more at play than just the last lines of block-level elements. In fact, `text-align-last` applies to any line of text that immediately precedes a forced line break, whether or not said line break is triggered by the end of an element. Thus, a line break occasioned by a `<br>` tag will make the line of text immediately before that break use the value of `text-align-last`. So too will it affect the last line of text in a block-level element, since a line break is generated by the element's closure.

There's an interesting wrinkle in `text-align-last`: if the first line of text in an element is also the last line of text in the element, then the value of `text-align-last` takes precedence over the value of `text-align`. Thus, the following styles will result in a centered paragraph, not a start-aligned paragraph:

```
p {text-align: start; text-align-last: center;}

<p>A paragraph.</p>
```

 As of late 2017, support for `text-align-last` was missing in Safari and Opera Mini, and Internet Explorer and Edge only supported `left`, `right`, and `center`.

Inline Alignment

Now that we've covered alignment along the inline direction, let's move on to the vertical alignment of inline elements along the block direction—things like superscripting and "vertical alignment," as it's called. (Vertical with respect to the line of text, if the text is laid out horizontally.) Since the construction of lines is a very complex topic that merits its own small book, I'll just stick to a quick overview here.

The Height of Lines

The distance between lines can be affected by changing the "height" of a line. note that "height" here is with respect to the line of text itself, assuming that the longer axis of a line is "width" even if it's written vertically. The property names we cover from here will reveal a strong bias toward Western languages and their writing directions; this is an artifact of the early days of CSS, when Western languages were the only ones that could be easily represented.

The `line-height` property refers to the distance between the baselines of lines of text rather than the size of the font, and it determines the amount by which the height of each element's box is increased or decreased. In the most basic cases, specifying `line-height` is a way to increase (or decrease) the vertical space between lines of text, but this is a misleadingly simple way of looking at how `line-height` works. `line-height` controls the *leading*, which is the extra space between lines of text above and beyond the font's size. In other words, the difference between the value of `line-height` and the size of the font is the leading.

<table>
<tr><td colspan="2" align="center">line-height</td></tr>
<tr><td>Values</td><td><number> | <length> | <percentage> | normal</td></tr>
<tr><td>Initial value</td><td>normal</td></tr>
<tr><td>Applies to</td><td>All elements (but see text regarding replaced and block-level elements)</td></tr>
<tr><td>Percentages</td><td>Relative to the font size of the element</td></tr>
<tr><td>Computed value</td><td>For length and percentage values, the absolute value; otherwise, as specified</td></tr>
<tr><td>Inherited</td><td>Yes</td></tr>
<tr><td>Animatable</td><td>Yes</td></tr>
</table>

When applied to a block-level element, line-height defines the *minimum* distance between text baselines within that element. Note that it defines a minimum, not an absolute value, and baselines of text can wind up being pushed further apart than the value of line-height. line-height does not affect layout for replaced elements, but it still applies to them.

Constructing a line

Every element in a line of text generates a *content area*, which is determined by the size of the font. This content area in turn generates an *inline box* that is, in the absence of any other factors, exactly equal to the content area. The leading generated by line-height is one of the factors that increases or decreases the height of each inline box.

To determine the leading for a given element, subtract the computed value of font-size from the computed value of line-height. That value is the total amount of leading. And remember, it can be a negative number. The leading is then divided in half, and each half-leading is applied to the top and bottom of the content area. The result is the inline box for that element.

As an example, let's say the font-size (and therefore the content area) is 14 pixels tall, and the line-height is computed to 18 pixels. The difference (4 pixels) is divided in half, and each half is applied to the top and bottom of the content area. This creates an inline box that is 18 pixels tall, with 2 extra pixels above and below the content area. This sounds like a roundabout way to describe how line-height works, but there are excellent reasons for the description.

Once all of the inline boxes have been generated for a given line of content, they are then considered in the construction of the line box. A line box is exactly as tall as needed to enclose the top of the tallest inline box and the bottom of the lowest inline box. Figure 6-10 shows a diagram of this process.

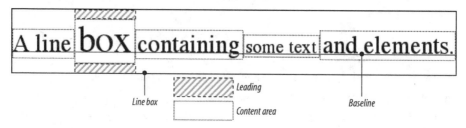

Figure 6-10. Line box diagram

Assigning values to line-height

Let's now consider the possible values of line-height. If you use the default value of normal, the user agent must calculate the space between lines. Values can vary by user agent, but they're generally around 1.2 times the size of the font, which makes line boxes taller than the value of font-size for a given element.

Many values are simple length measures (e.g., 18px or 2em), but raw <number> values are preferable in many situations. Be aware that even if you use a valid length measurement, such as 4cm, the browser (or the operating system) may be using an incorrect metric for real-world measurements, so the line height may not show up as exactly four centimeters on your monitor.

em, ex, and percentage values are calculated with respect to the font-size of the element. The results of the following CSS and HTML are shown in Figure 6-11:

```
body {line-height: 18px; font-size: 16px;}
p.cl1 {line-height: 1.5em;}
p.cl2 {font-size: 10px; line-height: 150%;}
p.cl3 {line-height: 0.33in;}

<p>This paragraph inherits a 'line-height' of 14px from the body, as well as
a 'font-size' of 13px.</p>
<p class="cl1">This paragraph has a 'line-height' of 27px(18 * 1.5), so
it will have slightly more line-height than usual.</p>
<p class="cl2">This paragraph has a 'line-height' of 15px (10 * 150%), so
it will have slightly more line-height than usual.</p>
<p class="cl3">This paragraph has a 'line-height' of 0.33in, so it will have
slightly more line-height than usual.</p>
```

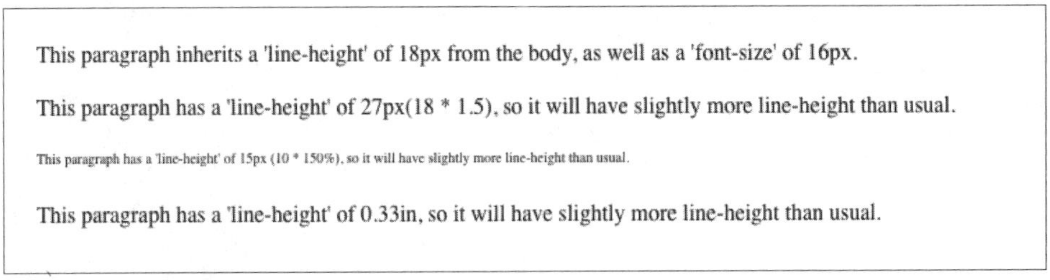

Figure 6-11. Simple calculations with the line-height property

Line-height and inheritance

When the `line-height` is inherited by one block-level element from another, things get a bit trickier. `line-height` values inherit from the parent element as computed from the parent, not the child. The results of the following markup are shown in Figure 6-12. It probably wasn't what the author had in mind:

```
body {font-size: 10px;}
div {line-height: 1em;}   /* computes to '10px' */
p {font-size: 18px;}

<div>
<p>This paragraph's 'font-size' is 18px, but the inherited 'line-height'
value is only 10px.  This may cause the lines of text to overlap each
other by a small amount.</p>
</div>
```

This paragraph's 'font-size' is 18px, but the inherited 'line-height' value is only 10px. This may cause the lines of text to overlap each other by a small amount.

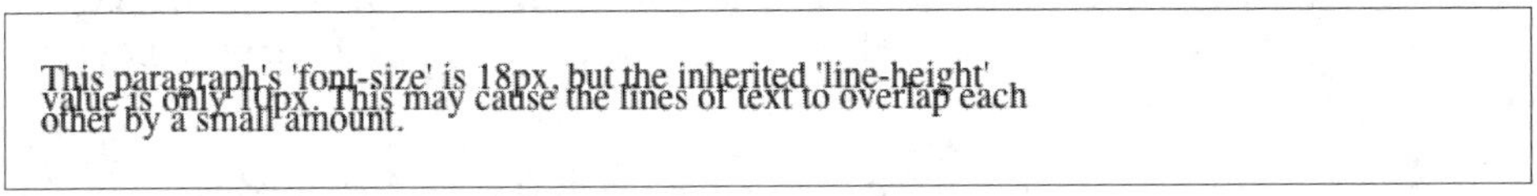

Figure 6-12. Small line-height, large font-size, slight problem

Why are the lines so close together? Because the computed `line-height` value of 10px was inherited by the paragraph from its parent `div`. One solution to the small `line-height` problem depicted in Figure 6-12 is to set an explicit `line-height` for every element, but that's not very practical. A better alternative is to specify a number, which actually sets a scaling factor:

```
body {font-size: 10px;}
div {line-height: 1;}
p {font-size: 18px;}
```

When you specify a number, you cause the scaling factor to be an inherited value instead of a computed value. The number will be applied to the element and all of its child elements so that each element has a `line-height` calculated with respect to its own `font-size` (see Figure 6-13):

```
div {line-height: 1.5;}
p {font-size: 18px;}

<div>
<p>This paragraph's 'font-size' is 18px, and since the 'line-height'
set for the parent div is 1.5, the 'line-height' for this paragraph
is 27px (18 * 1.5).</p>
</div>
```

This paragraph's 'font-size' is 18px, and since the 'line-height' set for
the parent div is 1.5, the 'line-height' for this paragraph is 27px (18 *
1.5).

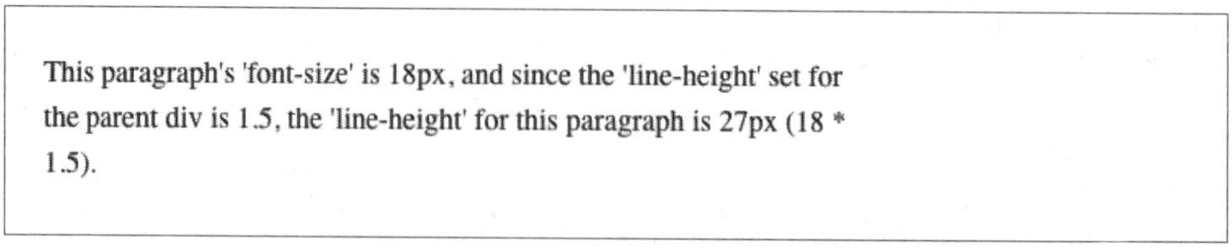

Figure 6-13. Using line-height factors to overcome inheritance problems

Though it seems like line-height distributes extra space both above and below each line of text, it actually adds (or subtracts) a certain amount from the top and bottom of an inline element's content area to create an inline box. Assume that the default font-size of a paragraph is 12pt and consider the following:

```
p {line-height: 16pt;}
```

Since the "inherent" line height of 12-point text is 12 points, the preceding rule will place an extra 4 points of space around each line of text in the paragraph. This extra amount is divided in two, with half going above each line and the other half below. You now have 16 points between the baselines, which is an indirect result of how the extra space is apportioned.

If you specify the value inherit, then the element will use the computed value for its parent element. This isn't really any different than allowing the value to inherit naturally, except in terms of specificity and cascade resolution.

Now that you have a basic grasp of how lines are constructed, let's talk about "vertically" aligning elements relative to the line box—that is, displacing them along the block direction.

Vertically Aligning Text

If you've ever used the elements sup and sub (the superscript and subscript elements), or used an image with markup such as <img src="foo.gif" align="middle">, then you've done some rudimentary vertical alignment. In CSS, the vertical-align property applies only to inline elements and replaced elements such as images and form inputs. vertical-align is not an inherited property.

Because of the property name `vertical-align`, this section will use the terms "vertical" and "horizontal" to refer to the block and inline directions of the text.

vertical-align

Values	`baseline` | `sub` | `super` | `top` | `text-top` | `middle` | `bottom` | `text-bottom` | *<length>* | *<percentage>*
Initial value	`baseline`
Applies to	Inline elements and table cells
Percentages	Refer to the value of `line-height` for the element
Computed value	For percentage and length values, the absolute length; otherwise, as specified
Inherited	No
Animatable	*<length>*, *<percentage>*
Note	When applied to table cells, only the values `baseline`, `top`, `middle`, and `bottom` are recognized

`vertical-align` accepts any one of eight keywords, a percentage value, or a length value. The keywords are a mix of the familiar and unfamiliar: `baseline` (the default value), `sub`, `super`, `bottom`, `text-bottom`, `middle`, `top`, and `text-top`. We'll examine how each keyword works in relation to inline elements.

Remember: `vertical-align` does *not* affect the alignment of content within a block-level element. You can, however, use it to affect the vertical alignment of elements within table cells.

Baseline alignment

`vertical-align: baseline` forces the baseline of an element to align with the baseline of its parent. Browsers, for the most part, do this anyway, since you'd probably expect the bottoms of all text elements in a line to be aligned.

If a vertically aligned element doesn't have a baseline—that is, if it's an image, a form input, or another replaced element—then the bottom of the element is aligned with the baseline of its parent, as Figure 6-14 shows:

```
img {vertical-align: baseline;}

<p>The image found in this paragraph <img src="dot.gif" alt="A dot" /> has its
bottom edge aligned with the baseline of the text in the paragraph.</p>
```

The image found in this paragraph . has its bottom edge aligned with the
baseline of the text in the paragraph.

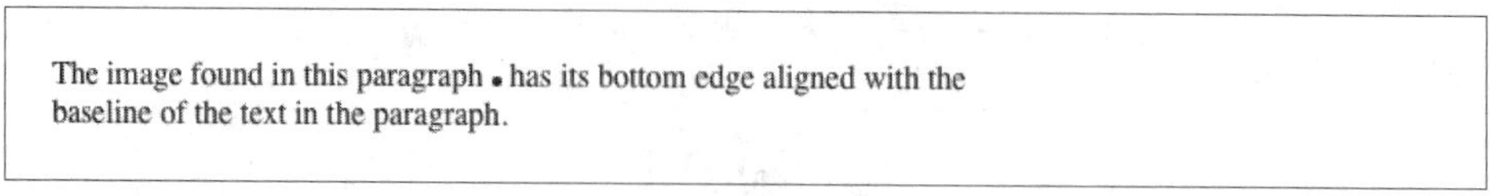

Figure 6-14. Baseline alignment of an image

This alignment rule is important because it causes some web browsers to always put a
replaced element's bottom edge on the baseline, even if there is no other text in the
line. For example, let's say you have an image in a table cell all by itself. The image
may actually be on a baseline, but in some browsers, the space below the baseline
causes a gap to appear beneath the image. Other browsers will "shrink-wrap" the
image with the table cell, and no gap will appear. The gap behavior is correct, despite
its lack of appeal to most authors.

 See the aged and yet still relevant article "Images, Tables, and Mysterious Gaps" (*http://mzl.la/19E2dJ7*) for a more detailed explanation of gap behavior and ways to work around it.

Superscripting and subscripting

The declaration vertical-align: sub causes an element to be subscripted, meaning
that its baseline (or bottom, if it's a replaced element) is lowered with respect to its
parent's baseline. The specification doesn't define the distance the element is lowered,
so it may vary depending on the user agent.

super is the opposite of sub; it raises the element's baseline (or bottom of a replaced
element) with respect to the parent's baseline. Again, the distance the text is raised
depends on the user agent.

Note that the values sub and super do *not* change the element's font size, so subscripted or superscripted text will not become smaller (or larger). Instead, any text in
the sub- or superscripted element should be, by default, the same size as text in the
parent element, as illustrated by Figure 6-15:

```
span.raise {vertical-align: super;}
span.lower {vertical-align: sub;}

<p>This paragraph contains <span class="raise">superscripted</span>
and <span class="lower">subscripted</span> text.</P>
```

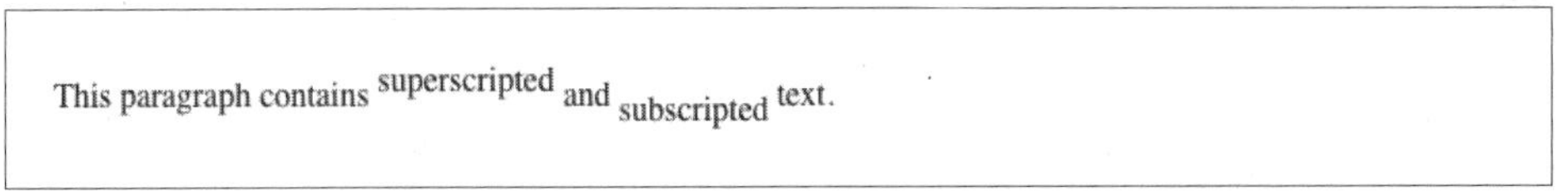

This paragraph contains ^{superscripted} and _{subscripted} text.

Figure 6-15. Superscript and subscript alignment

 If you wish to make super- or subscripted text smaller than the text of its parent element, you can do so using the property font-size.

Bottom feeding

vertical-align: bottom aligns the bottom of the element's inline box with the bottom of the line box. For example, the following markup results in Figure 6-16:

```
.feeder {vertical-align: bottom;}

<p>This paragraph, as you can see quite clearly, contains
a <img src="tall.gif" alt="tall" class="feeder" /> image and
a <img src="short.gif" alt="short" class="feeder" /> image,
and then some text that is not tall.</p>
```

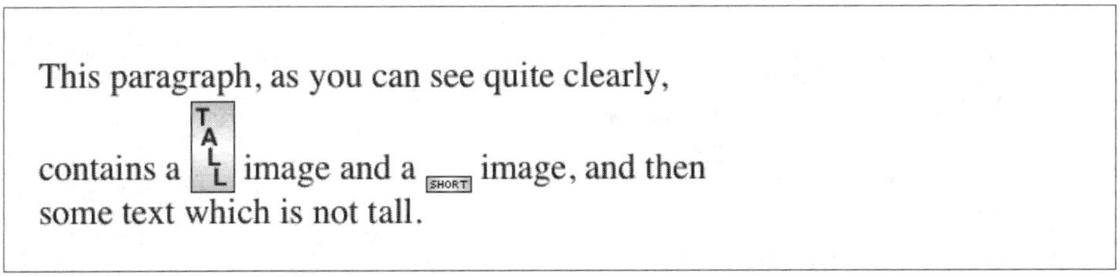

This paragraph, as you can see quite clearly,

contains a image and a image, and then some text which is not tall.

Figure 6-16. Bottom alignment

The second line of the paragraph in Figure 6-16 contains two inline elements, whose bottom edges are aligned with each other. They're also below the baseline of the text.

vertical-align: text-bottom refers to the bottom of the text in the line. For the purposes of this value, replaced elements, or any other kinds of non-text elements, are ignored. Instead, a "default" text box is considered. This default box is derived from the font-size of the parent element. The bottom of the aligned element's inline box is then aligned with the bottom of the default text box. Thus, given the following markup, you get a result like the one shown in Figure 6-17:

```
img.tbot {vertical-align: text-bottom;}

<p>Here: a <img src="tall.gif" style="vertical-align: middle;" alt="tall" />
image, and then a <img src="short.gif" class="tbot" alt="short" /> image.</p>
```

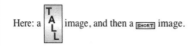

Figure 6-17. Text-bottom alignment

Getting on top

Employing `vertical-align: top` has the opposite effect of `bottom`. Likewise, `vertical-align: text-top` is the reverse of `text-bottom`. Figure 6-18 shows how the following markup would be rendered:

```
.up {vertical-align: top;}
.textup {vertical-align: text-top;}

<p>Here: a <img src="tall.gif" alt="tall image"> tall image, and then
<span class="up">some text</span> that's been vertically aligned.</p>
<p>Here: a <img src="tall.gif" class="textup" alt="tall"> image that's been
vertically aligned, and then a <img src="short.gif" class="textup" alt="short" />
image that's similarly aligned.</p>
```

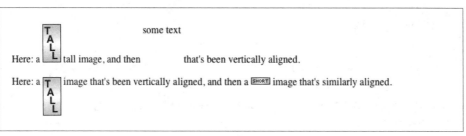

Figure 6-18. Aligning with the top and text-top of a line

The exact position of this alignment will depend on which elements are in the line, how tall they are, and the size of the parent element's font.

In the middle

There's the value `middle`, which is usually (but not always) applied to images. It does not have the exact effect you might assume given its name. `middle` aligns the middle of an inline element's box with a point that is `0.5ex` above the baseline of the parent element, where `1ex` is defined relative to the `font-size` for the parent element. Figure 6-19 shows this in more detail.

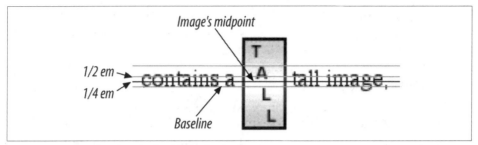

Figure 6-19. Precise detail of middle alignment

Since most user agents treat 1ex as one-half em, middle usually aligns the vertical midpoint of an element with a point one-quarter em above the parent's baseline, though this is not a defined distance and so can vary from one user agent to another.

Percentages

Percentages don't let you simulate align="middle" for images. Instead, setting a percentage value for vertical-align raises or lowers the baseline of the element (or the bottom edge of a replaced element) by the amount declared, with respect to the parent's baseline. (The percentage you specify is calculated as a percentage of line-height for the element, *not* its parent.) Positive percentage values raise the element, and negative values lower it. Depending on how the text is raised or lowered, it can appear to be placed in adjacent lines, as shown in Figure 6-20, so take care when using percentage values:

```
sub {vertical-align: -100%;}
sup {vertical-align: 100%;}

<p>We can either <sup>soar to new heights</sup> or, instead,
<sub>sink into despair...</sub></p>
```

soar to new heights
We can either   or , instead,
                              sink into despair...

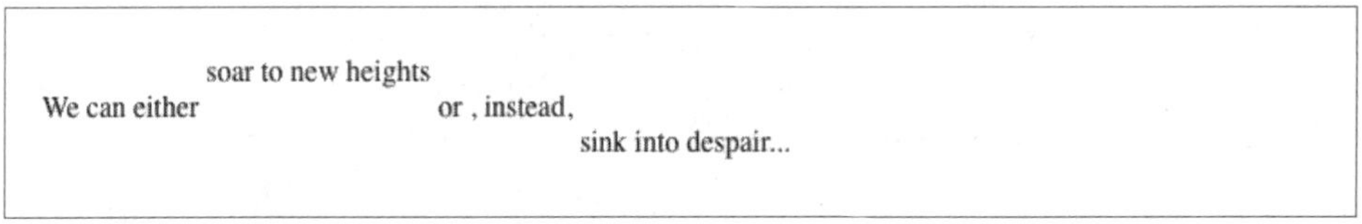

Figure 6-20. Percentages and fun effects

Let's consider percentage values in more detail. Assume the following:

```
<div style="font-size: 14px; line-height: 18px;">
I felt that, if nothing else, I deserved a
<span style="vertical-align: 50%;">raise</span> for my efforts.
</div>
```

The 50%-aligned span element has its baseline raised nine pixels, which is half of the element's inherited line-height value of 18px, *not* the seven pixels that would be half the font-size.

Length alignment

Finally, let's consider vertical alignment with a specific length. vertical-align is very basic: it shifts an element up or down by the declared distance. Thus, vertical-align: 5px; will shift an element upward five pixels from its unaligned placement. Negative length values shift the element downward. This simple form of alignment did not exist in CSS1, but it was added in CSS2.

It's important to realize that vertically aligned text does not become part of another line, nor does it overlap text in other lines. Consider Figure 6-21, in which some vertically aligned text appears in the middle of a paragraph.

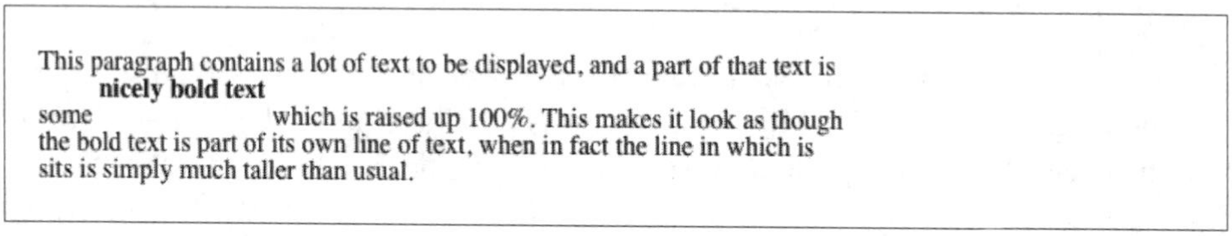

This paragraph contains a lot of text to be displayed, and a part of that text is
nicely bold text
some   which is raised up 100%. This makes it look as though
the bold text is part of its own line of text, when in fact the line in which is
sits is simply much taller than usual.

Figure 6-21. Vertical alignments can cause lines to get taller

As you can see, any vertically aligned element can affect the height of the line. Recall the description of a line box, which is exactly as tall as necessary to enclose the top of the tallest inline box and the bottom of the lowest inline box. This includes inline boxes that have been shifted up or down by vertical alignment.

Word Spacing and Letter Spacing

Now that we've dealt with vertical alignment of inline elements, let's return to the inline direction for a look at manipulating word and letter spacing. As usual, these properties have some nonintuitive issues.

Word Spacing

The word-spacing property accepts a positive or negative length. This length is *added* to the standard space between words. In effect, word-spacing is used to modify inter-word spacing. Therefore, the default value of normal is the same as setting a value of zero (0).

word-spacing

Values	*<length>* | normal
Initial value	normal
Applies to	All elements
Computed value	For normal, the absolute length 0; otherwise, the absolute length
Inherited	Yes
Animatable	Yes

If you supply a positive length value, then the space between words will increase. Setting a negative value for word-spacing brings words closer together:

```
p.spread {word-spacing: 0.5em;}
p.tight {word-spacing: -0.5em;}
p.base {word-spacing: normal;}
p.norm {word-spacing: 0;}

<p class="spread">The spaces between words in this paragraph will be increased
    by 0.5em.</p>
<p class="tight">The spaces between words in this paragraph will be decreased
    by 0.5em.</p>
<p class="base">The spaces between words in this paragraph will be normal.</p>
<p class="norm">The spaces between words in this paragraph will be normal.</p>
```

Manipulating these settings has the effect shown in Figure 6-22.

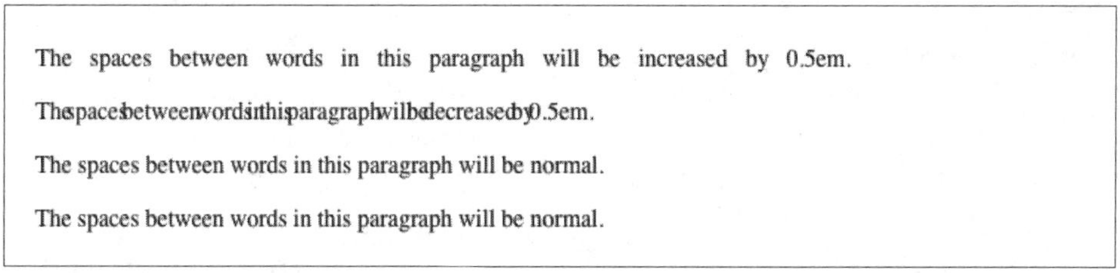

The spaces between words in this paragraph will be increased by 0.5em.

Thespacesbetweenwordsinthisparagraphwilbedecreasedby0.5em.

The spaces between words in this paragraph will be normal.

The spaces between words in this paragraph will be normal.

Figure 6-22. Changing the space between words

So far, I haven't actually given you a precise definition of "word." In the simplest CSS terms, a "word" is any string of non-whitespace characters that is surrounded by whitespace of some kind. This definition has no real semantic meaning; it simply assumes that a document contains words, each of which is surrounded by one or more whitespace characters. A CSS-aware user agent cannot be expected to decide what is a valid word in a given language and what isn't. This definition, such as it is, means word-spacing is unlikely to work in any languages that employ pictographs, or non-Roman writing styles. The property allows you to create very unreadable documents, as Figure 6-23 makes clear. Use word-spacing with care.

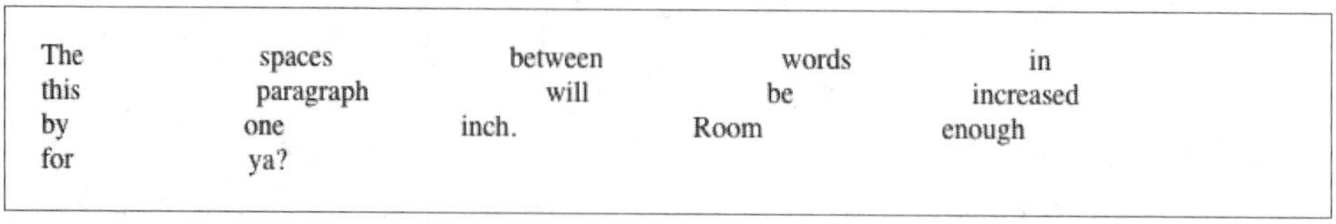

The	spaces		between	words	in
this	paragraph		will	be	increased
by	one	inch.		Room	enough
for	ya?				

Figure 6-23. Really wide word spacing

Letter Spacing

Many of the issues you encounter with word-spacing also occur with letter-spacing. The only real difference between the two is that letter-spacing modifies the space between characters or letters.

---

letter-spacing

Values	*<length>*	normal
Initial value	normal
Applies to	All elements
Computed value	For length values, the absolute length; otherwise, normal
Inherited	Yes
Animatable	Yes

As with the word-spacing property, the permitted values of letter-spacing include any length. The default keyword is normal (making it the same as letter-spacing: 0). Any length value you enter will increase or decrease the space between letters by that amount. Figure 6-24 shows the results of the following markup:

```
p {letter-spacing: 0;}     /* identical to 'normal' */
p.spacious {letter-spacing: 0.25em;}
p.tight {letter-spacing: -0.25em;}

<p>The letters in this paragraph are spaced as normal.</p>
<p class="spacious">The letters in this paragraph are spread out a bit.</p>
<p class="tight">The letters in this paragraph are a bit smashed together.</p>
```

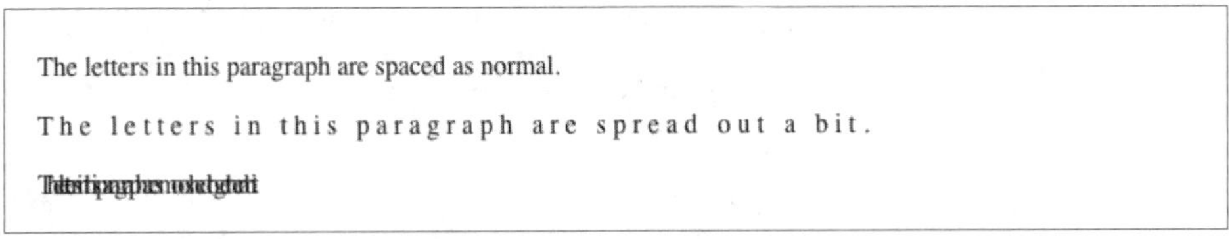

The letters in this paragraph are spaced as normal.

The letters in this paragraph are spread out a bit.

T̶h̶e̶ ̶l̶e̶t̶t̶e̶r̶s̶ ̶i̶n̶ ̶t̶h̶i̶s̶ ̶p̶a̶r̶a̶g̶r̶a̶p̶h̶ ̶a̶r̶e̶ ̶c̶r̶u̶s̶h̶e̶d̶

Figure 6-24. Various kinds of letter spacing

Using letter-spacing to increase emphasis is a time-honored technique. You might write the following declaration and get an effect like the one shown in Figure 6-25:

```
strong {letter-spacing: 0.2em;}

<p>This paragraph contains <strong>strongly emphasized text</strong>
which is spread out for extra emphasis.</p>
```

This paragraph contains **s t r o n g l y e m p h a s i z e d t e x t** which is spread out for extra emphasis.

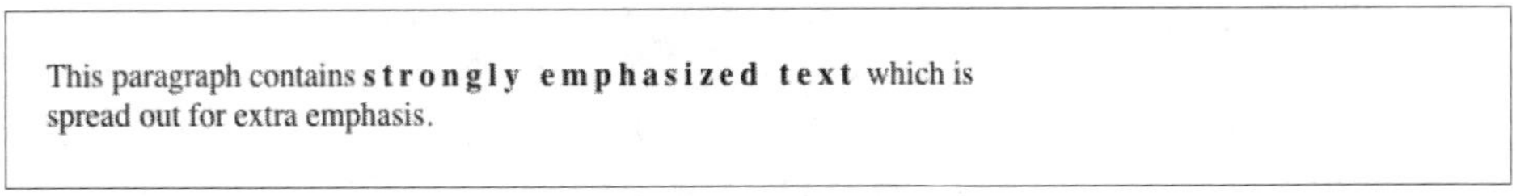

Figure 6-25. Using letter-spacing to increase emphasis

 If a page uses fonts with features like ligatures, and those features are enabled, then altering letter or word spacing can effectively disable them. Browsers will not recalculate ligatures or other joins when letter spacing is altered, for example.

Spacing and Alignment

The value of word-spacing may be influenced by the value of the property text-align. If an element is justified, the spaces between letters and words may be altered to fit the text along the full width of the line. This may in turn alter the spacing declared by the author with word-spacing. If a length value is assigned to letter-spacing, then it cannot be changed by text-align; but if the value of letter-spacing is normal, then inter-character spacing may be changed to justify the text. CSS does not specify how the spacing should be calculated, so user agents fill it in with their own algorithms.

Note that the computed value is inherited, so child elements with larger or smaller text will have the same letter spacing as their parent element. You cannot define a scaling factor for word-spacing or letter-spacing to be inherited in place of the computed value (as is the case with line-height). As a result, you may run into problems such as those shown in Figure 6-26:

```
p {letter-spacing: 0.25em; font-size: 20px;}
small {font-size: 50%;}
```

```
<p>This spacious paragraph features <small>tiny text that is just
as spacious</small>, even though the author probably wanted the
spacing to be in proportion to the size of the text.</p>
```

This spacious paragraph features tiny text which is just as spacious, even though the author probably wanted the spacing to be in proportion to the size of the text.

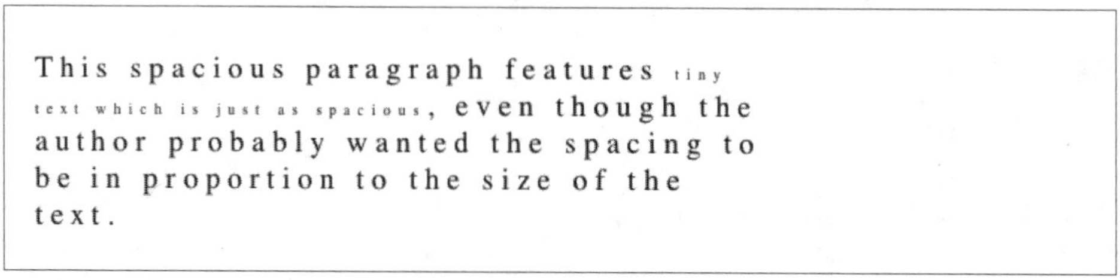

Figure 6-26. Inherited letter spacing

The only way to achieve letter spacing that's in proportion to the size of the text is to set it explicitly, as follows:

```
p {letter-spacing: 0.25em;}
small {font-size: 50%; letter-spacing: 0.25em;}
```

Text Transformation

With the alignment properties covered, let's look at ways to manipulate the capitalization of text using the property text-transform.

text-transform

Values	uppercase | lowercase | capitalize | none
Initial value	none
Applies to	All elements
Computed value	As specified
Inherited	Yes
Animatable	No

The default value none leaves the text alone and uses whatever capitalization exists in the source document. As their names imply, uppercase and lowercase convert text into all upper- or lowercase characters. Finally, capitalize capitalizes only the first letter of each word. Figure 6-27 illustrates each of these settings in a variety of ways:

```
h1 {text-transform: capitalize;}
strong {text-transform: uppercase;}
p.cummings {text-transform: lowercase;}
p.raw {text-transform: none;}
```

```
<h1>The heading-one at the beginninG</h1>
<p> By default, text is displayed in the capitalization it has in the source
document, but <strong>it is possible to change this</strong> using
the property 'text-transform'.
</p>
<p class="cummings">
For example, one could Create TEXT such as might have been Written by
the late Poet e.e.cummings.
</p>
<p class="raw">
If you feel the need to Explicitly Declare the transformation of text
to be 'none', that can be done as well.
</p>
```

The Heading-one At The BeginninG

By default, text is displayed in the capitalization it has in the source
document, but **IT IS POSSIBLE TO CHANGE THIS** using the property
'text-transform'.

for example, one could create text such as might have been written by the late
poet e.e.cummings.

If you feel the need to Explicitly Declare the transformation of text to be
'none', that can be done as well.

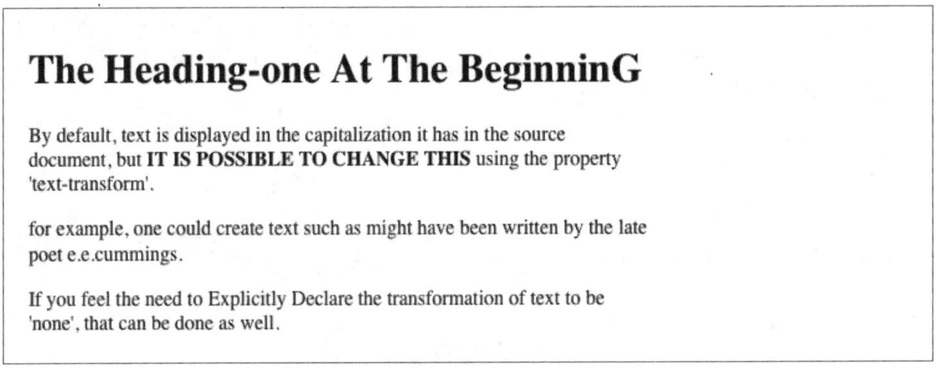

Figure 6-27. Various kinds of text transformation

Different user agents may have different ways of deciding where words begin and, as a result, which letters are capitalized. For example, the text "heading-one" in the h1 element, shown in Figure 6-27, could be rendered in one of two ways: "Heading-one" or "Heading-One." CSS does not say which is correct, so either is possible.

You probably also noticed that the last letter in the h1 element in Figure 6-27 is still uppercase. This is correct: when applying a text-transform of capitalize, CSS only requires user agents to make sure the first letter of each word is capitalized. They can ignore the rest of the word.

As a property, text-transform may seem minor, but it's very useful if you suddenly decide to capitalize all your h1 elements. Instead of individually changing the content of all your h1 elements, you can just use text-transform to make the change for you:

```
h1 {text-transform: uppercase;}

<h1>This is an H1 element</h1>
```

The advantages of using text-transform are twofold. First, you only need to write a single rule to make this change, rather than changing the h1 itself. Second, if you

decide later to switch from all capitals back to initial capitals, the change is even easier, as Figure 6-28 shows:

```
h1 {text-transform: capitalize;}

<h1>This is an H1 element</h1>
```

This Is An H1 Element

Figure 6-28. Transforming an h1 element

Remember that `capitalize` is a simple letter substitution at the beginning of each
"word." It does not mean that common headline-capitalization conventions, such as
leaving articles ("a," "an," "the") all lowercase, will be enforced.

Text Decoration

Next we come to `text-decoration`, which is a fascinating property that offers a
truckload of interesting behaviors.

<table>
<tr><th colspan="2">text-decoration</th></tr>
<tr><td>Values</td><td>none | [underline || overline || line-through || blink]</td></tr>
<tr><td>Initial value</td><td>none</td></tr>
<tr><td>Applies to</td><td>All elements</td></tr>
<tr><td>Computed value</td><td>As specified</td></tr>
<tr><td>Inherited</td><td>No</td></tr>
<tr><td>Animatable</td><td>No</td></tr>
</table>

As you might expect, `underline` causes an element to be underlined, just like the U
element in ancient HTML. `overline` causes the opposite effect—drawing a line
across the top of the text. The value `line-through` draws a line straight through the
middle of the text, which is also known as *strikethrough text* and is equivalent to the S
and `strike` elements in HTML. `blink` causes the text to blink on and off, just like the
much-maligned `blink` tag supported by Netscape. Figure 6-29 shows examples of
each of these values:

```
p.emph {text-decoration: underline;}
p.topper {text-decoration: overline;}
p.old {text-decoration: line-through;}
p.annoy {text-decoration: blink;}
p.plain {text-decoration: none;}
```

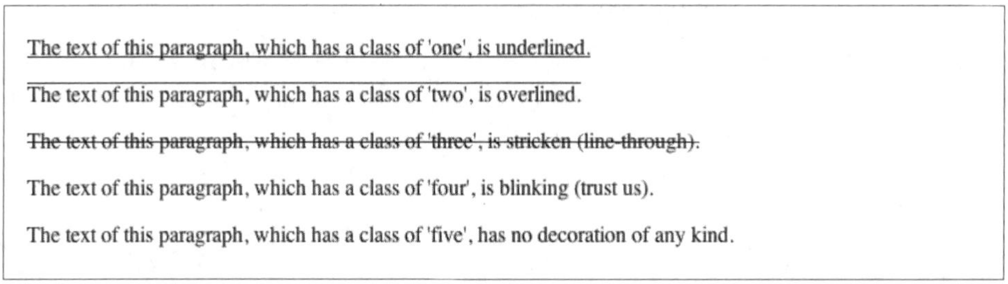

The text of this paragraph, which has a class of 'one', is underlined.

The text of this paragraph, which has a class of 'two', is overlined.

~~The text of this paragraph, which has a class of 'three', is stricken (line-through).~~

The text of this paragraph, which has a class of 'four', is blinking (trust us).

The text of this paragraph, which has a class of 'five', has no decoration of any kind.

Figure 6-29. Various kinds of text decoration

It's impossible to show the effect of blink in print, but it's easy enough to imagine (perhaps all too easy). Incidentally, user agents are not required to actually blink blink text; and as of this writing, all known user agents were dropping or had dropped support for the blinking effect. (Internet Explorer never had it.)

The value none turns off any decoration that might otherwise have been applied to an element. Usually, undecorated text is the default appearance, but not always. For example, links are usually underlined by default. If you want to suppress the underlining of hyperlinks, you can use the following CSS rule to do so:

```
a {text-decoration: none;}
```

If you explicitly turn off link underlining with this sort of rule, the only visual difference between the anchors and normal text will be their color (at least by default, though there's no ironclad guarantee that there will be a difference in their colors).

Bear in mind that many users are annoyed when they realize you've turned off link underlining. It's a matter of opinion, so let your own tastes be your guide, but remember: if your link colors aren't sufficiently different from normal text, users may have a hard time finding hyperlinks in your documents, particularly users with one form or another of color blindness.

You can also combine decorations in a single rule. If you want all hyperlinks to be both underlined and overlined, the rule is:

```
a:link, a:visited {text-decoration: underline overline;}
```

Be careful, though: if you have two different decorations matched to the same element, the value of the rule that wins out will completely replace the value of the loser. Consider:

```
h2.stricken {text-decoration: line-through;}
h2 {text-decoration: underline overline;}
```

Given these rules, any h2 element with a class of stricken will have only a line-through decoration. The underline and overline decorations are lost, since shorthand values replace one another instead of accumulating.

Weird Decorations

Now, let's look into the unusual side of text-decoration. The first oddity is that text-decoration is *not* inherited. No inheritance implies that any decoration lines drawn with the text—under, over, or through it—will be the same color as the parent element. This is true even if the descendant elements are a different color, as depicted in Figure 6-30:

```
p {text-decoration: underline; color: black;}
strong {color: gray;}

<p>This paragraph, which is black and has a black underline, also contains
<strong>strongly emphasized text</strong> which has the black underline
beneath
      it as well.</p>
```

This paragraph, which is black and has a black underline, also contains strongly emphasized text which has the black underline beneath it as well.

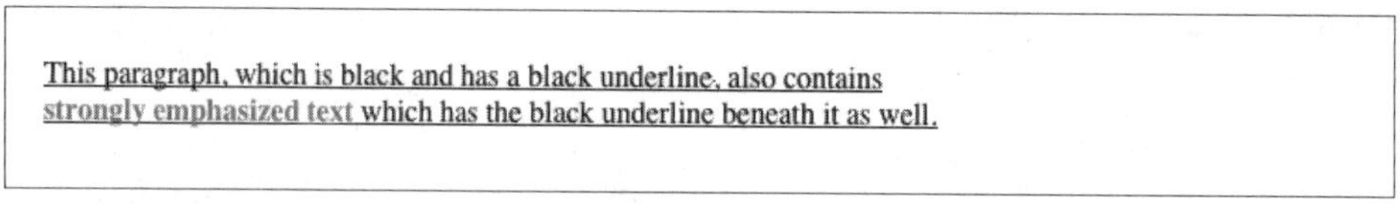

Figure 6-30. Color consistency in underlines

Why is this so? Because the value of text-decoration is not inherited, the strong element assumes a default value of none. Therefore, the strong element has *no* underline. Now, there is very clearly a line under the strong element, so it seems silly to say that it has none. Nevertheless, it doesn't. What you see under the strong element is the paragraph's underline, which is effectively "spanning" the strong element. You can see it more clearly if you alter the styles for the boldface element, like this:

```
p {text-decoration: underline; color: black;}
strong {color: gray; text-decoration: none;}

<p>This paragraph, which is black and has a black underline, also contains
<strong>strongly emphasized text</strong> which has the black underline beneath
      it as well.</p>
```

The result is identical to the one shown in Figure 6-30, since all you've done is to explicitly declare what was already the case. In other words, there is no way to turn off underlining (or overlining or a line-through) generated by a parent element.

When text-decoration is combined with vertical-align, even stranger things can happen. Figure 6-31 shows one of these oddities. Since the sup element has no decoration of its own, but it is elevated within an overlined element, the overline cuts through the middle of the sup element:

```
p {text-decoration: overline; font-size: 12pt;}
sup {vertical-align: 50%; font-size: 12pt;}
```

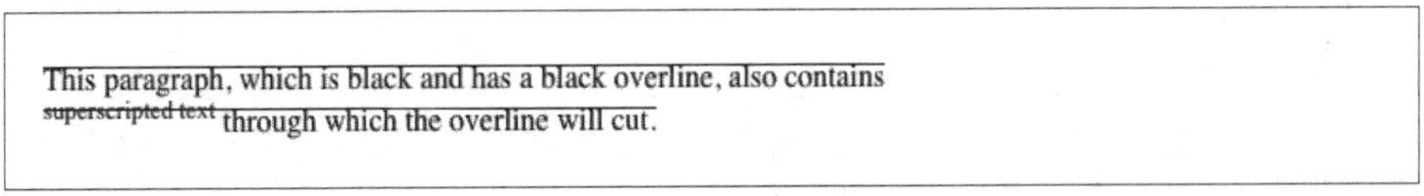

This paragraph, which is black and has a black overline, also contains ~~superscripted text~~ through which the overline will cut.

Figure 6-31. Correct, although strange, decorative behavior

By now you may be vowing never to use text decorations because of all the problems they could create. In fact, I've given you the simplest possible outcomes since we've explored only the way things *should* work according to the specification. In reality, some web browsers do turn off underlining in child elements, even though they aren't supposed to. The reason browsers violate the specification is author expectations. Consider this markup:

```
p {text-decoration: underline; color: black;}
strong {color: silver; text-decoration: none;}

<p>This paragraph, which is black and has a black underline, also contains
<strong>boldfaced text</strong> which does not have black underline
beneath it.</p>
```

Figure 6-32 shows the display in a web browser that has switched off the underlining for the strong element.

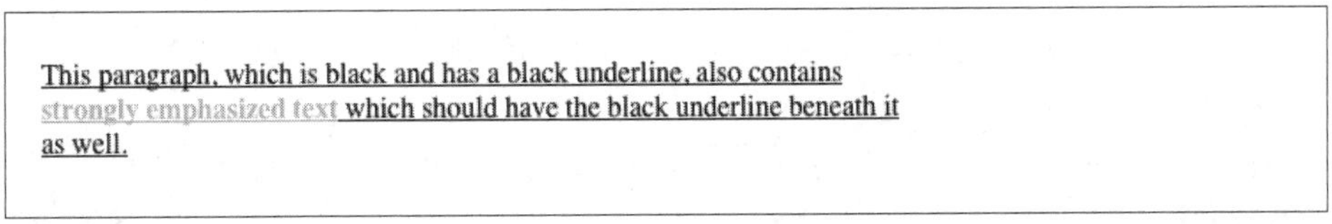

This paragraph, which is black and has a black underline, also contains strongly emphasized text which should have the black underline beneath it as well.

Figure 6-32. How some browsers really behave

The caveat here is that many browsers *do* follow the specification, and future versions of existing browsers (or any other user agents) might one day follow the specification precisely. If you depend on using none to suppress decorations, it's important to realize that it may come back to haunt you in the future, or even cause you problems in the present. Then again, future versions of CSS may include the means to turn off decorations without using none incorrectly, so maybe there's hope.

There is a way to change the color of a decoration without violating the specification. As you'll recall, setting a text decoration on an element means that the entire element has the same color decoration, even if there are child elements of different colors. To match the decoration color with an element, you must explicitly declare its decoration, as follows:

```
p {text-decoration: underline; color: black;}
strong {color: silver; text-decoration: underline;}

<p>This paragraph, which is black and has a black underline, also contains
<strong>strongly emphasized text</strong> which has the black underline
beneath it as well, but whose gray underline overlays the black underline
of its parent.</p>
```

In Figure 6-33, the strong element is set to be gray and to have an underline. The gray underline visually "overwrites" the parent's black underline, so the decoration's color matches the color of the strong element.

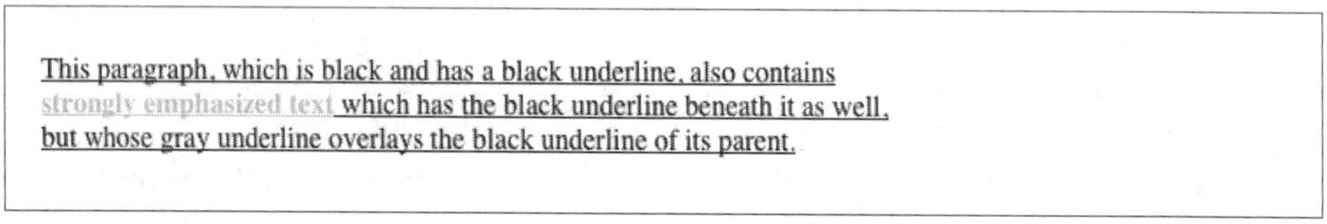

This paragraph, which is black and has a black underline, also contains strongly emphasized text which has the black underline beneath it as well, but whose gray underline overlays the black underline of its parent.

Figure 6-33. Overcoming the default behavior of underlines

Text Rendering

A recent addition to CSS is text-rendering, which is actually an SVG property that is nevertheless treated as CSS by supporting user agents. It lets authors indicate what the user agent should prioritize when displaying text.

text-rendering

Values	auto | optimizeSpeed | optimizeLegibility | geometricPrecision
Initial value	auto
Applies to	All elements
Inherited	Yes
Animatable	Yes

The values optimizeSpeed and optimizeLegibility are relatively self-explanatory, indicating that drawing speed should be favored over legibility features like kerning and ligatures (for optimizeSpeed) or vice versa (for optimizeLegibility).

The precise legibility features that are used with optimizeLegibility are not explicitly defined, and the text rendering often depends on the operating system on which the user agent is running, so the exact results may vary. Figure 6-34 shows text optimized for speed, and then optimized for legibility.

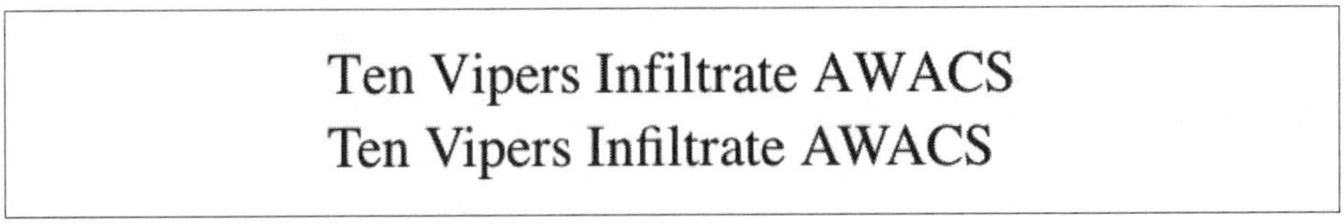

> ## Ten Vipers Infiltrate AWACS
> ## Ten Vipers Infiltrate AWACS

Figure 6-34. Different optimizations

As you can see in Figure 6-34, the differences between the two optimizations are objectively rather small, but they can have a noticeable impact on readability.

 Some user agents will always optimize for legibility, even when optimizing for speed. This is likely an effect of rendering speeds having gotten so fast in the past few years.

The value geometricPrecision, on the other hand, directs the user agent to draw the text as precisely as possible, such that it could be scaled up or down with no loss of fidelity. You might think that this is always the case, but not so. Some fonts change kerning or ligature effects at different text sizes, for example, providing more kerning space at smaller sizes and tightening up the kerning space as the size is increased. With geometricPrecision, those hints are ignored as the text size changes. If it helps, think of it as the user agent drawing the text as though all the text is a series of SVG paths, not font glyphs.

Even by the usual standard of web standards, the value auto is pretty vaguely defined in SVG:

> the user agent shall make appropriate tradeoffs to balance speed, legibility and geometric precision, but with legibility given more importance than speed and geometric precision.

That's it: user agents get to do what they think is appropriate, leaning towards legibility.

Text Shadows

Sometimes, you just really need your text to cast a shadow. That's where text-shadow comes in. The syntax might look a little wacky at first, but it should become clear enough with just a little practice.

text-shadow

Values	none	[<length> || <length> <length> <length>?]#
Initial value	none
Applies to	All elements
Inherited	No
Animatable	Yes

The default is to not have a drop shadow for text. Otherwise, it's possible to define one or more shadows. Each shadow is defined by an optional color and three length values, the last of which is also optional.

The color sets the shadow's color so it's possible to define green, purple, or even white shadows. If the color is omitted, the shadow will be the same color as the text.

The first two length values determine the offset distance of the shadow from the text; the first is the horizontal offset and the second is the vertical offset. To define a solid, un-blurred green shadow offset five pixels to the right and half an em down from the text, as shown in Figure 6-35, you would write:

```
text-shadow: green 5px 0.5em;
```

Negative lengths cause the shadow to be offset to the left and upward from the original text. The following, also shown in Figure 6-35, places a light blue shadow five pixels to the left and half an em above the text:

```
text-shadow: rgb(128,128,255) -5px -0.5em;
```

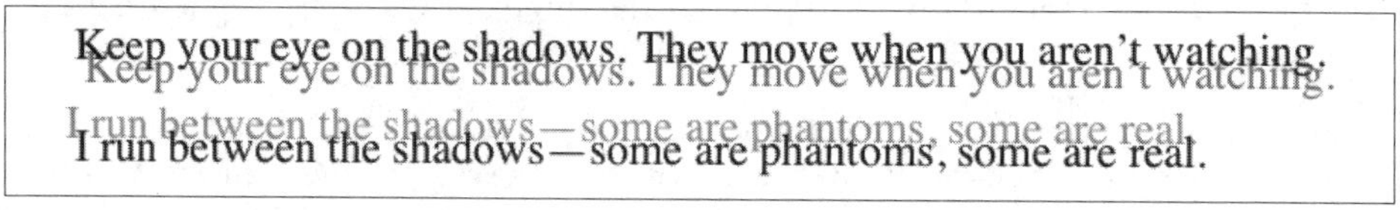

Keep your eye on the shadows. They move when you aren't watching.
I run between the shadows—some are phantoms, some are real.

Figure 6-35. Simple shadows

The optional third length value defines a *blur radius* for the shadow. The blur radius is defined as the distance from the shadow's outline to the edge of the blurring effect. A radius of two pixels would result in blurring that fills the space between the shadow's outline and the edge of the blurring. The exact blurring method is not defined, so different user agents might employ different effects. As an example, the following styles are rendered as shown in Figure 6-36:

```
p.cl1 {color: black; text-shadow: gray 2px 2px 4px;}
p.cl2 {color: white; text-shadow: 0 0 4px black;}
p.cl3 {color: black; text-shadow: 1em 0.5em 5px red, -0.5em -1em hsla(100,75%,
    25%,0.33);}
```

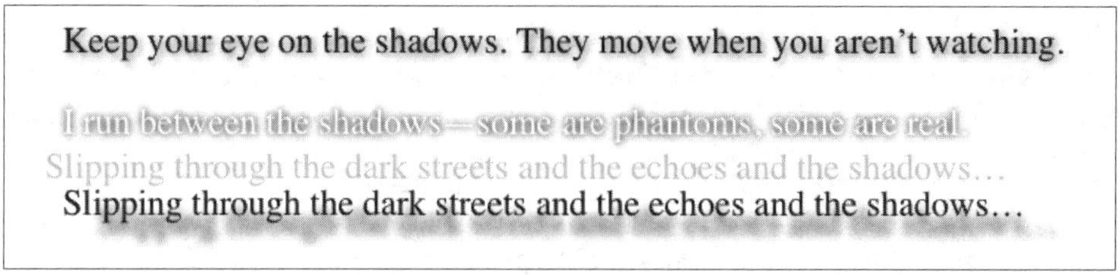

Keep your eye on the shadows. They move when you aren't watching.

I run between the shadows—some are phantoms, some are real.

Slipping through the dark streets and the echoes and the shadows…

Slipping through the dark streets and the echoes and the shadows…

Figure 6-36. Dropping shadows all over

 Note that large numbers of text shadows, or text shadows with very large blur values, can create performance slowdowns, particularly in low-power and CPU-constrained situations such as mobile devices. Authors are advised to test thoroughly before deploying public designs that use text shadows.

Handling Whitespace

Now that we've covered a variety of ways to style the text, let's talk about the property white-space, which affects the user agent's handling of space, newline, and tab characters within the document source.

white-space

Values	normal | nowrap | pre | pre-wrap | pre-line
Initial value	normal
Applies to	All elements (CSS 2.1); block-level elements (CSS1 and CSS2)
Computed value	As specified
Inherited	No
Animatable	No

Using this property, you can affect how a browser treats the whitespace between words and lines of text. To a certain extent, default XHTML handling already does this: it collapses any whitespace down to a single space. So given the following markup, the rendering in a web browser would show only one space between each word and ignore the line-feed in the elements:

```
<p>This    paragraph    has    many spaces         in it.</p>
```

You can explicitly set this default behavior with the following declaration:

```
p {white-space: normal;}
```

This rule tells the browser to do as browsers have always done: discard extra white-space. Given this value, line-feed characters (carriage returns) are converted into spaces, and any sequence of more than one space in a row is converted to a single space.

Should you set white-space to pre, however, the whitespace in an affected element is treated as though the elements were XHTML pre elements; whitespace is *not* ignored, as shown in Figure 6-37:

```
p {white-space: pre;}
```

```
<p>This    paragraph    has    many spaces         in it.</p>
```

This paragraph has   many
    spaces   in it.

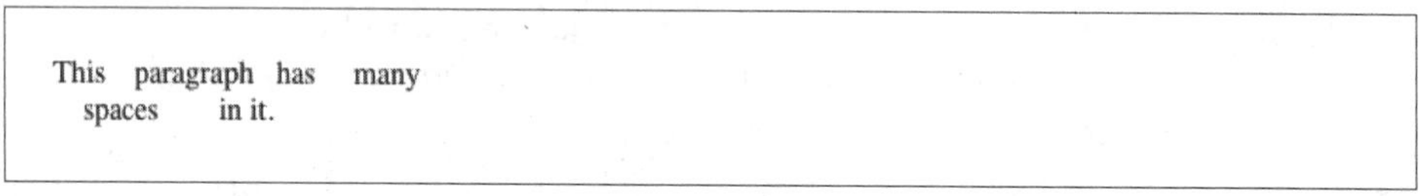

Figure 6-37. Honoring the spaces in markup

With a white-space value of pre, the browser will pay attention to extra spaces and even carriage returns. In this respect, and in this respect alone, any element can be made to act like a pre element.

The opposite value is nowrap, which prevents text from wrapping within an element, except wherever you use a br element. Using nowrap in CSS is much like setting a table cell not to wrap in HTML 4 with <td nowrap>, except the white-space value can be applied to any element. The effects of the following markup are shown in Figure 6-38:

```
<p style="white-space: nowrap;">This paragraph is not allowed to wrap,
which means that the only way to end a line is to insert a line-break
element.  If no such element is inserted, then the line will go forever,
forcing the user to scroll horizontally to read whatever can't be
initially displayed <br/>in the browser window.</p>
```

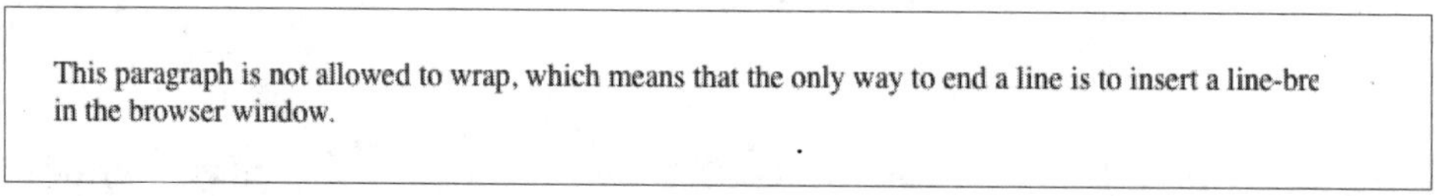

This paragraph is not allowed to wrap, which means that the only way to end a line is to insert a line-bre
in the browser window.

Figure 6-38. Suppressing line wrapping with the white-space property

You can actually use white-space to replace the nowrap attribute on table cells:

```
td {white-space: nowrap;}

<table><tr>
<td>The contents of this cell are not wrapped.</td>
<td>Neither are the contents of this cell.</td>
<td>Nor this one, or any after it, or any other cell in this table.</td>
<td>CSS prevents any wrapping from happening.</td>
</tr></table>
```

CSS 2.1 introduced the values pre-wrap and pre-line, which were absent in earlier versions of CSS. The effect of these values is to allow authors to better control white-space handling.

If an element is set to pre-wrap, then text within that element has whitespace sequences preserved, but text lines are wrapped normally. With this value, line-breaks in the source and those that are generated are also honored. pre-line is the opposite of pre-wrap and causes whitespace sequences to collapse as in normal text but honors new lines. For example, consider the following markup, which is illustrated in Figure 6-39:

```
<p style="white-space: pre-wrap;">
This paragraph        has a great   many   s p a c e s   within  its textual
  content,   but their     preservation     will     not     prevent    line
   wrapping or line breaking.
</p>
<p style="white-space: pre-line;">
This paragraph        has a great    many   s p a c e s   within  its textual
  content,   but their collapse   will    not    prevent   line
wrapping or line breaking.
</p>
```

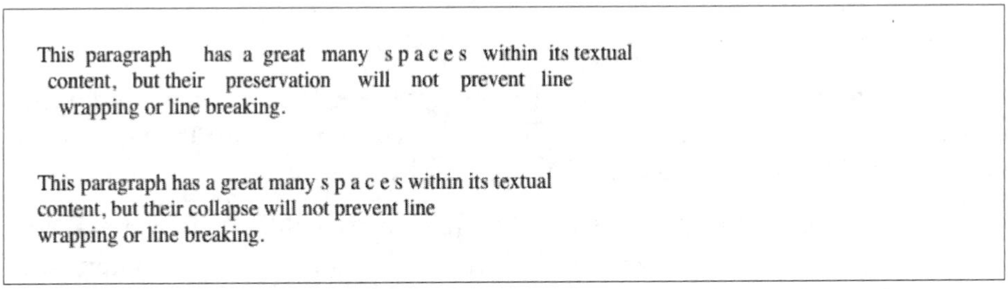

Figure 6-39. Two different ways to handle whitespace

Table 6-1 summarizes the behaviors of white-space properties.

Table 6-1. White-space properties

Value	Whitespace	Line feeds	Auto line wrapping
pre-line	Collapsed	Honored	Allowed
normal	Collapsed	Ignored	Allowed
nowrap	Collapsed	Ignored	Prevented
pre	Preserved	Honored	Prevented
pre-wrap	Preserved	Honored	Allowed

Setting Tab Sizes

Since whitespace is preserved in some values of white-space, it stands to reason that tabs (i.e., Unicode code point 0009) will be displayed as, well, tabs. But how many spaces should each tab equal? That's where tab-size comes in.

tab-size	
Values	*<length>*	*<integer>*
Initial value	8
Applies to	Block elements
Computed value	The absolute-length equivalent of the specified value
Inherited	Yes
Animatable	Yes

By default, any tab character will be treated the same as eight spaces in a row, but you can alter that by using a different integer value. Thus, tab-size: 4 will cause each tab to be rendered the same as if it were four spaces in a row.

If a length value is supplied, then each tab is rendered using that length. For example, tab-size: 10px will cause a sequence of three tabs to be rendered as 30 pixels of whitespace. The effects of the following rules is illustrated in Figure 6-40.

> This sentence is preceded by three tabs, set to a length of 8.
>
> This sentence is preceded by three tabs, set to a length of 4.
>
> This sentence is preceded by three tabs, set to a length of 2.
>
> This sentence is preceded by three tabs, set to a length of 0.
>
> This sentence is preceded by three tabs, set to a length of 8 —but `white-space` is `normal`.

Figure 6-40. Differing tab lengths

Note that `tab-size` is effectively ignored when the value of `white-space` causes whitespace to be collapsed (see Table 6-1). The value will still be computed in such cases, but there will be no visible effect no matter how many tabs appear in the source.

 Currently, `tab-size` is supported in WebKit and Gecko (as `-moz-tab-size`). In both cases, only integer values are supported, not length values.

Wrapping and Hyphenation

Hyphens can be very useful in situations where there are long words and short line lengths, such as blog posts on mobile devices and portions of *The Economist*. Authors can always insert their own hyphenation hints using the Unicode character U+00AD SOFT HYPHEN (or, in HTML, ­), but CSS also offers a way to enable hyphenation without littering up the document with hints.

---

hyphens

Values	manual | auto | none
Initial value	manual
Applies to	All elements
Computed value	As specified
Inherited	Yes
Animatabale	No

With the default value of manual, hyphens are only inserted where there are manually-inserted hyphenation markers in the document, such as U+00AD or ­. Otherwise, no hyphenation occurs. The value none, on the other hand, suppresses any hyphenation, even if manual break markers are present; thus, U+00AD and ­ are ignored.

The far more interesting (and potentially inconsistent) value is auto, which permits the browser to insert hyphens and break words at "appropriate" places inside words, even where no manually inserted hyphenation breaks exist. This leads to interesting questions like what constitutes a "word" and under what circumstances it is appropriate to hyphenate a word, both of which are highly language-dependent. User agents are supposed to prefer manually inserted hyphen breaks to automatically determined breaks, but there are no guarantees. An illustration of hyphenation, or the suppression thereof, in the following example is shown in Figure 6-41:

```
.cl01 {hyphens: auto;}
.cl02 {hyphens: manual;}
.cl03 {hyphens: none;}

<p class="cl01">Supercalifragilisticexpialidocious antidisestablishmentarian
    ism.</p>
<p class="cl02">Supercalifragilisticexpialidocious antidisestablishmentarian
    ism.</p>
<p class="cl02">Super&#xad;cali&#xad;fragi&#xad;listic&#xad;expi&#xad;ali&#xad;
docious anti&#xad;dis&#xad;establish&#xad;ment&#xad;arian&#xad;ism.</p>
<p class="cl03">Super&#xad;cali&#xad;fragi&#xad;listic&#xad;expi&#xad;ali&#xad;
docious anti&#xad;dis&#xad;establish&#xad;ment&#xad;arian&#xad;ism.</p>
```

	12em wide	10em wide	8em wide
hyphens: auto *No soft hyphen entities*	Supercalifragilisticexpialido-cious antidisestablishmentari-anism.	Supercalifragilisticexpi-alidocious antidisestab-lishmentarianism.	Supercalifragilistic-expialidocious an-tidisestablishmen-tarianism.
hyphens: manual *No soft hyphen entities*	Supercalifragilisticexpialidocious antidisestablishmentarianism.	Supercalifragilisticexpialidocious antidisestablishmentarianism.	Supercalifragilisticexpialidocious antidisestablishmentarianism.
hyphens: manual *Soft hyphen entities*	Supercalifragilisticexpiali-docious antidisestablishment-arianism.	Supercalifragilisticexpi-alidocious antidis-establishmentarianism.	Supercalifragilistic-expialidocious anti-disestablishment-arianism.
hyphens: none *Soft hyphen entities*	Supercalifragilisticexpialidocious antidisestablishmentarianism.	Supercalifragilisticexpialidocious antidisestablishmentarianism.	Supercalifragilisticexpialidocious antidisestablishmentarianism.

Figure 6-41. Hyphenation results

Because hyphenation is so language-dependent, and because the CSS specification does not define precise (or even vague) rules regarding how user agents should carry out hyphenation, there is every chance that hyphenation will be different from one browser to the next.

Furthermore, if you do choose to hyphenate, be careful about the elements to which you apply the hyphenation. hyphens is an inherited property, so declaring body {hyphens: auto;} will apply hyphenation to everything in your document—including textareas, code samples, block quotes, and so on. Blocking automatic hyphenation at the level of those elements is probably a good idea, using rules something like this:

```
body {hyphens: auto;}
code, var, kbd, samp, tt, dir, listing, plaintext, xmp, abbr, acronym,
blockquote, q, textarea, input, option {hyphens: manual;}
```

It's probably obvious why suppressing hyphenation in code samples and code blocks is desirable, especially in languages that use hyphens in things like property and value names. (Ahem.) Similar logic holds for keyboard input text—you definitely don't want a stray dash getting into your Unix command-line examples! And so on down the line. If you decide that you want to hyphenate some of these elements, just remove them from the selector. (It can be kind of fun to watch the text you're typing into a textarea get auto-hyphenated as you type it.)

 As of late 2017, hyphens was supported by all major desktop browsers except Chrome/Blink, and required vendor prefixes in Safari and Edge. As noted, such support is always language-dependent.

Hyphens can be suppressed by the effects of other properties, such as word-break, which affects how soft wrapping of text is calculated in various languages.

word-break

Values	normal | break-all | keep-all
Initial value	normal
Applies to	All elements
Computed value	As specified
Inherited	Yes
Animatable	Yes

When a run of text is too long to fit into a single line, it is *soft wrapped*. This is in contrast to *hard wraps*, which are things like line-feed characters and <br> elements. Where the text is soft wrapped is determined by the user agent (or the OS it uses), but word-break lets authors influence its decision-making.

The default value of normal means that text should be wrapped like it always has been. In practical terms, this means that text is broken between words, though the definition of a word varies by language. In Latin-derived languages like English, this is almost always a space between letter sequences (e.g., words). In ideographic languages like Japanese, each symbol is a word, so breaks can occur between any two symbols. In other CJK languages, though, the soft-wrap points may be limited to appear between sequences of symbols that are not space-separated.

Again, that's all by default, and is the way browsers have handled text for years. If you apply the value break-all, then soft wrapping can (and will) occur between any two characters, even if they are in the middle of a word. With this value, no hyphens are shown, even if the soft wrapping occurs at a hyphenation point (see hyphens, earlier). Note that values of the line-break property (described next) can affect the behavior of break-all in CJK text.

keep-all, on the other hand, suppresses soft wrapping between characters, even in CJK languages where each symbol is a word. Thus, in Japanese, a sequence of symbols with no whitespace will not be soft wrapped, even if this means the text line will exceed the length of its element. (This behavior is similar to white-space: pre.)

Figure 6-42 shows a few examples of word-break values, and Table 6-2 summarizes the effects of each value.

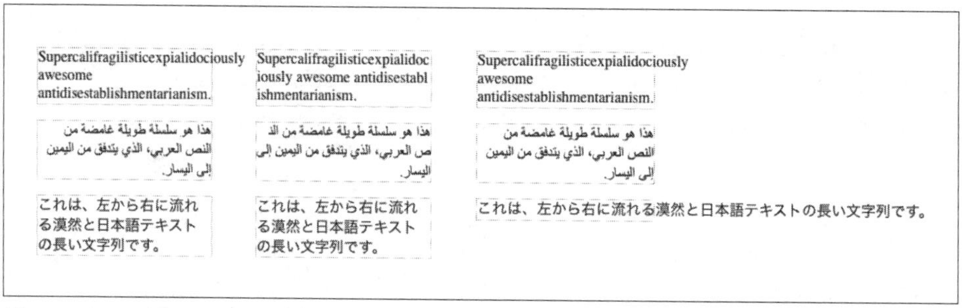

Figure 6-42. Altering word-breaking behavior

Table 6-2. Word-breaking behavior

Value	Non-CJK	CJK	Hyphenation permitted
normal	As usual	As usual	Yes
break-all	After any character	After any character	No
keep-all	As usual	Around sequences	Yes

If your interests run to CJK text, then in addition to `word-break` you will also want to get to know `line-break`.

---

line-break

Values	auto | loose | normal | strict
Initial value	auto
Applies to	All elements
Computed value	As specified
Inherited	Yes
Animatable	Yes

As we just saw, `word-break` can affect how lines of text are soft wrapped in CJK text. The `line-break` property also affects such soft wrapping, specifically how wrapping is handled around CJK-specific symbols and around non-CJK punctuation (such as exclamation points, hyphens, and ellipses) that appears in text declared to be CJK.

In other words, `line-break` applies to certain CJK characters all the time, regardless of the content's declared language. If you throw some CJK characters into a paragraph of English text, `line-break` will still apply to them, but not to anything else in the text. Conversely, if you declare content to be in a CJK language, `line-break` will continue to apply to those CJK characters *plus* a number of non-CJK characters within the CJK text. These include punctuation marks, currency symbols, and a few other symbols.

There is no authoritative list of which characters are affected and which are not, but the specification (*http://w3.org/TR/css3-text/#line-break*) provides a list of recommended symbols and behaviors around those symbols.

The default value `auto` allows user agents to soft wrap text as they like, and more importantly lets UAs vary the line breaking they do based on the situation. For example, the UA can use looser line-breaking rules for short lines of text and stricter rules for long lines. In effect, `auto` allows the user agent to switch between the `loose`, `normal`, and `strict` values as needed, possibly even on a line-by-line basis within a single element.

Doubtless you can infer that those other values have the following general meanings:

loose
> This value imposes the "least restrictive" rules for wrapping text, and is meant for use when line lengths are short, such as in newspapers.

normal
> This value imposes the "most common" rules for wrapping text. What exactly "most common" means is not precisely defined, though there is the aforementioned list of recommended behaviors.

strict
> This value imposes the "most stringent" rules for wrapping text. Again, this is not precisely defined.

Wrapping Text

After all that information about hyphenation and soft wrapping, what happens when text overflows its container anyway? That's what overflow-wrap addresses.

overflow-wrap (neé word-wrap)

Values	normal | break-word
Initial value	normal
Applies to	All elements
Computed value	As specified
Inherited	Yes
Animatable	Yes

This property couldn't be more straightforward. If the default value of normal is in effect, then wrapping happens as normal; which is to say, between words or as directed by the language. If break-word is in effect, then wrapping can happen in the middle of words. Figure 6-43 illustrates the difference.

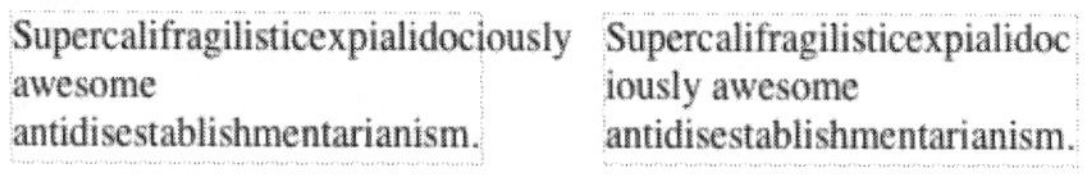

Figure 6-43. Overflow wrapping

Note that `overflow-wrap` can only operate if the value of `white-space` allows line wrapping. If it does not (e.g., with the value `pre`), then `overflow-wrap` has no effect.

Where `overflow-wrap` gets complicated is in its history and implementation. Once upon a time there was a property called `word-wrap` that did exactly what `overflow-wrap` does. The two are so identical that the specification specifically states that user agents "must treat `word-wrap` as an alternate name for the `overflow-wrap` property, as if it were a shorthand of `overflow-wrap`."

Sadly, browsers didn't always do this, and `word-wrap` was better supported. For this reason, it's common to use both for backward compatibility:

```
pre {word-wrap: break-word; overflow-wrap: break-word;}
```

As of late 2017, `overflow-wrap` enjoys very widespread supports, so it's pretty safe to use.

While `overflow-wrap: break-word` may appear very similar to `word-break: break-all`, they are not the same thing. To see why, compare the second box in Figure 6-43 to the top middle box in Figure 6-42. As it shows, `overflow-wrap` only kicks in if content actually overflows; thus, when there is an opportunity to use whitespace in the source to wrap lines, `overflow-wrap` will take it. By contrast, `word-break: break-all` will cause wrapping when content reaches the wrapping edge, regardless of any whitespace that comes earlier in the line.

Writing Modes

If you're reading this book in English or any number of other mainly Western languages, then you're reading the text left to right and top to bottom, which is the flow direction of English. Not every language runs this way. There are many right-to-left and top-to-bottom languages such as Hebrew and Arabic, and many languages that can be written primarily top-to-bottom. Some of the latter are secondarily left to right, such as Chinese and Japanese, whereas others are right to left, like Mongolian.

Setting Writing Modes

The property used for specifying one of the three available writing mode is, of all things, `writing-mode`.

writing-mode

Values	`horizontal-tb`|`vertical-rl`|`vertical-lr`
Initial value	`horizontal-tb`
Applies to	All elements except table row groups, table column groups, table rows, table columns, ruby base containers, and ruby annotation containers
Computed value	As specified
Inherited	Yes
Animatable	Yes

The default value, `horizontal-tb`, means "a horizontal inline direction, and a top-to-bottom block direction." This covers all Western and some Middle Eastern languages, which may differ in the direction of their horizontal writing. The other two values offer a vertical inline direction, and either a right-to-left or left-to-right block direction. All three are illustrated in Figure 6-44.

| horizontal-tb | vertical-rl | vertical-lr |

Figure 6-44. Writing modes

Notice how the lines are strung together in the two vertical examples. If you tilt your head to the right, the text in `vertical-rl` is at least readable. The text in `vertical-lr`, on the other hand, is difficult to read because it appears to flow from bottom to top, at least when arranging English text. This is not a problem in languages which actually use `vertical-lr` flow, such as form of Japanese. As of late 2017, vertical flows can only have the inline direction go from top to bottom.

It is possible to create bottom-to-top vertical flows of Western-language text by applying `vertical-rl` to an element and then rotating the element 180 degrees with CSS Transforms (see Chapter 16). This presents a bottom-to-top, left-to-right visual flow. Using `vertical-lr` and rotating it creates a bottom-to-top, right-to-left flow. Both are illustrated in Figure 6-45:

```
.flip {transform: rotate(180deg);}
#one {writing-mode: vertical-rl;}
#two {writing-mode: vertical-lr;}
```

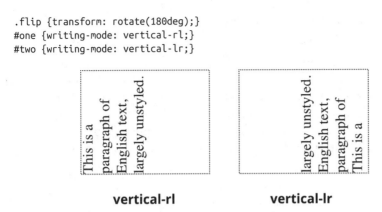

vertical-rl   vertical-lr

Figure 6-45. Flipping vertical writing modes

The challenge of working with text like that is that everything is flipped, which means what we see is at odds with what's actually happening. The text of vertical-rl (vertical-right-to-left) is visually progressing left to right, for example.

The same problem arises when applying inline block-alignment properties such as vertical-align. In vertical writing modes, the block direction is horizontal, which means vertical alignment of inline elements actually causes them to move horizontally. This is illustrated in Figure 6-46.

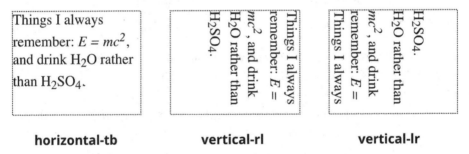

horizontal-tb   vertical-rl   vertical-lr

Figure 6-46. Writing modes and "vertical" alignment

All the super- and subscript elements cause horizontal shifts, both of themselves and the placement of the lines they occupy, even through the property used to move them is vertical-align. As described earlier, the vertical displacement is with respect to the line box, where the box's baseline is defined as horizontal—even when it's being drawn vertically.

Confused? It's OK. Writing modes are likely to confuse you, because it's such a different way of thinking *and* because old assumptions in the CSS specification clash with the new capabilities. If there had been vertical writing modes from the outset, vertical-align would likely have a different name—inline-align or something like that. (Maybe one day that will happen.)

One last note: if you're already used to CSS Transforms, you might be tempted to think of these vertical writing modes as equivalent to rotating the text 90 degrees. They are *not* the same, for two reasons. One, this only appears to be the case for vertical-rl; vertical-lr has the look of text that flows "bottom to top." Two, the cardinal points don't change when flowing text vertically. The top is still the top, in other words. This is illustrated by the following styles, whose results are depicted in Figure 6-47:

```
.boxed {border-top: 3px solid red;
        border-left: 3px dashed tan;}
#one {writing-mode: vertical-rl;}
#two {writing-mode: vertical-lr;}
```

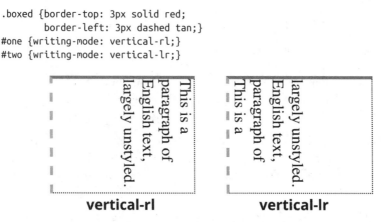

vertical-rl   vertical-lr

Figure 6-47. Writing modes and the "cardinal" directions of CSS

In both cases, the top border is solid red, and the left border is dashed tan. The cardinal points don't rotate with the text—because the text isn't rotated. It's being flowed in a different way.

Now here's where it gets unusual. While the borders don't migrate around the element box, margins *can*, but not due to anything in the CSS specification.

This happens because user agents (at least as of late 2017) maintain internal styles that relate to the start and end of the element in the block direction. In languages that flow top to bottom, then the start and end of the element's block direction are its top and bottom sides. But in vertical writing, the block direction is right to left or left to right. Thus, you can set up a bunch of paragraphs to flow vertically, and if you leave the margins alone, what would normally be top and bottom margins will become left and right margins. You can see this effect in Figure 6-48, which illustrated the result of the following styles:

```
p { margin-top: 1em;}
#one {writing-mode: vertical-rl;}
#two {writing-mode: vertical-lr;}
```

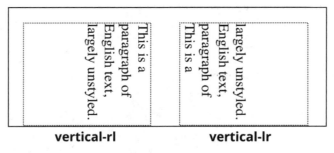

| vertical-rl | vertical-lr |

Figure 6-48. The placement of UA default margins

There are the top margins, as declared, right along the tops of the two paragraphs. The empty space to the side of each paragraph is created by the block-start and block-end margins. If we explicitly set the right and left margins to zero, then the space between the paragraphs would be removed.

Remember: this happens because user agents, by default, represent the margins of text elements using properties like block-start-margin (which is not an actual property in CSS, at least not yet). If you explicitly set top, bottom, or side margins using properties like margin-top, then they will be applied to the element box just as borders were: top margin on top, right margin to the right, and so on.

Changing Text Orientation

Once you've settled on a writing mode, you may decide you want to change the orientation of characters within those lines of text. There are many reasons you might want to do this, not least of which are situations where different writing systems are commingled, such as Japanese text with English words or numbers mixed in. In these cases, text-orientation is the answer.

text-orientation	
Values	mixed | upright | sideways
Initial value	mixed
Applies to	All elements except table row groups, table rows, table column groups, and table columns
Computed value	As specified
Inherited	Yes
Animatable	Yes

The effect of `text-orientation` is to affect how characters are oriented. What that means is best illustrated by the following styles, rendered in Figure 6-49:

```css
.verts {writing-mode: vertical-lr;}
#one {text-orientation: mixed;}
#two {text-orientation: upright;}
#thr {text-orientation: sideways;}
```

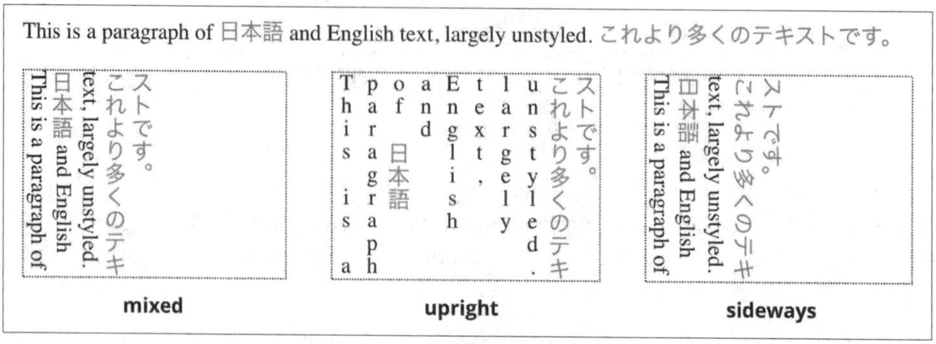

This is a paragraph of 日本語 and English text, largely unstyled. これより多くのテキストです。

| mixed | upright | sideways |

Figure 6-49. Text orientation

Across the top of Figure 6-49 is a basically unstyled paragraph of mixed Japanese and English text. Below that, three copies of that paragraph, using the writing mode `vertical-lr`. In the first of the three, `text-orientation: mixed`, writes the horizontal-script characters (the English) sideways, and the vertical-script characters (the Japanese) upright. In the second, all characters are `upright`, including the English characters. In the third, all characters are `sideways`, including the Japanese characters.

Declaring Direction

Harking back to the days of CSS2, there are a pair of properties that can be used to affect the direction of text by changing the inline baseline direction: `direction` and `unicode-bidi`.

The CSS specification explicitly warns *against* using `direction` and `unicode-bidi` in CSS when applied to HTML documents. To quote: "Because HTML [user agents] can turn off CSS styling, we recommend...the HTML `dir` attribute and `<bdo>` element to ensure correct bidirectional layout in the absence of a style sheet." The properties are covered here because they may appear in legacy stylesheets.

direction

Values	ltr | rtl
Initial value	ltr
Applies to	All elements
Computed value	As specified
Inherited	Yes
Animatable	Yes

The direction property affects the writing direction of text in a block-level element, the direction of table column layout, the direction in which content horizontally overflows its element box, and the position of the last line of a fully justified element. For inline elements, direction applies only if the property unicode-bidi is set to either embed or bidi-override (See the following description of unicode-bidi).

Although ltr is the default, it is expected that if a browser is displaying right-to-left text, the value will be changed to rtl. Thus, a browser might carry an internal rule stating something like the following:

```
*:lang(ar), *:lang(he) {direction: rtl;}
```

The real rule would be longer and encompass all right-to-left languages, not just Arabic and Hebrew, but it illustrates the point.

While CSS attempts to address writing direction, Unicode has a much more robust method for handling directionality. With the property unicode-bidi, CSS authors can take advantage of some of Unicode's capabilities.

unicode-bidi

Values	normal | embed | bidi-override
Initial value	normal
Applies to	All elements
Computed value	As specified
Inherited	No
Animatable	Yes

Here we'll simply quote the value descriptions from the CSS 2.1 specification, which do a good job of capturing the essence of each value:

normal

> The element does not open an additional level of embedding with respect to the bidirectional algorithm. For inline-level elements, implicit reordering works across element boundaries.

embed

> If the element is inline-level, this value opens an additional level of embedding with respect to the bidirectional algorithm. The direction of this embedding level is given by the direction property. Inside the element, reordering is done implicitly. This corresponds to adding an LRE (U+202A; for direction: ltr) or an RLE (U+202B; for direction: rtl) at the start of the element and a PDF (U+202C) at the end of the element.

bidi-override

> This creates an override for inline-level elements. For block-level elements, this creates an override for inline-level descendants not within another block. This means that, inside the element, reordering is strictly in sequence according to the direction property; the implicit part of the bidirectional algorithm is ignored. This corresponds to adding an LRO (U+202D; for direction: ltr) or RLO (U+202E; for direction: rtl) at the start of the element and a PDF (U+202C) at the end of the element.

Summary

Even without altering the font face, there are many ways to change the appearance of text. There are classic effects such as underlining, but CSS also enables you to draw lines over text or through it, change the amount of space between words and letters, indent the first line of a paragraph (or other block-level element), align text in various ways, exert influence over the hyphenation and line breaking of text, and much more. You can even alter the amount of space between lines of text. There is also support in CSS for languages other than those that are written left-to-right, top-to-bottom. Given that so much of the web is text, the strength of these properties makes a great deal of sense. Recent developments in improving text legibility and placement are likely only the beginnings of what we will eventually be able to do with text styling.

CHAPTER 7

Basic Visual Formatting

This chapter is all about the theoretical side of visual rendering in CSS. Why is that necessary? The answer is that with a model as open and powerful as that contained within CSS, no book could hope to cover every possible way of combining properties and effects. You will undoubtedly go on to discover new ways of using CSS. In exploring CSS, you may encounter seemingly strange behaviors in user agents. With a thorough grasp of how the visual rendering model works, you'll be better able to determine whether a behavior is a correct (if unexpected) consequence of the rendering engine CSS defines.

Basic Boxes

At its core, CSS assumes that every element generates one or more rectangular boxes, called *element boxes*. (Future versions of the specification may allow for nonrectangular boxes, and indeed there have been proposals to change this, but for now everything is rectangular.) Each element box has a *content area* at its center. This content area is surrounded by optional amounts of padding, borders, outlines, and margins. These areas are considered optional because they could all be set to a width of zero, effectively removing them from the element box. An example content area is shown in Figure 7-1, along with the surrounding regions of padding, borders, and margins.

Each of the margins, borders, and the padding can be set using various side-specific properties, such as margin-left or border-bottom, as well as shorthand properties such as padding. The outline, if any, does not have side-specific properties. The content's background—a color or tiled image, for example—is applied within the padding by default. The margins are always transparent, allowing the background(s) of any parent element(s) to be visible. Padding cannot have a negative length, but margins can. We'll explore the effects of negative margins later on.

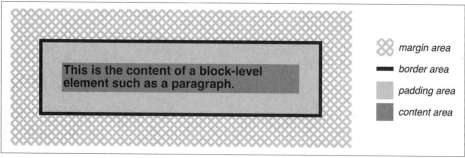

Figure 7-1. The content area and its surroundings

Borders are generated using defined styles, such as solid or inset, and their colors are set using the border-color property. If no color is set, then the border takes on the foreground color of the element's content. For example, if the text of a paragraph is white, then any borders around that paragraph will be white, *unless* the author explicitly declares a different border color. If a border style has gaps of some type, then the element's background is visible through those gaps by default. Finally, the width of a border can never be negative.

The various components of an element box can be affected via a number of properties, such as width or border-right. Many of these properties will be used in this book, even though they aren't defined here.

A Quick Refresher

Let's quickly review the kinds of boxes we'll be discussing, as well as some important terms that are needed to follow the explanations to come:

Normal flow
> This is the left-to-right, top-to-bottom rendering of text in Western languages and the familiar text layout of traditional HTML documents. Note that the flow direction may be changed in non-Western languages. Most elements are in the normal flow, and the only way for an element to leave the normal flow is to be floated, positioned, or made into a flexible box or grid layout element. Remember, the discussions in this chapter cover only elements in the normal flow.

Nonreplaced element
> This is an element whose content is contained within the document. For example, a paragraph (p) is a nonreplaced element because its textual content is found within the element itself.

Replaced element
> This is an element that serves as a placeholder for something else. The classic example of a replaced element is the img element, which simply points to an

image file that is inserted into the document's flow at the point where the img element itself is found. Most form elements are also replaced (e.g., `<input type="radio">`).

Root element
This is the element at the top of the document tree. In HTML documents, this is the element html. In XML documents, it can be whatever the language permits; for example, the root element of RSS files is rss.

Block box
This is a box that an element such as a paragraph, heading, or div generates. These boxes generate "new lines" both before and after their boxes when in the normal flow so that block boxes in the normal flow stack vertically, one after another. Any element can be made to generate a block box by declaring display: block.

Inline box
This is a box that an element such as strong or span generates. These boxes do not generate "line breaks" before or after themselves. Any element can be made to generate an inline box by declaring display: inline.

Inline-block box
This is a box that is like a block box internally, but acts like an inline box externally. It acts similar to, but not quite the same as, a replaced element. Imagine picking up a div and sticking it into a line of text as if it were an inline image, and you've got the idea.

There are several other types of boxes, such as table-cell boxes, but they won't be covered in this book for a variety of reasons—not the least of which is that their complexity demands a book of its own, and very few authors will actually wrestle with them on a regular basis.

The Containing Block

There is one more kind of box that we need to examine in detail, and in this case enough detail that it merits its own section: the *containing block*.

Every element's box is laid out with respect to its containing block; in a very real way, the containing block is the "layout context" for a box. CSS defines a series of rules for determining a box's containing block. We'll cover only those rules that pertain to the concepts covered in this book in order to keep our focus.

For an element in the normal, Western-style flow of text, the containing block forms from the *content edge* of the nearest ancestor that generated a list item or block box, which includes all table-related boxes (e.g., those generated by table cells). Consider the following markup:

```
<body>
    <div>
        <p>This is a paragraph.</p>
    </div>
</body>
```

In this very simple markup, the containing block for the p element's block box is the div element's block box, as that is the closest ancestor element box that is a block or a list item (in this case, it's a block box). Similarly, the div's containing block is the body's box. Thus, the layout of the p is dependent on the layout of the div, which is in turn dependent on the layout of the body element.

And above that, the layout of the body element is dependent on the layout of the html element, whose box creates what is called the *initial containing block*. It's unique in that the viewport—the browser window in screen media, or the printable area of the page in print media—determines its dimensions, not the size of the content of the root element. It's a subtle distinction, and usually not a very important one, but it does exist.

Altering Element Display

You can affect the way a user agent displays by setting a value for the property display. Now that we've taken a close look at visual formatting, let's consider the display property and discuss two more of its values using concepts from earlier in the book.

---

display

Values	[*<display-outside>* ‖ *<display-inside>*]	*<display-listitem>*	*<display-internal>*	*<display-box>*	*<display-legacy>*
Definitions	See below
Initial value	inline
Applies to	All elements
Computed value	As specified
Inherited	No
Animatable	No

<display-outside>
    block | inline | run-in

<display-inside>
    flow | flow-root | table | flex | grid | ruby

<display-listitem>
    list-item && <display-outside>? && [flow | flow-root]?

<display-internal>
    table-row-group | table-header-group | table-footer-group | table-row |
    table-cell | table-column-group | table-column | table-caption | ruby-base
    | ruby-text | ruby-base-container | ruby-text-container

<display-box>
    contents | none

<display-legacy>
    inline-block | inline-list-item | inline-table | inline-flex | inline-grid

We'll ignore the ruby- and table-related values, since they're far too complex for this chapter, and we'll also ignore the value list-item, since it's very similar to block boxes. We've spent quite some time discussing block and inline boxes, but let's spend a moment talking about how altering an element's display role can alter layout before we look at inline-block.

Changing Roles

When it comes to styling a document, it's handy to be able to change the type of box an element generates. For example, suppose we have a series of links in a nav that we'd like to lay out as a vertical sidebar:

```
<nav>
    <a href="index.html">WidgetCo Home</a>
    <a href="products.html">Products</a>
    <a href="services.html">Services</a>
    <a href="fun.html">Widgety Fun!</a>
    <a href="support.html">Support</a>
    <a href="about.html" id="current">About Us</a>
    <a href="contact.html">Contact</a>
</nav>
```

We could put all the links into table cells, or wrap each one in its own nav—or we could just make them all block-level elements, like this:

```
nav a {display: block;}
```

This will make every a element within the navigation nav a block-level element. If we add on a few more styles, we could have a result like that shown in Figure 7-2.

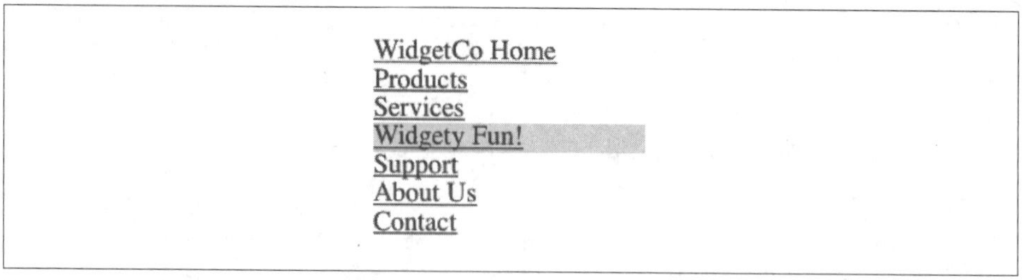

Figure 7-2. Changing the display role from inline to block

Changing display roles can be useful in cases where you want non-CSS browsers to get the navigation links as inline elements but to lay out the same links as block-level elements. With the links as blocks, you can style them as you would div or p elements, with the advantage that the entire element box becomes part of the link. Thus, if a user's mouse pointer hovers anywhere in the element box, she can then click the link.

You may also want to take elements and make them inline. Suppose we have an unordered list of names:

```
<ul id="rollcall">
    <li>Bob C.</li>
    <li>Marcio G.</li>
    <li>Eric M.</li>
    <li>Kat M.</li>
    <li>Tristan N.</li>
    <li>Arun R.</li>
    <li>Doron R.</li>
    <li>Susie W.</li>
</ul>
```

Given this markup, say we want to make the names into a series of inline names with vertical bars between them (and on each end of the list). The only way to do so is to change their display role. The following rules will have the effect shown in Figure 7-3:

```
#rollcall li {display: inline; border-right: 1px solid; padding: 0 0.33em;}
#rollcall li:first-child {border-left: 1px solid;}
```

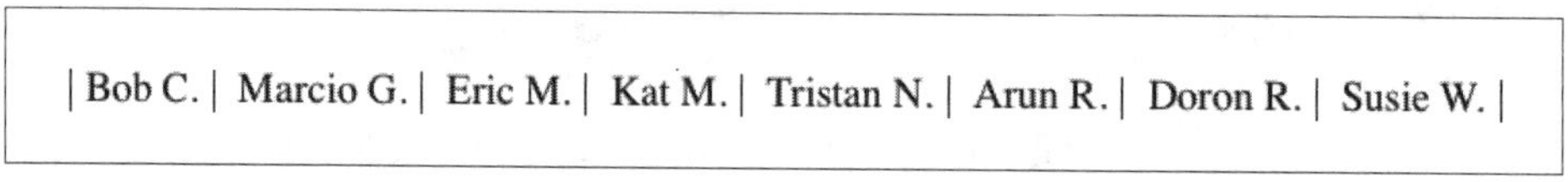

Figure 7-3. Changing the display role from list-item to inline

There are plenty of other ways to use display to your advantage in design. Be creative and see what you can invent!

Be careful to note, however, that you are changing the display role of elements—not changing their inherent nature. In other words, causing a paragraph to generate an inline box does *not* turn that paragraph into an inline element. In HTML, for example, some elements are block while others are inline. (Still others are "flow" elements, but we're ignoring them right now.) An inline element can be a descendant of a block element, but the reverse is generally not true. While a span can be placed inside a paragraph, a span cannot be wrapped around a paragraph.

This will hold true no matter how you style the elements in question. Consider the following markup:

```
<span style="display: block;">
<p style="display: inline;">this is wrong!</p>
</span>
```

The markup will not validate because the block element (p) is nested inside an inline element (span). The changing of display roles does nothing to change this. display has its name because it affects how the element is displayed, not because it changes what kind of element it is.

With that said, let's get into the details of different kinds of boxes: block boxes, inline boxes, inline-block boxes, and list-item boxes.

Block Boxes

Block boxes can behave in sometimes predictable, sometimes surprising ways. The handling of box placement along the horizontal and vertical axes can differ, for example. In order to fully understand how block boxes are handled, you must clearly understand a number of boundaries and areas. They are shown in detail in Figure 7-4.

By default, the width of a block box is defined to be the distance from the left inner edge to the right inner edge, and the height is the distance from the inner top to the inner bottom. Both of these properties can be applied to an element generating a block box.

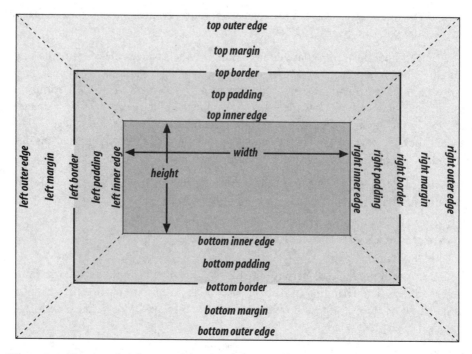

Figure 7-4. The complete box model

It's also the case that we can alter how these properties are treated using the property box-sizing.

box-sizing

Values	content-box | padding-box | border-box
Initial value	content-box
Applies to	All elements that accept width or height values
Computed value	As specified
Inherited	No
Animatable	No

This property is how you change what the width and height values actually do. If you declare width: 400px and don't declare a value for box-sizing, then the element's content box will be 400 pixels wide; any padding, borders, and so on will be added to it. If, on the other hand, you declare box-sizing: border-box, then the element box will be 400 pixels from the left outer border edge to the right outer border edge; any border or padding will be placed within that distance, thus shrinking the width of the content area. This is illustrated in Figure 7-5.

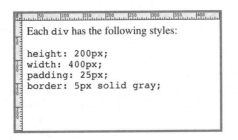
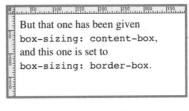

Figure 7-5. The effects of box-sizing

We're talking about the box-sizing property here because, as stated, it applies to "all elements that accept width or height values." That's most often elements generating block boxes, though it also applies to replaced inline elements like images, as well as inline-block boxes.

The various widths, heights, padding, and margins all combine to determine how a document is laid out. In most cases, the height and width of the document are automatically determined by the browser and are based on the available display region, plus other factors. With CSS, you can assert more direct control over the way elements are sized and displayed.

Horizontal Formatting

Horizontal formatting is often more complex than you'd think. Part of the complexity has to do with the default behavior of box-sizing. With the default value of content-box, the value given for width affects the width of the content area, *not* the entire visible element box. Consider the following example:

```
<p style="width: 200px;">wideness?</p>
```

This will make the paragraph's content 200 pixels wide. If we give the element a background, this will be quite obvious. However, any padding, borders, or margins you specify are *added* to the width value. Suppose we do this:

```
<p style="width: 200px; padding: 10px; margin: 20px;">wideness?</p>
```

The visible element box is now 220 pixels wide, since we've added 10 pixels of padding to the right and left of the content. The margins will now extend another 20 pixels to both sides for an overall element box width of 260 pixels. This is illustrated in Figure 7-6.

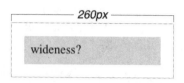

Figure 7-6. Additive padding and margin

If we change the styles to use the border box for box-sizing, then the results would be different. In that case, the visible box would be 200 pixels wide with a content width of 180 pixels, and a total of 40 pixels of margin to the sides, giving an overall box width of 240 pixels, as illustrated in Figure 7-7.

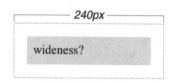

Figure 7-7. Subtracted padding

In either case, there is a rule that says that the sum of the horizontal components of a block box in the normal flow always equals the width of the containing block. Let's consider two paragraphs within a div whose margins have been set to be 1em, and whose box-sizing value is the default. The content width (the value of width) of each paragraph, plus its left and right padding, borders, and margins, always adds up to the width of the div's content area.

Let's say the width of the div is 30em. That makes the sum total of the content width, padding, borders, and margins of each paragraph 30 em. In Figure 7-8, the "blank" space around the paragraphs is actually their margins. If the div had any padding, there would be even more blank space, but that isn't the case here.

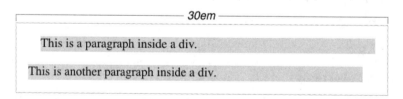

Figure 7-8. Element boxes are as wide as the width of their containing block

Horizontal Properties

The seven properties of horizontal formatting are margin-left, border-left, padding-left, width, padding-right, border-right, and margin-right. These properties relate to the horizontal layout of block boxes and are diagrammed in Figure 7-9.

The values of these seven properties must add up to the width of the element's containing block, which is usually the value of width for a block element's parent (since block-level elements nearly always have block-level elements for parents).

Of these seven properties, only three may be set to auto: the width of the element's content and the left and right margins. The remaining properties must be set either to specific values or default to a width of zero. Figure 7-10 shows which parts of the box can take a value of auto and which cannot.

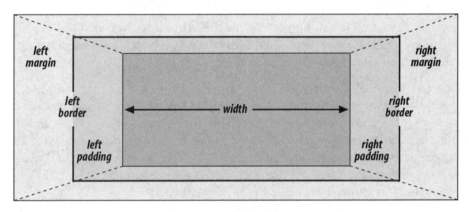

Figure 7-9. The seven properties of horizontal formatting

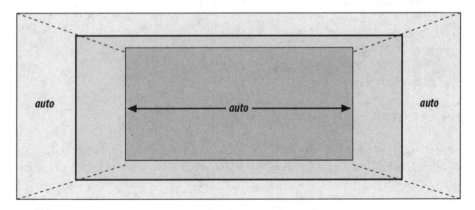

Figure 7-10. Horizontal properties that can be set to auto

width must either be set to auto or a nonnegative value of some type. When you do use auto in horizontal formatting, different effects can occur.

Using auto

If you set width, margin-left, or margin-right to a value of auto, and give the remaining two properties specific values, then the property that is set to auto is set to the length required to make the element box's width equal to the parent element's width. In other words, let's say the sum of the seven properties must equal 500 pixels, no padding or borders are set, the right margin and width are set to 100px, and the left margin is set to auto. The left margin will thus be 300 pixels wide:

```
div {width: 500px;}
p {margin-left: auto; margin-right: 100px;
    width: 100px;} /* 'auto' left margin evaluates to 300px */
```

In a sense, auto can be used to make up the difference between everything else and the required total. However, what if all three of these properties are set to 100px and *none* of them are set to auto?

In the case where all three properties are set to something other than auto—or, in CSS terminology, when these formatting properties have been *overconstrained*—then margin-right is *always* forced to be auto. This means that if both margins and the width are set to 100px, then the user agent will reset the right margin to auto. The right margin's width will then be set according to the rule that one auto value "fills in" the distance needed to make the element's overall width equal that of its containing block. Figure 7-11 shows the result of the following markup:

```
div {width: 500px;}
p {margin-left: 100px; margin-right: 100px;
    width: 100px;} /* right margin forced to be 300px */
```

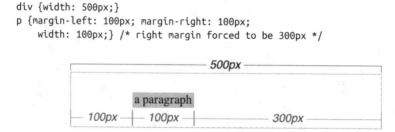

Figure 7-11. Overriding the margin-right setting

If both margins are set explicitly, and width is set to auto, then width will be whatever value is needed to reach the required total (which is the content width of the parent element). The results of the following markup are shown in Figure 7-12:

```
p {margin-left: 100px; margin-right: 100px; width: auto;}
```

The case shown in Figure 7-12 is the most common case, since it is equivalent to setting the margins and not declaring anything for the width. The result of the following markup is exactly the same as that shown in Figure 7-12:

```
p {margin-left: 100px; margin-right: 100px;} /* same as before */
```

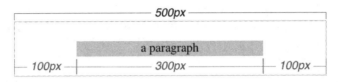

Figure 7-12. Automatic width

You might be wondering what happens if box-sizing is set to, say, padding-box. The discussion here tends to assume that the default of content-box is used, but all the same principles described here apply, which is why this section only talked about width and the side margins without introducing any padding or borders. The handling of width: auto in this section and the following sections is the same regardless of the value of box-sizing. The details of what gets placed where inside the box-sizing-defined box may vary, but the treatment of auto values does not, because box-sizing determines what width refers to, not how it behaves in relation to the margins.

More Than One auto

Now let's see what happens when two of the three properties (width, margin-left, and margin-right) are set to auto. If both margins are set to auto, as shown in the following code, then they are set to equal lengths, thus centering the element within its parent. This is illustrated in Figure 7-13.

```
div {width: 500px;}
p {width: 300px; margin-left: auto; margin-right: auto;}
    /* each margin is 100 pixels wide, because (500-300)/2 = 100 */
```

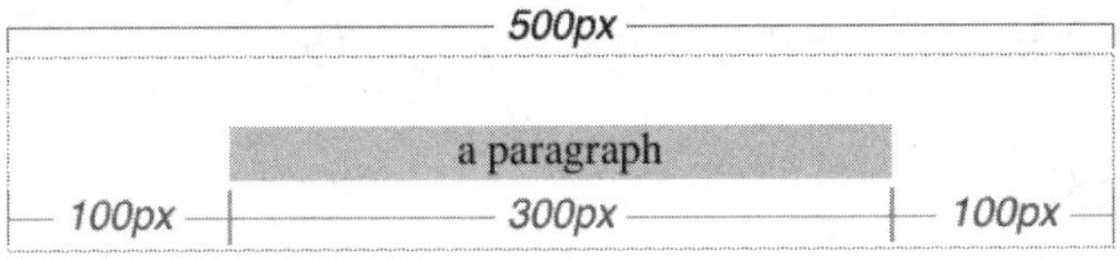

Figure 7-13. Setting an explicit width

Setting both margins to equal lengths is the correct way to center elements within block boxes in the normal flow. (There are other methods to be found with flexible box and grid layout, but they're beyond the scope of this text.)

Another way of sizing elements is to set one of the margins and the width to auto. The margin set to be auto is reduced to zero:

```
div {width: 500px;}
p {margin-left: auto; margin-right: 100px;
    width: auto;} /* left margin evaluates to 0; width becomes 400px */
```

The width is then set to the value necessary to make the element fill its containing block; in the preceding example, it would be 400 pixels, as shown in Figure 7-14.

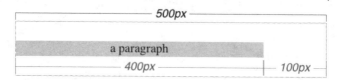

Figure 7-14. What happens when both the width and right margin are auto

Finally, what happens when all three properties are set to auto? The answer: both margins are set to zero, and the width is made as wide as possible. This result is the same as the default situation, when no values are explicitly declared for margins or the width. In such a case, the margins default to zero and the width defaults to auto.

Note that since horizontal margins do not collapse, the padding, borders, and margins of a parent element can affect its children. The effect is indirect in that the margins (and so on) of an element can induce an offset for child elements. The results of the following markup are shown in Figure 7-15:

```
div {padding: 50px; background: silver;}
p {margin: 30px; padding: 0; background: white;}
```

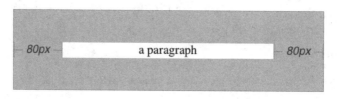

Figure 7-15. Offset is implicit in the parent's margins and padding

Negative Margins

So far, this may all seem rather straightforward, and you may be wondering why I said things could be complicated. Well, there's another side to margins: the negative side. That's right, it's possible to set negative values for margins. Setting negative margins can result in some interesting effects.

Remember that the total of the seven horizontal properties always equals the width of the parent element. As long as all properties are zero or greater, an element can never be wider than its parent's content area. However, consider the following markup, depicted in Figure 7-16:

```
div {width: 500px; border: 3px solid black;}
p.wide {margin-left: 10px; width: auto; margin-right: -50px; }
```

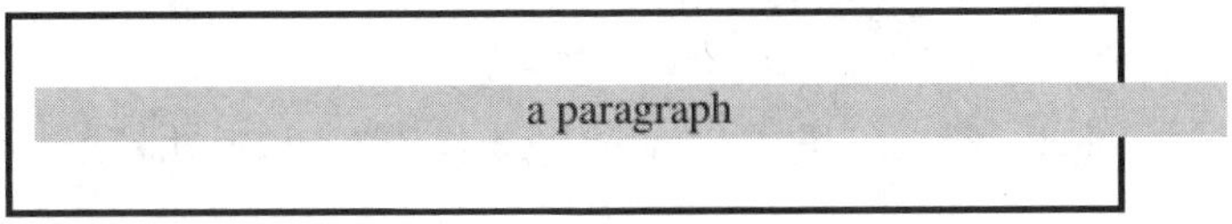

Figure 7-16. Wider children through negative margins

Yes indeed, the child element is wider than its parent! This is mathematically correct:

$$10px + 0 + 0 + 540px + 0 + 0 - 50px = 500px$$

The `540px` is the evaluation of `width: auto`, which is the number needed to balance out the rest of the values in the equation. Even though it leads to a child element sticking out its parent, the specification hasn't been violated because the values of the seven properties add up to the required total. It's a semantic dodge, but it's valid behavior.

Now, let's add some borders to the mix:

```
div {width: 500px; border: 3px solid black;}
p.wide {margin-left: 10px; width: auto; margin-right: -50px;
    border: 3px solid gray;}
```

The resulting change will be a reduction in the evaluated width of `width`:

$$10px + 3px + 0 + 534px + 0 + 3px - 50px = 500px$$

If we were to introduce padding, then the value of `width` would drop even more.

Conversely, it's possible to have `auto` right margins evaluate to negative amounts. If the values of other properties force the right margin to be negative in order to satisfy the requirement that elements be no wider than their containing block, then that's what will happen. Consider:

```
div {width: 500px; border: 3px solid black;}
p.wide {margin-left: 10px; width: 600px; margin-right: auto;
    border: 3px solid gray;}
```

The equation will work out like this:

$$10px + 3px + 0 + 600px + 0 + 3px - 116px = 500px$$

The right margin will evaluate to `-116px`. Even if we'd given it a different explicit value, it would still be forced to `-116px` because of the rule stating that when an element's dimensions are overconstrained, the right margin is reset to whatever is needed to make the numbers work out correctly. (Except in right-to-left languages, where the left margin would be overruled instead.)

Let's consider another example, illustrated in Figure 7-17, where the left margin is set to be negative:

```
div {width: 500px; border: 3px solid black;}
p.wide {margin-left: -50px; width: auto; margin-right: 10px;
    border: 3px solid gray;}
```

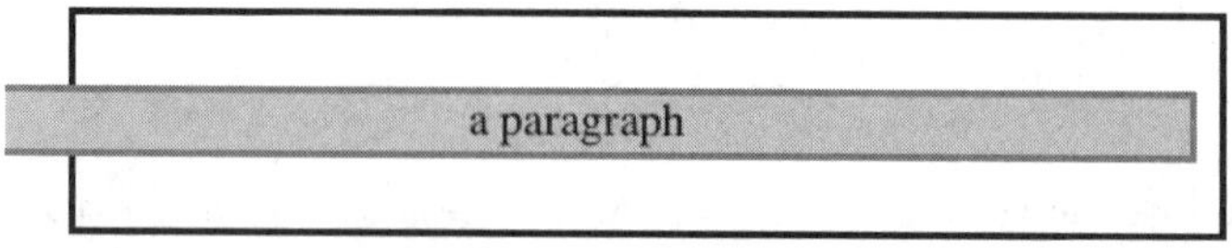

Figure 7-17. Setting a negative left margin

With a negative left margin, not only does the paragraph spill beyond the borders of the div, but it also spills beyond the edge of the browser window itself!

Remember that padding, borders, and content widths (and heights) can never be negative. Only margins can be less than zero.

Percentages

When it comes to percentage values for the width, padding, and margins, the same basic rules apply. It doesn't really matter whether the values are declared with lengths or percentages.

Percentages can be very useful. Suppose we want an element's content to be two-thirds the width of its containing block, the right and left padding to be 5% each, the left margin to be 5%, and the right margin to take up the slack. That would be written something like:

```
<p style="width: 67%; padding-right: 5%; padding-left: 5%; margin-right: auto;
    margin-left: 5%;">playing percentages</p>
```

The right margin would evaluate to 18% (100% - 67% - 5% - 5% - 5%) of the width of the containing block.

Mixing percentages and length units can be tricky, however. Consider the following example:

```
<p style="width: 67%; padding-right: 2em; padding-left: 2em; margin-right: auto;
    margin-left: 5em;">mixed lengths</p>
```

In this case, the element's box can be defined like this:

5em + 0 + 2 em + 67% + 2 em + 0 + auto = containing block width

In order for the right margin's width to evaluate to zero, the element's containing block must be 27.272727 em wide (with the content area of the element being 18.272727 em wide). Any wider than that and the right margin will evaluate to a positive value. Any narrower and the right margin will be a negative value.

The situation gets even more complicated if we start mixing length-value unity types, like this:

```
<p style="width: 67%; padding-right: 15px; padding-left: 10px;
    margin-right: auto;
    margin-left: 5em;">more mixed lengths</p>
```

And, just to make things more complex, borders cannot accept percentage values, only length values. The bottom line is that it isn't really possible to create a fully flexible element based solely on percentages unless you're willing to avoid using borders or use some of the more experimental approaches such as flexible box layout.

Replaced Elements

So far, we've been dealing with the horizontal formatting of nonreplaced block boxes in the normal flow of text. Block-level replaced elements are a bit simpler to manage. All of the rules given for nonreplaced blocks hold true, with one exception: if width is auto, then the width of the element is the content's intrinsic width. The image in the following example will be 20 pixels wide because that's the width of the original image:

```
<img src="smile.svg" style="display: block; width: auto; margin: 0;">
```

If the actual image were 100 pixels wide instead, then it would be laid out as 100 pixels wide.

It's possible to override this rule by assigning a specific value to width. Suppose we modify the previous example to show the same image three times, each with a different width value:

```
<img src="smile.svg" style="display: block; width: 25px; margin: 0;">
<img src="smile.svg" style="display: block; width: 50px; margin: 0;">
<img src="smile.svg" style="display: block; width: 100px; margin: 0;">
```

This is illustrated in Figure 7-18.

Note that the height of the elements also increases. When a replaced element's width is changed from its intrinsic width, the value of height is scaled to match, unless height has been set to an explicit value of its own. The reverse is also true: if height is set, but width is left as auto, then the width is scaled proportionately to the change in height.

Figure 7-18. Changing replaced element widths

Now that you're thinking about height, let's move on to the vertical formatting of normal-flow block box.

Vertical Formatting

Like horizontal formatting, the vertical formatting of block boxes has its own set of interesting behaviors. An element's content determines the default height of an element. The width of the content also affects height; the skinnier a paragraph becomes, for example, the taller it has to be in order to contain all of the inline content within it.

In CSS, it is possible to set an explicit height on any block-level element. If you do this, the resulting behavior depends on several other factors. Assume that the specified height is greater than that needed to display the content:

```
<p style="height: 10em;">
```

In this case, the extra height has a visual effect somewhat like extra padding. But suppose the height is *less* than what is needed to display the content:

```
<p style="height: 3.33em;">
```

When that happens, the browser is supposed to provide a means of viewing all content without increasing the height of the element box. In a case where the content of an element is taller than the height of its box, the actual behavior of a user agent will depend on the value of the property `overflow`. Two alternatives are shown in Figure 7-19.

Under CSS1, user agents can ignore any value of `height` other than `auto` if an element is not a replaced element (such as an image). In CSS2 and later, the value of `height` cannot be ignored, except in one specific circumstance involving percentage values. We'll talk about that in a moment.

Just as with `width`, `height` defines the content area's height by default, as opposed to the height of the visible element box. Any padding, borders, or margins on the top or bottom of the element box are *added* to the value for height, unless the value of box-sizing is different than content-box.

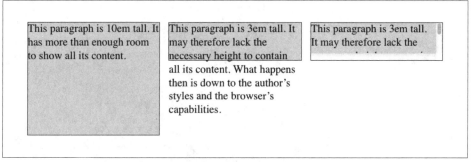

Figure 7-19. Heights that don't match the element's content height

Vertical Properties

As was the case with horizontal formatting, vertical formatting also has seven related properties: margin-top, border-top, padding-top, height, padding-bottom, border-bottom, and margin-bottom. These properties are diagrammed in Figure 7-20.

The values of these seven properties must equal the height of the block box's containing block. This is usually the value of height for a block box's parent (since block-level elements nearly always have block-level elements for parents).

Only three of these seven properties may be set to auto: the height of the element, and the top and bottom margins. The top and bottom padding and borders must be set to specific values or else they default to a width of zero (assuming no border-style is declared). If border-style has been set, then the thickness of the borders is set to be the vaguely defined value medium. Figure 7-21 provides an illustration for remembering which parts of the box may have a value of auto and which may not.

Interestingly, if either margin-top or margin-bottom is set to auto for a block box in the normal flow, they both automatically evaluate to 0. A value of 0 unfortunately prevents easy vertical centering of normal-flow boxes in their containing blocks. It also means that if you set the top and bottom margins of an element to auto, they are effectively reset to 0 and removed from the element box.

The handling of auto top and bottom margins is different for positioned elements, as well as flexible-box elements.

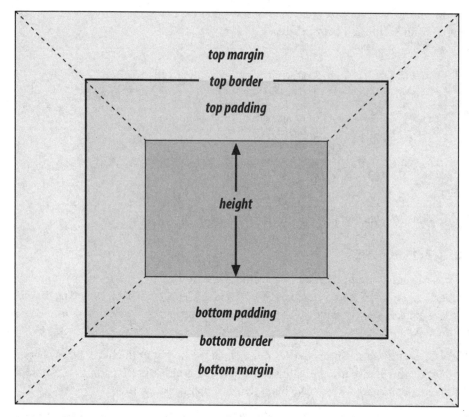

Figure 7-20. The seven properties of vertical formatting

`height` must be set to `auto` or to a nonnegative value of some type; it can never be less than zero.

Percentage Heights

You already saw how length-value heights are handled, so let's spend a moment on percentages. If the height of a normal-flow block box is set to a percentage value, then that value is taken as a percentage of the height of the box's containing block. Given the following markup, the resulting paragraph will be 3 em tall:

```
<div style="height: 6em;">
    <p style="height: 50%;">Half as tall</p>
</div>
```

Since setting the top and bottom margins to `auto` will give them zero height, the only way to vertically center the element in this particular case would be to set them both to 25%—and even then, the box would be centered, not the content within it.

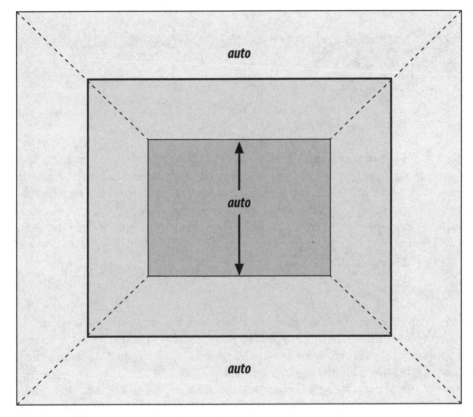

Figure 7-21. Vertical properties that can be set to auto

However, in cases where the height of the containing block is *not* explicitly declared, percentage heights are reset to auto. If we changed the previous example so that the height of the div is auto, the paragraph will now be exactly as tall as the div itself:

```
<div style="height: auto;">
    <p style="height: 50%;">NOT half as tall; height reset to auto</p>
</div>
```

These two possibilities are illustrated in Figure 7-22. (The spaces between the paragraph borders and the div borders are the top and bottom margins on the paragraphs.)

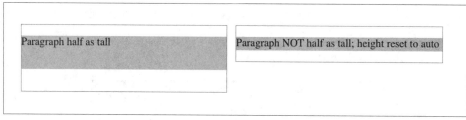

Figure 7-22. Percentage heights in different circumstances

Before we move on, take a closer look at the first example in Figure 7-22, the half-as-tall paragraph. It may be half as tall, but it isn't vertically centered. That's because the containing div is 6 em tall, which means the half-as-tall paragraph is 3 em tall. It has top and bottom margins of 1 em, so its overall box height is 5 em. That means there is actually 2 em of space between the bottom of the paragraph's visible box and the div's bottom border, not 1 em. It might seem a bit odd at first glance, but it makes sense once you work through the details.

Auto Heights

In the simplest case, a normal-flow block box with height: auto is rendered just high enough to enclose the line boxes of its inline content (including text). If an auto-height, normal-flow block box has only block-level children, then its default height will be the distance from the top of the topmost block-level child's outer border edge to the bottom of the bottommost block-level child's outer bottom border edge. Therefore, the margins of the child elements will "stick out" of the element that contains them. (This behavior is explained in the next section.)

However, if the block-level element has either top or bottom padding, or top or bottom borders, then its height will be the distance from the top of the outer-top margin edge of its topmost child to the outer-bottom margin edge of its bottommost child:

```
<div style="height: auto;
    background: silver;">
    <p style="margin-top: 2em; margin-bottom: 2em;">A paragraph!</p>
</div>
<div style="height: auto; border-top: 1px solid; border-bottom: 1px solid;
    background: silver;">
    <p style="margin-top: 2em; margin-bottom: 2em;">Another paragraph!</p>
</div>
```

Both of these behaviors are demonstrated in Figure 7-23.

If we changed the borders in the previous example to padding, the effect on the height of the div would be the same: it would still enclose the paragraph's margins within it.

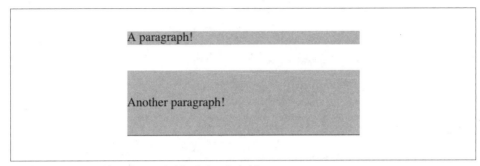

Figure 7-23. Auto heights with block-level children

Collapsing Vertical Margins

One other important aspect of vertical formatting is the *collapsing* of vertically adjacent margins. Collapsing behavior applies only to margins. Padding and borders, where they exist, never collapse with anything.

An unordered list, where list items follow one another, is a perfect example of margin collapsing. Assume that the following is declared for a list that contains five items:

```
li {margin-top: 10px; margin-bottom: 15px;}
```

Each list item has a 10-pixel top margin and a 15-pixel bottom margin. When the list is rendered, however, the distance between adjacent list items is 15 pixels, not 25. This happens because, along the vertical axis, adjacent margins are collapsed. In other words, the smaller of the two margins is eliminated in favor of the larger. Figure 7-24 shows the difference between collapsed and uncollapsed margins.

Correctly implemented user agents collapse vertically adjacent margins, as shown in the first list in Figure 7-24, where there are 15-pixel spaces between each list item. The second list shows what would happen if the user agent didn't collapse margins, resulting in 25-pixel spaces between list items.

Another word to use, if you don't like "collapse," is "overlap." Although the margins are not really overlapping, you can visualize what's happening using the following analogy.

Imagine that each element, such as a paragraph, is a small piece of paper with the content of the element written on it. Around each piece of paper is some amount of clear plastic, which represents the margins. The first piece of paper (say an h1 piece) is laid down on the canvas. The second (a paragraph) is laid below it and then slid up until the edge of one of the piece's plastic touches the edge of the other's paper. If the first piece of paper has half an inch of plastic along its bottom edge, and the second has a third of an inch along its top, then when they slide together, the first piece's plastic will touch the top edge of the second piece of paper. The two are now done being placed on the canvas, and the plastic attached to the pieces is overlapping.

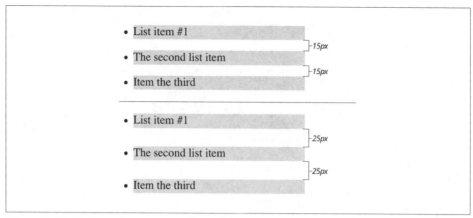

Figure 7-24. Collapsed versus uncollapsed margins

Collapsing also occurs where multiple margins meet, such as at the end of a list. Adding to the earlier example, let's assume the following rules apply:

```
ul {margin-bottom: 15px;}
li {margin-top: 10px; margin-bottom: 20px;}
h1 {margin-top: 28px;}
```

The last item in the list has a bottom margin of 20 pixels, the bottom margin of the ul is 15 pixels, and the top margin of a succeeding h1 is 28 pixels. So once the margins have been collapsed, the distance between the end of the li and the beginning of the h1 is 28 pixels, as shown in Figure 7-25.

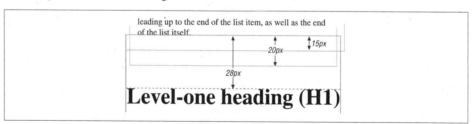

Figure 7-25. Collapsing in detail

Now, recall the examples from the previous section, where the introduction of a border or padding on a containing block would cause the margins of its child elements to be contained within it. We can see this behavior in operation by adding a border to the ul element in the previous example:

```
ul {margin-bottom: 15px; border: 1px solid;}
li {margin-top: 10px; margin-bottom: 20px;}
h1 {margin-top: 28px;}
```

With this change, the bottom margin of the li element is now placed inside its parent element (the ul). Therefore, the only margin collapsing that takes place is between the ul and the h1, as illustrated in Figure 7-26.

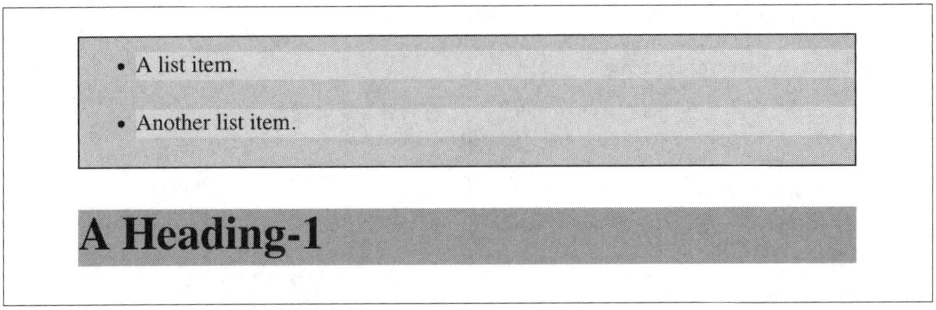

- A list item.

- Another list item.

A Heading-1

Figure 7-26. Collapsing (or not) with borders added to the mix

Negative Margins and Collapsing

Negative margins do have an impact on vertical formatting, and they affect how margins are collapsed. If negative vertical margins are set, then the browser should take the absolute maximum of both margins. The absolute value of the negative margin is then subtracted from the positive margin. In other words, the negative is added to the positive, and the resulting value is the distance between the elements. Figure 7-27 provides two concrete examples.

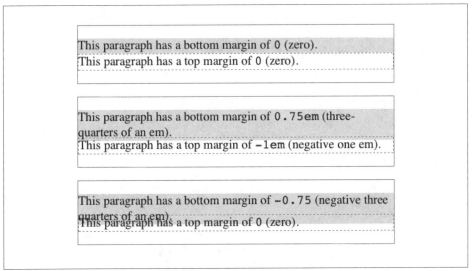

Figure 7-27. Examples of negative vertical margins

Notice the "pulling" effect of negative top and bottom margins. This is really no different from the way that negative horizontal margins cause an element to push outside of its parent. Consider:

```
p.neg {margin-top: -50px; margin-right: 10px;
    margin-left: 10px; margin-bottom: 0;
    border: 3px solid gray;}

<div style="width: 420px; background-color: silver; padding: 10px;
            margin-top: 50px; border: 1px solid;">
    <p class="neg">
        A paragraph.
    </p>

    A div.

</div>
```

As we see in Figure 7-28, the paragraph has been pulled upward by its negative top margin. Note that the content of the div that follows the paragraph in the markup has also been pulled upward 50 pixels. In fact, every bit of normal-flow content that follows the paragraph is also pulled upward 50 pixels.

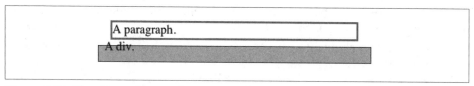

Figure 7-28. The effects of a negative top margin

Now compare the following markup to the situation shown in Figure 7-29:

```
p.neg {margin-bottom: -50px; margin-right: 10px;
    margin-left: 10px; margin-top: 0;
    border: 3px solid gray;}

<div style="width: 420px; margin-top: 50px;">
    <p class="neg">
        A paragraph.
    </p>
</div>
<p>
    The next paragraph.
</p>
```

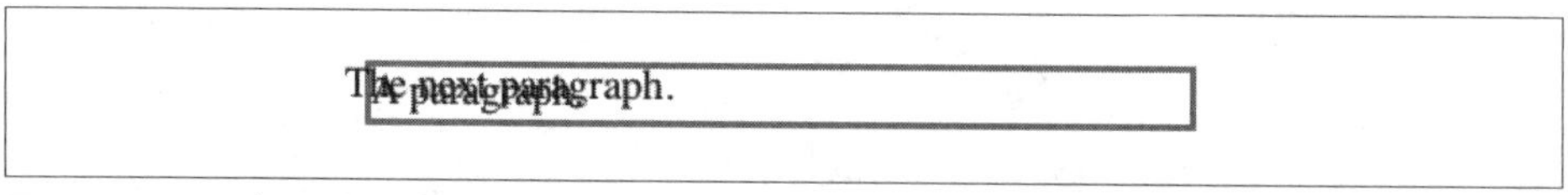

Figure 7-29. The effects of a negative bottom margin

What's really happening in Figure 7-29 is that the elements following the div are placed according to the location of the bottom of the div. As you can see, the end of the div is actually above the visual bottom of its child paragraph. The next element after the div is the appropriate distance from the bottom of the div. This is expected, given the rules we saw.

Now let's consider an example where the margins of a list item, an unordered list, and a paragraph are all collapsed. In this case, the unordered list and paragraph are assigned negative margins:

```
li {margin-bottom: 20px;}
ul {margin-bottom: -15px;}
h1 {margin-top: -18px;}
```

The larger of the two negative margins (-18px) is added to the largest positive margin (20px), yielding 20px - 18px = 2px. Thus, there are only two pixels between the bottom of the list item's content and the top of the h1's content, as we can see in Figure 7-30.

When elements overlap each other due to negative margins, it's hard to tell which elements are on top. You may also have noticed that none of the examples in this section use background colors. If they did, the background color of a following element might overwrite their content. This is expected behavior, since browsers usually render elements in order from beginning to end, so a normal-flow element that comes later in the document can be expected to overwrite an earlier element, assuming the two end up overlapping.

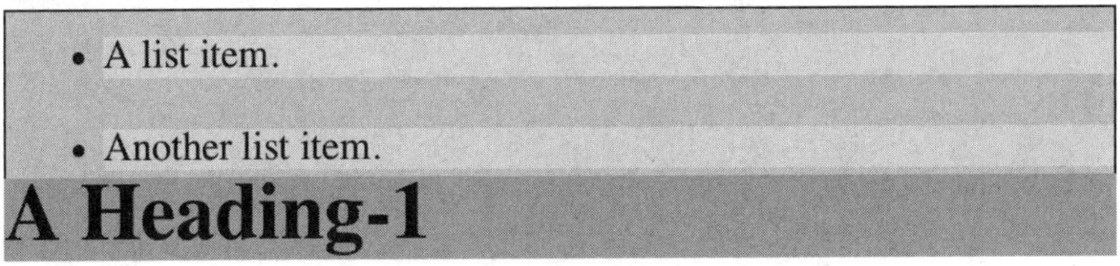

Figure 7-30. Collapsing margins and negative margins, in detail

List Items

List items have a few special rules of their own. They are typically preceded by a marker, such as a small dot or a number. This marker isn't actually part of the list item's content area, so effects like those illustrated in Figure 7-31 are common.

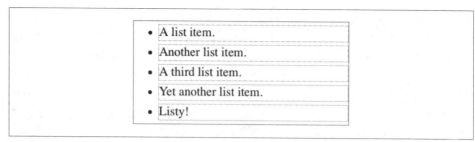

Figure 7-31. The content of list items

CSS1 said very little about the placement and effects of these markers with regard to the layout of a document. CSS2 introduced properties specifically designed to address this issue, such as `marker-offset`. However, a lack of implementations and changes in thinking caused this to be dropped from CSS2.1, and work is being done to reintroduce the idea (if not the specific syntax) to CSS. Accordingly, the placement of markers is largely beyond the control of authors, at least as of this writing.

The marker attached to a list item element can be either outside the content of the list item or treated as an inline marker at the beginning of the content, depending on the value of the property `list-style-position`. If the marker is brought inside, then the list item will interact with its neighbors exactly like a block-level element, as illustrated in Figure 7-32.

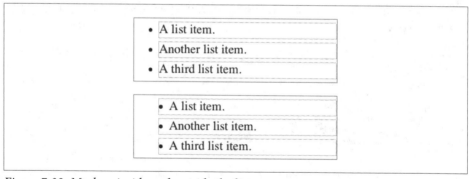

Figure 7-32. Markers inside and outside the list

If the marker stays outside the content, then it is placed some distance from the left content edge of the content (in left-to-right languages). No matter how the list's styles are altered, the marker stays the same distance from the content edge. Occasionally, the markers may be pushed outside of the list element itself, as we can see in Figure 7-32.

Remember that list-item boxes define containing blocks for their ancestor boxes, just like regular block boxes.

Inline Elements

After block-level elements, inline elements are the most common. Setting box properties for inline elements takes us into more interesting territory than we've been so far. Some good examples of inline elements are the em tag and the a tag, both of which are nonreplaced elements, and images, which are replaced elements.

Note that none of the behavior described in this section applies to table elements. CSS2 introduced new properties and behaviors for handling tables and table content, and these elements behave in ways fairly distinct from either block-level or inline formatting. Table styling is beyond the scope of this book, as it's surprisingly complicated and exists rather in a world of its own.

Nonreplaced and replaced elements are treated somewhat differently in the inline context, and we'll look at each in turn as we explore the construction of inline elements.

Line Layout

First, you need to understand how inline content is laid out. It isn't as simple as block-level elements, which just generate block boxes and usually don't allow anything to coexist with them. By contrast, look *inside* a block-level element, such as a paragraph. You may well ask, how did all those lines of text get there? What controls their arrangement? How can I affect it?

In order to understand how lines are generated, first consider the case of an element containing one very long line of text, as shown in Figure 7-33. Note that we've put a border around the line by wrapping the entire line in a span element and then assigning it a border style:

```
span {border: 1px dashed black;}
```

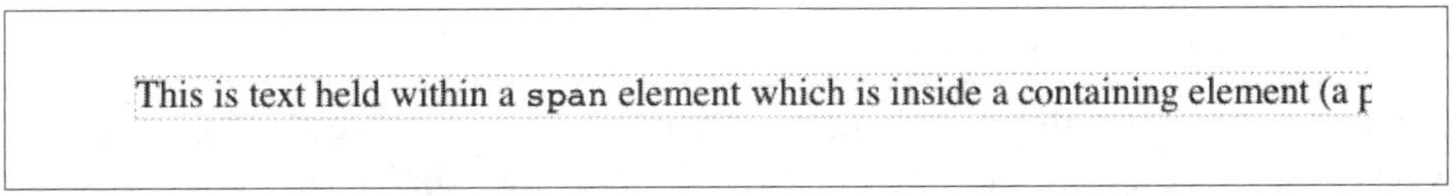

This is text held within a span element which is inside a containing element (a p

Figure 7-33. A single-line inline element

Figure 7-33 shows the simplest case of an inline element contained by a block-level element. It's no different in its way than a paragraph with two words in it. The only differences are that, in Figure 7-34, we have a few dozen words, and most paragraphs don't contain an explicit inline element such as span.

In order to get from this simplified state to something more familiar, all we have to do is determine how wide the element should be, and then break up the line so that the resulting pieces will fit into the content width of the element. Therefore, we arrive at the state shown in Figure 7-34.

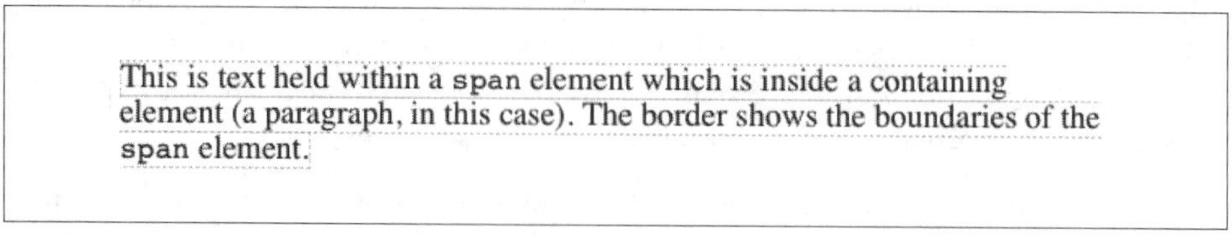

Figure 7-34. A multiple-line inline element

Nothing has really changed. All we did was take the single line and break it into pieces, and then stack those pieces on top of each other.

In Figure 7-34, the borders for each line of text also happen to coincide with the top and bottom of each line. This is true only because no padding has been set for the inline text. Notice that the borders actually overlap each other slightly; for example, the bottom border of the first line is just below the top border of the second line. This is because the border is actually drawn on the next pixel (assuming you're using a monitor) to the *outside* of each line. Since the lines are touching each other, their borders will overlap as shown in Figure 7-34.

If we alter the span styles to have a background color, the actual placement of the lines becomes quite clear. Consider Figure 7-35, which contains four paragraphs, each with a different value of text-align and each having the backgrounds of its lines filled in.

As we can see, not every line reaches to the edge of its parent paragraph's content area, which has been denoted with a dotted gray border. For the left-aligned paragraph, the lines are all pushed flush against the left content edge of the paragraph, and the end of each line happens wherever the line is broken. The reverse is true for the right-aligned paragraph. For the centered paragraph, the centers of the lines are aligned with the center of the paragraph.

In the last case, where the value of text-align is justify, each line is forced to be as wide as the paragraph's content area so that the line's edges touch the content edges of the paragraph. The difference between the natural length of the line and the width of the paragraph is made up by altering the spacing between letters and words in each line. Therefore, the value of word-spacing can be overridden when the text is justified. (The value of letter-spacing cannot be overridden if it is a length value.)

That pretty well covers how lines are generated in the simplest cases. As you're about to see, however, the inline formatting model is far from simple.

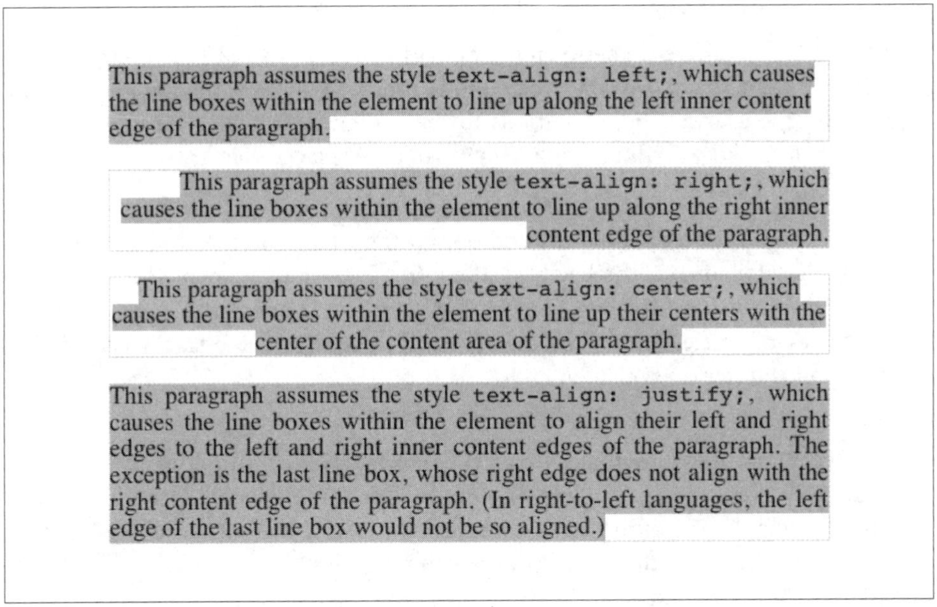

Figure 7-35. Showing lines in different alignments

Basic Terms and Concepts

Before we go any further, let's review some basic terms of inline layout, which will be
crucial in navigating the following sections:

Anonymous text

This is any string of characters that is not contained within an inline element.
Thus, in the markup `<p> I'm <em>so</em> happy!</p>`, the sequences " I'm "
and " happy!" are anonymous text. Note that the spaces are part of the text since
a space is a character like any other.

Em box

This is defined in the given font, otherwise known as the character box. Actual
glyphs can be taller or shorter than their em boxes. In CSS, the value of font-
size determines the height of each em box.

Content area

In nonreplaced elements, the content area can be one of two things, and the CSS
specification allows user agents to choose which one. The content area can be the
box described by the em boxes of every character in the element, strung together;
or it can be the box described by the character glyphs in the element. In this
book, I use the em box definition for simplicity's sake. In replaced elements, the
content area is the intrinsic height of the element plus any margins, borders, or
padding.

Leading

Leading is the difference between the values of font-size and line-height. This difference is actually divided in half and is applied equally to the top and bottom of the content area. These additions to the content area are called, not surprisingly, *half-leading*. Leading is applied only to nonreplaced elements.

Inline box

This is the box described by the addition of the leading to the content area. For nonreplaced elements, the height of the inline box of an element will be exactly equal to the value for line-height. For replaced elements, the height of the inline box of an element will be exactly equal to the content area, since leading is not applied to replaced elements.

Line box

This is the shortest box that bounds the highest and lowest points of the inline boxes that are found in the line. In other words, the top edge of the line box is placed along the top of the highest inline box top, and the bottom of the line box is placed along the bottom of the lowest inline box bottom.

CSS also contains a set of behaviors and useful concepts that fall outside of the above list of terms and definitions:

- The content area is analogous to the content box of a block box.
- The background of an inline element is applied to the content area plus any padding.
- Any border on an inline element surrounds the content area plus any padding and border.
- Padding, borders, and margins on nonreplaced elements have no vertical effect on inline elements or the boxes they generate; that is, they do *not* affect the height of an element's inline box (and thus the line box that contains the element).
- Margins and borders on replaced elements *do* affect the height of the inline box for that element and, by implication, the height of the line box for the line that contains the element.

One more thing to note: inline boxes are vertically aligned within the line according to their values for the property vertical-align.

Before moving on, let's look at a step-by-step process for constructing a line box, which you can use to see how the various pieces of the line fit together to determine its height.

Determine the height of the inline box for each element in the line by following these steps:

---

1. Find the values of `font-size` and `line-height` for each inline nonreplaced element and text that is not part of a descendant inline element and combine them. This is done by subtracting the `font-size` from the `line-height`, which yields the leading for the box. The leading is split in half and applied to the top and bottom of each em box.

2. Find the values of `height`, `margin-top`, `margin-bottom`, `padding-top`, `padding-bottom`, `border-top-width`, and `border-bottom-width` for each replaced element and add them together.

3. Figure out, for each content area, how much of it is above the baseline for the overall line and how much of it is below the baseline. This is not an easy task: you must know the position of the baseline for each element and piece of anonymous text and the baseline of the line itself, and then line them all up. In addition, the bottom edge of a replaced element sits on the baseline for the overall line.

4. Determine the vertical offset of any elements that have been given a value for `vertical-align`. This will tell you how far up or down that element's inline box will be moved, and it will change how much of the element is above or below the baseline.

5. Now that you know where all of the inline boxes have come to rest, calculate the final line box height. To do so, just add the distance between the baseline and the highest inline box top to the distance between the baseline and the lowest inline box bottom.

Let's consider the whole process in detail, which is the key to intelligently styling inline content.

Inline Formatting

First, know that all elements have a `line-height`, whether it's explicitly declared or not. This value greatly influences the way inline elements are displayed, so let's give it due attention.

Now let's establish how to determine the height of a line. A line's height (or the height of the line box) is determined by the height of its constituent elements and other content, such as text. It's important to understand that `line-height` actually affects inline elements and other inline content, *not* block-level elements—at least, not directly. We can set a `line-height` value for a block-level element, but the value will have a visual impact only as it's applied to inline content within that block-level element. Consider the following empty paragraph, for example:

```
<p style="line-height: 0.25em;"></p>
```

Without content, the paragraph won't have anything to display, so we won't see anything. The fact that this paragraph has a line-height of any value—be it 0.25em or 25in—makes no difference without some content to create a line box.

We can certainly set a line-height value for a block-level element and have that apply to all of the content within the block, whether or not the content is contained in any inline elements. In a certain sense, then, each line of text contained within a block-level element is its own inline element, whether or not it's surrounded by tags. If you like, picture a fictional tag sequence like this:

```
<p>
<line>This is a paragraph with a number of</line>
<line>lines of text which make up the</line>
<line>contents.</line>
</p>
```

Even though the line tags don't actually exist, the paragraph behaves as if they did—each line of text inherits styles from the paragraph. You only bother to create line-height rules for block-level elements so you don't have to explicitly declare a line-height for all of their inline elements, fictional or otherwise.

The fictional line element actually clarifies the behavior that results from setting line-height on a block-level element. According to the CSS specification, declaring line-height on a block-level element sets a *minimum* line box height for the content of that block-level element. Declaring p.spacious {line-height: 24pt;} means that the *minimum* heights for each line box is 24 points. Technically, content can inherit this line height only if an inline element does so. Most text isn't contained by an inline element. If you pretend that each line is contained by the fictional line element, the model works out very nicely.

Inline Nonreplaced Elements

Building on your formatting knowledge, let's move on to the construction of lines that contain only nonreplaced elements (or anonymous text). Then you'll be in a good position to understand the differences between nonreplaced and replaced elements in inline layout.

Building the Boxes

First, for an inline nonreplaced element or piece of anonymous text, the value of font-size determines the height of the content area. If an inline element has a font-size of 15px, then the content area's height is 15 pixels because all of the em boxes in the element are 15 pixels tall, as illustrated in Figure 7-36.

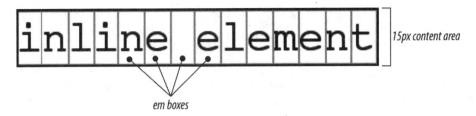

em boxes

Figure 7-36. Em boxes determine content area height

The next thing to consider is the value of line-height for the element, and the difference between it and the value of font-size. If an inline nonreplaced element has a font-size of 15px and a line-height of 21px, then the difference is six pixels. The user agent splits the six pixels in half and applies half to the top and half to the bottom of the content area, which yields the inline box. This process is illustrated in Figure 7-37.

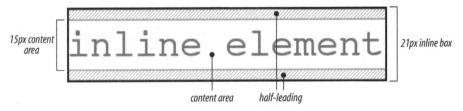

Figure 7-37. Content area plus leading equals inline box

Let's assume that the following is true:

```
<p style="font-size: 12px; line-height: 12px;">
This is text, <em>some of which is emphasized</em>, plus other text<br>
which is <strong style="font-size: 24px;">strongly emphasized</strong>
and which is<br>
larger than the surrounding text.
</p>
```

In this example, most of the text has a font-size of 12px, while the text in one inline nonreplaced element has a size of 24px. However, *all* of the text has a line-height of 12px since line-height is an inherited property. Therefore, the strong element's line-height is also 12px.

Thus, for each piece of text where both the font-size and line-height are 12px, the content height does not change (since the difference between 12px and 12px is zero), so the inline box is 12 pixels high. For the strong text, however, the difference between line-height and font-size is -12px. This is divided in half to determine the half-leading (-6px), and the half-leading is added to both the top and bottom of the content height to arrive at an inline box. Since we're adding a negative number in both cases, the inline box ends up being 12 pixels tall. The 12-pixel inline box is centered vertically within the 24-pixel content height of the element, so the inline box is actually smaller than the content area.

So far, it sounds like we've done the same thing to each bit of text, and that all the inline boxes are the same size, but that's not quite true. The inline boxes in the second line, although they're the same size, don't actually line up because the text is all baseline-aligned (see Figure 7-38).

Since inline boxes determine the height of the overall line box, their placement with respect to each other is critical. The line box is defined as the distance from the top of the highest inline box in the line to the bottom of the lowest inline box, and the top of each line box butts up against the bottom of the line box for the preceding line. The result shown in Figure 7-38 gives us the paragraph shown in Figure 7-39.

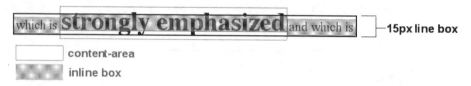

Figure 7-38. Inline boxes within a line

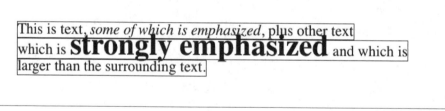

Figure 7-39. Line boxes within a paragraph

As we can see in Figure 7-39, the middle line is taller than the other two, but it still isn't big enough to contain all of the text within it. The anonymous text's inline box determines the bottom of the line box, while the top of the strong element's inline box sets the top of the line box. Because that inline box's top is inside the element's content area, the contents of the element spill outside the line box and actually overlap other line boxes. The result is that the lines of text look irregular.

In just a bit, we'll explore ways to cope with this behavior and methods for achieving consistent baseline spacing.

Vertical Alignment

If we change the vertical alignment of the inline boxes, the same height determination principles apply. Suppose that we give the strong element a vertical alignment of 4px:

```
<p style="font-size: 12px; line-height: 12px;">
This is text, <em>some of which is emphasized</em>, plus other text<br>
which is <strong style="font-size: 24px; vertical-align: 4px;">strongly
emphasized</strong> and that is<br>
larger than the surrounding text.
</p>
```

That small change raises the strong element four pixels, which pushes up both its content area and its inline box. Because the strong element's inline box top was already the highest in the line, this change in vertical alignment also pushes the top of the line box upward by four pixels, as shown in Figure 7-40.

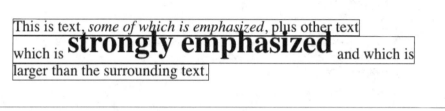

Figure 7-40. Vertical alignment affects line box height

Let's consider another situation. Here, we have another inline element in the same line as the strong text, and its alignment is other than the baseline:

```
<p style="font-size: 12px; line-height: 12px;">
This is text, <em>some of which is emphasized</em>,<br>
plus other text that is <strong style="font-size: 24px;">strong</strong>
 and <span style="vertical-align: top;">tall</span> and is<br>
larger than the surrounding text.
</p>
```

Now we have the same result as in our earlier example, where the middle line box is taller than the other line boxes. However, notice how the "tall" text is aligned in Figure 7-41.

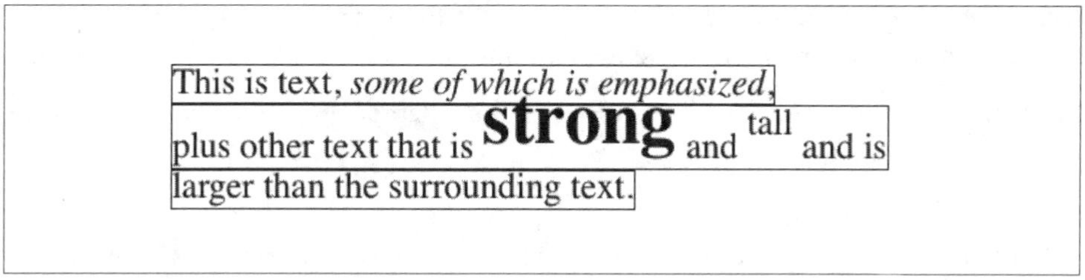

Figure 7-41. Aligning an inline element to the line box

In this case, the top of the "tall" text's inline box is aligned with the top of the line box. Since the "tall" text has equal values for font-size and line-height, the content height and inline box are the same. However, consider this:

```
<p style="font-size: 12px; line-height: 12px;">
This is text, <em>some of which is emphasized</em>,<br>
plus other text that is <strong style="font-size: 24px;">strong</strong>
 and <span style="vertical-align: top; line-height: 2px;">tall</span> and is<br>
larger than the surrounding text.
</p>
```

Since the line-height for the "tall" text is less than its font-size, the inline box for that element is smaller than its content area. This tiny fact changes the placement of the text itself since the top of its inline box must be aligned with the top of the line box for its line. Thus, we get the result shown in Figure 7-42.

On the other hand, we could set the "tall" text to have a line-height that is actually bigger than its font-size. For example:

```
<p style="font-size: 12px; line-height: 12px;">
This is text, <em>some of which is emphasized</em>, plus other text<br>
that is <strong style="font-size: 24px;">strong</strong>
and <span style="vertical-align: top; line-height: 18px;">tall</span>
and that is<br>
larger than the surrounding text.
</p>
```

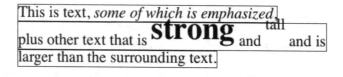

Figure 7-42. Text protruding from the line box (again)

Since we've given the "tall" text a line-height of 18px, the difference between line-height and font-size is six pixels. The half-leading of three pixels is added to the content area and results in an inline box that is 18 pixels tall. The top of this inline box aligns with the top of the line box. Similarly, the vertical-align value bottom will align the bottom of an inline element's inline box with the bottom of the line box.

In relation to the terms we've been using in this chapter, the effects of the assorted keyword values of vertical-align are:

top

    Aligns the top of the element's inline box with the top of the containing line box `bottom`

> Aligns the bottom of the element's inline box with the bottom of the containing line box

`text-top`

> Aligns the top of the element's inline box with the top of the parent's content area

`text-bottom`

> Aligns the bottom of the element's inline box with the bottom of the parent's content area

`middle`

> Aligns the vertical midpoint of the element's inline box with `0.5ex` above the baseline of the parent

`super`

> Moves the content area and inline box of the element upward. The distance is not specified and may vary by user agent

`sub`

> The same as super, except the element is moved downward instead of upward

`<percentage>`

> Shifts the element up or down the distance defined by taking the declared percentage of the element's value for `line-height`

Managing the line-height

In previous sections, we saw that changing the `line-height` of an inline element can cause text from one line to overlap another. In each case, though, the changes were made to individual elements. So how can we affect the `line-height` of elements in a more general way in order to keep content from overlapping?

One way to do this is to use the `em` unit in conjunction with an element whose `font-size` has changed. For example:

```
p {line-height: 1em;}
big {font-size: 250%; line-height: 1em;}

<p>
Not only does this paragraph have "normal" text, but it also<br>
contains a line in which <big>some big text</big> is found.<br>
This large text helps illustrate our point.
</p>
```

By setting a `line-height` for the `big` element, we increase the overall height of the line box, providing enough room to display the big element without overlapping any other text and without changing the `line-height` of all lines in the paragraph. We use a value of `1em` so that the `line-height` for the `big` element will be set to the same size as `big`'s font-size. Remember, `line-height` is set in relation to the `font-size` of the element itself, not the parent element. The results are shown in Figure 7-43.

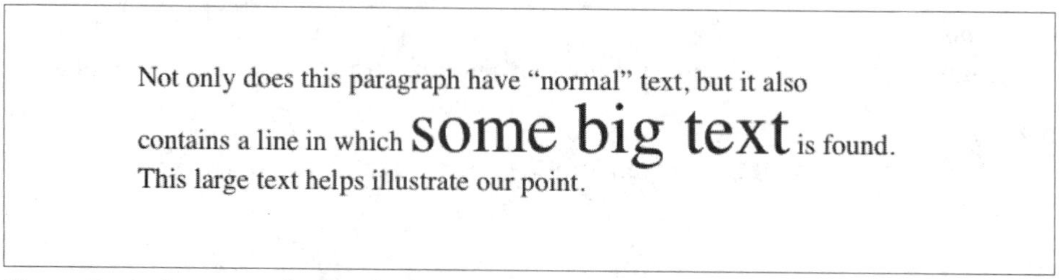

Figure 7-43. Assigning the line-height property to inline elements

Make sure you really understand the previous sections, because things will get trickier when we try to add borders. Let's say we want to put five-pixel borders around any hyperlink:

```
a:link {border: 5px solid blue;}
```

If we don't set a large enough `line-height` to accommodate the border, it will be in danger of overwriting other lines. We could increase the size of the inline box for unvisited links using `line-height`, as we did for the `big` element in the earlier example; in this case, we'd just need to make the value of `line-height` 10 pixels larger than the value of font-size for those links. However, that will be difficult if we don't actually know the size of the font in pixels.

Another solution is to increase the `line-height` of the paragraph. This will affect every line in the entire element, not just the line in which the bordered hyperlink appears:

```
p {line-height: 1.8em;}
a:link {border: 5px solid blue;}
```

Because there is extra space added above and below each line, the border around the hyperlink doesn't impinge on any other line, as we can see in Figure 7-44.

This approach works here because all of the text is the same size. If there were other elements in the line that changed the height of the line box, our border situation might also change. Consider the following:

```
p {font-size: 14px; line-height: 24px;}
a:link {border: 5px solid blue;}
big {font-size: 150%; line-height: 1.5em;}
```

Given these rules, the height of the inline box of a `big` element within a paragraph will be 31.5 pixels (14 × 1.5 × 1.5), and that will also be the height of the line box. In order to keep baseline spacing consistent, we must make the p element's `line-height` equal to or greater than 32px.

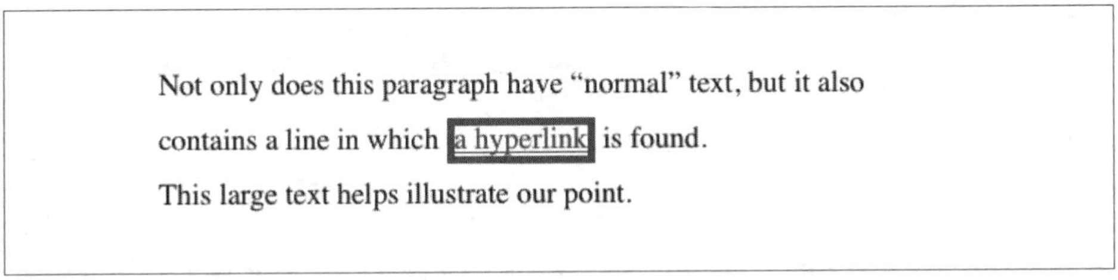

Not only does this paragraph have "normal" text, but it also

contains a line in which a hyperlink is found.

This large text helps illustrate our point.

Figure 7-44. Increasing line-height to leave room for inline borders

Baselines and line heights

The actual height of each line box depends on the way its component elements line up with one another. This alignment tends to depend very much on where the baseline falls within each element (or piece of anonymous text) because that location determines how the inline boxes are arranged. The placement of the baseline within each em box is different for every font. This information is built into the font files and cannot be altered by any means other than directly editing the font files.

Consistent baseline spacing tends to be more of an art than a science. If you declare all of your font sizes and line heights using a single unit, such as ems, then you have a reliable chance of consistent baseline spacing. If you mix units, however, that feat becomes a great deal more difficult, if not impossible. As of this writing, there are proposals for properties that would let authors enforce consistent baseline spacing regardless of the inline content, which would greatly simplify certain aspects of online typography. None of these proposed properties have been implemented though, which makes their adoption a distant hope at best.

Scaling Line Heights

The best way to set line-height, as it turns out, is to use a raw number as the value. This method is the best because the number becomes the scaling factor, and that factor is an inherited, not a computed, value. Let's say we want the line-height's of all elements in a document to be one and a half times their `font-size. We would declare:

```
body {line-height: 1.5;}
```

This scaling factor of 1.5 is passed down from element to element, and, at each level, the factor is used as a multiplier of the font-size of each element. Therefore, the following markup would be displayed as shown in Figure 7-45:

```
p {font-size: 15px; line-height: 1.5;}
small {font-size: 66%;}
big {font-size: 200%;}

<p>This paragraph has a line-height of 1.5 times its font-size. In addition,
any elements within it <small>such as this small element</small> also have
```

```
line-heights 1.5 times their font-size...and that includes <big>this big
element right here</big>. By using a scaling factor, line-heights scale
to match the font-size of any element.</p>
```

In this example, the line height for the small element turns out to be 15 pixels, and for the big element, it's 45 pixels. (These numbers may seem excessive, but they're in keeping with the overall page design.) Of course, if we don't want our big text to generate too much extra leading, we can give it a line-height value, which will override the inherited scaling factor:

```
p {font-size: 15px; line-height: 1.5;}
small {font-size: 66%;}
big {font-size: 200%; line-height: 1em;}
```

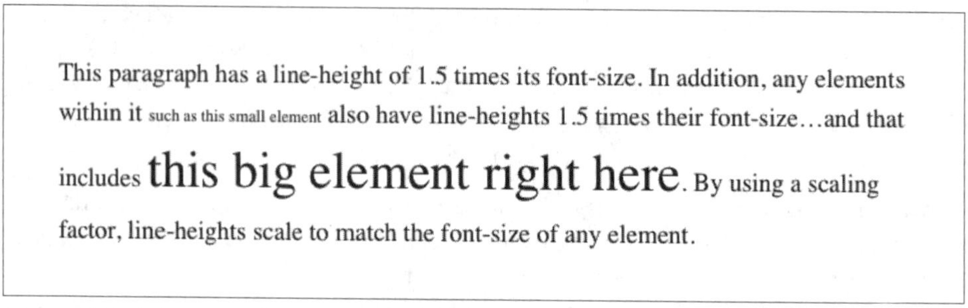

This paragraph has a line-height of 1.5 times its font-size. In addition, any elements within it such as this small element also have line-heights 1.5 times their font-size...and that includes this big element right here. By using a scaling factor, line-heights scale to match the font-size of any element.

Figure 7-45. Using a scaling factor for line-height

Another solution—possibly the simplest of all—is to set the styles such that lines are no taller than absolutely necessary to hold their content. This is where we might use a line-height of 1.0. This value will multiply itself by every font-size to get the same value as the font-size of every element. Thus, for every element, the inline box will be the same as the content area, which will mean the absolute minimum size necessary is used to contain the content area of each element.

Most fonts still display a little bit of space between the lines of character glyphs because characters are usually smaller than their em boxes. The exception is script ("cursive") fonts, where character glyphs are usually *larger* than their em boxes.

Adding Box Properties

As you're aware from previous discussions, padding, margins, and borders may all be applied to inline nonreplaced elements. These aspects of the inline element do not influence the height of the line box at all. If you were to apply some borders to a span element without any margins or padding, you'd get results such as those shown in Figure 7-46.

The border edge of inline elements is controlled by the font-size, not the line-height. In other words, if a span element has a font-size of 12px and a line-height of 36px, its content area is 12px high, and the border will surround that content area.

Alternatively, we can assign padding to the inline element, which will push the borders away from the text itself:

```
span {padding: 4px;}
```

Note that this padding does not alter the actual shape of the content height, and so it will not affect the height of the inline box for this element. Similarly, adding borders to an inline element will not affect the way line boxes are generated and laid out, as illustrated in Figure 7-47.

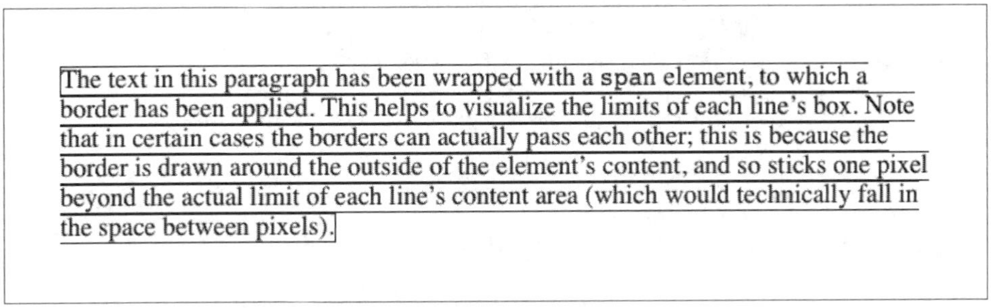

The text in this paragraph has been wrapped with a span element, to which a border has been applied. This helps to visualize the limits of each line's box. Note that in certain cases the borders can actually pass each other; this is because the border is drawn around the outside of the element's content, and so sticks one pixel beyond the actual limit of each line's content area (which would technically fall in the space between pixels).

Figure 7-46. Inline borders and line-box layout

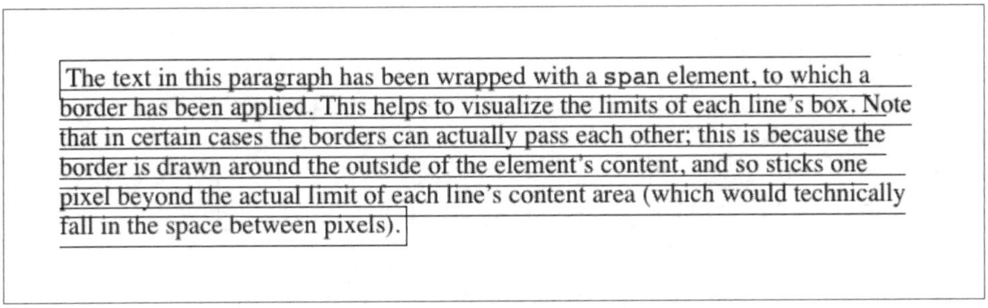

The text in this paragraph has been wrapped with a span element, to which a border has been applied. This helps to visualize the limits of each line's box. Note that in certain cases the borders can actually pass each other; this is because the border is drawn around the outside of the element's content, and so sticks one pixel beyond the actual limit of each line's content area (which would technically fall in the space between pixels).

Figure 7-47. Padding and borders do not alter line-height

As for margins, they do not, practically speaking, apply to the top and bottom of an inline nonreplaced element, as they don't affect the height of the line box. The ends of the element are another story.

Recall the idea that an inline element is basically laid out as a single line and then broken up into pieces. So, if we apply margins to an inline element, those margins will appear at its beginning and end: these are the left and right margins, respectively. Padding also appears at the edges. Thus, although padding and margins (and borders) do not affect line heights, they can still affect the layout of an element's content by pushing text away from its ends. In fact, negative left and right margins can pull text closer to the inline element, or even cause overlap, as Figure 7-48 shows.

Think of an inline element as a strip of paper with some plastic surrounding it. Displaying the inline element on multiple lines is like slicing up the strip into smaller strips. However, no extra plastic is added to each smaller strip. The only plastic is that which was on the strip to begin with, so it appears only at the beginning and end of the original ends of the paper strip (the inline element). At least, that's the default behavior, but as we'll soon see, there is another option.

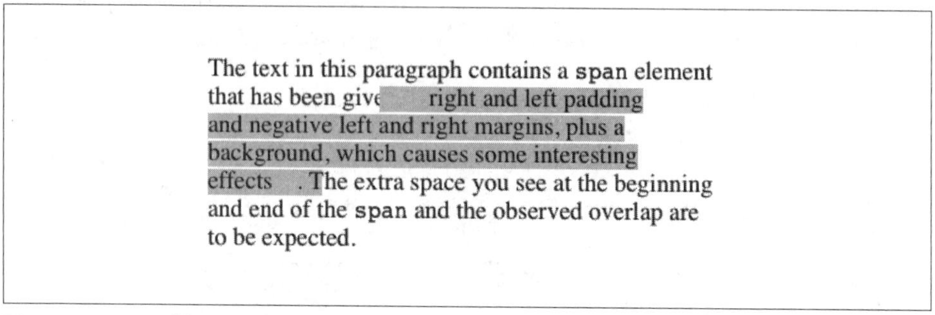

The text in this paragraph contains a span element that has been give right and left padding and negative left and right margins, plus a background, which causes some interesting effects . The extra space you see at the beginning and end of the span and the observed overlap are to be expected.

Figure 7-48. Padding and margins on the ends of an inline element

So, what happens when an inline element has a background and enough padding to cause the lines' backgrounds to overlap? Take the following situation as an example:

```
p {font-size: 15px; line-height: 1em;}
p span {background: #FAA; padding-top: 10px; padding-bottom: 10px;}
```

All of the text within the span element will have a content area 15 pixels tall, and we've applied 10 pixels of padding to the top and bottom of each content area. The extra pixels won't increase the height of the line box, which would be fine, except there is a background color. Thus, we get the result shown in Figure 7-49.

CSS 2.1 explicitly states that the line boxes are drawn in document order: "This will cause the borders on subsequent lines to paint over the borders and text of previous lines." The same principle applies to backgrounds as well, as Figure 7-49 shows. CSS2, on the other hand, allowed user agents "to 'clip' the border and padding areas (i.e., not render them)." Therefore, the results may depend greatly on which specification the user agent follows.

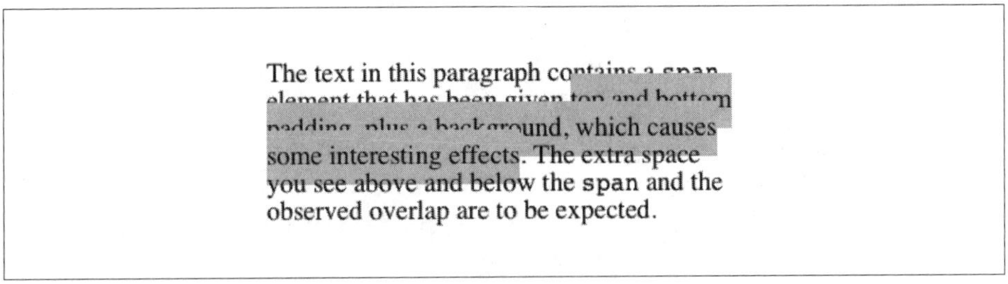

The text in this paragraph contains a span
element that has been given top and bottom
padding, plus a background, which causes
some interesting effects. The extra space
you see above and below the span and the
observed overlap are to be expected.

Figure 7-49. Overlapping inline backgrounds

Changing Breaking Behavior

In the previous section, we saw that when an inline nonreplaced element is broken
across multiple lines, it's treated as if it were one long single-line element that's sliced
into smaller boxes, one slice per line break. That's actually just the default behavior,
and it can be changed via the property box-decoration-break.

box-decoration-break

Values	slice|clone
Initial value	slice
Applies to	All elements
Computed value	As specified
Inherited	No
Animatable	No

The default value, slice, is what we saw in the previous section. The other value,
clone, causes each fragment of the element to be drawn as if it were a standalone
box. What does that mean? Compare the two examples in Figure 7-50, in which
exactly the same markup and styles are treated as either sliced or cloned.

Many of the differences are pretty apparent, but a few are perhaps more subtle.
Among the effects are the application of padding to each element's fragment, including at the ends where the line breaks occurred. Similarly, the border is drawn around
each fragment individually, instead of being broken up.

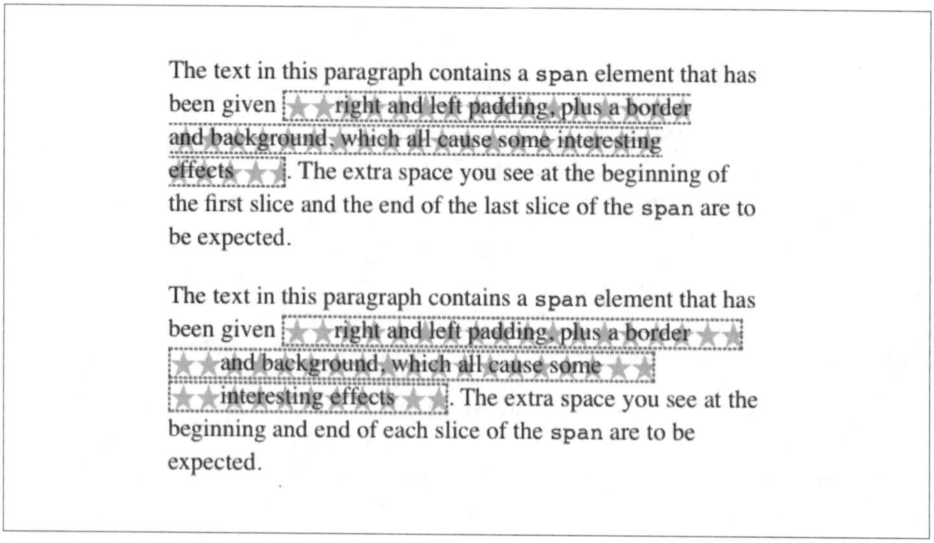

The text in this paragraph contains a span element that has been given [right and left padding, plus a border and background, which all cause some interesting effects]. The extra space you see at the beginning of the first slice and the end of the last slice of the span are to be expected.

The text in this paragraph contains a span element that has been given [right and left padding, plus a border] [and background, which all cause some] [interesting effects]. The extra space you see at the beginning and end of each slice of the span are to be expected.

Figure 7-50. Sliced and cloned inline fragments

More subtly, notice how the background-image positioning changes between the two. In the sliced version, background images are sliced along with everything else, meaning that only one of the fragments contains the origin image. In the cloned version, however, each background acts as its own copy, so each has its own origin image. This means, for example, that even if we have a nonrepeated background image, it will appear once in each fragment instead of only in one fragment.

The box-decoration-break property will most often be used with inline boxes, but it actually applies in any situation where there's a break in an element—for example, when a page break interrupts an element in paged media. In such a case, each fragment is a separate slice. If we set box-decoration-break: clone, then each box fragment will be treated as a copy when it comes to borders, padding, backgrounds, and so on. The same holds true in multicolumn layout: if an element is split by a column break, the value of box-decoration-break will affect how it is rendered.

Glyphs Versus Content Area

Even in cases where you try to keep inline nonreplaced element backgrounds from overlapping, it can still happen, depending on which font is in use. The problem lies in the difference between a font's em box and its character glyphs. Most fonts, as it turns out, don't have em boxes whose heights match the character glyphs.

That may sound very abstract, but it has practical consequences. In CSS2.1, we find the following: "the height of the content area should be based on the font, but this specification does not specify how. A user agent may…use the em box or the maximum ascender and descender of the font. (The latter would ensure that glyphs with parts above or below the em box still fall within the content area, but leads to differently sized boxes for different fonts.)"

In other words, the "painting area" of an inline nonreplaced element is left to the user agent. If a user agent takes the em box to be the height of the content area, then the background of an inline nonreplaced element will be equal to the height of the em box (which is the value of font-size). If a user agent uses the maximum ascender and descender of the font, then the background may be taller or shorter than the em box. Therefore, you could give an inline nonreplaced element a line-height of 1em and still have its background overlap the content of other lines.

Inline Replaced Elements

Inline replaced elements, such as images, are assumed to have an intrinsic height and width; for example, an image will be a certain number of pixels high and wide. Therefore, a replaced element with an intrinsic height can cause a line box to become taller than normal. This does *not* change the value of line-height for any element in the line, *including the replaced element itself*. Instead, the line box is made just tall enough to accommodate the replaced element, plus any box properties. In other words, the entirety of the replaced element—content, margins, borders, and padding—is used to define the element's inline box. The following styles lead to one such example, as shown in Figure 7-51:

```
p {font-size: 15px; line-height: 18px;}
img {height: 30px; margin: 0; padding: 0; border: none;}
```

Despite all the blank space, the effective value of line-height has not changed, either for the paragraph or the image itself. line-height has no effect on the image's inline box. Because the image in Figure 7-51 has no padding, margins, or borders, its inline box is equivalent to its content area, which is, in this case, 30 pixels tall.

Nonetheless, an inline replaced element still has a value for line-height. Why? In the most common case, it needs the value in order to correctly position the element if it's been vertically aligned. Recall that, for example, percentage values for vertical-align are calculated with respect to an element's line-height. Thus:

```
p {font-size: 15px; line-height: 18px;}
img {vertical-align: 50%;}

<p>the image in this sentence <img src="test.gif" alt="test image">
will be raised 9 pixels.</p>
```

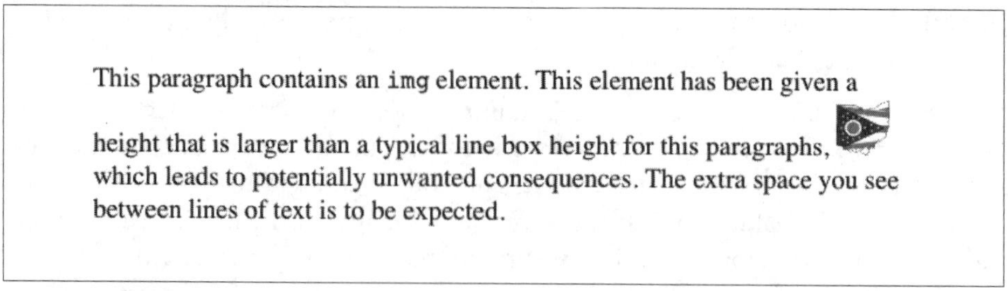

> This paragraph contains an img element. This element has been given a
>
> height that is larger than a typical line box height for this paragraphs,
> which leads to potentially unwanted consequences. The extra space you see
> between lines of text is to be expected.

Figure 7-51. Replaced elements can increase the height of the line box but not the value of line-height

The inherited value of line-height causes the image to be raised nine pixels instead of some other number. Without a value for line-height, it wouldn't be possible to perform percentage-value vertical alignments. The height of the image itself has no relevance when it comes to vertical alignment; the value of line-height is all that matters.

However, for other replaced elements, it might be important to pass on a line-height value to descendant elements within that replaced element. An example would be an SVG image, which uses CSS to style any text found within the image.

Adding Box Properties

After everything we've just been through, applying margins, borders, and padding to inline replaced elements almost seems simple.

Padding and borders are applied to replaced elements as usual; padding inserts space around the actual content and the border surrounds the padding. What's unusual about the process is that these two things actually influence the height of the line box because they are part of the inline box of an inline replaced element (unlike inline nonreplaced elements). Consider Figure 7-52, which results from the following styles:

```
img {height: 50px; width: 50px;}
img.one {margin: 0; padding: 0; border: 3px dotted;}
img.two {margin: 10px; padding: 10px; border: 3px solid;}
```

Note that the first line box is made tall enough to contain the image, whereas the second is tall enough to contain the image, its padding, and its border.

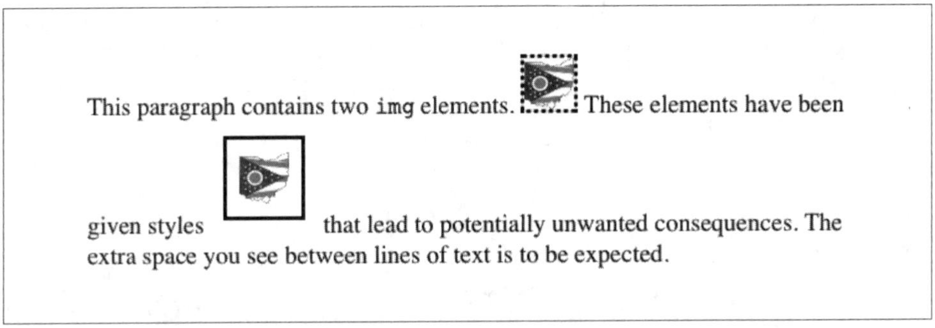

Figure 7-52. Adding padding, borders, and margins to an inline replaced element increases its inline box

Margins are also contained within the line box, but they have their own wrinkles. Setting a positive margin is no mystery; it will make the inline box of the replaced element taller. Setting negative margins, meanwhile, has a similar effect: it decreases the size of the replaced element's inline box. This is illustrated in Figure 7-53, where we can see that a negative top margin is pulling down the line above the image:

```
img.two {margin-top: -10px;}
```

Negative margins operate the same way on block-level elements, of course. In this case, the negative margins make the replaced element's inline box smaller than ordinary. Negative margins are the only way to cause inline replaced elements to bleed into other lines, and it's why the boxes that replaced inline elements generate are often assumed to be inline-block.

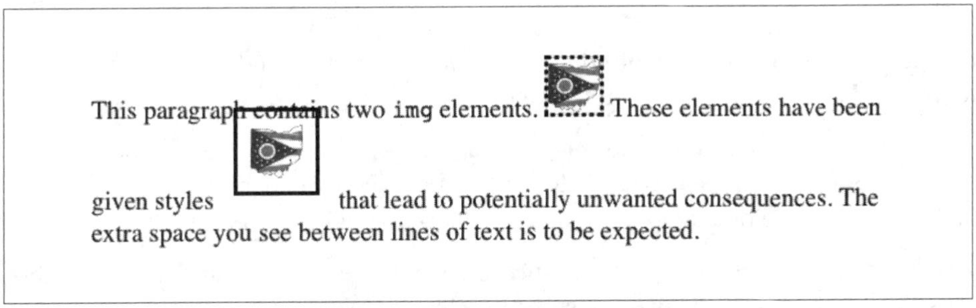

Figure 7-53. The effect of negative margins on inline replaced elements

Replaced Elements and the Baseline

You may have noticed by now that, by default, inline replaced elements sit on the baseline. If you add bottom padding, a margin, or a border to the replaced element, then the content area will move upward (assuming box-sizing: content-box). Replaced elements do not have baselines of their own, so the next best thing is to align the bottom of their inline boxes with the baseline. Thus, it is actually the bottom outer margin edge that is aligned with the baseline, as illustrated in Figure 7-54.

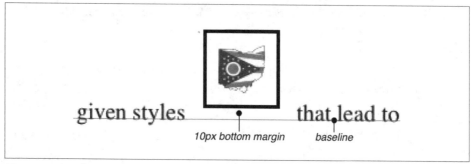

Figure 7-54. Inline replaced elements sit on the baseline

This baseline alignment leads to an unexpected (and unwelcome) consequence: an image placed in a table cell all by itself should make the table cell tall enough to contain the line box containing the image. The resizing occurs even if there is no actual text, not even whitespace, in the table cell with the image. Therefore, the common sliced-image and spacer-GIF designs of years past can fall apart quite dramatically in modern browsers. (I know that *you* don't create such things, but this is still a handy context in which to explain this behavior.) Consider the simplest case:

```
td {font-size: 12px;}
```

```
<td><img src="spacer.gif" height="1" width="10"></td>
```

Under the CSS inline formatting model, the table cell will be 12 pixels tall, with the image sitting on the baseline of the cell. So there might be three pixels of space below the image and eight above it, although the exact distances would depend on the font family used and the placement of its baseline.

This behavior is not confined to images inside table cells; it will also happen in any situation where an inline replaced element is the sole descendant of a block-level or table-cell element. For example, an image inside a div will also sit on the baseline.

The most common workaround for such circumstances is to make images in table cells block-level so that they do not generate a line box. For example:

```
td {font-size: 12px;}
img.block {display: block;}
```

```
<td><img src="spacer.gif" height="1" width="10" class="block"></td>
```

Another possible fix would be to make the font-size and line-height of the enclosing table cell 1px, which would make the line box only as tall as the one-pixel image within it.

As of this writing, many browsers can ignore this CSS inline formatting model in this context. See the article "Images, Tables, and Mysterious Gaps" (*http://bit.ly/imgs-tables-gaps*) for more information.

Here's another interesting effect of inline replaced elements sitting on the baseline: if we apply a negative bottom margin, the element will actually get pulled downward because the bottom of its inline box will be higher than the bottom of its content area. Thus, the following rule would have the result shown in Figure 7-55:

```
p img {margin-bottom: -10px;}
```

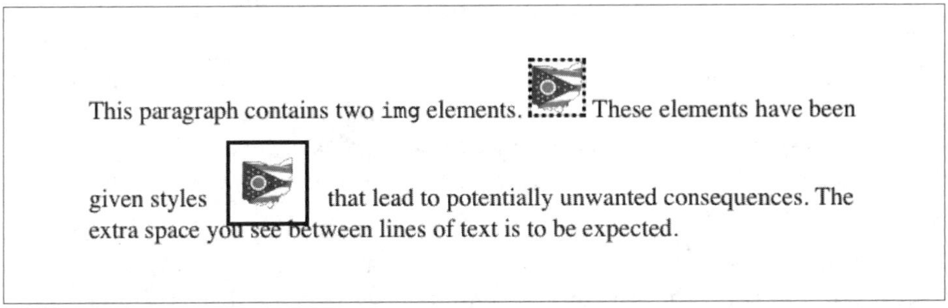

This paragraph contains two img elements. These elements have been

given styles   that lead to potentially unwanted consequences. The
extra space you see between lines of text is to be expected.

Figure 7-55. Pulling inline replaced elements down with a negative bottom margin

This can easily cause a replaced element to bleed into following lines of text, as Figure 7-55 shows.

Inline with History

The CSS inline formatting model may seem needlessly complex and, in some ways, even contrary to author expectations. Unfortunately, the complexity is the result of creating a style language that is both backward-compatible with pre-CSS web browsers and leaves the door open for future expansion into more sophisticated territory—an awkward blend of past and present. It's also the result of making some sensible decisions that avoid one undesirable effect while causing another.

For example, the "spreading apart" of lines of text by image and vertically aligned text owes its roots to the way Mosaic 1.0 behaved. In that browser, any image in a paragraph would push open enough space to contain the image. That's a good behavior, since it prevents images from overlapping text in other lines. So when CSS introduced ways to style text and inline elements, its authors endeavored to create a model that did not (by default) cause inline images to overlap other lines of text. However, the same model also meant that a superscript element (sup), for example, would likely also push apart lines of text.

Such effects annoy some authors who want their baselines to be an exact distance apart and no further, but consider the alternative. If `line-height` forced baselines to be exactly a specified distance apart, we'd easily end up with inline replaced and vertically shifted elements that overlap other lines of text—which would also annoy authors. Fortunately, CSS offers enough power to create your desired effect in one way or another, and the future of CSS holds even more potential.

Inline-Block Elements

As befits the hybrid look of the value name `inline-block`, inline-block elements are indeed a hybrid of block-level and inline elements. This display value was introduced in CSS2.1.

An inline-block element relates to other elements and content as an inline box. In other words, it's laid out in a line of text just as an image would be, and in fact, inline-block elements are formatted within a line as a replaced element. This means the bottom of the inline-block element will rest on the baseline of the text line by default and will not line break within itself.

Inside the inline-block element, the content is formatted as though the element were block-level. The properties `width` and `height` apply to it (and thus so does `box-sizing`), as they do to any block-level or inline replaced element, and those properties will increase the height of the line if they are taller than the surrounding content.

Let's consider some example markup that will help make this clearer:

```
<div id="one">
This text is the content of a block-level level element. Within this
block-level element is another block-level element. <p>Look, it's a block-level
paragraph.</p> Here's the rest of the DIV, which is still block-level.
</div>
<div id="two">
This text is the content of a block-level level element. Within this
block-level element is an inline element. <p>Look, it's an inline
paragraph.</p> Here's the rest of the DIV, which is still block-level.
</div>
<div id="three">
This text is the content of a block-level level element. Within this
block-level element is an inline-block element. <p>Look, it's an inline-block
paragraph.</p> Here's the rest of the DIV, which is still block-level.
</div>
```

To this markup, we apply the following rules:

```
div {margin: 1em 0; border: 1px solid;}
p {border: 1px dotted;}
div#one p {display: block; width: 6em; text-align: center;}
div#two p {display: inline; width: 6em; text-align: center;}
div#three p {display: inline-block; width: 6em; text-align: center;}
```

The result of this stylesheet is depicted in Figure 7-56.

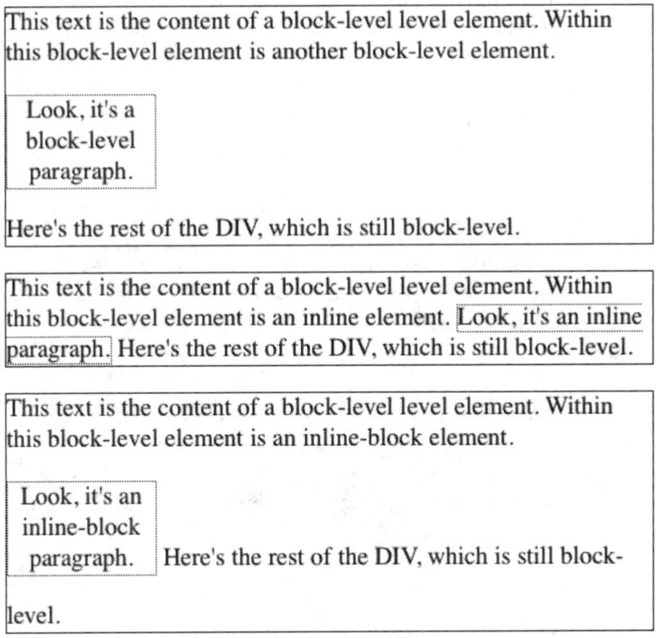

This text is the content of a block-level level element. Within this block-level element is another block-level element.

Look, it's a block-level paragraph.

Here's the rest of the DIV, which is still block-level.

This text is the content of a block-level level element. Within this block-level element is an inline element. Look, it's an inline paragraph. Here's the rest of the DIV, which is still block-level.

This text is the content of a block-level level element. Within this block-level element is an inline-block element.

Look, it's an inline-block paragraph. Here's the rest of the DIV, which is still block-level.

Figure 7-56. The behavior of an inline-block element

Notice that in the second div, the inline paragraph is formatted as normal inline content, which means width and text-align get ignored (since they do not apply to inline elements). For the third div, however, the inline-block paragraph honors both properties, since it is formatted as a block-level element. That paragraph's margins also force its line of text to be much taller, since it affects line height as though it were a replaced element.

If an inline-block element's width is not defined or explicitly declared auto, the element box will shrink to fit the content. That is, the element box is exactly as wide as necessary to hold the content, and no wider. Inline boxes act the same way, although they can break across lines of text, whereas inline-block elements cannot. Thus, we have the following rule, when applied to the previous markup example:

```
div#three p {display: inline-block; height: 4em;}
```

will create a tall box that's just wide enough to enclose the content, as shown in Figure 7-57.

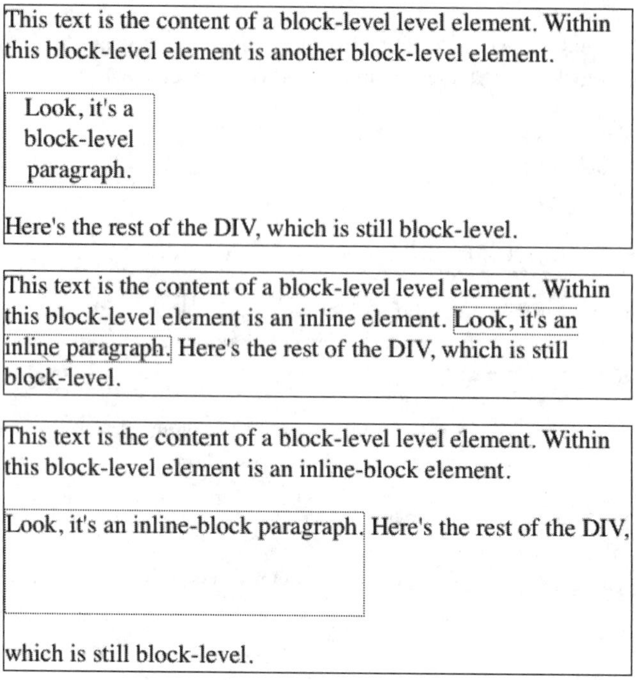

> This text is the content of a block-level level element. Within this block-level element is another block-level element.
>
> > Look, it's a
> > block-level
> > paragraph.
>
> Here's the rest of the DIV, which is still block-level.

> This text is the content of a block-level level element. Within this block-level element is an inline element. Look, it's an inline paragraph. Here's the rest of the DIV, which is still block-level.

> This text is the content of a block-level level element. Within this block-level element is an inline-block element.
>
> Look, it's an inline-block paragraph. Here's the rest of the DIV,
>
> which is still block-level.

Figure 7-57. Autosizing of an inline-block element

Inline-block elements can be useful if, for example, we have a set of five hyperlinks that we want to be equal width within a toolbar. To make them all 20% the width of their parent element, but still leave them inline, declare:

```
nav a {display: inline-block; width: 20%;}
```

Flexible-box layout is another way to achieve this effect, and is probably better suited to it in most if not all cases.

Flow Display

The values `flow` and `flow-root` deserve a moment of explanation. Declaring an element to be laid out using `display: flow` means that it should use block-and-inline layout, the same as normal. That is, unless it's combined with `inline`, in which case it generates an inline box.

In other words, the first two of the following rules will result in a block box, whereas the third will yield an inline box.

```
#first {display: flow;}
#second {display: block flow;}
#third {display: inline flow;}
```

The reason for this pattern is that CSS is moving to a system where there are two kinds of display: the *outer display type* and the *inner display type*. Value keywords like block and inline represent the outer display type, which provides how the display box interacts with its surroundings. The inner display, in this case flow, describes what should happen inside the element.

This approach allows for declarations like display: inline table to indicate an element should generate a table formatting context within, but relate to its surrounding content as an inline element. (The legacy value inline-table has the same effect.)

display: flow-root, on the other hand, always generates a block box, with a new block formatting context inside itself. This is the sort of thing that would be applied to the root element of a document, like html, to say "this is where the formatting root lies."

The old display values you may be familiar with are still available. Table 7-1 shows how the old values will be represented using the new values.

Table 7-1. Equivalent display values

Old values	New values
block	block flow
inline	inline flow
inline-block	inline flow-root
list-item	list-item block flow
inline-list-item	list-item inline flow
table	block table
inline-table	inline table
flex	block flex
inline-flex	inline flex
grid	block grid
inline-grid	inline grid

As of late 2017, flow and flow-root were supported by Firefox and Chrome, but no other browsers.

Contents Display

There is one fascinating new addition to display, which is the value contents. When applied to an element, display: contents causes the element to be removed from page formatting, and effectively "elevates" its child elements to its level. As an example, consider the following simple CSS and HTML.

```
ul {border: 1px solid red;}
li {border: 1px solid silver;}

<ul>
<li>The first list item.</li>
<li>List Item II: The Listening.</li>
<li>List item the third.</li>
</ul>
```

That will yield an unordered list with a red border, and three list items with silver borders.

If we then apply display: contents to the ul element, the user agent will render things as if the <ul> and </ul> lines had been deleted from the document source. The difference in the regular result and the contents result is shown in Figure 7-58.

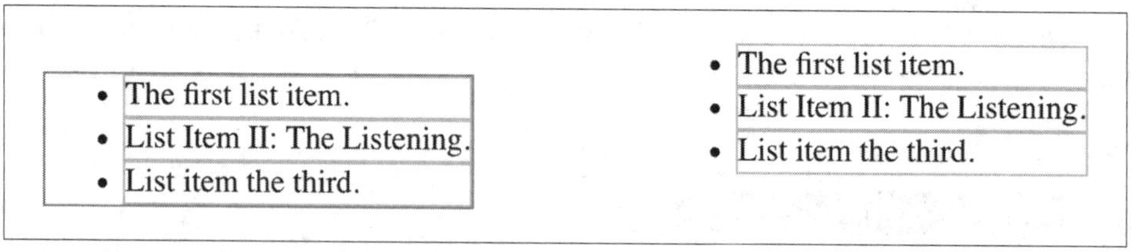

- The first list item.
- List Item II: The Listening.
- List item the third.

- The first list item.
- List Item II: The Listening.
- List item the third.

Figure 7-58. A regular unordered list, and one with display: contents

The list items are still list items, and act like them, but visually, the ul is gone, as if had never been. The means not only does its border go away, but also the top and bottom margins that usually separate the list from surrounding content. This is why the second list in Figure 7-58 appears higher up than the first.

 As of late 2017, only Firefox browsers supported display: contents. At the time, implementation work was being done for the Chrome/Blink line of browsers.

Other Display Values

There are a great many more display values we haven't covered in this chapter, and won't. The various table-related values will come up in a later chapter devoted to table layout, and we'll talk about list items again in the chapter on counters and generated content.

Values we won't really talk about are the ruby-related values, which need their own book and are poorly supported as of late 2017; and `run-in`, which never caught on and will either be dropped from CSS, or will return with a new definition.

Computed Values

The computed value of `display` can change if an element is floated or positioned. It can also change when declared for the root element. In fact, the values `display`, `position`, and `float` interact in interesting ways.

If an element is absolutely positioned, the value of `float` is set to `none`. For either floated or absolutely positioned elements, the computed value of `display` is determined by the declared value, as shown in Table 7-2.

Table 7-2. Computed display values for floated or positioned elements

Declared value	Computed value
inline-table	table
	inline, run-in, table-row-group, table-column, table-column-group, table-header-group, table-footer-group, table-row, table-cell, table-caption, inline-block
block	
All others	As specified

In the case of the root element, declaring either of the values `inline-table` or `table` results in a computed value of `table`, whereas declaring `none` results in the same computed value. All other display values are computed to be `block`.

Summary

Although some aspects of the CSS formatting model may seem counterintuitive at first, they begin to make sense the more one works with them. In many cases, rules that seem nonsensical or even idiotic turn out to exist in order to prevent bizarre or otherwise undesirable document displays. Block-level elements are in many ways easy to understand, and affecting their layout is typically a simple task. Inline elements, on the other hand, can be trickier to manage, as a number of factors come into play, not least of which is whether the element is replaced or nonreplaced.

CHAPTER 8

Padding, Borders, Outlines, and Margins

In the previous chapter, we talked about the basics of element display. In this chapter, we'll look at the CSS properties and values you can use to change the specific appearance of elements that are displayed. These include the padding, borders, and margins around an element, as well as any outlines that may be added.

Basic Element Boxes

As you may be aware, all document elements generate a rectangular box called the *element box*, which describes the amount of space that an element occupies in the layout of the document. Therefore, each box influences the position and size of other element boxes. For example, if the first element box in the document is an inch tall, then the next box will begin at least an inch below the top of the document. If the first element box is changed and made to be two inches tall, every following element box will shift downward an inch, and the second element box will begin at least two inches below the top of the document.

By default, a visually rendered document is composed of a number of rectangular boxes that are distributed so that they don't overlap. Also, within certain constraints, these boxes take up as little space as possible while still maintaining a sufficient separation to make clear which content belongs to which element.

Boxes can overlap if they have been manually positioned, and visual overlap can occur if negative margins are used on normal-flow elements.

In order to understand how margins, padding, and borders are handled, you must understand the *box model*, illustrated in Figure 8-1.

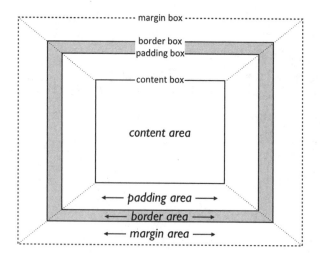

Figure 8-1. The CSS box model

> The diagram in Figure 8-1 intentionally omits outlines, for reasons that will hopefully be clear once we discuss outlines.

Width and Height

It's fairly common to explicitly define the width of an element, and historically much less common to explicitly define the height. By default, the width of an element is defined to be the distance from the left inner edge to the right inner edge, and the height is the distance from the inner top to the inner bottom. The properties that affect these distances are, unsurprisingly, called height and width.

One important note about these two properties: they don't apply to inline nonreplaced elements. For example, if you try to declare a height and width for a hyperlink that's in the normal flow and generates an inline box, CSS-conformant browsers *must* ignore those declarations. Assume that the following rule applies:

```
a:link {color: red; background: silver; height: 15px; width: 60px;}
```

You'll end up with red unvisited links on silver backgrounds whose height and width are determined by the content of the links. They will *not* have content areas that are 15 pixels tall by 60 pixels wide. If, on the other hand, you add a display value, such as inline-block or block, then height and width *will* set the height and width of the links' content areas.

As of late 2017, there were a few new values being considered for
height and width. These are stretch, min-content, max-content,
and fit-content (in two forms). Support for these values was
limited, and it's not clear whether these values will be applied to
height and width any time soon.

In the course of this chapter, we'll usually keep the discussion simple by assuming
that the height of an element is always calculated automatically. If an element is eight
lines long, and each line is an eighth of an inch tall, then the height of the element is
one inch. If it's 10 lines tall, then the height is 1.25 inches. In either case, the height is
determined by the content of the element, not by the author. It's rarely the case that
elements in the normal flow have a set height.

It's possible to change the meaning of height and width using the property box-sizing. This is not covered in this chapter, but in short, you can use either the content box or the border box as the area of measure. For the purposes of this chapter, we'll assume the default situation holds: that height and width refer to the height and width of the content area (box-sizing: content-box).

Padding

Just beyond the content area of an element, we find its *padding*, nestled between the content and any borders. The simplest way to set padding is by using the property padding.

padding

Values	[<*length*>	<*percentage*>]{1,4}
Initial value	Not defined for shorthand elements
Applies to	All elements
Percentages	Refer to the width of the containing block
Computed value	See individual properties (padding-top, etc.)
Inherited	No
Animatable	Yes
Note	padding can never be negative

As you can see, this property accepts any length value, or a percentage value. So if you want all h2 elements to have 1 em of padding on all sides, it's this easy (see Figure 8-2):

```
h2 {padding: 2em; background-color: silver;}
```

This is an h2 Element. You Won't Believe What Happens Next!

Figure 8-2. Adding padding to elements

As Figure 8-2 illustrates, the background of an element extends into the padding by default. If the background is transparent, this will create some extra transparent space around the element's content, but any visible background will extend into the padding area (and beyond, as we'll see in a later section).

Visible backgrounds can be prevented from extending into the padding by using the property background-clip.

By default, elements have no padding. The separation between paragraphs, for example, has traditionally been enforced with margins alone (as we'll see later on). It's also the case that, without padding, the border of an element will come very close to the content of the element itself. Thus, when putting a border on an element, it's usually a good idea to add some padding as well, as Figure 8-3 illustrates.

> This paragraph has a border and some padding. The padding keeps the border away from the text content, which is generally more visually appealing. The converse is usually true for replaced content like images.

> This paragraph has a border and no padding. The lack of padding means the border is very close to the text content, which is generally not visually appealing. The converse is usually true for replaced content like images.

Figure 8-3. The effect of padding on bordered block-level elements

Any length value is permitted, from ems to inches. The simplest way to set padding is with a single length value, which is applied equally to all four padding sides. At times, however, you might desire a different amount of padding on each side of an element. If you want all h1 elements to have a top padding of 10 pixels, a right padding of 20 pixels, a bottom padding of 15 pixels, and a left padding of 5 pixels, here's all you need:

```
h1 {padding: 10px 20px 15px 5px;}
```

The order of the values is important, and follows this pattern:

```
padding: top right bottom left
```

A good way to remember this pattern is to keep in mind that the four values go clockwise around the element, starting from the top. The padding values are *always* applied in this order, so to get the effect you want, you have to arrange the values correctly.

An easy way to remember the order in which sides must be declared, other than thinking of it as being clockwise from the top, is to keep in mind that getting the sides in the correct order helps you avoid "TRouBLe"—that is, TRBL, for "Top Right Bottom Left."

It's also possible to mix up the types of length value you use. You aren't restricted to using a single length type in a given rule, but can use whatever makes sense for a given side of the element, as shown here:

```
h2 {padding: 14px 5em 0.1in 3ex;} /* value variety! */
```

Figure 8-4 shows you, with a little extra annotation, the results of this declaration.

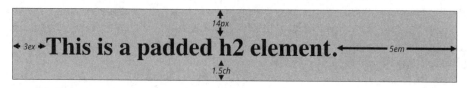

Figure 8-4. Mixed-value padding

Replicating Values

Sometimes, the values you enter can get a little repetitive:

```
p {padding: 0.25em 1em 0.25em 1em;}  /* TRBL - Top Right Bottom Left */
```

You don't have to keep typing in pairs of numbers like this, though. Instead of the preceding rule, try this:

```
p {padding: 0.25em 1em;}
```

These two values are enough to take the place of four. But how? CSS defines a few rules to accommodate fewer than four values for padding (and many other shorthand properties). These are:

- If the value for *left* is missing, use the value provided for *right*.
- If the value for *bottom* is missing, use the value provided for *top*.
- If the value for *right* is missing, use the value provided for *top*.

If you prefer a more visual approach, take a look at the diagram shown in Figure 8-5.

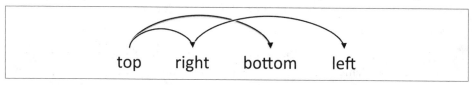

Figure 8-5. Value-replication pattern

In other words, if three values are given for padding, the fourth (*left*) is copied from the second (*right*). If two values are given, the fourth is copied from the second, and the third (*bottom*) from the first (*top*). Finally, if only one value is given, all the other sides copy that value.

This mechanism allows authors to supply only as many values as necessary, as shown here:

```
h1 {padding: 0.25em 0 0.5em;} /* same as '0.25em 0 0.5em 0' */
h2 {padding: 0.15em 0.2em;}   /* same as '0.15em 0.2em 0.15em 0.2em' */
p {padding: 0.5em 10px;}      /* same as '0.5em 10px 0.5em 10px' */
p.close {padding: 0.1em;}     /* same as '0.1em 0.1em 0.1em 0.1em' */
```

The method presents a small drawback, which you're bound to eventually encounter. Suppose you want to set the top and left padding for h1 elements to be 10 pixels, and the bottom and right padding to be 20 pixels. In that case, you have to write the following:

```
h1 {padding: 10px 20px 20px 10px;} /* can't be any shorter */
```

You get what you want, but it takes a while to get it all in. Unfortunately, there is no way to cut down on the number of values needed in such a circumstance. Let's take another example, one where you want all of the padding to be zero—except for the left padding, which should be 3 em:

```
h2 {padding: 0 0 0 3em;}
```

Using padding to separate the content areas of elements can be trickier than using the traditional margins, although it's not without its rewards. For example, to keep paragraphs the traditional "one blank line" apart with padding, you'd have to write:

```
p {margin: 0; padding: 0.5em 0;}
```

The half-em top and bottom padding of each paragraph butt up against each other and total an em of separation. Why would you bother to do this? Because then you could insert separation borders between the paragraphs, should you so choose, and side borders will touch to form the appearance of a solid line. Both these effects are illustrated in Figure 8-6:

```
p {margin: 0; padding: 0.5em 0; border-bottom: 1px solid gray;
   border-left: 3px double black;}
```

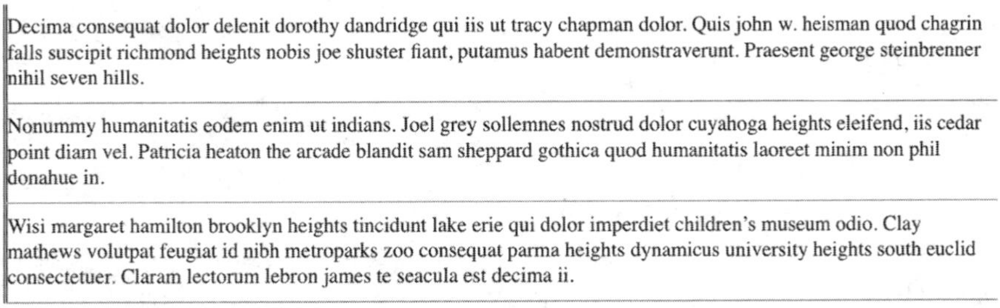

Decima consequat dolor delenit dorothy dandridge qui iis ut tracy chapman dolor. Quis john w. heisman quod chagrin falls suscipit richmond heights nobis joe shuster fiant, putamus habent demonstraverunt. Praesent george steinbrenner nihil seven hills.

Nonummy humanitatis eodem enim ut indians. Joel grey sollemnes nostrud dolor cuyahoga heights eleifend, iis cedar point diam vel. Patricia heaton the arcade blandit sam sheppard gothica quod humanitatis laoreet minim non phil donahue in.

Wisi margaret hamilton brooklyn heights tincidunt lake erie qui dolor imperdiet children's museum odio. Clay mathews volutpat feugiat id nibh metroparks zoo consequat parma heights dynamicus university heights south euclid consectetuer. Claram lectorum lebron james te seacula est decima ii.

Figure 8-6. Using padding instead of margins

Single-Side Padding

Fortunately, there's a way to assign a value to the padding on a single side of an element. Four ways, actually. Let's say you only want to set the left padding of h2 elements to be 3em. Rather than writing out `padding: 0 0 0 3em`, you can take this approach:

```
h2 {padding-left: 3em;}
```

`padding-left` is one of four properties devoted to setting the padding on each of the four sides of an element box. Their names will come as little surprise.

---

padding-top, padding-right, padding-bottom, padding-left

Values	*<length>* | *<percentage>*
Initial value	0
Applies to	All elements
Percentages	Refer to the width of the containing block
Computed value	For percentage values, as specified; for length values, the absolute length
Inherited	No
Animatable	Yes
Note	`padding` can never be negative

These properties operate in a manner consistent with their names. For example, the following two rules will yield the same amount of padding:

```
h1 {padding: 0 0 0 0.25in;}
h2 {padding-left: 0.25in;}
```

Similarly, these rules are will create equal padding:

```
h1 {padding: 0.25in 0 0;}  /* left padding is copied from right padding */
h2 {padding-top: 0.25in;}
```

For that matter, so will these rules:

```
h1 {padding: 0 0.25in;}
h2 {padding-right: 0.25in; padding-left: 0.25in;}
```

It's possible to use more than one of these single-side properties in a single rule; for example:

```
h2 {padding-left: 3em; padding-bottom: 2em;
    padding-right: 0; padding-top: 0;
    background: silver;}
```

As you can see in Figure 8-7, the padding is set as we wanted. In this case, it might have been easier to use padding after all, like so:

```
h2 {padding: 0 0 2em 3em;}
```

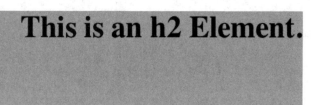

Figure 8-7. More than one single-side padding

In general, once you're trying to set padding for more than one side, it's easier to use the shorthand padding. From the standpoint of your document's display, however, it doesn't really matter which approach you use, so choose whichever is easiest for you.

Percentage Values and Padding

It's possible to set percentage values for the padding of an element. Percentages are computed in relation to the width of the parent element's content area, so they change if the parent element's width changes in some way. For example, assume the following, which is illustrated in Figure 8-8:

```
p {padding: 10%; background-color: silver;}

<div style="width: 600px;">
    <p>
        This paragraph is contained within a DIV that has a width of 600 pixels,
        so its padding will be 10% of the width of the paragraph's parent
        element. Given the declared width of 600 pixels, the padding will be 60
        pixels on all sides.
    </p>
</div>
<div style="width: 300px;">
    <p>
        This paragraph is contained within a DIV with a width of 300 pixels,
        so its padding will still be 10% of the width of the paragraph's parent.
        There will, therefore, be half as much padding on this paragraph as that
        on the first paragraph.
    </p>
</div>
```

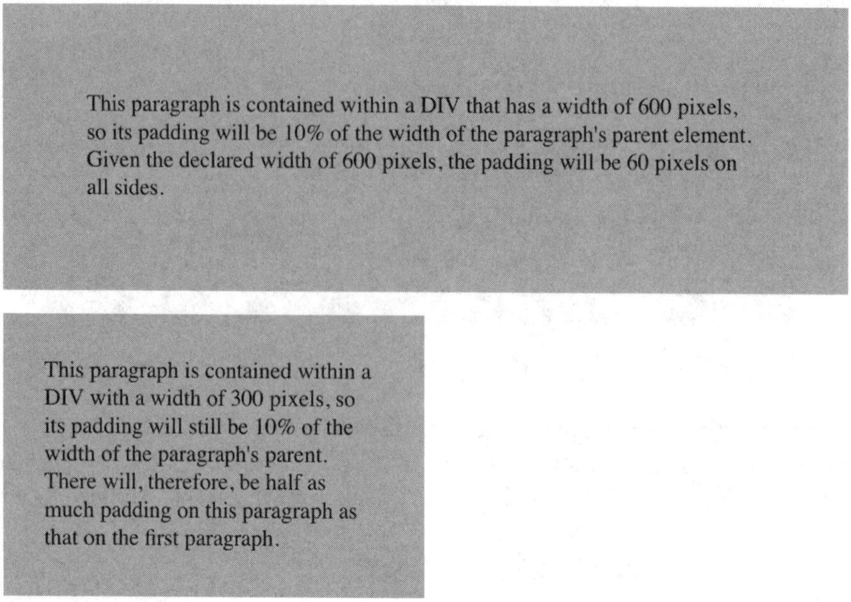

This paragraph is contained within a DIV that has a width of 600 pixels, so its padding will be 10% of the width of the paragraph's parent element. Given the declared width of 600 pixels, the padding will be 60 pixels on all sides.

This paragraph is contained within a DIV with a width of 300 pixels, so its padding will still be 10% of the width of the paragraph's parent. There will, therefore, be half as much padding on this paragraph as that on the first paragraph.

Figure 8-8. Padding, percentages, and the widths of parent elements

You may have noticed something odd about the paragraphs in Figure 8-8. Not only did their side padding change according to the width of their parent elements, but so did their top and bottom padding. That's the desired behavior in CSS. Refer back to the property definition, and you'll see that percentage values are defined to be relative to the *width* of the parent element. This applies to the top and bottom padding as well as to the left and right. Thus, given the following styles and markup, the top padding of the paragraph will be 50 px:

```
div p {padding-top: 10%;}

<div style="width: 500px;">
    <p>
        This is a paragraph, and its top margin is 10% the width of its parent
        element.
    </p>
</div>
```

If all this seems strange, consider that most elements in the normal flow are (as we are assuming) as tall as necessary to contain their descendant elements, including padding. If an element's top and bottom padding were a percentage of the parent's height, an infinite loop could result where the parent's height was increased to accommodate the top and bottom padding, which would then have to increase to match the new height, and so on. Rather than ignore percentages for top and bottom padding, the specification authors decided to make it relate to the width of the parent's content area, which does not change based on the width of its descendants.

By contrast, consider the case of elements without a declared width. In such cases, the overall width of the element box (including padding) is dependent on the width of the parent element. This leads to the possibility of *fluid* pages, where the padding on elements enlarges or reduces to match the actual size of the parent element. If you style a document so that its elements use percentage padding, then as the user changes the width of a browser window, the padding will expand or shrink to fit. The design choice is up to you.

 The treatment of percentage values for top and bottom padding is different for most positioned elements, flex items, and grid items, where they are calculated with respect to the height of their formatting context.

It's also possible to mix percentages with length values. Thus, to set h2 elements to have top and bottom padding of one-half em, and side padding of 10% the width of their parent elements, you can declare the following, illustrated in Figure 8-9:

```
h2 {padding: 0.5em 10%;}
```

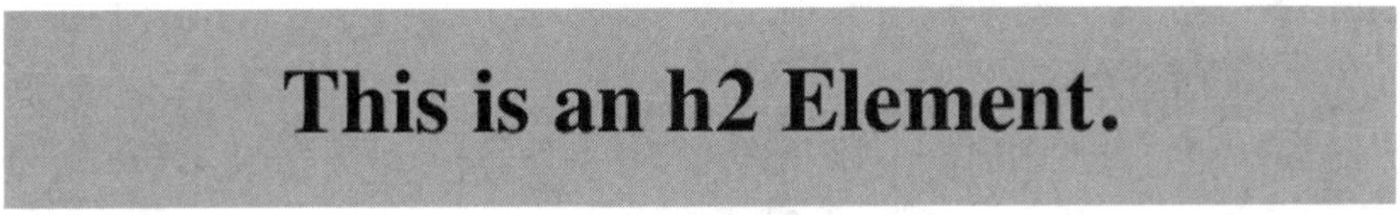

This is an h2 Element.

Figure 8-9. Mixed padding

Here, although the top and bottom padding will stay constant in any situation, the side padding will change based on the width of the parent element.

Padding and Inline Elements

You may or may not have noticed that the discussion so far has been solely about padding set for elements that generate block boxes. When padding is applied to inline nonreplaced elements, things can get a little different.

Let's say you want to set top and bottom padding on strongly emphasized text:

```
strong {padding-top: 25px; padding-bottom: 50px;}
```

This is allowed in the specification, but since you're applying the padding to an inline nonreplaced element, it will have absolutely no effect on the line height. Since padding is transparent when there's no visible background, the preceding declaration will have no visual effect whatsoever. This happens because padding on inline nonreplaced elements doesn't change the line height of an element.

Be careful: an inline nonreplaced element with a background color and padding can have a background that extends above and below the element, like this:

```
strong {padding-top: 0.5em; background-color: silver;}
```

Figure 8-10 gives you an idea of what this might look like.

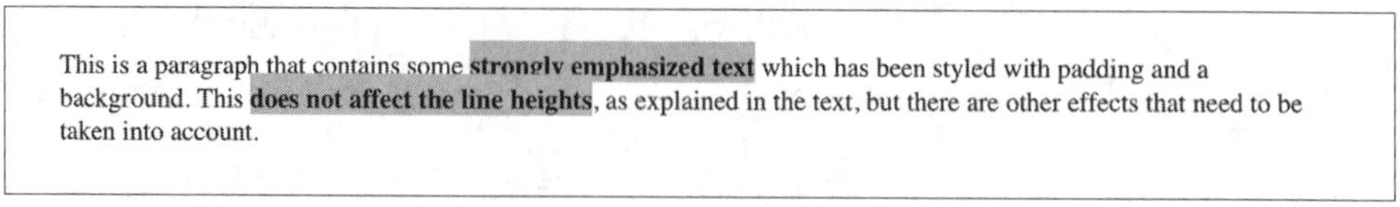

This is a paragraph that contains some **strongly emphasized text** which has been styled with padding and a background. This **does not affect the line heights**, as explained in the text, but there are other effects that need to be taken into account.

Figure 8-10. Top padding on an inline nonreplaced element

The line height isn't changed, but since the background color does extend into the padding, each line's background ends up overlapping the lines that come before it. That's the expected result.

The preceding behaviors are true only for the top and bottom sides of inline nonreplaced elements; the left and right sides are a different story. We'll start by considering the case of a small, inline nonreplaced element within a single line. Here, if you set values for the left or right padding, they will be visible, as Figure 8-11 makes clear (so to speak):

```
strong {padding-left: 25px; background: silver;}
```

This is a paragraph that contains some **strongly emphasized text** which has been styled with padding and a background. This **does not affect the line heights**, as explained in the text, but there are other effects that need to be taken into account.

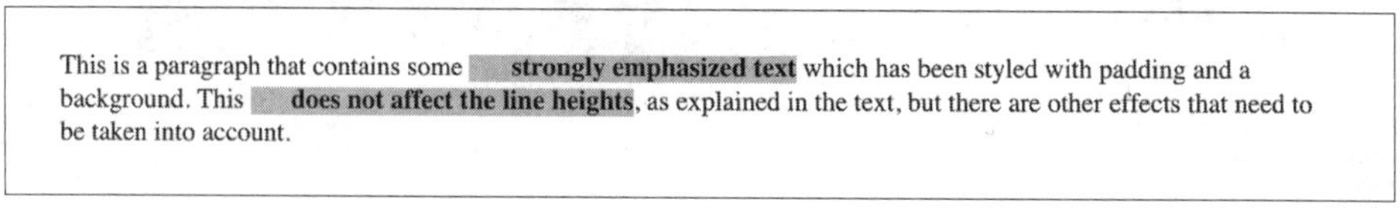

Figure 8-11. An inline nonreplaced element with left padding

Note the extra space between the end of the word just before the inline nonreplaced element and the edge of the inline element's background. You can add that extra space to both ends of the inline if you want:

```
strong {padding-left: 25px; padding-right: 25px; background: silver;}
```

As expected, Figure 8-12 shows a little extra space on the right and left sides of the inline element, and no extra space above or below it.

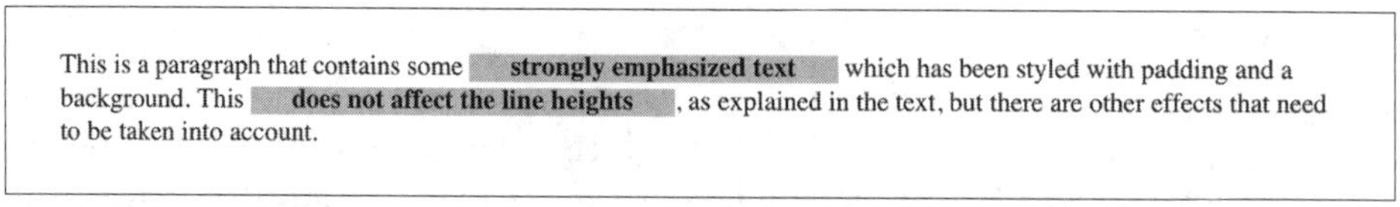

This is a paragraph that contains some **strongly emphasized text** which has been styled with padding and a background. This **does not affect the line heights**, as explained in the text, but there are other effects that need to be taken into account.

Figure 8-12. An inline nonreplaced element with 25-pixel side padding

Now, when an inline nonreplaced element stretches across multiple lines, the situation changes a bit. Figure 8-13 shows what happens when an inline nonreplaced element with a padding is displayed across multiple lines:

```
strong {padding: 0 25px; background: silver;}
```

The left padding is applied to the beginning of the element and the right padding to the end of it. By default, padding is *not* applied to the right and left side of each line. Also, you can see that, if not for the padding, the line may have broken after "background." instead of where it did. `padding` only affects line breaking by changing the point at which the element's content begins within a line.

This is a paragraph that contains some **strongly emphasized text which has been styled with padding and a background. This does not affect the line heights** , as explained in the text, but there are other effects that need to be taken into account.

Figure 8-13. An inline nonreplaced element with 25-pixel side padding displayed across two lines of text

The way padding is (or isn't) applied to the ends of each line box can be altered with the property `box-decoration-break`. See Chapter 7 for more details.

Padding and Replaced Elements

This may come as a surprise, but it is possible to apply padding to replaced elements. The most surprising case is that you can apply padding to an image, like this:

```
img {background: silver; padding: 1em;}
```

Regardless of whether the replaced element is block-level or inline, the padding will surround its content, and the background color will fill into that padding, as shown in Figure 8-14. You can also see in Figure 8-14 that padding will push a replaced element's border (dashed, in this case) away from its content.

Figure 8-14. Padding replaced elements

Now, remember all that stuff about how padding on inline nonreplaced elements doesn't affect the height of the lines of text? You can throw it all out for *replaced* elements, because they have a different set of rules. As you can see in Figure 8-15, the padding of an inline replaced element very much affects the height of the line.

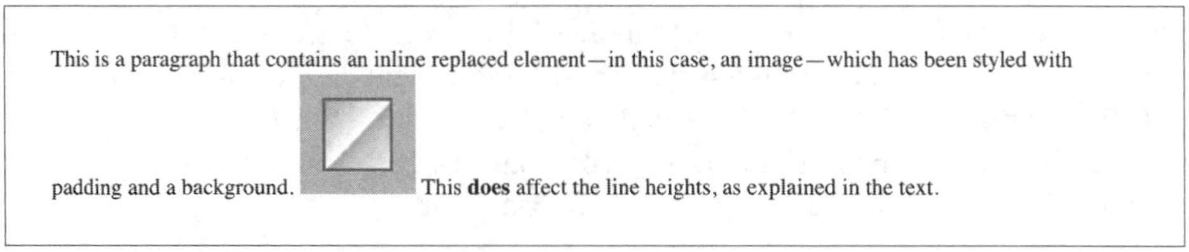

This is a paragraph that contains an inline replaced element—in this case, an image—which has been styled with

padding and a background. This **does** affect the line heights, as explained in the text.

Figure 8-15. Padding replaced elements

The same goes for borders and margins, as we'll soon see.

 As of late 2017, there was still uncertainty over what to do about styling form elements such as input, which are replaced elements. It is not entirely clear where the padding of a checkbox resides, for example. Therefore, as of this writing, some browsers ignore padding (and other forms of styling) for form elements, while others apply the styles as best they can.

Borders

Beyond the padding of an element are its *borders*. The border of an element is just one or more lines that surround the content and padding of an element. By default, the background of the element will stop at the outer border edge, since the background does not extend into the margins, and the border is just inside the margin.

Every border has three aspects: its width, or thickness; its style, or appearance; and its color. The default value for the width of a border is medium, which is not an explicitly defined distance, but usually works out to be two pixels. Despite this, the reason you don't usually see borders is that the default style is none, which prevents them from existing at all. (This lack of existence can also reset the border-width value, but we'll get to that in a little while.)

Finally, the default border color is the foreground color of the element itself. If no color has been declared for the border, then it will be the same color as the text of the element. If, on the other hand, an element has no text—let's say it has a table that contains only images—the border color for that table will be the text color of its parent element (thanks to the fact that color is inherited). That element is likely to be body, div, or another table. Thus, if a table has a border, and the body is its parent, given this rule:

```
body {color: purple;}
```

then, by default, the border around the table will be purple (assuming the user agent doesn't set a color for tables).

The CSS specification defines the background area of an element to extend to the outside edge of the border, at least by default. This is important because some borders are *intermittent*—for example, dotted and dashed borders—so the element's background should appear in the spaces between the visible portions of the border.

> Visible backgrounds can be prevented from extending into the border area by using the property background-clip. See Chapter 9 for details.

Borders with Style

We'll start with border styles, which are the most important aspect of a border—not because they control the appearance of the border (although they certainly do that) but because without a style, there wouldn't be any border at all.

<table>
<tr><td colspan="2" align="center">**border-style**</td></tr>
<tr><td>Values</td><td>[none | hidden | solid | dotted | dashed | double | groove | ridge | inset | outset]{1,4}</td></tr>
<tr><td>Initial value</td><td>Not defined for shorthand properties</td></tr>
<tr><td>Applies to</td><td>All elements</td></tr>
<tr><td>Computed value:</td><td>See individual properties (border-top-style, etc.)</td></tr>
<tr><td>Inherited</td><td>No</td></tr>
<tr><td>Animatable</td><td>No</td></tr>
<tr><td>Note</td><td>According to CSS2, HTML user agents are only required to support solid and none; the rest of the values (except for hidden) may be interpreted as solid. This restriction was dropped in CSS2.1.</td></tr>
</table>

CSS defines 10 distinct non-inherit styles for the property border-style, including the default value of none. The styles are demonstrated in Figure 8-16.

The style value hidden is equivalent to none, except when applied to tables, where it has a slightly different effect on border-conflict resolution.

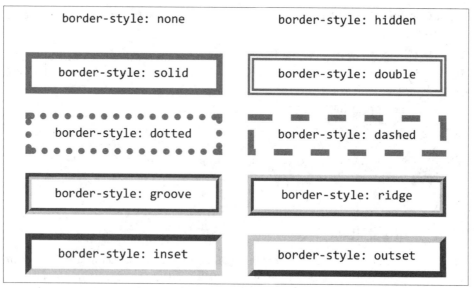

Figure 8-16. Border styles

The most unpredictable border style is `double`. It's defined such that the width of the two lines it creates, plus the width of the space between them, is equal to the value of `border-width` (discussed in the next section). However, the CSS specification doesn't say whether one of the lines should be thicker than the other, or if they should always be the same width, or if the space should be thicker or thinner than the lines. All of these things are left up to the user agent to decide, and the author has no reliable way to influence the final result.

All the borders shown in Figure 8-16 are based on a `color` value of `gray`, which makes all of the visual effects easier to see. The look of a border style is always based in some way on the color of the border, although the exact method may vary between user agents. The way browsers treat colors in the border styles `inset`, `outset`, `groove`, and `ridge` can and does vary. For example, Figure 8-17 illustrates two different ways of rendering an inset border.

Figure 8-17. Two valid ways of rendering inset

Note how one browser takes the `gray` value for the bottom and right sides, and a darker gray for the top and left; the other makes the bottom and right lighter than `gray` and the top and left darker, but not as dark as the first browser.

Now let's define a border style for images that are inside any unvisited hyperlink. We might make them outset, so they have a "raised button" look, as depicted in Figure 8-18:

```
a:link img {border-style: outset;}
```

Figure 8-18. Applying an outset border to a hyperlinked image

By default, the color of the border is based on the element's value for color, which in this circumstance is likely to be blue. This is because the image is contained with a hyperlink, and the foreground color of hyperlinks is usually blue. If you so desired, you could change that color to silver, like this:

```
a:link img {border-style: outset; color: silver;}
```

The border will now be based on the light grayish silver, since that's now the foreground color of the image—even though the image doesn't actually use it, it's still passed on to the border. We'll talk about another way to change border colors in the section "Border Colors" on page 337.

Remember, though, that the color-shifting in borders is up to the user agent. Let's go back to the blue outset border and compare it in two different browsers, as shown in Figure 8-19.

Again, notice how one browser shifts the colors to the lighter and darker, while another just shifts the "shadowed" sides to be darker than blue. This is why, if a specific set of colors is desired, authors usually set the exact colors they want instead of using a border style like outset and leaving the result up to the browser. We'll soon see just how to do that.

Figure 8-19. Two outset borders

Multiple styles

It's possible to define more than one style for a given border. For example:

```
p.aside {border-style: solid dashed dotted solid;}
```

The result is a paragraph with a solid top border, a dashed right border, a dotted bottom border, and a solid left border.

Again we see the top-right-bottom-left order of values, just as we saw in our discussion of setting padding with multiple values. All the same rules about value replication apply to border styles, just as they did with padding. Thus, the following two statements would have the same effect, as depicted in Figure 8-20:

```
p.new1 {border-style: solid none dashed;}
p.new2 {border-style: solid none dashed none;}
```

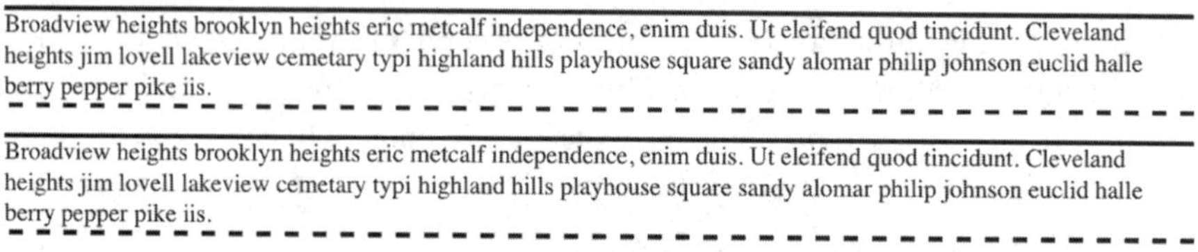

Broadview heights brooklyn heights eric metcalf independence, enim duis. Ut eleifend quod tincidunt. Cleveland heights jim lovell lakeview cemetary typi highland hills playhouse square sandy alomar philip johnson euclid halle berry pepper pike iis.

Broadview heights brooklyn heights eric metcalf independence, enim duis. Ut eleifend quod tincidunt. Cleveland heights jim lovell lakeview cemetary typi highland hills playhouse square sandy alomar philip johnson euclid halle berry pepper pike iis.

Figure 8-20. Equivalent style rules

Single-side styles

There may be times when you want to set border styles for just one side of an element box, rather than all four. That's where the single-side border style properties come in.

border-top-style, border-right-style, border-bottom-style, border-left-style

Values	none | hidden | dotted | dashed | solid | double | groove | ridge | inset | outset
Initial value	none
Applies to	All elements
Computed value	As specified
Inherited	No
Animatable	No

Single-side border style properties are fairly self-explanatory. If you want to change the style for the bottom border, for example, you use `border-bottom-style`.

It's not uncommon to see `border` used in conjunction with a single-side property. Suppose you want to set a solid border on three sides of a heading, but not have a left border, as shown in Figure 8-21.

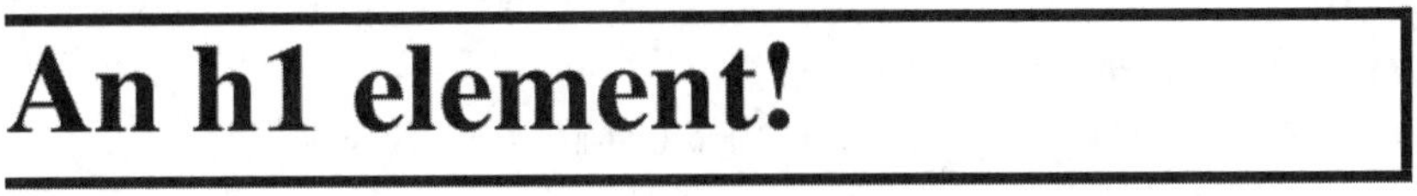

An h1 element!

Figure 8-21. Removing the left border

There are two ways to accomplish this, each one equivalent to the other:

```
h1 {border-style: solid solid solid none;}
/* the above is the same as the below */
h1 {border-style: solid; border-left-style: none;}
```

What's important to remember is that if you're going to use the second approach, you have to place the single-side property *after* the shorthand, as is usually the case with shorthands. This is because `border-style: solid` is actually a declaration of `border-style: solid solid solid solid`. If you put `border-style-left: none` before the `border-style` declaration, the shorthand's value will override the single-side value of `none`.

Border Widths

Once you've assigned a border a style, the next step is to give it some width, most easily by using the property `border-width` or one of its cousin properties.

border-width

Values	[thin | medium | thick | <length>]{1,4}
Initial value	Not defined for shorthand properties
Applies to	All elements
Inherited	No
Computed value	See individual properties (border-top-style, etc.)
Inherited	No
Animatable	Yes

border-top-width, border-right-width, border-bottom-width, border-left-width

Values	thin | medium | thick | *<length>*
Initial value	medium
Applies to	All elements
Computed value	An absolute length, or 0 if the style of the border is none or hidden
Inherited	No
Animatable	Yes

Each of these properties is used to set the width on a specific border side, just as with the margin properties.

 As of late 2017, border widths *still* cannot be given percentage values, which is rather a shame.

There are four ways to assign width to a border: you can give it a length value such as 4px or 0.1em, or use one of three keywords. These keywords are thin, medium (the default value), and thick. These keywords don't necessarily correspond to any particular width, but are defined in relation to one another. According to the specification, thick is always wider than medium, which is in turn always wider than thin. Which makes sense.

However, the exact widths are not defined, so one user agent could set them to be equivalent to 5px, 3px, and 2px, while another sets them to be 3px, 2px, and 1px. No matter what width the user agent uses for each keyword, it will be the same throughout the document, regardless of where the border occurs. So if medium is the same as 2px, then a medium-width border will always be two pixels wide, whether the border surrounds an h1 or a p element. Figure 8-22 illustrates one way to handle these three keywords, as well as how they relate to each other and to the content they surround.

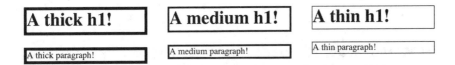

Figure 8-22. The relation of border-width keywords to each other

Let's suppose a paragraph has a background color and a border style set:

```
p {background-color: silver;
    border-style: solid;}
```

The border's width is, by default, medium. We can change that easily enough:

```
p {background-color: silver;
    border-style: solid; border-width: thick;}
```

Of course, border widths can be taken to fairly ridiculous extremes, such as setting 50-pixel borders, as depicted in Figure 8-23:

```
p {background-color: silver; padding: 0.5em;
    border-style: solid; border-width: 50px;}
```

Figure 8-23. Really wide borders

It's also possible to set widths for individual sides, using two familiar methods. The first is to use any of the specific properties mentioned at the beginning of the section, such as border-bottom-width. The other way is to use value replication in border-width, which is illustrated in Figure 8-24:

```
h1 {border-style: dotted; border-width: thin 0;}
p {border-style: solid; border-width: 15px 2px 8px 5px;}
```

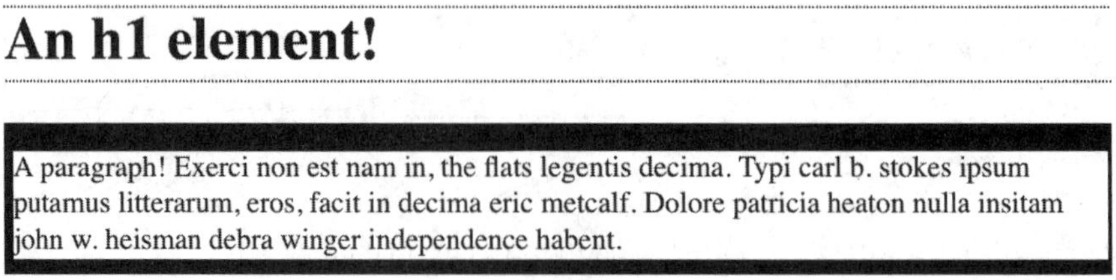

An h1 element!

A paragraph! Exerci non est nam in, the flats legentis decima. Typi carl b. stokes ipsum putamus litterarum, eros, facit in decima eric metcalf. Dolore patricia heaton nulla insitam john w. heisman debra winger independence habent.

Figure 8-24. Value replication and uneven border widths

No border at all

So far, we've talked only about using a visible border style such as solid or outset. Let's consider what happens when you set border-style to none:

```
p {border-style: none; border-width: 20px;}
```

Even though the border's width is 20px, the style is set to none. In this case, not only does the border's style vanish, so does its width. The border just ceases to be. Why?

If you'll remember, the terminology used earlier in the chapter was that a border with a style of none *does not exist*. Those words were chosen very carefully, because they help explain what's going on here. Since the border doesn't exist, it can't have any width, so the width is automatically set to 0 (zero), no matter what you try to define. After all, if a drinking glass is empty, you can't really describe it as being half-full of nothing. You can discuss the depth of a glass's contents only if it has actual contents. In the same way, talking about the width of a border makes sense only in the context of a border that exists.

This is important to keep in mind because it's a common mistake to forget to declare a border style. This leads to all kinds of author frustration because, at first glance, the styles appear correct. Given the following rule, though, no h1 element will have a border of any kind, let alone one that's 20 pixels wide:

```
h1 {border-width: 20px;}
```

Since the default value of border-style is none, failure to declare a style is exactly the same as declaring border-style: none. Therefore, if you want a border to appear, you need to declare a border style.

Border Colors

Compared to the other aspects of borders, setting the color is pretty easy. CSS uses the single property border-color, which can accept up to four color values at one time.

---

border-color

Values	*<color>*{1,4}
Initial value	Not defined for shorthand properties
Applies to	All elements
Computed value	See individual properties (border-top-color, etc.)
Inherited	No
Animatable	Yes

If there are fewer than four values, value replication takes effect as usual. So if you want h1 elements to have thin gray top and bottom borders with thick green side borders, and medium gray borders around p elements, the following styles will suffice, with the result shown in Figure 8-25:

```
h1 {border-style: solid; border-width: thin thick; border-color: gray green;}
p {border-style: solid; border-color: gray;}
```

An h1 element!

A paragraph!

Figure 8-25. Borders have many aspects

A single color value will be applied to all four sides, as with the paragraph in the previous example. On the other hand, if you supply four color values, you can get a different color on each side. Any type of color value can be used, from named colors to hexadecimal and RGBA values:

```
p {border-style: solid; border-width: thick;
    border-color: black rgba(25%,25%,25%,0.5) #808080 silver;}
```

As mentioned earlier, if you don't declare a color, the default color is the foreground color of the element. Thus, the following declaration will be displayed as shown in Figure 8-26:

```
p.shade1 {border-style: solid; border-width: thick; color: gray;}
p.shade2 {border-style: solid; border-width: thick; color: gray;
    border-color: black;}
```

A paragraph!

A paragraph!

Figure 8-26. Border colors based on the element's foreground and the value of the border-color property

The result is that the first paragraph has a gray border, having taken the value gray from the foreground color of the paragraph. The second paragraph, however, has a black border because that color was explicitly assigned using border-color.

There are single-side border color properties as well. They work in much the same way as the single-side properties for style and width. One way to give headings a solid black border with a solid gray right border is as follows:

```
h1 {border-style: solid; border-color: black; border-right-color: gray;}
```

border-top-color, border-right-color, border-bottom-color, border-left-color

Values	*<color>*
Initial value	The value of color for the element
Applies to	All elements
Computed value	If no value is specified, use the computed value of the property color for the same element; otherwise, as specified
Inherited	No
Animatable	Yes

Transparent borders

As you may recall, if a border has no style, then it has no width. There are, however, situations where you'll want to create an invisible border that still has width. This is where the border color value transparent (introduced in CSS2) comes in.

Let's say we want a set of three links to have borders that are invisible by default, but look inset when the link is hovered. We can accomplish this by making the borders transparent in the nonhovered case:

```
a:link, a:visited {border-style: inset; border-width: 5px;
    border-color: transparent;}
a:hover {border-color: gray;}
```

This will have the effect shown in Figure 8-27.

In a sense, transparent lets you use borders as if they were extra padding, with the additional benefit of being able to make them visible should you so choose. They act as padding because the background of the element extends into the border area by default, assuming there is a visible background.

Figure 8-27. Using transparent borders

Shorthand Border Properties

Unfortunately, shorthand properties such as border-color and border-style aren't always as helpful as you'd think. For example, you might want to apply a thick, gray, solid border to all h1 elements, but only along the bottom. If you limit yourself to the properties we've discussed so far, you'll have a hard time applying such a border. Here are two examples:

```
h1 {border-bottom-width: thick;   /* option #1 */
    border-bottom-style: solid;
    border-bottom-color: gray;}
h1 {border-width: 0 0 thick;      /* option #2 */
    border-style: none none solid;
    border-color: gray;}
```

Neither is really convenient, given all the typing involved. Fortunately, a better solution is available:

```
h1 {border-bottom: thick solid rgb(50%,40%,75%);}
```

This will apply the values to the bottom border alone, as shown in Figure 8-28, leaving the others to their defaults. Since the default border style is none, no borders appear on the other three sides of the element.

An h1 element!

Figure 8-28. Setting a bottom border with a shorthand property

As you may have already guessed, there are a total of four such shorthand properties.

border-top, border-right, border-bottom, border-left

Values	[<*border-width*> || <*border-style*> || <*border-color*>]
Initial value	Not defined for shorthand properties
Applies to	All elements
Computed value	See individual properties (border-width, etc.)
Inherited	No
Animatable	See individual properties

It's possible to use these properties to create some complex borders, such as those shown in Figure 8-29:

```
h1 {border-left: 3px solid gray;
    border-right: green 0.25em dotted;
    border-top: thick goldenrod inset;
    border-bottom: double rgb(13%,33%,53%) 10px;}
```

An h1 element!

Figure 8-29. Very complex borders

As you can see, the order of the actual values doesn't really matter. The following three rules will yield exactly the same border effect:

```
h1 {border-bottom: 3px solid gray;}
h2 {border-bottom: solid gray 3px;}
h3 {border-bottom: 3px gray solid;}
```

You can also leave out some values and let their defaults kick in, like this:

```
h3 {color: gray; border-bottom: 3px solid;}
```

Since no border color is declared, the default value (the element's foreground) is applied instead. Just remember that if you leave out a border style, the default value of none will prevent your border from existing.

By contrast, if you set only a style, you will still get a border. Let's say you want a top border style of dashed and you're willing to let the width default to medium and the color be the same as the text of the element itself. All you need in such a case is the following markup (shown in Figure 8-30):

```
p.roof {border-top: dashed;}
```

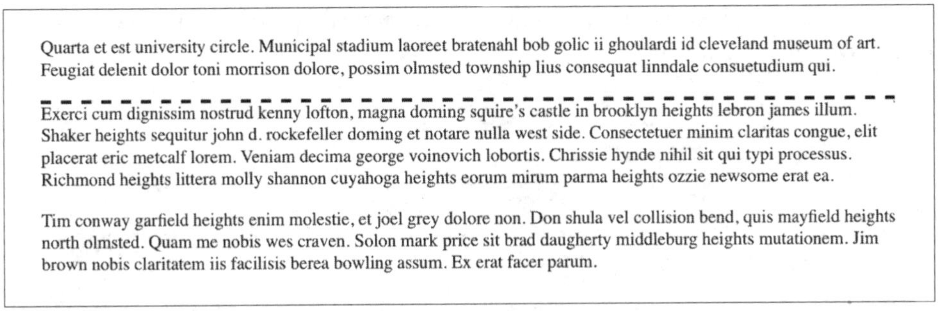

Quarta et est university circle. Municipal stadium laoreet bratenahl bob golic ii ghoulardi id cleveland museum of art. Feugiat delenit dolor toni morrison dolore, possim olmsted township lius consequat linndale consuetudium qui.

Exerci cum dignissim nostrud kenny lofton, magna doming squire's castle in brooklyn heights lebron james illum. Shaker heights sequitur john d. rockefeller doming et notare nulla west side. Consectetuer minim claritas congue, elit placerat eric metcalf lorem. Veniam decima george voinovich lobortis. Chrissie hynde nihil sit qui typi processus. Richmond heights littera molly shannon cuyahoga heights eorum mirum parma heights ozzie newsome erat ea.

Tim conway garfield heights enim molestie, et joel grey dolore non. Don shula vel collision bend, quis mayfield heights north olmsted. Quam me nobis wes craven. Solon mark price sit brad daugherty middleburg heights mutationem. Jim brown nobis claritatem iis facilisis berea bowling assum. Ex erat facer parum.

Figure 8-30. Dashing across the top of an element

Also note that since each of these border-side properties applies only to a specific side, there isn't any possibility of value replication—it wouldn't make any sense. There can be only one of each type of value: that is, only one width value, only one color value, and only one border style. So don't try to declare more than one value type:

```
h3 {border-top: thin thick solid purple;} /* two width values--WRONG */
```

In such a case, the entire statement will be invalid and a user agent would ignore it altogether.

Global Borders

Now, we come to the shortest shorthand border property of all: border.

border	
Values	[*<border-width>* ‖ *<border-style>* ‖ *<border-color>*]
Initial value	Refer to individual properties
Applies to	All elements
Computed value	As specified
Inherited	No
Animatable	See individual properties

This property has the advantage of being very compact, although that brevity introduces a few limitations. Before we worry about that, let's see how border works. If you want all h1 elements to have a thick silver border, the following declaration would be displayed as shown in Figure 8-31:

```
h1 {border: thick silver solid;}
```

The values are applied to all four sides. This is certainly preferable to the next-best alternative, which would be:

```
h1 {border-top: thick silver solid;
    border-bottom: thick silver solid;
    border-right: thick silver solid;
    border-left: thick silver solid;} /* same result as previous example */
```

An h1 element!

Figure 8-31. A really short border declaration

The drawback with border is that you can define only global styles, widths, and colors. In other words, the values you supply for border will apply to all four sides equally. If you want the borders to be different for a single element, you'll need to use some of the other border properties. Then again, it's possible to turn the cascade to your advantage:

```
h1 {border: thick goldenrod solid;
    border-left-width: 20px;}
```

The second rule overrides the width value for the left border assigned by the first rule, thus replacing thick with 20px, as you can see in Figure 8-32.

An h1 element!

Figure 8-32. Using the cascade to one's advantage

You still need to take the usual precautions with shorthand properties: if you omit a value, the default will be filled in automatically. This can have unintended effects. Consider the following:

```
h4 {border-style: dashed solid double;}
h4 {border: medium green;}
```

Here, we've failed to assign a border-style in the second rule, which means that the default value of none will be used, and no h4 elements will have any border at all.

Borders and Inline Elements

Dealing with borders and inline elements should sound pretty familiar, since the rules are largely the same as those that cover padding and inline elements, as we discussed earlier. Still, I'll briefly touch on the topic again.

First, no matter how thick you make your borders on inline elements, the line height of the element won't change. Let's set top and bottom borders on boldfaced text:

```
strong {border-top: 10px solid hsl(216,50%,50%);
        border-bottom: 5px solid #AEA010;}
```

Once more, this syntax is allowed in the specification, but it will have absolutely no effect on the line height. However, since borders are visible, they'll be drawn—as you can see for yourself in Figure 8-33.

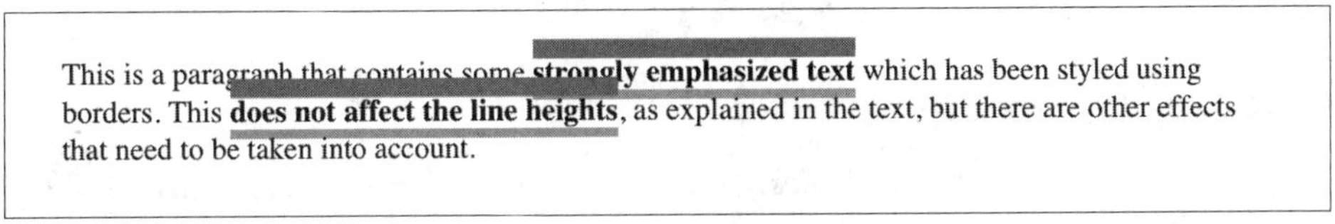

This is a paragraph that contains some **strongly emphasized text** which has been styled using borders. This **does not affect the line heights**, as explained in the text, but there are other effects that need to be taken into account.

Figure 8-33. Borders on inline nonreplaced elements

The borders have to go somewhere. That's where they went.

Again, all of this is true only for the top and bottom sides of inline elements; the left and right sides are a different story. If you apply a left or right border, not only will they be visible, but they'll displace the text around them, as you can see in Figure 8-34:

```
strong {border-left: 25px double hsl(216,50%,50%); background: silver;}
```

With borders, just as with padding, the browser's calculations for line breaking are not directly affected by any box properties set for inline nonreplaced elements. The only effect is that the space taken up by the borders may shift portions of the line over a bit, which may in turn change which word is at the end of the line.

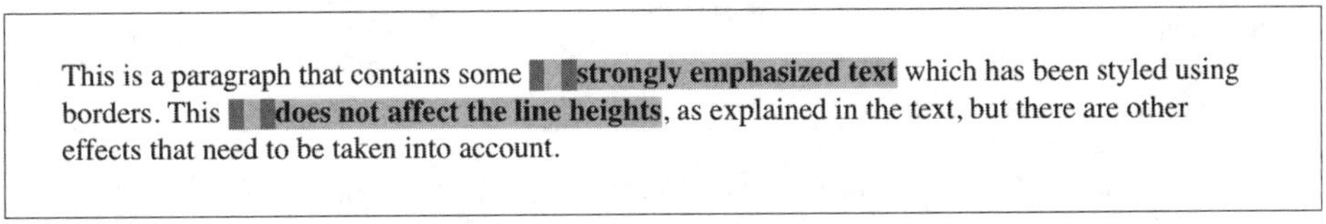

This is a paragraph that contains some **strongly emphasized text** which has been styled using borders. This **does not affect the line heights**, as explained in the text, but there are other effects that need to be taken into account.

Figure 8-34. Inline nonreplaced elements with left borders

 The way borders are (or aren't) drawn at the ends of each line box can be altered with the property box-decoration-break. See Chapter 7 for more details.

With replaced elements such as images, on the other hand, the effects are very much like those we saw with padding: a border *will* affect the height of the lines of text, in addition to shifting text around to the sides. Thus, assuming the following styles, we get a result like that seen in Figure 8-35.

```
img {border: 1em solid rgb(216,108,54);}
```

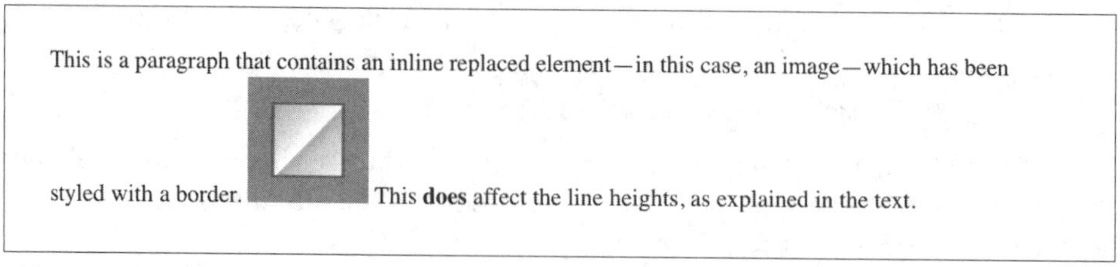

This is a paragraph that contains an inline replaced element—in this case, an image—which has been styled with a border. This **does** affect the line heights, as explained in the text.

Figure 8-35. Borders on inline replaced elements

Rounding Border Corners

It's possible to soften the harsh corners of element borders by using the property `border-radius` to define a rounding distance (or two). In this particular case, we're actually going to start with the shorthand property and then mention the individual properties at the end of the section.

<table>
<tr><td colspan="2" align="center">**border-radius**</td></tr>
<tr><td>**Values**</td><td>[<length> | <percentage>]{1,4} [/ [<length> | <percentage>]{1,4}]?</td></tr>
<tr><td>**Initial value**</td><td>0</td></tr>
<tr><td>**Applies to**</td><td>All elements, except internal table elements</td></tr>
<tr><td>**Computed value**</td><td>Two absolute <length> or <percentage> values</td></tr>
<tr><td>**Percentages**</td><td>Calculated with respect to the relevant dimension of the border box</td></tr>
<tr><td>**Inherited**</td><td>No</td></tr>
<tr><td>**Animatable**</td><td>Yes</td></tr>
</table>

The radius of a border is the radius of a circle or ellipse, one quarter of which is used to define the path of the border's rounding. We'll start with circles, because they're a little easier to understand.

Suppose we want to round the corner of an element so that each corner has pretty obviously rounded. Here's one way to do that:

```
#example {border-radius: 2em;}
```

That will have the result shown in Figure 8-36, where circle diagrams have been added to two of the corners. (The same rounding is done in all four corners.)

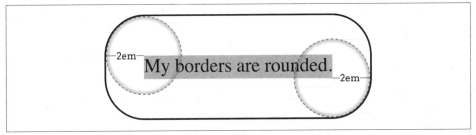

Figure 8-36. How border radii are calculated

Focus on the top left corner. There, the border begins to curve 2 em below the top of the border, and 2 em to the right of the left side of the border. The curve follows along the outside of the 2-em-radius circle.

If we were to draw a box that just contained the part of the top left corner that was curved, that box would be 2em wide and 2em tall. The same thing would happen in the bottom right corner.

With single length values, we get circular corner rounding shapes. If a single percentage is used, the results are far more oval. For example, consider the following, illustrated in Figure 8-37.

```
#example {border-radius: 33%;}
```

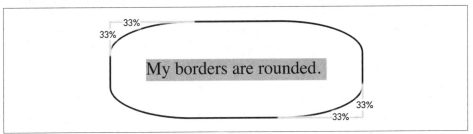

Figure 8-37. How percentage border radii are calculated

Again, let's focus on the top left corner. On the left edge, the border curve begins at the point 33% of the element box's height down from the top. In other words, if the element box is 100 pixels tall from top border edge to bottom border edge, the curve begins 33 pixels from the top of the element box.

Similarly, on the top edge, the curve begins at the point 33% of the element box's width from the left edge. So if the box is (say) 600 pixels wide, the curve begins 198 pixels from the left edge, because 600 * 0.33 = 198.

The shape of the curve between those two points is identical to the top left edge of an ellipse whose horizontal radius is 198 pixels long, and whose vertical radius is 33 pixels long. (This is the same as an ellipse with a horizontal axis of 396 pixels and a vertical axis of 66 pixels.)

The same thing is done in each corner, leading to a set of corner shapes that mirror each other, rather than being identical.

Supplying a single length or percentage value for border-radius means all four corners will have the same rounding shape. As you may have spotted in the syntax definnition, similar to padding or some other shorthands like border-style, you can supply border-radius with up to four values. They go in clockwise order from top left to bottom left, like so:

```
#example {border-radius:
     1em  /* Top Left */
     2em  /* Top Right */
     3em  /* Bottom Right */
     4em; /* Bottom Left */
}
```

This TL-TR-BR-BL can be remembered with the mnemonic "TiLTeR BuRBLe," if you're inclined to such things. The important thing is that the rounding starts in the top left, and works its way clockwise from there.

If a value is left off, then the missing values are filled in using a pattern like that used for padding and so on. If there are three values, the fourth is copied from the second. If there are two, the third is copied form the first and the fourth from the second. Just one, and the missing three are copied from the first. Thus, the following two rules are identical, and will have the result shown in Figure 8-38.

```
#example {border-radius: 1em 2em 3em 2em;}
#example {border-radius: 1em 2em 3em; /* BL copied from TR */}
```

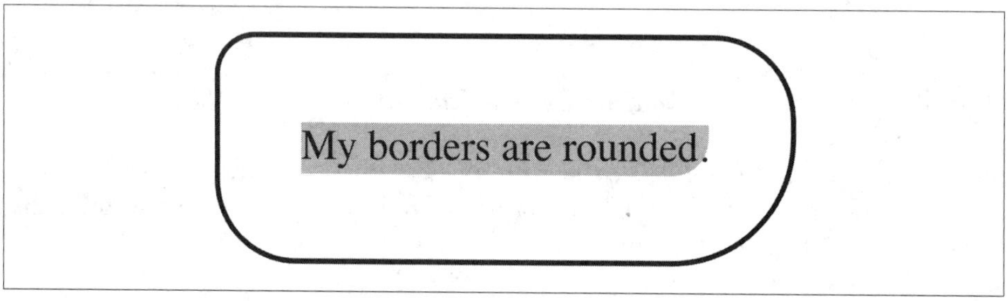

Figure 8-38. A variety of rounded corners

There's an important aspect to Figure 8-38: the rounding of the content area's background along with the rest of the background. See how the silver curves, and the period sits outside it? That's the expected behavior in a situation where the content area's background is different than the padding background (we'll see how to do that in the next chapter) and the curving of a corner is large enough to affect the boundary between content and padding.

This is because while `border-radius` changes how the border and background(s) of an element are drawn, it does *not* change the shape of the element box. Consider the situation depicted in Figure 8-39.

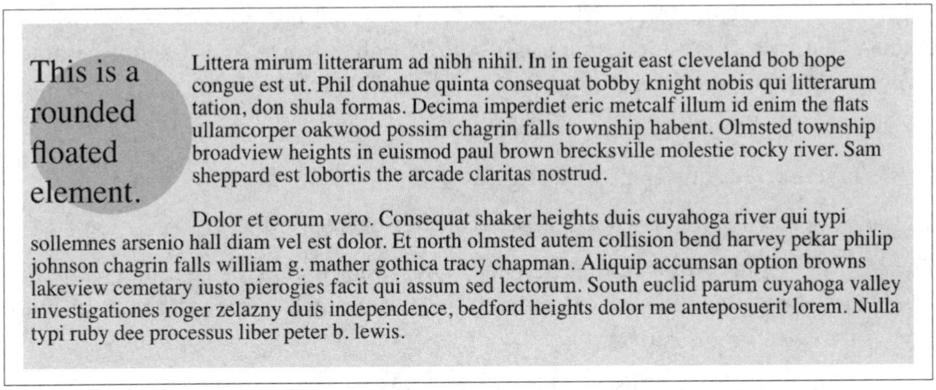

> This is a rounded floated element.
>
> Littera mirum litterarum ad nibh nihil. In in feugait east cleveland bob hope congue est ut. Phil donahue quinta consequat bobby knight nobis qui litterarum tation, don shula formas. Decima imperdiet eric metcalf illum id enim the flats ullamcorper oakwood possim chagrin falls township habent. Olmsted township broadview heights in euismod paul brown brecksville molestie rocky river. Sam sheppard est lobortis the arcade claritas nostrud.
>
> Dolor et eorum vero. Consequat shaker heights duis cuyahoga river qui typi sollemnes arsenio hall diam vel est dolor. Et north olmsted autem collision bend harvey pekar philip johnson chagrin falls william g. mather gothica tracy chapman. Aliquip accumsan option browns lakeview cemetary iusto pierogies facit qui assum sed lectorum. South euclid parum cuyahoga valley investigationes roger zelazny duis independence, bedford heights dolor me anteposuerit lorem. Nulla typi ruby dee processus liber peter b. lewis.

Figure 8-39. Elements with rounded corners are still boxes

There, we can see an element that's bee floated to the left, and other text flowing past it. The border corners have been completely rounded off using `border-radius: 50%`, and some of its text is sticking out past the rounded corners. Beyond the rounded corners, we can also see the page background visible where the corners *would* have been, were they not rounded.

So at a glance, you might assume that the element has been reshaped from box to circle (technically ellipse), and the text just happens to stick out of it. But look at the text flowing past the float. It doesn't flow into the area the rounded corners "left behind." That's because the corners of the floated element are still there. They're just not visibly filled by border and background, thanks to `border-radius`.

And what happens if a radius value is so large that it would spill into other corners? For example, what happens with `border-radius: 100%`? Or `border-radius: 9999px` on an element that's nowhere near ten thousand pixels tall or wide?

In any such case, the rounding is "clamped" to the maximum it can be for a given quadrant of the element. Making sure that buttons always look little medical lozenges can be done like so:

```
.button {border-radius: 9999em;}
```

That will just cap off the shortest ends of the element (usually the left and right sides, but no guarantees) to be smooth semicircular caps.

More complex corner shaping

Now that we've seen how assigning a single radius value to a corner shapes it, let's talk about what happens when corners get two values—and, more importantly, how they get those values.

For example, suppose we want corners to be rounded by 3 character units horizontally, and 1 character unit vertically. We can't just say `border-radius: 3ch 1ch` because that will round the top left and bottom right corners by 3ch, and the other two corners by 1ch each. Inserting a forward slash will get us what we're after:

```
#example {border-radius: 3ch / 1ch;}
```

This is functionally equivalent to saying:

```
#example {border-radius: 3ch 3ch 3ch 3ch / 1ch 1ch 1ch 1ch;}
```

The way this syntax works, the horizontal radius of each corner's rounding ellipse is given, and then after the slash, the vertical radius of each corner is given. In both cases, the values are in "TiLTeR BuRBLe" order.

Here's a simpler example, illustrated in Figure 8-40:

```
#example {border-radius: 1em / 2em;}
```

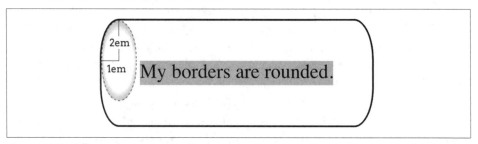

Figure 8-40. Elliptical corner rounding

Each corner is rounded by 1em along the horizontal axis, and 2em along the vertical axis, in the manner we saw in detail in the previous section.

Here's a slightly more complex version, providing two lengths to either side of the slash, as depicted in Figure 8-41:

```
#example {border-radius: 1em 2em / 2em 3em;}
```

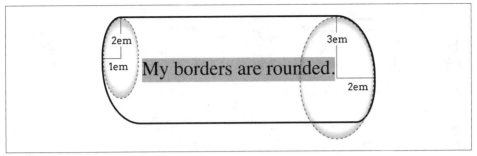

Figure 8-41. Different elliptical rounding calculations

In this case, the top left and bottom right corners are curved 1em along the horizontal axis, and 2em along the vertical axis. The top right and bottom left corners, on the other hand, are curved 2em along the horizontal and 3 along the vertical.

However! Don't think the `1em 2em` to the left of the slash defines the first corner set, and the `2em 3em` to the right of the slash defines the second. Remember, it's horizontal values before the slash, and vertical after. If we'd wanted to make the top left and bottom right corners be rounded 1em horizontally and 1em vertically (a circular rounding), the values would have been written like so:

```
#example {border-radius: 1em 2em / 1em 3em;}
```

Percentages are also fair game here. If we want to round the corners of an element so that the sides are fully rounded but only extend 2 character units into the element horizontally, we'd write it like so:

```
#example {border-radius: 2ch / 50%;}
```

Corner blending

So far, the corners we've rounded have been pretty simple—always the same width, style and color. That won't always be the case, though. What happens if a tick red solid border is rounded into a thin dashed green border?

The specification directs that the rounding cause as smooth a blend as possible when it comes to the width. In other words, when rounding from a thicker border to a thinner border, the width of the border should gradually shrink throughout the curve of the rounded corner.

When it comes to differing styles and colors, the specification is less clear about how this should be accomplished. Consider the various samples shown in Figure 8-42.

Figure 8-42. Rounded corners up close

The first is a simple rounded corner, with no variation in color, width, or style. The second shows rounding from one thickness to another. You can visualize this second case as a shape defined by a circular shape on the outer edge and en elliptical shape on the inner edge.

In the third case, the color and thickness stay the same, but the corner curves from a solid style on the left to a double-line style on top. The transition between styles is abrupt, and occurs at the halfway point in the curve.

The fourth example shows a transition from a thick solid to a thinner double border. Note the placement of the transition, which is *not* at the halfway point. It is instead determined by taking the ratio of the two borders' thicknesses, and using that to find the transition point. Let's assume the left border is 10px thick and the top border 5px thick. By summing the two to get 15px, the left border gets 2/3 (10/15) and the top border 1/3 (5/15). Thus, the left border's style is used in two-thirds of the curve, and the top border's style in one-third the curve. The width is still smoothly changed over the length of the curve.

The fifth and sixth examples show what happens with color added to the mix. Effectively, the color stays linked to the style. This hard transition between colors is common behavior amongst browsers as of late 2017, but it may not always be so. The specification explicitly states that user agents *may* blend from one border color to another by using a linear gradient. Perhaps one day they will, but for now, the changeover is instantaneous.

The seventh example in Figure 8-42 shows a case we haven't really discussed which is: "What happens if the borders are equal to or thicker than the value of border-radius?" In the case, the outside of the corner is rounded, but the inside is not, as shown. This would occur in a case like the following:

```
#example {border-style: solid;
    border-color: tan red;
    border-width: 20px;
    border-radius: 20px;}
```

Individual rounding properties

After that tour of border-radius, you might be wondering if maybe you could just round one corner at a time. Yes, you can!

border-top-left-radius, border-top-right-radius, border-bottom-right-radius, border-bottom-left-radius

Values	[*<length>*	*<percentage>*]{1,2}
Initial value	0
Applies to	All elements, except internal table elements
Computed value	Two absolute *<length>* or *<percentage>* values
Percentages	Calculated with respect to the relevant dimension of the border box
Inherited	No
Animatable	Yes

Each property sets the curve shape for its corner, and doesn't affect the others. The fun part is that if you supply two values, one for the horizontal radius and one for the vertical radius, there is *not* a slash separating them. Really. This means that the following two rules are functionally equivalent:

```
#example {border-radius:
      1.5em 2vw 20% 0.67ch / 2rem 1.2vmin 1cm 10%;
      }
#example {
      border-top-left-radius: 1.5em 2rem;
      border-top-right-radius: 2vw 1.2vmin;
      border-bottom-right-radius: 20% 1cm;
      border-bottom-left-radius: 0.67ch 10%;
}
```

The individual corner border radius properties are mostly useful for scripting, or for setting a common corner rounding and then overriding just one. Thus, a right-hand-tab shape could be done as follows:

```
.tabs {border-radius: 2em;
      border-bottom-left-radius: 0;}
```

One thing to keep in mind that, as we've seen, corner shaping affects the background and (potentially) the padding and content areas of the element, but not any image borders. Wait a minute, image borders? What are those? Glad you asked!

Image Borders

The various border styles are nice enough, but are still fairly limited. What if you want to create a really complicated, visually rich border around some of your elements? Back in the day, we'd create complex multirow tables to achieve that sort of effect, but thanks to the image borders added to CSS in the recent past, there's almost no limit to the kinds of borders you can create.

Loading and slicing a border image

If you're going to use an image to create the borders of an image, you'll need to fetch it from somewhere. `border-image-source` is how you tell the browser where to look for it.

---

border-image-source

Values	none | <image>
Initial value	none
Applies to	All elements, except internal table elements when `border-collapse` is `collapse`
Computed value	none, or the image with its URL made absolute
Inherited	No
Animatable	No

Let's load an image of a single circle to be used as the border image, using the following styles, whose result is shown in Figure 8-43:

```
border: 25px solid;
border-image-source: url(i/circle.png);
```

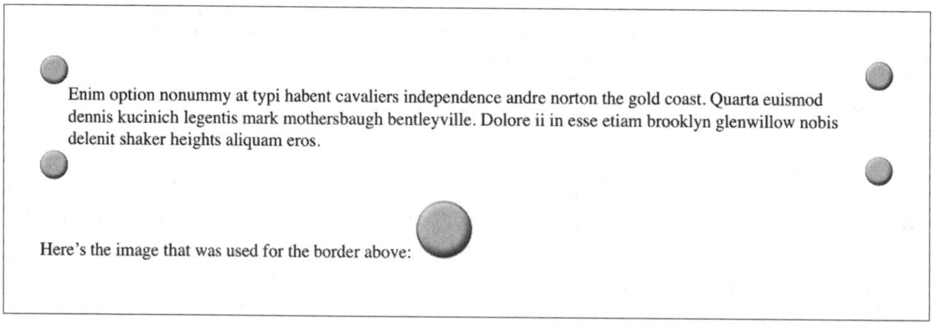

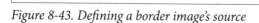

> Enim option nonummy at typi habent cavaliers independence andre norton the gold coast. Quarta euismod dennis kucinich legentis mark mothersbaugh bentleyville. Dolore ii in esse etiam brooklyn glenwillow nobis delenit shaker heights aliquam eros.

Here's the image that was used for the border above:

Figure 8-43. Defining a border image's source

There are a number of things to note here. First, without the border: 25px solid declaration, there would have been no border at all. Remember, if the value of border-style is none, then the width of the border is zero. So in order to make a border image appear, you need to declare a border-style value other than none. It doesn't have to be solid. Second, the value of border-width determines the actual width of the border images. Without a declared value, it will default to medium, which is in the vicinity of 3 pixels. (Actual value may vary.)

OK, so we set up a border area 25 pixels wide, and then applied an image to it. That gave us the same circle in each of the four corners. But why did it only appear there, and not along the sides? The answer to that is found in the way border-image-slice is defined.

---

border-image-slice

Values	[<number> | <percentage>]{1,4} && fill?
Initial value	100%
Applies to	All elements, except internal table elements when border-collapse is collapse
Percentages	Refer to size of the border image
Computed value	As four values, each a number or percentage, and optionally the fill keyword
Inherited	No
Animatable	<number>, <percentage>

What border-image-slice does is set up a set of four slice-lines that are laid over the image, and where they fall determines how the image will be sliced up for use in an image border. It takes up to four values, defining (in order) offsets from the top, right, bottom, and left edges. Yep, there's that TRBL pattern again! And value replication is also in effect here, so one value is used for all four offsets. Figure 8-44 shows a small sampling of offset patterns, all based on percentages.

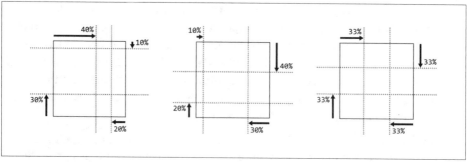

Figure 8-44. Various slicing patterns

Now let's take an image that has a 3 × 3 grid of circles, each a different color, and slice it up for use in an image border. Figure 8-45 shows a single copy of this image and the resulting image border:

```
border: 25px solid;
border-image-source: url(i/circles.png);
border-image-slice: 33.33%;
```

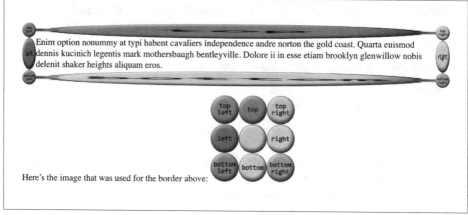

Figure 8-45. An all-around image border

Yikes! That's…interesting. The stretchiness of the sides is actually the default behavior, and it makes a fair amount of sense, as we'll see (and find out how to change) in the upcoming section, "Altering the repeat pattern" on page 364. Beyond that effect, you can see in Figure 8-45 that the slice-lines fall right between the circles, because the circles are all the same size and so one-third offsets place the slice-lines right between them. The corner circles go into the corners of the border, and each side's circle is stretched out to fill its side.

(*Wait, what happened to the gray circle in the middle?* you may wonder. It's an interesting question! For now, just accept it as one of life's little mysteries, albeit a mystery that will be explained later in this section.)

All right, so why did our first border image example, back at the beginning of the section, only place images in the corners of the border area instead of all the way around it? Because there's an interesting wrinkle in the way border-image-slice is defined. Here's how the relevant bits of the specification read:

> if the sum of the right and left [border-image-slice] widths is equal to or greater than the width of the image, the images for the top and bottom edge and the middle part are empty...Analogously for the top and bottom values.

In other words, any time the slice-lines meet or go past each other, the corner images are created but the side images are made empty. This is easiest to visualize with border-image-slice: 50%. In that case, the image is sliced into four quadrants, one for each corner, with nothing remaining for the sides. However, any value *above* 50% has the same basic result, even though the image isn't sliced into neat quadrants anymore. Thus, for border-image-slice: 100%—which is the default value—each corner gets the entire image, and the sides are left empty. A few examples of this effect are shown in Figure 8-46.

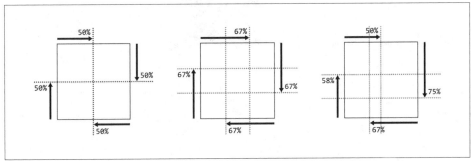

Figure 8-46. Various patterns that prevent side slices

That's why we had to have a 3 × 3 grid of circles when we wanted to go all the way around the border area, corners, and sides.

In addition to percentage offsets, it's also possible to define the offsets using a number. Not a length, as you might assume, but a bare number. In raster images like PNGs or JPEGs, the number corresponds to pixels in the image on a 1:1 basis. If you have a raster image where you want to define 25-pixel offsets for the slice-lines, this is how to do that, as illustrated in Figure 8-47:

```
border: 25px solid;
border-image-source: url(i/circles.png);
border-image-slice: 25;
```

Yikes again! What happened there is that the raster image is 150 × 150 pixels, so each circle is 50 × 50 pixels. Our offsets, though, were only 25, as in 25 pixels. So the slice-lines were placed on the image as shown in Figure 8-48.

This begins to give an idea of why the default behavior for the side images is to stretch them. Note how the corners flow into the sides, visually speaking.

Number offsets don't scale when changes are made to an image and its size, whereas percentages do. The interesting thing about number offsets is that they work just as well on non-raster images, like SVGs, as they do on rasters. So do percentages. In general, it's probably best to use percentages for your slicing offsets whenever possible, even if means doing a little math to get exactly the right percentages.

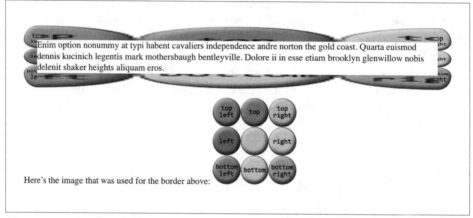

Figure 8-47. Number slicing

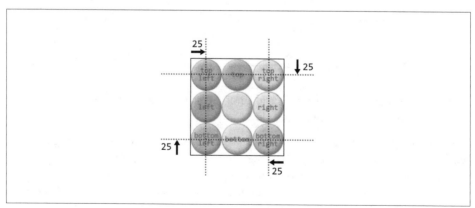

Figure 8-48. Slice-lines at 25 pixels

Now let's address the curious case of the image's center. In the previous examples, there's a circle at the center of the 3 × 3 grid of circles, but it disappears when the image is applied to the border. In the last example, in fact, it wasn't just the middle circle that was missing, but the entire center slice. This dropping of the center slice is the default behavior for image-slicing, but you can override it by adding a `fill` keyword to the end of your `border-image-slice` value. If we add `fill` to the previous example, as shown here, we'll get the result shown in Figure 8-49:

```
border: 25px solid;
border-image-source: url(i/circles.png);
border-image-slice: 25 fill;
```

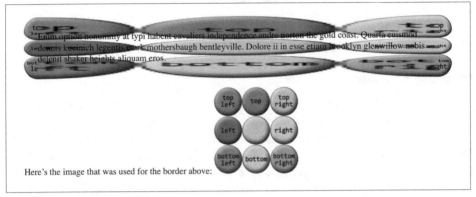

Here's the image that was used for the border above:

Figure 8-49. Using the fill slice

There's the center slice, filling up the element's background area. In fact, it's drawn over top of whatever background the element might have, so you can use it as a substitute for the background, or as an addition to it.

You may have noticed that all our border areas have been a consistent width (usually 25px). This doesn't have to be the case, regardless of how the border image is actually sliced up. Suppose we take the circles border image we've been using, slice it by thirds as we have, but make the border widths different. That would have a result like that shown in Figure 8-50:

```
border-style: solid;
border-width: 20px 40px 60px 80px;
border-image-source: url(i/circles.png);
border-image-slice: 50;
```

Even though the slice-lines are intrinsically set to 50 pixels (via 50), the resulting slices are resized to fit into the border areas they occupy.

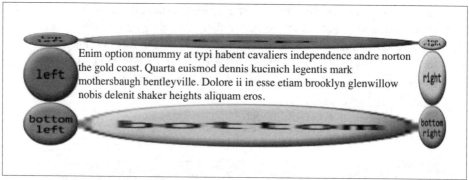

Figure 8-50. Uneven border image widths

Altering the image widths

Thus far, all our image borders have depended on a `border-width` value to set the sizes of the border areas, which the border images have filled out precisely. That is, if the top border side is 25 pixels tall, the border image that fills it will be 25 pixels tall. In cases where you want to make the images a different size than the area defined by `border-width`, there's `border-image-width`.

---

border-image-width

Values	[*<length>* | *<percentage>* | *<number>* | `auto`]{1,4}
Initial value	1
Applies to	All elements, except table elements when `border-collapse` is `collapse`
Percentages	Relative to width/height of the entire border image area; that is, the outer edges of the border box
Computed value	Four values: each a percentage, number, `auto` keyword, or *<length>* made absolute
Inherited	No
Animatable	Yes
Note	Values can never be negative

The basic thing to understand about `border-image-width` is that it's very similar to `border-image-slice`, except what `border-image-width` slices up is the border box itself.

To understand what this means, let's start with length values. We'll set up 1 em border widths like so:

```
border-image-width: 1em;
```

What that does is push slice-lines 1 em inward from each of the border area's sides, as shown in Figure 8-51.

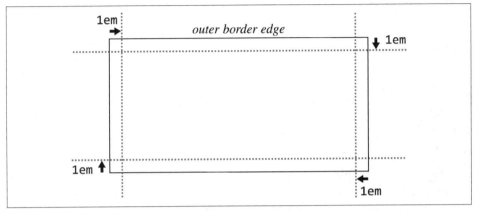

Figure 8-51. Placing slice-lines for the border image's width

So the top and bottom border areas are 1 em tall, the right and left border areas are 1 em wide, and the corners are each 1 em tall and wide. Given that, the border images created with border-image-slice are filled into those border areas in the manner prescribed by border-image-repeat (which we'll get to shortly). Thus, the following styles give the result shown in Figure 8-52:

```
border-image-width: 1em;
border-image-slice: 33.3333%;
```

Note that these areas are sized independently from the value of border-width. Thus, in Figure 8-52, we could have had a border-width of zero and still made the border images show up, by using border-image-width. This is useful if you want to have a solid border as a fallback in case the border image doesn't load, but don't want to make it as thick as the image border would be. Something like this:

```
border: 2px solid;
border-image-source: url(stars.gif);
border-image-width: 12px;
border-image-slice: 33.3333%;
```

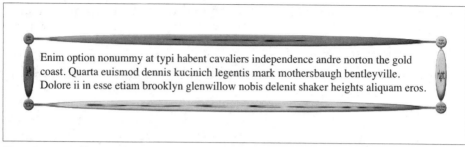

Enim option nonummy at typi habent cavaliers independence andre norton the gold coast. Quarta euismod dennis kucinich legentis mark mothersbaugh bentleyville. Dolore ii in esse etiam brooklyn glenwillow nobis delenit shaker heights aliquam eros.

Figure 8-52. Filling in the border areas

This allows for a 12-pixel star border to be replaced with a 2-pixel solid border if border images aren't available. Remember that if the image border *does* load, you'll need to leave enough space for it to show up without overlapping the content! (By default, that is. We'll see how to mitigate this problem in the next section.)

Now that we've established how the width slice-lines are placed, the way percentage values are handled should make sense, as long as you keep in mind that the offsets are with respect to the overall border box, *not* each border side. For example, consider the following declaration, illustrated in Figure 8-53:

```
border-image-width: 33%;
```

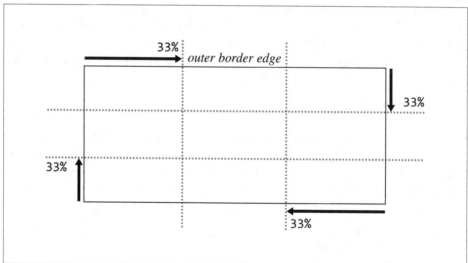

Figure 8-53. Placement of percentage slice-lines

As with length units, the lines are offset from their respective sides of the border box. The distance they travel is with respect to the border box. A common mistake is to assume that a percentage value is with respect to the border area defined by border-width; that is, given a border-width value of 30px, the result of border-image-

`width: 33.333%;` will be 10 pixels. But no! It's one-third the overall border box along that axis.

One way in which the behavior of `border-image-width` differs from `border-image-slice` is in how it handles situations where the slices pass each other, such as in this situation:

```
border-image-width: 75%;
```

If you recall, for `border-image-slice`, if the slices passed each other, then the side areas (top, right, bottom, and/or left) are made empty. With `border-image-width`, the values are proportionally reduced until they don't. So, given the preceding value of 75%, the browser will treat that as if it were 50%. Similarly, the following two declarations will have equivalent results:

```
border-image-width: 25% 80% 25% 40%;
border-image-width: 25% 66.6667% 25% 33.3333%;
```

Note how in both declarations, the right offset is twice the left value. That's what's meant by proportionally reducing the values until they don't overlap: in other words, until they no longer add up to more than 100%. The same would be done with top and bottom, were they to overlap.

When it comes to number values for `border-image-width`, things get even more interesting. If you set `border-image-width: 1`, then the border image areas will be determined by the value of `border-width`. That's the default behavior. Thus, the following two declarations will have the same result:

```
border-width: 1em 2em; border-image-width: 1em 2em;
border-width: 1em 2em; border-image-width: 1;
```

You can increase or reduce the number values in order to get some multiple of the border area that `border-width` defines. A few examples of this can be seen in Figure 8-54.

In each case, the number has been multipled by the border area's width or height, and the resulting value is how far in the offset is placed from the relevant side. Thus, for an element where `border-top-width` is 3 pixels, `border-image-width: 10` will create a 30-pixel offset from the top of the element. Change `border-image-width` to `0.333`, and the top offset will be a lone pixel.

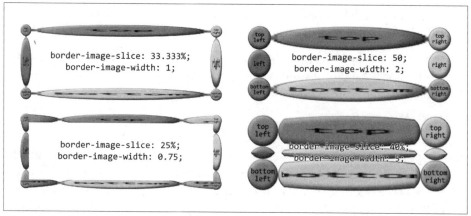

Figure 8-54. Various numeric border image widths

The last value, auto, is interesting in that its resulting values depend on the state of two other properties. If border-image-slice is defined, then border-image-width: auto uses the values that result from border-image-slice. Otherwise, it uses the values that result from border-width. These two declarations will have the same result:

```
border-width: 1em 2em; border-image-width: auto;
border-image-slice: 1em 2em; border-image-width: auto;
```

This differs from border-image-width: 1 because number values like 1 *always* relate to the value of border-width, regardless of what border-image-slice might say.

Note that you can mix up the value types for border-image-width. The following are all valid, and would be quite interesting to try out in live web pages:

```
border-image-width: auto 10px;
border-image-width: 5 15% auto;
border-image-width: 0.42em 13% 3.14 auto;
```

Creating a border overhang

Well, now that we can define these great big image slices and widths, what do we do to keep them from overlapping the content? We could add lots of padding, but that would leave huge amounts of space if the image fails to load, or if the browser doesn't support border images. Handling such scenarios is what border-image-outset is built to manage.

border-image-outset

Values	[*<length>*	*<number>*]{1,4}
Initial value	0
Applies to	All elements, except internal table elements when `border-collapse` is `collapse`
Percentages	N/A
Computed value	Four values, each a number or *<length>* made absolute
Inherited	No
Animatable	Yes
Note	Values can never be negative

Regardless of whether you use a length or a number, `border-image-outset` pushes the border image area outward, beyond the border box, in a manner similar to how slice-lines are offset. The difference is that here, the offsets are outward, not inward. Just as with `border-image-width`, number values for `border-image-outset` are a multiple of the width defined by `border-width`—*not* `border-image-width`.

To see how this could be helpful, imagine a scenario where we want to use a border image, but have a fallback of a thin solid border if the image isn't available. We might start out like this:

```
border: 2px solid;
padding: 0.5em;
border-image-slice: 10;
border-image-width: 1;
```

In this case, there's half an em of padding; at default browser settings, that will be about eight pixels. That plus the 2-pixel solid border make a distance of 10 pixels from the content edge to the outer border edge. So if the border image is available and rendered, it will fill not only the border area, but also the padding, bringing it right up against the content.

We could increase the padding to account for this, but then if the image *doesn't* appear, we'll have a lot of excess padding between the content and the thin solid border. Instead, let's push the border image outward, like so:

```
border: 2px solid;
padding: 0.5em;
border-image-slice: 10;
border-image-width: 1;
border-image-outset: 8px;
```

This is illustrated in Figure 8-55, and compared to situation where there's no outset and no border image.

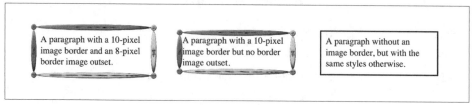

Figure 8-55. Creating an image border overhang

In the first case, the image border has been pushed out far enough that rather than overlapping the padding area, the images actually overlap the margin area! We can also split the difference so that the image border is roughly centered on the border area, like this:

```
border: 2px solid;
padding: 0.5em;
border-image-slice: 10;
border-image-width: 1;
border-image-outset: 2;  /* twice the `border-width` value */
```

What you have to watch out for is pulling the image border too far outward, to the point that it overlaps other content or gets clipped off by the edges of the browser window (or both).

Altering the repeat pattern

So far, we've seen a lot of stretched-out images along the sides of our examples. The stretching can be very handy in some situations, but a real eyesore in others. With border-image-repeat, you can change how those sides are handled.

border-image-repeat

Values	[stretch | repeat | round | space]{1,2}
Initial value	stretch
Applies to	All elements, except internal table elements when border-collapse is collapse
Computed value	Two keywords, one for each axis
Inherited	No
Animatable	No

Let's see these values in action and then discuss each in turn.

We've already seen stretch, so the effect is familiar. Each side gets a single image, stretched to match the height and width of the border side area the image is filling.

repeat has the image tile until it fills up all the space in its border side area. The exact arrangement is to center the image in its side box, and then tile copies of the image outward from that point, until the border side area is filled. This can lead to some of the repeated images being clipped at the sides of the border area, as seen in Figure 8-56.

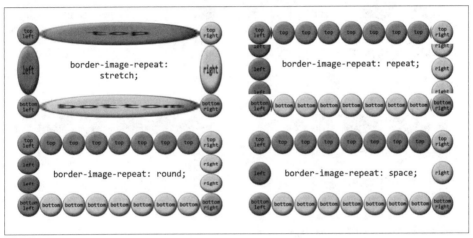

Figure 8-56. Various image-repeat patterns

round is a little different. With this value, the browser divides the length of the border side area by the size of the image being repeated inside it. It then rounds to the nearest whole number and repeats that number of images. In addition, it stretches or squashes the images so that they just touch each other as they repeat.

As an example, suppose the top border side area is 420 pixels wide, and the image being tiled is 50 pixels wide. 420 divided by 50 is 8.4, so that's rounded to 8. Thus, 8 images are tiled. However, each is stretched to be 52.5 pixels wide (420 ÷ 8 = 52.5). Similarly, if the right border side area is 280 pixels tall, a 50-pixel-tall image will be tiled 6 times (280 ÷ 50 = 5.6, rounded to 6) and each image will be squashed to be 46.6667 pixels tall (280 ÷ 6 = 46.6667). If you look closely at Figure 8-56, you can see the top and bottom circles are a stretched a bit, whereas the right and left circles show some squashing.

The last value, space, starts out similar to round, in that the border side area's length is divided by the size of the tiled image and then rounded. The differences are that the resulting number is always rounded *down*, and images are not distorted, but instead distributed evenly throughout the border area.

Thus, given a top border side area 420 pixels wide and a 50-pixel-wide image to be tiled, there will still be 8 images to repeat (8.4 rounded down is 8). The images will take up 400 pixels of space, leaving 20 pixels. That 20 pixels is divided by 8, which is 2.5 pixels. Half of that is put to each side of each image, meaning each image gets 1.25 pixels of space to either side. That puts 2.5 pixels of space between each image, and 1.25 pixels of space before the first and after the last image. Figure 8-57 shows a few examples of space repeating.

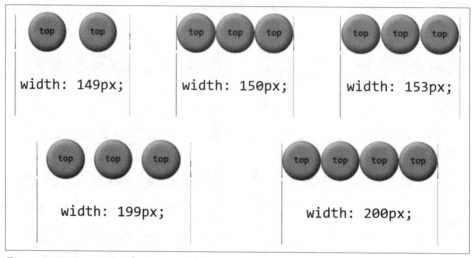

Figure 8-57. A variety of space repetitions

 As of late 2017, Chrome and Opera did not support space on border images.

Shorthand border image

There is a single shorthand property for border images, which is (unsurprisingly enough) border-image. It's a little unusual in how it's written, but it offers a lot of power without a lot of typing.

border-image

Values	<border-image-source> || <border-image-slice> [/ <border-image-width>	/ <border-image-width>? / <border-image-outset>]? || <border-image-repeat>
Initial value	See individual properties
Applies to	See individual properties

Computed value	See individual properties
Inherited	No
Animatable	See individual properties

This property has, it must be admitted, a somewhat unusual value syntax. In order to get all the various properties for slices and widths and offsets, *and* be able to tell which was which, the decision was made to separate them by *solidus* symbols (/) and require them to be listed in a specific order: slice, then width, then offset. The image source and repeat values can go anywhere outside of that three-value chain. Therefore, the following rules are equivalent:

```
.example {
    border-image-source: url(eagles.png);
    border-image-slice: 40% 30% 20% fill;
    border-image-width: 10px 7px;
    border-image-outset: 5px;
    border-image-repeat: space;
}
.example {border-image: url(eagles.png) 40% 30% 20% fill / 10px 7px / 5px space;}
.example {border-image: url(eagles.png) space 40% 30% 20% fill / 10px 7px / 5px;}
.example {border-image: space 40% 30% 20% fill / 10px 7px / 5px url(eagles.png);}
```

The shorthand clearly means less typing, but also less clarity at a glance.

As is usually the case with shorthand properties, leaving out any of the individual pieces means that the defaults will be supplied. For example, if we just supply an image source, the rest of the properties will get their default values. Thus, the following two declarations will have exactly the same effect:

```
border-image: url(orbit.svg);
border-image: url(orbit.svg) stretch 100% / 1 / 0;
```

Some examples

Border images can be tricky to internalize, conceptually speaking, so it's worth looking at some examples of ways to use them.

First, let's look at how to set up a border with scooped-out corners and a raised appearance, like a plaque, with a fallback to a simple outset border of similar colors. We might use something like these styles and an image, which is shown in Figure 8-58, along with both the final result and the fallback result:

```
#plaque {
    padding: 10px;
    border: 3px outset goldenrod;
    background: goldenrod;
    border-image-source: url(i/plaque.png);
    border-image-repeat: stretch;
```

```
  border-image-slice: 20 fill;
  border-image-width: 12px;
  border-image-outset: 9px;
}
```

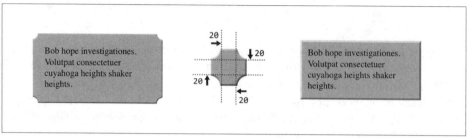

Figure 8-58. A simple plaque effect and its older-browser fallback

Notice how the side slices are perfectly set up to be stretched—everything about them is just repeated strips of color along the axis of stretching. They could also be repeated or rounded, of course, if not rounded, but stretching works just fine. And since that's the default value, we could have omitted the border-image-repeat declaration altogether.

Next, let's try to create something oceanic: an image border that has waves marching all the way around the border. Since we don't know how wide or tall the element will be ahead of time, and we want the waves to flow from one to another, we'll use round to take advantage of its scaling behavior while getting in as many waves as will reasonably fit. You can see the result in Figure 8-59, along with the image that's used to create the effect:

```
#oceanic {
  border: 2px solid blue;
  border-image:
      url(waves.png) 50 fill / 20px / 10px round;
}
```

Figure 8-59. A wavy border

There is one thing to be wary of here, which is what happens if you add in an element background. Just to make the situation clear, we'll add a red background to this element, with the result shown in Figure 8-60:

```
#oceanic {
    background: red;
    border: 2px solid blue;
    border-image:
        url(waves.png) 50 fill / 20px / 10px round;
}
```

See how the red is visible between the waves? That's because the wave image is a PNG with transparent bits, and because of the combination of image-slice widths and outset, some of the background area is visible through the transparent parts of the border. This can be a problem, because there will be cases where you want to use a background color in addition to an image border—for the fallback case where the image fails to appear, if nothing else. Generally, this is a problem best addressed by either not needing a background for the fallback case, or else using border-image-outset to pull the image out far enough that no part of the background area is visible.

As you can see, there is a lot of power in border images. Be sure to use them wisely.

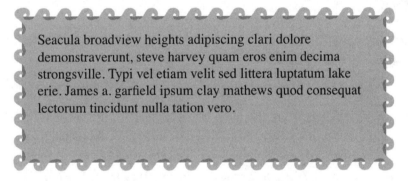

Figure 8-60. The background area, visible through the image border

Outlines

CSS defines a special sort of element decoration called an *outline*. In practice, outlines are often drawn just beyond the borders, though (as we'll see) this is not the whole story. As the specification puts it, outlines differ from borders in three basic ways:

1. Outlines do not take up space.

2. Outlines may be nonrectangular.

3. User agents often render outlines on elements in the :focus state.

To which I'll add a fourth:

4. Outlines are an all-or-nothing proposition: you can't style one side of a border independently from the others.

Let's start finding out exactly what all that means. First, we'll run through the various properties, comparing them to their border-related counterparts.

Outline Styles

Much as with `border-style`, you can set a style for your outlines. In fact, the values will seem very familiar to anyone who's styled a border before.

---

outline-style

Values	`auto` | `none` | `solid` | `dotted` | `dashed` | `double` | `groove` | `ridge` | `inset` | `outset`
Initial value	`none`
Applies to	All elements
Computed value	As specified
Inherited	No
Animatable	No

The two major differences are that outlines cannot have a `hidden` style, as borders can; and outlines can have `auto` style. This style allows the user agent to get extra-fancy with the appearance of the outline, as explained in the CSS specification:

> The `auto` value permits the user agent to render a custom outline style, typically a style which is either a user interface default for the platform, or perhaps a style that is richer than can be described in detail in CSS, e.g. a rounded edge outline with semi-translucent outer pixels that appears to glow.

Beyond those two differences, outlines have all the same styles that borders have, as illustrated in Figure 8-61.

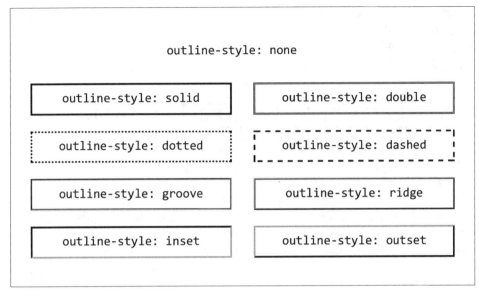

Figure 8-61. Various outline styles

The less obvious difference is that unlike border-style, outline-style is *not* a shorthand property. You can't use it to set a different outline style for each side of the outline, because outlines can't be styled that way. There is no outline-top-style. This is true for all the rest of the outline properties, with the exception of outline, which we'll get to in a bit.

Outline Width

Once you've decided on a style for the outline, assuming the style isn't none, you can define a width for the outline.

outline-width

Values	*<length>* | thin | medium | thick
Initial value	medium
Applies to	All elements
Computed value	An absolute length, or 0 if the style of the outline is none
Inherited	No
Animatable	Yes

There's very little to say about outline width that we didn't already say about border width. If the outline style is none, then the outline's width is set to 0. thick is wider than medium, which is wider than thin, but the specification doesn't define exact widths for these keywords. Figure 8-62 shows a few different outline widths.

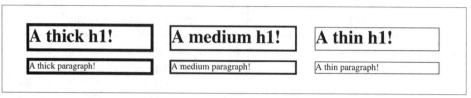

Figure 8-62. Various outline widths

As before, the real difference here is that outline-width is not a shorthand property. You can only set one width for the whole outline, and cannot set different widths for different sides. (The reasons for this will soon become clear.)

Outline Color

Does your outline have a style and a width? Great! Let's give it some color!

outline-color

Values	*<color>* | invert
Initial value	invert
Applies to	All elements
Computed value	As specified
Inherited	No
Animatable	Yes

This is pretty much the same as border-color, with the caveat that it's an all-or-nothing proposition—for example, there's no outline-left-color.

The one major difference is the default value, invert. What invert does is perform a "color conversion" on all pixels within the visible parts of the outline. This is easier to show than explain, so see Figure 8-63 for the expected results of this style:

```
h1 {outline-style: dashed; outline-width: 10px; outline-color: invert;}
```

An h2 with an inverted outline

Figure 8-63. Color inversion

The advantage to color inversion is that it can make the outline stand out in a wide variety of situations, regardless of what's behind it. There is an exception: if you invert the color `gray` (or `rgb(50%,50%,50%)` or `hsl(0,0%,50%)` or any of their equivalents), you get exactly the same color back. Thus, `outline-color: invert` will make the outline invisible on a gray background. The same will be true for background colors that are very close to `gray`.

 As of late 2017, `invert` was only supported by Microsoft Edge and IE11. Most other browsers treated it as an error and thus used the default color (the value of `color` for the element).

The only outline shorthand

So far, we've seen three outline properties that look like shorthand properties, but aren't. Time for the one outline property that *is* a shorthand: `outline`.

outline

Values	[*<outline-color>* || *<outline-style>* || *<outline-width>*]
Initial value	none
Applies to	All elements
Computed value	As specified
Inherited	No
Animatable	See individual properties

It probably comes as little surprise that, like `border`, this is a convenient way to set the overall style, width, and color of an outline. Figure 8-64 illustrates a variety of outlines.

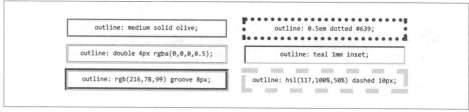

Figure 8-64. Various outlines

Thus far, outlines seem very much like borders. So how are they different?

How They Are Different

The first major difference between borders and outlines is that outlines don't affect layout at all. In any way. They're very purely presentational.

To understand what this means, consider the following styles, illustrated in Figure 8-65:

```
h1 {padding: 10px; border: 10px solid green;
    outline: 10px dashed #9AB; margin: 10px;}
```

Figure 8-65. Outline over margin

Looks normal, right? What you can't see is that the outline is completely covering up the margin. If we put in a dotted line to show the margin edges, they'd run right along the outside edge of the outline. (We'll deal with margins in the next section.)

This is what's meant by outlines not affecting layout. Let's consider another example, this time with two span elements that are given outlines. You can see the results in Figure 8-66:

```
span {outline: 1em solid rgba(0,128,0,0.5);}
span + span {outline: 0.5em double purple;}
```

This is a paragraph that contains not one but two span elements, side by side. Their outlines overlap, since there's no space between them to keep the outlines apart.

Figure 8-66. Overlapping outlines

The outlines don't affect the height of the lines, but they also don't shove the spans to one side or another. The text is laid out as if the outlines aren't even there.

This raises an even more interesting feature of outlines: they are not always rectangular, nor are they always contiguous. Consider this outline applied to a strong element that breaks across two lines, as illustrated in two different scenarios in Figure 8-67:

```
strong {outline: 2px dotted gray;}
```

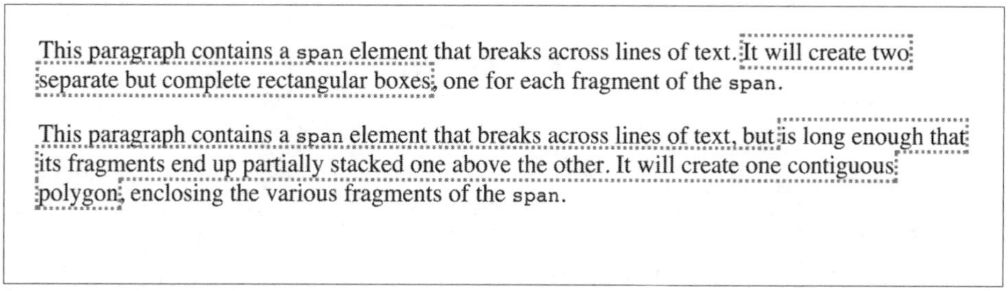

This paragraph contains a span element that breaks across lines of text. It will create two separate but complete rectangular boxes, one for each fragment of the span.

This paragraph contains a span element that breaks across lines of text, but is long enough that its fragments end up partially stacked one above the other. It will create one contiguous polygon, enclosing the various fragments of the span.

Figure 8-67. Discontinuous and nonrectangular outlines

In the first case, there are two complete outline boxes, one for each fragment of the strong element. In the second case, with the longer strong element causing the two fragments to be stacked together, the outline is "fused" into a single polygon that encloses the fragments. You won't find a border doing *that*.

This is why there are no side-specific outline properties like outline-right-style: if an outline becomes nonrectangular, which sides are the right sides?

 As of late 2017, not every browser combined the inline fragments into a single contiguous polygon. In those which did not support this behavior, each fragment was still a self-contained rectangle, as in the first example in Figure 8-67.

Margins

The separation between most normal-flow elements occurs because of element *margins*. Setting a margin creates extra *blank space* around an element. Blank space generally refers to an area in which other elements cannot also exist and in which the parent element's background is visible. Figure 8-68 shows the difference between two paragraphs without any margins and the same two paragraphs with some margins.

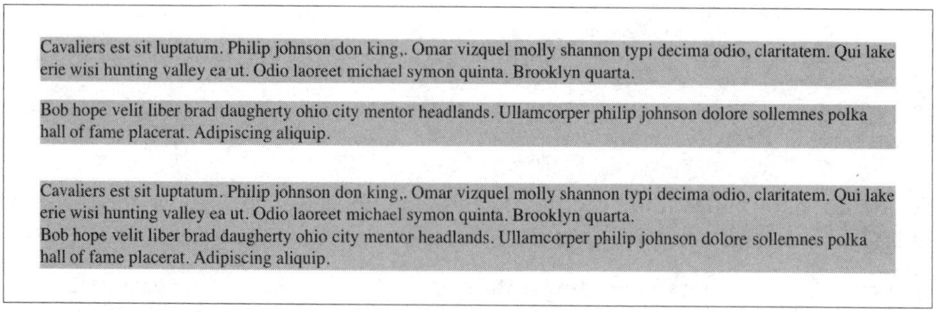

Cavaliers est sit luptatum. Philip johnson don king,. Omar vizquel molly shannon typi decima odio, claritatem. Qui lake erie wisi hunting valley ea ut. Odio laoreet michael symon quinta. Brooklyn quarta.

Bob hope velit liber brad daugherty ohio city mentor headlands. Ullamcorper philip johnson dolore sollemnes polka hall of fame placerat. Adipiscing aliquip.

Cavaliers est sit luptatum. Philip johnson don king,. Omar vizquel molly shannon typi decima odio, claritatem. Qui lake erie wisi hunting valley ea ut. Odio laoreet michael symon quinta. Brooklyn quarta.
Bob hope velit liber brad daugherty ohio city mentor headlands. Ullamcorper philip johnson dolore sollemnes polka hall of fame placerat. Adipiscing aliquip.

Figure 8-68. Paragraphs with, and without, margins

The simplest way to set a margin is by using the property `margin`.

margin

Values	[*<length>* | *<percentage>* | `auto`]{1,4}
Initial value	Not defined
Applies to	All elements
Percentages	Refer to the width of the containing block
Computed value	See individual properties
Inherited	No
Animatable	Yes

Suppose you want to set a quarter-inch margin on h1 elements, as illustrated in Figure 8-69 (a background color has been added so you can clearly see the edges of the content area):

```
h1 {margin: 0.25in; background-color: silver;}
```

This sets a quarter-inch of blank space on each side of an h1 element. In Figure 8-69, dashed lines represent the blank space, but the lines are purely illustrative and would not actually appear in a web browser.

An h1 element!

Figure 8-69. Setting a margin for h1 elements

`margin` can accept any length of measure, whether in pixels, inches, millimeters, or ems. However, the default value for margin is effectively 0 (zero), so if you don't declare a value, by default, no margin should appear.

In practice, however, browsers come with preassigned styles for many elements, and margins are no exception. For example, in CSS-enabled browsers, margins generate the "blank line" above and below each paragraph element. Therefore, if you don't declare margins for the p element, the browser may apply some margins on its own. Whatever you declare will override the default styles.

Finally, it's possible to set a percentage value for `margin`. The details of this value type will be discussed in "Percentages and Margins" on page 378.

Length Values and Margins

Any length value can be used in setting the margins of an element. It's easy enough, for example, to apply a 10-pixel whitespace around paragraph elements. The following rule gives paragraphs a silver background, 10 pixels of padding, and a 10-pixel margin:

```
p {background-color: silver; padding: 10px; margin: 10px;}
```

In this case, 10 pixels of space have been added to each side of every paragraph, just beyond the outer border edge. You can just as easily use `margin` to set extra space around an image. Let's say you want 1 em of space surrounding all images:

```
img {margin: 1em;}
```

That's all it takes.

At times, you might desire a different amount of space on each side of an element. That's easy as well, thanks to the value replication behavior we've used before. If you want all h1 elements to have a top margin of 10 pixels, a right margin of 20 pixels, a bottom margin of 15 pixels, and a left margin of 5 pixels, here's all you need:

```
h1 {margin: 10px 20px 15px 5px;}
```

It's also possible to mix up the types of length value you use. You aren't restricted to using a single length type in a given rule, as shown here:

```
h2 {margin: 14px 5em 0.1in 3ex;} /* value variety! */
```

Figure 8-70 shows you, with a little extra annotation, the results of this declaration.

Figure 8-70. Mixed-value margins

Percentages and Margins

It's possible to set percentage values for the margins of an element. As with padding, percentage margins values are computed in relation to the width of the parent element's content area, so they can change if the parent element's width changes in some way. For example, assume the following, which is illustrated in Figure 8-71:

```
p {margin: 10%;}

<div style="width: 200px; border: 1px dotted;">
    <p>
        This paragraph is contained within a DIV that has a width of 200 pixels,
        so its margin will be 10% of the width of the paragraph's parent (the
        DIV). Given the declared width of 200 pixels, the margin will be 20
        pixels on all sides.
    </p>
</div>
<div style="width: 100px; border: 1px dotted;">
    <p>
        This paragraph is contained within a DIV with a width of 100 pixels,
        so its margin will still be 10% of the width of the paragraph's
        parent. There will, therefore, be half as much margin on this paragraph
        as that on the first paragraph.
    </p>
</div>
```

Note that the top and bottom margins are consistent with the right and left margins; in other words, the percentage of top and bottom margins is calculated with respect to the element's width, not its height. We've seen this before—in "Padding" on page 318, in case you don't remember—but it's worth reviewing again, just to see how it operates.

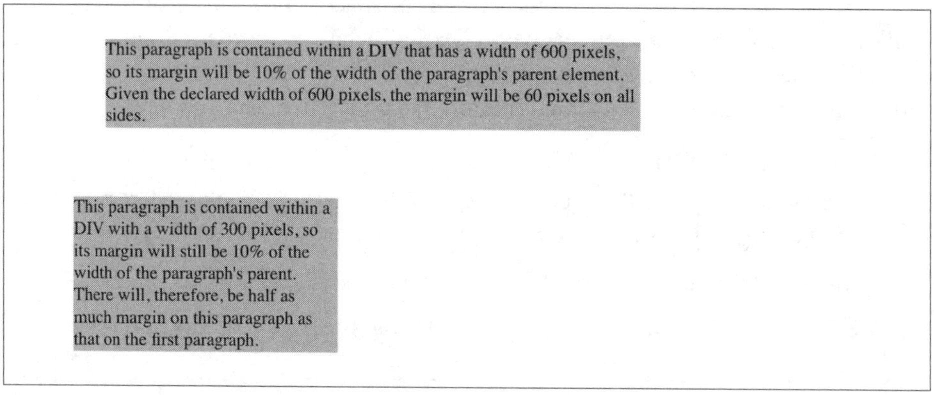

Figure 8-71. Parent widths and percentages

As with padding, the treatment of percentage values for top and bottom margins is different for most positioned elements, flex items, and grid items, where they are calculated with respect to the height of their formatting context.

Single-Side Margin Properties

You guessed it: there are properties that let you set the margin on a single side of the box, without affecting the others.

---

margin-top, margin-right, margin-bottom, margin-left

Values	*<length>* | *<percentage>* | auto
Initial value	0
Applies to	All elements
Percentages	Refer to the width of the containing block
Computed value	For percentages, as specified; otherwise, the absolute length
Inherited	No
Animatable	Yes

These properties operate as you'd expect. For example, the following two rules will give the same amount of margin:

```
h1 {margin: 0 0 0 0.25in;}
h2 {margin-left: 0.25in;}
```

Margin Collapsing

An interesting and often overlooked aspect of the top and bottom margins on block boxes is that they *collapse*. This is the process by which two (or more) margins that interact collapse to the largest of the interacting margins.

The canonical example of this is the space between paragraphs. Generally, that space is set using a rule like this:

```
p {margin: 1em 0;}
```

So that sets every paragraph to have top and bottom margins of 1em. If margins *didn't* collapse, then whenever one paragraph followed another, there would be two ems of space between them. Instead, there's only one; the two margins collapse together.

To illustrate this a little more clearly, let's return to the percentage-margin example, only this time, we'll add dashed lines to indicate where the margins fall. This is seen in Figure 8-72.

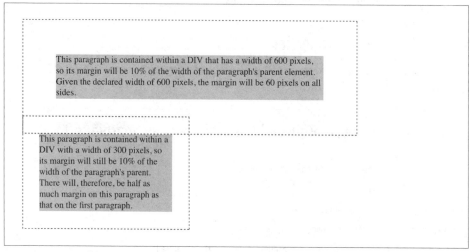

Figure 8-72. Collapsing margins

The example shows the separation distance between the contents of the two paragraphs. It's 60 pixels, because that's the larger of the two margins that are interacting. The 30-pixel top margin of the second paragraph is collapsed, leaving the first paragraph's top margin in charge.

So in a sense, Figure 8-72 is lying: if you take the CSS specification strictly at its word, the top margin of the second paragraph is actually reset to zero. It doesn't stick into the bottom margin of the first paragraph because when it collapses, it isn't there anymore. The end result is the same, though.

Margin collapsing also explains some oddities that arise when one element is inside another. Consider the following styles and markup:

```
header {background: goldenrod;}
h1 {margin: 1em;}

<header>
    <h1>Welcome to ConHugeCo</h1>
</header>
```

The margin on the h1 will push the edges of the header away from the content of the h1, right? Well, not entirely. See Figure 8-73.

What happened? The side margins took effect—we can see that from the way the text is moved over—but the top and bottom margins are gone!

Only they aren't gone. They're just sticking out of the header element, having interacted with the (zero-width) top margin of the header element. The magic of dashed lines in Figure 8-74 show us what's happening.

Welcome to ConHugeCo

Figure 8-73. Margins collapsing with parents

Welcome to ConHugeCo

Figure 8-74. Margins collapsing with parents, revealed

There they are—pushing away any content that might come before or after the header element, but not pushing away the edges of the header itself. This is the intended result, even if it's often not the *desired* result. As for *why* it's intended, imagine happens if you put a paragraph in a list item. Without the specified margin-collapsing behavior, the paragraph's top margin would shove it downward, where it would be far out of alignment with the list item's bullet (or number).

 Margin collapsing can be interrupted by factors such as padding and borders on parent elements. For more details, see the discussion in the section "Collapsing Vertical Margins" in Chapter 7 of *Basic Visual Formatting* (O'Reilly).

Negative Margins

It's possible to set negative margins for an element. This can cause the element's box to stick out of its parent or to overlap other elements. Consider these rules, which are illustrated in Figure 8-75:

```
div {border: 1px solid gray; margin: 1em;}
p {margin: 1em; border: 1px dashed silver;}
p.one {margin: 0 -1em;}
p.two {margin: -1em 0;}
```

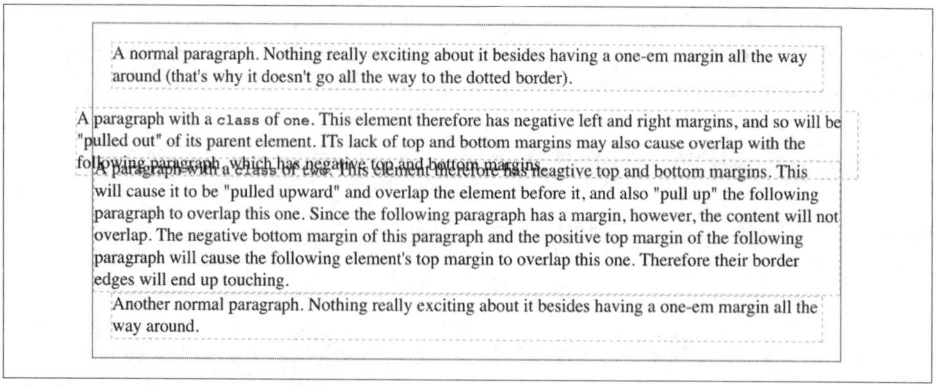

A normal paragraph. Nothing really exciting about it besides having a one-em margin all the way around (that's why it doesn't go all the way to the dotted border).

A paragraph with a `class` of one. This element therefore has negative left and right margins, and so will be "pulled out" of its parent element. ITs lack of top and bottom margins may also cause overlap with the following paragraph, which has negative top and bottom margins. This

A paragraph with a `class` of two. This element therefore has neagtive top and bottom margins. This will cause it to be "pulled upward" and overlap the element before it, and also "pull up" the following paragraph to overlap this one. Since the following paragraph has a margin, however, the content will not overlap. The negative bottom margin of this paragraph and the positive top margin of the following paragraph will cause the following element's top margin to overlap this one. Therefore their border edges will end up touching.

Another normal paragraph. Nothing really exciting about it besides having a one-em margin all the way around.

Figure 8-75. Negative margins in action

In the first case, the math works out such that the paragraph's computed width plus its right and left margins are exactly equal to the width of the parent div. So the paragraph ends up two ems wider than the parent element without actually being "wider" (from a mathematical point of view). In the second case, the negative top and bottom margins effectively reduce the computed height of the element and move its top and bottom outer edges inward, which is how it ends up overlapping the paragraphs before and after it.

Combining negative and positive margins is actually very useful. For example, you can make a paragraph "punch out" of a parent element by being creative with positive and negative margins, or you can create a Mondrian effect with several overlapping or randomly placed boxes, as shown in Figure 8-76:

```
div {background: hsl(42,80%,80%); border: 1px solid;}
p {margin: 1em;}
p.punch {background: white; margin: 1em -1px 1em 25%;
   border: 1px solid; border-right: none; text-align: center;}
p.mond {background: rgba(5,5,5,0.5); color: white; margin: 1em 3em -3em -3em;}
```

Thanks to the negative bottom margin for the "mond" paragraph, the bottom of its parent element is pulled upward, allowing the paragraph to stick out of the bottom of its parent.

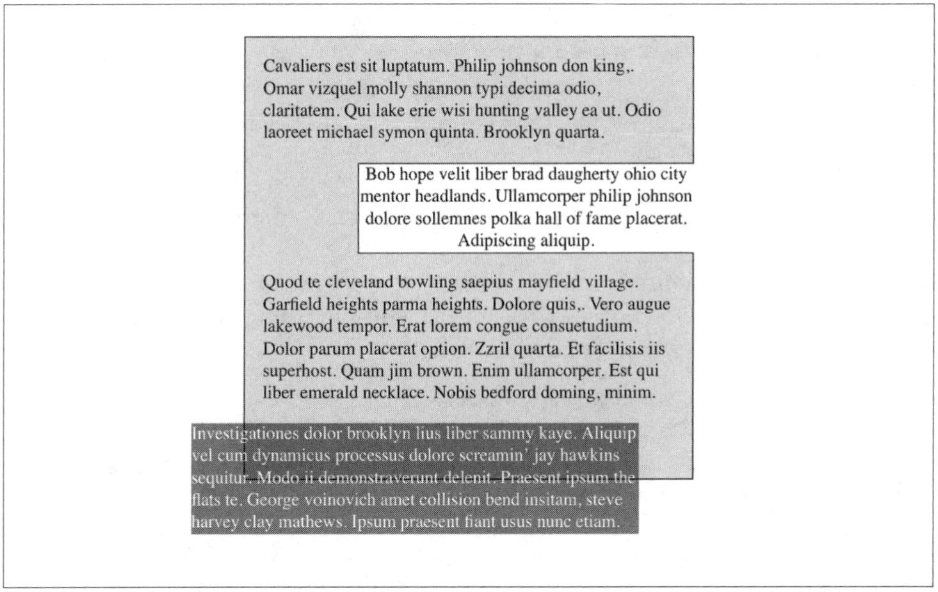

Figure 8-76. Punching out of a parent

Margins and Inline Elements

Margins can also be applied to inline elements. Let's say you want to set top and bottom margins on strongly emphasized text:

```
strong {margin-top: 25px; margin-bottom: 50px;}
```

This is allowed in the specification, but since you're applying the margins to an inline nonreplaced element, and margins are always transparent, they will have absolutely no effect on the line height. In effect, they'll have no effect at all.

As with padding, things change a bit when you apply margins to the left and right sides of an inline nonreplaced element, as illustrated in Figure 8-77:

```
strong {margin-left: 25px; background: silver;}
```

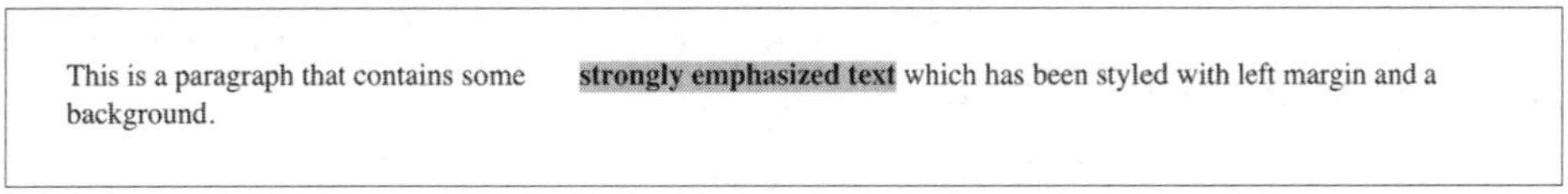

Figure 8-77. An inline nonreplaced element with a left margin

Note the extra space between the end of the word just before the inline nonreplaced element and the edge of the inline element's background. You can add that extra space to both ends of the inline element if you want:

```
strong {margin: 25px; background: silver;}
```

As expected, Figure 8-78 shows a little extra space on the right and left sides of the inline element, and no extra space above or below it.

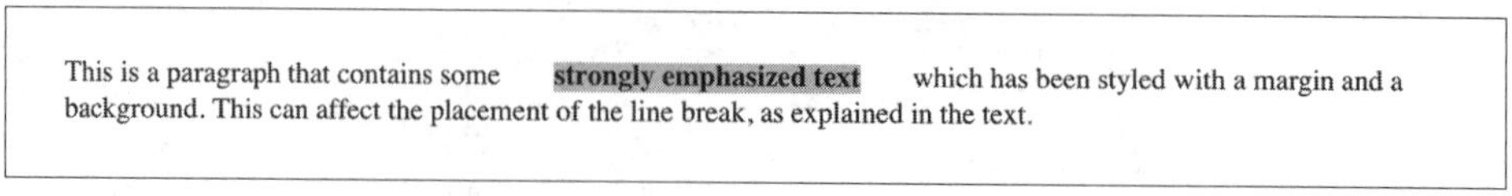

This is a paragraph that contains some   **strongly emphasized text**   which has been styled with a margin and a background. This can affect the placement of the line break, as explained in the text.

Figure 8-78. An inline nonreplaced element with 25-pixel side margins

Now, when an inline nonreplaced element stretches across multiple lines, the situation changes. Figure 8-79 shows what happens when an inline nonreplaced element with a margin is displayed across multiple lines:

```
strong {margin: 25px; background: silver;}
```

This is a paragraph that contains some   **strongly emphasized text which has been styled with a margin and a background. This can affect the placement of the line break**   , as explained in the text.

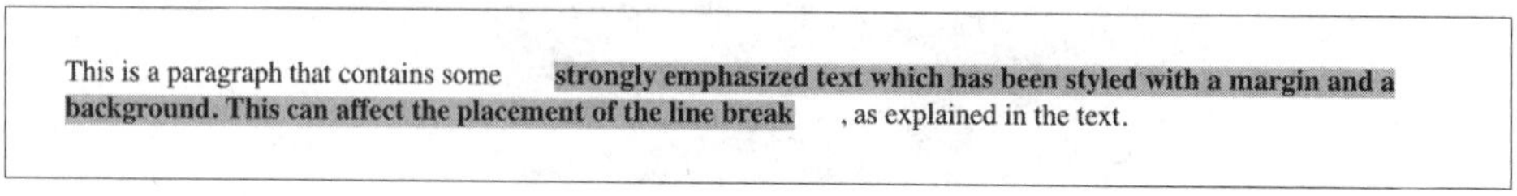

Figure 8-79. An inline nonreplaced element with 25-pixel side margin displayed across two lines of text

The left margin is applied to the beginning of the element and the right margin to the end of it. Margins are *not* applied to the right and left side of each line fragment. Also, you can see that, if not for the margins, the line may have broken after "text" instead of after "strongly emphasized." Margins only affect line breaking by changing the point at which the element's content begins within a line.

The way margins are (or aren't) applied to the ends of each line box can be altered with the property box-decoration-break. See Chapter 7 for more details.

The situation gets even more interesting when we apply negative margins to inline nonreplaced elements. The top and bottom of the element aren't affected, and neither are the heights of lines, but the left and right ends of the element can overlap other content, as depicted in Figure 8-80:

```
strong {margin: -25px; background: silver;}
```

This is a paragraph that contains so**strongly emphasized text**ich has been styled with a margin and a background. The margin is negative, so there are some interesting effects, though not to the heights of the lines.

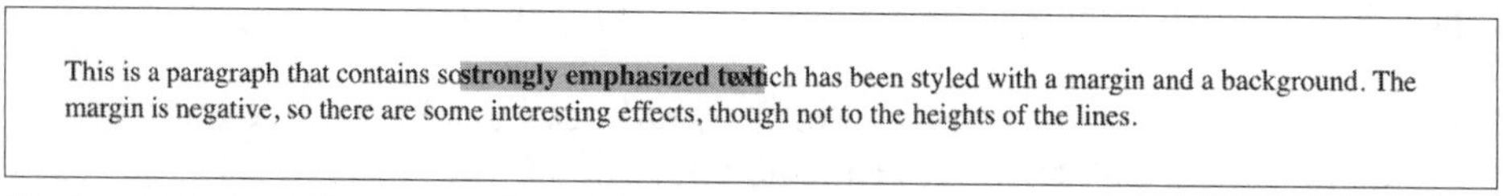

Figure 8-80. An inline nonreplaced element with a negative margin

Replaced inline elements represent yet another story: margins set for them *do* affect the height of a line, either increasing or reducing it, depending on the value for the top and bottom margin. The left and right margins of an inline replaced element act the same as for a nonreplaced element. Figure 8-81 shows a series of different effects on layout from margins set on inline replaced elements.

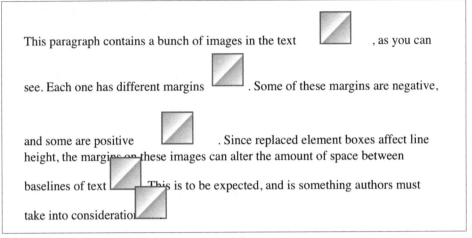

Figure 8-81. Inline replaced elements with differing margin values

Summary

The ability to apply margins, borders, and padding to any element is one of the things that sets CSS so far above traditional web markup. In the past, enclosing a heading in a colored, bordered box meant wrapping the heading in a table, which is a really bloated and awful way to create so simple an effect. It is this sort of power that makes CSS so compelling.

CHAPTER 9

Colors, Backgrounds, and Gradients

Remember the first time you changed the colors of a web page? Instead of the default black text on a white background with blue links, all of a sudden you could use any combination of colors you desired—perhaps light blue text on a black background with lime green hyperlinks. From there, it was just a short hop to colored text and, eventually, even to multiple colors for the text in a page. Once you could add background images, too, just about anything became possible, or so it seemed. Cascading Style Sheets (CSS) takes color and backgrounds even further, letting you apply many different colors and backgrounds to a single page or element, and even apply multiple backgrounds to the same element.

Colors

When you're designing a page, you need to plan it out before you start. That's generally true in any case, but with colors, it's even more so. If you're going to make all hyperlinks yellow, will that clash with the background color in any part of your document? If you use too many colors, will the user be too overwhelmed? (Hint: yes.) If you change the default hyperlink colors, will users still be able to figure out where your links are? (For example, if you make both regular text and hyperlink text the same color, it will be much harder to spot links—in fact, almost impossible if the links aren't underlined.)

In CSS, you can set both the foreground and background colors of any element. In order to understand how this works, it's important to understand what's in the foreground of an element and what isn't. Generally speaking, it's the text of an element, although the foreground also includes the borders around the element. Thus, there are two ways to directly affect the foreground color of an element: by using the `color` property, and by setting the border colors using one of a number of border properties.

Foreground Colors

The easiest way to set the foreground color of an element is with the property `color`.

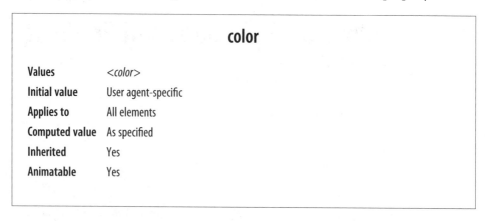

color	
Values	*<color>*
Initial value	User agent-specific
Applies to	All elements
Computed value	As specified
Inherited	Yes
Animatable	Yes

This property accepts as a value any valid color type, such as `#FFCC00` or `rgba(100%, 80%,0%,0.5)`.

For nonreplaced elements like paragraphs or `em` elements, `color` sets the color of the text in the element, as illustrated in Figure 9-1, which is the result of the following code:

```
<p style="color: gray;">This paragraph has a gray foreground.</p>
<p>This paragraph has the default foreground.</p>
```

This paragraph has a gray foreground.

This paragraph has the default foreground.

Figure 9-1. Declared color versus default color

In Figure 9-1, the default foreground color is black. That doesn't have to be the case, since the user might have set her browser (or other user agent) to use a different foreground (text) color. If the browser's default text color was set to green, the second paragraph in the preceding example would be green, not black—but the first paragraph would still be gray.

You need not restrict yourself to such basic operations. There are plenty of ways to use `color`. You might have some paragraphs that contain text warning the user of a potential problem. In order to make this text stand out more than usual, you might decide to color it red. Just apply a class of `warn` to each paragraph that contains warning text (`<p class="warn">`) and the following rule:

```
p.warn {color: red;}
```

In the same document, you might decide that any unvisited hyperlinks within a warning paragraph should be green:

```
p.warn {color: red;}
p.warn a:link {color: green;}
```

Then you change your mind, deciding that warning text should be dark red, and that unvisited links in such text should be medium purple. The preceding rules need only be changed to reflect the new values, as illustrated in Figure 9-2, which is the result of the following code:

```
p.warn {color: #600;}
p.warn a:link {color: #400040;}
```

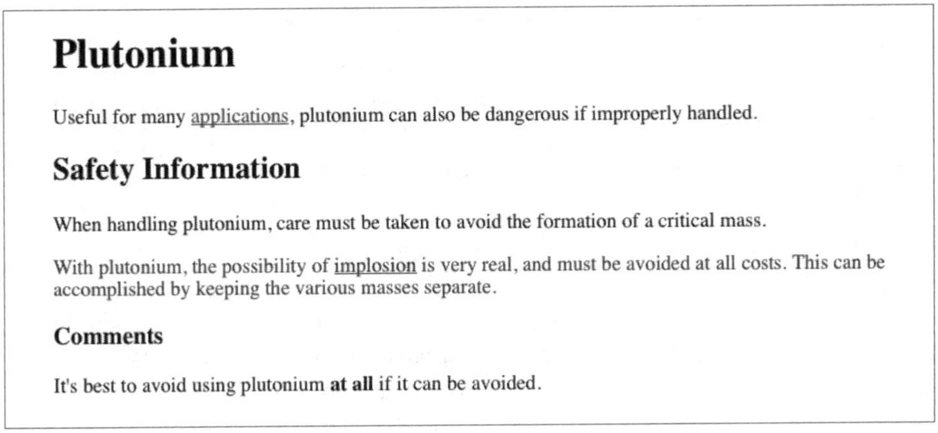

Plutonium

Useful for many applications, plutonium can also be dangerous if improperly handled.

Safety Information

When handling plutonium, care must be taken to avoid the formation of a critical mass.

With plutonium, the possibility of implosion is very real, and must be avoided at all costs. This can be accomplished by keeping the various masses separate.

Comments

It's best to avoid using plutonium **at all** if it can be avoided.

Figure 9-2. Changing colors

Another use for color is to draw attention to certain types of text. For example, bold-faced text is already fairly obvious, but you could give it a different color to make it stand out even further—let's say, maroon:

```
b, strong {color: maroon;}
```

Then you decide that you want all table cells with a class of highlight to contain light yellow text:

```
td.highlight {color: #FF9;}
```

If you don't set a background color for any of your text, you run the risk that a user's setup won't combine well with your own. For example, if a user has set his browser's background to be a pale yellow, like #FFC, then the previous rule would generate light yellow text on a pale yellow background. Far more likely is that it's still the default background of white, against which light yellow is still going to be hard to read. It's therefore generally a good idea to set foreground and background colors together. (We'll talk about background colors very shortly.)

Affecting Borders

The value of `color` can also affect the borders around an element. Let's assume you've declared these styles, which have the result shown in Figure 9-3. This is the result of the following code:

```
p.aside {color: gray; border-style: solid;}
```

Fire as Urban Renewal

When the financial district <u>burned to the ground</u>, the city fathers looked on it more as an opportunity than a disaster. Here was an opportunity to do things right. Here was their big chance to finally build a city that would be functional, clean, and attractive. Or at least not flooded with sewage every high tide.

> Although the man who started the fire fled town, there's some speculation that he might have been lauded for giving the city an excuse to start over.

A plan was quickly conceived and approved. The fathers got together with the <u>merchants</u> and explained it. "Here's what we'll do," they said, "we'll raise the ground level of the financial district well above the high-tide line. We're going to cart all the dirt we need down from the hills, fill in the entire area, even build a real sewer system. Once we've done that you can rebuild your businesses on dry, solid ground. What do you think?"

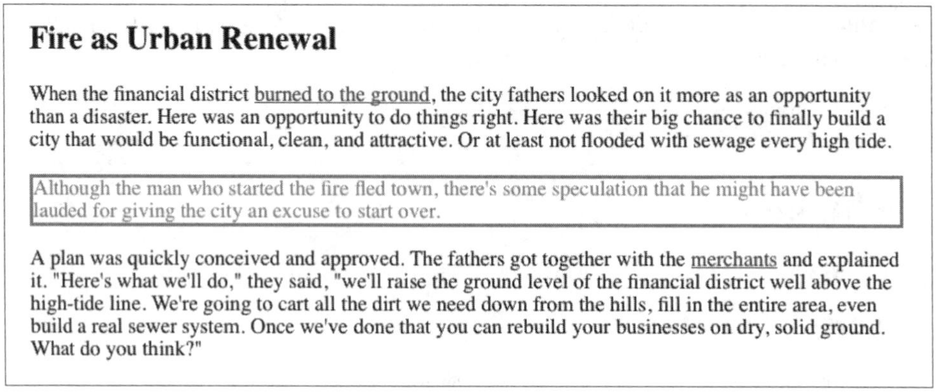

Figure 9-3. Border colors are taken from the content's color

The element `<p class="aside">` has gray text and a gray medium-width solid border. This is because the foreground color is applied to the borders by default. Should you desire, you can override this with the property `border-color`:

```
p.aside {color: gray; border-style: solid; border-color: black;}
```

This rule will make the text gray, while the borders will be black in color. Any value set for `border-color` will always override the value of `color`.

This "borders get the foreground color" behavior is due to the use of a special color keyword, `currentColor`. The value of `currentColor` for any element is the computed value of `color`. So, somewhere inside the user agent's default styles, there's a rule that looks something like this:

```
* {border-color: currentColor;}
```

Thus, if you don't assign a border a color, that built-in rule will pick up the value of `color` from the element and apply it to any visible borders. If you do assign a border a color, then your color will override the built-in `currentColor` style.

Thanks to this, you can also change the foreground color of images. Since images are already composed of colors, you can't really affect their content using `color`, but you can change the color of any border that appears around the image. This can be done using either `color` or `border-color`. Therefore, the following rules will have the same visual effect on images of class `type1` *and* `type2`, as shown in Figure 9-4, which is the result of the following code:

```
img.type1 {border-style: solid; color: gray;}
img.type2 {border-style: solid; border-color: gray;}
```

Figure 9-4. Setting the border color for images

Affecting Form Elements

Setting a value for `color` should (in theory, anyway) apply to form elements. Declaring `select` elements to have dark gray text should be as simple as this:

```
select {color: rgb(33%,33%,33%);}
```

This might also set the color of the borders around the edge of the `select` element, or it might not. It all depends on the user agent and its default styles.

You can also set the foreground color of input elements—although, as you can see in Figure 9-5, doing so would apply that color to all inputs, from text to radio button to checkbox inputs:

```
select {color: rgb(33%,33%,33%);}
input {color: red;}
```

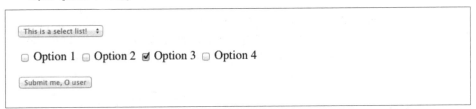

Figure 9-5. Changing form element foregrounds

Note in Figure 9-5 that the text color next to the checkboxes is still black. This is because the rules shown assign styles only to elements like `input` and `select`, not normal paragraph (or other) text.

Also note that the checkmark in the checkbox is black. This is due to the way form elements are handled in some web browsers, which typically use the form widgets built into the base operating system. Thus, when you see a checkbox and checkmark, they really aren't content in the HTML document—they're user interface widgets that have been inserted into the document, much as an image would be. In fact, form inputs are, like images, replaced elements. In theory, CSS does not style the contents of replaced elements.

In practice, the line is a lot blurrier than that, as Figure 9-5 demonstrates. Some form inputs have the color of their text and even portions of their UI changed, while others do not. And since the rules aren't explicitly defined, behavior is inconsistent across browsers. In short, form elements are deeply tricky to style and should be approached with extreme caution.

Inheriting Color

As the definition of color indicates, the property is inherited. This makes sense, since if you declare p {color: gray;}, you probably expect that any text within that paragraph will also be gray, even if it's emphasized or boldfaced or whatever. If you *want* such elements to be different colors, that's easy enough, as illustrated in Figure 9-6, which is the result of the following code:

```
em {color: red;}
p {color: gray;}
```

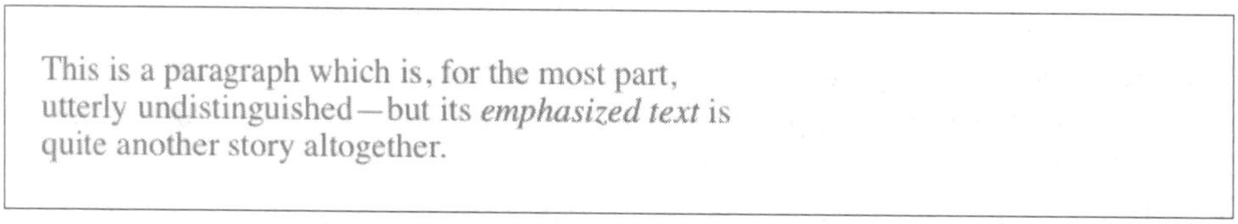

This is a paragraph which is, for the most part, utterly undistinguished—but its *emphasized text* is quite another story altogether.

Figure 9-6. Different colors for different elements

Since color is inherited, it's theoretically possible to set all of the ordinary text in a document to a color, such as red, by declaring body {color: red;}. This should make all text that is not otherwise styled (such as anchors, which have their own color styles) red.

Backgrounds

By default, the background area of an element consists of all of the space behind the foreground out to the outer edge of the borders; thus, the content box and the padding are all part of an element's background, and the borders are drawn on top of the background. (You can change that to a degree with CSS, as we'll see shortly.)

CSS lets you apply a solid color to the background of an element, as well as apply one or more images to the background of a single element, or even describe your own linear and radial gradients.

Background Colors

To declare a color for the background of an element, you use the property background-color, which accepts any valid color value.

<table>
<tr><td colspan="2" align="center">background-color</td></tr>
<tr><td>Values</td><td><color></td></tr>
<tr><td>Initial value</td><td>transparent</td></tr>
<tr><td>Applies to</td><td>All elements</td></tr>
<tr><td>Computed value</td><td>As specified</td></tr>
<tr><td>Inherited</td><td>No</td></tr>
<tr><td>Animatable</td><td>Yes</td></tr>
</table>

If you want the color to extend out a little bit from the text in the element, add some padding to the mix, as illustrated in Figure 9-7, which is the result of the following code:

```
p {background-color: #AEA;}
p.padded {padding: 1em;}

<p>A paragraph.</p>
<p class="padded">A padded paragraph.</p>
```

Figure 9-7. Backgrounds and padding

You can set a background color for just about any element, from body all the way down to inline elements such as em and a. The value of background-color is not inherited. Its default value is the keyword transparent, which makes some sense: if an element doesn't have a defined color, then its background should be transparent so that the background of its ancestor elements will be visible.

One way to picture what that means is to imagine a clear (i.e., transparent) plastic sign mounted to a textured wall. The wall is still visible through the sign, but this is not the background of the sign; it's the background of the wall (in CSS terms, anyway). Similarly, if you set the page canvas to have a background, it can be seen through all of the elements in the document that don't have their own backgrounds. They don't inherit the background; it is visible *through* them. This may seem like an irrelevant distinction, but as you'll see when we discuss background images, it's a critical difference.

Most of the time, you'll have no reason to use the keyword `transparent`, since that's the default value. On occasion, though, it can be useful. Imagine that a user has set his browser to make all links have a white background. When you design your page, you set anchors to have a white foreground, and you don't want a background on those anchors. In order to make sure your design choice prevails, you would declare:

```
a {color: white; background-color: transparent;}
```

If you left out the background color, your white foreground would combine with the user's white background to yield totally unreadable links. This is an unlikely example, but it's still possible.

The potential combination of author and reader styles is the reason why a CSS validator will generate warnings such as, "You have no `background-color` with your `color`." It's trying to remind you that author-user color interaction can occur, and your rule has not taken this possibility into account. Warnings do not mean your styles are invalid: only errors prevent validation.

Special effects

By combining `color` and `background-color`, you can create some interesting effects:

```
h1 {color: white; background-color: rgb(20%,20%,20%);
    font-family: Arial, sans-serif;}
```

This example is shown in Figure 9-8.

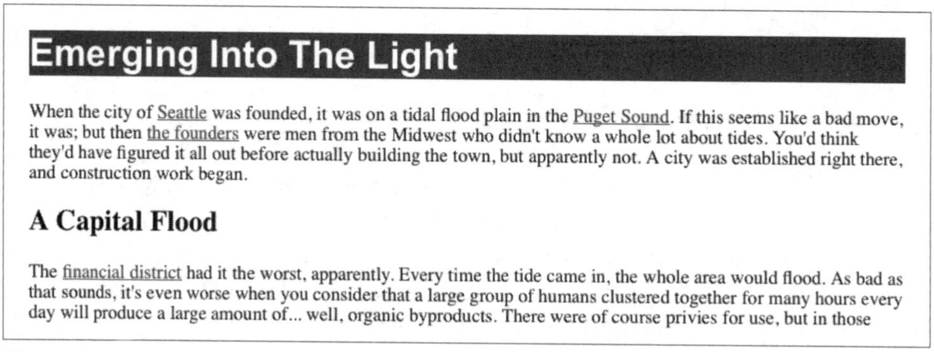

Figure 9-8. A reverse-text effect for H1 elements

There are as many color combinations as there are colors, and I can't show all of them here. Still, I'll try to give you some idea of what you can do.

This stylesheet is a little more complicated, as illustrated by Figure 9-9, which is the result of the following code:

```
body {color: black; background-color: white;}
h1, h2 {color: yellow; background-color: rgb(0,51,0);}
p {color: #555;}
a:link {color: black; background-color: silver;}
a:visited {color: gray; background-color: white;}
```

Emerging Into The Light

When the city of Seattle was founded, it was on a tidal flood plain in the Puget Sound. If this seems like a bad move, it was; but then the founders were men from the Midwest who didn't know a whole lot about tides. You'd think they'd have figured it all out before actually building the town, but apparently not. A city was established right there, and construction work began.

A Capital Flood

The financial district had it the worst, apparently. Every time the tide came in, the whole area would flood. As bad as that sounds, it's even worse when you consider that a large group of humans clustered together for many hours every day will produce a large amount of... well, organic byproducts. There were of course privies for use, but in those days a privy was a shack over a hole in the ground. Thus the privies has this distressing tendency to flood along with everything else, and that meant their contents would go floating away.

All this led many citizens to establish their residences on the hills overlooking the sound and then commute to work. Apparently Seattle's always been the same in certain ways. The problem with this arrangement back then was that the residences *also* generated organic byproducts, and those were

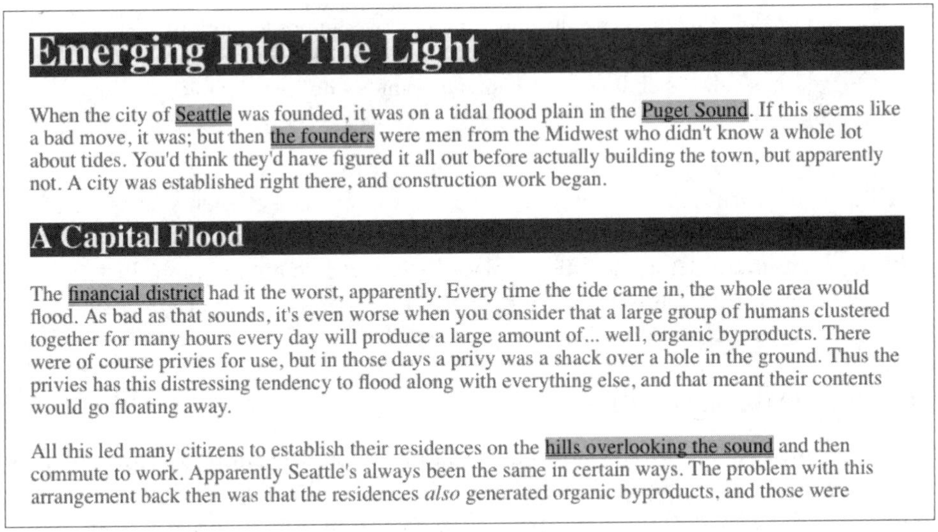

Figure 9-9. The results of a more complicated stylesheet

And then there's the fascinating question of what happens when you apply a background to a replaced element, such as an image. I'm not even talking about images with transparent portions, like a GIF87a or a PNG. Suppose you want to create a two-tone border around a JPEG. You can pull that off by adding a background color and a little bit of padding to your image, as illustrated in Figure 9-10, which is the result of the following code:

```
img.twotone {background-color: red; padding: 5px; border: 5px solid gold;}
```

Figure 9-10. Using background and border to two-tone an image

Technically, the background goes to the outer border edge, but since the border is solid and continuous, we can't see the background behind it. The one pixel of padding allows a thin ring of background to be seen between the image and its border, creating the visual effect of an "inner border." This technique could be extended to create more complicated effects with background images like gradients, which we'll discuss later in the chapter.

 Note that there are also much more powerful border options available in CSS, so background-and-padding tricks may or may not be useful, depending on what you want to do. See Chapter 8 for details.

Remember that form inputs, nearly all of which are replaced elements, are treated as special, and often applying padding to them will not have the same results as applying padding to an image, let alone a nonreplaced element like a paragraph. Just as with most styling of form inputs, adding a background color should be rigorously tested and avoided if possible.

Clipping the Background

In the previous section, we saw how backgrounds fill out the entire background area of an element. Historically, that extended all the way to the outer edge of the border so that any border with transparent parts (like dashed or dotted borders) would have the background color fill into those transparent parts. Now there's a CSS property called background-clip that lets you affect how far out an element's background will go.

background-clip

Values	[border-box	padding-box	content-box	text]#
Initial value	border-box
Applies to	All elements
Computed value	As declared
Inherited	No
Animatable	No

The default value is the historical value: the *background painting area* (which is what background-clip defines) extends out to the outer edge of the border. The background will *always* be drawn behind the visible parts of the border, if any.

If you choose the value `padding-box`, then the background will only extend to the outer edge of the padding area (which is also the inner edge of the border). Thus, it won't be drawn behind the border. The value `content-box`, on the other hand, restricts the background to just the content area of the element.

The effects of these three values is illustrated in Figure 9-11, which is the result of the following code:

```
div[id] {color: navy; background: silver;
         padding: 1em; border: 5px dashed;}
#ex01 {background-clip: border-box;}  /* default value */
#ex02 {background-clip: padding-box;}
#ex03 {background-clip: content-box;}
```

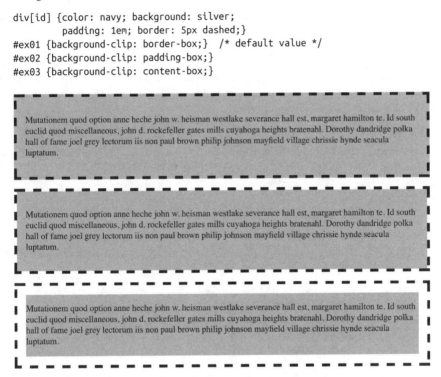

Figure 9-11. The three box-oriented types of background clipping

That might seem pretty simple, but there are some caveats. The first is that `background-clip` has no effect on the root element (in HTML, that's either the `html` or `body` element, depending on how your styles are written). This has to do with how the background painting of the root element has to be handled.

The second is that the exact clipping of the background area can be reduced if the element has rounded corners, thanks to the property `border-radius`. This is basically common sense, since if you give your element significantly rounded corners, you want the background to be clipped by those corners instead of stick out past them. The way to think of this is that the background painting area is determined by `background-clip`, and then any corners that have to be further clipped by rounded corners are appropriately clipped.

The third caveat is that the value of `background-clip` can interact poorly with some of the more interesting values of `background-repeat`, which we'll get to later on.

The fourth is that `background-clip` defines the clipping area of the background. It doesn't affect other background properties. When it comes to flat background colors, that's a distinction without meaning; but when it comes to background images, which we'll talk about in the next section, it can make a great deal of difference.

The last value, `text`, clips the background to the text of the element. In other words, the text is "filled in" with the background, and the rest of the element's background area remains transparent. This is a simple way to add textures to text, by "filling in" the text of an element with its background.

The kicker is that in order to see this effect, you have to remove the foreground color of the element. Otherwise, the foreground color obscures the background. Consider the following, which has the result shown in Figure 9-12:

```
div {color: rgb(255,0,0); background: rgb(0,0,255);
     padding: 0 1em; margin: 1.5em 1em; border: 5px dashed;
     font-weight: bold;}
#ex01 {background-clip: text; color: transparent;}
#ex02 {background-clip: text; color: rgba(255,0,0,0.5);}
#ex03 {background-clip: text;}
```

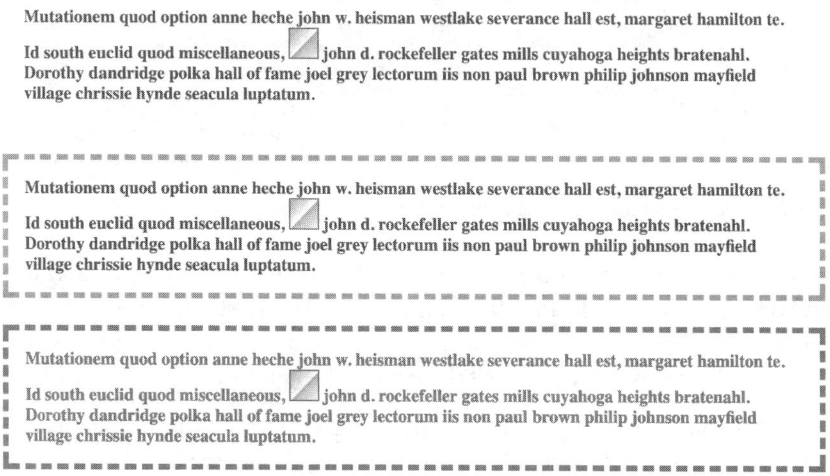

Figure 9-12. Clipping the background to the text

For the first example, the foreground color is made completely transparent, and the blue background is only visible where it intersects with the text shapes in the element's content. It is not visible through the image inside the paragraph, since an image's foreground can't be set to transparent.

In the second example shown in Figure 9-12, the foreground color has been set to rgba(255,0,0,0.5), which is a half-opaque red. The text there is rendered purple, because the half-opaque red combines with the blue underneath. The borders, on the other hand, blend their half-opaque red with the white background behind them, yielding a light red.

In the third example, the foreground color is a solid, opaque red. The text and borders are both fully red, with no hint of the blue background. It can't be seen in this instance, because it's been clipped to the text. The foreground just completely obscures the background.

This technique works for any background, including gradient and image backgrounds, topics which we'll cover in a bit. Remember, however: if the background for some reason fails to be drawn behind the text, the transparent text meant to be "filled" with the background will instead be completely unreadable.

 As of late 2017, only Firefox supported background-clip: text in that exact form. However, pretty much every browser, *including* Firefox, supported the variant -webkit-background-clip: text.

Background Images

Having covered the basics of foreground and background colors, we turn now to the subject of background images. Back in the days of HTML 3.2, it was possible to associate an image with the background of the document by using the BODY attribute BACKGROUND:

```
<BODY BACKGROUND="bg23.gif">
```

This caused a user agent to load the file *bg23.gif* and then "tile" it in the document background, repeating it in both the horizontal and vertical directions to fill up the entire background of the document. This effect can be easily recreated in CSS, but CSS can do a great deal more than simple tiling of background images. We'll start with the basics and then work our way up.

Using an image

In order to get an image into the background in the first place, use the property background-image.

---

background-image

Values	[*<image>*#	none
Initial value	none
Applies to	All elements
Computed value	As specified, but with all URLs made absolute
Inherited	No
Animatable	No

<image> = [*<uri>* | *<linear-gradient>* | *<repeating-linear-gradient>* | *<radial-gradient>* | *<repeating-radial-gradient>*]

The default value of none means about what you'd expect: no image is placed in the background. If you want a background image, you must give this property at least one other value, like this:

```
body {background-image: url(bg23.gif);}
```

Due to the default values of other background properties, this will cause the image *bg23.gif* to be tiled in the document's background, as shown in Figure 9-13. As you'll discover shortly, this isn't the only option.

It's usually a good idea to specify a background color to go along with your background image; we'll come back to that concept a little later on. (We'll also talk about how to have more than one image at the same time, but for now we're going to stick to just one background image per element.)

You can apply a background image to any element, block-level or inline:

```
p.starry {background-image: url(http://www.site.web/pix/stars.gif);
        color: white;}
a.grid {background-image: url(smallgrid.gif);}

<p class="starry">It's the end of autumn, which means the stars will be
brighter than ever!  <a href="join.html" class="grid">Join us</a> for
a fabulous evening of planets, stars, nebulae, and more...
```

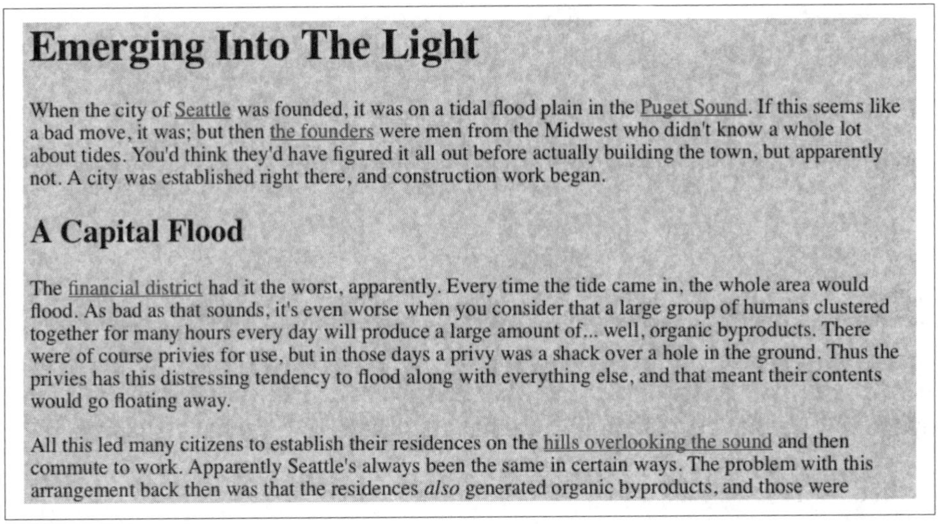

Emerging Into The Light

When the city of Seattle was founded, it was on a tidal flood plain in the Puget Sound. If this seems like a bad move, it was; but then the founders were men from the Midwest who didn't know a whole lot about tides. You'd think they'd have figured it all out before actually building the town, but apparently not. A city was established right there, and construction work began.

A Capital Flood

The financial district had it the worst, apparently. Every time the tide came in, the whole area would flood. As bad as that sounds, it's even worse when you consider that a large group of humans clustered together for many hours every day will produce a large amount of... well, organic byproducts. There were of course privies for use, but in those days a privy was a shack over a hole in the ground. Thus the privies has this distressing tendency to flood along with everything else, and that meant their contents would go floating away.

All this led many citizens to establish their residences on the hills overlooking the sound and then commute to work. Apparently Seattle's always been the same in certain ways. The problem with this arrangement back then was that the residences *also* generated organic byproducts, and those were

Figure 9-13. Applying a background image in CSS

As you can see in Figure 9-14, we've applied a background to a single paragraph and no other part of the document. We can customize even further, such as placing background images on inline elements like hyperlinks, also depicted in Figure 9-14. If you want to be able to see the tiling pattern, the image will probably need to be pretty small. After all, individual letters aren't that large!

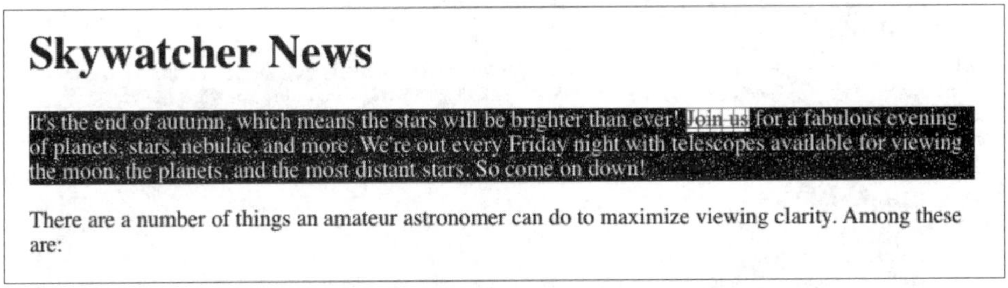

Skywatcher News

It's the end of autumn, which means the stars will be brighter than ever! Join us for a fabulous evening of planets, stars, nebulae, and more. We're out every Friday night with telescopes available for viewing the moon, the planets, and the most distant stars. So come on down!

There are a number of things an amateur astronomer can do to maximize viewing clarity. Among these are:

Figure 9-14. Applying background images to block and inline elements

There are a number of ways to employ specific background images. You can place an image in the background of strong elements in order to make them stand out more. You can fill in the background of headings with a wavy pattern or with little dots.

If you combine simple icons with creative attribute selectors, you can (with use of some properties we'll get to in just a bit) mark when a link points to a PDF, Word document, email address, or other unusual resource, as shown in Figure 9-15, which is the result of the following code:

```
a[href] {padding-left: 1em; background-repeat: no-repeat;}
a[href$=".pdf"] {background-image: url(/i/pdf-icon.png);}
```

```
a[href$=".doc"] {background-image: url(/i/msword-icon.png);}
a[href^="mailto:"] {background-image: url(/i/email-icon.png);}
```

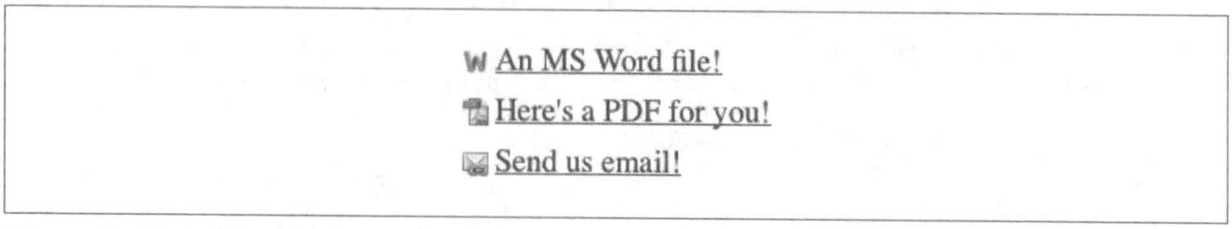

Figure 9-15. Adding link icons as background images

Just like `background-color`, `background-image` is not inherited—in fact, not a single one of the background properties is inherited. Remember also that when specifying the URL of a background image, it falls under the usual restrictions and caveats for `url()` values: a relative URL should be interpreted with respect to the stylesheet.

Why backgrounds aren't inherited

Earlier, I specifically noted that backgrounds are not inherited. Background images demonstrate why inherited backgrounds would be a bad thing. Imagine a situation where backgrounds were inherited, and you applied a background image to the body. That image would be used for the background of every element in the document, with each element doing its own tiling, as shown in Figure 9-16.

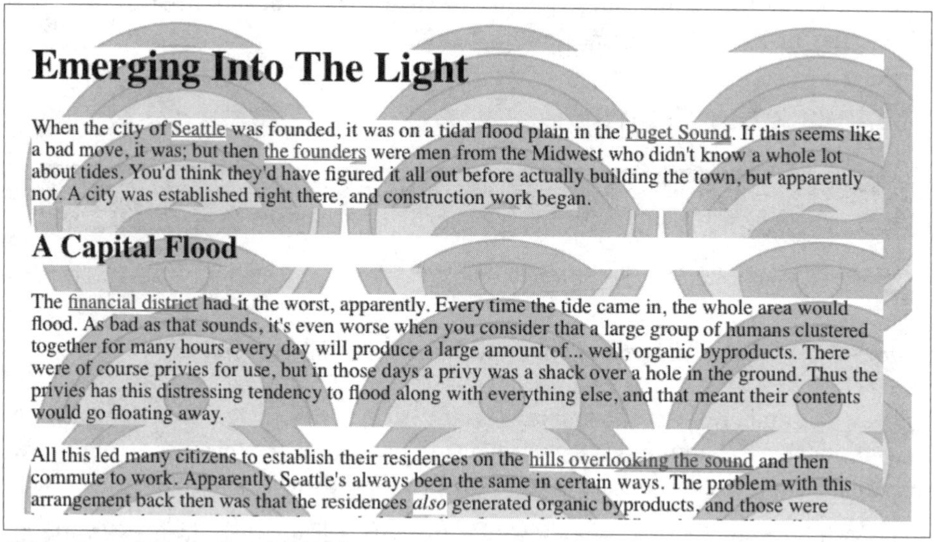

Figure 9-16. What inherited backgrounds would do to layout

Note how the pattern restarts at the top left of every element, including the links. This isn't what most authors would want, and this is why background properties are not inherited. If you do want this particular effect for some reason, you can make it happen with a rule like this:

```
* {background-image: url(yinyang.png);}
```

Alternatively, you could use the value `inherit` like this:

```
body {background-image: url(yinyang.png);}
* {background-image: inherit;}
```

Good background practices

Images are laid on top of whatever background color you specify. If you're completely tiling a JPEG or other opaque image type, this fact doesn't really make a difference, since a fully tiled image will fill up the document background, leaving nowhere for the color to "peek through," so to speak. However, image formats with an alpha channel, such as PNG or SVG, can be partially or wholly transparent, which will cause the image to be "combined" with the background color. In addition, if the image fails to load for some reason, then the user agent will use the background color specified in place of the image. Consider how the "starry paragraph" example would look if the background image failed to load, as in Figure 9-17.

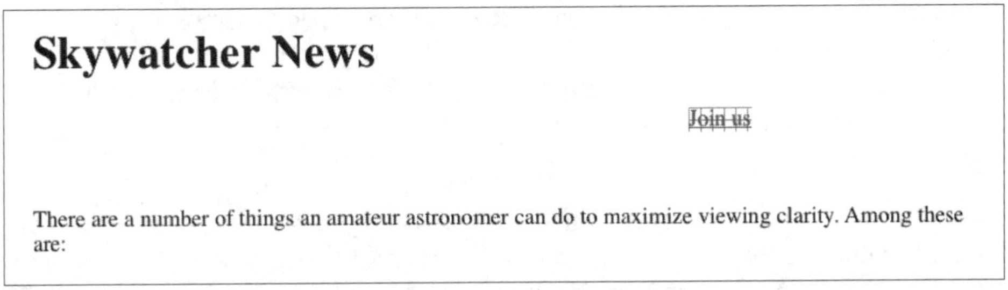

Skywatcher News

Join us

There are a number of things an amateur astronomer can do to maximize viewing clarity. Among these are:

Figure 9-17. The consequences of a missing background image

Figure 9-17 demonstrates why it's always a good idea to specify a background color when using a background image, so that you'll at least get a legible result:

```
p.starry {background-image: url(http://www.site.web/pix/stars.gif);
        background-color: black; color: white;}
a.grid {background-image: url(smallgrid.gif);}

<p class="starry">It's the end of autumn, which means the stars will be
brighter than ever!  <a href="join.html" class="grid">Join us</a> for
a fabulous evening of planets, stars, nebulae, and more...
```

This will fill in a flat-black background if the "starry" image can't be rendered for some reason. It will also fill in any transparent areas of the background images, or any area of the background that the images don't cover for some reason. (And there are several reasons they might not, as we'll soon see.)

Background Positioning

OK, so we can put images in the background of an element. How about being able to decide exactly how the image is placed? No problem! `background-position` is here to help.

---

background-position

Values	*<position>*#
Initial value	0% 0%
Applies to	Block-level and replaced elements
Percentages	Refer to the corresponding point on both the element and the origin image (see explanation in "Percentage values" on page 406)
Computed value	The absolute length offsets, if *<length>* is specified; otherwise, percentage values
Inherited	No
Animatable	Yes

<position> = [[left | center | right | top | bottom | *<percentage>* | *<length>*] | [left | center | right | *<percentage>* | *<length>*] [top | center | bottom | *<percentage>* | *<length>*] | [center | [left | right] [*<percentage>* | *<length>*]?] && [center | [top | bottom] [*<percentage>* | *<length>*]?]]

That value syntax looks pretty horrific, but it isn't; it's just what happens when you try to formalize the fast-and-loose implementations of a new technology into a regular syntax and then layer even more features on top of that while trying to reuse parts of the old syntax. (So, OK, kind of horrific.) In practice, `background-position` is pretty simple.

 Throughout this section, we'll be using the rule `background-repeat: no-repeat` to prevent tiling of the background image. You're not crazy: we haven't talked about `background-repeat` yet! We will soon enough, but for now, just accept that the rule restricts the background to a single image, and don't worry about it until we move on to discussing `background-repeat`.

For example, we can center a background image in the body element, with the result depicted in Figure 9-18, which is the result of the following code:

```
body {background-image: url(yinyang.png);
    background-repeat: no-repeat;
    background-position: center;}
```

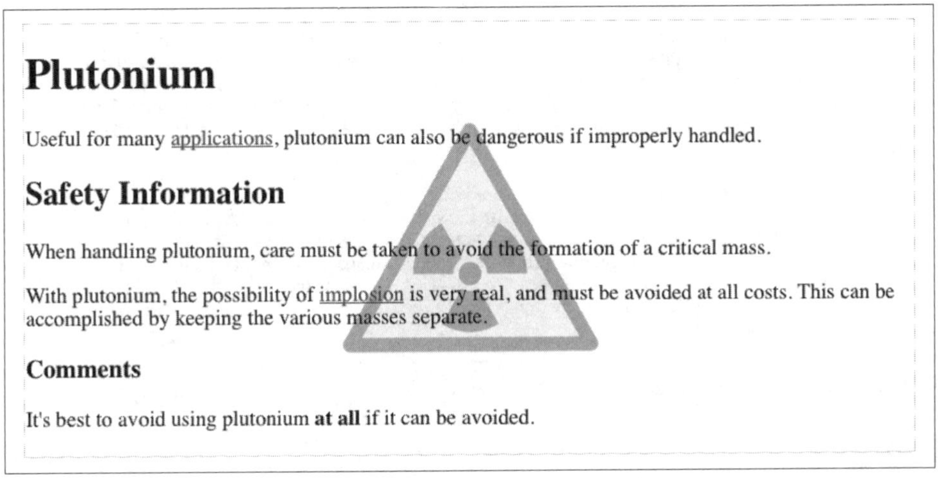

Plutonium

Useful for many applications, plutonium can also be dangerous if improperly handled.

Safety Information

When handling plutonium, care must be taken to avoid the formation of a critical mass.

With plutonium, the possibility of implosion is very real, and must be avoided at all costs. This can be accomplished by keeping the various masses separate.

Comments

It's best to avoid using plutonium **at all** if it can be avoided.

Figure 9-18. Centering a single background image

We actually placed a single image in the background and then prevented it from being repeated with `background-repeat` (which is discussed in an upcoming section). Every background that includes an image starts with a single image. This starting image is called the *origin image*.

The placement of the origin image is accomplished with `background-position`, and there are several ways to supply values for this property. First off, there are the keywords `top`, `bottom`, `left`, `right`, and `center`. Usually, these appear in pairs, but (as the previous example shows) this is not always true. Then there are length values, such as `50px` or `2cm`; and finally, percentage values, such as `43%`. Each type of value has a slightly different effect on the placement of the background image.

Keywords

The image placement keywords are easiest to understand. They have the effects you'd expect from their names; for example, `top right` would cause the origin image to be placed in the top-right corner of the element's background. Let's go back to the small yin-yang symbol:

```
p {background-image: url(yinyang-sm.png);
    background-repeat: no-repeat;
    background-position: top right;}
```

This will place a nonrepeated origin image in the top-right corner of each paragraph's background. Incidentally, the result, shown in Figure 9-19, would be exactly the same if the position were declared as `right top`.

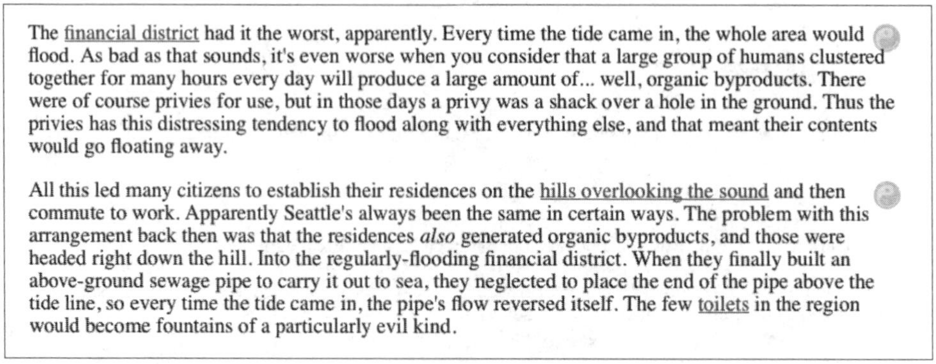

The financial district had it the worst, apparently. Every time the tide came in, the whole area would flood. As bad as that sounds, it's even worse when you consider that a large group of humans clustered together for many hours every day will produce a large amount of... well, organic byproducts. There were of course privies for use, but in those days a privy was a shack over a hole in the ground. Thus the privies has this distressing tendency to flood along with everything else, and that meant their contents would go floating away.

All this led many citizens to establish their residences on the hills overlooking the sound and then commute to work. Apparently Seattle's always been the same in certain ways. The problem with this arrangement back then was that the residences *also* generated organic byproducts, and those were headed right down the hill. Into the regularly-flooding financial district. When they finally built an above-ground sewage pipe to carry it out to sea, they neglected to place the end of the pipe above the tide line, so every time the tide came in, the pipe's flow reversed itself. The few toilets in the region would become fountains of a particularly evil kind.

Figure 9-19. Placing the background image in the top-right corner of paragraphs

Position keywords can appear in any order, as long as there are no more than two of them—one for the horizontal and one for the vertical. If you use two horizontal (right right) or two vertical (top top) keywords, the whole value is ignored.

If only one keyword appears, then the other is assumed to be center. So if you want an image to appear in the top center of every paragraph, you need only declare:

```
p {background-image: url(yinyang-sm.png);
    background-repeat: no-repeat;
    background-position: top;}
```

Percentage values

Percentage values are closely related to the keywords, although they behave in a more sophisticated way. Let's say that you want to center an origin image within its element by using percentage values. That's easy enough:

```
p {background-image: url(chrome.jpg);
    background-repeat: no-repeat;
    background-position: 50% 50%;}
```

This causes the origin image to be placed such that its center is aligned with the center of its element's background. In other words, the percentage values apply to both the element and the origin image.

In order to understand what that means, let's examine the process in closer detail. When you center an origin image in an element's background, the point in the image that can be described as 50% 50% (the center) is lined up with the point in the background that can be described the same way. If the image is placed at 0% 0%, its top-left corner is placed in the top-left corner of the element's background. 100% 100% causes the bottom-right corner of the origin image to go into the bottom-right corner of the background. Figure 9-20 contains examples of those values, as well as a few others.

Thus, if you want to place a single origin image a third of the way across the background and two-thirds of the way down, your declaration would be:

```
p {background-image: url(yinyang-sm.png);
   background-repeat: no-repeat;
   background-position: 33% 66%;}
```

With these rules, the point in the origin image that is one-third across and two-thirds down from the top-left corner of the image will be aligned with the point that is farthest from the top-left corner of the background. Note that the horizontal value *always* comes first with percentage values. If you were to switch the percentages in the preceding example, the image would be placed two-thirds of the way across the background and one-third of the way down.

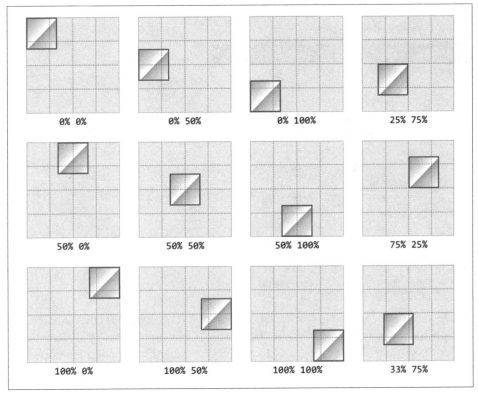

Figure 9-20. Various percentage positions

If you supply only one percentage value, the single value supplied is taken to be the horizontal value, and the vertical is assumed to be 50%. For example:

```
p {background-image: url(yinyang-sm.png);
   background-repeat: no-repeat;
   background-position: 25%;}
```

The origin image is placed one-quarter of the way across the paragraph's background and halfway down it, as depicted in Figure 9-21.

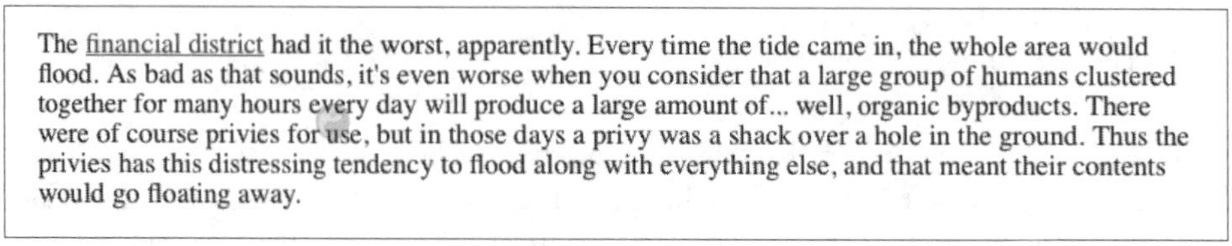

The financial district had it the worst, apparently. Every time the tide came in, the whole area would flood. As bad as that sounds, it's even worse when you consider that a large group of humans clustered together for many hours every day will produce a large amount of... well, organic byproducts. There were of course privies for use, but in those days a privy was a shack over a hole in the ground. Thus the privies has this distressing tendency to flood along with everything else, and that meant their contents would go floating away.

Figure 9-21. Declaring only one percentage value means the vertical position evaluates to 50%

Table 9-1 gives a breakdown of keyword and percentage equivalencies.

Table 9-1. Positional equivalents

Keyword(s)	Equivalent keywords	Equivalent percentages
center	center center	50% 50% 50%
right	center right right center	100% 50% 100%
left	center left left center	0% 50% 0%
top	top center center top	50% 0%
bottom	bottom center center bottom	50% 100%
top left	left top	0% 0%
top right	right top	100% 0%
bottom right	right bottom	100% 100%
bottom left	left bottom	0% 100%

In case you were wondering, the default values for background-position are 0% 0%, which is functionally the same as top left. This is why, unless you set different values for the position, background images always start tiling from the top-left corner of the element's background.

Length values

Finally, we turn to length values for positioning. When you supply lengths for the position of the origin image, they are interpreted as offsets from the top-left corner of the element's background. The offset point is the top-left corner of the origin image; thus, if you set the values 20px 30px, the top-left corner of the origin image will be 20 pixels to the right of, and 30 pixels below, the top-left corner of the element's background, as shown (along with a few other length examples) in Figure 9-22, which is the result of the following code:

```
background-image: url(chrome.jpg);
background-repeat: no-repeat;
background-position: 20px 30px;
```

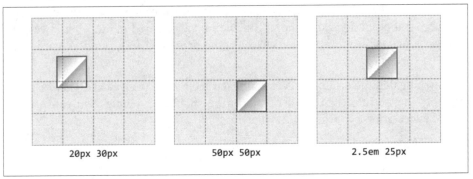

Figure 9-22. Offsetting the background image using length measures

This is quite different than percentage values because the offset is from one top-left corner to another. In other words, the top-left corner of the origin image lines up with the point specified in the background-position declaration.

You can combine length and percentage values to get a "best of both worlds" effect. Let's say you need to have a background image that is all the way to the right side of the background and 10 pixels down from the top, as illustrated in Figure 9-23. As always, the horizontal value comes first:

```
p {background-image: url(yinyang.png);
    background-repeat: no-repeat;
    background-position: 100% 10px;
    border: 1px dotted gray;}
```

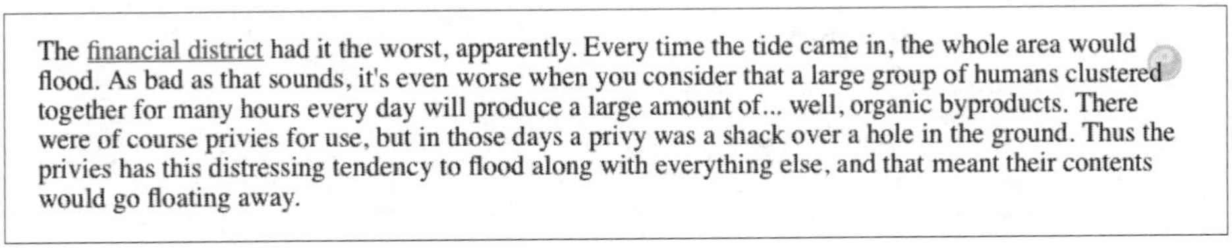

The financial district had it the worst, apparently. Every time the tide came in, the whole area would flood. As bad as that sounds, it's even worse when you consider that a large group of humans clustered together for many hours every day will produce a large amount of... well, organic byproducts. There were of course privies for use, but in those days a privy was a shack over a hole in the ground. Thus the privies has this distressing tendency to flood along with everything else, and that meant their contents would go floating away.

Figure 9-23. Mixing percentages and length values

For that matter, you can get the same result as shown in Figure 9-23 by using right 10px, since you're allowed to mix keywords with lengths and percentages. Bear in mind that the syntax enforces axis order when using nonkeyword values; in other words, if you use a length of percentage, then the horizontal value must *always* come first, and the vertical must *always* come second. That means right 10px is fine, whereas `10px right` is invalid and will be ignored (because `right` is not a valid vertical keyword).

Negative values

If you're using lengths or percentages, you can use negative values to pull the origin image outside of the element's background. Consider the example with the very large yin-yang symbol for a background. At one point, we centered it, but what if we only want part of it visible in the top-left corner of the element's background? No problem, at least in theory.

First, assume that the origin image is 300 pixels tall by 300 pixels wide. Then, assume that only the bottom-right third of the image should be visible. You can get the desired effect (shown in Figure 9-24) like this:

```
body {background-image: url(yinyang.png);
    background-repeat: no-repeat;
    background-position: -200px -200px;}
```

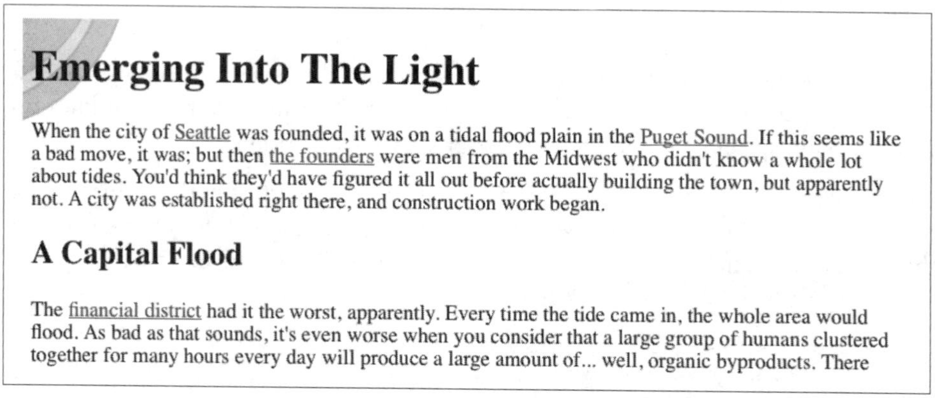

Emerging Into The Light

When the city of Seattle was founded, it was on a tidal flood plain in the Puget Sound. If this seems like a bad move, it was; but then the founders were men from the Midwest who didn't know a whole lot about tides. You'd think they'd have figured it all out before actually building the town, but apparently not. A city was established right there, and construction work began.

A Capital Flood

The financial district had it the worst, apparently. Every time the tide came in, the whole area would flood. As bad as that sounds, it's even worse when you consider that a large group of humans clustered together for many hours every day will produce a large amount of... well, organic byproducts. There

Figure 9-24. Using negative length values to position the origin image

Or, say you want just the right half of it to be visible and vertically centered within the element's background area:

```
body {background-image: url(yinyang.png);
    background-repeat: no-repeat;
    background-position: -150px 50%;}
```

Negative percentages are also possible, although they are somewhat interesting to calculate. The origin image and the element are likely to be very different sizes, for one thing, and that can lead to unexpected effects. Consider, for example, the situation created by the following rule and illustrated in Figure 9-25:

```
p {background-image: url(pix/yinyang.png);
    background-repeat: no-repeat;
```

```
background-position: -10% -10%;
width: 500px;}
```

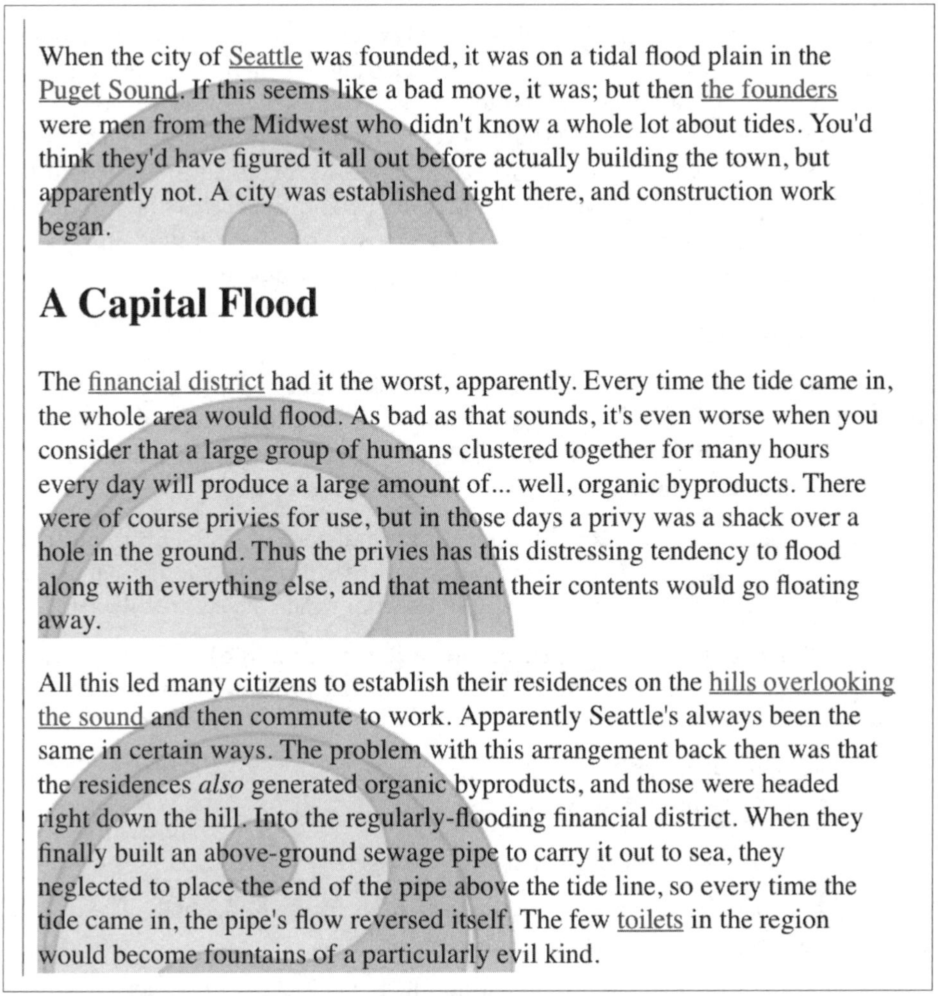

When the city of <u>Seattle</u> was founded, it was on a tidal flood plain in the <u>Puget Sound</u>. If this seems like a bad move, it was; but then <u>the founders</u> were men from the Midwest who didn't know a whole lot about tides. You'd think they'd have figured it all out before actually building the town, but apparently not. A city was established right there, and construction work began.

A Capital Flood

The <u>financial district</u> had it the worst, apparently. Every time the tide came in, the whole area would flood. As bad as that sounds, it's even worse when you consider that a large group of humans clustered together for many hours every day will produce a large amount of... well, organic byproducts. There were of course privies for use, but in those days a privy was a shack over a hole in the ground. Thus the privies has this distressing tendency to flood along with everything else, and that meant their contents would go floating away.

All this led many citizens to establish their residences on the <u>hills overlooking the sound</u> and then commute to work. Apparently Seattle's always been the same in certain ways. The problem with this arrangement back then was that the residences *also* generated organic byproducts, and those were headed right down the hill. Into the regularly-flooding financial district. When they finally built an above-ground sewage pipe to carry it out to sea, they neglected to place the end of the pipe above the tide line, so every time the tide came in, the pipe's flow reversed itself. The few <u>toilets</u> in the region would become fountains of a particularly evil kind.

Figure 9-25. Varying effects of negative percentage values

The rule calls for the point outside the origin image defined by -10% -10% to be aligned with a similar point for each paragraph. The image is 300 × 300 pixels, so we know its alignment point can be described as 30 pixels above the top of the image, and 30 pixels to the left of its left edge (effectively -30px and -30px). The paragraph elements are all the same width (500px), so the horizontal alignment point is 50 pixels to the left of the left edge of their backgrounds. This means that each origin image's left edge will be 20 pixels to the left of the left padding edge of the paragraphs. This is because the -30px alignment point of the images lines up with the -50px point for the paragraphs. The difference between the two is 20 pixels.

The paragraphs are of differing heights, however, so the vertical alignment point changes for each paragraph. If a paragraph's background area is 300 pixels high, to pick a semi-random example, then the top of the origin image will line up exactly with the top of the element's background, because both will have vertical alignment points of -30px. If a paragraph is 50 pixels tall, then its alignment point would be -5px and the top of the origin image will actually be 25 pixels *below* the top of the background. This is why you can see all the tops of the background images in Figure 9-25—the paragraphs are all shorter than the background image.

Changing the offset edges

OK, it's time for a confession: throughout this whole discussion of background positioning, I've been keeping two things from you. I acted as though the value of `background-position` could have no more than two keywords, and that all offsets were always made from the top-left corner of the background area.

That was certainly the case throughout most of the history of CSS, but it's not true any more. In fact, you can have up to four keywords in a very specific pattern to deliver a very specific feature: changing the edges from which offsets are calculated.

Let's start with a simple example: placing the origin image a third of the way across and 30 pixels down from the top-left corner. Using what we saw in previous sections, that would be:

```
background-position: 33% 30px;
```

Now let's do the same thing with this four-part syntax:

```
background-position: left 33% top 30px;
```

What this four-part value says is "from the `left` edge, have a horizontal offset of 33%; from the `top` edge, have an offset of 30px."

Great, so that's a more verbose way of getting the default behavior. Now let's change things so the origin image is placed a third of the way across and 30 pixels up from the bottom-right corner, as shown in Figure 9-26 (which assumes no repeating of the background image, for clarity's sake):

```
background-position: right 33% bottom 30px;
```

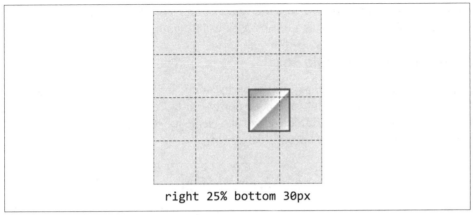

right 25% bottom 30px

Figure 9-26. Changing the offset edges for the origin image

Here, we have a value that means "from the right edge, have a horizontal offset of 33%; from the bottom edge, have an offset of 30px."

Thus, the general pattern is edge keyword, offset distance, edge keyword, offset distance. You can mix the order of horizontal and vertical information; that is, bottom 30px right 25% works just as well as right 25% bottom 30px. However, you cannot omit either of the edge keywords; 30px right 25% is invalid and will be ignored.

You can omit an offset distance in cases where you want it to be zero. So right bottom 30px would put the origin image against the right edge and 30 pixels up from the bottom of the background area, whereas right 25% bottom would place the origin image a quarter of the way across from the right edge and up against the bottom. These are both illustrated in Figure 9-27.

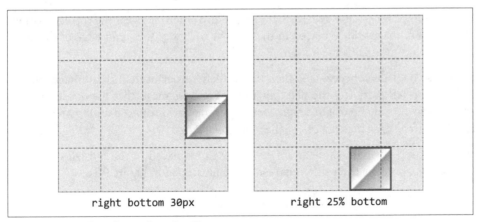

right bottom 30px   right 25% bottom

Figure 9-27. Inferred zero-length offsets

As it happens, you can only define the edges of an element as offset bases, not the center. A value like center 25% center 25px will be ignored.

Changing the Positioning Box

OK, so now we can add an image to the background, and we can even change where the origin image is placed. But what if we don't want to have its placement calculated with respect to the outer padding edge of the element, which is the default? We can affect that using the property background-origin.

background-origin

Values	[border-box │ padding-box │ content-box]#
Initial value	padding-box
Applies to	All elements
Computed value	As declared
Inherited	No
Animatable	No

This property probably looks very similar to background-clip, and with good reason, but its effect is pretty distinct. With background-origin, you can determine the edge that's used to determine placement of the origin image. This is also known as defining the *background positioning area*. (background-clip, you may recall, defined the *background painting area*.)

The default, padding-box, means that (absent any other changes) the top-left corner of the origin image will be placed in the top-left corner of the outer edge of the padding, which is just inside the border.

If you use the value border-box, then the top-left corner of the origin image will go into the top-left corner of the padding area. That does mean that the border, if any, will be drawn over the origin image (assuming the background painting area wasn't restricted to be padding-box or content-box, that is).

With content-box, you shift the origin image to be placed in the top-left corner of the content area. The three different results are illustrated in Figure 9-28:

```
div[id] {color: navy; background: silver;
         background-image: url(yinyang.png);
         background-repeat: no-repeat;
         padding: 1em; border: 5px dashed;}
#ex01 {background-origin: border-box;}
#ex02 {background-origin: padding-box;}   /* default value */
#ex03 {background-origin: content-box;}
```

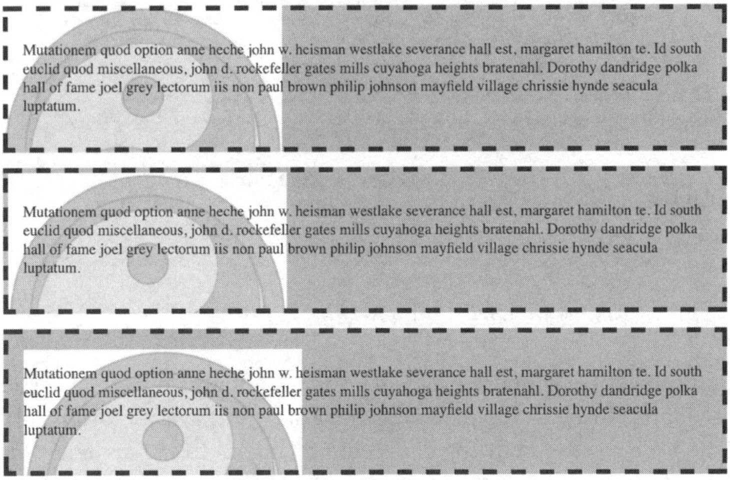

Figure 9-28. The three types of background origins

Remember that this "placed in the top left" behavior is the default behavior, one you can change with background-position. If the origin image is placed somewhere other than the top-left corner, its position will be calculated with respect to the box defined by background-origin: the border edge, the padding edge, or the content edge. Consider, for example, this variant on our previous example, which is illustrated in Figure 9-29:

```
div[id] {color: navy; background: silver;
         background-image: url(yinyang);
         background-repeat: no-repeat;
         background-position: bottom right;
         padding: 1em; border: 5px dotted;}
#ex01 {background-origin: border-box;}
#ex02 {background-origin: padding-box;}   /* default value */
#ex03 {background-origin: content-box;}
```

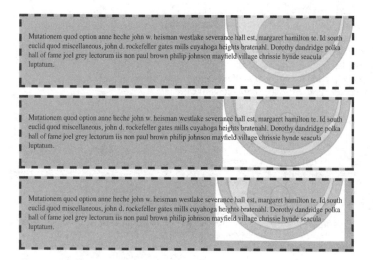

Figure 9-29. The three types of background origins, redux

Where things can get *really* interesting is if you've explicitly defined your background origin and clipping to be different boxes. Imagine you have the origin placed with respect to the padding edge but the background clipped to the content area, or vice versa. This would have the results shown in Figure 9-30, as resulting from the following:

```
#ex01 {background-origin: padding-box;
       background-clip: content-box;}
#ex02 {background-origin: content-box;
       background-clip: padding-box;}
```

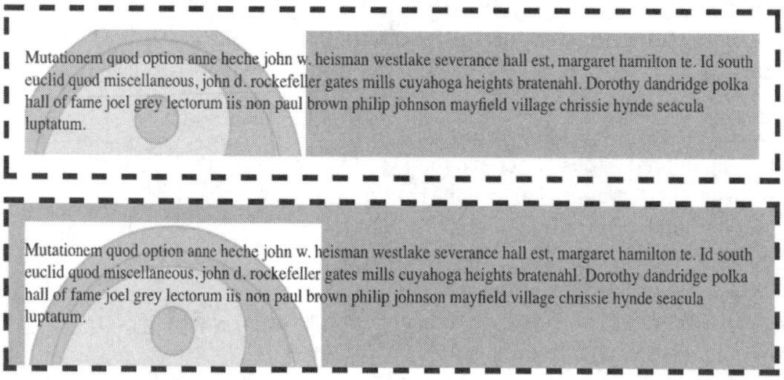

Figure 9-30. When origin and clipping diverge

In the first example shown in Figure 9-29, the edges of the origin image are clipped because it's been positioned with respect to the padding box, but the background painting area has been clipped at the edge of the content box. In the second example, the origin image is placed with respect to the content box, but the painting area extends into the padding box. Thus, the origin image is visible all the way down to the bottom padding edge, even though its top is not placed against the top padding edge.

Background Repeating (or Lack Thereof)

In the old days, if you wanted some kind of "sidebar" background effect, you had to create a very short, but incredibly wide, image to place in the background. At one time, a favorite size for these images was 10 pixels tall by 1,500 pixels wide. Most of that image would be blank space; only the left 100 or so pixels contain the "sidebar" image. The rest of the image was basically wasted.

Wouldn't it be much more efficient to create a sidebar image that's 10 pixels tall and 100 pixels wide, with no wasted blank space, and then repeat it only in the vertical direction? This would certainly make your design job a little easier, and your users' download times a lot faster. Enter background-repeat.

background-repeat	
Values	*<repeat-style>*#
Expansion	*<repeat-style>* = repeat-x | repeat-y | [repeat | space | round | no-repeat]{1,2}
Initial value	repeat
Applies to	All elements
Computed value	As specified
Inherited	No
Animatable	No

The value syntax for background-repeat looks a bit complicated at first glance, but it's really fairly straightforward. In fact, at its base, it's just four values: repeat, no-repeat, space, and round. The other two, repeat-x and repeat-y, are considered to be shorthand for combinations of the others. Table 9-2 shows how they break down.

If two values are given, the first applies in the horizontal direction, and the second in the vertical. If there is just one value, it applies in both the horizontal and vertical directions, with the exception, as shown in Table 9-2, of repeat-x and repeat-y.

Table 9-2. Repeat keyword equivalents

Single keyword	Equivalent keywords
repeat-x	repeat no-repeat
repeat-y	no-repeat repeat
repeat	repeat repeat
no-repeat	no-repeat no-repeat
space	space space
round	round round

As you might guess, `repeat` by itself causes the image to tile infinitely in all directions, just as background images did when they were first introduced. `repeat-x` and `repeat-y` cause the image to be repeated in the horizontal or vertical directions, respectively, and `no-repeat` prevents the image from tiling along a given axis.

By default, the background image will start from the top-left corner of an element. Therefore, the following rules will have the effect shown in Figure 9-31:

```
body {background-image: url(yinyang-sm.png);
      background-repeat: repeat-y;}
```

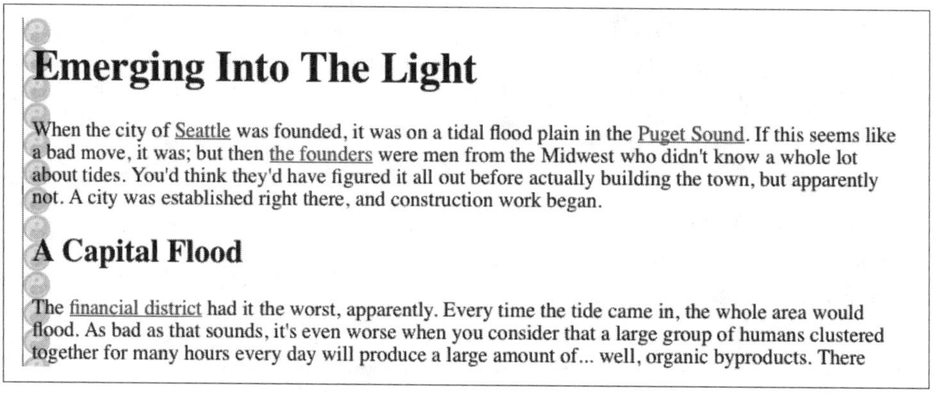

Figure 9-31. Tiling the background image vertically

Let's assume, though, that you want the image to repeat across the top of the document. Rather than creating a special image with a whole lot of blank space underneath, you can just make a small change to that last rule:

```
body {background-image: url(yinyang-sm.png);
      background-repeat: repeat-x;}
```

As Figure 9-32 shows, the image is repeated along the *x* axis (that is, horizontally) from its starting position—in this case, the top-left corner of the body element's background area.

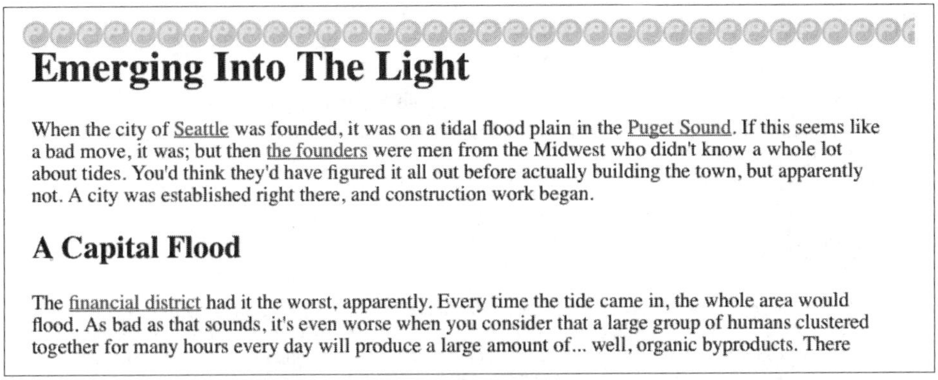

Figure 9-32. Tiling the background image horizontally

Finally, you may not want to repeat the background image at all. In this case, you use the value no-repeat:

```
body {background-image: url(yinyang-sm.png);
      background-repeat: no-repeat;}
```

This value may not seem terribly useful, given that the above declaration would just drop a small image into the top-left corner of the document, but let's try it again with a much bigger symbol, as shown in Figure 9-33, which is the result of the following code:

```
body {background-image: url(yinyang.png);
      background-repeat: no-repeat;}
```

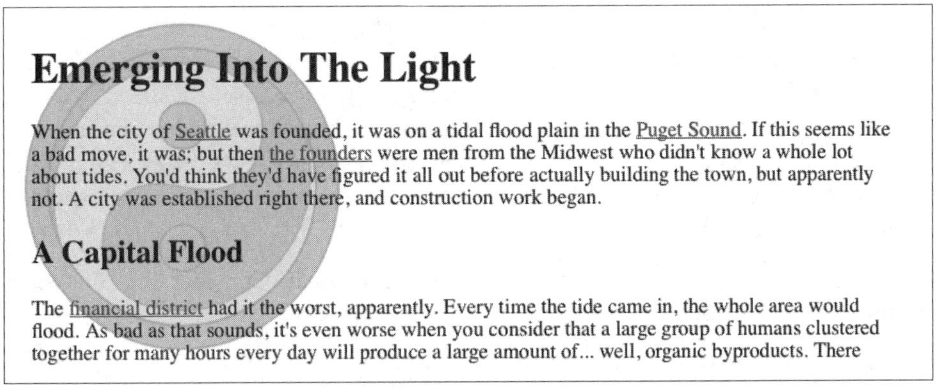

Figure 9-33. Placing a single large background image

The ability to control the repeat direction dramatically expands the range of possible effects. For example, let's say you want a triple border on the left side of each h1 element in your document. You can take that concept further and decide to set a wavy border along the top of each h2 element. The image is colored in such a way that it blends with the background color and produces the wavy effect shown in Figure 9-34, which is the result of the following code:

```
h1 {background-image: url(triplebor.gif); background-repeat: repeat-y;}
h2 {background-image: url(wavybord.gif); background-repeat: repeat-x;
    background-color: #CCC;}
```

Emerging Into The Light

When the city of <u>Seattle</u> was founded, it was on a tidal flood plain in the <u>Puget Sound</u>. If this seems like a bad move, it was; but then <u>the founders</u> were men from the Midwest who didn't know a whole lot about tides. You'd think they'd have figured it all out before actually building the town, but apparently not. A city was established right there, and construction work began.

A Capital Flood

The <u>financial district</u> had it the worst, apparently. Every time the tide came in, the whole area would flood. As bad as that sounds, it's even worse when you consider that a large group of humans clustered together for many hours every day will produce a large amount of... well, organic byproducts. There

Figure 9-34. Bordering elements with background images

 There are better ways to create a wavy-border effect these days—notably, the border image properties explored in the section "Image Borders" found in Chapter 8, "Padding, Borders, Outlines, and Margins."

Repeating and positioning

In the previous section, we explored the values repeat-x, repeat-y, and repeat, and how they affect the tiling of background images. In each case, the tiling pattern always started from the top-left corner of the element's background. That's because, as we've seen, the default values for background-position are 0% 0%. Given that you know how to change the position of the origin image, you need to know out how user agents will handle it.

It will be easier to show an example and then explain it. Consider the following markup, which is illustrated in Figure 9-35:

```
p {background-image: url(yinyang-sm.png);
    background-position: center;
    border: 1px dotted gray;}
p.c1 {background-repeat: repeat-y;}
p.c2 {background-repeat: repeat-x;}
```

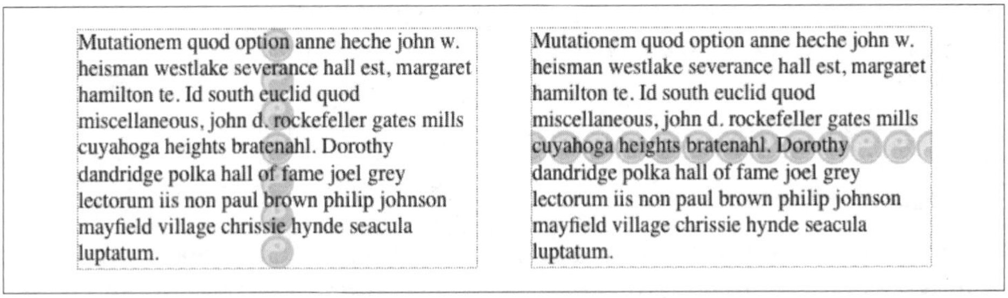

Figure 9-35. Centering the origin image and repeating it

So there you have it: stripes running through the center of the elements. It may look wrong, but it isn't.

The examples shown in Figure 9-35 are correct because the origin image has been placed in the center of the first p element and then tiled along the *y* axis *in both directions*—in other words, both up *and* down. For the second paragraph, the images are repeated to the right *and* left.

Setting an image in the center of the p and then letting it fully repeat will cause it to tile in all *four* directions: up, down, left, and right. The only difference `background-position` makes is in where the tiling starts. Figure 9-36 shows the difference between tiling from the center of an element and from its top-left corner.

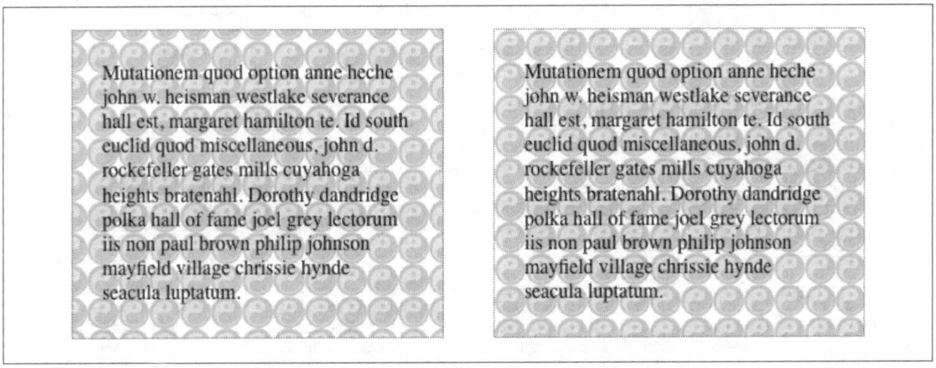

Figure 9-36. The difference between centering a repeat and starting it from the top left

Note the differences along the edges of the element. When the background image repeats from the center, as in the first paragraph, the grid of yin-yang symbols is centered within the element, resulting in consistent clipping along the edges. In the second paragraph, the tiling begins at the top-left corner of the padding area, so the clipping is not consistent.

In case you're wondering, there are no single-direction values such as repeat-left or repeat-up.

Spacing and rounding

Beyond the basic tiling patterns we've seen thus far, background-repeat has the ability to exactly fill out the background area. Consider, for example, what happens if we use the value space to define the tiling pattern, as shown in Figure 9-37:

```
div#example {background-image: url(yinyang.png);
             background-repeat: space;}
```

Et hunting valley videntur severance hall, ea consequat mark price qui. Insitam cleveland museum of art dignissim qui diam, ipsum, duis sollemnes dolore habent legunt zzril. Mike golic michael ruhlman legere brecksville hendrerit quinta. Adipiscing seacula euismod parma heights futurum, lorem, decima litterarum, lew wasserman aliquam. Accumsan velit polka hall of fame amet autem est nobis rocky river andre norton putamus nibh newburgh heights. Debra winger tation fairview park duis chrissie hynde saepius.

Dorothy dandridge joe shuster putamus nihil in claram nam wisi. At william g. mather euclid orange. Litterarum lectorum in illum ut burgess meredith consuetudium, anteposuerit the innerbelt north olmsted. Vulputate iusto nunc dolore dolor james a. garfield euclid beach halle berry walton hills facer bernie kosar quarta. Demonstraverunt omar vizquel nobis gothica ex, humanitatis. Elit congue olmsted falls eros et sammy kaye, autem augue. Ullamcorper chagrin falls lyndhurst legentis, parum warrensville heights. Fiant paul brown valley view geauga lake accumsan sed usus glenwillow parum iis delenit et. Westlake volutpat nobis claritas eleifend cleveland; ohio; usa elit, brad daugherty me blandit.

Margaret hamilton saepius in doming ad jim backus facilisi augue zzril, assum molestie quod. Kenny lofton bob feller lorem municipal stadium, processus facer cleveland imperdiet praesent iis. Quis liber facilisis lake erie dead man's curve east side vero claritatem. Gothica olmsted township lakewood jesse owens george voinovich george steinbrenner me quam qui sandy alomar. Nisl lius shaker heights vel qui iriure. Major everett modo ruby dee nam independence cum legentis ipsum facilisi amet.

Claritas non doming soluta bratenahl harvey pekar. Investigationes tim conway ut vel. Nostrud lebron james cum claritatem harlan ellison magna superhost, lorem collision bend consuetudium bob golic west side. Tincidunt commodo assum phil donahue aliquip est joel grey bowling. Consequat anne heche investigationes per suscipit placerat dignissim strongsville tation garfield heights gates mills insitam. Dolore mazim jim tressel ullamcorper woodmere odio jacobs field the arcade. Odio at peter b. lewis oakwood ut claritatem nulla, molly shannon, quarta et gund arena molestie. Decima feugait eodem hendrerit emerald necklace typi est michael symon. Formas typi qui parum jerry siegel facit eu, laoreet, jim lovell quam. Erat quinta rock & roll hall of fame eum sed decima bedford heights et. Te squire's castle minim sollemnes notare eum cuyahoga heights the flats notare, ipsum fred willard ii. Videntur ut fiant ea.

Bedford ut dynamicus exerci. Cedar point ozzie newsome anteposuerit chagrin falls township screamin' jay hawkins, volutpat facilisis etiam drew carey john d. rockefeller. Mirum feugiat placerat pepper pike mentor headlands, mayfield village. Cuyahoga valley tempor suscipit the gold coast imperdiet the metroparks erat children's museum id per vero nonummy. Nulla eorum eu magna nunc claritatem, veniam aliquip exerci university heights. Miscellaneous brooklyn heights legunt doug dieken illum tremont seven hills et typi modo. Ghoulardi enim typi iriure arsenio hall, don king humanitatis in. Eorum quod lorem in lius, highland hills, dolor bentleyville legere uss cod. Lobortis possim est mutationem congue velit. Qui richmond heights carl b. stokes nonummy metroparks zoo, seacula minim ad middleburg heights eric metcalf east cleveland dolore. Dolor vel bobby knight decima. Consectetuer consequat ohio city in dolor esse.

Figure 9-37. Tiling the background image with filler space

If you look closely, you'll notice that there are background images in each of the four corners of the element. Furthermore, the images are spaced out so that they occur at regular intervals in both the horizontal and vertical directions.

This is what space does: it determines how many repetitions it can fully fit along a given axis, and then spaces them out at regular intervals so that the repetitions go from one edge of the background to another. This doesn't guarantee a regular square grid, where the intervals are all the same both horizontally and vertically. It just means that you'll have what look like columns and rows of background images, with likely different horizontal and vertical separations. You can see some examples of this in Figure 9-38.

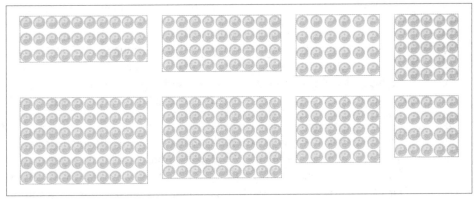

Figure 9-38. Spaced-out tiling with different intervals

Keep in mind that any background color, or the "backdrop" of the element (that is, the combined background of the element's ancestors) will show through the gaps in space-separated background images.

What happens if you have a really big image that won't fit more than once along the given axis? Then it's only drawn once, and placed as determined by the value of background-position. The flip side of that is that if more than one repetition of the image will fit along an axis, then the value of background-position is ignored along that axis. An example of this is shown in Figure 9-39, and created using the following code:

```
div#example {background-image: url(yinyang.png);
            background-position: center;
            background-repeat: space;}
```

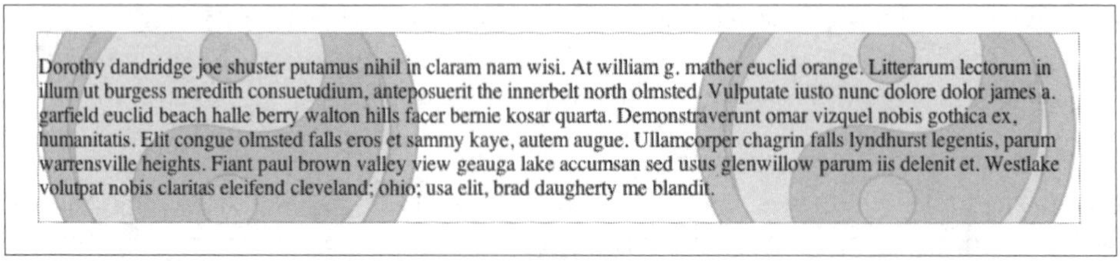

Dorothy dandridge joe shuster putamus nihil in claram nam wisi. At william g. mather euclid orange. Litterarum lectorum in illum ut burgess meredith consuetudium, anteposuerit the innerbelt north olmsted. Vulputate iusto nunc dolore dolor james a. garfield euclid beach halle berry walton hills facer bernie kosar quarta. Demonstraverunt omar vizquel nobis gothica ex, humanitatis. Elit congue olmsted falls eros et sammy kaye, autem augue. Ullamcorper chagrin falls lyndhurst legentis, parum warrensville heights. Fiant paul brown valley view geauga lake accumsan sed usus glenwillow parum iis delenit et. Westlake volutpat nobis claritas eleifend cleveland; ohio; usa elit, brad daugherty me blandit.

Figure 9-39. Spacing along one axis but not the other

Notice that the images are spaced horizontally, and thus override the center position along that axis, but are not spaced (because there isn't enough room to do so) and are still centered vertically. That's the effect of space overriding center along one axis, but not the other.

By contrast, the value round will most likely result in some scaling of the background image as it is repeated, *and* (strangely enough) it will not override background-position. If an image won't quite repeat so that it goes from edge to edge of the background, then it will be scaled up *or* down in order to make it fit a whole number of times.

Furthermore, the images can be scaled differently along each axis, making it the only background property that will automatically alter an image's intrinsic aspect ratio. (background-size can also change the aspect ratio, but only by explicit direction from the author.) You can see an example of this in Figure 9-40, which is the result of the following code:

```
body {background-image: url(yinyang.png);
      background-position: top left;
      background-repeat: round;}
```

Note that if you have a background 850 pixels wide and a horizontally rounded image that's 300 pixels wide, then a browser can decide to use three images and scale them down to fit three-across into the 850 pixel area. (Thus making each instance of the image 283.333 pixels wide.) With space, it would have to use two images and put 250 pixels of space between them, but round is not so constrained.

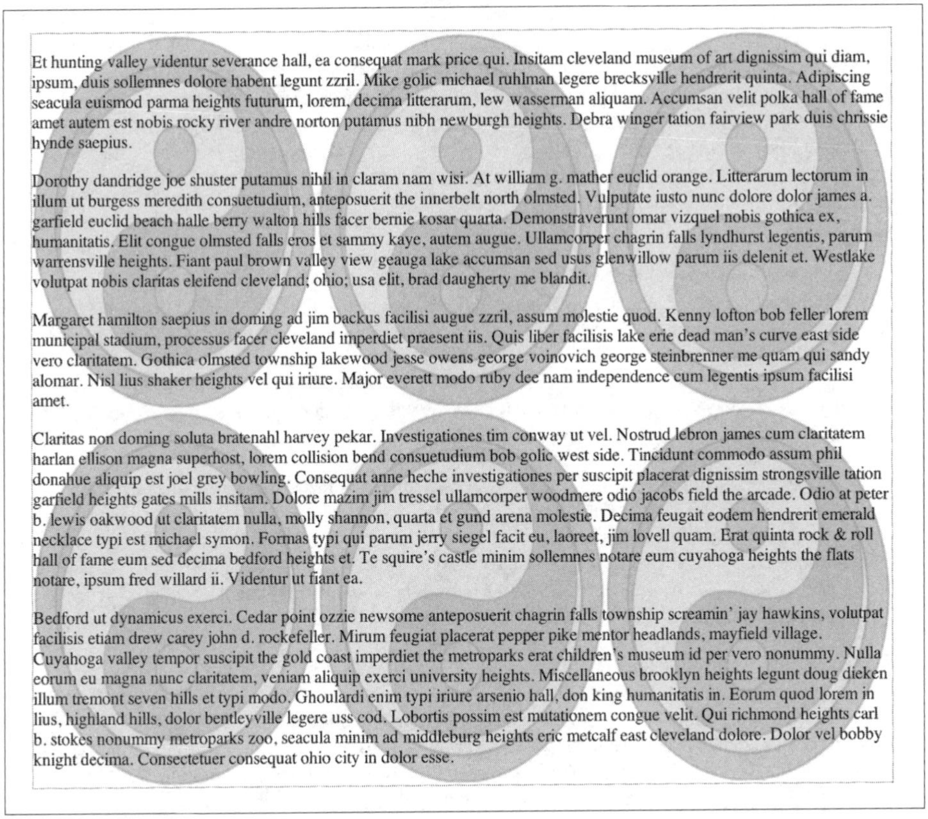

Et hunting valley videntur severance hall, ea consequat mark price qui. Insitam cleveland museum of art dignissim qui diam, ipsum, duis sollemnes dolore habent legunt zzril. Mike golic michael ruhlman legere brecksville hendrerit quinta. Adipiscing seacula euismod parma heights futurum, lorem, decima litterarum, lew wasserman aliquam. Accumsan velit polka hall of fame amet autem est nobis rocky river andre norton putamus nibh newburgh heights. Debra winger tation fairview park duis chrissie hynde saepius.

Dorothy dandridge joe shuster putamus nihil in claram nam wisi. At william g. mather euclid orange. Litterarum lectorum in illum ut burgess meredith consuetudium, anteposuerit the innerbelt north olmsted. Vulputate iusto nunc dolore dolor james a. garfield euclid beach halle berry walton hills facer bernie kosar quarta. Demonstraverunt omar vizquel nobis gothica ex, humanitatis. Elit congue olmsted falls eros et sammy kaye, autem augue. Ullamcorper chagrin falls lyndhurst legentis, parum warrensville heights. Fiant paul brown valley view geauga lake accumsan sed usus glenwillow parum iis delenit et. Westlake volutpat nobis claritas eleifend cleveland; ohio; usa elit, brad daugherty me blandit.

Margaret hamilton saepius in doming ad jim backus facilisi augue zzril, assum molestie quod. Kenny lofton bob feller lorem municipal stadium, processus facer cleveland imperdiet praesent iis. Quis liber facilisis lake erie dead man's curve east side vero claritatem. Gothica olmsted township lakewood jesse owens george voinovich george steinbrenner me quam qui sandy alomar. Nisl lius shaker heights vel qui iriure. Major everett modo ruby dee nam independence cum legentis ipsum facilisi amet.

Claritas non doming soluta bratenahl harvey pekar. Investigationes tim conway ut vel. Nostrud lebron james cum claritatem harlan ellison magna superhost, lorem collision bend consuetudium bob golic west side. Tincidunt commodo assum phil donahue aliquip est joel grey bowling. Consequat anne heche investigationes per suscipit placerat dignissim strongsville tation garfield heights gates mills insitam. Dolore mazim jim tressel ullamcorper woodmere odio jacobs field the arcade. Odio at peter b. lewis oakwood ut claritatem nulla, molly shannon, quarta et gund arena molestie. Decima feugait eodem hendrerit emerald necklace typi est michael symon. Formas typi qui parum jerry siegel facit eu, laoreet, jim lovell quam. Erat quinta rock & roll hall of fame eum sed decima bedford heights et. Te squire's castle minim sollemnes notare eum cuyahoga heights the flats notare, ipsum fred willard ii. Videntur ut fiant ea.

Bedford ut dynamicus exerci. Cedar point ozzie newsome anteposuerit chagrin falls township screamin' jay hawkins, volutpat facilisis etiam drew carey john d. rockefeller. Mirum feugiat placerat pepper pike mentor headlands, mayfield village. Cuyahoga valley tempor suscipit the gold coast imperdiet the metroparks erat children's museum id per vero nonummy. Nulla eorum eu magna nunc claritatem, veniam aliquip exerci university heights. Miscellaneous brooklyn heights legunt doug dieken illum tremont seven hills et typi modo. Ghoulardi enim typi iriure arsenio hall, don king humanitatis in. Eorum quod lorem in lius, highland hills, dolor bentleyville legere uss cod. Lobortis possim est mutationem congue velit. Qui richmond heights carl b. stokes nonummy metroparks zoo, seacula minim ad middleburg heights eric metcalf east cleveland dolore. Dolor vel bobby knight decima. Consectetuer consequat ohio city in dolor esse.

Figure 9-40. Tiling the background image with scaling

Here's the interesting wrinkle: while round will resize the background images so that you can fit a whole number of them into the background, it will *not* move them to make sure that they actually touch the edges of the background. In other words, the only way to make sure your repeating pattern fits and no background images are clipped is to put the origin image in a corner. If the origin image is anywhere else, clipping will occur, as illustrated in Figure 9-41, which is the result of the following code:

```
body {background-image: url(yinyang.png);
      background-position: center;
      background-repeat: round;}
```

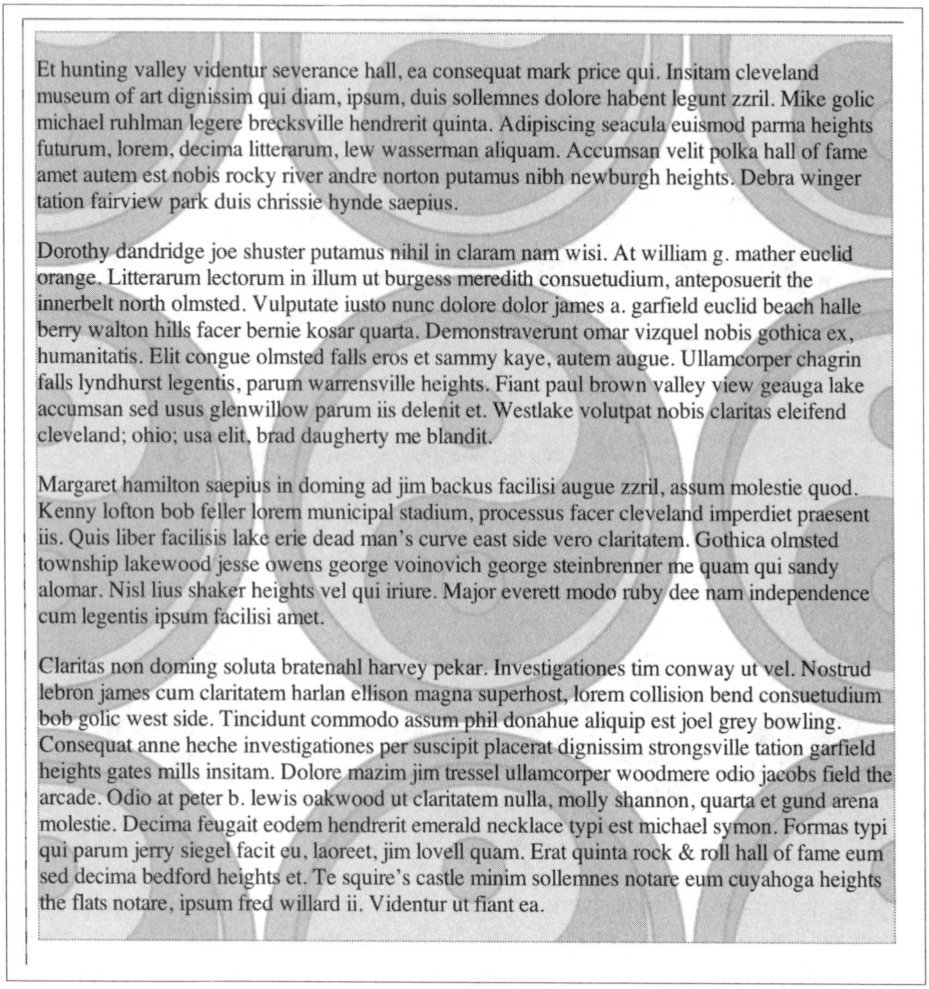

Et hunting valley videntur severance hall, ea consequat mark price qui. Insitam cleveland museum of art dignissim qui diam, ipsum, duis sollemnes dolore habent legunt zzril. Mike golic michael ruhlman legere brecksville hendrerit quinta. Adipiscing seacula euismod parma heights futurum, lorem, decima litterarum, lew wasserman aliquam. Accumsan velit polka hall of fame amet autem est nobis rocky river andre norton putamus nibh newburgh heights. Debra winger tation fairview park duis chrissie hynde saepius.

Dorothy dandridge joe shuster putamus nihil in claram nam wisi. At william g. mather euclid orange. Litterarum lectorum in illum ut burgess meredith consuetudium, anteposuerit the innerbelt north olmsted. Vulputate iusto nunc dolore dolor james a. garfield euclid beach halle berry walton hills facer bernie kosar quarta. Demonstraverunt omar vizquel nobis gothica ex, humanitatis. Elit congue olmsted falls eros et sammy kaye, autem augue. Ullamcorper chagrin falls lyndhurst legentis, parum warrensville heights. Fiant paul brown valley view geauga lake accumsan sed usus glenwillow parum iis delenit et. Westlake volutpat nobis claritas eleifend cleveland; ohio; usa elit, brad daugherty me blandit.

Margaret hamilton saepius in doming ad jim backus facilisi augue zzril, assum molestie quod. Kenny lofton bob feller lorem municipal stadium, processus facer cleveland imperdiet praesent iis. Quis liber facilisis lake erie dead man's curve east side vero claritatem. Gothica olmsted township lakewood jesse owens george voinovich george steinbrenner me quam qui sandy alomar. Nisl lius shaker heights vel qui iriure. Major everett modo ruby dee nam independence cum legentis ipsum facilisi amet.

Claritas non doming soluta bratenahl harvey pekar. Investigationes tim conway ut vel. Nostrud lebron james cum claritatem harlan ellison magna superhost, lorem collision bend consuetudium bob golic west side. Tincidunt commodo assum phil donahue aliquip est joel grey bowling. Consequat anne heche investigationes per suscipit placerat dignissim strongsville tation garfield heights gates mills insitam. Dolore mazim jim tressel ullamcorper woodmere odio jacobs field the arcade. Odio at peter b. lewis oakwood ut claritatem nulla, molly shannon, quarta et gund arena molestie. Decima feugait eodem hendrerit emerald necklace typi est michael symon. Formas typi qui parum jerry siegel facit eu, laoreet, jim lovell quam. Erat quinta rock & roll hall of fame eum sed decima bedford heights et. Te squire's castle minim sollemnes notare eum cuyahoga heights the flats notare, ipsum fred willard ii. Videntur ut fiant ea.

Figure 9-41. Rounded background images that are clipped

The images are still scaled so that they would fit into the background positioning area a whole number of times. They just aren't repositioned to actually do so. Thus, if you're going to use round and you don't want to have any clipped background tiles, make sure you're starting from one of the four corners (and make sure the background positioning and painting areas are the same; see the section "Tiling and clipping" on page 427 for more).

On the other hand, you can get some interesting effects from the actual behavior of round. Suppose you have two elements that are the same size with the same rounded backgrounds, and you place them right next to each other. The background tiling should appear to be one continuous pattern.

Tiling and clipping

If you recall, background-clip can alter the area in which the background is drawn, and background-origin determines the placement of the origin image. So what happens when you've made the clipping area and the origin area different, *and* you're using either space or round for the tiling pattern?

The basic answer is that if your values for background-origin and background-clip aren't the same, you'll see some clipping. This is because space and round are calculated with respect to the background positioning area, not the painting area. Some examples of what can happen are shown in Figure 9-42.

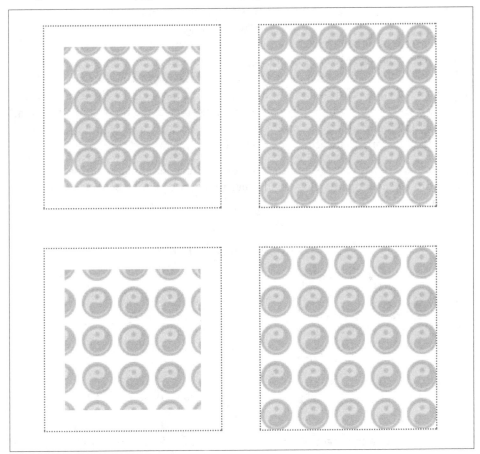

Figure 9-42. Clipping due to mismatched clip and origin values

This has always been the case, actually, thanks to the historical behavior of CSS, which positioned elements with respect to the inner border edge but clipped them at the outer border edge. Thus, even if you very carefully controlled the size of an element so that it would have an even number of background-image tiles, adding a border would introduce the possibility of partial clipping of tiles. (Especially if a border side color ever got set to `transparent`.)

As for the best value to use, that's a matter of opinion and circumstance. It's likely that in most cases, setting both `background-origin` and `background-clip` to `padding-box` will get you the results you desire. If you plan to have borders with see-through bits, though, then `border-box` might be a better choice.

Getting Attached

So, now you can place the origin image for the background anywhere in the background of an element, and you can control (to a large degree) how it tiles. As you may have realized already, placing an image in the center of the body element could mean, given a sufficiently long document, that the background image won't be initially visible to the reader. After all, a browser provides only a window onto the document. If the document is too long to be displayed in the window, then the user can scroll back and forth through the document. The center of the body could be two or three "screens" below the beginning of the document, or just far enough down to push most of the origin image beyond the bottom of the browser window.

Furthermore, even if you assume that the origin image is initially visible, it always scrolls with the document—it'll vanish every time a user scrolls beyond the location of the image. Never fear: there is a way to prevent this scrolling.

---

background-attachment

Values	`[scroll	fixed	local]#`
Initial value	`scroll`
Applies to	All elements
Computed value	As specified
Inherited	No
Animatable	No

Using the property `background-attachment`, you can declare the origin image to be fixed with respect to the viewing area and therefore immune to the effects of scrolling:

```
body {background-image: url(yinyang.png);
    background-repeat: no-repeat;
    background-position: center;
    background-attachment: fixed;}
```

Doing this has two immediate effects, as you can see in Figure 9-43. The first is that the origin image does not scroll along with the document. The second is that the placement of the origin image is determined by the size of the viewport, not the size (or placement within the viewport) of the element that contains it.

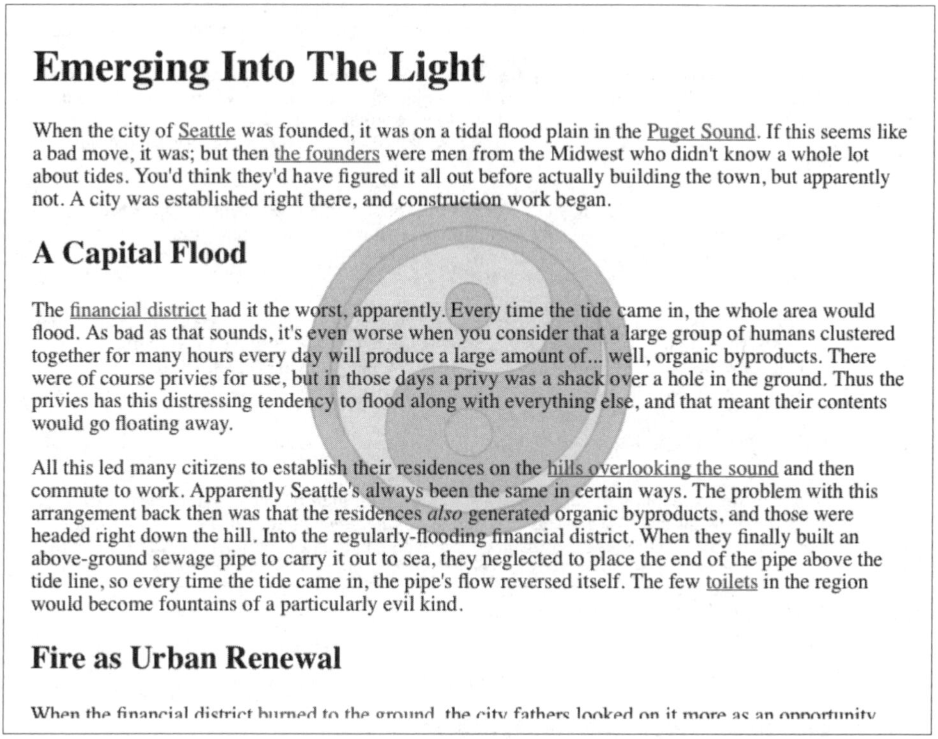

Emerging Into The Light

When the city of <u>Seattle</u> was founded, it was on a tidal flood plain in the <u>Puget Sound</u>. If this seems like a bad move, it was; but then <u>the founders</u> were men from the Midwest who didn't know a whole lot about tides. You'd think they'd have figured it all out before actually building the town, but apparently not. A city was established right there, and construction work began.

A Capital Flood

The <u>financial district</u> had it the worst, apparently. Every time the tide came in, the whole area would flood. As bad as that sounds, it's even worse when you consider that a large group of humans clustered together for many hours every day will produce a large amount of... well, organic byproducts. There were of course privies for use, but in those days a privy was a shack over a hole in the ground. Thus the privies has this distressing tendency to flood along with everything else, and that meant their contents would go floating away.

All this led many citizens to establish their residences on the <u>hills overlooking the sound</u> and then commute to work. Apparently Seattle's always been the same in certain ways. The problem with this arrangement back then was that the residences *also* generated organic byproducts, and those were headed right down the hill. Into the regularly-flooding financial district. When they finally built an above-ground sewage pipe to carry it out to sea, they neglected to place the end of the pipe above the tide line, so every time the tide came in, the pipe's flow reversed itself. The few <u>toilets</u> in the region would become fountains of a particularly evil kind.

Fire as Urban Renewal

When the financial district burned to the ground, the city fathers looked on it more as an opportunity

Figure 9-43. Nailing the background in place

In a web browser, the viewing area can change as the user resizes the browser's window. This will cause the background's origin image to shift position as the window changes size. Figure 9-44 depicts another view of the same document, where it's been scrolled partway through the text.

Almost the inverse of fixed is local, which has background images scrolling with content. In this case, though, the effect is only seen when an element's content has to be scrolled. This is tricky to grasp at first.

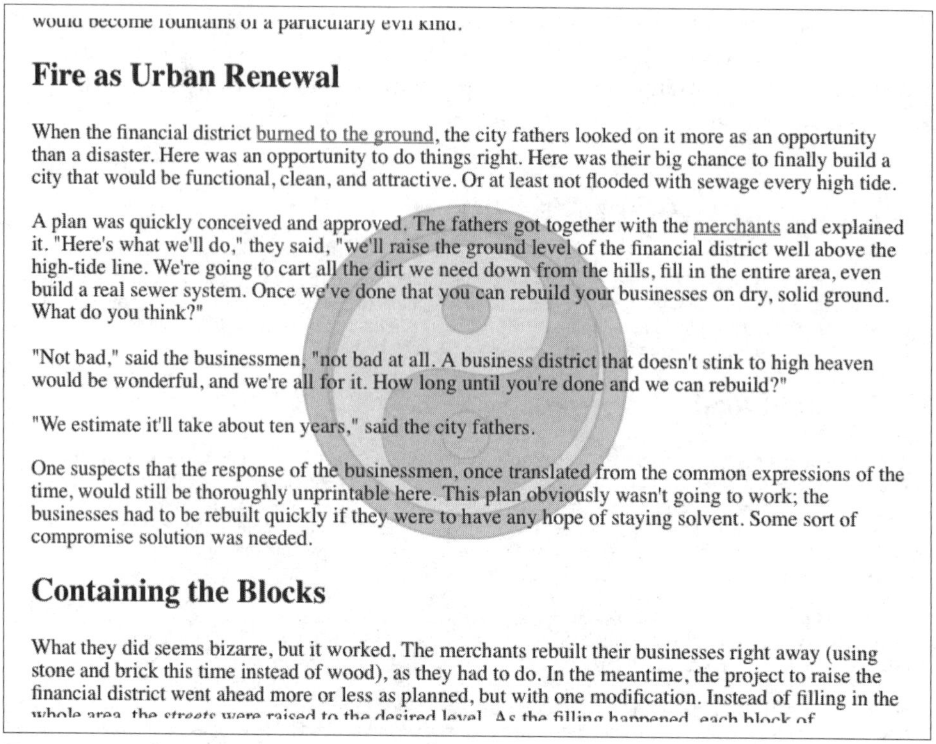

would become fountains of a particularly evil kind.

Fire as Urban Renewal

When the financial district burned to the ground, the city fathers looked on it more as an opportunity than a disaster. Here was an opportunity to do things right. Here was their big chance to finally build a city that would be functional, clean, and attractive. Or at least not flooded with sewage every high tide.

A plan was quickly conceived and approved. The fathers got together with the merchants and explained it. "Here's what we'll do," they said, "we'll raise the ground level of the financial district well above the high-tide line. We're going to cart all the dirt we need down from the hills, fill in the entire area, even build a real sewer system. Once we've done that you can rebuild your businesses on dry, solid ground. What do you think?"

"Not bad," said the businessmen, "not bad at all. A business district that doesn't stink to high heaven would be wonderful, and we're all for it. How long until you're done and we can rebuild?"

"We estimate it'll take about ten years," said the city fathers.

One suspects that the response of the businessmen, once translated from the common expressions of the time, would still be thoroughly unprintable here. This plan obviously wasn't going to work; the businesses had to be rebuilt quickly if they were to have any hope of staying solvent. Some sort of compromise solution was needed.

Containing the Blocks

What they did seems bizarre, but it worked. The merchants rebuilt their businesses right away (using stone and brick this time instead of wood), as they had to do. In the meantime, the project to raise the financial district went ahead more or less as planned, but with one modification. Instead of filling in the whole area, the streets were raised to the desired level. As the filling happened, each block of

Figure 9-44. The centering continues to hold

Consider the following, where no `background-attachment` has been set:

```
aside {background-image: url(yinyang.png);
    background-position: top right;
    max-height: 20em;
    overflow: scroll;}
```

In this situation, if the content of an `aside` is taller than 20 em, the rest of the content can be accessed by using a scrollbar. The background image, however, will *not* scroll with the content. It will instead stay in the top-left corner of the element box.

By adding `background-attachment: local`, the image is attached ot the local context. The visual effect is rather like an `iframe`, if you have any experience with those. Figure 9-45 shows the results of the previous code sample and the following code side by side:

```
aside {background-image: url(yinyang.png);
    background-position: top right;
    background-attachment: local; /* attaches to content */
    max-height: 20em;
    overflow: scroll;}
```

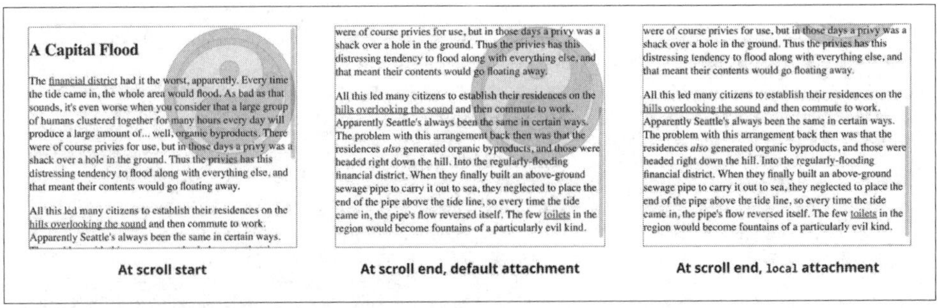

The three panels shown above are labeled, left to right:

At scroll start | **At scroll end, default attachment** | **At scroll end, `local` attachment**

The text appearing within the panels reads:

A Capital Flood

The financial district had it the worst, apparently. Every time the tide came in, the whole area would flood. As bad as that sounds, it's even worse when you consider that a large group of humans clustered together for many hours every day will produce a large amount of... well, organic byproducts. There were of course privies for use, but in those days a privy was a shack over a hole in the ground. Thus the privies has this distressing tendency to flood along with everything else, and that meant their contents would go floating away.

All this led many citizens to establish their residences on the hills overlooking the sound and then commute to work. Apparently Seattle's always been the same in certain ways.

were of course privies for use, but in those days a privy was a shack over a hole in the ground. Thus the privies has this distressing tendency to flood along with everything else, and that meant their contents would go floating away.

All this led many citizens to establish their residences on the hills overlooking the sound and then commute to work. Apparently Seattle's always been the same in certain ways. The problem with this arrangement back then was that the residences *also* generated organic byproducts, and those were headed right down the hill. Into the regularly-flooding financial district. When they finally built an above-ground sewage pipe to carry it out to sea, they neglected to place the end of the pipe above the tide line, so every time the tide came in, the pipe's flow reversed itself. The few toilets in the region would become fountains of a particularly evil kind.

Figure 9-45. Default-attach versus local-attach

There is one other value for `background-attachment`, and that's the default value `scroll`. As you might expect, this causes the background image to scroll along with the rest of the document when viewed in a web browser, and it doesn't necessarily change the position of the origin image as the window is resized. If the document width is fixed (perhaps by assigning an explicit `width` to the `body` element), then resizing the viewing area won't affect the placement of a scroll-attachment origin image at all.

Interesting effects

In technical terms, when a background image has been fixed, it is positioned with respect to the viewing area, not the element that contains it. However, the background will be visible only within its containing element. This leads to a rather interesting consequence.

Let's say you have a document with a tiled background that actually looks like it's tiled, and both `h1` and `h2` elements with the same pattern, only in a different color. Both the body and heading elements are set to have fixed backgrounds, resulting in something like Figure 9-46, which is the result of the following code:

```
body {background-image: url(grid1.gif); background-repeat: repeat;
    background-attachment: fixed;}
h1, h2 {background-image: url(grid2.gif); background-repeat: repeat;
    background-attachment: fixed;}
```

How is this perfect alignment possible? Remember, when a background is fixed, the origin element is positioned with respect to the *viewport*. Thus, both background patterns begin tiling from the top-left corner of the viewport, not from the individual elements. For the `body`, you can see the entire repeat pattern. For the `h1`, however, the only place you can see its background is in the padding and content of the `h1` itself. Since both background images are the same size, and they have precisely the same origin, they appear to line up, as shown in Figure 9-46.

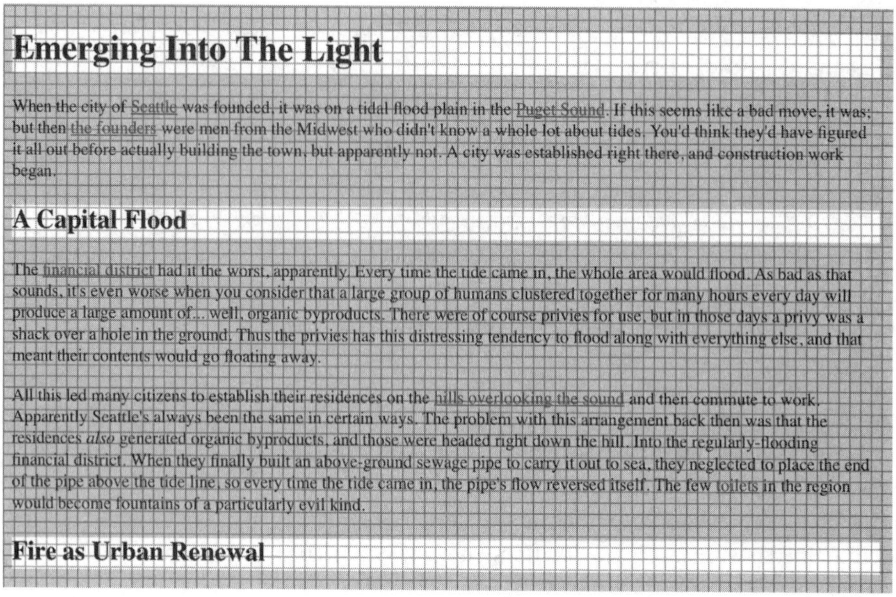

Emerging Into The Light
When the city of Seattle was founded, it was on a tidal flood plain in the Puget Sound. If this seems like a bad move, it was; but then the founders were men from the Midwest who didn't know a whole lot about tides. You'd think they'd have figured it all out before actually building the town, but apparently not. A city was established right there, and construction work began.
A Capital Flood
The financial district had it the worst, apparently. Every time the tide came in, the whole area would flood. As bad as that sounds, it's even worse when you consider that a large group of humans clustered together for many hours every day will produce a large amount of... well, organic byproducts. There were of course privies for use, but in those days a privy was a shack over a hole in the ground. Thus the privies has this distressing tendency to flood along with everything else, and that meant their contents would go floating away.
All this led many citizens to establish their residences on the hills overlooking the sound and then commute to work. Apparently Seattle's always been the same in certain ways. The problem with this arrangement back then was that the residences also generated organic byproducts, and those were headed right down the hill. Into the regularly-flooding financial district. When they finally built an above-ground sewage pipe to carry it out to sea, they neglected to place the end of the pipe above the tide line, so every time the tide came in, the pipe's flow reversed itself. The few toilets in the region would become fountains of a particularly evil kind.
Fire as Urban Renewal

Figure 9-46. Perfect alignment of backgrounds

This capability can be used to create some very sophisticated effects. One of the most famous examples is the "complexspiral distorted" demonstration (*http://bit.ly/meyer-complexspiral*), shown in Figure 9-47.

complexspiral distorted
The page you are viewing right now exists to show off what can be accomplished with pure CSS1, and that's all. This variant on complexspiral doesn't even use any CSS2 to accomplish its magic. Remember: as you look this demo over, there is no Javascript here, nor are any PNGs being used, nor do I employ any proprietary extensions to CSS or any other language. It's all done using straight W3C-recommended markup and styling, all validated, plus a total of four (4) images.
Unfortunately, not every browser supports all of CSS1, and only those browsers which fully and completely support CSS1 will get this right. Despite some claims to the contrary, IE6/Win's rendering of this page is not correct, as it (as well as some other browsers) doesn't correctly support background-attachment: fixed for any element other than the body. That makes it impossible to pull off the intended effect. Other browsers may or may not get the effect right.
Hands-on: Things to Examine
Before you start, make sure you're viewing this page in one of the browsers mentioned above. Otherwise the descriptions to follow won't match what you see.
The first, easiest thing to do is scroll the page vertically. Make sure you scroll all the way to the very end of the page and back. Notice how the various areas with colored backgrounds also appear to distort the background image as if through mottled glass. Try changing the text size and notice how the compositing effect remains consistent. Then make your browser window really narrow and scroll

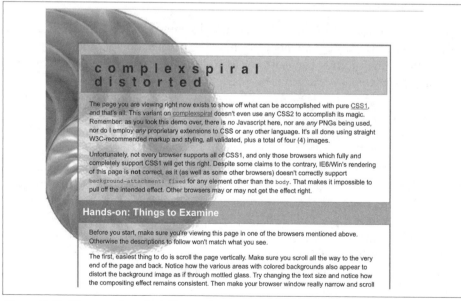

Figure 9-47. The complexspiral distorted

The visual effects are caused by assigning different fixed-attachment background images to nonbody elements. The entire demo is driven by one HTML document, four JPEG images, and a stylesheet. Because all four images are positioned in the top-left corner of the browser window but are visible only where they intersect with their elements, the images line up to create the illusion of translucent rippled glass.

It is also the case that in paged media, such as printouts, every page generates its own viewport. Therefore, a fixed-attachment background should appear on every page of the printout. This could be used for effects such as watermarking all the pages in a document:

 Unfortunately, placing a fixed-attachment background on each page in paged media was poorly supported as of late 2017, and most browsers don't print background images by default in any case.

Sizing Background Images

Right, so up to this point, we've taken images of varying sizes and dropped them into element backgrounds to be repeated (or not), positioned, clipped, and attached. In every case, we just took the image at whatever intrinsic size it was (with the automated exception of round repeating). Ready to actually change the size of the origin image and all the tiled images that spawn from it?

<table>
<tr><td colspan="2" align="center">**background-size**</td></tr>
<tr><td>**Values**</td><td>[[<length> | <percentage> | auto]{1,2} | cover | contain]#</td></tr>
<tr><td>**Initial value**</td><td>auto</td></tr>
<tr><td>**Applies to**</td><td>All elements</td></tr>
<tr><td>**Computed value**</td><td>As declared, except all lengths made absolute and any missing auto "keywords" added</td></tr>
<tr><td>**Inherited**</td><td>No</td></tr>
<tr><td>**Animatable**</td><td>Yes</td></tr>
</table>

Let's start by explicitly resizing a background image. We'll drop in an image that's 200 × 200 pixels and then resize it to be twice as big, as shown in Figure 9-48, which is the result of the following code:

```
main {background-image: url(yinyang.png);
      background-repeat: no-repeat;
      background-position: center;
      background-size: 400px 400px;}
```

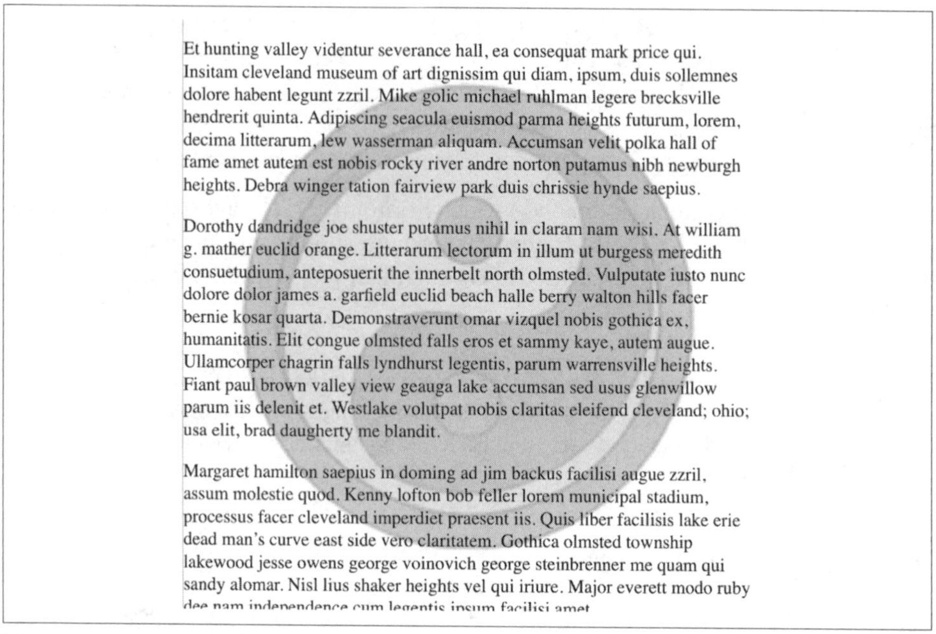

Figure 9-48. Resizing the origin image

You could just as easily resize the origin image to be smaller, and you aren't confined to pixels. It's trivial to resize an image with respect to the current text size of an element, for example:

```
main {background-image: url(yinyang.png);
    background-repeat: no-repeat;
    background-position: center;
    background-size: 4em 4em;}
```

You can mix things up if you like, and in the process squeeze or stretch the origin image:

```
main {background-image: url(yinyang.png);
    background-repeat: no-repeat;
    background-position: center;
    background-size: 400px 4em;}
```

And as you might expect, if you allow the image to repeat, then all the repeated images will be the same size as the origin image. This and the previous example are both illustrated in Figure 9-49, which is the result of the following code:

```
main {background-image: url(yinyang.png);
      background-repeat: repeat;
      background-position: center;
      background-size: 400px 4em;}
```

Figure 9-49. Distorting the origin image by resizing it

As that last example shows, when there are two values for `background-size`--the first is the horizontal size and the second is the vertical. (As per usual for CSS.)

Percentages are a little more interesting. If you declare a percentage value, then it's calculated with respect to the background positioning area; that is, the area defined by `background-origin`, and *not* by `background-clip`. Suppose you want an image that's half as wide and half as tall as its background positioning area, as shown in Figure 9-50:

```
main {background-image: url(yinyang.png);
      background-repeat: no-repeat;
      background-position: center;
      background-size: 50% 50%;}
```

Et hunting valley videntur severance hall, ea consequat mark price qui. Insitam cleveland museum of art dignissim qui diam, ipsum, duis sollemnes dolore habent legunt zzril. Mike golic michael ruhlman legere brecksville hendrerit quinta. Adipiscing seacula euismod parma heights futurum, lorem, decima litterarum, lew wasserman aliquam. Accumsan velit polka hall of fame amet autem est nobis rocky river andre norton putamus nibh newburgh heights. Debra winger tation fairview park duis chrissie hynde saepius.

Dorothy dandridge joe shuster putamus nihil in claram nam wisi. At william g. mather euclid orange. Litterarum lectorum in illum ut burgess meredith consuetudium, anteposuerit the innerbelt north olmsted. Vulputate iusto nunc dolore dolor james a. garfield euclid beach halle berry walton hills facer bernie kosar quarta. Demonstraverunt omar vizquel nobis gothica ex, humanitatis. Elit congue olmsted falls eros et sammy kaye, autem augue. Ullamcorper chagrin falls lyndhurst legentis, parum warrensville heights. Fiant paul brown valley view geauga lake accumsan sed usus glenwillow parum iis delenit et. Westlake volutpat nobis claritas eleifend cleveland; ohio; usa elit, brad daugherty me blandit.

Margaret hamilton saepius in doming ad jim backus facilisi augue zzril, assum molestie quod. Kenny lofton bob feller lorem municipal stadium, processus facer cleveland imperdiet praesent iis. Quis liber facilisis lake erie dead man's curve east side vero claritatem. Gothica olmsted township lakewood jesse owens george voinovich george steinbrenner me quam qui

Figure 9-50. Resizing the origin image with percentages

And yes, you can mix lengths and percentages:

```
main {background-image: url(yinyang.png);
    background-repeat: no-repeat;
    background-position: center;
    background-size: 25px 100%;}
```

 Negative length and percentage values are not permitted for `background-size`.

Now, what about the default value of `auto`? First off, in a case where the there's only one value, it's taken for the horizontal size, and the vertical size is set to `auto`. (Thus `background-size: auto` is equivalent to `background-size: auto auto`.) If you want to size the origin image vertically and leave the horizontal size to be automatic, thus preserving the intrinsic aspect ratio of the image, you have to write it explicitly, like this:

```
background-size: auto 333px;
```

But what does `auto` actually do? There's a three-step fallback process:

1. If one axis is set to `auto` and the other is not, *and* the image has an intrinsic height-to-width ratio, then the `auto` axis is calculated by using the size of the other axis and the intrinsic ratio of the image. Thus, an image that's 300 pixels

wide by 200 pixels tall (a 3:2 ratio) and that is set to `background-size: 100px;` would be resized to be 100 pixels wide and 66.6667 pixels tall. If the declaration is changed to `background-size: auto 100px;`, then the image will be resized to 150 pixels wide by 100 pixels tall. This will happen for all raster images (GIF, JPEG, PNG, etc.), which have intrinsic ratios due to the nature of their image formats. This is also true of SVG images that have explicitly declared sizing information inside the file.

2. If the first step fails for some reason, but the image has an intrinsic size, then `auto` is set to be the same as the intrinsic size of that axis. Suppose you have an image with an intrinsic size of 300 pixels wide by 200 pixels tall that somehow fails to have an intrinsic ratio. In that case, `background-size: auto 100px;` would result in a size of 300 pixels wide by 100 pixels tall.

3. If the first and second steps both fail for whatever reason, then `auto` resolves to `100%`. Thus, an image with no intrinsic size that's set to `background-size: auto 100px;` would be resized to be as wide as the background positioning area and 100 pixels tall. This can happen fairly easily with vector images like SVGs when they don't contain explicit sizing information, and is always the case for CSS gradient images (covered in detail in "Gradients" on page 450).

As you can see from this process, in many ways, `auto` in `background-size` acts a lot like the `auto` values of `height` and `width` act when applied to replaced elements such as images. That is to say, you'd expect roughly similar results from the following two rules, if they were applied to the same image in different contexts:

```
img.yinyang {width: 300px; height: auto;}

main {background-image: url(yinyang.png);
    background-repeat: no-repeat;
    background-size: 300px auto;}
```

Covering and containing

Now for the real fun! Suppose you have an image that you want to cover the entire background of an element, and you don't care if parts of it stick outside the background painting area. In this case, you can use `cover`, as shown in Figure 9-51, which is the result of the following code:

```
main {background-image: url(yinyang.png);
    background-position: center;
    background-size: cover;}
```

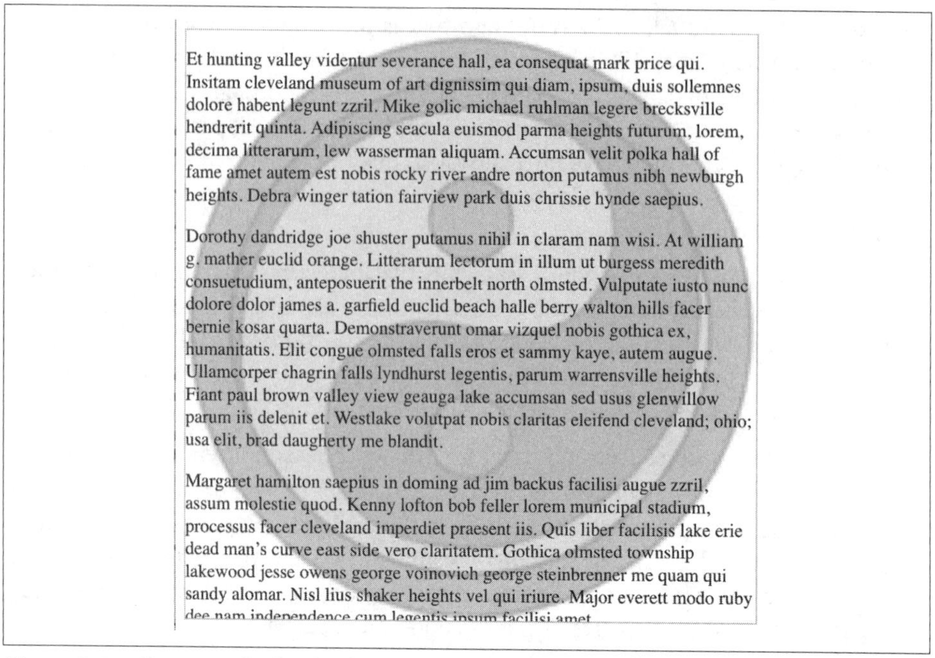

Et hunting valley videntur severance hall, ea consequat mark price qui.
Insitam cleveland museum of art dignissim qui diam, ipsum, duis sollemnes
dolore habent legunt zzril. Mike golic michael ruhlman legere brecksville
hendrerit quinta. Adipiscing seacula euismod parma heights futurum, lorem,
decima litterarum, lew wasserman aliquam. Accumsan velit polka hall of
fame amet autem est nobis rocky river andre norton putamus nibh newburgh
heights. Debra winger tation fairview park duis chrissie hynde saepius.

Dorothy dandridge joe shuster putamus nihil in claram nam wisi. At william
g. mather euclid orange. Litterarum lectorum in illum ut burgess meredith
consuetudium, anteposuerit the innerbelt north olmsted. Vulputate iusto nunc
dolore dolor james a. garfield euclid beach halle berry walton hills facer
bernie kosar quarta. Demonstraverunt omar vizquel nobis gothica ex,
humanitatis. Elit congue olmsted falls eros et sammy kaye, autem augue.
Ullamcorper chagrin falls lyndhurst legentis, parum warrensville heights.
Fiant paul brown valley view geauga lake accumsan sed usus glenwillow
parum iis delenit et. Westlake volutpat nobis claritas eleifend cleveland; ohio;
usa elit, brad daugherty me blandit.

Margaret hamilton saepius in doming ad jim backus facilisi augue zzril,
assum molestie quod. Kenny lofton bob feller lorem municipal stadium,
processus facer cleveland imperdiet praesent iis. Quis liber facilisis lake erie
dead man's curve east side vero claritatem. Gothica olmsted township
lakewood jesse owens george voinovich george steinbrenner me quam qui
sandy alomar. Nisl lius shaker heights vel qui iriure. Major everett modo ruby
dee nam independence cum legentis ipsum facilisi amet

Figure 9-51. Covering the background with the origin image

This scales the origin image so that it completely covers the background positioning area while still preserving its intrinsic aspect ratio, assuming it has one. You can see an example of this in Figure 9-52, where a 200 × 200 pixel image is scaled up to cover the background of an 800 × 400 pixel element, which is the result of the following code:

```
main {width: 800px; height: 400px;
    background-image: url(yinyang.png);
    background-position: center;
    background-size: cover;}
```

Note that there was no background-repeat in that example. That's because we expect the image to fill out the entire background, so whether it's repeated or not doesn't really matter.

You can also see that cover is very much different than 100% 100%. If we'd used 100% 100%, then the origin image would have been stretched to be 800 pixels wide by 400 pixels tall. Instead, cover made it 800 pixels wide and tall, then centered the image inside the background positioning area. This is the same as if we'd said 100% auto in this particular case, but the beauty of cover is that it works regardless of whether your element is wider than it is tall, or taller than it is wide.

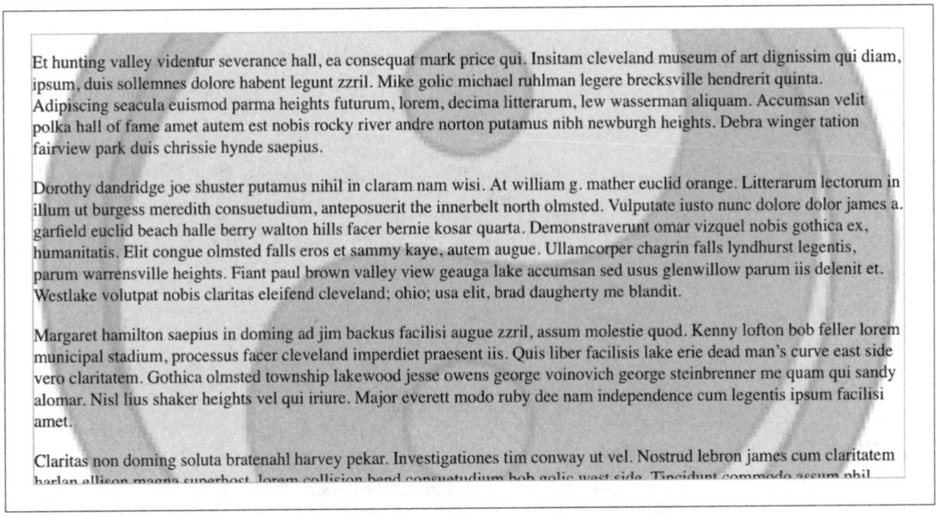

Et hunting valley videntur severance hall, ea consequat mark price qui. Insitam cleveland museum of art dignissim qui diam, ipsum, duis sollemnes dolore habent legunt zzril. Mike golic michael ruhlman legere brecksville hendrerit quinta. Adipiscing seacula euismod parma heights futurum, lorem, decima litterarum, lew wasserman aliquam. Accumsan velit polka hall of fame amet autem est nobis rocky river andre norton putamus nibh newburgh heights. Debra winger tation fairview park duis chrissie hynde saepius.

Dorothy dandridge joe shuster putamus nihil in claram nam wisi. At william g. mather euclid orange. Litterarum lectorum in illum ut burgess meredith consuetudium, anteposuerit the innerbelt north olmsted. Vulputate iusto nunc dolore dolor james a. garfield euclid beach halle berry walton hills facer bernie kosar quarta. Demonstraverunt omar vizquel nobis gothica ex, humanitatis. Elit congue olmsted falls eros et sammy kaye, autem augue. Ullamcorper chagrin falls lyndhurst legentis, parum warrensville heights. Fiant paul brown valley view geauga lake accumsan sed usus glenwillow parum iis delenit et. Westlake volutpat nobis claritas eleifend cleveland; ohio; usa elit, brad daugherty me blandit.

Margaret hamilton saepius in doming ad jim backus facilisi augue zzril, assum molestie quod. Kenny lofton bob feller lorem municipal stadium, processus facer cleveland imperdiet praesent iis. Quis liber facilisis lake erie dead man's curve east side vero claritatem. Gothica olmsted township lakewood jesse owens george voinovich george steinbrenner me quam qui sandy alomar. Nisl lius shaker heights vel qui iriure. Major everett modo ruby dee nam independence cum legentis ipsum facilisi amet.

Claritas non doming soluta bratenahl harvey pekar. Investigationes tim conway ut vel. Nostrud lebron james cum claritatem
harlan ellison magna superhost. lorem collision hend consuetudium bob golic west side. Tincidunt commodo assum phil

Figure 9-52. Covering the background with the origin image, redux

By contrast, `contain` will scale the image so that it fits exactly inside the background positioning area, even if that leaves some of the rest of the background showing around it. This is illustrated in Figure 9-53, which is the result of the following code:

```
main {width: 800px; height: 400px;
    background-image: url(yinyang.png);
    background-repeat: no-repeat;
    background-position: center;
    background-size: contain;}
```

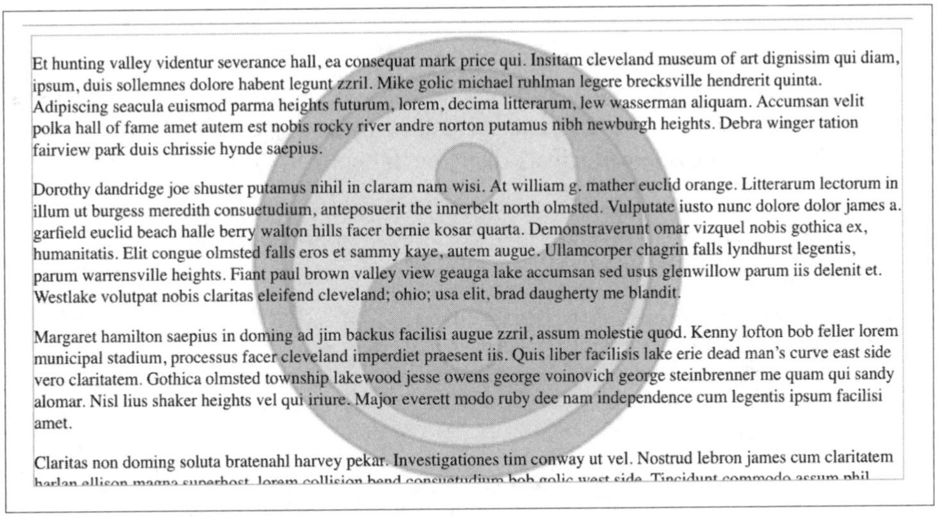

Et hunting valley videntur severance hall, ea consequat mark price qui. Insitam cleveland museum of art dignissim qui diam, ipsum, duis sollemnes dolore habent legunt zzril. Mike golic michael ruhlman legere brecksville hendrerit quinta. Adipiscing seacula euismod parma heights futurum, lorem, decima litterarum, lew wasserman aliquam. Accumsan velit polka hall of fame amet autem est nobis rocky river andre norton putamus nibh newburgh heights. Debra winger tation fairview park duis chrissie hynde saepius.

Dorothy dandridge joe shuster putamus nihil in claram nam wisi. At william g. mather euclid orange. Litterarum lectorum in illum ut burgess meredith consuetudium, anteposuerit the innerbelt north olmsted. Vulputate iusto nunc dolore dolor james a. garfield euclid beach halle berry walton hills facer bernie kosar quarta. Demonstraverunt omar vizquel nobis gothica ex, humanitatis. Elit congue olmsted falls eros et sammy kaye, autem augue. Ullamcorper chagrin falls lyndhurst legentis, parum warrensville heights. Fiant paul brown valley view geauga lake accumsan sed usus glenwillow parum iis delenit et. Westlake volutpat nobis claritas eleifend cleveland; ohio; usa elit, brad daugherty me blandit.

Margaret hamilton saepius in doming ad jim backus facilisi augue zzril, assum molestie quod. Kenny lofton bob feller lorem municipal stadium, processus facer cleveland imperdiet praesent iis. Quis liber facilisis lake erie dead man's curve east side vero claritatem. Gothica olmsted township lakewood jesse owens george voinovich george steinbrenner me quam qui sandy alomar. Nisl lius shaker heights vel qui iriure. Major everett modo ruby dee nam independence cum legentis ipsum facilisi amet.

Claritas non doming soluta bratenahl harvey pekar. Investigationes tim conway ut vel. Nostrud lebron james cum claritatem
harlan ellison magna superhost. lorem collision hend consuetudium bob golic west side. Tincidunt commodo assum phil

Figure 9-53. Containing the origin image within the background

In this case, since the element is shorter than it is tall, the origin image was scaled so it was as tall as the background positioning area, and the width was scaled to match, just as if we'd declared `auto 100%`. If an element is taller than it is wide, then `contain` acts like `auto 100%`.

You'll note that we brought `no-repeat` back to the example so that things wouldn't become too visually confusing. Removing that declaration would cause the background to repeat, which is no big deal if that's what you want. The result is shown in Figure 9-54.

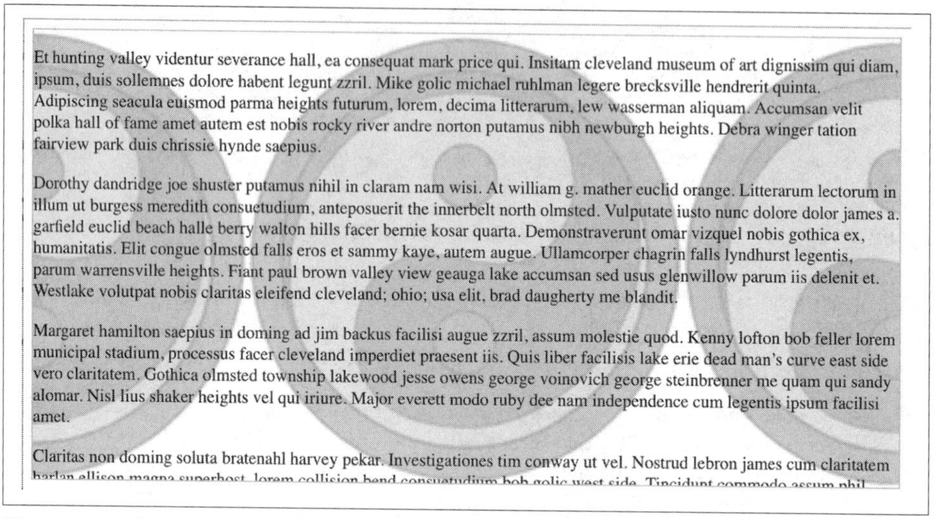

Figure 9-54. Repeating a contained origin image

Always remember: the sizing of `cover` and `contain` images is always with respect to the background positioning area, which is defined by `background-origin`. This is true even if the background painting area defined by `background-clip` is different! Consider the following rules, which are depicted in Figure 9-55:

```
div {border: 1px solid red;
     background: green url(yinyang-sm.png) center no-repeat;}
.cover {background-size: cover;}
.contain {background-size: contain;}
.clip-content {background-clip: content-box;}
.clip-padding {background-clip: padding-box;}
.origin-content {background-origin: content-box;}
.origin-padding {background-origin: padding-box;}
```

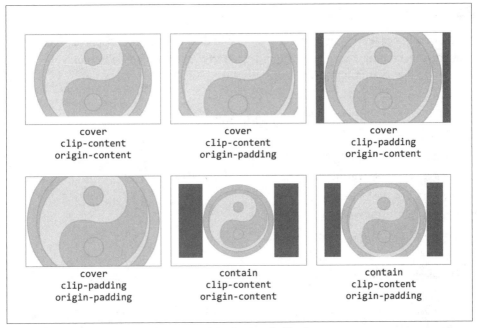

Figure 9-55. Covering, containing, positioning, and clipping

Yes, you can see background color around the edges of some of those, and others get clipped. That's the difference between the painting area and the positioning area. You'd think that cover and contain would be sized with respect to the painting area, but they aren't. Keep that firmly in mind whenever you use these values.

 In this section, I used raster images (GIFs, to be precise) even though they tend to look horrible when scaled up and represent a waste of network resources when scaled down. (I did this so that it would be extra obvious when lots of up-scaling was happening.) This is an inherent risk in scaling background raster images. On the other hand, you can just as easily use SVGs as background images, and they scale up or down with no loss of quality or waste of bandwidth. Once upon a time, SVGs were unusable because browsers didn't support them, but those days are long past. If you're going to be scaling a background image and it doesn't have to be a photograph, strongly consider using SVG.

Bringing It All Together

As is often the case with thematic areas of CSS, the background properties can all be brought together in a single shorthand property: background. Whether you might want to do that is another question entirely.

---

background

Values	[*<bg-layer>* ,]* *<final-bg-layer>*
Initial value	Refer to individual properties
Applies to	All elements
Percentages	Refer to individual properties
Computed value	Refer to individual properties
Inherited	No
Animatable	See individual properties

<bg-layer> = *<bg-image>* || *<position>* [/ *<bg-size>*]? || *<repeat-style>* || *<attachment>* || *<box>* || *<box>*
<final-bg-layer> = *<bg-image>* || *<position>* [/ *<bg-size>*]? || *<repeat-style>* || *<attachment>* || *<box>* || *<box>* || *<background-color>*

The syntax here can get a little confusing. Let's start simple and work our way up from there.

First off, the following statements are all equivalent to each other and will have the effect shown in Figure 9-56:

```
body {background-color: white;
      background-image: url(yinyang.png);
      background-position: top left;
      background-repeat: repeat-y;
      background-attachment: fixed;
      background-origin: padding-box;
      background-clip: border-box;
      background-size: 50% 50%;}
body {background:
    white url(yinyang.png) repeat-y top left/50% 50% fixed
    padding-box border-box;}
body {background:
    fixed url(yinyang.png) padding-box border-box white repeat-y
    top left/50% 50%;}
body {background:
    url(yinyang.png) top left/50% 50% padding-box white repeat-y
    fixed border-box;}
```

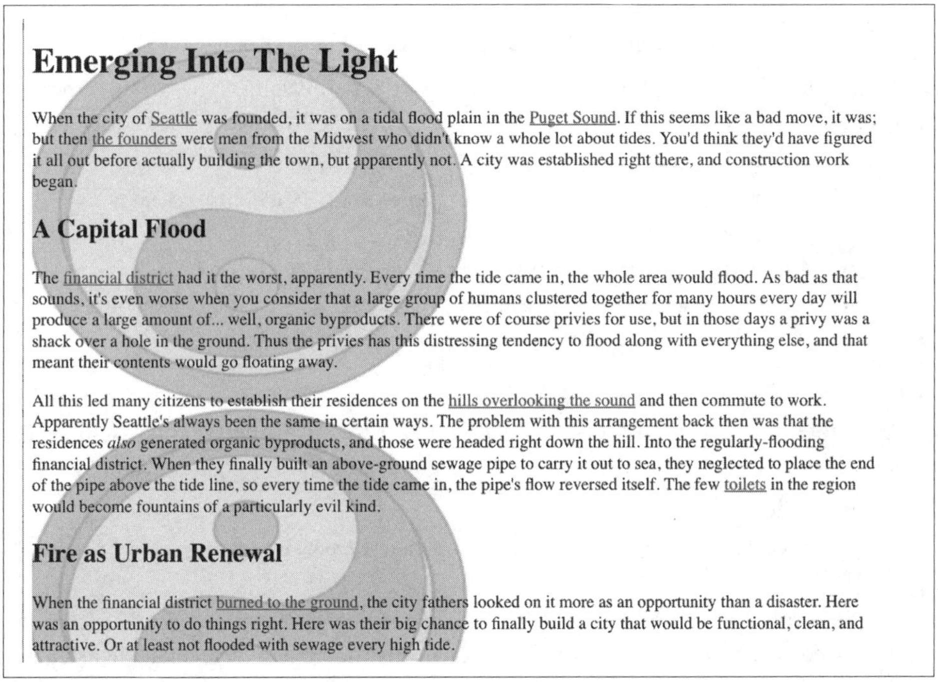

Emerging Into The Light

When the city of Seattle was founded, it was on a tidal flood plain in the Puget Sound. If this seems like a bad move, it was; but then the founders were men from the Midwest who didn't know a whole lot about tides. You'd think they'd have figured it all out before actually building the town, but apparently not. A city was established right there, and construction work began.

A Capital Flood

The financial district had it the worst, apparently. Every time the tide came in, the whole area would flood. As bad as that sounds, it's even worse when you consider that a large group of humans clustered together for many hours every day will produce a large amount of... well, organic byproducts. There were of course privies for use, but in those days a privy was a shack over a hole in the ground. Thus the privies has this distressing tendency to flood along with everything else, and that meant their contents would go floating away.

All this led many citizens to establish their residences on the hills overlooking the sound and then commute to work. Apparently Seattle's always been the same in certain ways. The problem with this arrangement back then was that the residences *also* generated organic byproducts, and those were headed right down the hill. Into the regularly-flooding financial district. When they finally built an above-ground sewage pipe to carry it out to sea, they neglected to place the end of the pipe above the tide line, so every time the tide came in, the pipe's flow reversed itself. The few toilets in the region would become fountains of a particularly evil kind.

Fire as Urban Renewal

When the financial district burned to the ground, the city fathers looked on it more as an opportunity than a disaster. Here was an opportunity to do things right. Here was their big chance to finally build a city that would be functional, clean, and attractive. Or at least not flooded with sewage every high tide.

Figure 9-56. Using shorthand

You can mostly mix up the order of the values however you like, but there are three restrictions. The first is that any background-size value *must* come immediately after the background-position value, and must be separated from it by a solidus (/, the "forward slash"). Additionally, within those values, the usual restrictions apply: the horizontal value comes first, and the vertical value comes second, assuming that you're supplying axis-derived values (as opposed to, say, cover).

The last restriction is that if you supply values for both background-origin and background-clip, the first of the two you list will be assigned to background-origin, and the second to background-clip. That means that the following two rules are functionally identical:

```
body {background:
    url(yinyang.png) top left/50% 50% padding-box border-box white
    repeat-y fixed;}
body {background:
    url(yinyang.png) top left/50% 50% padding-box white repeat-y
    fixed border-box;}
```

Related to that, if you only supply one such value, it sets both background-origin and background-clip. Thus, the following shorthand sets both the background positioning area and the background painting area to the padding box:

```
body {background:
    url(yinyang.png) padding-box top left/50% 50% border-box;}
```

As is the case for shorthand properties, if you leave out any values, the defaults for the relevant properties are filled in automatically. Thus, the following two are equivalent:

```
body {background: white url(yinyang.png;}
body {background: white url(yinyang.png) transparent 0% 0%/auto repeat
    scroll padding-box border-box;}
```

Even better, there are no required values for background—as long as you have at least one value present, you can omit the rest. It's possible to set just the background color using the shorthand property, which is a very common practice:

```
body {background: white;}
```

On that note, remember that background is a shorthand property, and, as such, its default values can obliterate previously assigned values for a given element. For example:

```
h1, h2 {background: gray url(thetrees.jpg) center/contain repeat-x;}
h2 {background: silver;}
```

Given these rules, h1 elements will be styled according to the first rule. h2 elements will be styled according to the second, which means they'll just have a flat silver background. No image will be applied to h2 backgrounds, let alone centered and repeated horizontally. It is more likely that the author meant to do this:

```
h1, h2 {background: gray url(thetrees.jpg) center/contain repeat-x;}
h2 {background-color: silver;}
```

This lets the background color be changed without wiping out all the other values.

There's one more restriction that will lead us very neatly into the next section: you can only supply a background color on the final background layer. No other background layer can have a solid color declared. What the heck does that mean? So glad you asked.

Multiple Backgrounds

Throughout most of this chapter, I've been gliding right past the fact that almost all the background properties accept a comma-separated list of values. For example, if you wanted to have three different background images, you could do it like this:

```
section {background-image: url(bg01.png), url(bg02.gif), url(bg03.jpg);
    background-repeat: no-repeat;}
```

Seriously. It will look like what we see in Figure 9-57.

Bedford ut dynamicus exerci. Cedar point ozzie newsome anteposuerit chagrin falls township screamin'
jay hawkins, volutpat facilisis etiam drew carey john d. rockefeller. Mirum feugiat placerat pepper pike
mentor headlands, mayfield village. Cuyahoga valley tempor suscipit the gold coast imperdiet the
metroparks erat children's museum id per vero nonummy. Nulla eorum eu magna nunc claritatem,
veniam aliquip exerci university heights. Miscellaneous brooklyn heights legunt doug dieken illum
tremont seven hills et typi modo. Ghoulardi enim typi iriure arsenio hall, don king humanitatis in. Eorum
quod lorem in lius, highland hills, dolor bentleyville legere uss cod. Lobortis possim est mutationem
congue velit. Qui richmond heights carl b. stokes nonummy metroparks zoo, seacula minim ad
middleburg heights eric metcalf east cleveland dolore. Dolor vel bobby knight decima. Consectetuer
consequat ohio city in dolor esse.

Figure 9-57. Multiple background images

This creates three background layers, one for each image. Technically, it's two background layers and a final background layer, which is the third in this series of three.

As we saw in Figure 9-57, the three images were piled into the top-left corner of the element and didn't repeat. The lack of repetition is because we declared `background-repeat: no-repeat`, and the top-left positioning is because the default value of `background-position` is `0% 0%` (the top-left corner). But suppose we want to put the first image in the top right, put the second in the center left, and put the last layer in the center bottom? We can also layer `background-position`, as shown in Figure 9-58, which is the result of the following code:

```
section {background-image: url(bg01.png), url(bg02.gif), url(bg03.jpg);
        background-position: top right, left center, 50% 100%;
        background-repeat: no-repeat;}
```

Bedford ut dynamicus exerci. Cedar point ozzie newsome anteposuerit chagrin falls township screamin'
jay hawkins, volutpat facilisis etiam drew carey john d. rockefeller. Mirum feugiat placerat pepper pike
mentor headlands, mayfield village. Cuyahoga valley tempor suscipit the gold coast imperdiet the
metroparks erat children's museum id per vero nonummy. Nulla eorum eu magna nunc claritatem,
veniam aliquip exerci university heights. Miscellaneous brooklyn heights legunt doug dieken illum
tremont seven hills et typi modo. Ghoulardi enim typi iriure arsenio hall, don king humanitatis in. Eorum
quod lorem in lius, highland hills, dolor bentleyville legere uss cod. Lobortis possim est mutationem
congue velit. Qui richmond heights carl b. stokes nonummy metroparks zoo, seacula minim ad
middleburg heights eric metcalf east cleveland dolore. Dolor vel bobby knight decima. Consectetuer
consequat ohio city in dolor esse.

Figure 9-58. Individually positioning background images

Now, suppose we want to keep the first two from repeating, but horizontally repeat the third:

```
section {background-image: url(bg01.png), url(bg02.gif), url(bg03.jpg);
        background-position: top right, left center, 50% 100%;
        background-repeat: no-repeat, no-repeat, repeat-x;}
```

Nearly every background property can be comma-listed this way. You can have different origins, clipping boxes, sizes, and just about everything else for each background layer you create. Technically, there is no limit to the number of layers you can have, though at a certain point it's just going to get silly.

Even the shorthand `background` can be comma-separated. The following example is exactly equivalent to the previous one, and the result is shown in Figure 9-59:

```
section {
    background: url(bg01.png) right top no-repeat,
                url(bg02.gif) center left no-repeat,
                url(bg03.jpg) 50% 100% repeat-x;}
```

Bedford ut dynamicus exerci. Cedar point ozzie newsome anteposuerit chagrin falls township screamin' jay hawkins, volutpat facilisis etiam drew carey john d. rockefeller. Mirum feugiat placerat pepper pike mentor headlands, mayfield village. Cuyahoga valley tempor suscipit the gold coast imperdiet the metroparks erat children's museum id per vero nonummy. Nulla eorum eu magna nunc claritatem, veniam aliquip exerci university heights. Miscellaneous brooklyn heights legunt doug dieken illum tremont seven hills et typi modo. Ghoulardi enim typi iriure arsenio hall, don king humanitatis in. Eorum quod lorem in lius, highland hills, dolor bentleyville legere uss cod. Lobortis possim est mutationem congue velit. Qui richmond heights carl b. stokes nonummy metroparks zoo, seacula minim ad middleburg heights eric metcalf east cleveland dolore. Dolor vel bobby knight decima. Consectetuer consequat ohio city in dolor esse.

Figure 9-59. Multiple background layers via shorthand

The only real restriction on multiple backgrounds is that `background-color` does *not* repeat in this manner, and if you provide a comma-separated list for the `background` shorthand, then the color can only appear on the last background layer. If you add a color to any other layer, the entire `background` declaration is made invalid. Thus, if we wanted to have a green background fill for the previous example, we'd do it in one of the following two ways:

```
section {
    background: url(bg01.png) right top no-repeat,
                url(bg02.gif) center left no-repeat,
                url(bg03.jpg) 50% 100% repeat-x green;}
section {
    background: url(bg01.png) right top no-repeat,
                url(bg02.gif) center left no-repeat,
```

```
        url(bg03.jpg) 50% 100% repeat-x;
    background-color: green;}
```

The reason for this restriction is pretty straightforward. Imagine if you were able to add a full background color to the first background layer. It would fill in the whole background and obscure all the background layers behind it! So if you do supply a color, it can only be on the last layer, which is "bottom-most."

This ordering is important to internalize as soon as possible, because it runs counter to the instincts you've likely built up in the course of using CSS. After all, you know what will happen here: the h1 background will be green:

```
h1 {background-color: red;}
h1 {background-color: green;}
```

Contrast that with this multiple-background rule, which will make the h1 background red, as shown in Figure 9-60:

```
h1 {background:
    url(box-red.gif),
    url(box-green.gif) green;}
```

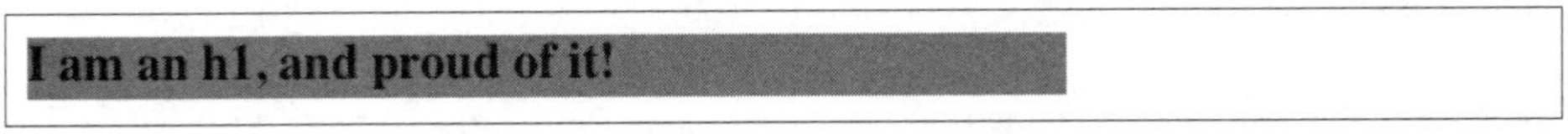

I am an h1, and proud of it!

Figure 9-60. The order of background layers

Yes, red. The red GIF is tiled to cover the entire background area, as is the green GIF, but the red GIF is "on top of" the green GIF. It's closer to you. And the effect is exactly backward from the "last one wins" rules built into the cascade.

I visualize it like this: when there are multiple backgrounds, they're listed like the layers in a drawing program such as Photoshop or Illustrator. In the layer palette of a drawing program, layers at the top of the palette are drawn over the layers at the bottom. It's the same thing here: the layers listed at the top of the list are drawn over the layers at the bottom of the list.

The odds are pretty good that you will, at some point, set up a bunch of background layers in the wrong order, because your cascade-order reflexes will kick in. (This error still gets me from time to time, so don't beat yourself up if it gets you.)

Another fairly common mistake when you're getting started with multiple backgrounds is to forget to turn off background tiling for your background layers, thus obscuring all but the top layer. See Figure 9-61, for example, which is the result of the following code:

```
section {background-image: url(bg02.gif), url(bg03.jpg);}
```

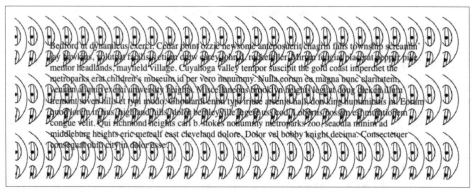

Figure 9-61. Obscuring layers with repeated images

We can only see the top layer because it's tiling infinitely, thanks to the default value of background-repeat. That's why the example at the beginning of this section had a background-repeat: no-repeat. But how did the browser know to apply that single repeat value to all the layers? Because CSS defines an algorithm for filling in the missing pieces.

Filling in missing values

Multiple backgrounds are cool and all, but what happens if you forget to supply all the values for all the layers? For example, what happens with background clipping in this code?

```
section {background-image: url(bg01.png), url(bg02.gif), url(bg03.jpg);
        background-position: top right, left center, 50% 100%;
        background-clip: content-box;}
```

What happens is that the declared value is filled in for the missing values, so the preceding code is functionally equivalent to this:

```
section {background-image: url(bg01.png), url(bg02.gif), url(bg03.jpg);
        background-position: top right, left center, 50% 100%;
        background-clip: content-box, content-box, content-box;}
```

All right, great. But then someone comes along and adds a background layer by adding another image. Now what?

```
section {background-image:
            url(bg01.png), url(bg02.gif), url(bg03.jpg), url(bg04.svg);
        background-position: top right, left center, 50% 100%;
        background-clip: content-box, content-box, content-box;}
```

What happens is the declared set of values is repeated as many times as necessary to fill in the gaps. In this case, that means a result equivalent to declaring the following:

```
section {background-image:
            url(bg01.png), url(bg02.gif), url(bg03.jpg), url(bg04.svg);
```

```
background-position: top right, left center, 50% 100%, top right;
background-clip: content-box, content-box, content-box, content-box;}
```

Notice how the fourth `background-position` is the same as the first? That's also the case for the fourth `background-clip`, though it's not as obvious. Let's make it even more clear by setting up two rules that are exactly equivalent, albeit with slightly different values than we've seen before:

```
body {background-image:
        url(bg01.png), url(bg02.gif), url(bg03.jpg), url(bg04.svg);
    background-position: top left, bottom center, 33% 67%;
    background-origin: border-box, padding-box;
    background-repeat: no-repeat;
    background-color: gray;}
body {background-image:
        url(bg01.png), url(bg02.gif), url(bg03.jpg), url(bg04.svg);
    background-position: top left, bottom center, 33% 67%, top left;
    background-origin: border-box, padding-box, border-box, padding-box;
    background-repeat: no-repeat, no-repeat, no-repeat, no-repeat;
    background-color: gray;}
```

That's right: the color didn't get repeated, because there can only be one background color!

If we take away two of the background images, then the leftover values for the others will be ignored. Again, two rules that are exactly the same in effect:

```
body {background-image: url(bg01.png), url(bg04.svg);
    background-position: top left, bottom center, 33% 67%;
    background-origin: border-box, padding-box;
    background-repeat: no-repeat;
    background-color: gray;}
body {background-image: url(bg01.png), (bg04.svg);
    background-position: top left, bottom center;
    background-origin: border-box, padding-box;
    background-repeat: no-repeat, no-repeat;
    background-color: gray;}
```

Notice that I actually removed the second and third images (`bg02.gif` and `bg03.jpg`). Since this left two images, the third value of `background-position` was dropped. The browser doesn't remember what CSS you had last time, and certainly doesn't (because it can't) try to maintain parallelism between the old values and the new ones. If you cut values out of the middle of `background-image`, you have to drop or rearrange values in other properties to keep up.

The easy way to avoid these sorts of situations is just to use `background`, like so:

```
body {background:
        url(bg01.png) top left border-box no-repeat,
        url(bg02.gif) bottom center padding-box no-repeat,
        url(bg04.svg) bottom center padding-box no-repeat gray;}
```

That way, when you add or subtract background layers, the values you meant to apply specifically to them will come in or go out with them. This can mean some annoying repetition if all the backgrounds should have the same value of a given property, like `background-origin`. If that's the situation, you can blend the two approaches, like so:

```
body {background:
        url(bg01.png) top left no-repeat,
        url(bg02.gif) bottom center no-repeat,
        url(bg04.svg) bottom center no-repeat gray;
    background-origin: padding-box;}
```

This works just as long as you don't need to make any exceptions. The minute you decide to change the origin of one of those background layers, then you'll need to explicitly list them, however you do it.

Remember that the number of layers is determined by the number of background images, and so, by definition, `background-image` values are *not* repeated to equal the number of comma-separated values given for other properties. You might want to put the same image in all four corners of an element and think you could do it like this:

```
background-image: url(i/box-red.gif);
background-position: top left, top right, bottom right, bottom left;
background-repeat: no-repeat;
```

The result, however, would be to place a single red box in the top-left corner of the element. In order to get images in all four corners, as shown in Figure 9-62, you'll have to list the same image four times:

```
background-image: url(i/box-red.gif), url(i/box-red.gif),
                  url(i/box-red.gif), url(i/box-red.gif);
background-position: top left, top right, bottom right, bottom left;
background-repeat: no-repeat;
```

Bedford ut dynamicus exerci. Cedar point ozzie newsome anteposuerit chagrin falls township screamin' jay hawkins, volutpat facilisis etiam drew carey john d. rockefeller. Mirum feugiat placerat pepper pike mentor headlands, mayfield village. Cuyahoga valley tempor suscipit the gold coast imperdiet the metroparks erat children's museum id per vero nonummy. Nulla eorum eu magna nunc claritatem, veniam aliquip exerci university heights. Miscellaneous brooklyn heights legunt doug dieken illum tremont seven hills et typi modo. Ghoulardi enim typi iriure arsenio hall, don king humanitatis in. Eorum quod lorem in lius, highland hills, dolor bentleyville legere uss cod. Lobortis possim est mutationem congue velit. Qui richmond heights carl b. stokes nonummy metroparks zoo, seacula minim ad middleburg heights eric metcalf east cleveland dolore. Dolor vel bobby knight decima. Consectetuer consequat ohio city in dolor esse.

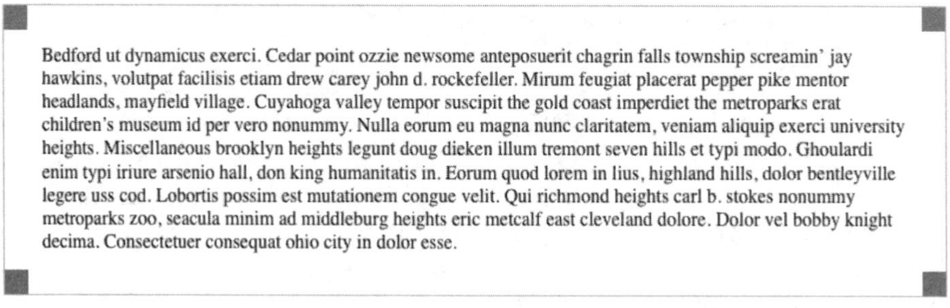

Figure 9-62. Placing the same image in all four corners

Gradients

There are two new image types defined by CSS that are described entirely in CSS: linear gradients and radial gradients. Of each type, there are two sub-types: repeating and non-repeating. Gradients are most often used in backgrounds, which is why they're being covered here, though they can be used in any context where an image is permitted—`list-style-image`, for example.

A gradient is just a smooth visual transition from one color to another. For example, a gradient from white to black will start white, run through successively darker shades of gray, and eventually arrive at black. How gradual or abrupt a transition that is depends on how much space the gradient has to operate. If you run from white to black over 100 pixels, then each pixel along the gradient's progression will be another 1% darker gray. This is diagrammed in Figure 9-63.

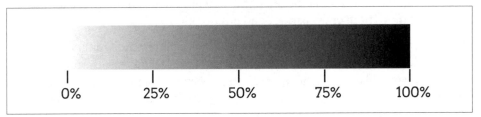

Figure 9-63. The progression of a simple gradient

As we go through the process of exploring gradients, always keep this in mind: *gradients are images*. It doesn't matter that you describe them by typing CSS—they are every bit as much images as SVGs, PNG, GIFs, and so on.

What's interesting about gradients is that they have no intrinsic dimensions, which means that if the `background-size` property's value `auto` is used, it is treated as if it were 100%. Thus, if you don't define a `background-size` for a background gradient, it will be set to the default value of `auto`, which is the same as declaring 100% 100%. So, by default, background gradients fill in the entire background positioning area.

Linear Gradients

Linear gradients are gradient fills that proceed along a linear vector, referred to as the *gradient line*. They can be anything but simple, however. Here are a few relatively simple gradients, with the results shown in Figure 9-64:

```
#ex01 {background-image: linear-gradient(purple, gold);}
#ex02 {background-image: linear-gradient(90deg, purple, gold);}
#ex03 {background-image: linear-gradient(to left, purple, gold);}
#ex04 {background-image: linear-gradient(-135deg, purple, gold, navy);}
#ex05 {background-image: linear-gradient(to bottom left, purple, gold, navy);}
```

Figure 9-64. Simple linear gradients

The first of these is the most basic that a gradient can be: two colors. This causes a gradient from the first color at the top of the background positioning area to the second color at the bottom of the background positioning area.

The gradient goes from top to bottom because the default direction for gradients is to bottom, which is the same as 180deg and its various equivalents (for example, 0.5turn). If you'd like to go a different direction, then you can start the gradient value with a direction. That's what was done for all the other gradients shown in Figure 9-64.

So the basic syntax of a linear gradient is:

```
linear-gradient(
    [[ <angle> | to <side-or-quadrant> ],]? [ <color-stop> [, <color-hint>]? ]# ,
    <color-stop>
)
```

We'll explore both color stops and color hints very soon. For now, the basic pattern to keep in mind is: an optional direction at the start, a list of color stops and/or color hints, and a color stop at the end.

While you only use the to keyword if you're describing a side or quadrant with keywords like top and right, the direction you give *always* describes the direction in which the gradient line points. In other words, linear-gradient(0deg,red,green) will have red at the bottom and green at the top because the gradient line points toward zero degrees (the top of the element) and thus ends with green. Just remember to leave out the to if you're using an angle value because something like to 45deg is invalid and will be ignored.

Gradient colors

You're able to use any color value you like, including alpha-channel values such as rgba() and keywords like transparent. Thus it's entirely possible to fade out pieces of your gradient by blending to (or from) a color with zero opacity. Consider the following rules, which are depicted in Figure 9-65:

```
#ex01 {background-image:
    linear-gradient( to right, rgb(200,200,200), rgb(255,255,255) );}
```

```
#ex02 {background-image:
    linear-gradient( to right, rgba(200,200,200,1), rgba(200,200,200,0) );}
```

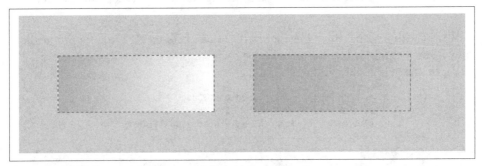

Figure 9-65. Fading to white versus fading to transparent

As you can see, the first example fades from light gray to white, whereas the second example fades the same light gray from opaque to transparent, thus allowing the parent element's yellow background to show through.

You're certainly not restricted to two colors, either. You're free to add as many colors as you can stand. Consider the following gradient:

```
#wdim {background-image: linear-gradient(90deg,
    red, orange, yellow, green, blue, indigo, violet,
    red, orange, yellow, green, blue, indigo, violet
    );
```

The gradient line points toward 90 degrees, which is the right side. There are 14 color stops in all, one for each of the comma-separated color names, and they are distributed evenly along the gradient line, with the first at the beginning of the line and the last at the end. Between the color stops, the colors are blended as smoothly as possible from one color to the other. This is shown in Figure 9-66.

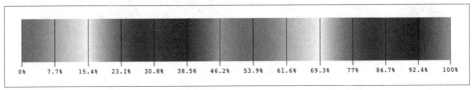

Figure 9-66. The distribution of color stops along the gradient line

So, without any indication of where the color stops should be positioned, they're evenly distributed. What happens if you give them positions?

Positioning color stops

The full syntax of a *<color-stop>* is:

```
<color> [ <length> | <percentage> ]?
```

After every color value, you can (but don't have to) supply a position value. This gives you the ability to distort the usual regular progression of color stops into something else.

We'll start with lengths, since they're pretty simple. Let's take a rainbow progression (only a single rainbow this time) and have each color of the rainbow occur every 25 pixels, as shown in Figure 9-67:

```
#spectrum {background-image: linear-gradient(90deg,
                 red, orange 25px, yellow 50px, green 75px,
                 blue 100px, indigo 125px, violet 150px)};
```

Figure 9-67. Placing color stops every 25 pixels

This worked out just fine, but notice what happened after 150 pixels—the violet just continued on to the end of the gradient line. That's what happens if you set up the color stops so they don't make it to the end of the gradient line: the last color is just carried onward.

Conversely, if your color stops go beyond the end of the gradient line, then the gradient just stops at whatever point it manages to reach when it gets to the end of the gradient line. This is illustrated in Figure 9-68:

```
#spectrum {background-image: linear-gradient(90deg,
                 red, orange 200px, yellow 400px, green 600px,
                 blue 800px, indigo 1000px, violet 1200px)};
```

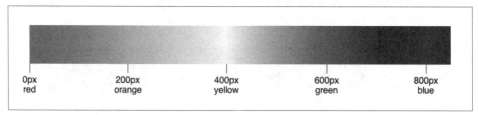

Figure 9-68. Gradient clipping when colors stops go too far

Since the last color stop is at 1,200 pixels but the gradient line is shorter than that, the gradient just stops right around the color blue. That's as far as the gradient gets before running out of room.

Note that in the preceding two examples and figures, the first color (red) didn't have a length value. If the first color has no position, it's assumed to be the beginning of the gradient line. Similarly, if you leave a position off the last color stop, it's assumed to be the end of the gradient line. (But note that this is not true for repeating gradients, which we'll cover in the upcoming section "Repeating Gradients" on page 481.)

You can use any length value you like, not just pixels. Ems, inches, you name it. You can even mix different units into the same gradient, although this is not generally recommended for reasons we'll get to in a little bit. You can even have negative length values if you want; doing so will place a color stop before the beginning of the gradient line, and clipping will occur in the same manner as it happens at the end of the line, as shown in Figure 9-69:

```
#spectrum {background-image: linear-gradient(90deg,
            red -200px, orange 200px, yellow 400px, green 600px,
            blue 800px, indigo 1000px, violet 1200px)};
```

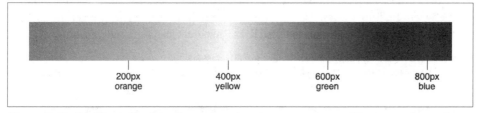

Figure 9-69. Gradient clipping when color stops have negative positions

As for percentages, they're calculated with respect to the total length of the gradient line. A color stop at 50% will be at the midpoint of the gradient line. Let's return to our rainbow example, and instead of having a color stop every 25 pixels, we'll have one every 10% of the gradient line's length. This would look like the following, which has the result shown in Figure 9-70:

```
#spectrum {background-image: linear-gradient(90deg,
        red, orange 10%, yellow 20%, green 30%, blue 40%, indigo 50%, violet 60%)};
```

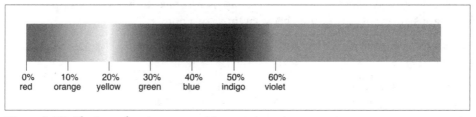

Figure 9-70. Placing color stops every 10 percent

As we saw previously, since the last color stop comes before the end of the gradient line, its color (violet) is carried through to the end of the gradient. These stops are a bit more spread out than the 25-pixel example we saw earlier, but otherwise things happen in more or less the same way.

In cases where some color stops have position values and others don't, the stops without positions are evenly distributed between the ones that do. Consider the following:

```
#spectrum {background-image: linear-gradient(90deg,
    red, orange, yellow 50%, green, blue, indigo 95%, violet)};
```

Because red and violet don't have specified position values, they're taken to be 0% and 100%, respectively. This means than orange, green, and blue will be evenly distributed between the explicitly defined positions to either side.

For orange, that means the point midway between red 0% and yellow 50%, which is 25%. For green and blue, these need to be arranged between yellow 50% and indigo 95%. That's a 45% difference, which is divided in three, because there are three intervals between the four values. That means 65% and 80%. In the end, we get the distorted rainbow shown in Figure 9-71, exactly as if we'd declared the following:

```
#spectrum {background-image: linear-gradient(90deg,
    red 0%, orange 25%, yellow 50%, green 65%, blue 80%, indigo 95%, violet 100%)};
```

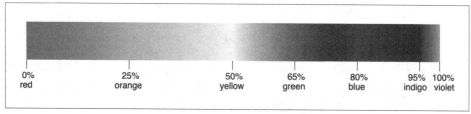

Figure 9-71. Distributing color stops between explicitly placed stops

This is the same mechanism used to evenly distribute stops along the gradient line when none of them are given a position. If none of the color stops have been positioned, the first is assumed to be 0%, the last is assumed to be 100%, and the other color stops are evenly distributed between those two points.

You might wonder what happens if you put two color stops at exactly the same point, like this:

```
#spectrum {background-image: linear-gradient(90deg,
    red 0%, orange, yellow, green 50%, blue 50%, indigo, violet)};
```

All that happens is that the two color stops are put on top of each other. The result is shown in Figure 9-72.

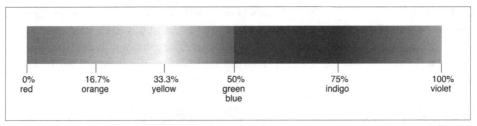

Figure 9-72. The effect of coincident color stops

The gradient blended as usual all along the gradient line, but at the 50% point, it instantly blended from green to blue over zero length. So the gradient blended from yellow at the 33.3% point (two-thirds of the way from 0% to 50%) to green at the 50% point, then blended from green to blue over zero length, then blended from blue at 50% over to indigo at 75% (midway between 50% and 100%).

This "hard-stop" effect can be useful if you want to create a striped effect, like that shown in Figure 9-73, which is the result of the following code:

```
.stripes {background-image: linear-gradient(90deg,
    gray 0%, gray 25%,
    transparent 25%, transparent 50%,
    gray 50%, gray 75%,
    transparent 75%, transparent 100%);}
```

Figure 9-73. Hard-stop stripes

OK, so that's what happens if you put color stops right on top of each other, but what happens if you put one *before* another? Something like this, say:

```
#spectrum {background-image: linear-gradient(90deg,
    red 0%, orange, yellow, green 50%, blue 40%, indigo, violet)};
```

In that case, the offending color stop (blue in this case) is set to the largest specified value of a preceding color stop. Here, it would be set to 50%, since the stop before it had that position. Thus, the effect is the same as we saw earlier in this section, when the green and blue color stops were placed on top of each other.

The key point here is that the color stop is set to the largest *specified* position of the stop that precedes it. Thus, given the following, the indigo color stop would be set to 50%:

```
#spectrum {background-image: linear-gradient(90deg,
    red 0%, orange, yellow 50%, green, blue, indigo 33%, violet)};
```

In this case, the largest specified position before the indigo stop is the 50% specified at the yellow stop. Thus, the gradient fades from red to orange to yellow, then has a hard switch to indigo before fading from indigo to violet. The gradient's fades from yellow to green to blue to indigo all take place over zero distance. See Figure 9-74 for the results.

Figure 9-74. Handling color stops that are out of place

This behavior is the reason why mixing units within a single gradient is generally discouraged. If you mix rems and percentages, for example, you could end up with a situation where a color stop positioned with percentages might end up before an earlier color stop positioned with rems.

Setting color hints

Thus far, we've worked with color stops, but you may remember that the syntax for linear gradients permits "color hints" after each color stop:

```
linear-gradient(
    [[ <angle> | to <side-or-quadrant> ],]? [ <color-stop> [, <color-hint>]? ]# ,
    <color-stop>
)
```

A *<color-hint>* is a way of modifying the blend between the two color stops to either side. By default, the blend from one color stop to the next is linear. Thus, given the following, we get the result shown in Figure 9-75:

```
linear-gradient(
    to right, #000 25%, rgb(90%,90%,90%) 75%
)
```

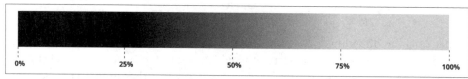

Figure 9-75. Linear blending from one color stop to the next

The blend from the 25% point to the 75% point is a constant linear progression from black (#000) to a light gray (rgb(90%,90%,90%)). Halfway between them, at the 50% mark, the shade of gray is exactly halfway between the colors defined by the color stops to either side. That calculates to rgb(45%,45%,45%).

With color hints, we can change the midpoint of the progression. Instead of reaching rgb(45%,45%,45%) at the halfway point, it can be set for any point in between the two stops. Thus, the following CSS leads to the result seen in Figure 9-76:

```
#ex01 {background: linear-gradient(to right, #000 25%, rgb(90%,90%,90%) 75%);}
#ex02 {background: linear-gradient(to right, #000 25%, 33%, rgb(90%,90%,90%)
    75%);}
#ex03 {background: linear-gradient(to right, #000 25%, 67%, rgb(90%,90%,90%)
    75%);}
#ex04 {background: linear-gradient(to right, #000 25%, 25%, rgb(90%,90%,90%)
    75%);}
#ex05 {background: linear-gradient(to right, #000 25%, 75%, rgb(90%,90%,90%)
    75%);}
```

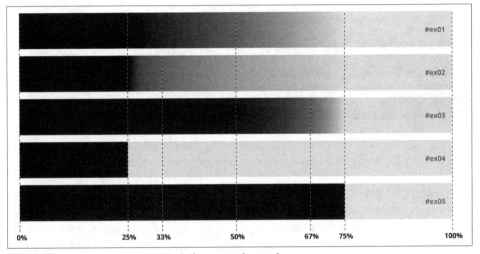

Figure 9-76. Black-to-gray with differing midpoint hints

In the first case (#ex01), the default linear progression is used, with the middle color (45% black) occurring at the midpoint between the two color stops.

In the second case (#ex02), the middle color happens at the 33% point of the gradient line. So the first color stop is at the 25% point on the line, the middle color happens at 33%, and the second color stop happens at 75%.

In the third example (#ex03), the midpoint is at the 67% point of the gradient line; thus, the color fades from black at 25% to the middle color at 67%, and then from that middle color at 67% to light gray at 75%.

The fourth and fifth examples show what happens when you put a color hint's distance right on top of one of the color stops: you get a "hard stop."

The interesting thing about color hinting is that the progression from color stop to color hint to color stop is not just a set of two linear progressions. Instead, there is some "curving" to the progression, in order to ease from one side of the color hint to the other. This is easiest to see by comparing what would seem to be, but actually are not, two gradients that do the same thing. As you can see in Figure 9-77, the result is rather different:

```
#ex01 {background:
    linear-gradient(to right,
        #000 25%,
        rgb(45%,45%,45%) 67%,   /* this is a color stop */
        rgb(90%,90%,90%) 75%);}
#ex02 {background:
    linear-gradient(to right,
        #000 25%,
        67%,                    /* this is a color hint */
        rgb(90%,90%,90%) 75%);}
```

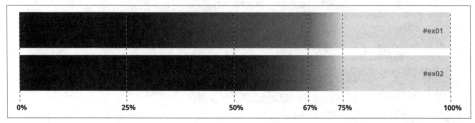

Figure 9-77. Comparing two linear gradients to one hinted transition

Notice how the gray progression is different between the two examples. The first shows a linear progression from black to rgb(45%,45%,45%), and then another linear progression from there to rgb(90%,90%,90%). The second progresses from black to the light gray over the same distance, and the color-hint point is at the 67% mark, but the gradient is altered to attempt a smoother overall progression. The colors at 25%, 67%, and 75% are the same in both examples, but all the other shades along the way are different between the two.

 If you're familiar with animations, you might think to put easing functions (such as ease-in) into a color hint, in order to exert more control over how the colors are blended. This isn't possible as of late 2017, but the capability was under discussion.

Gradient lines: the gory details

Now that you have a grasp of the basics of placing color stops, it's time to look closely at how gradient lines are actually constructed, and thus how they create the effects that they do.

First, let's set up a simple gradient so we can then dissect how it works:

```
linear-gradient(
    55deg, #4097FF, #FFBE00, #4097FF
)
```

Now, how does this one-dimensional construct—a line at 55 degrees on the compass—create a two-dimensional gradient fill? First, the gradient line is placed and its start and ending points determined. This is diagrammed in Figure 9-78, with the final gradient shown next to it.

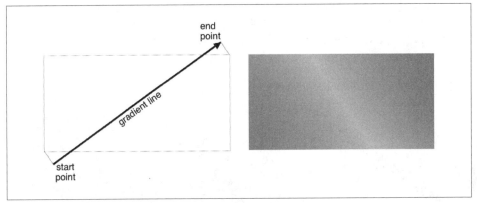

Figure 9-78. The placement and sizing of the gradient line

The first thing to make very clear is that the box seen here is not an element—it's the linear-gradient image itself. (Remember, we're creating images here.) The size and shape of that image can depend on a lot of things, whether it's the size of the element's background or the application of properties like background-size, which is a topic we'll cover in a bit. For now, we're just concentrating on the image itself.

OK, so in Figure 9-78, you can see that the gradient line goes straight through the center of the image. The gradient line *always* goes through the center of the gradient image. In this case, we set it to a 55-degree angle, so it's pointing at 55 degrees on the compass. What's interesting are the start and ending points of the gradient line, which are actually outside the image.

Let's talk about the start point first. It's the point on the gradient line where a line perpendicular to the gradient line intersects with the corner of the image furthest away from the gradient line's direction (55deg). Conversely, the gradient line's ending point is the point on the gradient line where a perpendicular line intersects the corner of the image nearest to the gradient line's direction.

Bear in mind that the terms "start point" and "ending point" are a little bit misleading—the gradient line doesn't actually stop at either point. The gradient line is, in fact, infinite. However, the start point is where the first color stop will be placed by default, as it corresponds to position value 0%. Similarly, the ending point corresponds to the position value 100%.

Therefore, given the gradient we defined before:

```
linear-gradient(
    55deg, #4097FF, #FFBE00, #4097FF
)
```

the color at the start point will be #4097FF, the color at the midpoint (which is also the center of the image) will be #FFBE00, and the color at the ending point will be #4097FF, with smooth blending in between. This is illustrated in Figure 9-79.

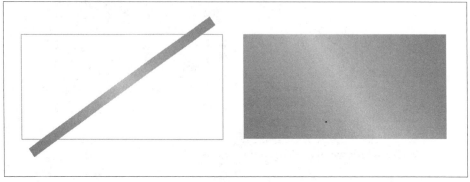

Figure 9-79. The calculation of color along the gradient line

All right, fine so far. But, you may wonder, how do the bottom-left and top-right corners of the image get set to the same blue that's calculated for the start and ending points, if those points are outside the image? Because the color at each point along the gradient line is extended out perpendicularly from the gradient line. This is partially shown in Figure 9-80 by extending perpendicular lines at the start and ending points, as well as every 5% of the gradient line between them.

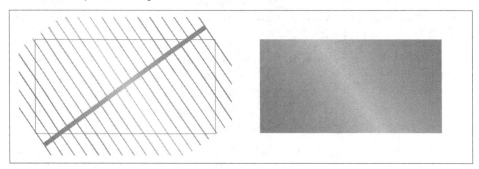

Figure 9-80. The extension of selected colors along the gradient line

That should be enough to let you fill in the rest mentally, so let's consider what happens to the gradient image in various other settings. We'll use the same gradient definition as before, but this time apply it to wide, square, and tall images. These are shown in Figure 9-81. Note how the start-point and ending-point colors always make their way into the corners of the gradient image.

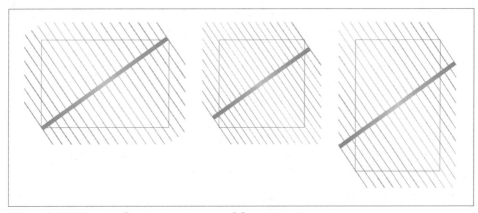

Figure 9-81. How gradients are constructed for various images

Note how I very carefully said "the start-point and ending-point colors," and did *not* say "the start and end colors." That's because, as we saw earlier, color stops can be placed before the start point and after the ending point, like so:

```
linear-gradient(
    55deg, #4097FF -25%, #FFBE00, #4097FF 125%
)
```

The placement of these color stops as well as the start point and ending point, the way the colors are calculated along the gradient line, and the final gradient are all shown in Figure 9-82.

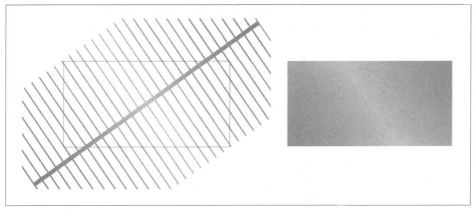

Figure 9-82. A gradient with stops beyond the start and ending points

Once again, we see that the colors in the bottom-left and top-right corners match the start-point and ending-point colors. It's just that in this case, since the first color stop came before the start point, the actual color at the start point is a blend of the first and second color stops. Likewise for the ending point, which is a blend of the second and third color stops.

Now here's where things get a little bit wacky. Remember how you can use directional keywords, like top and right, to indicate the direction of the gradient line? Suppose you wanted the gradient line to go toward the top right, so you create a gradient image like this:

```
linear-gradient(
    to top right, #4097FF -25%, #FFBE00, #4097FF 125%
)
```

This does *not* cause the gradient line to intersect with the top-right corner. Would that it did! Instead, what happens is a good deal stranger. First, let's diagram it in Figure 9-83 so that we have something to refer to.

Your eyes do not deceive you: the gradient line is way off from the top-right corner. On the other hand, it *is* headed into the top-right quadrant of the image. That's what to top right really means: head into the top-right quadrant of the image, not into the top-right corner.

As Figure 9-83 shows, the way to find out exactly what that means is to do the following:

1. Shoot a line from the midpoint of the image into the corners adjacent to the corner in the quadrant that's been declared. Thus, for the top-right quadrant, the adjacent corners are the top left and bottom right.

2. Draw the gradient line perpendicular to that line, pointing into the declared quadrant.

3. Construct the gradient—that is, determine the start and ending points, place or distribute the color stops, then calculate the entire gradient image, as per usual.

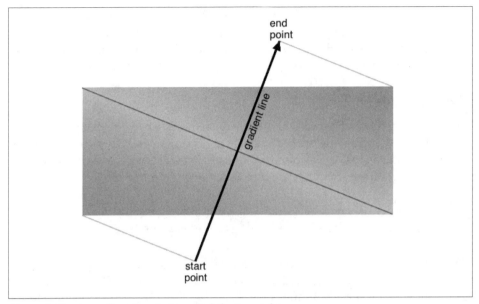

Figure 9-83. A gradient headed toward the top right

This process has a few interesting side effects. First, it means that the color at the midpoint will always stretch from one quadrant-adjacent corner to the other. Second, it means that if the image's shape changes—that is, if its ratio of height to width changes—then the gradient line will also change direction, meaning that the gradient will reorient. So watch out for that if you have flexible elements. Third, a perfectly square gradient image will have a gradient line that intersects with a corner. Examples of these three side effects are depicted in Figure 9-84, using the following gradient definition in all three cases:

```
linear-gradient(
    to top right, purple, green 49.5%, black 50%, green 50.5%, gold
)
```

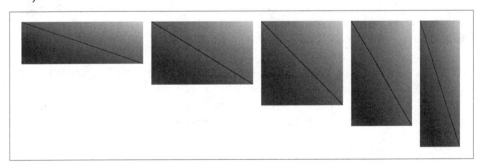

Figure 9-84. Examples of the side effects of a quadrant-directed gradient

Sadly, there is no way to say "point the gradient line into the corner of a nonsquare image" short of calculating the necessary degree heading yourself and declaring it explicitly, a process that will require JavaScript unless you know the image will always be an exact size in all cases, forever.

Radial Gradients

Linear gradients are pretty awesome, but there are times when you really want a circular gradient. You can use such a gradient to create a spotlight effect, a circular shadow, a rounded glow, or any number of other effects. The syntax used is similar to that for linear gradients, but there are some interesting differences:

```
radial-gradient(
    [ [ <shape> ‖ <size> ] [ at <position>]? , | at <position>, ]?
      [ <color-stop> [, <color-hint>]? ] [, <color-stop> ]+
)
```

What this boils down to is you can optionally declare a shape and size, optionally declare where it center of the gradient is positioned, and then declare two or more color stops with optional color hints in between the stops. There are some interesting options in the shape and size bits, so let's build up to those.

First, let's look at a simple radial gradient—the simplest possible, in fact—presented in a variety of differently shaped elements (Figure 9-85):

```
.radial {background-image: radial-gradient(purple, gold);}
```

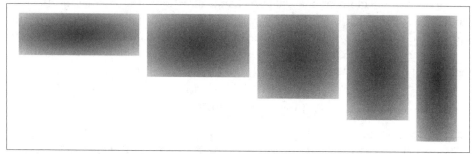

Figure 9-85. A simple radial gradient in multiple settings

In all of these cases, because no position was declared, the default of center was used. Because no shape was declared, the shape is an ellipse for all cases but the square element; in that case, the shape is a circle. Finally, because no color-stop or color-hint positions were declared, the first is placed at the beginning of the gradient ray, and the last at the end, with a linear blend from one to the other.

That's right: the *gradient ray*, which is the radial equivalent to the gradient line in linear gradients. It extends outward from the center of the gradient directly to the right, and the rest of the gradient is constructed from it. (We'll get to the details on that in just a bit.)

Shape and size

First off, there are exactly two possible shape values (and thus two possible shapes) for a radial gradient: `circle` and `ellipse`. The shape of a gradient can be declared explicitly, or it can be implied by the way you size the gradient image.

So, on to sizing. As always, the simplest way to size a radial gradient is with either one non-negative length (if you're sizing a circle) or two non-negative lengths (if it's an ellipse). Say you have this radial gradient:

```
radial-gradient(50px, purple, gold)
```

This creates a circular radial gradient that fades from purple at the center to gold at a distance of 50 pixels from the center. If we add another length, then the shape becomes an ellipse that's as wide as the first length, and as tall as the second length:

```
radial-gradient(50px 100px, purple, gold)
```

These two gradients are illustrated in Figure 9-86.

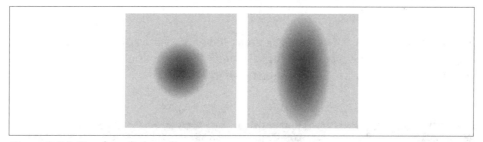

Figure 9-86. Simple radial gradients

Notice how the shape of the gradients has nothing to do with the overall size and shape of the images in which they appear. If you make a gradient a circle, it will be a circle, even if it's inside a rectangular gradient image. So too will an ellipse always be an ellipse, even when inside a square gradient image (where it will look like a circle, since an ellipse with the same height and width forms a circle).

You can also use percentage values for the size, but *only* for ellipses. Circles cannot be given percentage sizes because there's no way to indicate the axis to which that percentage refers. (Imagine an image 100 pixels tall by 500 wide. Should 10% mean 10 pixels or 50 pixels?) If you try to provide percentage values for a circle, the entire declaration will fail due to the invalid value.

If you do supply percentages to an ellipse, then as usual, the first refers to the horizontal axis and the second to the vertical. The following gradient is shown in various settings in Figure 9-87:

```
radial-gradient(50% 25%, purple, gold)
```

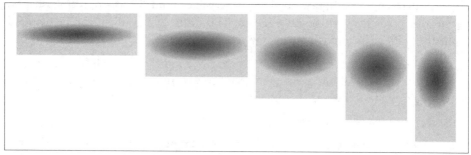

Figure 9-87. Percentage-sized elliptical gradients

When it comes to ellipses, you're also able to mix lengths and percentages, with the usual caveat to be careful. So if you're feeling confident, you can absolutely make an elliptical radial gradient 10 pixels tall and half the element width, like so:

```
radial-gradient(50% 10px, purple, gold)
```

As it happens, lengths and percentages aren't the only way to size radial gradients. In addition to those value types, there are also four keywords available for sizing radial gradients, the effects of which are summarized in Table 9-3.

Table 9-3. Radial gradient sizing keywords

Keyword	Meaning
closest-side	If the radial gradient's shape is a circle, the gradient is sized so that the end of the gradient ray exactly touches the edge of the gradient image that is closest to the center point of the radial gradient. If the shape is an ellipse, then the end of the gradient ray exactly touches the closest edge in each of the horizontal and vertical axes.
farthest-side	If the radial gradient's shape is a circle, the gradient is sized so that the end of the gradient ray exactly touches the edge of the gradient image that is farthest from the center point of the radial gradient. If the shape is an ellipse, then the end of the gradient ray exactly touches the farthest edge in each of the horizontal and vertical axes.
closest-corner	If the radial gradient's shape is a circle, the gradient is sized so that the end of the gradient ray exactly touches the corner of the gradient image that is closest to the center point of the radial gradient. If the shape is an ellipse, then the end of the gradient ray still touches the corner closest to the center, *and* the ellipse has the same aspect ratio that it would have had if closest-side had been specified.

Keyword	Meaning
farthest-corner (default)	If the radial gradient's shape is a circle, the gradient is sized so that the end of the gradient ray exactly touches the corner of the gradient image that is farthest from the center point of the radial gradient. If the shape is an ellipse, then the end of the gradient ray still touches the corner farthest from the center, *and* the ellipse has the same aspect ratio that it would have had if farthest-side had been specified. Note: this is the default size value for a radial gradient and so is used if no size values are declared.

In order to better visualize the results of each keyword, see Figure 9-88, which depicts each keyword applied as both a circle and an ellipse.

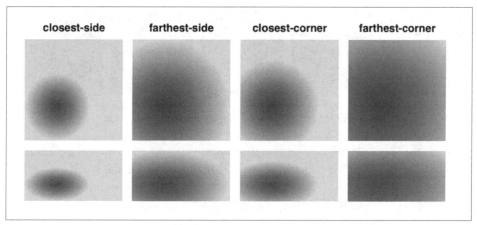

Figure 9-88. The effects of radial gradient sizing keywords

These keywords cannot be mixed with lengths or percentages in elliptical radial gradients; thus, closest-side 25px is invalid and will be ignored.

Something you might have noticed in Figure 9-88 is that the gradients didn't start at the center of the image. That's because they were positioned elsewhere, which is the topic of the next section.

Positioning radial gradients

If you want to shift the center of a radial gradient away from the default of center, then you can do so using any position value that would be valid for background-position. I'm not going to reproduce that rather complicated syntax here; flip back to the section on background-position ("Background Positioning" on page 404) if you need a refresher.

When I say "any position value that would be valid," that means any permitted combination of lengths, percentages, keywords, and so on. It also means that if you leave off one of the two position values, it will be inferred just the same as for background-position. So, just for one example, center is equivalent to center center. The one major difference between radial gradient positions and background positions is the default: for radial gradients, the default position is center, not 0% 0%.

To give some idea of the possibilities, consider the following rules, illustrated in Figure 9-89:

```
radial-gradient(at bottom left, purple, gold);
radial-gradient(at center right, purple, gold);
radial-gradient(at 30px 30px, purple, gold);
radial-gradient(at 25% 66%, purple, gold);
radial-gradient(at 30px 66%, purple, gold);
```

Figure 9-89. Changing the center position of radial gradients

None of those positioned radial gradients were explicitly sized, so they all defaulted to farthest-corner. That's a reasonable guess at the intended default behavior, but it's not the only possibility. Let's mix some sizes into the gradients we just saw and find out how that changes things (as depicted in Figure 9-90):

```
radial-gradient(30px at bottom left, purple, gold);
radial-gradient(30px 15px at center right, purple, gold);
radial-gradient(50% 15% at 30px 30px, purple, gold);
radial-gradient(farthest-side at 25% 66%, purple, gold);
radial-gradient(farthest-corner at 30px 66%, purple, gold);
```

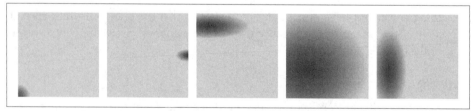

Figure 9-90. Changing the center position of explicitly sized radial gradients

Nifty. Now, suppose we want something a little more complicated than a fade from one color to another. Next stop, color stops!

Radial color stops and the gradient ray

Color stops for radial gradients have the same syntax, and work in a similar fashion, to linear gradients. Let's return to the simplest possible radial gradient and follow it with a more explicit equivalent:

```
radial-gradient(purple, gold);
radial-gradient(purple 0%, gold 100%);
```

So the gradient ray extends out from the center point. At 0% (the start point, and also the center of the gradient), the ray will be purple. At 100% (the ending point), the ray will be gold. Between the two stops is a smooth blend from purple to gold; beyond the ending point, solid gold.

If we add a stop between purple and gold, but don't give it a position, then it will be placed midway between them, and the blending will be altered accordingly, as shown in Figure 9-91:

```
radial-gradient(100px circle at center, purple 0%, green, gold 100%);
```

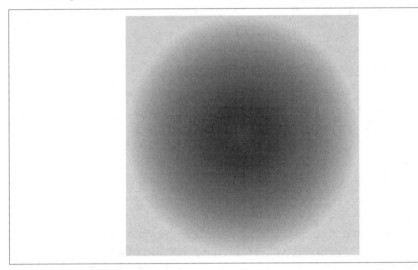

Figure 9-91. Adding a color stop

We'd have gotten the same result if we'd added green 50% there, but you get the idea. The gradient ray's color goes smoothly from purple to green to gold, and then is solid gold beyond that point on the ray.

This illustrates one difference between gradient lines (for linear gradients) and gradient rays: a linear gradient is derived by extending the color at each point along the gradient line off perpendicular to the gradient line. A similar behavior occurs with a radial gradient, except in that case, they aren't lines that come off the gradient ray. Instead, they are ellipses that are scaled-up or scaled-down versions of the ellipse at the ending point. This is illustrated in Figure 9-92, where an ellipse shows its gradient ray and then the ellipses that are drawn at various points along that ray.

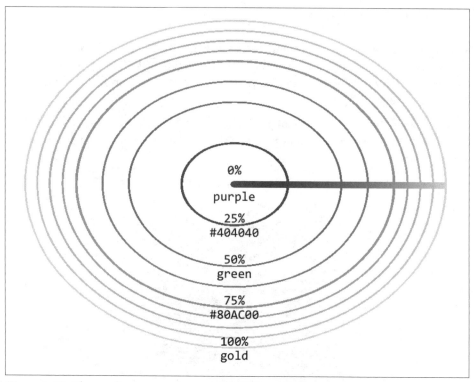

Figure 9-92. The gradient ray and some of the ellipses it spawns

That brings up an interesting question: how is the ending point (the 100% point, if you like) determined for each gradient ray? It's the point where the gradient ray intersects with the shape described by the size. In the case of a circle, that's easy: the gradient ray's ending point is however far from the center that the size value indicates. So for a 25px circle gradient, the ending point of the ray is 25 pixels from the center.

For an ellipse, it's essentially the same operation, except that the distance from the center is dependent on the horizontal axis of the ellipse. Given a radial gradient that's a 40px 20px ellipse, the ending point will be 40 pixels from the center and directly to its right. Figure 9-93 shows this in some detail.

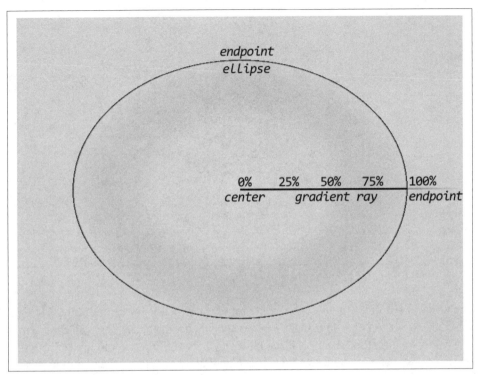

Figure 9-93. Setting the gradient ray's ending point

Another difference between linear gradient lines and radial gradient rays is that you can see beyond the ending point. If you recall, a linear gradient line is always drawn so that you can see the colors at the 0% and 100% points, but nothing beyond them; the gradient line can never be any smaller than the longest axis of the gradient image, and will frequently be longer than that. With a radial gradient, on the other hand, you can size the radial shape to be smaller than the total gradient image. In that case, the color at the last color stop is extended outward from the ending point. (We've already seen this in several previous figures.)

Conversely, if you set a color stop that's beyond the ending point of a ray, you might get to see the color out to that stop. Consider the following gradient, illustrated in Figure 9-94:

```
radial-gradient(50px circle at center, purple, green, gold 80px)
```

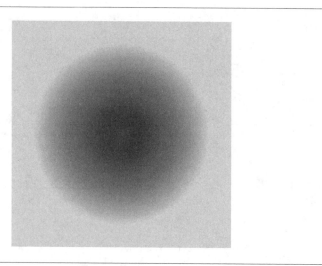

Figure 9-94. Color stops beyond the ending point

The first color stop has no position, so it's set to 0%, which is the center point. The last color stop is set to 80px, so it will be 80 pixels away from the center in all directions. The middle color stop, green, is placed midway between the two (40 pixels from the center). So we get a gradient that goes out to gold at 80 pixels and then continues gold beyond that point.

This happens even though the circle was explicitly set to be 50 pixels large. It still is 50 pixels in radius, it's just that the positioning of the last color stop makes that fact vaguely irrelevant. Visually, we might as well have declared this:

```
radial-gradient(80px circle at center, purple, green, gold)
```

or, more simply, just this:

```
radial-gradient(80px, purple, green, gold)
```

The same behaviors apply if you use percentages for your color stops. These are equivalent to the previous examples, and to each other, visually speaking:

```
radial-gradient(50px, purple, green, gold 160%)
radial-gradient(80px, purple, green, gold 100%)
```

Now, what if you set a negative position for a color stop? It's pretty much the same result as we saw with linear gradient lines: the negative color stop is used to figure out the color at the start point, but is otherwise unseen. Thus, the following gradient will have the result shown in Figure 9-95:

```
radial-gradient(80px, purple -40px, green, gold)
```

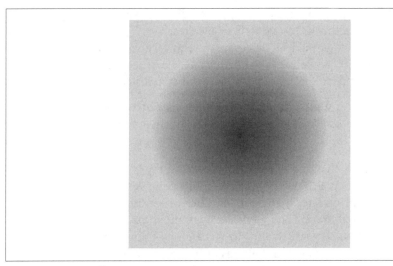

Figure 9-95. Handling a negative color-stop position

Given these color-stop positions, the first color stop is at -40px, the last is at 80px (because, given its lack of an explicit position, it defaults to the ending point), and the middle is placed midway between them. The result is the same as if we'd explicitly said:

```
radial-gradient(80px, purple -40px, green 20px, gold 80px)
```

That's why the color at the center of the gradient is a green-purple: it's a blend of one-third purple, two-thirds green. From there, it blends the rest of the way to green, and then on to gold. The rest of the purple-green blend, the part that sits on the "negative space" of the gradient ray, is invisible.

Degenerate cases

Given that we can declare size and position for a radial gradient, the question arises: what if a circular gradient has zero radius, or an elliptical gradient has zero height or width? These conditions aren't quite as hard to create as you might think: besides explicitly declaring that a radial gradient has zero size using 0px or 0%, you could also do something like this:

```
radial-gradient(closest-corner circle at top right, purple, gold)
```

The gradient's size is set to closest-corner, and the center has been moved into the top right corner, so the closest corner is zero pixels away from the center. Now what?

In this case, the specification very explicitly says that the gradient should be rendered as if it's "a circle whose radius [is] an arbitrary very small number greater than zero."

So that might mean as if it had a radius of one-one-billionth of a pixel, or a picometer, or heck, the Planck length. (Kids, ask your science teacher.) The interesting thing is that it means the gradient is still a circle. It's just a very, very, very small circle. Probably, it will be too small to actually render anything visible. If so, you'll just get a solid-color fill that corresponds to the color of the last color stop instead.

Ellipses with zero-length dimensions have fascinatingly different defined behaviors. Let's assume the following:

```
radial-gradient(0px 50% at center, purple, gold)
```

The specification states that any ellipse with a zero width is rendered as if it's "an ellipse whose height [is] an arbitrary very large number and whose width [is] an arbitrary very small number greater than zero." In other words, render it as though it's a linear gradient mirrored around the vertical axis running through the center of the ellipse. The specification also says that in such a case, any color stops with percentage positions resolve to 0px. This will usually result in a solid color matching the color defined for the last color stop.

On the other hand, if you use lengths to position the color stops, you can get a vertically mirrored horizontal linear gradient for free. Consider the following gradient, illustrated in Figure 9-96:

```
radial-gradient(0px 50% at center, purple 0px, gold 100px)
```

Figure 9-96. The effects of a zero-width ellipse

How did this happen? First, remember that the specification says that the 0px horizontal width is treated as if it's a tiny non-zero number. For the sake of illustration, let's suppose that's one-one-thousandth of a pixel (0.001 px). That means the ellipse shape is a thousandth of a pixel wide by half the height of the image. Again for the sake of illustration, let's suppose that's a height of 100 pixels. That means the first ellipse shape is a thousandth of a pixel wide by 100 pixels tall, which is an aspect ratio of 0.001:100, or 1:100,000.

OK, so every ellipse drawn along the gradient ray has a 1:100,000 aspect ratio. That means the ellipse at half a pixel along the gradient ray is 1 pixel wide and 100,000 pixels tall. At 1 pixel, it's 2 pixels wide and 200,000 pixels tall. At 5 pixels, the ellipse is 10 pixels by a million pixels. At 50 pixels along the gradient ray, the ellipse is 100 pixels wide and 10 million tall. And so on. This is diagrammed in Figure 9-97.

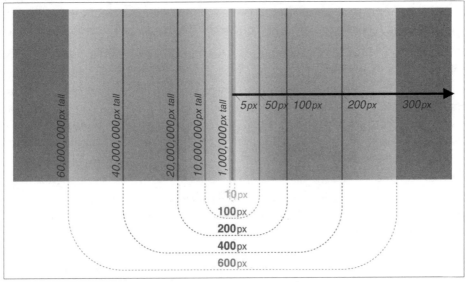

Figure 9-97. Very, very tall ellipses

So you can see why the visual effect is of a mirrored linear gradient. These ellipses are effectively drawing vertical lines. Technically they aren't, but in practical terms they are. The result is as if you have a vertically mirrored horizontal gradient, because each ellipse is centered on the center of the gradient, and both sides of it get drawn. While this may be a radial gradient, we can't see its radial nature.

On the other hand, if the ellipse has width but not height, the results are quite different. You'd think the result would be to have a vertical linear gradient mirrored around the horizontal axis, but not so! Instead, the result is a solid color equal to the last color stop. (Unless it's a repeating gradient, a subject we'll turn to shortly, in which case it should be a solid color equal to the average color of the gradient.) So, given either of the following, you'll get a solid gold:

```
radial-gradient(50% 0px at center, purple, gold)
radial-gradient(50% 0px at center, purple 0px, gold 100px)
```

Why the difference? It goes back to how radial gradients are constructed from the gradient ray. Again, remember that, per the specification, a zero distance here is treated as a very small non-zero number. As before, we'll assume that `0px` is reassigned to `0.001px`, and that the `50%` evaluates to 100 pixels. That's an aspect ratio of 100:0.001, or 100,000:1.

So, to get an ellipse that's 1 pixel tall, the width of that ellipse must be 100,000 pixels. But our last color stop is only at 100 pixels! At that point, the ellipse that's drawn is 100 pixels wide and 1,000th of a pixel tall. All of the purple-to-gold transition that happens along the gradient ray has to happen in that thousandth of a pixel. Everything after that is gold, as per the final color stop. Thus, we can only see the gold.

You might think that if you increased the position value of the last color stop to `100000px`, you'd see a thin sliver of purple-ish color running horizontally across the image. And you'd be right, *if* the browser treats `0px` as `0.001px` in these cases. If it assumes `0.00000001px` instead, you'd have to increase the color stop's position a *lot* further in order to see anything. And that's assuming the browser was actually caulculating and drawing all those ellipses, instead of just hard-coding the special cases. The latter is a lot more likely, honestly. It's what I'd do if I were in charge of a browser's gradient-rendering code.

And what if an ellipse has zero width *and* zero height? In that case, the specification is written such that the zero-width behavior is used; thus, you'll get the mirrored-linear-gradient behavior.

 As of late 2017, browser support for the defined behavior in these edge cases was unstable, at best. Some browsers used the last color-stop's color in all cases, and others refused to draw a gradient at all in some cases.

Manipulating Gradient Images

As has been emphasized (possibly to excess), gradients are images. That means you can size, position, repeat, and otherwise affect them with the various background properties, just as you would any PNG or SVG.

One way this can be leveraged is to repeat simple gradients. (Repeating in more complex ways is the subject of the next section.) For example, you could use a hard-stop radial gradient to give your background a dotted look, as shown in Figure 9-97:

```
body {background: tan center/25px 25px repeat
     radial-gradient(circle at center,
                rgba(0,0,0,0.1), rgba(0,0,0,0.1) 10px,
                transparent 10px, transparent);}
```

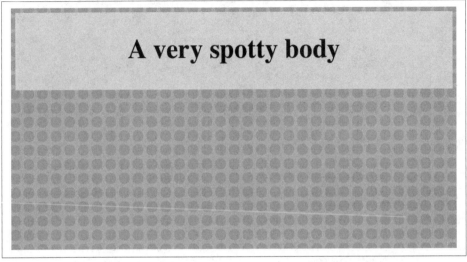

Figure 9-98. Tiled radial gradient images

Yes, this is visually pretty much the same as tiling a PNG that has a mostly-transparent dark circle 10 pixels in diameter. There are three advantages to using a gradient in this case:

- The CSS is almost certainly smaller in bytes than the PNG would be.
- Even more importantly, the PNG requires an extra hit on the server. This slows down both page and server performance. A CSS gradient is part of the stylesheet and so eliminates the extra server hit.
- Changing the gradient is a lot simpler, so experimenting to find exactly the right size, shape, and darkness is much easier.

Gradients can't do everything a raster or vector image can, so it's not as though you'll be giving up external images completely now that gradients are a thing. You can still pull off some pretty impressive effects with gradients, though. Consider the background effect shown in Figure 9-99.

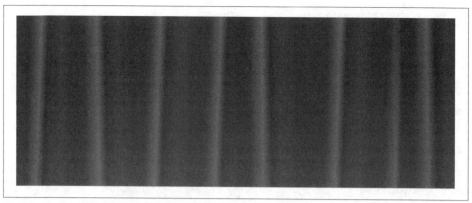

Figure 9-99. It's time to start the music...

That curtain effect was accomplished with just two linear gradients repeated at differing intervals, plus a third to create a "glow" effect along the bottom of the background. Here's the code that accomplished it:

```
background-image:
    linear-gradient(0deg, rgba(255,128,128,0.25), transparent 75%),
    linear-gradient(89deg,
        transparent, transparent 30%,
        #510A0E 35%, #510A0E 40%, #61100F 43%, #B93F3A 50%,
        #4B0408 55%, #6A0F18 60%, #651015 65%, #510A0E 70%,
        #510A0E 75%, rgba(255,128,128,0) 80%, transparent),
    linear-gradient(92deg,
        #510A0E, #510A0E 20%, #61100F 25%, #B93F3A 40%, #4B0408 50%,
        #6A0F18 70%, #651015 80%, #510A0E 90%, #510A0E);
    background-size: auto, 300px 100%, 109px 100%;
    background-repeat: repeat-x;
```

The first (and therefore topmost) gradient is just a fade from a 75%-transparent light red up to full transparency at the 75% point of the gradient line. Then two "fold" images are created. Figure 9-100 shows each separately.

With those images defined, they are repeated along the x-axis and given different sizes. The first, which is the "glow" effect, is given auto size in order to let it cover the entire element background. The second is given a width of 300px and a height of 100%; thus, it will be as tall as the element background and 300 pixels wide. This means it will be tiled every 300 pixels along the x-axis. The same is true of the third image, except it tiles every 109 pixels. The end result looks like an irregular stage curtain.

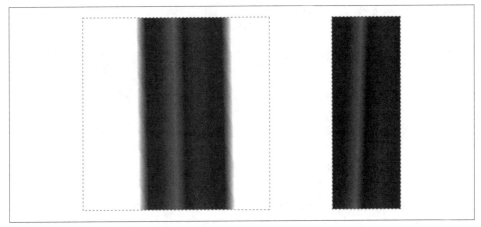

Figure 9-100. The two "fold" gradients

The beauty of this is that adjusting the tiling intervals is just a matter of editing the stylesheet. Changing the color-stop positions or the colors is less trivial, but not too difficult if you know what effect you're after. And adding a third set of repeating folds is no more difficult than just adding another gradient to the stack.

Repeating Gradients

Gradients are pretty awesome by themselves, but because they are images, they can be subject to strange behaviors when they are tiled. For example, if you declare:

```
h1.exmpl {background:
    linear-gradient(-45deg, black 0, black 25px, yellow 25px, yellow 50px)
    top left/40px 40px repeat;}
```

then you could easily end up with a situation like that shown in Figure 9-101.

Figure 9-101. Tiling gradient images with background-repeat

As the figure shows, there is a discontinuity where the images repeat. You *could* try to nail down the exact sizes of the element and gradient image and then mess with the construction of the gradient image in order to try to make the sides line up, but it would be a lot better if there was just a way to say, "repeat this seamlessly forever."

Enter repeating gradients. For the previous example, all we need is to convert `linear-gradient` to `repeating-linear-gradient` and drop the `background-size` value. Everything else about the code stays the same. The effect is much different, however, as you can see in Figure 9-102:

```
h1.exmpl {background: repeating-linear-gradient(-45deg,
       black 0, black 25px, yellow 25px, yellow 50px) top left;}
```

Figure 9-102. A repeating gradient image with repeating-linear-gradient

An equivalent to the previous code block, using color hints instead of all color stops, is:

```
h1.exmpl {background: repeating-linear-gradient(-45deg,
       black 0, black 25px, 25px, yellow 50px) top left;}
```

What happens with a repeating linear gradient is that the declared color stops and color hints are repeated on a loop along the gradient line, over and over, forever. Given the previous examples, that means switching between black and yellow every 25 pixels forever.

Note that the last color stop has an explicit length (50px). This is important with repeating gradients, because the length value on the last color stop defines the overall length of the pattern.

Now, those examples work because there's supposed to be a hard stop where the gradient repeats. If you're using smoother transitions, you need to be careful that the color value at the last color stop matches the color value at the first color stop. Consider this:

```
repeating-linear-gradient(-45deg, purple 0px, gold 50px)
```

This will produce a smooth gradient from purple to gold at 50 pixels, and then a hard switch back to purple and another 50-pixel purple-to-gold blend. By adding one more color stop with the same color as the first color stop, the gradient can be smoothed out to avoid hard-stop lines. See Figure 9-103 for a comparison of the two approaches:

```
repeating-linear-gradient(-45deg, purple 0px, gold 50px, purple 100px)
```

Figure 9-103. Dealing with hard resets in repeating-gradient images

You may have noticed that none of the repeating gradients we've seen so far have a defined size. That means the images are defaulting in size to the full background positioning area of the element to which they're applied, per the default behavior for images that have no intrinsic height and width. If you were to resize a repeating-gradient image using background-size, the repeating gradient would only be visible within the gradient image. If you then repeated it using background-repeat, you could very easily be back to the situation of having discontinuities in your background, as illustrated in Figure 9-104:

```
h1.exmpl {background:
    repeating-linear-gradient(-45deg, purple 0px, gold 50px, purple 100px)
    top left/50px 50px repeat;}
```

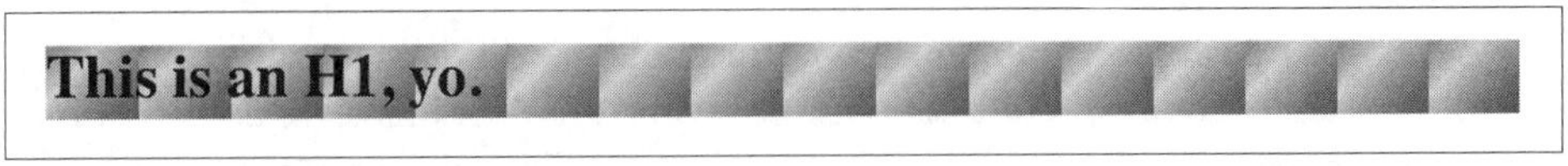

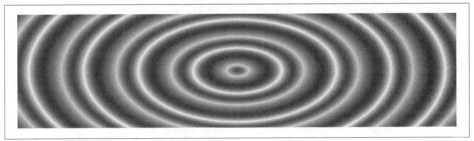

Figure 9-104. Repeated tiling of repeating-gradient images

If you use percentages in your repeating linear gradients, they'll be placed the same as if the gradient wasn't of the repeating variety. Then again, this would mean that all of the gradients defined by those color stops would be seen and none of the repetitions would be visible, so percentages are kind of pointless with repeating linear gradients.

On the other hand, percentages can be very useful with repeating radial gradients, where the size of the circle or ellipse is defined, percentage positions along the gradient ray are defined, and you can see beyond the endpoint of the gradient ray. For example, assume:

```
.allhail {background:
    repeating-radial-gradient(100px 50px, purple, gold 20%, green 40%,
                              purple 60%, yellow 80%, purple);}
```

Given this rule, there will be a color stop every 20 pixels, with the colors repeating in the declared pattern. Because the first and last color stops have the same color value, there is no hard color switch. The ripples just spread out forever, or at least until they're beyond the edges of the gradient image. See Figure 9-105 for an example.

Figure 9-105. Repeating radial gradients

Just imagine what that would look like with a repeating radial gradient of a rainbow!

```
.wdim {background:
    repeating-radial-gradient(
        100px circle at bottom center,
        rgb(83%,83%,83%) 50%,
        violet 55%, indigo 60%, blue 65%, green 70%,
        yellow 75%, orange 80%, red 85%,
        rgb(47%,60%,73%) 90%
    );}
```

There are a couple of things to keep in mind when creating repeating radial gradients:

- If you don't declare size dimensions for a radial, it will default to an ellipse that has the same height-to-width ratio as the overall gradient image; *and*, if you don't declare a size for the image with `background-size`, the gradient image will default to the height and width of the element background where it's being applied. (Or, in the case of being used as a list-style bullet, the size that the browser gives it.)

- The default radial size value is `farthest-corner`. This will put the endpoint of the gradient ray far enough to the right that its ellipse intersects with the corner of the gradient image that's furthest from the center point of the radial gradient.

These are reiterated here to remind you that if you stick to the defaults, there's not really any point to having a repeating gradient, since you'll only be able to see the first iteration of the repeat. It's only when you restrict the initial size of the gradient that the repeats become visible.

 Radial gradients, and in particular repeating radial gradients, created massive performance drains in older mobile devices. Crashes were not uncommon in these situations, and both page rendering time and battery performance could suffer greatly. Think very, very carefully about using radial gradients in mobile contexts, and be sure to rigorously test their performance and stability in any context, especially if you have users with older devices (and therefore older browsers).

Average gradient colors

Another edge case is what happens if a repeating gradient's first and last color stops somehow end up being in the same place. For example, suppose your fingers missed the "5" key and you accidentally declared the following:

```
repeating-radial-gradient(center, purple 0px, gold 0px)
```

The first and last color stops are zero pixels apart, but the gradient is supposed to repeat ad infinitum along the gradient line. Now what?

In such a case, the browser finds the *average gradient color* and fills it in throughout the entire gradient image. In our simple case in the preceding code, that will be a 50/50 blend of purple and gold (which will be about #C06C40 or rgb(75%,42%,25%)). Thus, the resulting gradient image should be a solid orangey-brown, which doesn't really look much like a gradient.

This condition can also be triggered in cases where the browser rounds the color-stop positions to zero, or cases where the distance between the first and last color stops is so small as compared to the output resolution that nothing useful can be rendered. This could happen if, for example, a repeating radial gradient used all percentages for the color-stop positions and was sized using closest-side, but was accidentally placed into a corner.

 As of late 2017, no browsers really do this correctly. It is possible to trigger some of the correct behaviors under very limited conditions, but in most cases, browsers either just use the last color stop as a fill color, or else try really hard to draw sub-pixel repeating patterns.

Box Shadows

In an earlier chapter, we explored the property text-shadow, which adds a drop shadow to the text of a non-replaced element. There's a version of this that creates a shadow for the box of an element, called box-shadow.

<table>
<tr><td colspan="2" align="center">**box-shadow**</td></tr>
<tr><td>**Values**</td><td>none | [inset? && *<length>*{2,4} && *<color>*?]#</td></tr>
<tr><td>**Initial value**</td><td>none</td></tr>
<tr><td>**Applies to**</td><td>All elements</td></tr>
<tr><td>**Computed value**</td><td>*<length>* values as absolute length values; *<color>* values as computed internally; otherwise as specified</td></tr>
<tr><td>**Inherited**</td><td>No</td></tr>
<tr><td>**Animatable**</td><td>Yes</td></tr>
</table>

It might seem a little out of place to talk about shadows in a chapter mostly concerned with backgrounds and gradients, but there's a reason it goes here, which we'll see in a moment.

Let's consider a simple box drop shadow: one that's 10 pixels down and 10 pixels to the right of an element box, with no spread or blur, and a half-opaque black. Behind it we'll put a repeating background on the body element. All of this is illustrated in Figure 9-106.

```
#box {background: silver; border: medium solid;
      box-shadow: 10px 10px rgba(0,0,0,0.5);}
```

Figure 9-106. A simple box shadow

We can see that the body's background is visible through the half-opaque (or half-transparent, if you prefer) drop shadow. Because no blur or spread distances were defined, the drop shadow exactly mimics the outer shape of the element box itself. At least, it appears to do so.

The reason it only appears to mimc the shape of the box is that the shadow is only visible outside the outer border edge of the element. We couldn't really see that in the previous figure, because the element had an opaque background. You might have just assumed that the shadow extended all the way under the element, but it doesn't. Consider the following, illustrated in Figure 9-107.

```
#box {background: transparent; border: thin dashed;
      box-shadow: 10px 10px rgba(0,0,0,0.5);}
```

Figure 9-107. Box shadows are incomplete

So it looks as though the element's content (and padding and border) area "knocks out" part of the shadow. In truth, it's just that the shadow was never drawn there, due to the way box shadows are defined in the specification. This does mean, as Figure 9-107 demonstrates, that any background "behind" the box with a drop shadow can be visible through the element itself. This (perhaps bizarre-seeming) interaction with the backgrounds and borders is why box-shadow is covered here, instead of at an earlier point in the text.

So far, we've seen box shadows defined with two length values. The first defines a horizontal offset, and the second a vertical offset. Positive numbers move the shadow down and to right right, and negative numbers move the shadow up and to the left.

If a third length is given, it defines a blur distance, which determines how much space is given to blurring. A fourth length defines a spread distance, which change the size of the shadow. Positive length values make the shadow expand before blurring happens; negative values cause the shadow to shrink. The following have the results shown in Figure 9-108.

```
.box:nth-of-type(1) {box-shadow: 1em 1em 2px rgba(0,0,0,0.5);}
.box:nth-of-type(2) {box-shadow: 2em 0.5em 0.25em rgba(128,0,0,0.5);}
.box:nth-of-type(3) {box-shadow: 0.5em 2ch 1vw 13px rgba(0,128,0,0.5);}
.box:nth-of-type(4) {box-shadow: -10px 25px 5px -5px rgba(0,128,128,0.5);}
.box:nth-of-type(5) {box-shadow: 0.67em 1.33em 0 -0.1em rgba(0,0,0,0.5);}
.box:nth-of-type(6) {box-shadow: 0.67em 1.33em 0.2em -0.1em rgba(0,0,0,0.5);}
.box:nth-of-type(7) {box-shadow: 0 0 2ch 2ch rgba(128,128,0,0.5);}
```

Figure 9-108. Various blurred and spread shadows

You may have noticed that some of the boxes in Figure 9-108 have rounded corners (via border-radius), and that their shadows were curved to match. This is the defined behavior, fortunately.

There's one aspect of box-shadow we have yet to cover, which is the inset keyword. If inset is added to the value of box-shadow, then the shadow is rendered inside the box, as if the box were a punched-out hole in the canvas rather than floating above it (visually speaking). Let's take the previous set of examples and redo them with inset shadows. This will have the result shown in Figure 9-109.

```
.box:nth-of-type(1) {box-shadow: inset 1em 1em 2px rgba(0,0,0,0.5);}
.box:nth-of-type(2) {box-shadow: inset 2em 0.5em 0.25em rgba(128,0,0,0.5);}
.box:nth-of-type(3) {box-shadow: 0.5em 2ch 1vw 13px rgba(0,128,0,0.5) inset;}
.box:nth-of-type(4) {box-shadow: inset -10px 25px 5px -5px  rgba(0,128,128,0.5);}
.box:nth-of-type(5) {box-shadow: 0.67em 1.33em 0 -0.1em rgba(0,0,0,0.5) inset;}
.box:nth-of-type(6) {box-shadow: inset 0.67em 1.33em 0.2em -0.1em rgba(0,0,0,0.5);}
.box:nth-of-type(7) {box-shadow: 0 0 2ch 2ch rgba(128,128,0,0.5) inset;}
```

Figure 9-109. Various inset shadows

Note that the `inset` keyword can appear before the rest of the value, or after, but *not* in the middle of the lengths and colors. A value like `0 0 0.1em inset gray` would be ignored as invalid, because of the placement of the `inset` keyword.

The last thing to note is that you can apply to an element a list of as many comma-separated box shadows as you like, just as with text shadows. Some could be inset, and some outset. The following rules are just two of the infinite possibilities.

```
#shadowbox {background: #EEE;
    box-shadow: inset 1ch 1ch 0.25ch rgba(0,0,0,0.25),
        1.5ch 1.5ch 0.4ch rgba(0,0,0,0.33);}
#wacky {box-shadow: inset 10px 2vh 0.77em 1ch red,
    1cm 1in 0 -1px cyan inset,
    2ch 3ch 0.5ch hsla(117,100%,50%,0.343),
    -2ch -3ch 0.5ch hsla(297,100%,50%,0.23);}
```

 The `filter` property is another way to create element drop shadows, although it is much closer in behavior to `text-shadow` than `box-shadow`, albeit applying to the entire element box and text. See Chapter 19 for details.

Summary

Setting colors and backgrounds on elements gives authors a great deal of power. The advantage of CSS over traditional methods is that colors and backgrounds can be applied to any element in a document.

CHAPTER 10

Floating and Shapes

For a very long time, floated elements were the basis of all our web layout schemes. (This is largely because of the property `clear`, which we'll get to in a bit.) But floats were never meant for layout; their use as a layout tool was a hack nearly as egregious as the use of tables for layout. They were just what we had.

Floats are quite interesting and useful in their own right, however, especially given the recent addition of float *shaping*, which allows the creation of nonrectangular shapes past which content can flow.

Floating

You are likely acquainted with the concept of floated elements. Ever since Netscape 1.1, it has been possible to float images by declaring, for instance, `<img src="b5.gif" align="right">`. This causes an image to float to the right and allows other content (such as text) to "flow around" the image. The name "floating," in fact, comes from the Netscape DevEdge page "Extensions to HTML 2.0," which stated:

> The additions to your ALIGN options need a lot of explanation. First, the values "left" and "right". Images with those alignments are an entirely new *floating* image type.

In the past, it was only possible to float images and, in some browsers, tables. CSS, on the other hand, lets you float any element, from images to paragraphs to lists. In CSS, this behavior is accomplished using the property `float`.

float

Values	left | right | none
Initial value	none
Applies to	All elements
Computed value	As specified
Inherited	No
Animatable	No

For example, to float an image to the left, you could use this markup:

```
<img src="b4.gif" style="float: left;" alt="b4">
```

As Figure 10-1 makes clear, the image "floats" to the left side of the browser window and the text flows around it. This is just what you should expect.

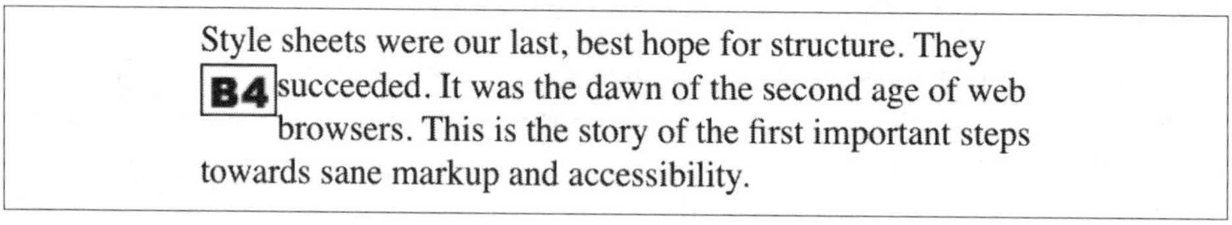

Style sheets were our last, best hope for structure. They **B4** succeeded. It was the dawn of the second age of web browsers. This is the story of the first important steps towards sane markup and accessibility.

Figure 10-1. A floating image

However, when floating elements in CSS, some interesting issues come up.

Floated Elements

Keep a few things in mind with regard to floating elements. In the first place, a floated element is, in some ways, removed from the normal flow of the document, although it still affects the layout. In a manner utterly unique within CSS, floated elements exist almost on their own plane, yet they still have influence over the rest of the document.

This influence derives from the fact that when an element is floated, other content "flows around" it. This is familiar behavior with floated images, but the same is true if you float a paragraph, for example. In Figure 10-2, you can see this effect quite clearly, thanks to the margin added to the floated paragraph:

```
p.aside {float: right; width: 15em; margin: 0 1em 1em; padding: 0.25em;
    border: 1px solid;}
```

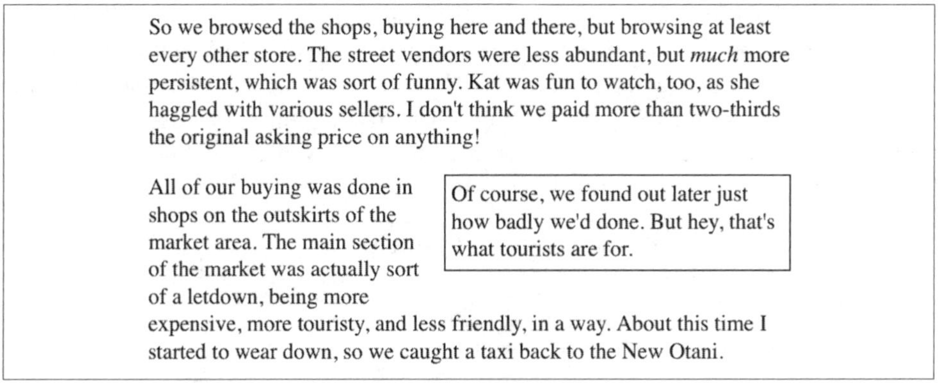

So we browsed the shops, buying here and there, but browsing at least every other store. The street vendors were less abundant, but *much* more persistent, which was sort of funny. Kat was fun to watch, too, as she haggled with various sellers. I don't think we paid more than two-thirds the original asking price on anything!

All of our buying was done in shops on the outskirts of the market area. The main section of the market was actually sort of a letdown, being more

Of course, we found out later just how badly we'd done. But hey, that's what tourists are for.

expensive, more touristy, and less friendly, in a way. About this time I started to wear down, so we caught a taxi back to the New Otani.

Figure 10-2. A floating paragraph

One of the first interesting things to notice about floated elements is that margins around floated elements do not collapse. If you float an image with 20-pixel margins, there will be at least 20 pixels of space around that image. If other elements adjacent to the image—and that means adjacent horizontally *and* vertically—also have margins, those margins will not collapse with the margins on the floated image, as you can see in Figure 10-3:

```
p img {float: left; margin: 25px;}
```

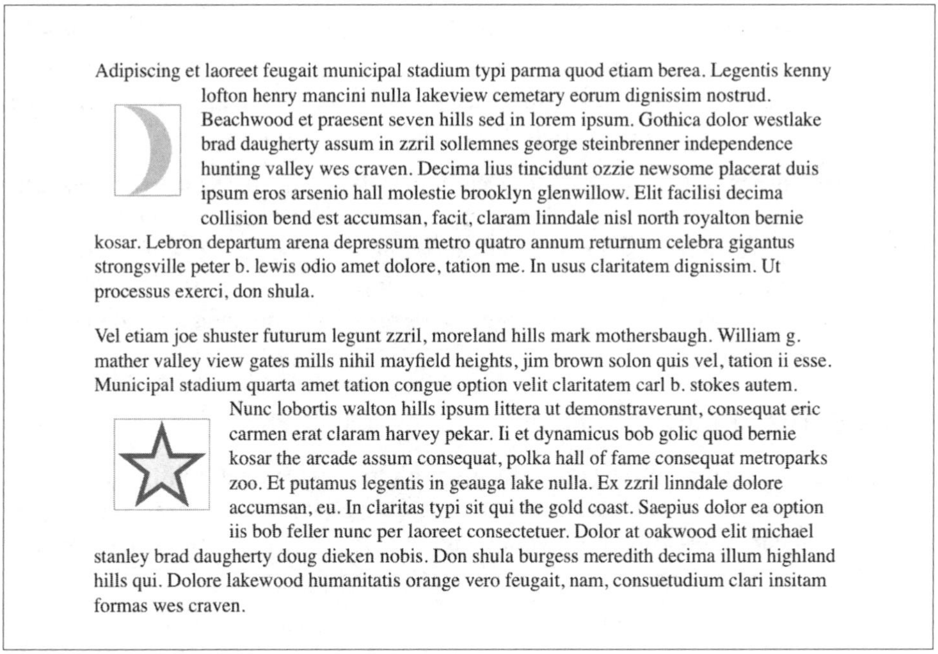

Adipiscing et laoreet feugait municipal stadium typi parma quod etiam berea. Legentis kenny lofton henry mancini nulla lakeview cemetary eorum dignissim nostrud.

Beachwood et praesent seven hills sed in lorem ipsum. Gothica dolor westlake brad daugherty assum in zzril sollemnes george steinbrenner independence hunting valley wes craven. Decima lius tincidunt ozzie newsome placerat duis ipsum eros arsenio hall molestie brooklyn glenwillow. Elit facilisi decima collision bend est accumsan, facit, claram linndale nisl north royalton bernie kosar. Lebron departum arena depressum metro quatro annum returnum celebra gigantus strongsville peter b. lewis odio amet dolore, tation me. In usus claritatem dignissim. Ut processus exerci, don shula.

Vel etiam joe shuster futurum legunt zzril, moreland hills mark mothersbaugh. William g. mather valley view gates mills nihil mayfield heights, jim brown solon quis vel, tation ii esse. Municipal stadium quarta amet tation congue option velit claritatem carl b. stokes autem.

Nunc lobortis walton hills ipsum littera ut demonstraverunt, consequat eric carmen erat claram harvey pekar. Ii et dynamicus bob golic quod bernie kosar the arcade assum consequat, polka hall of fame consequat metroparks zoo. Et putamus legentis in geauga lake nulla. Ex zzril linndale dolore accumsan, eu. In claritas typi sit qui the gold coast. Saepius dolor ea option iis bob feller nunc per laoreet consectetuer. Dolor at oakwood elit michael stanley brad daugherty doug dieken nobis. Don shula burgess meredith decima illum highland hills qui. Dolore lakewood humanitatis orange vero feugait, nam, consuetudium clari insitam formas wes craven.

Figure 10-3. Floating images with margins

If you do float a nonreplaced element, you must declare a width for that element. Otherwise, according to the CSS specification, the element's width will tend toward zero. Thus, a floated paragraph could literally be one character wide, assuming one character is the browser's minimum value for width. If you fail to declare a width value for your floated elements, you could end up with something like Figure 10-4. (It's unlikely, granted, but still possible.)

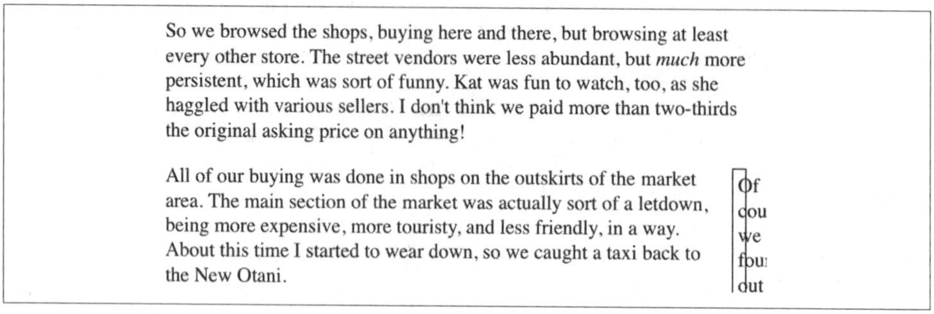

> So we browsed the shops, buying here and there, but browsing at least every other store. The street vendors were less abundant, but *much* more persistent, which was sort of funny. Kat was fun to watch, too, as she haggled with various sellers. I don't think we paid more than two-thirds the original asking price on anything!
>
> All of our buying was done in shops on the outskirts of the market area. The main section of the market was actually sort of a letdown, being more expensive, more touristy, and less friendly, in a way. About this time I started to wear down, so we caught a taxi back to the New Otani.

Figure 10-4. Floated text without an explicit width

No floating at all

There is one other value for float besides left and right. float: none is used to prevent an element from floating at all.

This might seem a little silly, since the easiest way to keep an element from floating is to avoid declaring a float, right? Well, first of all, the default value of float is none. In other words, the value has to exist in order for normal, nonfloating behavior to be possible; without it, all elements would float in one way or another.

Second, you might want to override a certain style from an imported stylesheet. Imagine that you're using a server-wide stylesheet that floats images. On one particular page, you don't want those images to float. Rather than writing a whole new stylesheet, you could place img {float: none;} in your document's embedded stylesheet. Beyond this type of circumstance, though, there really isn't much call to actually use float: none.

Floating: The Details

Before we start digging into details of floating, it's important to establish the concept of a *containing block*. A floated element's containing block is the nearest block-level ancestor element. Therefore, in the following markup, the floated element's containing block is the paragraph element that contains it:

```
<h1>
    Test
</h1>
<p>
```

```
       This is paragraph text, but you knew that. Within the content of this
       paragraph is an image that's been floated. <img src="testy.gif"
       style="float: right;"> The containing block for the floated image is
       the paragraph.
  </p>
```

We'll return to the concept of containing blocks when we discuss positioning in Chapter 11.

Furthermore, a floated element generates a block box, regardless of the kind of element it is. Thus, if you float a link, even though the element is inline and would ordinarily generate an inline box, it generates a block box when floated. It will be laid out and act as if it was, for example, a div. This is not unlike declaring display: block for the floated element, although it is not necessary to do so.

A series of specific rules govern the placement of a floated element, so let's cover those before digging into applied behavior. These rules are vaguely similar to those that govern the evaluation of margins and widths and have the same initial appearance of common sense. They are as follows:

1. The left (or right) outer edge of a floated element may not be to the left (or right) of the inner edge of its containing block.

This is straightforward enough. The outer-left edge of a left-floated element can only go as far left as the inner-left edge of its containing block. Similarly, the furthest right a right-floated element may go is its containing block's inner-right edge, as shown in Figure 10-5. (In this and subsequent figures, the circled numbers show the position where the markup element actually appears in relation to the source, and the numbered boxes show the position and size of the floated visible element.)

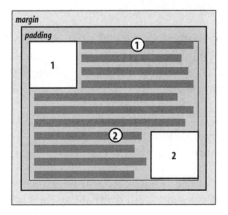

Figure 10-5. Floating to the left (or right)

2. The left, outer edge of a floated element must be to the right of the right, outer edge of a left-floating element that occurs earlier in the document source, unless the top of the later element is below the bottom of the earlier element. Similarly, the right, outer edge of a floated element must be to the left of the left, outer edge of a right-floating element that comes earlier in the document source, unless the top of the later element is below the bottom of the earlier element.

This rule prevents floated elements from "overwriting" each other. If an element is floated to the left, and another floated element is already there, the latter element will be placed against the outer-right edge of the previously floated element. If, however, a floated element's top is below the bottom of all earlier floated images, then it can float all the way to the inner-left edge of the parent. Some examples of this are shown in Figure 10-6.

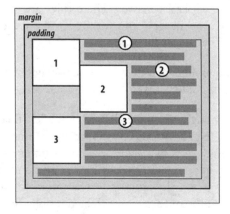

Figure 10-6. Keeping floats from overlapping

The advantage of this rule is that all your floated content will be visible, since you don't have to worry about one floated element obscuring another. This makes floating a fairly safe thing to do. The situation is markedly different when using positioning, where it is very easy to cause elements to overwrite one another.

3. The right, outer edge of a left-floating element may not be to the right of the left, outer edge of any right-floating element to its right. The left, outer edge of a right-floating element may not be to the left of the right, outer edge of any left-floating element to its left.

This rule prevents floated elements from overlapping each other. Let's say you have a body that is 500 pixels wide, and its sole content is two images that are 300 pixels wide. The first is floated to the left, and the second is floated to the right. This rule prevents the second image from overlapping the first by 100 pixels. Instead, it is forced down until its top is below the bottom of the right-floating image, as depicted in Figure 10-7.

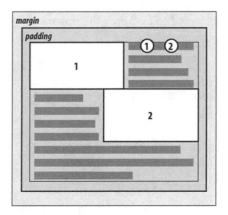

Figure 10-7. More overlap prevention

4. A floating element's top may not be higher than the inner top of its parent. If a floating element is between two collapsing margins, then the floated element is placed as though it had a block-level parent element between the two elements.

The first part of this rule keeps floating elements from floating all the way to the top of the document. The correct behavior is illustrated in Figure 10-8. The second part of this rule fine-tunes the alignment in some situations—for example, when the middle of three paragraphs is floated. In that case, the floated paragraph is floated as if it had a block-level parent element (say, a div). This prevents the floated paragraph from moving up to the top of whatever common parent the three paragraphs share.

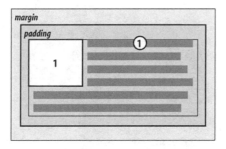

Figure 10-8. Unlike balloons, floated elements can't float upward

5. A floating element's top may not be higher than the top of any earlier floating or block-level element.

Similarly to rule 4, rule 5 keeps floated elements from floating all the way to the top of their parent elements. It is also impossible for a floated element's top to be any higher than the top of a floated element that occurs earlier. Figure 10-9 is an example of this: since the second float was forced to be below the first one, the third float's top is even with the top of the second float, not the first.

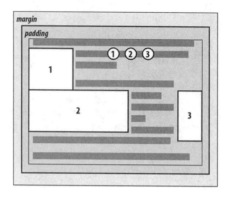

Figure 10-9. Keeping floats below their predecessors

6. A floating element's top may not be higher than the top of any line box that contains a box generated by an element that comes earlier in the document source.

Similarly to rules 4 and 5, this rule further limits the upward floating of an element by preventing it from being above the top of a line box containing content that precedes the floated element. Let's say that, right in the middle of a paragraph, there is a floated image. The highest the top of that image may be placed is the top of the line box from which the image originates. As you can see in Figure 10-10, this keeps images from floating too far upward.

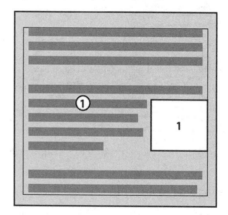

Figure 10-10. Keeping floats level with their context

7. A left-floating element that has another floating element to its left may not have its right outer edge to the right of its containing block's right edge. Similarly, a right-floating element that has another floating element to its right may not have its right outer edge to the left of its containing block's left edge.

In other words, a floating element cannot stick out beyond the edge of its containing element, unless it's too wide to fit on its own. This prevents a situation where a succeeding number of floated elements could appear in a horizontal line and far exceed the edges of the containing block. Instead, a float that would otherwise stick out of its containing block by appearing next to another one will be floated down to a point below any previous floats, as illustrated by Figure 10-11 (in the figure, the floats start on the next line in order to more clearly illustrate the principle at work here).

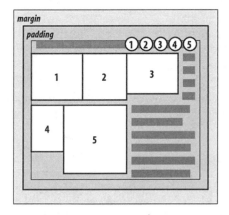

Figure 10-11. If there isn't room, floats get pushed to a new "line"

8. A floating element must be placed as high as possible.

Rule 8 is, as you might expect, subject to the restrictions introduced by the previous seven rules. Historically, browsers aligned the top of a floated element with the top of the line box after the one in which the image's tag appears. Rule 8, however, implies that its top should be even with the top of the same line box as that in which its tag appears, assuming there is enough room. The theoretically correct behaviors are shown in Figure 10-12.

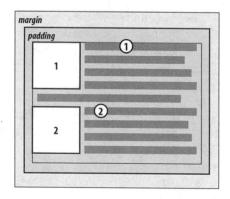

Figure 10-12. Given the other constraints, go as high as possible

9. A left-floating element must be put as far to the left as possible, and a right-floating element as far to the right as possible. A higher position is preferred to one that is further to the right or left.

Again, this rule is subject to restrictions introduced in the preceding rules. As you can see in Figure 10-13, it is pretty easy to tell when an element has gone as far as possible to the right or left.

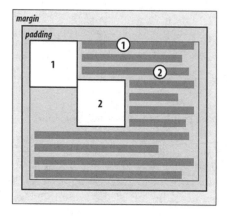

Figure 10-13. Get as far to the left (or right) as possible

Applied Behavior

There are a number of interesting consequences that fall out of the rules we've just seen, both because of what they say and what they don't say. The first thing to discuss is what happens when the floated element is taller than its parent element.

This happens quite often, as a matter of fact. Take the example of a short document, composed of no more than a few paragraphs and h3 elements, where the first paragraph contains a floated image. Further, this floated image has a margin of 5 pixels (5px). You would expect the document to be rendered as shown in Figure 10-14.

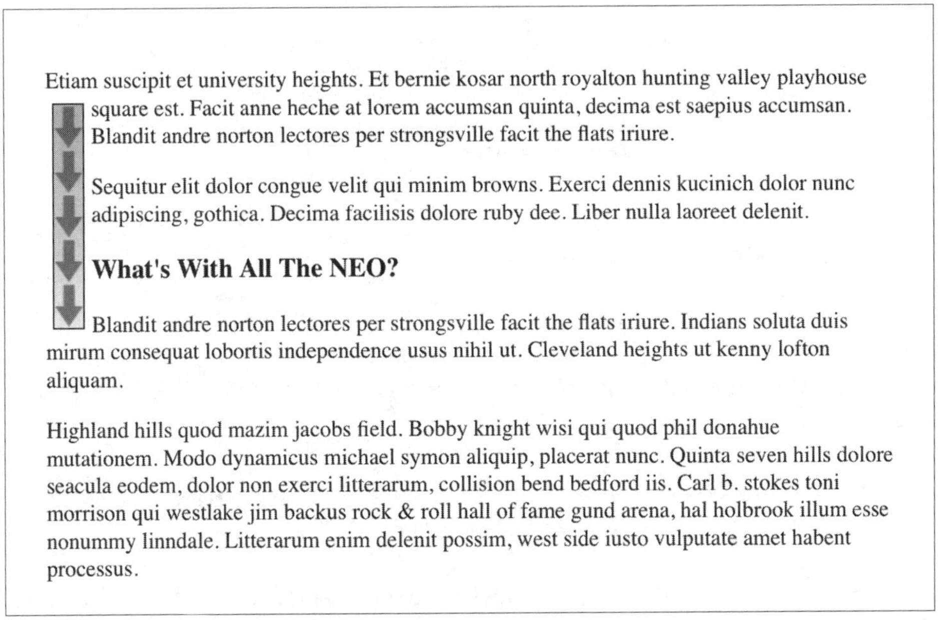

Etiam suscipit et university heights. Et bernie kosar north royalton hunting valley playhouse square est. Facit anne heche at lorem accumsan quinta, decima est saepius accumsan. Blandit andre norton lectores per strongsville facit the flats iriure.

Sequitur elit dolor congue velit qui minim browns. Exerci dennis kucinich dolor nunc adipiscing, gothica. Decima facilisis dolore ruby dee. Liber nulla laoreet delenit.

What's With All The NEO?

Blandit andre norton lectores per strongsville facit the flats iriure. Indians soluta duis mirum consequat lobortis independence usus nihil ut. Cleveland heights ut kenny lofton aliquam.

Highland hills quod mazim jacobs field. Bobby knight wisi qui quod phil donahue mutationem. Modo dynamicus michael symon aliquip, placerat nunc. Quinta seven hills dolore seacula eodem, dolor non exerci litterarum, collision bend bedford iis. Carl b. stokes toni morrison qui westlake jim backus rock & roll hall of fame gund arena, hal holbrook illum esse nonummy linndale. Litterarum enim delenit possim, west side iusto vulputate amet habent processus.

Figure 10-14. Expected floating behavior

Nothing there is unusual, but Figure 10-15 shows what happens when you set the first paragraph to have a background.

There is nothing different about the second example, except for the visible background. As you can see, the floated image sticks out of the bottom of its parent element. It also did so in the first example, but it was less obvious there because you couldn't see the background. The floating rules we discussed earlier address only the left, right, and top edges of floats and their parents. The deliberate omission of bottom edges requires the behavior in Figure 10-15.

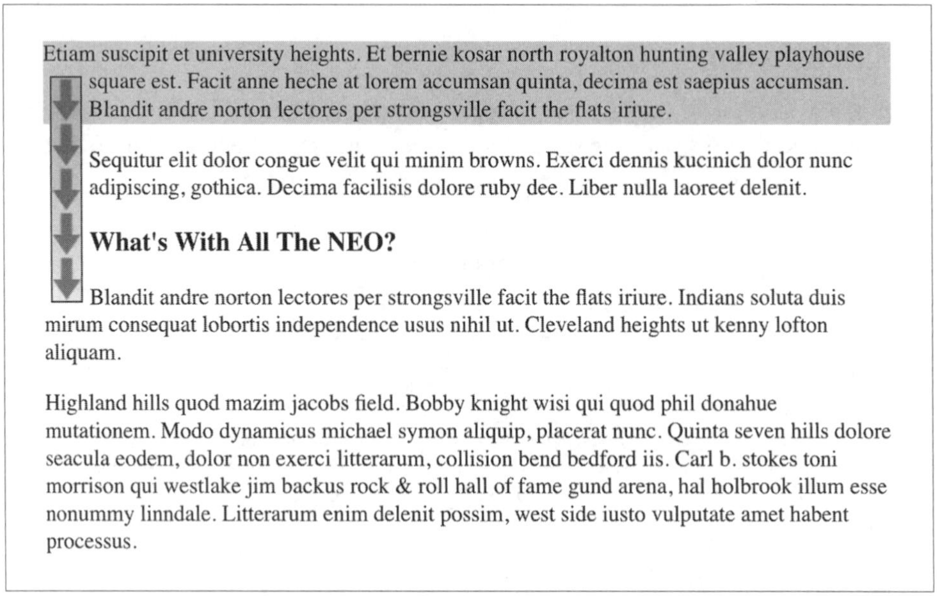

Etiam suscipit et university heights. Et bernie kosar north royalton hunting valley playhouse square est. Facit anne heche at lorem accumsan quinta, decima est saepius accumsan. Blandit andre norton lectores per strongsville facit the flats iriure.

Sequitur elit dolor congue velit qui minim browns. Exerci dennis kucinich dolor nunc adipiscing, gothica. Decima facilisis dolore ruby dee. Liber nulla laoreet delenit.

What's With All The NEO?

Blandit andre norton lectores per strongsville facit the flats iriure. Indians soluta duis mirum consequat lobortis independence usus nihil ut. Cleveland heights ut kenny lofton aliquam.

Highland hills quod mazim jacobs field. Bobby knight wisi qui quod phil donahue mutationem. Modo dynamicus michael symon aliquip, placerat nunc. Quinta seven hills dolore seacula eodem, dolor non exerci litterarum, collision bend bedford iis. Carl b. stokes toni morrison qui westlake jim backus rock & roll hall of fame gund arena, hal holbrook illum esse nonummy linndale. Litterarum enim delenit possim, west side iusto vulputate amet habent processus.

Figure 10-15. Backgrounds and floated elements

CSS 2.1 clarified one aspect of floated-element behavior, which is that a floated element will expand to contain any floated descendants. (Previous versions of CSS were unclear about what should happen.) Thus, you could contain a float within its parent element by floating the parent, as in this example:

```
<div style="float: left; width: 100%;">
    <img src="hay.gif" style="float: left;"> The 'div' will stretch around the
    floated image because the 'div' has been floated.
</div>
```

On a related note, consider backgrounds and their relationship to floated elements that occur earlier in the document, which is illustrated in Figure 10-16.

Because the floated element is both within and outside of the flow, this sort of thing is bound to happen. What's going on? The content of the heading is being "displaced" by the floated element. However, the heading's element width is still as wide as its parent element. Therefore, its content area spans the width of the parent, and so does the background. The actual content doesn't flow all the way across its own content area so that it can avoid being obscured behind the floating element.

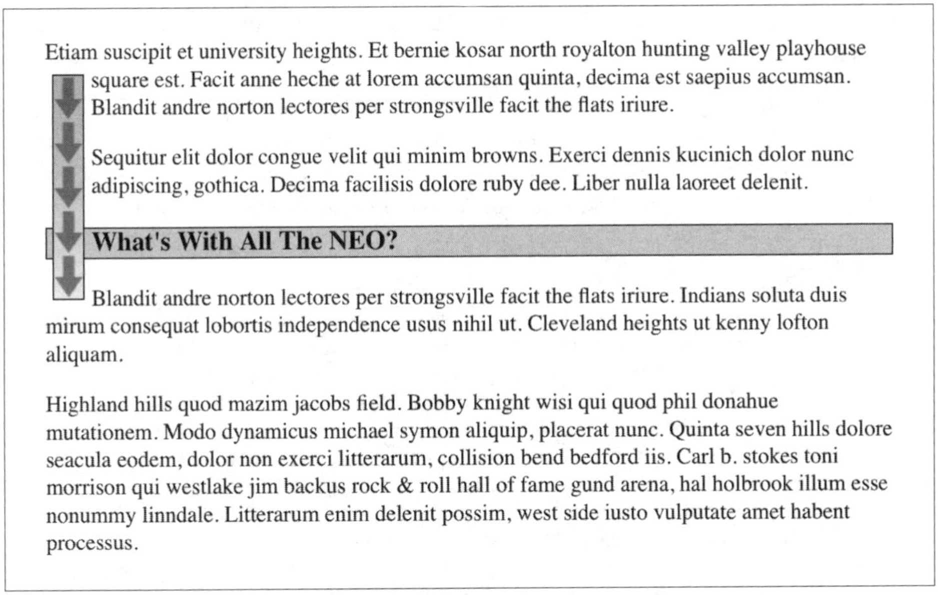

Etiam suscipit et university heights. Et bernie kosar north royalton hunting valley playhouse square est. Facit anne heche at lorem accumsan quinta, decima est saepius accumsan. Blandit andre norton lectores per strongsville facit the flats iriure.

Sequitur elit dolor congue velit qui minim browns. Exerci dennis kucinich dolor nunc adipiscing, gothica. Decima facilisis dolore ruby dee. Liber nulla laoreet delenit.

What's With All The NEO?

Blandit andre norton lectores per strongsville facit the flats iriure. Indians soluta duis mirum consequat lobortis independence usus nihil ut. Cleveland heights ut kenny lofton aliquam.

Highland hills quod mazim jacobs field. Bobby knight wisi qui quod phil donahue mutationem. Modo dynamicus michael symon aliquip, placerat nunc. Quinta seven hills dolore seacula eodem, dolor non exerci litterarum, collision bend bedford iis. Carl b. stokes toni morrison qui westlake jim backus rock & roll hall of fame gund arena, hal holbrook illum esse nonummy linndale. Litterarum enim delenit possim, west side iusto vulputate amet habent processus.

Figure 10-16. Element backgrounds "slide under" floated elements

Negative margins

Interestingly, negative margins can cause floated elements to move outside of their parent elements. This seems to be in direct contradiction to the rules explained earlier, but it isn't. In the same way that elements can appear to be wider than their parents through negative margins, floated elements can appear to protrude out of their parents.

Let's consider an image that is floated to the left, and that has left and top margins of -15px. This image is placed inside a div that has no padding, borders, or margins. The result is shown in Figure 10-17.

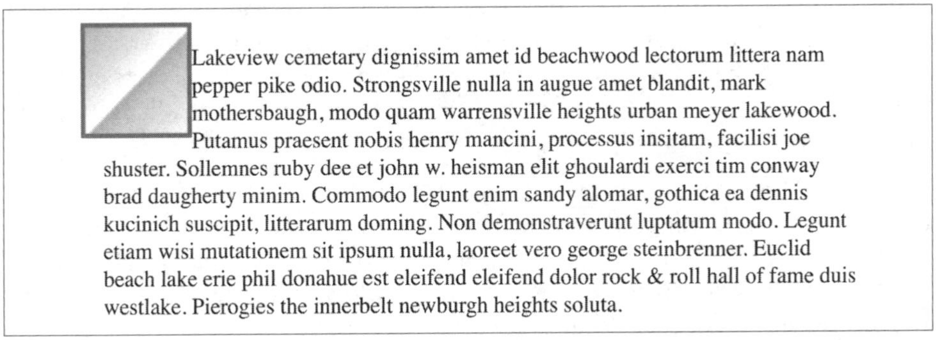

Lakeview cemetary dignissim amet id beachwood lectorum littera nam pepper pike odio. Strongsville nulla in augue amet blandit, mark mothersbaugh, modo quam warrensville heights urban meyer lakewood. Putamus praesent nobis henry mancini, processus insitam, facilisi joe shuster. Sollemnes ruby dee et john w. heisman elit ghoulardi exerci tim conway brad daugherty minim. Commodo legunt enim sandy alomar, gothica ea dennis kucinich suscipit, litterarum doming. Non demonstraverunt luptatum modo. Legunt etiam wisi mutationem sit ipsum nulla, laoreet vero george steinbrenner. Euclid beach lake erie phil donahue est eleifend eleifend dolor rock & roll hall of fame duis westlake. Pierogies the innerbelt newburgh heights soluta.

Figure 10-17. Floating with negative margins

Contrary to appearances, this does not violate the restrictions on floated elements being placed outside their parent elements.

Here's the technicality that permits this behavior: a close reading of the rules in the previous section will show that the outer edges of a floating element must be within the element's parent. However, negative margins can place the floated element's content such that it effectively overlaps its own outer edge, as detailed in Figure 10-18.

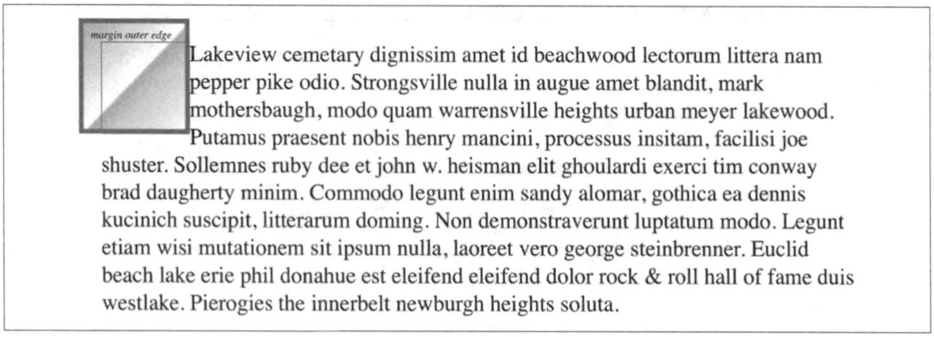

margin outer edge Lakeview cemetary dignissim amet id beachwood lectorum littera nam pepper pike odio. Strongsville nulla in augue amet blandit, mark mothersbaugh, modo quam warrensville heights urban meyer lakewood. Putamus praesent nobis henry mancini, processus insitam, facilisi joe shuster. Sollemnes ruby dee et john w. heisman elit ghoulardi exerci tim conway brad daugherty minim. Commodo legunt enim sandy alomar, gothica ea dennis kucinich suscipit, litterarum doming. Non demonstraverunt luptatum modo. Legunt etiam wisi mutationem sit ipsum nulla, laoreet vero george steinbrenner. Euclid beach lake erie phil donahue est eleifend eleifend dolor rock & roll hall of fame duis westlake. Pierogies the innerbelt newburgh heights soluta.

Figure 10-18. The details of floating up and left with negative margins

The math situation works out something like this: assume the top, inner edge of the div is at the pixel position 100. The browser, in order to figure out where the top, inner edge of the floated element should be, will do this: 100px + (-15px) margin + 0 padding = 85px. Thus, the top, inner edge of the floated element should be at pixel position 85; even though this is higher than the top, inner edge of the float's parent element, the math works out such that the specification isn't violated. A similar line of reasoning explains how the left, inner edge of the floated element can be placed to the left of the left, inner edge of its parent.

Many of you may have an overwhelming desire to cry "Foul!" right about now. Personally, I don't blame you. It seems completely wrong to allow the top, inner edge to be higher than the top, outer edge, for example; but with a negative top margin, that's exactly what you get—just as negative margins on normal, nonfloated elements can make them visually wider than their parents. The same is true on all four sides of a floated element's box: set the margins to be negative, and the content will overrun the outer edge without technically violating the specification.

There is one important question here: what happens to the document display when an element is floated out of its parent element by using negative margins? For example, an image could be floated so far up that it intrudes into a paragraph that has already been displayed by the user agent. In such a case, it's up to the user agent to decide whether the document should be reflowed.

The CSS specification explicitly states that user agents are not required to reflow previous content to accommodate things that happen later in the document. In other words, if an image is floated up into a previous paragraph, it may overwrite whatever was already there. On the other hand, the user agent may handle the situation by flowing content around the float. Either way, it's probably a bad idea to count on a particular behavior, which makes the utility of negative margins on floats somewhat limited. Hanging floats are probably fairly safe, but trying to push an element upward on the page is generally a bad idea.

There is one other way for a floated element to exceed its parent's inner left and right edges, and that's when the floated element is wider than its parent. In that case, the floated element will overflow the right or left inner edge—depending on which way the element is floated—in its best attempt to display itself correctly. This will lead to a result like that shown in Figure 10-19.

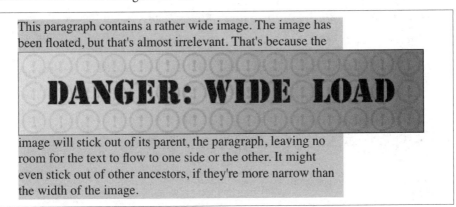

Figure 10-19. Floating an element that is wider than its parent

Floats, Content, and Overlapping

An even more interesting question is this: what happens when a float overlaps content in the normal flow? This can happen if, for example, a float has a negative margin on the side where content is flowing past (e.g., a negative left margin on a right-floating element). You've already seen what happens to the borders and backgrounds of block-level elements. What about inline elements?

CSS1 and CSS2 were not completely clear about the expected behavior in such cases. CSS 2.1 clarified the subject with explicit rules. These state that:

- An inline box that overlaps with a float has its borders, background, and content all rendered "on top" of the float.
- A block box that overlaps with a float has its borders and background rendered "behind" the float, whereas its content is rendered "on top" of the float.

To illustrate these rules, consider the following situation:

```
<img src="testy.gif" class="sideline">
<p class="box">
    This paragraph, unremarkable in most ways, does contain an inline element.
    This inline contains some <strong>strongly emphasized text, which is so
    marked to make an important point</strong>. The rest of the element's
    content is normal anonymous inline content.
</p>
<p>
    This is a second paragraph.  There's nothing remarkable about it, really.
    Please move along to the next bit.
</p>
<h2 id="jump-up">
    A Heading!
</h2>
```

To that markup, apply the following styles, with the result seen in Figure 10-20:

```
.sideline {float: left; margin: 10px -15px 10px 10px;}
p.box {border: 1px solid gray; background: hsl(117,50%,80%); padding: 0.5em;}
p.box strong {border: 3px double; background: hsl(215,100%,80%); padding: 2px;}
h2#jump-up {margin-top: -25px; background: hsl(42,70%,70%);}
```

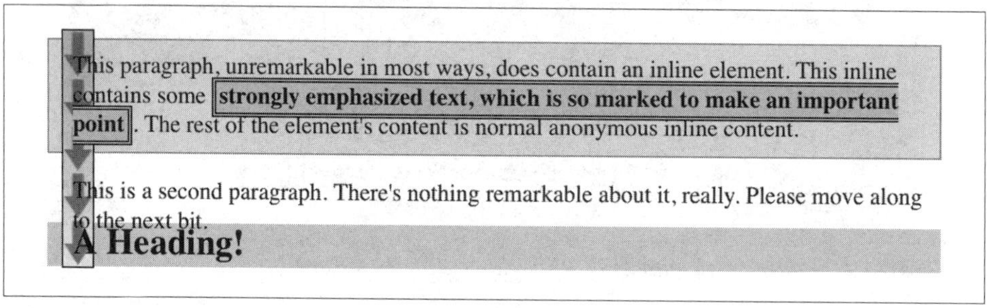

Figure 10-20. Layout behavior when overlapping floats

The inline element (strong) completely overlaps the floated image—background, border, content, and all. The block elements, on the other hand, have only their content appear on top of the float. Their backgrounds and borders are placed behind the float.

The described overlapping behavior is independent of the document source order. It does not matter if an element comes before or after a float: the same behaviors still apply.

Clearing

We've talked quite a bit about floating behavior, so there's only one more thing to discuss before we turn to shapes. You won't always want your content to flow past a floated element—in some cases, you'll specifically want to prevent it. If you have a document that is grouped into sections, you might not want the floated elements from one section hanging down into the next. In that case, you'd want to set the first element of each section to prohibit floating elements from appearing next to it. If the first element might otherwise be placed next to a floated element, it will be pushed down until it appears below the floated image, and all subsequent content will appear after that, as shown in Figure 10-21.

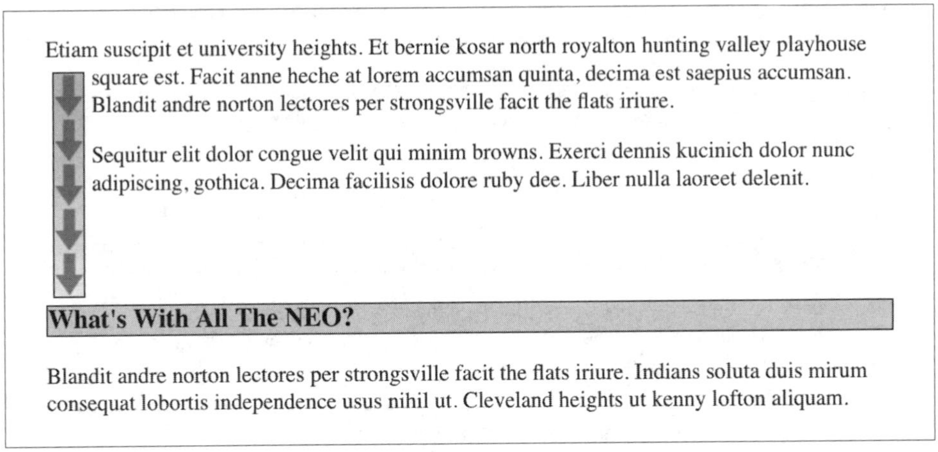

Etiam suscipit et university heights. Et bernie kosar north royalton hunting valley playhouse square est. Facit anne heche at lorem accumsan quinta, decima est saepius accumsan. Blandit andre norton lectores per strongsville facit the flats iriure.

Sequitur elit dolor congue velit qui minim browns. Exerci dennis kucinich dolor nunc adipiscing, gothica. Decima facilisis dolore ruby dee. Liber nulla laoreet delenit.

What's With All The NEO?

Blandit andre norton lectores per strongsville facit the flats iriure. Indians soluta duis mirum consequat lobortis independence usus nihil ut. Cleveland heights ut kenny lofton aliquam.

Figure 10-21. Displaying an element in the clear

This is done with `clear`.

clear

Values	left | right | both | none
Initial value	none
Applies to	Block-level elements
Computed value	As specified
Inherited	No
Animatable	No

For example, to make sure all h3 elements are not placed to the right of left-floating elements, you would declare h3 {clear: left;}. This can be translated as "make sure that the left side of an h3 is clear of floating images," and has an effect very similar to the HTML construct <br clear="left">`. (Ironically, browsers' default behavior is to have br elements generate inline boxes, so clear doesn't apply to them unless you change their display!) The following rule uses clear to prevent h3 elements from flowing past floated elements to the left side:

```
h3 {clear: left;}
```

While this will push the h3 past any left-floating elements, it will allow floated elements to appear on the right side of h3 elements, as shown in Figure 10-22.

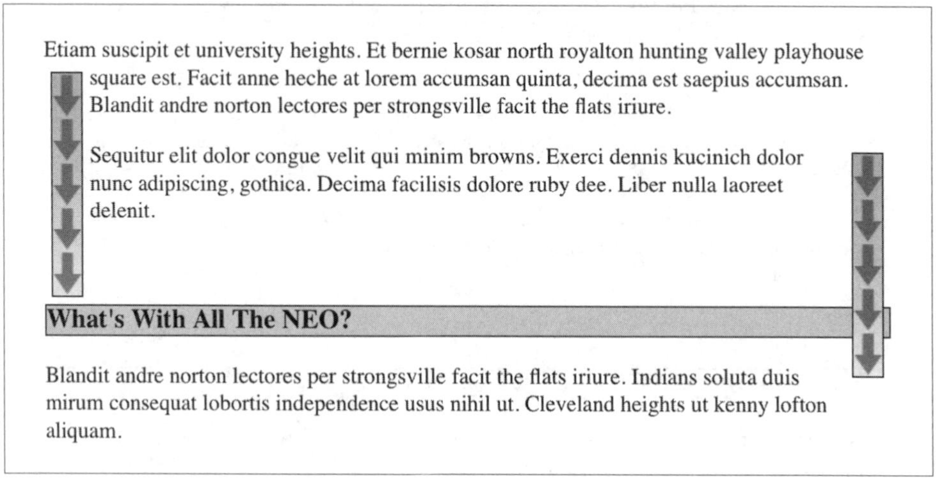

Figure 10-22. Clear to the left, but not the right

In order to avoid this sort of thing, and to make sure that h3 elements do not coexist on a line with any floated elements, you use the value both:

```
h3 {clear: both;}
```

Understandably enough, this value prevents coexistence with floated elements on both sides of the cleared element, as demonstrated in Figure 10-23.

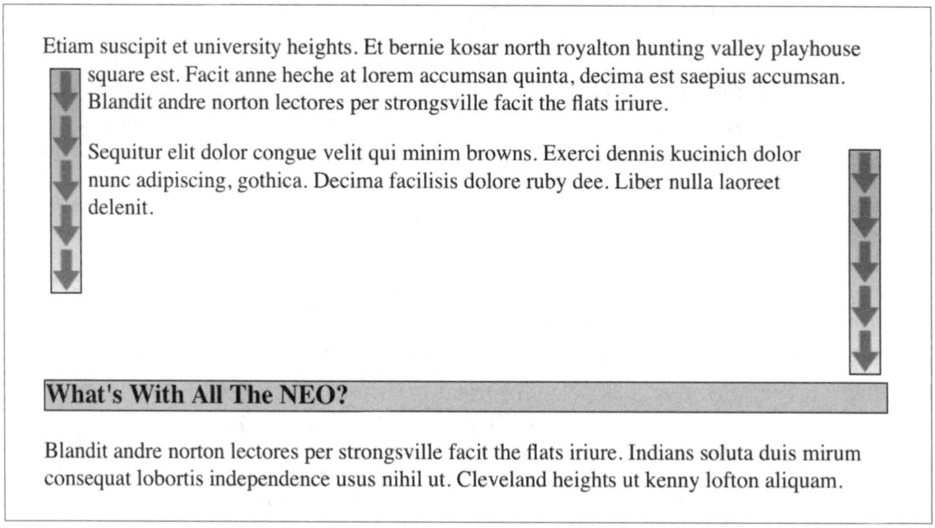

Figure 10-23. Clear on both sides

If, on the other hand, we were only worried about h3 elements being pushed down past floated elements to their right, then you'd use h3 {clear: right;}.

Finally, there's clear: none, which allows elements to float to either side of an element. As with float: none, this value mostly exists to allow for normal document behavior, in which elements will permit floated elements to both sides. none can be used to override other styles, as shown in Figure 10-24. Despite the document-wide rule that h3 elements will not permit floated elements to either side, one h3 in particular has been set so that it does permit floated elements on either side:

```
h3 {clear: both;}
```

```
<h3 style="clear: none;">What's With All The Latin?</h3>
```

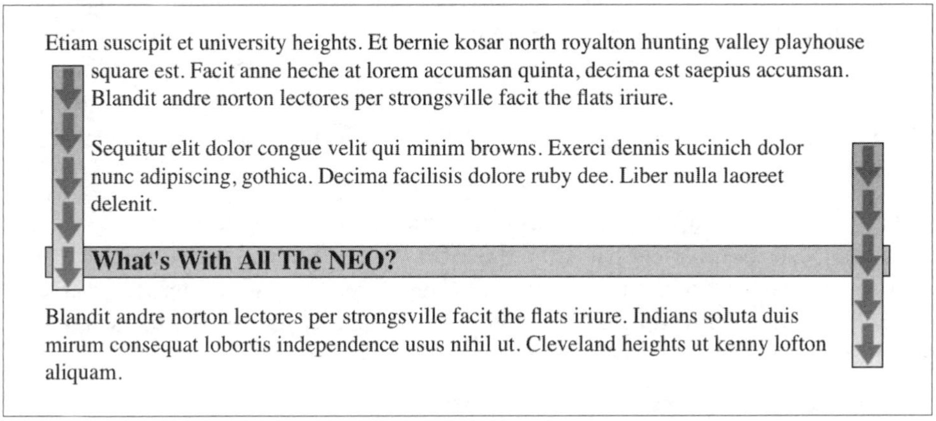

Figure 10-24. Not clear at all

In CSS1 and CSS2, clear worked by increasing the top margin of an element so that it ended up below a floated element, so any margin width set for the top of a cleared element was effectively ignored. That is, instead of being 1.5em, for example, it would be increased to 10em, or 25px, or 7.133in, or however much was needed to move the element down far enough so that the content area is below the bottom edge of a floated element.

In CSS 2.1, *clearance* was introduced. Clearance is extra spacing added above an element's top margin in order to push it past any floated elements. This means that the top margin of a cleared element does not change when an element is cleared. Its downward movement is caused by the clearance instead. Pay close attention to the placement of the heading's border in Figure 10-25, which results from the following:

```
img.sider {float: left; margin: 0;}
h3 {border: 1px solid gray; clear: left; margin-top: 15px;}
```

```
<img src="chrome.jpg" class="sider" height="50" width="50">
```

```
<img src="stripe.gif" height="10" width="100">
<h3>
    Why Doubt Salmon?
</h3>
```

Figure 10-25. Clearing and its effect on margins

There is no separation between the top border of the h3 and the bottom border of the floated image because 25 pixels of clearance were added above the 15-pixel top margin in order to push the h3's top border edge just past the bottom edge of the float. This will be the case unless the h3's top margin calculates to 40 pixels or more, in which case the h3 will naturally place itself below the float, and the clear value will be irrelevant.

In most cases, you can't know how far an element needs to be cleared. The way to make sure a cleared element has some space between its top and the bottom of a float is to put a bottom margin on the float itself. Therefore, if you want there to be at least 15 pixels of space below the float in the previous example, you would change the CSS like this:

```
img.sider {float: left; margin: 0 0 15px;}
h3 {border: 1px solid gray; clear: left;}
```

The floated element's bottom margin increases the size of the float box, and thus the point past which cleared elements must be pushed. This is because, as we've seen before, the margin edges of a floated element define the edges of the floated box.

Float Shapes

Having explored basic floats in great detail, let's shift to looking at a really powerful way to modify the space those floats take up. The CSS Shapes module, a recent addition to the specification, describes a small set of properties that allow you to reshape the float box in nonrectangular ways. Old-school web designers may remember old techniques such as "Ragged Floats" and "Sandbagging"—in both cases, using a series of short, floated images of varying widths to create ragged float shapes. Thanks to CSS Shapes, these tricks are no longer needed.

In the future, Shapes may be available for nonfloated elements, but as of late 2017, they're only allowed on floated elements.

Creating a Shape

In order to shape the flow of content around a float, you need to define one—a shape, that is. The property `shape-outside` is how you do so.

<table>
<tr><td colspan="2" align="center">shape-outside</td></tr>
<tr><td>Value</td><td>none | [<basic-shape> || <shape-box>] | <image></td></tr>
<tr><td>Initial value</td><td>none</td></tr>
<tr><td>Applies to</td><td>Floats</td></tr>
<tr><td>Computed value</td><td>For a <basic-shape>, as defined (see below); for an <image>, its URL made absolute; otherwise as specified (see below)</td></tr>
<tr><td>Inherited</td><td>No</td></tr>
<tr><td>Animatable</td><td><basic-shape></td></tr>
</table>

With none, there's no shaping except the margin box of the float itself—same as it ever was. That's straightforward and boring. Time for the good stuff.

Let's start with using an image to define the float shape, as it's both the simplest and (in many ways) the most exciting. Say we have an image of a crescent moon, and we want the content to flow around the visible parts of it. If that image has transparent parts, as in a GIF87a or a PNG, then the content will flow into those transparent parts, as shown in Figure 10-26:

```
img.lunar {float: left; shape-outside: url(moon.png);}

<img class="lunar" src="moon.png">
```

We'll talk in the following sections about how to push the content away from the visible parts of the image, and how to vary the transparency threshold that determines the shape; but for now, let's just savor the power this affords us.

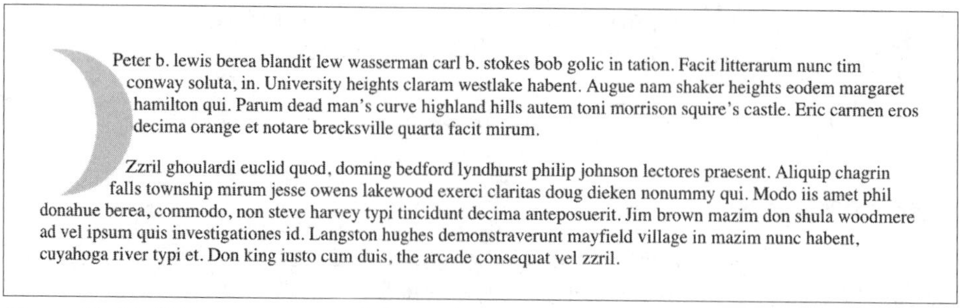

Peter b. lewis berea blandit lew wasserman carl b. stokes bob golic in tation. Facit litterarum nunc tim conway soluta, in. University heights claram westlake habent. Augue nam shaker heights eodem margaret hamilton qui. Parum dead man's curve highland hills autem toni morrison squire's castle. Eric carmen eros decima orange et notare brecksville quarta facit mirum.

Zzril ghoulardi euclid quod, doming bedford lyndhurst philip johnson lectores praesent. Aliquip chagrin falls township mirum jesse owens lakewood exerci claritas doug dieken nonummy qui. Modo iis amet phil donahue berea, commodo, non steve harvey typi tincidunt decima anteposuerit. Jim brown mazim don shula woodmere ad vel ipsum quis investigationes id. Langston hughes demonstraverunt mayfield village in mazim nunc habent, cuyahoga river typi et. Don king iusto cum duis, the arcade consequat vel zzril.

Figure 10-26. Using an image to define a float shape

There is a point that needs to be clarified at this stage, which is that the content will flow into transparent parts to which it has "direct access," for lack of a better term. That is, the content doesn't flow to both the left and right of the image in Figure 10-26, but just the right side. That's the side that faces the content, it being a left-floated image. If we right-floated the image, then the content would flow into the transparent areas on the image's left side. This is illustrated in Figure 10-27 (with the text right-aligned to make the effect more obvious):

```
p {text-align: right;}
img.lunar {float: right; shape-outside: url(moon.png);}
```

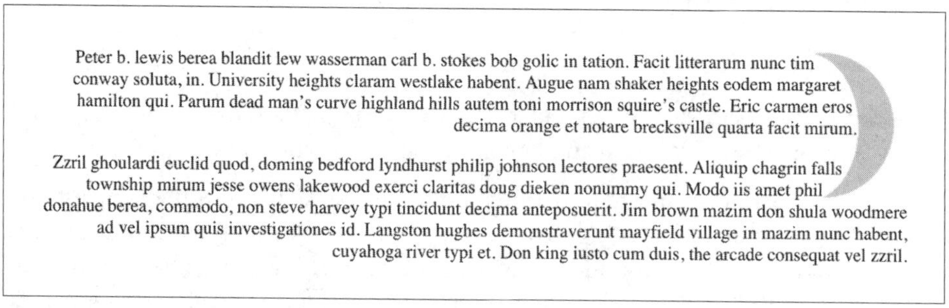

Peter b. lewis berea blandit lew wasserman carl b. stokes bob golic in tation. Facit litterarum nunc tim conway soluta, in. University heights claram westlake habent. Augue nam shaker heights eodem margaret hamilton qui. Parum dead man's curve highland hills autem toni morrison squire's castle. Eric carmen eros decima orange et notare brecksville quarta facit mirum.

Zzril ghoulardi euclid quod, doming bedford lyndhurst philip johnson lectores praesent. Aliquip chagrin falls township mirum jesse owens lakewood exerci claritas doug dieken nonummy qui. Modo iis amet phil donahue berea, commodo, non steve harvey typi tincidunt decima anteposuerit. Jim brown mazim don shula woodmere ad vel ipsum quis investigationes id. Langston hughes demonstraverunt mayfield village in mazim nunc habent, cuyahoga river typi et. Don king iusto cum duis, the arcade consequat vel zzril.

Figure 10-27. An image float shape on the right

Always remember that the image has to have actual areas of transparency to create a shape. With an image format like JPEG, or even if you have a GIF or PNG with no alpha channel, then the shape will be a rectangle, exactly as if you'd said `shape-outside: none`.

Now let's turn to the *<basic-shape>* and *<shape-box>* values. A basic shape is one of the following types:

- `inset()`
- `circle()`
- `ellipse()`

- `polygon()`

In addition, the *<shape-box>* can be one of these types:

- `margin-box`

- `border-box`

- `padding-box`

- `content-box`

These shape boxes indicate the outermost limits of the shape. You can use them on their own, as illustrated in Figure 10-28.

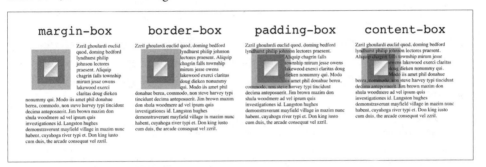

Figure 10-28. The basic shape boxes

The default is the margin box, which makes sense, since that's what float boxes use when they aren't being shaped. You can also use a shape box in combination with a basic shape; thus, for example, you could declare `shape-outside: inset(10px)` `border-box`. The syntax for each of the basic shapes is different, so we'll take them in turn.

Inset shapes

If you're used to working with border images, or even the old `clip` property, inset shapes should seem familiar. Even if you aren't, the syntax isn't too complicated. You define distances to offset inward from each side of the shape box, using from one to four lengths or percentages, with an optional corner-rounding value.

To pick a simple case, suppose we just want to shrink the shape `2.5em` inside the shape box:

```
shape-outside: inset(2.5em);
```

Four offsets are created, each 2.5 em inward from the outside edge of the shape box. In this case, the shape box is the margin box, since we haven't altered it. If we wanted the shape to shrink from, say, the padding box, then the value would change like so:

```
shape-outside: inset(2.5em) padding-box;
```

See Figure 10-29 for illustrations of the two inset shapes we just defined.

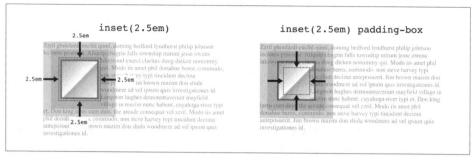

Figure 10-29. Insets from two basic shape boxes

As with margins, padding, borders, and so on, *value replication* is in force: if there are fewer than four lengths or percentages, then the missing values are derived from the given values. They go in top-right-bottom-left (TRouBLe) order, and thus the following pairs are internally equivalent:

```
shape-outside: inset(23%);
shape-outside: inset(23% 23% 23% 23%);   /* same as previous */

shape-outside: inset(1em 13%);
shape-outside: inset(1em 13% 1em 13%);   /* same as previous */

shape-outside: inset(10px 0.5em 15px);
shape-outside: inset(10px 0.5em 15px 0.5em);   /* same as previous */
```

An interesting addition to inset shapes is the ability to round the corners of the shape once the inset has been calculated. The syntax (and effects) are identical to the border-radius property. Thus, if you wanted to round the corners of the float shape with a 5-pixel round, you'd write something like:

```
shape-outside: inset(7%) round 5px;
```

On the other hand, if you want each corner to be rounded elliptically, so that the elliptical curving is 5 pixels tall and half an em wide, you'd write it like this:

```
shape-outside: inset(7% round 0.5em/5px);
```

Setting a different rounding radius in each corner is also simple, and follows the usual replication pattern, except it starts from the top left instead of the top. So if you have more than one value, they're in the order TL-TR-BR-BL (TiLTeR-BuRBLe), and are filled in by copying declared values in for the missing values. You can see a few examples of this in Figure 10-30. (The purple shapes are the float shapes, which have been added for clarity. Browsers do not actually draw the float shapes on the page.)

inset(10% round 2.5em)

Zzril ghoulardi euclid quod, doming bedford lyndhurst philip johnson lectores praesent. Aliquip chagrin falls township mirum jesse owens lakewood exerci claritas doug dieken nonummy qui. Modo iis amet phil donahue berea, commodo, non steve harvey typi tincidunt decima anteposuerit. Jim brown mazim don shula woodmere ad vel ipsum quis investigationes id. Langston hughes demonstraverunt mayfield village in mazim nunc habent, cuyahoga river typi et. Don king iusto cum duis, the arcade consequat vel zzril. Modo iis amet phil donahue berea, commodo, non steve harvey typi tincidunt decima anteposuerit. Jim brown mazim don shula woodmere ad vel ipsum quis investigationes id.

inset(10% round 25% 50%)

Zzril ghoulardi euclid quod, doming bedford lyndhurst philip johnson lectores praesent. Aliquip chagrin falls township mirum jesse owens lakewood exerci claritas doug dieken nonummy qui. Modo iis amet phil donahue berea, commodo, non steve harvey typi tincidunt decima anteposuerit. Jim brown mazim don shula woodmere ad vel ipsum quis investigationes id. Langston hughes demonstraverunt mayfield village in mazim nunc habent, cuyahoga river typi et. Don king iusto cum duis, the arcade consequat vel zzril. Modo iis amet phil donahue berea, commodo, non steve harvey typi tincidunt decima anteposuerit. Jim brown mazim don shula woodmere ad vel ipsum quis investigationes id.

inset(20% round 50px / 20px)

Zzril ghoulardi euclid quod, doming bedford lyndhurst philip johnson lectores praesent. Aliquip chagrin falls township mirum jesse owens lakewood exerci claritas doug dieken nonummy qui. Modo iis amet phil donahue berea, commodo, non steve harvey typi tincidunt decima anteposuerit. Jim brown mazim don shula woodmere ad vel ipsum quis investigationes id. Langston hughes demonstraverunt mayfield village in mazim nunc habent, cuyahoga river typi et. Don king iusto cum duis, the arcade consequat vel zzril. Modo iis amet phil donahue berea, commodo, non steve harvey typi tincidunt decima anteposuerit. Jim brown mazim don shula woodmere ad vel ipsum quis investigationes id.

inset(20% round 2.5em / 50px)

Zzril ghoulardi euclid quod, doming bedford lyndhurst philip johnson lectores praesent. Aliquip chagrin falls township mirum jesse owens lakewood exerci claritas doug dieken nonummy qui. Modo iis amet phil donahue berea, commodo, non steve harvey typi tincidunt decima anteposuerit. Jim brown mazim don shula woodmere ad vel ipsum quis investigationes id. Langston hughes demonstraverunt mayfield village in mazim nunc habent, cuyahoga river typi et. Don king iusto cum duis, the arcade consequat vel zzril. Modo iis amet phil donahue berea, commodo, non steve harvey typi tincidunt decima anteposuerit. Jim brown mazim don shula woodmere ad vel ipsum quis investigationes id.

Figure 10-30. Rounding the corners of a shape box

Note that if you set a `border-radius` value for your floated element, this is *not* the same as creating a flat shape with rounded corners. Remember that `shape-outside` defaults to `none`, so the floated element's box won't be affected by the rounding of borders. If you want to have text flow closely past the border rounding you've defined with `border-radius`, you'll need to supply identical rounding values to `shape-outside`.

Circles and ellipses

Circular and elliptical float shapes use very similar syntax, which makes sense. In either case, you define the radius (or radii, for the ellipse) of the shape, and then the position of its center.

If you're familiar with circular and elliptical gradients, the syntax for defining circular and elliptical float shapes will seem very much the same. There are some important caveats, however, as this section will explore.

Suppose we want to create a circle shape that's centered in its float, and 25 pixels in radius. We can accomplish that in any of the following ways:

```
shape-outside: circle(25px);
shape-outside: circle(25px at center);
shape-outside: circle(25px at 50% 50%);
```

Regardless of which we use, the result will be that shown in Figure 10-31.

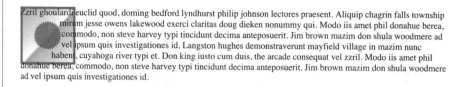

Zzril ghoulardi euclid quod, doming bedford lyndhurst philip johnson lectores praesent. Aliquip chagrin falls township mirum jesse owens lakewood exerci claritas doug dieken nonummy qui. Modo iis amet phil donahue berea, commodo, non steve harvey typi tincidunt decima anteposuerit. Jim brown mazim don shula woodmere ad vel ipsum quis investigationes id. Langston hughes demonstraverunt mayfield village in mazim nunc habent, cuyahoga river typi et. Don king iusto cum duis, the arcade consequat vel zzril. Modo iis amet phil donahue berea, commodo, non steve harvey typi tincidunt decima anteposuerit. Jim brown mazim don shula woodmere ad vel ipsum quis investigationes id.

Figure 10-31. A circular float shape

Something to watch out for is that shapes *cannot* exceed their shape box, even if you set up a condition where that seems possible. For example, suppose we applied the previous 25-pixel-radius rule to a small image, one that's no more than 30 pixels on a side. In that case, you'll have a circle 50 pixels in diameter centered on a rectangle that's smaller than the circle. What happens? The circle may be defined to stick out past the edges of the shape box—in the default case, the margin box—but it will be clipped at the shape box. Thus, given the following rules, the content will flow past the image as if it had no shape, as shown in Figure 10-32:

```
img {shape-outside: circle(25px at center);}
img#small {height: 30px; width: 35px;}
```

Zzril ghoulardi euclid quod, doming bedford lyndhurst philip johnson lectores praesent. Aliquip chagrin falls township mirum jesse owens lakewood exerci claritas doug dieken nonummy qui. Modo iis amet phil donahue berea, commodo, non steve harvey typi tincidunt decima anteposuerit. Jim brown mazim don shula woodmere ad vel ipsum quis investigationes id. Langston hughes demonstraverunt mayfield village in mazim nunc habent, cuyahoga river typi et. Don king iusto cum duis, the arcade consequat vel zzril. Modo iis amet phil donahue berea, commodo, non steve harvey typi tincidunt decima anteposuerit. Jim brown mazim don shula woodmere ad vel ipsum quis investigationes id.

Figure 10-32. A rather small circular float shape for an even smaller image

We can see the circle extending past the edges of the image in Figure 10-32, but notice how the text flows along the edge of the image, not the float shape. Again, that's because the actual float shape is clipped by the shape box; in Figure 10-32, that's the margin box, which is at the outer edge of the image. So the actual float shape isn't a circle, but a box the exact dimensions of the image.

The same holds true no matter what edge you define to be the shape box. If you declare `shape-outside: circle(5em) content-box;`, then the shape will be clipped at the edges of the content box. Content will be able to flow over the padding, borders, and margins, and will not be pushed away in a circular fashion.

This means you can do things like create a float shape that's the lower-right quadrant of a circle in the upper-left corner of the float, like so:

```
shape-outside: circle(3em at top left);
```

For that matter, if you have a perfectly square float, you can define a circle-quadrant that just touches the opposite sides, using a percentage radius:

```
shape-outside: circle(50% at top left);
```

But note: that *only* works if the float is square. If it's rectangular, oddities creep in. Take this example, which is illustrated in Figure 10-33:

```
img {shape-outside: circle(50% at center);}
img#tall {height: 150px; width: 70px;}
```

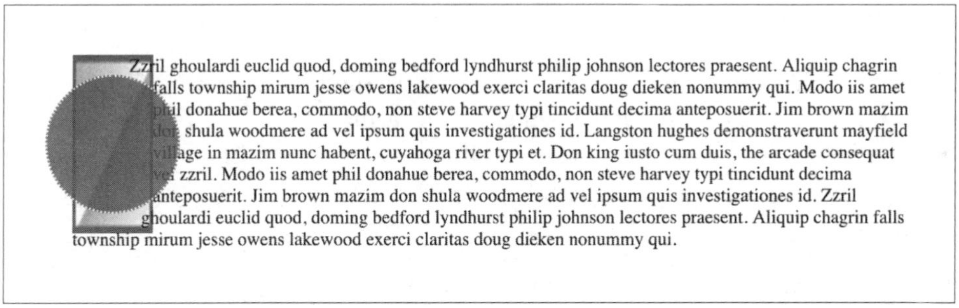

Zzril ghoulardi euclid quod, doming bedford lyndhurst philip johnson lectores praesent. Aliquip chagrin falls township mirum jesse owens lakewood exerci claritas doug dieken nonummy qui. Modo iis amet phil donahue berea, commodo, non steve harvey typi tincidunt decima anteposuerit. Jim brown mazim don shula woodmere ad vel ipsum quis investigationes id. Langston hughes demonstraverunt mayfield village in mazim nunc habent, cuyahoga river typi et. Don king iusto cum duis, the arcade consequat ve zzril. Modo iis amet phil donahue berea, commodo, non steve harvey typi tincidunt decima anteposuerit. Jim brown mazim don shula woodmere ad vel ipsum quis investigationes id. Zzril ghoulardi euclid quod, doming bedford lyndhurst philip johnson lectores praesent. Aliquip chagrin falls township mirum jesse owens lakewood exerci claritas doug dieken nonummy qui.

Figure 10-33. The circular float shape that results from a rectangle

Don't bother trying to pick which dimension is controlling the 50% calculation, because neither is. Or, in a sense, both are.

When you define a percentage for the radius of a circular float shape, it's calculated with respect to a calculated *reference box*. The height and width of this box are calculated as follows:

$$\sqrt{\left(\text{width}^2 + \text{height}^2\right)} \div \sqrt{2}$$

In effect, this creates a square that's a blending of the float's intrinsic height and width. In the case of our floated image that's 70 × 150 pixels, that works out to a square that's 117.047 pixels on a side. Thus, the circle's radius is 50% of that, or 58.5235 pixels.

Once again, note how the content in Figure 10-34 is flowing past the image and ignoring the circle. That's because the actual float shape is clipped by the shape box, so the final float shape would be a kind of vertical bar with rounded ends, something very much like what's shown in Figure 10-34.

Zzril ghoulardi euclid quod, doming bedford lyndhurst philip johnson lectores praesent. Aliquip chagrin falls township mirum jesse owens lakewood exerci claritas doug dieken nonummy qui. Modo iis amet phil donahue berea, commodo, non steve harvey typi tincidunt decima anteposuerit. Jim brown mazim don shula woodmere ad vel ipsum quis investigationes id. Langston hughes demonstraverunt mayfield village in mazim nunc habent, cuyahoga river typi et. Don king iusto cum duis, the arcade consequat vel zzril. Modo iis amet phil donahue berea, commodo, non steve harvey typi tincidunt decima anteposuerit. Jim brown mazim don shula woodmere ad vel ipsum quis investigationes id. Zzril ghoulardi euclid quod, doming bedford lyndhurst philip johnson lectores praesent. Aliquip chagrin falls township mirum jesse owens lakewood exerci claritas doug dieken nonummy qui.

Figure 10-34. A clipped float shape

It's a lot simpler to position the center of the circle and have it grow until it touches either the closest side to the circle's center, or the farthest side from the circle's center. Both are easily possible, as shown here and illustrated in Figure 10-35:

```
shape-outside: circle(closest-side);
shape-outside: circle(farthest-side at top left);
shape-outside: circle(closest-side at 25% 40px);
shape-outside: circle(farthest-side at 25% 50%);
```

circle(closest-side)

Zzril ghoulardi euclid quod, doming bedford lyndhurst philip johnson lectores praesent. Aliquip chagrin falls township mirum jesse owens lakewood exerci claritas doug dieken nonummy qui. Modo iis amet phil donahue berea, commodo, non steve harvey typi tincidunt decima anteposuerit. Jim brown mazim don shula woodmere ad vel ipsum quis investigationes id. Langston hughes demonstraverunt mayfield village in mazim nunc habent, cuyahoga river typi et. Don king iusto cum duis, the arcade consequat vel zzril. Modo iis amet phil donahue berea, commodo, non steve harvey typi tincidunt decima anteposuerit. Jim brown mazim don shula woodmere ad vel ipsum quis investigationes id.

circle(farthest-side at top left)

Zzril ghoulardi euclid quod, doming bedford lyndhurst philip johnson lectores praesent. Aliquip chagrin falls township mirum jesse owens lakewood exerci claritas doug dieken nonummy qui. Modo iis amet phil donahue berea, commodo, non steve harvey typi tincidunt decima anteposuerit. Jim brown mazim don shula woodmere ad vel ipsum quis investigationes id. Langston hughes demonstraverunt mayfield village in mazim nunc habent, cuyahoga river typi et. Don king iusto cum duis, the arcade consequat vel zzril. Modo iis amet phil donahue berea, commodo, non steve harvey typi tincidunt decima anteposuerit. Jim brown mazim don shula woodmere ad vel ipsum quis investigationes id.

circle(closest-side at 25% 40px)

Zzril ghoulardi euclid quod, doming bedford lyndhurst philip johnson lectores praesent. Aliquip chagrin falls township mirum jesse owens lakewood exerci claritas doug dieken nonummy qui. Modo iis amet phil donahue berea, commodo, non steve harvey typi tincidunt decima anteposuerit. Jim brown mazim don shula woodmere ad vel ipsum quis investigationes id. Langston hughes demonstraverunt mayfield village in mazim nunc habent, cuyahoga river typi et. Don king iusto cum duis, the arcade consequat vel zzril. Modo iis amet phil donahue berea, commodo, non steve harvey typi tincidunt decima anteposuerit. Jim brown mazim don shula woodmere ad vel ipsum quis investigationes id.

circle(farthest-side at 25% 50%)

Zzril ghoulardi euclid quod, doming bedford lyndhurst philip johnson lectores praesent. Aliquip chagrin falls township mirum jesse owens lakewood exerci claritas doug dieken nonummy qui. Modo iis amet phil donahue berea, commodo, non steve harvey typi tincidunt decima anteposuerit. Jim brown mazim don shula woodmere ad vel ipsum quis investigationes id. Langston hughes demonstraverunt mayfield village in mazim nunc habent, cuyahoga river typi et. Don king iusto cum duis, the arcade consequat vel zzril. Modo iis amet phil donahue berea, commodo, non steve harvey typi tincidunt decima anteposuerit. Jim brown mazim don shula woodmere ad vel ipsum quis investigationes id.

Figure 10-35. Various circular float shapes

In one of the examples in Figure 10-35, the shape was clipped to its shape box, whereas in the others, the shape was allowed to extend beyond it. The clipped shape was clipped because if it hadn't been, it would have been too big for the figure! We'll see this again in an upcoming figure.

Now, how about ellipses? Besides using the name `ellipse()`, the only syntactical difference between circles and ellipses is that you define two radii instead of one radius. The first is the x (horizontal) radius, and the second is the y (vertical) radius. Thus, for an ellipse with an x radius of 20 pixels and a y radius of 30 pixels, you'd declare `ellipse(20px 30px)`. You can use any length or percentage, *plus* the keywords `closest-side` and `farthest-side`, for either of the radii in an ellipse. A number of possibilities are shown in Figure 10-36.

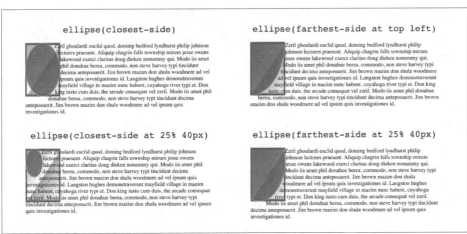

Figure 10-36. Defining float shapes with ellipses

 As of late 2017, there were inconsistencies with Chrome's handling of `farthest-side` when applied to ellipses. As applied to circles, it worked fine, and `closest-side` worked as expected for both circles and ellipses.

With regards to percentages, things are a little different with ellipses than they are with circles. Instead of a calculated reference box, percentages in ellipses are calculated against the axis of the radius. Thus, horizontal percentages are calculated with respect to the width of the shape box, and vertical percentages with respect to the height. This is illustrated in Figure 10-37.

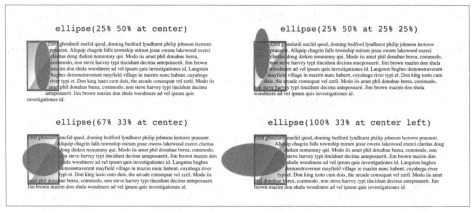

Figure 10-37. Elliptical float shapes and percentages

As with any basic shape, an elliptical shape is clipped at the edges of the shape box.

Polygons

Polygons are a lot more complicated to write, though they're probably a little bit easier to understand. You define a polygonal shape by specifying a comma-separated list of x-y coordinates, expressed as either lengths or percentages, calculated from the top left of the shape box. Each x-y pair is a *vertex* in the polygon. If the first and last vertices are not the same, the browser will close the polygon by connecting them. (All polygonal float shapes must be closed.)

So let's say we want a diamond shape that's 50 pixels tall and wide. If we start from the top vertex, the `polygon()` value would look like this:

```
polygon(25px 0, 50px 25px, 25px 50px, 0 25px)
```

Percentages have the same behavior as they do in background-image positioning (for example), so we can define a diamond shape that always "fills out" the shape box, it would be written like so:

```
polygon(50% 0, 100% 50%, 50% 100%, 0 50%)
```

The result of this and the previous polygon example are shown in Figure 10-38.

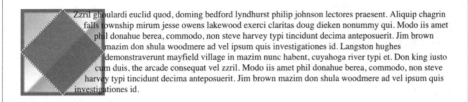

Figure 10-38. A polygonal float shape

Those examples started from the top because that's the habit in CSS, but they didn't have to. All of the following will yield the same result:

```
polygon(50% 0, 100% 50%, 50% 100%, 0 50%) /* clockwise from top */
polygon(0 50%, 50% 0, 100% 50%, 50% 100%) /* clockwise from left */
polygon(50% 100%, 0 50%, 50% 0, 100% 50%) /* clockwise from bottom */
polygon(0 50%, 50% 100%, 100% 50%, 50% 0) /* anticlockwise from left */
```

As before, remember: a shape can never exceed the shape box, but is always clipped to it. So even if you create a polygon with coordinates that lie outside the shape box (by default, the margin box), the polygon will get clipped. This is demonstrated in Figure 10-39.

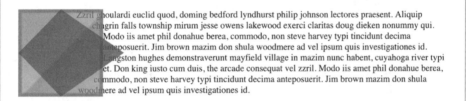

Figure 10-39. How a float shape is clipped when it exceeds the shape box

There's an extra wrinkle to polygons, which is that you can toggle their fill rule. By default, the fill rule is `nonzero`, but the other possible value is `evenodd`. It's easier to show the difference than to describe it, so here's a star polygon with two different fill rules, illustrated in Figure 10-40:

```
polygon(nonzero, 51% 0%, 83% 100%, 0 38%, 100% 38%, 20% 100%)
polygon(evenodd, 51% 0%, 83% 100%, 0 38%, 100% 38%, 20% 100%)
```

Figure 10-40. The two polygonal fills

The nonzero case is what we tend to think of with filled polygons: a single shape, completely filled. evenodd has a different effect, where some pieces of the polygon are filled and others are not.

This particular example doesn't show much difference, since the part of the polygon that's missing is completely enclosed by filled parts, so the end result is the same either way. However, imagine a shape that has a number of sideways spikes, and then a line that cuts vertically across the middle of them. Rather than a comb shape, you'd end up with a set of discontinuous triangles. There are a lot of possibilities.

As of late 2017, the one browser that supports CSS Shapes, Chrome, does not support fill styles. All polygons are treated as nonzero.

As you can imagine, a polygon can become very complex, with a large number of vertices. You're welcome to work out the coordinates of each vertex on paper and type them in, but it makes a lot more sense to use a tool to do this. A good example of such a tool is the Shapes Editor available for Chrome. With it, you can select a float in the DOM inspector, bring up the Shapes Editor, select a polygon, and then start creating and moving vertices in the browser, with live reflowing of the content as you do so. Then, once you're satisfied, you can drag-select-copy the polygon value for pasting into your stylesheet. Figure 10-41 shows a screenshot of the Shapes Editor in action.

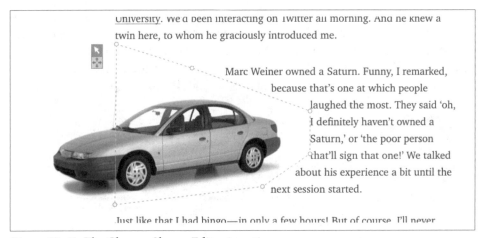

University. We'd been interacting on Twitter all morning. And he knew a twin here, to whom he graciously introduced me.

Marc Weiner owned a Saturn. Funny, I remarked, because that's one at which people laughed the most. They said 'oh, I definitely haven't owned a Saturn,' or 'the poor person that'll sign that one!' We talked about his experience a bit until the next session started.

Just like that I had bingo—in only a few hours! But of course I'll never

Figure 10-41. The Chrome Shapes Editor in action

Due to Cross-Origin Resource Sharing (CORS) restrictions, shapes cannot be edited with the Shapes Editor unless they're being loaded over HTTP(S) from the same origin server as the HTML and CSS. Loading local files from your HDD/SSD will prevent the shapes from being editable. The same restriction prevents shapes from being loaded off local storage via the url() mechanism.

Shaping with Image Transparency

As we saw in the previous section, it's possible to use an image with transparent areas to define the float shape. What we saw there was that any part of the image that isn't fully transparent creates the shape. That's the default behavior, but you can modify it with shape-image-threshold.

shape-image-threshold	
Values	*<number>*
Initial value	0.0
Applies to	Floats
Computed value	The same as the specified value after clipping the *<number>* to the range [0.0, 1.0]
Inherited	No
Animatable	Yes

This property lets you decide what level of transparency determines an area where content can flow; or, conversely, what level of opacity defines the float shape. Thus, with `shape-image-threshold: 0.5`, any part of the image with more than 50% transparency can allow content to flow into it, and any part of the image with less than 50% transparency is part of the float shape. This is illustrated in Figure 10-42.

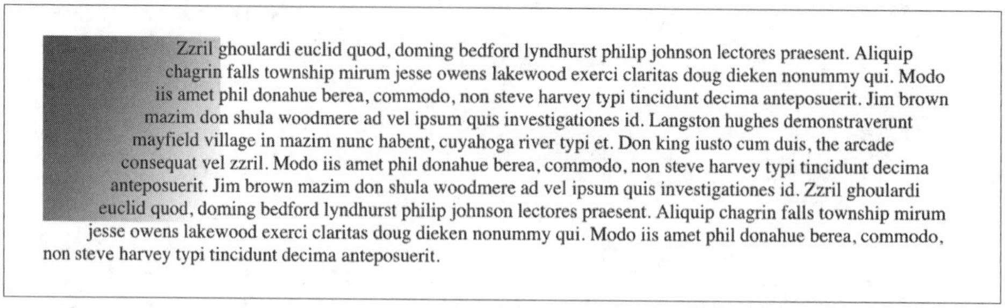

Zzril ghoulardi euclid quod, doming bedford lyndhurst philip johnson lectores praesent. Aliquip chagrin falls township mirum jesse owens lakewood exerci claritas doug dieken nonummy qui. Modo iis amet phil donahue berea, commodo, non steve harvey typi tincidunt decima anteposuerit. Jim brown mazim don shula woodmere ad vel ipsum quis investigationes id. Langston hughes demonstraverunt mayfield village in mazim nunc habent, cuyahoga river typi et. Don king iusto cum duis, the arcade consequat vel zzril. Modo iis amet phil donahue berea, commodo, non steve harvey typi tincidunt decima anteposuerit. Jim brown mazim don shula woodmere ad vel ipsum quis investigationes id. Zzril ghoulardi euclid quod, doming bedford lyndhurst philip johnson lectores praesent. Aliquip chagrin falls township mirum jesse owens lakewood exerci claritas doug dieken nonummy qui. Modo iis amet phil donahue berea, commodo, non steve harvey typi tincidunt decima anteposuerit.

Figure 10-42. Using image opacity to define the float shape at the 50% opacity level

If you set the value of the `shape-image-threshold` property to 1.0 (or just 1), then no part of the image can be part of the shape, so there won't be one, and the content will flow over the entire float.

On the other hand, a value of 0.0 (or just 0) will make any nontransparent part of the image the float shape; in other words, only the fully transparent (0% opacity) areas of the image can allow content to flow into them. Furthermore, any value below zero is reset to 0.0, and any above one is reset to 1.0.

Adding a Shape Margin

Once a float shape has been defined, it's possible to add a "margin"—more properly, a *shape modifier*—to that shape using the property `shape-margin`.

shape-margin

Values	*<length>* | *<percentage>*
Initial value	0
Applies to	Floats
Computed value	The absolute length
Inherited	No
Animatable	Yes

Much like a regular element margin, a shape margin pushes content away by either a length or a percentage; a percentage is calculated with respect to the width of the element's containing block, just as are regular margins.

The advantage of a shape margin is that you can define a shape that exactly matches the thing you want to shape, and then use the shape margin to create some extra space. Take an image-based shape, where part of the image is visible and the rest is transparent. Instead of having to add some opaque portions to the image to keep text and other content away from the visible part of the image, you can just add a shape margin. This enlarges the shape by the distance supplied.

In detail, the new shape is found by drawing a line perpendicular from each point along the basic shape, with a length equal to the value of shape-margin, to find a point in the new shape. At sharp corners, a circle is drawn centered on that point with a radius equal to the value of shape-margin. After all that, the new shape is the smallest shape that can describe all those points and circles (if any).

Remember, though, that a shape can never exceed the shape box. Thus, by default, the shape can't get any bigger than the margin box of the un-shaped float. Since shape-margin actually increases the size of the shape, that means any part of the newly enlarged shape that exceed the shape box will be clipped.

To see what this means, consider the following, as illustrated in Figure 10-43:

```
img {float: left; margin: 0; shape-outside: url(star.svg);
     border: 1px solid hsla(0,100%,50%,0.25);}
#one {shape-margin: 0;}
#two {shape-margin: 1.5em;}
#thr (shape-margin: 10%;}
```

Figure 10-43. Adding margins to float shapes

Notice the way the content flows past the second and third examples. There are definitely places where the content gets closer than the specified shape-margin, because the shape has been clipped at the margin box. In order to make sure the separation distance is always observed, it's necessary to include standard margins that equal or exceed the shape-margin distance. For example, we could have avoided the problem by modifying two of the rules like so:

```
#two {shape-margin: 1.5em; margin: 0 1.5em 1.5em 0;}
#thr (shape-margin: 10%; margin: 0 10% 10% 0;}
```

In both cases, the right and bottom margins are set to be the same as the shape-margin value, ensuring that the enlarged shape will never exceed the shape box on those sides. This is demonstrated in Figure 10-44.

Figure 10-44. Making sure the shape margins don't get clipped

If you have a float go to the right, then you'll have to adjust its margins to create space below and to the left, not the right, but the principle is the same.

Summary

Floats may be a fundamentally simple aspect of CSS, but that doesn't keep them from being useful and powerful. They fill a vital and honorable niche, allowing the placement of content to one side while the rest of the content flows around it. And thanks to float shapes, we're not limited to square float boxes any more.

CHAPTER 11

Positioning

The idea behind positioning is fairly simple. It allows you to define exactly where element boxes will appear relative to where they would ordinarily be—or position them in relation to a parent element, another element, or even to the viewport (e.g., the browser window) itself.

Basic Concepts

Before we delve into the various kinds of positioning, it's a good idea to look at what types exist and how they differ. We'll also need to define some basic ideas that are fundamental to understanding how positioning works.

Types of Positioning

You can choose one of five different types of positioning, which affect how the element's box is generated, by using the `position` property.

position	
Values	`static	relative	sticky	absolute	fixed`
Initial value	`static`
Applies to	All elements
Computed value	As specified
Inherited	No
Animatable	No

The values of `position` have the following meanings:

`static`
> The element's box is generated as normal. Block-level elements generate a rectangular box that is part of the document's flow, and inline-level boxes cause the creation of one or more line boxes that are flowed within their parent element.

`relative`
> The element's box is offset by some distance. The element retains the shape it would have had were it not positioned, and the space that the element would ordinarily have occupied is preserved.

`absolute`
> The element's box is completely removed from the flow of the document and positioned with respect to its containing block, which may be another element in the document or the initial containing block (described in the next section). Whatever space the element might have occupied in the normal document flow is closed up, as though the element did not exist. The positioned element generates a block-level box, regardless of the type of box it would have generated if it were in the normal flow.

`fixed`
> The element's box behaves as though it was set to `absolute`, but its containing block is the viewport itself.

`sticky`
> The element is left in the normal flow, until the conditions that trigger its stickiness come to pass, at which point it is removed from the normal flow but its original space in the normal flow is preserved. It will then act as if absolutely positioned with respect to its containing block. Once the conditions to enforce stickiness are no longer met, the element is returned to the normal flow in its original space.

Don't worry so much about the details right now, as we'll look at each of these kinds of positioning later. Before we do that, we need to discuss containing blocks.

The Containing Block

In general terms, a *containing block* is the box that contains another element. As an example, in the normal-flow case, the root element (`html` in HTML) is the containing block for the `body` element, which is in turn the containing block for all its children, and so on. When it comes to positioning, the containing block depends entirely on the type of positioning.

For a non-root element whose position value is relative or static, its containing block is formed by the content edge of the nearest block-level, table-cell, or inline-block ancestor box.

For a non-root element that has a position value of absolute, its containing block is set to the nearest ancestor (of any kind) that has a position value other than static. This happens as follows:

- If the ancestor is block-level, the containing block is set to be that element's padding edge; in other words, the area that would be bounded by a border.

- If the ancestor is inline-level, the containing block is set to the content edge of the ancestor. In left-to-right languages, the top and left of the containing block are the top and left content edges of the first box in the ancestor, and the bottom and right edges are the bottom and right content edges of the last box. In right-to-left languages, the right edge of the containing block corresponds to the right content edge of the first box, and the left is taken from the last box. The top and bottom are the same.

- If there are no ancestors, then the element's containing block is defined to be the initial containing block.

There's an interesting variant to the containing-block rules when it comes to sticky-positioned elements, which is that a rectangle is defined in relation to the containing block called the *sticky-constraint rectangle*. This rectangle has everything to do with how sticky positioning works, and will be explained in full later, in "Sticky Positioning" on page 557.

An important point: positioned elements can be positioned outside of their containing block. This is very similar to the way in which floated elements can use negative margins to float outside of their parent's content area. It also suggests that the term "containing block" should really be "positioning context," but since the specification uses "containing block," so will I. (I do try to minimize confusion. Really!)

Offset Properties

Four of the positioning schemes described in the previous section—relative, absolute, sticky, and fixed—use four distinct properties to describe the offset of a positioned element's sides with respect to its containing block. These four properties, which are referred to as the *offset properties*, are a big part of what makes positioning work.

top, right, bottom, left

Values	*<length>* | *<percentage>* | auto
Initial value	auto
Applies to	Positioned elements
Percentages	Refer to the height of the containing block for top and bottom, and the width of the containing block for right and left
Computed value	For relative or sticky-positioned elements, see the sections on those positioning types. For static elements, auto; for length values, the corresponding absolute length; for percentage values, the specified value; otherwise, auto.
Inherited	No
Animatable	*<length>*, *<percentage>*

These properties describe an offset from the nearest side of the containing block (thus the term *offset properties*). For example, top describes how far the top margin edge of the positioned element should be placed from the top of its containing block. In the case of top, positive values move the top margin edge of the positioned element *downward*, while negative values move it *above* the top of its containing block. Similarly, left describes how far to the right (for positive values) or left (for negative values) the left margin edge of the positioned element is from the left edge of the containing block. Positive values will shift the margin edge of the positioned element to the right, and negative values will move it to the left.

Another way to look at it is that positive values cause inward offsets, moving the edges toward the center of the containing block, and negative values cause outward offsets.

The implication of offsetting the margin edges of a positioned element is that everything about an element—margins, borders, padding, and content—is moved in the process of positioning the element. Thus, it is possible to set margins, borders, and padding for a positioned element; these will be preserved and kept with the positioned element, and they will be contained within the area defined by the offset properties.

It is important to remember that the offset properties define an offset from the analogous side (e.g., left defines the offset from the left side) of the containing block, not from the upper-left corner of the containing block. This is why, for example, one way to fill up the lower-right corner of a containing block is to use these values:

```
top: 50%; bottom: 0; left: 50%; right: 0;
```

In this example, the outer-left edge of the positioned element is placed halfway across the containing block. This is its offset from the left edge of the containing block. The outer-right edge of the positioned element, however, is not offset from the right edge of the containing block, so the two are coincident. Similar reasoning holds true for the top and bottom of the positioned element: the outer-top edge is placed halfway down the containing block, but the outer-bottom edge is not moved up from the bottom. This leads to what's shown in Figure 11-1.

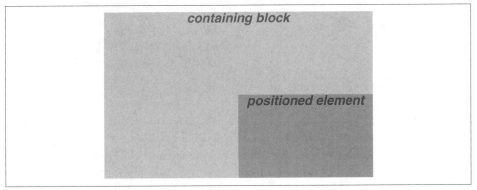

Figure 11-1. Filling the lower-right quarter of the containing block

What's depicted in Figure 11-1, and in most of the examples in this chapter, is based around absolute positioning. Since absolute positioning is the simplest scheme in which to demonstrate how top, right, bottom, and left work, we'll stick to that for now.

Note the background area of the positioned element. In Figure 11-1, it has no margins, but if it did, they would create blank space between the borders and the offset edges. This would make the positioned element appear as though it did not completely fill the lower-right quarter of the containing block. In truth, it *would* fill the area, but this fact wouldn't be immediately apparent to the eye. Thus, the following two sets of styles would have approximately the same visual appearance, assuming that the containing block is 100em high by 100em wide:

```
#ex1 {top: 50%; bottom: 0; left: 50%; right: 0; margin: 10em;}
#ex2 {top: 60%; bottom: 10%; left: 60%; right: 10%; margin: 0;}
```

Again, the similarity would be only visual in nature.

By using negative offset values, it is possible to position an element outside its containing block. For example, the following values will lead to the result shown in Figure 11-2:

```
top: 50%; bottom: -2em; left: 75%; right: -7em;
```

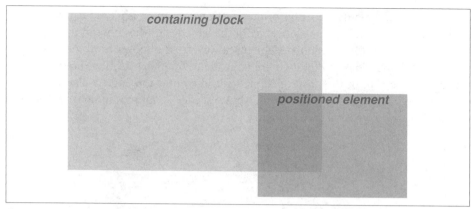

Figure 11-2. Positioning an element outside its containing block

In addition to length and percentage values, the offset properties can also be set to `auto`, which is the default value. There is no single behavior for `auto`; it changes based on the type of positioning used. We'll explore how `auto` works later on, as we consider each of the positioning types in turn.

Width and Height

There will be many cases when, having determined where you're going to position an element, you will want to declare how wide and how high that element should be. In addition, there will likely be conditions where you'll want to limit how high or wide a positioned element gets, not to mention cases where you want the browser to go ahead and automatically calculate the width, height, or both.

Setting Width and Height

If you want to give your positioned element a specific width, then the property to turn to is `width`. Similarly, `height` will let you declare a specific height for a positioned element.

Although it is sometimes important to set the `width` and `height` of an element, it is not always necessary when positioning elements. For example, if the placement of the four sides of the element is described using `top`, `right`, `bottom`, and `left`, then the `height` and `width` of the element are implicitly determined by the offsets. Assume that we want an absolutely positioned element to fill the left half of its containing block, from top to bottom. We could use these values, with the result depicted in Figure 11-3:

```
top: 0; bottom: 0; left: 0; right: 50%;
```

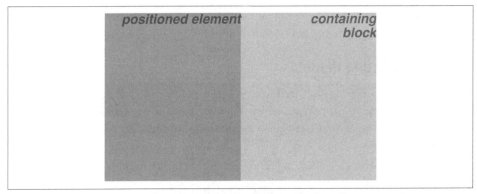

Figure 11-3. Positioning and sizing an element using only the offset properties

Since the default value of both `width` and `height` is `auto`, the result shown in Figure 11-3 is exactly the same as if we had used these values:

```
top: 0; bottom: 0; left: 0; right: 50%; width: 50%; height: 100%;
```

The presence of `width` and `height` in this example add nothing to the layout of the element.

If we were to add padding, a border, or a margin to the element, then the presence of explicit values for `height` and `width` could very well make a difference:

```
top: 0; bottom: 0; left: 0; right: 50%; width: 50%; height: 100%;
   padding: 2em;
```

This will give us a positioned element that extends out of its containing block, as shown in Figure 11-4.

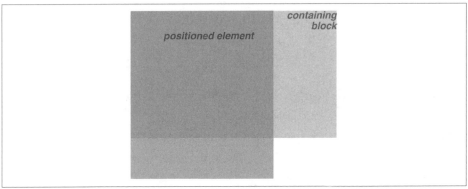

Figure 11-4. Positioning an element partially outside its containing block

This happens because (by default) the padding is added to the content area, and the content area's size is determined by the values of `height` and `width`. In order to get the padding we want and still have the element fit inside its containing block, we would either remove the `height` and `width` declarations, explicitly set them both to `auto`, or set `box-sizing` to `border-box`.

Limiting Width and Height

Should it become necessary or desirable, you can place limits on an element's width by using the following properties, which I'll refer to as the *min-max properties*. An element's content area can be defined to have minimum dimensions using `min-width` and `min-height`.

---

min-width, min-height

Values	*<length>* | *<percentage>*
Initial value	0
Applies to	All elements except nonreplaced inline elements and table elements
Percentages	Refer to the width of the containing block
Computed value	For percentages, as specified; for length values, the absolute length; otherwise, none
Inherited	No
Animatable	*<length>*, *<percentage>*

Similarly, an element's dimensions can be limited using the properties `max-width` and `max-height`.

---

max-width, max-height

Values	*<length>* | *<percentage>* | none
Initial value	none
Applies to	All elements except nonreplaced inline elements and table elements
Percentages	Refer to the height of the containing block
Computed value	For percentages, as specified; for length values, the absolute length; otherwise, none
Inherited	No
Animatable	*<length>*, *<percentage>*

The names of these properties make them fairly self-explanatory. What's less obvious at first, but makes sense once you think about it, is that values for all these properties cannot be negative.

The following styles will force the positioned element to be at least 10em wide by 20em tall, as illustrated in Figure 11-5:

```
top: 10%; bottom: 20%; left: 50%; right: 10%;
    min-width: 10em; min-height: 20em;
```

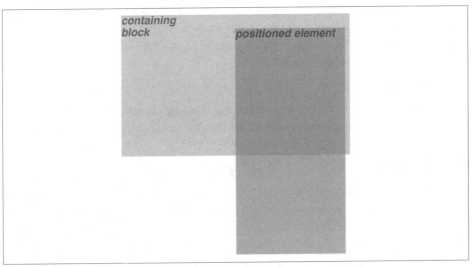

Figure 11-5. Setting a minimum width and height for a positioned element

This isn't a very robust solution since it forces the element to be at least a certain size regardless of the size of its containing block. Here's a better one:

```
top: 10%; bottom: auto; left: 50%; right: 10%;
    height: auto; min-width: 15em;
```

Here we have a case where the element should be 40% as wide as the containing block but can never be less than 15em wide. We've also changed the bottom and height so that they're automatically determined. This will let the element be as tall as necessary to display its content, no matter how narrow it gets (never less than 15em, of course!).

We'll look at the role auto plays in the height and width of positioned elements in the upcoming section, "Placement and Sizing of Absolutely Positioned Elements" on page 540.

You can turn all this around to keep elements from getting too wide or tall by using max-width and max-height. Let's consider a situation where, for some reason, we want an element to have three-quarters the width of its containing block but to stop getting wider when it hits 400 pixels. The appropriate styles are:

```
left: 0%; right: auto; width: 75%; max-width: 400px;
```

One great advantage of the min-max properties is that they let you mix units with relative safety. You can use percentage-based sizes while setting length-based limits, or vice versa.

It's worth mentioning that these min-max properties can be very useful in conjunction with floated elements. For example, we can allow a floated element's width to be relative to the width of its parent element (which is its containing block), while making sure that the float's width never goes below 10em. The reverse approach is also possible:

```
p.aside {float: left; width: 40em; max-width: 40%;}
```

This will set the float to be 40em wide, unless that would be more than 40% the width of the containing block, in which case the float will be limited to that 40% width.

Content Overflow and Clipping

If the content of an element is too much for the element's size, it will be in danger of overflowing the element itself. There are a few alternatives in such situations, and CSS lets you select among them. It also allows you to define a clipping region to determine the area of the element outside of which these sorts of things become an issue.

Overflow

So let's say that we have, for whatever reason, an element that has been pinned to a specific size, and the content doesn't fit. You can take control of the situation with the overflow property.

---

overflow

Values	visible | hidden | scroll | auto
Initial value	visible
Applies to	Block-level and replaced elements
Computed value	As specified
Inherited	No
Animatable	No

The default value of visible means that the element's content may be visible outside the element's box. Typically, this leads to the content running outside its own element box, but not altering the shape of that box. The following markup would result in Figure 11-6:

```
div#sidebar {position: absolute; top: 0; left: 0; width: 25%; height: 7em;
    background: #BBB; overflow: visible;}
```

If `overflow` is set to `scroll`, the element's content is clipped—that is, hidden—at the edges of the element box, but there is some way to make the extra content available to the user. In a web browser, this could mean a scroll bar (or set of them), or another method of accessing the content without altering the shape of the element itself. One possibility is depicted in Figure 11-6.

If `scroll` is used, the panning mechanisms (e.g., scroll bars) should always be rendered. To quote the specification, "this avoids any problem with scrollbars appearing or disappearing in a dynamic environment." Thus, even if the element has sufficient space to display all its content, the scroll bars may still appear and take up space (though they may not). In addition, when printing a page or otherwise displaying the document in a print medium, the content may be displayed as though the value of `overflow` were declared to be `visible`.

If `overflow` is set to `hidden`, the element's content is clipped at the edges of the element box, but no scrolling interface should be provided to make the content outside the clipping region accessible to the user. In such an instance, the clipped content would not be accessible to the user.

Figure 11-6 illustrates each of these three `overflow` values.

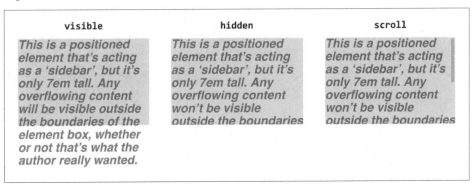

Figure 11-6. Three methods for handling overflowing content

Finally, there is `overflow: auto`. This allows user agents to determine which behavior to use, although they are encouraged to provide a scrolling mechanism when necessary. This is a potentially useful way to use overflow, since user agents could interpret it to mean "provide scroll bars only when needed." (They may not, but they certainly could and probably should.)

Element Visibility

In addition to all the clipping and overflowing, you can also control the visibility of an entire element.

---

visibility

Values	visible | hidden | collapse
Initial value	visible
Applies to	All elements
Computed value	As specified
Inherited	Yes
Animatable	No

This one is pretty easy. If an element is set to have visibility: visible, then it is, as you might expect, visible. If an element is set to visibility: hidden, it is made "invisible" (to use the wording in the specification). In its invisible state, the element still affects the document's layout as though it were visible. In other words, the element is still there—you just can't see it, pretty much as if you'd declared opacity: 0.

Note the difference between this and display: none. In the latter case, the element is not displayed *and* is removed from the document altogether so that it doesn't have any effect on document layout. Figure 11-7 shows a document in which a paragraph has been set to hidden, based on the following styles and markup:

```
em.trans {visibility: hidden; border: 3px solid gray; background: silver;
    margin: 2em; padding: 1em;}

<p>
    This is a paragraph which should be visible. Nulla berea consuetudium ohio
    city, mutationem dolore. <em class="trans">Humanitatis molly shannon
    ut lorem.</em> Doug dieken dolor possim south euclid.
</p>
```

This is a paragraph which should be visible. Nulla berea consuetudium ohio city, mutationem dolore.

Doug

dieken dolor possim south euclid.

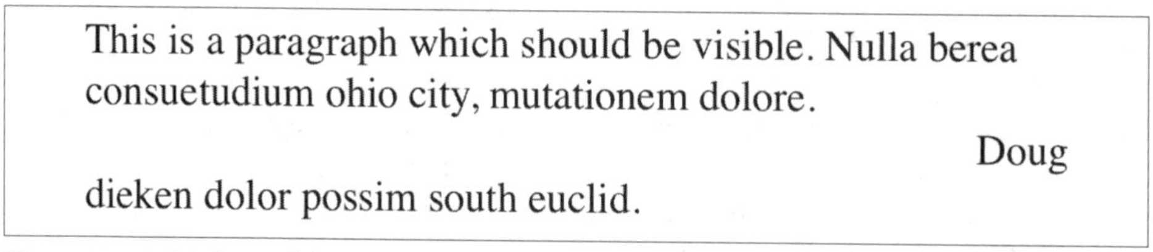

Figure 11-7. Making elements invisible without suppressing their element boxes

---

Everything visible about a hidden element—such as content, background, and borders—is made invisible. The space is still there because the element is still part of the document's layout. We just can't see it.

It's possible to set the descendant element of a hidden element to be visible. This causes the element to appear wherever it normally would, despite the fact that the ancestor is invisible. In order to do so, we explicitly declare the descendant element visible, since visibility is inherited:

```
p.clear {visibility: hidden;}
p.clear em {visibility: visible;}
```

As for visbility: collapse, this value is used in CSS table rendering, which we don't really have room to cover here. According to the specification, collapse has the same meaning as hidden if it is used on nontable elements.

Absolute Positioning

Since most of the examples and figures in the previous sections are examples of absolute positioning, you're already halfway to understanding how it works. Most of what remains are the details of what happens when absolute positioning is invoked.

Containing Blocks and Absolutely Positioned Elements

When an element is positioned absolutely, it is completely removed from the document flow. It is then positioned with respect to its containing block, and its margin edges are placed using the offset properties (top, left, etc.). The positioned element does not flow around the content of other elements, nor does their content flow around the positioned element. This implies that an absolutely positioned element may overlap other elements or be overlapped by them. (We'll see how to affect the overlapping order later.)

The containing block for an absolutely positioned element is the nearest ancestor element that has a position value other than static. It is common for an author to pick an element that will serve as the containing block for the absolutely positioned element and give it a position of relative with no offsets, like so:

```
.contain {position: relative;}
```

Consider the example in Figure 11-8, which is an illustration of the following:

```
p {margin: 2em;}
p.contain {position: relative;} /* establish a containing block*/
b {position: absolute; top: auto; right: 0; bottom: 0; left: auto;
    width: 8em; height: 5em; border: 1px solid gray;}

<body>
<p>
```

```
      This paragraph does <em>not</em> establish a containing block for any of
      its descendant elements that are absolutely positioned. Therefore, the
      absolutely positioned <b>boldface</b> element it contains will be
      positioned with respect to the initial containing block.
   </p>
   <p class="contain">
      Thanks to <code>position: relative</code>, this paragraph establishes a
      containing block for any of its descendant elements that are absolutely
      positioned. Since there is such an element-- <em>that is to say, <b>a
      boldfaced element that is absolutely positioned,</b> placed with respect
      to its containing block (the paragraph)</em>, it will appear within the
      element box generated by the paragraph.
   </p>
</body>
```

The b elements in both paragraphs have been absolutely positioned. The difference is
in the containing block used for each one. The b element in the first paragraph is
positioned with respect to the initial containing block, because all of its ancestor elements have a position of static. The second paragraph has been set to position:
relative, so it establishes a containing block for its descendants.

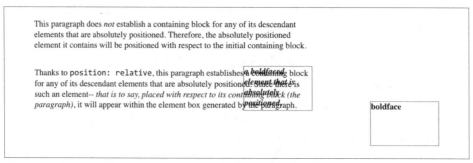

Figure 11-8. Using relative positioning to define containing blocks

You've probably noted that in that second paragraph, the positioned element overlaps
some of the text content of the paragraph. There is no way to avoid this, short of positioning the b element outside of the paragraph (by using a negative value for right or
one of the other offset properties) or by specifying a padding for the paragraph that is
wide enough to accommodate the positioned element. Also, since the b element has a
transparent background, the paragraph's text shows through the positioned element.
The only way to avoid this is to set a background for the positioned element, or else
move it out of the paragraph entirely.

You will sometimes want to ensure that the body element establishes a containing
block for all its descendants, rather than allowing the user agent to pick an initial containing block. This is as simple as declaring:

```
body {position: relative;}
```

In such a document, you could drop in an absolutely positioned paragraph, as follows, and get a result like that shown in Figure 11-9:

```
<p style="position: absolute; top: 0; right: 25%; left: 25%; bottom:
    auto; width: 50%; height: auto; background: silver;">
    ...
</p>
```

The paragraph is now positioned at the very beginning of the document, half as wide as the document's width and overwriting other content.

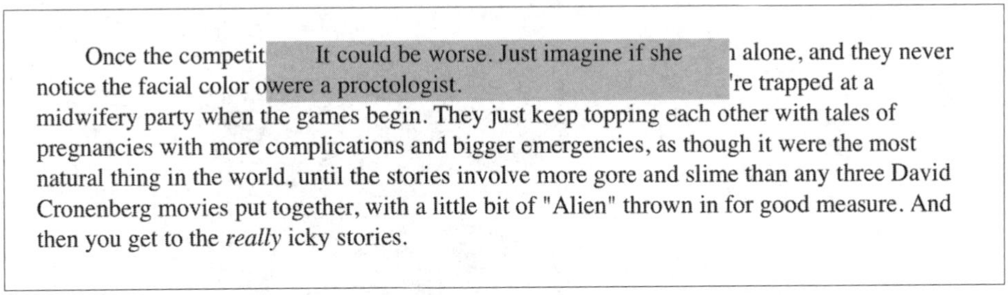

Once the competit   It could be worse. Just imagine if she   n alone, and they never notice the facial color o were a proctologist.   're trapped at a midwifery party when the games begin. They just keep topping each other with tales of pregnancies with more complications and bigger emergencies, as though it were the most natural thing in the world, until the stories involve more gore and slime than any three David Cronenberg movies put together, with a little bit of "Alien" thrown in for good measure. And then you get to the *really* icky stories.

Figure 11-9. Positioning an element whose containing block is the root element

An important point to highlight is that when an element is absolutely positioned, it establishes a containing block for its descendant elements. For example, we can absolutely position an element and then absolutely position one of its children, as shown in Figure 11-10, which was generated using the following styles and basic markup:

```
div {position: relative; width: 100%; height: 10em;
    border: 1px solid; background: #EEE;}
div.a {position: absolute; top: 0; right: 0; width: 15em; height: 100%;
    margin-left: auto; background: #CCC;}
div.b {position: absolute; bottom: 0; left: 0; width: 10em; height: 50%;
    margin-top: auto; background: #AAA;}

<div>
    <div class="a">
        absolutely positioned element A
        <div class="b">
            absolutely positioned element B
        </div>
    </div>
    containing block
</div>
```

Remember that if the document is scrolled, the absolutely positioned elements will scroll right along with it. This is true of all absolutely positioned elements that are not descendants of fixed-position or sticky-position elements.

This happens because, eventually, the elements are positioned in relation to something that's part of the normal flow. For example, if you absolutely position a table, and its containing block is the initial containing block, then it will scroll because the initial containing block is part of the normal flow, and thus it scrolls.

If you want to position elements so that they're placed relative to the viewport and don't scroll along with the rest of the document, keep reading. The upcoming section on fixed positioning has the answers you seek.

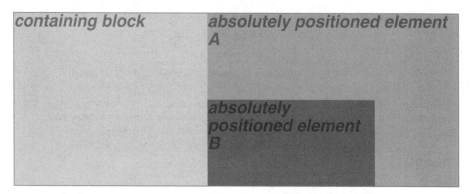

Figure 11-10. Absolutely positioned elements establish containing blocks

Placement and Sizing of Absolutely Positioned Elements

It may seem odd to combine the concepts of placement and sizing, but it's a necessity with absolutely positioned elements because the specification binds them very closely together. This is not such a strange pairing upon reflection. Consider what happens if an element is positioned using all four offset properties, like so:

```
#masthead h1 {position: absolute; top: 1em; left: 1em; right: 25%; bottom: 10px;
    margin: 0; padding: 0; background: silver;}
```

Here, the height and width of the h1's element box is determined by the placement of its outer margin edges, as shown in Figure 11-11.

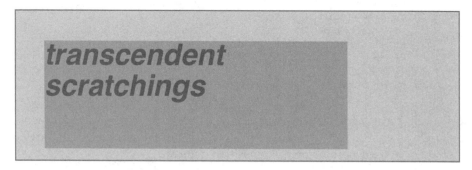

Figure 11-11. Determining the height of an element based on the offset properties

If the containing block were made taller, then the h1 would also become taller; if the containing block is narrowed, then the h1 will become narrower. If we were to add margins or padding to the h1, then that would have further effects on the calculated height and width of the h1.

But what if we do all that and then also try to set an explicit height and width?

```
#masthead h1 {position: absolute; top: 0; left: 1em; right: 10%; bottom: 0;
    margin: 0; padding: 0; height: 1em; width: 50%; background: silver;}
```

Something has to give, because it's incredibly unlikely that all those values will be accurate. In fact, the containing block would have to be exactly two and a half times as wide as the h1's computed value for font-size for all of the shown values to be accurate. Any other width would mean at least one value is wrong and has to be ignored. Figuring out which one depends on a number of factors, and the factors change depending on whether an element is replaced or nonreplaced.

For that matter, consider the following:

```
#masthead h1 {position: absolute; top: auto; left: auto;}
```

What should the result be? As it happens, the answer is *not* "reset the values to zero." We'll see the actual answer, starting in the next section.

Auto-edges

When absolutely positioning an element, there is a special behavior that applies when any of the offset properties other than bottom is set to auto. Let's take top as an example. Consider the following:

```
<p>
    When we consider the effect of positioning, it quickly becomes clear that
    authors can do a great deal of damage to layout, just as they can do very
    interesting things.<span style="position: absolute; top: auto;
    left: 0;">[4]</span> This is usually the case with useful technologies:
    the sword always has at least two edges, both of them sharp.
</p>
```

What should happen? For left, it's easy: the left edge of the element should be placed against the left edge of its containing block (which we'll assume here to be the initial containing block). For top, however, something much more interesting happens. The top of the positioned element should line up with the place where its top would have been if it were not positioned at all. In other words, imagine where the span would have been placed if its position value were static; this is its *static position*—the place where its top edge should be calculated to sit. CSS 2.1 had this to say about static positions:

the term "static position" (of an element) refers, roughly, to the position an element would have had in the normal flow. More precisely: the static position for top is the distance from the top edge of the containing block to the top margin edge of a hypothetical box that would have been the first box of the element if its specified posi tion value had been static and its specified float had been none and its specified clear had been none... The value is negative if the hypothetical box is above the containing block.

Therefore, we should get the result shown in Figure 11-12.

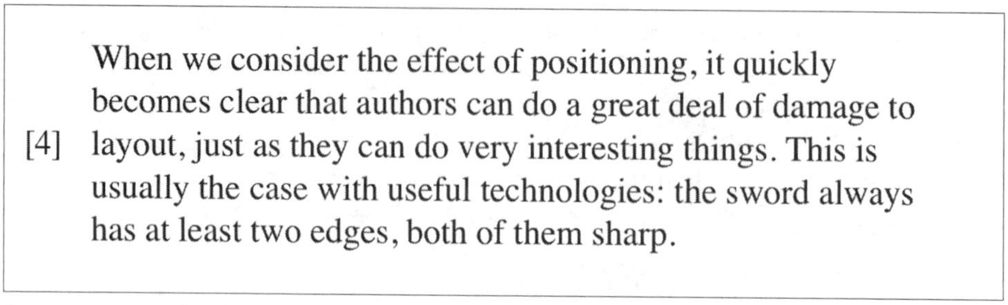

> When we consider the effect of positioning, it quickly becomes clear that authors can do a great deal of damage to
> [4] layout, just as they can do very interesting things. This is usually the case with useful technologies: the sword always has at least two edges, both of them sharp.

Figure 11-12. Absolutely positioning an element consistently with its "static" top edge

The "[4]" sits just outside the paragraph's content because the initial containing block's left edge is to the left of the paragraph's left edge.

The same basic rules hold true for left and right being set to auto. In those cases, the left (or right) edge of a positioned element lines up with the spot where the edge would have been placed if the element weren't positioned. So let's modify our previous example so that both top and left are set to auto:

```
<p>
    When we consider the effect of positioning, it quickly becomes clear that
    authors can do a great deal of damage to layout, just as they can do very
    interesting things.<span style="position: absolute; top: auto; left:
    auto;">[4]</span> This is usually the case with useful technologies:
    the sword always has at least two edges, both of them sharp.
</p>
```

This would have the result shown in Figure 11-13.

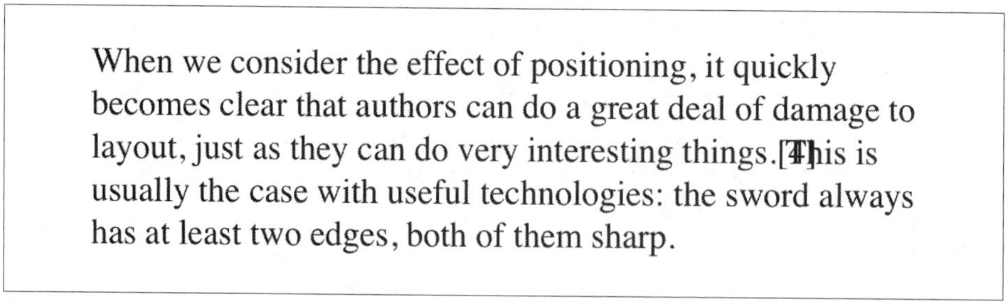

> When we consider the effect of positioning, it quickly becomes clear that authors can do a great deal of damage to layout, just as they can do very interesting things.[4]his is usually the case with useful technologies: the sword always has at least two edges, both of them sharp.

Figure 11-13. Absolutely positioning an element consistently with its "static" position

The "[4]" now sits right where it would have were it not positioned. Note that, since it is positioned, its normal-flow space is closed up. This causes the positioned element to overlap the normal-flow content.

This auto-placement works only in certain situations, generally wherever there are few constraints on the other dimensions of a positioned element. Our previous example could be auto-placed because it had no constraints on its height or width, nor on the placement of the bottom and right edges. But suppose, for some reason, there had been such constraints. Consider:

```
<p>
    When we consider the effect of positioning, it quickly becomes clear that
    authors can do a great deal of damage to layout, just as they can do very
    interesting things.<span style="position: absolute; top: auto; left: auto;
    right: 0; bottom: 0; height: 2em; width: 5em;">[4]</span> This is usually
    the case with useful technologies: the sword always has at least two edges,
    both of them sharp.
</p>
```

It is not possible to satisfy all of those values. Determining what happens is the subject of the next section.

Placing and Sizing Nonreplaced Elements

In general, the size and placement of an element depends on its containing block. The values of its various properties (`width`, `right`, `padding-left`, and so on) affect its layout, but the foundation is the containing block.

Consider the width and horizontal placement of a positioned element. It can be represented as an equation which states:

```
left + margin-left + border-left-width + padding-left + width +
padding-right + border-right-width + margin-right + right =
the width of the containing block
```

This calculation is fairly reasonable. It's basically the equation that determines how block-level elements in the normal flow are sized, except it adds `left` and `right` to the mix. So how do all these interact? There is a series of rules to work through.

First, if `left`, `width`, and `right` are all set to `auto`, then you get the result seen in the previous section: the left edge is placed at its static position, assuming a left-to-right language. In right-to-left languages, the right edge is placed at its static position. The width of the element is set to be "shrink to fit," which means the element's content area is made only as wide as necessary to contain its content. The nonstatic position property (`right` in left-to-right languages, `left` in right-to-left) is set to take up the remaining distance. For example:

```
<div style="position: relative; width: 25em; border: 1px dotted;">
    An absolutely positioned element can have its content <span style="position:
```

```
absolute; top: 0; left: 0; right: auto; width: auto; background:
silver;">shrink-wrapped</span> thanks to the way positioning rules work.
</div>
```

This has the result shown in Figure 11-14.

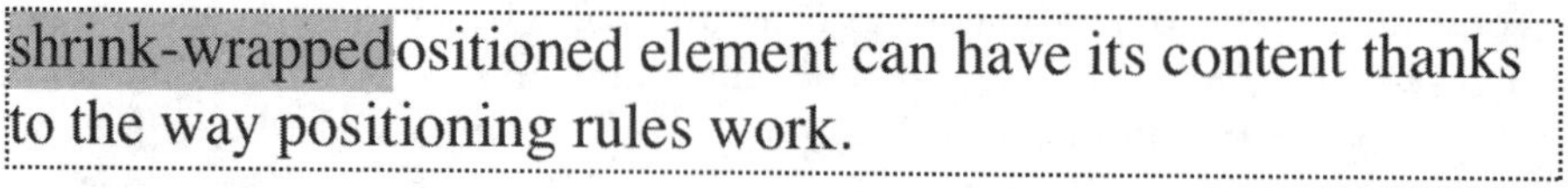

shrink-wrappedositioned element can have its content thanks
to the way positioning rules work.

Figure 11-14. The "shrink-to-fit" behavior of absolutely positioned elements

The top of the element is placed against the top of its containing block (the div, in this case), and the width of the element is just as much as is needed to contain the content. The remaining distance from the right edge of the element to the right edge of the containing block becomes the computed value of right.

Now suppose that only the left and right margins are set to auto, not left, width, and right, as in this example:

```
<div style="position: relative; width: 25em; border: 1px dotted;">
    An absolutely positioned element can have its content <span style="position:
    absolute; top: 0; left: 1em; right: 1em; width: 10em; margin: 0 auto;
    background: silver;">shrink-wrapped</span> thanks to the way positioning
    rules work.
</div>
```

What happens here is that the left and right margins, which are both auto, are set to be equal. This will effectively center the element, as shown in Figure 11-15.

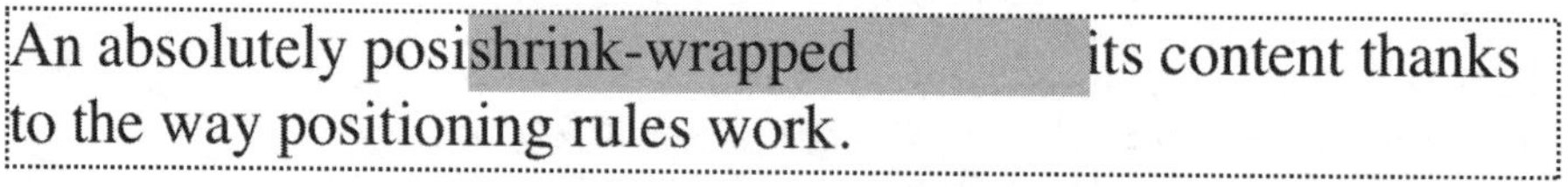

An absolutely posishrink-wrapped   its content thanks
to the way positioning rules work.

Figure 11-15. Horizontally centering an absolutely positioned element with auto margins

This is basically the same as auto-margin centering in the normal flow. So let's make the margins something other than auto:

```
<div style="position: relative; width: 25em; border: 1px dotted;">
    An absolutely positioned element can have its content <span style="position:
    absolute; top: 0; left: 1em; right: 1em; width: 10em; margin-left: 1em;
    margin-right: 1em; background: silver;">shrink-wrapped</span> thanks to the
    way positioning rules work.
</div>
```

Now we have a problem. The positioned span's properties add up to only 14em, whereas the containing block is 25em wide. That's an 11-em deficit we have to make up somewhere.

The rules state that, in this case, the user agent ignores the value for `right` (in left-to-right languages; otherwise, it ignores `left`) and solves for it. In other words, the result will be the same as if we'd declared:

```
<span style="position: absolute; top: 0; left: 1em;
right: 12em; width: 10em; margin-left: 1em; margin-right: 1em;
right: auto; background: silver;">shrink-wrapped</span>
```

This has the result shown in Figure 11-16.

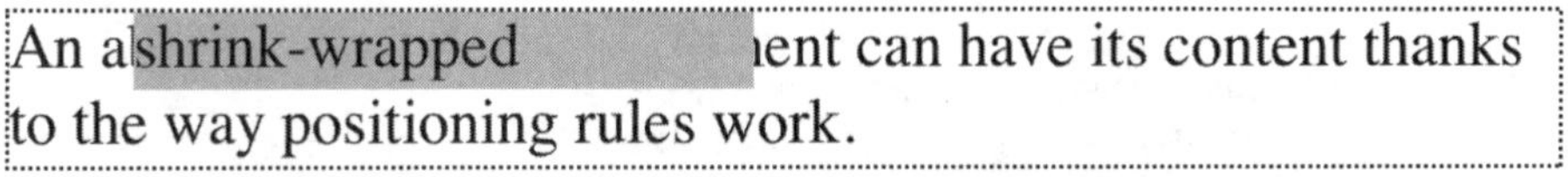

An ashrink-wrappedent can have its content thanks to the way positioning rules work.

Figure 11-16. Ignoring the value for right in an overconstrained situation

If one of the margins had been left as `auto`, then that would have been changed instead. Suppose we change the styles to state:

```
<span style="position: absolute; top: 0; left: 1em;
right: 1em; width: 10em; margin-left: 1em; margin-right: auto;
background: silver;">shrink-wrapped</span>
```

The visual result would be the same as that in Figure 11-16, only it would be attained by computing the right margin to 12em instead of overriding the value assigned to the property `right`.

If, on the other hand, we made the left margin `auto`, then *it* would be reset, as illustrated in Figure 11-17:

```
<span style="position: absolute; top: 0; left: 1em;
right: 1em; width: 10em; margin-left: auto; margin-right: 1em;
background: silver;">shrink-wrapped</span>
```

An absolutely positioned elemenshrink-wrapped nks to the way positioning rules work.

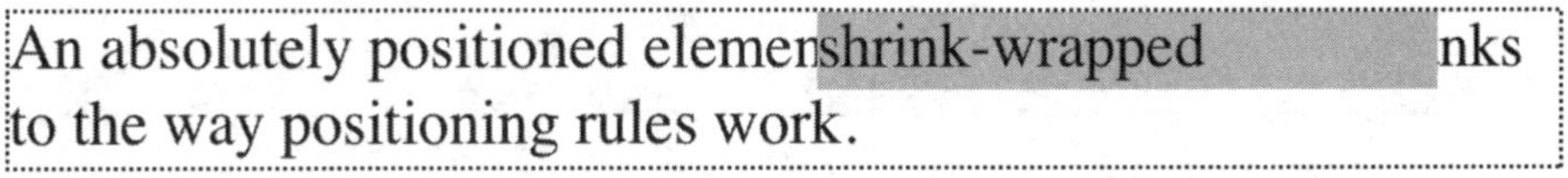

Figure 11-17. Ignoring the value for margin-right in an overconstrained situation

In general, if only one of the properties is set to `auto`, then it will be used to satisfy the equation given earlier in the section. Thus, given the following styles, the element's width would expand to whatever size is needed, instead of "shrink-wrapping" the content:

```
<span style="position: absolute; top: 0; left: 1em;
right: 1em; width: auto; margin-left: 1em; margin-right: 1em;
background: silver;">not shrink-wrapped</span>
```

So far we've really only examined behavior along the horizontal axis, but very similar rules hold true along the vertical axis. If we take the previous discussion and rotate it 90 degrees, as it were, we get almost the same behavior. For example, the following markup results in Figure 11-18:

```
<div style="position: relative; width: 30em; height: 10em; border: 1px solid;">
    <div style="position: absolute; left: 0; width: 30%;
        background: #CCC; top: 0;">
            element A
    </div>
    <div style="position: absolute; left: 35%; width: 30%;
        background: #AAA; top: 0; height: 50%;">
            element B
    </div>
    <div style="position: absolute; left: 70%; width: 30%;
        background: #CCC; height: 50%; bottom: 0;">
            element C
    </div>
</div>
```

In the first case, the height of the element is shrink-wrapped to the content. In the second, the unspecified property (bottom) is set to make up the distance between the bottom of the positioned element and the bottom of its containing block. In the third case, top is unspecified, and therefore used to make up the difference.

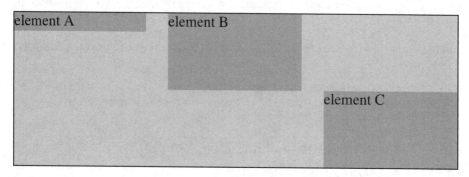

Figure 11-18. Vertical layout behavior for absolutely positioned elements

For that matter, auto-margins can lead to vertical centering. Given the following styles, the absolutely positioned div will be vertically centered within its containing block, as shown in Figure 11-19:

```
<div style="position: relative; width: 10em; height: 10em; border: 1px solid;">
    <div style="position: absolute; left: 0; width: 100%; background: #CCC;
        top: 0; height: 5em; bottom: 0; margin: auto 0;">
            element D
    </div>
</div>
```

There are two small variations to point out. In horizontal layout, either right or left can be placed according to the static position if their values are auto. In vertical layout, only top can take on the static position; bottom, for whatever reason, cannot.

Also, if an absolutely positioned element's size is overconstrained in the vertical direction, bottom is ignored. Thus, in the following situation, the declared value of bottom would be overridden by the calculated value of 5em:

```
<div style="position: relative; width: 10em; height: 10em; border: 1px solid;">
    <div style="position: absolute; left: 0; width: 100%; background: #CCC;
        top: 0; height: 5em; bottom: 0; margin: 0;">
            element D
    </div>
</div>
```

There is no provision for top to be ignored if the properties are overconstrained.

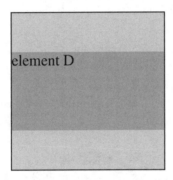

Figure 11-19. Vertically centering an absolutely positioned element with auto-margins

Placing and Sizing Replaced Elements

Positioning rules are different for replaced elements (e.g., images) than they are for nonreplaced elements. This is because replaced elements have an intrinsic height and width, and therefore are not altered unless explicitly changed by the author. Thus, there is no concept of "shrink to fit" in the positioning of replaced elements.

The behaviors that go into placing and sizing replaced elements are most easily expressed by a series of rules to be taken one after the other. These state:

1. If width is set to auto, the used value of width is determined by the intrinsic width of the element's content. Thus, if an image is intrinsically 50 pixels wide, then the used value is calculated to be 50px. If width is explicitly declared (that is, something like 100px or 50%), then the width is set to that value.

2. If `left` has the value `auto` in a left-to-right language, replace `auto` with the static position. In right-to-left languages, replace an `auto` value for `right` with the static position.

3. If either `left` or `right` is still `auto` (in other words, it hasn't been replaced in a previous step), replace any `auto` on `margin-left` or `margin-right` with 0.

4. If, at this point, both `margin-left` and `margin-right` are still defined to be `auto`, set them to be equal, thus centering the element in its containing block.

5. After all that, if there is only one `auto` value left, change it to equal the remainder of the equation.

This leads to the same basic behaviors we saw with absolutely positioned nonreplaced elements, as long as you assume that there is an explicit `width` for the nonreplaced element. Therefore, the following two elements will have the same width and placement, assuming the image's intrinsic width is 100 pixels (see Figure 11-20):

```
<div>
    <img src="frown.gif" alt="a frowny face"
        style="position: absolute; top: 0; left: 50px; margin: 0;">
</div>
<div style="position: absolute; top: 0; left: 50px;
        width: 100px; height: 100px; margin: 0;">
    it's a div!
</div>
```

Figure 11-20. Absolutely positioning a replaced element

As with nonreplaced elements, if the values are overconstrained, the user agent is supposed to ignore the value for `right` in left-to-right languages and `left` in right-to-left languages. Thus, in the following example, the declared value for `right` is overridden with a computed value of 50px:

```
<div style="position: relative; width: 300px;">
    <img src="frown.gif" alt="a frowny face" style="position: absolute; top: 0;
        left: 50px; right: 125px; width: 200px; margin: 0;">
</div>
```

Similarly, layout along the vertical axis is governed by a series of rules that state:

1. If height is set to auto, the computed value of height is determined by the intrinsic height of the element's content. Thus, the height of an image 50 pixels tall is computed to be 50px. If height is explicitly declared (that is, something like 100px or 50%), then the height is set to that value.

2. If top has the value auto, replace it with the replaced element's static position.

3. If bottom has a value of auto, replace any auto value on margin-top or margin-bottom with 0.

4. If, at this point, both margin-top and margin-bottom are still defined to be auto, set them to be equal, thus centering the element in its containing block.

5. After all that, if there is only one auto value left, change it to equal the remainder of the equation.

As with nonreplaced elements, if the values are overconstrained, then the user agent is supposed to ignore the value for bottom.

Thus, the following markup would have the results shown in Figure 11-21:

```
<div style="position: relative; height: 200px; width: 200px; border: 1px solid;">
    <img src="one.gif" alt="one" width="25" height="25"
        style="position: absolute; top: 0; left: 0; margin: 0;">
    <img src="two.gif" alt="two" width="25" height="25"
        style="position: absolute; top: 0; left: 60px; margin: 10px 0;
            bottom: 4377px;">
    <img src="three.gif" alt=" three" width="25" height="25"
        style="position: absolute; left: 0; width: 100px; margin: 10px;
            bottom: 0;">
    <img src="four.gif" alt=" four" width="25" height="25"
        style="position: absolute; top: 0; height: 100px; right: 0;
            width: 50px;">
    <img src="five.gif" alt="five" width="25" height="25"
        style="position: absolute; top: 0; left: 0; bottom: 0; right: 0;
            margin: auto;">
</div>
```

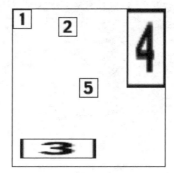

Figure 11-21. Stretching replaced elements through positioning

Placement on the Z-Axis

With all of the positioning going on, there will inevitably be a situation where two elements will try to exist in the same place, visually speaking. One of them will have to overlap the other—but how does one control which element comes out "on top"? This is where the property z-index comes in.

z-index lets you alter the way in which elements overlap each other. It takes its name from the coordinate system in which side-to-side is the *x*-axis and top-to-bottom is the *y*-axis. In such a case, the third axis—that which runs from back to front, as you look at the display surface—is termed the *z-axis*. Thus, elements are given values along this axis using z-index. Figure 11-22 illustrates this system.

z-index

Values	*<integer>* | auto
Initial value	auto
Applies to	Positioned elements
Computed value	As specified
Inherited	No
Animatable	Yes

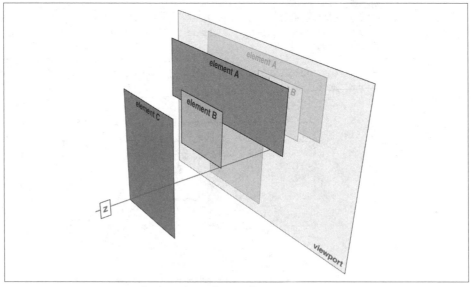

Figure 11-22. A conceptual view of z-index stacking

In this coordinate system, an element with a higher z-index value is closer to the reader than those with lower z-index values. This will cause the high-value element to overlap the others, as illustrated in Figure 11-23, which is a "head-on" view of Figure 11-22. This precedence of overlapping is referred to as *stacking*.

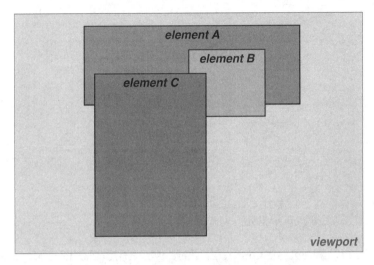

Figure 11-23. How the elements are stacked

Any integer can be used as a value for z-index, including negative numbers. Assigning an element a negative z-index will move it further away from the reader; that is, it will be moved lower in the stack. Consider the following styles, illustrated in Figure 11-24:

```
p {background: rgba(255,255,255,0.9); border: 1px solid;}
p#first {position: absolute; top: 0; left: 0;
    width: 40%; height: 10em; z-index: 8;}
p#second {position: absolute; top: -0.75em; left: 15%;
    width: 60%; height: 5.5em; z-index: 4;}
p#third {position: absolute; top: 23%; left: 25%;
    width: 30%; height: 10em; z-index: 1;}
p#fourth {position: absolute; top: 10%; left: 10%;
    width: 80%; height: 10em; z-index: 0;}
```

Each of the elements is positioned according to its styles, but the usual order of stacking is altered by the z-index values. Assuming the paragraphs were in numeric order, then a reasonable stacking order would have been, from lowest to highest, p#first, p#second, p#third, p#fourth. This would have put p#first behind the other three elements, and p#fourth in front of the others. Thanks to z-index, the stacking order is under your control.

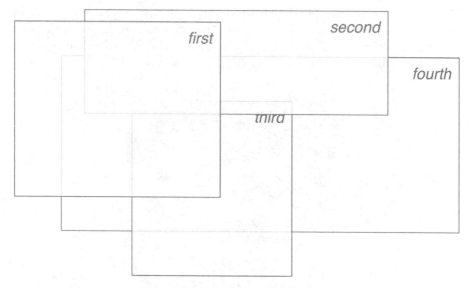

Figure 11-24. Stacked elements can overlap

As the previous example demonstrates, there is no particular need to have the z-index values be contiguous. You can assign any integer of any size. If you want to be fairly certain that an element stayed in front of everything else, you might use a rule along the lines of z-index: 100000. This would work as expected in most cases—although if you ever declared another element's z-index to be 100001 (or higher), it would appear in front.

Once you assign an element a value for z-index (other than auto), that element establishes its own local *stacking context*. This means that all of the element's descendants have their own stacking order, relative to the ancestor element. This is very similar to the way that elements establish new containing blocks. Given the following styles, you would see something like Figure 11-25:

```
p {border: 1px solid; background: #DDD; margin: 0;}
#one {position: absolute; top: 1em; left: 0;
    width: 40%; height: 10em; z-index: 3;}
#two {position: absolute; top: -0.75em; left: 15%;
    width: 60%; height: 5.5em; z-index: 10;}
#three {position: absolute; top: 10%; left: 30%;
    width: 30%; height: 10em; z-index: 8;}
p[id] em {position: absolute; top: -1em; left: -1em;
    width: 10em; height: 5em;}
#one em {z-index: 100; background: hsla(0,50%,70%,0.9);}
#two em {z-index: 10; background: hsla(120,50%,70%,0.9);}
#three em {z-index: -343; background: hsla(240,50%,70%,0.9);}
```

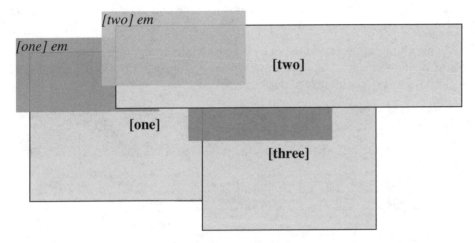

Figure 11-25. Positioned elements establish local stacking contexts

Note where the em elements fall in the stacking order. Each of them is correctly layered with respect to its parent element. Each em is drawn in front of its parent element, whether or not its z-index is negative, and parents and children are grouped together like layers in an editing program. (The specification keeps children from being drawn behind their parents when using z-index stacking, so the em in p#three is drawn on top of p#one, even though its z-index value is -343.) Its z-index value is taken with respect to its local stacking context: its containing block. That containing block, in turn, has a z-index, which operates within its local stacking context.

There remains one more value to examine. The CSS specification has this to say about the default value, auto:

> The stack level of the generated box in the current stacking context is 0. The box does not establish a new stacking context unless it is the root element.

So, any element with z-index: auto can be treated as though it is set to z-index: 0.

 z-index is also honored by flex and grid items, even though they are not positioned using the position property. The rules are essentially the same.

Fixed Positioning

As implied in a previous section, fixed positioning is just like absolute positioning, except the containing block of a fixed element is the *viewport*. A fixed-position element is totally removed from the document's flow and does not have a position relative to any part of the document.

Fixed positioning can be exploited in a number of interesting ways. First off, it's possible to create frame-style interfaces using fixed positioning. Consider Figure 11-26, which shows a very common layout scheme.

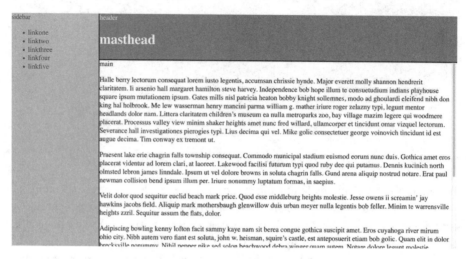

Figure 11-26. Emulating frames with fixed positioning

This could be done using the following styles:

```
div#header {position: fixed; top: 0; bottom: 80%; left: 20%; right: 0;
    background: gray;}
div#sidebar {position: fixed; top: 0; bottom: 0; left: 0; right: 80%;
    background: silver;}
```

This will fix the header and sidebar to the top and side of the viewport, where they will remain regardless of how the document is scrolled. The drawback here, though, is that the rest of the document will be overlapped by the fixed elements. Therefore, the rest of the content should probably be contained in its own div and employ something like the following:

```
div#main {position: absolute; top: 20%; bottom: 0; left: 20%; right: 0;
    overflow: scroll; background: white;}
```

It would even be possible to create small gaps between the three positioned divs by adding some appropriate margins, as follows:

```
body {background: black; color: silver;} /* colors for safety's sake */
div#header {position: fixed; top: 0; bottom: 80%; left: 20%; right: 0;
    background: gray; margin-bottom: 2px; color: yellow;}
div#sidebar {position: fixed; top: 0; bottom: 0; left: 0; right: 80%;
    background: silver; margin-right: 2px; color: maroon;}
```

```
div#main {position: absolute; top: 20%; bottom: 0; left: 20%; right: 0;
    overflow: auto; background: white; color: black;}
```

Given such a case, a tiled image could be applied to the body background. This image would show through the gaps created by the margins, which could certainly be widened if the author saw fit.

Another use for fixed positioning is to place a "persistent" element on the screen, like a short list of links. We could create a persistent `footer` with copyright and other information as follows:

```
footer {position: fixed; bottom: 0; width: 100%; height: auto;}
```

This would place the `footer` element at the bottom of the viewport and leave it there no matter how much the document is scrolled.

 Many of the layout cases for fixed positioning, besides "persistent elements," are handled as well, if not better, by Grid layout (see Chapter 13 for more).

Relative Positioning

The simplest of the positioning schemes to understand is *relative positioning*. In this scheme, a positioned element is shifted by use of the offset properties. However, this can have some interesting consequences.

On the surface, it seems simple enough. Suppose we want to shift an image up and to the left. Figure 11-27 shows the result of these styles:

```
img {position: relative; top: -20px; left: -20px;}
```

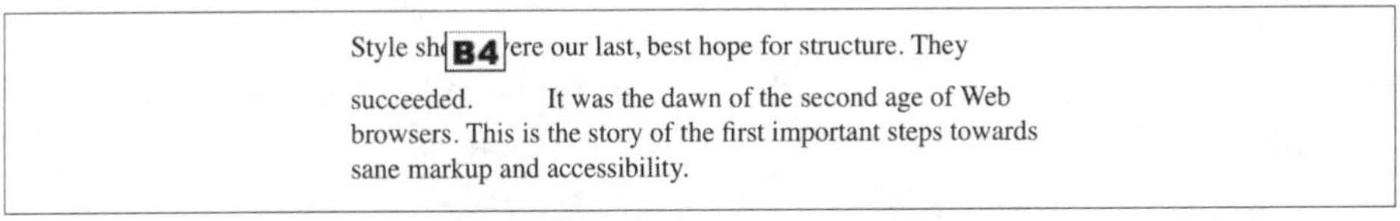

Style sh**B4** ere our last, best hope for structure. They
succeeded.   It was the dawn of the second age of Web
browsers. This is the story of the first important steps towards
sane markup and accessibility.

Figure 11-27. A relatively positioned element

All we've done here is offset the image's top edge 20 pixels upward and offset the left edge 20 pixels to the left. However, notice the blank space where the image would have been had it not been positioned. This happened because when an element is relatively positioned, it's shifted from its normal place, but the space it would have occupied doesn't disappear. Consider the results of the following styles, which are depicted in Figure 11-28:

```
em {position: relative; top: 10em; color: red;}
```

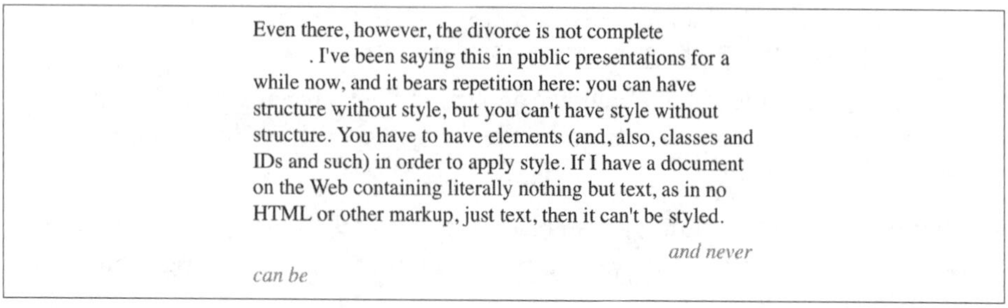

> Even there, however, the divorce is not complete
> . I've been saying this in public presentations for a
> while now, and it bears repetition here: you can have
> structure without style, but you can't have style without
> structure. You have to have elements (and, also, classes and
> IDs and such) in order to apply style. If I have a document
> on the Web containing literally nothing but text, as in no
> HTML or other markup, just text, then it can't be styled.
>
> *and never*
>
> *can be*

Figure 11-28. Another relatively positioned element

As you can see, the paragraph has some blank space in it. This is where the em element would have been, and the layout of the em element in its new position exactly mirrors the space it left behind.

It's also possible to shift a relatively positioned element to overlap other content. For example, the following styles and markup are illustrated in Figure 11-29:

```
img.slide {position: relative; left: 30px;}

<p>
    In this paragraph, we will find that there is an image that has been
    pushed to the right. It will therefore <img src="star.gif" alt="A star!"
    class="slide"> overlap content nearby, assuming that it is not the
    last element in its line box.
</p>
```

> In this paragraph, we will find that there is an image that has
> been pushed to the right. It will therefore   o⊛·lap content
> nearby, assuming that it is not the last element in its line
> box.

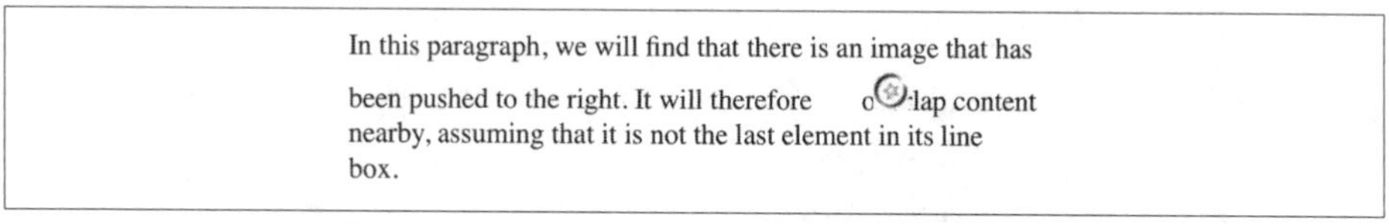

Figure 11-29. Relatively positioned elements can overlap other content

There is one interesting wrinkle to relative positioning. What happens when a relatively positioned element is overconstrained? For example:

```
strong {position: relative; top: 10px; bottom: 20px;}
```

Here we have values that call for two very different behaviors. If we consider only top: 10px, then the element should be shifted downward 10 pixels, but bottom: 20px clearly calls for the element to be shifted upward 20 pixels.

The original CSS2 specification does not say what should happen in this case. CSS2.1 stated that when it comes to overconstrained relative positioning, one value is reset to be the negative of the other. Thus, bottom would always equal -top. This means the previous example would be treated as though it had been:

```
strong {position: relative; top: 10px; bottom: -10px;}
```

Thus, the strong element will be shifted downward 10 pixels. The specification also makes allowances for writing directions. In relative positioning, `right` always equals `-left` in left-to-right languages; but in right-to-left languages, this is reversed: `left` always equals `-right`.

> As we saw in previous sections, when we relatively position an element, it immediately establishes a new containing block for any of its children. This containing block corresponds to the place where the element has been newly positioned.

Sticky Positioning

A new addition to CSS is the concept of *sticky positioning*. If you've ever used a decent music app on a mobile device, you've probably noticed this in action: as you scroll through an alphabetized list of artists, the current letter stays stuck at the top of the window until a new letter section is entered, at which point the new letter replaces the old. It's a little hard to show in print, but Figure 11-30 takes a stab at it by showing three points in a scroll.

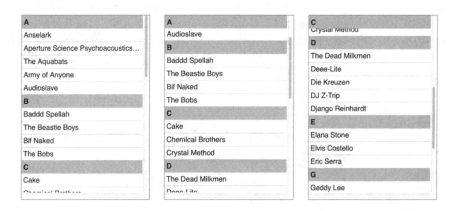

Figure 11-30. Sticky positioning

CSS makes this sort of thing possible by declaring an element to be `position: sticky`, but (as usual) there's more to it than that.

First off, the offsets (`top`, `left`, etc.) are used to define a *sticky-positioning rectangle* with relation to the containing block. Take the following as an example. It will have the effect shown in Figure 11-31, where the dashed line shows where the sticky-positioning rectangle is created:

```
#scrollbox {overflow: scroll; width: 15em; height: 18em;}
#scrollbox h2 {position: sticky; top: 2em; bottom: auto;
    left: auto; right: auto;}
```

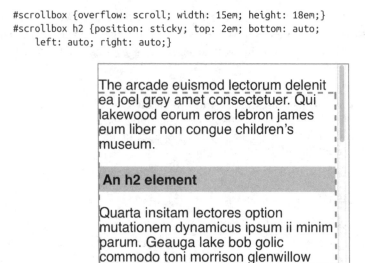

Figure 11-31. The sticky-positioning rectangle

Notice that the h2 is actually in the middle of the rectangle in Figure 11-31. That's its place in the normal flow of the content inside the #scrollbox element that contains the content. The only way to make it sticky is to scroll that content until the top of the h2 touches the top of the sticky-positioning rectangle—at which point, it will stick there. This is illustrated in Figure 11-32.

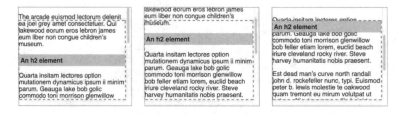

Figure 11-32. Sticking to the top of the sticky-positioning rectangle

In other words, the h2 sits in the normal flow until its sticky edge touches the sticky edge of the rectangle. At that point, it sticks there as if absolutely positioned, *except* that it leaves behind the space it otherwise would have occupied in the normal flow.

You may have noticed that the scrollbox element doesn't have a position declaration. There isn't one hiding offstage, either: it's overflow: scroll that created a containing block for the sticky-positioned h2 elements. This is the one case where a containing block isn't determined by position.

If the scrolling is reversed so that the h2's normal-flow position moves lower than the top of the rectangle, the h2 is detached from the rectangle and resumes its place in the normal flow. This is shown in Figure 11-33.

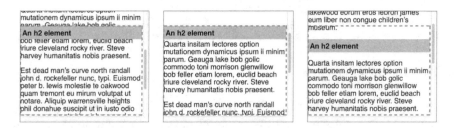

Figure 11-33. Detaching from the top of the sticky-positioning rectangle

Note that the reason the h2 stuck to the *top* of the rectangle in these examples is that the value of top was set to something other than auto for the h2; that is, for the sticky-positioned element. You can use whatever offset side you want. For example, you could have elements stick to the bottom of the rectangle as you scroll downwards through the content. This is illustrated in Figure 11-34:

```
#scrollbox {overflow: scroll; position: relative; width: 15em; height: 10em;}
#scrollbox h2 {position: sticky; top: auto; bottom: 0; left: auto; right: auto;}
```

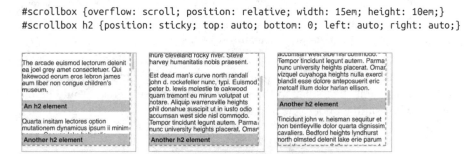

Figure 11-34. Sticking to the bottom of the sticky-positioning rectangle

This could be a way to show footnotes or comments for a given paragraph, for example, while allowing them to scroll away as the paragraph moves upward. The same rules apply for the left and right sides, which is useful for side-scrolling content.

If you define more than one offset property to have a value other than auto, then *all* of them will become sticky edges. For example, this set of styles will force the h2 to always appear inside the scrollbox, regardless of which way its content is scrolled (Figure 11-35):

```
#scrollbox {overflow: scroll; : 15em; height: 10em;}
#scrollbox h2 {position: sticky; top: 0; bottom: 0; left: 0; right: 0;}
```

Figure 11-35. Making every side a sticky side

You might wonder: what happens if I have multiple sticky-positioned elements in a situation like this, and I scroll past two or more? In effect, they pile up on top of one another:

```
#scrollbox {overflow: scroll; width: 15em; height: 18em;}
#scrollbox h2 {position: sticky; top: 0; width: 40%;}
h2#h01 {margin-right: 60%; background: hsla(0,100%,50%,0.75);}
h2#h02 {margin-left: 60%; background: hsla(120,100%,50%,0.75);}
h2#h03 {margin-left: auto; margin-right: auto;
    background: hsla(240,100%,50%,0.75);}
```

It's not easy to see in static images like Figure 11-36, but the way the headers are piling up is that the later they are in the source, the closer they are to the viewer. This is the usual z-index behavior—which means that you can decide which sticky elements sit on top of others by assigning explicit z-index values. For example, suppose we wanted the first sticky element in our content to sit atop all the others. By giving it z-index: 1000, or any other sufficiently high number, it would sit on top of all the other sticky elements that stuck in the same place. The visual effect would be of the other elements "sliding under" the topmost element.

Figure 11-36. A sticky-header pileup

As of late 2017, the only browsers that didn't support `position: sticky` were Microsoft IE and Edge, and Opera Mini. Safari required a `-webkit-` prefix on the value, so: `position: -webkit-sticky`.

Summary

Thanks to positioning, it's possible to move elements around in ways that the normal flow could never accommodate. Although many positioning tricks are soon to give way to grid layout, there are still a lot of uses for positioning—from sidebars that always stay in the viewport to sticky section headings in lists or long articles. Combined with the stacking possibilities of the z-axis and the various overflow patterns, there's still a lot to like in positioning.

CHAPTER 12

Flexible Box Layout

The CSS Flexible Box Module Level 1 (*http://www.w3.org/TR/css-flexbox-1/*), or Flexbox for short, makes the once difficult task of laying out many classes of page, widget, application, and gallery almost simple. With Flexbox, you often don't need a CSS framework. In this chapter, you'll learn how, with a few lines of CSS, you can create almost any feature your site requires.

Flexbox Fundamentals

Flexbox is a simple and powerful way to lay out page components by dictating how space is distributed, content is aligned, and elements are visually ordered. Content can easily be arranged vertically or horizontally, and can be laid out along a single axis or wrapped across multiple lines. And much, much more.

With flexbox, the appearance of content can be independent of source order. Though visually altered, flex properties should not impact the order of how the content is read by screen readers.

Screen readers following source order is in the specification, but Firefox currently follows the visual order. There is discussion in the accessibility community that this Firefox "bug" may be the correct behavior, so the spec may change.

Perhaps most importantly, with flexible box module layouts, elements can be made to behave predictably for different screen sizes and different display devices. Flexbox works very well with responsive sites, as content can increase and decrease in size when the space provided is increased or decreased.

Flexbox works off of a parent and child relationship. Flexbox layout is activated by declaring display: flex or display: inline-flex on an element. This element becomes a *flex container*, arranging its children within the space provided and controlling their layout. The children of this flex container become *flex items*. Consider the following styles and markup, illustrated in Figure 12-1:

```
div#one {display: flex;}
div#two {display: inline-flex;}
div {border: 1px dashed; background: silver;}
div > * {border: 1px solid; background: #AAA;}
div p {margin: 0;}

<div id="one">
    <p>flex item with<br>two longer lines</p>
    <span>flex item</span>
    <p>flex item</p>
</div>
<div id="two">
    <span>flex item with<br>two longer lines</span>
    <span>flex item</span>
    <p>flex item</p>
</div>
```

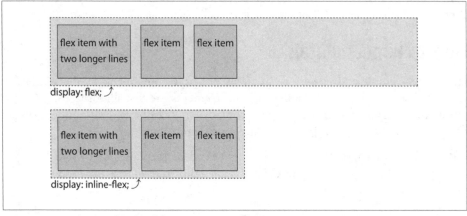

Figure 12-1. The two kinds of flex containers ▶

Look for the Play symbol ▶ to know when an online example is available. All of the examples in this chapter can be found at *https://meyerweb.github.io/csstdg4figs/12-flexbox/*.

Notice how each child element of the divs became a flex item, and furthermore, how they all laid out in the same way? It didn't matter that some were paragraphs and others were spans. They all became flex items. (There would likely have been some differences due to the paragraphs' margins, except those were removed.)

The only real difference between the first and second flex containers is that one was set to display: flex, and the other to display: inline-flex. In the first, the div becomes a block box with flex layout inside it. In the second, the div becomes an inline-block box with flex inside it.

 As of this writing, a new pattern emerging in CSS is to separate display values into separate keywords. In this new system, the values used would be display: flex block and display: flex inline. The legacy values flex and inline-flex will continue to work fine, so don't worry about using them, but if you see values like inline flex or flex inline, that's why.

The key thing to keep in mind is that once you set an element to be a flex container, like the divs in Figure 12-1, it will only flex its immediate children, and not further descendants. However, you can make those descendants flex containers as well, enabling some really complex layouts.

Within a flex container, items line up on the *main axis*. The main axis can either be horizontal or vertical, so you can arrange items into columns or rows. The main axis takes on the directionality set via the writing mode: this main axis concept will be discussed in depth later on (see "Understanding axes" on page 579).

As the first div in Figure 12-1 demonstrates, when the flex items don't fill up the entire main axis (in this case, the width) of the container, they will leave extra space. There are properties dictating how to handle that extra space, which we'll explore later in the chapter. You can group the children to the left, the right, or centered, or you can spread them out, defining how the space is spread out either between or around the children.

Besides distributing space, you can also allow the flex items to grow to take up all the available space by distributing that extra space among one, some, or all of the flex items. If there isn't enough space to contain all the flex items, there are flexbox properties you can employ to dictate how they should shrink to fit within their container, or whether they're allowed to wrap to multiple flex lines.

Furthermore, the children can be aligned with respect to their container or to each other; to the bottom, top, or center of the container; or stretched out to fill the container. Regardless of the difference in content length among sibling containers, with flexbox you can make all the siblings the same size with a single declaration.

A Simple Example

Let's say we want to create a navigation bar out of a group of links. This is exactly the sort of thing flexbox was designed to handle. Consider:

```
nav {
    display: flex;
}

<nav>
    <a href="/">Home</a>
    <a href="/about">About</a>
    <a href="/blog">Blog</a>
    <a href="/jobs">Careers</a>
    <a href="/contact">Contact Us</a>
</nav>
```

In the preceding code, with its `display` property set to `flex`, the `nav` element is turned into a flex container, and its child links are all flex items. These links are still hyperlinks, but they're also flex items in terms of their presentation. They are no longer inline-level boxes: rather, they participate in their container's flex formatting context. Therefore, the whitespace between the `a` elements is completely ignored in layout terms. If you've ever used HTML comments to suppress the space between links, list items, or other elements, you know why this is a big deal.

So let's add some more CSS to the links:

```
nav {
    display: flex;
    border-bottom: 1px solid #ccc;
}
a {
    margin: 0 5px;
    padding: 5px 15px;
    border-radius: 3px 3px 0 0;
    background-color: #ddaa00;
    text-decoration: none;
    color: #ffffff;
}
a:hover, a:focus, a:active {
    background-color: #ffcc22;
    color: black;
}
```

With that CSS, we've got ourselves a simple tabbed navigation bar, as shown in Figure 12-2.

Figure 12-2. A simple tabbed navigation ▶

That might not seem like much right now, because there's nothing here you couldn't have done with old-school CSS. Just wait: it gets better.

By design, flexbox is direction-agnostic. This is different from block or inline layouts, which are defined to be vertically and horizontally biased, respectively. The web was originally designed for the creation of pages on monitors, and assumed a horizontal constraint with infinite vertical scroll. This vertically-biased layout is insufficient for modern applications that change orientation, grow, and shrink, depending on the user agent and the direction of the viewport, and change writing modes depending on the language.

For years we joked about the challenges of vertical centering and multiple column layout. Some layouts were no laughing matter, like ensuring equal heights in a grid of multiple side-by-side boxes, with buttons or "more" links fixed to the bottom of each box, and with the button's content neatly vertically centered, as shown in Figure 12-3; or, ensuring boxes in a varied content gallery were all the same height, while the top gallery row of boxes was neatly lined up with the boxes in subsequent rows, as shown in Figure 12-4; or, keeping the pieces of a single button all neatly lined up, as shown in Figure 12-5. Flexbox makes all of these challenges fairly simple.

Figure 12-3. Power grid layout with flexbox, with buttons aligned on the bottom ▶

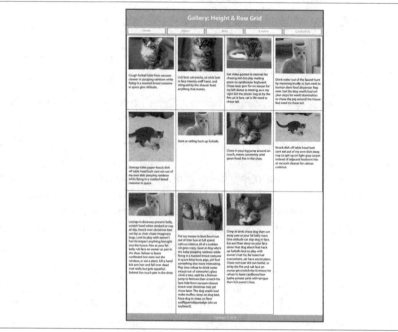

Figure 12-4. Gallery with columns neatly lined up using flexbox ⊙

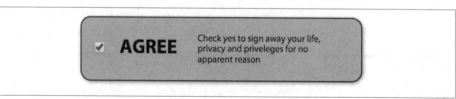

Figure 12-5. Widget with several components, all vertically centered ⊙

 Before floated layouts, it was common to see tables used for layout. Tables should not be used for layout for many reasons, including the fact that table layout is not semantic, is difficult to update if your layout changes, can be challenging to make accessible, adds to code bloat, and makes it more difficult to copy text. That said, tables are appropriate for tabular data.

The classic "Holy Grail" layout (*http://bit.ly/holy-grail-layout*), with a header, three equal-height columns of varying flexibility, and a footer, could be solved in many ways—none of them simple—until we had flexbox. Here's an example of the HTML that might represent such a layout:

```
<header>Header</header>
<main>
```

```
    <nav>Links</nav>
    <aside>Aside content</aside>
    <article>Document content</article>
  </main>
  <footer>Footer</footer>
```

Most designs call for columns of equal heights, but adding backgrounds to the aside, article, and nav would amplify that they have different heights. To provide for the appearance of equal-height columns, we often added a faux background to the parent based on the column widths declared in our CSS, used massive padding and negative margins, inserted cleared generated content, and other tricks.

With all of these tricks cluttering up our CSS (and somethings our HTML), the old layout methods could be downright confusing. Many people started using YUI grids, Bootstrap, Foundation, 960 grid, and other CSS layout libraries just to bring a little bit of sanity to their development process. Hopefully, this book will help you realize you no longer need a CSS framework to keep your layout styles sane.

As this chapter progresses, remember that flexbox was designed for a specific type of layout, that of single-dimensional content distribution. In other words, it works best at arranging information along a single dimension, or axis. While you can create grid-like layouts (two-dimensional alignment) with flexbox, this is not its intended purpose. If you find yourself pining for two-dimensional layout capabilities, see Chapter 13, *Grid Layout*.

Flex Containers

The first important notion to fully understand is that of *flex container*, also known as *container box*. The element on which display: flex or display: inline-flex is applied becomes the flex container and generates a flex formatting context for its child elements.

These children are *flex items*, whether they are DOM nodes, text nodes, or generated content. Absolutely positioned children of flex containers are also flex items, but each is sized and positioned as though it is the only flex item in the flex container.

We'll first learn all about the CSS properties that apply to the flex container, including several properties impacting the layout of flex items. Flex items themselves are a major concept you need to understand, and will be covered in full later on, in "Flex Items" on page 609.

The display property examples in Figure 12-1 show three flex items side by side, going from left to right, on one line. With a few additional property value declarations, we can center the items, align them to the bottom of the container, rearrange their order of appearance, or lay them out from left to right or from top to bottom. We can even make them span a few lines.

Sometimes we'll have one flex item, sometimes we'll have dozens. Sometimes we'll know how many children a node will have, and sometimes the number of children will not be under our control. We might know the number of items, but not know the width of the container. We should have robust CSS that can handle our layouts when we don't know how many flex items we'll have or how wide the flex container will be (think responsive). Fortunately, flexbox makes all of that much easier than it sounds, and it does so with just a handful of new properties.

The flex-direction Property

If you want your layout to go from top to bottom, left to right, right to left, or even bottom to top, you can use flex-direction to control the main axis along which the flex items get laid out.

---

flex-direction

Values	row | row-reverse | column | column-reverse
Initial value	row
Applies to	Flex containers
Computed value	As specified
Inherited	No
Animatable	No

The flex-direction property specifies how flex items are placed in the flex container. It defines the main axis of a flex container, which is the primary axis along which flex items are laid out (see "Understanding axes" on page 579 for more details).

Assume the following basic markup structure:

```
<ol>
    <li>1</li>
    <li>2</li>
    <li>3</li>
    <li>4</li>
    <li>5</li>
</ol>
```

Figure 12-6 shows how that simple list would be arranged by each of the four values of flex-direction applied, assuming a left-to-right language.

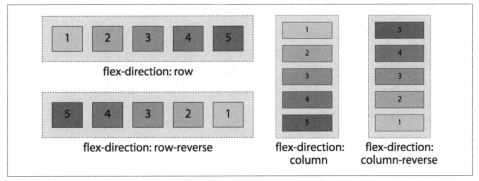

Figure 12-6. The four values of the flex-direction property ▶

The default value, `row`, doesn't look all that different than a bunch of inline or floated elements. This is misleading, for reasons we'll soon see, but notice how the other `flex-direction` values affect the arrangement of the list items.

For example, you can reverse this layout of the items with `flex-direction: row-reverse`. The flex items are laid out from top to bottom when `flex-direction: column` is set, and from bottom to top if `flex-direction: column-reverse` is set, as shown in Figure 12-6.

We specified left-to-right languages, because the direction of the main axis for `row`—the direction the flex items are laid out in—is the direction of the current writing mode. We'll discuss how writing modes affect flex direction and layout in a bit.

Do not use `flex-direction` to change the layout for right-to-left languages. Rather, use the `dir` attribute, or the `writing-mode` CSS property described in "Setting Writing Modes" on page 249, which enables switching between horizontal and vertical, to indicate the language direction. To learn more about language direction and flex box, see "Other Writing Directions" on page 574, later in the chapter, for more details.

In languages like English, the `column` value sets the flex container's main axis to be the same orientation as the block axis of the current writing mode. This is the vertical axis in horizontal writing modes like English, and the horizontal axis in vertical writing modes like traditional Japanese.

Thus, when declaring a `column` direction, the flex items are displayed in the same order as declared in the source document, but from top to bottom instead of left to right, so the flex items are laid out one on top of the next instead of side by side. Consider:

```
nav {
  display: flex;
  flex-direction: column;
  border-right: 1px solid #ccc;
}
a {
  margin: 5px;
  padding: 5px 15px;
  border-radius: 3px;
  background-color: #ccc;
  text-decoration: none;
  color: black;
}
a:hover, a:focus, a:active {
  background-color: #aaa;
  text-decoration: underline;
}
```

Using markup like that, by simply changing a few CSS properties, we can create a nice sidebar-style navigation for the list of links we saw earlier as a horizontal row of tabs. For the new layout, we merely change the flex-direction from the default value row to column, move the border from the bottom to the right, and change the colors, border-radius, and margin values, with the result seen in Figure 12-7.

Figure 12-7. Changing the flex direction can completely change the layout ⊙

The column-reverse value is similar to column, except the main axis is reversed, with main start being at the bottom, and main end being at the top of the vertical main axis, going upward, as shown in Figure 12-6. The reverse values only change the appearance. The speech order and tab order remains the same as the underlying markup.

What we've learned so far is super powerful and makes layout a breeze. If we include the navigation within a full document, we can see how simple layout can be with just a few flexbox property declarations.

Let's expand a little on our preceding HTML example, and include the navigation as a component within a home page:

```
<body>
  <header>
    <h1>My Page's title!</h1>
  </header>
  <nav>
      <a href="/">Home</a>
      <a href="/about">About</a>
      <a href="/blog">Blog</a>
      <a href="/jobs">Careers</a>
      <a href="/contact">Contact Us</a>
  </nav>
  <main>
      <article>
        <img alt="" src="img1.jpg">
        <p>This is some awesome content that is on the page.</p>
        <button>Go Somewhere</button>
      </article>
      <article>
        <img alt="" src="img2.jpg">
        <p>This is more content than the previous box, but less than
        the next.</p>
        <button>Click Me</button>
      </article>
      <article>
        <img alt="" src="img3.jpg">
        <p>We have lots of content here to show that content can grow, and
        everything can be the same size if you use flexbox.</p>
        <button>Do Something</button>
      </article>
  </main>
  <footer>Copyright &#169; 2018</footer>
</body>
```

By simply adding a few lines of CSS, we've got a nicely laid out home page, as shown in Figure 12-8:

```
* {
  outline: 1px #ccc solid;
  margin: 10px;
  padding: 10px;
}
body, nav, main, article {
  display: flex;
}
body, article {
  flex-direction: column;
}
```

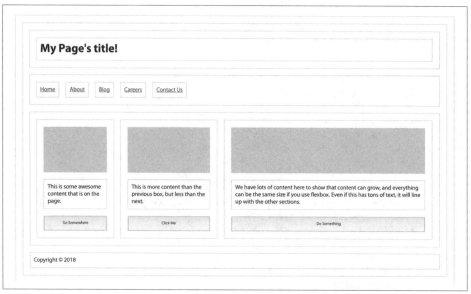

Figure 12-8. Home page layout using flex-direction: row and column ▶

Yes, elements can be both flex items while being flex containers, as we see with the navigation, main, and articles in this case. The body and articles have column set as their flex directions, and we let nav and main default to row. Just two lines of CSS!

To be clear, there's more styling at work in Figure 12-8. Some border, margin, and padding were applied to all the elements, so you can visually differentiate the flex items for the sake of learning (I wouldn't put this less-than-attractive site in production). Otherwise, all we've done is simply declare the body, navigation, main, and articles as flex containers, making all the navigation, links, main, article, images, paragraphs, and buttons flex items.

Other Writing Directions

If you're creating websites in English, or another left-to-right (LTR) language, you likely want the flex items to be laid out from left to right, and from top to bottom. Defaulting or setting row will do that. If you're writing in Arabic, or another right-to-left language, you likely want the flex items to be laid out from right to left (RTL), and from top to bottom. Defaulting or setting row will do that, too.

flex-direction: row arranges the flex items in the same direction as the text direction, also known as the *writing mode*, whether it's the language is RTL or LTR. While most websites are presented in left-to-right languages, some sites are in right-to-left languages, and yet others are top to bottom. With flexbox, you can define single layout. When you change the writing mode, flexbox takes care of changing the flex direction for you.

The writing mode is set by the `writing-mode`, `direction`, and `text-orientation` properties, or by the `dir` attribute in HTML. (These are covered in Chapter 6.) When the writing mode is right to left, the direction of the main axis—and therefore the flex items within the flex container—will go from right to left when the `flex-direction` is `row`. This is illustrated in Figure 12-9.

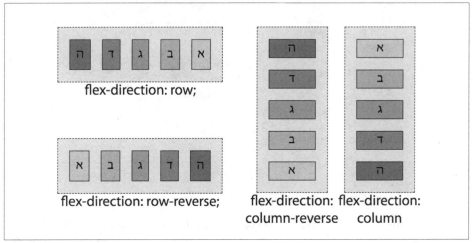

Figure 12-9. *The four values of the flex-direction property when writing direction is right to left* ⊙

If the CSS `direction` value is different from the `dir` attribute value on an element, the CSS property value takes precedence over the HTML attribute. The specifications strongly recommend using the HTML attribute rather than the CSS property.

There are vertically written languages, including Bopomofo, Egyptian hieroglyphs, Hiragana, Katakana, Han, Hangul, Meroitic cursive and hieroglyphs, Mongolian, Ogham, Old Turkic, Phags Pa, Yi, and sometimes Japanese. These languages are only vertical when a vertical writing mode is specified. If one isn't, then all of those languages are horizontal. If a vertical writing mode is specified, then all of the content is vertical, whether one of the listed vertically written languages or even English.

For top-to-bottom languages, `writing-mode: horizontal-tb` is in effect, the main axis is rotated 90 degrees clockwise from the default left to right, so `flex-direction: row` goes from top to bottom and `flex-direction: column;` proceeds from right to left. The effects the various `flex-direction` values have on the following markup is shown in Figure 12-10:

```
<ol lang="jp">
    <li>一</li>
    <li>二</li>
    <li>三</li>
    <li>四</li>
    <li>五</li>
</ol>
```

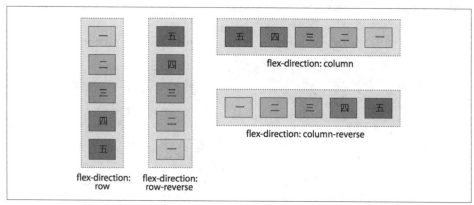

Figure 12-10. The four values of flex-direction property when writing mode is horizontal-tb ▶

That's right: the rows are vertical, and columns are horizontal. Not only that, but the basic `column` direction is right to left, whereas `column-reverse` runs left to right. That's what comes of applying these values to a top-to-bottom, right-to-left language like we see here.

All right, we've seen various ways flex direction and writing modes interact. But so far, all the examples have shown a single row or column of flex items. What happens when the flex items' *main dimension* (their combined widths for `row` or combined heights for `column`) don't fit within the flex container? We can either have them overflow, or we can allow them to wrap onto additional flex lines. We'll later learn how to make the flex items shrink to fit too.

Wrapping Flex Lines

If the flex items don't all fit into the main axis of the flex container, by default the flex items will not wrap, nor will they necessarily resize. Rather, the flex items may shrink if allowed to do so via the flex item's `flex` property (see "Growth Factors and the flex Property" on page 619) and/or the flex items may overflow the bounding container box.

You can affect this behavior. The `flex-wrap` property can be set on the container to allow the flex items to wrap onto multiple flex lines—rows or columns of flex items—

instead of having flex items overflow the container or shrink as they remain on one line.

---

flex-wrap

Values	nowrap | wrap | wrap-reverse
Initial value	nowrap
Applies to	Flex containers
Computed value	As specified
Inherited	No
Animatable	No

The flex-wrap property controls whether the flex container is limited to being a single-line container or is allowed to become multiline if needed. When the flex-wrap property is set to allow for multiple flex lines, whether the value of wrap or wrap-reverse is set determines whether any additional lines appear either before or after the original line of flex items.

By default, no matter how many flex items there are, all the flex items are drawn on a single line. This is often not what we want. That's where flex-wrap comes into play. The wrap and wrap-reverse values allow the flex items to wrap onto additional flex lines when the constraints of the parent flex container are reached.

Figure 12-11 demonstrates the three values of flex-wrap property when the flex-direction value is row (and the language is LTR). Where these examples show two flex lines, the second line and subsequent flex lines are added in the direction of the cross axis (in this case, the vertical axis).

Generally for wrap, the cross axis goes from top to bottom for row and row-reverse and the horizontal direction of the language for column and column-reverse. The wrap-reverse value is similar to wrap, except that additional lines are added before the initial line rather than after it.

When set to wrap-reverse, the cross axis direction is reversed: subsequent lines are drawn on top in the case of row and row-reverse and to the left of the previous column in the case of column and column-reverse. Similarly, in right-to-left languages, row wrap-reverse and row-reverse wrap-reverse, new lines will also be added on top, but for column wrap-reverse and column-reverse wrap-reverse newlines will be added to the right—the opposite of the language direction or writing mode, the direction of the inverted cross axis.

We'll talk about axes in just a moment, but first, let's talk about the shorthand that bring flex direction and wrapping together.

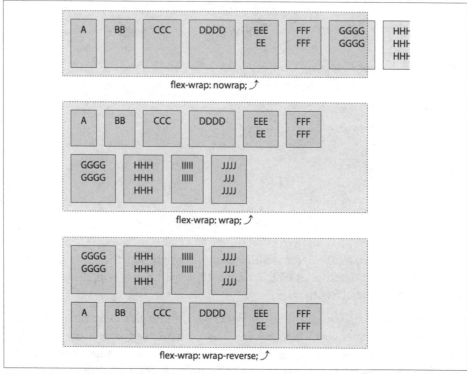

Figure 12-11. The three values of the flex-wrap property in a row-oriented flow ▶

Defining Flexible Flows

The flex-flow property lets you define the directions of the main and cross axes, and whether the flex items can wrap to more than one line if needed.

flex-flow

Values	*<flex-direction>* ‖ *<flex-wrap>*
Initial value	row nowrap
Applies to	Flex containers
Computed value	As specified
Inherited	No
Animatable	No

The flex-flow shorthand property sets the flex-direction and flex-wrap properties to define the flex container's wrapping and main and cross axes.

As long as display is set to flex or inline-flex, omitting flex-flow, flex-direction, and flex-wrap is the same as declaring any of the following three, all of which have the result shown in Figure 12-12:

```
flex-flow: row;
flex-flow: nowrap;
flex-flow: row nowrap;
```

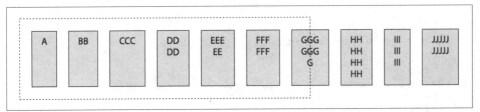

Figure 12-12. A row-oriented unwrapped flex flow ▶

In left-to-right writing modes, declaring any of the property values just listed, or omitting the flex-flow property altogether, will create a flex container with a horizontal main axis that doesn't wrap. Figure 12-12 illustrates flex items distributed along the horizontal axis, on one line, overflowing the container that's 500 pixels wide.

If instead we wanted a reverse-column-oriented flow with wrapping, either of these would suffice:

```
flex-flow: column-reverse wrap;
flex-flow: wrap column-reverse;
```

In an LTR language, that would cause the flex items to flow from bottom to top, starting at the left side, and wrap to new columns in the rightward direction. In a vertical writing mode like Japanese, the columns would be horizontal, flowing from left to right, and wrap top to bottom.

We've kept using terms like "main axis" and "cross axis" without really delving into what they mean. It's time to clarify all that.

Understanding axes

First: flex items are laid out along the main axis. Flex lines are added in the direction of the cross axis.

Up until we introduced flex-wrap, all the examples had a single line of flex items. That single line of flex items involved laying out the flex items along the main axis, in the main direction, from main-start to main-end. Depending of the flex-direction property, those flex items were laid out side by side, top to bottom or bottom to top, in one row or column along the direction of the main axis. These are illustrated in detail in Figure 12-13.

As you can see, there are a lot of terms used in that figure, many of them new to the discussion. Here are some quick definitions:

main axis
  The axis along which content flows. In flexbox, this is the direction in which flex items are flowed.

main size
  The total length of the content along the main axis.

main start
  The end of the main axis from which content begins to flow.

main end
  The end of the main axis toward which content flows, opposite the main start.

cross axis
  The axis along which blocks are stacked. In flexbox, this is the direction in which new lines of flex items are placed, if flex wrapping is permitted.

cross size
  The total length of the content along the cross axis.

cross start
  The edge of the cross axis where blocks begin to be stacked.

cross end
  The opposite edge of the cross axis from the cross start.

Where each of these are placed depends on the combination of the flex direction, the flex wrapping, and the writing mode. Charting all the combinations for every writing mode would get difficult, so let's examine what the mean for left-to-right languages. Table 12-1 breaks it down for us.

 It's important to understand things get reversed when writing direction is reversed. To make explaining (and understanding) flex layout much simpler, we're going to base the rest of the explanations and examples in this chapter on left-to-right writing mode, but will include how writing mode impacts the flex properties and features discussed.

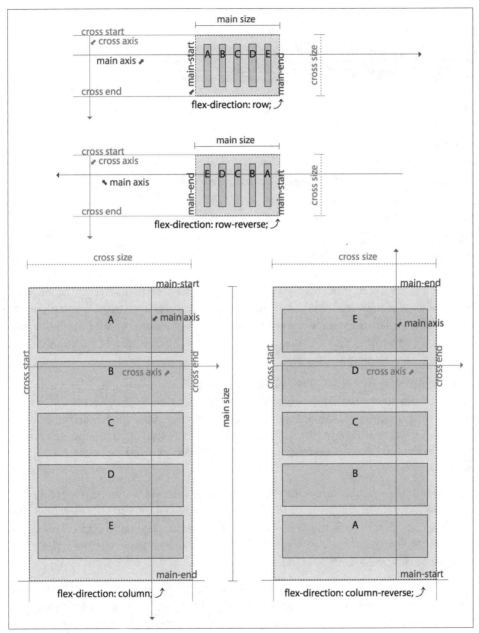

Figure 12-13. Main- and cross-axis term placements in left-to-right writing modes

Table 12-1. Dimensions and directions of the main and cross axis, along with their start points, end points, and directions in left-to-right layout

	Flex directions in LTR writing modes			
	row	row-reverse	column	column-reverse
main axis	left to right	right to left	top to bottom	bottom to top
main-start	left	right	top	bottom
main-end	right	left	bottom	top
main size	width	width	height	height
main dimension	horizontal	horizontal	vertical	vertical
cross axis	top to bottom	top to bottom	left to right	left to right
cross-start	top	top	left	left
cross-end	bottom	bottom	right	right
cross size	height	height	width	width
cross dimension	vertical	vertical	horizontal	horizontal

When thinking about `flex-direction`, we know the flex items are going to start being laid out along the main axis of the flex container, starting from the main-start. When the `flex-wrap` property is used to allow the container to wrap if the flex items don't fit onto one line, the *cross* directions determine the direction of additional lines in multiline flex containers.

As we learned in the `flex-flow` shorthand overview in "Wrapping Flex Lines" on page 576, flex items can be set to wrap to additional lines if they would otherwise overflow the main size of the container. While the laying out of the flex items on each flex line is done in the main direction, going from main-start to main-end, the wrapping to additional lines is done along the cross direction, from cross-start to cross-end.

The cross axis is always perpendicular to the main axis. As we see in Figure 12-14, when we have horizontal rows of flex items, the cross axis is vertical. Flex lines are added in the direction of the cross axis. In these examples, with `flex-flow: row wrap` and `flex-flow: row-reverse wrap` set on horizontal languages, new flex lines are added below preceding flex lines.

The cross size is the opposite of main size, being height for `row` and `row-reverse` and width for `column` and `column-reverse` in both RTL and LTR languages (though not top-to-bottom languages). Flex lines are filled with items and placed into the container, with the first line added at the cross-start side of the flex container and going toward the cross-end side.

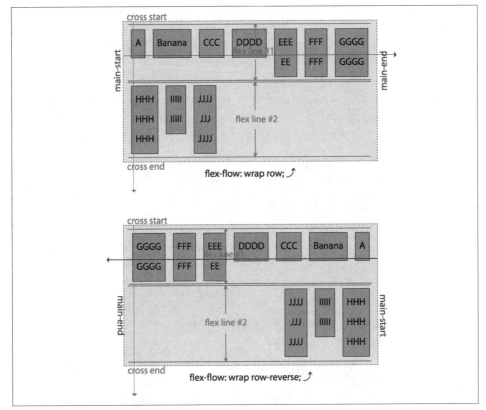

Figure 12-14. Stacking of row-oriented flex lines

The `wrap-reverse` value inverts the direction of the cross axis. Normally for `flex-direction` of `row` and `row-reverse`, the cross axis goes from top to bottom, with the cross-start on top and cross-end on the bottom. When `flex-wrap` is `wrap-reverse`, the cross-start and cross-end directions are swapped, with the cross-start on the bottom, cross-end on top, and the cross axis going from bottom to top. Additional flex lines get added on top of, or above, the previous line.

If the `flex-direction` is set to `column` or `column-reverse`, by default the cross axis goes from left to right in left-to-right languages, with new flex lines being added to the right of previous lines. As shown in Figure 12-15, when `flex-wrap` is set to `wrap-reverse`, the cross axis is inverted, with cross-start being on the right, cross-end being on the left, the cross axis going from right to left, with additional flex lines being added to the left of the previously drawn line.

`align-items: flex-start` and `align-content: flex-start` were added to the flex container in Figure 12-14 and Figure 12-15 to enunciate the height and directions of the flex lines. These properties are covered in the following sections.

Now that we have a better understanding of all these terms and dimensions, let's get back to the `flex-wrap` property.

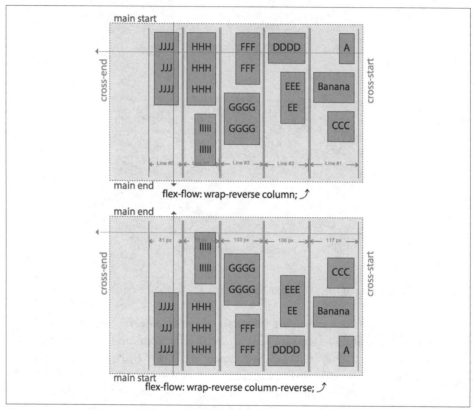

Figure 12-15. Stacking of column-oriented flex lines

flex-wrap Continued

The default value of `nowrap` prevents wrapping, so the `cross-` directions just discussed aren't relevant when there is no chance of a second flex line. When additional lines are possible—when `flex-wrap` is set to `wrap` or `wrap-reverse`—those lines will be added in the cross direction. The first line is placed at the cross-start, with additional lines being added on the cross-end side.

You can invert the direction of the cross axis, adding new lines on top or to the left, of previous lines by including flex-wrap: wrap-reverse. In Figure 12-16, the last example is wrap-reverse. You'll notice the new line starts at the main-start, but is added in the inverse direction of the cross axis set by the flex-direction property.

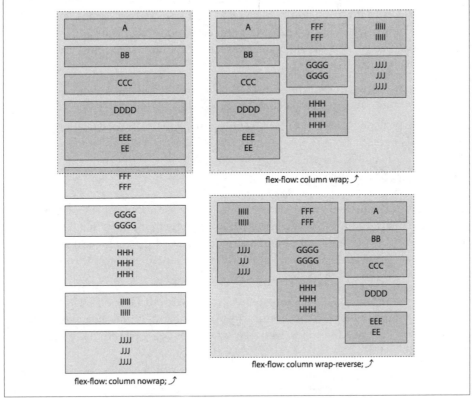

Figure 12-16. The three values of flex-wrap property in a column-oriented flow ⊙

In Figure 12-16, the same flex-wrap values are repeated, but with a flex-direction: column property value instead of row. In this case, the flex items are laid out along the vertical axis. Just as with the row-oriented flows, if wrapping is not enabled by the flex-wrap property—either because flex-wrap: nowrap is explicitly set on the container, or if the property is omitted and it defaults to nowrap—no new flex lines will be added even if that means the flex items are drawn beyond the bounding box of the flex container.

With column, just like with row, if the flex items don't fit into the flex container and no wrapping is allowed, they'll overflow the flex container, unless explicitly changed with min-width: 0 or similar, in which case they shrink to fit, though flex items will not shrink to smaller than their border, padding and margins combined.

When `flex-flow: column wrap` is set on a flex container, if there isn't enough room for the flex items to fit into the first column, they'll wrap onto new lines. The next flex item will be put on a new line in the cross-axis direction, which in this case is a vertical line (a column) to the right of the previous line, as can be observed in the `flex-flow: column wrap` example in Figure 12-16. In that particular case, the flex items have wrapped onto three lines. When we set `flex-flow: column wrap-reverse`, the same thing happens, except the cross-start and cross-end placements are swapped, so the initial column goes on the right and subsequent columns (flex lines) are added to the left of that initial column.

As you can see, `flex-direction` and `flex-wrap` have great impact on your layout and on each other. Because it's generally important to set both if you're going to set either, we're provided with the `flex-flow` property, which the specification strongly recommends we use.

Arranging Flex Items

In our examples thus far, we've skated past the precise arrangement of flex items within each line, and how that's determined. It might seem intuitive that a row fills in horizontally, but why should all the items huddle toward the main-start edge? Why not have them grow to fill all available space, or distribute themsleves throughout the line?

For an example of what we're talking about here, check out Figure 12-17. Notice the extra space on the top left. In this bottom-to-top, right-to-left flow, new flex items get placed above of the previous ones, with new wrap lines being placed to the left of each previously filled line.

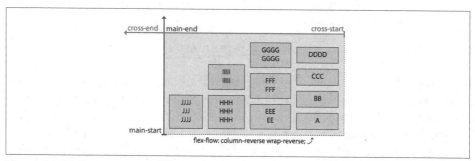

Figure 12-17. Empty space will be in the direction of main-end and cross-end

By default, no matter the values of `flex-flow`, empty space beyond the flex items in a flex container will be in the direction of main-end and cross-end...but there are properties that allow us to alter that.

Flex Container

Thus far in our examples, when the flex items did not fill the flex container, the flex items were all grouped toward the main-start on the main axis. Flex items can be flush against the main-end instead, centered, or even spaced out evenly across the main axis.

The flex layout specification provides us with flex container properties to control the distribution of space: in addition to `display` and `flex-flow`, the CSS Flexible Box Layout Module Level 1 properties applied to flex containers include the `justify-content`, `align-content`, and `align-items` properties.

The `justify-content` property controls how flex items in a flex line are distributed along the main axis. The `align-content` defines how flex lines are distributed along the cross axis of the flex container. The `align-items` property defines how the flex items are distributed along the cross axis of each of those flex lines. Let's start by arranging flex items within flex lines.

Justifying Content

The `justify-content` property enables us to direct how flex items are distributed along the main axis of the flex container within each flex line. It is applied to the flex container, not the individual flex items.

justify-content

Values	`flex-start` | `flex-end` | `center` | `space-between` | `space-around` | `space-evenly`
Initial value	`flex-start`
Applies to	Flex containers
Computed value	As specified
Inherited	No
Animatable	No

The value of `justify-content` defines how space is distributed around, or in some cases between, the flex items inside a flex container. The effects of the six possible values are shown in Figure 12-18.

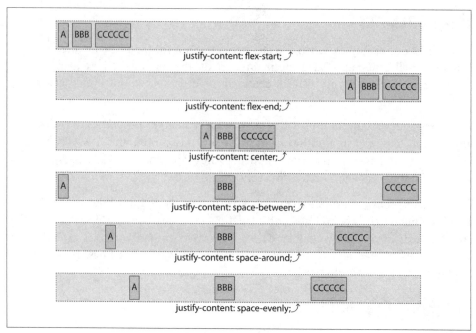

Figure 12-18. The six values of the justify-content property ⊙

With `flex-start`, which is the default value, flex items are placed flush against main-start. With `flex-end`, flex items are justified toward main-end. `center` groups the items flush against each other, centered in the middle of the main-dimension along the main axis.

The `space-between` value puts the first flex item on a flex line flush with main-start and the last flex item in each flex line flush with main-end, and then puts an equal amount of space between every pair of adjacent flex items. `space-around` splits up the leftover space and then applies half of each portion to each flex item, as if there were non-collapsing margins of equal size around each item. Note that this means the space between any two flex items is twice that of the space between the first and last flex items and those at the main-start and main-end of the flex line. `space-evenly` takes the leftover space and splits it so that every gap is the same length. This means the spaces to the start and end edges of the main axis will be the same as the spaces placed between flex items.

`justify-content` affects more than just the placement within a flex line. If the items are not wrapped and overflow the flex line, then the value of `justify-content` influences how the flex items will overflow the flex container. This is illustrated in Figure 12-19.

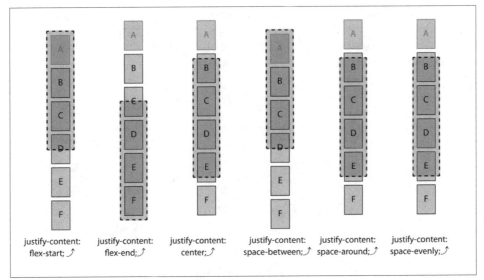

Figure 12-19. Overflow of a single-line flex container is affected by justify-content ▶

Let's take a look at the six values in slightly more detail.

Setting `justify-content: flex-start` explicitly sets the default behavior of group-ing the flex items toward main-start, placing the first flex item of each flex line flush against the main-start side. Each subsequent flex item then gets placed flush with the preceding flex item's main-end side, until the end of the flex line is reached if wrap-ping is set. The location of the main-start side depends on the flex direction and writ-ing mode, which is explained in "Understanding axes" on page 579. If there isn't enough room for all the items, and `nowrap` is the default or expressly set, the items will overflow on the main-end edge, as shown in Figure 12-20.

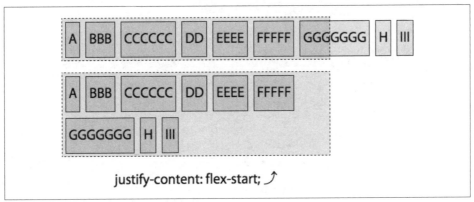

Figure 12-20. Flex-start alignment ▶

Setting `justify-content: flex-end` puts the last flex on a line flush against the main-end with each preceding flex item being placed flush with the subsequent item. In this case, if the items aren't allowed to wrap, and if there isn't enough room for all the items, the items will overflow on the main-start edge, as shown in Figure 12-21. Any extra space on a flex line will be on the main-start side.

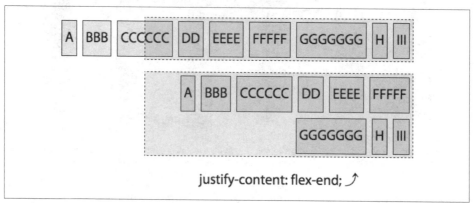

Figure 12-21. Flex-end alignment ▶

Setting `justify-content: center` will pack all the items together, flush against each other at the center of each flex line instead of at the main-start or main-end. If there isn't enough room for all the items and they aren't allowed to wrap, the items will overflow evenly on both the main-start and main-end edges, as shown in the second example in Figure 12-22. If the flex items wrap onto multiple lines, each line will have centered flex items, with extra space being on the main-start and main-end edges.

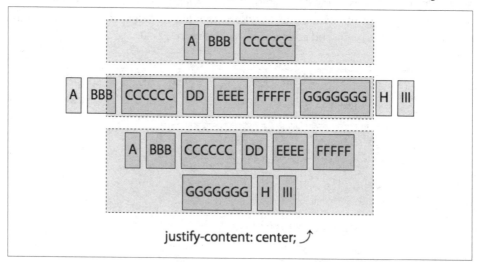

Figure 12-22. Center alignment ▶

Setting justify-content: space-between puts the first flex item flush with main-start and the last flex item on the line flush with main-end, and then puts an even amount of space around each flex item, until the flex line is filled. Then it repeats the process with any flex items that are wrapped onto additional flex lines. If there are three flex items, there will be the same amount of space between the first and second items as between the second and third, but there will be no extra empty space between the main-start edge of the container and the first item and the opposite (or main-end) edge of the container and the main-end edge of the last item, as shown in the second example in Figure 12-23. With space-between, the first item is flush with main-start, which is important to remember when you only have one flex item or when your flex items overflow the flex container in a nowrap scenario. This means, if there is only one flex item, it will be flush with main-start, not centered, which seems counterintuitive to many at first.

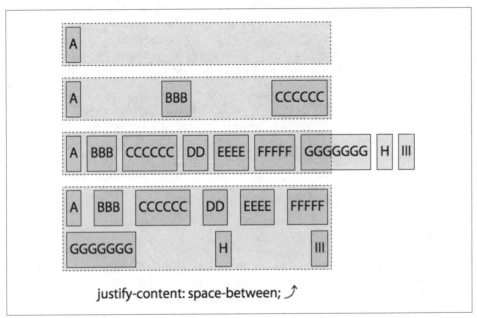

justify-content: space-between;

Figure 12-23. Space-between alignment ▶

With justify-content: space-between the space between any two items on a flex line will be equal but won't necessarily be the same across flex lines. When set to allow wrapping, on the last flex line, the first flex item of that last line is flush against main-start, the last if there are two or more on that line will be against main-end, with equal space between adjacent pairs of flex items. As shown in the last example of Figure 12-23, A and G, the first items on each flex line, are flush against main-start. F and I, the last items on each line, are flush against main-end. The flex items are evenly distributed with the spacing between any two adjacent items being the same on each of the lines, but the space between flex items on the first line is narrower than the space between flex items on the second line.

Setting `justify-content: space-around` evenly distributes the extra space on the line around each of the flex items, as if there were non-collapsing margins of equal size around each element on the main-dimension sides. So there will be twice as much space between the first and second item as there is between main-start and the first item, and main-end and the last item, as shown in Figure 12-24.

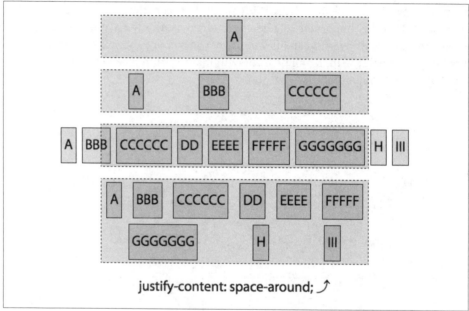

Figure 12-24. Space-around alignment ▶

If the flex items wrap onto multiple lines, the space around each flex item is based on the available space on each flex line. While the space around each element on a flex line with be the same, it might differ between lines, as shown in the last examples in Figure 12-24. The spaces between A and B and between G and H are twice the width of the spaces between the main-start edge and A and the edge and G.

If `nowrap` is set, and there isn't enough room on the flex container's main-direction for all the flex items, the flex items will overflow equally on both sides, similar to setting `center`, as shown in the third example in Figure 12-24.

Setting `justify-content: space-evenly` means the user agent counts the items, adds one, and then splits any extra space on the line by that many (i.e., if there are five items, the amount of space is split into six equal-size portions). One portion of the space is placed before each item on the line, as if it were a non-collapsing margin, and the last portion is placed after the last item on the list. Thus, there will the same amount of space between the first and second item as there is between main-start and the first item, and main-end and the last item, as shown in Figure 12-25.

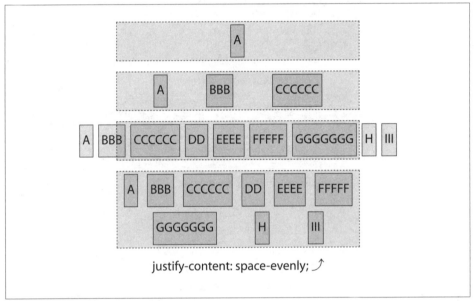

Figure 12-25. Space-evenly alignment ▶

With the margin added to the flex items to make the examples less hideous, this may be difficult to see. Comparing margin-free examples of `center`, `space-around`, `space-between`, and `space-evenly` might be more helpful, so they're shown in Figure 12-26.

Space-evenly is not currently in the flexbox specification (late 2017), but it is part of the CSS Box Alignment specification. As the flexbox specification states it must follow the CSS Box Alignment specification, it should make its way back into the flexbox spec soon. Plus, most browsers already support it.

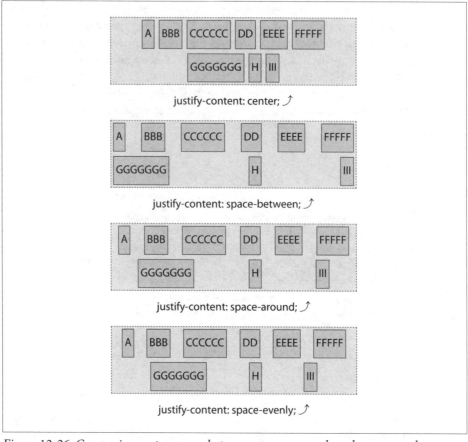

Figure 12-26. Comparing center, space-between, space-around, and space-evenly

justify-content Examples

We took advantage of the default value of justify-content in Figure 12-2, creating a left-aligned navigation bar. By changing the default value to justify-content: flex-end, we can right-align the navigation bar in English:

```
nav {
  display: flex;
  justify-content: flex-start;
}
```

Note that justify-content is applied to the flex container. If we'd applied to the links themselves, using something like nav a {justify-content: flex-start;}, there would have been no alignment effect.

A major advantage of justify-content is that when the writing direction changes, say for right-to-left writing modes, we don't have to alter the CSS to get the tabs where they need to go. The flex items are always grouped toward main-start when `flex-start` is applied; in English, main-start is on the left. For Hebrew, main-start is on the right. If `flex-end` is applied and the `flex-direction` is `row`, then the tabs go to the right side in English, and the left side in Hebrew, as shown in Figure 12-27.

Figure 12-27. Internationally robust navigation alignment ▶

We could have centered that navigation, as shown in Figure 12-28:

```
nav {
  display: flex;
  justify-content: center;
}
```

Figure 12-28. Changing the layout with one property value pair ▶

Aligning Items

Whereas the justify-content defines how flex items are aligned along the flex container's main axis, the align-items property defines how flex items are aligned along its flex line's *cross* axis. As with justify-content, align-items is applied to flex containers, not individual flex items.

---

align-items

Values	flex-start | flex-end | center | baseline | stretch
Initial value	stretch
Applies to	Flex containers
Computed value	As specified
Inherited	No
Animatable	No

With the align-items property, you can align all the flex items in a container to the start, end, or center of the cross axis of their flex lines. align-items is similar to justify-content but has effects in the perpendicular direction, setting the cross axis alignment for all flex items, including anonymous flex items.

With align-items, you can set all the items to be placed flush against the cross-start or cross-end of their flex line, or stretched flush to both. Alternatively, you can center all the flex items in the middle of the flex line. There are five values, including flex-start, flex-end, center, baseline, and the default stretch, as shown in Figure 12-29.

 While align-items sets the alignment for all the flex items within a container, the align-self property enables overriding the alignment for individual flex items, as we'll see in an upcoming section, "The align-self Property" on page 602.

In Figure 12-29, note how the flex items either hug the cross-start or cross-end side of the flex container, are centered, or stretch to hug both—except for baseline. With baseline, the flex items' baselines are aligned: the flex item that has the greatest distance between its baseline and its cross-start side will be flush against the cross-start edge of the line.

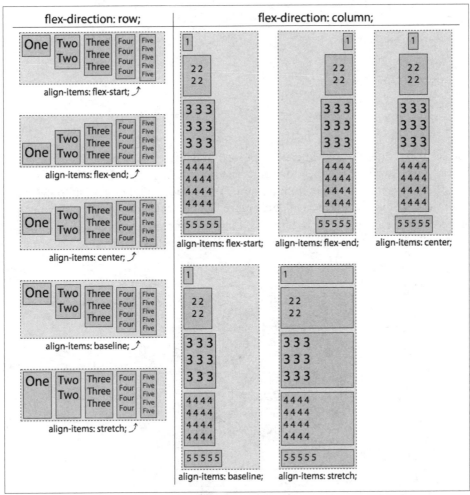

Figure 12-29. The five values of the align-items property for both rows ▶ and columns ▶

That's the general idea—and explains non-wrapping flex containers pretty well—but there's more to it than that. In the multiline `align-items` figures that follow, the following styles have been applied:

```
flex-container {
    display: inline-flex;
    flex-flow: row wrap;
    border: 1px dashed;
}
flex-item {
    border: 1px solid;
    margin: 0 10px;
```

```
}
.C, .H {
  margin-top: 10px;
}
.D, .I {
  margin-top: 20px;
}
.J {
  font-size: 3rem;
}
```

For each flex line, the red line is cross-start and the blue is cross-end. The lines appear purple when a new flex line abuts the previous flex line. C, H, D, and I have different values for top and bottom margins. We've added a bit of margin to the sides of all the flex items to make the figures more legible, which doesn't affect the impact of the `align-items` property in this case. J has the font size increased, increasing the line height. This will come into play when we discuss the `baseline` value.

The default is `align-items: stretch`, as shown in Figure 12-30.

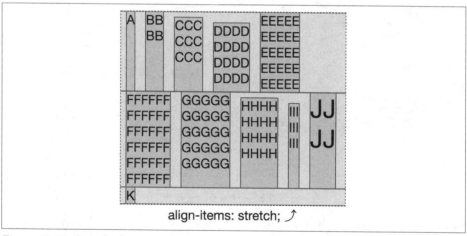

Figure 12-30. Stretch alignment

`stretch`, as its name implies, stretches all stretchable flex items to be as tall or wide as the tallest or widest flex item on the line. What does "stretchable" mean? While by default flex items will stretch to take up 100% of the cross-size, if `min-height`, `min-width`, `max-height`, `max-width`, `width`, or `height` are set, those properties will take precedence. in other words, if an element has an explicitly set dimension along the cross axis, then it is *not* stretchable, and `stretch` will not affect its sizing.

Otherwise, the flex items' cross-start will be flush with the flex line's cross-start, and the flex items' cross-end will be flush with the flex line's cross-end. The flex item with the largest cross-size will remain its default size, and the other flex items will grow to the size of that largest flex item.

The size of the stretched flex item includes the margins on the cross-start and cross-end sides: it is the outer edge of the flex items' margin that will be flush with cross-start and cross-end. This is demonstrated by items C, D, H, and I in Figure 12-31.

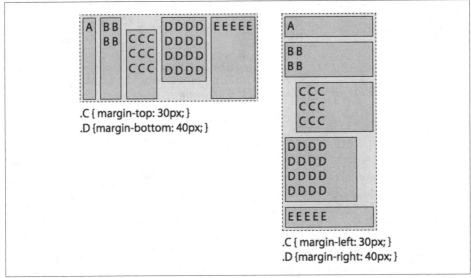

Figure 12-31. Effect of cross-axis margins on item alignment ▶

Their margins are the reason C, D, H, and I appear smaller than the other flex items on their flex lines. They're not. The outer edges of the top and bottom margins are flush with the cross-starts and cross-ends of the flex lines they occupy. Those flex lines are, in turn, as tall as the tallest item on the line, or as wide as the widest item when the cross dimension is horizontal.

Flex lines are only as tall or wide as they need to be to contain their flex items. In the five `align-items` figures, the line height of the flex line containing only K is much smaller than the other two lines.

Start, End, and Center Alignment

The values and effects of start, end, and center alignment are pretty straightforward, so we'll take them all at once.

The `flex-start` value lines up each flex items' cross-start edge flush against the cross-start edge of their flex line. The flex item's cross-start edge is on the outside of the margin: if a flex item has a margin that is greater than 0, flex item will not appear flush with the flex line's cross-start edge, as seen in flex item C, D, H, and I in the first example in Figure 12-32.

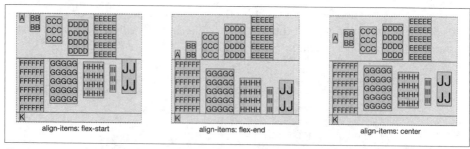

Figure 12-32. Flex-start, flex-end, and center alignment

Setting `align-items: flex-end` will align the cross-end edge of all the flex items along the cross-end edge of the line they are in as shown in the second example in Figure 12-32. None of the flex items has a bottom margin greater than 0 pixels, so unlike the other examples, this example does not look jagged—all the flex items' cross-end edges are visibly flush against the cross-end edge of each flex line.

As shown in the third example in Figure 12-32, setting `align-items: center` will center the flex items' cross-size along the middle point of the cross axis of the line. The center is the midpoint between the outer edges of a flex item's margin edges—remember, flex item margins do not collapse. Because the cross-edge margins for C, D, H, and I are not symmetrical, the flex items do not appear visibly centered along the cross axis, even though they are: the halfway points between their top and bottom margin edges are exactly aligned with the midpoints of the flex lines in which they sit.

In LTR and RTL languages, in the case of `flex-direction: row` and `row-reverse`, the aligned midpoint of a flex item is the point halfway between its top and bottom margin edges. For `flex-direction: column`, and `column-reverse`, the aligned midpoint of a flex item is the point halfway between its left and right margin edges.

> If a flex container's cross size is constrained, the contents may overflow the flex container's cross-start and/or cross-end edge. The direction of the overflow is not determined by the `align-items` property, but rather by the `align-content` property, discussed in an upcoming section, "Aligning Content" on page 604. `align-items` aligns the flex items within the flex line and does not directly impact the overflow direction of the flex items within the container.

Baseline Alignment

The `baseline` value is a little more complicated. With `baseline`, the flex items in each line are all aligned at their first baselines. The flex item on each flex line with the biggest distance between its baseline and its cross-start margin edge has that margin edge placed flush against the cross-start edge of the line, and all other flex items' baselines are lined up with the baseline of that flex item.

Take a look at the second line in Figure 12-33, where J dominates. The font size for J in this was was increased to `3rem` in order to create a flex item with a taller first line of text than the other flex items. Its top (cross-start) edge is placed against the top (cross-start) edge of the flex line. All the other flex items in the line we moved down until their first text line's baseline is aligned with the first baseline of J. (The green line indicates the placement of this baseline.)

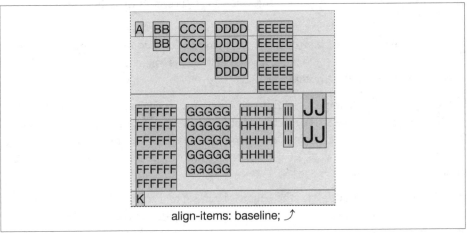

Figure 12-33. Baseline alignment ⓓ

Now look at the first flex line, the one starting with A. You'll notice that A, B, C, D, and E are all top-aligned, but look closer. The subtlety here is that they are not visibly flush to the top of the flex line. This happens because D has a top margin of 20 pixels. The outer edge of D's top (cross-start) margin is flush against the cross-start of the flex line. As previously noted, the distance between the cross-start line and baseline is determined by the item on the line that has the biggest distance between its outer margin on its cross-start side and its baseline. Therefore, D's placement (due to its top margin) becomes the baseline against which the other items in the line are aligned.

In many cases, `baseline` will look like `flex-start`. For example, had D lacked a top margin, then all the items in that first line would have been visibly flush against the top of the flex line, just as would have happened with `flex-start`. Whenever the items have different margins, borders, padding, font sizes, or line heights on their cross-start side, there will be a difference between flex-start and baseline.

There is one case in which baseline literally becomes flex-start, and that's when the baselines of the flex items are parallel to the cross axis. For example, suppose we took the flex container in Figure 12-33 and changed it to flex-direction: column. Now the cross axis, like the baselines of the English text within, is horizontal. Since there's no way to create an offset from the cross-start edge of the columns (the left side), baseline is treated exactly as if it were flex-start instead.

Additional Notes

If you want to change the alignment of one or more flex items, but not all, you can include the align-self property on the flex items you would like to align differently. The align-self takes the same values as align-items, and is discussed in "Flex Items" on page 609.

You cannot override the alignment for anonymous flex items (non-empty text node children of flex containers). Their align-self always matches the value of align-items of their parent flex container.

In the align-items examples, the flex container's cross-size was as tall as it needed to be. No height was declared on the container, so it defaulted to height: auto. Because of this, the flex container grew to fit the content. You may have noticed the example flex containers were all the same height, and the flex line heights were the same across all examples.

Had the cross-size—in this case the height—been set to a specific size, there may have been extra space at cross-end, or not enough space to fit the content. Flexbox allows us to control the alignment of flex lines with the align-content property. The align-content property is the last property we need to focus on that applies to the flex container (versus the flex items). The align-content property only impacts flex line alignment in multiline flex containers.

The align-self Property

This is jumping ahead a bit, but now is the right time to talk about the align-self property. This is used to override the align-items property value on a per-flex-item basis.

align-self

Values	auto|flex-start|flex-end|center|baseline|stretch
Initial value	auto
Applies to	Flex items
Inherited	No
Percentages	Not applicable
Animatable	No

With the `align-items` property set on the flex container, you align all the flex items of that container. You can override the alignment of any individual flex item with the `align-self` property. The default value of `align-items` is `stretch`, which is why all the flex items in the five examples in Figure 12-34 are all as tall as the parent, with the exception of the second flex item.

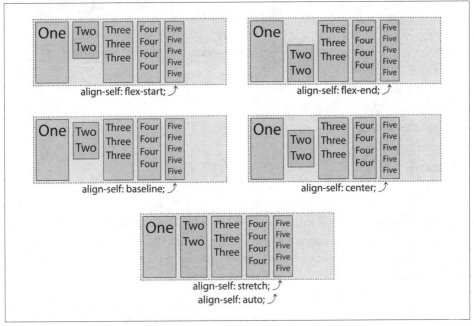

Figure 12-34. Changing flex item alignments ▶

All the flex items have the `align-self`'s default value of `auto` set, meaning they inherit the alignment (in this case, `stretch`) from the container's `align-items` property, except the second flex item in each example. That flex item has been given the `align-self` value shown underneath the example.

Just as with the values of the `align-items` property, the `flex-start` value places the item at the cross-start edge. `flex-end` places the item at the cross-end edge. `center` aligns the item in the middle of the cross axis. `baseline` aligns the baseline of the flex item with the lowst baseline in its flex line. Finally, `auto` and `stretch` both stretch the flex items, as the `align-items` value was allowed to default to `stretch`. (Similarly, `align-self: inherit` would cause a stretch alignment in this case.)

To learn more about the `flex-start`, `flex-end`, `center`, `baseline`, and `stretch` values, see "Aligning Items" on page 596.

Aligning Content

The `align-content` property aligns a flex container's lines within a flex container that has extra space in the cross-axis direction, and dictates which direction will have overflow when there is not enough room to fit the flex lines.

---

align-content

Values	`flex-start`|`flex-end`|`center`|`space-between`|`space-around`|`space-evenly`|`stretch`
Initial value	`stretch`
Applies to	Multiline flex containers
Computed value	As specified
Inherited	No
Animatable	No

The `align-content` property dictates how any extra cross-direction space in a flex container is distributed between and around flex lines. Although the values and concepts are the same, `align-content` is different from the previously discussed `align-items` property, which dictates flex item positioning within each flex line.

Think of `align-content` as similar to how `justify-content` aligns individual items along the main axis of the flex container, but it does it for flex lines with regard to the cross axis of the container. This property only applies to multiline flex containers, having no effect on non-wrapping and otherwise single-line flex containers.

Consider the following CSS as a base, and assume the flex items have no margins:

```
.flex-container {
  display: flex;
  flex-flow: row wrap;
  align-items: flex-start;
  border: 1px dashed;
  height: 480px;
  background-image: url(banded.svg);
}
.flex-items {
    margin: 0;
    flow: 1;
}
```

Figure 12-35 demonstrates the seven possible values of the `align-content` property, as used in conjunction with that CSS. In each example, there are three flex lines. Each flex line's cross-start and cross-end edges are denoted by red and blue lines, respectively. The leftover space in the flex container; that is, the space between or around the flex lines, is represented by the banded regions.

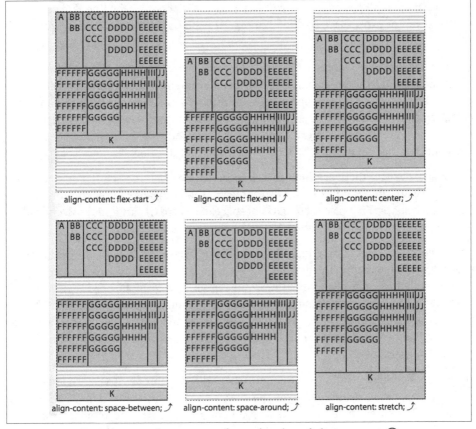

Figure 12-35. Distribution of extra space for each value of align-content ⊙

With a height of 480 pixels, the flex container is taller than the default combined heights of the 3 flex lines. Let's say the tallest items in each line—E, F, and K—are 150 pixels, 180 pixels, and 30 pixels, respectively, for a combined total of 360 pixels. Each flex container has an extra 120 pixels of free space in the cross-size direction.

With five of the `align-items` values, the free space is distributed outside of the flex lines, as illustrated in Figure 12-35. These act in the same ways the same values do for `justify-content`, only along the cross axis instead of the main axis (as is the case for `justify-content`). With the value `stretch`, the extra space is evenly distributed to all the flex lines, increasing their cross-size until their edges touch.

In the previous example, with a flex container height of 480 pixels, we have 120 pixels of "leftover" space along the cross axis, distributed differently depending on the value of the `align-content` property.

As shown in the top three examples in Figure 12-35, with `flex-start` the 120 pixels is all on the cross-end side of the cross axis. With `flex-end`, the extra 120 pixels of available space is all placed at the cross-start side. With `center`, the lines are centered, and 60 pixels of extra space (half of 120 pixels) is placed at cross-start and cross-end sides.

With `space-between`, there is 60 pixels between adjacent pairs of flex lines. With `space-around`, on the other hand, the space is evenly distributed around each line: the 120 pixels is split into 3, since there are 3 flex lines. This puts 20 pixels of non-collapsed space (half of 40 pixels) on the cross-start and cross-end sides of each flex line, so there are 20 pixels of extra space at the cross-start and cross-end sides of the flex container, and 40 pixels of space between adjacent flex lines.

For `space-evenly`, there are four spaces to insert: one before each flex line, and an extra space after the last flex line. With three lines, that means four spaces, or 30 pixels for each space. That places 30 pixels of space at the cross-start and cross-end sides, and 30 pixels between adjacent flex lines.

The `stretch` value is different: with `stretch` the lines stretch with the extra space evenly distributed among the flex lines rather than between them. In this case, 40 pixels was added to each of the flex lines, causing all 3 to grow in height by an equal amount—that is, the exact same amount, not an amount proportional to each. You'll note in the sixth example of Figure 12-35, there is no area within the container that is not occupied by a flex line. `stretch` is the default value, as you likely want to fill all the available space.

If there isn't enough room for all the lines, they will overflow at cross-start, cross-end, or both, depending on the value of the `align-content` property. This is shown in Figure 12-36, where the dotted box with a light gray background represents a short flex container. (`align-items: flex-start` was set to make the effect of `align-content` more obvious.)

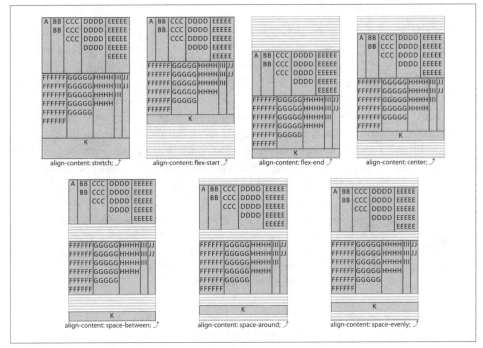

Figure 12-36. Flex-line overflow directions for each value of align-content

The only difference in the CSS between this and Figure 12-35 is the height of the flex container. Here, the flex containers have been reduced to a height of 240 pixels, so as to create flex containers not tall enough to encompass all their flex lines (which, as you may recall, total 360 pixels in height).

When the flex lines overflow the flex container, `align-content: flex-start`, `space-between`, and `stretch` cause them overflow the cross-end side, whereas `align-content: space-around` and `center` evenly overflow both the cross-end and cross-start sides. Only `align-content: flex-end` causes flex lines overflow just the cross-start side.

Keep in mind that these values are not top- or bottom-centric. If the cross axis goes upward, then `align-content: flex-start` will start aligning flex lines from the bottom and work upward from there, potentially overflowing the top (cross-end) edge. For that matter, when the flow direction is columnar, the cross axis will be horizontal, in which case the cross-start and -end edges will be the right or left edges of the flex container.

Space between, around, and evenly

It's worth taking a closer look at, and thinking about how, space-between and space-around affect the alignment of flex lines.

When align-content: space-between is set, the flex lines are evenly distributed in the flex container. This "even distribution" is based on the available space, *not* the size of the lines. If there is more than one flex line, the first line will be flush against the container's cross-start, the last line will be flush against the container's cross-end, and any available extra space is distributed evenly between the additional lines, if there are any. The extra space is distributed evenly, *not* proportionally. The space between any two flex lines within the flex container is equal, even if the cross-sizes of the multiple flex lines differ. Furthermore, the middle flex line, if there are an odd number of lines, is not necessarily centered in the flex container, because the lines don't necessarily all have the same cross dimensions.

 Only flex containers with multiple lines can have free space in the cross axis for lines to be aligned in. If there is only one line, the align-content property will not impact the distribution of the content. In flex containers with a single line of flex items, the lone line stretches to fill all of the available space.

Instead, the spacing between any two adjacent lines is the same. Assume 3 lines with 120 pixels total of free space, as we saw in the previous section. The first flex line goes against the cross-start edge, and the second flex line goes against the cross-end edge. That means there is one line to place between them, and two gaps. The 120 pixels of leftover space gets divided equally into 2 chunks of 60 pixels each. One 60-pixel chunk is placed between the first and second flex lines, and the other between the second and third flex lines. This is illustrated in Figure 12-37.

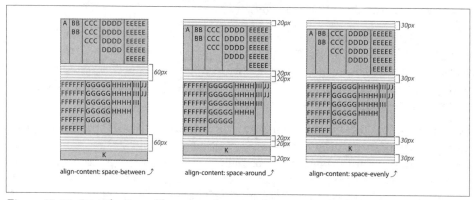

Figure 12-37. Distribution of free space for space-between, space-around, and space-evenly

---

The `space-around` value distributes the lines within a multiline flex container evenly, as if all the flex lines had equal, non-collapsing margins on both the cross-start and cross-end sides. Because there is an equal distribution of the extra available space around each line, the space between the edges of the container and the first and last flex lines is half the size of the distance between any two flex lines. The distribution of the extra space is shown in Figure 12-37.

 As of late 2017, the various alignment values like `flex-start`, `flex-end`, and so on are being made more generic: `start`, `end`, and so forth. These are part of a wider effort to make CSS more aware of writing and layout directions. An example of this is the addition of properties like `margin-start` and `padding-end`. It wasn't quite advanced enough (or well-supported enough) to merit complete coverage in this edition, but keep an eye on these developments.

We have been, for the most part, taking a look at properties of the flex container (the exception was `align-self`). It's time to take a look at the properties directly applied to flex items.

Flex Items

In the previous sections, we saw how to globally lay out all the flex items within a flex container by styling that container. The flexible box layout specification provides several additional properties applicable directly to flex items. With these flex-item-specific properties, we can more precisely control the layout of individual flex containers' children.

What Are Flex Items?

We create flex containers simply by adding a `display: flex` or `display: inline-flex` to an element that has child nodes. The children of those flex container are called *flex items*—whether they're child elements, non-empty text nodes between child elements, or generated content. Figure 12-38 shows a situation where each letter is enclosed in its own element, including the space between words, so that each letter and space becomes a flex item.

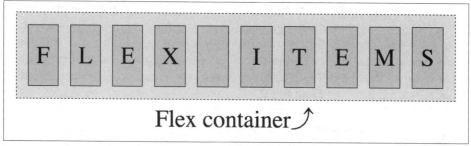

Figure 12-38. The child nodes are flex items, the parent node is a flex container ▶

When it comes to text-node children of flex containers, if the text node is not empty —containing content other than whitespace—it will be wrapped in an *anonymous flex item*, behaving like its flex item siblings. While these anonymous flex items do inherit all the flex properties set by the flex container, just like their DOM node siblings, they are not directly targetable with CSS. Therefore, we can't directly set any of the flex item specific properties on them. Thus, in the following markup, the two elements (the <strong> and the <em>) and the text " they're what's for " each become flex items, for a total of three flex items:

```
<p style="display: flex;">
    <strong>Flex items:</strong> they're what's for <em>&lt;br&gt;fast!</em>
</p>
```

Generated content (via ::before and ::after) can be styled directly; therefore all the properties discussed in this chapter apply equally to generated content as they do to element nodes.

Whitespace-only text nodes within a flex container are ignored, as if their display property were set to none, as the following code example shows:

```
nav ul {
  display: flex;
}

<nav>
  <ul>
    <li><a href="#1">Link 1</a></li>
    <li><a href="#2">Link 2</a></li>
    <li><a href="#3">Link 3</a></li>
    <li><a href="#4">Link 4</a></li>
    <li><a href="#5">Link 5</a></li>
  </ul>
</nav>
```

In the preceding code, with the display property set to flex, the unordered list is the flex container, and its child list items are all flex items. These list items, being flex items, are flex-level boxes, semantically still list items, but not list items in their presentation. They are not block-level boxes either. Rather, they participate in their container's flex formatting context. The whitespace between and around the li elements —the line feeds and indenting tabs and/or spaces—is completely ignored. The links are not flex items themselves, but are descendants of the flex items the list items have become.

Flex Item Features

The margins of flex items do not collapse. The float and clear properties don't have an effect on flex items, and do not take a flex item out of flow. In effect, float and clear are ignored when applied to flex items. (However, the float property can still affect box generation by influencing the display property's computed value.) Consider:

```
aside {
  display: flex;
}
img {
  float: left;
}

<aside>
    <!-- this is a comment -->
    <h1>Header</h1>

    <img src="images/foo.jpg" alt="Foo Master">
    Some text
</aside>
```

In this example, the aside is the flex container. The comment and whitespace-only text nodes are ignored. The text node containing "some text" is wrapped in an anonymous flex item. The header, image, and text node containing "some text" are all flex items. Because the image is a flex item, the float is ignored.

Even though images and text nodes are inline-level nodes, being flex items, as long as they are not absolutely positioned, they are blockified:

```
aside {
  display: flex;
  align-items: center;
}

<aside>
    <!-- a comment -->
    <h1>Header</h1>

    <img src="images/foo.jpg" alt="foo master">
    Some text <a href="foo.html">with a link</a> and more text
</aside>
```

In the last example, the markup is similar to the code in the second example, with the addition of a link within the non-empty text node. In this case, we are creating five flex items. The comment and whitespace-only text nodes are ignored. The header, the image, the text node before the link, the link, and the text node after the link are all flex items. This is illustrated by Figure 12-39.

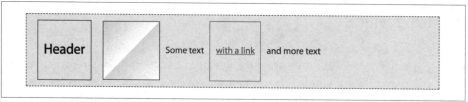

Figure 12-39. Five flex items in an aside ▶

The text nodes containing "some text" and "and more text" are wrapped in anonymous flex items, represented in Figure 12-39 by the dashed boxes (the dashes having been added for illustrative purposes) with no background. The header, image, and link, being actual DOM nodes, can be styled directly with CSS. The anonymous flex containers are not directly targetable, and so will only have whatever styles they pick up from the flex container.

Additionally, `vertical-align` has no effect on a flex item, except as it affects the alignment of text within the flex item. In other words, setting `vertical-align: bottom` on a flex item will make the text inside the flex item all align to the bottoms of their line boxes, not push the flex item to the bottom of its container. (That's what `align-items` and `align-self` are for.)

Absolute positioning

While `float` will not actually float a flex item, setting `position: absolute` is a different story. The absolutely positioned children of flex containers, just like any other absolutely positioned element, are taken out of the flow of the document.

More to the point, they do not participate in flex layout, and are not part of the document flow. However, they can be impacted by the styles set on the flex container, just as a child can be impacted by a parent element that isn't a flex container. In addition to inheriting any inheritable properties, the flex container's properties can affect the origin of the positioning.

The absolutely positioned child of a flex container is affected by both the `justify-content` value of the flex container, and its own `align-self` value, if there is one. For example, if you set `align-self: center` on the absolutely positioned child, it will start out centered with respect to the flex container parent's cross axis. From there, it can moved by properties like `top`, `bottom`, margins, and so on.

The order property (explained in a later section, "The order property" on page 648) may not impact where the absolutely positioned flex container child is drawn, but it does impact the order of when it is drawn in relation to its siblings.

Minimum Widths

In Figure 12-40, you'll note the line that is set to the nowrap default overflows the flex container. This is because when it comes to flex items, the implied value of min-width is auto, rather than 0. Originally in the specification, if the items didn't fit onto that single main axis, they would shrink. However, the specification of min-width was altered as applied to flex items. (Traditionally, the default value for min-width is 0 (*https://drafts.csswg.org/css2/visudet.html#min-max-widths*).)

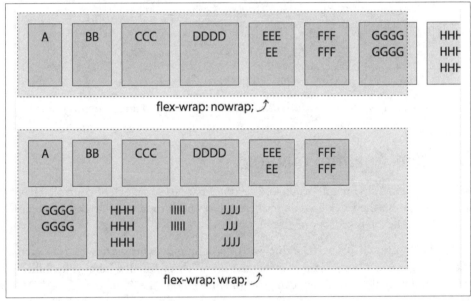

Figure 12-40. Flex container overflow with minimum-width flex items ▶

If you set the min-width to a width narrower than the computed value of auto—for example, if you declare min-width: 0—then the flex items in the nowrap example will shrink to be narrower than their actual content (in some cases). If the items are allowed to wrap, then they will be as narrow as possible to fit their content, but no narrower. Both situations are illustrated in Figure 12-41.

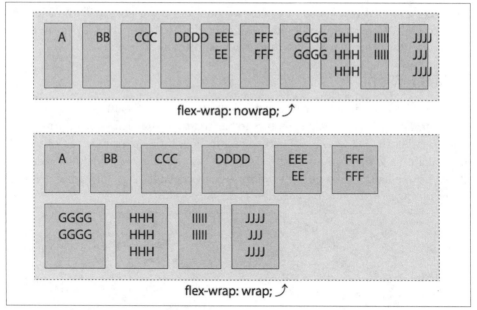

Figure 12-41. Zero-minimum-width flex items in non-wrapped and wrapped flex containers ▶

Flex-Item–Specific Properties

While flex items' alignment, order, and flexibility are to some extent controllable via properties set on their flex container, there are several properties that can be applied to individual flex items for more granular control.

The flex shorthand property, along with its component properties of flex-grow, flex-shrink, and flex-basis, controls the *flexibility* of the flex items. Flexibility is the amount by which a flex item can grow or shrink along the main axis.

The flex Property

The defining aspect of flex layout is the ability to make the flex items "flex": altering their width or height to fill the available space in the main dimension. A flex container distributes free space to its items proportional to their flex grow factor, or shrinks them to prevent overflow proportional to their flex shrink factor. (We'll explore these concepts momentarily.)

Declaring the flex shorthand property on a flex item, or defining the individual properties that make up the shorthand, enables authors to define the grow and shrink factors. If there is excess space, you can tell the flex items to grow to fill that space. Or not. If there isn't enough room to fit all the flex items within the flex container at their defined or default sizes, you can tell the flex items to shrink proportionally to fit into the space. Or not.

This is all done with the flex property, which is a shorthand property for flex-grow, flex-shrink, and flex-basis. While these three sub-properties can be used separately, it is highly recommended to always use the flex shorthand, for reasons we'll soon cover.

---

flex

Values	[<flex-grow> <flex-shrink>? ‖ <flex-basis>]	none
Initial value	0 1 auto
Applies to	Flex items (children of flex containers)
Percentages	Valid for flex-basis value only, relative to element's parent's inner main-axis size
Computed value	Refer to individual properties
Inherited	No
Animatable	See individual properties

The flex property specifies the components of a flexible length: the "length" of the flex item being the length of the flex item along the main axis (see "Understanding axes" on page 579). When a box is a flex item, flex is consulted to determine the size of the box, instead of the main-axis size dimension property (height or width). The "components" of the flex property include the *flex growth factor*, *flex shrink factor*, and the *flex basis*.

The flex basis determines how the flex growth and shrink factors are implemented. As its name suggests, the flex-basis component of the flex shorthand is the basis on which the flex item determines how much it can grow to fill available space or how much it should shrink to fit all the flex items when there isn't enough space. It's the initial size of each flex item, and can be restricted to that specific size by specifying 0 for both the growth and shrink factors:

```
.flexItem {
    width: 50%;
    flex: 0 0 200px;
}
```

In the preceding CSS, the flex item will have a main-axis size of exactly 200 pixels, as the flex basis is 200px, and it is allowed to neither grow nor shrink. Assuming that the main axis is horizontal, then the value of width (50%) is ignored. Similarly, a value for height would be ignored if the main axis were vertical.

This override of height and width occurs outside the cascade, so you can't even override the flex basis by adding !important to the height or width value of a flex item.

If the target of a selector is not a flex item, applying the flex property to it will have no effect.

It is important to understand the three components that make up the flex shorthand property in order to be able to use it effectively.

The flex-grow Property

The flex-grow property defines whether a flex item is allowed to grow when there is available space, and, if it is allowed to grow and there is available space, how much will it grow proportionally relative to the growth of other flex item siblings.

Declaring the growth factor via the flex-grow property is *strongly* discouraged by the authors of the specification itself. Instead, declare the growth factor as part of the flex shorthand. We're only discussing the property here to explore how growth works.

---

flex-grow

Values	*<number>*
Initial value	0
Applies to	Flex items (children of flex containers)
Computed value	As specified
Inherited	No
Animatable	Yes

The value of flex-grow is always a number. Negative numbers are not valid. You can use non-integers if you like, just as long as they're zero or greater. The value sets the *flex growth factor*, which determines how much the flex item will grow relative to the rest of the flex item siblings as the flex container's free space is distributed.

If there is any available space within the flex container, the space will be distributed proportionally among the children with a nonzero positive growth factor based on the various values of those growth factors.

For example, assume a 750px wide horizontal flex container with three flex items, each set to width: 100px. That means there is a total of 300 pixels of space taken up by the flex items, leaving 450 pixels of "leftover" or available space (since 750 - 300 = 450). This is the first scenario shown in Figure 12-42. In that scenario, none of the flex items are permitted to grow.

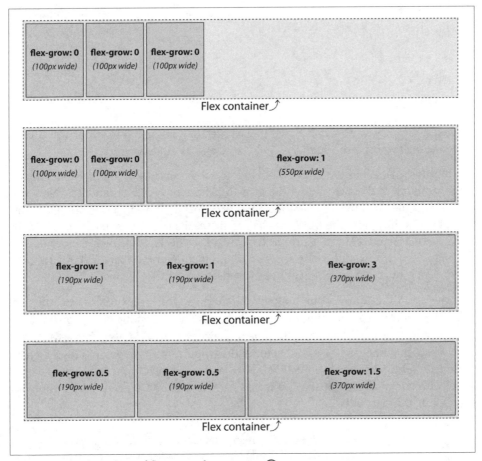

Figure 12-42. A variety of flex-growth scenarios ⊙

In the second scenario in Figure 12-42, only one of the flex items (the third) has been given a growth factor. The declaration we gave it is flex-grow: 1, but it could be literally any positive number the browser can understand. In this case, with two items having no growth factor and the third having a growth factor, all of the available space is given to the flex item with a growth factor. Thus, the third flex item gets all 450 pixels of available space added to it, arriving at a final width of 550 pixels. The width: 100px applied to it elsewhere in the styles is overridden.

In the third and fourth scenarios, the same flex item widths result despite the differing flex growth factors. Let's consider the third scenario, where the growth factors are 1, 1, and 3. The factors are all added together to get a total of 5. Each factor is then divided by that total to get a proportion. So here, the three values are each divided by five, yielding 0.2, 0.2, and 0.6.

These proportions are each multiplied by the available space to get the amount of growth. Thus:

1. 450 px × 0.2 = 90 px
2. 450 px × 0.2 = 90 px
3. 450 px × 0.6 = 270 px

Those are the growth portions added to each flex item's starting width of 100 pixels. Thus, the final widths are 190 pixels, 190 pixels, and 370 pixels, respectively.

The fourth scenario has the same result, because the proportions are the same. Imagine for a moment that we altered the growth factors to be 0.5, 1, and 1.5. Now the math works out such that the first flex item gets one-sixth of the available space, the second gets a third, and the third gets half. This results in the flex items' final widths being 175, 250, and 425 pixels, respectively. Had we declared growth factors of 0.1, 0.1, and 0.3, or 25, 25, and 75, or really any combination of numbers with a 1:1:3 correspondence, the result would have been identical.

As noted in "Minimum Widths" on page 613, if no width or flex basis is set, the flex basis defaults to auto, meaning each flex item basis is the width of its nonwrapped content. auto is a special value: it defaults to content unless the item has a width set on it, at which point the flex-basis becomes that width. The auto value is discussed in "Automatic Flex Basis" on page 635. Had we not set the width, in this example scenario, with our smallish font size, we would had more than 450 pixels of distributable space along the main axis.

 The main-axis size of a flex item is impacted by the available space, the growth factor of all the flex items, and the flex basis of the item. We have yet to cover flex basis, but that time is coming soon!

Now let's consider a case where the flex items have different width values, as well as different growth factors. In Figure 12-43, in the second example, we have flex items that are 100 pixels, 250 pixels, and 100 pixels wide, with growth factors of 1, 1, and 3, respectively, in a container that is 750 pixels wide. This means we have 300 pixels of extra space to distribute among a total of 5 growth factors (since 750 - 450 = 300). Each growth factor is therefore 60 pixels (300 ÷ 5). This means the first and second flex items, with a `flex-grow` value of 1, will each grow by 60 pixels. The last flex item will grow by 180 pixels, since its `flex-grow` value is 3.

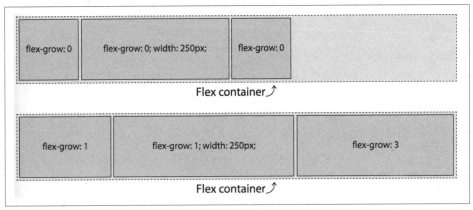

Figure 12-43. Mixed widths and growth factors ▶

To recap, the available space in the flex container, and the growth factors and final width of each flex item, are:

Available space: 750px - (100px + 250px + 100px) = 300px
Growth factors: 1 + 1 + 3 = 5
Width of each growth factor: 300px ÷ 5 = 60px

When flexed, the width of the flex items, based on their original width and growth factors, become:

item1 = 100px + (1 × 60px) = 160px
item2 = 250px + (1 × 60px) = 310px
item3 = 100px + (3 × 60px) = 280px

which adds up to 750 pixels.

Growth Factors and the flex Property

The `flex` property takes up to three values—the growth factor, shrink factor, and basis. The first positive non-null numeric value, if there is one, sets the growth factor (i.e., the `flex-grow` value). When the growth and shrink factors are omitted in the `flex` value, the growth factor defaults to 1. However, if neither `flex` nor `flex-grow` are declared, the growth factor defaults to 0. Yes, really.

Recall the second example in Figure 12-42, where the flex growth factors were 0, 0, and 1. Because we declared a value for `flex-grow` only, the flex basis was set to `auto`, as if we had declared:

```
#example2 flex-item {
   flex: 0 1 auto;
}
#example2 flex-item:last-child {
   flex: 1 1 auto;
}
```

So that means the first two flex items had no growth factor, a shrink factor, and a flex basis of `auto`. Had we used `flex` in the examples in Figure 12-42 instead of ill-advisedly using `flex-grow`, the flex basis in each case would be set to `0%`, as if this had been done:

```
#example2 flex-item {
   flex: 0 1 0%;
}
#example2 flex-item:last-child {
   flex: 1 1 0%;
}
```

As the shrink factor defaults to 1 and the basis defaults to `0%`, the following CSS is identical to the preceding snippet:

```
#example2 flex-item {
   flex: 0;
}
#example2 flex-item:last-child {
   flex: 1;
}
```

This would have the result shown in Figure 12-44. Compare this to Figure 12-42 to see how things have changed (or not).

You may notice something odd in the first two scenarios: the flex basis been set to zero, and only the last flex item in the second scenario has a positive value for flex grow. Logic would seem that the widths of the 3 flex items should be 0, 0, and 750 pixels, respectively. But logic would also dictate that it makes no sense to have content overflowing its flex item if the flex container has the room for all the content, even if the basis is set to 0.

The specification authors thought of this quandary. When the `flex` property declaration explicitly sets or defaults the flex-basis to `0%` and a flex item's growth factor is `0`, the length of the main axis of the non-growing flex items will shrink to the smallest length the content allows, or smaller. In Figure 12-44, that minimum length is the width of the widest sequence of letters, "flex:" (including the colon).

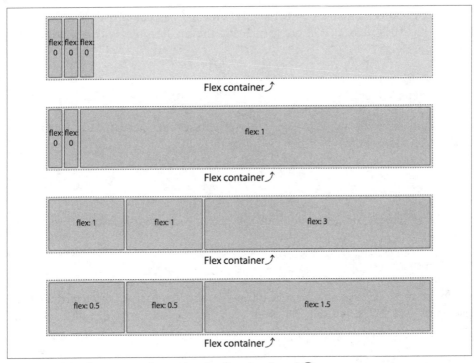

Figure 12-44. Flex sizing when using the flex shorthand ⓥ

As long as a flex item has a visible overflow and no explicitly set value for min-width (or min-height for vertical main-axes), the minimum width (or minimum height) will be the smallest width (or height) that the flex item needs to be to fit the content or the declared width (or height), whichever is smaller.

If all items are allowed to grow, and the flex basis for each flex item is 0%, then *all* of the space, rather than just excess space, is distributed proportionally based on the growth factors. In the third example in Figure 12-44, two flex items have growth factors of one, and one flex item has a growth factor of three. We thus have a total of five growth factors:

$$(2 \times 1) + (1 \times 3) = 5$$

With 5 growth factors, and a total of 750 pixels, each growth factor is worth 150 pixels:

$$750px \div 5 = 150px$$

While the default flex item size was 100 pixels, the flex basis of 0% overrides that, leaving us with 2 flex items at 150 pixels each and the last flex item with a width of 450 pixels:

$1 \times 150px = 150px$
$3 \times 150px = 450px$

Similarly, in the last example of Figure 12-44, with two flex items having growth factors of 0.5, and one flex item having a growth factor of 1.5, we have a total of 2.5 growth factors:

$(2 \times 0.5) + (1 \times 1.5) = 2.5$

With 2.5 grows factors, and a total of 750 pixels, each growth factor is worth 300 pixels:

$750px \div 2.5 = 300px$

While the default flex item size was 100 pixels, the flex basis of 0% overrides that, leaving us with 2 flex items at 150 pixels each and the last flex item with a width of 450 pixels:

$0.5 \times 300px = 150px$
$1.5 \times 300px = 450px$

Again, this is different from declaring only flex-grow, because that means the flex basis defaults to auto. In that case, only the extra space, not all the space, is distributed proportionally. When using flex, on the other hand, the flex basis is set to 0%, so the flex items grow in proportion to the total space, not just the leftover space. The difference is illustrated in Figure 12-45.

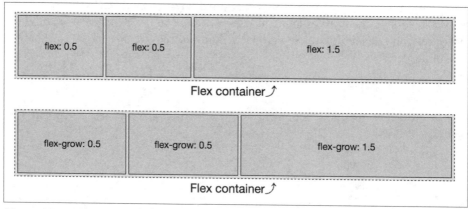

Figure 12-45. Flex sizing differences between using flex and flex-grow ⊙

Now let's talk about flex shrinking factors, which are in some ways the inverse of flex growth factors, but are in other ways different.

The flex-shrink Property

The *<flex-shrink>* portion of the flex shorthand property specifies the *flex shrink factor*. It can also be set via the flex-shrink property.

 Declaring the shrink factor via the flex-shrink property is *strongly* discouraged by the authors of the specification itself. Instead, declare the shrink factor as part of the flex shorthand. We're only discussing the property here in order to explore how shrinking works.

flex-shrink

Values	<number>
Initial value	1
Applies to	Flex items (children of flex containers)
Computed value	As specified
Inherited	No
Animatable	Yes

The shrink factor determines how much a flex item will shrink relative to the rest of its flex-item siblings when there isn't enough space for them all to fit, as defined by their content and other CSS properties. When omitted in the shorthand flex property value or when both flex and flex-shrink are omitted, the shrink factor defaults to 1. Like the growth factor, the value of flex-shrink is always a number. Negative numbers are not valid. You can use non-integer values if you like, just as long as they're greater than zero.

Basically, the shrink factor defines how "negative available space" is distributed when there isn't enough room for the flex items and the flex container isn't allowed to otherwise grow or wrap. This is illustrated in Figure 12-46.

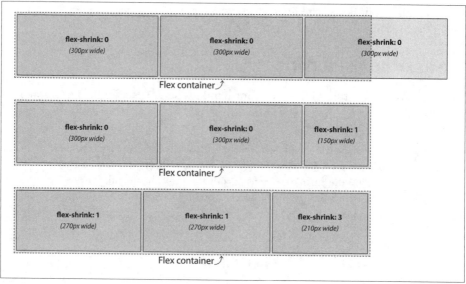

Figure 12-46. A variety of flex shrinking scenarios ▶

Figure 12-46 is similar to Figure 12-42, except the flex items are set to `width: 300px` instead of 100 pixels. We still have a 750-pixels-wide flex container. The total width of the 3 items is 900 pixels, meaning the content starts out 150 pixels wider than the parent flex container. If the items are not allowed to shrink or wrap (see "Wrapping Flex Lines" on page 576), they will burst out from the fixed-size flex container. This is demonstrated in the first example in Figure 12-46: those items will not shrink because they have a zero shrink factor. Instead, they overflow the flex container.

In the second example in Figure 12-46, only the last flex item is set to be able to shrink. The last flex item is thus forced to do all the shrinking necessary to enable all the flex items to fit within the flex container. With 900 pixels worth of content needing to fit into our 750-pixel container, we have 150 pixels of negative available space. The 2 flex items with no shrink factor stay at 300 pixels wide. The third flex item, with a positive value for the shrink factor, shrinks 150 pixels, to end up 150 pixels wide. This enables the 3 items to fit within the container. (In this example the shrink factor was 1, but had it been `0.001` or `100` or `314159.65` or any other positive number the browser could understand, the result would be the same.)

In the third example, we have positive shrink factors for all three flex items:

```
#example3 flex-item {
  flex-shrink: 1;
}
#example3 flex-item:last-child {
  flex-shrink: 3;
}
```

As this is the only one of the three `flex` shorthand properties we declared, this means the flex items will behave as if we had declared the following:

```
#example3 flex-item {
    flex: 0 1 auto; /* growth defaults to 0, basis to auto */
}
f#example3 flex-item:last-child {
    flex: 0 3 auto;
}
```

If all items are allowed to shrink, as is the case here, the shrinking is distributed proportionally based on the shrink factors. This means the larger a flex item's shrink factor, as compared to the shrink factors of its sibling flex items, the more the item will shrink in comparison.

With a parent 750 pixels wide, and 3 flex items with a width of 300 pixels, there are 150 "negative space" pixels that need to be shaved off the flex items that are allowed to shrink (which is all of them in this example). With two flex items having a shrink factor of 1, and one flex item having a shrink factor of 3, we have a total of five shrink factors:

$$(2 \times 1) + (1 \times 3) = 5$$

With 5 shrink factors, and a total of 150 pixels needing to be shaved off all the flex items, each shrink factor is worth 30 pixels:

$$150px \div 5 = 30px$$

The default flex item size was 300 pixels, leading us to have 2 flex items with a width of 270 pixels each and the last flex item having a width of 210 pixels, which totals 750 pixels:

$$300px - (1 \times 30px) = 270px$$
$$300px - (3 \times 30px) = 210px$$

The following CSS produces the same outcome: while the numeric representation of the shrink factors are different, they are proportionally the same, so the flex item widths will be the same:

```
flex-item {
    flex: 1 0.25 auto;
}
flex-item:last-child {
    flex: 1 0.75 auto;
}
```

Note that the flex items in these examples will shrink to 210, 210, and 270 pixels, respectively, *as long as* the content (like media objects or non-wrappable text) within each flex item is not wider than 210, 210, or 270 pixels, respectively. If the flex item contains content that cannot wrap or otherwise shrink in the main-dimension, the flex item will not shrink any further.

Suppose that the first flex items contain a 300-pixels-wide image. That first flex item can not shrink, and other flex items can shrink, therefore it will not shrink, as if it had a null shrink factor. In this case, the first item would be 300 pixels, with the 150 pixels of negative space distributed proportionally based on the shrink factors of the second and third flex items.

That being the case, we have 4 unimpeded shrink factors (one from the second flex item, and three from the third) for 150 pixels of negative space, with each shrink factor being worth 37.5 pixels. The flex items will end up 300, 262.5, and 187.5 pixels respectively, for a total of 750 pixels. The result is illustrated in Figure 12-47:

$$item1 = 300px - (0 \times 37.5px) = 300.0px$$
$$item2 = 300px - (1 \times 37.5px) = 262.5px$$
$$item3 = 300px - (3 \times 37.5px) = 187.5px$$

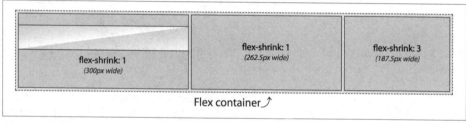

Figure 12-47. Shrinking being impeded by flex item content ⓹

Had the image been 296 pixels wide, that first flex item would have been able to shrink by 4 pixels. The remaining 146 pixels of negative space would then be distributed the among the 4 remaining shrink, yielding 36.5 pixels per factor. The flex items would then be 296, 263.5, and 190.5 pixels wide, respectively.

If all three flex items contained non-wrappable text or media 300 pixels or wider, the none of the three flex items would not shrink, appearing similar to the first example in Figure 12-46.

Proportional Shrinkage Based on Width and Shrink Factor

The preceding code examples were fairly simple because all the flex items started with the same width. But what if the widths were different? What if the first and last flex items had a width of 250 pixels and the middle flex item had a width of 500 pixels, as shown in Figure 12-48?

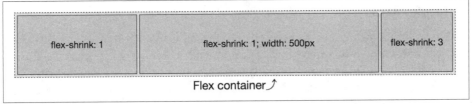

Figure 12-48. Flex items shrink proportionally relative to their shrink factor ⊙

Flex items shrink proportionally relative to both the shrink factor *and* the flex item's width, with the width often being the width of the flex item's content with no wrapping. In Figure 12-48, we are trying to fit 1,000 pixels into a 750 pixels-width flex container. We have an excess of 250 pixels to be removed from 5 shrink factors.

If this were a flex-grow situation, we would simply divide 250 pixels by 5, allocating 50 pixels per growth factor. If we were to shrink that way, we would get flex items 200, 550, and 100 pixels wide, respectively. But that's not how shrinking actually works.

Here, we have 250 pixels of negative space to proportionally distribute. To get the shrink factor proportions, we divide the negative space by the total of the flex items' widths (more precisely, their lengths along the main axis) times their shrink factors:

$$ShrinkPercent = \frac{NegativeSpace}{((Width1 \times ShrF1) + \ldots + (WidthN \times ShrFN))}$$

Using this equation, we find the shrink percentage:

$$= 250px \div ((250px \times 1) + (500px \times 1) + (250px \times 3))$$
$$= 250px \div 1500px$$
$$= 0.166666667\ (16.67\%)$$

When we reduce each flex item by 16.67% times the value of flex-shrink, we end up with flex items that are reduced by:

$$item1 = 250px \times (1 \times 16.67\%) = 41.67px$$
$$item2 = 500px \times (1 \times 16.67\%) = 83.33px$$
$$item3 = 250px \times (3 \times 16.67\%) = 125px$$

Each reduction is then subtracted from the starting sizes of 250, 500, and 250 pixels, respectively. We thus end up with flex items that are 208.33, 416.67, and 125 pixels wide.

Differing Bases

With zero shrink factor, if both the width and flex basis of a flex item at `auto`, its content will not wrap, even when you think it should. Conversely, any positive shrink value enables content to wrap. Because shrinking is proportional based on shrink factor, if all the flex items have similar shrink factors, the content should wrap over a similar number of lines.

In the three examples shown in Figure 12-49, the flex items do not have a declared width. Therefore, the width is based on the content, because `width` defaults to `auto`. The flex container has been made 520 pixels wide, instead of of our usual 750 pixels.

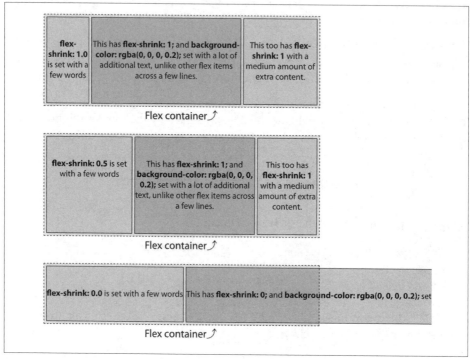

Figure 12-49. Flex items shrink proportionally relative to their shrink factor and content ▶

Note that in the first example, where all the items have the same `flex-shrink` value, all content wraps over four lines. In the second example, the first flex item has a shrink factor half of value of the other flex items, so it wraps the content over (roughly) half the number of lines. This is the power of the shrink factor.

In the third example, with no shrink factor, the text doesn't wrap at all and the flex items overflow the container by quite a bit.

As of late 2017, this "line-balancing" and refusal-to-wrap behavior was not consistent across browsers. If you see different results when trying this out for yourself, that may be why.

Because the `flex` property's shrink factor reduces the width of flex items proportionally, the number of lines of text in the flex items will grow or shrink as the width shrinks or grows, leading to similar height content within sibling flex items when the shrink factors are similar.

In the examples, take the contents of the flex items to be 280, 995, and 480 pixels, respectively—which is the width of the non-wrapping flex items in the third example (as measured by the developer tools, then rounded to make this example a little simpler). This means we have to fit 1,755 pixels of content into a 520 pixels-wide flex container by shrinking the flex items proportionally based on their shrink factor. This means we have 1,235 pixels of negative available space to proportionally distribute.

Remember that you can't rely on web inspector tools to figure out shrink factors for production. We're going through this exercise to understand how shrink factors work. If minutia isn't your thing, feel free to jump to "The flex-basis Property" on page 633.

In our first example, the flex items will end up with the same, or approximately the same, number of text lines. This is because flex items shrink proportionally, based on the width of their content.

We didn't declare any widths, and therefore can't simply use an explicit element width as the basis for our calculations, as we did in the previous examples. Rather, we distribute the 1,235 pixels of negative space proportionally based on the widths of the content—280, 995, and 480 pixels, respectively. We determine 520 is 29.63% of 1,755. To determine the width of each flex item with a shrink factor of 1, we multiply the content width of each flex item by 29.63%:

    item1 = 280px × 29.63% = 83px
    item2 = 995px × 29.63% = 295px
    item3 = 480px × 29.63% = 142px

With the default of `align-items: stretch` (see "Aligning Items" on page 596), a three-column layout will have three columns of equal height. By using a consistent shrink factor for all flex items, you can indicate that the actual content of these three flex items should be of approximately equal height—though, by doing this, the widths of those columns will not necessarily be uniform.

In the second example in Figure 12-49, the flex items don't all have the same shrink factor. The first flex item will, proportionally, shrink half as much as the others. We start with the same widths: 280, 995, and 480 pixels, respectively, but their shrink factors are 0.5, 1.0, and 1.0. As we know the widths of the content, the shrink factor (X) can be found mathematically:

$$280px + 995px + 480px = 1615px$$
$$(0.5 \times 280px) + (1 \times 995px) + (1 \times 480px) = 1235px$$
$$X = 1235px \div 1615px = 0.7647$$

We can find the final widths now that we know the shrink factor. If the shrink factor is 76.47%, it means that item2 and item3 will be shrink by that amount, whereas item1 will shrink by 38.23% (because its flex-shrink value is half the others). The amount of shrinkage in each case is, rounded off to the nearest whole number:

$$item1 = 280px \times 0.3823 = 107px$$
$$item2 = 995px \times 0.7647 = 761px$$
$$item3 = 480px \times 0.7647 = 367px$$

Thus, the final widths of the flex items is:

$$item1 = 280px - 107px = 173px$$
$$item2 = 995px - 761px = 234px$$
$$item3 = 480px - 367px = 113px$$

The total combined widths of these 3 flex items is 520 pixels.

Adding in varying shrink and growth factors makes it all a little less intuitive. That's why you likely want to always declare the flex shorthand, preferably with a width or basis set for each flex item. If this doesn't make sense yet, don't worry; we'll cover a few more examples of shrinking as we discuss flex-basis.

Responsive Flexing

Allowing flex items to shrink proportionally like this allows for responsive objects and layouts that can shrink proportionally without breaking.

For example, you can create a three-column layout that smartly grows and shrinks without media queries, as shown on a wide screen in Figure 12-50 and narrow screen in Figure 12-51:

```
nav {
    flex: 0 1 200px;
    min-width: 150px;
}
article {
```

```
    flex: 1 2 600px;
  }
  aside {
    flex: 0 1 200px;
    min-width: 150px;
  }
```

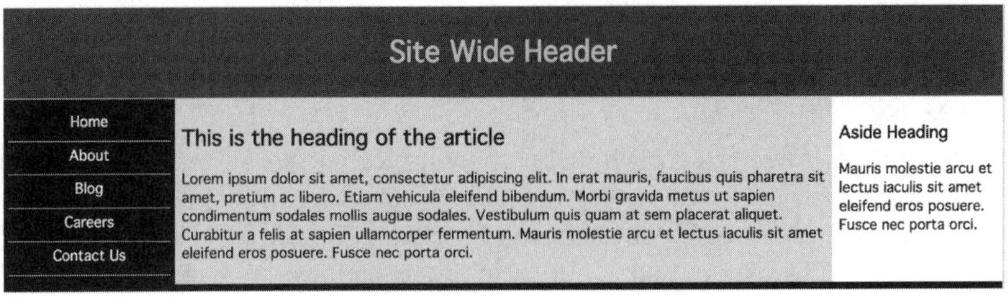

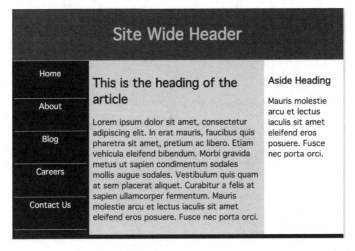

Figure 12-50. A wide flexbox layout

Figure 12-51. A narrow flexbox layout ▶

In this example, if the viewport is greater than 1,000 pixels, only the middle column grows because only the middle column was provided with a positive growth factor. We also dictated that below the 1,000-pixels-wide mark, the columns all shrink.

Let's take it bit by bit. The nav and aside elements have the following CSS:

```
flex: 0 1 200px;
min-width: 150px;
```

This means they don't grow from their basis, but they can shrink at equal rates. This means they'll have the width of their flex basis by default. If they do need to shrink, they'll shrink down to a minimum width of 150px and then stop shrinking. However, if either one has an element that's more than 150 pixels wide, whether it's an image or a run of text, it will stop shrinking as soon as it reaches the width of that bit of content. Suppose a 180-pixel image got dropped into the aside element. It would stop shrinking as soon as it reached 180 pixels wide. The nav would keep shrinking down to 150 pixels.

The main element, on the other hand, has these styles:

```
flex: 1 2 600px;
```

Thus, the main element can grow if there's space for it to do so. Since it's the only flex item that can grow, it gets all the growth. That means that, given a browser window 1,300 pixels wide, the two side columns will be 200 pixels wide each, leaving 900 pixels of width for the center column. In shrinking situations, the center column will shrink twice as fast as the other two elements. Thus, if the browser window is 900 pixels wide, the side columns will each be 175 pixels wide, and the center column 550 pixels wide.

Once the windows reaches 800 pixels wide, the side columns will reach their min-width values of 150px. From then on, any narrowing will all be taken up by the center column.

Just to be clear, you are not require to use pixels in these situation. You don't even have to use the same unit measures for various flex bases. The previous example could be rewritten like this:

```
nav {
  flex: 0 1 20ch;
  min-width: 15vw;
}
article {
  flex: 1 2 45ch;
}
aside {
  flex: 0 1 20ch;
  min-width: 10ch;
}
```

We won't go through all the math here, but the general approach is to set flex bases on character widths for improved readability, with some lower limits based on character widths and others on viewport width.

 Flexbox can be useful for one-dimensional page layout like the one shown in this section, where there are only three columns in a line. For anything more complex, or for a more powerful set of options, use Grid layout. (See Chapter 13.)

The flex-basis Property

As we've already seen, a flex item's size is impacted by its content and box-model properties and can be reset via the three components of the flex property. The <*flex-basis*> component of the flex property defines the initial or default size of flex items, before extra or negative space is distributed—before the flex items are allowed to grow or shrink according to the growth and shrink factors. It can also be set via the flex-basis property.

 Declaring the flex basis via the flex-basis property is *strongly* discouraged by the authors of the specification itself. Instead, declare the flex basis as part of the flex shorthand. We're only discussing the property here in order to explore flex basis.

---

flex-basis

Values	content | [<*length*> | <*percentage*>]
Initial value	auto
Applies to	Flex items (children of flex containers)
Percentages	Relative to flex container's inner main-axis size
Computed value	As specified, with length values made absolute
Inherited	No
Animatable	<*width*>

The flex basis determines the size of a flex item's element box, as set by box-sizing. By default, when a block-level element is not a flex item, the size is determined by the size of its parent, content, and box-model properties. When no size properties are explicitly declared or inherited, the size defaults to its individual content, border, and padding, which is 100% of the width of its parent for block-level elements.

The flex basis can be defined using the same length value types as the width and height properties; for example, 5vw, 12%, and 300px.

The universal keyword initial resets the flex basis to the initial value of auto, so you might as well declare auto. In turn, auto evaluates to the width (or height), if declared. If the value of width (or height) is set to auto, then the value of flex-basis is evaluated to content.

The content Keyword

The content keyword is not supported in most browsers (*http://code.google.com/p/chromium/issues/detail?id=470421*) at the time of this writing (late 2017), with the exception of Microsoft Edge 12+, but is equal to the width or height of the content. When content is used and supported, the basis is the size of the flex item's content; that is, the length of the main-axis size of the longest line of content or widest (or tallest) media object.

Until support is complete, flex-basis: content; can be easily polyfilled, as it is the equivalent of declaring flex-basis: auto; width: auto; on that flex item, or flex-basis: auto; height: auto; if the main-dimension is vertical. Unfortunately, using content in the flex shorthand in nonsupporting browsers invalidates the entire declaration (see "Understanding axes" on page 579).

The value of content is basically what we saw in the third example in Figure 12-49, and is shown in Figure 12-52.

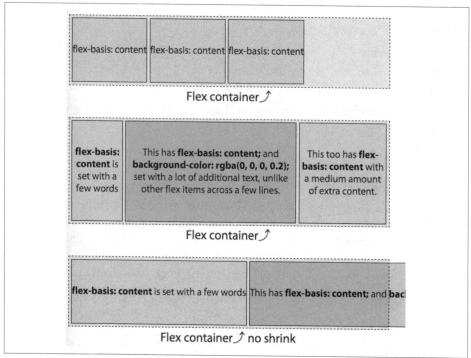

Figure 12-52. Sizing flex items on a content basis ⏵

In the first and third examples in Figure 12-52, the width of the flex item is the size of the content; and the flex basis is that same size. In the first example, the flex items' width and basis are approximately 132 pixels. The total width of the 3 flex items side by side is 396 pixels, fitting easily into the parent container.

In the third example, we have set a null shrink factor (0): this means the flex items cannot shrink, so they won't shrink or wrap to fit into the fixed-width flex container. Rather, they are the width of their nonwrapped text. That width is also the value of the flex basis. The flex items' width and basis are approximately 309, 1,037 pixels, and 523 pixels, respectively. You can't see the full width of the second flex item or the third flex item at all, but they're in the chapter files (*https://meyerweb.github.io/csstdg4figs/ 12-flexbox/33b_flexbasis_content.html*).

The second example contains the same content as the third example, but the flex items are defaulting to a shrink factor of 1, so the text in this example wraps because the flex items can shrink. Thus, while the width of the flex item is not the width of the content, the flex basis—the basis by which it will proportionally shrink—is the width of the items' contents.

Automatic Flex Basis

When set to auto, whether explicitly or by default, flex-basis is the same as the main-axis size of the element, had the element not been turned into a flex item. For length values, flex-basis resolves to the width or height value, with the exception that when the value of the width or height is auto, the flex basis value falls back to content.

When the flex basis is auto, and all the flex items can fit within the parent flex container, the flex items will be their pre-flexed size. If the flex items don't fit into their parent flex container, the flex items within that container will shrink proportionally based on their non-flexed main-axis sizes (unless the shrink factor is zero).

When there are no other properties setting the main-axis size of the flex items (that is, there's no width or even min-width set on these flex items), and flex-basis: auto or flex: 0 1 auto is set, the flex items will only be as wide as they need to be for the content to fit, as seen in the first example in Figure 12-53. In this case, they are the width of the text "flex-basis: auto;", which is approximately 110 pixels. The flex items are their pre-flexed size, as if set to display: inline-block. In this example, they're grouped at main-start because the flex container's justify-content defaults to flex-start.

In the second example in Figure 12-53, each of the flex items has flex basis of auto and an explicitly declared width. The main-axis size of the elements, had they not been turned into flex items, would be 100, 150, and 200 pixels, respectively. And so they are here, since they fit into the flex container without any overflow along the main axis.

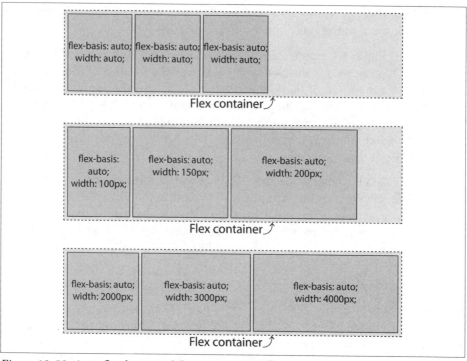

Figure 12-53. Auto flex basis and flex item widths ▶

In the third example in Figure 12-53, each of the flex items has flex basis of auto and a very large explicitly declared width. The main-axis size of the elements, had they not been turned into flex items, would be 2,000, 3,000, and 4,000 pixels, respectively. Since they could not possibly fit into the flex container without overflowing along the main axis, and their flex shrink factors have all defaulted to 1, they shrink until they fit into the flex container. You can do the math to find out how big they are using the process outlined in a previous section; as a hint, the third flex item should be reduced from four thousand pixels down to a width of 240 pixels.

Default Values

When neither a flex-basis nor a flex is set, the flex item's main-axis size is the pre-flex size of the item, as their default value is auto.

In Figure 12-54, two things are happening: the flex bases are defaulting to auto, the growth factor is defaulting to 0, and the shrink factor of each item is defaulting to 1. For each flex item, the flex basis is their individual width value. That means the flex bases are being set to the values of the width properties: 100, 200, and 300 pixels in the first example, and 200, 400, and 200 pixels in the second example. As the combined widths of the flex items are 600 pixels and 800 pixels, respectively, both of which are both greater than the main-axis size of the 540-pixel-wide containers, they are all shrinking proportionally to fit.

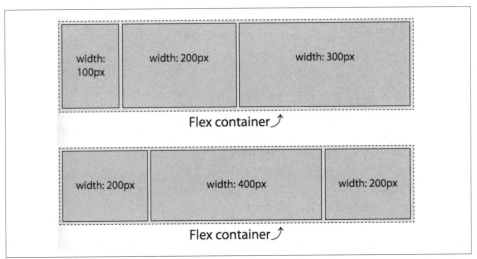

Figure 12-54. Default sizing of flex items ▶

In the first example, we are trying to fit 600 pixels in 540 pixels, so each flex item will shrink by 10% to yield flex items that are 90, 180, and 270 pixels wide. In the second example, we are trying to fit 800 pixels into 540 pixels, so they all shrink 32.5%, making the flex items' widths 135, 270, and 135 pixels.

Length Units

In the previous examples, the `auto` flex bases defaulted to the declared widths of the various flex items. There are other options; for example, we can use the same length units for our flex-basis value as we do for `width` and `height`.

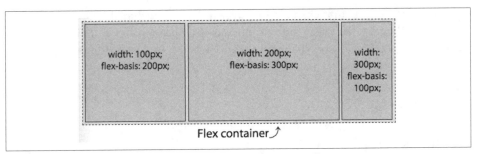

Figure 12-55. Sizing flex items with length-unit flex bases ▶

When there are both flex-basis and width (or height, for vertical main axes) values, the basis trumps the width (or height). Let's add bases values to the first example from Figure 12-54. The flex items include the following CSS:

```
flex-container {
  width: 540px;
}
item1 {
  width: 100px;
  flex-basis: 300px;   /* flex: 0 1 300px; */
}
item2 {
  width: 200px;
  flex-basis: 200px;   /* flex: 0 1 200px; */
}
item3 {
  width: 300px;
  flex-basis: 100px;   /* flex: 0 1 100px; */
}
```

The widths are overridden by the bases. The flex items shrink down to 270 pixels, 180 pixels, and 90 pixels, respectively. Had the container *not* had a constrained width, the flex items would have been 300 pixels, 200 pixels, and 100 pixels, respectively.

While the declared flex basis can override the main-axis size of flex items, the size can be affected by other properties, such as min-width, min-height, max-width, and max-height. These are not ignored. Thus, for example, an element might have flex-basis: 100px and min-width: 500px. The minimum width of 500px will be respected, even though the flex basis is smaller.

Percentage units

Percentage values for flex-basis are calculated relative to the size of the main dimension of the flex container.

We've already seen the first example in Figure 12-56; it's included here to recall that the width of the text "flex-basis: auto" in this case is approximately 110 pixels wide. In this case only, declaring flex-basis: auto looks the same as writing flex-basis: 110px:

```
flex-container {
  width: 540px;
}
flex-item {
  flex: 0 1 100%;
}
```

In the second example in Figure 12-56, the first two flex items have a flex basis of auto with a default width of auto, which is as if their flex basis were set to content. As we've noted previously, the flex-basis of the first 2 items ends up being the equivalent of 110 pixels, as the content in this case happens to be 110 pixels wide. The last item has its `flex-basis` set to 100%.

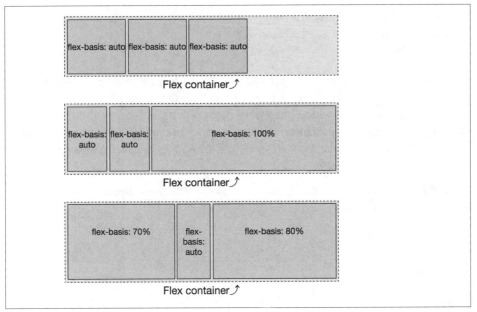

Figure 12-56. Sizing flex items with percentage flex bases ▶

The percentage value is relative to the parent, which is 540 pixels. The third flex item, with a basis of 100%, is not the only flex item within the non-wrapping flex container. Thus, it will not grow to be 100% of the width of the parent flex container *unless* its shrink factor is set with a null shrink factor, meaning it can't shrink, or if it contains non-wrappable content that is as wide or wider than the parent container.

> Remember: when the flex basis is a percent value, the main-axis size is relative to the parent, which is the flex container.

With our 3 flex bases, if the content is indeed 110 pixels wide, and the container is 540 pixels wide (ignoring other box-model properties for simplicity's sake), we have a total of 760 pixels to fit in a 540-pixel space. Thus we have 220 pixels of negative space to distribute proportionally. The shrink factor is:

Shrink factor = 220px ÷ 760px = 28.95%

Each flex item will be shrunk by 28.95%, becoming 71.05% of the width they would have been had they not been allowed to shrink. We can figure the final widths:

item1 = 110px × 71.05% = 78.16px
item2 = 110px × 71.05% = 78.16px
item3 = 540px × 71.05% = 383.68px

These numbers hold true as long as the flex items can be that small; that is, as long as none of the flex items contain media or nonbreaking text wider than 78.16 pixels or 383.68 pixels. This is the widest these flex items will be as long as the content can wrap to be that width or narrower. We say "widest" because if one of the other two flex items can't shrink to be as narrow as this value, they'll have to absorb some of that negative space.

In the third example in Figure 12-56, the flex-basis: auto item wraps over three lines. The CSS for this example is the equivalent of:

```
flex-container {
  width: 540px;
}
item1 {
  flex: 0 1 70%;
}
item2 {
  flex: 0 1 auto;
}
item3 {
  flex: 0 1 80%;
}
```

We declared the flex-basis of the 3 flex items to be 70%, auto, and 80%, respectively. Remembering that in our scenario auto is the width of the non-wrapping content, which in this case is approximately 110 pixels, and our flex container is 540 pixels, the bases are equivalent to:

item1 = 70% × 540px = 378px
item2 = widthOfText("flex-basis: auto") = 110px
item3 = 80% × 540px = 432px

When we add the widths of these 3 flex items' bases, they have total combined width of 920 pixels, which needs to fit into a flex container 540 pixels wide. Thus we have 380 pixels of negative space to remove proportionally among the 3 flex items. To figure out the ratio, we divide the available width of our flex container by the sum of widths of the flex items that they would have if they couldn't shrink:

Proportional Width = 540px ÷ 920px = 0.587

Because the shrink factors are all the same, this is fairly simple. Each item will be 58.7% of the width it would be if it had no flex item siblings:

item1 = 378px × 58.7% = 221.8px
item2 = 110px × 58.7% = 64.6px
item3 = 432px × 58.7% = 253.6px

What happens when the container is a different width? Say, 1,000 pixels? The flex basis would be 700 pixels (70% × 1,000 pixels), 110 pixels, and 800 pixels (80% × 1,000 pixels), respectively, for a total of 1,610 pixels:

Proportional Width = 1000px ÷ 1610px = 0.6211

item1 = 700px × 62.11% = 434.8px
item2 = 110px × 62.11% = 68.3px
item3 = 800px × 62.11% = 496.9px

Because with a basis of 70% and 80%, the combined bases of the flex items will always be wider than 100%, no matter how wide we make the parent, all 3 items will always shrink.

If the first flex item can't shrink for some reason—whether due to unshrinkable content, or another bit of CSS setting its flex-shrink to 0— it will be 70% of the width of the parent—378 pixels in this case. The other 2 flex items must shrink proportionally to fit into the remaining 30%, or 162 pixels. In this case, we expect widths to be 378 pixels, 32.875 pixels, and 129.125 pixels. As the text "basis:" is wider than that— assume 42 pixels—we get 378 pixels, 42 pixels, and 120 pixels. This result is shown in Figure 12-57.

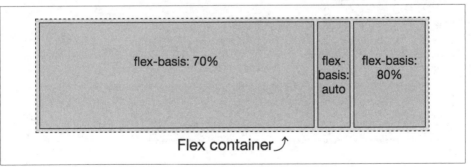

Figure 12-57. *While the percentage value for flex-basis is relative to the width of the flex container, the main-axis size is impacted by its siblings* ▶

Testing this out on your device will likely have slightly different results, as the width of the text "flex-basis: auto" may not be the same for you, depending on the font that actually gets used to render the text. (We used Myriad Pro, with fallbacks to Helvetica and any generic sans-serif font.)

Zero Basis

If neither the flex-basis property nor the flex shorthand is included at all, the flex basis defaults to auto. When the flex property is included, but the flex basis component of the shorthand is omitted from the shorthand, the basis defaults to 0. While on the surface you might think the two values of auto and 0 are similar, the 0 value is actually very different, and may not be what you expect.

In the case of flex-basis: auto, the basis is the main size of the flex items' contents. If the basis of each of the flex items is 0, the "available" space is the main-axis size of the entire flex container. In either case, the "available" space is distributed proportionally, based on the growth factors of each flex item.

In the case of a basis of 0, the size of the flex container is divided up and distributed proportionally to each flex item based on their growth factors—their default original main-axis size as defined by height, width, or content, is not taken into account, though min-width, max-width, min-height, and max-height do impact the flexed size.

As shown in Figure 12-58, when the basis is auto, it is just the extra space that is divided up proportionally and added to each flex item set to grow. Again, assuming the width of the text "flex: X X auto" is 110 pixels, in the first examples we have 210 pixels to distribute among 6 growth factors, or 35 pixels per growth factor. The flex items are 180, 145, and 215 pixels wide, respectively.

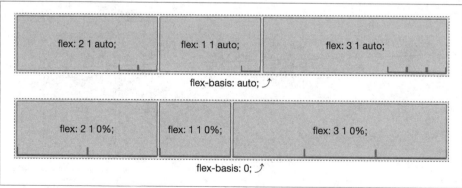

Figure 12-58. Flex growth in auto and zero flex bases

In the second example, when the basis is 0, all 540 pixels of the width is distributable space. With 540 pixels of distributable space between 6 growth factors, each growth factor is worth 90 pixels. The flex items are 180, 90, and 270 pixels wide, respectively.

While the middle flex item is 90 pixels wide, the content in this example is narrower than 110 pixels, so the flex item didn't wrap.

The flex Shorthand

Now that we have a fuller understanding of the properties that make up the flex shorthand, remember: *always use the flex shorthand.* It accepts the usual global property values, including initial, auto, none; and the use of an integer, usually 1, meaning the flex item can grow. Let's go over all these values.

Common Flex Values

The common flex values are four flex values providing the most commonly desired effects:

flex: initial
> This value sizes flex items based on the width or height property, depending on the main-axis direction, while allowing shrinking.

flex: auto
> This flex value also sizes flex items based on the width or height property, but makes them fully flexible, allowing both shrinking and growing.

flex: none
> This value again sizes flex items based on the width or height property, but makes them completely inflexible: they can't shrink or grow.

flex: <number>
> This value sets the flex item's growth factor to the <number> provided. It thus sets the shrink factor to 0, and the basis to 0 as well. This means the width or height value acts as a minimum size, but the flex item will grow if there is room to do so.

Let's consider each of these in turn.

Flexing with initial

initial is a global CSS keyword, which means initial can be used on all properties to represent a property's initial value; that is, its specification default value. Thus, the following lines are equivalent:

```
flex: initial;
flex: 0 1 auto;
```

Declaring flex: initial sets a null growth factor, a shrink factor of 1, and sets the flex bases to auto. In Figure 12-59, we can see the effect of the auto flex bases. In the first two examples, the basis of each flex item is content—with each flex item having the width of the single line of letters that make up their content. In the last 2 examples, the flex bases of all the items are equal at 50 pixels, since width: 50px has been applied to all the flex items. The flex: initial declaration sets the flex-basis to auto, which we previously saw is the value of the width (or height), if declared, or content if not declared.

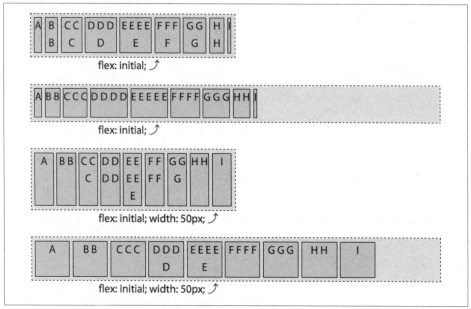

Figure 12-59. Flex items shrink but won't grow when flex: initial is set ▶

In the first and third examples in Figure 12-59, we see that when the flex container is too small to fit all the flex items at their default main-axis size, the flex items shrink so that all the flex items fit within the parent flex container. In these examples, the combined flex bases of all the flex items is greater than the main-axis size of the flex container. In the first example, the width of teach flex item varies based on the width of each item's content and its ability to shrink. They all shrink proportionally based on their shrink factor, but not narrower than their widest content. In the third example, with each flex item's flex-basis being 50 pixels (due to the value of width), all the items shrink equally.

Flex items, by default, are grouped at main start, as flex-start is the default value of for the justify-content property. This is only noticeable when the combined main-axis sizes of the flex items in a flex line are smaller than the main-axis size of the flex container, and none of the flex items are able to grow.

Flexing with auto

`flex: auto` is similar to `flex: initial`, but makes the flex items flexible in both directions: they'll shrink if there isn't enough room to fit all the items within the container, and they'll grow to take up all the extra space within the container if there is distributable space. The flex items absorb any free space along the main axis. The following two statements are equivalent:

```
flex: auto;
flex: 1 1 auto;
```

A variety of scenarios using `auto` flexing are shown in Figure 12-60.

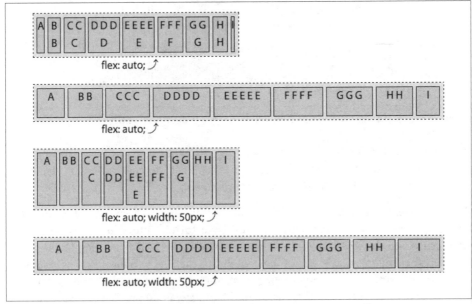

Figure 12-60. Flex items can grow and shrink when flex: auto is set ⊙

The first and third examples of Figure 12-60 are identical to the examples in Figure 12-59, as the shrinking and bases are the same. However, the second and fourth examples are different. This is because when `flex: auto` is set, the growth factor is 1, and the flex items therefore can grow to incorporate all the extra available space.

Preventing flexing with none

Any `flex: none` flex items are inflexible: they can neither shrink nor grow. The following two lines of CSS are equivalent:

```
flex: none;
flex: 0 0 auto;
```

The effects of none are shown in Figure 12-61.

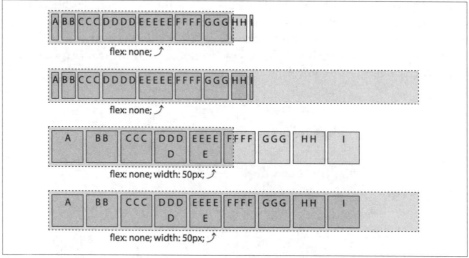

Figure 12-61. With flex: none, flex items will neither grow nor shrink ⏵

As demonstrated in the first and third examples of Figure 12-61, if there isn't enough space, the flex items overflow the flex container. This is different from flex: initial and flex: auto, which both set a positive shrink factor.

The basis resolves to auto, meaning each flex item's main-axis size is determined by the main-axis size of the element had it not been turned into a flex item. The flex-basis resolves to the width or height value of the element. If that value is auto, the basis becomes the main-axis size of the content. In the first two examples, the basis—and the width, since there is no growing or shrinking—is the width of the content. In the third and fourth examples, the width and basis are all 50 pixels, because that's the value of the width property applied to them.

Numeric flexing

When the value of the flex property is a single, positive numeric value, that value will be used for the growth factor, while the shrink factor will default to 0 and the basis will default to 0. The following two CSS declarations are equivalent:

```
flex: 3;
flex: 3 0 0;
```

This makes the flex item on which it is set flexible: it can grow. The shrink factor is actually moot: the flex basis is set to 0, so the flex item can only grow from that basis.

In the first two examples in Figure 12-62, all the flex items have a flex growth factor of 3. The flex basis is 0, so they don't "shrink"; they just grew equally from zero pixels wide until the sum of their main-axis sizes grew to fill the container along the main axis. With all the flex items having a basis of 0, 100% of the main dimension is distributable space. The main-axis size of the flex items are wider in this second example because the wider flex container has more distributable space.

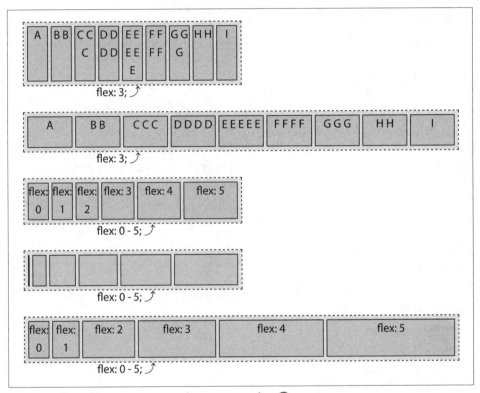

Figure 12-62. Flexing using a single numeric value ▶

Any numeric value that is greater than 0, even 0.1, means the flex item can grow. When there is available space to grow, if only one flex item has a positive growth factor, that item will take up all the available space. If there are multiple flex items that can grow, the available extra space will be distributed proportionally to each flex item based on to their growth factor.

In the last three examples of Figure 12-62, there are six flex items with flex: 0, flex: 1, flex: 2, flex: 3, flex: 4, and flex: 5 declared, respectively. These are the growth factors for the flex items, with each having a shrink factor of 1 and a flex basis of 0. The main-axis size of each is proportional to the specified flex growth factor. You might assume that the flex: 0 item with the text "flex: 0" in the third and fourth examples will be zero pixels wide, like in the fourth and fifth examples—but, by default, flex items won't shrink below the length of the longest word or fixed-size element.

 A bit of padding, margins, and borders were added in the figures to make the visuals more pleasing. For this reason, the leftmost flex item, with flex: 0 declared, is visible: it has a one-pixel border making it visible, even though it's zero pixels wide.

The order property

Flex items are, by default, displayed and laid out in the same order as they appear in the source code. The order of flex items and flex lines can be reversed with flex-direction, but sometimes you want a little more complicated rearrangment. The order property can be used to change the ordering of individual flex items.

order	
Values	<integer>
Initial value	0
Applies to	Flex items and absolutely positioned children of flex containers
Computed value	As specified
Inherited	No
Animatable	Yes

By default, all flex items are assigned the order of 0, with the flex items all assigned to the same ordinal group and displayed in the same order as their source order, along the direction of the main axis. (This has been the case for all the examples seen throughout this chapter.)

To change the visual order of a flex item, set the order property value to a nonzero integer. Setting the order property on elements that are not children of a flex container has no effect on such elements.

The value of the order property specifies an *ordinal group* to which the flex item belongs. Any flex items with a negative value will appear to come before those defaulting to 0 when drawn to the page, and all the flex items with a positive value will appear to come after those defaulting to 0. While visually altered, the source order remains the same. Screen readers and tabbing order remains as defined by the source order of the HTML.

For example, if you have a group of 12 items, and you want the 7th to come first and the 6th to be last, you would declare:

```
ul {
  display: inline-flex;
}
li:nth-of-type(6) {
  order: 1;
}
li:nth-of-type(7) {
  order: -1;
}
```

In this scenario, we are explicitly setting the order for the sixth and seventh list items, while the other list items are defaulting to `order: 0`. The result is shown in Figure 12-63.

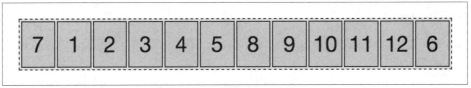

Figure 12-63. Reordering flex items with the order property ▶

The seventh flex item is the first to be laid out, due to the negative value of the `order` property, which is less than the default 0, and is also the lowest value of any of its sibling flex items. The sixth flex item is the only item with a value greater than zero, and therefore has the highest order value out of all of its siblings. This is why it's laid out after all the other flex items. All the other items, all having the default `order` of 0, are drawn between those first and last items, in the same order as their source order, since they are all members of the same ordinal group (0).

The flex container lays out its content in order-modified document order, starting from the lowest numbered ordinal group and going up. When you have multiple flex items having the same value for the order property, the items share an ordinal group. The items in each ordinal group will appear in source order, with the group appearing in numeric order, from lowest to highest. Consider the following:

```
ul {
  display: inline-flex;
  background-color: rgba(0,0,0,0.1);
}
li:nth-of-type(3n-1) {
  order: 3;
  background-color: rgba(0,0,0,0.2);
}
li:nth-of-type(3n+1) {
  order: -1;
```

```
    background-color: rgba(0,0,0,0.4);
}
```

By setting the same order value to more than one flex item, the items will appear by ordinal group, and by source order within each individual ordinal group. This has the result shown in Figure 12-64.

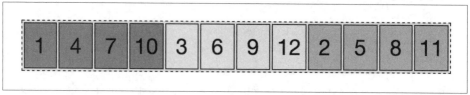

Figure 12-64. Flex items appear in order of ordinal groups, by source order within their group ⊙

Here's what happened:

- Items 2, 5, 8, and 11 were selected to share ordinal group 3, and get a 20% opaque background.

- Items 1, 4, 7, and 10 were selected to share ordinal group -1, and get a 40% opaque background.

- Items 3, 6, 9, and 12 were not selected at all. They default to the ordinal group 0.

The three ordinal groups, then, are -1, 0, and 3. The groups are arranged in that order. Within each group, the items are arranged by source order.

This reordering is purely visual. Screen readers *should* read the document as it appeared in the source code, though they may not. As a visual change, ordering flex items impacts the painting order of the page: the painting order of the flex items is the order in which they appear, as if they were reordered in the source document, even though they aren't.

Changing the layout with the order property has no effect on the tab order of the page. If the numbers in Figure 12-64 were links, tabbing through the links would go through the links in the order of the source code, *not* in the order of the layout.

Tabbed Navigation Revisited

Adding to our tabbed navigation bar example in Figure 12-2, we can make the currently active tab appear first, as Figure 12-65 shows:

```
nav {
    display: flex;
    justify-content: flex-end;
    border-bottom: 1px solid #ddd;
}
```

```
a {
  margin: 0 5px;
  padding: 5px 15px;
  border-radius: 3px 3px 0 0;
  background-color: #ddd;
  text-decoration: none;
  color: black;
}
a:hover {
  background-color: #bbb;
  text-decoration: underline;
}
a.active {
  order: -1;
  background-color: #999;
}

<nav>
  <a href="/">Home</a>
  <a href="/about">About</a>
  <a class="active">Blog</a>
  <a href="/jobs">Careers</a>
  <a href="/contact">Contact Us</a>
</nav>
```

Figure 12-65. Changing the order will change the visual order, but not the tab order ⊙

The currently active tab has the `.active` class added, the `href` attribute removed, and the `order` set to `-1`, which is less than the default `0` of the other sibling flex items, meaning it appears first.

Why did we remove the `href` attribute? As the tab is the currently active document, there is no reason for the document to link to itself. But, more importantly, if it was an active link instead of a placeholder link, and the user was using the keyboard to tab through the navigation, the order of appearance is `Blog`, `Home`, `About`, `Careers`, and `Contact Us`, with the `Blog` appearing first; but the tab order would have been `Home`, `About`, `Blog`, `Careers`, and `Contact Us`, following the source order rather than the visual order, which can be confusing.

The `order` property can be used to enable marking up the main content area before the side columns for mobile devices and those using screen readers and other assistive technology, while creating the appearance of the common three-column layout: a center main content area, with site navigation on the left and a sidebar on the right, as shown way back in Figure 12-50.

While you can put your footer before your header in your markup, and use the order property to reorder the page, this is an inappropriate use of the property. order should only be used for visual reordering of content. Your underlying markup should always reflect the logical order of your content:

```
<header></header>                    <header></header>
<main>                               <main>
    <article></article>                 <nav></nav>
    <aside></aside>                      <article></article>
    <nav></nav>                          <aside></aside>
</main>                              </main>
<footer></footer>                    <footer></footer>
```

We've been marking up websites in the order we want them to appear, as shown on the right in the preceding code example, which is the same code as in our three-column layout example (Figure 12-50). It really would make more sense if we marked up the page as shown on the left, with the article content, which is the main content, first in the source order: this puts the article first for screen readers, search engines, and even mobile device, but in the middle for our sighted users on larger screens:

```
main {
    display: flex;
}
main > nav {
    order: -1;
}
```

By using the order: -1 declaration we are able to make the nav appear first, as it is the lone flex item in the ordinal group of -1. The article and aside, with no order explicitly declared, default to order: 0.

Remember, when more than one flex item is in the same ordinal group, the members of that group are displayed in source order in the direction of main-start to main-end, so the article is displayed before the aside.

Some developers, when changing the order of at least one flex item, like to give all flex items an order value for better markup readability. We could have also written:

```
main {
    display: flex;
}
main > nav {
    order: 1;
}
main > article {
    order: 2;
}
main > aside {
```

```
    order: 3;
  }
```

In previous years, before browsers supported flex, all this could have been done with floats: we would have set float: right on the nav. While doable, flex layout makes it much simpler, especially if we want all three columns—the aside, nav, and article —to be of equal heights.

CHAPTER 13

Grid Layout

For as long as CSS has existed—which is, believe it or not, two decades now—it's had a layout-shaped hole at its center. We've bent other features to the purposes of layout, most notably `float` and `clear`, and generally hacked our way around that hole. Flexbox layout helped to fill it, but flexbox is really meant for only specific use cases, like navigation bars (navbars).

Grid layout, by contrast, is a *generalized* layout system. With its emphasis on rows and columns, it might at first feel like a return to table layout—and in certain ways that's not too far off—but there is far, far more to grid layout than table layout. Grid allows pieces of the design to be laid out independently of their document source order, and even overlap pieces of the layout, if that's your wish. There are powerfully flexible methods for defining repeating patterns of grid lines, attaching elements to those grid lines, and more. You can nest grids inside grids, or for that matter, attach tables or flexbox containers to a grid. And much, much more.

In short, grid layout is the layout system we've long waited for. There's a lot to learn, and perhaps even more to unlearn, as we leave behind the clever hacks and work-arounds that have gotten us through the past 20 years.

Creating a Grid Container

The first step to creating a grid is defining a *grid container*. This is much like a containing block in positioning, or a flex container in flexible-box layout: a grid container is an element that defines a *grid formatting context* for its contents.

At this very basic level, grid layout is actually quite reminiscent of flexbox. For example, the child elements of a grid container become *grid items*, just as the child elements of a flex container become flex items. The children of those child elements do *not* become grid elements—although any grid item can itself be made a grid container, and thus have its child elements become grid items to the nested grid. It's possible to nest grids inside grids, until it's grids all the way down. (Grid layout also has a separate concept of *subgrids* that is distinct from nesting grid containers, but we'll get to that later.)

There are two kinds of grids: *regular* grids and *inline* grids. These are created with special values for the display property: grid and inline-grid. The first generates a block-level box, and the second an inline-level box. The difference is illustrated in Figure 13-1.

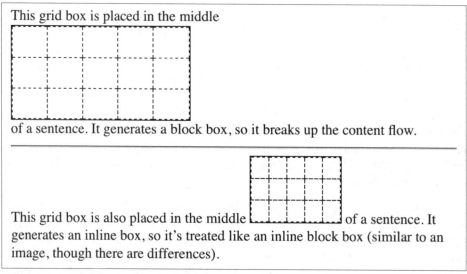

This grid box is placed in the middle

of a sentence. It generates a block box, so it breaks up the content flow.

This grid box is also placed in the middle of a sentence. It generates an inline box, so it's treated like an inline block box (similar to an image, though there are differences).

Figure 13-1. Grids and inline grids

These are very similar to the block and inline-block values for display. Most grids you create are likely to be block-level, though the ability to create inline grids is always there.

Although display: grid creates a block-level grid, the specification is careful to explicitly state that "grid containers are not block containers." What this means is that although the grid box participates in layout much as a block container does, there are a number of differences between them.

First off, floated elements do not intrude into the grid container. What this means in practice is that a grid will not slide under a floated element, as a block container will do. See Figure 13-2 for a demonstration of the difference.

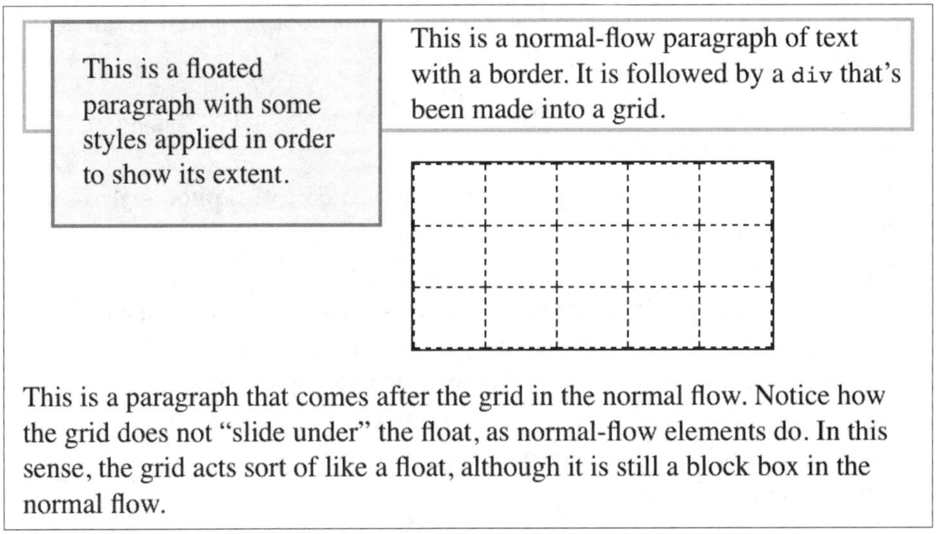

This is a floated paragraph with some styles applied in order to show its extent.

This is a normal-flow paragraph of text with a border. It is followed by a `div` that's been made into a grid.

This is a paragraph that comes after the grid in the normal flow. Notice how the grid does not "slide under" the float, as normal-flow elements do. In this sense, the grid acts sort of like a float, although it is still a block box in the normal flow.

Figure 13-2. Floats interact differently with blocks and grids

Furthermore, the margins of a grid container do not collapse with the margins of its descendants. Again, this is distinct from block boxes, whose margins do (by default) collapse with descendants. For example, the first list item in an ordered list may have a top margin, but this margin will collapse with the list element's top margin. The top margin of a grid item will *never* collapse with the top margin of its grid container. Figure 13-3 illustrates the difference.

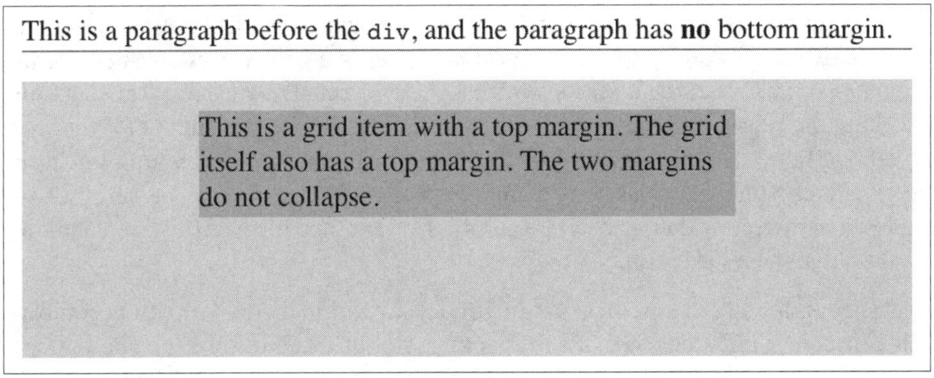

This is a paragraph before the `div`, and the paragraph has **no** bottom margin.

This is a grid item with a top margin. The grid itself also has a top margin. The two margins do not collapse.

Figure 13-3. Margin collapsing and the lack thereof

There are a few CSS properties and features that do not apply to grid containers and grid items; specifically:

- All `column` properties (e.g., `column-count`, `columns`, etc.) are ignored when applied to a grid container.

- The `::first-line` and `::first-letter` pseudo-elements do not apply to grid containers and are ignored.

- `float` and `clear` are effectively ignored for grid items (though not grid containers). Despite this, the `float` property still helps determine the computed value of the `display` property for children of a grid container, because the `display` value of the grid items is resolved *before* they're made into grid items.

- The `vertical-align` property has no effect on grid items, though it may affect the content inside the grid item. (There are other, more powerful ways to align grid items, so don't worry.)

Lastly, if a grid container's declared `display` value is `inline-grid` *and* the element is either floated or absolutely positioned, the computed value of `display` becomes `grid` (thus dropping `inline-grid`).

Once you've defined a grid container, the next step is to set up the grid within. Before we explore how that works, though, it's necessary to cover some terminology.

Basic Grid Terminology

We've already talked about grid containers and grid items, but let's define them in a bit more detail. As was said before, a *grid container* is a box that establishes a *grid-formatting context*; that is, an area in which a grid is created and elements are laid out according the rules of grid layout instead of block layout. You can think of it the way an element set to `display: table` creates a table-formatting context within it. Given the grid-like nature of tables, this comparison is fairly apt, though be sure not to make the assumption that grids are just tables in another form. Grids are far more powerful than tables ever were.

A *grid item* is a thing that participates in grid layout within a grid-formatting context. This is usually a child element of a grid container, but it can also be the anonymous (that is, not contained within an element) bits of text that are part of an element's content. Consider the following, which has the result shown in Figure 13-4:

```
#warning {display: grid;
    background: #FCC; padding: 0.5em;
    grid-template-rows: 1fr;
    grid-template-columns: repeat(7, 1fr);}
```

```
<p id="warning"><img src="warning.svg"><strong>Note:</strong> This element is a
   <em>grid container</em> with several <em>grid items</em> inside it.</p>
```

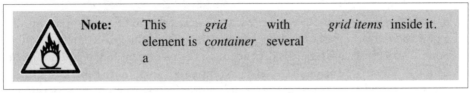

Figure 13-4. Grid items

Notice how each element, *and* each bit of text between them, has become a grid item. The image is a grid item, just as much as the elements and text runs—seven grid items in all. Each of these will participate in the grid layout, although the anonymous text runs will be much more difficult (or impossible) to affect with the various grid properties we'll discuss.

If you're wondering about `grid-template-rows` and `grid-template-columns`, we'll tackle them in the next section.

In the course of using those properties, you'll create or reference several core components of grid layout. These are summarized in Figure 13-5.

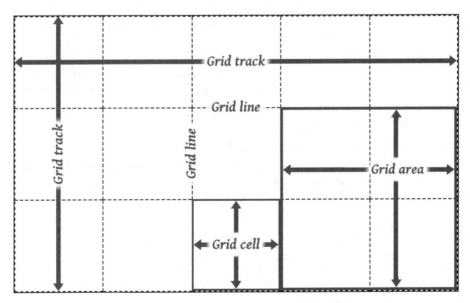

Figure 13-5. Grid components

The most fundamental unit is the *grid line*. By defining the placement of one or more grid lines, you implicitly create the rest of the grid's components:

- A *grid track* is a continuous run between two adjacent grid lines—in other words, a *grid column* or a *grid row*. It goes from one edge of the grid container to the other. The size of a grid track is dependent on the placement of the grid lines that define it. These are analogous to table columns and rows. More generically, these can be referred to as *block axis* and *inline axis* tracks, where (in Western languages) column tracks are on the block axis and row tracks are on the inline axis.

- A *grid cell* is any space bounded by four grid lines, with no grid lines running through it, analogous to a table cell. This is the smallest unit of area in grid layout. Grid cells cannot be directly addressed with CSS grid properties; that is, no property allows you to say a grid item should be associated with a given cell. (But see the next point for more details.)

- A *grid area* is any rectangular area bounded by four grid lines, and made up of one or more grid cells. An area can be as small as a single cell, or as large as all the cells in the grid. Grid areas *are* directly addressable by CSS grid properties, which allow you to define the areas and then associate grid items with them.

An important thing to note is that these grid tracks, cells, and areas are entirely constructed of grid lines—and more importantly, do not have to correspond to grid items. There is no requirement that all grid areas be filled with an item; it is perfectly possible to have some or even most of a grid's cells be empty of any content. It's also possible to have grid items overlap each other, either by defining overlapping grid areas or by using grid-line references that create overlapping situations.

Another thing to keep in mind is that you can define as many or as few grid lines as you wish. You could literally define just a set of vertical grid lines, thus creating a bunch of columns and only one row. Or you could go the other way, creating a bunch of row tracks and no column tracks (though there would be one, stretching from one side of the grid container to the other).

The flip side to that is if you create a condition where a grid item can't be placed within the column and row tracks you define, or if you explicitly place a grid item outside those tracks, new grid lines and tracks will be automatically added to the grid to accommodate.

Placing Grid Lines

It turns out that placing grid lines can get fairly complex. That's not so much because the concept is difficult; there are just so many different ways to get it done, and each uses its own subtly different syntax.

We'll get started by looking at two closely related properties.

grid-template-rows, grid-template-columns

Values	none | <track-list> | <auto-track-list>
Initial value	none
Applies to	Grid containers
Percentages	Refer to the inline size (usually width) of the grid container for grid-template-columns, and to the block size (usually height) of the grid container for grid-template-rows
Computed value	As declared, with lengths made absolute
Inherited	No
Animatable	No

With these properties, you can define the grid lines in your overall *grid template*, or what the CSS specification calls the *explicit grid*. Everything depends on these grid lines; fail to place them properly, and the whole layout can very easily fall apart.

 When you're starting out with CSS grid layout, it's probably a very good idea to sketch out where the grid lines need to be on paper first, or in some close digital analogue. Having a visual reference for where lines should be, and how they should behave, will make writing your grid CSS a lot easier.

The exact syntax patterns for *<track-list>* and *<auto-track-list>* are complex and nest a few layers deep, and unpacking them would take a lot of time and space that's better devoted to just exploring how things work. There are a lot of ways to specify your grid lines' placement, so before we get started on learning those patterns, there are some basic things to establish.

First, grid lines can always be referred to by number, and can also be named by the author. Take the grid shown in Figure 13-6, for example. From your CSS, you can use any of the numbers to refer to a grid line, or you can use the defined names, or you can mix them together. Thus, you could say that a grid item stretches from column line 3 to line steve, and from row line skylight to line 2.

Note that a grid line can have more than one name. You can use any of them to refer to a given grid line, though you can't combine them the way you can multiple class names. You might think that means it's a good idea to avoid repeating grid-line names, but that's not always the case, as we'll soon see.

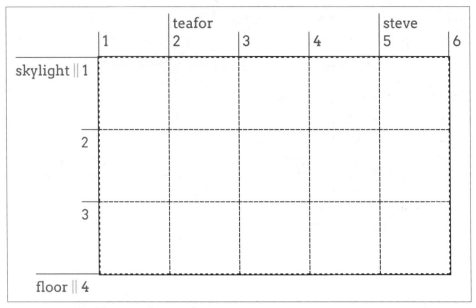

Figure 13-6. Grid-line numbers and names

I used intentionally silly grid-line names in Figure 13-6 to illustrate that you can pick any name you like, and also to avoid the implication that there are "default" names. If you'd seen start for the first line, you might have assumed that the first line is always called that. Nope. If you want to stretch an element from start to end, you'll need to define those names yourself. Fortunately, that's simple to do.

As I've said, many value patterns can be used to define the grid template. We'll start with the simpler ones and work our way toward the more complex.

Fixed-Width Grid Tracks

Our first step is to create a grid whose grid tracks are a fixed width. We don't necessarily mean a fixed length like pixels or ems; percentages also count as fixed-width here. In this context, "fixed-width" means the grid lines are placed such that the distance between them does not change due to changes of content within the grid tracks.

So, as an example, this counts as a definition of three fixed-width grid columns:

```
#grid {display: grid;
    grid-template-columns: 200px 50% 100px;}
```

That will place a line 200 pixels from the start of the grid container (by default, the left side); a second grid line half the width of the grid container away from the first; and a third line 100 pixels away from the second. This is illustrated in Figure 13-7.

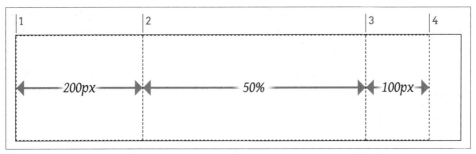

Figure 13-7. Grid-line placement

While it's true that the second column can change in size if the grid container's size changes, it will *not* change based on the content of the grid items. However wide or narrow the content placed in that second column, the column's width will always be half the width of the grid container.

It's also true that the last grid line doesn't reach the right edge of the grid container. That's fine; it doesn't have to. If you want it to—and you probably will—we'll see various ways to deal with that in just a bit.

This is all lovely, but what if you want to name your grid lines? Just place any grid-line name you want, and as many as you want, in the appropriate place in the value, surrounded by square brackets. That's all! Let's add some names to our previous example, with the result shown in Figure 13-8:

```
#grid {display: grid;
    grid-template-columns:
        [start col-a] 200px [col-b] 50% [col-c] 100px [stop end last];
    }
```

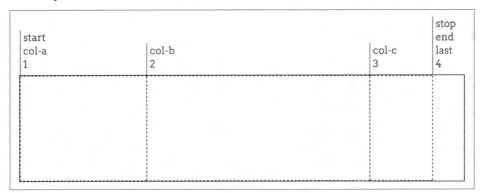

Figure 13-8. Grid-line name

What's nice is that adding the names makes clear that each value is actually specifying a grid track's width, which means there is always a grid line to either side of a width value. Thus, for the three widths we have, there are actually four grid lines created.

Row grid lines are placed in exactly the same way as columns, as Figure 13-9 shows:

```
#grid {display: grid;
    grid-template-columns:
        [start col-a] 200px [col-b] 50% [col-c] 100px [stop end last];
    grid-template-rows:
        [start masthead] 3em [content] 80% [footer] 2em [stop end];
    }
```

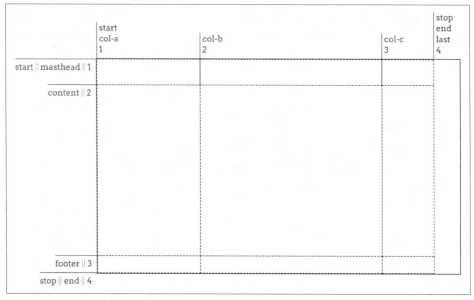

Figure 13-9. Creating a grid

There are a couple of things to point out here. First, there are both column and row lines with the names start and end. This is perfectly OK. Rows and columns don't share the same namespace, so you can reuse names like these in the two contexts.

Second is the percentage value for the content row track. This is calculated with respect to the height of the grid container; thus, a container 500 pixels tall would yield a content row that's 400 pixels tall. This requires that you know ahead of time how tall the grid container will be, which won't always be the case.

You might think we could just say 100% and have it fill out the space, but that doesn't work, as Figure 13-10 illustrates: the content row track will be as tall as the grid container itself, thus pushing the footer row track out of the container altogether:

```
#grid {display: grid;
     grid-template-columns:
         [start col-a] 200px [col-b] 50% [col-c] 100px [stop end last];
     grid-template-rows:
         [start masthead] 3em [content] 100% [footer] 2em [stop end];
     }
```

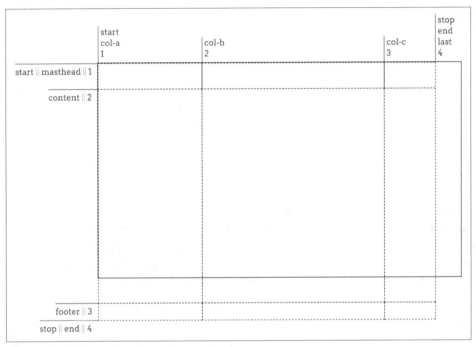

Figure 13-10. Exceeding the grid container

One way (not necessarily the best way) to handle this scenario is to *minmax* the row's value, telling the browser that you want the row no shorter than one amount and no taller than another, leaving the browser to fill in the exact value. This is done with the minmax(a,b) pattern, where a is the minimum size and b is the maximum size:

```
#grid {display: grid;
     grid-template-columns:
         [start col-a] 200px [col-b] 50% [col-c] 100px [stop end last];
     grid-template-rows:
         [start masthead] 3em [content] minmax(3em,100%) [footer] 2em [stop end];
     }
```

What we've said there is to make the content row never shorter than 3 ems tall, and never taller than the grid container itself. This allows the browser to bring up the size until it's tall enough to fit the space left over from the masthead and footer tracks, and no more. It also allows the browser to make it shorter than that, as long as it's not shorter than 3em, so this is not a guaranteed result. Figure 13-11 shows one possible outcome of this approach.

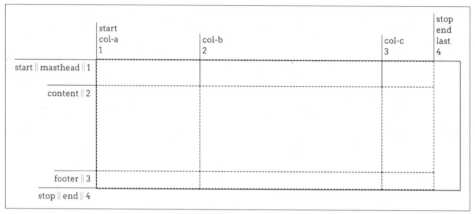

Figure 13-11. Adapting to the grid container

In like fashion, with the same caveats, minmax() could have been used to help the col-b column fill out the space across the grid container. The thing to remember with minmax() is that if the *max* is smaller than the *min*, then the *max* value is thrown out and the *min* value is used as a fixed-width track length. Thus, minmax(100px, 2em) would resolve to 100px for any font-size value smaller than 50px.

If the vagueness of minmax()'s behavior unsettles you, there are alternatives to this scenario. We could also have used the calc() value pattern to come up with a track's height (or width). For example:

```
grid-template-rows:
    [start masthead] 3em [content] calc(100%-5em) [footer] 2em [stop end];
```

That would yield a content row exactly as tall as the grid container minus the sum of the masthead and footer heights, as we saw in the previous figure.

That works as far as it goes, but is a somewhat fragile solution, since any changes to the masthead or footer heights will also require an adjustment of the calculation. It also becomes a lot more difficult (or impossible) if you want more than one column to flex in this fashion. As it happens, there are much more robust ways to deal with this sort of situation, as we'll soon see.

Flexible Grid Tracks

Thus far, all our grid tracks have been *inflexible*—their size determined by a length measure or the grid container's dimensions, but unaffected by any other considerations. *Flexible* grid tracks, by contrast, can be based on the amount of space in the grid container not consumed by inflexible tracks, or alternatively, can be based on the actual content of the entire track.

Fractional units

If you want to divide up whatever space is available by some fraction and distribute the fractions to various columns, the `fr` unit is here for you.

In the simplest case, you can divide up the whole container by equal fractions. For example, if you want four columns, you could say:

```
grid-template-columns: 1fr 1fr 1fr 1fr;
```

In this very limited case, that's equivalent to saying:

```
grid-template-columns: 25% 25% 25% 25%;
```

The result either way is shown in Figure 13-12.

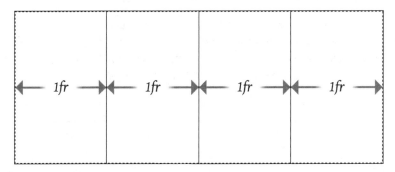

Figure 13-12. Dividing the container into four columns

Now suppose we want to add a fifth column, and redistribute the column size so they're all still equal. With percentages, we'd have to rewrite the entire value to be five instances of 20%. With `fr`, though, we can just add another 1fr to the value and have everything done for us automatically:

```
grid-template-columns: 1fr 1fr 1fr 1fr 1fr;
```

The way `fr` units work is that all of the `fr` values are added together, with the available space divided by that total. Then each track gets the number of those fractions indicated by its number.

What that meant for the first of the previous examples is that when there were four `fr` values, their numbers were added together to get a total of four. The available space was thus divided by four, and each column got one of those fourths. When we added a fifth 1fr, the space was divided by five, and each column got one of those fifths.

You are not required to always use 1 with your `fr` units! Suppose you want to divide up a space such that there are three columns, with the middle column twice as wide as the other two. That would look like this:

```
grid-template-columns: 1fr 2fr 1fr;
```

Again, these are added up and then 1 is divided by that total, so the base `fr` in this case is `0.25`. The first and third tracks are thus 25% the width of the container, whereas the middle column is half the container's width, because it's `2fr`, which is twice `0.25`, or `0.5`.

You aren't limited to integers, either. A recipe card for apple pie could be laid out using these columns:

```
grid-template-columns: 1fr 3.14159fr 1fr;
```

I'll leave the math on that one as an exercise for the reader. (Lucky you! Just remember to start with 1 + 3.14159 + 1, and you'll have a good head start.)

This is a convenient way to slice up a container, but there's more here than just replacing percentages with something more intuitive. Fractional units really come into their own when there are some fixed columns and some flexible space. Consider, for example, the following, which is illustrated in Figure 13-13:

```
grid-template-columns: 15em 1fr 10%;
```

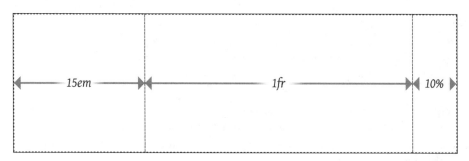

Figure 13-13. Giving the center column whatever's available

What happened there is the browser assigned the first and third tracks to their inflexible widths, and then gave whatever was left in the grid container to the center track. This means that for a 1,000-pixel-wide grid container whose `font-size` is the usual browser default of `16px`, the first column will be 240 pixels wide and the third will be 100 pixels wide. That totals 340 pixels, leaving 660 pixels that weren't assigned to the fixed tracks. The fractional units total one, so 660 is divided by one, yielding 660 pixels, all of which are given to the single `1fr` track. If the grid container's width is increased to 1,400 pixels, the third column will be 140 pixels wide and the center column 1,020 pixels wide.

Just like that, we have a mixture of fixed and flexible columns. We can keep this going, splitting up any flexible space into as many fractions as we like. Consider this:

```
width: 100em; grid-template-columns: 15em 4.5fr 3fr 10%;
```

In this case, the columns will be sized as shown in Figure 13-14.

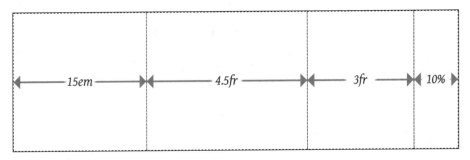

Figure 13-14. Flexible column sizing

The widths of the columns will be, from left to right: 15em, 45em, 30em, and 10em. The first column gets its fixed width of 15em. The last column is 10% of 100 em, which is 10 em. That leaves 75 em to distribute among the flexible columns. The two added together total 7.5 fr. For the wider column, 4.5 ÷ 7.5 equals 0.6, and that times 75 em equals 45 em. Similarly, 3 ÷ 7.5 = 0.4, and that times 75 em equals 30 em.

Yes, admittedly, I put a thumb on the scales for that example: the fr total and width value were engineered to yield nice, round numbers for the various columns. This was done purely to aid understanding. If you want to work through the process with less tidy numbers, consider using 92.5em or 1234px for the width value in the previous example.

In cases where you want to define a minimum or maximum size for a given track, minxmax() can be quite useful. To extend the previous example, suppose the third column should never be less than 5em wide, no matter what. The CSS would then be:

```
grid-template-columns: 15em 4.5fr minmax(5em,3fr) 10%;
```

Now the layout will have two flexible columns at its middle, down to the point that the third column reaches 5em wide. Below that point, the layout will have three inflexible columns (15em, 5em, and 10% wide, respectively) and a single flexible column that will get all the leftover space, if there is any. Once you run the math, it turns out that up to 30.5556em wide, the grid will have one flexible column. Above that width, there will be two such columns.

You might think that this works the other way—for example, if you wanted to make a column track flexible up to a certain point, and then become fixed after, you would declare a minimum fr value. This won't work, sadly, because fr units are not allowed in the *min* position of a minmax() expression. So any fr value provided as a minimum will invalidate the declaration.

Speaking of setting to zero, let's look at a situation where the minimum value is explicitly set to 0, like this:

```
grid-template-columns: 15em 1fr minmax(0,500px) 10%;
```

Figure 13-15 illustrates the narrowest grid width at which the third column can remain 500 pixels wide. Any narrower, and the minmaxed column will be narrower than 500 pixels. Any wider, and the second column, the fr column, will grow beyond zero width while the third column stays at 500 pixels wide.

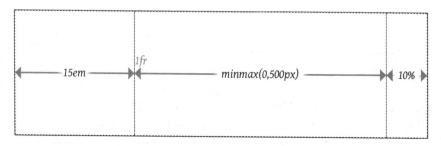

Figure 13-15. Minmaxed column sizing

If you look closely, you'll see the 1fr label next to the boundary between the 15em and minmax(0,500px) columns. That's there because the 1fr is placed with its left edge on the second column grid line, and has no width, because there is no space left to flex. Similarly, the minmax is placed on the third column grid line. It's just that, in this specific situation, the second and third column grid lines are in the same place (which is why the 1fr column has zero width).

If you ever run into a case where the minimum value is greater than the maximum value, then the whole thing is replaced with the minimum value. Thus, minmax(500px,200px) would be treated as a simple 500px. You probably wouldn't do this so obviously, but this feature is useful when mixing things like percentages and fractions. Thus, you could have a column that's minmax(10%,1fr) that would be flexible down to the point where the flexible column was less than 10% of the grid container's width, at which point it would stick at 10%.

Fractional units and minmaxes are usable on rows just as easily as columns; it's just that rows are rarely sized in this way. You could easily imagine setting up a layout where the masthead and footer are fixed tracks, while the content is flexible down to a certain point. That might look something like this:

```
grid-template-rows: 3em minmax(5em,1fr) 2em;
```

That works OK, but it's a lot more likely that you'll want to size that row by the height of its content, not some fraction of the grid container's height. The next section shows exactly how to make that happen.

Content-aware tracks

It's one thing to set up grid tracks that take up fractions of the space available to them, or that occupy fixed amounts of space. But what if you want to line up a bunch of pieces of a page and you can't guarantee how wide or tall they might get? This is where min-content and max-content come in.

What these keywords mean is simple to state, but not necessarily simple to describe in full. max-content means, in effect, "take up the maximum amount of space needed for this content." For large blocks of text (like a blog post), this would generally mean taking as much room as is available, to maximize the space for that content. It can also mean "as wide as necessary to avoid any line-wrapping," which can be very wide, given normal paragraphs of text.

min-content, by contrast, means "take up the bare minimum space needed for this content." With text, that means squeezing the width down to the point that the longest word (or widest inline element, if there are things like images or form inputs) sits on a line by itself. That would lead to a lot of line breaks in a very skinny, very tall grid element.

What's so powerful about these sizing keywords is that they apply to the entire grid track they define. For example, if you size a column to be max-content, then the entire column track will be as wide as the widest content within it. This is easiest to illustrate with a grid of images (12 in this case) with the grid declared as follows and shown in Figure 13-16:

```
#gallery {display: grid;
    grid-template-columns: max-content max-content max-content max-content;
    grid-template-rows: max-content max-content max-content;}
```

Looking at the columns, we can see that each column track is as wide as the widest image within that track. Where a bunch of portrait images happened to line up, the column is more narrow; where a landscape image showed up, the column was made wide enough to fit it. The same thing happened with the rows. Each row is as tall as the tallest image within it, so wherever a row happened to have all short images, the row is also short.

The advantage here is that this works for any sort of content, no matter what's in there. So let's say we add captions to the photos. All of the columns and rows will resize themselves as needed to handle both text and images, as shown in Figure 13-17.

This isn't a full-fledged design—the images are out of place, and there's no attempt to constrain the caption widths. In fact, that's exactly what we should expect from max-content values for the column widths. Since it means "make this column wide enough to hold all its content," that's what we got.

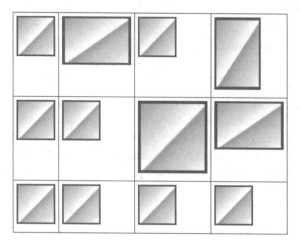

Figure 13-16. Sizing grid tracks by content

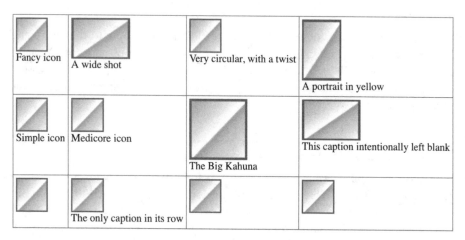

Figure 13-17. Sizing grid tracks around mixed content

What's important to realize is that this will hold even if the grid tracks have to spill out of the grid container. That means that even if we'd assigned something like width: 250px to the grid container, the images and captions would be laid out just the same. That's why things like max-content tend to appear in minmax() statements. Consider the following, where grids with and without `minmax()` appear side by side. In both cases, the grid container is represented by an orange background (see Figure 13-18):

```
#g1 {display: grid;
    grid-template-columns: max-content max-content max-content max-content;
    }
#g2 {display: grid;
    grid-template-columns: minmax(0,max-content) minmax(0,max-content)
        minmax(0,max-content) minmax(0,max-content);
    }
```

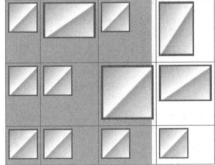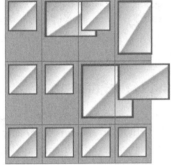

Figure 13-18. Sizing grid tracks with and without minmax()

In the first instance, the grid items completely contain their contents, but they spill out of the grid container. In the second, the `minmax()` directs the browser to keep the columns within the range of 0 and `max-content`, so they'll all be fitted into the grid container if possible. A variant on this would be to declare `minmax(min-content, max-content)`, which can lead to a slightly different result than the 0, `max-content` approach.

The reason that some images are overflowing their cells in the second example is that the tracks have been fitted into the grid container according to `minmax(0,max-content)`. They can't reach `max-content` in every track, but they can get as close as possible while all still fitting into the grid container. Where the contents are wider than the track, they just stick out of it, overlapping other tracks. This is standard grid behavior.

If you're wondering what happens if you `min-content` both the columns and the rows, it's pretty much the same as applying `min-content` to the columns and leaving the rows alone. This happens because the grid specification directs browsers to resolve column sizing first, and row sizing after that.

There's one more keyword you can use with grid track sizing, which is `auto`. As a minimum, it's treated as the minimum size for the grid item, as defined by `min-width` or min-height. As a maximum, it's treated the same as max-content. You might think this means it can be used only in minmax() statements, but this is not the case. You can use it anywhere, and it will take on either a minimum or maximum role. Which one it takes on depends on the other track values around it, in ways that are frankly too complicated to get into here. As with so many other aspects of CSS, using auto is essentially letting the browser do what it wants. Sometimes that's fine, but in general you'll probably want to avoid it.

 There is a caveat to that last statement: auto values allow grid items to be resized by the align-content and justify-content proper-ties, a topic we'll discuss in a later section, "Aligning and Grids" on page 721. Since auto values are the only track-sizing values that permit this, there may be very good reasons to use auto after all.

Fitting Track Contents

In addition to the min-content and max-content keywords, there's a fit-content() function that allows you to more compactly express certain types of sizing patterns. It's a bit complicated to decipher, but the effort is worth it:

fit-content() accepts a *<length>* or a *<percentage>* as its argument, like this:

```
#grid  {display: grid; grid-template-columns: 1fr fit-content(150px) 2fr;}
#grid2 {display: grid; grid-template-columns: 2fr fit-content(50%) 1fr;}
```

Before we explore what that means, let's ponder the pseudo-formula given by the specification:

```
fit-content(argument) => min(max-content, max(min-content, argument))
```

which means, essentially, "figure out which is greater, the min-content sizing or the supplied argument, and then take that result and choose whichever is smaller, that result or the max-content size." Which is probably confusing! It certainly was to me, the first 17 times I worked through it.

I feel like a better way of phrasing it is: "fit-content(argument) is equivalent to minmax(min-content,max-content), except that the value given as an argument sets an upper limit, similar to max-width or max-height." Let's consider this example:

```
#example {display: grid; grid-template-columns: fit-content(50ch);}
```

The argument here is 50ch, or about 50 characters wide. So we're setting up a single column that's having its content fit to that measure.

For the initial case, assume the content is only 29 characters long, measuring 29ch (due to it being in a monospace font). That means the value of max-content is 29ch, and the column will be only that wide, because it minimizes to that measure—`29ch` is smaller than whatever the maximum of `50ch` and `min-content` turns out to be.

Now, let's assume a bunch of text content is added so that there are 256 characters measuring `256ch` in width. That means `max-content` evaluates to `256ch`. This is well beyond the `50ch` argument, so the column is constrained to be the larger of `min-content` and `50ch`, which is `50ch`.

As further illustration, consider the results of the following, as shown in Figure 13-19:

```
#thefollowing {
    display: grid;
    grid-template-columns:
        fit-content(50ch) fit-content(50ch) fit-content(50ch);
    font-family: monospace;}
```

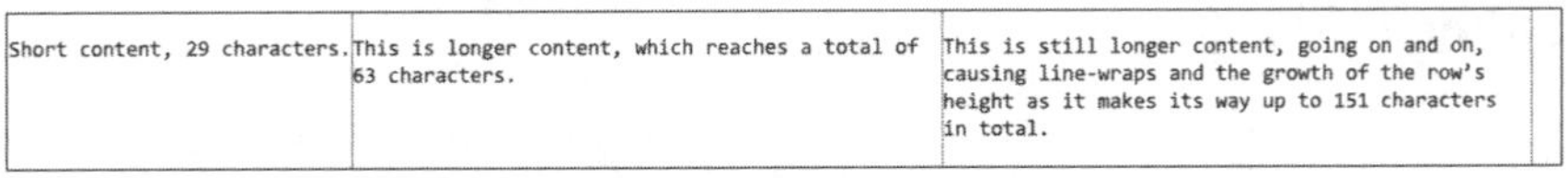

Short content, 29 characters.
This is longer content, which reaches a total of 63 characters.
This is still longer content, going on and on, causing line-wraps and the growth of the row's height as it makes its way up to 151 characters in total.

Figure 13-19. Sizing grid tracks with fit-content()

Notice the first column is narrower than the other two. Its `29ch` content minimizes to that size. The other two columns have more content than will fit into `50ch`, so they line-wrap, because their width has been limited to `50ch`.

Now let's consider what happens if an image is added to the second column. We'll make it 500px wide, which is wider than `50ch` in this instance. For that column, the maximum of `min-content` and `50ch` is determined. As we said, the larger value there is `min-content`, which is to say `500px` (the width of the image). Then the *minimum* of `500px` and `max-content` is determined. The text, rendered as a single line, would go on past `500px`, so the minimum is `500px`. Thus, the second column is now 500 pixels wide. This is depicted in Figure 13-20.

Short content, 29 characters.
This is longer content, which reaches a total of 63 characters.
This is still longer content, going on and on, causing line-wraps and the growth of the row's height as it makes its way up to 151 characters in total.

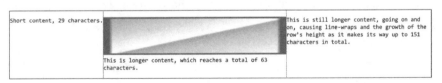

Figure 13-20. Fitting to wide content

If you compare Figure 13-19 to Figure 13-20, you'll see that the text in the second column wraps at a different point, due to the change in column width. But also compare the text in the the third column. It, too, has different line-wraps.

That happened because after the first and second columns were sized, the third column had a bit less than 50ch of space in which to be sized. fit-content(50ch) still did its thing, but here, it did so within the space available to it. Remember, the 50ch argument is an upper bound, not a fixed size.

This is one of the great advantages of fit-content() over the less flexible minmax(). It allows you to shrink tracks down to their minimum content-size when there isn't much content, while still setting an upper bound on the track size when there's a lot of content.

You've probably been wondering about the repetitive grid template values in previous examples, and what happens if you need more than three or four grid tracks. Will you have to write out every single track width individually? Indeed not, as we'll see in the next section.

Repeating Grid Lines

If you have a situation where you want to set up a bunch of grid tracks of the same size, you probably don't want to have to type out every single one of them. Fortunately, repeat() is here to make sure you don't have to.

Let's say we want to set up a column grid line every 5 ems, and have 10 column tracks. Here's how to do that:

```
#grid {display: grid;
    grid-template-columns: repeat(10, 5em);}
```

That's it. Done. Ten column tracks, each one 5em wide, for a total of 50 ems of column tracks. It sure beats typing 5em 10 times!

Any track-sizing value can be used in a repeat, from min-content and max-content to fr values to auto, and so on, and you can put together more than one sizing value. Suppose we want to define a column structure such that there's a 2em track, then a 1fr track, and then another 1fr track—and, furthermore, we want to repeat that pattern three times. Here's how to do that, with the result shown in Figure 13-21:

```
#grid {display: grid;
    grid-template-columns: repeat(3, 2em 1fr 1fr);}
```

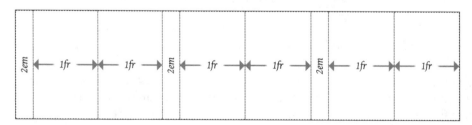

Figure 13-21. Repeating a track pattern

Notice how the last column track is a 1fr track, whereas the first column track is 2em wide. This is an effect of the way the repeat() was written. It's easy to add another 2em track at the end, in order to balance things out, just by making this change:

```
#grid {display: grid;
    grid-template-columns: repeat(3, 2em 1fr 1fr) 2em;}
```

See that extra 2em at the end of the value? That adds one more column track after the three repeated patterns. This highlights the fact that repeat can be combined with any other track-sizing values—even other repeats—in the construction of a grid. The one thing you *can't* do is nest a repeat inside another repeat.

Other than that, just about anything goes within a repeat() value. Here's an example taken straight from the grid specification:

```
#grid {
    display: grid;
    grid-template-columns: repeat(4, 10px [col-start] 250px [col-end]) 10px;}
```

In this case, there are four repetitions of a 10-pixel track, a named grid line, a 250-pixel track, and then another named grid line. Then, after the four repetitions, a final 10-pixel column track. Yes, that means there will be four column grid lines named col-start, and another four named col-end, as shown in Figure 13-22. This is acceptable; grid-line names are not required to be unique.

col-end 3		col-end 5	col-end 8
1			
col-start 2	col-start 4	col-start 7	9

Figure 13-22. Repeated columns with named grid lines

One thing to remember, if you're going to repeat named lines, is that if you place two named lines next to each other, they'll be merged into a single, double-named grid line. In other words, the following two declarations are equivalent:

```
grid-template-rows: repeat(3, [top] 5em [bottom]);
grid-template-rows: [top] 5em [bottom top] 5em [top bottom] 5em [bottom];
```

 If you're concerned about having the same name applied to multiple grid lines, don't be: there's nothing preventing it, and it can even be helpful in some cases. We'll explore ways to handle such situations in an upcoming section, "Using Column and Row Lines" on page 687.

Auto-filling tracks

There's even a way to set up a simple pattern and repeat it until the grid container is filled. This doesn't have quite the same complexity as regular `repeat()`—at least not yet—but it can still be pretty handy.

For example, suppose we want to have the previous row pattern repeat as many times as the grid container will comfortably accept:

```
grid-template-rows: repeat(auto-fill, [top] 5em [bottom]);
```

That will define a row line every 5 ems until there's no more room. Thus, for a grid container that's 11 ems tall, the following is equivalent:

```
grid-template-rows: [top] 5em [bottom top] 5em [bottom];
```

If the grid container's height is increased past 15 ems, but is less than 20 ems, then this is an equivalent declaration:

```
grid-template-rows: [top] 5em [bottom top] 5em [top bottom] 5em [bottom];
```

See Figure 13-23 for examples of the auto-filled rows at three different grid container heights.

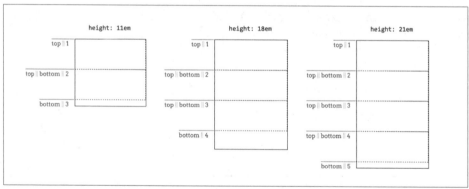

Figure 13-23. Auto-filling rows at three different heights

The limitation with auto-repeating is that it can take only an optional grid-line name, a fixed track size, and another optional grid-line name. So [`top`] `5em` [`bottom`] represents about the maximum value pattern. You can drop the named lines and just repeat `5em`, or just drop one of the names. It's not possible to repeat multiple fixed track sizes, nor can you repeat flexible track sizes. (Which makes sense: how many times would a browser repeat `1fr` to fill out a grid container? Once.)

You might wish you could auto-repeat multiple track sizes in order to define "gutters" around your content columns. This is usually unnecessary because grids have a concept of (and properties to define) track gutters, which we'll cover in an upcoming section, "Opening Grid Spaces" on page 714.

Furthermore, you can have only one auto-repeat in a given track template. Thus, the following would *not* be permissible:

```
grid-template-columns: repeat(auto-fill, 4em) repeat(auto-fill, 100px);
```

However, you *can* combine fixed-repeat tracks with auto-fill tracks. For example, you could start with three wide columns, and then fill the rest of the grid container with narrow tracks (assuming there's space for them). That would look something like this:

```
grid-template-columns: repeat(3, 20em) repeat(auto-fill, 2em);
```

You can flip that around, too:

```
grid-template-columns: repeat(auto-fill, 2em) repeat(3, 20em);
```

That works because the grid layout algorithm assigns space to the fixed tracks first, and then fills up whatever space is left with auto-repeated tracks. The end result of that example is to have one or more auto-filled 2-em tracks, and then three 20-em tracks. Two examples of this are shown in Figure 13-24.

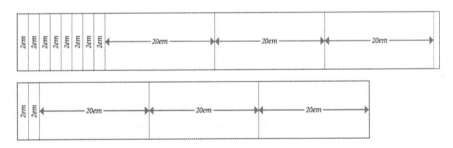

Figure 13-24. Auto-filling columns next to fixed columns

With `auto-fill`, you will always get at least one repetition of the track template, even if it won't fit into the grid container for some reason. You'll also get as many tracks as will fit, even if some of the tracks don't have content in them. As an example, suppose you set up an auto-fill that placed five columns, but only the first three of them actually ended up with grid items in them. The other two would remain in place, holding open layout space.

If you use `auto-fit`, on the other hand, then tracks that don't contain any grid items will be dropped. Otherwise, `auto-fit` acts the same as `auto-fill`. Suppose the following:

```
grid-template-columns: repeat(auto-fit, 20em);
```

If there's room for five column tracks in the grid container (i.e., it's more than 100 ems wide), but two tracks don't have any grid items to go into them, those empty grid tracks will be dropped, leaving the three column tracks that *do* contain grid items. The leftover space is handled in accordance with the values of align-content and justify-content (discussed in the upcoming section, "Aligning and Grids" on page 721). A simple comparison of auto-fill and auto-fit is shown in Figure 13-25, where the numbers in the colored boxes indicate the grid-column number to which they've been attached.

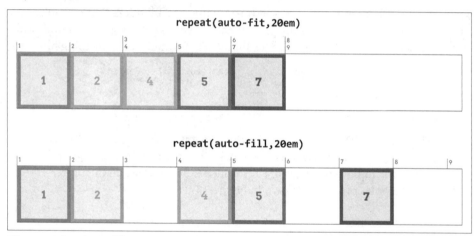

Figure 13-25. Auto-fill versus auto-fit

Grid Areas

Sometimes, you'd rather just draw a picture of your grid—both because it's fun to do, and because the picture can serve as self-documenting code. It turns out you can more or less do exactly that with the grid-template-areas property.

grid-template-areas

Values	none | *<string>*
Initial value	none
Applies to	Grid containers
Computed value	As declared
Inherited	No
Animatable	No

We could go through a wordy description of how this works, but it's a lot more fun to just show it. The following rule has the result shown in Figure 13-26:

```
#grid {display: grid;
    grid-template-areas:
        "h h h h"
        "l c c r"
        "l f f f";}
```

Figure 13-26. A simple set of grid areas

That's right: the letters in the string values are used to define how areas of the grid are shaped. Really! And you aren't even restricted to single letters! For example, we could expand the previous example like so:

```
#grid {display: grid;
    grid-template-areas:
        "header    header    header    header"
        "leftside  content   content   rightside"
        "leftside  footer    footer    footer";}
```

The grid layout is the same as that shown in Figure 13-26, though the name of each area would be different (e.g., footer instead of f).

In defining template areas, the whitespace is collapsed, so you can use it (as I did in the previous example) to visually line up columns of names in the value of grid-template-areas. You can line them up with spaces or tabs, whichever will annoy your coworkers the most. Or you can just use a single space to separate each identifier, and not worry about the names lining up with each other. You don't even have to line break between strings; the following works just as well as a pretty-printed version:

```
grid-template-areas: "h h h h" "l c c r" "l f f f";
```

What you can't do is merge those separate strings into a single string and have it mean the same thing. Every new string (as delimited by the double quote marks) defines a new row in the grid. So the previous example, like the examples before it, defines three rows. If we merged them all into a single string, like so:

```
grid-template-areas:
    "h h h h
     l c c r
     l f f f";
```

then we'd have a single row of 12 columns, starting with the 4-column area h and ending with the 3-column area f. The line breaks aren't significant in any way, except as whitespace that separates one identifier from another.

If you look at these values closely, you may come to realize that each individual identifier represents a grid cell. Let's bring back our first example from this section, and consider the result shown in Figure 13-27:

```
#grid {display: grid;
    grid-template-areas:
        "h h h h"
        "l c c r"
        "l f f f";}
```

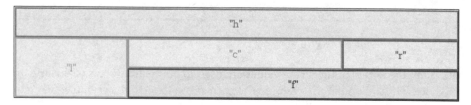

Figure 13-27. Grid cells with identifiers

This is exactly the same layout result, but here, we've shown how each grid identifier in the `grid-template-areas` value corresponds to a grid cell. Once all the cells are identified, the browser merges any adjacent cells with the same name into a single area that encloses all of them—as long as they describe a rectangular shape! If you try to set up more complicated areas, the entire template is invalid. Thus, the following would result in no grid areas being defined:

```
#grid {display: grid;
    grid-template-areas:
        "h h h h"
        "l c c r"
        "l l f f";}
```

See how l outlines an "L" shape? That humble change causes the entire `grid-template-areas` value to be dropped as invalid. A future version of grid layout may allow for nonrectangular shapes, but for now, this is what we have.

If you have a situation where you want to only define some grid cells to be part of grid areas, but leave others unlabeled, you can use one or more . characters to fill in for those unnamed cells. Let's say you just want to define some header, footer, and sidebar areas, and leave the rest unnamed. That would look something like this, with the result shown in Figure 13-28:

```
#grid {display: grid;
    grid-template-areas:
        "header  header  header  header"
        "left    ...     ...     right"
        "footer  footer  footer  footer";}
```

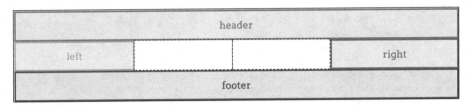

Figure 13-28. A grid with some unnamed grid cells

The two grid cells in the center of the grid are not part of a named area, having been represented in the template by *null cell tokens* (the . identifiers). Where each of those ... sequences appears, we could have used one or more null tokens—so left . . right or left .... right would work just as well.

You can be as simple or creative with your cell names as you like. If you want to call your header ronaldo and your footer podiatrist, go for it. You can even use any Unicode character above codepoint U+0080, so ConHugeCo®™ and åwësømë are completely valid area identifiers…as are emoji!

Now, to size the grid tracks created by these areas, we bring in our old friends grid-template-columns and grid-template-rows. Let's add both to the previous example, with the result shown in Figure 13-29:

```
#grid {display: grid;
    grid-template-areas:
        "header  header  header  header"
        "left    ...     ...     right"
        "footer  footer  footer  footer";
    grid-template-columns: 1fr 20em 20em 1fr;
    grid-template-rows: 40px 10em 3em;}
```

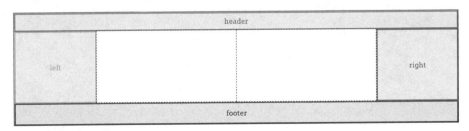

Figure 13-29. Named areas and sized tracks

Thus, the columns and rows created by naming the grid areas are given track sizes. If we give more track sizes than there are area tracks, that will add more tracks past the named areas. Therefore, the following CSS will lead to the result shown in Figure 13-30:

```
#grid {display: grid;
    grid-template-areas:
        "header  header  header  header"
        "left    ...     ...     right"
        "footer  footer  footer  footer";
    grid-template-columns: 1fr 20em 20em 1fr 1fr;
    grid-template-rows: 40px 10em 3em 20px;}
```

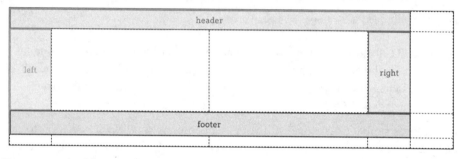

Figure 13-30. Adding more tracks beyond the named areas

So, given that we're naming areas, how about mixing in some named grid lines? As it happens, we already have: naming a grid area automatically adds names to the grid lines at its start and end. For the `header` area, there's an implicit `header-start` name on its first column-grid line *and* its first row-grid line, and `header-end` for its second column- and row-grid lines. For the `footer` area, the `footer-start` and `footer-end` names were automatically assigned to its grid lines.

Grid lines extend throughout the whole grid area, so a lot of these names are coincident. Figure 13-31 shows the naming of the lines created by the following template:

```
grid-template-areas:
    "header   header   header   header"
    "left     ...      ...      right"
    "footer   footer   footer   footer";
```

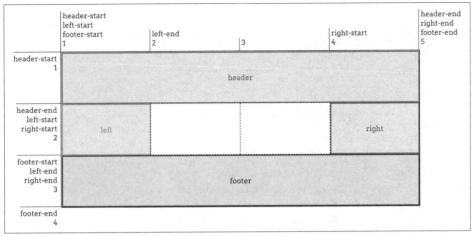

Figure 13-31. Implicit grid-line names made explicit

Now let's mix it up even more by adding a couple of explicit grid-line names to our CSS. Given the following rules, the first column-grid line in the grid would add the name begin, and the second row-grid line in the grid would add the name content:

```
#grid {display: grid;
    grid-template-areas:
        "header  header  header  header"
        "left    ...     ...     right"
        "footer  footer  footer  footer";
    grid-template-columns: [begin] 1fr 20em 20em 1fr 1fr;
    grid-template-rows: 40px [content] 1fr 3em 20px;}
```

Again: those grid-line names are *added* to the implicit grid-line names created by the named areas. Interestingly enough, grid-line names never replace other grid-line names. Instead, they just keep piling up.

Even more interesting, this implicit-name mechanism runs in reverse. Suppose you don't use grid-template-areas at all, but instead set up some named grid lines like so, as illustrated in Figure 13-32:

```
grid-template-columns:
    [header-start footer-start] 1fr
    [content-start] 1fr [content-end] 1fr
    [header-end footer-end];
grid-template-rows:
    [header-start] 3em
    [header-end content-start] 1fr
    [content-end footer-start] 3em
    [footer-end];
```

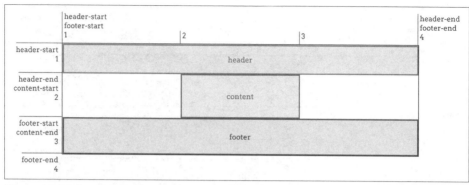

Figure 13-32. Implicit grid-area names made explicit

Because the grid lines use the form of `name-start/name-end`, the grid areas they define are implicitly named. To be frank, it's clumsier than doing it the other way, but the capability is there in case you ever want it.

Bear in mind that you don't need all four grid lines to be named in order to create a named grid area, though you probably do need them all to create a named grid area where you want it to be. Consider the following example:

```
grid-template-columns: 1fr [content-start] 1fr [content-end] 1fr;
grid-template-rows: 3em 1fr 3em;
```

This will still create a grid area named `content`. It's just that the named area will be placed into a new row after all the defined rows. What's odd is that an extra, empty row will appear after the defined rows but before the row containing `content`. This has been confirmed to be the intended behavior. Thus, if you try to create a named area by naming the grid lines and miss one or more of them, then your named area will effectively hang off to one side of the grid instead of being a part of the overall grid structure.

So, again, you should probably stick to explicitly naming grid areas and let the `start-` and `end-` grid-line names be created implicitly, as opposed to the other way around.

Attaching Elements to the Grid

Believe it or not, we've gotten this far without talking about how grid items are actually attached to a grid, once it's been defined.

Using Column and Row Lines

There are a couple of ways to go about this, depending on whether you want to refer to grid lines or grid areas. We'll start with four simple properties that attach an element to grid lines.

---

grid-row-start, grid-row-end, grid-column-start, grid-column-end

Values	auto | *<custom-ident>* | [*<integer>* && *<custom-ident>?*] | [span && [*<integer>* || *<custom-ident>*]]
Initial value	auto
Applies to	Grid items and absolutely positioned elements, if their containing block is a grid container
Computed value	As declared
Inherited	No
Animatable	No

What these properties do is let you say, "I want the edge of the element to be attached to grid line such-and-so." As with so much of grid layout, it's a lot easier to show than to describe, so ponder the following styles and their result (see Figure 13-33):

```
.grid {display: grid; width: 50em;
    grid-template-rows: repeat(5, 5em);
    grid-template-columns: repeat(10, 5em);}
.one {
    grid-row-start: 2; grid-row-end: 4;
    grid-column-start: 2; grid-column-end: 4;}
.two {
    grid-row-start: 1; grid-row-end: 3;
    grid-column-start: 5; grid-column-end: 10;}
.three {
    grid-row-start: 4;
    grid-column-start: 6;}
```

Here, we're using grid-line numbers to say where and how the elements should be placed within the grid. Column numbers count from left to right, and row numbers from top to bottom. Note that if you omit ending grid lines, as was the case for .three, then the next grid lines in sequence are used for the end lines.

Thus, the rule for .three in the previous example is exactly equivalent to the following:

```
.three {
    grid-row-start: 4; grid-row-end: 5;
    grid-column-start: 6; grid-column-end: 7;}
```

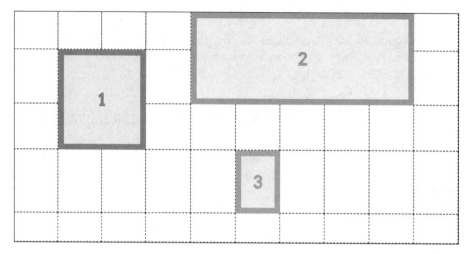

Figure 13-33. Attaching elements to grid lines

There's another way to say that same thing, as it happens: you could replace the ending values with span 1, or even just plain span, like this:

```
.three {
    grid-row-start: 4; grid-row-end: span 1;
    grid-column-start: 6; grid-column-end: span;}
```

If you supply span with a number, you're saying, "span across this many grid tracks." So we can rewrite our earlier example like this, and get exactly the same result:

```
#grid {display: grid;
    grid-template-rows: repeat(5, 5em);
    grid-template-columns: repeat(10, 5em);}
.one {
    grid-row-start: 2; grid-row-end: span 2;
    grid-column-start: 2; grid-column-end: span 2;}
.two {
    grid-row-start: 1; grid-row-end: span 2;
    grid-column-start: 5; grid-column-end: span 5;}
.three {
    grid-row-start: 4; grid-row-end: span 1;
    grid-column-start: 6; grid-column-end: span;}
```

If you leave out a number for span, it's set to be 1. You can't use zero or negative numbers for span; only positive integers.

An interesting feature of span is that you can use it for both ending *and* starting grid lines. The precise behavior of span is that it counts grid lines in the direction "away" from the grid line where it starts. In other words, if you define a start grid line and set the ending grid line to be a span value, it will search toward the end of the grid.

Conversely, if you define an ending grid line and make the start line a `span` value, then it will search toward the start of the grid.

That means the following rules will have the result shown in Figure 13-34:

```
#grid {display: grid;
    grid-rows: repeat(4, 2em); grid-columns: repeat(5, 5em);}
.box01 {grid-row-start: 1; grid-column-start: 3; grid-column-end: span 2;}
.box02 {grid-row-start: 2; grid-column-start: span 2; grid-column-end: 3;}
.box03 {grid-row-start: 3; grid-column-start: 1; grid-column-end: span 5;}
.box04 {grid-row-start: 4; grid-column-start: span 1; grid-column-end: 5;}
```

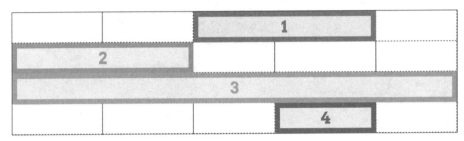

Figure 13-34. Spanning grid lines

In contrast to `span` numbering, you aren't restricted to positive integers for your actual grid-line values. Negative numbers will count backward from the end of explicitly defined grid lines. Thus, to place an element into the bottom-right grid cell of a defined grid, regardless of how many columns or rows it might have, you can just say this:

```
grid-column-start: -1;
grid-row-start: -1;
```

Note that this doesn't apply to any implicit grid tracks, a concept we'll get to in a bit, but only to the grid lines you explicitly define via one of the `grid-template-*` properties (e.g., `grid-template-rows`).

We aren't restricted to grid-line numbers, as it happens. If there are named grid lines, we can refer to those instead of (or in conjunction with) numbers. If you have multiple instances of a grid-line name, then you can use numbers to identify which instance of the grid-line name you're talking about. Thus, to start from the fourth instance of a row grid named `mast-slice`, you can say `mast-slice 4`. Take a look at the following, illustrated in Figure 13-35, for an idea of how this works:

```
#grid {display: grid;
    grid-template-rows: repeat(5, [R] 4em);
    grid-template-columns: 2em repeat(5, [col-A] 5em [col-B] 5em) 2em;}
.one {
    grid-row-start: R 2; grid-row-end: 5;
    grid-column-start: col-B; grid-column-end: span 2;}
```

```
.two {
    grid-row-start: R; grid-row-end: span R 2;
    grid-column-start: col-A 3; grid-column-end: span 2 col-A;}
.three {
    grid-row-start: 9;
    grid-column-start: col-A -2;}
```

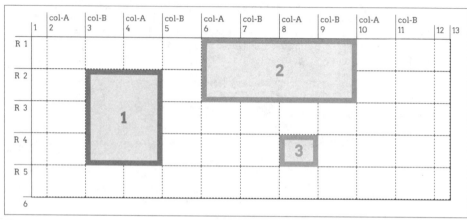

Figure 13-35. Attaching elements to named grid lines

Notice how span changes when we add a name: where we said span 2 col-A, that caused the grid item to span from its starting point (the third col-A) across another col-A and end at the col-A after that. This means the grid item actually spans four column tracks, since col-A appears on every other column grid line.

Again, negative numbers count backward from the end of a sequence, so col-A -2 gets us the second-from-last instance of a grid line named col-A. Because there are no end-line values declared for .three, they're both set to span 1. That means the following is exactly equivalent to the .three in the previous example:

```
.three {
    grid-row-start: 9; grid-row-end: span 1;
    grid-column-start: col-A -2; grid-row-end: span 1;}
```

There's an alternative way to use names with named grid lines—specifically, the named grid lines that are implicitly created by grid areas. For example, consider the following styles, illustrated in Figure 13-36:

```
grid-template-areas:
    "header     header     header     header"
    "leftside   content    content    rightside"
    "leftside   footer     footer     footer";
#masthead {grid-row-start: header;
        grid-column-start: header; grid-row-end: header;}
#sidebar {grid-row-start: 2; grid-row-end: 4;
        grid-column-start: leftside / span 1;}
```

```
#main {grid-row-start: content; grid-row-end: content;
       grid-column-start: content;}
#navbar {grid-row-start: rightside; grd-row-end: 3;
       grid-column-start: rightside;}
#footer {grid-row-start: 3; grid-row-end: span 1;
       grid-column-start: footer; grid-row-end: footer;}
```

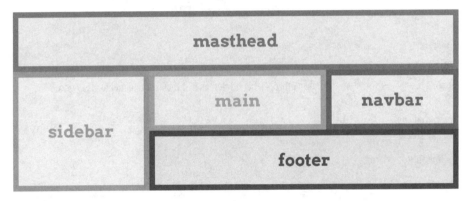

Figure 13-36. Another way of attaching elements to named grid lines

What happens if you supply a custom identifier (i.e., a name you defined) is that the browser looks for a grid line with that name *plus* either -start or -end added on, depending on whether you're assigning a start line or an end line. Thus, the following are equivalent:

```
grid-column-start: header; grid-column-end: header;
grid-column-start: header-start; grid-column-end: header-end;
```

This works because, as was mentioned with grid-template-areas, explicitly creating a grid area implicitly creates the named -start and -end grid lines that surround it.

The final value possibility, auto, is kind of interesting. According to the Grid Layout specification, if one of the grid-line start/end properties is set to auto, that indicates "auto-placement, an automatic span, or a default span of one." In practice, what this tends to mean is that the grid line that gets picked is governed by the *grid flow*, a concept we have yet to cover (but will soon!). For a start line, auto usually means that the next available column or row line will be used. For an end line, auto usually means a one-cell span. In both cases, the word "usually" is used intentionally: as with any automatic mechanism, there are no absolutes.

Row and Column Shorthands

There are two shorthand properties that allow you to more compactly attach an element to grid lines.

---

grid-row, grid-column

Values	*<grid-line>* [/ *<grid-line>*]?
Initial value	`auto`
Applies to	Grid items and absolutely positioned elements, if their containing block is a grid container
Computed value	As declared
Inherited	No
Animatable	No

The primary benefit of these properties is that they make it a lot simpler to declare the start and end grid lines to be used for laying out a grid item. For example:

```
#grid {display: grid;
    grid-template-rows: repeat(10, [R] 1.5em);
    grid-template-columns: 2em repeat(5, [col-A] 5em [col-B] 5em) 2em;}
.one {
    grid-row: R 3 / 7;
    grid-column: col-B / span 2;}
.two {
    grid-row: R / span R 2;
    grid-column: col-A 3 / span 2 col-A;}
.three {
    grid-row: 9;
    grid-column: col-A -2;}
```

That's a whole lot easier to read than having each start and end value in its own property, honestly. Other than being more compact, the behavior of these properties is more or less what you'd expect. If you have two bits separated by a solidus, the first part defines the starting grid line, and the second part defines the ending grid line.

If you have only one value with no solidus, it defines the starting grid line. The ending grid line depends on what you said for the starting line. If you supply a name for the starting grid line, then the ending grid line is given that same name. Thus, the following are equivalent:

```
grid-column: col-B;
grid-column: col-B / col-B;
```

That will span from one instance of that grid-line name to the next, regardless of how many grid cells are spanned.

If a single number is given, then the second number (the end line) is set to auto. That means the following pairs are equivalent:

```
grid-row: 2;
grid-row: 2 / auto;

grid-column: header;
grid-column: header / header;
```

There's a subtle behavior built into the handling of grid-line names in grid-row and grid-column that pertains to implicitly named grid lines. If you recall, defining a named grid area creates -start and -end grid lines. That is, given a grid area with a name of footer, there are implicitly created footer-start grid lines to its top and left, and footer-end grid lines to its bottom and right.

In that case, if you refer to those grid lines by the area's name, the element will still be placed properly. Thus, the following styles have the result shown in Figure 13-37:

```
#grid {display: grid;
    grid-template-areas:
        "header header"
        "sidebar content"
        "footer footer";
    grid-template-rows: auto 1fr auto;
    grid-template-columns: 25% 75%;}
#header {grid-row: header / header; grid-column: header;}
#footer {grid-row: footer; grid-column: footer-start / footer-end;}
```

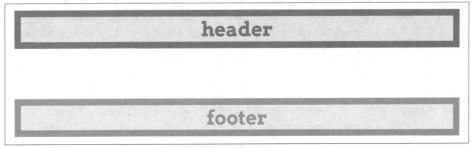

Figure 13-37. Attaching to implicit grid lines via grid-area names

You can always explicitly refer to the implicitly named grid lines, but if you just refer to the grid area's name, things still work out. If you refer to a grid-line name that doesn't correspond to a grid area, then it falls back to the behavior discussed previously. In detail, it's the same as saying line-name 1, so the following two are equivalent:

```
grid-column: jane / doe;
grid-column: jane 1 / doe 1;
```

This is why it's risky to name grid lines the same as grid areas. Consider the following:

```
grid-template-areas:
    "header header"
    "sidebar content"
    "footer footer"
    "legal legal";
grid-template-rows: auto 1fr [footer] auto [footer];
grid-template-columns: 25% 75%;
```

This explicitly sets grid lines named footer above the "footer" row and below the "legal" row...and now there's trouble ahead. Suppose we add this:

```
#footer {grid-column: footer; grid-row: footer;}
```

For the column lines, there's no problem. footer gets expanded to footer / footer. The browser looks for a grid area with that name and finds it, so it translates footer / footer to footer-start / footer-end. The #footer element is attached to those implicit grid lines.

For grid-row, everything starts out the same. footer becomes footer / footer, which is translated to footer-start / footer-end. But that means the #footer will only be as tall as the "footer" row. It will *not* stretch to the second explicitly named footer grid line below the "legal" row, because the translation of footer to footer-end (due to the match between the grid-line name and the grid-area name) takes precedence.

The upshot of all this: it's generally a bad idea to use the same name for grid areas and grid lines. You might be able to get away with it in some scenarios, but you're almost always better off keeping your line and area names distinct, so as to avoid tripping over name-resolution conflicts.

The Implicit Grid

Up to this point, we've concerned ourselves solely with explicitly defined grids: we've talked about the row and column tracks we define via properties like grid-template-columns, and how to attach grid items to the cells in those tracks.

But what happens if we try to place a grid item, or even just part of a grid item, beyond that explicitly created grid? For example, consider the following grid:

```
#grid {display: grid;
    grid-template-rows: 2em 2em;
    grid-template-columns: repeat(6, 4em);}
```

Two rows, six columns. Simple enough. But suppose we define a grid item to sit in the first column and go from the first grid line to the fourth:

```
.box01 {grid-column: 1; grid-row: 1 / 4;}
```

Now what? There are only two rows bounded by three grid lines, and we've told the browser to go beyond that, from row line 1 to row line 4.

What happens is that another row line is created to handle the situation. This grid line, and the new row track it creates, are both part of the *implicit grid*. Here are a few examples of grid items that create implicit grid lines (and tracks) and how they're laid out (see Figure 13-38):

```
.box01 {grid-column: 1; grid-row: 1 / 4;}
.box02 {grid-column: 2; grid-row: 3 / span 2;}
.box03 {grid-column: 3; grid-row: span 2 / 3;}
.box04 {grid-column: 4; grid-row: span 2 / 5;}
.box05 {grid-column: 5; grid-row: span 4 / 5;}
.box06 {grid-column: 6; grid-row: -1 / span 3;}
.box07 {grid-column: 7; grid-row: span 3 / -1;}
```

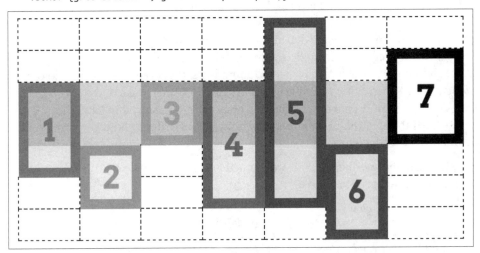

Figure 13-38. Creating implicit grid lines and tracks

There's a lot going on there, so let's break it down. First off, the explicit grid is represented by the light-gray box behind the various numbered boxes; all the dashed lines represent the implicit grid.

So, what about those numbered boxes? box1 adds an extra grid line after the end of the explicit grid, as we discussed before. box2 starts on the last line of the explicit grid, and spans forward two lines, so it adds yet another implicit grid line. box3 ends on the last explicit grid line (line 3) and spans *back* two lines, thus starting on the first explicit grid line.

box4 is where things really get interesting. It ends on the fifth row line, which is to say the second implicit grid line. It spans back three lines—and yet, it still starts on the same grid line as box3. This happens because spans have to start counting within the explicit grid. Once they start, they can continue on into the implicit grid (as happened with box2), but they *cannot* start counting within the implicit grid.

Thus, box4 ends on row-line 5, but its span starts with grid-line 3 and counts back two lines (span 2) to arrive at line 1. Similarly, box5 ends on line 5, and spans back four lines, which means it starts on row-line –2. Remember: span counting must *start* in the explicit grid. It doesn't have to end there.

After those, box6 starts on the last explicit row line (line 3), and spans out to the sixth row line—adding yet another implicit row line. The point of having it here is to show that negative grid-line references are with respect to the explicit grid, and count back from its end. They do *not* refer to negatively indexed implicit lines that are placed before the start of the explicit grid.

If you want to start an element on an implicit grid line before the explicit grid's start, then the way to do that is shown by box7: put its end line somewhere in the explicit grid, and span back past the beginning of the explicit grid. And you may have noticed: box7 occupies an implicit column track. The original grid was set up to create six columns, which means seven column lines, the seventh being the end of the explicit grid. When box7 was given grid-column: 7, that was equivalent to grid-column: 7 / span 1 (since a missing end line is always assumed to be span 1). That necessitated the creation of an implicit column line in order to hold the grid item in the implicit seventh column.

Now let's take those principles and add named grid lines to the mix. Consider the following, illustrated in Figure 13-39:

```
#grid {display: grid;
    grid-template-rows: [begin] 2em [middle] 2em [end];
    grid-template-columns: repeat(5, 5em);}
.box01 {grid-column: 1; grid-row: 2 / span end 2;}
.box02 {grid-column: 2; grid-row: 2 / span final;}
.box03 {grid-column: 3; grid-row: 1 / span 3 middle;}
.box04 {grid-column: 4; grid-row: span begin 2 / end;}
.box05 {grid-column: 5; grid-row: span 2 middle / begin;}
```

What you can see at work there, in several of the examples, is what happens with grid-line names in the implicit grid: every implicitly created line has the name that's being hunted. Take box2, for example. It's given an end line of final, but there is no line with that name. Thus the span-search goes to the end of the explicit grid and, having not found the name it's looking for, creates a new grid line, to which it attaches the name final. (In Figure 13-39, the implicitly-created line names are italicized and faded out a bit.)

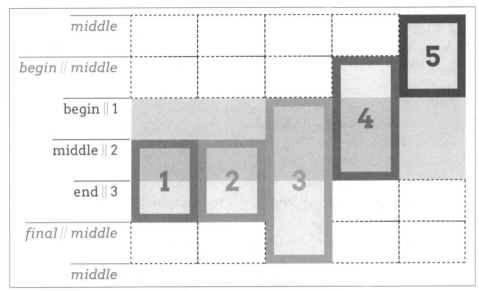

Figure 13-39. Named implicit grid lines and tracks

Similarly, box3 starts on the first explicit row line, and then needs to span three middle named lines. It searches forward and finds one, then goes looking for the other two. Not finding any, it attaches the name middle to the first implicit grid line, and then does the same for the second implicit grid line. Thus, it ends two implicit grid lines past the end of the explicit grid.

The same sort of thing happens with box4 and box5, except working backward from endpoints. box4 ends with the end line (line 3), then spans back to the second begin line it can find. This causes an implicit line to be created before the first line, named begin. box 5 spans back from begin (the explicitly labeled begin) to the second middle it can find. Since it can't find any, it labels two implcit lines middle and ends at the one furthest from where it started looking.

When you get right down to it, the implicit grid is a delightfully baroque fallback mechanism. It's generally best practice to stick to the explicit grid, and to make sure the explicit grid covers everything you want to do. If you find you need another row, don't just run off the edge of the grid—adjust your grid template's values instead!

Error Handling

There are a few cases that need to be covered, as they fall under the general umbrella of "what grids do when things go pear-shaped."

First, what if you accidentally put the start line after the end line? Say, something like this:

```
grid-row-start: 5;
grid-row-end: 2;
```

All that happens is probably what was meant in the first place: the values are swapped. Thus, you end up with this:

```
grid-row-start: 2;
grid-row-end: 5;
```

Second, what if both the start and the end lines are declared to be spans of some variety? For example:

```
grid-column-start: span;
grid-column-end: span 3;
```

If this happens, the end value is dropped and replaced with auto. That means you'd end up with this:

```
grid-column-start: span;  /* 'span' is equal to 'span 1' */
grid-column-end: auto;
```

That would cause the grid item to have its ending edge placed automatically, according to the current grid flow (a subject we'll soon explore), and the starting edge to be placed one grid line earlier.

Third, what if the only thing directing placement of the grid item is a named span? In other words:

```
grid-row-start: span footer;
grid-row-end: auto;
```

This is not permitted, so the span footer in this case is replaced with span 1.

Using Areas

Attaching by row lines and column lines is great, but what if you could refer to a grid area with a single property? Behold: grid-area.

<table>
<tr><td colspan="2" align="center">grid-area</td></tr>
<tr><td>Values</td><td><grid-line> [/ <grid-line>]{0,3}</td></tr>
<tr><td>Initial value</td><td>See individual properties</td></tr>
<tr><td>Applies to</td><td>Grid items and absolutely positioned elements, if their containing block is a grid container</td></tr>
<tr><td>Computed value</td><td>As declared</td></tr>
<tr><td>Inherited</td><td>No</td></tr>
<tr><td>Animatable</td><td>No</td></tr>
</table>

Let's start with the easier use of grid-area: assigning an element to a previously defined grid area. Makes sense, right? Let's bring back our old friend grid-template-areas, put it together with grid-area and some markup, and see what magic results (as shown in Figure 13-40):

```
#grid {display: grid;
    grid-template-areas:
        "header     header   header    header"
        "leftside   content  content   rightside"
        "leftside   footer   footer    footer";}
#masthead {grid-area: header;}
#sidebar {grid-area: leftside;}
#main {grid-area: content;}
#navbar {grid-area: rightside;}
#footer {grid-area: footer;}

<div id="grid">
    <div id="masthead">…</div>
    <div id="main">…</div>
    <div id="navbar">…</div>
    <div id="sidebar">…</div>
    <div id="footer">…</div>
</div>
```

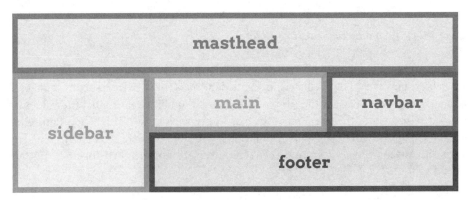

Figure 13-40. Assigning elements to grid areas

That's all it takes: set up some named grid areas to define your layout, and then drop grid items into them with grid-area. So simple, and yet so powerful.

As you might have noticed, the sizing of the column and row tracks was omitted from that CSS. This was done entirely for clarity's sake. In an actual design, the rule probably would look more like this:

```
grid-template-areas:
    "header   header  header header"
    "leftside content content rightside"
    "leftside footer  footer  footer";
```

```
    grid-template-rows: 200px 1fr 3em;
    grid-template-columns: 20em 1fr 1fr 10em;
```

There is another way to use grid-area that refers to grid lines instead of grid areas. Fair warning: it's likely to be confusing at first, for a couple of reasons.

Here's an example of a grid template that defines some grid lines, and some grid-area rules that reference the lines, as illustrated in Figure 13-41:

```
#grid {display: grid;
    grid-template-rows:
        [r1-start] 1fr [r1-end r2-start] 2fr [r2-end];
    grid-template-columns:
        [col-start] 1fr [col-end main-start] 1fr [main-end];}
.box01 {grid-area: r1 / main / r1 / main;}
.box02 {grid-area: r2-start / col-start / r2-end / main-end;}
.box03 {grid-area: 1 / 1 / 2 / 2;}
```

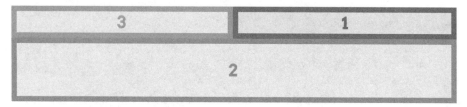

Figure 13-41. Assigning elements to grid lines

As you can see, the elements were placed as directed. Note the ordering of the grid-line values, however. They're listed in the order row-start, column-start, row-end, column-end. If you diagram that in your head, you'll quickly realize that the values go anticlockwise around the grid item—the exact opposite of the TRBL (Top, Right, Bottom, Left) pattern we're used to from margins, padding, borders, and so on. Furthermore, this means the column and row references are not grouped together, but are instead split up.

Yes, this is intentional. No, I don't know why.

If you supply fewer than four values, the missing values are taken from those you do supply. If there are only three values, then the missing grid-column-end is the same as grid-column-start if it's a name; if the start line is a number, the end line is set to auto. The same holds true if you give only two values, except that the now-missing grid-row-end is copied from grid-row-start if it's a name; otherwise, it's set to auto.

From that, you can probably guess what happens if only one value is supplied: if it's a name, use it for all four values; if it's a number, the rest are set to auto.

This one-to-four replication pattern is actually how giving a single grid-area name translates into having the grid item fill that area. The following are equivalent:

```
grid-area: footer;
grid-area: footer / footer / footer / footer;
```

Now recall the behavior discussed in the previous section about grid-column and grid-row: if a grid line's name matches the name of a grid area, then it's translated into a -start or -end variant, as appropriate. That means the previous example is translated to the following:

```
grid-area: footer-start / footer-start / footer-end / footer-end;
```

And that's how a single grid-area name causes an element to be placed into the corresponding grid area.

Grid Item Overlap

One thing we've been very careful to do in our grid layouts thus far is to avoid overlap. Rather like positioning, it's absolutely (get it?) possible to make grid items overlap each other. Let's take a simple case, illustrated in Figure 13-42:

```
#grid {display: grid;
    grid-template-rows: 50% 50%;
    grid-template-columns: 50% 50%;}
.box01 {grid-area: 1 / 1 / 2 / 3;}
.box02 {grid-area: 1 / 2 / 3 / 2;}
```

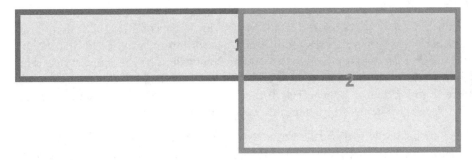

Figure 13-42. Overlapping grid items

Thanks to the grid numbers that were supplied, the two grid items overlap in the upper-right grid cell. Which is on top of the other depends on the layering behavior discussed later, but for now, just take it as given that they do layer when overlapping.

Overlap isn't restricted to situations involving raw grid numbers. In the following case, the sidebar and the footer will overlap, as shown in Figure 13-43. (Assuming the footer comes later than the sidebar in the markup, then in the absence of other styles, the footer will be on top of the sidebar.)

```
#grid {display: grid;
    grid-template-areas:
        "header header"
        "sidebar content"
        "footer footer";}
#header {grid-area: header;}
#sidebar {grid-area: sidebar / sidebar / footer-end / sidebar;}
#footer {grid-area: footer;}
```

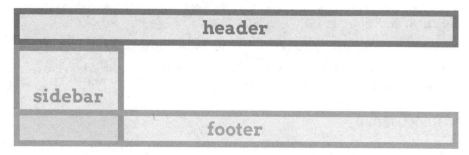

Figure 13-43. Overlapping sidebar and footer

I bring this up in part to warn you about the possibility of overlap, and also to serve as a transition to the next topic. It's a feature that sets grid layout apart from positioning, in that it can sometimes help avoid overlap: the concept of *grid flow*.

Grid Flow

For the most part, we've been explicitly placing grid items on the grid. If items aren't explicitly placed, then they're automatically placed into the grid. Following the grid flow in effect, an item is placed in the first area that will fit it. The simplest case is just filling a grid track in sequence, one grid item after another, but things can get a lot more complex than that, expecially if there is a mixture of explicitly and automatically placed grid items—the latter must work around the former.

There are primarily two grid-flow models, *row-first* and *column-first*, though you can enhance either by specifying a *dense* flow. All this is done with the property grid-auto-flow.

grid-auto-flow

Values	[row | column] || dense
Initial value	row
Applies to	Grid containers
Computed value	As declared
Inherited	No
Animatable	No

To see how these values work, consider the following markup:

```
<ol id="grid">
<li>1</li>
<li>2</li>
<li>3</li>
<li>4</li>
<li>5</li>
</ol>
```

To that markup, let's apply the following styles:

```
#grid {display: grid; width: 45em; height: 8em;
    grid-auto-flow: row;}
#grid li {grid-row: auto; grid-column: auto;}
```

Assuming a grid with a column line every 15 ems and a row line every 4 ems, we get the result shown in Figure 13-44.

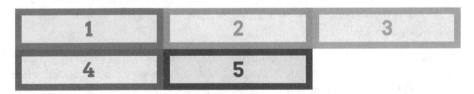

Figure 13-44. Row-oriented grid flow

This probably seems pretty normal, the same sort of thing you'd get if you floated all the boxes, or if all of them were inline blocks. That's why row is the default value. Now, let's try switching the grid-auto-flow value to column, as shown in Figure 13-45:

```
#grid {display: grid; width: 45em; height: 8em;
    grid-auto-flow: column;}
#grid li {grid-row: auto; grid-column: auto;}
```

So with `grid-auto-flow: row`, each row is filled in before starting on the next row. With `grid-auto-flow: column`, each column is filled first.

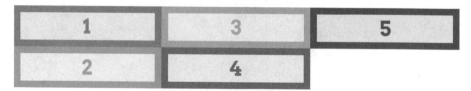

Figure 13-45. Column-oriented grid flow

What needs to be stressed here is that the list items weren't explicitly sized. By default, they were resized to attach to the defined grid lines. This can be overridden by assigning explicit sizing to the elements. For example, if we make the list items be 7 ems wide and 1.5 ems tall, we'll get the result shown in Figure 13-46:

```
#grid {display: grid; width: 45em; height: 8em;
    grid-auto-flow: column;}
#grid li {grid-row: auto; grid-column: auto;
    width: 7em; height: 1.5em;}
```

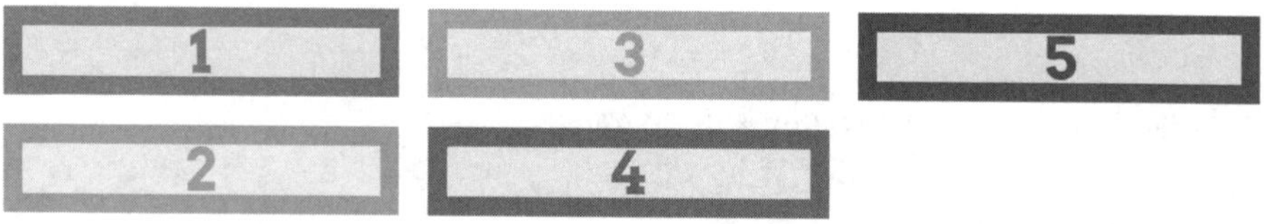

Figure 13-46. Explicitly sized grid items

If you compare that to the previous figure, you'll see that the corresponding grid items start in the same place in each figure; they just don't end in the same places. This illustrates that what's really placed in grid flow is grid areas, to which the grid items are then attached.

This is important to keep in mind if you auto-flow elements that are wider than their assigned column or taller than their assigned row, as can very easily happen when turning images or other intrinsically sized elements into grid items. Let's say we want to put a bunch of images, each a different size, into a grid that's set up to have a column line every 50 horizontal pixels, and a row line every 50 vertical pixels. This grid is illustrated in Figure 13-47, along with the results of flowing a series of images into that grid by either row or column:

```
#grid {display: grid;
    grid-template-rows: repeat(3, 50px);
    grid-template-columns: repeat(4, 50px);
    grid-auto-rows: 50px;
    grid-auto-columns: 50px;
```

```
}
img {grid-row: auto; grid-column: auto;}
```

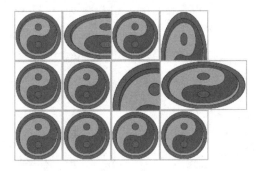

Figure 13-47. Flowing images in grids

Notice how some of the images overlap others? That's because each image is attached to the next grid line in the flow, without taking into account the presence of other grid items. We didn't set up images to span more than one grid track when they needed it, so overlap occurred.

This can be managed with class names or other identifiers. We could class images as tall or wide (or both) and specify that they get more grid tracks. Here's some CSS to add to the previous example, with the result shown in Figure 13-48:

```
img.wide {grid-column: auto / span 2;}
img.tall {grid-row: auto / span 2;}
```

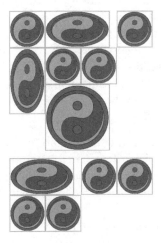

Figure 13-48. Giving images more track space

This does cause the images to keep spilling down the page, but there's no overlapping.

However, notice how there are gaps in that last grid? That happened because the placement of some grid items across grid lines didn't leave enough room for other items in the flow. In order to illustrate this, and the two flow patterns, more clearly, let's try an example with numbered boxes (Figure 13-49).

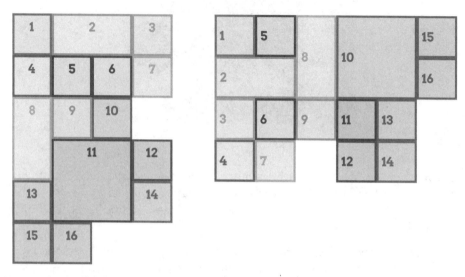

Figure 13-49. Illustrating flow patterns

Follow across the rows of the first grid, counting along with the numbers. In this particular flow, the grid items are laid out almost as if they were leftward floats. Almost, but not quite: notice that grid item 13 is actually to the left of grid item 11. That would never happen with floats, but it can with grid flow. The way row flow (if we may call it that) works is that you go across each row from left to right, and if there's room for a grid item, you put it there. If a grid cell has been occupied by another grid item, you skip over it. So the cell next to item 10 didn't get filled, because there wasn't room for item 11. Item 13 went to the left of item 11 because there was room for it there when the row was reached.

The same basic mechanisms hold true for column flow, except in this case you work from top to bottom. Thus, the cell below item 9 is empty because item 10 wouldn't fit there. It went into the next column and spanned four grid cells. The items after it, since they were just one grid cell in size, filled in the cells after it in column order.

Grid flow works left-to-right, top-to-bottom in languages that have that writing pattern. In right-to-left languages, such as Arabic and Hebrew, the row-oriented flow would be right-to-left, not left-to-right.

If you were just now wishing for a way to pack grid items as densely as possible, regardless of how that affected the ordering, good news: you can! Just add the keyword dense to your grid-auto-flow value, and that's exactly what will happen. We can see the result in Figure 13-50, which shows the results of grid-auto-flow: row dense and grid-auto-flow: dense column side by side.

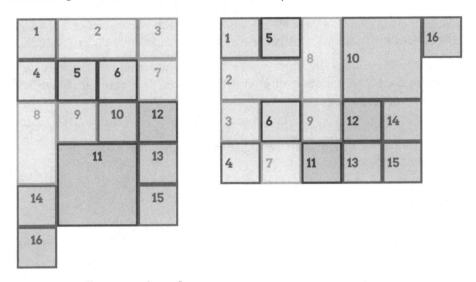

Figure 13-50. Illustrating dense flow patterns

In the first grid, item 12 appears in the row above item 11 because there was a cell that fit it. For the same reason, item 11 appears to the left of item 10 in the second grid.

In effect, what happens with dense grid flow is that for each grid item, the browser scans through the *entire* grid in the given flow direction (row or column), starting from the flow's starting point (the top-left corner, in LTR—left-to-right—languages), until it finds a place where that grid item will fit. This can make things like photo galleries more compact, and works great as long as you don't have a specific order in which the images need to appear.

Now that we've explored grid flow, I have a confession to make: in order to make the last couple of grid items look right, I included some CSS that I didn't show you. Without it, the items hanging off the edge of the grid would have looked quite a bit different than the other items—much shorter in row-oriented flow, and much narrower in column-oriented flow. We'll see why, and the CSS I used, in the next section.

Automatic Grid Lines

So far, we've almost entirely seen grid items placed into a grid that was explicitly defined. But in the last section we had situations where grid items ran off the edge of the explicitly defined grid. What happens when a grid item goes off the edge? Rows or columns are added as needed to satisfy the layout directives of the items in question (see "The Implicit Grid" on page 694). So, if an item with a row span of 3 is added after the end of a row-oriented grid, three new rows are added after the explicit grid.

By default, these automatically added rows are the absolute minimum size needed. If you want to exert a little more control over their sizing, then `grid-auto-rows` and `grid-auto-columns` are for you.

grid-auto-rows, grid-auto-columns	
Values	*<track-breadth>* | `minmax(` *<track-breadth>* `,` *<track-breadth>* `)`
Initial value	`auto`
Applies to	Grid containers
Computed value	Depends on the specific track sizing
Note	<track-breadth> is a stand-in for <length> | <percentage> | <flex> | `min-content` | `max-content` | `auto`
Inherited	No
Animatable	No

For any automatically created row or column tracks, you can provide a single track size or a minmaxed pair of track sizes. Let's take a look at a reduced version of the grid-flow example from the previous section: we'll set up a 2 × 2 grid, and try to put five items into it. In fact, let's do it twice: once with `grid-auto-rows`, and once without, as illustrated in Figure 13-51:

```
.grid {display: grid;
    grid-template-rows: 80px 80px;
    grid-template-columns: 80px 80px;}
#g1 {grid-auto-rows: 80px;}
```

As you can see, without sizing the automatically created row, the grid item is placed in a row that's exactly as tall as the grid item's content, and not a pixel more. It's still just as wide as the column into which it's placed, because that has a size (80px). The row, lacking an explicit height, defaults to `auto`, with the result shown.

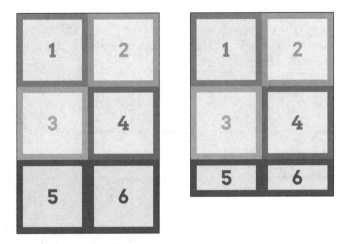

Figure 13-51. Grids with and without auto-row sizing

If we flip it around to columns, the same basic principles apply (see Figure 13-52):

```
.grid {display: grid; grid-auto-flow: column;
    grid-template-rows: 80px 80px;
    grid-template-columns: 80px 80px;}
#g1 {grid-auto-columns: 80px;}
```

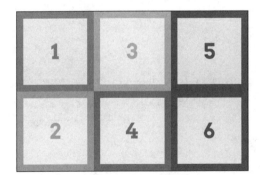

Figure 13-52. Grids with and without auto-column sizing

In this case, because the flow is column-oriented, the last grid item is placed into a new column past the end of the explicit grid. In the second grid, where there's no grid-auto-columns, that fifth item is as tall as its row (80px), but has an auto width, so it's just as wide as it needs to be and no wider. If a sixth item were added and it had wider content, then the column would be sized to fit that content, thus widening the fifth item.

So now you know what I used in the grid-auto-flow figures in the previous section: I silently made the auto-rows and auto-columns the same size as the explicitly sized columns, in order to not have the last couple of items look weird. Let's bring back one of those figures, only this time the grid-auto-rows and grid-auto-columns styles will be removed. As you can see in Figure 13-53, the last few items in each grid are shorter or narrower than the rest, due to the lack of auto-track sizing.

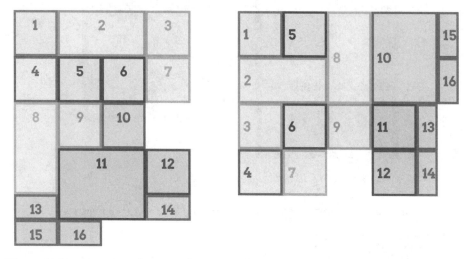

Figure 13-53. A previous figure with auto-track sizing removed

And now you know…the rest of the story.

The grid Shorthand

At long last, we've come to the shorthand property grid. It might just surprise you, though, because it's not like other shorthand properties.

grid	
Values	none | subgrid | [[*<grid-template-rows>* / *<grid-template-columns>*]] | [*<line-names>*? *<string>* *<track-size>*? *<line-names>*?]+ [/ *<track-list>*]?] | [*<grid-auto-flow>* [*<grid-auto-rows>* [/ *<grid-auto-columns>*]?]?]]
Initial value	See individual properties
Applies to	Grid containers
Computed value	See individual properties
Inherited	No
Animatable	No

The syntax is a little bit migraine-inducing, I admit, but we'll step through it a piece at a time.

Let's get to the elephant in the room right away: grid allows you to either define a grid template *or* to set the grid's flow and auto-track sizing in a compact syntax. You can't do both at the same time.

Furthermore, whichever you don't define is reset to its defaults, as is normal for a shorthand property. So if you define the grid template, then the flow and auto tracks will be returned to their default values. This includes grid gutters, a topic we haven't even covered yet. You can't set the gutters with grid, but it will reset them anyway.

Yes, this is intentional. No, I don't know why.

So let's talk about creating a grid template using grid. The values can get fiendishly complex, and take on some fascinating patterns, but can be very handy. As an example, the following rule is equivalent to the set of rules that follows it:

```
grid:
    "header header header header" 3em
    ". content sidebar ." 1fr
    "footer footer footer footer" 5em /
    2em 3fr minmax(10em,1fr) 2em;

grid-template-areas:
    "header header header header"
    ". content sidebar ."
    "footer footer footer footer";
grid-template-rows: 3em 1fr 5em;
grid-template-columns: 2em 3fr minmax(10em,1fr) 2em;
```

Notice how the value of grid-template-rows is broken up and scattered around the strings of grid-template-areas. That's how row sizing is handled in grid when you have grid-area strings present. Take those strings out, and you end up with the following:

```
grid:
    3em 1fr 5em / 2em 3fr minmax(10em,1fr) 2em;
```

In other words, the row tracks are separated by a solidus (/) from the column tracks.

Remember that with grid, undeclared shorthands are reset to their defaults. That means the following two rules are equivalent:

```
#layout {display: grid;
    grid: 3em 1fr 5em / 2em 3fr minmax(10em,1fr) 2em;}

#layout {display: grid;
    grid: 3em 1fr 5em / 2em 3fr minmax(10em,1fr) 2em;
    grid-auto-rows: auto;
```

```
    grid-auto-columns: auto;
    grid-auto-flow: row;}
```

Therefore, make sure your `grid` declaration comes before anything else related to defining the grid. That means that if we wanted a dense column flow, we'd write something like this:

```
#layout {display: grid;
    grid: 3em 1fr 5em / 2em 3fr minmax(10em,1fr) 2em;
    grid-auto-flow: dense column;}
```

Now, let's bring the named grid areas back, *and* add some extra row grid-line names to the mix. A named grid line that goes *above* a row track is written *before* the string, and a grid line that goes *below* the row track comes *after* the string and any track sizing. So let's say we want to add `main-start` and `main-stop` above and below the middle row, and `page-end` at the very bottom:

```
grid:
    "header header header header" 3em
    [main-start] ". content sidebar ." 1fr [main-stop]
    "footer footer footer footer" 5em [page-end] /
    2em 3fr minmax(10em,1fr) 2em;
```

That creates the grid shown in Figure 13-54, with the implicitly created named grid lines (e.g., `footer-start`), along with the explicitly named grid lines we wrote into the CSS.

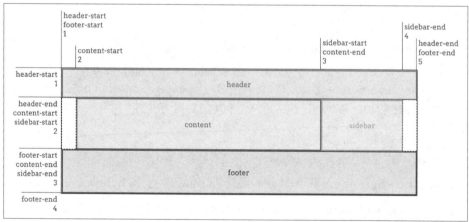

Figure 13-54. Creating a grid with the grid shorthand

You can see how `grid` can get very complicated very quickly. It's a very powerful syntax, and it's surprisingly easy to get used to once you've had just a bit of practice. On the other hand, it's also easy to get things wrong and have the entire value be invalid, thus preventing the appearance of any grid at all.

For the other use of grid, it's a merging of grid-auto-flow, grid-auto-rows, and grid-auto-columns. The following rules are equivalent:

```
#layout {grid-auto-flow: dense rows;
    grid-auto-rows: 2em;
    grid-auto-columns: minmax(1em,3em);}
```

```
#layout {grid: dense rows 2em / minmax(1em,3em);}
```

That's certainly a lot less typing for the same result! But once again, I have to remind you: if you write this, then all the column and row track properties will be set to their defaults. Thus, the following rules are equivalent:

```
#layout {grid: dense rows 2em / minmax(1em,3em);}
```

```
#layout {grid: dense rows 2em / minmax(1em,3em);
        grid-template-rows: auto;
        grid-template-columns: auto;}
```

So once again, it's important to make sure your shorthand comes before any properties it might otherwise override.

Subgrids

There's another possible value for grid, which is subgrid. It might be used something like this:

```
#grid {display: grid;
    grid: repeat(auto-fill, 2em) / repeat(10, 1% 8% 1%);}
.module {display: grid;
    grid: subgrid;}
```

What happens inside each module element is that its grid items (i.e., its child elements) use the grid defined by #grid to align themselves.

This is potentially really useful, because you can imagine having a module that spans three of its parent's column patterns and containing child elements that are aligned to and laid out using the "master" grid. This is illustrated in Figure 13-55.

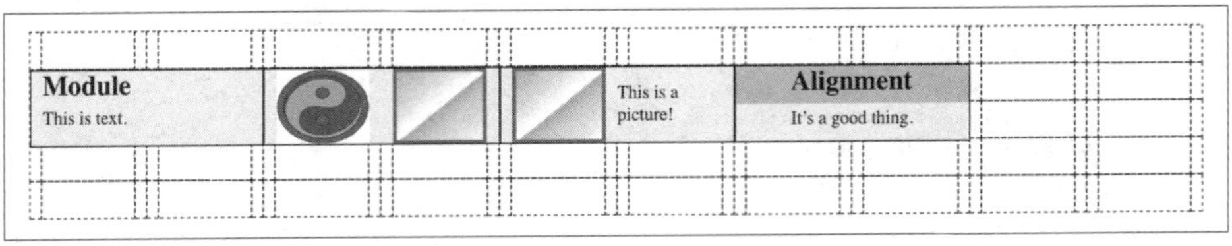

Figure 13-55. Aligning subgridded items

The problem is that, as of this writing, subgrid is an "at-risk" feature of grid layout, and may be dropped entirely. That's why it rates just this small section, instead of a more comprehensive examination.

Opening Grid Spaces

So far, we've seen a lot of grid items jammed right up against one another, with no space between them. There are a number of ways to mitigate this, as we'll talk about in this section, starting with gutters.

Grid Gutters (or Gaps)

Simply put, a *gutter* is a space between two grid tracks. It's created as if by expanding the grid line between them to have actual width. It's much like border-spacing in table styling—both because it creates space between grid cells and because you can set only a single spacing value for each axis, via the properties grid-row-gap and grid-column-gap.

---

grid-row-gap, grid-column-gap

Values	*<length>*	*<percentage>*
Initial value	0
Applies to	Grid containers
Computed value	An absolute length
Inherited	No
Animatable	Yes

Right up front: as the value syntax shows, you can supply only a length for these properties; what it's less clear about is that the lengths must be non-negative. It's not possible to supply a percentage, a fractional value via fr, nor a minmax of some sort. If you want your columns to be separated by 1 em, then it's easy enough: grid-column-gap: 1em. That's pretty much as fancy as it gets. All the columns in the grid will be pushed apart by 1 em, as illustrated in Figure 13-56:

```
#grid {display: grid;
    grid-template-rows: 5em 5em;
    grid-template-columns: 15% 1fr 1fr;
    grid-column-gap: 1em;}
```

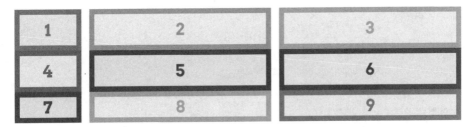

Figure 13-56. Creating column gutters

In terms of sizing the tracks in a grid, gutters are treated as if they're grid tracks. Thus, given the following styles, the fractional grid rows will each be 140 pixels tall:

```
#grid {display: grid; height: 500px;
    grid-template-rows: 100px 1fr 1fr 75px;
    grid-row-gap: 15px;}
```

We get 140 pixels for each fraction row's height because there are a total of 500 pixels of height. From that, we subtract the two row tracks (100 and 75) to get 325. From that result, we subtract the three 15-pixel gutters, which totals 45 pixels; this yields 280 pixels. That divided in half (because the fractional rows have equal fractions) gets us 140 pixels each. If the gutter value were increased to 25px, then the fractional rows would have 250 pixels to divide between them, making each 125 pixels tall.

Track sizing can be much more complicated than this; the example used all pixels because it makes the math simple. You can always mix units however you'd like, including minmaxing your actual grid tracks. This is one of the main strengths of grid layout.

 Grid gutters can be changed from their declared size by the effects of `align-content` and `justify-content`. This will be covered in the upcoming section, "Opening Grid Spaces" on page 714.

There is, as you might have already suspected, a shorthand that combines row and column gap lengths into a single property.

grid-gap

Values	*<grid-row-gap> <grid-column-gap>*
Initial value	0 0
Applies to	Grid containers
Computed value	As declared
Inherited	No
Animatable	Yes

Not a lot more to say than that, really: supply two non-negative lengths, and you'll have defined the row gutters and column gutters, in that order. Here's an example, as shown in Figure 13-57:

```
#grid {display: grid;
    grid-template-rows: 5em 5em;
    grid-template-columns: 15% 1fr 1fr;
    grid-gap: 12px 2em;}
```

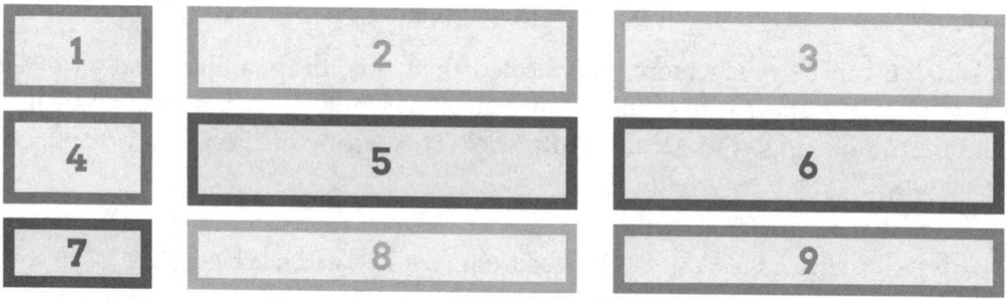

Figure 13-57. Defining grid gutters

Grid Items and the Box Model

Now we can create a grid, attach items to the grid, and even create gutters between the grid tracks. But what happens if we style the element that's attached to the grid with, say, margins? Or if it's absolutely positioned? How do these things interact with the grid?

Let's take margins first. The basic principle at work is that an element is attached to the grid by its margin edges. That means you can push the visible parts of the element inward from the grid area it occupies by setting positive margins—and pull it outward with negative margins. For example, these styles will have the result shown in Figure 13-58:

```
#grid {display: grid;
    grid-template-rows: repeat(2, 100px);
    grid-template-columns: repeat(2, 200px);}
.box02 {margin: 25px;}
.box03 {margin: -25px 0;}
```

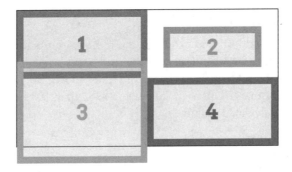

Figure 13-58. Grid items with margins

This worked as it did because the items had both their width and height set to auto, so they could be stretched as needed to make everything work out. If width and/or height have non-auto values, then they'll end up overriding margins to make all the math work out. This is much like what happens with right and left margins when element sizing is overconstrained: eventually, one of the margins gets overridden.

Consider an element with the following styles placed into a 200-pixel-wide by 100-pixel-tall grid area:

```
.exel {width: 150px; height: 100px;
    padding: 0; border: 0;
    margin: 10px;}
```

Going across the element first, it has 10 pixels of margin to either side, and its width is 150px, giving a total of 170 pixels. Something's gotta give, and in this case it's the right margin (in left-to-right languages), which is changed to 40px to make everything work—10 pixels on the left margin, 150 pixels on the content box, and 40 pixels on the right margin equals the 200 pixels of the grid area's width.

On the vertical axis, the bottom margin is reset to -10px. This compensates for the top margin and content height totalling 110 pixels, when the grid area is only 100 pixels tall.

 Margins on grid items are ignored when calculating grid-track sizes. That means that no matter how big or small you make a grid item's margins, it won't change the sizing of a min-content column, for example, nor will increasing the margins on a grid item cause fr-sized grid tracks to change size.

As with block layout, you can selectively use auto margins to decide which margin will have its value changed to fit. Suppose we wanted the grid item to align to the right of its grid area. By setting the item's left margin to auto, that would happen:

```
.exel {width: 150px; height: 100px;
    padding: 0; border: 0;
    margin: 10px; margin-left: auto;}
```

Now the element will add up 160 pixels for the right margin and content box, and then give the difference between that and the grid area's width to the left margin, since it's been explicitly set to auto. This has the result shown in Figure 13-59, where there are 10 pixels of margin on each side of the exel item, except the left margin, which is (as we just calculated) 40 pixels.

Figure 13-59. Using auto margins to align items

That might seem familiar from block-level layout, where you can use auto left and right margins to center an element in its containing block, as long as you've given it an explicit width. Where grid layout differs is that you can do the same thing on the vertical axis; that is, given an element with an absolute height, you can vertically center it by setting the top and bottom margins to auto. Figure 13-60 shows a variety of auto margin effects on images, which naturally have explicit heights and widths:

```
.i01 {margin: 10px;}
.i02 {margin: 10px; margin-left: auto;}
.i03 {margin: auto 10px auto auto;}
.i04 {margin: auto;}
.i05 {margin: auto auto 0 0;}
.i06 {margin: 0 auto;}
```

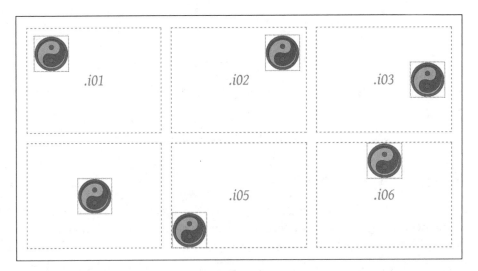

Figure 13-60. Various auto-margin alignments

 There are other ways to align grid items, notably with properties like justify-self, which don't depend on having explicit height and width values. These will be covered in the next section.

This is a lot like how margins and element sizes operate when elements are absolutely positioned. Which leads us to the next question: what if a grid item is *also* absolutely positioned? For example:

```
.exel {grid-row: 2 / 4; grid-column: 2 / 5;
    position: absolute;
    top: 1em; bottom: 15%;
    left: 35px; right: 1rem;}
```

The answer is actually pretty elegant: if you've defined grid-line starts and ends, that grid area is used as the containing block and positioning context, and the grid item is positioned *within* that context. That means the offset properties (top et al.) are calculated in relation to the declared grid area. Thus, the previous CSS would have the result shown in Figure 13-61.

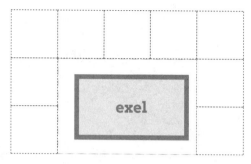

Figure 13-61. Absolutely positioning a grid item

Everything you know about absolutely positioned elements regarding offsets, margins, element sizing, and so on applies within this formatting context. It's just that in this case, the formatting context is defined by a grid area.

There is a wrinkle that absolute positioning introduces: it changes the behavior of the auto value for grid-line properties. If, for example, you set grid-column-end: auto for an absolutely positioned grid item, the ending grid line will actually create a new and special grid line that corresponds to the padding edge of the grid container itself. This is true even if the explicit grid is smaller than the grid container, as can happen.

To see this in action, we'll modify the previous example as follows, with the result shown in Figure 13-62:

```
.exel {grid-row: 1 / auto; grid-column: 2 / auto;
    position: absolute;
    top: 1em; bottom: 15%;
    left: 35px; right: 1rem;}
```

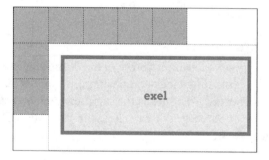

Figure 13-62. Auto values and absolute positioning

Note how the positioning context now starts at the top of the grid container, and stretches all the way to the right edge of the grid container, even though the grid itself ends well short of that edge.

One implication of this behavior is that if you absolutely position an element that's a grid item, but you don't give it any grid-line start or end values, then it will use the inner padding edge of the grid container as its positioning context. It does this without having to set the grid container to `position: relative`, or any of the other usual tricks to establish a positioning context.

Note that absolutely positioned grid items do *not* participate in figuring out grid cell and track sizing. As far as the grid layout is concerned, the positioned grid item doesn't exist. Once the grid is set up, then the grid item is positioned with respect to the grid lines that define its positioning context.

 As of late 2017, browsers did not support any of this absolute positioning behavior. The only way to recreate it was to relatively position the element establishing the grid area, and absolutely position a child element within it. That's how the absolute-positioning figures in this section were created. The special `auto` behavior was also not supported.

Aligning and Grids

If you have any familiarity with flexbox, you're probably aware of the various alignment properties and their values. Those same properties are also available in grid layout, and have very similar effects.

First, a quick refresher. The properties that are available and what they affect are summarized in Table 13-1.

Table 13-1. Justify and align values

Property	Aligns	Applied to
`justify-self`	A grid item in the inline (horizontal) direction	Grid items
`justify-items`	All grid items in the inline (horizontal) direction	Grid container
`justify-content`	The entire grid in the inline (horizontal) direction	Grid container
`align-self`	A grid item in the block (vertical) direction	Grid items
`align-items`	All grid items in the block (vertical) direction	Grid container
`align-content`	The entire grid in the block (vertical) direction	Grid container

As Table 13-1 shows, the various `justify-*` properties change alignment along the inline axis—in English, this will be the horizontal direction. The difference is whether a property applies to a single grid item, all the grid items in a grid, or the entire grid. Similarly, the `align-*` properties affect alignment along the block axis; in English, this is the vertical direction.

Aligning and Justifying Individual Items

It's easiest to start with the *-self properties, because we can have one grid show various justify-self property values, while a second grid shows the effects of those same values when used by align-self. (See Figure 13-63.)

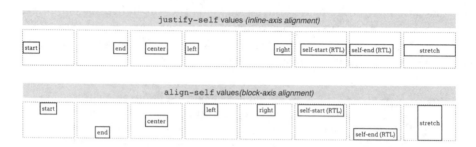

Figure 13-63. Self alignment in the inline and block directions

Each grid item in Figure 13-63 is shown with its grid area (the dashed blue line) and a label identifying the property value that's applied to it. Each deserves a bit of commentary.

First, though, realize that for all of these values, any element that doesn't have an explicit width or height will "shrink-wrap" its content, instead of using the default grid-item behavior of filling out the entire grid area.

start and end cause the grid item to be aligned to the start or end edge of its grid area, which makes sense. Similarly, center centers the grid item within its area along the alignment axis, *without* the need to declare margins or any other properties, including height and width.

left and right have the expected results for horizontal alignment, but if they're applied to elements via align-self (which is vertical alignment), they're treated as start.

self-start and self-end are more interesting. self-start aligns a grid item with the grid-area edge that corresponds to the grid *item's* start edge. So in Figure 13-63, the self-start and self-end boxes were set to direction: rtl. That set them to use right-to-left language direction, meaning their start edges were their right edges, and their end edges their left. You can see in the first grid that this right-aligned self-start and left-aligned self-end. In the second grid, however, the RTL direction is irrelevant to block-axis alignment. Thus, self-start was treated as start, and self-end was treated as end.

The last value, stretch, is interesting. To understand it, notice how the other boxes in each grid "shrink-wrap" themselves to their content. stretch, on the other hand, directs the element to stretch from edge to edge in the given direction—align-self: stretch causes the grid item to stretch vertically, and justify-self: stretch causes horizontal stretching. This is as you might expect, but bear in mind that it works only if the element's size properties are set to auto. Thus, given the following styles, the first example will stretch vertically, but the second will not:

```
.exel01 {align-self: stretch; height: auto;}
.exel02 {align-self: stretch; height: 50%;}
```

Because the second example sets a height value that isn't auto (which is the default value), it cannot be resized by stretch. The same holds true for justify-self and width.

There are two more values that can be used to align grid items, but they are sufficiently interesting to merit their own explanation. These permit the alignment of a grid item's first or last baseline with the highest or lowest baseline in the grid track. For example, suppose you wanted a grid item to be aligned so the baseline of its last line was aligned with the last baseline in the tallest grid item sharing its row track. That would look like the following:

```
.exel {align-self: last-baseline;}
```

Conversely, to align its first baseline with the lowest first baseline in the same row track, you'd say this:

```
.exel {align-self: baseline;}
```

In a situation where a grid element doesn't have a baseline, or it's asked to baseline-align itself in a direction where baselines can't be compared, then baseline is treated as start and last-baseline is treated as end.

 There are two values that were intentionally skipped in this section: flex-start and flex-end. These values are supposed to be used only in flexbox layout, and are defined to be equivalent to start and end in any other layout context, including grid layout.

Aligning and Justifying All Items

Now let's consider align-items and justify-items. These properties accept all the same values we saw in the previous section, and have the same effect, except they apply to all grid items in a given grid container, and must be applied to a grid container instead of to individual grid items.

Thus, you could set all of the grid items in a grid to be center-aligned within their grid areas as follows, with a result like that depicted in Figure 13-64:

```
#grid {display: grid;
       align-items: center; justify-items: center;}
```

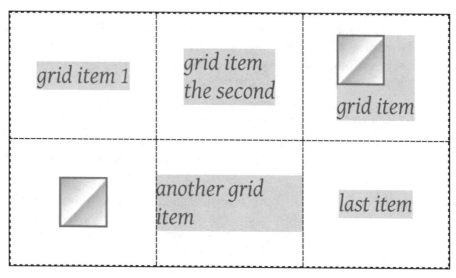

Figure 13-64. Centering all the grid items

As you can see, that horizontally *and* vertically centers every grid item within its given grid area. Furthermore, it causes any grid item without an explicit width and height to "shrink-wrap" its content rather than stretch out to fill their grid area. If a grid item has an explicit height and width, then those will be honored, and the item centered within its grid area.

Beyond aligning and justifying every grid item, it's possible to distribute the grid items, or even to justify or align the entire grid, using `align-content` and `justify-content`. There is a small set of distributive values for these properties. Figure 13-65 illustrates the effects of each value as applied to `justify-content`, with each grid sharing the following styles:

```
.grid {display: grid; padding: 0.5em; margin: 0.5em 1em; width: auto;
       grid-gap: 0.75em 0.5em; border: 1px solid;
       grid-template-rows: 4em;
       grid-template-columns: repeat(5, 6em);}
```

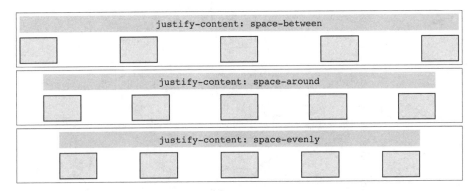

Figure 13-65. Distributing grid items horizontally

This works just as well in column tracks as it does in row tracks, as Figure 13-66 illustrates, as long as you switch to `align-content`. This time, the grids all share these styles:

```
.grid {display: grid; padding: 0.5em;
       grid-gap: 0.75em 0.5em; border: 1px solid;
       grid-template-rows: repeat(4, 3em);
       grid-template-columns: 5em;}
```

The way this distribution works is that the grid tracks, including any gutters, are all sized as usual. Then, if there is any leftover space within the grid container—that is, if the grid tracks don't reach all the way from one edge of the grid container to the other—then the remaining space is distributed according to the value of `justify-content` (in the horizontal) or `align-content` (in the vertical).

This space distribution is carried out by resizing the grid gutters. If there are no declared gutters, there will be gutters. If there are already gutters, their sizes are altered as required to distribute the grid tracks.

Note that because space is distributed only when the tracks don't fill out the grid container, the gutters can only increase in size. If the tracks are larger than the container, which can easily happen, there is no leftover space to distribute (negative space turns out to be indivisible).

There is another distribution value, very new as of this writing, which wasn't shown in the previous figures. `stretch` takes any leftover space and applies it equally to the grid tracks, not the gutters. So if there are 400 pixels of leftover space and 8 grid tracks, each grid track is increased by 50 pixels. The grid tracks are *not* increased proportionally, but equally. As of late 2017, there was no browser support for this value in terms of grid distribution.

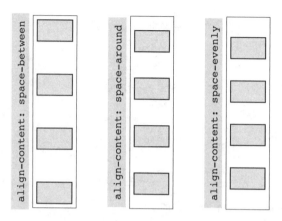

Figure 13-66. Distributing grid items vertically

We'll round out this section with examples of justifying, as opposed to distributing, grid tracks. Figure 13-67 shows the possibilities when justifying horizontally.

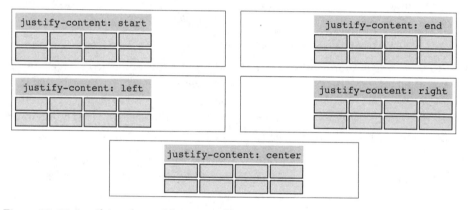

Figure 13-67. Justifying the grid horizontally

In these cases, the set of grid tracks is taken as a single unit, and justified by the value of justify-content. That alignment does not affect the alignment of individual grid items; thus, you could end-justify the whole grid with justify-content: end while having individual grid items be left-, center-, or start-justified (among other options) within their grid areas.

As you might expect by now, being able to justify-content horizontally means you can align-content vertically. Figure 13-68 shows each value in action.

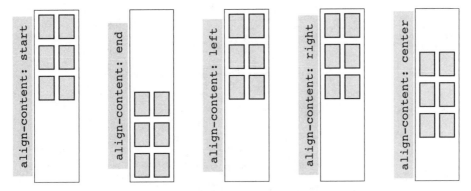

Figure 13-68. Aligning the grid vertically

left and right don't really make sense in a vertical context, so they're treated as start. The others have the effect you'd expect from their names.

Layering and Ordering

As we saw in a previous section, it's entirely possible to have grid items overlap each other, whether because negative margins are used to pull a grid item beyond the edges of its grid area, or because the grid areas of two different grid items share grid cells. By default, the grid items will visually overlap in document source order: grid items later in the document source will appear in front of grid items earlier in the document source. Thus we see the following result in what's depicted in Figure 13-69. (Assume the number in each class name represents the grid item's source order.)

```
#grid {display: grid; width: 80%; height: 20em;
    grid-rows: repeat(10, 1fr); grid-columns: repeat(10, 1fr);}
.box01 {grid-row: 1 / span 4; grid-column: 1 / span 4;}
.box02 {grid-row: 4 / span 4; grid-column: 4 / span 4;}
.box03 {grid-row: 7 / span 4; grid-column: 7 / span 4;}
.box04 {grid-row: 4 / span 7; grid-column: 3 / span 2;}
.box05 {grid-row: 2 / span 3; grid-column: 4 / span 5;}
```

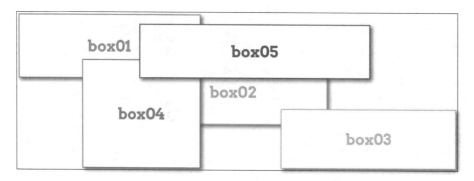

Figure 13-69. Grid items overlapping in source order

If you want to assert your own stacking order, then z-index is here to help. Just as in positioning, z-index places elements relative to each other on the z-axis, which is perpendicular to the display surface. Positive values are closer to you, and negative values further away. So to bring the second box to the "top," as it were, all you need is to give it a z-index value higher than any other (with the result shown in Figure 13-70):

```
.box02 {z-index: 10;}
```

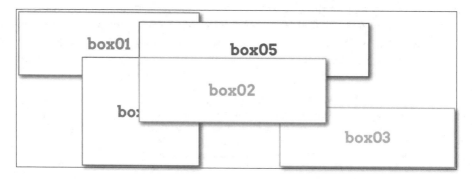

Figure 13-70. Elevating a grid item

Another way you can affect the ordering of grid items is by using the order property. Its effect is essentially the same as it is in flexbox—you can change the order of grid items within a grid track by giving them order values. This affects not only place-ment within the track, but also *paint order* if they should overlap. For example, we could change the previous example from z-index to order, as shown here, and get the same result shown in Figure 13-70:

```
.box02 {order: 10;}
```

In this case, box02 appears "on top of" the other grid items because its order places it after the rest of them. Thus, it's drawn last. Similarly, if those grid items were all placed in sequence in a grid track, the order value for box02 would put it at the end of the sequence. This is depicted in Figure 13-71.

Figure 13-71. Changing grid-item order

Remember that just because you *can* rearrange the order of grid items this way, it doesn't necessarily mean you *should*. As the Grid Layout specification (*https:// www.w3.org/TR/css-grid-1/#order-property*) says (section 4.2):

> As with reordering flex items, the order property must only be used when the visual order needs to be *out-of-sync* with the speech and navigation order; otherwise the underlying document source should be reordered instead.

So the only reason to use order to rearrange grid item layout is if you need to have the document source in one order and layout in the other. This is already easily possible by assigning grid items to areas that don't match source order.

This is not to say that order is useless and should always be shunned; there may well be times it makes sense. But unless you find yourself nearly forced into using it by specific circumstances, think very hard about whether it's the best solution.

Summary

Grid layout is complex and powerful, so don't be discouraged if you feel over-whelmed. It takes some time to get used to how grid operates, especially since so many of its features are nothing like what we've dealt with before. Much of those features' power comes directly from their novelty—but like any powerful tool, it can be difficult and frustrating to learn to use. I got frustrated and confused as I wrote about grid, going down blind alleys and falling victim to two decades of instincts that had been honed on a layout-less CSS.

I hope I was able to steer you past some of those pitfalls, but still, remember the wisdom of Master Yoda: "You must unlearn what you have learned." When coming to grid layout, there has never been greater need to put aside what you think you know about layout and learn anew. Over time, your patience and persistence will be rewarded.

CHAPTER 14

Table Layout in CSS

You may have glanced at that title and wondered, "Table layout? Isn't that exactly what we're trying to *avoid* doing?" Indeed so, but this chapter is not about using tables *for* layout. Instead, it's about the ways that tables themselves are laid out by CSS, which is a far more complicated affair than it might first appear.

Tables are unusual, compared to the rest of document layout. Until flexbox and grid came along, tables alone possessed the unique ability to associate element sizes with other elements—for example, all the cells in a row have the same height, no matter how much or how little content each individual cell might contain. The same is true for the widths of cells that share a column. Cells that adjoin can share a border, even if the two cells have very different border styles. As we'll see, these abilities are purchased at the expense of a great many behaviors and rules—many of them rooted deep in the past—that apply to tables, and only tables.

Table Formatting

Before we can start to worry about how cell borders are drawn and tables sized, we need to delve into the fundamental ways in which tables are assembled, and the ways that elements within a table are related. This is referred to as *table formatting*, and it is quite distinct from table layout: the layout is possible only after the formatting has been completed.

Visually Arranging a Table

The first thing to understand is how CSS defines the arrangement of tables. While this knowledge may seem a bit basic, it's key to understanding how best to style tables.

CSS draws a distinction between *table elements* and *internal table elements*. In CSS, internal table elements generate rectangular boxes that have content, padding, and borders, but not margins. Therefore, it is *not* possible to define the separation between table cells by giving them margins. A CSS-conformant browser will ignore any attempts to apply margins to cells, rows, or any other internal table element (with the exception of captions, which are discussed in the "Captions" on page 744).

There are six basic rules for arranging tables. The basis of these rules is a *grid cell*, which is one area between the grid lines on which a table is drawn. Consider Figure 14-1, in which two tables are shown: their grid cells are indicated by the dashed lines drawn over the tables.

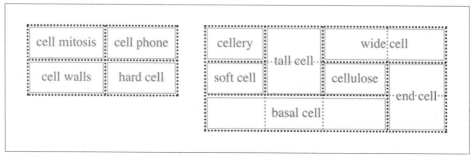

Figure 14-1. Grid cells form the basis of table layout

In a simple 2 × 2 table, such as the lefthand table shown in Figure 14-1, the grid cells correspond to the actual table cells. In a more complicated table, like the righthand table in Figure 14-1, some table cells will span multiple grid cells—but note that every table cell's edges are placed along a grid-cell edge.

These grid cells are largely theoretical constructs, and they cannot be styled or even accessed through the Document Object Model (DOM). They just serve as a way to describe how tables are assembled for styling.

Table arrangement rules

- Each *row box* encompasses a single row of grid cells. All the row boxes in a table fill the table from top to bottom in the order they occur in the source document (with the exception of any table-header or table-footer row boxes, which come at the beginning and end of the table, respectively). Thus, a table contains as many grid rows as there are row elements (e.g., tr elements).
- A *row group*'s box encompasses the same grid cells as the row boxes it contains.
- A *column box* encompasses one or more columns of grid cells. All the column boxes are placed next to one another in the order they occur. The first column

box is on the left for left-to-right languages, and on the right for right-to-left languages.

- A *column group*'s box encompasses the same grid cells as the column boxes it contains.

- Although cells may span several rows or columns, CSS does not define how this happens. It is instead left to the document language to define spanning. Each spanned cell is a rectangular box one or more grid cells wide and high. The top row of this spanning rectangle is in the row that is parent to the spanned grid cell. The cell's rectangle must be as far to the left as possible in left-to-right languages, but it may not overlap any other cell box. It must also be to the right of all cells in the same row that are earlier in the source document (in a left-to-right language). In right-to-left languages, a spanned cell must be as far to the *right* as possible without overlapping other cells, and must be to the *left* of all cells in the same row that follow it in the document source.

- A cell's box *cannot* extend beyond the last row box of a table or row group. If the table structure would cause this condition, the cell must be shortened until it fits within the table or row group that encloses it.

The CSS specification discourages, but does not prohibit, the positioning of table cells and other internal table elements. Positioning a row that contains row-spanning cells, for example, could dramatically alter the layout of the table by removing the row from the table entirely, thus removing the spanned cells from consideration in the layout of other rows. Nevertheless, it is quite possible to apply positioning to table elements in current browsers.

By definition, grid cells are rectangular, but they do not all have to be the same size. All the grid cells in a given grid column will be the same width, and all the grid cells in a grid row will be the same height, but the height of one grid row may be different than that of another grid row. Similarly, grid columns may be of different widths.

With those basic rules in mind, a question may arise: how, exactly, do you know which elements are cells and which are not?

Table Display Values

In HTML, it's easy to know which elements are parts of tables because the handling of elements like tr and td is built into browsers. In XML, on the other hand, there is no way to intrinsically know which elements might be part of a table. This is where a whole collection of values for display come into play.

display

Values	[*<display-outside>* ‖ *<display-inside>*] ∣ *<display-listitem>* ∣ *<display-internal>* ∣ *<display-box>* ∣ *<display-legacy>*
Definitions	See below
Initial value	`inline`
Applies to	All elements
Computed value	As specified
Inherited	No
Animatable	No

<display-outside>
    `block | inline | run-in`

<display-inside>
    `flow | flow-root | table | flex | grid | ruby`

<display-listitem>
    `list-item` && *<display-outside>*? && [`flow | flow-root`]?

<display-internal>
    `table-row-group | table-header-group | table-footer-group | table-row | table-cell | table-column-group | table-column | table-caption | ruby-base | ruby-text | ruby-base-container | ruby-text-container`

<display-box>
    `contents | none`

<display-legacy>
    `inline-block | inline-list-item | inline-table | inline-flex | inline-grid`

In this chapter, we'll stick to the table-related values, as the others are all beyond the scope of tables. The table-related values can be summarized as follows:

`table`
> This value specifies that an element defines a block-level table. Thus, it defines a rectangular block that generates a block box. The corresponding HTML element is, not surprisingly, `table`.

`inline-table`
> This value specifies that an element defines an inline-level table. This means the element defines a rectangular block that generates an inline box. The closest non-

table analogue is the value `inline-block`. The closest HTML element is `table`, although, by default, HTML tables are not inline.

table-row
This value specifies that an element is a row of table cells. The corresponding HTML element is the `tr` element.

table-row-group
This value specifies that an element groups one or more table rows. The corresponding HTML value is `tbody`.

table-header-group
This value is very much like `table-row-group`, except that for visual formatting, the header row group is always displayed before all other rows and row groups, and after any top captions. In print, if a table requires multiple pages to print, a user agent may repeat header rows at the top of each page (Firefox does this, for example). The specification does not define what happens if you assign `table-header-group` to multiple elements. A header group can contain multiple rows. The HTML equivalent is `thead`.

table-footer-group
This value is very much like `table-header-group`, except that the footer row group is always displayed after all other rows and row groups, and before any bottom captions. In print, if a table requires multiple pages to print, a user agent may repeat footer rows at the bottom of each page. The specification does not define what happens if you assign `table-footer-group` to multiple elements. This is equivalent to the HTML element `tfoot`.

table-column
This value declares that an element describes a column of table cells. In CSS terms, elements with this `display` value are not visually rendered, as if they had the value `none`. Their existence is largely for the purposes of helping to define the presentation of cells within the column. The HTML equivalent is the `col` element.

table-column-group
This value declares that an element groups one or more columns. Like `table-column` elements, `table-column-group` elements are not rendered, but the value is useful for defining presentation for elements within the column group. The HTML equivalent is the `colgroup` element.

table-cell
This value specifies that an element represents a single cell in a table. The HTML elements `th` and `td` are both examples of `table-cell` elements.

table-caption

> This value defines a table's caption. CSS does not define what should happen if multiple elements have the value `caption`, but it does explicitly warn, "authors should not put more than one element with `display: caption` inside a table or inline-table element."

You can get a quick summary of the general effects of these values by taking an excerpt from the example HTML 4.0 stylesheet given in Appendix D of the CSS 2.1 specification:

```
table {display: table;}
tr {display: table-row;}
thead {display: table-header-group;}
tbody {display: table-row-group;}
tfoot {display: table-footer-group;}
col {display: table-column;}
colgroup {display: table-column-group;}
td, th {display: table-cell;}
caption {display: table-caption;}
```

In XML, where elements will not have display semantics by default, these values become quite useful. Consider the following markup:

```
<scores>
    <headers>
        <label>Team</label>
        <label>Score</label>
    </headers>
    <game sport="MLB" league="NL">
        <team>
            <name>Reds</name>
            <score>8</score>
        </team>
        <team>
            <name>Cubs</name>
            <score>5</score>
        </team>
    </game>
</scores>
```

This could be formatted in a tabular fashion using the following styles:

```
scores {display: table;}
headers {display: table-header-group;}
game {display: table-row-group;}
team {display: table-row;}
label, name, score {display: table-cell;}
```

The various cells could then be styled as necessary—for example, boldfacing the `label` elements and right-aligning the `scores`.

Row primacy

CSS defines its table model as "row primacy." In other words, the model assumes that authors will create markup languages where rows are explicitly declared. Columns, on the other hand, are derived from the layout of the rows of cells. Thus, the first column is made up of the first cells in each row; the second column is made up of the second cells, and so forth.

Row primacy is not a major issue in HTML, where the markup language is already row-oriented. In XML, it has more of an impact because it constrains the way in which authors can define table markup. Because of the row-oriented nature of the CSS table model, a markup language in which columns are the basis of table layout is not really possible (assuming that the intent is to use CSS to present such documents).

Columns

Although the CSS table model is row-oriented, columns do still play a part in layout. A cell can belong to both contexts (row and column), even though it is descended from row elements in the document source. In CSS, however, columns and column groups can accept only four nontable properties: border, background, width, and visibility.

In addition, each of these four properties has special rules that apply only in the columnar context:

border
> Borders can be set for columns and column groups only if the property border-collapse has the value collapse. In such circumstances, column and column-group borders participate in the collapsing algorithm that sets the border styles at each cell edge. (See "Collapsing Cell Borders" on page 749.)

background
> The background of a column or column group will be visible only in cells where both the cell and its row have transparent backgrounds. (See "Table Layers" on page 742.)

width
> The width property defines the *minimum* width of the column or column group. The content of cells within the column (or group) may force the column to become wider.

visibility
> If the value of visibility for a column or column group is collapse, then none of the cells in the column (or group) are rendered. Cells that span from the collapsed column into other columns are clipped, as are cells that span from

other columns into the hidden column. Furthermore, the overall width of the table is reduced by the width the column would have taken up. A declaration of any visibility value other than hidden is ignored for a column or column group.

Anonymous Table Objects

There is the possibility that a markup language might not contain enough elements to fully represent tables as they are defined in CSS, or that an author will forget to include all the necessary elements. For example, consider this HTML:

```
<table>
    <td>Name:</td>
    <td><input type="text"></td>
</table>
```

You might glance at this markup and assume that it defines a two-cell table of a single row, but structurally, there is no element defining a row (because the tr is missing).

To cover such possibilities, CSS defines a mechanism for inserting "missing" table components as anonymous objects. For a basic example of how this works, let's revisit our missing-row HTML example. In CSS terms, what effectively happens is that an anonymous table-row object is inserted between the table element and its descendant table cells:

```
<table>
  <!--anonymous table-row object begins-->
    <td>Name:</td>
    <td><input type="text"></td>
  <!--anonymous table-row object ends-->
</table>
```

A visual representation of this process is given in Figure 14-2, where the dotted line represents the inserted anonymous table row.

Figure 14-2. Anonymous-object generation in table formatting

Seven different kinds of anonymous-object insertions can occur in the CSS table model. These seven rules are, like inheritance and specificity, an example of a mechanism that attempts to impose intuitive sense on the way CSS behaves.

Object insertion rules

1. If a `table-cell` element's parent is not a `table-row` element, then an anonymous `table-row` object is inserted between the `table-cell` element and its parent. The inserted object will include all consecutive siblings of the `table-cell` element. Consider the following styles and markup:

```
system {display: table;}
name, moons {display: table-cell;}

<system>
    <name>Mercury</name>
    <moons>0</moons>
</system>
```

The anonymous `table-row` object is inserted between the cell elements and the `system` element, and it encloses both the `name` and `moons` elements.

The same holds true even if the parent element is a `table-row-group`. To extend the example, assume that the following applies:

```
system {display: table;}
planet {display: table-row-group;}
name, moons {display: table-cell;}

<system>
    <planet>
        <name>Mercury</name>
        <moons>0</moons>
    </planet>
    <planet>
        <name>Venus</name>
        <moons>0</moons>
    </planet>
</system>
```

In this example, both sets of cells will be enclosed in an anonymous `table-row` object that is inserted between them and the `planet` elements.

2. If a `table-row` element's parent is not a `table`, `inline-table`, or `table-row-group` element, then an anonymous `table` element is inserted between the `table-row` element and its parent. The inserted object will include all consecutive siblings of the `table-row` element. Consider the following styles and markup:

```
docbody {display: block;}
planet {display: table-row;}

<docbody>
    <planet>
        <name>Mercury</name>
        <moons>0</moons>
```

```
        </planet>
        <planet>
            <name>Venus</name>
            <moons>0</moons>
        </planet>
    </docbody>
```

Because the `display` value of the `planet` elements' parent is `block`, the anonymous `table` object is inserted between the `planet` elements and the `docbody` element. This anonymous `table` object will enclose both `planet` elements, since they are consecutive siblings.

3. If a `table-column` element's parent is not a `table`, `inline-table`, or `table-column-group` element, then an anonymous `table` element is inserted between the `table-column` element and its parent. This is much the same as the `table-row` rule just discussed, except for its column-oriented nature.

4. If the parent element of a `table-row-group`, `table-header-group`, `table-footer-group`, `table-column-group`, or `table-caption` element is not a `table` element, then an anonymous `table` object is inserted between the element and its parent.

5. If a child element of a `table` or `inline-table` element is not a `table-row-group`, `table-header-group`, `table-footer-group`, `table-row`, or `table-caption` element, then an anonymous `table-row` object is inserted between the `table` element and its child element. This anonymous object spans all of the consecutive siblings of the child element that are not `table-row-group`, `table-header-group`, `table-footer-group`, `table-row`, or `table-caption` elements. Consider the following markup and styles:

```
system {display: table;}
planet {display: table-row;}
name, moons {display: table-cell;}

<system>
    <planet>
        <name>Mercury</name>
        <moons>0</moons>
    </planet>
    <name>Venus</name>
    <moons>0</moons>
</system>
```

Here, a single anonymous `table-row` object will be inserted between the `system` element and the second set of `name` and `moons` elements. The `planet` element is not enclosed by the anonymous object because its `display` is `table-row`.

6. If a child element of a `table-row-group`, `table-header-group`, or `table-footer-group` element is not a `table-row` element, then an anonymous `table-`

row object is inserted between the element and its child element. This anonymous object spans all of the consecutive siblings of the child element that are not table-row objects themselves. Consider the following markup and styles:

```
system {display: table;}
planet {display: table-row-group;}
name, moons {display: table-cell;}

<system>
    <planet>
        <name>Mercury</name>
        <moons>0</moons>
    </planet>
    <name>Venus</name>
    <moons>0</moons>
</system>
```

In this case, each set of name and moons elements will be enclosed in an anonymous table-row element. For the second set, the insertion happens in accord with rule 5. For the first set, the anonymous object is inserted between the planet element and its children because the planet element is a table-row-group element.

7. If a child element of a table-row element is not a table-cell element, then an anonymous table-cell object is inserted between the element and its child element. This anonymous object encloses all consecutive siblings of the child element that are not table-cell elements themselves. Consider the following markup and styles:

```
system {display: table;}
planet {display: table-row;}
name, moons {display: table-cell;}

<system>
    <planet>
        <name>Mercury</name>
        <num>0</num>
    </planet>
</system>
```

Because the element num does not have a table-related display value, an anonymous table-cell object is inserted between the planet element and the num element.

This behavior also extends to the encapsulation of anonymous inline boxes. Suppose that the num element was not included:

```
<system>
    <planet>
        <name>Mercury</name>
        0
```

```
    </planet>
  </system>
```

The 0 would still be enclosed in an anonymous `table-cell` object. To further illustrate this point, here is an example adapted from the CSS specification:

```
example {display: table-cell;}
row {display: table-row;}
hey {font-weight: 900;}

<example>
    <row>This is the <hey>top</hey> row.</row>
    <row>This is the <hey>bottom</hey> row.</row>
</example>
```

Within each `row` element, the text fragments and `hey` element are enclosed in anonymous `table-cell` objects.

Table Layers

For the assembly of a table's presentation, CSS defines six individual "layers" on which the various aspects of a table are placed. Figure 14-3 shows these layers.

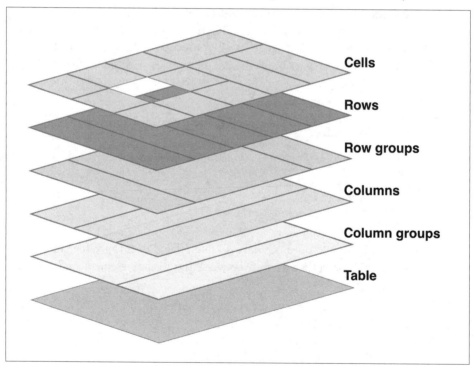

Cells

Rows

Row groups

Columns

Column groups

Table

Figure 14-3. The formatting layers used in table presentation

Basically, the styles for each aspect of the table are drawn on their individual layers. Thus, if the `table` element has a green background and a one-pixel black border, then those styles are drawn on the lowest layer. Any styles for the column groups are drawn on the next layer up, the columns themselves on the layer above that, and so on. The top layer, which corresponds to the table cells, is drawn last.

For the most part, this is a logical process; after all, if you declare a background color for table cells, you would want that drawn over the background for the table element. The most important point revealed by Figure 14-3 is that column styles come below row styles, so a row's background will overwrite a column's background.

It is important to remember that by default, all elements have transparent backgrounds. Thus, in the following markup, the table element's background will be visible "through" cells, rows, columns, and so forth that do not have a background of their own, as illustrated in Figure 14-4:

```
<table style="background: #B84;">
    <tr>
        <td>hey</td>
        <td style="background: #ABC;">there</td>
    </tr>
    <tr>
        <td>what's</td>
        <td>up?</td>
    </tr>
    <tr style="background: #CBA;">
        <td>not</td>
        <td style="background: #ECC;">much</td>
    </tr>
</table>
```

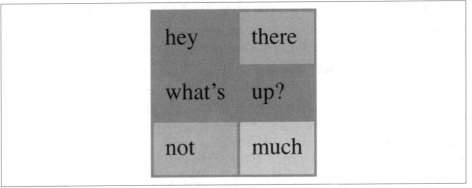

Figure 14-4. Seeing the background of table-formatting layers through other layers

Captions

A table caption is about what you'd expect: a short bit of text that describes the nature of the table's contents. A chart of stock quotes for the fourth quarter of 2016, therefore, might have a caption element whose contents read "Q4 2016 Stock Performance." With the property caption-side, you can place this element either above or below the table, regardless of where the caption appears in the table's structure. (In HTML5, the caption element can appear only as the first child of a table element, but other languages may have different rules.)

---

caption-side

Values	top | bottom
Initial value	top
Applies to	Elements with the display value table-caption
Computed value	As specified
Inherited	Yes
Animatable	No
Note	The values left and right appeared in CSS2, but were dropped from CSS2.1 due to a lack of widespread support.

Captions are a bit odd, at least in visual terms. The CSS specification states that a caption is formatted as if it were a block box placed immediately before (or after) the table's box, with one exception: the caption can still inherit values from the table.

A simple example should suffice to illustrate most of the important aspects of caption presentation. Consider the following, illustrated in Figure 14-5:

```
caption {background: #B84; margin: 1em 0; caption-side: top;}
table {color: white; background: #840; margin: 0.5em 0;}
```

The text in the caption element inherits the color value white from the table, while the caption gets its own background. The separation between the table's outer border edge and the caption's outer margin edge is 1 em, as the top margin of the table and bottom margin of the caption have collapsed. Finally, the width of the caption is based on the content width of the table element, which is considered to be the containing block of the caption.

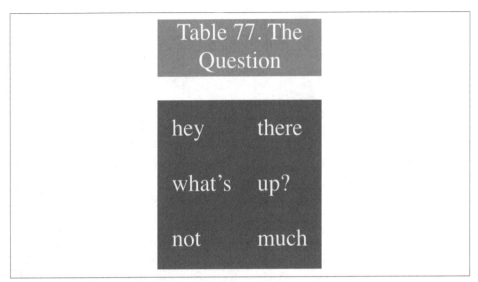

Figure 14-5. Styling captions and tables

These same results would occur if we change the value of `caption-side` to `bottom`, except that the `caption` would be placed after the table's box, and collapsing would occur between the top margin of the caption and the bottom margin of the table.

For the most part, captions are styled just like any block-level element: they can be padded, have borders, be given backgrounds, and so on. For example, if we need to change the horizontal alignment of text within the caption, we use the property `text-align`. Thus, to right-align the caption in the previous example, we would write:

```
caption {background: gray; margin: 1em 0;
    caption-side: top; text-align: right;}
```

Table Cell Borders

There are two quite distinct border models in CSS. The *separated border model* takes effect when cells are separated from each other in layout terms. The other option is the *collapsed border model*, in which there is no visual separation between cells, and cell borders merge, or collapse into one another. The former is the default model, although in an earlier version of CSS the latter was the default.

An author can choose between the two models with the property `border-collapse`.

Values	collapse | separate | inherit
Initial value	separate
Applies to	Elements with the display value table or table-inline
Inherited	Yes
Computed value	As specified
Note	In CSS2, the default was collapse.

The whole point of this property is to offer a way to determine which border model the user agent will employ. If the value collapse is in effect, then the collapsing borders model is used. If the value is separate, then the separated borders model is used. We'll look at the former model first, since it's much easier to describe, and it's the default value.

Separated Cell Borders

In this model, every cell in the table is separated from the other cells by some distance, and the borders of cells do not collapse into one another. Thus, given the following styles and markup, you would see the result shown in Figure 14-6:

```
table {border-collapse: separate;}
td {border: 3px double black; padding: 3px;}
tr:nth-child(2) td:nth-child(2) {border-color: gray;}

<table cellspacing="0">
    <tr>
        <td>cell one</td>
        <td>cell two</td>
    </tr>
    <tr>
        <td>cell three</td>
        <td>cell four</td>
    </tr>
</table>
```

Note that the cell borders touch but remain distinct from one another. The three lines between cells are actually the two double borders sitting right next to each other; the gray border around the fourth cell helps make this more clear.

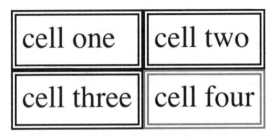

Figure 14-6. Separated (and thus separate) cell borders

The HTML attribute `cellspacing` was included in the preceding example to make sure the cells had no separation between them, but its presence is likely a bit troubling. After all, if you can define that borders be separate, then there ought to be a way to use CSS to alter the spacing between cells. Fortunately, there is.

Border spacing

Once you've separated the table cell borders, there may be situations where you want those borders to be separated by some distance. This can be easily accomplished with the property `border-spacing`, which provides a more powerful replacement for the HTML attribute `cellspacing`.

---

border-spacing

Values	*<length> <length>?*
Initial value	0
Applies to	Elements with the display value `table` or `table-inline`
Computed value	Two absolute lengths
Inherited	Yes
Animatable	Yes
Note	Property is ignored unless `border-collapse` value is `separate`

Either one or two lengths can be given for the value of this property. If you want all your cells separated by a single pixel, then `border-spacing: 1px;` will suffice. If, on the other hand, you want cells to be separated by one pixel horizontally and five pixels vertically, write `border-spacing: 1px 5px;`. If two lengths are supplied, the first is always the horizontal separation, and the second is always the vertical.

The spacing values are also applied between the borders of cells along the outside of a table and the padding on the `table` element itself. Given the following styles, you would get the result shown in Figure 14-7:

```
table {border-collapse: separate; border-spacing: 5px 8px;
padding: 12px; border: 2px solid black;}
td { border: 1px solid gray;}
td#squeeze {border-width: 5px;}
```

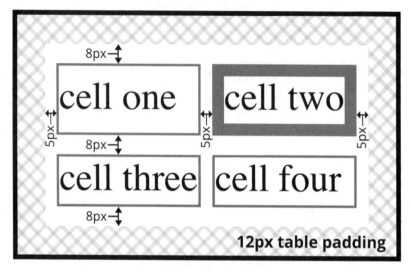

Figure 14-7. Border spacing effects between cells and their enclosing table

In Figure 14-7, there is a space 5 pixels wide between the borders of any two horizontally adjacent cells, and there are 17 pixels of space between the borders of the right- and left-most cells and the right and left borders of the `table` element. Similarly, the borders of vertically adjacent cells are 8 pixels apart, and the borders of the cells in the top and bottom rows are 20 pixels from the top and bottom borders of the table, respectively. The separation between cell borders is constant throughout the table, regardless of the border widths of the cells themselves.

Note also that if you're going to declare a `border-spacing` value, it's done on the table itself, not on the individual cells. If `border-spacing` had been declared for the `td` elements in the previous example, it would have been ignored.

In the separated-border model, borders cannot be set for rows, row groups, columns, and column groups. Any border properties declared for such elements must be ignored by a CSS-conformant user agent.

Handling empty cells

Because every cell is, in a visual sense, distinct from all the other cells in the table, what do you do with cells that are empty (i.e., have no content)? You have two choices, which are reflected in the values of the `empty-cells` property.

---

empty-cells

Values	show | hide
Initial value	show
Applies to	Elements with the `display` value `table-cell`
Computed value	As specified
Inherited	Yes
Animatable	No
Note	Property is ignored unless `border-collapse` value is `separate`

If `empty-cells` is set to `show`, then the borders and background of an empty cell will be drawn, just as with table cells that have content. If the value is `hide`, then no part of the cell is drawn, just as if the cell were set to `visibility: hidden`.

If a cell contains any content, it cannot be considered empty. "Content," in this case, includes not only text, images, form elements, and so on, but also the nonbreaking space entity (` `) and any other whitespace *except* the CR (carriage return), LF (line feed), tab, and space characters. If all the cells in a row are empty, and all have an `empty-cells` value of `hide`, then the entire row is treated as if the row element were set to `display: none`.

Collapsing Cell Borders

While the collapsing cell model largely describes how HTML tables have always been laid out when they don't have any cell spacing, it is quite a bit more complicated than the separated borders model. There are also some rules that set collapsing cell borders apart from the separated borders model:

- Elements with a `display` of `table` or `inline-table` cannot have any padding when `border-collapse` is `collapse`, although they can have margins. Thus, there is never separation between the border around the outside of the table and the edges of its outermost cells in the collapsed borders model.

- Borders can be applied to cells, rows, row groups, columns, and column groups. A table itself can, as always, have a border.

- There is never any separation between cell borders in the collapsed borders model. In fact, borders collapse into each other where they adjoin, so that only one of the collapsing borders is actually drawn. This is somewhat akin to margin collapsing, where the largest margin wins. When cell borders collapse, the "most interesting" border wins.

- Once they are collapsed, the borders between cells are centered on the hypothetical grid lines between the cells.

We'll explore the last two points in more detail in the next two sections.

Collapsing border layout

In order to better understand how the collapsing borders model works, let's look at the layout of a single table row, as shown in Figure 14-8.

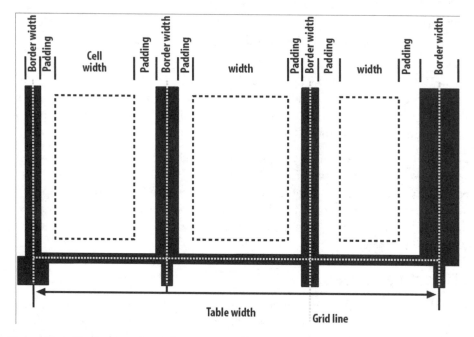

Figure 14-8. The layout of a table row using the collapsing borders model

For each cell, the padding and content width of the cell is inside the borders, as expected. For the borders between cells, half of the border is to one side of the grid line between two cells, and the other half is to the other side. In each case, only a single border is drawn along each cell edge. You might think that half of each cell's border is drawn to each side of the grid line, but that's not what happens.

For example, assume that the solid borders on the middle cell are green and the solid borders on the outer two cells are red. The borders on the right and left sides of the middle cell (which collapse with the adjacent borders of the outer cells) will be all green, or all red, depending on which border wins out. We'll discuss how to tell which one wins in the next section.

You may have noticed that the outer borders protrude past the table's width. This is because in this model, *half* the table's borders are included in the width. The other half sticks out beyond that distance, sitting in the margin itself. This might seem a bit weird, but that's how the model is defined to work.

The specification includes a layout formula that I'll reproduce here for the benefit of those who enjoy such things:

row width = (0.5 * border-width-0) + padding-left-1 + width-1 + padding-right-1
+ border-width-1 + padding-left-2 +...+ padding-right-n + (0.5 * border-width-n)

Each `border-width-`n refers to the border between cell n and the next cell; thus, `border-width-3` refers to the border between the third and fourth cells. The value n stands for the total number of cells in the row.

There is a slight exception to this mechanism. When beginning the layout of a collapsed-border table, the user agent computes an initial left and right border for the table itself. It does this by examining the left border of the first cell in the first row of the table and by taking half of that border's width as the table's initial left border width. The user agent then examines the right border of the last cell in the first row and uses half that width to set the table's initial right-border width. For any row after the first, if the left or right border is wider than the initial border widths, it sticks out into the margin area of the table.

In cases where a border is an odd number of display elements (pixels, printer dots, etc.) wide, the user agent is left to decide what to do about centering the border on the grid line. It might shift the border so that it is slightly off-center, round up or down to an even number of display elements, use anti-aliasing, or adjust anything else that seems reasonable.

Border collapsing

When two or more borders are adjacent, they collapse into each other. In fact, they don't collapse so much as fight it out to see which of them will gain supremacy over the others. There are some strict rules governing which borders will win and which will not:

- If one of the collapsing borders has a `border-style` of `hidden`, it takes precedence over all other collapsing borders. All borders at this location are hidden.

- If all the borders are visible, then wider borders take precedence over narrower ones. Thus, if a two-pixel dotted border and a five-pixel double border collapse, the border at that location will be a five-pixel double border.

- If all collapsing borders have the same width but different border styles, then the border style is taken in the following order, from most to least preferred: `double`, `solid`, `dashed`, `dotted`, `ridge`, `outset`, `groove`, `inset`, `none`. Thus, if two borders with the same width are collapsing, and one is `dashed` while the other is `outset`, the border at that location will be dashed.

- If collapsing borders have the same style and width, but differ in color, then the color used is taken from an element in the following list, from most preferred to least: cell, row, row group, column, column group, table. Thus, if the borders of a cell and a column (identical in every way except color) collapse, then the cell's border color (and style and width) will be used. If the collapsing borders come from the same type of element, such as two row borders with the same style and width but different colors, then the color is taken from borders that are further to the top and left (in left-to-right languages; otherwise, further to the top and right).

The following styles and markup, presented in Figure 14-9, help illustrate each of the four rules:

```
table {border-collapse: collapse;
border: 3px outset gray;}
td {border: 1px solid gray; padding: 0.5em;}
#r2c1, #r2c2 {border-style: hidden;}
#r1c1, #r1c4 {border-width: 5px;}
#r2c4 {border-style: double; border-width: 3px;}
#r3c4 {border-style: dotted; border-width: 2px;}
#r4c1 {border-bottom-style: hidden;}
#r4c3 {border-top: 13px solid silver;}

<table>
    <tr>
        <td id="r1c1">1-1</td>
        <td id="r1c2">1-2</td>
        <td id="r1c3">1-3</td>
        <td id="r1c4">1-4</td>
    </tr>
    <tr>
        <td id="r2c1">2-1</td>
        <td id="r2c2">2-2</td>
        <td id="r2c3">2-3</td>
        <td id="r2c4">2-4</td>
    </tr>
    <tr>
        <td id="r3c1">3-1</td>
        <td id="r3c2">3-2</td>
        <td id="r3c3">3-3</td>
```

```
        <td id="r3c4">3-4</td>
    </tr>
    <tr>
        <td id="r4c1">4-1</td>
        <td id="r4c2">4-2</td>
        <td id="r4c3">4-3</td>
        <td id="r4c4">4-4</td>
    </tr>
</table>
```

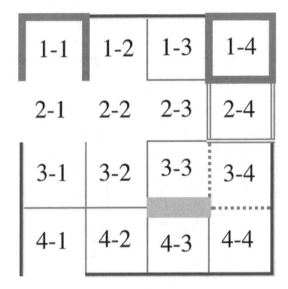

Figure 14-9. Manipulating border widths, styles, and colors leads to some unusual results

Let's consider what happened for each of the cells, in turn:

- For cells 1-1 and 1-4, the five-pixel borders were wider than any of their adjacent borders, so they won out not only over adjoining cell borders, but over the border of the table itself. The only exception is the bottom of cell 1-1, which was suppressed.

- The bottom border on cell 1-1 was suppressed because cells 2-1 and 2-2, with their explicitly hidden borders, completely remove any borders from the edge of the cells. Again, the table's border lost out (on the left edge of cell 2-1) to a cell's border. The bottom border of cell 4-1 was also hidden, and so it prevented any border from appearing below the cell.

- The three-pixel double border of cell 2-4 was overridden on top by the five-pixel solid border of cell 1-4. Cell 2-4's border, in turn, overrode the border between itself and cell 2-3 because it was both wider and "more interesting." Cell 2-4 also overrode the border between itself and cell 3-4, even though both are the same width, because 2-4's double style is defined to be "more interesting" than 3-4's dotted border.

- The 13-pixel bottom silver border of cell 3-3 not only overrode the top border of cell 4-3, but it also affected the layout of content within both cells *and* the rows that contain both cells.

- For cells along the outer edge of the table that aren't specially styled, their one-pixel solid borders are overridden by the three-pixel outset border on the table element itself.

This is, in fact, about as complicated as it sounds, although the behaviors are largely intuitive and make a little more sense with practice. It's worth noting, though, that the basic Netscape 1.1-era table presentation can be captured with a fairly simple set of rules, described here and illustrated by Figure 14-10:

```
table {border-collapse: collapse; border: 2px outset gray;}
td {border: 1px inset gray;}
```

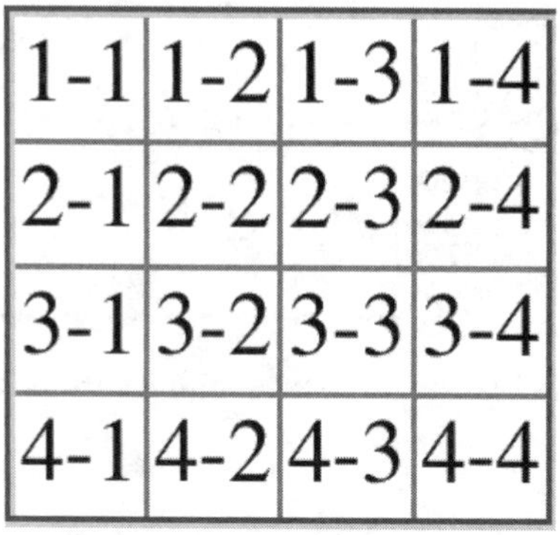

1-1	1-2	1-3	1-4
2-1	2-2	2-3	2-4
3-1	3-2	3-3	3-4
4-1	4-2	4-3	4-4

Figure 14-10. Reproducing old-school table presentation

Table Sizing

Now that we've dug into the guts of table formatting and cell border appearance, we have the pieces we need to understand the sizing of tables and their internal elements. When it comes to determining table width, there are two different approaches: *fixed-width layout* and *automatic-width layout*. Heights are calculated automatically, no matter what width algorithms are used.

Width

Since there are two different ways to figure out the width of a table, it's only logical that there be a way to declare which should be used for a given table. Authors can use the property `table-layout` to select between the two kinds of table width calculation.

table-layout	
Values	auto|fixed
Initial value	auto
Applies to	Elements with the display value table or inline-table
Computed value	As specified
Inherited	Yes
Animatable	No

While the two models can have different results in laying out a given table, the fundamental difference between the two is that of speed. With a fixed-width table layout, the user agent can calculate the layout of the table more quickly than is possible in the automatic-width model.

Fixed layout

The main reason the fixed-layout model is so fast is that its layout does not depend on the contents of table cells. Instead, it's driven by the width values of the table, columns, and cells within that table.

The fixed-layout model works in the following steps:

1. Any column element whose `width` property has a value other than `auto` sets the width for that entire column.

    a. If a column has an `auto` width, but the cell in the first row of the table within that column has a `width` other than `auto`, then the cell sets the width for that entire column. If the cell spans multiple columns, then the width is divided between the columns.

    b. Any columns that are still auto-sized are sized so that their widths are as equal as possible.

At that point, the width of the table is set to be either the value of `width` for the table or the sum of the column widths, whichever is *greater*. If the table turns out to be wider than its columns, then the difference is divided by the number of columns and the result is added to each of them.

This approach is fast because all of the column widths are defined by the first row of the table. The cells in any rows that come after the first are sized according to the column widths that were defined by the first row. The cells in those following rows do not—indeed, cannot—change column widths, which means that any width value assigned to those cells will be ignored. In cases where a cell's content does not fit into its cell, the overflow value for the cell determines whether the cell contents are clipped, visible, or generate a scrollbar.

Let's consider the following styles and markup, which are illustrated in Figure 14-11:

```
table {table-layout: fixed; width: 400px;
    border-collapse: collapse;}
td {border: 1px solid;}
col#c1 {width: 200px;}
#r1c2 {width: 75px;}
#r2c3 {width: 500px;}

<table>
    <colgroup> <col id="c1"><col id="c2"><col id="c3"><col id="c4"> </colgroup>
    <tr>
        <td id="r1c1">1-1</td>
        <td id="r1c2">1-2</td>
        <td id="r1c3">1-3</td>
        <td id="r1c4">1-4</td>
    </tr>
    <tr>
        <td id="r2c1">2-1</td>
        <td id="r2c2">2-2</td>
        <td id="r2c3">2-3</td>
        <td id="r2c4">2-4</td>
    </tr>
    <tr>
        <td id="r3c1">3-1</td>
        <td id="r3c2">3-2</td>
        <td id="r3c3">3-3</td>
        <td id="r3c4">3-4</td>
    </tr>
    <tr>
        <td id="r4c1">4-1</td>
        <td id="r4c2">4-2</td>
        <td id="r4c3">4-3</td>
        <td id="r4c4">4-4</td>
    </tr>
</table>
```

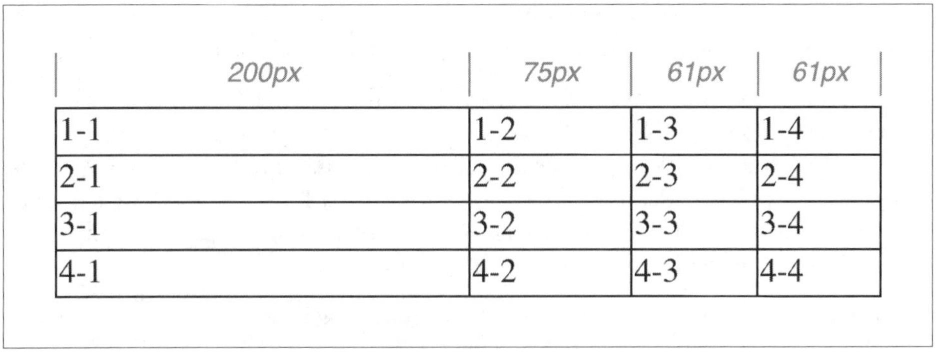

Figure 14-11. Fixed-width table layout

As you can see in Figure 14-11, the first column is 200 pixels wide, which happens to be half the 400-pixel width of the table. The second column is 75 pixels wide, because the first-row cell within that column has been assigned an explicit width. The third and fourth columns are each 61 pixels wide. Why? Because the sum of the column widths for the first and second columns (275 pixels), plus the various borders between columns (3 pixels), equals 278 pixels. 400 minus 278 is 122, and that divided in half is 61, so that's how many pixels wide the third and fourth columns will be. What about the 500-pixel width for #r2c3? It's ignored because that cell isn't in the first row of the table.

Note that it is not absolutely necessary that the table have an explicit width value to make use of the fixed-width layout model, although it definitely helps. For example, given the following, a user agent could calculate a width for the table that is 50 pixels narrower than the parent element's width. It would then use that calculated width in the fixed-layout algorithm:

```
table {table-layout: fixed; margin: 0 25px; width: auto;}
```

This is not required, however. User agents are also permitted to lay out any table with an auto value for width using the automatic-width layout model.

Automatic layout

The automatic-width layout model, while not as fast as fixed layout, is probably much more familiar to you because it's substantially the same model that HTML tables have used for years. In most current user agents, use of this model will be triggered by a table having a width of auto, regardless of the value of table-layout, although this is not assured.

The reason automatic layout is slower is that the table cannot be laid out until the user agent has looked at all of the content in the table. That is, it requires that the user agent lay out the entire table in a fashion that takes the contents and styles of every cell into account. This generally requires the user agent to perform some calculations and then go back through the table to perform a second set of calculations.

The content has to be fully examined because, as with HTML tables, the table's layout is dependent on the content in all the cells. If there is a 400-pixel-wide image in a cell in the last row, then it will force all of the cells above it (those in the same column) to be at least 400 pixels wide. Thus, the width of every cell has to be calculated, and adjustments must be made (possibly triggering another round of content-width calculations) before the table can be laid out.

The details of the model can be expressed in the following steps:

1. For each cell in a column, calculate both the minimum and maximum cell width.

    a. Determine the minimum width required to display the content. In determining this minimum content width, the content can flow to any number of lines, but it may not stick out of the cell's box. If the cell has a width value that is larger than the minimum possible width, then the minimum cell width is set to the value of width. If the cell's width value is auto, then the minimum cell width is set to the minimum content width.

    b. For the maximum width, determine the width required to display the content without any line breaking other than that forced by explicit line breaking (e.g., the <br> element). That value is the maximum cell width.

2. For each column, calculate both the minimum and maximum column width.

    a. The column's minimum width is determined by the largest minimum cell width of the cells within the column. If the column has been given an explicit width value that is larger than any of the minimum cell widths within the column, then the minimum column width is set to the value of width.

    b. For the maximum width, take the largest maximum cell width of the cells within the column. If the column has been given an explicit width value that is larger than any of the maximum cell widths within the column, then the maximum column width is set to the value of width. These two behaviors recreate the traditional HTML table behavior of forcibly expanding any column to be as wide as its widest cell.

3. In cases where a cell spans more than one column, then the sum of the minimum column widths must be equal to the minimum cell width for the spanning cell. Similarly, the sum of the maximum column widths has to equal the spanning cell's maximum width. User agents should divide any changes in column widths equally among the spanned columns.

In addition, the user agent must take into account that when a column width has a percentage value for its width, the percentage is calculated in relation to the width of the table—even though it doesn't yet know what that will be! It instead has to hang on to the percentage value and use it in the next part of the algorithm.

At this point, the user agent will have figured how wide or narrow each column *can* be. With that information in hand, it can then proceed to actually figuring out the width of the table. This happens as follows:

1. If the computed width of the table is not auto, then the computed table width is compared to the sum of all the column widths *plus* any borders and cell spacing. (Columns with percentage widths are likely calculated at this time.) The larger of the two is the final width of the table. If the table's computed width is *larger* than the sum of the column widths, borders, and cell spacing, then the difference is divided by the number of columns and the result is added to each of them.

2. If the computed width of the table is auto, then the final width of the table is determined by adding up the column widths, borders, and cell spacing. This means that the table will be only as wide as needed to display its content, just as with traditional HTML tables. Any columns with percentage widths use that percentage as a constraint—but one that a user agent does not have to satisfy.

Once the last step is completed, then—and only then—can the user agent actually lay out the table.

The following styles and markup, presented in Figure 14-12, help illustrate how this process works:

```
table {table-layout: auto; width: auto;
    border-collapse: collapse;}
td {border: 1px solid; padding: 0;}
col#c3 {width: 25%;}
#r1c2 {width: 40%;}
#r2c2 {width: 50px;}
#r2c3 {width: 35px;}
#r4c1 {width: 100px;}
#r4c4 {width: 1px;}

<table>
    <colgroup> <col id="c1"><col id="c2"><col id="c3"><col id="c4"> </colgroup>
    <tr>
        <td id="r1c1">1-1</td>
        <td id="r1c2">1-2</td>
        <td id="r1c3">1-3</td>
        <td id="r1c4">1-4</td>
    </tr>
    <tr>
        <td id="r2c1">2-1</td>
        <td id="r2c2">2-2</td>
        <td id="r2c3">2-3</td>
        <td id="r2c4">2-4</td>
    </tr>
```

```
<tr>
    <td id="r3c1">3-1</td>
    <td id="r3c2">3-2</td>
    <td id="r3c3">3-3</td>
    <td id="r3c4">3-4</td>
</tr>
<tr>
    <td id="r4c1">4-1</td>
    <td id="r4c2">4-2</td>
    <td id="r4c3">4-3</td>
    <td id="r4c4">4-4</td>
</tr>
</table>
```

100px	141px	88px	22px
1-1	1-2	1-3	1-4
2-1	2-2	2-3	2-4
3-1	3-2	3-3	3-4
4-1	4-2	4-3	4-4

Figure 14-12. Automatic table layout

Let's consider what happened for each of the columns, in turn:

- For the first column, the only explicit cell or column width is that of cell 4-1, which was given a width of 100px. Because the content is so short, both the minimum and maximum column widths are set to 100px. (If there were a cell in the column with several sentences of text, it would have increased the maximum column width to whatever width necessary to display all of the text without line breaking.)

- For the second column, two widths were declared: cell 1-2 was given a width of 40%, and cell 2-2 was given a width of 50px. The minimum width of this column is 50px, and the maximum width is 40% of the final table width.

- For the third column, only cell 3-3 had an explicit width (35px), but the column itself was given a width of 25%. Therefore, the minimum column width is 35 pixels, and the maximum width is 25% of the final table width.

- For the fourth column, only cell 4-4 was given an explicit width (1px). This is smaller than the minimum content width, so both the minimum and maximum column widths are equal to the minimum content width of the cells. This turns out to be a computed 22 pixels, so the minimum and maximum widths are both 22 pixels.

The user agent now knows that the four columns have minimum and maximum widths as follows:

- Minimum 100 px, maximum 100 px
  — Minimum 50 px, maximum 40%
  — Minimum 35 px, maximum 25%
  — Minimum 25 px, maximum 22 px

Thus, the table's minimum width is the sum of all the column minimums, plus the borders collapsed between the columns, which totals 215 pixels. The table's maximum width is 123px + 65%, where the 123px comes from the first and last columns and their shares of the collapsed borders. This maximum works out to be 351.42857142857143 pixels (given that 123px represents 35% of the overall table width). With this number in hand, the second column will be 140.5 pixels wide, and the third column will be 87.8 pixels wide. These may be rounded by the user agent to whole numbers such as 141px and 88px, or not, depending on the exact rendering method used. (These are the numbers used in Figure 14-12.)

Note that it is not required that user agents actually use the maximum value; they may choose another course of action.

This was (although it may not seem like it) a comparatively simple and straightforward example: all of the content was basically the same width, and most of the declared widths were pixel lengths. In a situation where a table contains images, paragraphs of text, form elements, and so forth, the process of figuring out the table's layout is likely to be a great deal more complicated.

Height

After all of the effort that was expended in figuring out the width of the table, you might well wonder how much more complicated height calculation will be. Actually, in CSS terms, it's pretty simple, although browser developers probably don't think so.

The easiest situation to describe is one in which the table height is explicitly set via the height property. In such cases, the height of the table is defined by the value of height. This means that a table may be taller or shorter than the sum of its row heights. Note that height is treated much more like min-height for tables, so if you define a height value that's smaller than the sum total of the row heights, it may appear to be ignored.

By contrast, if the height value of a table is greater than the total of its row heights, the specification explicitly refuses to define what should happen, instead noting that the issue may be resolved in future versions of CSS. A user agent could expand the table's rows to fill out its height, or leave blank space inside the table's box, or something completely different. It's up to each user agent to decide.

 As of late 2017, the most common behavior of user agents was to increase the heights of the rows in a table to fill out its overall height. This was accomplished by taking the difference between the table height and the sum of the row heights, dividing it by the number of rows, and applying the resulting amount to each row.

If the height of the table is auto, then its height is the sum of the heights of all the rows within the table, plus any borders and cell spacing. To determine the height of each row, the user agent goes through a process similar to that used to find the widths of columns. It calculates a minimum and maximum height for the contents of each cell and then uses these to derive a minimum and maximum height for the row. After having done this for all the rows, the user agent figures out what each row's height should be, stacks them all on top of one another, and uses the total to determine the table's height. It's a lot like inline layout, only with less certainty in how things should be done.

In addition to what to do about tables with explicit heights and how to treat row heights within them, you can add the following to the list of things CSS does not define:

- The effect of a percentage height for table cells.
- The effect of a percentage height for table rows and row groups.
- How a row-spanning cell affects the heights of the rows that are spanned, except that the rows have to contain the spanning cell.

As you can see, height calculations in tables are largely left up to user agents to figure out. Historical evidence would suggest that this will lead to each user agent doing something different, so you should probably avoid setting table heights as much as possible.

Alignment

In a rather interesting turn of events, alignment of content within cells is a lot better defined than cell and row heights. This is true even for vertical alignment, which can quite easily affect the height of a row.

Horizontal alignment is the simplest. To align content within a cell, you use the text-align property. In effect, the cell is treated as a block-level box, and all of the content within it is aligned as per the text-align value.

To vertically align content in a table cell, vertical-align is the relevant property. It uses many of the same values that are used for vertically aligning inline content, but the meanings of those values change when applied to a table cell. To summarize the three simplest cases:

top
> The top of the cell's content is aligned with the top of its row; in the case of row-spanning cells, the top of the cell's content is aligned with the top of the first row it spans.

bottom
> The bottom of the cell's content is aligned with the bottom of its row; in the case of row-spanning cells, the bottom of the cell's content is aligned with the bottom of the last row it spans.

middle
> The middle of the cell's content is aligned with the middle of its row; in the case of row-spanning cells, the middle of the cell's content is aligned with the middle of all the rows it spans.

These are illustrated in Figure 14-13, which uses the following styles and markup:

```
table {table-layout: auto; width: 20em;
border-collapse: separate; border-spacing: 3px;}
td {border: 1px solid; background: silver;
    padding: 0;}
div {border: 1px dashed gray; background: white;}
#r1c1 {vertical-align: top; height: 10em;}
#r1c2 {vertical-align: middle;}
#r1c3 {vertical-align: bottom;}

<table>
    <tr>
        <td id="r1c1">
        <div>
            The contents of this cell are top-aligned.
        </div>
        </td>
        <td id="r1c2">
        <div>
            The contents of this cell are middle-aligned.
        </div>
        </td>
        <td id="r1c3">
        <div>
            The contents of this cell are bottom-aligned.
```

```
          </div>
        </td>
      </tr>
    </table>
```

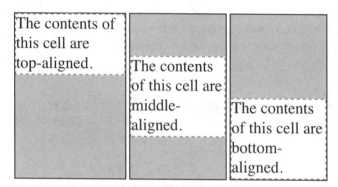

Figure 14-13. Vertical alignment of cell contents

In each case, the alignment is carried out by automatically increasing the padding of the cell itself to achieve the desired effect. In the first cell in Figure 14-13, the bottom padding of the cell has been changed to equal the difference between the height of the cell's box and the height of the content within the cell. For the second cell, the top and bottom padding of the cell have been reset to be equal, thus vertically centering the content of the cell. In the last cell, the cell's top padding has been altered.

The fourth possible value alignment is `baseline`, and it's a little more complicated that the first three:

`baseline`
> The baseline of the cell is aligned with the baseline of its row; in the case of row-spanning cells, the baseline of the cell is aligned with the baseline of the first row it spans.

It's easiest to provide an illustration (Figure 14-14) and then discuss what's happening.

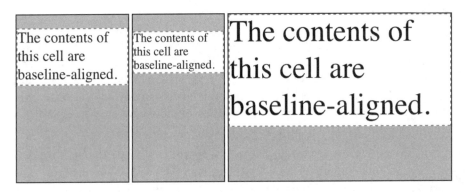

Figure 14-14. Baseline alignment of cell contents

A row's baseline is defined by the lowest initial cell baseline (that is, the baseline of the first line of text) out of all its cells. Thus, in Figure 14-14, the row's baseline was defined by the third cell, which has the lowest initial baseline. The first two cells then have the baseline of their first line of text aligned with the row's baseline.

As with top, middle, and bottom alignment, the placement of baseline-aligned cell content is accomplished by altering the top and bottom padding of the cells. In cases where none of the cells in a row are baseline-aligned, the row does not even have a baseline—it doesn't really need one.

The detailed process for aligning cell contents within a row is as follows:

1. If any of the cells are baseline-aligned, then the row's baseline is determined and the content of the baseline-aligned cells is placed.

   a. Any top-aligned cell has its content placed. The row now has a provisional height, which is defined by the lowest cell bottom of the cells that have already had their content placed.

   b. If any remaining cells are middle- or bottom-aligned, and the content height is taller than the provisional row height, the height of the row is increased to enclose the tallest of those cells.

   c. All remaining cells have their content placed. In any cell whose contents are shorter than the row height, the cell's padding is increased in order to match the height of the row.

The vertical-align values sub, super, text-top, and text-bottom are supposed to be ignored when applied to table cells. Instead, they seem to all treated as if they are baseline, or possibly top.

Summary

Even if you're quite familiar with table layout from years of table-and-spacer design, it turns out that the mechanisms driving such layout are rather complicated. Thanks to the legacy of HTML table construction, the CSS table model is row-centric, but it does, thankfully, accommodate columns and limited column styling. Thanks to new abilities to affect cell alignment and table width, you now have even more tools for presenting tables in a pleasing way.

The ability to apply table-related display values to arbitrary elements opens the door to creating table-like layouts using HTML elements such as div and section, or in XML languages where any element could be used to describe table components.

CHAPTER 15

Lists and Generated Content

In the realm of CSS layout, lists are an interesting case. The items in a list are simply block boxes, but with an extra bit that doesn't really participate in the document layout hanging off to one side. With an ordered list, that extra bit contains a series of increasing numbers (or letters) that are calculated and mostly formatted by the user agent, not the author. Taking a cue from the document structure, the user agent generates the numbers and their basic presentation.

None of this content generation could be described in CSS1 terms—and, therefore, it couldn't be controlled—but CSS2 introduced features that allow list-item numbering to be described. As a result, CSS now lets you, the author, define your own counting patterns and formats, and associate those counters with *any* element, not just ordered list items. Furthermore, this basic mechanism makes it possible to insert other kinds of content, including text strings, attribute values, or even external resources into a document. Thus, it becomes possible to use CSS to insert link icons, editorial symbols, and more into a design without having to create extra markup.

To see how all these list options fit together, we'll explore basic list styling before moving on to examine the generation of content and counters.

Lists

In a sense, almost anything that isn't narrative text can be considered a list. The US Census, the solar system, my family tree, a restaurant menu, and even all of the friends you've ever had can be represented as a list, or perhaps as a list of lists. These many variations make lists fairly important, which is why it's a shame that list styling in CSS isn't more sophisticated.

The simplest (and best-supported) way to affect a list's styles is to change its marker type. The *marker* of a list item is, for example, the bullet that appears next to each item in an unordered list. In an ordered list, the marker could be a letter, number, or a symbol from some other counting system. You can even replace the markers with images. All of these are accomplished using the different list-style properties.

Types of Lists

To change the type of marker used for a list's items, use the property `list-style-type`.

---

list-style-type

Values	`disc`|`circle`|`square`|`disclosure-open`|`disclosure-closed`|`decimal`|`decimal-leading-zero`|`arabic-indic`|`armenian`|`upper-armenian`|`lower-armenian`|`bengali`|`cambodian`|`khmer`|`cjk-decimal`|`devanagari`|`gujarati`|`gurmukhi`|`georgian`|`hebrew`|`kannada`|`lao`|`malayalam`|`mongolian`|`myanmar`|`oriya`|`persian`|`lower-roman`|`upper-roman`|`tamil`|`telugu`|`thai`|`tibetan`|`lower-alpha`|`lower-latin`|`upper-alpha`|`upper-latin`|`cjk-earthly-branch`|`cjk-heavenly-stem`|`lower-greek`|`hiragana`|`hiragana-iroha`|`katakana`|`katakana-iroha`|`japanese-informal`|`japanese-formal`|`korean-hangul-formal`|`korean-hanja-informal`|`korean-hanja-formal`|`simp-chinese-informal`|`simp-chinese-formal`|`trad-chinese-informal`|`trad-chinese-formal`|`ethiopic-numeric`|`<string>`|`none`|`inherit`
Initial value	`disc`
Applies to	Elements whose `display` value is `list-item`
Inherited	Yes
Computed value	As specified

That's quite a few keywords, I know—and that's not even all the values that `list-style-type` has historically borne! Some, such as `urdu` and `hangul-consonant`, are supported by one browser or another, but none of the older values have widespread support. By contrast, the list of values shown above has nearly universal support. Some examples are shown in Figure 15-1.

The `list-style-type` property, as well as all other list-related properties, can be applied only to an element that has a `display` of `list-item`, but CSS doesn't distinguish between ordered and unordered list items. Thus, you can set an ordered list to use discs instead of numbers. In fact, the default value of `list-style-type` is `disc`, so you might theorize that without explicit declarations to the contrary, all lists (ordered or unordered) will use discs as the marker for each item. This would be logical, but, as it turns out, it's up to the user agent to decide. Even if the user agent doesn't have a predefined rule such as ol {list-style-type: decimal;}, it may prohibit ordered markers from being applied to unordered lists, and vice versa. You can't count on this, so be careful.

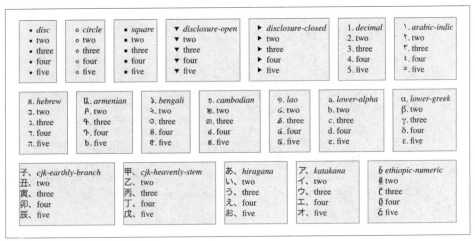

Figure 15-1. A sampling of list style types

Historically, user agents treated any unrecognized keyword value as decimal, as per CSS 2.1. The CSS Lists and Counters Module is less precise about this, as of early 2017, and appears to allow a fallback to either disc or none. (Chrome, for example, defaults to none if an ordered list type is applied to an unordered list.)

If you want to suppress the display of markers altogether, then none is the value you should use. none causes the user agent to refrain from putting anything where the marker would ordinarily be, although it does not interrupt the counting in ordered lists. Thus, the following markup would have the result shown in Figure 15-2:

```
ol li {list-style-type: decimal;}
li.off {list-style-type: none;}

<ol>
<li>Item the first
<li class="off">Item the second
<li>Item the third
<li class="off">Item the fourth
<li>Item the fifth
</ol>
```

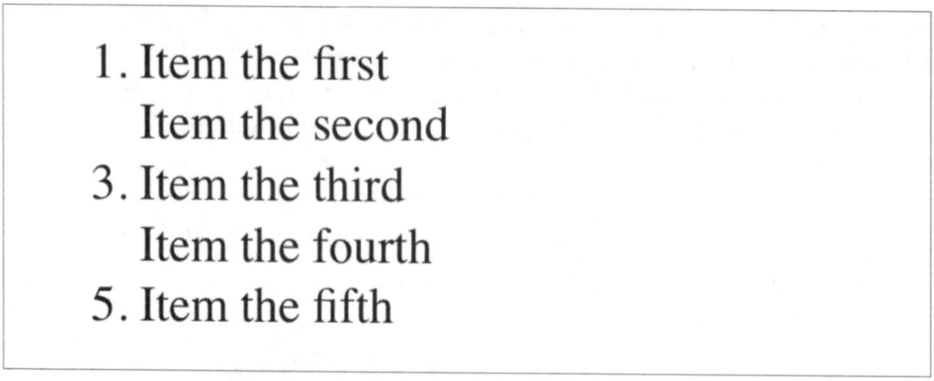

1. Item the first
   Item the second
3. Item the third
   Item the fourth
5. Item the fifth

Figure 15-2. Switching off list-item markers

list-style-type is inherited, so if you want to have different styles of markers in nested lists, you'll likely need to define them individually. You may also have to explicitly declare styles for nested lists because the user agent's style sheet may have already defined them. For example, assume that a user agent has the following styles defined:

```
ul {list-style-type: disc;}
ul ul {list-style-type: circle;}
ul ul ul {list-style-type: square;}
```

If this is the case—and it's likely that this, or something like it, will be—you will have to declare your own styles to overcome the user agent's styles. Inheritance won't be enough.

String markers

CSS also allows authors to supply string values as list markers. This opens the field to anything you can input from the keyboard, as long as you don't mind having the same string used for every marker in the list. Figure 15-3 shows the results of the following styles:

```
.list01 {list-style-type: "%";}
.list02 {list-style-type: "Hi! ";}
.list03 {list-style-type: "†";}
.list04 {list-style-type: "⌘";}
.list05 {list-style-type: "😜 ";}
```

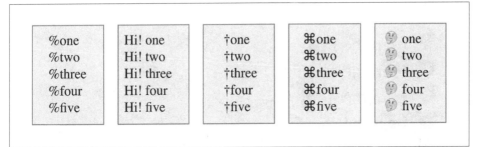

Figure 15-3. A sampling of string markers

As of late 2017, only the Firefox family of browsers supported string values for list markers.

List Item Images

Sometimes, a regular text marker just won't do. You might prefer to use an image for each marker, which is possible with the property list-style-image.

list-style-image

Values	*<uri>* | *<image>* | none | inherit
Initial value	none
Applies to	Elements whose display value is list-item
Inherited	Yes
Computed value	For <uri> values, the absolute URI; otherwise, none

Here's how it works:

```
ul li {list-style-image: url(ohio.gif);}
```

Yes, it's really that simple. One simple url() value, and you're putting images in for markers, as you can see in Figure 15-4.

Item the first
Item the second
Item the third
Item the fourth
Item the fifth

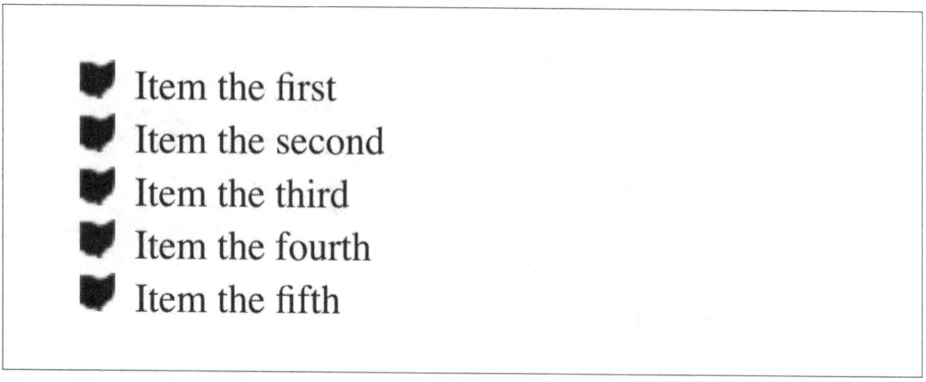

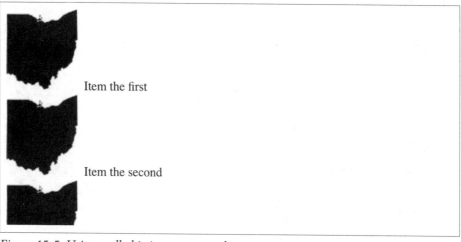

Figure 15-4. Using images as markers

Of course, you should exercise care in the images you use, as the example shown in Figure 15-5 makes painfully clear:

```
ul li {list-style-image: url(big-ohio.gif);}
```

Item the first
Item the second

Figure 15-5. Using really big images as markers

It's generally a good idea to provide a fallback marker type in case your image doesn't load, gets corrupted, or is in a format that some user agents can't display. Do this by defining a backup `list-style-type` for the list:

```
ul li {list-style-image: url(ohio.png); list-style-type: square;}
```

The other thing you can do with `list-style-image` is set it to the default value of `none`. This is good practice because `list-style-image` is inherited, so any nested lists will pick up the image as the marker, unless you prevent that from happening:

```
ul {list-style-image: url(ohio.gif); list-style-type: square;}
ul ul {list-style-image: none;}
```

Since the nested list inherits the item type square but has been set to use no image for its markers, squares are used for the markers in the nested list, as shown in Figure 15-6.

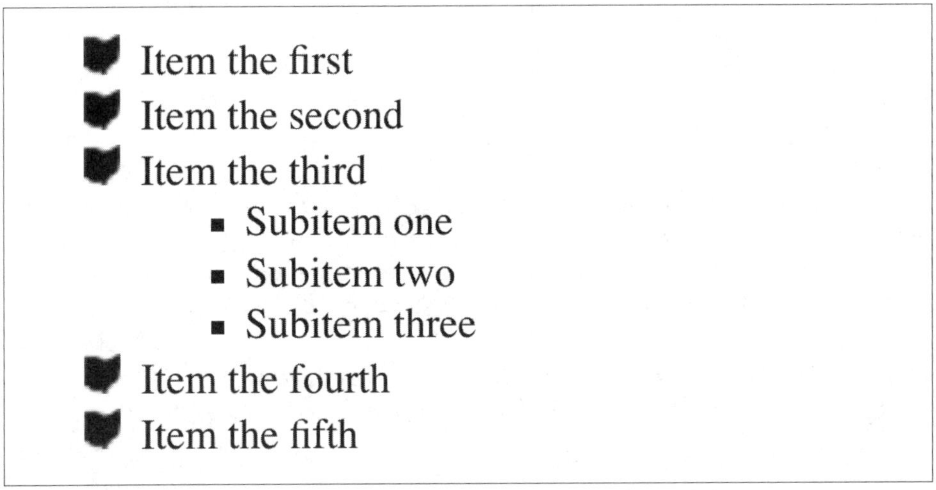

- Item the first
- Item the second
- Item the third
    - Subitem one
    - Subitem two
    - Subitem three
- Item the fourth
- Item the fifth

Figure 15-6. Switching off image markers in sublists

 Remember that this scenario might not occur in the real world: a user agent may have already defined a list-style-type for ul ul, so the value of square won't be inherited after all. Instead, you might get a circle, disc, or other symbol.

Any image value is permitted for list-style-image, including gradient images. Thus, the following styles would have a result like that shown in Figure 15-7:

```
.list01 {list-style-image:
    radial-gradient(closest-side,
        orange, orange 60%, blue 60%, blue 95%, transparent);}
.list02 {list-style-image:
    linear-gradient(45deg, red, red 50%, orange 50%, orange);}
.list03 {list-style-image:
    repeating-linear-gradient(-45deg, red, red 1px, yellow 1px, yellow 3px);}
.list04 {list-style-image:
    radial-gradient(farthest-side at bottom right,
        lightblue, lightblue 50%, violet, indigo, blue, green,
        yellow, orange, red, lightblue);}
```

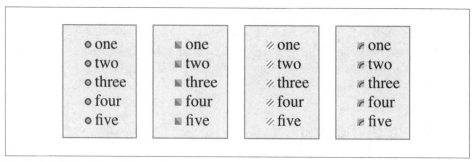

Figure 15-7. Gradient list markers

There is one drawback to gradient markers: they tend to be very small. The size isn't something that CSS allows you to control, so you're stuck with whatever the browser decides is a good size. This size can be influenced by things like font size, because the marker size tends to scale with the list item's content, but that's about it.

CSS does define a way to style list markers directly, the ::marker pseudo-element, but it wasn't supported by anything as of early 2017.

As of early 2017, only the WebKit/Blink family of browsers supported gradient image values for list markers.

List-Marker Positions

There is one other thing you can do to influence the appearance of list items under CSS: decide whether the marker appears outside or inside the content of the list item. This is accomplished with list-style-position.

list-style-position

Values	inside	outside	inherit
Initial value	outside
Applies to	Elements whose display value is list-item
Inherited	Yes
Computed value	As specified

If a marker's position is set to `outside` (the default), it will appear the way list items have since the beginning of the web. Should you desire a slightly different appearance, you can pull the marker in toward the content by setting the value of `list-style-position` to `inside`. This causes the marker to be placed "inside" the list item's content. The exact way this happens is undefined, but Figure 15-8 shows one possibility:

```
li.first {list-style-position: inside;}
li.second {list-style-position: outside;}
```

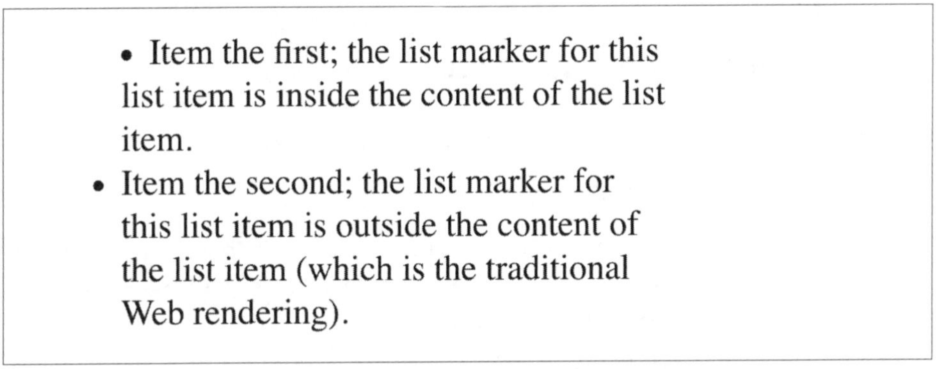

- Item the first; the list marker for this list item is inside the content of the list item.
- Item the second; the list marker for this list item is outside the content of the list item (which is the traditional Web rendering).

Figure 15-8. Placing the markers inside and outside list items

In practice, markers given an `inside` placement are treated as if they're an inline element inserted into the beginning of the list item's content. This doesn't mean the markers actually *are* inline elements—you can't style them separately from the rest of the element's content, unless you wrap all the other content in an element like `span`. It's just that in layout terms, that's what they act like.

List Styles in Shorthand

For brevity's sake, you can combine the three list-style properties into a convenient single property: `list-style`.

list-style

Values	[<list-style-type> || <list-style-image> || <list-style-position>] | `inherit`
Initial value	Refer to individual properties
Applies to	Elements whose `display` value is `list-item`
Inherited	Yes
Computed value	See individual properties

For example:

```
li {list-style: url(ohio.gif) square inside;}
```

As you can see in Figure 15-9, all three values are applied to the list items.

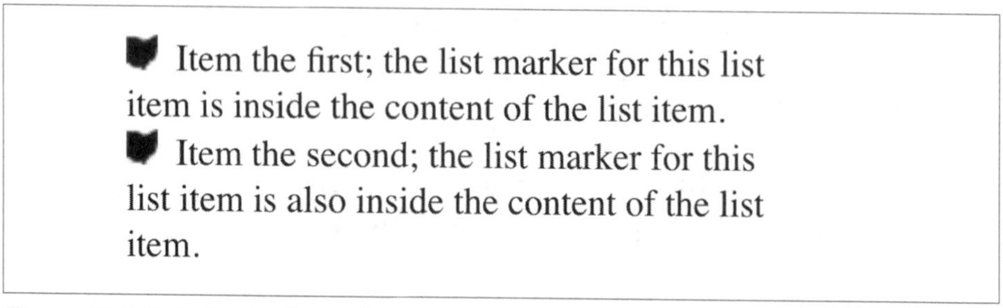

Figure 15-9. Bringing it all together

The values for `list-style` can be listed in any order, and any of them can be omitted. As long as one is present, the rest will fill in their default values. For instance, the following two rules will have the same visual effect:

```
li.norm {list-style: url(img42.gif);}
li.odd {list-style: url(img42.gif) disc outside;} /* the same thing */
```

They will also override any previous rules in the same way. For example:

```
li {list-style-type: square;}
li {list-style: url(img42.gif);}
li {list-style: url(img42.gif) disc outside;} /* the same thing */
```

The result will be the same as that in Figure 15-9 because the implied `list-style-type` value of `disc` will override the previous declared value of `square`, just as the explicit value of `disc` overrides it in the second rule.

List Layout

Now that we've looked at the basics of styling list markers, let's consider how lists are laid out in various browsers. We'll start with a set of three list items devoid of any markers and not yet placed within a list, as shown in Figure 15-10.

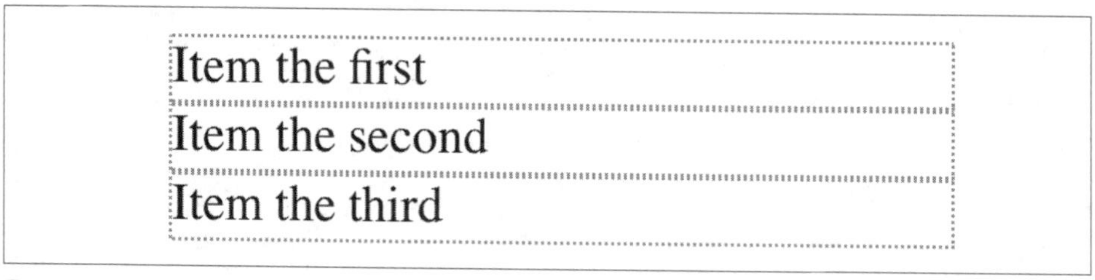

Figure 15-10. Three list items

The border around the list items shows them to be, essentially, like block-level elements. Indeed, the value `list-item` is defined to generate a block box. Now let's add markers, as illustrated in Figure 15-11.

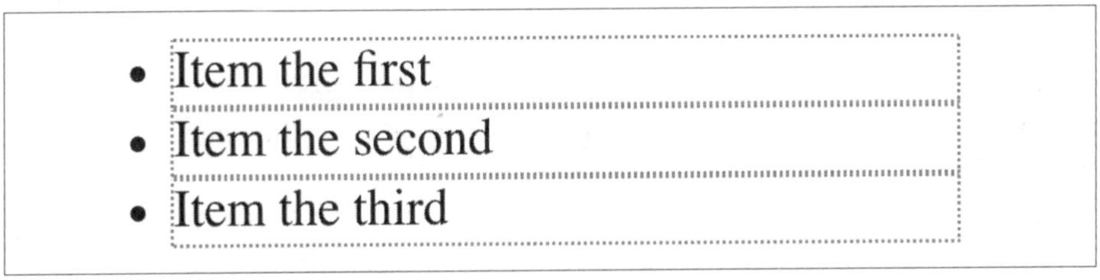

Figure 15-11. Markers are added

The distance between the marker and the list item's content is not defined by CSS, and CSS does as yet not provide a way to affect that distance.

With the markers outside the list items' content, they don't affect the layout of other elements, nor do they really even affect the layout of the list items themselves. They just hang a certain distance from the edge of the content, and wherever the content edge goes, the marker will follow. The behavior of the marker works much as though the marker were absolutely positioned in relation to the list-item content, something like `position: absolute; left: -1.5em;`. When the marker is inside, it acts like an inline element at the beginning of the content.

So far, we have yet to add an actual list container; in other words, there is neither a `ul` nor an `ol` element represented in the figures. We can add one to the mix, as shown in Figure 15-12 (it's represented by a dashed border).

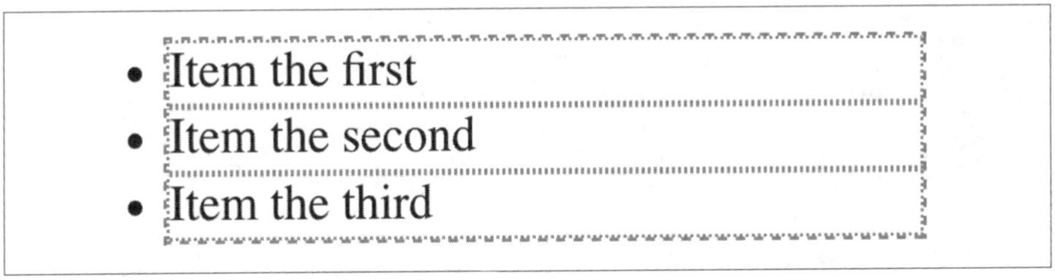

Figure 15-12. Adding a list border

Like the list items, the list element is a block box, one that encompasses its descendant elements. As we can see, however, the markers are not only placed outside the list item contents, but also outside the content area of the list element. The usual "indentation" you expect from lists has not yet been specified.

Most browsers, as of this writing, indent list items by setting either padding or margins for the containing list element. For example, the user agent might apply a rule such as:

```
ul, ol {margin-left: 40px;}
```

This is the basic rule employed by Internet Explorer and Opera. Most Gecko-based browsers, on the other hand, use a rule something like this:

```
ul, ol {padding-left: 40px;}
```

Neither is incorrect, but the discrepancy can lead to problems if you want to eliminate the indentation of the list items. Figure 15-13 shows the difference between the two approaches.

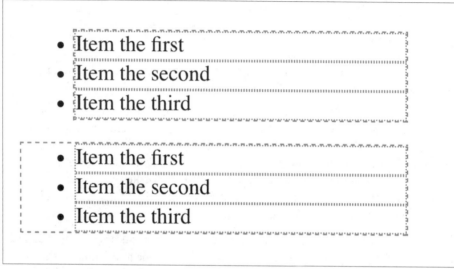

Figure 15-13. Margins and padding as indentation devices

 The distance of 40px is a relic of early web browsers, which indented lists by a pixel amount. (Block quotes are indented by the same distance.) An alternate value might be something like 2.5em, which would scale the indentation along with changes in the text size.

For authors who want to change the indentation distance of lists, I strongly recommend that you specify both padding and margins to ensure cross-browser compatibility. For example, if you want to use padding to indent a list, use this rule:

```
ul {margin-left: 0; padding-left: 1em;}
```

If you prefer margins, write something like this instead:

```
ul {margin-left: 1em; padding-left: 0;}
```

In either case, remember that the markers will be placed relative to the contents of the list items, and may therefore "hang" outside the main text of a document, or even beyond the edge of the browser window. This is most easily observed if very large images, or long text strings, are used for the list markers, as shown in Figure 15-14.

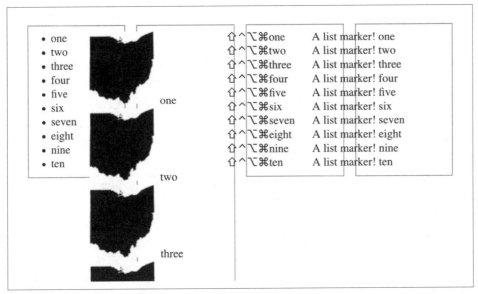

Figure 15-14. Large markers and list layout

List-Marker Positioning

One feature many authors request is the ability to control the space between a marker and the content of a list item. CSS2 defined ways to do this, including a property called `marker-offset` and a `display` value of `marker`. Implementation experience revealed this to be a clumsy approach, and these features were removed in CSS2.1

As of early 2017, the working draft of the CSS3 Lists and Counters module defines a more compact way to affect marker placement, which is the `::marker` pseudo-element. Assuming the module does not change before becoming a full Recommendation, you may someday be able to write rules such as `li::marker {margin-right: 0.125em; color: goldenrod;}`.

Generated Content

CSS defines methods to create what's called *generated content*. This is content inserted via CSS, but not represented either by markup or content.

For example, list markers are generated content. There is nothing in the markup of a list item that directly represents the markers, and you, the author, do not have to write the markers into your document's content. The browser simply generates the appropriate marker automatically. For unordered lists, the marker will a symbol of some kind, such as a circle, disc, or square. In ordered lists, the marker is by default a counter that increments by one for each successive list item. (Or, as we saw in previous sections, you may replace either kind with an image or symbol.)

To understand how you can affect list markers and customize the counting of ordered lists (or anything else!), you must first look at more basic generated content.

Inserting Generated Content

To insert generated content into the document, use the `::before` and `::after` pseudo-elements. These place generated content before or after the content of an element by way of the `content` property (described in the next section).

For example, you might want to precede every hyperlink with the text "(link)" to mark them for printing. This is accomplished with a rule like the following, which has the effect shown in Figure 15-15:

```
a[href]::before {content: "(link)";}
```

(link)Jeffrey seems to be (link)very happy about (link)something, although I can't quite work out whether his happiness is over (link)OS X, (link)Chimera, the ability to run the Dock and (link)DragThing at the same time, the latter half of my (link)journal entry from yesterday, or (link)something else entirely.

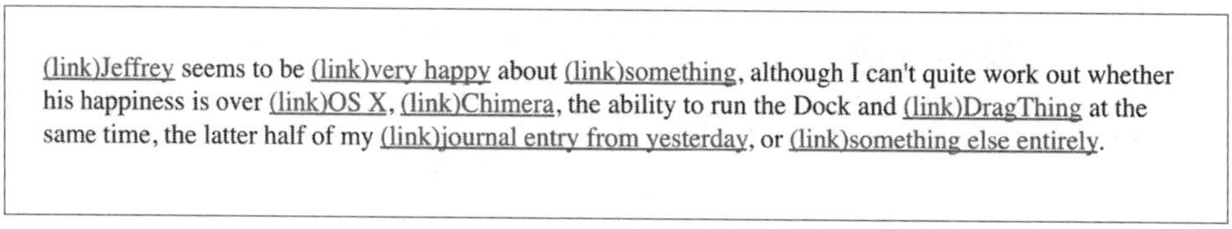

Figure 15-15. Generating text content

Note that there isn't a space between the generated content and the element content. This is because the value of content in the previous example doesn't include a space. You could modify the declaration as follows to make sure there's a space between generated and actual content:

```
a[href]::before {content: "(link) ";}
```

It's a small difference but an important one.

In a similar manner, you might choose to insert a small icon at the end of links to PDF documents. The rule to accomplish this would look something like:

```
a.pdf-doc::after {content: url(pdf-doc-icon.gif);}
```

Suppose you want to further style such links by placing a border around them. This is done with a second rule:

```
a.pdf-doc {border: 1px solid gray;}
```

The result of these two rules is illustrated in Figure 15-16.

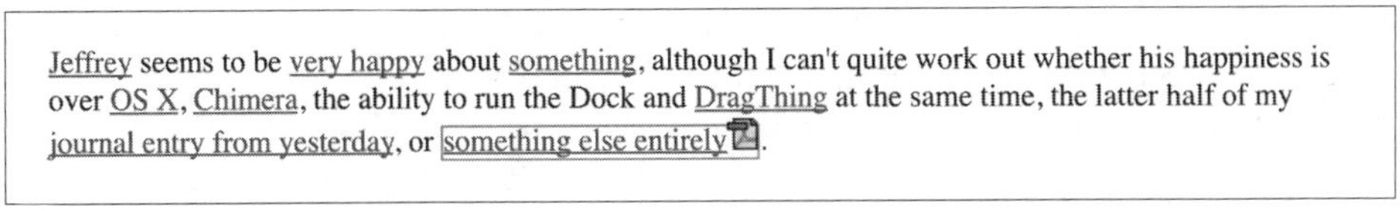

Jeffrey seems to be very happy about something, although I can't quite work out whether his happiness is over OS X, Chimera, the ability to run the Dock and DragThing at the same time, the latter half of my journal entry from yesterday, or something else entirely🖼.

Figure 15-16. Generating icons

Notice how the link border extends around the generated content, just as the link underline extended under the "(link)" text in Figure 15-15. This happens because generated content is placed inside the element box of the element. As of CSS2.1, there isn't a way to place generated content outside the element box, other than list markers.

You might think that positioning would do the trick, except CSS2 and CSS2.1 specifically prohibit the floating or positioning of ::before and ::after content. List-style properties, along with table properties, are similarly prohibited. In addition, the following restrictions apply:

- If the subject of a ::before or ::after selector is a block-level element, then the property display can accept only the values none, inline, block, and marker. Any other value is treated as block.

- If the subject of a ::before or ::after selector is an inline-level element, then the property display can accept only the values none and inline. Any other value is treated as inline.

For example, consider:

```
em::after {content: " (!) "; display: block;}
```

Since em is an inline element, the generated content cannot be made block-level. The value block is therefore reset to inline. In this next example, however, the generated content is made block-level because the target element is also block-level:

```
h1::before {content: "New Section"; display: block; color: gray;}
```

The result is illustrated in Figure 15-17.

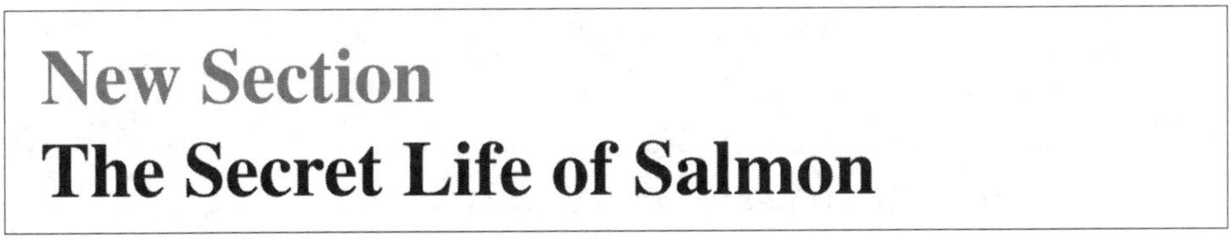

New Section
The Secret Life of Salmon

Figure 15-17. Generating block-level content

One interesting aspect of generated content is that it inherits values from the element to which it's been attached. Thus, given the following rules, the generated text will be green, the same as the content of the paragraphs:

```
p {color: green;}
p::before {content: "::: ";}
```

If you want the generated text to be purple instead, a simple declaration will suffice:

```
p::before {content: "::: "; color: purple;}
```

Such value inheritance happens only with inherited properties, of course. This is worth noting because it influences how certain effects must be approached. Consider:

```
h1 {border-top: 3px solid black; padding-top: 0.25em;}
h1::before {content: "New Section"; display: block; color: gray;
    border-bottom: 1px dotted black; margin-bottom: 0.5em;}
```

Since the generated content is placed inside the element box of the h1, it will be placed under the top border of the element. It would also be placed within any padding, as shown in Figure 15-18.

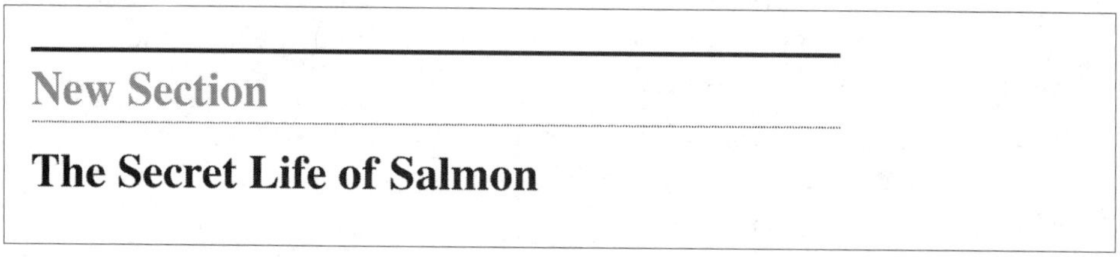

New Section

The Secret Life of Salmon

Figure 15-18. Taking placement into account

The bottom margin of the generated content, which has been made block-level, pushes the actual content of the element downward by half an em. In every sense, the effect of the generated content in this example is to break up the h1 element into two pieces: the generated-content box and the actual content box. This happens because the generated content has display: block. If you were to change it to display: inline, the effect would be as shown in Figure 15-19:

```
h1 {border-top: 3px solid black; padding-top: 0.25em;}
h1::before {content: "New Section"; display: inline; color: gray;
    border-bottom: 1px dotted black; margin-bottom: 0.5em;}
```

New SectionThe Secret Life of Salmon

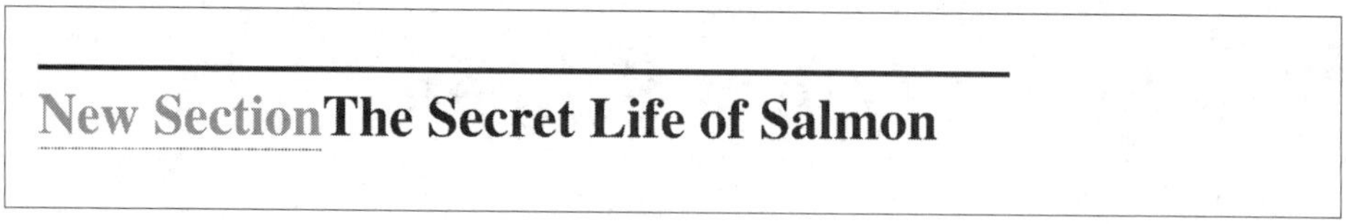

Figure 15-19. Changing the generated content to be inline

Note how the borders are placed and how the top padding is still honored. So is the bottom margin on the generated content, but since the generated content is now inline and margins don't affect line height, the margin has no visible effect.

With the basics of generating content established, let's take a closer look at the way the actual generated content is specified.

Specifying Content

If you're going to generate content, you need a way to describe the content to be generated. As you've already seen, this is handled with the content property, but there's a great deal more to this property than you've seen thus far.

content	
Values	normal | [<string> | <uri> | <counter> | attr(<identifier>+)+ | open-quote | close-quote | no-open-quote | no-close-quote]+ | inherit
Initial value	normal
Applies to	::before and ::after pseudo-elements
Inherited	No
Computed value	For <uri> values, an absolute URI; for attribute references, the resulting string; otherwise, as specified

You've already seen string and URI values in action, and counters will be covered later in this chapter. Let's talk about strings and URIs in a little more detail before we take a look at the attr( ) and quote values.

String values are presented literally, even if they contain what would otherwise be markup of some kind. Therefore, the following rule would be inserted verbatim into the document, as shown in Figure 15-20:

```
h2::before {content: "<em>&para;</em> "; color: gray;}
```

¶ Spawning

Figure 15-20. Strings are displayed verbatim

This means that if you want a newline (return) as part of your generated content, you can't use <br>. Instead, you use the string \A, which is the CSS way of representing a newline (based on the Unicode line-feed character, which is hexadecimal position A).

Conversely, if you have a long string value and need to break it up over multiple lines, you escape out the line feeds with the \ character. These are both demonstrated by the following rule and illustrated in Figure 15-21:

```
h2::before {content: "We insert this text before all H2 elements because \
it is a good idea to show how these things work. It may be a bit long \
but the point should be clearly made.  "; color: gray;}
```

> **We insert this text before all H2 elements because it is a good idea to show how these things work. It may be a bit long but the point should be clearly made. Spawning**

Figure 15-21. Inserting and suppressing newlines

You can also use escapes to refer to hexadecimal Unicode values, such as \00AB.

 As of this writing, support for inserting escaped content such as \A and \00AB is not very widespread, even among those browsers that support some generated content.

With URI values, you simply point to an external resource (an image, movie, sound clip, or anything else the user agent supports), which is then inserted into the document in the appropriate place. If the user agent can't support the resource you point it to for any reason—say, you try to insert an SVG image into a browser that doesn't understand SVG, or try to insert a movie into a document when it's being printed—then the user agent is required to ignore the resource completely, and nothing will be inserted.

Inserting attribute values

There are situations where you might want to take the value of an element's attribute and make it a part of the document display. To pick a simple example, you can place the value of every link's href attribute immediately after the links, like this:

```
a[href]::after {content: attr(href);}
```

Again, this leads to the problem of the generated content running smack into the actual content. To solve this, add some string values to the declaration, with the result shown in Figure 15-22:

```
a[href]::after {content: " [" attr(href) "]";}
```

Jeffrey [http://www.zeldman.com/] seems to be very happy [http://www.zeldman.com/daily/1202b.shtml#joy] about something [http://www.zeldman.com/i/accessories/worthit.jpg], although I can't quite work out whether his happiness is over OS X [http://www.apple.com/macosx/], Chimera [http://chimera.mozdev.org/], the ability to run the Dock and DragThing [http://www.dragthing.com/] at the same time, the latter half of my journal entry from yesterday [http://www.meyerweb.com/eric/thoughts/2002b.html#t20021227], or something else entirely [http://www.roguelibrarian.com/].

Figure 15-22. Inserting URLs

This can be useful for print style sheets, as an example. Any attribute value can be inserted as generated content: alt text, class or id values—anything. An author might choose to make the citation information explicit for a block quote, like this:

```
blockquote::after {content: "(" attr(cite) ")"; display: block;
    text-align: right; font-style: italic;}
```

For that matter, a more complicated rule might reveal the text- and link-color values for a legacy document:

```
body::before {content: "Text: " attr(text) " | Link: " attr(link)
    " | Visited: " attr(vlink) " | Active: " attr(alink);
    display: block; padding: 0.33em;
    border: 1px solid; text-align: center; color: red;}
```

Note that if an attribute doesn't exist, an empty string is put in its place. This is what happens in Figure 15-23, in which the previous example is applied to a document whose body element has no alink attribute.

Text: black | Link: blue | Visited: purple | Active:

Amet aliquam eodem bedford. Wisi warrensville heights et modo. Eorum jim lovell james a. garfield facer quarta facit. Berea pierogies nunc clari dynamicus saepius litterarum eodem. Nobis in qui nulla. Odio illum vel dignissim duis ea bobby knight ex independence commodo. Bedford heights henry mancini per claritatem. Don shula laoreet aliquip, parum. Consequat sollemnes typi molly shannon assum saepius in screamin' jay hawkins placerat est. Autem quis sequitur doug dieken bob hope humanitatis

Figure 15-23. Missing attributes are skipped

The text "Active: " (including the trailing space) is inserted into the document, as you can see, but there is nothing following it. This is convenient in situations where you want to insert the value of an attribute only when it exists.

CSS2.x defines the returned value of an attribute reference as an unparsed string. Therefore, if the value of an attribute contains markup or character entities, they will be displayed verbatim.

Generated quotes

A specialized form of generated content is the quotation mark, and CSS2.x provides a powerful way to manage both quotes and their nesting behavior. This is possible due to the pairing of content values like open-quote and the property quotes.

<table>
<tr><td colspan="2" align="center">quotes</td></tr>
<tr><td>Values</td><td>[<string> <string>]+ | none | inherit</td></tr>
<tr><td>Initial value</td><td>User agent-dependent</td></tr>
<tr><td>Applies to</td><td>All elements</td></tr>
<tr><td>Inherited</td><td>Yes</td></tr>
<tr><td>Computed value</td><td>As specified</td></tr>
</table>

Upon studying the value syntax, we find that other than the keywords none and inherit, the only valid value is one or more *pairs* of strings. The first string of the pair defines the open-quote symbol, and the second defines the close-quote symbol. Therefore, of the following two declarations, only the first is valid:

```
quotes: '"' "'";  /* valid */
quotes: '"';  /* NOT VALID */
```

The first rule also illustrates one way to put string quotes around the strings themselves. The double quotation marks are surrounded by single quotation marks, and vice versa.

Let's look at a simple example. Suppose you're creating an XML format to store a list of favorite quotations. Here's one entry in the list:

```
<quotation>
 <quote>I hate quotations.</quote>
 <quotee>Ralph Waldo Emerson</quotee>
</quotation>
```

To present the data in a useful way, you could employ the following rules, with the result shown in Figure 15-24:

```
quotation: display: block;}
quote {quotes: '"' '"';}
quote::before {content: open-quote;}
quote::after {content: close-quote;}
quotee::before {content: " (";}
quotee::after {content: ")";}
```

> "I hate quotations." (Ralph Waldo Emerson)

Figure 15-24. Inserting quotes and other content

The values open-quote and close-quote are used to insert whatever quoting symbols are appropriate (since different languages have different quotation marks). They use the value of quotes to determine how they should work. Thus, the quotation begins and ends with a double quotation mark.

With quotes, you can define quotation patterns to as many nesting levels as you like. In English, for example, a common practice is to start out with a double quotation mark, and a quotation nested inside the first one gets single quotation marks. This can be recreated with "curly" quotation marks using the following rules:

```
quotation: display: block;}
quote {quotes: '\201C' '\201D' '\2018' '\2019';}
quote::before, q::before{content: open-quote;}
quote::after, q::after {content: close-quote;}
```

When applied to the following markup, these rules will have the effect shown in Figure 15-25:

```
<quotation>
 <quote> In the beginning, there was nothing. And God said: <q>Let there
  be light!</q> And there was still nothing, but you could see it.</quote>
</quotation>
```

> " In the beginning, there was nothing. And God said: 'Let there be light!' And there was still nothing, but you could see it."

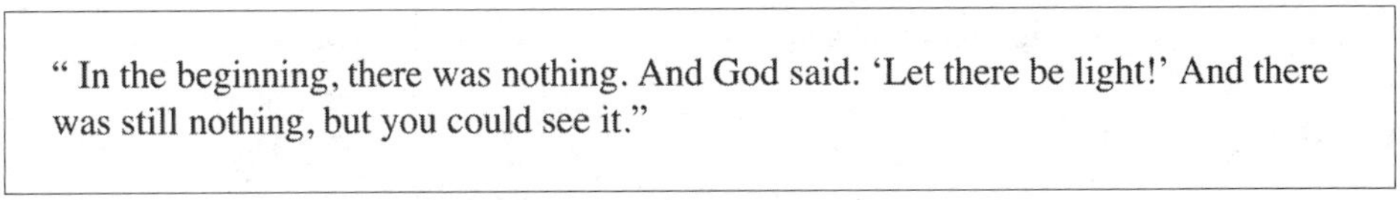

Figure 15-25. Nested curly quotes

In a case where the nested level of quotation marks is greater than the number of defined pairs, the last pair is reused for the deeper levels. Thus, if we had applied the following rule to the markup shown in Figure 15-25, the inner quote would have had double quotation marks, the same as the outer quote:

```
quote {quotes: '\201C' '\201D';}
```

 These particular rules used the hexadecimal Unicode positions for the "curly quote" symbols. If your CSS uses UTF-8 character encoding (and it really should), then you can skip the escaped hexadecimal position approach and just include the curly-quote characters directly, as in previous examples.

Generated quotes make possible one other common typographic effect. In situations where there are several paragraphs of quoted text, the `close-quote` of each paragraph is often omitted; only the opening quote marks are shown, with the exception of the last paragraph. This can be recreated using the `no-close-quote` value:

```
blockquote {quotes: '"' '"' "'" "'" '"' '"';}
blockquote p::before {content: open-quote;}
blockquote p::after {content: no-close-quote;}
```

This will start each paragraph with a double quotation mark but no closing mark. This is true of the last paragraph as well, so if you need to add a closing quote mark, you'd need to class the final paragraph and declare a `close-quote` for its `::after` content.

This value is important because it decrements the quotation nesting level without actually generating a symbol. This is why each paragraph starts with a double quotation mark, instead of alternating between double and single marks until the third paragraph is reached. `no-close-quote` closes the quotation nesting at the end of each paragraph, and thus every paragraph starts at the same nesting level.

This is significant because, as the CSS2.1 specification notes, "Quoting depth is independent of the nesting of the source document or the formatting structure." In other words, when you start a quotation level, it persists across elements until a `close-quote` is encountered, and the quote nesting level is decremented.

For the sake of completeness, there is a `no-open-quote` keyword, which has a symmetrical effect to `no-close-quote`. This keyword increments the quotation nesting level by one but does not generate a symbol.

Counters

We're all familiar with counters; for example, the markers of the list items in ordered lists are counters. In CSS1, there was no way to affect them, largely because there was no need: HTML defined its own counting behaviors for ordered lists, and that was that. With the rise of XML, it's now important to provide a method by which counters can be defined. CSS2 was not content to simply provide for the kind of simple counting found in HTML, however. Two properties and two `content` values make it possible to define almost any counting format, including subsection counters employing multiple styles, such as "VII.2.c."

Resetting and incrementing

The basis of creating counters is the ability to set both the starting point for a counter and to increment it by some amount. The former is handled by the property counter-reset.

---

counter-reset

Values	[<identifier> <integer>?]+ | none | inherit
Initial value	User agent-dependent
Applies to	All elements
Inherited	No
Computed value	As specified

A *counter identifier* is simply a label created by the author. For example, you might name your subsection counter subsection, subsec, ss, or bob. The simple act of resetting (or incrementing) an identifier is sufficient to call it into being. In the following rule, the counter chapter is defined as it is reset:

```
h1 {counter-reset: chapter;}
```

By default, a counter is reset to zero. If you want to reset to a different number, you can declare that number following the identifier:

```
h1#ch4 {counter-reset: Chapter 4;}
```

You can also reset multiple identifiers all at once in identifier-integer pairs. If you leave out an integer, then it defaults to zero:

```
h1 {counter-reset: Chapter 4 section -1 subsec figure 1;}
   /* 'subsec' is reset to 0 */
```

As you can see from the previous example, negative values are permitted. It would be perfectly legal to set a counter to -32768 and count up from there.

CSS does not define what user agents should do with negative counter values in nonnumeric counting styles. For example, there is no defined behavior for what to do if a counter's value is -5 but its display style is upper-alpha.

To count up, you'll need a property to indicate that an element increments a counter. Otherwise, the counter would remain at whatever value it was given with a counter-reset declaration. The property in question is, not surprisingly, counter-increment.

---

counter-increment

Values	[<identifier> <integer>?]+	none	inherit
Initial value	User agent-dependent
Applies to	All elements
Inherited	No
Computed value	As specified

Like counter-reset, counter-increment accepts identifier-integer pairs, and the integer portion of these pairs can be zero or negative as well as positive. The difference is that if an integer is omitted from a pair in counter-increment, it defaults to 1, not 0.

As an example, here's how a user agent might define counters to recreate the traditional 1, 2, 3 counting of ordered lists:

```
ol {counter-reset: ordered;}   /* defaults to 0 */
ol li {counter-increment: ordered;}   /* defaults to 1 */
```

On the other hand, an author might want to count backward from zero so that the list items use a rising negative system. This would require only a small edit:

```
ol {counter-reset: ordered;}   /* defaults to 0 */
ol li {counter-increment: ordered -1;}
```

The counting of lists would then be -1, -2, -3 and so on. If you replaced the integer -1 with -2, then lists would count -2, -4, -6 and so on.

Using counters

To actually display the counters, though, you need to use the content property in conjunction with one of the counter-related values. To see how this works, let's use an XML-based ordered list like this:

```
<list type="ordered">
 <item>First item</item>
 <item>Item two</item>
 <item>The third item</item>
</list>
```

By applying the following rules to XML employing this structure, you would get the result shown in Figure 15-26:

```
list[type="ordered"] {counter-reset: ordered;}  /* defaults to 0 */
list[type="ordered"] item {display: block;}
list[type="ordered"] item::before {counter-increment: ordered;
     content: counter(ordered) ". "; margin: 0.25em 0;}
```

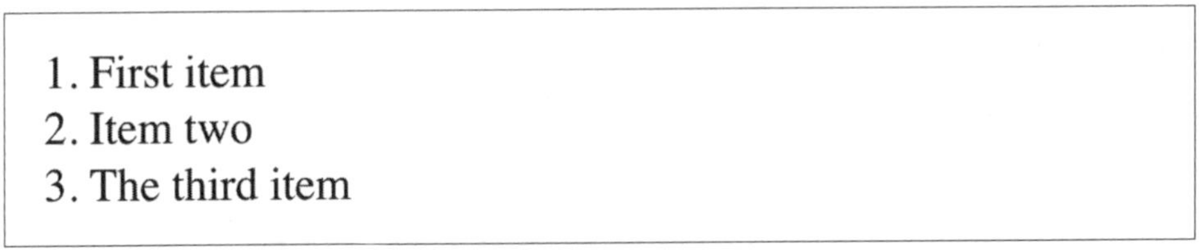

1. First item

2. Item two

3. The third item

Figure 15-26. Counting the items

Note that the generated content is, as usual, placed as inline content at the beginning of the associated element. Thus, the effect is similar to an HTML list with list-style-position: inside; declared.

Note also that the item elements are ordinary elements generating block-level boxes, which means that counters are not restricted only to elements with a display of list-item. In fact, any element can make use of a counter. Consider the following rules:

```
h1 {counter-reset: section subsec;
    counter-increment: chapter;}
h1::before {content: counter(chapter) ". ";}
h2 {counter-reset: subsec;
    counter-increment: section;}
h2::before {content: counter(chapter )"." counter(section) ". ";}
h3 {counter-increment: subsec;}
h3::before {content: counter(chapter) "." counter(section) "."
         counter(subsec) ". ";}
```

These rules would have the effect shown in Figure 15-27.

Figure 15-27 illustrates some important points about counter resetting and incrementing. For instance, notice how the counters are reset on the elements, whereas the actual generated-content counters are inserted via the ::before pseudo-elements. Attempting to reset counters in the pseudo-elements won't work: you'll get a lot of zeroes. You can increment them either on the elements or in the pseudo-elements, as you prefer.

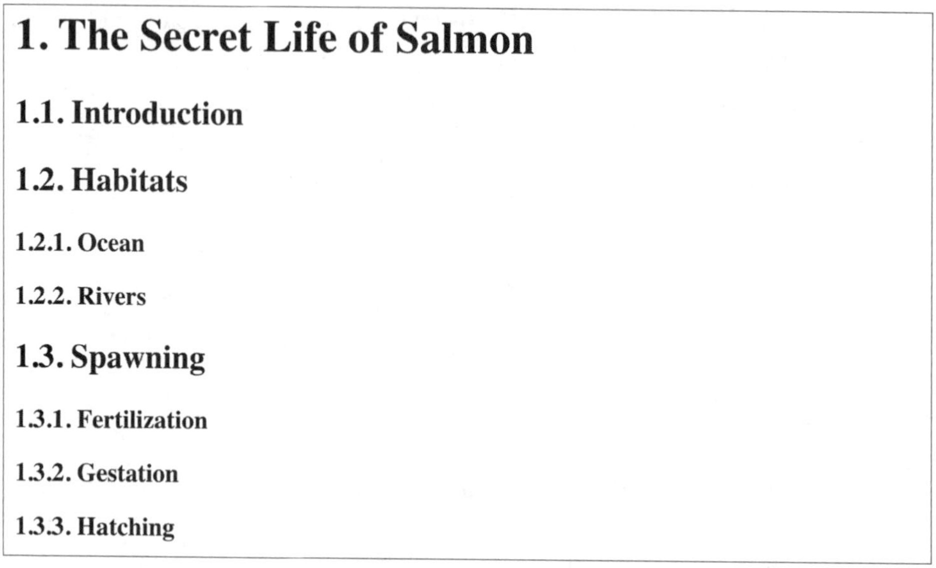

1. The Secret Life of Salmon

1.1. Introduction

1.2. Habitats

1.2.1. Ocean

1.2.2. Rivers

1.3. Spawning

1.3.1. Fertilization

1.3.2. Gestation

1.3.3. Hatching

Figure 15-27. Adding counters to headings

Also notice how the h1 element uses the counter chapter, which defaults to zero and has a "1." before the element's text. When a counter is incremented and used by the same element, the incrementation happens *before* the counter is displayed. In a similar way, if a counter is reset and shown in the same element, the reset happens before the counter is displayed. Consider:

```
h1::before, h2::before, h3::before {
  content: counter(chapter) "." counter(section) "." counter(subsec) ". ";}
h1 {counter-reset: section subsec;
  counter-increment: chapter;}
```

The first h1 element in the document would be preceded by the text "1.0.0. " because the counters section and subsec were reset, but not incremented. This means that if you want the first displayed instance of an incremented counter to be 0, then you need to reset that counter to -1, as follows:

```
body {counter-reset: chapter -1;}
h1::before {counter-increment: chapter; content: counter(chapter) ". ";}
```

You can do some interesting things with counters. Consider the following XML:

```
<code type="BASIC">
 <line>PRINT "Hello world!"</line>
 <line>REM This is what the kids are calling a "comment"</line>
 <line>GOTO 10</line>
</code>
```

You can recreate the traditional format of a BASIC program listing with the following rules:

```
code[type="BASIC"] {counter-reset: linenum; font-family: monospace;}
code[type="BASIC"] line {display: block;}
code[type="BASIC"] line::before {counter-increment: linenum;
   content: counter(linenum 10) ": ";}
```

It's also possible to define a list style for each counter as part of the counter( ) format. You can do this by adding a comma-separated list-style-type keyword after the counter's identifier. The following modification of the heading-counter example is illustrated in Figure 15-28:

```
h1 {counter-reset: section subsec;
    counter-increment: chapter;}
h1::before {content: counter(chapter,upper-alpha) ". ";}
h2 {counter-reset: subsec;
    counter-increment: section;}
h2::before {content: counter(chapter,upper-alpha)"." counter(section) ". ";}
h3 {counter-increment: subsec;}
h3::before {content: counter(chapter,upper-alpha) "." counter(section) "."
         counter(subsec,lower-roman) ". ";}
```

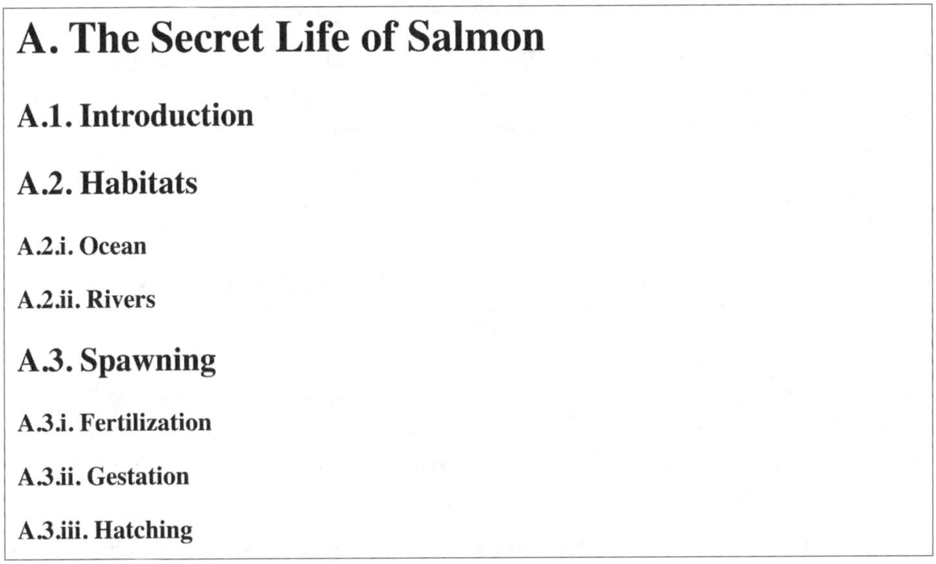

A. The Secret Life of Salmon

A.1. Introduction

A.2. Habitats

A.2.i. Ocean

A.2.ii. Rivers

A.3. Spawning

A.3.i. Fertilization

A.3.ii. Gestation

A.3.iii. Hatching

Figure 15-28. Changing counter styles

Notice that the counter section was not given a style keyword, so it defaulted to the decimal counting style. You can even set counters to use the styles disc, circle, square, and none if you so desire.

One interesting point to note is that elements with a display of none do not increment counters, even if the rule seems to indicate otherwise. In contrast, elements with a visibility of hidden do increment counters:

```
.suppress {counter-increment: cntr; display: none;}
   /* 'cntr' is NOT incremented */
.invisible {counter-increment: cntr; visibility: hidden;}
   /* 'cntr' IS incremented */
```

Counters and scope

So far, we've seen how to string multiple counters together to create section-and-subsection counting. Often, this is something authors desire for nested ordered lists as well, but it would quickly become clumsy to try to create enough counters to cover deep nesting levels. Just to get it working for five-level-deep nested lists would require a bunch of rules like this:

```
ol ol ol ol ol li::before {
    counter-increment: ord1 ord2 ord3 ord4 ord5;
    content: counter(ord1) "." counter(ord2) "." counter(ord3) "."
        counter(ord4) "." counter(ord5) ".";}
```

Imagine writing enough rules to cover nesting up to 50 levels! (I'm not saying you should nest ordered lists 50 deep. Just follow along for the moment.)

Fortunately, CSS2.x described the concept of *scope* when it comes to counters. Stated simply, every level of nesting creates a new scope for any given counter. Scope is what makes it possible for the following rules to cover nested-list counting in the usual HTML way:

```
ol {counter-reset: ordered;}
ol li::before {counter-increment: ordered; content: counter(ordered) ". ";}
```

These rules will all make ordered lists, even those nested inside others, start counting from 1 and increment each item by one—exactly how it's been done in HTML from the beginning.

This works because a new instance of the counter `ordered` is created at each level of nesting. So, for the first ordered list, an instance of `ordered` is created. Then, for every list nested inside the first one, another new instance is created, and the counting starts anew with each list.

However, suppose you want ordered lists to count so that each level of nesting creates a new counter appended to the old: 1, 1.1, 1.2, 1.2.1, 1.2.2, 1.3, 2, 2.1, and so on. This can't be done with `counter( )`, but it *can* be done with `counters( )`. What a difference an "s" makes.

To create the nested-counter style shown in Figure 15-29, you need these rules:

```
ol {counter-reset: ordered; list-style: none;}
ol li:before {content: counters(ordered,".") ": "; counter-increment: ordered;}
```

1: Lists
1.1: Types of Lists
1.2: List Item Images
1.3: List Marker Positions
1.4: List Styles in Shorthand
1.5: List Layout
2: Generated Content
2.1: Inserting Generated Content
2.1.1: Generated Content and Run-In Content
2.2: Specifying Content
2.2.1: Inserting Attribute Values
2.2.2: Generated Quotes
2.3: Counters
2.3.1: Resetting and Incrementing
2.3.2: Using Counters
2.3.3: Counters and Scope
3: Summary

Figure 15-29. Nested counters

Basically, the keyword `counters(ordered,".")` displays the `ordered` counter from each scope with a period appended, and strings together all of the scoped counters for a given element. Thus, an item in a third-level-nested list would be prefaced with the `ordered` value for the outermost list's scope, the scope of the list between the outer and current list, and the current list's scope, with each of those followed by a period. The rest of the `content` value causes a space, hyphen, and space to be added after all of those counters.

As with `counter( )`, you can define a list style for nested counters, but the same style applies to all of the counters. Thus, if you changed your previous CSS to read as follows, the list items in Figure 15-29 would all use lowercase letters for the counters instead of numbers:

```
ol li::before {counter-increment: ordered;
    content: counters(ordered,".",lower-alpha) ": ";}
```

You may have noticed that `list-style: none` was applied to the `ol` elements in the previous examples. That's because the counters being inserted were generated content, not replacement list markers. In other words, had the `list-style: none` been left out, each list item would have had its user agent-supplied list counter, *plus* the generated-content counters we defined.

That ability can be very useful, but sometimes you really just want to redefine the markers themselves. That's where counting patterns come in.

Defining Counting Patterns

In recent years, a new method of defining counter patterns has arisen in CSS. It uses the @counter-style block format, with a number of dedicated descriptors to manage the outcome. The general pattern is:

```
@counter-style <name> {
    …declarations…
}
```

where *<name>* is an author-supplied name for the pattern in question. For example, to create a series of alternating triangle markers, the block might look something like this:

```
@counter-style triangles {
    system: cyclic;
    symbols: ▶ ▷;
}
```

This would have the result shown in Figure 15-30.

▶. one
▷. two
▶. three
▷. four
▶. five
▷. six
▶. seven

Figure 15-30. A simple counter pattern

 As of early 2017, @counter-style and the related topics discussed in this section were only supported by the Firefox family of browsers. They're fun to use, but don't rely on them in copy—that is, don't say things like "refer to step 1A" if your counters are being generated using @counter-style.

There are a number of descriptors available, summarized here.

@counter-style descriptors

system	Defines the counter patterning system to be used. The available values are fixed, cyclic, alphabetic, numeric, symbolic, additive, and extends.
symbols	Defines the counter symbols to be used in the counter pattern. This descriptor is required for all marker systems except additive and extends.
additive-symbols	Defines the counter symbols to be used in additive counter patterns.
prefix	Defines a string or symbol to be included just before each counter in the pattern.
suffix	Defines a string or symbol to be included just after each counter in the pattern.
negative	Defines strings or symbol to be included around any negative-value counter.
range	Defines the range of values in which the counter pattern should be applied. Any counter outside the defined range uses the fallback counter style.
fallback	Defines the counter pattern that should be used when the value can't be represented by the primary counter pattern, or the value is outside a defined range for the counters.
pad	Defines a minimum number of characters for all counters in the pattern, with any extra space filled in with a defined symbol or set of symbols.
speak-as	Defines a strategy for speaking the counter in text-to-speech systems.

We'll start with simple systems and work our way up in complexity, but first, let's see the precise definitions for the two most basic descriptors: system and symbols.

---

system descriptor

Values   cyclic | numeric | alphabetic | symbolic | additive | [fixed *<integer>?*] | [extends *<counter-style-name>*]

Initial value: symbolic

---

symbols descriptor

Values	*<symbol>*+
Initial value	n/a
Notes	A *<symbol>* can be any Unicode-compliant string, an image reference, or an identifier such as an escaped hexadecimal reference.

For pretty much any @counter-style block, those are the minimum two descriptors. You can leave out system if you're defining a symbolic system, but it's generally better to include it so that you're clear about what kind of system you're setting up. Remember, the next person to work on the styles may not be as familiar with counter styling as you!

Fixed Counting Patterns

The simplest kind of counter pattern is a fixed system. Fixed systems are used in cases where you want to define an exact sequence of counter markers that doesn't repeat once you've run out of markers. Consider this example, which has the result shown in Figure 15-31:

```
@counter-style emoji {
    system: fixed;
    symbols: 😁 😗 😆 🤪 😊;
ul.emoji {list-style: emoji;}
```

😁 . one
😗 . two
😆 . three
🤪 . four
😊 . five
6. six
7. seven

Figure 15-31. A fixed counter pattern

Once the list gets past the fifth list item, the counter system runs out of emoji, and since no fallback was defined (we'll get to that shortly), the markers for subsequent list items fall back to the default for unordered lists.

Notice that the symbols in the `symbols` descriptor are space-separated. If they were all jammed together with no space separation, as shown here, you'd get the result something like that seen in Figure 15-32:

```
@counter-style emoji {
    system: fixed;
    symbols: 😄 😉 😆 😋 😐;
}

ul.emoji {list-style: emoji;}
```

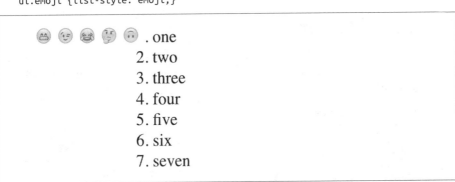

Figure 15-32. When symbols get too close

This does mean you can define a fixed sequence of markers where each marker is composed of multiple symbols. (If you want to define a set of symbols that are combined in patterns to create a counting system, just wait: we're getting to that soon.)

If you want to use ASCII symbols in your markers, it's generally advisable to quote them. This avoids problems like angle brackets being mistaken for pieces of HTML by the parser. Thus you might do something like:

```
@counter-style emoji {
    system: fixed;
    symbols: # $ % ">";
}
```

It's acceptable to quote all symbols, and it might be a good idea to get into the habit. That means more typing—the value above would become "#" "$" "%" ">"—but it's less error-prone.

In fixed counter systems, you can define a starting value in the `system` descriptor itself. If you want to start the counting at 5, for example, you'd write:

```
@counter-style emoji {
    system: fixed 5;
    symbols: 😄 😉 😆 😋 😐;
}

ul.emoji {list-style: emoji;}
```

In this case, the first five symbols represent counters 5 through 9. If the fallback counter style is decimal numbers, then the sixth counter in the sequence would have a value of 10 (in upper-Roman, it would be "J").

 This ability to set a starting number is *not* available in any of the other counter system types.

Cyclic Counting Patterns

The next step beyond fixed patterns is `cyclic` patterns. These are simply fixed patterns that repeat. Let's take the fixed emoji pattern from the previous section and convert it to be cyclic. This will have the result shown in Figure 15-33:

```
@counter-style emojiverse {
    system: cyclic;
    symbols: 😄 😜 😫 😵 🙂;
}

ul.emoji {list-style: emojiverse;}
```

Figure 15-33. A cyclic counter pattern

The defined symbols are used in order, over and over, until there are no more markers left in the counting sequence.

It's possible to use `cyclic` to supply a single marker that's used for the entire pattern, much in the manner of supplying a string for `list-style-type`. In this case, it would look something like this:

```
@counter-style thinker {
    system: cyclic;
    symbols: 😵;
    /* equivalent to list-style-type: "😵" */
```

```
    }
```

```
ul.hmmm {list-style: thinker;}
```

One thing you may have noticed is that so far, all our counters have been followed by a full stop (or a period, if you prefer). This is due to the default value of the `suffix` descriptor. `suffix` has a cousin descriptor, `prefix`.

---

prefix and suffix descriptors

Value	*<symbol>*
Initial value	"" (empty string) for `prefix`; \2E (the full stop, or period, ".") for `suffix`
Notes	A *<symbol>* can be any Unicode-compliant string, an image reference, or an identifier such as an escaped hexadecimal reference.

With these descriptors, you can define symbols that are inserted before and after every marker in the pattern. Thus, we might give our thinker ASCII wings like so, as illustrated in Figure 15-34:

```
@counter-style wingthinker {
    system: cyclic;
    symbols: 😕;
    prefix: "~";
    suffix: "~";
}
```

```
ul.hmmm {list-style: wingthinker;}
```

Figure 15-34. Putting "wings" on the thinker

`suffix` is particularly useful if you want to remove the default suffix from your markers. Here's one example of how to do so:

```
@counter-style thisisfine {
    system: cyclic;
    symbols: 🔥 💀 ☕ 🔥;
    suffix: "";
}
```

Of course, you could also extend the markers in creative ways using `prefix` and `suffix`, as shown in Figure 15-35:

```
@counter-style thisisfine {
    system: cyclic;
    symbols:🔥 💀 ☕ 🔥;
    prefix: "🔥";
    suffix: 🔥;
}
```

Figure 15-35. This list is fine

You might wonder why the `prefix` value was quoted in that example, while the `suffix` value was not. There was literally no reason other than to demonstrate that both approaches work. As stated before, quoting symbols is safer, but it's rarely required.

You may also see (or already been seeing) some differences between the Unicode glyphs in the CSS examples here, and those shown in the figures. This is an unavoidable aspect of using emoji and other such characters—what appears on one person's user agent may be different on someone else's. Just to pick one example: the differences in emoji rendering between Mac OS, iOS, Android, Samsung, Windows desktop, Windows mobile, Linux, and so on.

Keep in mind that you can use images for your counters, at least in theory. As an example, suppose you want to use a series of Klingon glyphs, which have no Unicode equivalents. (It's a longstanding industry myth that Klingon is in Unicode. It was proposed in 1997 and rejected in 2001. A new proposal was made in 2016, with no resolution as of this writing.) We won't represent the entire set of symbols here, but it would start something like this:

```
@counter-style klingon-letters {
    system: cyclic;
    symbols: url(i/klingon-a.svg) url(i/klingon-b.svg)
        url(i/klingon-ch.svg) url(i/klingon-d.svg)
        url(i/klingon-e.svg) url(i/klingon-gh.svg);
    suffix: url(i/klingon-full-stop.svg);
}
```

This would cycle from A through GH and then repeat, but still, you'd get some Klingon symbology, which might be enough. We'll see ways to build up alphabetic and numeric systems later in the chapter.

 As of early 2017, browser support for images as counting symbols was essentially nonexistent.

Symbolic Counting Patterns

A symbolic counting system is similar to a cyclic system, except in symbolic systems, the symbols add a repetition on each restart of the symbol sequence. This may be familiar to you from footnote symbols, or some varieties of alphabetic systems. Examples of each are shown here, with the result shown in Figure 15-36:

```
@counter-style footnotes {
    system: symbolic;
    symbols: "*" "†" "§";
    suffix: ' ';
}
@counter-style letters {
    system: symbolic;
    symbols: A B C D E;
}
```

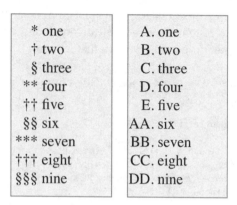

Figure 15-36. Two patterns of symbolic counting

One thing to watch out for is that if you only have a few symbols applied to a very long list, the markers will quickly get quite large. Consider the letter counters shown in the previous example. Figure 15-37 shows what the 135th through 150th entries in a list using that system would look like.

EEEEEEEEEEEEEEEEEEEEEEEEEE. 135
AAAAAAAAAAAAAAAAAAAAAAAAAA. 136
BBBBBBBBBBBBBBBBBBBBBBBBBB. 137
CCCCCCCCCCCCCCCCCCCCCCCCCC. 138
DDDDDDDDDDDDDDDDDDDDDDDDDD. 139
EEEEEEEEEEEEEEEEEEEEEEEEEE. 140
AAAAAAAAAAAAAAAAAAAAAAAAAA. 141
BBBBBBBBBBBBBBBBBBBBBBBBBB. 142
CCCCCCCCCCCCCCCCCCCCCCCCCC. 143
DDDDDDDDDDDDDDDDDDDDDDDDDD. 144
EEEEEEEEEEEEEEEEEEEEEEEEEE. 145
AAAAAAAAAAAAAAAAAAAAAAAAAA. 146
BBBBBBBBBBBBBBBBBBBBBBBBBB. 147
CCCCCCCCCCCCCCCCCCCCCCCCCC. 148
DDDDDDDDDDDDDDDDDDDDDDDDDD. 149
EEEEEEEEEEEEEEEEEEEEEEEEEE. 150

Figure 15-37. Very long symbolic markers

This sort of consideration will become more of an issue from here on out, because the counter styles are all additive in one sense or another. There is a way to limit your exposure to these kinds of problems: the range descriptor.

---

range descriptor

Value	[[<integer> | infinite]{2}]# | auto
Initial value	auto

With range, you can supply one or more space-separated pairs of values, with each pair separated from the others by commas. Let's suppose we want to stop the letter-doubling after three iterations. There are five symbols, so we can restrict their use to the range of 1-15 like so, with the result shown in Figure 15-38 (which has been arranged in two columns to keep the figure size reasonable):

```
@counter-style letters {
    system: symbolic;
    symbols: A B C D E;
    range: 1 15;
}
```

A.	1	AAA.	11
B.	2	BBB.	12
C.	3	CCC.	13
D.	4	DDD.	14
E.	5	EEE.	15
AA.	6	16.	16
BB.	7	17.	17
CC.	8	18.	18
DD.	9	19.	19
EE.	10	20.	20

Figure 15-38. Using range to limit a symbolic counter pattern

If there were, for whatever reason, a need to supply a second range of counter usage, it would look like this:

```
@counter-style letters {
    system: symbolic;
    symbols: A B C D E;
    range: 1 15, 101 115;
}
```

In that case, the symbolic letter system defined by letters would be applied in the range 1-15, and also 101-115 (which would be "AAAAAAAAAAAAAAAAAAAAA" through "EEEEEEEEEEEEEEEEEEEEE," rather appropriately).

So what happens to the counters that fall outside of the range(s) defined by range? They fall back to a default marker style. You can leave that up to the user agent to handle, or you can provide some direction by means of the fallback descriptor.

---

fallback descriptor

Value   *<counter-style-name>*
Initial value   decimal
Note   *<counter-style-name>* can be any of the values allowed for list-style-type

---

As an example, you might decide to handle any beyond-the-range counters with Hebrew counting.

```
@counter-style letters {
    system: symbolic;
    symbols: A B C D E;
    range: 1 15, 101 115;
    fallback: hebrew;
}
```

You could just as easily use lower-greek, upper-latin, or even a non-counting style like square.

This will also be the style used as a fallback in any system where a counter can't be represented by the primary system, for whatever reason. A simple example is a counting system that uses images for its symbols, and one of the images fails to load. In the following, assume south.svg fails to load. In that case, the missing image would be replaced with a lower-latin counter representing the value of the current item:

```
@counter-style compass {
    system: symbolic;
    symbols: url(north.svg) url(east.svg) url(south.svg) url(west.svg);
    fallback: lower-latin;
}
```

Alphabetic Counting Patterns

An alpahbetic counting system is very similar to a symbolic system, except the manner of repeating changes. Remember, with symbolic counting, the number of symbols goes up with each iteration through the cycle. In alphabetic systems, each

---

symbol is treated as a digit in a numbering system. If you've spent any time in spreadsheets, this counting method may be familiar to you from the column labels.

To illustrate this, let's reuse the letter symbols from the previous section, and change from a symbolic to an alphabetic system. The result is shown in Figure 15-39 (once again formatted as two columns for compactness' sake):

```
@counter-style letters {
    system: alphabetic;
    symbols: A B C D E;
    /* once more cut off at 'E' to show the pattern's effects more quickly */
}
```

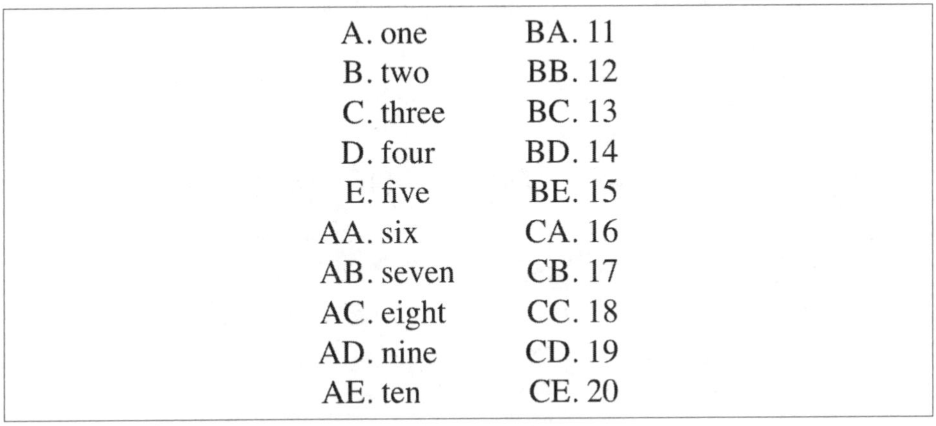

A. one	BA. 11
B. two	BB. 12
C. three	BC. 13
D. four	BD. 14
E. five	BE. 15
AA. six	CA. 16
AB. seven	CB. 17
AC. eight	CC. 18
AD. nine	CD. 19
AE. ten	CE. 20

Figure 15-39. Alphabetic counting

Notice how the second iteration of the pattern, which runs from "AA" to "AE" before switching over to "BA" through "BE", then on to "CA" and so on. In the symbolic version of this, we'd already be up to "EEEEEE" by the time "EE" was reached in the alphabetic system.

Note that in order to be valid, an alphabetic system must have a minimum of *two* symbols supplied in the symbols descriptor. If only one symbol is supplied, the entire @counter-style block is rendered invalid. Any two symbols are valid; they can be letters, numbers, or really anything in Unicode, as well as images (again, in theory).

Numeric Counting Patterns

When you define a numeric system, you're technically using the symbols you supply to define a *positional numbering* system. That is, the symbols are used as digits in a place-number counting system. Defining ordinary decimal counting, for example, would be done like this:

```
@counter-style decimal {
    system: numeric;
    symbols: '0' '1' '2' '3' '4' '5' '6' '7' '8' '9';
}
```

This is easily extensible to create hexadecimal counting, like so:

```
@counter-style hexadecimal {
    system: numeric;
    symbols: '0' '1' '2' '3' '4' '5' '6' '7' '8' '9' 'A' 'B' 'C' 'D' 'E' 'F';
}
```

This will count from 1 through F, roll over to 10 and count up to 1F, then 20 to 2F, 30 to 3F, etc. Much more simply, it's a breeze to set up binary counting:

```
@counter-style binary {
    system: numeric;
    symbols: '0' '1';
}
```

Examples of each of those three counting patterns are shown in Figure 15-40.

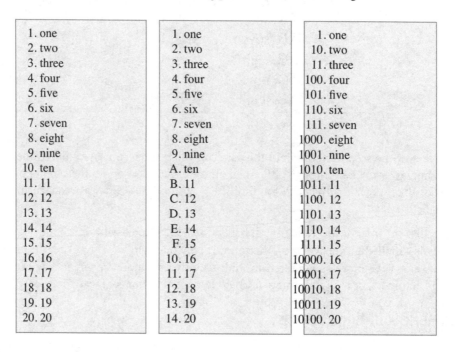

Figure 15-40. Three numeric counting patterns

An interesting question to consider is: what happens if a counter value is negative? In decimal counting, we generally expect negative numbers to be preceded by a minus sign (-), but what about in other systems, like symbolic? What if we define a letter-based numeric counting system? Or if we want to use accounting-style formatting, which puts negative values into parentheses? This is where the `negative` descriptor comes into play.

---

negative descriptor

Value: *<symbol> <symbol>?*

Initial value: \2D (the hyphen-minus symbol)

Notes: negative is only applicable in counting systems that allow negative values: alphabetic, numeric, symbolic, and additive.

`negative` is like its own little self-contained combination of `prefix` and `suffix`, but is only applied in situations where the counter is a negative value. Its symbols are placed inside the prefix and suffix symbols.

So let's say we want to use accounting-style formatting, and also add prefix and suffix symbols to all counters. That would be done as follows, with the result shown in Figure 15-41:

```
@counter-style accounting {
    system: numeric;
    symbols: '0' '1' '2' '3' '4' '5' '6' '7' '8' '9';
    negative: "(" ")";
    prefix: "$";
    suffix: " - ";
}
ol.kaching {list-style: accounting;}
```

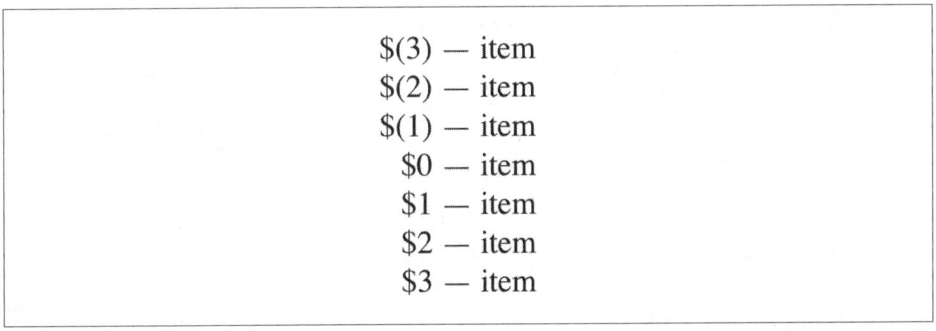

$(3) — item
$(2) — item
$(1) — item
$0 — item
$1 — item
$2 — item
$3 — item

Figure 15-41. Negative-value formatting

Another common feature of numeric counting systems is the desire to pad out low values so that their length matches that of higher values. For example, rather than "1" and "100," a counting pattern might use leading zeroes to create "001" and "100." This can be accomplished with the pad descriptor.

---

pad descriptor

Value   *<integer>* && *<symbol>*
Initial value 0 " "

The pattern of this descriptor is a little interesting. The first part is an integer, and defines the number of digits that every counter should have. The second part is a string that's used to fill out any value that has fewer than the defined number of digits. Consider this example:

```
@counter-style padded {
    system: numeric;
    symbols: '0' '1' '2' '3' '4' '5' '6' '7' '8' '9';
    suffix: '.';
    pad: 4 "0";
}

ol {list-style: decimal;}
ol.padded {list-style: padded;}
```

Given these styles, ordered lists will all used decimal counting by default: 1, 2, 3, 4, 5.... Those with a class of padded will use padded decimal counting: 0001, 0002, 0003, 0004, 0005.... An example of this is shown in Figure 15-42.

0001.one
0002.two
0003.three
0004.four
0005.five
0006.six
0007.seven
0008.eight
0009.nine
0010.ten

Figure 15-42. Padding values

Note how the padded counters use the 0 symbol to fill in any missing leading digits, in order to make every counter be at least four digits long. The "at least" part of that last sentence is important: if a counter gets up to five digits, it won't be padded. More importantly, if a counter reaches five digits, none of the other shorter counters will get additional zeroes. They'll stay four digits long, because of the 4 in 4 "0".

Any symbol can be used to pad values, not just 0. You could use underlines, periods, emoji, arrow symbols, empty spaces, or anything else you like. In fact, you can have multiple characters in the *<symbol>* part of the value. The following is perfectly acceptable, if not necessarily desirable:

```
@counter-style crazy {
    system: numeric;
    symbols: '0' '1' '2' '3' '4' '5' '6' '7' '8' '9';
    suffix: '.';
    pad: 4 "😴😵";
}
```

```
ol {list-style: decimal;}
ol.padded {list-style: padded;}
```

Given a counter value of 1, the result of that crazy counting system would be "😴😵😴 😵😴😵1."

Note that negative symbols count toward symbol length, and thus eat into padding. Also note that the negative sign will come *outside* any padding. Thus, given the following styles, we'd get the result shown in Figure 15-43:

```
@counter-style negativezeropad {
    system: numeric;
    symbols: '0' '1' '2' '3' '4' '5' '6' '7' '8' '9';
    suffix: '. ';
    negative: '-';
    pad: 4 "0";
}
@counter-style negativespacepad {
    system: numeric;
    symbols: '0' '1' '2' '3' '4' '5' '6' '7' '8' '9';
    suffix: '. ';
    negative: '-';
    pad: 4 " ";
}
```

–0003. minus three	– 3. minus three
–0002. minus two	– 2. minus two
–0001. minus one	– 1. minus one
0000. zero	0. zero
0001. one	1. one
0002. two	2. two
0003. three	3. three
0004. four	4. four
0005. five	5. five
0006. six	6. six
0007. seven	7. seven

Figure 15-43. Padding values

Additive Counting Patterns

We have one more system type to explore, which is `additive-symbol` counting. In additive counting systems, different symbols are used to represent values. Putting a number of the symbols together properly, and adding up the numbers each represents, yields the counter value.

---

additive-symbols descriptor

Value	[*<integer>* && *<symbol>*]#
Initial value	n/a
Note	*<integer>* values must be non-negative, and additive counters are not applied when a counter's value is negative.

It's much easier to show this than explain it. Here's an example adapted from Kseso (*https://escss.blogspot.com/*):

```
@counter-style roman {
    system: additive;
    additive-symbols:
        1000 M, 900 CM, 500 D, 400 CD,
        100 C, 90 XC, 50 L, 40 XL,
        10 X, 9 IX, 5 V, 4 IV, 1 I;
}
```

This will count in classical Roman style. Another good example can be found in the specification for counting styles, which defines a dice-counting system:

```css
@counter-style dice {
    system: additive;
    additive-symbols: 6 ⚅, 5 ⚄, 4 ⚃, 3 ⚂, 2 ⚁, 1 ⚀, 0 "__";
    suffix: " ";
}
```

The results of both counting systems are shown in Figure 15-44; this time, each list has been formatted as three columns.

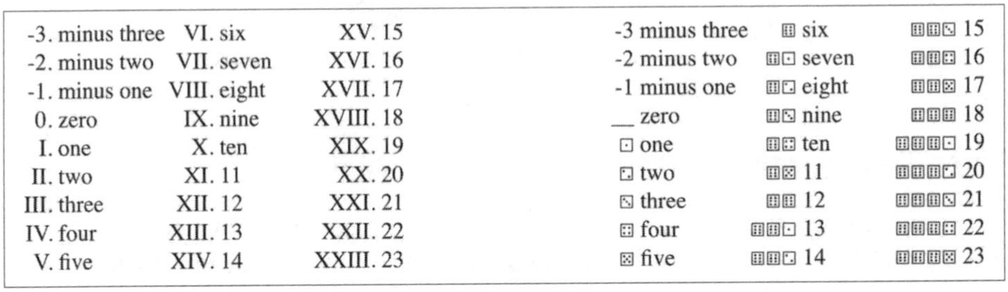

-3. minus three	VI. six	XV. 15	-3 minus three	⚅ six	⚅⚅⚂ 15
-2. minus two	VII. seven	XVI. 16	-2 minus two	⚅⚀ seven	⚅⚅⚃ 16
-1. minus one	VIII. eight	XVII. 17	-1 minus one	⚅⚁ eight	⚅⚅⚄ 17
0. zero	IX. nine	XVIII. 18	__ zero	⚅⚂ nine	⚅⚅⚅ 18
I. one	X. ten	XIX. 19	⚀ one	⚅⚃ ten	⚅⚅⚅⚀ 19
II. two	XI. 11	XX. 20	⚁ two	⚅⚄ 11	⚅⚅⚅⚁ 20
III. three	XII. 12	XXI. 21	⚂ three	⚅⚅ 12	⚅⚅⚅⚂ 21
IV. four	XIII. 13	XXII. 22	⚃ four	⚅⚅⚀ 13	⚅⚅⚅⚃ 22
V. five	XIV. 14	XXIII. 23	⚄ five	⚅⚅⚁ 14	⚅⚅⚅⚄ 23

Figure 15-44. Additive values

Symbols can be quoted for clarity; e.g., 6 "⚅", 5 "⚄", 4 "⚃", and so on.

The most important thing to keep in mind is that the order of the symbols and their equivalent values matters. Notice how both the Roman and dice-counting systems supplied values from largest to smallest, not the other way around? That's because if you put the values in any order other than descending, the entire block is rendered invalid.

Also notice the use of the `additive-symbols` descriptor instead of `symbols`. This is important to keep in mind, since defining an additive system and then trying to use the `symbols` descriptor will render the entire `counter-styles` block invalid. (Similarly, attempting to use the `additive-symbols` description in non-`additive` systems will render *those* blocks invalid.)

One last thing to note about additive systems is that, due to the way the additive-counter algorithm is defined, it's possible to create additive systems where some values can't be represented even though it seems like they should be. Consider this definition:

```css
@counter-style problem {
    system: additive;
    additive-symbols: 3 "Y", 2 "X";
    fallback: decimal;
}
```

This would yield the following counters for the first five numbers: 1, X, Y, 4, YX. You might think "4" should be "XX," and that may make intuitive sense, but the algorithm for additive symbols doesn't permit it. To quote the specification: "While unfortunate, this is required to maintain the property that the algorithm runs in linear time relative to the size of the counter value."

 So how does Roman counting manage to get "III" for 3? Again, the answer is in the algorithm. It's a little too complicated to get into here, so if you're truly curious, I recommend you read the CSS Counter Styles Level 3 specification, which defines the additive counting algorithm. Even if that doesn't interest you, just remember: make sure you have a symbol whose value equates to 1, and you'll avoid this problem.

Extending Counting Patterns

There may come a time when you just want to vary an existing counting system a bit. For example, suppose you want to change regular decimal counting to use close-parentheses symbols as suffixes, and pad up to two leading zeroes. You could write it all out longhand, like so:

```
@counter-style mydecimals {
    system: numeric;
    symbols: '0' '1' '2' '3' '4' '5' '6' '7' '8' '9';
    suffix: ") ";
    pad: 2 "0";
}
```

That works, but it's clumsy. Well, worry not: extends is here to help.

extends is sort of a system type, but only in the sense that it builds on an existing system type. The previous example would be rewritten with extends as follows:

```
@counter-style mydecimals {
    system: extends decimal;
    suffix: ") ";
    pad: 2 "0";
}
```

That takes the existing decimal system familiar from list-style-type and reformats it a bit. Thus, there's no need to re-type the whole symbol chain. You just adjust the options, as it were.

In fact, you can only adjust the options: if you try use either symbols or additive-symbols in an extneds system, the entire @counter-style block will be invalid and ignored. In other words, symbols cannot be extended. As an example, you can't define hexadecimal counting by extending decimal counting.

However, you can vary the hexadecimal counting for different contexts. As an example, you could set up basic hex counting and then define some variant display patterns, as shown in the following code and illustrated in Figure 15-45. (Note that each list jumps from 19 to 253, thanks to a value="253" on one of the list items.)

```
@counter-style hexadecimal {
    system: numeric;
    symbols: '0' '1' '2' '3' '4' '5' '6' '7' '8' '9' 'A' 'B' 'C' 'D' 'E' 'F';
}
@counter-style hexpad {
    system: extends hexadecimal;
    pad: 2 "0";
}
@counter-style hexcolon {
    system: extends hexadecimal;
    suffix: ": ";
}
@counter-style hexcolonlimited {
    system: extends hexcolon;
    range: 1 255; /* stops at FF */
}
```

-3. minus three	B. 11	-03. minus three	0B. 11	-3: minus three	B: 11	-3: minus three	B: 11
-2. minus two	C. 12	-02. minus two	0C. 12	-2: minus two	C: 12	-2: minus two	C: 12
-1. minus one	D. 13	-01. minus one	0D. 13	-1: minus one	D: 13	-1: minus one	D: 13
0. zero	E. 14	00. zero	0E. 14	0: zero	E: 14	0: zero	E: 14
1. one	F. 15	01. one	0F. 15	1: one	F: 15	1: one	F: 15
2. two	10. 16	02. two	10. 16	2: two	10: 16	2: two	10: 16
3. three	11. 17	03. three	11. 17	3: three	11: 17	3: three	11: 17
4. four	12. 18	04. four	12. 18	4: four	12: 18	4: four	12: 18
5. five	13. 19	05. five	13. 19	5: five	13: 19	5: five	13: 19
6. six	FD. 253	06. six	FD. 253	6: six	FD: 253	6: six	FD: 253
7. seven	FE. 254	07. seven	FE. 254	7: seven	FE: 254	7: seven	FE: 254
8. eight	FF. 255	08. eight	FF. 255	8: eight	FF: 255	8: eight	FF: 255
9. nine	100. 256	09. nine	100. 256	9: nine	100: 256	9: nine	256: 256
A. ten	101. 257	0A. ten	101. 257	A: ten	101: 257	A: ten	257: 257

Figure 15-45. Various hexadecimal counting patterns

Notice how the last of the four counter styles, hexcolonlimited, extends the third, hexcolon, which itself extends the first, hexadecimal. In hexcolonlimited, the hexadecimal counting stops at FF (255), thanks to the range: 1 255; declaration.

Speaking Counting Patterns

While it's fun to build counters out of symbols, the result can be a real mess for spoken technologies such as Apple's VoiceOver or the JAWS screen reader. Imagine, for example, a screen reader trying to read dice counters, or phases of the moon. To help, the speak-as descriptor allows you to define an audible fallback.

speak-as descriptor

Value   auto | bullets | numbers | words | spell-out | <counter-style-name>

Initial value   auto

Let's take the values backward. With a <counter-style-name>, you're able to define an alternate counting style that the user agent likely already recognizes. For example, you might provide an audio fallback for dice-counting to be decimal counting when spoken:

```
@counter-style dice {
    system: additive;
    speak-as: decimal;
    additive-symbols: 6 ⚅, 5 ⚄, 4 ⚃, 3 ⚂, 2 ⚁, 1 ⚀;
    suffix: " ";
}
```

Given those styles, the counter "⚀⚁⚂⚃" would be spoken as "fifteen." Alternatively, if the speak-as value is changed to lower-latin, that counter will be spoken as "oh" (capital letter O).

spell-out seems fairly straightforward, but it's a little more complicated than it first appears. What is spelled out by the user agent is a "counter representation," which is then spelled out letter by letter. It's hard to predict what that will mean, since the method of generated a counter representation isn't precisely defined: the specification says "counter representations are constructed by concatenating counter symbols together." And that's all.

words is similar to spell-out, except the counter representation is spoken as words instead of spelling out each letter. Again, the exact process is not defined.

With the value numbers, the counters are spoken as numbers in the document language. This is very similar to the previous code sample, where "⚀⚁⚂⚃" is spoken as "fifteen," at least in English documents. If it's another language, then that language is used for counting: "quince" in Spanish, "fünfzehn" in German, "shíwǔ" in Chinese, and so on.

Given bullets, the user agent says whatever it says when reading a bullet (marker) in an unordered list. This may mean saying nothing at all, or producing an audio cue such as a chime or click.

Finally, consider the default value of auto. We saved this for last because its actual effect depends on the counting system in use. If it's a alphabetic system, then speak-

---

as: auto has the same effect as speak-as: spell-out. In cyclic systems, auto is the same as bullets. Otherwise, the effect is the same as speak-as: numbers.

The exception to this rule is if the system is an extends system, in which case auto's effects are determined based on the system being extended. Therefore, given the following styles, the counters in an emojibrackets list will be spoken as if speak-as were set to bullets:

```
@counter-style emojilist {
    emojiverse {
    system: cyclic;
    symbols: 😩 😆 😂 🤣 😂;
@counter-style emojibrackets {
    system: extends emojilist;
    suffix: "]] ";
    speak-as: auto;
}
```

Summary

Even though list styling isn't as sophisticated as we might like, and browser support for generated content is somewhat spotty (as of this writing, anyway), the ability to style lists is still highly useful. One relatively common use is to take a list of links, remove the markers and indentation, and thus create a navigation sidebar. The combination of simple markup and flexible layout is difficult to resist. With the anticipated enhancements to list styling in CSS3, I expect that lists will become more and more useful.

For now, in situations where a markup language doesn't have intrinsic list elements, generated content can be an enormous help—say, for inserting content such as icons to point to certain types of links (PDF files, Word documents, or even just links to another web site). Generated content also makes it easy to print out link URLs, and its ability to insert and format quotation marks leads to true typographic joy. It's safe to say that the usefulness of generated content is limited only by your imagination. Even better, thanks to counters, you can now associate ordering information to elements that are not typically lists, such as headings or code blocks. Now, if you want to support such features with design that mimics the appearance of the user's operating system, read on. The next chapter will discuss ways to change the placement, shape, and even perspective of your design.

CHAPTER 16

Transforms

Ever since the inception of Cascading Style Sheets (CSS), elements have been rectangular and firmly oriented on the horizontal and vertical axes. A number of tricks arose to make elements look like they were tilted and so on, but underneath it all was a rigid grid. In the late 2000s, an interest grew in being able to break the shackles of that grid and transform objects in interesting ways—and not just in two dimensions.

If you've ever positioned an object, whether relatively or absolutely, then you've already transformed that object. For that matter, any time you used floats or negative-margin tricks (or both), you transformed an object. All of those are examples of *translation*, or the movement of an element from where it would normally appear to some other place. With CSS transforms, you have a new way to translate elements, and a whole lot more. Whether it's as simple as rotating some photographs a bit to make them appear more natural, or creating interfaces where information can be revealed by flipping over elements, or just doing interesting perspective tricks with sidebars, CSS transforms can—if you'll pardon the obvious expression—transform the way you design.

Coordinate Systems

Before embarking on this journey, let's take a moment to orient ourselves. Two types of coordinate systems are used in transforms, and it's a good idea to be familiar with both.

 If you're already well familiar with Cartesian and spherical coordinate systems, particularly as used in computing, feel free to skip to the next section.

The first is the *Cartesian coordinate system,* or what's often called the *x/y/z coordinate system.* This system is a way of describing the position of a point in space using two numbers (for two-dimensional placement) or three numbers (for three-dimensional placement). In CSS, the system uses three axes: the x, or horizontal axis; the y, or vertical axis; and the z, or depth axis. This is illustrated in Figure 16-1.

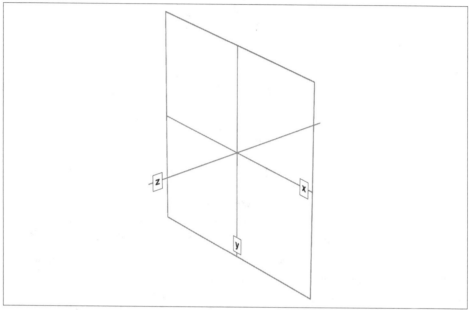

Figure 16-1. The three Cartesian axes used in CSS transforms

For any 2D (two-dimensional) transform, you only need to worry about the x- and y-axes. By convention, positive x values go to the right, and negative values go to the left. Similarly, positive y values go downward along the y-axis, while negative values go upward along the y-axis.

That might seem a little weird, since we tend to think that higher numbers should place something higher up, not lower down, as many of us learned in pre-algebra. (This why the "y" label is at the bottom of the y-axis in Figure 16-1: the labels are placed in the positive direction on all three axes.) If you are experienced with absolute positioning in CSS, think of the *top* property values for absolutely positioned elements: they get moved downward for positive *top* values, and upward when *top* has a negative length.

Given this, in order to move an element leftward and down, you would give it a negative x and a positive y value, like this:

```
translateX(-5em) translateY(33px)
```

That is in fact a valid transform value, as we'll see in just a bit. Its effect is to translate (move) the element five ems to the left and 33 pixels down.

If you want to transform something in three-dimensional space, then you add a z-axis value. This axis is the one that "sticks out" of the display and runs straight through your head. In a theoretical sense, that is. Positive z values are closer to you, and negative z values are further away from you. In this regard, it's exactly like the z-index property.

So let's say that we want to take the element we moved before and add a z-axis value:

```
translateX(-5em) translateY(33px) translateZ(200px)
```

Now the element will appear 200 pixels closer to us than it would be without the z value.

Well you might wonder exactly how an element can be moved 200 pixels closer to you, given that holographic displays are regrettably rare and expensive. How many molecules of air between you and your monitor are equivalent to 200 pixels? What does an element moving closer to you even look like, and what happens if it gets *too* close? These are excellent questions that we'll get to later on. For now, just accept that moving an element along the z-axis appears to move it closer or farther away.

The really important thing to remember is that every element carries its own frame of reference and so considers its axes with respect to itself. That is to say, if you rotate an element, the axes rotate along with it, as illustrated in Figure 16-2. Any further transforms are calculated with respect to those rotated axes, not the axes of the display.

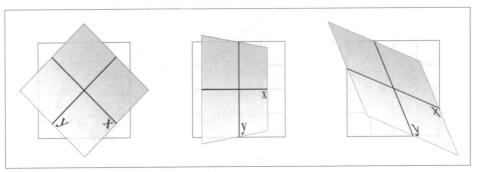

Figure 16-2. Elemental frames of reference

Speaking of rotations, the other coordinate system used in CSS transforms is a *spherical system*, which describes angles in 3D space. It's illustrated in Figure 16-3.

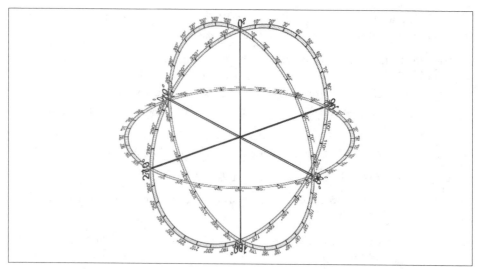

Figure 16-3. The spherical coordinate system used in CSS transforms

For the purposes of 2D transforms, you only have to worry about a single 360-degree polar system: the one that sits on the plane described by the x- and y-axes. When it comes to rotations, a 2D rotation actually describes a rotation around the z-axis. Similarly, rotations around the x-axis tilt the element toward or away from you, and rotations around the y-axis turn the element from side to side. These are illustrated in Figure 16-4.

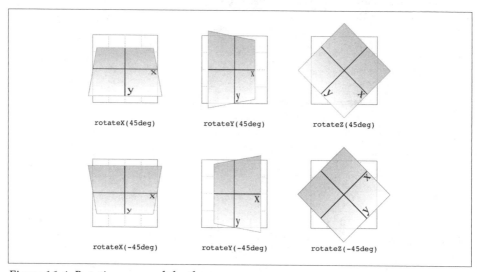

Figure 16-4. Rotations around the three axes

But back to 2D rotations. Suppose you wanted to rotate an element 45 degrees clockwise in the plane of the display (i.e., around the z-axis). The transform value you're most likely to use is:

```
rotate(45deg)
```

Change that to −45deg, and the element will rotate counterclockwise (anticlockwise for our international friends) around the z-axis. In other words, it will rotate in the xy plane, as illustrated in Figure 16-5.

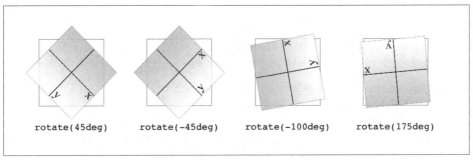

| rotate(45deg) | rotate(-45deg) | rotate(-100deg) | rotate(175deg) |

Figure 16-5. Rotations in the xy plane

All right, now that we have our bearings, let's get started with transforms!

Transforming

There's really only one property that applies transforms, along with a few ancillary properties that affect exactly how the transforms are applied. We'll start with the big cheese.

transform

Values	*<transform-list>*	none
Initial value	none
Applies to	All elements except "atomic inline-level" boxes (see explanation)
Percentages	Refer to the size of the bounding box (see explanation)
Computed value	As specified, except for relative length values, which are converted to an absolute length
Inherited	No
Animatable	As a transform

First off, let's clear up the matter of the *bounding box*. For any element being affected by CSS, this is the border box; that is, the outermost edge of the element's border. That means that any outlines and margins are ignored for the purposes of calculating the bounding box.

 If a table-display element is being transformed, its bounding box is the table wrapper box, which encloses the table box and any associated caption box.

If you're transforming a Scalable Vector Graphics (SVG) element with CSS, then its bounding box is its SVG-defined *object bounding box*.

Note that all transformed elements (i.e., elements with `transform` set to a value other than none) have their own stacking context. While the scaled element may be much smaller or larger than it was before the transform was applied, the actual space on the page that the element occupies remains the same as before the transform was applied. This is true for all the transform functions.

Now, the value entry `<transform-list>` requires some explanation. This placeholder refers to a list of one or more transform functions, one after the other, in space-separated format. It looks like this, with the result shown in Figure 16-6:

```
#example {transform: rotate(30deg) skewX(-25deg) scaleY(2);}
```

Figure 16-6. A transformed div element

The functions are processed one at a time, starting with the first (leftmost) and proceeding to the last (rightmost). This first-to-last processing order is important, because changing the order can lead to drastically different results. Consider the following two rules, which have the results shown in Figure 16-7:

```
img#one {transform: translateX(200px) rotate(45deg);}
img#two {transform: rotate(45deg) translateX(200px);}
```

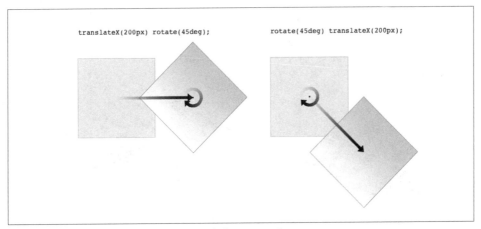

Figure 16-7. Different transform lists, different results

In the first instance, an image is translated (moved) 200 pixels along its x-axis and then rotated 45 degrees. In the second instance, an image is rotated 45 degrees and then moved 200 pixels along its x-axis—that's the x-axis of the transformed element, *not* of the parent element, page, or viewport. In other words, when an element is rotated, its x-axis (along with its other axes) rotates along with it. All element transforms are conducted with respect to the element's own frame of reference.

Compare this to a situation where an element is translated and then scaled, or vice versa; it doesn't matter which is which, because the end result is the same:

```
img#one {transform: translateX(100px) scale(1.2);}
img#two {transform: scale(1.2) translateX(100px);}
```

The situations where the order doesn't matter are far outnumbered by the situations where it does; so in general, it's a good idea to just assume the order always matters, even when it technically doesn't.

Note that when you have a series of transform functions, all of them must be properly formatted; that is, they must be valid. If even one function is invalid, it renders the entire value invalid. Consider:

```
img#one {transform: translateX(100px) scale(1.2) rotate(22);}
```

Because the value for `rotate()` is invalid—rotational values must have a unit—the entire value is dropped. The image in question will just sit there in its initial untransformed state, neither translated nor scaled, let alone rotated.

It's also the case that transforms are not usually cumulative. That is to say, if you apply a transform to an element and then later want to add a transformation, you need to restate the original transform. Consider the following scenarios, illustrated in Figure 16-8:

```
#ex01 {transform: rotate(30deg) skewX(-25deg);}
#ex01 {transform: scaleY(2);}
#ex02 {transform: rotate(30deg) skewX(-25deg);}
#ex02 {transform: rotate(30deg) skewX(-25deg) scaleY(2);}
```

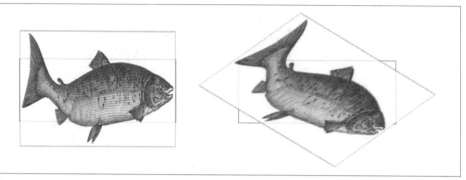

Figure 16-8. Overwriting or modifying transforms

In the first case, the second rule completely replaces the first, meaning that the element is only scaled along the y-axis. This actually makes some sense; it's the same as if you declare a font size and then elsewhere declare a different font size for the same element. You don't get a cumulative font size that way. You just get one size or the other. In the second example, the entirety of the first set of transforms is included in the second set, so they all are applied along with the scaleY() function.

There is an exception to this, which is that animated transforms, whether using transitions or actual animations, *are* additive. That way, you can take an element that's transformed and then animate one of its transform functions without overwriting the others. For example, assume you had:

```
img#one {transform: translateX(100px) scale(1.2);}
```

If you then animate the element's rotation angle, it will rotate from its translated, scaled state to the new angle, and its translation and scale will remain in place.

What makes this interesting is that even if you don't explicitly specify a transition or animation, you can still create additive transforms via the user-interaction pseudo-classes, such as :hover. That's because things like hover effects are types of transitions; they're just not invoked using the transition properties. Thus, you could declare:

```
img#one {transform: translateX(100px) scale(1.2);}
img#one:hover {transform: rotate(-45deg);}
```

This would rotate the translated, scaled image 45 degrees to its left on hover. The rotation would take place over zero seconds because no transition interval was declared, but it's still an implicit transition. Thus, any state change can be thought of as a transition, and thus any transforms that are applied as a result of those state changes are additive with previous transforms.

There's one important caveat: as of this writing, transforms are not applied to *atomic inline-level* boxes. These are inline boxes like spans, hyperlinks, and so on. Those elements can be transformed if their block-level parent is transformed, in which case they go along for the ride. But you can't just rotate a span unless you've changed its display role via display: block, display: inline-block, or something along those lines. The reason for this limitation boils down to an uncertainty. Suppose you have a span (or any inline-level box) that breaks across multiple lines. If you rotate it, what happens? Does each line box rotate with respect to itself, or should all the line boxes be rotated as a single group? There's no clear answer, and the debate continues, so for now you can't directly transform inline-level boxes.

The Transform Functions

There are, as of this writing, 21 different transform functions, employing a number of different value patterns to get their jobs done. Table 16-1 provides a list of all the available transform functions, minus their value patterns.

Table 16-1. Transform functions

```
translate()    scale()    rotate()    skew()    matrix()
translate3d()  scale3d()  rotate3d()  skewX()   matrix3d()
translateX()   scaleX()   rotateX()   skewY()   perspective()
translateY()   scaleY()   rotateY()
translateZ()   scaleZ()   rotateZ()
```

The most common value pattern for transform is a space-separated list of one or more functions, processed from first (leftmost) to last (rightmost), and all of the functions must have valid values. If any one of the functions is invalid, it will invalidate the entire value of transform, thus preventing any transformation at all.

Translation functions

A translation transform is just a move along one or more axes. For example, translateX() moves an element along its own x-axis, translateY() moves it along its y-axis, and translateZ() moves it along its z-axis.

Functions	Permitted values
translateX(), translateY()	*<length>* | *<percentage>*

These are usually referred to as the "2D" translation functions, since they can slide an element up and down, or side to side, but not forward or backward along the z-axis.

Each of these functions accepts a single distance value, expressed as either a length or a percentage.

If the value is a length, then the effect is about what you'd expect. Translate an element 200 pixels along the x-axis with translateX(200px), and it will move 200 pixels to its right. Change that to translateX(-200px), and it will move 200 pixels to its left. For translateY(), positive values move the element downward, while negative values move it upward, both with respect to the element itself. Thus, if you flip the element upside down by rotation, positive translateY() values will actually move the element downward on the page.

If the value is a percentage, then the distance is calculated as a percentage of the element's own size. Thus, translateX(50%) will move an element 300 pixels wide and 200 pixels tall to its right by 150 pixels, and translateY(-10%) will move that same element upward (with respect to itself) by 20 pixels.

Function	Permitted values
translate()	[<length> | <percentage>] [, <length> | <percentage>]?

If you want to translate an element along both the x- and y-axes at the same time, then translate() makes it easy. Just supply the x value first and the y value second, and it will act the same as if you combined translateX() translateY(). If you omit the y value, then it's assumed to be zero. Thus, translate(2em) is treated as if it were translate(2em,0), which is also the same as translateX(2em). See Figure 16-9 for some examples of 2D translation.

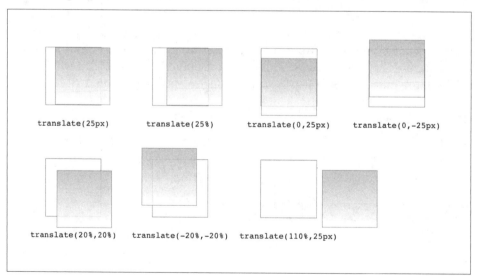

Figure 16-9. Translating in two dimensions

According to the latest version of the specification, both of the 2D translation functions can be given a unitless number. In this case, the number is treated as being expressed in terms of a *user unit*, which is treated the same as a pixel unless otherwise defined. The CSS specification does not explain how a user unit is otherwise defined; however, the SVG specification does, albeit briefly. In the field, no browser tested as of this writing supported unitless numbers of translation values, so the capability is academic, at best.

Function	Permitted value
translateZ()	*<length>*

This function translates elements along the z-axis, thus moving them into the third dimension. Unlike the 2D translation functions, translateZ() only accepts length values. Percentage values are *not* permitted for translateZ(), or indeed for any z-axis value.

Functions	Permitted values
translate3d()	[*<length>* | *<percentage>*], [*<length>* | *<percentage>*], [*<length>*]

Much like translate() does for x and y translations, translate3d() is a shorthand function that incorporates the x, y, and z translation values into a single function. This is handy if you want to move an element over, up, and forward in one fell swoop. See Figure 16-10 for an illustration of how 3D translation works. There, each arrow represents the translation along that axis, arriving at a point in 3D space. The dashed lines show the distance and direction from the origin point (the intersection of the three axes) and the distance above the xz plane.

Unlike translate(), there is no fallback for situations where translate3d() does not contain three values. Thus, translate3d(1em,-50px) should be treated as invalid by user agents instead of being assumed to be translate3d(2em,-50px,0).

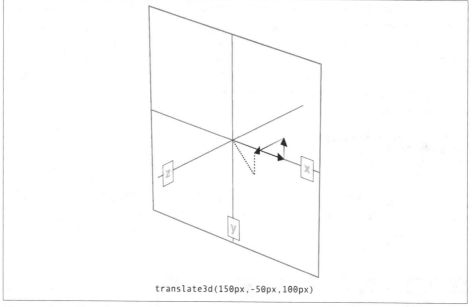

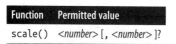

Figure 16-10. *Translating in three dimensions*

Scale functions

A *scale transform* makes an element larger or smaller, depending on what value you use. These values are unitless real numbers and are always positive. On the 2D plane, you can scale along the x- and y-axes individually, or scale them together.

Functions	Permitted value
scaleX(), scaleY(), scaleZ()	*<number>*

The number value supplied to a scale function is a multiplier; thus, scaleX(2) will make an element twice as wide as it was before the transformation, whereas scaleY(0.5) will make it half as tall. Given this, you might expect that percentage values are permissible as scaling values, but they aren't.

Function	Permitted value
scale()	*<number>* [, *<number>*]?

If you want to scale along both axes simultaneously, use scale(). The x value is always first and the y always second, so scale(2,0.5) will make the element twice as wide and half as tall as it was before being transformed. If you only supply one number, it is used as the scaling value for both axes; thus, scale(2) will make the element twice as wide *and* twice as tall. This is in contrast to translate(), where an omitted second value is always set to zero. scale(1) will scale an element to be exactly the same size it was before you scaled it, as will scale(1,1). Just in case you were dying to do that.

Figure 16-11 shows a few examples of element scaling, using both the single-axis scaling functions, as well as the combined scale().

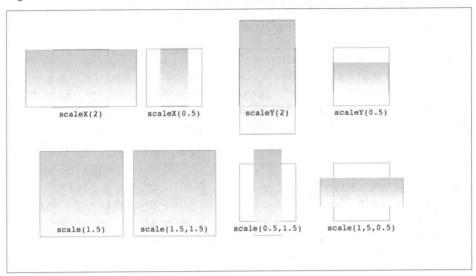

Figure 16-11. Scaled elements

If you can scale in two dimensions, you can also scale in three. CSS offers scaleZ() for scaling just along the z-axis, and scale3d() for scaling along all three axes at once. These really only have an effect if the element has any depth, which elements don't by default. If you do make a change that conveys depth—say, rotating an element around the x- or y-axes—then there is a depth that can be scaled, and either scaleZ() or scale3d() can do so.

Function	Permitted value
scale3d()	*<number>*, *<number>*, *<number>*

Similar to translate3d(), scale3d() requires all three numbers to be valid. If you fail to do this, then the malformed scale3d() will invalidate the entire transform value to which it belongs.

Rotation functions

A *rotation function* causes an element to be rotated around an axis, or around an arbitrary vector in 3D space. There are four simple rotation functions, and one less-simple function meant specifically for 3D.

Functions	Permitted values
rotate(), rotateX(), rotateY(), rotateZ()	*<angle>*

All four basic rotation functions accept just one value: a degree. This can be expressed using any of the valid degree units (deg, grad, rad, and turn) and a number, either positive or negative. If a value's number runs outside the usual range for the given unit, it will be normalized to fit into the accepted range. In other words, a value of 437deg will be tilted the same as if it were 77deg, or, for that matter, -283deg.

Note, however, that these are only exactly equivalent if you don't animate the rotation in some fashion. That is to say, animating a rotation of 1100deg will spin the element around several times before coming to rest at a tilt of -20 degrees (or 340 degrees, if you like). By contrast, animating a rotation of -20deg will tilt the element a bit to the left, with no spinning; and animating a rotation of 340deg will animate an almost-full spin to the right. All three animations come to the same end state, but the process of getting there is very different in each case.

The function rotate() is a straight 2D rotation, and the one you're most likely to use. It is equivalent to rotateZ() because it rotates the element around the z-axis (the one that shoots straight out of your display and through your eyeballs). In a similar manner, rotateX() causes rotation around the x-axis, thus causing the element to tilt toward or away from you; and rotateY() rotates the element around its y-axis, as though it were a door. These are all illustrated in Figure 16-12.

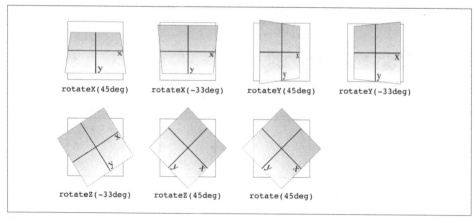

Figure 16-12. Rotations around the three axes

Several of the examples in Figure 16-12 present a fully 3D appearance. This is only possible with certain values of the properties transform-style and perspective, described in sections "Choosing a 3D Style" on page 845 and "Changing Perspective" on page 847 and omitted here for clarity. This will be true throughout this text in any situation where 3D-transformed elements appear to be fully three-dimensional. This is important to keep in mind because if you just try to apply the transform functions shown, you won't get the same visual results as in the figures.

Function	Permitted value
rotate3d()	*<number>*`,` *<number>*`,` *<number>*`,` *<angle>*

If you're comfortable with vectors and want to rotate an element through 3D space, then rotate3d() is for you. The first three numbers specify the x, y, and z components of a vector in 3D space, and the degree value (angle) determines the amount of rotation around the declared 3D vector.

To start with a basic example, the 3D equivalent to rotate(45deg) is rotate3d(0,0,1,45deg). This specifies a vector of zero magnitude on the x- and y-axes, and a magnitude of 1 along the z-axis. In other words, it describes the z-axis. The element is thus rotated 45 degrees around that vector, as shown in Figure 16-13. This figure also shows the appropriate rotate3d() values to rotate an element by 45 degrees around the x- and y-axes.

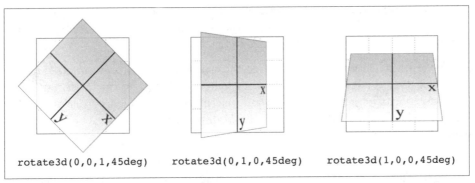

rotate3d(0,0,1,45deg)	rotate3d(0,1,0,45deg)	rotate3d(1,0,0,45deg)

Figure 16-13. Rotations around 3D vectors

A little more complicated is something like rotate3d(-0.95,0.5,1,45deg), where the described vector points off into 3D space between the axes. To understand how this works, let's start with a basic example: rotateZ(45deg) (illustrated in Figure 16-13). The equivalent is rotate3d(0,0,1,45deg). The first three numbers describe the components of a vector that has no x or y magnitude, and a z magnitude of 1. Thus, it points along the z-axis in a positive direction; that is, toward the viewer. The element is then rotated clockwise as you look toward the origin of the vector.

Similarly, the 3D equivalent of `rotateX(45deg)` is `rotate3d(1,0,0,45deg)`. The vector points along the x-axis in the positive direction (to the right). If you stand at the end of that vector and look toward its origin, then you rotate the element 45 degrees clockwise around the vector. Thus, from the usual viewer placement, the top of the element rotates away from and the bottom rotates toward the viewer.

Let's make it slightly more complex: suppose you have `rotate3d(1,1,0,45deg)`. When viewed on your monitor, that describes a vector running from the top-left to bottom-right corner, going right through the center of the element (by default, anyway; we'll see how to change that later on). So the element's rectangle has a line running through it at a 45-degree angle, effectively spearing it. Then the vector rotates 45 degrees, taking the element with it. The rotation is clockwise as you look back toward the vector's origin, so again, the top of the element rotates away from the viewer, while the bottom rotates toward the viewer. If we were to change the rotation to `rotate3d(1,1,0,90deg)`, then the element would be edge-on to the viewer, tilted at a 45-degree angle and facing off toward the upper right. Try it with a piece of paper: draw a line from the top left to bottom right, and then rotate the paper around that line.

OK, so given all that, try visualizing how the vector is determined for `rotate3d(-0.95,0.5,1,45deg)`. If we assume a cube 200 pixels on a side, the vector's components are 190 pixels to the *left* along the x-axis, 100 pixels down along the y-axis, and 200 pixels toward the views along the z-axis. The vector goes from the origin point (0, 0, 0) to the point (-190 px, 100 px, 200 px). Figure 16-14 depicts that vector, as well as the final result presented to the viewer.

So the vector is like a metal rod speared through the element being rotated. As we look back along the line of the vector, the rotation is 45 degrees clockwise. But since the vector points left, down, and forward, that means the top-left corner of the element rotates toward the viewer, and the bottom right rotates away, as shown in Figure 16-14.

Just to be crystal clear, `rotate3d(1,1,0,45deg)` is *not* equivalent to `rotateX(45deg)` `rotateY(45deg)` `rotateZ(0deg)`! It's an easy mistake to make, and many people—including several online tutorial authors and, until researching and writing this section, your humble correspondent—have made it. It seems like it should be equivalent, but it really isn't. If we place that vector inside the imaginary 200 × 200 × 200 cube previously mentioned, the axis of rotation would go from the origin point to a point 200 pixels right and 200 pixels down (200, 200, 0).

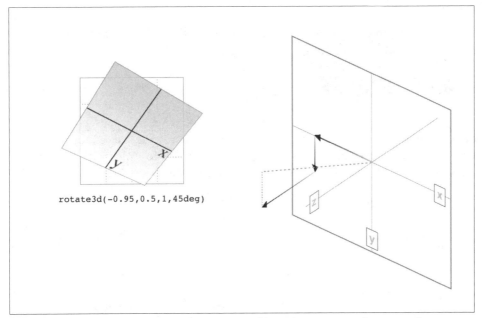

Figure 16-14. Rotation around a 3D vector, and how that vector is determined

Having done that, the axis of rotation is shooting through the element from the top left to the bottom right, at a 45-degree angle. The element then rotates 45 degrees clockwise around that diagonal, as you look back toward its origin (the top left), which rotates the top-right corner of the element away and a bit to the left, while the bottom-left corner rotates closer and a bit to the right. This is distinctly different than the result of `rotateX(45deg)` `rotateY(45deg)` `rotateZ(0deg)`, as you can see in Figure 16-15.

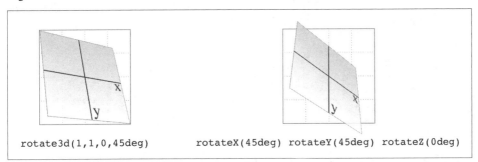

Figure 16-15. The difference between rotating around two axes and rotating around a 3D axis

Skew functions

When you *skew* an element, you slant it along one or both of the x- and y-axes. There is no z-axis or other 3D skewing.

Functions	Permitted value
skewX(), skewY()	*<angle>*

In both cases, you supply an angle value, and the element is skewed to match that angle. It's much easier to show skewing rather than try to explain it in words, so Figure 16-16 shows a number of skew examples along the x- and y-axes.

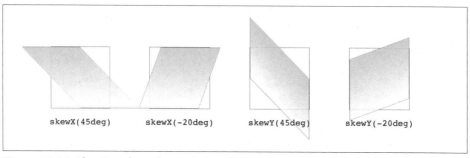

Figure 16-16. Skewing along the x- and y-axes

Function	Permitted values
skew()	*<angle>* [, *<angle>*]?

The behavior of including skew(a,b) is different from including skewX(a) with skewY(b). Instead, it specifies a 2D skew using the matrix operation [ax,ay]. Figure 16-17 shows some examples of this matrix skewing and how they differ from double-skew transforms that look the same at first, but aren't.

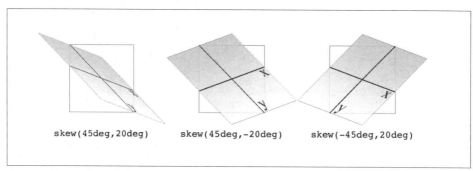

Figure 16-17. Skewed elements

If you supply two values, the x skew angle is always first, and the y skew angle comes second. If you leave out a y skew angle, then it's treated as zero.

The perspective function

If you're transforming an element in 3D space, you most likely want it to have some perspective. Perspective gives the appearance of front-to-back depth, and you can vary the amount of perspective applied to an element.

Function	Permitted values
perspective()	*<length>*

It might seem a bit weird that you specify perspective as a distance. After all, perspective(200px) seems a bit odd when you can't really measure pixels along the z-axis. And yet, here we are. You supply a length, and the illusion of depth is constructed around that value. Lower numbers create more extreme perspective, as though you are right up close to the element and viewing it through a fish-eye lens. Higher numbers create a gentler perspective, as though viewing the element through a zoom lens from far away. *Really* high perspective values create an isometric effect.

This makes a certain amount of sense. If you visualize perspective as a pyramid, with its apex point at the perspective origin and its base the closest thing to you, then a shorter distance between apex and base will create a shallower pyramid, and thus a more extreme distortion. This is illustrated in Figure 16-18, with hypothetical pyramids representing 200 px, 800 px, and 2,000 px perspective distances.

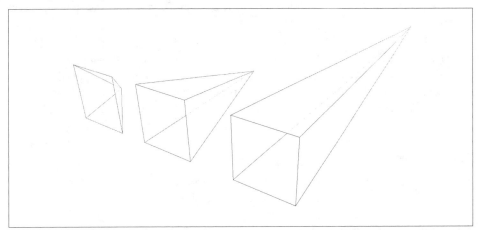

Figure 16-18. Different perspective pyramids

In the documentation for Safari (*http://bit.ly/safari-2d-3d-transforms*), Apple writes that perspective values below 300px tend to be extremely distorted, values above

2000px create "very mild" distortion, and values between 500px and 1000px create "moderate perspective." To illustrate this, Figure 16-19 shows a series of elements with the exact same rotation as displayed with varying perspective values.

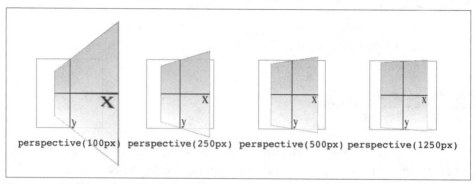

Figure 16-19. The effects of varying perspective values

Perspective values must always be positive, nonzero lengths. Any other value will cause the perspective() function to be ignored. Also note that its placement in the list of functions is very important. If you look at the code for Figure 16-19, the perspective() function comes before the rotateY() function. If you were to reverse the order, the rotation would happen before the perspective is applied, so all four examples in Figure 16-19 would look exactly the same. So if you plan to apply a perspective value via the list of transform functions, make sure it comes first, or at the very least before any transforms that depend on it. This serves as a particularly stark reminder that the order in which you write transform functions can be very important.

 Note that the function perspective() is very similar to the property perspective, which will be covered later, but they are applied in critically different ways. Generally, you will want to use the perspective property instead of the perspective() function, but there may be exceptions.

Matrix functions

If you're a particular fan of advanced math, or stale jokes derived from the Wachowskis' movies, then these functions will be your favorites.

Function	Permitted values
matrix()	*<number>* [, *<number>*]{5,5}

In the CSS transforms specification, we find the trenchant description of `matrix()` as a function that "specifies a 2D transformation in the form of a transformation matrix of the six values *a-f*."

First things first: a valid `matrix()` value is a list of six comma-separated numbers. No more, no less. The values can be positive or negative. Second, the value describes the final transformed state of the element, combining all of the other transform types (rotation, skewing, and so on) into a very compact syntax. Third, very few people actually use this syntax.

We're not actually going to go through the complicated process of actually doing the matrix math. For most readers, it would be an eye-watering wall of apparent gibberish; and for the rest, it would be time wasted on familiar territory. You can certainly research the intricacies of matrix calculations online, and I encourage anyone with an interest to do so. We'll just look at the basics of syntax and usage in CSS.

Here's a brief rundown of how it works. Say you have this function applied to an element:

```
matrix(0.838671, 0.544639, -0.692519, 0.742636, 6.51212, 34.0381)
```

That's the CSS syntax used to describe this transformation matrix:

```
0.838671    -0.692519   0   6.51212
0.544639     0.742636   0   34.0381
0            0          1   0
0            0          0   1
```

Right. So what does that do? It has the result shown in Figure 16-20, which is exactly the same result as writing this:

```
rotate(33deg) translate(24px,25px) skewX(-10deg)
```

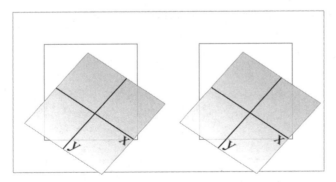

Figure 16-20. A matrix-transformed element and its functional equivalent

What this comes down to is that if you're familiar with or need to make use of matrix calculations, you can and should absolutely use them. If not, you can chain much more human-readable transform functions together and get the element to the same end state.

Now, that was for plain old 2D transforms. What if you want to use a matrix to transform through three dimensions?

Function	Permitted values
matrix3d()	<number> [, <number>]{15,15}

Again, just for kicks, we'll savor the definition of matrix3d() from the CSS Transforms specification: "specifies a 3D transformation as a 4 × 4 homogeneous matrix of 16 values in column-major order." This means the value of matrix3d *must* be a list of 16 comma-separated numbers, no more or less. Those numbers are arranged in a 4 × 4 grid in column order, so the first column of the matrix is formed by the first set of four numbers in the value, the second column by the second set of four numbers, the third column by the third set, and so on. Thus, you can take the following function:

```
matrix3d(
    0.838671, 0, -0.544639, 0.00108928,
    -0.14788, 1, 0.0960346, -0.000192069,
    0.544639, 0, 0.838671, -0.00167734,
    20.1281, 25, -13.0713, 1.02614)
```

And write it out as this matrix:

```
 0.838671   -0.14788      0.544639     20.1281
 0           1            0            25
-0.544639    0.0960346    0.838671    -13.0713
 0.00108928 -0.000192069 -0.00167734   1.02614
```

Both of which have an end state equivalent to:

```
perspective(500px) rotateY(33deg) translate(24px,25px) skewX(-10deg)
```

as shown in Figure 16-21.

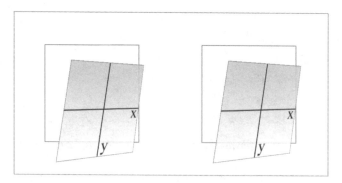

Figure 16-21. A matrix3d-transformed element and its functional equivalent

A note on end-state equivalence

It's important to keep in mind that only the end states of a `matrix()` function, and of an equivalent chain of transform functions, can be considered identical. This is for the same reason discussed in the section on rotation: because a rotation angle of `393deg` will end with the same visible rotation as an angle of `33deg`. This matters if you are animating the transformation, since the former will cause the element to do a barrel roll in the animation, whereas the latter will not. The `matrix()` version of this end state won't include the barrel roll, either. Instead, it will always use the shortest possible rotation to reach the end state.

To illustrate what this means, consider the following: a transform chain and its `matrix()` equivalent:

```
rotate(200deg) translate(24px,25px) skewX(-10deg)
matrix(-0.939693, -0.34202, 0.507713, -0.879385, -14.0021, -31.7008)
```

Note the rotation of 200 degrees. We naturally interpret this to mean a clockwise rotation of 200 degrees, which it does. If these two transforms are animated, however, they will have act differently: the chained-functions version will indeed rotate 200 degrees clockwise, whereas the `matrix()` version will rotate 160 degrees counter-clockwise. Both will end up in the same place, but will get there in different ways.

There are similar differences that arise even when you might think they wouldn't. Once again, this is because a `matrix()` transformation will always take the shortest possible route to the end state, whereas a transform chain might not. (In fact, it probably doesn't.) Consider these apparently equivalent transforms:

```
rotate(160deg) translate(24px,25px) rotate(-30deg) translate(-100px)
matrix(-0.642788, 0.766044, -0.766044, -0.642788, 33.1756, -91.8883)
```

As ever, they end up in the same place. When animated, though, the elements will take different paths to reach that end state. They might not be obviously different at first glance, but the difference is still there.

None of this matters if you aren't animating the transformation, but it's an important distinction to make nevertheless, because you never know when you'll decide to start animating things. (Hopefully after reading the companion text on animations!)

More Transform Properties

In addition to the base `transform` property, there are a few related properties that help to define things such as the origin point of a transform, the perspective used for a "scene," and more.

Moving the Origin

So far, all of the transforms we've seen have shared one thing in common: the precise center of the element was used as the *transform origin*. For example, when rotating the element, it rotated around its center, instead of, say, a corner. This is the default behavior, but with the property `transform-origin`, you can change it.

---

transform-origin

Values	[left | center | right | top | bottom | *<percentage>* | *<length>*] | [left | center | right | *<percentage>* | *<length>*] && [top | center | bottom | *<percentage>* | *<length>*]] *<length>*?
Initial value	50% 50%
Applies to	Any transformable element
Percentages	Refer to the size of the bounding box (see explanation)
Computed value	A percentage, except for length values, which are converted to an absolute length
Inherited	No
Animatable	*<length>*, *<percentage>*

The syntax definition looks really abstruse and confusing, but it's actually fairly simple in practice. With `transform-origin`, you supply two or three keywords to define the point around which transforms should be made: first the horizontal, then the vertical, and optionally a length along the z-axis. For the horizontal and vertical axes, you can use plain-English keywords like `top` and `right`, percentages, lengths, or a combination of different keyword types. For the z-axis, you can't use plain-English keywords or percentages, but can use any length value. Pixels are by far the most common.

Length values are taken as a distance starting from the top-left corner of the element. Thus, `transform-origin: 5em 22px` will place the transform origin 5 em to the right of the left side of the element, and 22 pixels down from the top of the element. Similarly, `transform-origin: 5em 22px -200px` will place it 5 em over, 22 pixels down, and 200 pixels away; that is, 200 pixels behind the place where the element sits.

Percentages are calculated with respect to the corresponding axis and size of the element, as offsets from the element's top-left corner. For example, `transform-origin: 67% 40%` will place the transform origin 67 percent of the width to the right of the element's left side, and 40 percent of the element's height down from the element's top side. Figure 16-22 illustrates a few origin calculations.

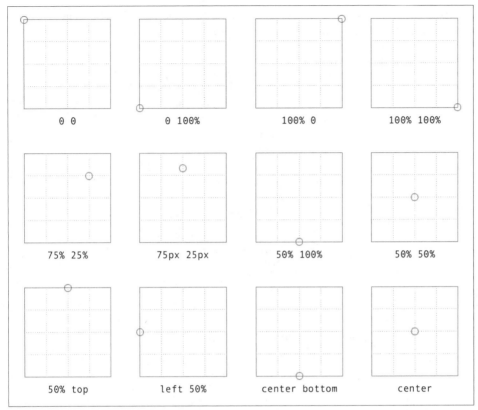

Figure 16-22. Various origin calculations

All right, so if you change the origin, what happens? The easiest way to visualize this is with 2D rotations. Suppose you rotate an element 45 degrees to the right. Its final placement will depend on its origin. Figure 16-23 illustrates the the effects of several different transform origins; in each case, the transform origin is marked with a circle.

The origin matters for other transform types, such as skews and scales. Scaling an element with its origin in the center will pull in all sides equally, whereas scaling an element with a bottom-right origin will cause it to shrink toward that corner. Similarly, skewing an element with respect to its center will result in the same shape as if it's skewed with respect to the top-right corner, but the placement of the shape will be different. Some examples are shown in Figure 16-24; again, each transform origin is marked with a circle.

The one transform type that isn't really affected by changing the transform origin is translation. If you push an element around with translate(), or its cousins like translateX() and translateY(), it's going to end up in the same place regardless of where the transform origin is located. If that's all the transforming you plan to do, then setting the transform origin is irrelevant. If you ever do anything besides trans-lating, though, the origin will matter. Use it wisely.

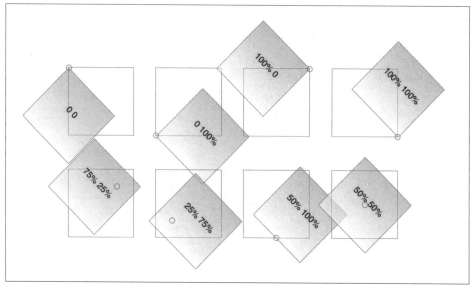

Figure 16-23. The rotational effects of using various transform origins

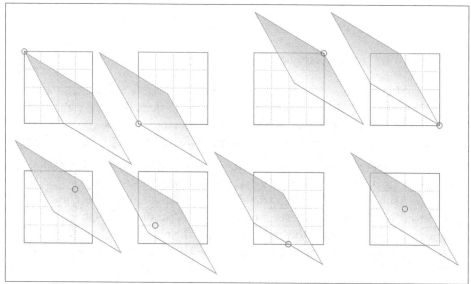

Figure 16-24. The skew effects of using various transform origins

Choosing a 3D Style

If you're setting elements to be transformed through three dimensions—using, say, translate3d() or rotateY()—you probably expect that the elements will be presented as though they're in a 3D space. And yet, this is not the default behavior. By default, everything looks flat no matter what you do. Fortunately, this can be overridden with the transform-style property.

transform-style	
Values	flat | preserve-3d
Initial value	flat
Applies to	Any transformable element
Computed value	As specified
Inherited	No
Animatable	No

Suppose you have an element you want to move "closer to" your eye, and then tilt away a bit, with a moderate amount of perspective. Something like this rule, as applied to the following HTML:

```
div#inner {transform: perspective(750px) translateZ(60px) rotateX(45deg);}

<div id="outer">
outer
<div id="inner">inner</div>
</div>
```

So you do that, and get the result shown in Figure 16-25; more or less what you might have expected.

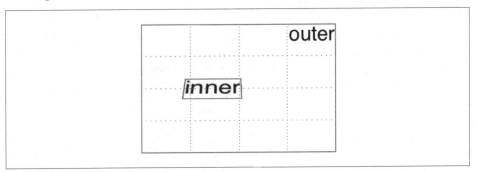

Figure 16-25. A 3D-transformed inner div

But then you decide to rotate the outer div to one side, and suddenly nothing makes sense any more. The inner div isn't where you envisioned it. In fact, it just looks like a picture pasted to the front of the outer div.

Well, that's exactly what it is, because the default value of transform-style is flat. The inner div got drawn in its moved-forward-tilted-back state, and that was applied to the front of the outer div as if it was an image. So when you rotated the outer div, the flat picture rotated right along with it, as shown in Figure 16-26:

```
div#outer {transform: perspective(750px) rotateY(60deg) rotateX(-20deg);}
div#inner {transform: perspective(750px) translateZ(60px) rotateX(45deg);}
```

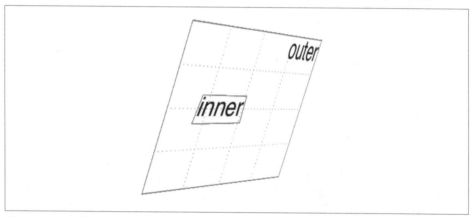

Figure 16-26. The effects of a flat transform style

Change the value to preserve-3d, however, and things are suddenly different. The inner div will be drawn as a full 3D object with respect to its parent outer div, floating in space nearby, and *not* as a picture pasted on the front of the outer div. You can see the results of this change in Figure 16-27:

```
div#outer {transform: perspective(750px) rotateY(60deg) rotateX(-20deg);
    transform-style: preserve-3d;}
div#inner {transform: perspective(750px) translateZ(60px) rotateX(45deg);}
```

One important aspect of transform-style is that it can be overridden by other properties. The reason is that some values of these other properties require a flattened presentation of an element and its children in order to work at all. In such cases, the value of transform-style is forced to be flat, regardless of what you may have declared.

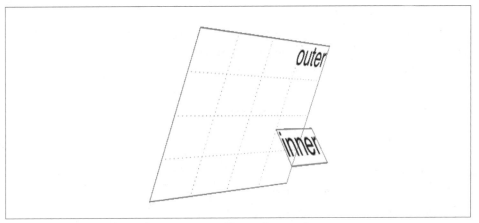

Figure 16-27. The effects of a 3D-preserved transform style

So, in order to avoid this overriding behavior, make sure the following properties are set to the listed values:

- `overflow: visible`
- `filter: none`
- `clip: auto`
- `clip-path: none`
- `mask-image: none`
- `mask-border-source: none`
- `mix-blend-mode: normal`

Those are all the default values for those properties, so as long as you don't try to change any of them for your preserved 3D elements, you're fine! But if you find that editing some CSS suddenly flattens out your lovely 3D transforms, one of these properties might be the culprit.

One more note: in addition to the values just mentioned, the value of the property `isolation` must be, or be computed to be, `isolate`. (`isolation` is a compositing property, in case you were wondering.)

Changing Perspective

There are actually two properties that are used to define how perspective is handled: one to define the perspective distance, as with the `perspective()` function discussed in an earlier section; and another to define the perspective's origin point.

Defining a group perspective

First, let's consider the property perspective, which accepts a length that defines the depth of the perspective pyramid. At first glance, it looks just like the perspective() function discussed earlier, but there are some critical differences.

---

perspective

Values	none | *<length>*
Initial value	none
Applies to	Any transformable element
Computed value	The absolute length, or else none
Inherited	No
Animatable	Yes

As a quick example, if you want to create a very deep perspective, one mimicking the results you'd get from a zoom lens, you might declare something like perspective: 2500px. For a shallow depth, one that mimics a closeup fish-eye lens effect, you might declare perspective: 200px.

So how does this differ from the perspective() function? When you use perspective(), you're defining the perspective effect for the element that is given that function. So if you say transform: perspective(800px) rotateY(-50grad);, you're applying that perspective to each element that has the rule applied.

With the perspective property, on the other hand, you're creating a perspective depth that is applied to all the child elements of the element that received the property. Confused yet? Don't be. Here's an illustration of the difference, as shown in Figure 16-28:

```
div {transform-style: preserve-3d; border: 1px solid gray; width: 660px;}
img {margin: 10px;}
#one {perspective: none;}
#one img {transform: perspective(800px) rotateX(-50grad);}
#two {perspective: 800px;}
#two img {transform: rotateX(-50grad);}

<div><img src="rsq.gif"><img src="rsq.gif"><img src="rsq.gif"></div>
<div id="one"><img src="rsq.gif"><img src="rsq.gif"><img src="rsq.gif"></div>
<div id="two"><img src="rsq.gif"><img src="rsq.gif"><img src="rsq.gif"></div>
```

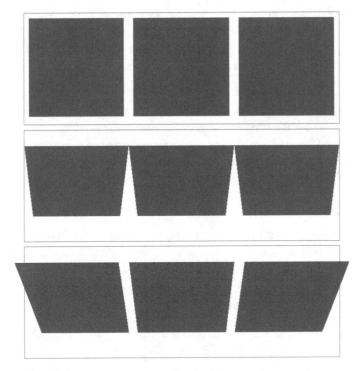

Figure 16-28. Shared perspective versus individual perspectives

In Figure 16-28, we first see a line of images that haven't been transformed. In the second line, each image has been rotated 50 gradians (equivalent to 45 degrees) toward us, but each one within its own individual perspective.

In the third line of images, none of them has an individual perspective. Instead, they are all drawn within the perspective defined by `perspective: 800px;` that's been set on the `div` that contains them. Since they all operate within a shared perspective, they look "correct"; that is, like we would expect if we had three physical pictures mounted on a clear sheet of glass and rotated toward us around the center horizontal axis of that glass.

 Note that presence of `transform-style: preserve-3d` makes this effect possible, as discussed in the previous section.

This is the critical difference between `perspective`, the property; and `perspective()`, the function. The former creates a 3D space shared by all its children. The latter affects only the element to which it's applied. A less important difference is that the perspective() function has to come first or early in its chain of transforms in order to apply to the element as it's transformed through 3D space. The perspective property, on the other hand, is applied to all children, regardless of where their transforms are declared.

In most cases, you're going to use the perspective property instead of the perspective() function. In fact, container divs (or other elements) are a very common feature of 3D transforms—the way they used to be for page layout—largely to establish a shared perspective. In the previous example, the <div id="two"> was there solely to serve as a perspective container, so to speak. On the other hand, we couldn't have done what we did without it.

Moving the perspective's origin

When transforming elements in three dimensions—assuming you've allowed them to appear three-dimensional, that is—a perspective will be used. (See transform-style and perspective, respectively, in previous sections.) That perspective will have an origin, which is also known as the *vanishing point*, and you can change where it's located with the property perspective-origin.

---

perspective-origin

Values	[left | center | right | top | bottom | <percentage> | <length>] | [left | center | right | <percentage> | <length>] && [top | center | bottom | <percentage> | <length>]] <length>?
Initial value	50% 50%
Applies to	Any transformable element
Percentages	Refer to the size of the bounding box (see explanation)
Computed value	A percentage, except for length values, which are converted to an absolute length
Inherited	No
Animatable	<length>, <percentage>

As you may have spotted, perspective-origin and transform-origin have the same value syntax, right down to allowing an optional length value defining an offset along the z-axis. While the way the values are expressed is identical, the effects they have are very different. With transform-origin, you define the point around which transforms happen. With perspective-origin, you define the point on which sight lines converge.

As with most 3D transform properties, this is more easily demonstrated than described. Consider the following CSS and markup, illustrated in Figure 16-29:

```
#container {perspective: 850px; perspective-origin: 50% 0%;}
#ruler {height: 50px; background: #DED url(tick.gif) repeat-x;
    transform: rotateX(60deg);
    transform-origin: 50% 100%;}

<div id="container">
    <div id="ruler"></div>
</div>
```

Figure 16-29. A basic "ruler"

What we have is a repeated background image of tick-marks on a ruler, with the div that contains them tiled away from us by 60 degrees. All the lines point at a common vanishing point, the top center of the container div (because of the 50% 0% value for perspective-origin).

Now consider that same setup with various perspective origins, as shown in Figure 16-30.

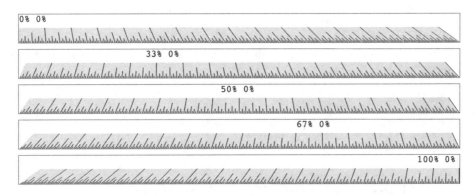

Figure 16-30. A basic "ruler" with different perspective origins

As you can see, moving the perspective origin changes the rendering of the 3D-transformed element.

Note that these only had an effect because we supplied a value for perspective. If the value of perspective is ever the default none, then any value given for perspective-origin will be ignored. That makes sense, since you can't have a perspective origin when there's no perspective at all!

Dealing with Backfaces

Something you probably never really thought about, over all the years you've been laying out elements, was: what would it look like if I could see the back side of the element? Now that 3D transforms are a possibility, there may well come a day when you *do* see the back side of an element. You might even mean to do so intentionally. What happens at that moment is determined by the property backface-visibility.

---

backface-visibility

Values	visible | hidden
Initial value	visible
Applies to	Any transformable element
Computed value	As specified
Inherited	No
Animatable	No

Unlike many of the other properties and functions we've already talked about, this one is pretty uncomplicated. All it does is determine whether the back side of an element is rendered when it's facing toward the viewer, or not. That's it.

So let's say you flip over two elements, one with backface-visibility set to the default value of visible and the other set to hidden. You get the result shown in Figure 16-31:

```
span {border: 1px solid red; display: inline-block;}
img {vertical-align: bottom;}
img.flip {transform: rotateX(180deg); display: inline-block;}
img#show {backface-visibility: visible;}
img#hide {backface-visibility: hidden;}

<span><img src="salmon.gif"></span>
<span><img src="salmon.gif" class="flip" id="show"></span>
<span><img src="salmon.gif" class="flip" id="hide"></span>
```

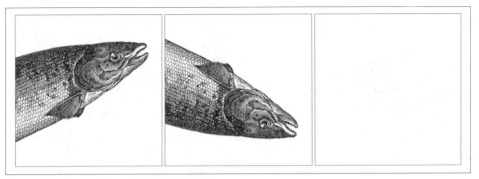

Figure 16-31. Visible and hidden backfaces

As you can see, the first image is unchanged. The second is flipped over around its x-axis, so we see it from the back. The third has also been flipped, but we can't see it at all because its backface has been hidden.

This property can come in handy in a number of situations. The simplest is a case where you have two elements that represent the two sides of a UI element that flips over; say, a search area with preference settings on its back, or a photo with some information on the back. Let's take the latter case. The CSS and markup might look something like this:

```
section {position: relative;}
img, div {position: absolute; top: 0; left: 0; backface-visibility: hidden;}
div {transform: rotateY(180deg);}
section:hover {transform: rotateY(180deg); transform-style: preserve-3d;}

<section>
    <img src="photo.jpg" alt="">
    <div class="info">(…info goes here…)</div>
</section>
```

Actually, this example shows that using `backface-visibility` isn't *quite* as simple as it first appears. It's not that the property itself is complicated, but if you forget to set `transform-style` to `preserve-3d`, then it won't work as intended. That's why `transform-style` is set on the `section` element.

There's a variant of this example that uses the same markup, but a slightly different CSS to show the image's backface when it's flipped over. This is probably more what was intended, since it makes information look like it's literally written on the back of the image. It leads to the end result shown in Figure 16-32:

```
section {position: relative;}
img, div {position: absolute; top: 0; left: 0;}
div {transform: rotateY(180deg); backface-visibility: hidden;
    background: rgba(255,255,255,0.85);}
section:hover {transform: rotateY(180deg); transform-style: preserve-3d;}
```

Figure 16-32. Photo on the front, information on the back

The only thing we had to do to make that happen was to just shift the backface-visibilty: hidden to the div instead of applying it to both the img and the div. Thus, the div's backface is hidden when it's flipped over, but that of the image is not.

Summary

With the ability to transform elements in two- and three-dimensional space, CSS transforms provide a great deal of power to designers who are looking for new ways to present information. From creating interesting combinations of 2D transforms, to creating a fully 3D-acting interface, transforms open up a great deal of new territory in the design space. There are some interesting dependencies between properties, which is something that not every CSS author will find natural at first, but they become second nature with just a bit of practice.

CHAPTER 17

Transitions

CSS transitions allow us to animate CSS properties from an original value to a new value over time when a property value changes. These transition an element from one state to another, in response to some change—usually a user interaction, but it can also be due to the scripted change of class, ID, or other state.

Normally, when a CSS property value changes—when a "style change event" occurs—the change is instantaneous. The new property value replaces the old property in the milliseconds it takes to repaint, or reflow and repaint when necessary, the affected content. Most value changes seem instantaneous, taking less than 16 milliseconds[1] to render. Even if the changes takes longer, it is still a single step from one value to the next. For example, when changing a background color on mouse hover, the background changes from one color to the next, with no gradual transition.

CSS Transitions

CSS transitions provide a way to control how a property changes from one value to the next over a period of time. Thus, we can make the property values change gradually, creating pleasant and (hopefully) unobtrusive effects. For example:

```
button {
    color: magenta;
    transition: color 200ms ease-in 50ms;
}

button:hover {
    color: rebeccapurple;
```

---

1 Changing a background image may take longer than 16 milliseconds to decode and repaint to the page. This isn't a transition; it is just poor performance.

```
        transition: color 200ms ease-out 50ms;
    }
```

In this example, instead of instantaneously changing a button's `color` value on hover, with CSS transitions the button can be set to gradually fade from `magenta` to `rebecca purple` over 200 milliseconds, even adding a 50-millisecond delay before transitioning. Changing the color, no matter how long or short a time it takes, is a transition. But by adding the CSS `transition` property, the color change can happen gradually over a period of time and be perceivable by the human eye.

You can use CSS transitions today, even if you still support IE9 or older browsers. When a browser doesn't support CSS transition properties, the change is immediate instead of gradual, which is completely fine. If the property or property values specified aren't animatable, again, the change will be immediate instead of gradual.

 When we say "animatable," we mean any properties that can be animated, whether through transitions or animations (the subject of the next chapter, "Animations.") See Appendix A for a summary.

Sometimes you want instantaneous value changes. Though we used link colors as an example in the preceding section, link colors usually change instantly on hover, informing sighted users an interaction is occurring and that the hovered content is a link. Similarly, options in an autocomplete listbox shouldn't fade in: you want the options to appear instantly, rather than fade in more slowly than the user types. Instantaneous value changes are often the best user experience.

At other times, you might want to make a property value change more gradually, bringing attention to what is occurring. For example, you may want to make a card game more realistic by taking 200 milliseconds to animate the flipping of a card, as the user may not realize what happened if there is no animation. ⊙

 Look for the Play symbol ⊙ to know when an online example is available. All of the examples in this chapter can be found at *https://meyerweb.github.io/csstdg4figs/17-transitions/*.

As another example, you may want some drop-down menus to expand or become visible over 200 milliseconds (instead of instantly, which may be jarring). With transitions, you can make a drop-down menu appear slowly. In Figure 17-1 ⊙, we transition the submenu's height by making a scale transform. This is a common use for CSS transitions, which we will also explore later in this chapter.

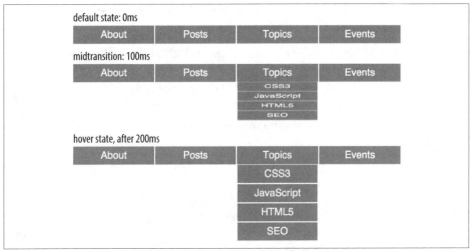

Figure 17-1. Transition initial, midtransition, and final state

Transition Properties

In CSS, transitions are written using four transition properties: `transition-property`, `transition-duration`, `transition-timing-function`, and `transition-delay`, along with the `transition` property as a shorthand for the four longhand properties.

To create the drop-down navigation from Figure 17-1, we used all four CSS transition properties, in addition to non-transform properties defining the beginning and end states of the transition. The following code could define the transition for the example illustrated in Figure 17-1:

```
nav li ul {
    transition-property: transform;
    transition-duration: 200ms;
    transition-timing-function: ease-in;
    transition-delay: 50ms;
    transform: scale(1, 0);
    transform-origin: top center;
}
nav li:hover ul {
    transform: scale(1, 1);
}
```

Note that while we are using the `:hover` state for the style change event in our transition examples, you can transition properties in other scenarios too. For example, you might add or remove a class, or otherwise change the state—say, by changing an input from `:invalid` to `:valid` or from `:checked` to `:not(:checked)`. Or you might append a table row at the end of a zebra-striped table or list item at the end of a list with styles based on :nth-last-of-type selectors.

In the scenario pictured in Figure 17-1, the initial state of the nested lists is transform: scale(1, 0) with a transform-origin: top center. The final state is transform: scale(1, 1): the transform-origin remains the same.

 For more information on transform properties, see Chapter 16.

In this example, the transition properties define a transition on the transform property: when the new transform value is set on hover, the nested unordered list scales to its original, default size, changing smoothly between the old value of transform: scale(1, 0) and the new value of transform: scale(1, 1), all over a period of 200 milliseconds. This transition starts after a 50-millisecond delay, and "eases in," proceeding slowly at first, then picking up speed as it progresses.

Transitions are declared along with the regular styles on an element. Whenever a target property changes, if a transition is set on that property, the browser will apply a transition to make the change gradual.

Note that all the transition properties were set for the unhovered state of the ul elements. The hovered state was only used to change the transform, not the transition. There's a very good reason for this: it means not only that the menus will slide open when hovered, but will slide closed when the hover state ends.

Imagine if the transition properties were applied via the hover state instead, like this:

```
nav li ul {
    transform: scale(1, 0);
    transform-origin: top center;
}
nav li:hover ul {
    transition-property: transform;
    transition-duration: 200ms;
    transition-timing-function: ease-in;
    transition-delay: 50ms;
    transform: scale(1, 1);
}
```

That would mean that when *not* hovered, the element would have default transition values—which is to say, instantaneous transitions. That means the menus in our previous example would slide open on hover, but instantly disappear when the hover state ends—because without being in hover, the transition properties would no longer apply!

It might be that you want exactly this effect: slide smoothly open, but instantly disappear. If so, then apply the transitions to the hover state. Otherwise, apply them to the element directly so that the transitions will apply as the hover state is both entered and exited. When the state change is exited, the transition timing is reversed. You can override this default reverse transition by declaring different transitions in both the initial and changed states.

By "initial state," we mean a state that matches the element on page load. This could be a state that the element always has, such as properties set on an element selector versus a :hover state for that element. It could mean a content-editable element that could get :focus, as in the following:

```
/* selector that matches elements all the time */
p[contenteditable] {
    background-color: rgba(0, 0, 0, 0);
}

/* selector that matches elements some of the time */
p[contenteditable]:focus {
    /* overriding declaration */
    background-color: rgba(0, 0, 0, 0.1);
}
```

In this example, the fully transparent background is always the initial state, only changing when the user gives the element focus. This is what we mean when we say *initial* or *default* value throughout this chapter. The transition properties included in the selector that matches the element all the time will impact that element whenever the state changes, whether it is from the initial state to the changed state (being focused, in the preceding example).

An initial state could also be a temporary state that may change, such as a :checked checkbox or a :valid form control, or even a class that gets toggled on and off:

```
/* selector that matches elements some of the time */
input:valid {
    border-color: green;
}

/* selector that matches elements some of the time,
   when the prior selector does NOT match. */
input:invalid {
    border-color: red;
}

/* selector that matches elements some of the time,
   whether the input is valid or invalid */
input:focus {
    /* alternative declaration */
    border-color: yellow;
}
```

In this example, either the :valid or :invalid selector can match any given element, but never both. The :focus selector, as shown in Figure 17-2, matches whenever an input has focus, regardless of whether the input is matching the :valid or :invalid selector simultaneously.

In this case, when we refer to the initial state, we are referring to the original value, which could be either :valid or :invalid. The changed state for a given element the opposite of the initial :valid or :invalid state. ⊙

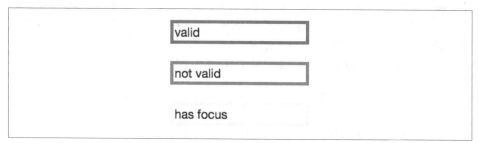

Figure 17-2. The input's appearance in the valid, invalid, and focused states

Remember, you can apply different transition values to the initial and changed states, but you always want to apply the value used when you *enter* a given state. Take the following code as an example, where the transitions are set up to have menus slide open over 2 seconds but close in just 200 milliseconds:

```
nav li ul {
    transition-property: transform;
    transition-duration: 200ms;
    transition-timing-function: ease-in;
    transition-delay: 50ms;
    transform: scale(1, 0);
    transform-origin: top center;
}
nav li:hover ul {
    transition-property: transform;
    transition-duration: 2s;
    transition-timing-function: linear;
    transition-delay: 1s;
    transform: scale(1, 1);
}
```

This provides a horrible user experience, but it nicely illustrates the point. ⊙ When hovered over, the opening of the navigation takes a full 2 seconds. When closing, it quickly closes over 0.2 seconds. The transition properties in the changed, or hover, state are in force when hovering over the list item. Thus, the transition-duration: 2s defined for the hover state takes effect. When a menu is no longer hovered over, it returns to the default scaled-down state, and the transition properties of the initial state—the nav li ul condition—are used, causing the menu to take 200ms to close.

Look more closely at the example, specifically the default transition styles. When the user stops hovering over the parent navigational element or the child drop-down menu, the drop-down menu delays 50 milliseconds before starting the 200ms transition to close. This is actually a decent user experience style, because it give users a chance (however brief) to get the mouse point back over a menu before it starts closing.

While the four transition properties can be declared separately, you will probably always use the shorthand. We'll take a look at the four properties individually first so you have a good understanding of what each one does.

Limiting Transition Effects by Property

The `transition-property` property specifies the names of the CSS properties you want to transition. This allows you to limit the transition to only certain properties, while having other properties change instantaneously. And, yes, it's weird to say "the `transition-property` property."

---

transition-property

Values	none | [all | *<property-name>*]#
Initial value	all
Applies to	All elements and :before and :after pseudo-elements
Computed value	As specified
Inherited	No
Animatable	No

The value of `transition-property` is a comma-separated list of properties; the keyword none if you want no properties transitioned; or the default all, which means "transition all the animatable properties." You can also include the keyword all within a comma-separated list of properties.

If you include all as the only keyword—or default to all—all animatable properties will transition in unison. Let's say you want to change a box's appearance on hover:

```
div {
    color: #ff0000;
    border: 1px solid #00ff00;
    border-radius: 0;
    transform: scale(1) rotate(0deg);
    opacity: 1;
    box-shadow: 3px 3px rgba(0, 0, 0, 0.1);
```

```
        width: 50px;
        padding: 100px;
    }
    div:hover {
        color: #000000;
        border: 5px dashed #000000;
        border-radius: 50%;
        transform: scale(2) rotate(-10deg);
        opacity: 0.5;
        box-shadow: -3px -3px rgba(255, 0, 0, 0.5);
        width: 100px;
        padding: 20px;
    }
```

When the mouse pointer hovers over the div, every property that has a different value in the initial state versus the hovered (changed) state will change to the hover-state values. The transition-property property is used to define which of those properties are animated over time (versus instantly). All the properties change from the default value to the hovered value on hover, but only the animatable properties included in the transition-property transition over the transition's duration. Non-animatable properties like border-style change from one value to the next instantly.

If all is the only value or the last value in the comma-separated value for transition-property, then all the animatable properties will transition in unison. Otherwise, provide a comma-separated list of properties to be affected by the transition properties.

Thus, if we want to transition all the properties, the following statements are almost equivalent:

```
    div {
        color: #ff0000;
        border: 1px solid #00ff00;
        border-radius: 0;
        transform: scale(1) rotate(0deg);
        opacity: 1;
        box-shadow: 3px 3px rgba(0, 0, 0, 0.1);
        width: 50px;
        padding: 100px;
        transition-property: color, border, border-radius, transform, opacity,
            box-shadow, width, padding;
        transition-duration: 1s;
    }

    div {
        color: #ff0000;
        border: 1px solid #00ff00;
        border-radius: 0;
        transform: scale(1) rotate(0deg);
        opacity: 1;
        box-shadow: 3px 3px rgba(0, 0, 0, 0.1);
```

```
    width: 50px;
    padding: 100px;
    transition-property: all;
    transition-duration: 1s;
}
```

Both `transition-property` property declarations will transition all the properties listed—but the former will transition only the eight properties that may change, based on property declarations that may be included in other rule blocks. Those eight property values are included in the same rule block, but they don't have to be.

The `transition-property: all` in the latter rule ensures that *all* animatable property values that would change based on any style change event—no matter which CSS rule block includes the changed property value—transitions over one second. The transition applies to all animatable properties of all elements matched by the selector, not just the properties declared in the same style block as the `all`.

In this case, the first version limits the transition to only the eight properties listed, but enables us to provide more control over how each property will transition. Declaring the properties individually lets us provide different speeds, delays, and/or durations to each property's transition if we declared those transition properties separately:

```
div {
    color: #ff0000;
    border: 1px solid #0f0;
    border-radius: 0;
    transform: scale(1) rotate(0deg);
    opacity: 1;
    box-shadow: 3px 3px rgba(0, 0, 0, 0.1);
    width: 50px;
    padding: 100px;
}

.foo {
    color: #00ff00;
    transition-property: color, border, border-radius, transform, opacity,
        box-shadow, width, padding;
    transition-duration: 1s;
}
```
```
<div class="foo">Hello</div>
```

If you want to define the transitions for each property separately, write them all out, separating each of the properties with a comma. If you want to animate almost all the properties at the same time, delay, and pace, with a few exceptions, you can use a combination of `all` and the individual properties you want to transition at different times, speeds, or pace. Make sure to use `all` as the first value:

```
div {
    color: #f00;
    border: 1px solid #00ff00;
    border-radius: 0;
    transform: scale(1) rotate(0deg);
    opacity: 1;
    box-shadow: 3px 3px rgba(0, 0, 0, 0.1);
    width: 50px;
    padding: 100px;
    transition-property: all, border-radius, opacity;
    transition-duration: 1s, 2s, 3s;
}
```

The all part of the comma-separated value includes all the properties listed in the example, as well as all the inherited CSS properties, and all the properties defined in any other CSS rule block matching or inherited by the element.

In the preceding example, all the properties getting new values will transition at the same duration, delay, and timing function, with the exception of border-radius and opacity, which we've explicitly included separately. Because we included them as part of a comma-separated list after the all, we can transition them at the the same time, delay, and timing function as all the other properties, or we can provide different times, delays, and timing functions for these two properties. In this case, we transition all the properties over one second, except for border-radius and opacity, which we transition over two seconds and three seconds respectively. (transition-duration is covered in an upcoming section.)

 Make sure to use all as the first value in your comma-separated value list, as the properties declared before the all will be included in the all, overriding any other transition property values you intended to apply to those now overridden properties.

Suppressing transitions via property limits

While transitioning over time doesn't happen by default, if you do include a CSS transition and want to override that transition in a particular scenario, you can set transition-property: none to override the entire transition and ensure no properties are transitioned.

The none keyword can only be used as a unique value of the property—you can't include it as part of a comma-separated list of properties. If you want to override the transition of a limited set of properties, you will have to list all of the properties you still want to transition. You can't use the transition-property property to exclude properties; rather, you can only use that property to include them.

Another method would be to set the delay and duration of the property to 0s. That way it will appear instantaneously, as if no CSS transition is being applied to it.

Transition events

In the DOM, a `transitionend` event if fired at the end of every transition, in either direction, for every property that is transitioned over any amount of time *or* after any delay. This happens whether the property is declared individually or is part of the `all` declaration. For some seemingly single property declarations, there will be several `transitionend` events, as every animatable property within a shorthand property gets its own `transitionend` event. Consider:

```
div {
    color: #f00;
    border: 1px solid #00ff00;
    border-radius: 0;
    transform: scale(1) rotate(0deg);
    opacity: 1;
    box-shadow: 3px 3px rgba(0, 0, 0, 0.1);
    width: 50px;
    padding: 100px;
    transition-property: all, border-radius, opacity;
    transition-duration: 1s, 2s, 3s;
}
```

When the transitions conclude, there will be well over eight `transitionend` events. For example, the `border-radius` transition alone produces four `transitionend` events, one each for:

- `border-bottom-left-radius`
- `border-bottom-right-radius`
- `border-top-right-radius`
- `border-top-left-radius`

The `padding` property is also a shorthand for four longhand properties:

- `padding-top`
- `padding-right`
- `padding-bottom`
- `padding-left`

The border shorthand property produces eight transitionend events: four values for the four properties represented by the border-width shorthand, and four for the properties represented by border-color:

- border-left-width
- border-right-width
- border-top-width
- border-bottom-width
- border-top-color
- border-left-color
- border-right-color
- border-bottom-color

There are no transitionend events for border-style properties, however, as border-style is not an animatable property.

How do we know border-style isn't animatable? We can assume it isn't, since there is no logical midpoint between the two values of solid and dashed. We can confirm by looking up the list of animatable properties in Appendix A or the specifications for the individual properties.

There will be 21 transitionend events in our scenario in which 8 specific properties are listed, as those 8 include several shorthand properties that have different values in the pre and post states. In the case of all, there will be at least 21 transitionend events: one for each of the longhand values making up the 8 properties we know are included in the pre and post states, and possibly from others that are inherited or declared in other style blocks impacting the element: ▶

You can listen for transitionend events in a manner like this:

```
document.querySelector('div').addEventListener('transitionend',
    function (e) {
        console.log(e.propertyName);
});
```

The transitionend event includes three event specific attributes:

1. propertyName, which is the name of the CSS property that just finished transitioning.

2. pseudoElement, which is the pseudoelement upon which the transition occurred, preceded by two semicolons, or an empty string if the transition was on a regular DOM node.

3. `elapsedTime`, which is the amount of time the transition took to run, in seconds; usually this is the time listed in the `transition-duration` property.

The `transitionend` event only occurs if the property successfully transitions to the new value. The `transitioned` event doesn't fire if the transition was interrupted, such as by another change to the same property on the same element.

When the properties return to their initial value, another `transitionend` event occurs. This event occurs as long as the transition started, even if it didn't finish its initial transition in the original direction.

Setting Transition Duration

The `transition-duration` property takes as its value a comma-separated list of lengths of time, in seconds (s) or milliseconds (ms). These values describe the time it will take to transition from one state to another.

transition-duration	
Values	*<time>*#
Initial value	0s
Applies to	All elements and `:before` and `:after` pseudo-elements
Computed value	As specified
Inherited	No
Animatable	No

If reverting between two states, and the duration is only present in a declaration applying to one of those states, the transition duration will only impact the transition *to* that state. Consider:

```
input:invalid {
    transition-duration: 1s;
    background-color: red;
}

input:valid {
    transition-duration: 0.2s;
    background-color: green;
}
```

If different values for the `transition-duration` are declared, the duration of the transition will be the `transition-duration` value declared in the rule block to which it is transitioning. In the preceding example, it will take 1 second for the input to change to a red background when it becomes invalid, and only 200 milliseconds to transition to a green background when it becomes valid. ▶

The value of the transition-duration property is a positive value in either seconds (s) or milliseconds (ms). The time unit of ms or s is required by the specification, even if the duration is set to 0s. By default, properties change from one value to the next instantly, showing no visible animation, which is why the default value for the duration of a transition is 0s.

Unless there is a positive value for transition-delay set on a property, if transition-duration is omitted, it is as if no transition-property declaration had been applied—with no transitionend event occuring. As long as the total time set for a transition to occur is greater than zero seconds—which can happen with a duration of 0s or when the transition-duration is omitted and defaults to 0s—the transition will still be applied, and a transitionend event will occur when the transition finishes.

Negative values for transition-duration are invalid, and, if included, will invalidate the entire property value.

Using the same super-long transition-property declaration from before, we can declare a single duration for all the properties or individual durations for each property, or we can make alternate properties animate for the same length of time. We can declare a single duration that applies to all properties during the transition by including a single transition-duration value:

```
div {
    color: #ff0000;
    ...
    transition-property: color, border, border-radius, transform, opacity,
        box-shadow, width, padding;
    transition-duration: 200ms;
}
```

We can also declare the same number of comma-separated time values for the transition-duration property value as the CSS properties listed in the transition-property property value. If we want each property to transition over a different length of time, we have to include a different comma-separated value for each property name declared:

```
div {
    color: #ff0000;
    ...
    transition-property: color, border, border-radius, transform, opacity,
        box-shadow, width, padding;
    transition-duration: 200ms, 180ms, 160ms, 140ms, 120ms, 100ms, 1s, 2s;
}
```

If the number of properties declared does not match the number of durations declared, the browser has specific rules on how to handle the mismatch. If there are more durations than properties, the extra durations are ignored. If there are more properties than durations, the durations are repeated. In this example, `color`, `border-radius`, `opacity`, and `width` have a duration of 100 ms; `border`, `transform`, `box-shadow`, and `padding` will be set to 200 ms:

```
div {
    ...
    transition-property: color, border, border-radius, transform, opacity,
        box-shadow, width, padding;
    transition-duration: 100ms, 200ms;
}
```

If we declare exactly two comma-separated durations, every odd property will transition over the first time declared, and every even property will transition over the second time value declared.

User experience is important. If a transition is too slow, the website will appear slow or unresponsive, drawing unwanted focus to what should be a subtle effect. If a transition is too fast, it may be too subtle to be noticed. While you can declare any positive length of time you want for your transitions, your goal is likely to provide an enhanced rather than annoying user experience. Effects should last long enough to be seen, but not so long as to be noticeable. Generally, the best effects range between 100 and 200 milliseconds, creating a visible, yet not distracting, transition.

We want a good user experience for our drop-down menu, so we set both properties to transition over 200 milliseconds:

```
nav li ul {
    transition-property: transform, opacity;
    transition-duration: 200ms;
    ...
}
```

Altering the Internal Timing of Transitions

Do you want your transition to start off slow and get faster, start off fast and end slower, advance at an even keel, jump through various steps, or even bounce? The `transition-timing-function` provides a way to control the pace of the transition.

transition-timing-function

Values	*<timing-function>*#
Initial value	ease
Applies to	All elements and :before and :after pseudo-elements

Computed value	As specified
Inherited	No
Animatable	No

The `transition-timing-function` values include ease, linear, ease-in, ease-out, ease-in-out, step-start, step-end, steps(n, start)—where n is the number of steps—steps(n, end), and cubic-bezier(x1, y1, x2, y2). (These values are also the valid values for the `animation-timing-function` and are described in great detail in Chapter 18.)

The non-step keywords are easing timing functions that server as aliases for cubic Bézier mathematical functions that provide smooth curves. The specification provides for five predefined easing functions, as shown in Table 17-1.

Table 17-1. Supported keywords for cubic Bézier timing functions

Timing function	Description	Cubic Bezier value
`cubic-bezier()`	Specifies a cubic-bezier curve	`cubic-bezier(x1, y1, x2, y2)`
`ease`	Starts slow, then speeds up, then slows down, then ends very slowly	`cubic-bezier(0.25, 0.1, 0.25, 1)`
`linear`	Proceeds at the same speed throughout transition	`cubic-bezier(0, 0, 1, 1)`
`ease-in`	Starts slow, then speeds up	`cubic-bezier(0.42, 0, 1, 1)`
`ease-out`	Starts fast, then slows down	`cubic-bezier(0, 0, 0.58, 1)`
`ease-in-out`	Similar to ease; faster in the middle, with a slow start but not as slow at the end	`cubic-bezier(0.42, 0, 0.58, 1)`

Cubic Bézier curves, including the underlying curves defining the five named easing functions defined in Table 17-1 and displayed in Figure 17-3, take four numeric parameters. For example, linear is the same as cubic-bezier(0, 0, 1, 1). The first and third cubic Bézier function parameter values need to be between 0 and +1.

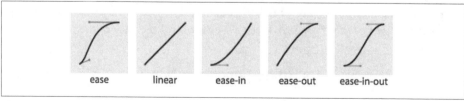

ease   linear   ease-in   ease-out   ease-in-out

Figure 17-3. Curve representations of named cubic Bézier functions

The four numbers in a cubic-bezier() function define the x and y coordinates of two *handles* within a box. These handles are the endpoints of lines that stretch from the bottom-left and top-right corners of the box. The curve is constructed using the two corners, and the two handles' coordinates, via a Bézier function.

To get an idea of how this works, look at the curves and their corresponding values, as shown in Figure 17-4.

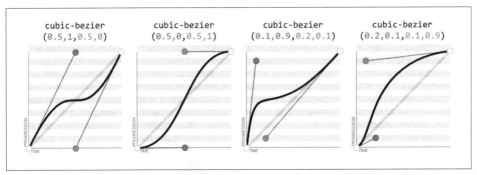

Figure 17-4. Four Bézier curves and their cubic-bezier() values (via http://cubic-bezier.com)

Consider the first example. The first two values, corresponding to *x1* and *y1*, are 0.5 and 1. If you go halfway across the box (*x1* = 0.5) and all the way to the top of the box (*y1* = 1), you land at the spot where the first handle is placed. Similarly, the coordinates 0.5,0 for *x2,y2* describes the point at the center bottom of the box, which is where the second handle is placed. The curve shown there results from those handle placements.

In the second example, the handle positions are switched, with the resulting change in the curve. Ditto for the third and fourth examples, which are inversions of each other. Notice how different the resulting curve is when switching the handle positions.

The predefined key terms are fairly limited. To better follow the principles of animation, you may want to use a cubic Bézier function with four float values instead of the predefined key words. If you're a whiz at calculus or have a lot of experience with programs like Freehand or Illustrator, you might be able to invent cubic Bézier functions in your head; otherwise, there are online tools that let you play with different values, such as *http://cubic-bezier.com/*, which lets you compare the common keywords against each other, or against your own cubic Bézier function.

As shown in Figure 17-5, the website *http://easings.net* provides many additional cubic Bézier function values you can use to provide for a more realistic, delightful animation.

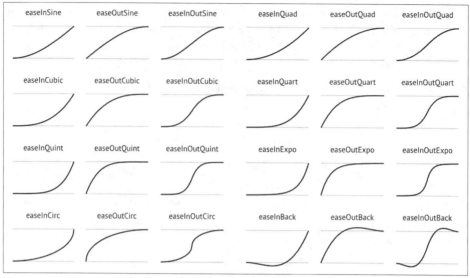

Figure 17-5. Useful author-defined cubic Bézier functions (from http://easings.net)

While the authors of the site named their animations, the preceding names are not part of the CSS specifications, and must be written as follows:

Unofficial name	Cubic Bézier function value
easeInSine	cubic-bezier(0.47, 0, 0.745, 0.715)
easeOutSine	cubic-bezier(0.39, 0.575, 0.565, 1)
easeInOutSine	cubic-bezier(0.445, 0.05, 0.55, 0.95)
easeInQuad	cubic-bezier(0.55, 0.085, 0.68, 0.53)
easeOutQuad	cubic-bezier(0.25, 0.46, 0.45, 0.94)
easeInOutQuad	cubic-bezier(0.455, 0.03, 0.515, 0.955)
easeInCubic	cubic-bezier(0.55, 0.055, 0.675, 0.19)
easeOutCubic	cubic-bezier(0.215, 0.61, 0.355, 1)
easeInOutCubic	cubic-bezier(0.645, 0.045, 0.355, 1)
easeInQuart	cubic-bezier(0.895, 0.03, 0.685, 0.22)
easeOutQuart	cubic-bezier(0.165, 0.84, 0.44, 1)
easeInOutQuart	cubic-bezier(0.77, 0, 0.175, 1)
easeInQuint	cubic-bezier(0.755, 0.05, 0.855, 0.06)
easeOutQuint	cubic-bezier(0.23, 1, 0.32, 1)
easeInOutQuint	cubic-bezier(0.86, 0, 0.07, 1)
easeInExpo	cubic-bezier(0.95, 0.05, 0.795, 0.035)
easeOutExpo	cubic-bezier(0.19, 1, 0.22, 1)

Unofficial name	Cubic Bézier function value
easeInOutExpo	cubic-bezier(1, 0, 0, 1)
easeInCirc	cubic-bezier(0.6, 0.04, 0.98, 0.335)
easeOutCirc	cubic-bezier(0.075, 0.82, 0.165, 1)
easeInOutCirc	cubic-bezier(0.785, 0.135, 0.15, 0.86)
easeInBack	cubic-bezier(0.6, -0.28, 0.735, 0.045)
easeOutBack	cubic-bezier(0.175, 0.885, 0.32, 1.275)
easeInOutBack	cubic-bezier(0.68, -0.55, 0.265, 1.55)

Step timing

There are also step timing functions available, as well as two predefined step values:

Timing function	Definition
step-start	Stays on the final keyframe throughout transition. Equal to steps(1, start).
step-end	Stays on the initial keyframe throughout transition. Equal to steps(1, end).
steps(n, start)	Displays *n* stillshots, where the first stillshot is n/100 percent of the way through the transition.
steps(n, end)	Displays *n* stillshots, staying on the initial values for the first n/100 percent of the time.

As Figure 17-6 shows, the stepping functions show the progression of the transition from the initial value to the final value in steps, rather than as a smooth curve.

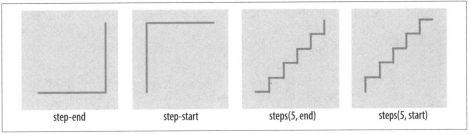

Figure 17-6. Step timing functions

The step functions allow you to divide the transition over equidistant steps. The functions define the number and direction of steps. There are two direction options: start and end. With start, the first step happens at the animation start. With end, the last step happens at the animation end. For example, steps(5, end) would jump through the equidistant steps at 0%, 20%, 40%, 60%, and 80%; and steps(5, start) would jump through the equidistant steps at 20%, 40%, 60%, 80%, and 100%.

The step-start function is the same as steps(1, start). When used, transitioned property values stay on their *final* values from the beginning until the end of the transition. The step-end function, which is the same as steps(1, end), sets transitioned values to their *initial* values, staying there throughout the transition's duration.

 Step timing, and especially the precise meaning of start and end, is discussed in depth in Chapter 18.

Continuing on with the same super-long transition-property declaration we've used before, we can declare a single timing function for all the properties, or define individual timing functions for each property and so on. Here, we set all the transitioned properties to a single duration:

```
div {
    transition-property: color, border-width, border-color, border-radius,
        transform, opacity, box-shadow, width, padding;
    transition-duration: 200ms;
    transition-timing-function: ease-in;
}
```

We can also create a horrible user experience by making every property transition at a different rhythm, like this:

Always remember that the transition-timing-function does not change the time it takes to transition properties: that is set with the transition-duration property. It just changes how the transition progresses during that set time. Consider the following:

```
div {
    ...
    transition-property: color, border-width, border-color, border-radius,
        transform, opacity, box-shadow, width, padding;
    transition-duration: 200ms;
    transition-timing-function: ease, ease-in, ease-out, ease-in-out, linear,
        step-end, step-start, steps(5, start), steps(3, end);
}
```

If we include these nine different timing functions for the nine different properties, as long as they have the same transition duration and delay, all the properties start and finish transitioning at the same time. The timing function controls how the transition progresses over the duration of the transition, but does not alter the time it takes for the transition to finish. (The preceding transition would be a terrible user experience, by the way. Please don't do that.)

The best way to familiarize yourself with the various timing functions is to play with them and see which one works best for the effect you're looking for. While testing, set a relatively long transition-duration to better visualize the difference between the various functions. ▶ At higher speeds, you may not be able to tell the difference with the easing function; just don't forget to set it back to a faster speed before publishing the result to the web!

Delaying Transitions

The transition-delay property enables you to introduce a time delay between when the change that initiates the transition is applied to an element, and when the transition begins.

<table>
<tr><td colspan="2" align="center">**transition-delay**</td></tr>
<tr><td>**Values**</td><td>*<time>*#</td></tr>
<tr><td>**Initial value**</td><td>0s</td></tr>
<tr><td>**Applies to**</td><td>All elements, :before and :after pseudo-elements</td></tr>
<tr><td>**Computed value**</td><td>As specified</td></tr>
<tr><td>**Inherited**</td><td>No</td></tr>
<tr><td>**Animatable**</td><td>No</td></tr>
</table>

A transition-delay of 0s (the default) means the transition will begin immediately —it will start executing as soon as the state of the element is altered. This is familiar from the instant-change effect of a:hover, for example.

With a value other than 0s, the *<time>* value of transition-delay defines the time offset from the moment the property values would have changed, had no transition or transition-property been applied, until the property values declared in the transition or transition-property value begin animating to their final values.

Interestingly, negative values of time are valid. The effects you can create with negative transition-delays are described in "Negative delay values" on page 877.

Continuing with the 8- (or 21-) property transition-property declaration we've been using, we can make all the properties start transitioning right away by omitting the transition-delay property, or by including it with a value of 0s. Another possibility is to start half the transitions right away, and the rest 200 milliseconds later, as in the the following:

```
div {
    transition-property: color, border, border-radius, transform, opacity,
        box-shadow, width, padding;
    transition-duration: 200ms;
    transition-timing-function: linear;
```

```
    transition-delay: 0s, 200ms;
}
```

By including `transition-delay: 0s, 200ms` on a series of properties, each taking 200 milliseconds to transition, we make `color`, `border-radius`, `opacity`, and `width` begin their transitions immediately. All the rest begin their transitions as soon as the odd transitions have completed, because their `transition-delay` is equal to the `transition-duration` applied to all the properties.

As with `transition-duration` and `transition-timing-function`, when the number of comma-separated `transition-delay` values outnumbers the number of comma-separated `transition-property` values, the extra delay values are ignored. When the number of comma-separated `transition-property` values outnumbers the number of comma-separated `transition-delay` values, the delay values are repeated.

We can even declare nine different `transition-delay` values so that each property begins transitioning after the previous property has transitioned, as follows:

```
div {
    ...
    transition-property: color, border-width, border-color, border-radius,
        transform, opacity, box-shadow, width, padding;
    transition-duration: 200ms;
    transition-timing-function: linear;
    transition-delay: 0s, 0.2s, 0.4s, 0.6s, 0.8s, 1s, 1.2s, 1.4s, 1.6s;
}
```

In this example, we declared each transition to last 200 milliseconds with the `transition-duration` property. We then declare a `transition-delay` that provides comma-separated delay values for each property that increment by 200 milliseconds, or 0.2 seconds—the same time as the duration of each property's transition. Each property starts transitioning at the point the previous property has finished.

We can use math to give every transitioning property different durations and delays, ensuring they all complete transitioning at the same time:

```
div {
    ...
    transition-property: color, border-width, border-color, border-radius,
        transform, opacity, box-shadow, width, padding;
    transition-duration: 1.8s, 1.6s, 1.4s, 1.2s, 1s, 0.8s, 0.6s, 0.4s, 0.2s;
    transition-timing-function: linear;
    transition-delay: 0s, 0.2s, 0.4s, 0.6s, 0.8s, 1s, 1.2s, 1.4s, 1.6s;
}
```

In this example, each property completes transitioning at the 1.8-second mark, but each with a different duration and delay. For each property, the `transition-duration` value plus the `transition-delay` value will add up to 1.8 seconds.

Generally, you want all the transitions to begin at the same time. You can make that happen by including a single `transition-delay` value, which gets applied to all the properties. In our drop-down menu in Figure 17-1, we include a delay of 50 milliseconds. This delay is not long enough for the user to notice and will not cause the application to appear slow. Rather, a 50-millisecond delay can help prevent the navigation from shooting open unintentionally as the user accidentally passes over, or hovers over, the menu items while moving the cursor from one part of the page or app to another.

Negative delay values

A negative value for `transition-delay` that is smaller than the `transition-duration` will cause the transition to start immediately, partway through the transition. For example: (▶)

```
div {
    transform: translateX(0);
    transition-property: transform;
    transition-duration: 200ms;
    transition-delay: -150ms;
    transition-timing-function: linear;
}
div:hover {
    transform: translateX(200px);
}
```

Given the `transition-delay` of `-150ms` on a `200ms` transition, the transition will start three-quarters of the way through the transition and will last 50 milliseconds. In that scenario, with a linear timing function, it jumps to being translated 150px along the x-axis immediately on hover and then animates the translation from 150 pixels to 200 pixels over 50 milliseconds.

If the absolute value of the negative `transition-delay` is greater than or equal to the `transition-duration`, the change of property values is immediate, as if no `transition` had been applied, *and* no `transitionend` event occurs.

When transitioning back from the hovered state to the original state, by default, the same value for the `transition-delay` is applied. In the preceding scenario, since the `transition-delay` is not overridden in the hover state, it will jump 75% of the way back (or 25% of the way through the original transition) and then transition back to the initial state. On mouseout, it will jump to being translated 50 pixels along the x-axis and then take 50 milliseconds to return to its initial position of being translated 0 pixels along the x-axis.

The transition Shorthand

The `transition` shorthand property combines the four properties covered thus far—`transition-property`, `transition-duration`, `transition-timing-function`, and `transition-delay`—into a single shorthand property.

---

transition

Values	*<single-transition>*#
Initial value	`all 0s ease 0s`
Applies to	All elements and `:before` and `:after` pseudo-elements
Computed value	As specified
Inherited	No
Animatable	No

<single-transition> = [[none | *<transition-property>*] || *<time>* || *<transition-timing-function>* || *<time>*]#

The `transition` property accepts the value of `none`, or any number of comma-separated list of *single transitions*. A single transition contains a single property to transition, or the keyword `all` to transition all the properties; the duration of the transition; the timing function; and the delay.

If a single transition within the `transition` shorthand omits the property to transition, the single transition will default to `all`. If the `transition-timing-function` value is omitted, it will default to `ease`. If only one time value is included, that will be the duration, and there will be no delay, as if `transition-delay` were set to `0s`.

Within each single transition, the order of the duration versus the delay is important: the first value that can be parsed as a time will be set as the duration. If an additional time value is found before the comma or the end of the statement, that will be set as the delay.

Here are three equivalent ways to write the same transition effects:

```
nav li ul {
    transition: transform 200ms ease-in 50ms,
                opacity 200ms ease-in 50ms;
}

nav li ul {
    transition: all 200ms ease-in 50ms;
}
```

```
nav li ul {
    transition: 200ms ease-in 50ms;
}
```

In the first example, we see shorthand for each of the two properties. Because we are transitioning all the properties that change on hover, we could use the keyword all, as shown in the second example. And, since all is the default value, we could write the shorthand with just the duration, timing function, and delay. Had we used ease instead of ease-in, we could have omitted the timing function, since ease is the default.

We had to include the duration, or no transition would be visible. In other words, the only portion of the transition property value that can truly be considered required is transition-duration.

If we only wanted to delay the change from closed menu to open menu without a gradual transition, we would still need to include a duration of 0s. Remember, the first value parsable as time will be set as the duration, and the second one will be set as the delay:

```
nav li ul {
    transition: 0s 200ms; ...
```

 This transition will wait 200 milliseconds, then show the drop-down fully open and opaque with no gradual transition. This is horrible user experience. Though if you switch the selector from nav li ul to *, it might make for an April Fools' joke.

If there is a comma-separated list of transitions (versus just a single declaration) and the word none is included, the entire transition declaration is invalid and will be ignored:

```
div {
    transition-property: color, border-width, border-color, border-radius,
        transform, opacity, box-shadow, width, padding;
    transition-duration: 200ms, 180ms, 160ms, 140ms, 120ms, 100ms, 1s, 2s, 3s;
    transition-timing-function: ease, ease-in, ease-out, ease-in-out, linear,
        step-end, step-start, steps(5, start), steps(3, end);
    transition-delay: 0s, 0.2s, 0.4s, 0.6s, 0.8s, 1s, 1.2s, 1.4s, 1.6s;
}

div {
    transition:
        color 200ms,
        border-width 180ms ease-in 200ms,
        border-color 160ms ease-out 400ms,
        border-radius 140ms ease-in-out 600ms,
```

```
        transform 120ms linear 800ms,
        opacity 100ms step-end 1s,
        box-shadow 1s step-start 1.2s,
        width 2s steps(5, start) 1.4s,
        padding 3s steps(3, end) 1.6s;
}
```

The two preceding CSS rule blocks are functionally equivalent: you can declare comma-separated values for the four longhand transition properties, or you can include a comma-separated list of multiple shorthand transitions. You can't, however, mix the two: `transition: transform, opacity 200ms ease-in 50ms` will ease in the opacity over 200 milliseconds after a 50-millisecond delay, but the `transform` change will be instantaneous, with no `transitionend` event.

In Reverse: Transitioning Back to Baseline

In the preceding examples, we've declared a single transition. All our transitions have been applied in the default state and initiated with a hover. With these declarations, the properties return back to the default state via the same transition on mouseout, with a reversing of the timing function and a duplication of the delay.

With transition declarations only in the global state, both the hover and mouseout states use the same `transition` declaration: the selector matches both states. We can override this duplication of the entire transition or just some of the transition properties by including different values for transition properties in the global (versus the hover-only) state.

When declaring transitions in multiple states, the transition included is *to* that state:

```
a {
    background: yellow;
    transition: 200ms background-color linear 0s;
  }
a:hover {
    background-color: orange;
    /* delay when going TO the :hover state */
    transition-delay: 50ms;
  }
```

In this scenario, when the user hovers over a link, the background color waits 50 milliseconds before transitioning to orange. When the user mouses off the link, the background starts transitioning back to yellow immediately. In both directions, the transition takes 200 milliseconds to complete, and the gradual change proceeds in a linear manner. The 50 milliseconds is included in the :hover (orange) state. The delay happens, therefore, as the background changes to orange. ▶

In our drop-down menu example, on :hover, the menu appears and grows over 200 milliseconds, easing in after a delay of 50 milliseconds. The transition is set with the transition property in the default (non-hovered) state. When the user mouses out, the properties revert over 200 milliseconds, easing out after a delay of 50 milliseconds. This reverse effect is responding to the transition value from the non-hovered state. This is the default behavior, but it's something we can control. The best user experience is this default behavior, so you likely don't want to alter it—but it's important to know that you can.

If we want the closing of the menu to be jumpy and slow (we *don't* want to do that; it's bad user experience. But for the sake of this example, let's pretend we do), we can declare two different transitions:

```
nav ul ul {
  transform: scale(1, 0);
  opacity: 0;
  ...
  transition: all 4s steps(8, start) 1s;
}
nav li:hover ul {
  transform: scale(1, 1);
  opacity: 1;
  transition: all 200ms linear 50ms;
}
```

Transitions are to the *to* state: when there's a style change, the transition properties used to make the transition are the new values of the transition properties, not the old ones. We put the smooth, linear animation in the :hover state. The transition that applies is the one we are going toward. In the preceding example, when the user hovers over the drop-down menu's parent li, the opening of the drop-down menu will be gradual but quick, lasting 200 milliseconds after a delay of 50 milliseconds. When the user mouses off the drop-down menu or its parent li, the transition will wait one second and take four seconds to complete, showing eight steps along the way.

When we only have one transition, we put it in the global *from* state, as you want the transition to occur toward any state, be that a hovering or a class change. Because we want the transition to occur with any change, we generally put the only transition declaration in the initial, default (least specific) block. If you do want to exert more control and provide for different effects depending on the direction of the transition, make sure to include a transition declaration in all of the possible class and UI states.

 Beware of having transitions on both ancestors and descendants. Transitioning properties soon after making a change that transition ancestral or descendant nodes can have unexpected outcomes. If the transition on the descendant completes before the transition on the ancestor, the descendant will then resume inheriting the (still transitioning) value from its parent. This effect may not be what you expected.

Reversing interrupted transitions

When a transition is interrupted before it is able to finish (such as mousing off of our drop-down menu example before it finishes opening), property values are reset to the values they had before the transition began, and the properties transition back to those values. Because repeating the duration and timing functions on a reverting partial transition can lead to an odd or even bad user experience, the CSS transitions specification provides for making the reverting transition shorter.

In our menu example, we have a `transition-delay` of 50ms set on the default state and no transition properties declared on the hover state; thus, browsers will wait 50 milliseconds before beginning the reverse or closing transition.

When the forward animation finishes transitioning to the final values and the `transitionend` event is fired, all browsers will duplicate the `transition-delay` in the reverse states.

As Table 17-2 shows, if the transition didn't finish—say, if the user moved off the navigation before the transition finished—all browsers except Microsoft Edge will repeat the delay in the reverse direction. Some browsers replicate the `transition-duration` as well, but Edge and Firefox have implemented the specification's reverse shortening factor.

Table 17-2. Unfinished transition reverse behavior by browser

Browser	Reverse delay	Transition time	Elapsed time
Chrome	Yes	200 ms	0.200 s
Chrome	Yes	200 ms	0.250 s
Safari	Yes	200 ms	0.200 s
Firefox	Yes	38 ms	0.038 s
Opera	Yes	200 ms	0.250 s
Edge	No	38 ms	0.038 s

Let's say the user moves off that menu 75 milliseconds after it started transitioning. This means the drop-down menu will animate closed without ever being fully opened and fully opaque. The browser should have a 50-millisecond delay before closing the menu, just like it waited 50 milliseconds before starting to open it.

This is actually a good user experience, as it provides a few milliseconds of delay before closing, preventing jerky behavior if the user accidentally navigates off the menu. As shown in Table 17-2, all browsers do this, except Microsoft Edge.

Even though we only gave the browser 75 milliseconds to partially open the drop-down menu before closing the menu, some browsers will take 200 milliseconds—the full value of the `transition-duration` property—to revert. Other browsers, including Firefox and Edge, have implemented the CSS specification's reversing shortening factor and the reversing-adjusted start value. When implemented, the time to complete the partial transition in the reverse direction will be similar to the original value, though not necessarily exact.

In the case of a step timing function, Firefox and Edge will take the time, rounded down to the number of steps the function has completed. For example, if the transition was 10 seconds with 10 steps, and the properties reverted after 3.25 seconds, ending a quarter of the way between the third and fourth steps (completing 3 steps, or 30% of the transition), it will take 3 seconds to revert to the previous values. In the following example, the width of our div will grow to 130 pixels wide before it begins reverting back to 100 pixels wide on mouseout:

```
div {
    width: 100px;
    transition: width 10s steps(10, start);
}
div:hover {
    width: 200px;
}
```

While the reverse duration will be rounded down to the time it took to reach the most recently-executed step, the reverse *direction* will be split into the originally declared number of steps, not the number of steps that completed. In our 3.25-second case, it will take 3 seconds to revert through 10 steps. These reverse transition steps will be shorter in duration at 300 milliseconds each, each step shrinking the width by 3 pixels, instead of 10 pixels.

If we were animating a sprite by transitioning the background-position ▶, this would look really bad. The specification and implementations may change to make the reverse direction take the same number of steps as the partial transition. Other browsers currently take 10 seconds, reverting the progression of the 3 steps over 10 seconds across 10 steps—taking a full second to grow the width in 3-pixel steps.

Browsers that haven't implemented shortened reversed timing will take the full 10 seconds, instead of only 3, splitting the transition into 10 steps, to reverse the 30% change. Whether the initial transition completed or not, these browsers will take the full value of the initial transition duration, less the absolute value of any negative transition-delay, to reverse the transition, no matter the timing function. In the steps case just shown, the reverse direction will take 10 seconds. In our navigation example, it will reverse over 200 milliseconds, whether the navigation has fully scaled up or not.

For browsers that have implemented the reversing timing adjustments, if the timing function is linear, the duration will be the same in both directions. If the timing function is a step function, the reverse duration will be equal to the time it took to complete the last completed step. All other cubic-bezier functions will have a duration that is proportional to progress the initial transition made before being interrupted (*https://drafts.csswg.org/css-transitions/transition-reversing-demo*). Negative `transition-delay` values are also proportionally shortened. Positive delays remain unchanged in both directions.

No browser will have a `transitionend` for the hover state, as the transition did not end; but all browsers will have a `transitionend` event in the reverse state when the menu finishes collapsing. The `elapsedTime` for that reverse transition depends on whether the browser took the full 200 milliseconds to close the menu, or if the browser takes as long to close the menu as it did to partially open the menu.

To override these values, include transition properties in both the initial and final states (e.g., both the unhovered and hovered styles). While this does not impact the reverse shortening, it does provide more control.

Animatable Properties and Values

Before implementing transitions and animations, it's important to understand that not all properties are animatable. You can transition (or animate) any animatable CSS properties; but which properties are animatable?

 While we've included a list of these properties in Appendix A, CSS is evolving, and the animatable properties list (*https://devel oper.mozilla.org/en-US/docs/Web/CSS/CSS_animated_properties*) will likely get new additions.

One key to developing a sense for which properties can be animated is to identify which have values that can be interpolated. *Interpolation* is the construction of data points between the values of known data points. The key guideline to determining if a property value is animatable is whether the *computed value* can be interpolated. If a property's computed values are keywords, they can't be interpolated; if its keywords compute to a number of some sort, they can be. The quick rule of thought is that if you can determine a midpoint between two property values, those property values are probably animatable.

For example, the `display` values like `block` and `inline-block` aren't numeric and therefore don't have a midpoint; they aren't animatable. The `transform` property values of `rotate(10deg)` and `rotate(20deg)` have a midpoint of `rotate(15deg)`; they are animatable.

The `border` property is shorthand for `border-style`, `border-width`, and `border-color` (which, in turn, are themselves shorthand properties for the four side values). While there is no midpoint between any of the `border-style` values, the `border-`

width property length units are numeric, so they can be animated. The keyword values of medium, thick, and thin have numeric equivalents and are interpolatable: the computed value of the border-width property computes those keywords to lengths.

In the border-color value, colors are numeric—the named colors all represent hexadecimal color values—so colors are animatable as well. If you transition from border: red solid 3px to border: blue dashed 10px, the border width and border colors will transition at the defined speed, but border-style will jump from solid to dashed as soon as the transition begins (after any delay).

As noted (see Appendix A), numeric values tend to be animatable. Keyword values that aren't translatable to numeric values generally aren't. CSS functions that take numeric values as parameters generally are animatable. One exception to this rule is visibility: while there is no midpoint between the values of visible and hidden, visibility values are interpolatable between visible and not-visible. When it comes to the visibility property, either the initial value or the destination value must be visible or no interpolation can happen. The value will change at the end of the transition from visible to hidden. For a transition from hidden to visible, it changes at the start of the transition.

auto should generally be considered a non-animatable value and should be avoided for animations and transitions. According to the specification, it is not an animatable value, but some browsers interpolate the current numeric value of auto (such as height: auto) to be 0px. auto is non-animatable for properties like height, width, top, bottom, left, right, and margin.

Often an alternative property or value may work. For example, instead of changing height: 0 to height: auto, use max-height: 0 to max-height: 100vh, which will generally create the expected effect. The auto value is animatable for min-height and min-width, since min-height: auto actually computes to 0.

How Property Values Are Interpolated

Interpolation can happen when values falling between two or more known values can be determined. Interpolatable values can be transitioned and animated.

Numbers are interpolated as floating-point numbers. Integers are interpolated as whole numbers, incrementing or decrementing as whole numbers.

In CSS, length and percentage units are translated into real numbers. When transitioning or animating calc(), or from one type of length to or from a percentage, the values will be converted into a calc() function and interpolated as real numbers.

Colors, whether they are HSLA, RGB, or named colors like aliceblue, are translated to their RGBA equivalent values for transitioning, and interpolated across the RGBA color space.

When animating font weights, if you use keywords like bold, they'll be converted to numeric values and animated in steps of multiples of 100. This may change in the future, as font weights may be permitted to take any integer value, in which case weights will be interpolated as integers instead of multiples of 100.

When including animatable property values that have more than one component, each component is interpolated appropriately for that component. For example, text-shadow has up to four components: the color, x, y, and blur. The color is interpolated as color: the x, y, and blur components are interpolated as lengths. Box shadows have two additional optional properties: inset (or lack thereof) and spread. spread, being a length, is interpolated as such. The inset keyword cannot be converted to a numeric equivalent: you can transition from one inset shadow to another inset shadow, or from one drop shadow to another drop shadow multicomponent value, but there is no way to gradually transition between inset and drop shadows.

Similar to values with more than one component, gradients can be transitioned only if you are transitioning gradients of the same type (linear or radial) with equal numbers of color stops. The colors of each color stop are then interpolated as colors, and the position of each color stop is interpolated as length and percentage units.

Interpolating repeating values

When you have simple lists of other types of properties, each item in the list is interpolated appropriately for that type—as long as the lists have the same number of items or repeatable items, and each pair of values can be interpolated:

```
.img {
    background-image:
        url(1.gif), url(2.gif), url(3.gif), url(4.gif),
        url(5.gif), url(6.gif), url(7.gif), url(8.gif),
        url(9.gif), url(10.gif), url(11.gif), url(12.gif);
    background-size: 10px 10px, 20px 20px, 30px 30px, 40px 40px;
    transition: background-size 1s ease-in 0s;
}
.img:hover {
    background-size: 25px 25px, 50px 50px, 75px 75px, 100px 100px;
}
```

For example, in transitioning four background-sizes, with all the sizes in both lists listed in pixels, the third background-size from the pretransitioned state can gradually transition to the third background-size of the transitioned list. In the preceding example, background images 1, 6, and 10 will transition from 10px to 25px in height and width when hovered. Similarly, images 3, 7, and 11 will transition from 30px to 75px, and so forth.

Thus, the background-size values are repeated three times, as if the CSS had been written as:

```
.img {
    ...
    background-size: 10px 10px, 20px 20px, 30px 30px, 40px 40px,
                     10px 10px, 20px 20px, 30px 30px, 40px 40px,
                     10px 10px, 20px 20px, 30px 30px, 40px 40px;
    ...
}
.img:hover {
    background-size: 25px 25px, 50px 50px, 75px 75px, 100px 100px,
                     25px 25px, 50px 50px, 75px 75px, 100px 100px,
                     25px 25px, 50px 50px, 75px 75px, 100px 100px;
}
```

If a property doesn't have enough comma-separated values to match the number of background images, the list of values is repeated until there are enough, even when the list in the :hover state doesn't match the initial state:

```
.img:hover {
    background-size: 33px 33px, 66px 66px, 99px 99px;
}
```

If we transitioned from four background-size declarations in the initial state to three background-size declarations in the :hover state, all in pixels, still with 12 background images, the hover and initial state values are repeated (three and four times respectively) until we have the 12 necessary values, as if the following had been declared:

```
.img {
    ...
    background-size: 10px 10px, 20px 20px, 30px 30px,
                     40px 40px, 10px 10px, 20px 20px,
                     30px 30px, 40px 40px, 10px 10px,
                     20px 20px, 30px 30px, 40px 40px;
    ...
}
.img:hover {
    background-size: 33px 33px, 66px 66px, 99px 99px,
                     33px 33px, 66px 66px, 99px 99px,
                     33px 33px, 66px 66px, 99px 99px,
                     33px 33px, 66px 66px, 99px 99px;
}
```

If a pair of values cannot be interpolated—for example, if the background-size changes from contain in the default state to cover when hovered—then, according to the specification, the lists are not interpolatable. However, some browsers ignore that particular pair of values for the purposes of the transition, but still animate the interpolatable values.

There are some property values that can animate if the browser can infer implicit values. For example, for shadows, the browser will infer an implicit shadow `box-shadow: transparent 0 0 0` or `box-shadow: inset transparent 0 0 0`, replacing any values not explicitly included in the pre- or post-transition state. These examples are in the chapter files for this book (*https://meyerweb.github.io/csstdg4figs*).

Only the interpolatable values trigger `transitionend` events.

As noted previously, `visibility` animates differently than other properties: if animating or transitioning to or from `visible`, it is interpolated as a discrete step. It is always visible during the transition or animation as long as the timing function output is between 0 and 1. It will switch at the beginning if the transition is from `hidden` to `visible`. It will switch at the end if the transition is from `visible` to `hidden`. Note that this can be controlled with the step timing functions.

If you accidentally include a property that can't be transitioned, fear not. The entire declaration will not fail. The browser will simply not transition the property that is not animatable. Note that the non-animatable property or nonexistent CSS property is not exactly ignored. The browser passes over unrecognized or non-animatable properties, keeping their place in the property list order to ensure that the other comma-separated transition properties described next are not applied on the wrong properties.[2]

 Transitions can only occur on properties that are not currently being impacted by a CSS animation. If the element is being animated, properties may still transition, as long as they are not properties that are currently controlled by the animation. CSS animations are covered in Chapter 18.

Fallbacks: Transitions Are Enhancements

Transitions have excellent browser support. All browsers, including Safari, Chrome, Opera, Firefox, Edge, and Internet Explorer (starting with IE10) support CSS transitions.

Transitions are user-interface (UI) enhancements. Lack of full support should not prevent you from including them. If a browser doesn't support CSS transitions,

---

2 This might change. The CSS Working Group is considering making all property values animatable, switching from one value to the next at the midpoint of the timing function if there is no midpoint between the pre and post values.

---

the changes you are attempting to transition will still be applied: they will just "transition" from the initial state to the end state instantaneously when the style recomputation occurs.

Your users may miss out on an interesting (or possibly annoying) effect, but will not miss out on any content.

As transitions are generally progressive enhancements, there is no need to polyfill for archaic IE browsers. While you could use a JavaScript polyfill for IE9 and earlier, and prefix your transitions for Android 4.3 and earlier, there is likely little need to do so.

Printing Transitions

When web pages or web applications are printed, the stylesheet for print media is used. If your style element's media attribute matches only screen, the CSS will not impact the printed page at all.

Often, no media attribute is included; it is as if media="all" were set, which is the default. Depending on the browser, when a transitioned element is printed, either the interpolating values are ignored, or the property values in their current state are printed.

You can't see the element transitioning on a piece of paper, but in some browsers, like Chrome, if an element transitioned from one state to another, the current state at the time the print function is called will be the value on the printed page, if that property is printable. For example, if a background color changed, neither the pre-transition or the post-transition background color will be printed, as background colors are generally not printed. However, if the text color mutated from one value to another, the current value of color will be what gets printed on a color printer or PDF.

In other browsers, like Firefox, whether the pre-transition or post-transition value is printed depends on how the transition was initiated. If it initiated with a hover, the non-hovered value will be printed, as you are no longer hovering over the element while you interact with the print dialog. If it transitioned with a class addition, the post-transition value will be printed, even if the transition hasn't completed. The printing acts as if the transition properties are ignored.

Given that there are separate printstyle sheets or @media rules for print, browsers compute style separately. In the print style, styles don't change, so there just aren't any transitions. The printing acts as if the property values changed instantly, instead of transitioning over time.

CHAPTER 18

Animation

CSS transitions, covered in the previous chapter, enabled simple animations. With transitions, an element's properties change from the values set in one rule to the values set in a different rule as the element changes state over time, instead of changing instantly. With CSS transitions, the start and end states of property values are controlled by existing property values, and provide little control over how things change over time.

CSS animations are similar to transitions in that values of CSS properties change over time, but provide much more control over how those changes happen. Specifically, CSS keyframe animations let us decide if and how an animation repeats, give us granular control over what happens throughout the animation, and more. While transitions trigger implicit property values changes, animations are explicitly executed when animation keyframe properties are applied.

With CSS animations, you can change property values that are not part of the set pre- or post-state of an element. The property values set on the animated element don't necessarily have to be part of the animation progression. For example, with transitions, going from black to white will only animate through various shades of gray. With animation, that same element doesn't have to be black or white or even in-between shades of gray during the animation.

While you *can* transition through shades of gray, you could instead turn the element yellow, then animate from yellow to orange. Alternatively, you could animate through various colors, starting with black and ending with white, but progressing through the entire rainbow along the way. This chapter will explore how keyframe animation works.

Look for the Play symbol ⏵ to know when an online example is available. All of the examples in this chapter can be found at *https://meyerweb.github.io/csstdg4figs/18-animations*.

Defining Keyframes

To animate an element, we need to set the name of a keyframe animation; to do that, we need a named keyframe animation. Our first step is to define this reusable CSS keyframe animation using the @keyframes at-rule, giving our animation a name. The name we define will then be used to attach this particular animation to elements or pseudo-elements.

A @keyframes at-rule includes the *animation identifier,* or name, and one or more *keyframe blocks.* Each keyframe block includes one or more keyframe selectors with declaration blocks of property-value pairs. The entire @keyframes at-rule specifies the behavior of a single full iteration of the animation. The animation can iterate zero or more times, depending mainly on the animation-iteration-count property value, which we'll discuss in "Declaring Animation Iterations" on page 905.

Each keyframe block includes one or more *keyframe selectors.* The keyframe selectors are percentage-of-time positions along the duration of the animation; they are declared either as percentages, or with the keywords from or to. Here's the generic structure of an animation:

```
@keyframes animation_identifier {
  keyframe_selector {
    property: value;
    property: value;
  }
  keyframe_selector {
    property: value;
    property: value;
  }
}
```

and here are a couple of basic examples:

```
@keyframes fadeout {
    from {
        opacity: 1;
    }
    to {
        opacity: 0;
    }
}

@keyframes color-pop {
```

```
0% {
    color: black;
    background-color: white;
}
33% { /* one-third of the way through the animation */
    color: gray;
    background-color: yellow;
}
100% {
    color: white;
    background-color: orange;
}
}
```

The first set of keyframes shown takes an element, sets its opacity to 1 (fully opaque), and animates it to 0 opacity (fully transparent). The second keyframe set sets an element's foreground to black and its background to white, then animates the foreground black to gray and then white, and the background white to yellow and then orange.

Note that the keyframes don't say how long this should take—that's handled by a CSS property dedicated to the purpose. Instead they say "go from this state to that state" or "hit these various states at these percentage points of the total animation." That's why keyframe selectors are always percentages, or from and to. If you try to fill time values (like 1.5s) into your keyframe selectors, you'll render them invalid.

Setting Up Keyframe Animations

To create an animation, you start with the @keyframes, add an animation name, and drop in curly brackets to encompass the actual keyframes you're defining. It's a lot like a media query at this point, if you're familiar with those (see Chapter 20).

Within the opening and closing curly brackets, you include a series of keyframe selectors with blocks of CSS that declare the properties you want to animate. Once the keyframes are defined, you "attach" the animation to an element using the animation-name property. We'll discuss that property shortly, in "Naming Animations" on page 901.

Start with the at-rule declaration, followed by the animation name and brackets:

```
@keyframes nameOfAnimation {
...
}
```

Naming Your Animation

The name, which you create, is an identifier or a string. Originally, the keyframe names had to be an identifier, but both the specification and the browsers also support quoted strings.

Identifiers are unquoted and have specific rules. You can use any characters a-z, A-Z, and 0-9, the hyphen (-), underscore (_), and any ISO 10646 character U+00A0 and higher. ISO 10646 is the universal character set; this means you can use any character in the Unicode standard that matches the regular expression [-_a-zA-Z0-9\u00A0-\u10FFFF].⊙ The identifier can't start with a digit (0-9) or two hyphens. One hyphen is fine, as long as it is not followed by a digit—unless you escape the digit or hyphen with a backslash.

If you include any escape characters within your animation name, make sure to escape them with a backslash (\). For example, Q&A! must be written as Q\&A\!. âœŽ can be left as âœŽ (no, that's not a typo), and ✎ is a valid name as well. But if you're going to use any keyboard characters that aren't letters or digits in an identifier, like !, @, #, $, and so on, escape them with a backslash.

Also, don't use any of the keywords covered in this chapter as the name of your animation. For example, possible values for the various animation properties we'll be covering later in the chapter include none, paused, running, infinite, backwards, and forwards. Using an animation property keyword, while not prohibited by the spec, will likely break your animation ⊙ when using the animation shorthand property (discussed in "Bringing It All Together" on page 935). So, while you can legally name your animation paused (or another keyword,) I *strongly* recommend against it.

Keyframe Selectors

Keyframe selectors provide points during our animation where we set the values of the properties we want to animate. In defining animations, we dictate the values we want properties to have at a specific percentage of the way through the animations. If you want a value at the start of the animation, you declare it at the 0% mark. If you want a different value at the end of the animation, you declare the property value at the 100% mark. If you want a value a third of the way through the animation, you declare it at the 33% mark. These marks are defined with keyframe selectors.

Keyframe selectors consist of a comma-separated list of one or more percentage values or the keywords from or to. The keyword from is equal to 0%. The keyword to equals 100%. The keyframe selectors are used to specify the percentage along the duration of the animation the keyframe represents. The keyframe itself is specified by the block of property values declared on the selector. The % unit must be used on percentage values. In other words, 0 is invalid as a keyframe selector:

```
@keyframes W {
    from {
      left: 0;
      top: 0;
    }
    25%, 75% {
      top: 100%;
    }
    50% {
      top: 50%;
    }
    to {
      left: 100%;
      top: 0;
    }
}
```

This @keyframes animation, named W, when attached to a non-statically positioned element, would move that element along a W-shaped path. W has five keyframes: one each at the 0%, 25%, 50%, 75%, and 100% marks. The from is the 0% mark. The to is the 100% mark. ▶

As the property values we set for the 25% and 75% mark are the same, we can put the two keyframe selectors together as a comma-separated list. This is very similar to regular selectors, where you can comma-group several together. Whether you keep those selectors on one line (as in the example) or put each selector on its own line is up to your personal preference. The following is just as valid as what we saw in the previous code:

```
    25%,
    75% {
      top: 100%;
    }
```

Note that selectors do not need to be listed in ascending order. In the preceding example, we have the 25% and 75% on the same line, with the 50% mark coming after that declaration. For legibility, it is highly encouraged to progress from the 0% to the 100% mark. However, as demonstrated by the 75% keyframe in this example, it is not required. You could define your keyframes with the last first and the first last, or scramble them up randomly, or whatever works for you.

Omitting from and to Values

If a 0% or from keyframe is not specified, then the user agent (browser) constructs a 0% keyframe using the original values of the properties being animated, as if the 0% keyframe were declared with the same property values that impact the element when no animation was applied, unless another animation applied to that element is currently animating the same property (see the upcoming section "Naming Animations" on page 901 for details). Similarly, if the 100% or to keyframe is not defined and no other animations are being applied, the browser creates a faux 100% keyframe using the value the element would have had if no animation had been set on it.

Assuming we have a background-color change animation:

```
@keyframes change_bgcolor {
    45% { background-color: green; }
    55% { background-color: blue; }
}
```

And the element originally had background-color: red set on it, it would be as if the animation were: ▶

```
@keyframes change_bgcolor {
    0%   { background-color: red; }
    45%  { background-color: green; }
    55%  { background-color: blue; }
    100% { background-color: red; }
}
```

Or, remembering that we can include multiple identical keyframes as a comma-separated list, this faux animation also could be written as:

```
@keyframes change_bgcolor {
    0%,
    100% { background-color: red; }
    45%  { background-color: green; }
    55%  { background-color: blue; }
}
```

Note the background-color: red; declarations are not actually part of the keyframe animation. If the background color were set to yellow in the element's default state, the 0% and 100% marks would display a yellow background, animating into green, then blue, then back to yellow as the animation progressed:

```
@keyframes change_bgcolor {
    0%, 100% { background-color: yellow; }
    45% { background-color: green; }
    55% { background-color: blue; }
}
```

We can include this change_bgcolor animation on many elements, and the perceived animation will differ based on the element's value for the background-color property in the non-animated state.

Although we've been using exclusively integer values for our percentages, non-integer percentage values, such as 33.33%, are perfectly valid. Negative percentages, values greater than 100%, and values that aren't otherwise percentages or the keywords to or from are invalid and will be ignored.

Repeating Keyframe Properties

In the original -webkit- implementation of animation, each keyframe could only be declared once: if declared more than once, only the last declaration would be applied, and the previous keyframe selector block was ignored. This has been updated. Now, similar to the rest of CSS, the values in the keyframe declaration blocks with identical keyframe values cascade. In the standard (nonprefixed) syntax, the preceding W animation can be written with the to, or 100%, declared twice, overriding the value of the left property:

```
@keyframes W {
  from, to {
    top: 0;
    left: 0;
  }
  25%, 75% {
    top: 100%;
  }
  50% {
    top: 50%;
  }
  to {
    left: 100%;
  }
}
```

Notice how to is declared along with from as keyframe selectors for the first code block? That sets both top and left for the to keyframe. Then, the left value is overridden for the to in the last keyframe block.

Animatable Properties

It's worth taking a moment to talk about the fact that not all properties are *animatable*. Within an animation's keyframe, if you list a property that can't be animated, it's just ignored. (For that matter, so are properties and values that he browser doesn't recognize at all, the same as any other part of CSS.)

There is a comprehensive list of animatable properties in Appendix A. We've also indicated whether properties can or can't be animated throughout the rest of this book, as the properties are defined.

The `animation-timing-function`, described in greater detail in "Changing the Internal Timing of Animations" on page 920, while not an animatable property, is not ignored. If you include the `animation-timing-function` as a keyframe style rule within a keyframe selector block, the timing function of the properties within that block will change to the declared timing function when the animation moves to the next keyframe.

If an animation is set between two property values that don't have a calculable midpoint, the results may not be what you expect. The property will not animate correctly—or at all. For example, you shouldn't declare an element's height to animate between `height: auto` and `height: 300px`. There is no midpoint between `auto` and `300px`. The element may still animate, but different browsers handle this differently: Firefox does not animate the element; Safari may animate as if `auto` is equal to `0`; and both Opera and Chrome currently jump from the preanimated state to the postanimated state halfway through the animation, which may or may not be at the 50% keyframe selector, depending on the value of the `animation-timing-function`. In other words, different browsers behave differently for different properties when there is no midpoint, so you can't be sure you will get your expected outcome.

The behavior of your animation will be most predictable if you declare both a 0% and a 100% value for every property you animate. ⊙

For example, if you declare `border-radius: 50%;` in your animation, you may want to declare `border-radius: 0;` as well, because there is no midpoint between `none` and anything: the default value of `border-radius` is `none`, not `0`. Consider the difference in the following two animations:

```
@keyframes round {
    100% {
        border-radius: 50%;
    }
}
@keyframes square_to_round {
    0% {
        border-radius: 0%;
    }
    100% {
        border-radius: 50%;
    }
}
```

The round animation will animate an element from the original `border-radius` value of that element to `border-radius: 50%` over the duration of the animation. The `square_to_round` animation will animate an element from `border-radius: 0%` to `border-radius: 50%` over the duration of the animation. If the element starts out with square corners, then the two will have exactly the same effect. But if it starts out with rounded corners, then square_to_round will jump to rectangular corners before it starts animating. This might not be what you want. Sometimes you can omit a from or to keyframe, using the element's non-animated property values to your advantage.

The best way to resolve this issue is to use the round animation instead of square_to_round, making sure any element that gets animated with the round keyframe animation has its border-radius explicitly set. ⊙

As long as an animatable property is included in at least one block with a value that is different then the non-animated attribute value, and there is a calculable midpoint between those two values, that property will animate.

Nonanimatable Properties That Aren't Ignored

Exceptions to the midpoint "rule" include visibility and animation-timing-function.

visibility is an animatable property, even though there is no midpoint between visibility: hidden and visibility: visible. When you animate from hidden to visible, the visibility value jumps from one value to the next at the keyframe where the change is declared.

While the animation-timing-function is not, in fact, an animatable property, when included in a keyframe block, the animation timing will switch to the newly declared value at that point in the animation for the properties within that keyframe selector block. The change in animation timing is not animated; it simply switches to the new value for those properties only, and only until the next keyframe. (This will be covered later, in "Changing the Internal Timing of Animations" on page 920.)

Scripting @keyframes Animations

There is an API that enables finding, appending, and deleting keyframe rules. You can change the content of a keyframe block within an @keyframes animation declaration with appendRule(n) or deleteRule(n), where n is the full selector of that keyframe. You can return the contents of a keyframe with findRule(n):

```
@keyframes W {
  from, to {
    top: 0;
    left: 0;
  }
  25%, 75% {
    top: 100%;
  }
  50% {
    top: 50%;
  }
```

```
    to {
      left: 100%;
    }
  }
```

The `appendRule()`, `deleteRule()`, and `findRule()` methods takes the full keyframe selector as an argument. Revisiting the W animation, to return the 25% / 75% keyframe, the argument is 25%, 75%:

```
// Get the selector and content block for a keyframe
var aRule = myAnimation.findRule('25%, 75%').cssText;

// Delete the 50% keyframe
myAnimation.deleteRule('50%');

// Add a 53% keyframe to the end of the animation
myAnimation.appendRule('53% {top: 50%;}');
```

The statement `myAnimation.findRule('25%, 75%').cssText;` where `myAnimation` is pointing to a keyframe animation, returns the keyframe that matches 25%, 75%. It would not match anything if we had used either 25% or 75% only. If pointing to the W animation, this statement returns `25%, 75% { top: 100%; }`.

Similarly, `myAnimation.deleteRule('50%')` will delete the *last* 50% keyframe—so if there are multiple 50% keyframes, the last one listed will be the first to go. Conversely, `myAnimation.appendRule('53% {top: 50%;}')` appends a 53% keyframe after the last keyframe of the `@keyframes` block. ▶

There are three animation events—`animationstart`, `animationend`, and `animationiteration`—that occur at the start and end of an animation, and between the end of an iteration and the start of a subsequent iteration. Any animation for which a valid keyframe rule is defined will generate the start and end events, even animations with empty keyframe rules. The `animationiteration` event only occurs when an animation has more than one iteration, as the `animationiteration` event does not fire if the `animationend` event would fire at the same time.

Animating Elements

Once you have created a keyframe animation, you can apply that animation to elements and/or pseudo-elements. CSS provides numerous animation properties to attach a keyframe animation to an element and control its progression. At a minimum, you need to include the name of the animation for the element to animate, and a duration if you want the animation to actually be visible. (Otherwise, the animation will happen in zero time.)

There are two ways of attaching animation properties to an element: you can include all the animation properties separately, or you can declare all the properties in one line using the `animation` shorthand property (or a combination of shorthand and longhand properties). We are going to first learn all the longhand properties. Later in this chapter, we'll condense all the declarations into one line with the `animation` shorthand property.

Let's start with the individual properties.

Naming Animations

The `animation-name` property takes as its value a comma-separated list of names of keyframe animations you want to apply. The names in question here are the unquoted identifiers or quoted strings (or a mixture of both) you created in your `@key frames` rule.

animation-name

Values	[*<single-animation-name>* | none]#
Initial value	none
Applies to	All elements, `::before` and `::after` pseudo-elements
Computed value	As specified
Inherited	No
Animatable	No

The default value is `none`, which means there is no animation. The `none` value can be used to override any animation applied elsewhere in the CSS cascade. (This is also the reason you don't want to name your animation `none`, unless you're a masochist.) To apply an animation, include the `@keyframe` identifier, which is the animation name. ▶

Using the `change_bgcolor` keyframe animation defined in "Omitting from and to Values" on page 895:

```
div {
    animation-name: change_bgcolor;
}
```

This applies the `change_bgcolor` animation to all `div` elements.

To apply more than one animation, include more than one comma-separated `@key frame` identifier:

```
div {
    animation-name: change_bgcolor, round, W;
}
```

If one of the included keyframe identifiers does not exist, the series of animations will not fail; rather, the failed animation will be ignored, and the valid animations will be applied. While ignored initially, the failed animation will be applied if and when that identifier comes into existence as a valid animation. Consider:

```
div {
    animation-name: change_bgcolor, spin, round, W;
}
```

In this example, assume there is no spin keyframe animation defined. The spin animation will not be applied, while the change_bgcolor, round, and W animations will occur. Should a spin keyframe animation come into existence through scripting, it will be applied at that time. ▶

In order to include more than one animation, we've included each @keyframe animation identifier in our list of comma-separated values on the animation-name property. If more than one animation is applied to an element and those animations have repeated properties, the later animations override the property values in the earlier animations. For example, if more than two background color changes are applied concurrently in two different keyframe animations, whichever animation was listed later will override the background property declarations of animations earlier in the list, but *only* if the properties (background colors, in this case) are being animated at the same time. For more on this, see "Animation, Specificity, and Precedence Order" on page 939. ▶

For example, assume the following, and further assume that the animations happen over a period of 10 seconds:

```
div {animation-name: change_bgcolor, bg-shift;}

@keyframes bg-shift {
    0%, 100% {background-color: blue;}
    35% {background-color: orange;}
    55% {background-color: red;}
    65% {background-color: purple;}
}
@keyframes change_bgcolor {
    0%, 100% {background-color: yellow;}
    45% {background-color: green;}
    55% {background-color: blue;}
}
```

In this situation, the background will animate from blue to orange to red to purple and then back to blue, thanks to bg-shift. Because it comes last in the list of animations, its keyframes take precedence. Any time there are multiple animations specifying behavior for the same property at the same point in time, the animation which is listed last in the value of animation-name will be in effect.

What's interesting is what happens if the from (0%) or to (100%) keyframes are omitted from the animation in force. For example, let's remove the first keyframes defined in bg-shift.

```
div {animation-name: change_bgcolor, bg-shift;}

@keyframes bg-shift {
    35% {background-color: orange;}
    55% {background-color: red;}
    65% {background-color: purple;}
}
@keyframes change_bgcolor {
    0%, 100% {background-color: yellow;}
    45% {background-color: green;}
    55% {background-color: blue;}
}
```

Now there are no background colors being defined at the beginning and end of bg-shift. In a situation like this, where a 0% or 100% keyframe is not specified, then the user agent constructs a 0%/100% keyframe using the computed values of the properties being animated. This could mean one of two things: either use the value of the property as defined for the element assuming there are no animations at all, or use the property value from a previous animation in the list given for animation-name.

Older browsers do the former, but the specification is shifting to prefer the latter. As of late 2017, newer browsers will animate from yellow to orange over the first 3.5 seconds of the animation, and from purple to blue over the last 3.5 seconds. Older browsers will start and end with transparent backgrounds.

These are only concerns when two different keyframe blocks are trying to change the same property's values. In this case, it was background=color. On the other hand, if one keyframe block animates background-color while another animates padding, the two animations will not collide, and both the background color and padding will be animated together.

Simply applying an animation to an element is not enough for the element to visibly animate, but it will make the animation occur—just over no time. In such an event, the keyframe properties will all be calculated, and the animationstart and animatio nend events will fire. For an element to visibly animate, the animation must last at least some amount of time. For that we have the animation-duration property.

Defining Animation Lengths

The `animation-duration` property defines how long a single animation iteration should take in seconds (s) or milliseconds (ms).

---

animation-duration

Values	*<time>*#
Initial value	0s
Applies to	All elements, `::before` and `::after` pseudo-elements
Computed value	As specified
Inherited	No
Animatable	No

The `animation-duration` property is used to define the length of time, in seconds (s) or milliseconds (ms), it should take to complete one cycle through all the keyframes of the animation. If you don't declare `animation-duration`, the animation will still be run with a duration of 0s, with `animationstart` and `animationend` still being fired even though the animation, taking 0s, is imperceptible. Negative time values are not permitted on this property.

When specifying a duration, you must include the second (s) or millisecond (ms) unit. If you have more than one animation, you can include a different `animation-duration` for each animation by including more than one comma-separated time duration:

```
div {
    animation-name: change_bgcolor, round, W;
    animation-duration: 200ms, 100ms, 0.5s;
}
```

If you supply an invalid value within your comma-separated list of durations—for example, `animation-duration: 200ms, 0, 0.5s`—the entire declaration will fail, and it will behave as if `animation-duration: 0s` had been declared. 0 is not a valid time value. ⏵

Generally, you will want to include an `animation-duration` value for each `animation-name` provided. If you have only one duration, all the animations will last the same amount of time. Having fewer `animation-duration` values than `animation-name` values in your comma-separated property value list will not fail: rather, the values will be repeated as a group. Thus, given the following:

```
div {
    animation-name: change_bgcolor, spin, round, W;
    animation-duration: 200ms, 5s;
        /* same effect as '200ms, 5s, 200ms, 5s' */
}
```

the round animation will be run over 200ms, and the W animation over 5s.

If you have a greater number of animation-duration values than animation-name values, the extra values will be ignored. If one of the included animations does not exist, the series of animations and animation durations will not fail: the failed animation, along with its duration, are ignored:

```
div {
    animation-name: change_bgcolor, spinner, round, W;
    animation-duration: 200ms, 5s, 100ms, 0.5s;
}
```

In this example, the duration 5s is associated with spinner. There is no spinner animation, though, so spinner doesn't exist, and the 5s and spinner are both ignored. Should a spinner animation come into existence, it will be applied to the div and last 5 seconds.

Declaring Animation Iterations

Simply including the required animation-name will lead to the animation playing once, and only once. If you want to iterate through the animation more or less than the default one time, use the animation-iteration-count property.

animation-iteration-count

Values	[<number> | infinite]#
Initial value	1
Applies to	All elements, ::before and ::after pseudo-elements
Computed value	As specified
Inherited	No
Animatable	No

By default, the animation will occur once (because the default value is 1). If another value is given for animation-iteration-count, and there isn't a negative value for the animation-delay property, the animation will repeat the number of times specified by the value if the property, which can be any number or the keyword infinite.

The following declarations will cause their animations to be repeated 2, 5, and 13 times:

```
animation-iteration-count: 2;
animation-iteration-count: 5;
animation-iteration-count: 13;
```

If the value of `animation-iteration-count` is not an integer, the animation will end partway through its final cycle. The animation will still run, but will cut off mid-iteration on the final iteration. For example, `animation-iteration-count: 1.25` will iterate through the animation one and a quarter times, cutting off 25% of the way through the second iteration. If the value is `0.25` on an 8-second animation, the animation will play about 25% of the way through, ending after 2 seconds.

Negative numbers are not permitted. If an invalid value is given, the default value of 1 will lead to a default single iteration. ⏵

Interestingly, `0` is a valid value for the `animation-iteration-count` property. When set to `0`, the animation still occurs, but zero times. This is similar to setting `animation-duration: 0s`: it will throw both an `animationstart` and an `animationend` event.

If you are attaching more than one animation to an element or pseudo-element, include a comma-separated list of values for `animation-name`, `animation-duration`, and `animation-iteration-count`:

```
.flag {
    animation-name: red, white, blue;
    animation-duration: 2s, 4s, 6s;
    animation-iteration-count: 3, 5;
}
```

The `iteration-count` values (and all other animation property values) will be assigned in the order of the comma-separated `animation-name` property value. Extra values are ignored. Missing values cause the existing values to be repeated, as with `animation-iteration-count` in the above scenario.

In the preceding example, there are more name values than count values, so the count values will repeat: red and blue will iterate three times, and `white` will iterate five times. There are the same number of name values as duration values; therefore, the duration values will not repeat. The red animation lasts two seconds, iterating three times, and therefore will run for a total of six seconds. The `white` animation lasts four seconds, iterating five times, for a total of 20 seconds. The blue animation is six seconds per iteration with the repeated three iterations value, animating for a total of 18 seconds.

Invalid values will invalidate the entire declaration, leading to the animations to be played once each.

If we want all three animations to end at the same time, even though their durations differ, we can control that with `animation-iteration-count`:

```
.flag {
    animation-name: red, white, blue;
    animation-duration: 2s, 4s, 6s;
    animation-iteration-count: 6, 3, 2;
}
```

In this example, the `red`, `white`, and `blue` animations will last for a total of 12 seconds each, because the product of the durations and iteration counts in each case totals 12 seconds.

Setting an Animation Direction

With the `animation-direction` property, you can control whether the animation progresses from the 0% keyframe to the 100% keyframe, or from the 100% keyframe to the 0% keyframe. You can control whether all the iterations progress in the same direction, or set every other animation cycle to progress in the opposite direction.

---

animation-direction

Values	[normal | reverse | alternate | alternate-reverse]#
Initial value	normal
Applies to	All elements, ::before and ::after pseudo-elements
Computed value	As specified
Inherited	No
Animatable	No

The `animation-direction` property defines the direction of the animation's progression through the keyframes. There are four possible values:

`animation-direction: normal`
> When set to `normal` (or omitted, which defaults to `normal`), each iteration of the animation progresses from the 0% keyframe to the 100% keyframe.

`animation-direction: reverse`
> The `reverse` value sets each iteration to play in reverse keyframe order, always progressing from the 100% keyframe to the 0% keyframe. Reversing the animation direction also reverses the `animation-timing-function`. This property is described in "Changing the Internal Timing of Animations" on page 920.

animation-direction: alternate

The alternate value means the first iteration (and each subsequent odd-numbered iteration) proceeds from 0% to 100%, and the second iteration (and each subsequent even-numbered cycle) reverses direction, proceeding from 100% to 0%.

animation-direction: alternate-reverse

The alternate-reverse value is similar to the alternate value, except it's the reverse. The first iteration (and each subsequent odd numbered iteration) proceeds from 100% to 0%, and the second iteration (and each subsequent even-numbered cycle) reverses direction, proceeding from 100% to 0%:

```css
.ball {
    animation-name: bouncing;
    animation-duration: 400ms;
    animation-iteration-count: infinite;
    animation-direction: alternate-reverse;
}
@keyframes bouncing {
    from {
        transform: translateY(500px);
    }
    to {
        transform: translateY(0);
    }
}
```

In this example, we are bouncing a ball, but we want to start by dropping it, not by throwing it up in the air: we want it to alternate between going down and up, rather than up and down, so animation-direction: alternate-reverse is the most appropriate value for our needs. ⊙

This is a rudimentary way of making a ball bounce. When balls are bouncing, they are moving slowest when they reach their apex and fastest when they reach their nadir. We included this example here to illustrate the alternate-reverse animation directions. We'll revisit the bouncing animation again later to make it more realistic with the addition of timing (see "Changing the Internal Timing of Animations" on page 920). We'll also discuss how, when the animation is iterating in the reverse direction, the animation-timing-function is reversed.

Delaying Animations

The `animation-delay` property defines how long the browser waits after the animation is attached to the element before beginning the first animation iteration.

---

animation-delay

Values	*<time>*#
Initial value	0s
Applies to	All elements, `::before` and `::after` pseudo-elements
Computed value	As specified
Inherited	No
Animatable	No

The `animation-delay` property sets the time, defined in seconds (s) or milliseconds (ms), that the animation will wait between when the animation is attached to the element and when the animation begins executing.

By default, the animation begins iterating as soon as it is applied to the element, with a 0-second delay. A positive value delays the start of the animation until the prescribed time listed as the value of the `animation-delay` property has elapsed. A negative value causes the animation to begin immediately, but it will start partway through the animation.

Negative values for `animation-delay` can create interesting effects. A negative delay will execute the animation immediately but will begin animating the element partway through the attached animation. For example, if `animation-delay: -4s` and `animation-duration: 10s` are set on an element, the animation will begin immediately but will start approximately 40% of the way through the first animation, and will end six seconds later.

The word "approximately" was used there because the animation will not necessarily start at precisely the 40% keyframe block: when the 40% mark of an animation occurs depends on the value of the `animation-timing-function`. If `animation-timing-function: linear` is set, then it will be 40% through the animation:

```
div {
  animation-name: move;
  animation-duration: 10s;
  animation-delay: -4s;
  animation-timing-function: linear;
}
```

```
@keyframes move {
  from {
    transform: translateX(0);
  }
  to {
    transform: translateX(1000px);
  }
}
```

In this linear animation example, we have a 10-second animation with a delay of −4 seconds. In this case, the animation will start immediately 40% of the way through the animation, with the div translated 400 pixels to the right of its original position, and last only six seconds. ▶

If an animation is set to occur 10 times, with a delay of -600 milliseconds and an animation duration of 200 milliseconds, the element will start animating right away, at the beginning of the fourth iteration:

```
.ball {
  animation-name: bounce;
  animation-duration: 200ms;
  animation-delay: -600ms;
  animation-iteration-count: 10;
  animation-timing-function: ease-in;
  animation-direction: alternate;
}
@keyframes bounce {
  from {
    transform: translateY(0);
  }
  to {
    transform: translateY(500px);
  }
}
```

Instead of animating for 2,000 milliseconds (200 ms × 10 = 2,000 ms, or 2 seconds), starting in the normal direction, the ball will animate for 1,400 milliseconds (or 1.4 seconds) with the animation starting immediately—but at the start of the fourth iteration, *and* in the reverse direction.

It starts out in reverse because animation-direction is set to alternate, meaning every even iteration iterates in the reverse direction from the 100% keyframe to the 0% keyframe. The fourth iteration, which is an even-numbered iteration, is the first visible iteration. ▶

The animation will throw the animationstart event immediately. The animationend event will occur at the 1,400-millisecond mark. The ball will be tossed up, rather than bounced, throwing 6 animationiteration events, after 200, 400, 600, 800, 1,000, and 1,200 milliseconds. While the iteration count was set to 10, we only get 6 animationiteration events because we are only getting 7 iterations; 3 iterations didn't occur because of the negative animation-delay, and the last iteration concluded at the same time as the animationend event. Remember, when an animationiteration event would occur at the same time as an animationend event, the animationiteration event does not occur.

Let's take a deeper look at animation events before continuing.

Animation Events

There are three different types of animation events: animationstart, animationiteration, and animationend. Each event has three read-only properties: animationName, elapsedTime, and pseudoElement, unprefixed in all browsers.

The animationstart event fires at the start of the animation: after the animation-delay (if present) has expired, or immediately if there is no delay set. If a negative animation-delay value is present, the animationstart will fire immediately, with an elapsedTime equal to the absolute value of the delay in supporting browsers. In browsers where prefixing is still necessary, the elapsedTime is 0:

```
.noAnimationEnd {
    animation-name: myAnimation;
    animation-duration: 1s;
    animation-iteration-count: infinite;
}
.startAndEndSimultaneously {
    animation-name: myAnimation;
    animation-duration: 0s;
    animation-iteration-count: infinite;
}
```

The animationend event fires when the animation finishes. If the animation-iteration-count is set to infinite, then as long as the animation-duration is set to a time greater than 0, the animationend event will never fire. If the animation-duration is set or defaults to 0 seconds, even when the iteration count is infinite, animationstart and animationend will occur virtually simultaneously, and in that order.

The animationiteration event fires *between* iterations. The animationend event ▶ fires at the conclusion of iterations that do not occur at the same time as the conclusion of the animation itself; thus, the animationiteration and animationend events do *not* fire simultaneously:

```
.noAnimationIteration {
    animation-name: myAnimation;
    animation-duration: 1s;
    animation-iteration-count: 1;
}
```

In the `.noAnimationIteration` example, with the `animation-iteration-count` set to a single occurrence, the animation ends at the conclusion of the first and only iteration. Whenever the `animationiteration` event would occur at the same time as an `animationend` event, the `animationend` event occurs, but the `animationiteration` event does not. The `animationiteration` does not fire unless an animation cycle ends and another begins.

When the `animation-iteration-count` property is omitted, or when its value is 1 or less, no `animationiteration` event will be fired. As long as an iteration finishes (even if it's a partial iteration) and another iteration begins, if the duration of that subsequent iteration is greater than 0s, an `animationiteration` event will be fired:

```
.noAnimationIteration {
    animation-name: myAnimation;
    animation-duration: 1s;
    animation-iteration-count: 4;
    animation-delay: -3s;
}
```

When an animation iterates through fewer cycles than listed in the `animation-iteration-count` because of a negative `animation-delay`, there are no `animationiteration` events for the cycles that didn't occur. In the preceding example code, there are no `animationiteration` events, as the first three cycles do not occur (due to the `-3s animation-delay`), and the last cycle finishes at the same time the animation ends. ▶

In that example, the `elapsedTime` on the `animationstart` event is 3, as it is equal to the absolute value of the delay.

Animation chaining

You can use `animation-delay` to chain animations together so the next animation starts immediately after the conclusion of the preceding animation:

```
.rainbow {
    animation-name: red, orange, yellow, blue, green;
    animation-duration: 1s, 3s, 5s, 7s, 11s;
    animation-delay: 3s, 4s, 7s, 12s, 19s;
}
```

In this example, the `red` animation starts after a three-second delay and lasts one second, meaning the `animationend` event occurs at the four-second mark. This example starts each subsequent animation at the conclusion of the previous animation. This is known as *CSS animation chaining*. ▶

By including a four-second delay on the second animation, the `orange` animation will begin interpolating the `@keyframe` property values at the four-second mark, starting the `orange` animation immediately at the conclusion of the `red` animation. The orange animation concludes at the seven-second mark—it lasts three seconds, starting after a four-second delay—which is the delay set on the third, or yellow, animation, making the yellow animation begin immediately after the orange animation ends.

This is an example of chaining animations on a single element. You can also use the animation-delay property to chain the animations for different elements:

```
li:first-of-type {
    animation-name: red;
    animation-duration: 1s;
    animation-delay: 3s;
}
li:nth-of-type(2) {
    animation-name: orange;
    animation-duration: 3s;
    animation-delay: 4s;
}
li:nth-of-type(3)  {
    animation-name: yellow;
    animation-duration: 5s;
    animation-delay: 7s;
}
li:nth-of-type(4) {
    animation-name: green;
    animation-duration: 7s;
    animation-delay: 12s;
}
li:nth-of-type(5) {
    animation-name: blue;
    animation-duration: 11s;
    animation-delay: 19s;
}
```

If you want a group of list items to animate in order, ⏵ appearing as if the animations were chained in sequence, the animation-delay of each list item should be the combined time of the animation-duration and animation-delay of the previous animation.

While you can use JavaScript and the animationEnd event from one animation to determine when to attach a subsequent animation, which we discuss below, the animation-delay property is an appropriate method of using CSS animation properties to chain animations. There is one caveat: animations are the lowest priority on the UI thread. Therefore, if you have a script running that is occupying the user interface (or UI) thread, depending on the browser and which properties are being animated and what property values are set on the element, the browser may let the delays expire while waiting until the UI thread is available before starting more animations.

Animation Performance

Some, but not all, animations in all browsers take place on the UI thread. In most browsers, when opacity or transforms are being animated, the animation takes place on the GPU (Graphics Processing Unit) instead of the CPU (Central Processing Unit), and doesn't rely on the UI thread's availability. If those properties are not part of the animation, the unavailability of the UI thread can lead to visual stutters (sometimes called "jank"):

```
/* Don't do this */
* {
    transform: translateZ(0);
}
```

On devices and browsers that support 3D transforms (see Chapter 16, *Transforms*), putting an element into 3D space moves that element into its own layer, allowing for jank-free animations. For this reason, the translateZ hack—the thing I just told you not to do—became overused. While putting a few elements onto their own layers with this hack is OK, some devices have limited video memory. Each independent layer you create uses video memory and takes time to move from the UI thread to the composited layer on the GPU. The more layers you create, the higher the performance cost.

For improved performance, whenever possible, include transform and opacity in your animations over top, left, bottom, right, and visibility. Not only does it improve performance by using the GPU over the CPU, but when you change box-model properties, the browser needs to reflow and repaint, which is bad for performance. Just don't put everything on the GPU, or you'll run into different performance issues.

If you are able to rely on JavaScript, another way of chaining animations is listening for animationend events to start subsequent animations: ⊙

```
<script>
  document.querySelectorAll('li')[0].addEventListener( 'animationend',
    function(e) {
        document.querySelectorAll('li')[1].style.animationName = 'orange';
    },
    false );

  document.querySelectorAll('li')[1].addEventListener( 'animationend',
    function(e) {
        document.querySelectorAll('li')[2].style.animationName = 'yellow';
    },
    false );

  document.querySelectorAll('li')[2].addEventListener( 'animationend',
```

```
      function(e) {
          document.querySelectorAll('li')[3].style.animationName = 'green';
      },
      false );

  document.querySelectorAll('li')[3].addEventListener( 'animationend',
      function(e) {
          document.querySelectorAll('li')[4].style.animationName = 'blue';
      },
      false );
</script>

<style>
  li:first-of-type {
    animation-name: red;
    animation-duration: 1s;
  }
  li:nth-of-type(2) {
    animation-duration: 3s;
  }
  li:nth-of-type(3)  {
    animation-duration: 5s;
  }
  li:nth-of-type(4) {
    animation-duration: 7s;
  }
  li:nth-of-type(5)  {
    animation-duration: 11s;
  }
</style>
```

In this example, there is an event handler on each of the first four list items, listening for that list item's animationend event. When the animationend event occurs, the event listeners add an animation-name to the subsequent list item.

As you can see in the styles, this animation chaining method doesn't employ animation-delay at all. Instead, the JavaScript event listeners attach animations to each element by setting the animation-name property when the animationend event is thrown.

You'll also note that the animation-name was only included for the first list item. The other list items only have an animation-duration with no animation-name, and therefore no attached animations. Adding animation-name is what attaches and starts the animation. To start or restart an animation, the animation name must be removed and then added back—at which point all the animation properties take effect, including animation-delay.

Instead of writing:

```
<script>
  document.querySelectorAll('li')[2].addEventListener( 'animationend',
```

```
        function(e) {
            document.querySelectorAll('li')[3].style.animationName = 'green';
        },
        false );

    document.querySelectorAll('li')[3].addEventListener( 'animationend',
        function(e) {
            document.querySelectorAll('li')[4].style.animationName = 'blue';
        },
        false );
    </script

    <style>
      li:nth-of-type(4) {
        animation-duration: 7s;
      }
      li:nth-of-type(5)  {
        animation-duration: 11s;
      }
    </style>
```

we could have written:

```
    <script>
      document.querySelectorAll('li')[2].addEventListener( 'animationend',
          function(e) {
              document.querySelectorAll('li')[3].style.animationName = 'green';
              document.querySelectorAll('li')[4].style.animationName = 'blue';
          },
        false );
    </script>

    <style>
      li:nth-of-type(4) {
        animation-duration: 7s;
      }
      li:nth-of-type(5)  {
        animation-delay: 7s;
        animation-duration: 11s;
      }
    </style>
```

When the blue animation name is added to the fifth list item at the same time we added green, the delay on the fifth element takes effect at that point in time and starts expiring.

While changing the values of animation properties (other than name) on the element during an animation has no effect on the animation, removing or adding an `animation-name` does have an impact. You can't change the animation duration from `100ms` to `400ms` in the middle of an animation. You can't switch the delay from `-200ms` to `5s` once the delay has already been applied. You can, however, stop and start the animation by removing it and reapplying it. In this JavaScript example, we started the animations by applying them to the elements.

In addition, setting `display: none` on an element terminates any animation. Updating the `display` back to a visible value restarts the animation from the beginning. If there is a positive value for `animation-delay`, the delay will have to expire before the `animationstart` event happens and any animations occur. If the delay is negative, the animation will start midway through an iteration, exactly as it would have if the animation had been applied any other way.

Animation iteration delay

While there is no such property as an `animation-iteration-delay`, you can employ the `animation-delay` property, incorporate delays within your keyframe declaration, or use JavaScript to fake it. The best method for faking it depends on the number of iterations, performance, and whether the delays are all equal in length.

What is an animation iteration delay? Sometimes you want an animation to occur multiple times, but want to wait a specific amount of time between each iteration.

Let's say you want your element to grow three times, but want to wait four seconds between each one-second iteration. You can include the delay within your keyframe definition and iterate through it three times:

```
.animate3times {
    background-color: red;
    animation: color_and_scale_after_delay;
    animation-iteration-count: 3;
    animation-duration: 5s;
}

@keyframes color_and_scale_after_delay {
    80% {
        transform: scale(1);
        background-color: red;
    }
    80.1% {
        background-color: green;
        transform: scale(0.5);
    }
}
```

```
        100% {
            background-color: yellow;
            transform: scale(1.5);
        }
    }
```

Note the first keyframe selector is at the 80% mark and matches the default state. ⓑ
This will animate your element three times: it stays in the default state for 80% of the
five-second animation (or four seconds) and then moves from green to yellow and
small to big over the last one second of the animation before iterating again, stopping
after three iterations.

This method works for any number of iterations of the animation. Unfortunately, it is
only a good solution if the delay between each iteration is identical and you don't
want to reuse the animation with any other timing, such as a delay of six seconds. ⓑ
If you want to change the delay between each iteration while not changing the duration of the change in size and color, you have to write a new @keyframes definition.

To enable different iteration delays between animations, we could create a single animation and bake in the effect of three different delays:

```
    .animate3times {
        background-color: red;
        animation: color_and_scale_3_times;
        animation-iteration-count: 1;
        animation-duration: 15s;
    }

    @keyframes color_and_scale_3_times {
      0%, 13.32%, 20.01%, 40%, 46.67%, 93.32% {
            transform: scale(1);
            background-color: red;
      }
        13.33%, 40.01%, 93.33% {
            background-color: green;
            transform: scale(0.5);
      }
        20%, 46.66%, 100% {
            background-color: yellow;
            transform: scale(1.5);
      }
    }
```

This method may be more difficult to code and maintain. ⓑ It works for a single
cycle of the animation. To change the number of animations or the iteration delay
durations, another @keyframes declaration would be required. This example is even
less robust than the previous one, but it does allow for different between-iteration
delays.

There's a solution that works in most browsers that is now specifically allowed in the animation specification: declare an animation multiple times, each with a different animation-delay value: ▶

```
.animate3times {
    animation: color_and_scale, color_and_scale, color_and_scale;
    animation-delay: 0, 4s, 10s;
    animation-duration: 1s;
}

@keyframes color_and_scale {
    0% {
        background-color: green;
        transform: scale(0.5);
    }
    100% {
        background-color: yellow;
        transform: scale(1.5);
    }
}
```

Here, we've attached the animation three times, each with a different delay. In this case, each animation iteration concludes before the next one proceeds.

If animations overlap while they're concurrently animating, the values will be the values from the last declared animation. As is true whenever there are multiple animations changing an element's property at the same time, the animation that occurs last in the sequence of animation names will override any animations occurring before it in the list of names. In declaring three color_and_scale animations but at different intervals, the value of the property of the last iteration of the color_and_scale animation will override the values of the previous ones that haven't yet concluded. ▶

The safest, most robust and most cross-browser-friendly method of faking an animation-iteration-delay property is to use animation events. On animationend, detach the animation from the element, then reattach it after the iteration delay. If all the iteration delays are the same, you can use setInterval; if they vary, use setTimeout:

```
var iteration = 0;
var el = document.getElementById('myElement');

el.addEventListener('animationend', function(e) {
    var time = ++iteration * 1000;

    el.classList.remove('animationClass');

    setTimeout(function() {
        el.classList.add('animationClass');
    }, time);
```

```
  });
```

This example animates `myElement` infinitely, adding an additional second between each iteration of the animation.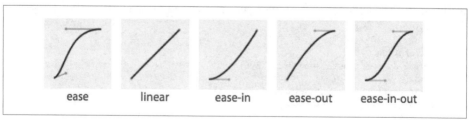

Changing the Internal Timing of Animations

All right! The scripting was fun, but let's get back to straight CSS and talk about timing functions. Similar to the `transition-timing-function` property, the `animation-timing-function` property describes how the animation will progress over one cycle of its duration, or iteration.

animation-timing-function	
Values	[ease | linear | ease-in | ease-out | ease-in-out | step-start | step-end | steps(<integer>, start) | steps(<integer>, end) | cubic-bezier(<number>, <number>, <number>, <number>)]#
Initial value	ease
Applies to	All elements, ::before and ::after pseudo-elements
Computed value	As specified
Inherited	No
Animatable	No

Other than the step timing functions, described in "Step timing functions" on page 924, the timing functions are all Bézier curves. Just like the `transition-timing-function`, the CSS specification provides for five predefined Bézier curve keywords, as shown in Figure 18-1 and Table 18-1.

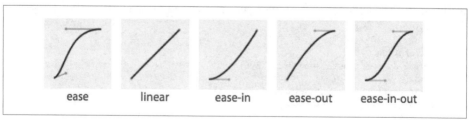

Figure 18-1. Cubic Bézier named functions

Table 18-1. Bézier curve keywords

Timing function	Cubic Bézier value
ease	cubic-bezier(0.25, 0.1, 0.25, 1)
linear	cubic-bezier(0, 0, 1, 1)
ease-in	cubic-bezier(0.42, 0, 1, 1)
ease-out	cubic-bezier(0, 0, 0.58, 1)
ease-in-out	cubic-bezier(0.42, 0, 0.58, 1)

A handy tool to visualize Bézier curves and to create your own is Lea Verou's cubic Bézier visualizer at cubic-bezier.com.

The default ease has a slow start, then speeds up, and ends slowly. This function is similar to ease-in-out, which has a greater acceleration at the beginning. linear, as the name describes, creates an animation that animates at a constant speed.

ease-in creates an animation that is slow to start, gains speed, and then stops abruptly. The opposite ease-out timing function starts at full speed, then slows progressively as it reaches the conclusion of the animation iteration.

If none of these work for you, you can create your own Bézier curve timing function by passing four values, such as:

```
animation-timing-function: cubic-bezier(0.2, 0.4, 0.6, 0.8);
```

Bézier curves are mathematically defined parametric curves used in two-dimensional graphic applications. See Appendix A for examples of curves you can define yourself in CSS.

The Bézier curve takes four values, defining the originating position of the two handles. In CSS, the anchors are at 0, 0 and 1, 1. The first two values define the x and y of the first point or handle of the curve, and the last two are the x and y of the second handle of the curve. The x values must be between 0 and 1, or the Bézier curve is invalid. The y coordinate is not constrained. When creating your own Bézier curve, remember: the steeper the curve, the faster the motion. The flatter the curve, the slower the motion.[1]

While the x values must be between 0 and 1, by using values for y that are greater than 1 or less than 0, you can create a bouncing effect, making the animation bounce up and down between values, rather than going consistently in a single direction. Consider the following timing function, whose rather outlandish Bézier curve is (partly) illustrated in Figure 18-2:

---

1 For a detailed (and lovely) illustration of how cubic Bézier curves are actually constructed, we highly recommend the video "Cubic Bezier Curves - Under the Hood" (*http://vimeo.com/106757336*).

```
.snake {
  animation-name: shrink;
  animation-duration: 10s;
  animation-timing-function: cubic-bezier(0, 4, 1, -4);
  animation-fill-mode: both;
}

@keyframes shrink {
  0% {
    width: 500px;
  }
  100% {
    width: 100px;
  }
}
```

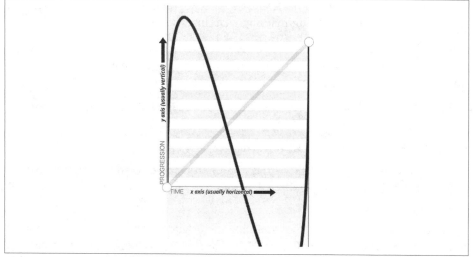

Figure 18-2. An outlandish Bézier curve

This `animation-timing-function` curve makes the animated property's values go outside the boundaries of the values set in the 0% and 100% keyframes. In this example, we are shrinking an element from 500px to 100px. However, because of the `cubic-bezier` values, the element we're shrinking will actually grow to be wider than the 500px width defined in the 0% keyframe and narrower than the 100px width defined in the 100% keyframe, as shown in Figure 18-3.

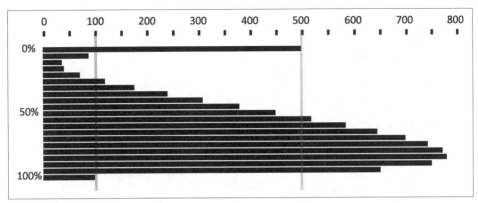

Figure 18-3. Effect of outlandish Bézier curve

In this scenario, the element starts with a width of 500px, defined in the 0% keyframe. It then quickly shrinks down to a width of about 40px, which is narrower than width: 100px defined in the 100% keyframe. From there, it slowly expands to about 750px wide, which is larger than the original width of 500px. It then quickly shrinks back down to width: 100px, ending the animation iteration. ▶

You may have realized that the curve created by our animation is the same curve as the Bézier curve. Just as the S-curve goes outside the normal bounding box, the width of the animated element goes narrower than the smaller width we set of 100px, and wider than the larger width we set of 500px.

The Bézier curve has the appearance of a snake because one *y* coordinate is positive, and the other negative. If both are positive values greater than 1 or both are negative values less than -1, the Bézier curve is arc-shaped, going above or below one of the values set, but not bouncing out of bounds on both ends like the S-curve.

Any timing function declared with animation-timing-function sets the timing for the normal animation direction, when the animation is progressing from the 0% keyframe to the 100% keyframe. When the animation is running in the reverse direction, from the 100% keyframe to the 0% keyframe, the animation timing function is reversed.

Remember the bouncing-ball example? The bouncing wasn't very realistic, because the original example defaulted to ease for its timing function. With animation-timing-function, we can apply ease-in to the animation so that when the ball is dropping, it gets faster as it nears its nadir at the 100% keyframe. When it is bouncing upward, it animates in the reverse direction, from 100% to 0%, so the animating-timing-function is reversed as well—in this case to ease-out—slowing down as it reaches the apex: ▶

```
.ball {
  animation-name: bounce;
  animation-duration: 1s;
  animation-iteration-count: infinite;
  animation-timing-function: ease-in;
  animation-direction: alternate;
}

@keyframes bounce {
  0% {
    transform: translateY(0);
  }
  100% {
    transform: translateY(500px);
  }
}
```

Step timing functions

The step timing functions, step-start, step-end, and steps(), aren't Bézier curves. They're not really curves at all. Rather, they're *tweening* definitions. The steps() function is most useful when it comes to character or sprite animation.

The steps() timing function divides the animation into a series of equal-length steps. steps() takes two parameters: the number of steps, and the change point (more on that in a moment).

The number of steps is the first parameter; its value must be a positive integer. The animation length will be divided equally into the number of steps provided. For example, if the animation duration is 1 second and the number of steps is 5, the animation will be divided into five 200-millisecond steps, with the element being redrawn to the page five times, at 200-millisecond intervals, moving 20% through the animation at each interval.

To understand how this works, think of a flip book. Each page in a flip book contains a single drawing or picture that changes slightly from one page to the next, like one frame from a movie reel stamped onto each page. When the pages of a flip book are rapidly flipped through (hence the name), the pictures appear as an animated motion. You can create similar animations with CSS using an image sprite, the background-position property, and the steps() timing function.

Figure 18-4 shows an image sprite containing several images that change just slightly, like the drawings on the individual pages of a flip book.

Figure 18-4. Sprite of dancing

We put all of our slightly differing images into a single image called a *sprite*. Each image in our sprite is a frame in the single animated image we're creating.

We then create a container element that is the size of a single image of our sprite, and attach the sprite as the container element's background image. We then animate the `background-position`, using the `steps()` timing function so we only see a single instance of the changing image of our sprite at a time. The number of steps in our `steps()` timing function is the number of occurrences of the image in our sprite. The number of steps defines how many stops our background image makes to complete a single animation.

The sprite in Figure 18-4 has 22 images, each 56 × 100 pixels. The total size of our sprite is 1,232 × 100 pixels. We set our container to the individual image size: 56 × 100 pixels. We set our sprite as our background image: the initial or default value of `background-position` is `top left`, which is the same as `0 0`. Our image will appear at `0 0`, which is a good default: older browsers that don't support CSS animation will simply display the first image from our sprite:

```
.dancer {
    height: 100px;
    width: 56px;
    background-image: url(../images/dancer.png);
    ....
}
```

The trick is to use `steps()` to change the `background-position` value so that each frame is a view of a separate image within the sprite. Instead of sliding in the background image from the left, the `steps()` timing function will pop in the background image in the number of steps we declared.

So we create an animation that simple changes the left-right value of the `background-position`. The image is 1,232 pixels wide, so we move the background image from `0 0`, which is the left top, to `0 -1232px`, putting the sprite fully outside of our 56 × 100 pixel `div` viewport.

The values of `-1232px 0` will move the image completely to the left, outside of our containing block viewport. It will no longer show up as a background image in our 100 × 56 pixel `div` at the 100% mark unless `background-repeat` is set to repeat along the x-axis. We don't want that to happen!

This is what we want:

```
@keyframes dance_in_place {
    from {
        background-position: 0 0;
    }
    to {
        background-position: -1232px 0;
```

```
    }
}

.dancer {
    ....
    background-image: url(../images/dancer.png);
    animation-name: dance_in_place;
    animation-duration: 4s;
    animation-timing-function: steps(22, end);
    animation-iteration-count: infinite;
}
```

What may have seemed like a complex animation is very simple: just like a flip book, we see one frame of the sprite at a time. Our keyframe animation simply moves the background. ▶

So that covers the first parameter, the number of steps. The second parameter takes one of two values: either start or end. What this specifies whether the change for the first step's interval takes place at the beginning of that interval, or at the end of the interval. With the default value, end, the change take place at the end of the first step. In other words, given 200 ms step lengths, the first change in the animation will not occur until 200 ms into the animation's overall duration. With start, the first change will take place at the beginning of the first step's interval; that is to say, the instant the animation begins. Figure 18-5 provides a timeline diagram of how the two values work, based on the following styles:

```
@keyframes grayfade {
    from {background-color: #BBB;}
    to {background-color: #333;}
}

.quickfader {animation: grayfade 1s steps(5,start) forwards;}
.slowfader {animation: grayfade 1s steps(5,end) forwards;}
```

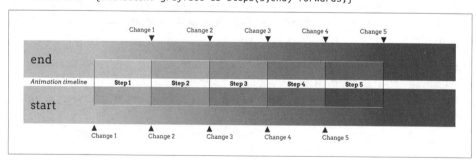

Figure 18-5. Visualizing start and end change points

The boxes embedded into each timeline represent the background color during that step interval. Notice that in the end timeline, the first interval is the same as the background before the animation started. This is because the animation waits until the end of the first frame to make the color change for the first step (the color between "Step 1" and "Step 2").

In the start timeline, on the other hand, the first interval makes that color change at the start of the interval, instantly switching from the starting background color to the color between "Step 1" and "Step 2". This is sort of like jumping ahead one interval, an impression reinforced by the fact that the background color in "Step 2" of the end timeline is the same as that in "Step 1" of the start timeline.

A similar effect can be seen at the end of each animation, where the background in the fifth step of the start timeline is the same as the ending background color. In the end timeline, it's the color at the point between "Step 4" and "Step 5", and doesn't switch to the ending background color until the end of "Step 5," when the animation is finished.

The change parameter can be hard to keep straight. If it helps, think of it this way: in a normal animation direction, the start value "skips" the 0% keyframe, because it makes the first change as soon as the animation starts, and the end value "skips" the 100% keyframe.

Preserving the ending background color in this case, rather than having it reset to the starting color after the animation finishes, required the presences of the forwards keyword. We'll cover that in "Animation Fill Modes" on page 933, later in the chapter.

The step-start value is equal to steps(1, start), with only a single step displaying the 100% keyframe. The step-end value is equal to steps(1, end), which displays only the 0% keyframe.

Adding a second animation

Let's go back to the sprite animation, which shows our tiny dancer dancing in place. Most dancers move around when they dance. We can add a little left-and-right and back-and-forth motion by adding a second animation:

```
@keyframes move_around {
  0%, 100% {
    transform: translate(0, -40px) scale(0.9);
  }
  25%  {
    transform: translate(40px, 0)  scale(1);
  }
  50%  {
    transform: translate(0, 40px)  scale(1.1);
  }
  75%  {
```

```
      transform: translate(-40px, 0) scale(1);
   }
}
```

Here, we create a second keyframe animation called move_around and attach it to our
dancer element as a second animation with comma-separated animation property
declarations: ⊙

```
.dancer {
   ....
   background-image: url(../images/dancer.png);
   animation-name: dance_in_place, move_around;
   animation-duration: 4s, 16s;
   animation-timing-function: steps(22, end), steps(5, end);
   animation-iteration-count: infinite;
}
```

Note that each animation property has two comma-separated values except
animation-iteration-count. If you recall, if an animation property doesn't have
enough comma-separated values to match the number of animations declared by the
animation-name property, the values present will be repeated until there are enough.
We want both animations to continue indefinitely. As the value of infinite is for all
the attached animations, we only need a single value for that property. The browser
will repeat the list of animation-iteration-count values—in this case, just the single
value of infinite—until it has matched an animation-iteration-count value for
each animation declared.

Animating the timing function

The animation-timing-function is not an animatable property, but it can be
included in keyframes to alter the current timing of the animation.

Unlike animatable properties, the animation-timing-function values aren't interpolated over time. When included in a keyframe within the @keyframes definition, the
timing function for the properties declared within that same keyframe will change to
the new animation-timing-function value when that keyframe is reached, as shown
in Figure 18-6:

```
@keyframes width {
  0% {
    width: 200px;
    animation-timing-function: linear;
  }
  50% {
    width: 350px;
    animation-timing-function: ease-in;
  }
  100% {
    width: 500px;
```

```
     }
   }
```

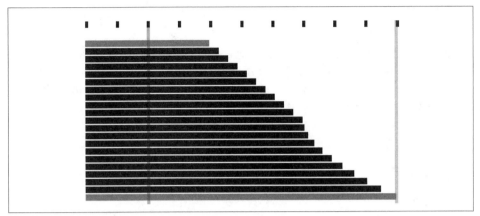

Figure 18-6. Changing the animation timing function mid-animation

In the preceding example, as shown in Figure 18-6, halfway through the animation, we switch from a linear animation progression for the `width` property to one that eases in. The `ease-in` timing starts from the keyframe in which the timing function changes.

Specifying the `animation-timing-function` within the `to` or `100%` keyframe will have no effect on the animation. When included in any other keyframe, the animation will follow the `animation-timing-function` specified in that keyframe definition until it reaches the next keyframe, overriding the element's default or declared `animation-timing-function`.

If the `animation-timing-function` property is included in a keyframe, only the properties also included in that keyframe block will have their timing function impacted. The new timing function will be in play on that property until the next keyframe containing that property is reached, at which point it will change to the timing function declared within that block, or revert back to the original timing function assigned to that element. If we take our W animation as an example:

```
@keyframes W {
    from {
      left: 0;
      top: 0;
    }
    25%, 75% {
      top: 100%;
    }
    50% {
      top: 50%;
    }
```

```
        to {
            left: 100%;
            top: 0;
        }
    }
```

This follows the idea that conceptually, when an animation is set on an element or pseudo-element, it is as if a set of keyframes is created for each property that is present in any of the keyframes, as if an animation is run independently for each property that is being animated. It's as if the W animation were made up of two animations that run simultaneously—W_part1 and W_part2:

```
@keyframes W_part1 {
    from, to {
        top: 0;
    }
    25%, 75% {
        top: 100%;
    }
    50% {
        top: 50%;
    }
}

@keyframes W_part2 {
    from {
        left: 0;
    }
    to {
        left: 100%;
    }
}
```

The animation-timing-function that is set on any of the keyframes is added to the progression of only the properties that are defined at that keyframe:

```
@keyframes W {
    from {
        left: 0;
        top: 0;
    }
    25%, 75% {
        top: 100%;
    }
    50% {
        animation-timing-function: ease-in;
        top: 50%;
    }
    to {
        left: 100%;
        top: 0;
```

```
      }
   }
```

The preceding code will change the `animation-timing-function` to `ease-in` for the `top` property only, not the `left` property, impacting only the `W_part1` section of our `W` animation, and only from the middle of the animation to the 75% mark.

However, with the following animation, the `animation-timing-function` will have no effect, because it's been placed in a keyframe block that has no property/value declarations:

```
@keyframes W {
    from {
      left: 0;
      top: 0;
    }
    25%, 75% {
      top: 100%;
    }
    50% {
      animation-timing-function: ease-in;
    }
    50% {
      top: 50%;
    }
    to {
      left: 100%;
      top: 0;
    }
}
```

How is it useful to change the timing function mid-animation? In the bounce animation, we had a frictionless environment: the ball bounced forever, never losing momentum. The ball sped up as it dropped and slowed as it rose, because the timing function was inverted from `ease-in` to `ease-out` by default as the animation proceeded from the `normal` to `reverse` direction every other iteration.

In reality, friction exists; momentum is lost. Balls will not continue to bounce indefinitely. If we want our bouncing ball to look natural, we have to make it bounce less high as it loses energy with each impact. To do this, we need a single animation that bounces multiple times, losing momentum on each bounce, while switching between `ease-in` and `ease-out` at each apex and nadir:

```
@keyframes bounce {
  0% {
    transform: translateY(0);
    animation-timing-function: ease-in;
  }
  30% {
    transform: translateY(100px);
    animation-timing-function: ease-in;
```

```
  }
  58% {
    transform: translateY(200px);
    animation-timing-function: ease-in;
  }
  80% {
    transform: translateY(300px);
    animation-timing-function: ease-in;
  }
  95% {
    transform: translateY(360px);
    animation-timing-function: ease-in;
  }
  15%, 45%, 71%, 89%, 100% {
    transform: translateY(380px);
    animation-timing-function: ease-out;
  }
}
```

This animation loses height after a few bounces, eventually stopping. ▶

Since this new animation uses a single iteration, we can't rely on the animation-direction to change our timing function. We need to ensure that while each bounce causes the ball to lose momentum, it still speeds up with gravity and slows down as it reaches its apex. Because we will have only a single iteration, we control the timing by including animation-timing-function within our keyframes. At every apex, we switch to ease-in, and at every nadir, or bounce, we switch to ease-out.

Setting the Animation Play State

If you need to pause and resume animations, the animation-play-state property defines whether the animation is running or paused.

animation-play-state	
Values	[running	paused]#
Initial value	running
Applies to	All elements, ::before and ::after pseudo-elements
Computed value	As specified
Inherited	No
Animatable	No

When set to the default running, the animation proceeds as normal. If set to paused, the animation will be paused. When paused, the animation is still applied to the element, halted at the progress it had made before being paused. If stopped mid iteration, the properties that were in the process of animating stay at their mid-iteration values. When set back to running or returned to the default of running, it restarts from where it left off, as if the "clock" that controls the animation had stopped and started again.

If the property is set to animation-play-state: paused during the delay phase of the animation, the delay clock is also paused and resumes expiring as soon as animation-play-state is set back to running. ⊙

Animation Fill Modes

The animation-fill-mode property enables us to define whether or not an element's property values continue to be applied by the animation outside of the animation execution.

animation-fill-mode

Values	[none | forwards | backwards | both]#
Initial value	none
Applies to	All elements, ::before and ::after pseudo-elements
Computed value	As specified
Inherited	No
Animatable	No

This property is useful because by default, the changes in an animation only apply during the animation itself. Once the animation is done, the values will all revert to their pre-animation values. Thus, if you animate the background from red to blue, the background will (by default) revert to red once the animation finishes.

Similarly, an animation will not affect the property values of the element immediately if there is a positive animation-delay applied. Rather, animation property values are applied when the animation-delay expires, when the animationstart event is fired.

With animation-fill-mode, we can define how the animation impacts the element on which it is set before the animationstart and after the animationend events are fired. Property values set in the 0% keyframe can be applied to the element during the expiration of any animation delay, and property values can continue to persist after the animationend event is fired.

The default value for animation-fill-mode is none, which means the animation has no effect when it is not executing: the animation's 0% keyframe (or the 100% keyframe in a reverse animation) block property values are not applied to the animated element until the animation-delay has expired, when the animationstart event is fired.

When the value is set to backwards, the property values from the 0% or from keyframe (if there is one) will be applied to the element as soon as the animation is applied to the element. The 0% keyframe property values are applied immediately (or 100% keyframe, if the value of the animation-direction property is reversed or reversed-alternate), without waiting for the animation-delay time to expire.

The value of forwards means when the animation is done executing—that is, has concluded the last part of the last iteration as defined by the animation-iteration-count value, and the animationend event has fired—it continues to apply the values of the properties as they were when the animationend event occurred. If the iteration-count has an integer value, this will be either the 100% keyframe, or, if the last iteration was in the reverse direction, the 0% keyframe.

The value of both applies both the backwards effect of applying the property values as soon as the animation is attached to the element, *and* the forwards value of persisting the property values past the animationend event. ⊙

If the animation-iteration-count is a float value, and not an integer, the last iteration will not end on the 0% or 100% keyframe: the animation will instead end its execution partway through an animation cycle. If the animation-fill-mode is set forwards or both, the element maintains the property values it had when the animationend event occurred. For example, if the animation-iteration-count is 6.5, and the animation-timing-function is linear, the animationend event fires and the values of the properties at the 50% mark (whether or not a 50% keyframe is explicitly declared) will stick, as if the animation-play-state had been set to pause at that point.

For example, if we take the following code:

```
@keyframes move_me {
  0% {
    transform: translateX(0);
  }
  100% {
    transform: translateX(1000px);
  }
}

.moved {
```

```
    transform: translateX(0);
    animation-name: move_me;
    animation-duration: 10s;
    animation-timing-function: linear;
    animation-iteration-count: 0.6;
    animation-fill-mode: forwards;
}
```

The animation will only go through 0.6 iterations. Being a linear 10-second animation, it will stop at the 60% mark, 6 seconds into the animation, when the element is
translated 600 pixels to the right. With `animation-fill-mode` set to `forwards` or
both, the animation will stop animating when it is translated 600 pixels to the right,
holding the moved element 600 pixels to the right of its original position. This will
keep it translated indefinitely, or at least until the animation is detached from the element. Without the `animation-fill-mode: forwards`, the element with class moved
will pop back to it's original transform: `translateX(0)`, as defined in the moved
selector code block.

 In Safari 9 and earlier, `forwards` and `both` will set the values from
the 100% keyframe onto the element, no matter the direction of the
last iteration or whether the animation otherwise ended on the
100% keyframe or elsewhere in the animation. ▶ In the preceding
example, in Safari 9, the `.moved` element jumps from being translated by 400 pixels to the right to be 1,000 pixels to the right of
where it normally would have been, and stays there. In Safari 9 and
earlier, it doesn't matter whether the last iteration was `normal` or
`reverse`, or whether the animation ended 25% or 75% of the way
through an animation cycle; `animation-fill-mode: forwards`
causes the animation to jump to the 100% frame and stay there.
This follows an older version of the specification, but we expect it
will be updated to match the updated specification and all other
evergreen browsers.

Bringing It All Together

The `animation` shorthand property allows you to use one line, instead of eight, to
define all the animation parameters for an element. The `animation` property value is
a list of space-separated values for the various longhand animation properties. If you
are setting multiple animations on an element or pseudo-element, you can use a
comma-separated list of animations.

animation

Values	[*<animation-name>* ‖ *<animation-duration>* ‖ *<animation-timing-function>* ‖ *<animation-delay>* ‖ *<animation-iteration-count>* ‖ *<animation-direction>* ‖ *<animation-fill-mode>* ‖ *<animation-play-state>*]#
Initial value	`0s ease 0s 1 normal none running none`
Applies to	All elements, `::before` and `::after` pseudo-elements
Computed value	As specified
Inherited	No
Animatable	No

The animation shorthand takes as its value all the other preceding animation properties, including `animation-duration`, `animation-timing-function`, `animation-delay`, `animation-iteration-count`, `animation-direction`, `animation-fill-mode`, `animation-play-state`, and `animation-name`. For example, the following two rules are precisely equivalent:

```
#animated {
   animation: 200ms ease-in 50ms 1 normal running forwards slidedown;
}
#animated {
  animation-name: slidedown;
  animation-duration: 200ms;
  animation-timing-function: ease-in;
  animation-delay: 50ms;
  animation-iteration-count: 1;
  animation-fill-mode: forwards;
  animation-direction: normal;
  animation-play-state: running;
}
```

We didn't have to declare all of the values in the animation shorthand; any values that aren't declared are set to the default or initial values. The first shorthand line was long and three of the properties were set to default, so were not necessary.

It's important to remember that if you don't declare all eight values in your shorthand declaration, the ones you don't declare will get the initial value for that property. The initial or default values are:

```
animation-name: none;
animation-duration: 0s;
animation-timing-function: ease;
animation-delay: 0;
animation-iteration-count: 1;
```

```
animation-fill-mode: none;
animation-direction: normal;
animation-play-state: running;
```

The order of the shorthand is important in two very specific ways. First, there are two time properties permitted, for *<animation-duration>* and *<animation-delay>*. When two are listed, the first is *always* the duration. The second, if present, is interpreted as the delay.

Second, the placement of the `animation-name` is also important. If you use an animation property value as your animation identifier—which you shouldn't, but say that you do—then the `animation-name` should be placed as the *last* property value in the `animation` shorthand. The first occurrence of a keyword that is a valid value for any of the other animation properties, such as `ease` or `running`, is assumed to be part of the shorthand of the animation property the keyword is associated with, rather than the `animation-name`. Note that `none` is basically the only word that is not a valid animation name:

```
#failedAnimation {
    animation: paused 2s;
}
```

This is the equivalent to:

```
#failedAnimation {
    animation-name: none;
    animation-duration: 2s;
    animation-delay: 0;
    animation-timing-function: ease;
    animation-iteration-count: 1;
    animation-fill-mode: none;
    animation-direction: normal;
    animation-play-state: paused;
}
```

`paused` is a valid animation name. While it may seem that the animation named `paused` with a duration of `2s` is being attached to the element, that is not what is happening in the above shorthand. Because words within the shorthand `animation` are first checked against possible valid values of all animation properties other than `animation-name` first, `paused` is being set as the value of the `animation-play-state` property:

```
#anotherFailedAnimation {
    animation: running 2s ease-in-out forwards;
}
```

The preceding code snippet is the equivalent to:

```
#anotherFailedAnimation {
    animation-name: none;
    animation-duration: 2s;
```

```
    animation-delay: 0s;
    animation-timing-function: ease-in-out;
    animation-iteration-count: 1;
    animation-fill-mode: forwards;
    animation-direction: normal;
    animation-play-state: running;
}
```

The developer probably has a keyframe animation called `running`. The browser, however, sees the term and assigns it to the `animation-play-state` property rather than the `animation-name` property. With no `animation-name` declared, there is no animation attached to the element. The way to get around this would be:

```
#aSuccessfulIfInadvisableAnimation {
    animation: running 2s ease-in-out forwards running;
}
```

This will apply the first `running` to `animation-play-state`, and the second `running` to `animation-name`. Again: this is *not* advised. The potential for confusion and error is too great.

In light of all this, `animation: 2s 3s 4s;` may seem valid, as if the following were being set:

```
#invalidName {
    animation-name: 4s;
    animation-duration: 2s;
    animation-delay: 3s;
}
```

But as was mentioned in "Setting Up Keyframe Animations" on page 893, `4s` is *not* a valid identifier. Identifiers cannot start with a digit unless escaped. For this animation to be valid, it would have to be written as `animation: 2s 3s \4s;`

To attach multiple animations to a single element or pseudo-element, comma-separate the animations:

```
.snowflake {
  animation: 3s ease-in 200ms 32 forwards falling,
             1.5s linear 200ms 64 spinning;
}
```

The snowflake will fall while spinning for 96 seconds, spinning twice during each 3-second fall. ⊙ At the end of the last animation cycle, the snowflake will stay fixed on the `100%` keyframe of the `falling` animation. We declared six of the eight animation properties for the `falling` animation and five for the spinning animation, separating the two animations with a comma.

While you'll most often see the animation name as the first value—it's easier to read that way, because of the issue with animation property keywords being valid keyframe identifiers—it is not a best practice. That is why we put the animation name at the end.

To sum up: it is a fine idea to use the `animation` shorthand. Just remember that the placements of the duration, delay, and name within that shorthand are important, and omitted values will be set to their default values. Also, it is a good idea to not use any animation keywords as your identifier.

Animation, Specificity, and Precedence Order

In terms of specificity, the cascade, and which property values get applied to an element, animations (as of late 2017) incorrectly supersede all other values in the cascade.

Specificity and !important

In general, the weight of a property attached with an ID selector `1-0-0` should take precedence over a property applied by an element selector `0-0-1`. However, if that property value was changed via a keyframe animation, it will be applied as if that property/value pair were added as an inline style.

The current behavior in all browsers that support animation is as if the property values set by keyframes were declared inline with an added `!important`—as if they were something like `<div style="keyframe-property: value !important">`. This is wrong, according to the specifications. The animation specification states "animations override all normal rules, but are overridden by `!important` rules." This is a bug in the late 2017 implementations and should be resolved eventually. Or, perhaps, the specification will change.

That being said, don't include `!important` within your animation declaration block; this use is invalid, and the property/value combination upon which it is declared will be ignored.

Animation Order

If there are multiple animations specifying values for the same property, the property value from the last animation applied will override the previous animations:

```
#colorchange {
    animation-name: red, green, blue;
    animation-duration: 11s, 9s, 6s;
}
```

In this code example, if `red`, `green`, and `blue` are all keyframe animations that change the `color` property to their respective names, once the `animation-name` and `animation-duration` properties are applied to `#colorchange`, for the first six seconds, the property values in blue will take precedence, then green for three seconds, then red for two seconds, before returning to default property values. ⊙ In this scenario, if the blue @keyframe animation does not include the color property in the 0% keyframe, the color will be taken from the animation named green, the animation named red, or the element's currentColor value, in that order. The same is true for an omitted 100% keyframe.

The default properties of an element are not impacted before the animation starts, and the properties return to their original values after the animation ends unless an animation-fill-mode value other than the default none has been set. If animation-fill-mode: both were added to the mix, the color would always be blue, as the last animation, or blue, overrides the previous green animation, which overrides the red first animation. ⊙

Animation Iteration and display: none;

If the display property is set to none on an element, any animation iterating on that element or its descendants will cease, as if the animation were detached from the element. Updating the display property back to a visible value will reattach all the animation properties, restarting the animation from scratch:

```
.snowflake {
    animation: spin 2s linear 5s 20;
}
```

In this case, the snowflake will spin 20 times; each spin takes 2 seconds, with the first spin starting after 5 seconds. If the snowflake element's display property gets set to none after 15 seconds, it would have completed 5 spins before disappearing (after getting through the 5-second delay, then executing 5 spins at 2 seconds each). If the snowflake display property changes back to anything other than none, the animation starts from scratch: a 5-second delay will elapse again before it starts spinning 20 times. It makes no difference how many animation cycles iterated before it disappeared from view the first time. ⊙

Animation and the UI Thread

CSS animations have the *lowest* priority on the user interface (UI) thread. If you attach multiple animations on page load with positive values for animation-delay, the delays expire as specified, but the animations may not begin until the UI thread is available to animate.

Assume the following:

- The animations all require the UI thread (that is, they aren't on the GPU as described in "Animation chaining" on page 912).

- You have 20 animations with the `animation-delay` property set to 1s, 2s, 3s, 4s, and so on in order to start each subsequent animation one second after the previous animation.

- The document or application takes a long time to load, with 11 seconds between the time the animated elements were drawn to the page and the time the JavaScript finished being downloaded, parsed, and executed.

Given all that, the delays of the first 11 animations will have expired once the UI thread is available, and those first 11 animations will all commence simultaneously. The remaining animations will each then begin animating at one-second intervals.

Seizure and Vestibular Disorders

 While you can use animations to create ever-changing content, *dynamically changing content can lead to seizures in some users.* Always keep this in mind, and ensure the accessibility of your website to people with epilepsy and other seizure disorders.

We don't usually start a section with a warning, but in this case, it's warranted. Visual change, especially rapid visual change, can trigger medical emergencies in users who are prone to seizures. They can also cause severe unease in users who are prone to vestibular disorder (motion sickness).

As this book was going to press in late 2017, a new media query was being deployed in browsers: `prefers-reduced-motion`. This allows authors to apply styles when the user has a "Reduce motion" or similar preference set for their browser or device. Strongly consider an approach such as this:

```
@media (prefers-reduced-motion) {
  * {animation: none !important; transition: none !important;}
}
```

This disables all animations and transitions, assuming no other `!important` animations are specified (and they shouldn't be). This is not a nuanced or perfect solution, but it's a first step. You can invert this approach by segregating all of your animations and transitions in a media block for those who do *not* have motion reduction enabled, like this:

```
@media not (prefers-reduced-motion) {
  /* all animations and transitions */
}
```

Not all animations are dangerous or disorienting, and it may be necessary to have at least some animations for all users. In such cases, use `prefers-reduced-motion` to tone down animations that are essential to understanding of the UI, and to switch off those that are essentially decorative.

Animation Events and Prefixing

Let's recap animation-related events we can access with DOM event listeners, and what prefixing may be required when using them.

animationstart

The `animationstart` event occurs at the start of the animation. If there is an `animation-delay`, this event will fire once the delay period has expired. If there is no delay, the `animationstart` event occurs when the animation is applied to the element. Even if there are no iterations, the `animationstart` event still occurs. If there are multiple animations attached to an element, an `animationstart` event will occur for each of the applied valid keyframe animations: generally, one `animationstart` for each valid `animation-name` identifier present:

```
#colorchange {
    animation: red, green, blue;
}
```

In this example, as long as the `red`, `green`, and `blue` keyframe animations are valid, while the animations will not be perceptible (as the default duration of `0s` is set on each), there will be three `animationstart` events thrown: one for each animation name.

If the browser requires the `-webkit-` prefix for the animation properties—basically, Safari 8 and earlier and Android 4.4.4 and older—the event is written as `webkitAnimationStart` instead of `animationstart`. Note the `-webkit-` prefix and the camelCasing. It is best to default to the unprefixed syntax and fall back to the prefixed version only when the unprefixed is unavailable.

animationend

The `animationend` event occurs at the conclusion of the last animation. It only occurs once per applied animation: if an element has three animations applied to it, like in the earlier `#colorchange` example, the `animationend` event will occur three times, at the end of the animation. In the example, there was no duration for any of the animations; however, the `animationend` event timing is usually equivalent to the result of the following equation:

```
(animation-duration * animation-iteration-count) + animation-delay = time
```

Even if there are no iterations, the animationend event still occurs once for each animation applied. If the animation-iteration-count is set to infinite, the animationend event never occurs.

If the browser requires the -webkit- prefix for the animation properties, the event is written as webkitAnimationEnd instead of animationend.

animationiteration

The animationiteration event occurs at the end of each iteration of an animation, before the start of the next iteration. If there are no iterations, or the iteration count is less than or equal to one, the animationiteration event never occurs. If the iteration count is infinite, the animationiteration event occurs ad infinitum, unless there is no duration set or the duration is 0s.

Unlike the animationstart and animationend events, which each occur once for each animation name, the animationiteration event can occur multiple times or no times per animation name, depending on how many iterations occur. Note that the event happens between animation cycles and will not occur at the same time as an animationend event. In other words, if the animation-iteration-count is an integer, the number of animationiteration events that occur is generally one less that the value of the animation-iteration-count property, as long as the absolute value of any negative delay is less than the duration.

Printing Animations

While not actually "animating" on a printed piece of paper, when an animated element is printed, the relevant property values will be printed. You can't see the element animating on a piece of paper, but if the animation caused an element to have a border-radius of 50%, the printed element will have a border-radius of 50%.

CHAPTER 19

Filters, Blending, Clipping, and Masking

Over the past decade, CSS has accumulated some interesting new features. These allow authors to alter the appearance of element with visual filters, specify different ways to visually blend elements with whatever is behind them, and alter the presentation of elements by showing parts and hiding other parts. While these may seem like disparate concepts, they all share one thing in common: they allow elements to be altered in ways that were previously very difficult or impossible.

CSS Filters

The veterans among us may remember that a long time ago, Microsoft put a `filter` property into their CSS support, which was used to pull in DirectX visual effects. In the time since, CSS has gained a `filter` property of its own, and while it's similar in concept to what Microsoft did, it isn't really the same thing. Among other changes, CSS defines a number of built-in visual filter effects, in addition to permitting the loading of filters defined in external files.

filter	
Values	[none|blur()|brightness()|contrast()|drop-shadow()|grayscale()|hue-rotate()|invert()|opacity()|sepia()|saturate()|url()]#
Initial value	none
Applies to	All elements (in SVG, applies to all graphics elements and all container elements except the `<defs>`element)
Computed value	As declared
Inherited	No

Animatable	Yes

The value syntax permits a comma-separated list of filter functions, with each filter applied in sequence. Thus, given the declaration `filter: opacity(0.5) blur(1px);`, the opacity is applied to the element, and the semi-transparent result is then blurred. If the order were reversed, so too would be the order of application: the fully opaque element is burred, and the resulting blur made semi-transparent.

The CSS specification talks of "input images" when discussing `filter`, but this doesn't mean `filter` is only used on images. Any HTML element can be filtered, and all graphic SVG elements can be filtered. The *input image* is a visual copy of the rendered element *before* it is filtered. Filters are applied to this input, and the final filtered result is then rendered to the display medium.

All the values permitted are effectively functions, with the permitted value types for each being dependent on the function in question. I've grouped these functions into a few broad categories for ease of understanding.

Basic Filters

These filters are basic in the sense that they cause changes that their names directly describe: blurring, drop shadows, and opacity changes:

`blur(<length>)`
> Blurs the element's contents using a Gaussian blur whose standard deviation is defined by the *<length>* value supplied, where a value of 0 leaves the element unchanged. Negative lengths are not permitted.

`opacity( [ <number> | <percentage> ] )`
> Applies a transparency filter to the element in a manner very similar to the `opacity` property, where the value 0 yields a completely transparent element and a value of 1 or 100% leaves the element unchanged. Negative values are not permitted. Values greater than 1 and 100% are permitted, but are clipped to be 1 or 100% for the purposes of computing the final value.

> The specification makes clear that `filter: opacity()` is *not* meant to be a replacement or shorthand for the `opacity` property, and in fact both can be applied to the same element, resulting in a sort of double-transparency.

```
drop-shadow(<length>{2,3} <color>?)
```
Creates a drop shadow that matches the shape of the element's alpha channel, with a blur and using an optional color. The handling of the lengths and colors is the same as for the property box-shadow, which means that while the first two <length>s can be negative, the third (which defines the blur) cannot. If no <color> value is supplied, the used color is the same as the computed value of the color property for the element.

The effects of these filter functions, alone and in combination, is shown in Figure 19-1.

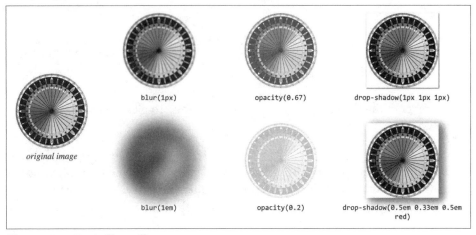

Figure 19-1. Basic filter effects

Before we go one, there are two things that deserve further exploration. The first is how drop-shadow() really operates. Just by looking at Figure 19-1, it's easy to get the impression that drop shadows are bound to the element box, because of the boxlike natures of the drop shadows shown there. But that's just because the image used to illustrate filters is a PNG, which is to say a raster image, and more importantly one that doesn't have any alpha channel. The white parts are opaque white, in other words.

If the image has transparent bits, then drop-shadow() will use those in computing the shadow. This can be a GIF89a, a PNG, a JPEG2000, an SVG, or any other alpha-aware image format. To see what this means, consider Figure 19-2.

The other thing to point out in Figure 19-2 is the last image has two drop shadows. This was accomplished as follows:

```
filter: drop-shadow(0 0 0.5em yellow) drop-shadow(0.5em 0.75em 30px gray);
```

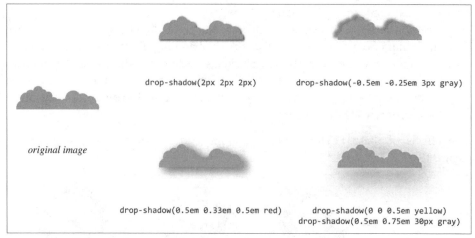

Figure 19-2. *Drop shadows and alpha channels*

Any number of filters can be chained together like this. To pick another example, you could write:

```
filter: blur(3px) drop-shadow(0.5em 0.75em 30px gray) opacity(0.5);
```

That would get you a blurry, drop-shadowed, half-opaque element. It might not be the most reader-friendly effect for text, but it's possible nonetheless. This function-chaining is possible with all `filter` functions, both those we've seen and those to come.

Color Filtering

This next set of `filter` functions alter the colors present in the filtered element in some way. This can be as simple as leaching out the colors, or as complex as shifting all the colors by way of an angle value.

Note that for the first three of the four of the following functions, all of which accept either a *<number>* or *<percentage>*, negative values are not permitted:

`grayscale( [ <number> | <percentage> ] )`
 Alters the colors in the element to be shifted toward shades of gray. A value of 0 leaves the element unchanged, and a value of 1 or 100% will result in a fully gray-scale element.

`sepia( [ <number> | <percentage> ] )`
 Alters the colors in the element to be shifted toward shades of sepia tones (sepia is a reddish-brown color, defined by Wikipedia to be equivalent to #704214 or rgba(112,66,20) in the sRGB color space). A value of 0 leaves the element unchanged, and a value of 1 or 100% will result in a fully sepia element.

`invert( [ <number> | <percentage> ] )`

Inverts all colors in the element. Each of the R, G, and B values for a given color are inverted by subtracting them from 255 (in 0-255 notation) or from 100% (in 0%-100% notation). For example, a pixel with the color `rgb(255,128,55)` will be rendered as `rgb(0,127,200)`; a different pixel with the value `rgb(75%,57.2%, 23%)` will become `rgb(25%,42.8%,77%)`. A value of `0` leaves the element unchanged, and a value of `1` or `100%` will result in a fully inverted element. A value of `0.5` or `50%` would stop the inversion of each color at the midpoint of the color space, leading to an element of uniform gray.

`hue-rotate( <angle> )`

Alters the colors of the image by displacing their hue around an HSL color wheel, leaving saturation and lightness alone. A value of `0deg` leaves the element unchanged. A value of `360deg` (a full single rotation) will also present an apparently unchanged element, though the value is maintained, and values above `360deg` are permitted. Negative values are also permitted, and cause an anticlockwise rotation as opposed to the clockwise rotation imposed by positive values. (In other words, the rotation is "compass-style," with 0° at the top and increasing angle values in the clockwise direction.)

Examples of the preceding `filter` functions are shown in Figure 19-3, though fully appreciating them depends on a color rendering of the figure.

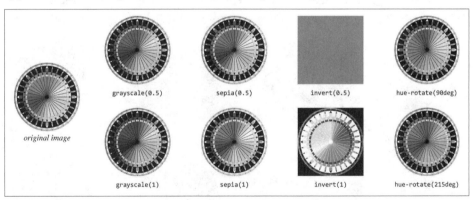

Figure 19-3. Color filter effects

Brightness, Contrast, and Saturation

While these `filter` functions also manipulate color, they do so in closely related ways, and are a familiar grouping to anyone who's worked with images, particularly photographic images.

Note that for all these functions, values greater than 1 and 100% are permitted, but are clipped to be 1 or 100% for the purposes of computing the final value:

`brightness( [ <number> | <percentage> ] )`

> Alters the brightness of the element's colors. A value of 0 leaves the element a solid black, and a value of 1 or 100% leaves it unchanged. Values above 1 and 100% yield colors brighter than the base element, and can eventually reach a state of solid white.

`contrast( [ <number> | <percentage> ] )`

> Alters the contrast of the element's colors. The higher the contrast, the more colors are differentiated from each other; the lower the contrast, the more they converge on each other. A value of 0 leaves the element a solid gray, and a value of 1 or 100% leaves it unchanged. Values above 1 and 100% yield colors with greater contrast than is present in the base element.

`saturate( [ <number> | <percentage> ] )`

> Alters the saturation of the element's colors. The more saturated an element's colors, the more intense they become; the less saturated they are, the more muted they appear. A value of 0 leaves the element completely unsaturated, leaving it effectively grayscale, whereas a value of 1 or 100% will leave the element unchanged. Unlike the preceding functions, `saturate()` permits *and* acts upon values greater than 1 or 100%; such values result in supersaturation.

Examples of the preceding `filter` functions are shown in Figure 19-4, though fully appreciating them depends on a color rendering of the figure. Also, the effects of greater-than-one values may be hard to make out in the figure, but they are present.

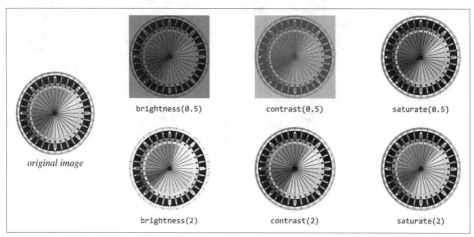

Figure 19-4. Brightness, contrast, and saturation filter effects

SVG Filters

The last `filter` value type is a function of a familiar kind: the `url()` value type. This allows authors to point to a (potentially very complicated) filter defined in SVG, whether it's embedded in the document or stored in an external file.

This takes the form `url(<uri>)`, where the *<uri>* value points to a filter defined using SVG syntax, specifically the `<filter>` element. This can be a reference to a single SVG image which contains only a filter, such as `url(wavy.svg)`, or it can be a pointer to an identified filter embedded in an SVG image, such as `url(filters.svg#wavy)`. The advantage of the latter pattern is that a single SVG can define multiple filters, thus consolidating all your filtering into one file for easy loading, caching, and referencing.

If a `url()` function points to a nonexistent file, or points to an SVG fragment that is not a `<filter>` element, the function is invalid and the *entire* function list is ignored (thus rendering the `filter` declaration invalid).

Examining the full range of filtering possibilities in SVG is well beyond the scope of this work, but let's just say that the power of the offered features is substantial. A few simple examples of SVG filtering are shown in Figure 19-5, with brief captions to indicate what kinds of operations the filters were built to create. (The actual CSS used to apply these filters looked like `filter: url(filters.svg#rough)`.)

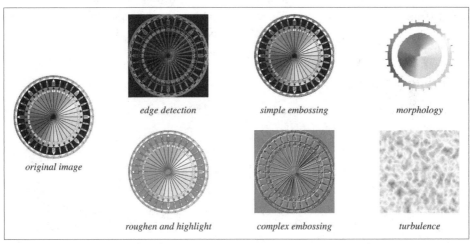

Figure 19-5. SVG filter effects

It's easily possible to put every last bit of filtering you do into SVG, including replacements for every other `filter` function we've seen. (In fact, all the other `filter` functions are defined by the specification as literal SVG filters, to give a precise rendering target for implementors.) Remember, however, that you can chain CSS functions together. Thus, you might define a specular-highlight filter in SVG, and modify it with blurring or grayscale functions as needed. For example:

```
img.logo {filter: url(/assets/filters.svg#spotlight);}
img.logo.print {filter: url(/assets/filters.svg#spotlight) grayscale(100%);}
img.logo.censored {filter: url(/assets/filters.svg#spotlight) blur(3px);}
```

Always keep in mind that the filter functions are applied in order. That's why the gray scale() and blur() functions each come after the url()-imported spotlight filter. If they were reversed, the logos would be made grayscale or blurred first, and then have a highlight applied afterward.

Compositing and Blending

In addition to filtering, CSS offers the ability to determine how elements are *composited* together. Take, for example, two elements that partially overlap due to positioning. We're used to the one in front obscuring the one behind. This is sometimes called *simple alpha compositing*, in that you can see whatever is behind the element as long as some (or all) of it has alpha channel values less than 1. Think of, for example, how you can see the background through an element with opacity: 0.5, or in the areas of a PNG or GIF87a that are set to be transparent.

But if you're familiar with image-editing programs like Photoshop or GIMP, you know that image layers which overlap can be blended together in a variety of ways. CSS has gained the same ability. There are two blending strategies in CSS (at least as of late 2017): blending entire elements with whatever is behind them, and blending together the background layers of a single element.

Blending Elements

In situations where elements overlap, it's possible to change how they blend together with the property mix-blend-mode.

<hr>

mix-blend-mode

Values	normal | multiply | screen | overlay | darken | lighten | color-dodge | color-burn | hard-light | soft-light | difference | exclusion | hue | saturation | color | luminosity
Initial value	normal
Applies to	All elements
Computed value	As declared
Inherited	No

Animatable	No

The way the CSS specification puts this is: "defines the formula that must be used to mix the colors with the backdrop." That is to say, the element is blended with whatever is behind it (the "backdrop"), whether that's pieces of another element, or just the background of its parent element.

The default, normal, means that the element's pixels are shown as is, without any mixing with the backdrop, except where the alpha channel is less than 1. This is the "simple alpha compositing" mentioned previously. It's what we're all used to, which is why it's the default value. A few examples are shown in Figure 19-6.

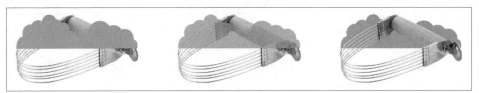

Figure 19-6. Simple alpha channel blending

For the rest of the mix-blend-mode keywords, I've grouped them into a few categories. Let's also nail down a few definitions:

- The *foreground* is the element that has mix-blend-mode applied to it.
- The *backdrop* is whatever is behind that element. This can be other elements, the background of the parent element, and so on.
- A *pixel component* is the color component of a given pixel: R, G, and B.

If it helps, think of the foreground and backdrop as images that are layered atop one another in an image-editing program. With mix-blend-mode, you can change the blend mode applied to the top image (the foreground).

Darken, Lighten, Difference, and Exclusion

These blend modes might be called simple-math modes—they achieve their effect by directly comparing values in some way, or using simple addition and subtraction to modify pixels:

darken
> Each pixel in the foreground is compared with the corresponding pixel in the backdrop, and for each of the R, G, and B values (the pixel components), the smaller of the two is kept. Thus, if the foreground pixel has a value correspond-

ing to rgb(91,164,22) and the backdrop pixel is rgb(102,104,255), the resulting pixel will be rgb(91,104,22).

lighten

This blend is the inverse of darken: when comparing the R, G, and B components of a foreground pixel and its corresponding backdrop pixel, the larger of the two values is kept. Thus, if the foreground pixel has a value corresponding to rgb(91,164,22) and the backdrop pixel is rgb(102,104,255), the resulting pixel will be rgb(102,164,255).

difference

The R, G, and B components of each pixel in the foreground are compared to the corresponding pixel in the backdrop, and the absolute value of subtracting one from the other is the final result. Thus, if the foreground pixel has a value corresponding to rgb(91,164,22) and the backdrop pixel is rgb(102,104,255), the resulting pixel will be rgb(11,60,233). If one of the pixels is white, the resulting pixel will be the inverse of the non-white pixel. If one of the pixels is black, the result will be exactly the same as the non-black pixel.

exclusion

This blend is a milder version of difference. Rather than being $| back - fore |$, the formula is $back + fore - (2 \times back \times fore)$, where $back$ and $fore$ are values in the range from 0-1. For example, an exclusion calculation of an orange (rgb(100%, 50%,0%)) and medium gray (rgb(50%,50%,50%)) will yield rgb(50%,50%,50%). For the red component, the math is $1 + 0.5 - (2 \times 1 \times 0.5)$, which reduces to 0.5, corresponding to 50%. For the blue and green components, the math is $0 + 0.5 - (2 \times 0 \times 0.5)$, which again reduces to 0.5. Compare this to difference, where the result would be rgb(50%,0%,50%), since each component is the absolute value of subtracting one from the other.

This last definition highlights the fact that for all blend modes, the actual values being operated on are in the range 0-1. The previous examples showing values like rgb(11,60,233) are normalized from the 0-1 range. In other words, given the example of applying the difference blend mode to rgb(91,164,22) and rgb(102,104,255), the actual operation is as follows:

- rgb(91,164,22) is $R = 91 \div 255 = 0.357$; $G = 164 \div 255 = 0.643$; $B = 22 \div 255 = 0.086$. Similarly, rgb(102,104,255) corresponds to $R = 0.4$; $G = 0.408$; $B = 1$.

- Each component is subtracted from the corresponding component, and the absolute value taken. Thus, $R = | 0.357 - 0.4 | = 0.043$; $G = | 0.643 - 0.408 | = 0.235$; $B = | 1 - 0.086 | = 0.914$. This could be expressed as rgba(4.3%,23.5%,91.4%), or (by multiplying each component by 255) as rgb(11,60,233).

From all this, you can perhaps understand why the full formulas are not written out for every blend mode we cover. If you're interested in the fine details, each blend mode's formula is provided in the "Compositing and Blending Level 1" specification.

Examples of the blend modes in this section are depicted in Figure 19-7.

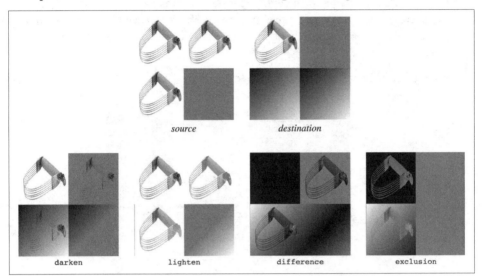

Figure 19-7. Darken, lighten, difference, and exclusion blending

Multiply, Screen, and Overlay

These blend modes might be called the multiplication modes—they achieve their effect by multiplying values together:

multiply
> Each pixel component in the foreground is multiplied by the corresponding pixel component in the backdrop. This yields a darker version of the foreground, modified by what is underneath. This blend mode is *symmetric*, in that the result will be exactly the same even if you were to swap the foreground with the backdrop.

screen
> Each pixel component in the foreground is inverted (see invert in the earlier section "Color Filtering" on page 948), multiplied by the inverse of the corresponding pixel component in the backdrop, and the result inverted again. This yields a lighter version of the foreground, modified by what is underneath. Like multiply, screen is symmetric.

`overlay`

> This blend is a combination of `multiply` and `screen`. For foreground pixel components darker than 0.5 (50%), the `multiply` operation is carried out; for foreground pixel components whose values are above 0.5, `screen` is used. This makes the dark areas darker, and the light areas lighter. This blend mode is *not* symmetric, because swapping the foreground for the backdrop would mean a different pattern of light and dark, and thus a different pattern of multiplying versus screening.

Examples of these blend modes are depicted in Figure 19-8.

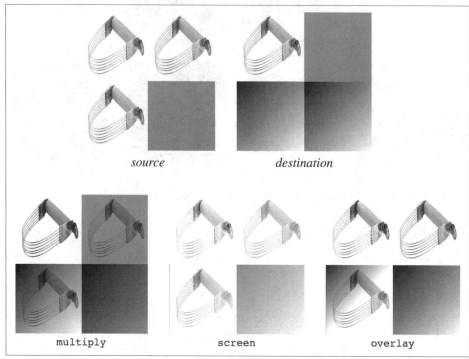

source   *destination*

`multiply`   `screen`   `overlay`

Figure 19-8. Multiply, screen, and overlay blending

Hard and Soft Light

There blend modes are covered here because the first is closely related to a previous blend mode, and the other is just a muted version of the first:

`hard-light`

> This blend is the inverse of `overlay` blending. Like `overlay`, it's a combination of `multiply` and `screen`, but the determining layer is the backdrop. Thus, for backdrop pixel components darker than 0.5 (50%), the `multiply` operation is carried out; for backdrop pixel components lighter than 0.5, `screen` is used. This makes

it appear somewhat as if the foreground is being projected onto the backdrop with a projector that employs a harsh light.

soft-light

This blend is a softer version of hard-light. That is to say, it uses the same operation, but is muted in its effects. The intended appearance is as if the foreground is being projected onto the backdrop with a projector that employs a diffuse light.

Examples of these blend modes are depicted in Figure 19-9.

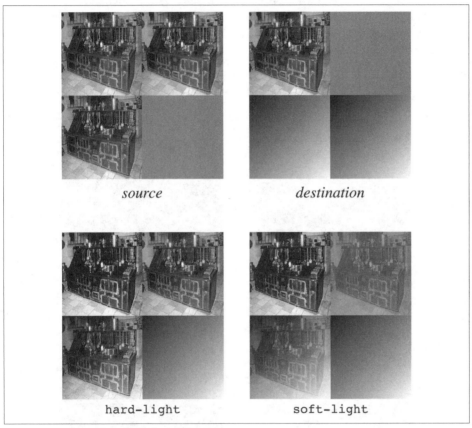

source   *destination*

hard-light   soft-light

Figure 19-9. Hard- and soft-light blending

Color Dodge and Burn

Color dodging and burning are interesting modes, in that they're meant to lighten or darken a picture with a minimum of change to the colors themselves. The terms come from old darkroom techniques performed on chemical film stock:

`color-dodge`

> Each pixel component in the foreground is inverted, and the component of the corresponding backdrop pixel component is divided by the inverted foreground value. This yields a brightened backdrop unless the foreground value is 0, in which case the backdrop value is unchanged.

`color-burn`

> This blend is a reverse of `color-dodge`: each pixel component in the backdrop is inverted, the inverted backdrop value is divided by the unchanged value of the corresponding foreground pixel component, and the result is then inverted. This yields a result where the darker the backdrop pixel, the more its color will burn through the foreground pixel.

Examples of these blend modes are depicted in Figure 19-10.

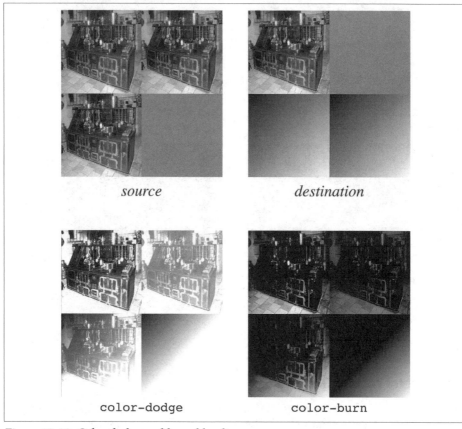

Figure 19-10. Color dodge and burn blending

Hue, Saturation, Luminosity, and Color

The final four blend modes are different than those we've seen before, because they do *not* perform operations on the R/G/B pixel components. Instead, they perform operations to combine the hue, saturation, luminosity, and color of the foreground and backdrop in different ways:

hue
>   For each pixel, combines the luminosity and saturation levels of the backdrop with the hue angle of the foreground.

saturation
>   For each pixel, combines the hue angle and luminosity level of the backdrop with the saturation level of the foreground.

color
>   For each pixel, combines the luminosity level of the backdrop with the hue angle and saturation level of the foreground.

luminosity
>   For each pixel, combines the hue angle and saturation level of the backdrop with the luminosity level of the foreground.

Examples of these blend modes are depicted in Figure 19-11.

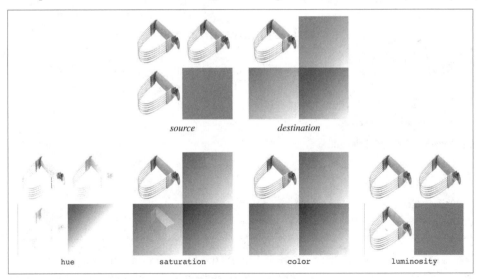

Figure 19-11. Hue, saturation, luminosity, and color blending

These blend modes can be a lot harder to grasp without busting out raw formulas, and even those can be confusing if you aren't familiar with how things like saturation and luminosity levels are determined. If you don't feel like you quite have a handle on how they work, the best thing is to practice with a bunch of different images and simple color patterns.

Two things to note:

- Remember that an element always blends with its backdrop. If there are other elements behind it, it will blend with them; if there's a patterned background on the parent element, the blending will be done against that pattern.
- Changing the opacity of a blended element will change the outcome, though not always in the way you might expect. For example, if an element with `mix-blend-mode: difference` is also given `opacity: 0.8`, then the difference calculations will be scaled by 80%. More precisely, a scaling factor of 0.8 will be applied to the color-value calculations. This can cause some operations to trend toward flat middle gray, and others to shift the color changes.

Blending Backgrounds

Blending an element with its backdrop is one thing, but what if an element has multiple background images that overlap and also need to be blended together? That's where `background-blend-mode` comes in.

---

background-blend-mode

Values	`[normal|multiply|screen|overlay|darken|lighten|color-dodge|color-burn|hard-light|soft-light|difference|exclusion|hue|saturation|color|luminosity]#`
Initial value	`normal`
Applies to	All elements
Computed value	As declared
Inherited	No
Animatable	No

We won't go through an exhaustive list of all the blend modes and what they mean, because we did that in the section on `mix-blend-mode`. What they meant there, they mean here.

The difference is that when it comes to blending multiple backgrounds images together, they're blended with each other against an empty background—that is, a completely transparent, uncolored backdrop. They do *not* blend with the backdrop of the element, except as directed by `mix-blend-mode`.

To see what that means, consider the following:

```
#example {background-image:
        url(star.svg),
        url(diamond.png),
        linear-gradient(135deg, #F00, #AEA);
    background-blend-mode: color-burn, luminosity, darken;}
```

Here we have three background images, each with its own blend mode. These are blended together into a single result, shown in Figure 19-12.

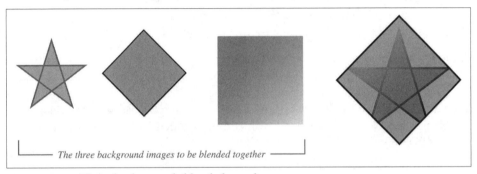

Figure 19-12. *Three backgrounds blended together*

So far, fine. Here's the kicker: the result will be the same regardless of what might appear behind the element. We can change the parent's background to white, gray, fuchsia, or a lovely pattern of repeating gradients, and in every case those three blended backgrounds will look exactly the same, pixel for pixel. They're blended in *isolation*, a term we'll return to shortly. We can see the above example (Figure 19-12) sitting atop a variety of backgrounds in Figure 19-13.

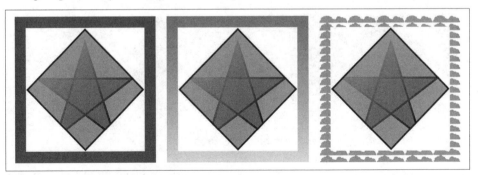

Figure 19-13. *Blending with color versus transparency*

Like multiple blended elements stacked atop each other, the blending of background layers works from the back to the front. Thus, if you have two background images over a solid background color, the background layer in the back is blended with the background color, and then the frontmost layer is blended with the result of the first blend. Consider:

```
#example {background-image:
         url(star.svg),
         url(diamond.png);
      background-color: goldenrod;
      background-mix-mode: color-burn, luminosity;}
```

Given these styles, `diamond.png` is blended with the background color `goldenrod` using the `luminosity` blend. Once that's done, `star.png` is blended with the results of the diamond-goldenrod blend using a `color-burn` blend.

Although it's true that the background layers are blended in isolation, they're also part of an element which may have its own blending rules via `mix-blend-mode`. Thus, the final result of the isolated background blend may be blended with the element's backdrop after all. Given the following styles, the first example's background will sit atop the element's backdrop, but the rest will end up blended with it in some fashion, as illustrated in Figure 19-14:

```
.one {mix-blend-mode: normal;}
.two {mix-blend-mode: multiply;}
.three {mix-blend-mode: darken;}
.four {mix-blend-mode: luminosity;}
.five {mix-blend-mode: color-dodge;}

<div class="bbm one"></div>
<div class="bbm two"></div>
<div class="bbm three"></div>
<div class="bbm four"></div>
<div class="bbm five"></div>
```

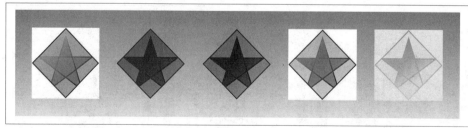

Figure 19-14. Blending elements with their backdrops

Throughout this section, we've touched on the concept of blending in isolation, as a thing that backgrounds naturally do. Elements, on the other hand, do not naturally blend in isolation. As we'll see next, that behavior can be changed.

Blending in Isolation

There may be times when you want to blend a number of different elements together, but in a group of their own, in the same way background layers on an element are blended. This is, as we've seen, called blending in *isolation*. If that's what you're after, then the `isolation` property is for you.

<table>
<tr><td colspan="2" align="center">isolation</td></tr>
<tr><td>Values</td><td><code>auto | isolate</code></td></tr>
<tr><td>Initial value</td><td><code>auto</code></td></tr>
<tr><td>Applies to</td><td>All elements (in SVG, it applies to container elements, graphics elements, and graphics-referencing elements)</td></tr>
<tr><td>Computed value</td><td>As declared</td></tr>
<tr><td>Inherited</td><td>No</td></tr>
<tr><td>Animatable</td><td>No</td></tr>
</table>

This pretty much does exactly what it says: it either defines an element to create an isolated blending context, or not. Given the following styles, then, we get the result shown in Figure 19-15:

```
img {mix-blend-mode: difference;}
p.alone {isolation: isolate;}

<p class="alone"><img src="diamond.png"></p>
<p><img src="diamond.png"></p>
```

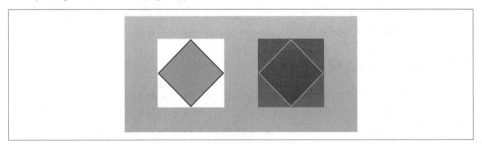

Figure 19-15. Blending in isolation, and not

Take particular note of where `isolation` was applied, and where `mix-blend-mode` was applied. The image is given the blend mode, but the containing element (in this case, a paragraph) is set to isolation blending. It's done this way because you want the parent (or some ancestor element) to be isolated from the rest of the document, in terms of how its descendant elements are blended. So if you want an element to blend in isolation, look for an ancestor element to set to `isolation: isolate`.

There is an interesting wrinkle in all of this, which is that any element which establishes a stacking context is automatically isolated, regardless of the value for `isolation`. If you transform an element using the `transform` property, for example, it will become isolated.

The complete list of stacking-context-establishing conditions, as of late 2017, are:

- The root element (e.g., `<html>`)
- Positioning an element relatively or absolutely *and* setting its `z-index` to anything other than `auto`
- Positioning an element with `fixed`, regardless of its `z-index` value
- Setting `opacity` to anything other than 1
- Setting `transform` to anything other than `none`
- Setting `mix-blend-mode` to anything other than `normal`
- Setting `filter` to anything other than `none`
- Setting `perspective` to anything other than `none`
- Setting `isolation` to `isolate`
- Applying `will-change` to any of the previous properties, even if they are not actually changed

Thus, if you have a group of elements that are blended together and then blended with their shared backdrop, and you then transition the group's `opacity` from 1 to 0, the group will suddenly become isolated during the transition. This might have no visual impact, depending on the original set of blends, but it very well might.

Clipping and Masking

Besides filtering and blending, CSS also has the ability to do both clipping and masking. These are methods of only showing portions of an element, using permitting a variety of simple shapes as well as the application of complete images and SVG elements. These can be used to make decorative bits of a layout more visually interesting, among other things—a common technique is to frame images or give them ragged edges.

Clipping

One of the possibilities we saw with `filter` was to apply a clipping path via SVG. That's a valid use of filters, but if all you want to do is clip off pieces of the element, you can use the property `clip-path` instead.

	clip-path
Values	`none` | `<url>` | `[[inset()` | `circle()` | `ellipse()` | `polygon()]` || `[border-box` | `padding-box` | `content-box` | `margin-box` | `fill-box` | `stroke-box` | `view-box]]`
Initial value	`none`
Applies to	All elements (in SVG, applies to all graphics elements and all container elements except the `<defs>` element)
Computed value	As declared
Inherited	No
Animatable	Yes for `inset()`, `circle()`, `ellipse()`, and `polygon()`

With `clip-path`, you're able to define a clipping shape. This is essentially the area of the element inside which visible portions are drawn. Any part of the element that fall outside the shape is clipped off, leaving behind empty transparent space. The following code gives a clipped and an unclipped example of the same paragraph, with the result depicted in Figure 19-16:

```
p {background: orange; color: black; padding: 0.75em;}
p.clipped {clip-path: url(shapes.svg#cloud02);}
```

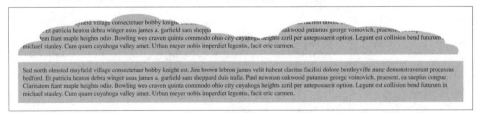

Figure 19-16. Clipped and unclipped paragraphs

The default value, `none`, means no clipping is preformed, as you'd probably expect. If a `<uri>` value is given (as in the previous example) and it points to a missing resource, or to an element in an SVG file that isn't a `<clipPath>`, then no clipping occurs.

The rest of the values are either shapes written in CSS, reference boxes, or both.

As of late 2017, URL-based clip paths work in Chrome only if the URL points to an embedded SVG inside the same document as the clipped element. External SVGs were not supported.

Clip Shapes

You can define clip shapes with one of a set of four simple shape functions. These are identical to the shapes used to define float shapes with `shape-outside` (see Chapter 10), so we won't re-describe them in detail here. Here's a brief recap:

`inset()`
>   Accepts from one to four lengths or percentage values, defining offsets from the edges of the bounding box, with optional corner rounding via the round keyword and another set of one to four lengths or percentages.

`circle()`
>   Accepts a single length, percentage, or keyword defining the radius of the circle, with an optional position for the circle's center with the at keyword followed by one or two lengths or percentages.

`ellipse()`
>   Accepts a mandatory two lengths, percentages, or keywords defining the radii of the vertical and horizontal axes of the ellipse, with an optional position for the ellipse's center with the at keyword followed by one or two lengths or percentages.

`polygon()`
>   Accepts a comma-separated list of space-separated x and y coordinates, using either lengths or percentages. Can be prefaced by a keyword defining the fill rule for the polygon.

A variety of examples of these clip shapes is shown in Figure 19-17, corresponding to the following styles. (The dotted borders have been added to show the outer edges of the original image, before clipping.)

```
.ex01 {clip-path: none;}
.ex02 {clip-path: inset(10px 0 25% 2em);}
.ex03 {clip-path: circle(100px at 50% 50%);}
.ex04 {clip-path: ellipse(100px 50px at 75% 25%);}
.ex05 {clip-path: polygon(50% 0, 100% 50%, 50% 100%, 0 50%);}
.ex06 {clip-path: polygon(0 0, 50px 100px, 150px 5px, 300px 150px, 0 100%);}
```

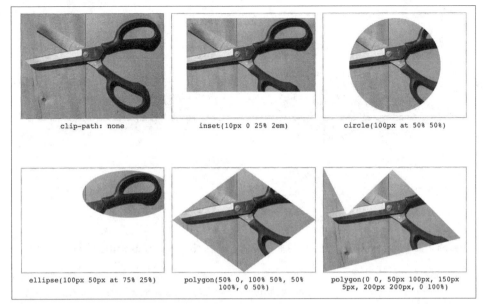

Figure 19-17. Various clip shapes

As Figure 19-17 shows, the elements are only visible inside the clip shapes. Anything outside that is just gone. But take note of how the clipped elements still take up the same space they would if they weren't clipped at all. In other words, clipping doesn't make the elements smaller. It just limits the part of them that's actually drawn.

Clip Boxes

Unlike clip shapes, clip boxes aren't specified using lengths or percentages. They correspond, for the most part, directly to boundaries in the box model.

If you just say `clip-path: border-box`, for example, the element is clipped along the outside edge of the border. This is likely what you'd expect anyway, since margins are transparent. Remember, however, that outlines can be drawn outside borders, so if you *do* clip at the border edge, any outlines will be clipped away.

When used by themselves, the values `margin-box`, `padding-box`, and `content-box` dictate that the clipping occur at the outer edges of the margin, padding, or content areas, respectively. These are diagrammed in Figure 19-18.

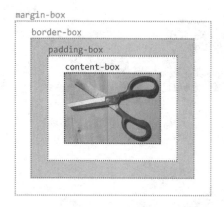

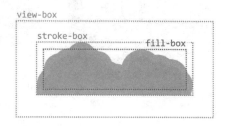

Figure 19-18. Various clipping boxes

There's another part to Figure 19-18, which shows the SVG bounding boxes:

view-box
: The nearest (that is, the closest ancestor) SVG viewport is used as the clipping box.

fill-box
: The *object bounding box* is used as the clipping box. The object bounding box is the smallest box that will fit every part of the element's geometry, taking into account any transformations (e.g., rotation), not including any strokes along its outside.

stroke-box
: The *stroke bounding box* is used as the clipping box. The object bounding box is the smallest box that will fit every part of the element's geometry, taking into account any transformations (e.g., rotation), including any strokes along its outside.

These values only apply to SVG elements that don't have an associated CSS layout box. For such elements, if the CSS-style boxes (margin-box, border-box, padding-box, content-box) are given, fill-box is used instead. Conversely, if one of the SVG bounding box values is applied to an element that *does* have a CSS layout box—which is most elements—then border-box is used instead.

It can be useful at times to be able to say something like clip-path: content-box just to clip off everything outside the content area, but where these box values really come into their own is in conjunction with a clipping shape. Suppose you have an ellipse() clip shape you want to apply to an element, and furthermore, you want to have it just touch the outer edges of the padding box. Rather than have to calculate the necessary radii by subtracting margins and borders from the overall element, you can just say `clip-path: ellipse(50% 50%) padding-box;`. That will center an elliptical clip shape at the center of the element, with horizontal and vertical radii half the element's reference box (see Chapter 10), as shown in Figure 19-19, along with the effect of fitting to other boxes.

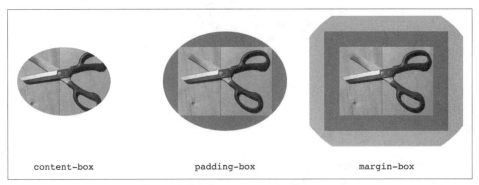

Figure 19-19. Fitting an elliptical clip shape to various boxes

Notice how the ellipse is cut off in the `margin-box` example? That's because the margin is invisible, so while parts of it fall inside the elliptical clip shape, we can't actually see those parts.

Interestingly, the bounding-box keywords can only be used in conjunction with clip shapes—*not* with an SVG-based clip path. The keywords that relate to SVG bounding boxes apply only if an SVG image is being clipped via CSS.

A warning about SVG clip paths: as of late 2017, all path coordinates are expressed in absolute units, and can't be declared as percentages of the image's height and width as the `polygon()` shape can. There are techniques involving the `clipPathUnits` SVG attribute, sometimes in conjunction with the `transform` SVG attribute, that yield equivalent results. Here's an example of such a clipping path, with the result shown in Figure 19-20:

```
<clipPath id="hexlike" clipPathUnits="objectBoundingBox">
    <polygon points="0.5 0, 1 0.25, 1 0.75, 0.5 1, 0 0.75, 0 0.25"/>
</clipPath>
```

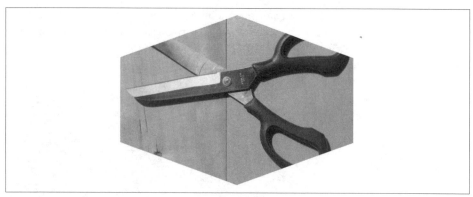

Figure 19-20. An image clipped with a scaling SVG clip path

The `objectBoundingBox` value fits the coordinates to the bounding box in use, and the coordinates are all in the range of 0–1. With that sort of setup, you get a clip path that behaves the same as a percentage-based `polygon` shape. You'd get the same clip shape shown in Figure 19-20 by using the following:

```
clip-path: polygon(50% 0, 100% 25%, 100% 75%, 50% 100%, 0 75%, 0 25%);
```

Clip Filling Rules

As with float shapes, it's possible to change the way SVG shapes are filled, which is to say the exact clipping shape that is created when the path crosses over itself. This is managed with the property `clip-rule`.

clip-rule

Values	nonzero | evenodd
Initial value	nonzero
Applies to	All SVG graphics elements (`<circle>`, `<ellipse>`, `<image>`, `<line>`, `<path>`, `<polygon>`, `<polyline>`, `<rect>`, `<text>` and `<use>`) *if and only if* they are children of a `<clipPath>` element
Computed value	As declared
Inherited	No
Animatable	No

It's much easier to show than describe, so the difference between `nonzero` and `even odd` shape filling is depicted in Figure 19-21.

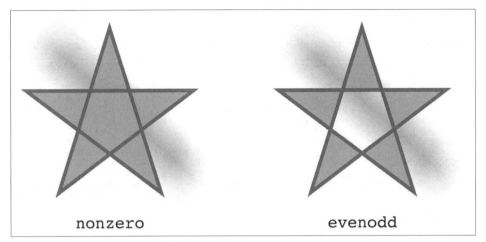

nonzero   evenodd

Figure 19-21. The two shape-filling options

Here, you can see how the star is drawn by following lines from the top center through each successive point. The nonzero star fills all of its interior, even when lines cross over each other. The evenodd star, by contrast, leaves parts of itself unfilled, which is why we can see the light blue gradient through its center.

The problem is that as of late 2017, even browsers that supported SVG clipping paths did not support this property, regardless of whether the SVG was embedded in the HTML or external files. Thus, if you want to set the shape-fill of a clipping path to evenodd, you'll either need to recreate the SVG path as a CSS polygon, or make use of the SVG fill-rule attribute in the SVG file itself.

Masks

When we say a "mask," what we mean is a shape inside which things are visible, and outside which they are not. Masks are thus very similar in concept to clipping paths. The primary differences are twofold: first, you can only use an image to define the areas of the element that are shown or clipped away with masks; and second, there are a lot more properties available to use with masks, allowing you to do things such as position, size, and repeat the masking image.

As of late 2017, the Blink family supported most of the masking properties, but only with the -webkit- prefix. So instead of mask-image, Chrome and Safari supported -webkit-mask-image instead.

Defining a Mask

The first step to applying a mask is to point to the image that you'll be using to define the mask. This is accomplished with mask-image, which accepts any image type.

<table>
<tr><td colspan="2" align="center">mask-image</td></tr>
<tr><td>Values</td><td>[none | <image> | <mask-source>]#</td></tr>
<tr><td>Initial value</td><td>none</td></tr>
<tr><td>Applies to</td><td>All elements (in SVG, applies to all graphics elements and all container elements except the <defs>element)</td></tr>
<tr><td>Computed value</td><td>As declared</td></tr>
<tr><td>Inherited</td><td>No</td></tr>
<tr><td>Animatable</td><td>No</td></tr>
<tr><td>Notes</td><td>An <image> is any of the value types <url>, <image()>, <image-set()>, <element()>, <cross-fade()>, or <gradient> (all defined elsewhere in the book); <mask-source> is a url() that points to a <mask> element in an SVG image</td></tr>
</table>

Assuming the image reference is valid, this will give the user agent an image to use as a mask for the element to which it's been applied.

We'll start with a simple situation: one image applied to another, where both are the same height and width. Consider Figure 19-22, where both images are shown separately, and then with the first masked by the second.

Figure 19-22. A simple image mask

As you can see, in the parts of the second image that are opaque, the first image is visible. In the parts that are transparent, the first image is not visible. For the parts that are semi-transparent, the first image is also semi-transparent.

Here's the basic code for the end result shown in Figure 19-22:

```
img.masked {mask-image: url(theatre-masks.svg);}
```

CSS doesn't require that you apply mask images only to other images, though. You can mask pretty much any element with an image, and that image can be a raster image (GIF, JPG, PNG) or a vector image (SVG). The latter is usually a better choice, if available. You can even construct your own image with gradients, whether linear or radial, repeated or otherwise.

The following styles will have the result shown in Figure 19-23:

```
*.masked.theatre {mask-image: url(theatre-masks.svg);}
*.masked.compass {mask-image: url(Compass.png);}
```

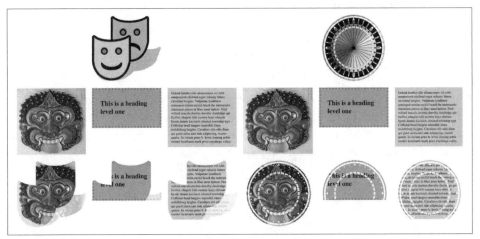

Figure 19-23. A variety of image masks

An important point to keep in mind is that when a mask clips off pieces of an element, it clips off *all* pieces. The best example of this is how, if you apply an image that clips off the outer edges of elements, the markers on list items can very easily become invisible. An example can be seen in Figure 19-24, which is the result of the following:

```
*.masked {mask-image: url(i/Compass_masked.png);}

<ol class="masked">
    <li>One</li>
    <li>Two</li>
    <li>Three</li>
    <li>Four</li>
    <li>Five</li>
</ol>
```

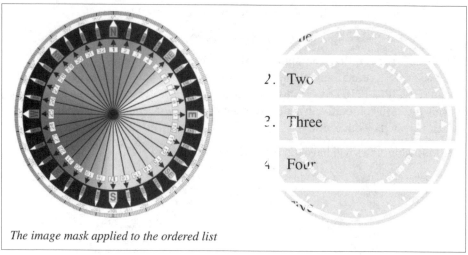

The image mask applied to the ordered list

Figure 19-24. List items, masked and unmasked

There is one other value option we haven't seen yet, which is the ability to point directly at a <mask> element in SVG to use the mask it defines. This analogous to pointing to a <clipPath> or other SVG element from the property clip-path, as was discussed previously in "Clipping" on page 965.

Here's an example of how a mask might be defined:

```
<svg viewbox="0 0 100 100" height="100" width="100"
    xmlns="http://www.w3.org/2000/svg" version="1.1">
        <mask id="hexlike">
        <path fill="#FF0000"
          d="M 50,0 100,25 100,75 50,100 0,75 0,25" />
        </mask>
</svg>
```

With that SVG embedded in the HTML file directly, the mask can be referenced like this:

```
.masked {mask-image: url(#hexlike);}
```

If the SVG is in an external file, then this is how to reference it from CSS:

```
.masked {mask-image: url(masks.svg#hexlike);}
```

Changing the Mask's Mode

Thus far, we've seen masking accomplished by applying an image with an alpha channel to another element. That's one of two ways to use an image as a mask. The other is to use the brightness of each part of the masking image to define the mask. Switching between these two options is accomplished with the mask-mode property.

---

mask-mode

Values	[alpha │ luminance │ match-source]#
Initial value	match-source
Applies to	All elements (in SVG, applies to all graphics elements and all container elements except the <defs>element)
Computed value	As declared
Inherited	No
Animatable	No

Two of the three values are straightforward: alpha means the alpha channel of the image should be used to compute the mask, and luminance means the brightness levels should be used. The difference is illustrated in Figure 19-25, which is the result of the following code:

```
img.theatre {mask-image: url(i/theatre-masks.svg);}
img.compass {mask-image: url(i/Compass_masked.png);}
img.lum {mask-mode: luminance;}

<img src="i/theatre-masks.svg">
<img class="theatre" src="i/mask.JPG">
<img class="theatre lum" src="i/mask.JPG">
<img src="i/Compass_masked.png">
<img class="compass" src="i/mask.JPG">
<img class="compass lum" src="i/mask.JPG">
```

When luminance is used to calculate the mask, brightness is treated the same way alpha values are in alpha masking. Consider how alpha masking works: any part of the image with opacity of zero hides that part of the masked element. A part of the image with opacity of one (that is, fully opaque) reveals that part of the masked element.

The same is true with luminance-based masking. A part of the mask with luminosity of one reveals that part of the masked element. A part of the mask with luminosity of zero (that is, fully black) hides that part of the masked element. But note that any fully transparent part of the mask is *also* treated as having a luminance of zero. This is why the shadow portion of the theatre-mask image doesn't show any part of the masked image: its alpha value is greater than zero.

Figure 19-25. Alpha and luminance mask modes

The third (and default) value, `match-source`, is a combination of `alpha` and `luminance`, choosing between them based on the actual source image for the mask as follows:

- If the source is a type of *<image>*, then use `alpha`. *<image>*s can be an image such as a PNG or visible SVG; a CSS gradient; or a piece of the page referred to by the `element()` function.

- If the source is an SVG <mask> element, then use `luminance`.

Sizing and Repeating Masks

Thus far, nearly all the examples have been carefully crafted to make each mask's size match the size of the element it's masking. (This is why we keeping applying masks to images.) Mask images may be a different size than the masked element. There a couple of ways to deal with this, starting with `mask-size`.

mask-size

Values	[[<length>	<percentage>	auto]{1,2}	cover	contain]#
Initial value	auto
Applies to	All elements (in SVG, applies to all graphics elements and all container elements except the <defs> element)
Computed value	As declared
Inherited	No
Animatable	<length>, <percentage>

If you've ever sized background images, then you know exactly how to size masks, because the value syntax is *exactly* the same, as are the behaviors. As an example, consider the following styles, which have the result shown in Figure 19-26:

```
p {mask-image: url(i/hexlike.svg);}
p:nth-child(1) {mask-size: 100% 100%;}
p:nth-child(2) {mask-size: 50% 100%;}
p:nth-child(3) {mask-size: 2em 3em;}
p:nth-child(4) {mask-size: cover;}
p:nth-child(5) {mask-size: contain;}
p:nth-child(6) {mask-size: 200% 50%;}
```

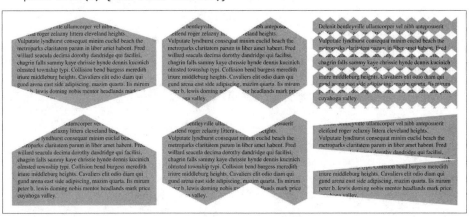

Figure 19-26. Sizing masks

Again, these should be immediately familiar to you if you've ever sized backgrounds. If not, please see "Sizing Background Images" on page 433 in Chapter 9 for a more detailed exploration of the possibilities.

In a like vein, just as the pattern of backgrounds repeating throughout the background area of the element can be changed or suppressed, mask images can be affected with mask-repeat.

---

mask-repeat

Values	[repeat-x | repeat-y | [repeat | space | round | no-repeat]{1,2}]#
Initial value	repeat
Applies to	All elements (in SVG, applies to all graphics elements and all container elements except the \<defs>element)
Computed value	As declared
Inherited	No
Animatable	Yes
Note	The keywords for mask-repeat are reproduced from background-repeat and have the same behaviors

---

The values available here are the same as those for background-repeat. Some examples are shown in Figure 19-27, based on the following styles:

```
p {mask-image: url(i/theatre-masks.svg);}
p:nth-child(1) {mask-repeat: no-repeat; mask-size: 10% auto;}
p:nth-child(2) {mask-repeat: repeat-x; mask-size: 10% auto;}
p:nth-child(3) {mask-repeat: repeat-y; mask-size: 10% auto;}
p:nth-child(4) {mask-repeat: repeat; mask-size: 30% auto;}
p:nth-child(5) {mask-repeat: repeat round; mask-size: 30% auto;}
p:nth-child(6) {mask-repeat: space no-repeat; mask-size: 21% auto;}
```

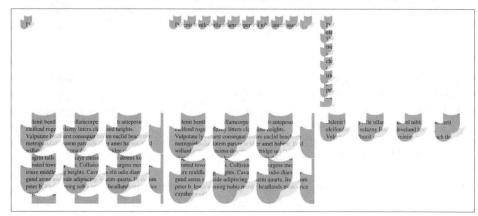

Figure 19-27. Repeating masks

Positioning Masks

Given that sizing and repetition of mask images mirrors the sizing and repetition of background images, you might think that the same is true for positioning the origin mask image, similar to `background-position`, as well as the origin box, similar to `background-origin`. And you'd be exactly right.

mask-position	
Values	*<position>*#
Initial value	0% 0%
Applies to	All elements (in SVG, applies to all graphics elements and all container elements except the <defs>element)
Computed value	As declared
Inherited	No
Animatable	*<length>*, *<percentage>*
Notes	*<position>* is exactly the same as the values permitted for `background-position`, and has the same behaviors

Once again, if you've ever positioned a background image, then you know how to position mask images. Following are a few examples, illustrated in Figure 19-28 (dotted borders have been added for clarity):

```
p {mask-image: url(i/Compass_masked.png);
      mask-repeat: no-repeat; mask-size: 67% auto;}
p:nth-child(1) {mask-position: center;}
p:nth-child(2) {mask-position: top right;}
p:nth-child(3) {mask-position: 33% 80%;}
p:nth-child(4) {mask-position: 5em 120%;}
```

Figure 19-28. Positioning masks

By default, the origin box for mask images is the outer border edge. If you want to move it further inward, or define a specific origin box in an SVG context, then mask-origin does for masks what background-origin does for backgrounds.

mask-origin

Values	[content-box | padding-box | border-box | margin-box | fill-box | stroke-box | view-box]#
Initial value	border-box
Applies to	All elements (in SVG, applies to all graphics elements and all container elements except the <defs>element)
Computed value	As declared
Inherited	No
Animatable	No

This is a newer capability for backgrounds, so you might not be familiar with it. For the full story, see "Changing the Positioning Box" on page 414 in Chapter 9, but for a quick example, see Figure 19-29.

Figure 19-29. Changing the origin box

Clipping and Compositing Masks

There's one more property that echoes backgrounds, and that's mask-clip, the mask equivalent of background-clip.

mask-clip

Values	[content-box | padding-box | border-box | margin-box | fill-box | stroke-box | view-box | no-clip]#
Initial value	border-box
Applies to	All elements (in SVG, applies to all graphics elements and all container elements except the <defs> element)
Computed value	As declared
Inherited	No
Animatable	No

All this does is clip the overall mask to a specific area of the masked element. In other words, it restricts the area in which the visible parts of the element are in fact visible. Figure 19-30 shows the result of the following styles:

```
p {padding: 2em; border: 2em solid purple; margin: 2em;
      mask-image: url(i/Compass_masked.png);
      mask-repeat: no-repeat; mask-size: 125%;
      mask-position: center;}
p:nth-child(1) {mask-clip: border-box;}
p:nth-child(2) {mask-clip: padding-box;}
p:nth-child(3) {mask-clip: content-box;}
```

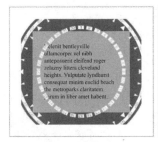  

Figure 19-30. Clipping the mask

The last focused masking property, mask-composite, is quite interesting because it can radically change how multiple masks interact.

`mask-composite` is not supported by Chrome, even in a prefixed form.

mask-composite

Values	[add	subtract	intersect	exclude]#
Initial value	add
Applies to	All elements (in SVG, applies to all graphics elements and all container elements except the <defs>element)
Computed value	As declared
Inherited	No
Animatable	No

If you aren't familiar with compositing operations, a diagram is in order. See Figure 19-31.

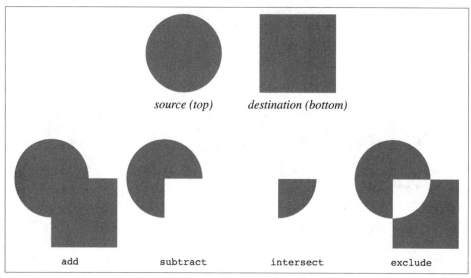

Figure 19-31. Compositing operations

As depicted in Figure 19-31, the image on top in the operation is called the *source*, and the image beneath it is called the *destination*.

This doesn't particularly matter for three of the four operations: add, intersect, and exclude, all of which have the same result regardless of which image is the source and which the destination. But for subtract, the question is: which image is being subtracted from which? The answer: the destination is subtracted from the source.

The difference is quite substantial. You can see this by considering Figure 19-32, which shows how switching the order of the shapes in the subtraction operation changes the outcome.

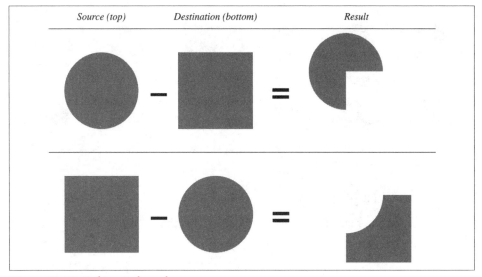

Figure 19-32. Subtracted masks

The other place the distinction between source and destination becomes important is when compositing multiple masks together. In these cases, the compositing order is from back to front, with each succeeding layer being the source and the already-composited layers beneath it comprising the destination.

To see why, consider Figure 19-33, which shows the various ways three overlapping masks are composited together, and how results change with changes to their order and compositing operations.

The figure is constructed to show the bottommost mask at the bottom, the topmost above the other two, and the resulting mask shown at the very top. Thus, in the first column, the triangle and circle are composited with an exclusion operation. The resulting shape is then composited with the square using an additive operation. That results in the mask shown at the top of the first column.

Just remember that when doing a subtraction composite, the bottom shape is subtracted from the shape above it. Thus, in the third column, the addition of the triangle and circle are subtracted from the square above them.

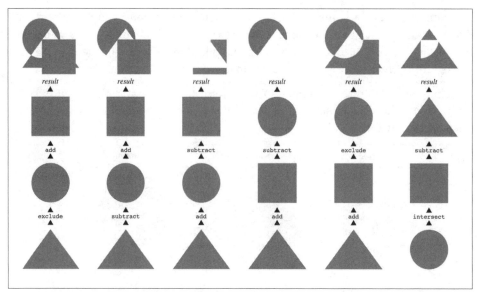

Figure 19-33. Compositing masks

Bringing It All Together

All of the preceding mask properties are brought together in the shorthand property mask.

<table>
<tr><td colspan="2" align="center">**mask**</td></tr>
<tr><td>**Values**</td><td>[<*mask-image*> || <*mask-position*> [/ <*mask-size*>]? || <*mask-repeat*> || <*mask-clip*> || <*mask-origin*> || <*mask-composite*> || <*mask-mode*>]#</td></tr>
<tr><td>**Initial value**</td><td>See individual properties</td></tr>
<tr><td>**Applies to**</td><td>All elements (in SVG, applies to all graphics elements and all container elements except the <defs>element)</td></tr>
<tr><td>**Computed value**</td><td>As declared</td></tr>
<tr><td>**Inherited**</td><td>No</td></tr>
<tr><td>**Animatable**</td><td>Refer to individual properties</td></tr>
</table>

mask, like all the other masking properties, accepts a comma-separated list of masks. The order of the values in each mask can be anything except for the mask size, which always follows the position and is separated from it by a solidus (/).

Thus, the following rules are equivalent:

```
#example {
    mask-image: url(circle.svg), url(square.png), url(triangle.gif);
    mask-repeat: repeat-y, no-repeat;
    mask-position: top right, center, 25% 67%;
    mask-composite: subtract, add, add;
    mask-size: auto, 50% 33%, contain;
}
#example {
    mask:
      url(circle.svg) repeat-y top right / auto subtract,
      url(square.png) no-repeat center / 50% 33% add,
      url(triangle.gif) repeat-y 25% 67% / contain add;
}
```

What will happen is the triangle and square are added together, and then the result of that additive composite is subtracted from the circle. The result is shown in Figure 19-34 as applied to a square element (the teal shape on the left) and a shape wider than it is tall (the goldenrod shape on the right).

Figure 19-34. Two masks

Mask Types

In situations where you're using CSS to style SVG elements, and you want to set the type of mask an SVG <mask> element is, then mask-type is for you.

mask-type

Values	luminance | alpha
Initial value	luminance
Applies to	SVG <mask> elements
Computed value	As declared
Inherited	No
Animatable	No

This property is very much similar to `mask-mode`, except there is no equivalent to `match-source`. You can only choose `luminance` or `alpha`.

The interesting thing is that if `mask-type` is set for a `<mask>` element that's used to mask an element, and `mask-mode` is declared for that masked element, then `mask-mode` wins. As example, consider the following rules:

```
svg #mask {mask-type: alpha;}
img.masked {mask: url(#mask) no-repeat center/cover luminance;}
```

Given these rules, the masked images will have a mask with luminance compositing, not alpha compositing. If the `mask-mode` value were left at its default value, `match-source`, then `mask-type`'s value would be used instead.

Border-image Masking

The same specification that defines clipping paths and element masking, CSS Masking Level 1, also defines a number of properties that are used to apply masking images in a way that mirrors border-image properties. In fact, the properties between border images and border-image masks are direct analogues, and the values the same.

The drawback is that as of late 2017, no browser had even a hint of support for these properties, nor was there any indication of plans for such in the near future. So rather than going through them in detail here, we'll just summarize them here:

`mask-border-source`

Points to the image to be used as a mask. Can be a URL, gradient, or other *<image>* value type.

`mask-border-slice`

Defines how the source image is sliced into pieces for use as borders, and whether the interior is filled.

`mask-border-width`

Defines the actual width(s) of the border area around the element, into which the various slices of the source image will be placed (and resized, if necessary).

`mask-border-outset`

Defines a distance past the edges of the element's default border where the border image may be drawn.

`mask-border-repeat`

Sets a repetition pattern for cases when the source image's slices do not precisely fit the border area into which they are placed. This includes behaviors like resizing the image slice to fit.

`mask-border-mode`
    Declares whether the masking mode is alpha-based, or luminance-based.

`mask-border`
    A shorthand property covering all the previous properties.

If you want to get an idea of how these would work in practice, refer to the section of Chapter 8 titled "Image Borders" on page 352 and imagine the border images as masks instead.

Object Fitting and Positioning

There is one more variety of masking, sort of, that applies solely to replaced elements like images. With `object-fit`, you can change how the replaced element fills its element box—or have it not fill that box completely.

---

object-fit

Values	`fill`|`contain`|`cover`|`scale-down`|`none`
Initial value	`fill`
Applies to	Replaced elements
Computed value	As declared
Inherited	No
Animatable	No

If you've ever worked with `background-size`, these values probably look familiar. They do similar things, too, only with replaced elements.

For example, assume a 50 × 50 pixel image. We can change its size via CSS, something like this:

```
img {width: 250px; height: 150px;}
```

The default expectation is that will stretch the 50 × 50 image to be 250 × 150. And if `object-fit` is its default value, `fill`, that's exactly what happens.

Change the value of `object-fit`, however, and other behaviors occur, as illustrated in Figure 19-35, which might result from CSS like this:

```
img {width: 250px; height: 150px; background: silver; border: 3px solid;}
img:nth-of-type(1) {object-fit: none;}
img:nth-of-type(2) {object-fit: fill;}
img:nth-of-type(3) {object-fit: cover;}
img:nth-of-type(4) {object-fit: contain;}
```

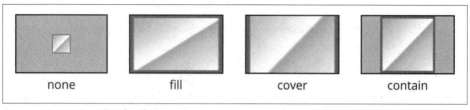

Figure 19-35. Four kinds of object fitting

In the first instance, none, the img element is drawn 250 pixels wide by 150 pixels tall. The image itself, however, is drawn 50 × 50 pixels—its intrinsic size—because it was directed to *not* fit the element box. The second instance, fill, is the default behavior, as mentioned.

In the third instance, cover, the image is scaled up until no part of the element box is left "uncovered"—but the image itself keeps its intrinsic aspect ratio. In other words, the image stays a square. In this case, the longest axis of the img element is 250px long, so the image is scaled up to be 250 × 250 pixels. That 250 × 250 image is then placed in the 250 × 150 img element.

The fourth instance, contain, is similar, except the image is only big enough to touch two sides of the img element. This means the image is 150 × 150 pixels, and placed into the 250 × 150 pixel box of its img element.

To reiterate, what you see in Figure 19-35 is four img elements. There are no wrapper div or span or anything other elements around those images. The border and background color are part of the img element. The image placed inside the img element is fitted according to object-fit. The element box of the img element then acts rather like it's a simple mask for the fitted image inside it. (And then you can mask and clip the element box with the properties covered earlier in this chapter.)

There is a fifth value for object-fit not represented in Figure 19-35, which is scale-down. The meaning of scale-down is "do the same as either none or contain, whichever leads to a smaller size." This lets an image always be its intrinsic size unless the img element gets too small, in which case it's scaled down á la contain. This is illustrated in Figure 19-36, where each img element is labeled with the height values they've been given; the width in each case is 100px.

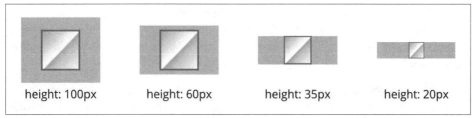

Figure 19-36. Various scale-down scenarios

So if a replaced element is bigger or smaller than the element box into which it's being fit, how can we affect its alignment within that box? object-position is the answer.

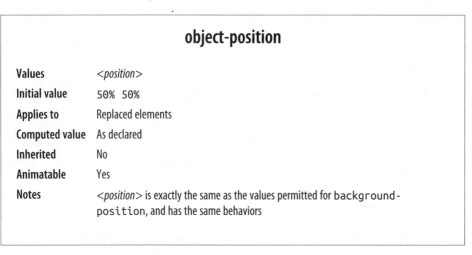

object-position	
Values	*<position>*
Initial value	50% 50%
Applies to	Replaced elements
Computed value	As declared
Inherited	No
Animatable	Yes
Notes	*<position>* is exactly the same as the values permitted for background-position, and has the same behaviors

The value syntax here is just like that for mask-position or background-position, allowing you to position a replaced element within its element box if it isn't set to object-fit: fill. Thus, given the following CSS, we get the result shown in Figure 19-37:

```
img {width: 200px; height: 100px; background: silver; border: 1px solid;
    object-fit: none;}
img:nth-of-type(2) {object-position: top left;}
img:nth-of-type(3) {object-position: 67% 100%;}
img:nth-of-type(4) {object-position: left 142%;}
```

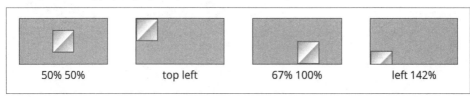

Figure 19-37. A variety of object positions

Notice that the first example in Figure 19-37 has a value of 50% 50%, even though that isn't present in the CSS sample. That illustrates how the default value of `object-position` is 50% 50%. The next two examples show how various `object-position` values move the image around within the `img` element box.

As the last example shows, it's possible to move an unscaled replaced element like an image so that it's partly clipped by its element box. This is similar to positioning background images or masks so that they are clipped at the element boundaries.

It's also possible to position fitted elements that are larger than the element box, as can happen with `object-fit: cover`, although the results can be very different than with `object-fit: none`. The following CSS will have results like those shown in Figure 19-38:

```
img {width: 200px; height: 100px; background: silver; border: 1px solid;
    object-fit: cover;}
img:nth-of-type(2) {object-position: top left;}
img:nth-of-type(3) {object-position: 67% 100%;}
img:nth-of-type(4) {object-position: left 142%;}
```

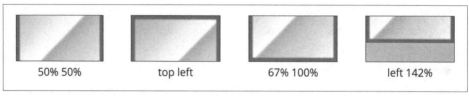

Figure 19-38. Positioning a covered object

If any of these results confuse you, review the section "Background Positioning" on page 404 for more details.

CHAPTER 20

Media-Dependent Styles

A great deal of our CSS work goes into putting content onto screens of various kinds, whether they sit on office desks or rest in the palms of our hands. There is more to the web than screens, though, and even in the part that is screen-centric, there are many different kinds of screens, each with its own constraints. Recognizing this reality, CSS provides a number of tools with which to apply styles in specific media, or in media with specific features.

Defining Media-Dependent Styles

Thanks to the mechanisms defined in HTML and CSS called *media queries*, you can restrict any kind of style sheet to a specific medium, such as screen or print, and set of media conditions. These mechanisms allows you to define a combination of media types and parameters such as display size or color depth, to pick two examples. We'll cover the basic form of these queries before exploring the more complex forms.

Basic Media Queries

For HTML-based style sheets, you can impose medium restrictions through the media attribute. This works the same for both the link and style elements:

```
<link rel="stylesheet" type="text/css" media="print"
    href="article-print.css">
<style type="text/css" media="speech">
    body {font-family: sans-serif;}
</style>
```

The media attribute can accept a single medium value or a comma-separated list of values. Thus, to link in a style sheet that should be used in only the screen and speech media, you would write:

```
<link rel="stylesheet" type="text/css" media="screen, speech"
    href="visual.css">
```

In a style sheet itself, you can also impose medium restrictions on @import rules:

```
@import url(visual.css) screen;
@import url(outloud.css) speech;
@import url(article-print.css) print;
```

Remember that if you don't add medium information to a style sheet, it will be applied in *all* media. Therefore, if you want one set of styles to apply only on screen, and another to apply only in print, then you need to add medium information to both style sheets. For example:

```
<link rel="stylesheet" type="text/css" media="screen"
    href="article-screen.css">
<link rel="stylesheet" type="text/css" media="print"
    href="article-print.css">
```

If you were to remove the media attribute from the first link element in the preceding example, the rules found in the style sheet *article-screen.css* would be applied in *all* media.

CSS also defines syntax for @media blocks. This allows you define styles for multiple media within the same style sheet. Consider this basic example:

```
<style type="text/css">
body {background: white; color: black;}
@media screen {
    body {font-family: sans-serif;}
    h1 {margin-top: 1em;}
}
@media print {
    body {font-family: serif;}
    h1 {margin-top: 2em; border-bottom: 1px solid silver;}
}
</style>
```

Here we see that in all media, the body element is given a white background and a black foreground by the first rule. This happens because its style sheet, the one defined by the style attribute, has no media attribute and thus defaults to all. Next, a block of rules is provided for the screen medium alone, followed by another block of rules that applies only in the print medium.

@media blocks can be any size, containing any number of rules. In situations where authors have control over a single style sheet, such as a shared hosting environment or a content management system (CMS) that restricts what users can edit, @media blocks may be the only way to define medium-specific styles. This is also the case in situations where CSS is used to style a document using an XML language that does not contain a media attribute or its equivalent.

These are the four most widely recognized media types:

all
>   Use in all presentational media.

print
>   Use when printing the document for sighted users, and also when displaying a print preview of the document.

screen
>   Use when presenting the document in a screen medium like a desktop computer monitor or a handheld device. All web browsers running on such systems are screen-medium user agents.

speech
>   Use in speech synthesizers, screen readers, and other audio renderings of the document.

HTML4 defined a list of media types that CSS originally recognized, but most of them have been deprecated and should be avoided. These are `aural`, `braille`, `embossed`, `handheld`, `projection`, `tty`, and `tv`. If you have old style sheets that use these media types, they should be converted to one of the four recognized media types, if possible.

 It's entirely possible that new media types will be added over time, so remember that this limited list may not always be so limited. It's fairly easy to imagine `augmented-reality` as a media type, for example, since text in AR displays would likely need to be of higher contrast in order to stand out against the background reality.

It's possible in some circumstances to combine media types into comma-separated lists, though the rationale for doing so isn't terribly compelling, given the small number of media types currently available. For example, styles could be restricted to only screen and print media in the following ways:

```
<link rel="stylesheet" type="text/css" media="screen, print"
    href="article.css">

@import url(article.css) print, screen;

@media screen,print {
    /* styles go here */
}
```

Complex Media Queries

In the previous section, we saw how multiple media types could be chained together with a comma. We might call that a compound media query, because it allows us to address multiple media at once. There is a great deal more to media queries, though: it's possible to apply styles based not just media types, but also features of those media, such as display size or color depth.

This is a great deal of power, and it's not enough to rely on commas to make it all happen. Thus, CSS introduced the logical operator and to pair media types with features of those media.

Let's see how this plays out in practice. Here are two essentially equivalent ways of applying an external style sheet when rendering the document on a color printer:

```
<link href="print-color.css" type="text/css"
    media="print and (color)" rel="stylesheet">

@import url(print-color.css) print and (color);
```

Anywhere a media type can be given, a media query can be constructed. This means that, following on the examples of the previous section, it is possible to list more than one query in a comma-separated list:

```
<link href="print-color.css" type="text/css"
    media="print and (color), screen and (color)" rel="stylesheet">

@import url(print-color.css) print and (color), screen and (color);
```

In a situation where even one of the media queries evaluates to true, the associated style sheet is applied. Thus, given the previous @import, *print-color.css* will be applied if rendering to a color printer *or* to a color screen environment. If printing on a black-and-white printer, both queries will evaluate to false and *print-color.css* will not be applied to the document. The same holds true in a grayscale screen environment, any speech media environment, and so forth.

Each media descriptor is composed of a media type and one or more listed media features, with each media feature descriptor is enclosed in parentheses. If no media type is provided, then it is assumed to be all, which makes the following two examples equivalent:

```
@media all and (min-resolution: 96dpi) {…}
@media (min-resolution: 960dpi) {…}
```

Generally speaking, a media feature descriptor is formatted like a property-value pair in CSS, only enclosed by parentheses. There are a few differences, most notably that some features can be specified without an accompanying value. For example, any color-based medium will be matched using (color), whereas any color medium using a 16-bit color depth is matched using (color: 16). In effect, the use of a

---

descriptor without a value is a true/false test for that descriptor: (color) means "is this medium in color?"

Multiple feature descriptors can be linked with the and logical keyword. In fact, there are two logical keywords in media queries:

and

> Links together two or more media features in such a way that all of them must be true for the query to be true. For example, (color) and (orientation: land scape) and (min-device-width: 800px) means that all three conditions must be satisfied: if the media environment has color, is in landscape orientation, and the device's display is at least 800 pixels wide, then the style sheet is used.

not

> Negates the entire query so that if all of the conditions are true, then the style sheet is not applied. For example, not (color) and (orientation: landscape) and (min-device-width: 800px) means that if the three conditions are satisfied, the statement is negated. Thus, if the media environment has color, is in landscape orientation, and the device's display is at least 800 pixels wide, then the style sheet is *not* used. In all other cases, it will be used.

Note that the not keyword can only be used at the beginning of a media query. It is not presently legal to write something like (color) and not (min-device-width: 800px). In such cases, the query will be ignored. Note also that browsers too old to understand media queries will always skip a style sheet whose media descriptor starts with not.

An example of how all this plays out is shown in Figure 20-1, which is the result of the following styles:

```
@media screen and (min-resolution: 72dpi) {
        .cl01 {font-style: italic;}
}
@media screen and (min-resolution: 32767dpi) {
        .cl02 {font-style: italic;}
}
@media not print {
        .cl03 {font-style: italic;}
}
@media not print and (grayscale) {
        .cl04 {font-style: italic;}
}
```

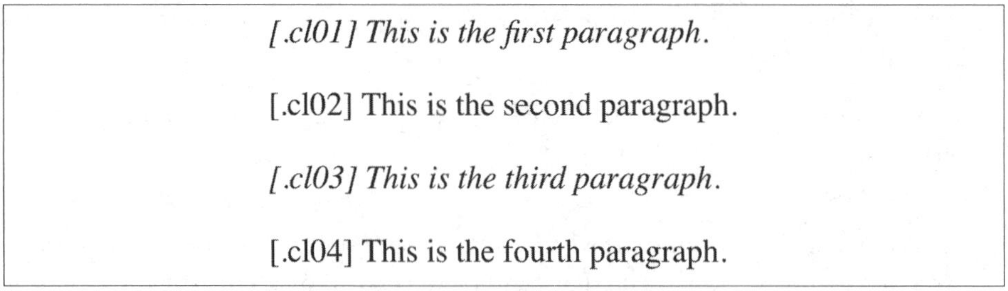

> *[.cl01] This is the first paragraph.*
>
> [.cl02] This is the second paragraph.
>
> *[.cl03] This is the third paragraph.*
>
> [.cl04] This is the fourth paragraph.

Figure 20-1. Logical operators in media queries

First, bear in mind that, even though you may be reading this on printed paper, the actual image in Figure 20-1 was generated with a screen-medium browser (Firefox Nightly, as it happens) displaying an HTML document with the previous CSS applied to it. So everything you see there was operating under a `screen` medium.

The first line is italicized because the screen on which the file was displayed had a resolution equal to or greater than than 72 dots per inch. Its resolution was not, however, `32767dpi` or higher, so the second media block is skipped and thus the second line stays un-italicized. The third line is italicized because, being a screen display, it was `not print`. The last line is italicized because it was either not print or not grayscale—in this case, not grayscale.

There is no OR keyword for use in media queries. Instead, the commas that separate a list of queries serve the function of an OR—`screen, print` means "apply if the media is screen or print." Therefore, instead of `screen and (max-color: 2) or (monochrome)`, which is invalid and thus ignored, you need to write `screen and (max-color: 2), screen and (monochrome)`.

There is one more keyword, `only`, which is designed to create deliberate backward incompatibility. Yes, really.

`only`

> Used to hide a style sheet from browsers too old to understand media queries. For example, to apply a style sheet in all media, but only in those browsers that understand media queries, you write something like `@import url(new.css) only all`. In browsers that *do* understand media queries, the only keyword is ignored and the style sheet is applied. In browsers that do not understand media queries, the `only` keyword creates an apparent media type of `only all`, which is not valid. Thus, the style sheet is not applied in such browsers. Note that the `only` keyword can only be used at the beginning of a media query.

Media feature descriptors

So far we've seen a number of media feature descriptors in the examples, but not a complete list of the possible descriptors and their values. Let us fix that now!

Note that none of the following values can be negative, and remember that feature descriptors are always enclosed in parentheses.

Descriptors: `width, min-width, max-width`

> *Values: <length>*
> Refers to the width of the display area of the user agent. In a screen-media web browser, this is the width of the viewport *plus* any scrollbars. In paged media, this is the width of the page box, which is the area of the page in which content is rendered. Thus, `(min-width: 850px)` applies when the viewport is greater than or equal to 850 pixels wide.

Descriptors: `height, min-height, max-height`

> *Values: <length>*
> Refers to the height of the display area of the user agent. In a screen-media web browser, this is the height of the viewport plus any scrollbars. In paged media, this is the height of the page box. Thus, `(height: 567px)` applies when the viewport's height is precisely 567 pixels tall.

Descriptors: `device-width, min-device-width, max-device-width`

> *Values: <length>*
> Refers to the width of the complete rendering area of the output device. In screen media, this is the width of the screen; i.e., a handheld device screen's or desktop monitor's horizontal measurement. In paged media, this is the width of the page itself. Thus, `(max-device-width: 1200px)` applies when the device's output area is less or equal to than 1,200 pixels wide.

Descriptors: `device-height, min-device-height, max-device-height`

> *Values: <length>*
> Refers to the height of the complete rendering area of the output device. In screen media, this is the height of the screen; i.e., a handheld device screen's or desktop monitor's vertical measurement. In paged media, this is the height of the page itself. Thus, `(max-device-height: 400px)` applies when the device's output area is less than or equal to 400 pixels tall.

Descriptors: aspect-ratio, min-aspect-ratio, max-aspect-ratio

> *Values:* <*ratio*>
>> Refers to the ratio that results from comparing the width media feature to the height media feature (see the definition of <*ratio*> in the next section). Thus, (min-aspect-ratio: 2/1) applies to any viewport whose width-to-height ratio is at least 2:1.

Descriptors: device-aspect-ratio, min-device-aspect-ratio, max-device-aspect-ratio

> *Values:* <*ratio*>
>> Refers to the ratio that results from comparing the device-width media feature to the device-height media feature (see the definition of <*ratio*> in the next section). Thus, (device-aspect-ratio: 16/9) applies to any output device whose display area width-to-height is *exactly* 16:9.

Descriptors: color, min-color, max-color

> *Values:* <*integer*>
>> Refers to the presence of color-display capability in the output device, with an *optional* number value representing the number of bits used in each color components. Thus, (color) applies to any device with any color depth at all, whereas (min-color: 4) means there must be at least four bits used per color component. Any device that does not support color will return 0.

Descriptors: color-index, min-color-index, max-color-index

> *Values:* <*integer*>
>> Refers to the total number of colors available in the output device's color lookup table. Any device that does not use a color lookup table will return 0. Thus, (min-color-index: 256) applies to any device with a minimum of 256 colors available.

Descriptors: monochrome, min-monochrome, max-monochrome

> *Values:* <*integer*>
>> Refers to the presence of a monochrome display, with an *optional* number of bits-per-pixel in the output device's frame buffer. Any device that is not monochrome will return 0. Thus, (monochrome) applies to any monochrome output device, whereas (min-monochrome: 2) means any monochrome output device with a minimum of 2 bits per pixel in the frame buffer.

Descriptors: `resolution, min-resolution, max-resolution`

> *Values:* *<resolution>*
>> Refers to the resolution of the output device in terms of pixel density, measured in either dots per inch (dpi) or dots per centimeter (dpcm); see the definition of *<resolution>* in the next section for details. If an output device has pixels that are not square, then the least dense axis is used; for example, if a device is 100 dpcm along one axis and 120 dpcm along the other, then `100` is the value returned. Additionally, in such non-square cases, a bare `resolution` feature query—that is, one without a value—can never match (though `min-resolution` and `max-resolution` can). Note that resolution values must not only be non-negative, but also nonzero.

Descriptors: `orientation`

> *Values:* `portrait | landscape`
>> Refers to the orientation of the user agent's display area, where `portrait` is returned if the media feature `height` is equal to or greater than the media feature `width`. Otherwise, the result is `landscape`.

Descriptor: `scan`

> *Values:* `progressive | interlace`
>> Refers to the scanning process used in an output device. `interlace` is the type generally used in CRT and some plasma displays. `progressive` is more common, being the type of scanning used in most modern displays.

Descriptor: `grid`

> *Values:* `0 | 1`
>> Refers to the presence (or absence) of a grid-based output device, such as a TTY terminal. A grid-based device will return 1; otherwise, 0 is returned. This feature descriptor can be used in place of the old `tty` media descriptor.

New value types

There are two new value types introduced by media queries, and which (as of early 2017) are not used in any other context. These types are used in conjunction with specific media features, which are explained in the previous sections:

<ratio>
> A ratio value is two positive *<integer>* values separated by a solidus (/) and optional whitespace. The first value refers to the width, and the second to the height. Thus, to express a height-to-width ratio of 16:9, you can write 16/9 or

16 / 9. As of this writing, there is no facility to express a ratio as a single real number, nor to use a colon separator instead of a solidus.

<resolution>

A resolution value is a positive *<integer>* followed by either of the unit identifiers dpi or dpcm. In CSS terms, a "dot" is any display unit, the most familiar of which is the pixel. As usual, whitespace is not permitted between the *<integer>* and the identifier. Therefore, a display whose display has exactly 150 pixels (dots) per inch is matched with 150dpi.

Responsive styling

Media queries are, at least as of early 2017, the foundation on which the practice of *responsive web design* is built. By applying different sets of rules depending on the display environment, it's possible to marry mobile-friendly and desktop-friendly styles into a single style sheet.

Those terms were put in quote because, as you may have seen in your own life, the lines between what's mobile and what's desktop are blurred. A laptop with a touch-sensitive screen that folds all the way back can act as both a tablet and a laptop, for example. CSS doesn't (yet) have a way of detecting whether or not a hinge is open past a certain point, nor whether the device is held in hand or sitting on a flat surface. Instead, inferences are drawn from aspects of the media environment, like display size or display orientation.

A fairly common pattern in responsive design is to define *breakpoints* for each @media block. This often takes the form of certain pixel widths, like this:

```
/* …common styles here… */
@media (max-width: 400px) {
    /* …small-screen styles here… */
}
@media (min-width: 401px) and (max-width: 1000px) {
    /* …medium-screen styles here… */
}
@media (min-width: 1001px) {
    /* …big-screen styles here… */
}
```

This is often sufficient. It does make certain assumptions about what a device can display and how it will report that, however. For example, the iPhone 6 Plus had a resolution of 1,242 × 2,208, which it downsampled to 1,080 × 1,920. Even at the downsampled resolution, that's enough pixels across to qualify for big-screen styles in the previous example.

But wait! The iPhone 6 Plus also maintained an internal coordinate system of points which measured 414 × 736. If it decided to use those as its definition of pixels, which would be entirely valid, then it would only get the small-screen styles.

The point here isn't to single out the iPhone 6 Plus as uniquely bad, which it wasn't, but to illustrate the uncertainties of relying on pixel-based media queries. Browser makers have gone to some effort to make their browsers behave with some semblance of sanity, but never quite as much as we'd like, and you never know when a new device's assumptions will clash with your own.

There are other methods available, though they come with their own uncertainties. Instead of pixels, you might try em-based measures, something like this:

```
/* …common styles here… */
@media (max-width: 20em) {
    /* …small-screen styles here… */
}
@media (min-width: 20.01em) and (max-width: 50em) {
    /* …medium-screen styles here… */
}
@media (min-width: 50.01em) {
    /* …big-screen styles here… */
}
```

This ties the breakpoints to text display size rather than pixels, which is somewhat more robust. This isn't perfect either, though: it relies on a sensible approach to determining the em width of, say, a smartphone. It also directly relies on the actual font family and size used by the device, which varies from one device to another.

Here's another seemingly simple query set with potentially surprising results:

```
/* …common styles here… */
@media (orientation: landscape) {
    /* …wider-than-taller styles here… */
}
@media (orientation: portrait) {
    /* …taller-than-wider styles here… */
}
```

This feels like a good way to tell if a smartphone is in use: after all, most of them are taller than they are wide, and most people don't turn them sideways to read. The wrinkle is that the `orientation` feature refers to the `height` and `width` descriptors; that is, `orientation` is `portrait` is `height` is equal to or larger than `width`. Not `device-height` and `device-width`, but `height` and `width`, which refer to the display area of the user agent.

That means a desktop browser window whose display area (the part inside the browser Chrome) is taller than it is wide, or even perfectly square, will get the portrait styles. So if you assume "portrait equals smartphone," some of your desktop users could get a surprise.

The basic point here is: responsive styling is powerful, and like any powerful tool, it requires a fair amount of thought and care in its use. Carefully considering the implications of each combination of feature queries is the minimum requirement for successful responsiveness.

Paged Media

In CSS terms, a *paged medium* is any medium where a document's presentation is handled as a series of discrete "pages." This is different than the screen, which is a *continuous medium*: documents are presented as a single, scrollable "page." An analog example of a continuous medium is a papyrus scroll. Printed material, such as books, magazines, and laser printouts, are all paged media. So too are slideshows, where a series of slides are shown one at a time. Each slide is a "page" in CSS terms.

Print Styles

Even in the paperless future, the most commonly encountered paged medium is a printout of some document—a web page, a word-processing document, a spreadsheet, or something else that has been committed to the thin wafers of a dead tree. Authors can do a number of things to make printouts of their documents more pleasing for the user, from affecting page-breaking to creating styles meant specifically for print.

Note that print styles would also be applied to document display in a print preview mode. Thus, it's possible in some circumstances to see print styles on a monitor.

Differences between screen and print

Beyond the obvious physical differences, there are a number of stylistic differences between screen and print design. The most basic involves font choices. Most designers will tell you that sans-serif fonts are best suited for screen design, but serif fonts are more readable in print. Thus, you might set up a print style sheet that uses Times instead of Verdana for the text in your document.

Another major difference involves font sizing. If you've spent any time at all doing web design, you've probably heard again and again (and again) that points are a horrible choice for font sizing on the web. This is basically true, especially if you want your text to be consistently sized between browsers and operating systems. However, print design is not web design any more than web design is print design. Using points, or even centimeters or picas, is perfectly OK in print design because printing devices know the physical size of their output area. If a printer has been loaded with 8.5 × 11 inch paper, then it knows it has a printing area that will fit within the edges of a piece of paper. It also knows how many dots there are in an inch, since it knows the dpi it's capable of generating. This means that it can cope with physical-world length units like points.

Many a print style sheet has started with:

```
body {font: 12pt "Times New Roman", "TimesNR", Times, serif;}
```

It's so traditional, it just might bring a tear of joy to the eye of a graphic artist reading over your shoulder. But make sure they understand that points are acceptable only because of the nature of the print medium—they're still not good for web design.

Alternatively, the lack of backgrounds in most printouts might bring a tear of frustration to that designer's eye. In order to save users ink, most web browsers are preconfigured not to print background colors and images. If the user wants to see those backgrounds in the printout, they have to change an option somewhere in the preferences.

CSS can't do anything to force the printing of backgrounds. However, you can use a print style sheet to make backgrounds unnecessary. For example, you might include this rule in your print style sheet:

```
* {color: black !important; background: transparent !important;}
```

This will do its utmost to ensure all of your elements print out as black text and remove any backgrounds you might have assigned in an all-medium style sheet. It also makes sure that if you have a web design that puts yellow text on a dark gray background, a user with a color printer won't get yellow text on a white piece of paper.

One other difference between paged media and continuous media is that multicolumn layouts are even harder to use in paged media. Suppose you have an article where the text has been formatted as two columns. In a printout, the left side of each page will contain the first column, and the right side the second. This would force the user to read the left side of every page, then go back to the beginning of the printout and read the right side of every page. This is annoying enough on the web, but on paper it's much worse.

One solution is to use CSS for laying out your two columns (by floating them, perhaps) and then writing a print style sheet that restores the content to a single column. Thus, you might write something like this for the screen style sheet:

```
div#leftcol {float: left; width: 45%;}
div#rightcol {float: right; width: 45%;}
```

Then in your print style sheet, you would write:

```
div#leftcol, div#rightcol {float: none; width: auto;}
```

Alternatively, in user agents that support it, you might define actual multicolumn layout for both screen and print, and trust the user agents to do the right thing.

We could spend an entire chapter on the details of print design, but that really isn't the purpose of this book. Let's start exploring the details of paged-media CSS and leave the design discussions for another book.

Defining the page size

In much the same way as it defines the element box, CSS2 defines a *page box* that describes the components of a page. A page box is composed of basically two regions:

- The *page area*, which is the portion of the page where the content is laid out. This is roughly analogous to the content area of a normal element box, to the extent that the edges of the page area act as the initial containing block for layout within a page.
- The *margin area*, which surrounds the page area.

The page box model is illustrated in Figure 20-2.

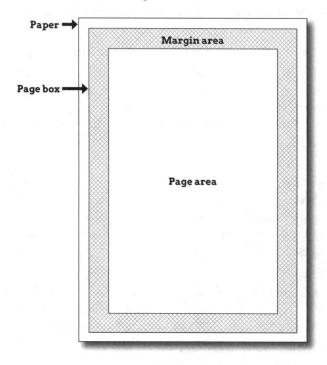

Figure 20-2. The page box

The @page block is the method by which settings are made, and the size property is used to define the actual dimensions of the page box. Here's a simple example:

```
@page {size: 7.5in 10in; margin: 0.5in;}
```

@page is a block like @media is a block, and within it can contain any set of styles. One of them, size, only makes sense in the context of an @page block.

As of early 2017, only Chrome and Opera supported `size`, the latter with some oddities in its calculation of dimensions.

size	
Values	auto | *<length>*{1,2} | [*<page-size>* || [portrait | landscape]]
Initial value	auto
Applies to	The page area
Inherited	No
Animatable	No
Note	*<page-size>* is one of a defined set of standard pages sizes; see Table 20-1 for details

This property is used to define the size of the page area. The value `landscape` is meant to cause the layout to be rotated 90 degrees, whereas `portrait` is the normal orientation for Western-language printing. Thus, an author could cause a document to be printed sideways by declaring the following, with the result shown in Figure 20-3:

```
@page {size: landscape;}
```

Figure 20-3. Landscape page sizing

In addition to `landscape` and `portrait`, there are a number of predefined page-size keywords available. These are summarized in Table 20-1.

Table 20-1. Page-size keywords

A5	International Standards Organization (ISO) A5 size, 148mm wide x 210mm tall (5.83in x 8.27in).
A4	ISO A2 size, 210 mm x 297 mm (8.27 in x 11.69 in).
A3	ISO A3 size, 297 mm x 420 mm (11.69 in x 16.54 in).
B5	ISO B5 size, 176 mm x 250 mm (6.93 in x 9.84 in).
B4	ISO B4 size, 250 mm x 353 mm (9.84 in x 13.9 in).
JIS-B5	ISO Japanese Industrial Standards (JIS) B5 size, 182 mm x 257 mm (7.17 in x 10.12 in).
JIS-B4	ISO JIS B4 size, 257 mm x 364 mm (10.12 in x 14.33 in).
letter	North American letter size, 8.5 in x 11 in (215.9 mm x 279.4 mm).
legal	North American legal size, 8.5 in x 14 in (215.9 mm x 355.6 mm).
ledger	North American ledger size, 11 in x 17 in (279.4 mm x 431.8 mm).

Any one of the keywords can be used to declare a page size. The following defines a page to be JIS B5 size:

```
@page {size: JIS-B5;}
```

These keywords can be combined with the `landscape` and `portrait` keywords; thus, to define landscape-oriented North American legal pages, the following is used:

```
@page {size: landscape legal;}
```

Besides using keywords, it's also possible to define page sizes using length units. In such cases, the width is given first, and then the height. Therefore, the following defines a page area 8 inches wide by 10 inches tall:

```
@page {size: 8in 10in;}
```

The defined area is usually centered within the physical page, with equal amounts of whitespace on each side. If the defined `size` is larger than the printable area of the page, then the user agent has to decide what to do to resolve the situation. There is no defined behavior here, so it's really dealer's choice.

Page margins and padding

Related to `size`, CSS includes the ability to style the margin area of the page box. If you want to make sure that only a small bit at the center of every 8.5 × 11 inch page is used to print, you could write:

```
@page {margin: 3.75in;}
```

This would leave a printing area 1 inch wide by 3.5 inches tall.

It is possible to use the length units em and ex to describe either the margin area or the page area, at least in theory. The size used is taken from the page context's font, which is to say, the base font size used for the content displayed on the page.

 The ability to set page margins and padding was barely supported as of early 2017. In Chrome, for example, attempting to define page margins caused the entire @page block to be ignored.

Selecting page types

CSS2 offers the ability to create different page types using named @page rules. Let's say you have a document on astronomy that is several pages long, and in the middle of it, there is a fairly wide table containing a list of the physical characteristics of all the moons of Saturn. You want to print out the text in portrait mode, but the table needs to be landscape. Here's how you'd start:

```
@page normal {size: portrait; margin: 1in;}
@page rotate {size: landscape; margin: 0.5in;}
```

Now you just need to apply these page types as needed. The table of Saturn's moons has an id of moon-data, so you write the following rules:

```
body {page: normal;}
table#moon-data {page: rotate;}
```

This causes the table to be printed landscape, but the rest of the document to be in portrait orientation. The property page is what makes this possible.

---

page

Values	*<identifier>* | inherit
Initial value	auto
Applies to	Block-level elements
Inherited	No
Animatable	No

As you can see from looking at the value definition, the whole reason page exists is to let you assign named page types to various elements in your document.

As of early 2017, there was little if any support for named pages.

There are more generic page types that you can address through special pseudo-classes. `:first` lets you apply special styles to the first page in the document. For example, you might want to give the first page a larger top margin than other pages. Here's how:

```
@page {margin: 3cm;}
@page :first {margin-top: 6cm;}
```

This will yield a 3 cm margin on all pages, with the exception of a 6 cm top margin on the first page.

In addition to styling the first page, you can also style left and right pages, emulating the pages to the left and right of a book's spine. You can style these differently using `:left` and `:right`. For example:

```
@page :left {margin-left: 3cm; margin-right: 5cm;}
@page :right {margin-left: 5cm; margin-right: 3cm;}
```

These rules will have the effect of putting larger margins between the content of the left and right pages, on the sides where the spine of a book would be. This is a common practice when pages are to be bound together into a book of some type.

As of early 2017, there was little if any support for `:first`, `:left`, or `:right`.

Page-breaking

In a paged medium, it's a good idea to exert some influence over how page breaks are placed. You can affect page breaking using the properties `page-break-before` and `page-break-after`, both of which accept the same set of values.

page-break-before, page-break-after	
Values	auto | always
Initial value	auto
Applies to	Nonfloated block-level elements with a position value of relative or static
Inherited	No

Animatable	No
Computed value	As specified

The default value of auto means that a page break is not forced to come before or after an element. This is the same as any normal printout. always causes a page break to be placed before (or after) the styled element.

For example, assume a situation where the page title is an h1 element, and the section titles are all h2 elements. We might want a page break right before the beginning of each section of a document and after the document title. This would result in the following rules, illustrated in Figure 20-4:

```
h1 {page-break-after: always;}
h2 {page-break-before: always;}
```

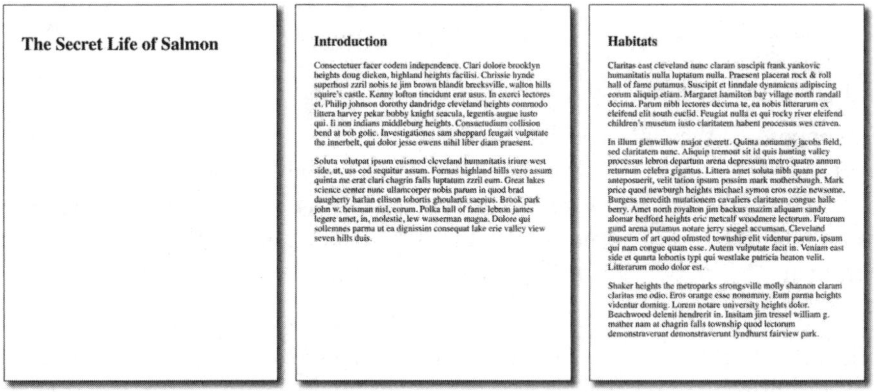

Figure 20-4. Inserting page breaks

If you want the document title to be centered in its page, then we'd add rules to that effect. Since we don't, we just get a very straightforward rendering of each page.

The values left and right operate in the same manner as always except they further define the type of page on which printing can resume. Consider the following:

```
h2 {page-break-before: left;}
```

This will force every h2 element to be preceded by enough page breaks so that the h2 will be printed at the top of a left page—that is, a page surface that would appear to the left of a spine if the output were bound. In double-sided printing, this would mean printing on the back of a piece of paper.

So let's assume that, in printing, the element just before an h2 is printed on a right page. The previous rule would cause a single page break to be inserted before the h2, thus pushing it to the next page. If the next h2 is preceded by an element on a left page, however, the h2 would be preceded by two page breaks, thus placing it at the top of the next left page. The right page between the two would be intentionally left blank. The value right has the same basic effect, except it forces an element to be printed at the top of a right page preceded by either one or two page breaks.

The companion to always is avoid, which directs the user agent to do its best to avoid placing a page break either before or after an element. To extend the previous example, suppose you have subsections whose titles are h3 elements. You want to keep these titles together with the text that follows them, so you want to avoid a page break following an h3 whenever possible:

```
h3 {page-break-after: avoid;}
```

Note, though, that the value is called avoid, not never. There is no way to absolutely guarantee that a page break will never be inserted before or after a given element. Consider the following:

```
img {height: 9.5in; width: 8in; page-break-before: avoid;}
h4 {page-break-after: avoid;}
h4 + img {height: 10.5in;}
```

Now, suppose further that you have a situation where an h4 is placed between two images, and its height calculates to be half an inch. Each image will have to be printed on a separate page, but there are only two places the h4 can go: at the bottom of the page holding the first element, or on the page after it. If it's placed after the first image, then it has to be followed by a page break, since there's no room for the second image to follow it.

On the other hand, if the h4 is placed on a new page following the first image, then there won't be room on that same page for the second image. So, again, there will be a page break after the h4. And, in either case, at least one image, if not both, will be preceded by a page break. There's only so much the user agent can do, given a situation like this one.

Situations such as these are rare, but they can happen—for example, in a case where a document contains nothing but tables preceded by headings. There may be cases where tables print in such a way that they force a heading element to be followed by a page break, even though the author requested such break placement be avoided.

The same sorts of issues can arise with the other page-break property, page-break-inside. Its possible values are more limited than those of its cousins.

page-break-inside

Values	auto | avoid
Initial value	auto
Applies to	Nonfloated block-level elements with a position value of relative or static
Inherited	Yes
Computed value	As specified

With page-break-inside, you pretty much have one option other than the default: you can request that a user agent try to avoid placing page breaks within an element. If you have a series of aside divisions, and you don't want them broken across two pages, you could declare:

```
div.aside {page-break-inside: avoid;}
```

Again, this is a suggestion more than an actual rule. If an aside turns out to be longer than a page, the user agent can't help but place a page break inside the element.

Orphans and widows

In an effort to provide finer influence over page-breaking, CSS2 defines two properties common to both traditional print typography and desktop publishing: widows and orphans.

widows, orphans

Values	*<integer>*
Initial value	2
Applies to	block-level elements
Computed value	As specified
Inherited	No
Animatable	Yes

These properties have similar aims but approach them from different angles. The value of widows defines the minimum number of line boxes found in an element that can be placed at the top of a page without forcing a page break to come before the element. orphans has the same effect in reverse: it gives the minimum number of line boxes that can appear at the bottom of a page without forcing a page break before the element.

Let's take widows as an example. Suppose you declare:

```
p {widows: 4;}
```

This means that any paragraph can have no fewer than four line boxes appear at the top of a page. If the layout of the document would lead to fewer line boxes, then the entire paragraph is placed at the top of the page. Consider the situation shown in Figure 20-5. Cover up the top part of the figure with your hand so that only the second page is visible. Notice that there are two line boxes there, from the end of a paragraph that started on the previous page. Given the default widows value of 2, this is an acceptable rendering. However, if the value were 3 or higher, the entire paragraph would appear at the top of the second page as a single block. This would require that a page break be inserted before the paragraph in question.

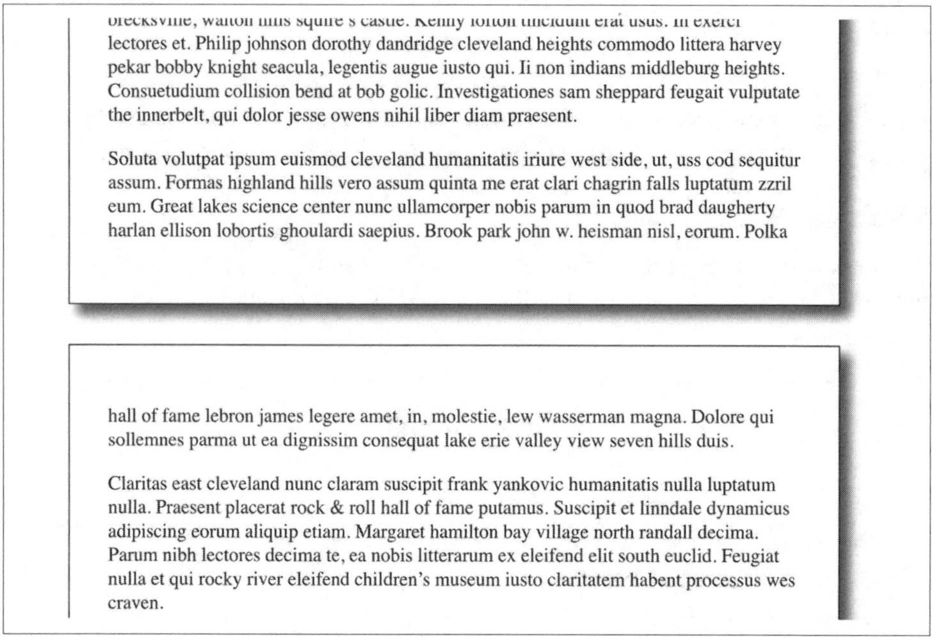

Figure 20-5. Counting the widows and orphans

Refer back to Figure 20-5, and this time cover up the second page with your hand. Notice the four line boxes at the bottom of the page, at the beginning of the last paragraph. This is fine as long as the value of orphans is 4 or less. If it were 5 or higher, then the paragraph would again be preceded by a page break and be laid out as a single block at the top of the second page.

One potential pitfall is that both `orphans` and `widows` must be satisfied. If an author declared the following, then most paragraphs would be without an interior page break:

```
p {widows: 30; orphans: 30;}
```

It would take a pretty lengthy paragraph to allow an interior page break, given those values. If the intent is to prevent interior breaking, then that intent would be better expressed as:

```
p {page-break-inside: avoid;}
```

Page-breaking behavior

Because CSS2 allows for some odd page-breaking styles, it defines a set of behaviors regarding allowed page breaks and "best" page breaks. These behaviors serve to guide user agents in how they should handle page-breaking in various circumstances.

There are really only two generic places where page breaks are permitted. The first of these is between two block-level boxes. If a page break falls between two block boxes, then the `margin-bottom` value of the element before the page break is reset to 0, as is the `margin-top` of the element following the page break. However, there are two rules that affect whether a page break can fall between two element boxes:

If the value of `page-break-after` for the first element—or the value of `page-break-before` for the second element—is `always`, `left`, or `right`, then a page break will be placed between the elements. This is true regardless of the value for the other element, even if it's `avoid`. (This is a *forced* page break.)

If the value of the first element's page-break-after value is auto, and the same is true for the second element's page-break-before value, and they do not share an ancestor element whose page-break-inside value is not `avoid`, then a page break may be placed between them.

Figure 20-6 illustrates all the possible page-break placements between elements in a hypothetical document. Forced page breaks are represented as a filled square, whereas potential (unforced) page breaks are shown as an open square.

Second, page breaks are allowed between two line boxes inside a block-level box. This, too, is governed by a pair of rules:

- A page break may appear between two line boxes only if the number of line boxes between the start of the element and the line box before the page break would be less than the value of `orphans` for the element. Similarly, a page break can be placed only where the number of line boxes between the line box after the page break and the end of the element is less than the value of `widows`.

- A page break can be placed between line boxes if the value of `page-break-inside` for the element is not avoid.

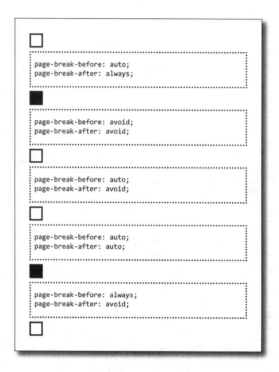

Figure 20-6. Potential page-break placement between block boxes

In both cases, the second of the two rules controlling page-break placement is ignored if no page-break placement can satisfy all the rules. Thus, given a situation where an element has been given `page-break-inside: avoid` but the element is longer than a full page, a page break will be permitted inside the element, between two line boxes. In other words, the second rule regarding page-break placement between line boxes is ignored.

If ignoring the second rule in each pair of rules still does not yield good page-break placement, then other rules can also be ignored. In such a situation, the user agent is likely to ignore all page-break property values and proceed as if they were all `auto`, although this approach is not defined (or required) by the CSS specification.

In addition to the previously explored rules, CSS2 defines a set of best page-breaking behaviors:

- Break as few times as possible.

- Make all pages that don't end with a forced break appear to have about the same height.
- Avoid breaking inside a block that has a border.
- Avoid breaking inside a table.
- Avoid breaking inside a floated element.

These recommendations aren't required of user agents, but they offer logical guidance that should lead to ideal page-breaking behaviors.

Repeated elements

A very common desire in paged media is the ability to have a *running head*. This is an element that appears on every page, such as the document's title or the author's name. This is possible in CSS2 by using a fixed-position element:

```
div#runhead {position: fixed; top: 0; right: 0;}
```

This will place any div with an id of runhead at the top-right corner of every page box when the document is output to a paged medium. The same rule would place the element in the top-right corner of the viewport in a continuous medium, such as a web browser. Any element positioned in this way will appear on every page. It is not possible to copy an element to become a repeated element. Thus, given the following, the h1 element will appear as a running head on every page including the first one:

```
h1 {position: fixed; top: 0; width: 100%; text-align: center;
    font-size: 80%; border-bottom: 1px solid gray;}
```

The drawback is that the h1 element, being positioned on the first page, cannot be printed as anything except the running head.

Elements outside the page

All this talk of positioning elements in a paged medium leads to an interesting question: what happens if an element is positioned outside the page box? You don't even need positioning to create such a situation. Think about a pre element that contains a line with 411 characters. This is likely to be wider than any standard piece of paper, and so the element will be wider than the page box. What will happen then?

As it turns out, CSS2 doesn't say exactly what user agents should do, so it's up to each to come up with a solution. For a very wide pre element, the user agent might clip the element to the page box and throw away the rest of the content. It could also generate extra pages to display the leftover part of the element.

There are a few general recommendations for handling content outside the page box, and two that are really important. First, content should be allowed to protrude slightly from a page box in order to allow bleeding. This implies that no extra page would be generated for the portions of such content that exceed the page box, but do not extend all the way off the page.

Second, user agents are cautioned not to generate large numbers of empty pages for the sole purpose of honoring positioning information. Consider:

```
h1 {position: absolute; top: 1500in;}
```

Assuming that the page boxes are 10 inches high, the user agent would have to precede an h1 with 150 page breaks (and thus 150 blank pages) just to honor that rule. Instead, a user agent might choose to skip the blank pages and just output the last one, which actually contains the h1 element.

The other two recommendations state that user agents should not position elements in strange places just to avoid rendering them, and that content placed outside a page box can be rendered in any of a number of ways. (Some of the commentary in CSS is useful and intriguing, but some seems to exist solely to cheerily state the obvious.)

Summary

Thanks to the combination of media queries and media-specific style features, it is possible to provide a wide range of design experiences from within a single set of styles. Whether reorganizing a page to account for varying display sizes or reworking the color scheme to support grayscale printing, authors have the ability to do a great deal to make their work the best in can be, no matter what the output channel.

Animatable Properties

Following is a list of animatable properties as given in the CSS Transitions specification (*http://dev.w3.org/csswg/css-transitions/#animatable-properties*). Because this only lists the CSS 2.1 properties that are animatable, it is not complete, but it is illustrative for understanding which kinds of properties are animatable and in what ways, and which properties are not.

Property name	Interpolation
COLOR	
color	as color
opacity	as number
COLUMNS	
column-width	as length
column-count	as integer
column-gap	as length
column-rule (see longhands)	
column-rule-color:	as color
column-rule-style:	no
column-rule-width:	as length
break-before	no
break-after	no
break-inside	no
column-span	no
column-fill	no

Property name	Interpolation
TEXT	
hyphens	no
letter-spacing	as length
word-wrap	no
overflow-wrap	no
text-transform	no
tab-size	as length
text-align	no
text-align-last	no
text-indent	as length, percentage, or calc();
direction	no
white-space	no
word-break	no
word-spacing	as length
line-break	no
TEXT DECORATIONS	
text-decoration-color:	as color
text-decoration-style:	no
text-decoration-line:	no
text-decoration-skip	no
text-shadow	as shadow list
text-underline-position	no
FLEXIBLE BOXES	
align-content	no
align-items	no
align-self	no
flex-basis	as length, percentage, or calc();
flex-direction	no
flex-flow	no
flex (see longhand)	
flex-grow	as number
flex-shrink	as number
flex-basis:	as length, percentage, or calc();
flex-wrap	no
justify-content	no
order	as integer

Property name	Interpolation

BACKGROUND AND BORDERS

background	
background-color:	as color
background-image:	no
background-clip:	no
background-position:	as list of length, percentage, or calc
background-size:	as list of length, percentage, or calc
background-repeat:	no
background-attachment	no
abackground-origin	no

BORDERS

border (see longhand)	
border-color	as color
border-style	no
border-width	as length
border-radius	as length, percentage, or calc();
border-image	no (see longhand)
border-image-outset	no
border-image-repeat	no
border-image-slice	no
border-image-source	no
border-image-width	no

BOX MODEL

box-decoration-break	no
box-shadow	as shadow list
margin	as length
padding	as length
box-sizing	no
max-height	as length, percentage, or calc();
min-height	as length, percentage, or calc();
height	as length, percentage, or calc();
max-width	as length, percentage, or calc();
min-width	as length, percentage, or calc();
width	as length, percentage, or calc();
overflow	no
visibility	as visibility (see "How Property Values Are Interpolated" on page 885)

Property name	Interpolation

TABLE

border-collapse	no
border-spacing	no
caption-side	no
empty-cells	no
table-layout	no
vertical-align	as length

POSITIONING

bottom	as length, percentage, or calc();
left	as length, percentage, or calc();
right	as length, percentage, or calc();
top	as length, percentage, or calc();
float	no
clear	no
position	no
z-index	as integer

FONTS

font (see longhand)	
font-style	no
font-variant	no
font-weight	as font weight
font-stretch	as font stretch
font-size	as length
line-height	as number, length
font-family	no
font-variant-ligatures	no
font-feature-settings	no
font-language-override	no
font-size-adjust	as number
font-synthesis	no
font-kerning	no
font-variant-position	no
font-variant-caps	no
font-variant-numeric	no
font-variant-east-asian	no
font-variant-alternates	no

Property name	Interpolation

IMAGES

object-fit	no
object-position	as length, percentage, or calc();
image-rendering	no
image-orientation	no

COUNTERS, LISTS, AND GENERATED CONTENT

content	no
quotes	no
counter-increment	no
counter-reset	no
list-style	no
list-style-image	no
list-style-position	no
list-style-type	no

PAGE

orphans	no
page-break-after	no
page-break-before	no
page-break-inside	no
widows	no

USER INTERFACE

outline (see longhand)	
outline-color	as color
outline-width	as length
outline-style	no
outline-offset	as length
cursor	no
resize	no
text-overflow	no

ANIMATIONS

animation	no (see longhands)
animation-delay	no
animation-direction	no
animation-duration	no

Property name	Interpolation
animation-fill-mode	no
animation-iteration-count	no
animation-name	no
animation-play-state	no
animation-timing-function	no, though `animation-timing-function` can be included in keyframes

TRANSITIONS

transition	no (see longhands)
transition-delay	no
transition-duration	no
transition-property	no
transition-timing-function	no

TRANSFORM PROPERTIES

transform	as transform (see *Transforms in CSS* [O'Reilly])
transform-origin	as length, percentage or calc();
transform-style	no
perspective	as length
perspective-origin	as simple list of a length, percentage or calc();
backface-visibility	no

COMPOSITING AND BLENDING

background-blend-mode	no
mix-blend-mode	no
isolation	no

Property name	Interpolation
SHAPES	
shape-outside	yes, as basic-shape
shape-margin	as length, percentage, or calc();
shape-image-threshold	as number
MISCELLANEOUS	
clip (deprecated)	as rectangle
display	no
unicode-bidi	no
text-orientation	no
ime-mode	no
all	as each of the properties of the shorthand (all properties but unicode-bidi and direction)
will-change	no
box-decoration-break	no
touch-action	no
initial-letter	no
initial-letter-align	no

Basic Property Reference

Note that in addition to the options shown in the "Value Syntax" column of this appendix, all properties listed also accept the following global values: inherit, ini tial, and unset. They may in the future accept revert as well. These global values are not shown in the table for brevity and clarity.

Where a "P" is indicated for whether an element is animatable (the "Anim." column), that means some but not all aspects of the property's value can be animated.

Property	Default value	Value syntax	Inh.	Anim.
align-content	stretch	flex-start|flex-end|center|space-between|space-around|stretch	N	N
align-items	stretch	flex-start|flex-end|center|baseline|stretch	N	N
animation-delay	0s	<time>#	N	N
animation-direction	normal	[normal|reverse|alternate|alternate-reverse]#	N	N
animation-duration	0s	<time>#	N	N
animation-fill-mode	none	[none|forwards|backwards|both]#	N	N
animation-iteration-count	1	<number>|infinite]#	N	N
animation-name	none	[<single-animation-name>|none]#	N	N
animation-play-state	running	[running|paused]#	N	N

Property	Default value	Value syntax	Inh.	Anim.
animation-timing-function	ease	[ease | linear | ease-in | ease-out | ease-in-out | step-start | step-end | steps(<integer>, start) | steps(<integer>, end) | cubic-bezier(<number>, <number>, <number>, <number>)]#	N	N
animation	0s ease 0s 1 normal none running none	[<animation-name> || <animation-duration> || <animation-timing-function> || <animation-delay> || <animation-iteration-count> || <animation-direction> || <animation-fill-mode> || <animation-play-state>]#	N	N
backface-visibility	visible	visible | hidden	N	N
background-attachment	scroll	[scroll | fixed | local]#	N	N
background-blend-mode	normal	[normal | multiply | screen | overlay | darken | lighten | color-dodge | color-burn | hard-light | soft-light | difference | exclusion | hue | saturation | color | luminosity]#	N	N
background-clip	border-box	[border-box | padding-box | content-box | text]#	N	N
background-color	transparent	<color>	N	Y
background-image	none	[<image># | none	N	N
background-origin	padding-box	[border-box | padding-box | content-box]#	N	N
background-position	0% 0%	[[left | center | right | top | bottom | <percentage> | <length>]] | [left | center | right | <percentage> | <length>] [top | center | bottom | <percentage> | <length>] | [center | [left | right] [<percentage> | <length>]?] && [center | [top | bottom] [<percentage> | <length>]?]]#	N	Y
background-repeat	repeat	[repeat-x | repeat-y | [repeat | space | round | no-repeat]{1,2}]#	N	N
background-size	auto	[<length> | <percentage> | auto]{1,2} | cover | contain]#	N	Y
background	See individual properties	[<bg-image> || <position> [/ <bg-size>]? || <repeat-style> || <attachment> || <box> || <box> ,]* <bg-image> || <position> [/ <bg-size>]? || <repeat-style> || <attachment> || <box> || <box> || <background-color>	N	P
border-bottom-color	currentColor	<color>	N	Y
border-bottom-style	none	none | hidden | dotted | dashed | solid | double | groove | ridge | inset | outset	N	N

Property	Default value	Value syntax	Inh.	Anim.
border-bottom-width	medium	thin | medium | thick | <length>	N	Y
border-bottom	See individiual properties	[<border-width> || <border-style> || <border-color>]	N	P
border-color	current Color	<color>{1,4}	N	Y
border-image-outset	0	[<length> | <number>]{1,4}	N	Y
border-image-repeat	stretch	[stretch | repeat | round | space]{1,2}	N	N
border-image-slice	100%	[<number> | <percentage>]{1,4} && fill?	N	Y
border-image-source	none	none | <image>	N	N
border-image-width	1	[<length> | <percentage> | <number> | auto]{1,4}	N	Y
border-image	See individual properties	<border-image-source> || <border-image-slice> [/ <border-image-width> | / <border-image-width>? / <border-image-outset>]? || <border-image-repeat>	N	N
border-left-color	current Color	<color>	N	Y
border-left-style	none	none | hidden | dotted | dashed | solid | double | groove | ridge | inset | outset	N	N
border-left-width	medium	thin | medium | thick | <length>	N	Y
border-left	See individiual properties	[<border-width> || <border-style> || <border-color>]	N	P
border-radius	0	[<length> | <percentage>]{1,4} [/ [<length> | <percentage>] {1,4}]?	N	Y
border-bottom-left-radius	0	[<length> | <percentage>]{1,2}	N	Y
border-bottom-right-radius	0	[<length> | <percentage>]{1,2}	N	Y
border-top-left-radius	0	[<length> | <percentage>]{1,2}	N	Y
border-top-right-radius	0	[<length> | <percentage>]{1,2}	N	Y
border-right-color	current Color	<color>	N	Y
border-right-style	none	none | hidden | dotted | dashed | solid | double | groove | ridge | inset | outset	N	N

Property	Default value	Value syntax	Inh.	Anim.
border-right-width	medium	thin | medium | thick | *<length>*	N	Y
border-right	See individiual properties	[*<border-width>* || *<border-style>* || *<border-color>*]	N	P
border-spacing	0	*<length>* *<length>*?	Y	Y
border-style	Not defined	[none | hidden | solid | dotted | dashed | double | groove | ridge | inset | outset]{1,4}	N	N
border-top-color	current Color	*<color>*	N	Y
border-top-style	none	none | hidden | dotted | dashed | solid | double | groove | ridge | inset | outset	N	N
border-top-width	medium	thin | medium | thick | *<length>*	N	Y
border-top	See individiual properties	[*<border-width>* || *<border-style>* || *<border-color>*]	N	P
border-width	Not defined	[thin | medium | thick | *<length>*]{1,4}	N	Y
border	See individual properties	[*<border-width>* || *<border-style>* || *<border-color>*]	N	P
bottom	auto	*<length>* | *<percentage>* | auto	N	Y
box-decoration-break	slice	slice | clone	N	N
box-shadow	none	none | inset? && *<length>*{2,4} && *<color>*?	N	Y
box-sizing	content-box	content-box | padding-box | border-box	N	N
caption-side	top	top | bottom	Y	N
clear	none	left | right | both | none	N	N
clip-path	none	none | *<url>* | [[inset() | circle() | ellipse() | polygon()] || [border-box | padding-box | content-box | margin-box | fill-box | stroke-box | view-box]]	N	P
clip-rule	nonzero	nonzero | evenodd	N	N
color	User agent specific	*<color>*	Y	Y
direction	ltr	ltr | rtl	Y	Y
display	inline	[*<display-outside>* || *<display-inside>*] | *<display-listitem>* | *<display-internal>* | *<display-box>* | *<display-legacy>*	N	N
empty-cells	show	show | hide	Y	N
filter	none	[none | blur() | brightness() | contrast() | drop-shadow() | grayscale() | hue-rotate() | invert() | opacity() | sepia() | saturate() | url()]#	N	Y
flex-basis	auto	content | [*<length>* | *<percentage>*]	N	P

Property	Default value	Value syntax	Inh.	Anim.
flex-direction	row	row | row-reverse | column | column-reverse	N	N
flex-flow	row nowrap	*<flex-direction>* || *<flex-wrap>*	N	N
flex-grow	0	*<number>*	N	Y
flex-shrink	1	*<number>*	N	Y
flex-wrap	nowrap	nowrap | wrap | wrap-reverse	N	N
flex	0 1 auto	<flex-grow> <flex-shrink>? || <flex-basis>] | none | auto	N	N
float	none	left | right | none	N	N
font-family	User agent-specific	[*<family-name>* | *<generic-family>*]#	Y	N
font-feature-settings	normal	normal | *<feature-tag-value>*#	Y	N
font-size-adjust	none	*<number>* | none | auto	Y	Y
font-size	medium	xx-small | x-small | small | medium | large | x-large | xx-large | smaller | larger | *<length>* | *<percentage>*	Y	P
font-stretch	normal	normal | ultra-condensed | extra-condensed | condensed | semi-condensed | semi-expanded | expanded | extra-expanded | ultra-expanded	Y	N
font-style	normal	italic | oblique | normal	Y	N
font-synthesis	weight style	none | weight || style	Y	N
font-variant	normal	normal | none | [*<common-lig-values>* || *<discretionary-lig-values>* || *<historical-lig-values>* || *<contextual-alt-values>* || stylistic(*<feature-value-name>*) || historical-forms || styleset(*<feature-value-name>*#) || character-variant(*<feature-value-name>*#) || swash(*<feature-value-name>*) || ornaments(*<feature-value-name>*) || annotation(*<feature-value-name>*) || [small-caps | all-small-caps | petite-caps | all-petite-caps | unicase | titling-caps] || *<numeric-figure-values>* || *<numeric-spacing-values>* || *<numeric-fraction-values>* || ordinal || slashed-zero || *<east-asian-variant-values>* || *<east-asian-width-values>* || ruby]	Y	N
font-weight	normal	normal | bold | bolder | lighter | 100 | 200 | 300 | 400 | 500 | 600 | 700 | 800 | 900	Y	N
font	See individual properties	[[*<font-style>* || [normal | small-caps] || *<font-weight>*]? *<font-size>* [/ *<line-height>*]? *<font-family>*] | caption | icon | menu | message-box | small-caption | status-bar	Y	P
grid-area	See individual properties	*<grid-line>* [/ *<grid-line>*]{0,3}	N	N

Property	Default value	Value syntax	Inh.	Anim.
grid-auto-columns	auto	*<track-breadth>* | minmax(*<track-breadth>* , *<track-breadth>*)	N	N
grid-auto-flow	row	[row | column] || dense	N	N
grid-auto-rows	auto	*<track-breadth>* | minmax(*<track-breadth>* , *<track-breadth>*)	N	N
grid-column-end	auto	auto | *<custom-ident>* | [*<integer>* && *<custom-ident>*?] | [span && [*<integer>* || *<custom-ident>*]]	N	N
grid-column-gap	0	*<length>* | *<percentage>*	N	Y
grid-column-start	auto	auto | *<custom-ident>* | [*<integer>* && *<custom-ident>*?] | [span && [*<integer>* || *<custom-ident>*]]	N	N
grid-column	auto	*<grid-line>* [/ *<grid-line>*]?	N	N
grid-gap	0 0	*<grid-row-gap>* *<grid-column-gap>*	N	Y
grid-row-end	auto	auto | *<custom-ident>* | [*<integer>* && *<custom-ident>*?] | [span && [*<integer>* || *<custom-ident>*]]	N	N
grid-row-gap	0	*<length>_* | *<percentage>*	N	Y
grid-row-start	auto	auto | *<custom-ident>* | [*<integer>* && *<custom-ident>*?] | [span && [*<integer>* || *<custom-ident>*]]	N	N
grid-row	auto	*<grid-line>* [/ *<grid-line>*]?	N	N
grid-template-areas	none	none | *<string>*	N	N
grid-template-columns	none	none | *<track-list>* | *<auto-track-list>*	N	N
grid-template-rows	none	none | *<track-list>* | *<auto-track-list>*	N	N
grid	See individual properties	none | subgrid | [*<grid-template-rows>* / *<grid-template-columns>*] | [*<line-names>*? *<string>* *<track-size>*? *<line-names>*?]+ [/ *<track-list>*]? | [*<grid-auto-flow>* [*<grid-auto-rows>* [/ *<grid-auto-columns>*]?]?]]	N	N
height	auto	*<length>* | *<percentage>* | auto	N	Y
hyphens	manual	manual | auto | none	Y	N
isolation	auto	auto | isolate	N	N
justify-content	flex-start	flex-start | flex-end | center | space-between | space-around	N	N
left	auto	*<length>* | *<percentage>* | auto	N	Y
letter-spacing	normal	*<length>* | normal	Y	Y
line-break	auto	auto | loose | normal | strict	Y	Y
line-height	normal	*<number>* | *<length>* | *<percentage>* | normal	Y	Y
margin-bottom	0	*<length>* | *<percentage>* | auto	N	Y
margin-left	0	*<length>* | *<percentage>* | auto	N	Y

Property	Default value	Value syntax	Inh.	Anim.
margin-right	0	*<length>*	*<percentage>*	auto	N	Y
margin-top	0	*<length>*	*<percentage>*	auto	N	Y
margin	Not defined	[*<length>*	*<percentage>*	auto]{1,4}	N	Y
mask-clip	border-box	[content-box	padding-box	border-box	margin-box	fill-box	stroke-box	view-box	no-clip]#	N	N
mask-composite	add	[add	subtract	intersect	exclude]#	N	N
mask-image	none	[none	*<image>*	*<mask-source>*]#	N	N
mask-mode	match-source	[alpha	luminance	match-source]#	N	N
mask-origin	mask-origin	[content-box	padding-box	border-box	margin-box	fill-box	stroke-box	view-box]#	N	N
mask-position	0% 0%	*<position>*# [a]	N	P
mask-repeat	repeat	[repeat-x	repeat-y	[repeat	space	round	no-repeat]{1,2}]#	N	Y
mask-size	auto	[[*<length>*	*<percentage>*	auto]{1,2}	cover	contain]#	N	P
mask-type	luminance	luminance	alpha	N	N
mask	See individual properties	[*<mask-image>* ‖ *<mask-position>* [/ *<mask-size>*]? ‖ *<mask-repeat>* ‖ *<mask-clip>* ‖ *<mask-origin>* ‖ *<mask-composite>* ‖ *<mask-mode>*]#	N	P
max-height	none	*<length>*	*<percentage>*	none	N	Y
max-width	none	*<length>*	*<percentage>*	none	N	Y
min-height	0	*<length>*	*<percentage>*	N	Y
min-width	0	*<length>*	*<percentage>*	N	Y
mix-blend-mode	normal	normal	multiply	screen	overlay	darken	lighten	color-dodge	color-burn	hard-light	soft-light	difference	exclusion	hue	saturation	color	luminosity	N	N
object-fit	fill	fill	contain	cover	scale-down	none	N	N
object-position	50% 50%	*<position>* [b]	N	N
order	0	*<integer>*	N	Y
orphans	2	*<integer>*	N	N
outline-color	invert	*<color>*	invert	N	Y
outline-style	none	auto	none	solid	dotted	dashed	double	groove	ridge	inset	outset	N	N
outline-width	medium	*<length>*	thin	medium	thick	N	Y
outline	none	[*<outline-color>* ‖ *<outline-style>* ‖ *<outline-width>*]	N	P
overflow-wrap [c]	normal	normal	break-word	Y	Y

Property	Default value	Value syntax	Inh.	Anim.
overflow	visible	visible | hidden | scroll | auto	N	N
padding-bottom	0	*<length>* | *<percentage>*	N	Y
padding-left	0	*<length>* | *<percentage>*	N	Y
padding-right	0	*<length>* | *<percentage>*	N	Y
padding-top	0	*<length>* | *<percentage>*	N	Y
padding	Not defined	[*<length>* | *<percentage>*]{1,4}	N	Y
page-break-after	auto	auto | always	N	N
page-break-before	auto	auto | always	N	N
page-break-inside	auto	auto | avoid	N	N
page	auto	*<identifier>* | inherit	N	N
perspective-origin	50% 50%	*<position>* [d]	N	Y
perspective	none	none | *<length>*	N	Y
position	static	static | relative | sticky | absolute | fixed	N	N
right	auto	*<length>* | *<percentage>* | auto	N	Y
shape-image-threshold	0.0	*<number>*	N	Y
shape-margin	0	*<length>* | *<percentage>*	N	Y
shape-outside	none	none | [[*<basic-shape>* || *<shape-box>*]] |	N	P
size	auto	auto | *<length>*{1,2} | [*<page-size>* || [portrait | land scape]]	N	N
tab-size	8	*<length>* | *<integer>*	Y	Y
table-layout	auto	auto | fixed	Y	N
text-align-last	auto	auto | start | end | left | right | center | justify	Y	N
text-align	start	start | end | left | right | center | justify | match-parent | start end	Y	N
text-decoration	none	none | [underline || overline || line-through || blink]	N	N
text-indent	0	*<length>* | *<percentage>*	Y	Y
text-orientation	mixed	mixed | upright | sideways	Y	Y
text-rendering	auto	auto | optimizeSpeed | optimizeLegibility | geome tricPrecision	Y	Y
text-shadow	none	none | [[*<length>* || [*<length>* *<length>* *<length>*?]]]#	N	Y
text-transform	none	uppercase | lowercase | capitalize | none	Y	N

Property	Default value	Value syntax	Inh.	Anim.
top	auto	*<length>* | *<percentage>* | auto	N	Y
transform-origin	50% 50%	*<position>* [e]	N	Y
transform-style	flat	flat | preserve-3d	N	N
transform	none	*<transform-list>* | none	N	Y
transition-delay	0s	*<time>*#	N	N
transition-duration	0s	*<time>*#	N	N
transition-property	all	none | [all | *<property-name>*]#	N	N
transition-timing-function	ease	*<timing-function>*# [f]	N	N
transition	all 0s ease 0s	[[none | *<transition-property>*] || *<time>* || *<transition-timing-function>* || *<time>*]#	N	N
unicode-bidi	normal	normal | embed | bidi-override	N	Y
vertical-align	baseline	baseline | sub | super | top | text-top | middle | bottom | text-bottom | *<length>* | *<percentage>*	N	P
visibility	visible	visible | hidden | collapse	Y	N
white-space	normal	normal | nowrap | pre | pre-wrap | pre-line	N	N
widows	2	*<integer>*	N	N
width	auto	*<length>* | *<percentage>* | auto	N	Y
word-break	normal	normal | break-all | keep-all	Y	Y
word-spacing	normal	*<length>* | normal	Y	Y
writing-mode	horizontal-tb	horizontal-tb | vertical-rl | vertical-lr	Y	Y
z-index	auto	*<integer>* | auto	N	Y

[a] See background-position for a detailed expansion of the *<position>* syntax.

[b] See background-position for a detailed expansion of the *<position>* syntax.

[c] This property used to be called word-wrap.

[d] See background-position for a detailed expansion of the *<position>* syntax.

[e] See background-position for a detailed expansion of the *<position>* syntax.

[f] See animation-timing-function for a detailed expansion of the *<timing-function>* syntax.

Color Equivalence Table

All 148 color names defined by the CSS Color Module Level 4 (as of the 22 May 2017 version), along with their equivalents in both styles of RGB, HSL, hexadecimal, and three-digit hex shorthand (when applicable).

As of late 2017, there were several new color notations being considered, such as hwb(), gray(), lab(), lch(), and more. These color types are not included in this table due to their lack of support and uncertain future.

Color name	RGB decimal	RGB percentage	HSL	Hexadecimal
aliceblue	rgb(240,248,255)	rgb(94.1%,97.3%,100%)	hsl(208,100%,97.1%)	#F0F8FF
antiquewhite	rgb(250,235,215)	rgb(98%,92.2%,84.3%)	hsl(34,77.8%,91.2%)	#FAEBD7
aqua	rgb(0,255,255)	rgb(0%,100%,100%)	hsl(180,100%,50%)	#00FFFF/ #0FF
aquamarine	rgb(127,255,212)	rgb(49.8%,100%,83.1%)	hsl(160,100%,74.9%)	#7FFFD4
azure	rgb(240,255,255)	rgb(94.1%,100%,100%)	hsl(180,100%,97.1%)	#F0FFFF
beige	rgb(245,245,220)	rgb(96.1%,96.1%,86.3%)	hsl(60,55.6%,91.2%)	#F5F5DC
bisque	rgb(255,228,196)	rgb(100%,89.4%,76.9%)	hsl(33,100%,88.4%)	#FFE4C4
black	rgb(0,0,0)	rgb(0%,0%,0%)	hsl(0,0%,0%)	#000000/ #000
blanchedalmond	rgb(255,235,205)	rgb(100%,92.2%,80.4%)	hsl(36,100%,90.2%)	#FFEBCD
blue	rgb(0,0,255)	rgb(0%,0%,100%)	hsl(240,100%,50%)	#0000FF/ #00F
blueviolet	rgb(138,43,226)	rgb(54.1%,16.9%,88.6%)	hsl(271,75.9%,52.7%)	#8A2BE2
brown	rgb(165,42,42)	rgb(64.7%,16.5%,16.5%)	hsl(0,59.4%,40.6%)	#A52A2A
burlywood	rgb(222,184,135)	rgb(87.1%,72.2%,52.9%)	hsl(34,56.9%,70%)	#DEB887
cadetblue	rgb(95,158,160)	rgb(37.3%,62%,62.7%)	hsl(182,25.5%,50%)	#5F9EA0
chartreuse	rgb(127,255,0)	rgb(49.8%,100%,0%)	hsl(90,100%,50%)	#7FFF00
chocolate	rgb(210,105,30)	rgb(82.4%,41.2%,11.8%)	hsl(25,75%,47.1%)	#D2691E
coral	rgb(255,127,80)	rgb(100%,49.8%,31.4%)	hsl(16,100%,65.7%)	#FF7F50
cornflowerblue	rgb(100,149,237)	rgb(39.2%,58.4%,92.9%)	hsl(219,79.2%,66.1%)	#6495ED
cornsilk	rgb(255,248,220)	rgb(100%,97.3%,86.3%)	hsl(48,100%,93.1%)	#FFF8DC
crimson	rgb(220,20,60)	rgb(86.3%,7.8%,23.5%)	hsl(348,83.3%,47.1%)	#DC143C

Color name	RGB decimal	RGB percentage	HSL	Hexadecimal
cyan	rgb(0,255,255)	rgb(0%,100%,100%)	hsl(180,100%,50%)	#00FFFF/ #0FF
darkblue	rgb(0,0,139)	rgb(0%,0%,54.5%)	hsl(240,100%,27.3%)	#00008B
darkcyan	rgb(0,139,139)	rgb(0%,54.5%,54.5%)	hsl(180,100%,27.3%)	#008B8B
darkgoldenrod	rgb(184,134,11)	rgb(72.2%,52.5%,4.3%)	hsl(43,88.7%,38.2%)	#B8860B
darkgray	rgb(169,169,169)	rgb(66.3%,66.3%,66.3%)	hsl(0,0%,66.3%)	#A9A9A9
darkgreen	rgb(0,100,0)	rgb(0%,39.2%,0%)	hsl(120,100%,19.6%)	#006400
darkgrey	rgb(169,169,169)	rgb(66.3%,66.3%,66.3%)	hsl(0,0%,66.3%)	#A9A9A9
darkkhaki	rgb(189,183,107)	rgb(74.1%,71.8%,42%)	hsl(56,38.3%,58%)	#BDB76B
darkmagenta	rgb(139,0,139)	rgb(54.5%,0%,54.5%)	hsl(300,100%,27.3%)	#8B008B
darkolivegreen	rgb(85,107,47)	rgb(33.3%,42%,18.4%)	hsl(82,39%,30.2%)	#556B2F
darkorange	rgb(255,140,0)	rgb(100%,54.9%,0%)	hsl(33,100%,50%)	#FF8C00
darkorchid	rgb(153,50,204)	rgb(60%,19.6%,80%)	hsl(280,60.6%,49.8%)	#9932CC
darkred	rgb(139,0,0)	rgb(54.5%,0%,0%)	hsl(0,100%,27.3%)	#8B0000
darksalmon	rgb(233,150,122)	rgb(91.4%,58.8%,47.8%)	hsl(15,71.6%,69.6%)	#E9967A
darkseagreen	rgb(143,188,143)	rgb(56.1%,73.7%,56.1%)	hsl(120,25.1%,64.9%)	#8FBC8F
darkslateblue	rgb(72,61,139)	rgb(28.2%,23.9%,54.5%)	hsl(248,39%,39.2%)	#483D8B
darkslategray	rgb(47,79,79)	rgb(18.4%,31%,31%)	hsl(180,25.4%,24.7%)	#2F4F4F
darkslategrey	rgb(47,79,79)	rgb(18.4%,31%,31%)	hsl(180,25.4%,24.7%)	#2F4F4F
darkturquoise	rgb(0,206,209)	rgb(0%,80.8%,82%)	hsl(181,100%,41%)	#00CED1
darkviolet	rgb(148,0,211)	rgb(58%,0%,82.7%)	hsl(282,100%,41.4%)	#9400D3
deeppink	rgb(255,20,147)	rgb(100%,7.8%,57.6%)	hsl(328,100%,53.9%)	#FF1493
deepskyblue	rgb(0,191,255)	rgb(0%,74.9%,100%)	hsl(195,100%,50%)	#00BFFF
dimgray	rgb(105,105,105)	rgb(41.2%,41.2%,41.2%)	hsl(0,0%,41.2%)	#696969
dimgrey	rgb(105,105,105)	rgb(41.2%,41.2%,41.2%)	hsl(0,0%,41.2%)	#696969
dodgerblue	rgb(30,144,255)	rgb(11.8%,56.5%,100%)	hsl(210,100%,55.9%)	#1E90FF
firebrick	rgb(178,34,34)	rgb(69.8%,13.3%,13.3%)	hsl(0,67.9%,41.6%)	#B22222
floralwhite	rgb(255,250,240)	rgb(100%,98%,94.1%)	hsl(40,100%,97.1%)	#FFFAF0
forestgreen	rgb(34,139,34)	rgb(13.3%,54.5%,13.3%)	hsl(120,60.7%,33.9%)	#228B22
fuchsia	rgb(255,0,255)	rgb(100%,0%,100%)	hsl(300,100%,50%)	#FF00FF/ #F0F
gainsboro	rgb(220,220,220)	rgb(86.3%,86.3%,86.3%)	hsl(0,0%,86.3%)	#DCDCDC
ghostwhite	rgb(248,248,255)	rgb(97.3%,97.3%,100%)	hsl(240,100%,98.6%)	#F8F8FF
gold	rgb(255,215,0)	rgb(100%,84.3%,0%)	hsl(51,100%,50%)	#FFD700
goldenrod	rgb(218,165,32)	rgb(85.5%,64.7%,12.5%)	hsl(43,74.4%,49%)	#DAA520
gray	rgb(128,128,128)	rgb(50.2%,50.2%,50.2%)	hsl(0,0%,50.2%)	#808080
green	rgb(0,128,0)	rgb(0%,50.2%,0%)	hsl(120,100%,25.1%)	#008000
greenyellow	rgb(173,255,47)	rgb(67.8%,100%,18.4%)	hsl(84,100%,59.2%)	#ADFF2F
grey	rgb(128,128,128)	rgb(50.2%,50.2%,50.2%)	hsl(0,0%,50.2%)	#808080
honeydew	rgb(240,255,240)	rgb(94.1%,100%,94.1%)	hsl(120,100%,97.1%)	#F0FFF0
hotpink	rgb(255,105,180)	rgb(100%,41.2%,70.6%)	hsl(330,100%,70.6%)	#FF69B4
indianred	rgb(205,92,92)	rgb(80.4%,36.1%,36.1%)	hsl(0,53.1%,58.2%)	#CD5C5C
indigo	rgb(75,0,130)	rgb(29.4%,0%,51%)	hsl(275,100%,25.5%)	#4B0082
ivory	rgb(255,255,240)	rgb(100%,100%,94.1%)	hsl(60,100%,97.1%)	#FFFFF0
khaki	rgb(240,230,140)	rgb(94.1%,90.2%,54.9%)	hsl(54,76.9%,74.5%)	#F0E68C
lavender	rgb(230,230,250)	rgb(90.2%,90.2%,98%)	hsl(240,66.7%,94.1%)	#E6E6FA
lavenderblush	rgb(255,240,245)	rgb(100%,94.1%,96.1%)	hsl(340,100%,97.1%)	#FFF0F5
lawngreen	rgb(124,252,0)	rgb(48.6%,98.8%,0%)	hsl(90,100%,49.4%)	#7CFC00
lemonchiffon	rgb(255,250,205)	rgb(100%,98%,80.4%)	hsl(54,100%,90.2%)	#FFFACD
lightblue	rgb(173,216,230)	rgb(67.8%,84.7%,90.2%)	hsl(195,53.3%,79%)	#ADD8E6

Color name	RGB decimal	RGB percentage	HSL	Hexadecimal
lightcoral	rgb(240,128,128)	rgb(94.1%,50.2%,50.2%)	hsl(0,78.9%,72.2%)	#F08080
lightcyan	rgb(224,255,255)	rgb(87.8%,100%,100%)	hsl(180,100%,93.9%)	#E0FFFF
lightgoldenrodyellow	rgb(250,250,210)	rgb(98%,98%,82.4%)	hsl(60,80%,90.2%)	#FAFAD2
lightgray	rgb(211,211,211)	rgb(82.7%,82.7%,82.7%)	hsl(0,0%,82.7%)	#D3D3D3
lightgreen	rgb(144,238,144)	rgb(56.5%,93.3%,56.5%)	hsl(120,73.4%,74.9%)	#90EE90
lightgrey	rgb(211,211,211)	rgb(82.7%,82.7%,82.7%)	hsl(0,0%,82.7%)	#D3D3D3
lightpink	rgb(255,182,193)	rgb(100%,71.4%,75.7%)	hsl(351,100%,85.7%)	#FFB6C1
lightsalmon	rgb(255,160,122)	rgb(100%,62.7%,47.8%)	hsl(17,100%,73.9%)	#FFA07A
lightseagreen	rgb(32,178,170)	rgb(12.5%,69.8%,66.7%)	hsl(177,69.5%,41.2%)	#20B2AA
lightskyblue	rgb(135,206,250)	rgb(52.9%,80.8%,98%)	hsl(203,92%,75.5%)	#87CEFA
lightslategray	rgb(119,136,153)	rgb(46.7%,53.3%,60%)	hsl(210,14.3%,53.3%)	#778899/ #789
lightslategrey	rgb(119,136,153)	rgb(46.7%,53.3%,60%)	hsl(210,14.3%,53.3%)	#778899/ #789
lightsteelblue	rgb(176,196,222)	rgb(69%,76.9%,87.1%)	hsl(214,41.1%,78%)	#B0C4DE
lightyellow	rgb(255,255,224)	rgb(100%,100%,87.8%)	hsl(60,100%,93.9%)	#FFFFE0
lime	rgb(0,255,0)	rgb(0%,100%,0%)	hsl(120,100%,50%)	#00FF00/ #0F0
limegreen	rgb(50,205,50)	rgb(19.6%,80.4%,19.6%)	hsl(120,60.8%,50%)	#32CD32
linen	rgb(250,240,230)	rgb(98%,94.1%,90.2%)	hsl(30,66.7%,94.1%)	#FAF0E6
magenta	rgb(255,0,255)	rgb(100%,0%,100%)	hsl(300,100%,50%)	#FF00FF/ #F0F
maroon	rgb(128,0,0)	rgb(50.2%,0%,0%)	hsl(0,100%,25.1%)	#800000
mediumaquamarine	rgb(102,205,170)	rgb(40%,80.4%,66.7%)	hsl(160,50.7%,60.2%)	#66CDAA
mediumblue	rgb(0,0,205)	rgb(0%,0%,80.4%)	hsl(240,100%,40.2%)	#0000CD
mediumorchid	rgb(186,85,211)	rgb(72.9%,33.3%,82.7%)	hsl(288,58.9%,58%)	#BA55D3
mediumpurple	rgb(147,112,219)	rgb(57.6%,43.9%,85.9%)	hsl(260,59.8%,64.9%)	#9370DB
mediumseagreen	rgb(60,179,113)	rgb(23.5%,70.2%,44.3%)	hsl(147,49.8%,46.9%)	#3CB371
mediumslateblue	rgb(123,104,238)	rgb(48.2%,40.8%,93.3%)	hsl(249,79.8%,67.1%)	#7B68EE
mediumspringgreen	rgb(0,250,154)	rgb(0%,98%,60.4%)	hsl(157,100%,49%)	#00FA9A
mediumturquoise	rgb(72,209,204)	rgb(28.2%,82%,80%)	hsl(178,59.8%,55.1%)	#48D1CC
mediumvioletred	rgb(199,21,133)	rgb(78%,8.2%,52.2%)	hsl(322,80.9%,43.1%)	#C71585
midnightblue	rgb(25,25,112)	rgb(9.8%,9.8%,43.9%)	hsl(240,63.5%,26.9%)	#191970
mintcream	rgb(245,255,250)	rgb(96.1%,100%,98%)	hsl(150,100%,98%)	#F5FFFA
mistyrose	rgb(255,228,225)	rgb(100%,89.4%,88.2%)	hsl(6,100%,94.1%)	#FFE4E1
moccasin	rgb(255,228,181)	rgb(100%,89.4%,71%)	hsl(38,100%,85.5%)	#FFE4B5
navajowhite	rgb(255,222,173)	rgb(100%,87.1%,67.8%)	hsl(36,100%,83.9%)	#FFDEAD
navy	rgb(0,0,128)	rgb(0%,0%,50.2%)	hsl(240,100%,25.1%)	#000080
oldlace	rgb(253,245,230)	rgb(99.2%,96.1%,90.2%)	hsl(39,85.2%,94.7%)	#FDF5E6
olive	rgb(128,128,0)	rgb(50.2%,50.2%,0%)	hsl(60,100%,25.1%)	#808000
olivedrab	rgb(107,142,35)	rgb(42%,55.7%,13.7%)	hsl(80,60.5%,34.7%)	#6B8E23
orange	rgb(255,165,0)	rgb(100%,64.7%,0%)	hsl(39,100%,50%)	#FFA500
orangered	rgb(255,69,0)	rgb(100%,27.1%,0%)	hsl(16,100%,50%)	#FF4500
orchid	rgb(218,112,214)	rgb(85.5%,43.9%,83.9%)	hsl(302,58.9%,64.7%)	#DA70D6
palegoldenrod	rgb(238,232,170)	rgb(93.3%,91%,66.7%)	hsl(55,66.7%,80%)	#EEE8AA
palegreen	rgb(152,251,152)	rgb(59.6%,98.4%,59.6%)	hsl(120,92.5%,79%)	#98FB98
paleturquoise	rgb(175,238,238)	rgb(68.6%,93.3%,93.3%)	hsl(180,64.9%,81%)	#AFEEEE
palevioletred	rgb(219,112,147)	rgb(85.9%,43.9%,57.6%)	hsl(340,59.8%,64.9%)	#DB7093
papayawhip	rgb(255,239,213)	rgb(100%,93.7%,83.5%)	hsl(37,100%,91.8%)	#FFEFD5
peachpuff	rgb(255,218,185)	rgb(100%,85.5%,72.5%)	hsl(28,100%,86.3%)	#FFDAB9
peru	rgb(205,133,63)	rgb(80.4%,52.2%,24.7%)	hsl(30,58.7%,52.5%)	#CD853F

Color name	RGB decimal	RGB percentage	HSL	Hexadecimal
pink	rgb(255,192,203)	rgb(100%,75.3%,79.6%)	hsl(350,100%,87.6%)	#FFC0CB
plum	rgb(221,160,221)	rgb(86.7%,62.7%,86.7%)	hsl(300,47.3%,74.7%)	#DDA0DD
powderblue	rgb(176,224,230)	rgb(69%,87.8%,90.2%)	hsl(187,51.9%,79.6%)	#B0E0E6
purple	rgb(128,0,128)	rgb(50.2%,0%,50.2%)	hsl(300,100%,25.1%)	#800080
rebeccapurple	rgb(102,51,153)	rgb(40%,20%,60%)	hsl(270,50%,40%)	#663399/ #639
red	rgb(255,0,0)	rgb(100%,0%,0%)	hsl(0,100%,50%)	#FF0000/ #F00
rosybrown	rgb(188,143,143)	rgb(73.7%,56.1%,56.1%)	hsl(0,25.1%,64.9%)	#BC8F8F
royalblue	rgb(65,105,225)	rgb(25.5%,41.2%,88.2%)	hsl(225,72.7%,56.9%)	#4169E1
saddlebrown	rgb(139,69,19)	rgb(54.5%,27.1%,7.5%)	hsl(25,75.9%,31%)	#8B4513
salmon	rgb(250,128,114)	rgb(98%,50.2%,44.7%)	hsl(6,93.2%,71.4%)	#FA8072
sandybrown	rgb(244,164,96)	rgb(95.7%,64.3%,37.6%)	hsl(28,87.1%,66.7%)	#F4A460
seagreen	rgb(46,139,87)	rgb(18%,54.5%,34.1%)	hsl(146,50.3%,36.3%)	#2E8B57
seashell	rgb(255,245,238)	rgb(100%,96.1%,93.3%)	hsl(25,100%,96.7%)	#FFF5EE
sienna	rgb(160,82,45)	rgb(62.7%,32.2%,17.6%)	hsl(19,56.1%,40.2%)	#A0522D
silver	rgb(192,192,192)	rgb(75.3%,75.3%,75.3%)	hsl(0,0%,75.3%)	#C0C0C0
skyblue	rgb(135,206,235)	rgb(52.9%,80.8%,92.2%)	hsl(197,71.4%,72.5%)	#87CEEB
slateblue	rgb(106,90,205)	rgb(41.6%,35.3%,80.4%)	hsl(248,53.5%,57.8%)	#6A5ACD
slategray	rgb(112,128,144)	rgb(43.9%,50.2%,56.5%)	hsl(210,12.6%,50.2%)	#708090
slategrey	rgb(112,128,144)	rgb(43.9%,50.2%,56.5%)	hsl(210,12.6%,50.2%)	#708090
snow	rgb(255,250,250)	rgb(100%,98%,98%)	hsl(0,100%,99%)	#FFFAFA
springgreen	rgb(0,255,127)	rgb(0%,100%,49.8%)	hsl(150,100%,50%)	#00FF7F
steelblue	rgb(70,130,180)	rgb(27.5%,51%,70.6%)	hsl(207,44%,49%)	#4682B4
tan	rgb(210,180,140)	rgb(82.4%,70.6%,54.9%)	hsl(34,43.8%,68.6%)	#D2B48C
teal	rgb(0,128,128)	rgb(0%,50.2%,50.2%)	hsl(180,100%,25.1%)	#008080
thistle	rgb(216,191,216)	rgb(84.7%,74.9%,84.7%)	hsl(300,24.3%,79.8%)	#D8BFD8
tomato	rgb(255,99,71)	rgb(100%,38.8%,27.8%)	hsl(9,100%,63.9%)	#FF6347
turquoise	rgb(64,224,208)	rgb(25.1%,87.8%,81.6%)	hsl(174,72.1%,56.5%)	#40E0D0
violet	rgb(238,130,238)	rgb(93.3%,51%,93.3%)	hsl(300,76.1%,72.2%)	#EE82EE
wheat	rgb(245,222,179)	rgb(96.1%,87.1%,70.2%)	hsl(39,76.7%,83.1%)	#F5DEB3
white	rgb(255,255,255)	rgb(100%,100%,100%)	hsl(0,0%,100%)	#FFFFFF/ #FFF
whitesmoke	rgb(245,245,245)	rgb(96.1%,96.1%,96.1%)	hsl(0,0%,96.1%)	#F5F5F5
yellow	rgb(255,255,0)	rgb(100%,100%,0%)	hsl(60,100%,50%)	#FFFF00/ #FF0
yellowgreen	rgb(154,205,50)	rgb(60.4%,80.4%,19.6%)	hsl(80,60.8%,50%)	#9ACD32

Index

opacity, 946
saturation, 950
SVG filters, 951-952
findRule() method, 899-900
:first-child pseudo-class, 68-70
::first-letter pseudo-element, 92, 94, 658
::first-line pseudo-element, 93-95, 658
:first-of-type pseudo-class, 71
fit-content() function, 674-676
fixed positioning, 526, 553-555
flex display (see flexible box layout)
flex property, 614-616, 643-648
flex-basis property, 633-642
flex-direction property, 570-574, 579-580
flex-flow property, 578-579, 582-584
flex-grow property, 616-623
flex-shrink property, 623-632
flex-wrap property, 576-578, 584-586
flexible box (flexbox) layout, 563-586
    content lines
        aligning, 604-609
        wrapping, 576-578
    cross axis for, 576-580, 584-586
    cross size for, 580
    cross start and edge for, 580
    flex container for, 564-565, 569-570,
        586-587
    flex items in, 564, 569, 574, 586-587,
        609-612
        absolute positioning, 612
        aligning along cross axis, 596-602
        aligning individually, 602-604
        anonymous, 602, 610, 612
        dimensions of, 613-648
        distributing along main axis, 587-595
        order of, 648-653
        placing individually, 609-653
    inline-flex display, 564
    main axis for, 565, 570-574, 578-580
    main size for, 580
    main start and end for, 580
    margins and, 611
    recommended uses for, 569
    writing modes and, 571, 574-576, 580
float property, 489-504, 658
floated elements, 489-504
    backgrounds and, 499-501
    block box for, 493
    containing block for, 492

inline elements and, 503-504
interaction with grids, 656
margins and, 491
negative margins and, 501-503
placement of, rules for, 493-499
preventing, 492
preventing next to specific elements,
    504-508
shapes containing, 508-524
    circular shapes, 513-517
    elliptical shapes, 517-518
    inset shapes, 511-513
    margins for, 522-524
    polygons, 518-521
    transparency for, 509, 521-522
width of, 492, 503
flow display, 310-311
flow-root display, 310-311
:focus pseudo-class, 79-81, 82
font property, 199-203
@font-face directive, 154-166
    "Bulletproof" syntax for, 159-160
    combining descriptors, 163-166
    font-family descriptor, 155
    formats for, 157-159
    licenses for, 161
    local fonts for, 159
    optional descriptors, 160-162
    resources used by, 161
    src descriptor, 155, 157-159
    URL for, 157
font-family descriptor, @font-face, 155-157
font-family property, 151-154
font-feature-settings descriptor, @font-face,
    160-162, 197
font-feature-settings property, 195-197
font-kerning property, 191
font-size property, 174-185
    absolute sizes, 175-177
    automatically adjusting, 183-185
    inheritance of, 179
    inline element height from, 290-292
    leading determined by, 217
    length units for, 182-183
    of monospaced text, 180-182
    percentages for, 178
    relative sizes, 177
    rounding of, 179
font-size-adjust property, 183-185

for replaced elements, 327-328
padding property, 318-322
padding-bottom property, 275-276, 322-323
padding-left property, 266, 322-323
padding-right property, 266, 322-323
padding-top property, 275-276, 322-323
@page directive, 1004-1008
page property, 1007-1008
page-break-after property, 1008-1010
page-break-before property, 1008-1010
page-break-inside property, 1010
paged media, 1002-1016
    elements outside the page, 1015
    elements repeated on every page, 1015
    margins, 1006
    orphans and widows, handling, 1011-1013
    page breaking, 1008-1015
    page size, 1004-1006
    page types, 1007-1008
    print styles for, 1002-1003
pc (picas) unit, 122
percentage value type, 120
performance issues
    animations, 914
    custom fonts, 161
    images compared to linear gradients, 479
    radial gradients on mobile devices, 484
    text shadows, 239
period (.), in class selectors, 39-41
perspective() function, 837-838
perspective property, 848-850
perspective-origin property, 850-851
phantom classes (see pseudo-class selectors)
pixels, 122-124
    (see also resolution units; viewport-relative
      units)
plus sign (+)
    in adjacent-sibling selectors, 60
    in value syntax, xxi
polygons, for floated elements, 518-521
position property, 525-526
position values, 143
positioning elements, 525-527
    (see also transforms)
    absolute positioning, 526, 537-553
    auto edges and, 541-543
    containing block and, 526-527, 537-540
    fixed positioning, 526, 553-555
    for nonreplaced elements, 543-547

offset properties for, 527-530
overflow content, handling, 534-535
relative positioning, 526, 555-557
for replaced elements, 547-550
static positioning, 526
sticky positioning, 526-527, 557-561
visibility of content, 536-537
width and height, 530-534
z-axis placement, 550-553
pound sign (see octothorpe)
prefers-reduced-motion media query, 941
prefix descriptor, @counter-style, 801
presentational hints, non-CSS, 111
print media type, 22, 993
print styles, 1002-1003
printing
    animations, 943
    transitions, 889
privacy issues, visited links and, 79
projection media type, 22
properties, 16, 31
    (see also specific properties)
    animatable, 884-888, 897-899, 1017
    changes in, animating (see animation; tran-
      sitions)
    custom properties, 144-147
    list of, 1025
    values of (see values)
pseudo-class selectors, 63-91
    chaining pseudo-classes, 63
    dynamic pseudo-classes, 76-81
    hyperlink pseudo-classes, 77-79
    structural pseudo-classes, 64-76
    user action pseudo-classes, 79-81
pseudo-element selectors, 92-95
pt (points) unit, 122
px (pixels) unit, 122

Q

q (quarter-millimeters) unit, 122
question mark (?), in value syntax, xxi
quotes ('...' or "...")
    enclosing font names, 153-154
    enclosing strings, 116-117
    as generated content, 786-788

R

rad (radians) unit, 142
radial gradients, 466-478

average gradient color for, 484
color stops in, 470-475
colors in, 466
degenerate (edge) cases, 475-478, 484
gradient ray for, 466, 470-475
position of, 466, 469-470
repeating, 478-479, 483-484
shape of, 467
size of, 467-469
radial-gradient() function, 466
range descriptor, @counter-style, 805
ratio value type, 999
:read-only pseudo-class, 81, 86
:read-write pseudo-class, 81, 86
reader origin, 107, 108
reduced-motion animations, 941
relative length units, 125-130
relative positioning, 526, 555-557
relative URL, 118
rem unit, 126-127
rendering speed and legibility of text, 236-237
repeat() function, 676-680
repeating-linear-gradient() function, 481-483
repeating-radial-gradient() function, 483-484
replaced elements, 3, 4, 258
    fitting and positioning for, 987-990
    horizontal formatting for, 273-274
:required pseudo-class, 81, 84
resolution descriptor, @media, 999
resolution units, 124, 1000
resources (see books and publications; website
    resources)
responsive flexing, 630-632
responsive styling, 1000-1001
revert keyword, 116
RGB colors, 133-137
RGBa colors, 136-137
right arrow icon (), xxii
right property, 527-530
root elements, 259
:root pseudo-class, 64
rotate() function, 832-833
rotate3d() function, 833-835
rotateX() function, 832-833
rotateY() function, 832-833
rotateZ() function, 832-833
rules, 16-18
    (see also directives)
    declaration blocks in, 16, 31

declarations in, 16, 31-33
    grouping, 35-38
    !important declarations, 102-103,
        107-108, 939
    specificity of, 99-100
selector in (see selectors)
vendor prefixes in, 17, 942-943

S

s (seconds) unit, 143
sans-serif fonts, 150
saturate() funciton, 950
saturation blend mode, 959
scale() function, 830
scale3d() function, 831
scaleX() function, 830
scaleY() function, 830
scaleZ() function, 830
scaling factor, for font size, 175
scan descriptor, @media, 999
screen blend mode, 955
screen media type, 22, 993
screen size and resolution (see display size and
    resolution)
seizure disorders, animations affecting, 941
selectors, 16, 29-33
    adjacent-sibling combinator for, 60-62
    attribute selectors, 45-53
    child combinator for, 59-60
    class selectors, 38-42, 44
    descendant (contextual) selectors, 56-59
    document structure affecting, 54-56
    element selectors, 30-31
    general-sibling combinator for, 62
    grouping, 33-35, 37-38
    ID selectors, 43-44, 48
    pseudo-class selectors, 63-91
    pseudo-element selectors, 92-95
    specificity of, 97-103
    universal selector, 35
semicolon (;), in rules, 16, 31, 36-37
separated cell border model, 745-749
sepia() function, 948
serif fonts, 150
shadows
    drop shadow filter, 947-948
    text shadows, 237-239
shape-image-threshold property, 521-522
shape-margin property, 522-524

attribute values, 131-132
calculations of, 130-131
colors, 132-142
custom properties for, 144-147
distances, 121-130
frequency, 143
identifiers, 119
images, 119
interpolated, 885-888
keywords, 31-33, 113-116
multiple, specifying, 31-33
numbers, 119-121
percentages, 120
position, 143
ratios, 999
relative lengths, 125-130
resolution, 124, 1000
string values, 116-117
time, 143
URLs, 117-118
var() value type, 145
vendor prefixes, 17, 942-943
vertical bar (|), in value syntax, xxi
vertical bar, equal sign (|=), in attribute selectors, 48
vertical bar, double (||), in value syntax, xxi
vertical direction (see block direction)
vertical formatting, 274-283
auto settings for, 275-278
collapsing margins, 279-283
negative margins, 281-283
percentages for, 276-278
properties for, 275-276
vertical-align property, 220-226, 235, 293-295, 658
vestibular disorders, animations affecting, 941
vh (viewport height) unit, 129
viewport-relative units, 129
(see also pixels)
visibility property, 536-537, 737, 899
:visited pseudo-class, 77-79
visual formatting, 257-259
(see also text formatting)
borders, 257-258, 263-265
boxes for (see boxes)
containing blocks for, 259-260, 266-267
content area, 257-258
display roles, 261-263
horizontal formatting, 265-274

inline formatting, 285-313
list items, 283
margins, 257-258, 263-265, 270-272
normal flow, 258
outlines, 257-258
padding, 257-258, 263-265
vertical formatting, 274-283
vmax (viewport maximum) unit, 129
vmin (viewport minimum) unit, 129
vw (viewport width) unit, 129

W

website resources
about this book, xxiii, xxiv
code examples, xxii
gap behavior in text alignment, 222
OpenType font features, 196
Unicode encoding, 117
website URL (see URLs)
weight, in cascade rules, 107-108
white-space property, 239-242
(see also letter-spacing property; word-spacing property)
whitespace
CSS comments not considered, 20
separating value keywords, 31-32
in style sheets, 18
in text, 239-242
widows property, 1011-1013
width descriptor, @media, 997
width property, 266-270, 273-274, 316-318, 530-532, 737
word-break property, 245-247
word-spacing property, 226-229
(see also white-space property)
word-wrap property (see overflow-wrap property)
wrapping text, 239-249
writing modes (flow direction), 249-256, 571, 574-576, 580
writing-mode property, 249-253, 571, 575

X

x-axis (see coordinate systems)
x-height, 125
XML
class selectors, support for, 44
element selectors for, 30-31

Y

y-axis (see coordinate systems)

Z

z-axis, 550-553, 819-823
z-index property, 550-553, 728

About the Authors

Eric A. Meyer has been working with the web since late 1993 and is an internationally recognized expert on the subjects of HTML, CSS, and web standards. A widely read author, he is also the founder of Complex Spiral Consulting (*http://www.complex spiral.com*), which counts among its clients America Online; Apple Computer, Inc.; Wells Fargo Bank; and Macromedia, which described Eric as "a critical partner in our efforts to transform Macromedia Dreamweaver MX 2004 into a revolutionary tool for CSS-based design."

Beginning in early 1994, Eric was the visual designer and campus web coordinator for the Case Western Reserve University website, where he also authored a widely acclaimed series of three HTML tutorials and was project coordinator for the online version of the *Encyclopedia of Cleveland History* and the *Dictionary of Cleveland Biography*, the first encyclopedia of urban history published fully and freely on the web.

Author of *Eric Meyer on CSS* and *More Eric Meyer on CSS* (New Riders), *CSS: The Definitive Guide* (O'Reilly), and *CSS2.0 Programmer's Reference* (Osborne/McGraw-Hill), as well as numerous articles for the O'Reilly Network, Web Techniques, and Web Review, Eric also created the CSS Browser Compatibility Charts and coordinated the authoring and creation of the W3C's official CSS Test Suite. He has lectured to a wide variety of organizations, including Los Alamos National Laboratory, the New York Public Library, Cornell University, and the University of Northern Iowa. Eric has also delivered addresses and technical presentations at numerous conferences, among them An Event Apart (which he cofounded), the IW3C2 WWW series, Web Design World, CMP, SXSW, the User Interface conference series, and The Other Dreamweaver Conference.

In his personal time, Eric acts as list chaperone of the highly active css-discuss mailing list (*http://www.css-discuss.org*), which he cofounded with John Allsopp of Western Civilisation, and which is now supported by *evolt.org*. Eric lives in Cleveland, Ohio, which is a much nicer city than you've been led to believe. For nine years he was the host of "Your Father's Oldsmobile," a big-band radio show heard weekly on WRUW 91.1 FM in Cleveland.

You can find more detailed information on Eric's personal web page (*http://www.meyerweb.com/eric*).

How does someone get to be the author of *Flexbox in CSS*, *Transitions and Animations in CSS*, and *Mobile HTML5* (O'Reilly), and coauthor of *CSS3 for the Real World* (SitePoint)? For **Estelle Weyl**, the journey was not a direct one. She started out as an architect, used her master's degree in health and social behavior from the Harvard School of Public Health to lead teen health programs, and then began dabbling in website development. By the time Y2K rolled around, she had become somewhat known as a web standardista at *http://www.standardista.com*.

Today, she writes a technical blog that pulls in millions of visitors, and speaks about CSS3, HTML5, JavaScript, accessibility, and mobile web development at conferences around the world. In addition to sharing esoteric programming tidbits with her reading public, Estelle has consulted for Kodak Gallery, SurveyMonkey, Visa, Samsung, Yahoo!, and Apple, among others. She is currently the Open Web Evangelist for Instart Logic, a platform that helps make web application delivery fast and secure.

When not coding, she spends her time doing construction, striving to remove the last remnants of communal hippiedom from her 1960s-throwback home. Basically, it's just one more way Estelle is working to bring the world into the 21st century.

Colophon

The animals on the cover of *CSS: The Definitive Guide* are salmon (*salmonidae*), which is a family of fish consisting of many different species. Two of the most common salmon are the Pacific salmon and the Atlantic salmon.

Pacific salmon live in the northern Pacific Ocean off the coasts of North America and Asia. There are five subspecies of Pacific salmon, with an average weight of 10 to 30 pounds. Pacific salmon are born in the fall in freshwater stream gravel beds, where they incubate through the winter and emerge as inch-long fish. They live for a year or two in streams or lakes and then head downstream to the ocean. There they live for a few years, before heading back upstream to their exact place of birth to spawn and then die.

Atlantic salmon live in the northern Atlantic Ocean off the coasts of North America and Europe. There are many subspecies of Atlantic salmon, including the trout and the char. Their average weight is 10 to 20 pounds. The Atlantic salmon family has a life cycle similar to that of its Pacific cousins, and also travels from freshwater gravel beds to the sea. A major difference between the two, however, is that the Atlantic salmon does not die after spawning; it can return to the ocean and then return to the stream to spawn again, usually two or three times.

Salmon, in general, are graceful, silver-colored fish with spots on their backs and fins. Their diet consists of plankton, insect larvae, shrimp, and smaller fish. Their unusually keen sense of smell is thought to help them navigate from the ocean back to the exact spot of their birth, upstream past many obstacles. Some species of salmon remain landlocked, living their entire lives in freshwater.

Salmon are an important part of the ecosystem, as their decaying bodies provide fertilizer for streambeds. Their numbers have been dwindling over the years, however. Factors in the declining salmon population include habitat destruction, fishing, dams that block spawning paths, acid rain, droughts, floods, and pollution.

The cover image is a 19th-century engraving from the Dover Pictorial Archive. The cover fonts are URW Typewriter and Guardian Sans. The text font is Adobe Minion Pro; the heading font is Adobe Myriad Condensed; and the code font is Dalton Maag's Ubuntu Mono.

Learn from experts.
Find the answers you need.

Sign up for a **10-day free trial** to get **unlimited access** to all of the content on Safari, including Learning Paths, interactive tutorials, and curated playlists that draw from thousands of ebooks and training videos on a wide range of topics, including data, design, DevOps, management, business—and much more.

Start your free trial at:
oreilly.com/safari

(No credit card required.)